Contemporary
Management
Accounting

Contemporary Management Accounting

Albie Brooks
VICTORIA UNIVERSITY

Judy Oliver
SWINBURNE UNIVERSITY

Gillian Vesty
UNIVERSITY OF MELBOURNE

Leslie G. Eldenburg
UNIVERSITY OF ARIZONA

Susan Wolcott
WOLCOTTLYNCH ASSOCIATES, USA

WILEY

John Wiley & Sons Australia, Ltd

This edition published 2008 by
John Wiley & Sons Australia, Ltd
42 McDougall Street, Milton Qld 4064

Typeset in 10.5/12.5 Dante MT Regular

Australian edition © John Wiley & Sons Australia, Ltd 2008

US edition © 2005 by John Wiley & Sons, Inc.
All rights reserved.

Authorised adaptation of *Cost Management: Measuring,
Monitoring and Motivating Performance* (ISBN 978 0 471 20549 4),
published by John Wiley & Sons, Inc., New York, United
States of America. © 2005 in the United States of America
by John Wiley & Sons Inc. All rights reserved.

The moral rights of the authors have been asserted.

National Library of Australia
Cataloguing-in-Publication data

Brooks, Albie.
 Contemporary management accounting.

 Bibliography.
 Includes index.

 ISBN 978 0 470 81005 7 (pbk.).

 1. Managerial accounting. I. Oliver, Judy. II. Vesty,
Gillian. III. Title.

658.1511

Cover and internal design images: © Image Source

Edited by Miriana Dasovic

Typeset in India by Aptara

Printed in Singapore by
Craft Print International Ltd

10 9 8 7 6 5 4 3 2 1

About the authors

Albie Brooks

Albie Brooks, BCom, DipEd, PhD, FCPA, is a senior lecturer in accounting at Victoria University, where he has taught for 15 years. He teaches predominantly in the areas of management accounting and business research methods. His research interests include management accounting innovation issues, corporate governance issues and accounting education. With Judy Oliver, he was recipient of the 2003 Vice-Chancellor's Award for Teaching Excellence in the Faculty of Business and Law.

Judy Oliver

Judy Oliver, BBus, MBus, CA, is a senior lecturer in accounting at Swinburne University. She teaches management accounting at both the undergraduate and postgraduate levels. With Albie Brooks, she was the recipient of the 2003 Vice-Chancellor's Award for Teaching Excellence in the Faculty of Business and Law.

Gillian Vesty

Gillian Vesty, BBus, MBus (Res), RN, is a lecturer in accounting at the University of Melbourne. She teaches management accounting at both the undergraduate and postgraduate levels. In 2006, Gillian received a Dean's Certificate of Excellent Postgraduate Teaching. Extensive background experience in the healthcare sector has contributed to Gillian's research interests in management accounting control system change in public hospitals. More recently, Gillian has expanded her research portfolio to include sustainability management accounting.

Brief contents

Contents

Preface

Contemporary Management Accounting is an Australasian adaptation of the US text *Cost Management: Measuring, Monitoring, and Motivating Performance*. The original text focused on helping students learn through the application of cost and management accounting methods to a variety of organisational settings, and provided a diverse, strong set of student tasks at the end of each chapter.

Our aim with this adaptation is to build on the strengths of the original text, and provide an interesting and regionally relevant text for both students and instructors that encourages student engagement with the discipline of management accounting. We do this by:

- introducing the value chain framework in chapter 1 and using this framework to explore a range of management accounting issues.
- providing contemporary, relevant and interesting scene setters at the start of each chapter as a vehicle for introducing some of the issues explored within that chapter. The scene setters use real organisations and provide a rich context from which to explore the issues within the chapter. The scene setters can also be used as a basis for class discussion and/or extension work.
- focusing on management accounting information for decision making.
- including a set of articles at the back of the book. For each chapter, there is one article relevant to the issues explored in the chapter. These articles provide a link between the chapter content, practice and research.
- presenting the text in a user-friendly style with the use of diagrams for illustrative purposes and comprehensive examples throughout the chapters.
- including a chapter that focuses specifically on sustainability management accounting and is linked to other chapters in the text.
- grouping together the three chapters more focused on management accounting for financial reporting, namely chapters 13, 14 and 15. These chapters relate to job costing and process costing for financial reporting, and compare absorption, variable and throughput costing. This enables the remainder of the text to proceed without the specific influences of financial reporting.
- structuring and writing the text in a student-friendly manner.

Contemporary Management Accounting brings together conventional cost and management accounting tools and practices with more recent developments in the discipline. We believe the title *Contemporary Management Accounting* encapsulates much of what the text is about — providing decision-useful management accounting information suitable for the organisational environment.

Chapter focus

Chapter 1: The role of accounting information in management decision making

Chapter 1 provides an overview of organisational decision making and introduces students to the use of management accounting information in decision making. It gives a brief history of management accounting and outlines key influences on the structure of management accounting systems. Techniques for identifying and using relevant information are reviewed. A model for developing higher-quality decisions is introduced. We then provide an introduction to some key terms, and detail the value chain as a framework for considering a range of management accounting issues.

Chapter 2: Cost concepts

This chapter introduces accounting terms that relate to cost behaviour and explain the cost function. We discuss limitations of the information produced by cost functions, and problems with uncertainties and bias in developing cost functions. This focus allows students to consider the quality of information as they learn cost accounting methods. We present and illustrate techniques that are used to describe cost behaviour (engineered estimates, analysis at the account level, two-point method and regression analysis). Scatter plots are introduced as a way of providing additional information about cost behaviour. Linear and non-linear cost functions are presented.

Chapter 3: A costing framework

In this chapter we first explore the concepts of cost objects, and direct and indirect costs. We then outline a costing framework, and use this framework to explore cost allocation issues with a particular focus on the service sector. Then we use the costing framework in a support department setting to explore the direct, step-down and reciprocal methods of allocation. The chapter appendixes compare the single- and dual-rate allocation methods, and use Excel Solver to solve simultaneous equations under the reciprocal method.

Chapter 4: Activity analysis and management

Activity analysis for costing and management are introduced in this chapter. Comparisons are drawn between ABC-derived costs and conventionally derived costs. We introduce the ABC cost hierarchy and explore the benefits, cost and limitations of ABC and ABM. With a focus on more recent developments in costing, we illustrate time-driven ABC. Both service firm settings and manufacturing settings are used throughout.

Chapter 5: The strategic management of costs and revenues

Chapter 5 explores a range of issues relating to the strategic management of costs and revenues including value chain analysis and continuous cost improvement, just-in-time (JIT) manufacturing, total quality management (TQM) and costs of quality, target costing principles and techniques, kaizen costing and alternative pricing methods. Each of these is explored as a tool for achieving longer-term efficiency gains and profitability improvement.

Chapter 6: Cost–volume–profit (CVP) analysis

Single and multiple product examples are used to explore the development and application of CVP information, before and after taxes. The margin of safety and operating leverage are introduced and then used to analyse operational risk. Examples show how CVP information is used for both decision-making and monitoring purposes. Spreadsheets with input sections and cell referencing are introduced in the chapter appendix so that students can easily perform sensitivity analysis.

Chapter 7: Budgeting

Budgeting issues are explored as a tool for both short-term and long-term planning. We outline the role of the master budget and demonstrate the compilation of key components of the master budget. We then describe and illustrate the role of the cash budget, and examine how budgets are used as performance benchmarks through the application of static and flexible budgets. We also discuss participative, zero-based, rolling, ABC and kaizen budgets. Behavioural aspects of budgeting are explored, as are the effects of uncertainties and bias in budget information.

Chapter 8: Relevant costs for decision making

Non-routine decisions — special order, make or buy, keep or drop, product emphasis, and maximising constrained resources decisions — are covered in the first half of chapter 8. As the chapter progresses, we consider the impact of uncertainties and limitations of non-routine operating decisions as well as information quality issues. The second half of the chapter discusses and illustrates issues associated with joint costing using physical output, sales value at split-off point, net realisable value and constant gross margin NRV methods

Chapter 9: Investment decisions

Net present value analysis, internal rate of return and other capital budgeting techniques (payback and accounting rate of return) are described, compared and contrasted in this chapter. These are explored in the context of a process for addressing capital budgeting decisions. Examples with increasing complexity are used to examine capital budgeting decisions involving income taxes. Uncertainties, sensitivity analysis and bias in capital budget information are emphasised. Inflation effects are considered in the chapter appendix using both the real rate and nominal rate methods.

Chapter 10: Standard costs and variance analysis

The development and use of direct and overhead cost standards and variances are presented in this chapter. We explore how standards are established, how variances are calculated and then analysed, and how manufacturing cost variances are closed off at the end of the period. In the chapter appendix, profit-related variances (revenue variances and contribution margin-related variances) are described and calculated.

Chapter 11: Performance evaluation and compensation

Agency theory and responsibility accounting are introduced to explore the assignment of decision-making authority and responsibility. Performance evaluation measures (ROI, residual income and EVA) are compared and contrasted. We then explore the nature of compensation and its role in motivating and influencing managerial decision-making performance. Transfer pricing issues are addressed through a consideration and comparison of different transfer pricing methods.

Chapter 12: Strategy and the balanced scorecard

This chapter emphasises the strategic decision-making model introduced in chapter 1, highlighting the role of long-term strategic decision making. The balanced scorecard is presented as a method for combining financial and non-financial performance measures to gauge progress and motivate employees. We then explore the role and use of strategy maps as a recent development in the balanced scorecard. The strengths and weaknesses of the balanced scorecard are discussed, including uncertainties about the best choice of measures, mistakes in implementation, and the effects of bias on performance measure choices.

Chapter 13: Job costing for financial reporting

Chapter 13 introduces job costing as it relates to the financial reporting process. The first part of the chapter demonstrates the flow of costs through the manufacturing process and calculates the inventoriable product cost for customised products. Actual versus normal methods of job costing are compared, and calculations for overapplied and underapplied overhead are explained. We also include a discussion of the costs of spoilage, rework and scrap in job costing, describing opportunity costs that arise from poor quality. The chapter concludes with the uses and limitations of job costing for financial reporting.

Chapter 14: Process costing for financial reporting

This chapter presents process costing methods using FIFO and weighted average. We develop a single format that is used to calculate equivalent units for both the FIFO and weighted average methods. This format also helps students understand the difference between the two methods. In addition, accounting methods for spoilage arising in mass production are illustrated. We then explore the uses and limitations of process cost information. Finally, the use of standard costing in mass production is examined in the chapter appendix.

Chapter 15: Absorption, variable and throughput costing

Absorption, variable, and throughput income statements are compared and contrasted. Factors that affect the choice of fixed overhead allocation rates (theoretical, practical, normal and budgeted capacity) are explored. The uses and limitations of information produced by these three income statements are discussed. Several examples address the incentives under absorption costing for managers to improve this period's income by building up inventories.

Chapter 16: Sustainability management accounting

The emerging global sustainability landscape has increased the scrutiny on organisational environmental and social practices. This chapter introduces the concepts of sustainability, sustainability management and sustainability management accounting. Key sustainability management accounting tools are described. Examples of how sustainability management accounting can provide managers with strategically relevant information for sustainability performance reporting and management decision making are provided. The aim is to increase student awareness of the global sustainability paradigm and the role that sustainability management accounting can play.

Chapter features

Contemporary Management Accounting uses a number of pedagogical features and a common structure in each chapter to enhance teaching and learning. Each chapter contains:

- a brief introduction and set of learning objectives, which also serve as the basis of the chapter summary at the end of each chapter.
- a scene setter at the start of each chapter to explore some of the issues arising within the chapter. Each scene setter has been specifically written for this text using local and international companies and organisations.
- the use of comprehensive examples throughout.
- a chapter summary at the end of each chapter.
- self-study problems with suggested solution outlines for students to check their progress and understanding.
- graded tasks at the end of each chapter, classified into discussion questions, exercises, and problems.

Supplements: The teaching and learning package

Contemporary Management Accounting features a full range of teaching and learning resources. Driven by the same principles of the textbook, these materials provide a consistent and well-integrated set of learning materials.

Lecturer resources

Lecturers will be able to utilise the **Solutions manual**, **Instructor's manual**, **Test bank**, **Computerised test bank** and **PowerPoint** presentations for their teaching requirements. In addition to these supplements, lecturers will be able to access WileyPlus, a new online resource that integrates text and media, allowing lecturers to customise their course with the following tools:

- *Course administration* tools help lecturers manage their course and integrate Wiley website resources with course management systems, thereby helping lecturers keep all class materials in one location.

- A *Prepare and present* tool contains all lecturer resources. Lecturers can easily adapt, customise and add to these resources to meet the needs of their particular course.
- An *Assignment* area is a powerful tool that allows lecturers to assign online homework and quizzes comprised of end-of-chapter textbook questions. Lecturers save time because results are automatically graded and recorded in an instructor gradebook. Students benefit from the option to receive immediate feedback on their work, allowing them to quickly gauge their understanding of course content.
- An *Instructor's gradebook* will keep track of student progress and allow lecturers to analyse individual and overall class understanding of course concepts.

Instructor's manual

Designed to help lecturers maximise student learning, the instructor's manual offers teaching suggestions for each chapter of the main text, and explains content presentation in a more collaborative learning environment. The instructor's manual provides alternative syllabi, ways to organise course materials, and suggestions for teaching each chapter.

Test bank

The test bank is a comprehensive testing package that allows lecturers to prepare examinations according to chapter objectives, learning skills and content. It includes traditional types of questions (e.g. true/false, multiple-choice, matching, computational, and short-answer), as well as open-ended problems similar to those in the textbook.

Computerised test bank

The computerised test bank allows lecturers to create and print multiple versions of the same test by scrambling the order of all the different types of questions found in the test bank. It even allows answers to be scrambled within a particular multiple-choice question. Lecturers can modify and customise test questions by changing existing problems or adding their own. The computerised test bank is available in Respondus and Examview.

Solutions manual

The solutions manual contains detailed solutions to end-of-chapter questions, exercises and problems. The solutions provide more than just answers — they guide students through the required computational and thinking processes.

PowerPoint presentation

These electronic lecture aids allow adopters of the text to visually present key concepts found in each chapter of the main text. Intended as a lecture guideline, the PowerPoint slides present material in a concise 'bullet' format that enables easy note-taking.

Blackboard and WebCT

Blackboard and WebCT offer an integrated set of course management tools that enable lecturers to easily design, develop and manage web-based and web-enhanced courses.

Student resources

Contemporary Management Accounting students will be provided with a wealth of assessment-related materials to help develop their understanding of course concepts and increase their ability to solve problems. Students will find student practice quizzes with correct responses and page references helpful for learning. In addition to this, WileyPlus will provide online interactive assignment questions that can be used for both formal and informal assessment tasks.

Please contact your John Wiley & Sons sales consultant for more information on all these resources.

Steps for better thinking

Steps for better thinking is a decision-making model you may find useful as a pedagogical tool when reading the chapter and attempting the end-of-chapter activities. The model can be referred to when you:

- analyse chapter-opening scene setters
- work through the steps and details of the comprehensive examples
- attempt the end-of-chapter exercises and problems.

■ FOUNDATION Knowledge and skills

The foundation of *steps for better thinking* consists of the knowledge and basic skills needed to deal with a problem.

■ STEP 1 Identify the problem, relevant information and uncertainties

This step involves identifying relevant information and uncertainties. Recognising uncertainties is also an extremely important part of managerial decision making, as managers sometimes fail to adequately identify major uncertainties. This failure, in turn, causes them to make decisions without adequate analysis or to be overly confident in their decisions.

■ STEP 2 Explore interpretations and connections

This step includes recognising and controlling biases, more thoroughly considering uncertainties, and interpreting information from different viewpoints. For this kind of assessment, we must be adept at recognising and evaluating assumptions, gauging the quality of information and putting ourselves in others' shoes. We can think of step 2 as analysing the strengths and weaknesses of different alternatives. This is often the most time-consuming and important step when addressing open-ended problems. Too often, decision makers are hasty and fail to thoroughly analyse the information related to a problem; they jump to a conclusion. Careful attention to step 2 activities increases the probability of making the best decision.

■ STEP 3 Prioritise alternatives and implement conclusions

Step 3 involves making trade-offs and choosing the best possible alternative, then efficiently implementing it. For managers, these activities include ensuring that the organisation's values, core competencies and strategies are adequately considered. Efficient implementation includes motivating performance within the organisation.

■ STEP 4 Envision and direct strategic innovation

This step is necessary because open-ended problems cannot be solved with absolute certainty, and because the economic environment changes. Management decisions require monitoring and possible revision during implementation and subsequently, as new events unfurl. The most gifted decision makers act strategically to recognise change and new threats, and also to visualise new opportunities.

> **Step 4:** Envisioning
>
> **Step 3:** Prioritising
>
> **Step 2:** Exploring
>
> **Step 1:** Identifying
>
> **Foundation:** Knowing

Source: © 2002, Wolcott, SK, 'Steps for better thinking: a developmental problem-solving process'.
Available online at www.WolcottLynch.com.

Contemporary Management Accounting has been designed with you — the student —in mind. The design is our attempt to provide you with a textbook that both communicates the subject matter and facilitates learning. We have tried to accomplish these goals through the following elements.

5

Chapter opening double-page spread

The double-page spread includes an 'In brief' chapter opener that provides a brief overview of the content presented in the chapter and lists the expected learning objectives for the chapter.

The strategic management of costs and revenues

IN BRIEF
Managers and accountants make decisions about long-term organisational strategies as well as short-term operating plans. These strategies and plans include mutually dependent decisions about how to control costs and price products. Managers increasingly adopt practices such as target costing and just-in-time (JIT) inventory management to help them improve efficiency and achieve profitability goals. Cost measurements help managers make these types of decisions.

After studying this chapter, you should be able to:

1. Explain the value chain activities that provide for continuous cost improvement.
2. Explain the concepts of just-in-time (JIT) manufacturing, total quality management (TQM) and the theory of constraints (TOC).
3. Understand target costing principles and techniques.
4. Explain the concept of kaizen costing and how it compares to target costing.
5. Describe the characteristics of life cycle costing.
6. Describe pricing methods and how cost-based prices and market-based prices are managed.
7. Understand the uses and limitations of cost-based and market-based pricing.
8. Explain any additional factors that might affect prices.
9. Appreciate how pricing models apply to not-for-profit and government entities.

Sony, Microsoft and Nintendo: the game console war

The computer game industry can be highly profitable for companies such as Sony, Microsoft and Nintendo, who are all battling for a share of the $30 billion a year global game market. In Australia three-quarters of all households have a device for playing console games, and $1 billion is spent annually on games. In the last decade Sony, the market leader, has sold more than 200 million PlayStation consoles globally and has held significant power over setting prices for the console game market. When Microsoft entered the market in 2001, it lost more than $2 billion on its Xbox consoles. Over time, Microsoft has reduced the prices of its Xbox consoles to remain competitive with the Sony PlayStation 2 (PS2). In 2002, analysts predicted that the Xbox would sell at a loss for three years or more. In spite of these losses, Microsoft has continued to spend more than $2 billion investing in the market and trying to draw a wider audience for its new-generation Xbox 360 console, which was released in early 2006.

Such losses represent a standard practice in the videogame console industry. Manufacturers rely on income from software sales and licensing to subsidise their hardware costs. Managers plan for losses immediately after launching a new console design but expect to generate profits over the console's life. Historically, a particular console design lasts about five years before being replaced by a new design. Thus, managers expect repeated cycles of loss followed by profit. The generation of profits is made more difficult by pricing issues, as the price companies could charge its customers for the consoles is often limited by competition.

Sources: Information from Australian IT 2006, 'Fast start for Wii', 14 December, australianIT.com.au; Becker, D & Wilcox, J 2001, 'Will Xbox drain Microsoft?', CNET news, news.com.com, 6 March; Hill, J 2006, 'Xbox targets a wider audience', The Age, 23 March, www.theage.com.au; Kanellos, M 2006, 'PlayStation 3 component prices: Why so high?', CNET news, news.com.com; Moses, A 2006, 'PS3 better late than never', Sydney Morning Herald, 4 December, www.smh.com.au; Ramsay, R 2006a, '100 000 Xbox 360s sold in Oz', Gamespot, 25 October, au.gamespot.com/news; Ramsay, R 2006b, 'Wii breaks Aussie sales records', Gamespot, 13 December, au.gamespot.com/news; Tran, KTL 2002, 'Microsoft vows to spend $2 billion to restore Xbox game's momentum', Wall Street Journal Online, 21 May.

Issues from this scene setter to look for in the chapter include:

- The techniques such as value chain analysis and just-in-time (JIT) manufacturing that might be taken by companies such as Sony, Microsoft and Nintendo to reduce their game console costs.
- How the principles of target costing can assist with the decision to invest or continue to invest in the game console market.
- How decisions in competitive markets such as the game console industry might rely on techniques such as lifecycle costing.
- How cost-based or market-based pricing might affect company profits.
- How other factors, such as the customer demand for product (for example, demand for the new Nintendo Wii), might affect the sales forecasting and produce pricing of Microsoft's and Sony's game consoles.

Value chain activities for continuous cost improvement

The link between costs and prices has become increasingly important with global competition. Managers and accountants must simultaneously manage both. Successful entities continuously improve their cost efficiency, charge competitive prices and focus on long-term organisational strategies. Over the long term, profitable organisations continuously seek ways to become more efficient, reduce costs and improve interactions with suppliers and customers. A variety of methods — such as value chain and supply chain analysis, just-in-time (JIT) production and managing quality costs — are available for analysing and improving the systems used to produce and deliver goods and services. We begin this chapter by learning several specific methods used to reduce costs, and then we explore pricing methods.

Value chain and supply chain analysis

As discussed in chapter 1, analysis of the value chain can lead to improved relationships between the entity and others in the chain, creating an extended organisation that can respond flexibly to dynamic and competitive environments. The analysis of value-added or non-value-added activities within the entity and in relation to suppliers and customers can lead to business decisions that either eliminate non-value-added activities or improve value. Value chain analysis can also lead to improved communication, as individuals in each part of the process begin to share their abilities, needs and requirements with others in the value chain.

The chapter scene setter aims to motivate students by presenting an interesting real-world business or industry that applies the principles and concepts that are developed in the chapter.

The key issues in the scene setter are listed and provide a learning guide for students to follow when reading the chapter.

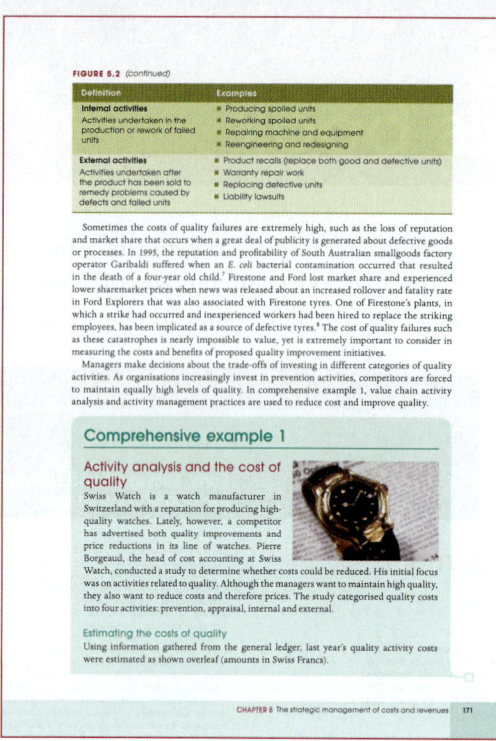

FIGURE 5.2 (continued)

Definition	Examples
Internal activities Activities undertaken in the production or rework of failed units	■ Producing spoiled units ■ Reworking spoiled units ■ Repairing machine and equipment ■ Reengineering and redesigning
External activities Activities undertaken after the product has been sold to remedy problems caused by defects and failed units	■ Product recalls (replace both good and defective units) ■ Warranty repair work ■ Replacing defective units ■ Liability lawsuits

Sometimes the costs of quality failures are extremely high, such as the loss of reputation and market share that occurs when a great deal of publicity is generated about defective goods or processes. In 1995, the reputation and profitability of South Australian smallgoods factory operator Garibaldi suffered when an *E. coli* bacterial contamination occurred that resulted in the death of a four-year old child.[7] Firestone and Ford lost market share and experienced lower sharemarket prices when news was released about an increased rollover and fatality rate in Ford Explorers that was also associated with Firestone tyres. One of Firestone's plants, in which a strike had occurred and inexperienced workers had been hired to replace the striking employees, has been implicated as a source of defective tyres.[8] The cost of quality failures such as these catastrophes is nearly impossible to value, yet is extremely important to consider in measuring the costs and benefits of proposed quality improvement initiatives.

Managers make decisions about the trade-offs of investing in different categories of quality activities. As organisations increasingly invest in prevention activities, competitors are forced to maintain equally high levels of quality. In comprehensive example 1, value chain activity analysis and activity management practices are used to reduce cost and improve quality.

Comprehensive example 1

Activity analysis and the cost of quality

Swiss Watch is a watch manufacturer in Switzerland with a reputation for producing high-quality watches. Lately, however, a competitor has advertised both quality improvements and price reductions in its line of watches. Pierre Borgeaud, the head of cost accounting at Swiss Watch, conducted a study to determine whether costs could be reduced. His initial focus was on activities related to quality. Although the managers want to maintain high quality, they also want to reduce costs and therefore prices. The study categorised quality costs into four activities: prevention, appraisal, internal and external.

Estimating the costs of quality

Using information gathered from the general ledger, last year's quality activity costs were estimated as shown overleaf (amounts in Swiss Francs).

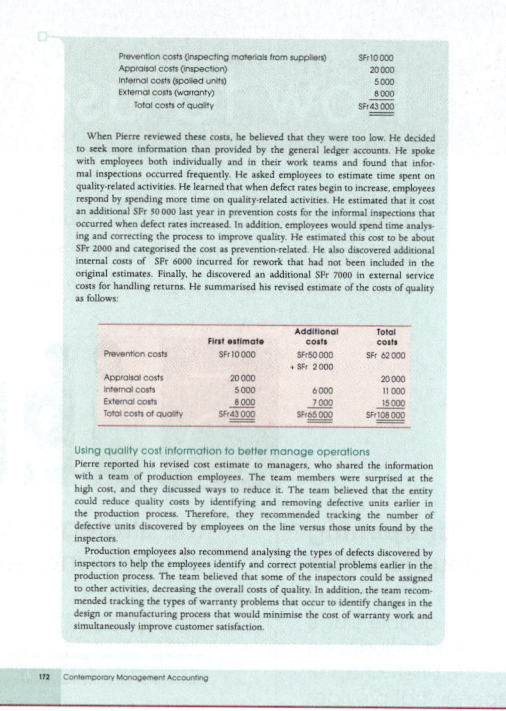

Prevention costs (inspecting materials from suppliers)	SFr 10 000
Appraisal costs (inspection)	20 000
Internal costs (spoiled units)	5 000
External costs (warranty)	8 000
Total costs of quality	SFr 43 000

When Pierre reviewed these costs, he believed that they were too low. He decided to seek more information than provided by the general ledger accounts. He spoke with employees both individually and in their work teams and found that informal inspections occurred frequently. He asked employees to estimate time spent on quality-related activities. He learned that when defect rates begin to increase, employees respond by spending more time on quality-related activities. He estimated that it cost an additional SFr 50 000 last year in prevention costs for the informal inspections that occurred when defect rates increased. In addition, employees would spend time analysing and correcting the process to improve quality. He estimated this cost to be about SFr 2000 and categorised the cost as prevention-related. He also discovered additional internal costs of SFr 6000 incurred for rework that had not been included in the original estimates. Finally, he discovered an additional SFr 7000 in external service costs for handling returns. He summarised his revised estimate of the costs of quality as follows:

	First estimate	Additional costs	Total costs
Prevention costs	SFr 10 000	SFr 50 000 + SFr 2 000	SFr 62 000
Appraisal costs	20 000		20 000
Internal costs	5 000	6 000	11 000
External costs	8 000	7 000	15 000
Total costs of quality	SFr 43 000	SFr 65 000	SFr 108 000

Using quality cost information to better manage operations

Pierre reported his revised cost estimate to managers, who shared the information with a team of production employees. The team members were surprised at the high cost, and they discussed ways to reduce it. The team believed that the entity could reduce quality costs by identifying and removing defective units earlier in the production process. Therefore, they recommended tracking the number of defective units discovered by employees on the line versus those units found by the inspectors.

Production employees also recommend analysing the types of defects discovered by inspectors to help the employees identify and correct potential problems earlier in the production process. The team believed that some of the inspectors could be assigned to other activities, decreasing the overall costs of quality. In addition, the team recommended tracking the types of warranty problems that occur to identify changes in the design or manufacturing process that would minimise the cost of warranty work and simultaneously improve customer satisfaction.

Comprehensive examples

After the presentation of a major cost accounting method, a realistic example in an organisational setting (with interactions between accountants and managers) demonstrates the method and introduces factors relevant to decision-making processes. These examples enhance student learning, clarify the business context and raise issues addressed by accountants, managers and others.

Frequently in the book, one business setting is used several times in a chapter to highlight and apply a different method or application.

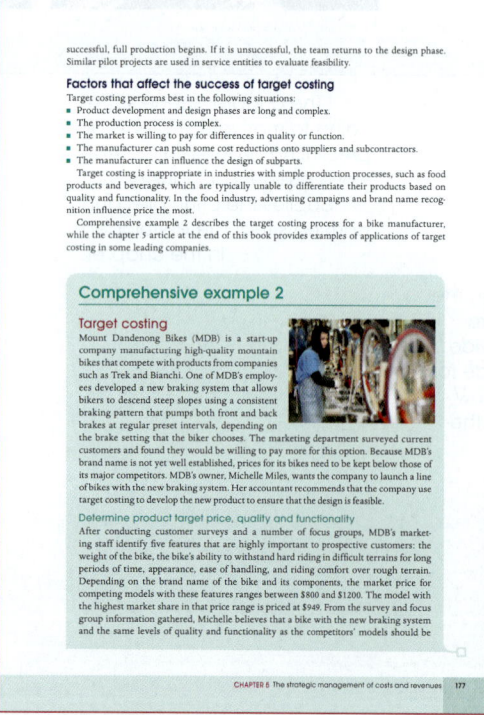

successful, full production begins. If it is unsuccessful, the team returns to the design phase. Similar pilot projects are used in service entities to evaluate feasibility.

Factors that affect the success of target costing

Target costing performs best in the following situations:
■ Product development and design phases are long and complex.
■ The production process is complex.
■ The market is willing to pay for differences in quality or function.
■ The manufacturer can push some cost reductions onto suppliers and subcontractors.
■ The manufacturer can influence the design of subparts.

Target costing is inappropriate in industries with simple production processes, such as food products and beverages, which are typically unable to differentiate their products based on quality and functionality. In the food industry, advertising campaigns and brand name recognition influence price the most.

Comprehensive example 2 describes the target costing process for a bike manufacturer, while the chapter 5 article at the end of this book provides examples of applications of target costing in some leading companies.

Comprehensive example 2

Target costing

Mount Dandenong Bikes (MDB) is a start-up company manufacturing high-quality mountain bikes that compete with products from companies such as Trek and Bianchi. One of MDB's employees developed a new braking system that allows bikers to descend steep slopes using a consistent braking pattern that pumps both front and back brakes at regular preset intervals, depending on the brake setting that the biker chooses. The marketing department surveyed current customers and found they would be willing to pay more for this option. Because MDB's brand name is not yet well established, prices for its bikes need to be kept below those of its major competitors. MDB's owner, Michelle Miles, wants the company to launch a line of bikes with the new braking system. Her accountant recommends that the company use target costing to develop the new product to ensure that the design is feasible.

Determine product target price, quality and functionality

After conducting customer surveys and a number of focus groups, MDB's marketing staff identify five features that are highly important to prospective customers: the weight of the bike, the bike's ability to withstand hard riding in difficult terrains for long periods of time, appearance, ease of handling, and riding comfort over rough terrain. Depending on the brand name of the bike and its components, the market price for competing models with these features ranges between $800 and $1200. The model with the highest market share in that price range is priced at $949. From the survey and focus group information gathered, Michelle believes that a bike with the new braking system and the same levels of quality and functionality as the competitors' models should be

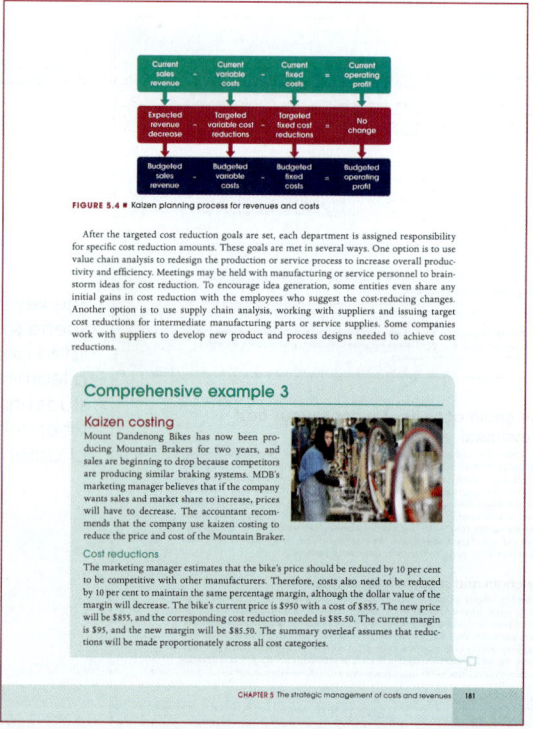

FIGURE 5.4 ■ Kaizen planning process for revenues and costs

After the targeted cost reduction goals are set, each department is assigned responsibility for specific cost reduction amounts. These goals are met in several ways. One option is to use value chain analysis to redesign the production or service process to increase overall productivity and efficiency. Meetings may be held with manufacturing or service personnel to brainstorm ideas for cost reduction. To encourage idea generation, some entities even share any initial gains in cost reduction with the employees who suggest the cost-reducing changes. Another option is to use supply chain analysis, working with suppliers and issuing target cost reductions for intermediate manufacturing parts or service supplies. Some companies work with suppliers to develop new product and process designs needed to achieve cost reductions.

Comprehensive example 3

Kaizen costing

Mount Dandenong Bikes has now been producing Mountain Brakers for two years, and sales are beginning to drop because competitors are producing similar braking systems. MDB's marketing manager believes that if the company wants sales and market share to increase, prices will have to decrease. The accountant recommends that the company use kaizen costing to reduce the price and cost of the Mountain Braker.

Cost reductions

The marketing manager estimates that the bike's price should be reduced by 10 per cent to be competitive with other manufacturers. Therefore, costs also need to be reduced by 10 per cent to maintain the same percentage margin, although the dollar value of the margin will decrease. The bike's current price is $950 with a cost of $855. The new price will be $855, and the corresponding cost reduction needed is $85.50. The current margin is $95, and the new margin will be $85.50. The summary overleaf assumes that reductions will be made proportionately across all cost categories.

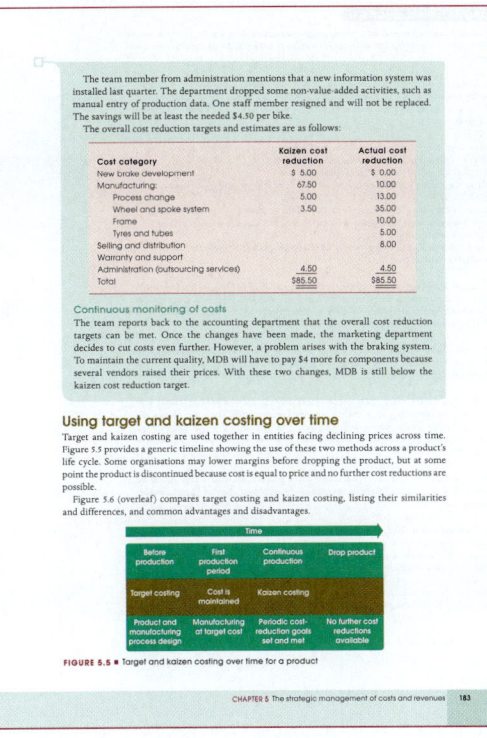

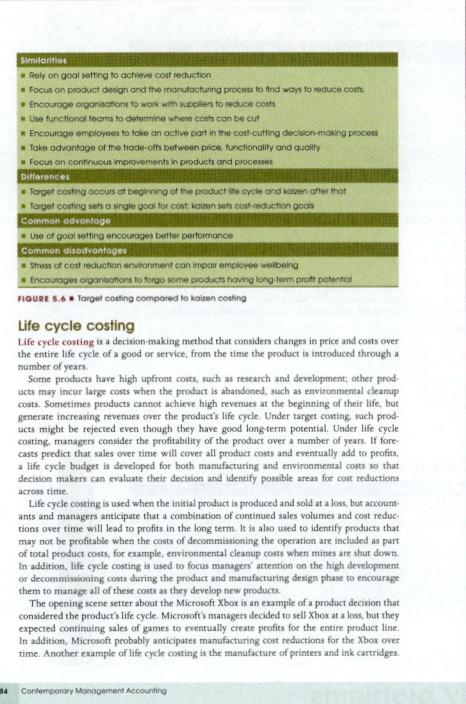

Figures and visual presentation of information

Highly visual figures illustrate and summarise important information in the chapter.

Summary

The chapter summary is organised by the learning objectives presented at the beginning of the chapter, and provides an overview of all key cost accounting methods and concepts. It is a visual tool for students, intended as an overview when they begin a chapter and as a review when they complete it.

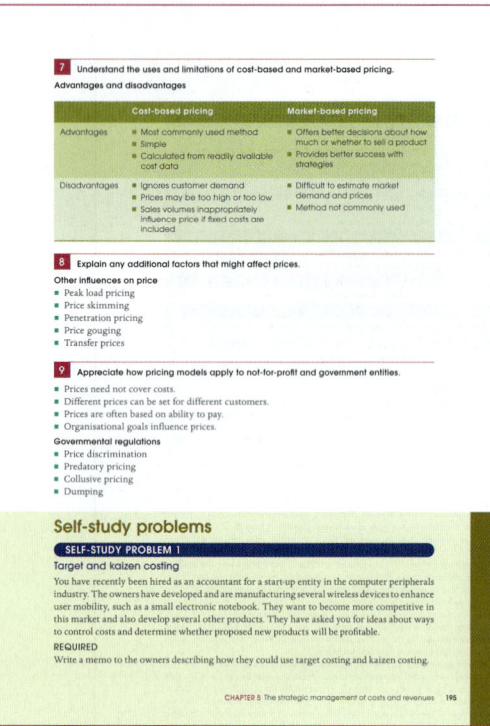

7 Understand the uses and limitations of cost-based and market-based pricing.

Advantages and disadvantages

	Cost-based pricing	Market-based pricing
Advantages	• Most commonly used method • Simple • Calculated from readily available cost data	• Offers better decisions about how much or whether to sell a product • Provides better success with strategies
Disadvantages	• Ignores customer demand • Prices may be too high or too low • Sales volumes inappropriately influence price if fixed costs are included	• Difficult to estimate market demand and prices • Method not commonly used

8 Explain any additional factors that might affect prices.

Other influences on price
• Peak load pricing
• Price skimming
• Penetration pricing
• Price gouging
• Transfer prices

9 Appreciate how pricing models apply to not-for-profit and government entities.

• Prices need not cover costs.
• Different prices can be set for different customers.
• Prices are often based on ability to pay.
• Organisational goals influence prices.

Governmental regulations
• Price discrimination
• Predatory pricing
• Collusive pricing
• Dumping

Self-study problems

SELF-STUDY PROBLEM 1

Target and kaizen costing

You have recently been hired as an accountant for a start-up entity in the computer peripherals industry. The owners have developed and are manufacturing several wireless devices to enhance user mobility, such as a small electronic notebook. They want to become more competitive in this market and also develop several other products. They have asked you for ideas about ways to control costs and determine whether proposed new products will be profitable.

REQUIRED

Write a memo to the owners describing how they could use target costing and kaizen costing.

CHAPTER 5 The strategic management of costs and revenues 195

Solution to self-study problem 1

Many possible approaches may be taken to write a memo on these topics. The body of one possible memo follows. Note that the memo is written to inform and help the managers of the entity make a decision.

You asked for my recommendations about ways to control costs and to determine whether proposed new products will be profitable. In this memo I briefly describe two techniques — target costing and kaizen costing — that could be implemented to achieve these goals.

Target costing. Target costing helps determine whether a proposed new product will be profitable. This technique involves the following steps:
• Estimate the market price of the proposed product.
• Given the market price, determine what the cost must be to achieve our desired profitability.
• Estimate the costs of producing the product. If the estimated cost exceeds the target cost, search for ways to reduce costs. Drop the product idea if it is not feasible to achieve the target cost.
• For potentially feasible new products, conduct pilot production projects to further evaluate estimated costs.

The biggest advantage of target costing is that it would help us focus on ways to design products and manufacturing processes to meet our profitability goals. If costs are too high, we will be forced to look for ways to reduce them, which might also lead us to make changes to the proposed features of a new product.

The target costing process would also help us involve everyone in the organisation in making product decisions and setting cost goals. This involvement would encourage employees to 'buy in' to the target costs, which will help us achieve them.

Kaizen costing. Kaizen costing helps control costs over the life of a product, taking into account the fact that selling prices decline over some product's life. The process for kaizen costing is similar to the process described for target costing. We would estimate the future selling prices of our existing products and determine the cost we need to achieve for our desired profit.

Kaizen costing would help us make decisions about products we wish to continue. If we cannot find ways to reduce costs to achieve desired profitability, then we should consider dropping it.

Risks. I believe that both of these methods would help us meet our goals. However, you should be aware of three major risks:
• Both methods involve a great deal of estimation for prices and costs. The rapid change in our industry presents a high risk of errors in our estimates that might prevent us from achieving our profitability goals.
• Teams of personnel from marketing, engineering, production and accounting would be needed for implementation. It will be critical for everyone to work toward

196 Contemporary Management Accounting

Self-study problems

Each chapter provides one or two self-study problems that address the most important content introduced in the chapter and are similar to the end-of-chapter exercises. Each self-study problem is accompanied by a solution that guides students through the calculations and thinking processes.

Exercises

Exercises focus primarily on ensuring that students learn to properly apply cost accounting methods.

(c) The price for economy grade feed can be computed in two steps:

$$\text{Elasticity of demand} = -\ln(1 - 0.40) \div \ln(1 + 0.10) = -5.36$$

$$\text{Profit-maximising price} = [-5.36 \div (-5.36 + 1)] \times \$10 = \$12.30$$

(d) The price in part (c) is only a guideline for pricing. The elasticity formulas are sensitive to error, so the profit-maximising prices are used only as guidelines. Torquay Produce Suppliers could reduce the price of economy grade feed slowly and see how volumes and profits change.

(e) (i) The relevant cost of filling the special order is the variable cost, which in this problem is the cost of materials: $10 per tonne × 200 tonnes = $2000.
(ii) Under the general quantitative decision rule for special orders, the minimum acceptable price is the variable cost. The minimum acceptable price would be $10 per tonne.

Questions

5.1 What is a just-in-time manufacturing system? Why would organisations choose to adopt it?
5.2 Explain the similarities and differences among target costing, kaizen costing and life cycle costing.
5.3 Identify three products for which target costing and kaizen costing could be used. Identify three products for which target costing and kaizen costing would be inappropriate.
5.4 Describe the four types of quality-related activities.
5.5 Explain the target costing cycle, and discuss the decision criteria used to determine whether a product will be manufactured using a target costing approach.
5.6 Explain cost-based pricing and give an example that shows how prices would be determined using this method.
5.7 Explain market-based pricing and explain where managers and accountants can find information that would help them set prices using this type of approach.
5.8 Supply chain analysis focuses particularly on one aspect of value chain analysis. Explain how supply chain analysis is performed and how it relates to value chain analysis.
5.9 List some common advantages and disadvantages for target and kaizen costing.
5.10 If fixed costs are included in the marked-up costs used in setting cost-based prices, a problem may occur when demand declines. Describe this problem.
5.11 Explain why not-for-profit entities do not always set prices so that their operating costs are recovered.

Exercises

5.12 Categorising quality activities Following is a list of quality-related activities.

QUALITY ACTIVITY
(a) Inspection of units when they are 100 per cent complete to remove defective units
(b) Designing a process with as few parts as possible to reduce the chance of defects
(c) Warranty costs for defective products returned to the factory for rework
(d) Reworking spoiled units before they leave the factory
(e) Costs to defend the entity against lawsuits for damages caused by defective products
(f) Tracking number of defects for each manufacturing team and posting daily defect rates on a plant-wide bulletin board

198 Contemporary Management Accounting

(g) Redesigning a manufacturing process to lower the rate of defects

REQUIRED
Mark each activity according to whether it pertains to the internal cost of prevention (P), appraisal (A), internal (I), or external (E) costs

5.13 Market-based price (elasticity formula) Lickety Split sells ice cream cones in a variety of flavours. Data for a recent week appear here:

Revenue (1000 cones @ $1.75 per cone)		$1750
Cost of ingredients	$640	
Rent	500	
Store attendant	600	1740
Pre-tax profit		$ 10

The manager estimates that if she were to increase the price of cones from $1.75 to $1.93 each, weekly volume would be cut to 850 cones due to competition from other nearby ice cream shops.

REQUIRED
Estimate the profit-maximising price per cone.

5.14 Market-based prices (elasticity formula) Arnie's Flowers is a small Mt Macedon florist shop. Arnie sells flowers for bouquets, and she also prepares and delivers flower arrangements.

REQUIRED
(a) Arnie is trying to decide how much to charge for a new type of rose that wholesales for $0.40 per bud. She ran a special on a similar rose last month and discovered that a 20 per cent discount on the usual price increased sales by about 35 per cent. What would you suggest as a starting price for the rose? Explain.
(b) Arnie has been wondering whether she has been charging the right prices on some of her specialty bouquets. She has been using a mark-up for all specialty items of 200 per cent (that is, she charges three times wholesale cost). Arnie estimates that a 10 per cent increase in price on such items would decrease her unit sales by about 12 per cent. Perform calculations to estimate a profit-maximising mark-up. Based on your calculation, do you think she should increase or decrease her mark-up? Explain.

5.15 JIT production Big Bertram uses the just-in-time method to manufacture golf clubs. The manufacturing schedule for the clubs is developed as customers place orders. Each club is made within a cell where five workers have production stations. The raw materials are delivered to the cell as needed. Each worker in the cell performs one step in the manufacturing process and then inspects the club before giving it to the next person. When a club is finished, it is set on a finished goods rack, which is sent to the packaging department at regular intervals.

REQUIRED
(a) What do we call a manufacturing system such as the one used by Big Bertram?
(b) Describe general advantages of this type of system.
(c) The supplier that manufactures the weights that are inserted in each club head would like to monitor Big Bertram's inventory levels through the Internet so that its new software program could release deliveries at appropriate times. List qualitative factors that might affect Big Bertram's decision about this proposal.

5.16 Quality costs using ABC versus traditional costing New-Rage Cosmetics uses a traditional cost accounting system to allocate quality control costs uniformly to all products at a rate of 14.5 per cent of direct labour cost. Monthly direct labour cost for Satin Sheen

CHAPTER 5 The strategic management of costs and revenues 199

Questions

Questions provide an opportunity to test student understanding of the concepts presented in the chapter and encourage considered comment. The questions will provide students with practice in using the terminology and cost accounting techniques learned in the chapter.

Inset textbook page (left)

(c) List qualitative factors that might be relevant to Blade Runner's managers as they decide on any product or process changes. List as many factors as you can.

(d) For each of the planned cost reductions, discuss uncertainties about whether the entity will achieve the planned cost reduction.

Problems

5.23 Cost reduction; JIT; value chain analysis Budget Cupboards produces kitchen and bathroom cupboards that incorporate unusual functions (such as specialty drawers for knives and kitchen tools) and kitchen appliance holders that pop up from under the countertop. Competition in this industry has recently increased. Budget's management wants to cut costs for its basic cupboard models and then cut prices.

REQUIRED

(a) The following table lists potential areas for cost reduction. Two potential cost reductions are provided for the first area listed (design phase). For each of the remaining areas, identify two potential ways that Budget Cupboard's management could reduce costs.

Potential area for cost reduction	Potential cost reductions	
	(i)	(ii)
Example: Design phase	Work with suppliers to reduce direct materials costs	Redesign cupboards to use fewer parts
Manufacturing process		
Administration		
Changes in quality or functionality		

(b) Budget Cupboards does not currently use just-in-time production or value chain analysis. Describe several advantages of using these methods when price competition increases.

5.24 Target and kaizen costing; uncertainties; manager incentives Suppose you are having a conversation with Sandy, another student in this course. Sandy is confused about the differences and similarities between target costing and kaizen costing.

Another student, Kevin, overhears your conversation with Sandy and insists that neither of these methods is beneficial. Kevin argues that some entities run into financial problems using these methods because their managers manipulated the cost estimates to appear however they wanted. If the managers wanted to launch a new product or keep an old one, they made sure their cost estimates supported their decision.

REQUIRED

(a) In your own words, explain how target costing and kaizen costing are the same and how they are different.

(b) Compare the information needed to apply the target costing and kaizen costing methods.
  (i) List the types of relevant information needed for each method.
  (ii) List the uncertainties in the relevant information for each method.

(c) Discuss ways in which managers might be able to create biased estimates under a target or kaizen costing system.

CHAPTER 5 The strategic management of costs and revenues **203**

Problems

These activities build upon students' established knowledge of the topic and encourage them to evaluate, calculate, compare and interpret a range of scenarios in which management accounting information is used by managers.

Articles

An end-of-book appendix contains a number of relevant and interesting articles that accompany every chapter in the text. The articles will enhance student understanding of management accounting concepts and procedures while introducing key information (taken from magazines and other media sources) associated with each topic.

Inset article page

CHAPTER 1

Slave to the supply chain

Conflicting supply chain models are exerting an undue influence on some business sectors.

Just when business thinks it's got it all worked out, markets go and change. The supply chain initiatives of the past decade, which used information technology and managerial techniques to transform, or re-engineer, companies are being re-thought. Changes at the customer end are making distribution strategies more problematic.

Except, perhaps, in Australia. Of the country's two big supermarket chains, Woolworths' imitation of United States retail giant Wal-Mart has proven more successful than Coles Myer's strategy, which is more an emulation of British retailers. But their supply chain strategies have not only determined their companies' fates, they have also made the environment for suppliers onerous. Most suppliers are being asked to deliver with greater frequency, in effect taking on the retailers' inventory costs. They have little control over volumes, and are being asked to adhere to strict protocols. No negotiations are available.

This produces a heavy emphasis on taking costs from existing practices, rather than system-wide innovation. Associate professor Bryan Lukas, head of the marketing and management department at the University of Melbourne, says the main retailers have been 'tightening the screws' on their suppliers. This, he says, is the opposite philosophy to that applied by car manufacturer Toyota, widely accepted as the best exponent of production efficiency and innovation in the world.

'Toyota offers land to suppliers on favourable conditions. The suppliers see Toyota as an extension of their livelihood, and are willing to give ideas and suggestions [about improving the system]. In Australia, the relationships are short-term and hard-nosed. If you have a good idea, why would you give it to them when you are going to be screwed anyway?'

The cost savings can be sizeable. According to John Lydon, a principal and supply chain specialist for consultants McKinsey & Co, consumer products companies have taken about 20 per cent of costs out of their supply chains in the past five years. By contrast, the mining and energy sectors have made few gains, despite having about a third of their cost base in the supply chain. '[The mining companies] are not involved in shipping and that has led to great supply inefficiencies,' he says.

But a supply chain battle based on squeezing suppliers is likely to be an endeavour with declining utility. Savings inevitably become more difficult to achieve unless there is innovation across the whole system. One response is to move into other industries. Mark Reynolds, senior practice manager for consulting firm Accenture, says Woolworths is becoming a de facto trucking company for suppliers, doing frequent deliveries from the factory gate.

Coles Myer takes another approach, sending one truck a week with one load. 'Coles Myer is doing a milk run. It is wildly successful. It is taking a bottom-up approach, and Woolworths, a top-down approach. They are simply managing the fleet. The big trend is to go to the factory gate, but only Coles and Woolworths have the scale to do that.'

Australia is well behind what is happening internationally, mainly because of the heavy concentration of the industry base. Greg Cudahy, Accenture's global head of supply chain practice, says companies are using multiple supply chains more often, depending on the customer. In some instances, even deliberate scarcity is created. Cudahy cites the example of a Streets ice cream that was deliberately released in volumes fixed so it would run out. 'You have "stock outs" with intent. There is a scarcity benefit to only having a limited number.'

The problem is increased complexity in customer behaviour. Lukas says the supply chain 'is the last frontier of marketing, without a doubt'. John Gattorna, author of Living Supply Chains

and an academic at the Macquarie Graduate School of Management, says markets are fragmenting. 'It is causing some confusion among suppliers that now have to think deeply about which combination of products, sales channels, pricing and physical fulfilment to use. Some companies are going in the opposite direction and trying to make their businesses easier to manage by seeking to standardise processes, technology and channels. All of which just leads eventually to more exceptions, and therefore, higher costs-to-serve.'

The solution is to segment the market for a product or service along 'behavioural lines', Gattorna says. 'Human behaviour is not as chaotic as first thought. There are never more than three or four really dominant types of buying behaviour in the market for any product or service category. There might be up to 16 or so variants, but never more than three or four at a time.'

Gattorna says one type of behaviour, 'continuous replenishment', is where the customer seeks a trusting relationship. Price is not as important as being predictable and regular. The main requirement is to stay close to the customer and to share forecasts. Margins are usually high and customer retention paramount.

A second type, 'lean supply', where the emphasis is on consistent lowest-price products delivered regularly to schedule, are something different. There is no consideration of brand or a relationship. The imperative is to make accurate forecasts of demand that bring the benefits of scale, and other synergies.

Agile supply chains are a third type. 'We are being besieged by a new breed of very demanding customer who turns up unannounced and wants the world, and very quickly,' Gattorna says. 'They don't have any loyalties other than to themselves because they want instant gratification, and they put a lot of pressure on the supplier to get their way. These customers can be managed, but you can't let them intimidate you.'

He says in this case it is necessary to build in additional capacity which may at times be standing idle, an additional cost. 'You therefore have to charge more to get a fair return on investment and maintain margins. Fashion fits very well into this type of supply chain.'

The fourth type of supply chain is the 'fully flexible' system. 'This is where customers find themselves with major problems of a pressing nature, and they look to the supplier to lead with innovative solutions. Price is not an issue.'

Gattorna says designing and operating all four supply chains requires developing four combinations of 'organisational structures, processes, key performance indicators, internal communications, training programs, and, above all, the same number of leadership styles.' He says some of the sub-cultures have difficulty co-existing because they are opposites.

'Therein lies the challenge. It all boils down to the ability of companies to mirror on the inside of the company what they see on the outside in the marketplace — the biggest rewards going to those finding practical ways to do this. Only a few have achieved this to date: Zara, the Spanish fashion retailer and manufacturer; Li & Fung, the Hong Kong supply chain management company; and the Foster's Group, which is starting to implement this type of strategy.'
Source: James, D 2006, BRW, 5 October, p. 52.

CHAPTER 2

Tell bean counters your variable is fixed

It's early summer, and it's just about time to devise your strategy for the annual marketing budget ritual. That means planning for next year and perhaps struggling to find spending givebacks this year so the corporate brass can make their third- and fourth-quarter numbers.

Budgeting is a numbing numbers game, with long hours squinting at a monitor tweaking spreadsheets building in hidden fat you can give back later without hurting your program. But

Acknowledgements

We would like to thank our families for their support and encouragement throughout the writing of the text. We would also like to thank the team at Wiley including Darren Taylor for his faith and support and Morag Kobez-Halvorson for her editorial work, cooperative spirit and just being a star. Thank you also to Marie and Trevor for their hospitality in the early phases of this project. Finally, we thank our students who have continually challenged us and contributed to our own development as educators.

The authors and publisher would like to thank the following copyright holders, organisations and individuals for permission to reproduce copyright material in this book.

Images

• Newspix: **pp. 3**/Bob Finlayson; **165**/Adam Smith; **305, 308**/Brett Hartwig; **447**/Heath Missen; **607**/Brad Newman • Photodisc: **pp. 27, 35, 42, 50, 73, 84, 221, 251, 303, 355, 487, 502, 571, 573, 575, 581, 585, 589, 612, 615** • Corbis Australia: **p. 81**/Mia Song; **p. 672**/Richard T Nowitz • Photolibrary/Science Photo Library: **pp. 87, 91, 93, 97** • © Purestock: **pp. 125, 363** • © Creatas: **p. 144** • Getty Images: **pp. 169**/AFP/Yoshikazu Tsuno; **171**/Time Life Pictures/ Zeva Oelbaum; **211**/Toshifumi Kitamura; **323**/Jose Azel; **393; 456, 459, 461, 468**/Stone/David Joel; **664**/Bay Ismoyo • AAP Image: **pp. 177, 181, 256, 262, 267, 271**/AP Photo/Wally Santana; **531**/Steve Thurlow • © Digital Stock/Corbis Corporation: **pp. 188, 300, 623, 651, 668** • © John Wiley & Sons Australia/Taken by Kari Ann Tapp: **p. 297** • © Corbis: **pp. 318, 319**/Robert Pickett; **pp. 534, 540, 545**/© Erika Koch/zefa • Image Disk Photography: **pp. 411, 412, 415, 416, 418** • © Copyright Clearance Centre: **p. 496** (top) • © University California San Francisco Campus Life Services Strategy Map 2006–07 http://cas.ucsf.edu/balancedscorecard/pdfs/ CLSStrategyMap2K6V5.0.pdf: **p. 498** • © Digital Vision: **pp. 565, 659** • © Visy Recycling: **p. 647** • © Environment Protection Authority, Victoria 2007: **p. 670** • © EyeWire Images: **p. 678** • © WME Magazine: **p. 775** (top).

Text

• John Wiley & Sons Australia, *Accounting: business reporting for decision making*, Jacqueline Birt et al., p. 50, ISBN 0470804734: **pp. 119–20** • Kaplan, Robert S, Atkinson, Anthony A, *Advanced Management Accounting*, 3rd edition, © 1998, pp. 120, 121, 122. Reprinted by permission of Pearson Education, Inc., Upper Saddle River, NJ: **pp. 132–5** • © Medicare Australia Health Insurance Commission Annual Report 2002/03, p. 10: **pp. 496–7** • © ICAA Table 3: Reasons for increased CSR, appears on page 10 of the Institute's publication *Extended Performance Reporting: A review of Empirical Studies*: **p. 655** • © Australian Securities Exchange Limited ABN 98008624691 (ASX) 2006. All rights reserved. This material is reproduced with the permission of ASX: **pp. 656, 657** • Table: Dow Jones Sustainability Indexes, Supersector Leaders 2006/07 © SAM Group Holding AG www.Sustainability-indexes.com: **p. 658** • BHP Billiton Limited: **p. 659**/ © BHP Billiton Limited, www.bhpbilliton.com, May 2004; **694–7**/Reprinted by permission of BHP Billiton Corporate Sustainability Assessment Results — SAM Benchmarking Report • Sustainability Reporting Guidelines. Version 3.0. October 2006. Stichting Global Reporting Initiative. Amsterdam, The Netherlands. www.globalreporting.org: **pp. 660–3** • © John Wiley & Sons UK: **pp. 666, 677**/'The sustainability balanced scorecard', *Business strategy & environment*, pp. 277, 278, F Figge, T Hahn, S Schaltegger & M Wagner. Reproduced with permission • © Australian Academy of Science/Nova http://www.science.org.au/ nova/034/034key.htm: **p. 672** • This article was published in 'The use of environmental management accounting (EMA) for identifying environmental costs', Christine Jasch, *Journal of Cleaner Productions*, 11, p. 674: **pp. 673–4** • © Environment Victoria Table 4.0 taken from the Environment Victoria report, 'Supermarket bag packing: a comparative time trial', Feb. 2007, p. 6: **p. 686** • Journalists Copyright: **pp. 702–3**/'Slave to the supply chain', David James, *BRW*, 05/10/06 http://global.factiva.com.ezp01.library.qut.edu.au/aa/default.aspx?pp=Print&hc=Publication; **750–2**/'Everyone gets a share', Emily Ross, *BRW*, 19/01/06 • Reprinted with permission, published by the American Marketing Association, 'Tell bean counters your variable is fixed', Bob Donath, *Marketing News*. p. 14, 19 June 2000: **pp. 703–4** • © Copyright Clearance Centre: **pp. 705–10**/'Distinguishing between direct and indirect costs is crucial for internet companies', Lawrence A Gordon & Martin P Loeb; **710–20**/'Using activity-based costing to assess channel/customer profitability', by DeWayne L Searcy, in *Management Accounting Quarterly*, Winter 2004, vol. 5; **721–7**/*Management Accounting Quarterly* by Dan Swenson, Shahid Ansari, Jan Bell & Il-Woon Kim, Winter 2003, vol. 4, no. 2, pp. 12–17; **728–33**/'Who needs budgets? You do', Penelope S Greenberg & Ralph H Greenberg, *Strategic Finance*, August 2006, pp. 41–5, accessed via online database; **733–9**; **740–3**/'Tie your capital to your strategic plan', HR Migliore & DE McCracken, *Strategic Finance*, June 2001, vol. 82 issue 12, p. 38, from online database; **743–50**/'Standard costing is alive and well at Parker Brass', *Management Accounting Quarterly*, Winter 2000, pp. 1–9; **753–6**/'The balanced scorecard at Philips Electronics', A Gumbus & B Lyons, *Strategic Finance*, November 2002; **757–61**/'RFID: The changes it will bring', Ariel Markelevich & Ronald Bell, *Strategic Finance*. Montvale: August 2006, vol. 88, issue 2, p. 46; **767–75**/'Making better decisions', T Corbett, *CMA Management*, November 1999, accessed via online database • 'Low cost, high hopes', TS Sakran, *Fortune*, 8 July 2006, vol. 154, issue 3, pp. 14–15, © 2006 Cable News Network LP, A Time Warner Company. All rights reserved: **pp. 727–8** • © John Wiley & Sons, Inc.: **pp. 761–7**/'From mass production to mass customization: postponement of inventory differentiation', from the *Journal of Corporate Accounting & Finance*, 2005, pages 61–65. GA Graman & DM Bukovinsky 2005. Reprinted with permission of John Wiley & Sons Inc. • 'Resource efficiency audit: the baseline vs the bottomline', *WME Magazine*, September 2006, pp. 27–30: **pp. 775–80**

Every effort has been made to trace ownership of copyright material. Information that will help to rectify any error or omission in subsequent editions will be welcome. In such cases, please contact the Permissions Section of John Wiley & Sons Australia, Ltd who will arrange for the payment of the usual fee.

The role of accounting information in management decision making

IN BRIEF

Managers use cost and management accounting information to help them make different types of decisions. These include developing organisational strategies, creating operating plans, and monitoring and motivating organisational performance. Higher-quality decisions are achieved by using higher-quality relevant information and decision-making practices. The value chain provides us with a suitable framework from which to explore a range of management decisions as well as providing a suitable framework for many of the issues raised in the remainder of the text.

After studying this chapter, you should be able to:

1 Describe the types of decisions managers make for an organisation.

2 Outline the role of cost and management accounting information in management decision making.

3 Explain how managers can make higher-quality decisions using accounting information.

4 Explain the value chain framework and its applications in management accounting.

aussieBum: if you doubt yourself, wear something else

Australian fashion designer Sean Ashby commenced his men's swimwear and clothing business aussieBum five years ago. A keen swimmer and surfer, he was unable to find a good pair of men's cossies and used his life savings of $20 000 to make a series of prototypes, buy materials and commence manufacturing in Australia. Despite rejection from local retailers who did not see the potential for aussieBum to compete with international brands, Ashby has proven critics wrong. He had no choice but to take his business online, with instant exposure to the international markets. They are now taking thousands of orders a day.

Since the company's inception, Ashby says that aussieBum has 'taken on its own little cult revolution', with celebrities such as Ewan McGregor, Billy Connolly and David Beckham fans of the aussieBum brand. Even Kylie Minogue sported men in aussieBum cossies on the film clip for her song 'Slow'. The marketing thrust behind Ashby's aussieBum is to live the dream — 'the dream to be independent and present our gear in a way that gets noticed. We don't apologise for pushing the boundaries … We have a saying at aussieBum — If you doubt yourself, wear something else'.[1]

The company has doubled in size every year over the past five years and continues to grow by 20 per cent every quarter. In 2005, aussieBum earned more than $5 million in sales and carried no debt. Currently, 90 per cent of aussieBum's sales are to international customers. The aussieBum brand now takes pride of place in stores such as Selfridges in the UK; Brown Thomas in Ireland; La Maison Stores in Canada; Alpha Male in Melrose Drive, Los Angeles; KaDeWa in Germany; as well as others in Spain, The Netherlands, Sweden, Poland and Russia. As well as direct department store sales, aussieBum's Internet retail orders are booming, with aussieBum being distributed to more than 70 countries. In fact, it is the Internet sales that management really wants to push. This further enables aussieBum to deal directly with its customers. The export performance of aussieBum is all the more impressive given that the level of trade export in clothing manufacturing is low and showing a downward trend.

Most of the raw materials are sourced from Italy and China. And by manufacturing in Australia, aussieBum hopes to promote Australia's culture and relaxed lifestyle as well as eliminate restrictions that might come with outsourcing production to other countries. Moreover, producing locally (through independent manufacturers) provides flexibility and a reduced timeframe in getting new products to market. With a heavy emphasis on innovative product design, aussieBum pays close attention to the design phase of the product process.

Sources: Information from AusIndustry 2005, *Aussie cossies kick butt overseas*, AusIndustry success story, Department of Industry, Tourism and Resources, www.ausindustry.gov.au; IBISWorld 2006, *Clothing manufacturing in Australia*, IBISWorld industry report, 11 December; Pascuzzi, C 2006, 'Today aussieBum, tomorrow the world', Mediasearch Music Film & Fashion in Australia, www.mediasearch.com.au; Spicer, R 2006, 'Developing your exports', *Dynamic Business Magazine*, September 2006, www.dynamicexport.com.au.

Issues from this scene setter to look for in the chapter include:

■ How management might make decisions.

■ The accounting information used in making decisions about matters such as pricing and production levels.

■ Where entities should focus their attention across the entire design/production/ distribution (value chain) processes.

■ Key factors driving organisational costs.

Management decision making

People at different levels within an entity continuously make many different kinds of decisions. These range from broad decisions, such as the markets pursued by the organisation, to detailed decisions, such as how to respond to a customer on the telephone. Figure 1.1 presents an overview of the decisions that managers make in organisations. It also suggests the role that information systems have in measuring, monitoring and motivating performance. We will briefly discuss each of the components illustrated in figure 1.1.

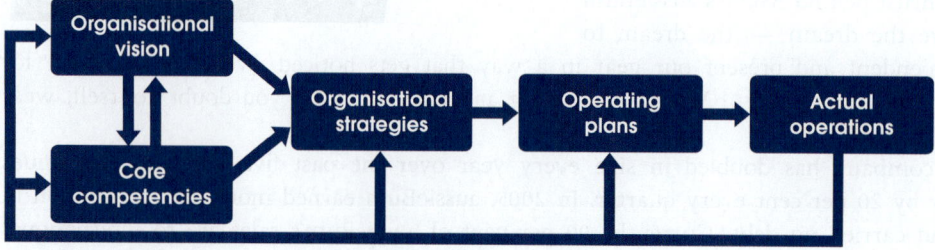

Measure, monitor and motivate

FIGURE 1.1 ■ Overview of management decision making

Organisational vision

The most far-reaching decision managers make is to identify and shape the organisation's vision. The **organisational vision** is the core purpose and ideology of the entity, which guides the entity's overall direction and approaches toward its various stakeholder groups. Stakeholder groups include: shareholders/owners, employees, customers and suppliers, lenders, local communities and the broader society. Organisational success increases when employees understand the organisational vision and work collectively to achieve it. To clarify and communicate the vision to employees and other stakeholders, managers sometimes divide the vision into one or more written statements. The definitions of these statements vary from entity to entity. In general, a vision statement is a theoretical description of what the organisation should become. A mission statement is a high-level declaration of the organisation's purpose. A core values statement is a summary of the beliefs that define the organisation's culture. Some managers also publish codes of conduct or statements describing the organisation's social or environmental responsibilities.

Organisational core competencies

Organisational core competencies are the entity's strengths relative to competitors. The organisational vision and core competencies are closely related. To create value for stakeholders, an organisation must have strengths relative to competitors. The vision should build on existing and achievable strengths.

Organisational strategies

Organisational strategies are the tactics that managers use to take advantage of core competencies while working towards the organisational vision. Although the term **strategies** can mean different things to different people and organisations, it commonly relates to providing direction and guiding long-term decisions. To monitor strategic progress, managers establish and monitor long-term goals such as market leadership or high-quality customer service.

Broad-based organisational strategies are commonly classified as:

- low-cost, where the emphasis is on competing on cost
- product differentiation, where the emphasis is on competing on points of difference such as quality of service or product attributes.

Operating plans

Operating plans involve specific short-term decisions that shape the organisation's day-to-day activities such as drawing cash from a bank line of credit, hiring an employee or ordering materials. Operating plans often include specific performance objectives such as budgeted revenues and costs.

Actual operations

Actual operations are the various actions taken and results achieved over a period of time. Actual operations include customer orders received, revenues earned, number of employees hired, costs incurred, units of goods or services produced, cash received and paid, and so on. Data about actual operations are collected and measured by the organisation's information system and then used to monitor and motivate performance.

Measuring, monitoring and motivating performance

Managers need information to help them make the types of decisions indicated in figure 1.1. For example, managers need information about costs to help them decide whether to sell a particular product or what price to set. They also need information to measure actual operations so that they can monitor the success of their decisions and motivate employees to work towards the organisational vision. Decisions are monitored by comparing actual operating results to plans (such as budgets) and to long-term goals. Desirable employee behaviour is often motivated by tying employee performance evaluation and pay to long-term or short-term results. An organisation's information system can be designed to measure and report information used for decision making as well as for monitoring and motivating.

While organisational information systems will commonly have a number of components, with each focusing on specific support (for example, human resources information, technology information, marketing information, production information and accounting-related information), our focus in this book is on the role of cost and management accounting information.

Cost and management accounting for decision making

Cost accounting information is used for both management and financial accounting activities. The Institute of Management Accountants (IMA) defines **cost accounting** as 'a technique or method for determining the cost of a project, process, or thing'.[2] Cost accounting is commonly regarded as the precursor to the more recently developed term *management accounting*, which has a somewhat broader perspective.

Cost accounting information often serves as an input into broader management accounting and financial accounting systems. In this way, cost accounting is often viewed as a subset of management accounting in particular, and financial accounting to a limited extent. **Management accounting** is the process of gathering, summarising and reporting financial and non-financial information used internally by managers to make decisions. An example of cost accounting information that is also management accounting information is a breakdown of customer service costs by both product line and average cost per customer service call. **Financial accounting** is the process of preparing and reporting financial information used most frequently by decision makers outside of the entity, such as shareholders and creditors. An example of cost accounting information that is also financial accounting information is the valuation of ending inventory shown on the balance sheet.

Managers use many types of information to help them make decisions. Information can be gathered formally or informally. Formal methods include point-of-service optical character readers, such as those used when customers purchase merchandise at retail stores. Such systems track inventory levels, geographic distribution of sales, trends, the relationship between prices and sales, and so on. Informal methods are also important for collecting information from inside or outside the organisation. For example, individuals inside a company often gather product pricing information by reading industry trade journals or examining competitor's websites.

Most organisations have many databases that contain information collected formally or informally from internal or external sources. Access to database information is often restricted to specific individuals. In addition, much valuable information is not readily accessible because it is held in the minds of employees. This information, called *intellectual capital*, is not formally captured by the information system. Thus, it is difficult for decision makers, even within an organisation, to gain access to all of the information they might wish to use. It is easy to argue that managers should obtain more and better information to help them make decisions. However, the benefit must exceed the cost of generating information.

To facilitate internal decision making (often a role for management accounting) and meet external reporting requirements (a key role of financial accounting), accounting departments within organisations use software to generate a variety of internal and external reports that summarise or highlight information. An **internal report** is a document that presents information for use only inside an organisation. An **external report** is a document that presents information predominantly for use outside an organisation. Figure 1.2 summarises common types of internal and external reports.

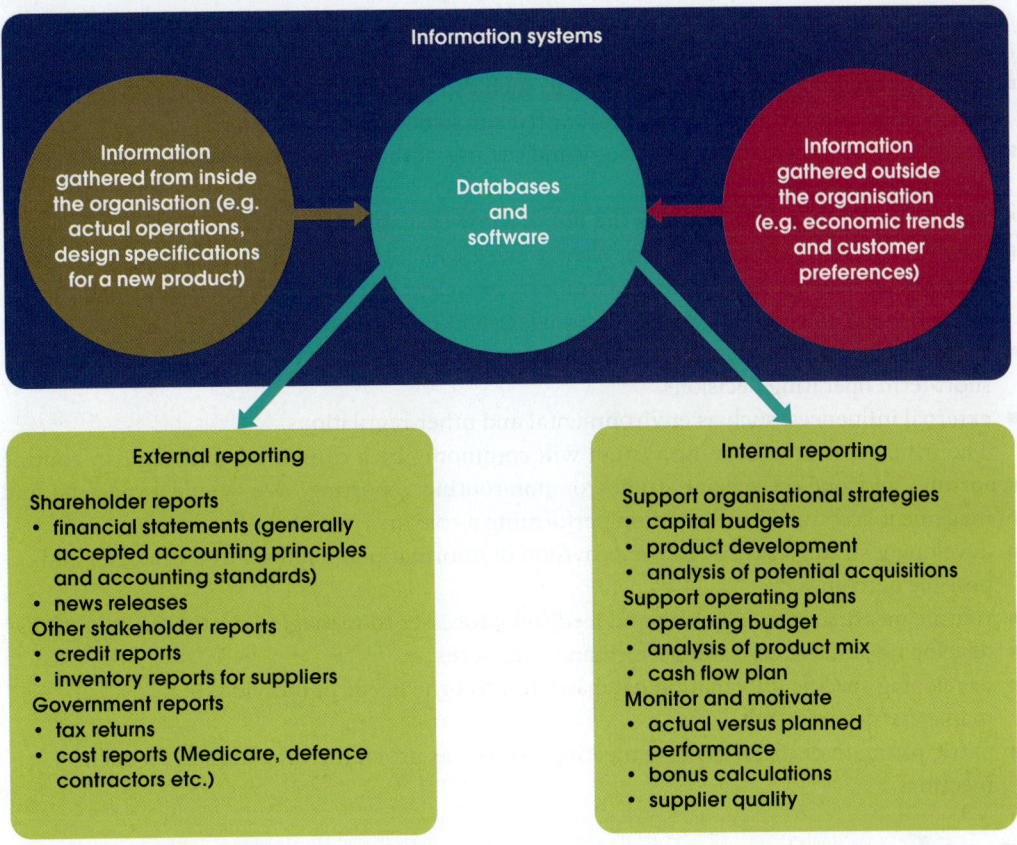

Information systems

Information gathered from inside the organisation (e.g. actual operations, design specifications for a new product)

Databases and software

Information gathered outside the organisation (e.g. economic trends and customer preferences)

External reporting

Shareholder reports
- financial statements (generally accepted accounting principles and accounting standards)
- news releases

Other stakeholder reports
- credit reports
- inventory reports for suppliers

Government reports
- tax returns
- cost reports (Medicare, defence contractors etc.)

Internal reporting

Support organisational strategies
- capital budgets
- product development
- analysis of potential acquisitions

Support operating plans
- operating budget
- analysis of product mix
- cash flow plan

Monitor and motivate
- actual versus planned performance
- bonus calculations
- supplier quality

FIGURE 1.2 ■ Examples of internal and external reports

Internal reports are designed to provide information for a variety of management decisions. Some internal reports, such as monthly sales summaries, are issued regularly. Other internal reports, such as the analysis of a potential business acquisition, are generated for one-time use and commonly serve a special purpose.

External reports can be distributed to different constituencies for many purposes. Some external reports, such as income tax returns, are mandatory. Others are discretionary, such as a news release about a joint venture agreement. Some reports, such as financial statements given to a supplier to obtain credit, facilitate business activities.

Although reports are developed for a specific audience, they may be used for other purposes. For example, internal reports such as quarterly sales data can be shared with people outside the organisation. Similarly, external reports such as financial statements are sometimes used within the organisation. In addition, organisations use reports prepared outside the organisation (for example, by consultants or vendors) for internal decision making.

Key influences on management accounting system structure

Like any system, the management accounting system requires input, processing and output stages. The management accounting system is likely to be linked to the financial accounting system (as outlined earlier) but will commonly also have its own domain and reporting mechanisms to meet the needs of managers. While any management accounting system will comprise a number of components (such as costing, performance measurement and evaluation, and budgeting), some of the key influences on the nature of the management accounting system might include:

- organisational structure, which relates to such things as the level of centralisation versus decentralisation and how hierarchical or flat the structure is
- availability of information technology and the use of that technology as part of the information system interface
- organisational strategies, such as the use of a low-cost strategy or differentiation strategy
- how the management accounting role is viewed *within* the organisation, which relates to whether management accounting assumes a proactive or reactive role, an information-provider-only role or an information-provider-and-decision-maker role
- types of decisions managers are confronted with, such as long-term strategic decisions and short-term operating decisions
- external influences, such as environmental and other regulations.

The management accounting system will commonly be a combination of regular, routine reporting; and one-off special studies or non-routine reporting. We would expect to find management accounting information performing a role in:

- developing strategies through the provision of information on alternative strategies and possible outcomes
- routine measuring, monitoring and feedback processes to managers relating to operations
- developing suitable cost and performance measures
- developing specific information databases to meet the needs of individual managers/departments
- participating in decision-making meetings as well as providing information for such meetings.

Cost and management accounting, yesterday and tomorrow

Cost accounting techniques date back to the industrial revolution and became popular in the early 1800s. As organisation size increased, the need for measuring, monitoring and motivating performance grew. By the mid 1800s, cost accounting practices were well developed. For example, in the United States, railroad accountants calculated the cost per ton-mile and operating expenses per dollar of revenue. One of the earliest detailed costing systems was developed for the steel mills of Andrew Carnegie (US steel manufacturer and philosopher), for which material and labour cost information was produced on a daily basis. Then, in the early 1900s, organisations were required to provide external reports such as financial statements and tax returns. Because the cost of keeping two sets of books for separate information requirements was relatively high, cost accounting focused primarily on information for income tax returns and financial statements.

From the early 1900s until the mid 1970s, cost accounting practices changed very little. However, as the business environment became more global, competition increased. In turn, demand grew for more sophisticated cost accounting information, and terms such as *management accounting* were used to encapsulate the range of activities now undertaken. Recent technological innovation has enabled cost accountants to develop previously infeasible cost and management accounting systems. Today, cost and accounting information is used for a variety of purposes, including internal decision making, measuring and monitoring performance at all levels, and aligning employee and stakeholder goals. Furthermore, managers now use cost accounting information to analyse the profitability of customers and to coordinate transactions with suppliers — extending traditional cost accounting beyond the walls of the entity.

As organisations continue to change and adapt to their environment, management accounting will similarly need to adapt to the changing organisational environment. This is critical if management accounting as a function, and management accountants as professionals, are to continue to add value to their organisations. Throughout this book, we explore a range of management accounting techniques, tools and practices relevant to organisations. Some of these techniques, tools and practices have been around for a long time (such as standard costing, cost–volume–profit analysis and capital budgeting), while others are more recent developments (such as the balanced scorecard, activity-based costing and sustainability management accounting). Further developments in management accounting tools will undoubtedly surface. Ultimately, the challenge for management accountants and the management accounting function is to ensure that the organisational decision-making needs are appropriately matched with the available management techniques, tools and practices.

The detail and quality of organisational data have improved in recent years. Historically, organisations used one accounting system that gathered information for financial statements. These data, prepared using generally accepted accounting principles (GAAP), were used for both external and internal reporting. This type of information was not always ideal for management decision making. As a result, resources were often poorly allocated, leading to operating and investment inefficiencies.

Recent information system developments have focused on business intelligence (BI). The internet and BI software provide opportunities for managers to save costs and improve profitability in the following ways:
- integrating systems:
  - throughout an organisation
  - between an organisation and its customers and suppliers
- improving management of:
  - customer relationships
  - supply chains
  - work teams within an organisation.

We should make some distinction between management accountants as professionals within organisations and the management accounting function. Most organisations will have a management accounting function in one form or another. In some organisations, this function might be performed by a variety of differently qualified and trained staff such as accountants (financial or management), costing clerks, engineers, and other staff with management training or experience. In some cases, the label *management accountant* might not even be used, but the management accounting work is still performed as a function. More often, though, the label *management accountant*, or some similar label such as *resource analyst* or *internal management consultant*, would be used. Whatever the terminology adopted, the management accounting function needs to be performed. Much of this book relates to the techniques, tools and practices that commonly comprise the management accounting function.

Relevant information for decision making

A key focus of management accounting is the provision of information for decision making. This requires the ability to distinguish between information that is relevant to a decision and information that is not. **Relevant information** helps the decision maker to evaluate and choose among alternative courses of action. Relevant information concerns the future and varies with the action taken. On the other hand, **irrelevant information** does not vary with the action taken and therefore is not useful for decision making. Although the information may be accurate, it simply does not help the decision maker evaluate the alternatives. Managers are less efficient and make lower-quality decisions when they allow irrelevant information to inappropriately influence their choices.

Whether a given type of information is relevant or irrelevant depends on the decision and other factors. Suppose a student is deciding whether to sign up for a particular university course. If the student has selected a degree program and wishes to graduate as quickly as possible, relevant information includes whether the course counts towards graduation. However, if the student's goal is to take courses in a variety of disciplines to explore possible degree programs, then it might be irrelevant whether the course will help meet graduation requirements.

Throughout the book, we will encounter a range of different types of decisions that require the identification of relevant information. For example, the concept of relevant costs is explored in a decision context in chapter 8, while the use of relevant cash flows is explored in chapter 9. Identifying relevant information is a useful skill that requires practice, and we will work on developing this skill throughout this textbook. We will also encounter different treatments of cost data in decision-making contexts. This is often referred to as *different cost for different purposes*, meaning the decision at hand and the nature of the cost object determine the cost data required and how such data might be used.

Management accounting information and the quality of decision making

Management accounting information is commonly used in decision-making, and this raises two issues: (1) the quality and relevance of the management accounting information; and (2) the quality of the decision-making processes in use within the organisation. Higher-quality decisions result from better information as well as from better decision processes. Organisations often use complex and sophisticated information systems to gather and organise information for decision making. Because of this sophistication, some decision makers are mistakenly confident that the information they use is correct, and they ignore uncertainty. Other decision makers, recognising that uncertainties always cloud decisions, go to the other extreme: instead of relying on imperfect information, they use only their intuition to make important business decisions. Neither of these approaches is optimal. Figure 1.3 summarises the path to higher-quality decisions.

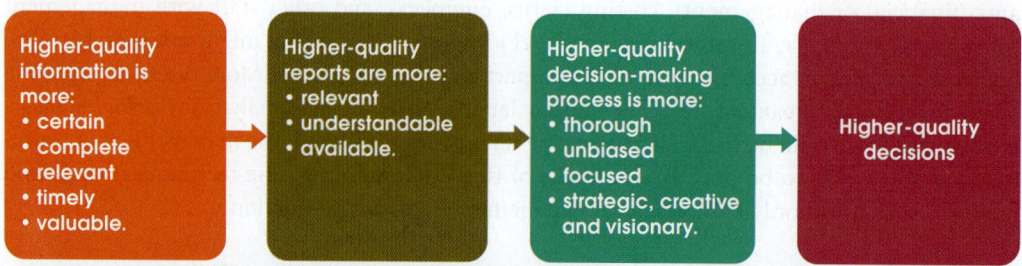

FIGURE 1.3 ■ Path to higher-quality management decisions

Higher-quality information will generally have fewer uncertainties if it is based on viable assumptions. Nonetheless, it is still imperfect and may be in various forms, including financial and non-financial information. It should be complete, timely and directly relevant to the decision. Two issues are worthy of specific mention here.

First, decision-useful information needs to have considered the impact of any opportunity costs on the decision. **Opportunity costs** are the benefits forgone when we choose one alternative over the next best alternative. Although such costs might be more difficult to quantify, they still need to be considered when evaluating alternative courses of action.

Second, the benefits derived from the information collected to support the decision-making process need to exceed the cost of collection. (The evaluation of such costs and benefits is commonly referred to as **cost–benefit analysis**.) This is particularly important when trying to make the information systems more complex say (for example, in order to improve the reliability of product cost data). The extra precision derived from the increased complexity needs to warrant the cost of changes to the system.

Value chain analysis: a framework for management accounting

In the mid 1980s, Harvard Professor Michael Porter introduced the idea of the generic **value chain**. A value chain can be described as the key activities engaged in by the organisation or industry. We can view the value chain on two levels: at the industry level, and at the (more common) organisational level.

At the industry level, the value chain comprises the key industry components based on the key activities within the industry. Figure 1.4 shows a sample industry-based value chain for the wine industry. Particular entities may choose to participate in the entire industry, in only part of the industry (say, as a vineyard operator such as competitor B), or across most of the value chain (which would make it a vertically integrated entity such as competitor A).

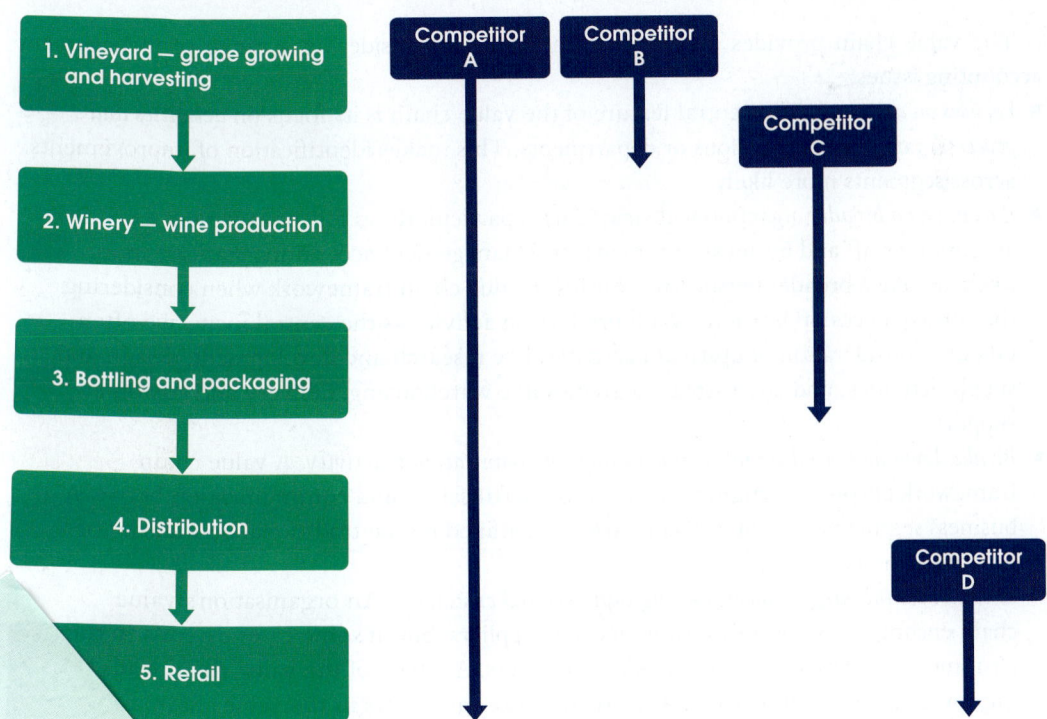

▼ Sample industry-based value chain for the wine industry

Adapted from Shank and Govindarajan 1992, 'Strategic cost management and the value chain', *Journal of Cost Management*, pp. 5–21.

The value chain at the organisational level is the more common view of the value chain. The organisational value chain is usually viewed as a combination of key and support activities. Figure 1.5 provides a sample value chain showing the key components.

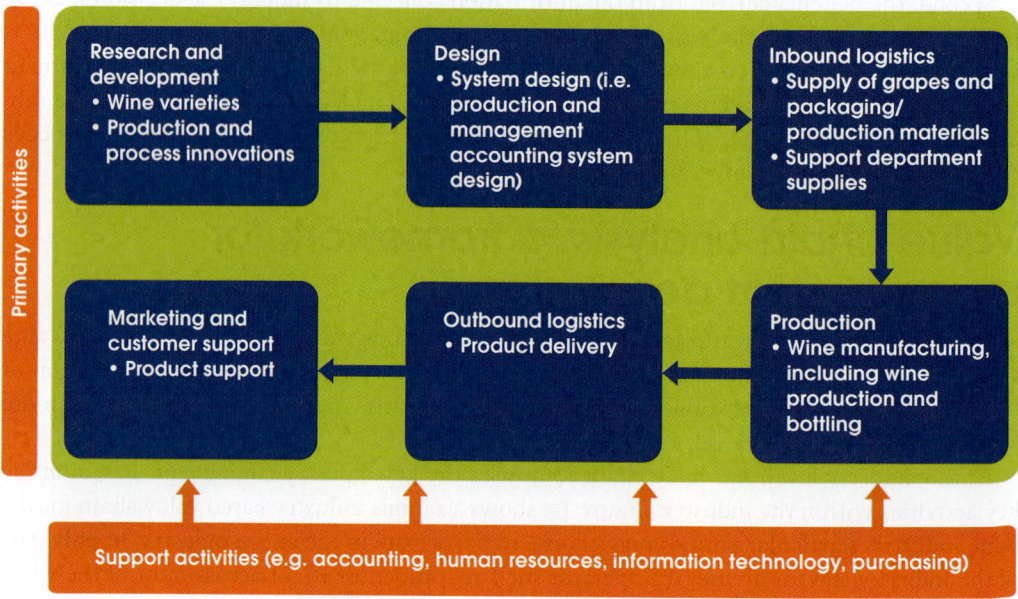

FIGURE 1.5 ■ Sample organisational value chain for a winery

The value chain provides a suitable framework for considering a range of management accounting issues:

- *Focuses on activities.* The central feature of the value chain is its focus on *activities and processes* rather than functions or departments. This makes identification of improvements across segments more likely.
- *Encourages a broader organisational view.* This is particularly so for management accounting staff and business unit managers. Management accounting staff are more likely to take a broader perspective if using a value chain framework when considering the consequences of decisions. With production activity as the central focus, we often talk of a consideration of upstream activities like research and development, design and supply activities; and downstream activities like warehousing, delivery and customer support.
- *Breaks down more traditional representations of organisational activity.* A value chain framework encourages higher levels of cross-fertilisation and communication between business segments, so that decisions are not confined by the traditional boundaries of functional areas.
- *Externalises thinking by incorporating suppliers and customers.* An organisation's value chain encompasses not only customers and suppliers, but in some cases extends to the customers' customers and the suppliers' suppliers. Analysis of the value chain leads to improved relationships between the organisation and others in the value chain, creating an extended organisation that can flexibly respond to dynamic and competitive environments. In other words, value chains explicitly recognise that no organisation operates in isolation from suppliers and customers.

- *Reinforces other initiatives such as activity-based costing (ABC).* With the focus on activities, a value chain framework provides a sound foundation for exploring activity-based costing (which is covered in chapter 4). ABC uses activities as the foundation of product and service costing. In this sense, activities are the fundamental cost object. We will explore cost objects and cost drivers in the next section. Moreover, a value chain framework complements other recent initiatives like strategic cost management, which refers to the simultaneous focus on reducing costs and strengthening an organisation's strategic position.[3] This commonly involves taking a longer-term view of cost management and decision making.

- *Provides a foundation for outsourcing and strategic alliance decisions.* A value chain framework serves as the foundation for considering decisions such as outsourcing of particular parts of the value chain and for considering the formation of strategic alliances with say a distributor. In this way, the value chain serves as a strategic tool.

- *Supports initiatives like supply chain analysis.* As organisations work to increase profitability, improving their relationships with suppliers becomes a priority. Improvements can be identified through supply chain analysis. The **supply chain** is the flow of resources from the initial suppliers through the delivery of goods and services to customers and clients. The initial suppliers may be inside or outside the organisation. Negotiating lower costs with suppliers is a straightforward way to reduce costs. Suppliers may be willing to reduce prices, particularly for organisations willing to sign long-term purchase commitments. Occasionally, organisations work with suppliers to help them reduce their costs so that the savings can be passed along.

  Accountants analyse supply chains by determining inventory level requirements, starting with customer demand for products or services. Opportunities to reduce cost and improve quality are identified through tracking and analysing use patterns of raw materials, supplies, finished goods and shipped goods. Vendors are included in inventory management decisions as part of this process. With close cooperation, inventory levels can be managed to reduce the quantitative costs of insurance and storage and the qualitative costs of quality changes and timeliness of delivery. The chapter 1 article at the end of this book explores some of the issues that are associated with supply chain analysis.

- *Categorises activities as value-added and non-value-added.* Value chain analysis involves studying each step in the business process to determine whether some activities can be eliminated because they do not add value. This analysis extends to suppliers and customers, and includes shared planning, inventory, human resources, information technology systems, and even corporate cultures. Eventually, the analysis leads to business decisions for improving value.

  Before activities in the value chain can be improved or eliminated, they must be identified and then categorised as value-added or non-value-added. A **value-added activity** is one that is necessary and that the customer/client is prepared to pay for, while a **non-value-added activity** is one that is wasteful (unnecessary) and that the customer/client would not normally be prepared to pay for. Some organisations use four categories, recognising both that it may be possible to improve value-added activities and that time may be needed to eliminate non-value-added activities. Figure 1.6 (overleaf) presents these four categories with examples of actions that managers could take to improve value. The process of analysing and categorising activities also improves communication, as individuals in each part of the process begin to share their abilities, needs and requirements with others in the value chain.

Activity classification	Action to improve value
A necessary activity that cannot be improved upon at this time	None
A necessary activity that could be changed to improve the process	Modify the process to improve value *Example:* Plant layout could be changed so that materials handling activities are reduced.
An unnecessary activity that can eventually be eliminated by changing the process	Eventually eliminate the unnecessary activity *Example:* Eliminate manual recording of employee hours using time cards. A new payroll system is eventually implemented. Plastic identity cards with magnetic strips are swiped through time clocks. The system electronically tracks hours worked and processes wages and salaries.
An unnecessary activity that can quickly be eliminated by changing the process	Immediately eliminate the unnecessary activity *Example:* In team manufacturing, inspection of units completed can be eliminated if each team member inspects each unit before it passes to the next team member.

FIGURE 1.6 ■ Classification of value-added and non-value-added activities

Cost objects and cost drivers

Throughout this textbook, a range of new terms and their meanings as they relate to management accounting and decision making will be introduced. Two concepts that are relatively fundamental to much of the book are cost objects and cost drivers. A **cost object** is a thing or activity for which we measure costs. For example, it might be a product or service, a production activity, a customer, a project — or even the entire organisation. A knowledge of the costs of these cost objects can serve a range of different purposes, many of which we will explore throughout the book. **Cost drivers** are the inputs or activities that cause changes in the total cost of a cost object, and they can be defined according to the level within the organisation that is our point of interest. We will explore the role of cost drivers in cost allocation and product/service cost determination later in the book. For now, our attention is on cost drivers at the organisational level. A number of different classification models exist. We will explore one here that classifies cost drivers as structural or executional.[4] Figure 1.7 contains a list of commonly identified structural and executional cost drivers.

Structural cost drivers are those that relate to the underlying economic structure of the organisation. Commonly, the status of such cost drivers are determined by decisions taken by senior management, and each is likely to have a significant effect on organisational costs. Executional cost drivers relate to the ability of the organisation to do what it does successfully. For executional cost drivers, more is usually better — for example, the greater the level of workforce involvement, the better.

Structural cost drivers	Executional cost drivers
Scale — investment in key parts of the business such as research and development, manufacturing or marketing and customer support	**Workforce involvement** — a workforce commitment to continuous improvement (it is the responsibility of senior management to create and maintain such an environment)
Scope — degree of vertical integration or extent of involvement in the value chain	**Total quality management (TQM)** — a management and workforce commitment to product and process quality
Experience — levels of knowledge and experience relating to initiatives and organisational actions (i.e. have we done this before?)	**Capacity utilisation** — available capacity and how it is utilised
Technology — nature and extent of process technologies employed by the organisation	**Plant/process layout efficiency** — how well the plant or process technologies are designed and structured
	Product configuration — design or formulation of the product
Complexity — extent of the organisation's product/service line	**Linkages with suppliers and customers** — how good the relationships are with customers and suppliers

FIGURE 1.7 ■ Classification of organisational-level cost drivers

Source: Adapted from Shank and Govindarajan 1992, 'Strategic cost management and the value chain', *Journal of Cost Management*, pp. 5–21.

Summary

1 Describe the types of decisions managers make for an organisation.

Overview of management decision making

Measure, monitor and motivate

2 Outline the role of cost and management accounting information in management decision making.

(a) Internal and external reporting

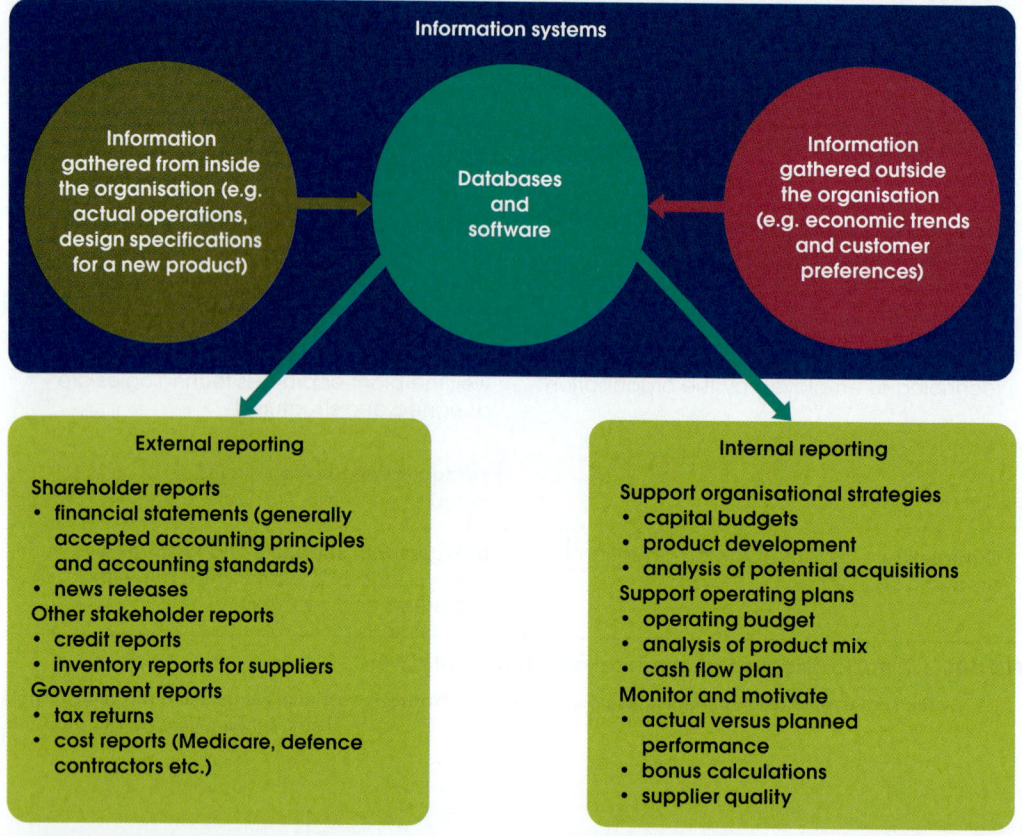

(b) Key influences on management accounting structure

(c) Relevant information for decision making

Relevant information

Helps decision makers evaluate and choose among alternative courses of action by:

(i) considering the future   (ii) varying with the action taken.

Includes incremental (avoidable) information (costs or cash flows).

Irrelevant information

- Not useful for decision making   ■ Includes unavoidable cash flows

3 Explain how managers can make higher-quality decisions using accounting information.

(a) Path to higher-quality management decisions

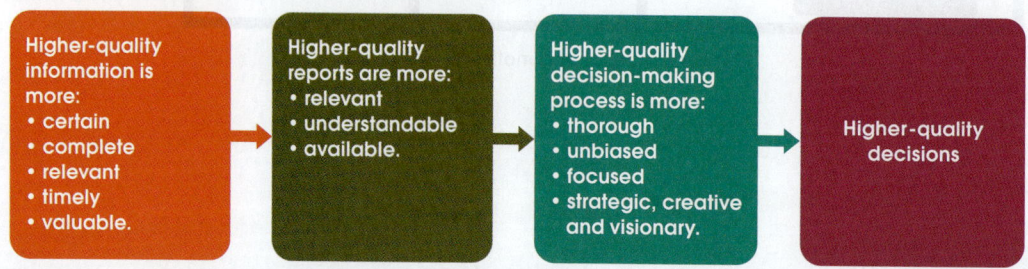

(b) Decision-useful information involves a consideration of:

- opportunity costs
- cost–benefit analysis.

4 Explain the value chain framework and its applications in management accounting.

A value chain can be described as the key activities engaged in by the organisation or industry.

Sample industry-based value chain for the wine industry

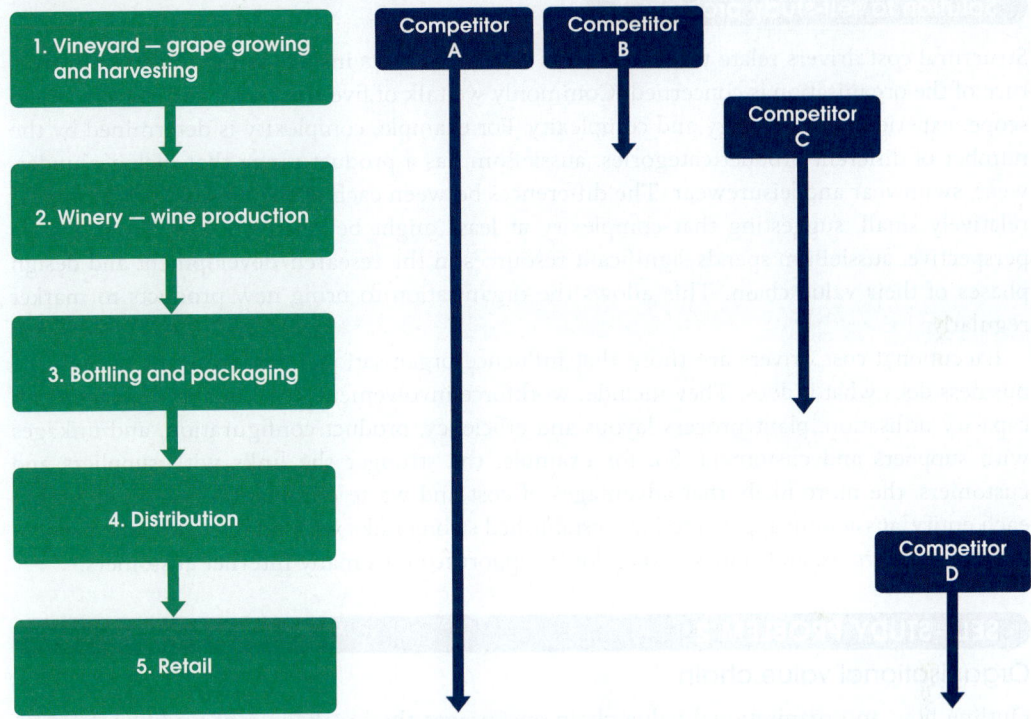

Sample organisational value chain for a winery

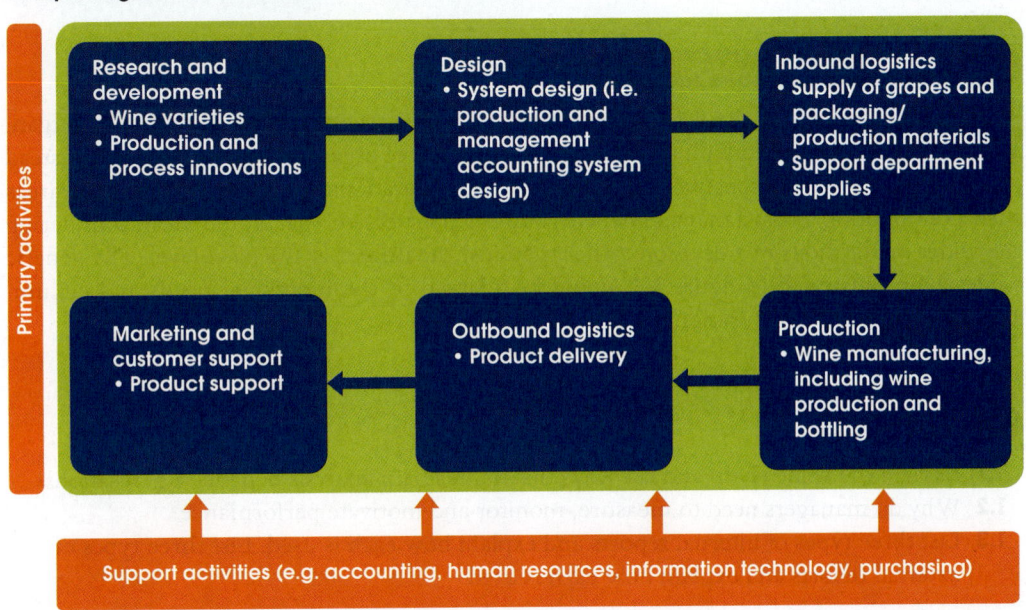

Self-study problems

SELF-STUDY PROBLEM 1

Organisational cost drivers

With reference to the scene setter aussieBum at the start of this chapter, distinguish between structural and executional cost drivers.

Solution to self-study problem 1

Structural cost drivers relate to those factors that cause costs insofar as the underlying structure of the organisation is concerned. Commonly we talk of five structural cost drivers: scale, scope, experience, technology and complexity. For example, complexity is determined by the number of different product categories. aussieBum has a product range that includes underwear, swimwear and leisurewear. The differences between each of the product ranges appear relatively small, suggesting that complexity at least might be relatively low. From a scale perspective, aussieBum spends significant resources in the research/development and design phases of their value chain. This allows the organisation to bring new products to market regularly.

Executional cost drivers are those that influence organisational cost in terms of how the business does what it does. They include: workforce involvement, total quality management, capacity utilisation, plant/process layout and efficiency, product configuration, and linkages with suppliers and customers. So, for example, the stronger the links with suppliers and customers, the more likely that advantages of cost and waste elimination can occur within each entity. aussieBum appears to have established strong links with retail customers, particularly those overseas, and enjoys strong, loyal support from its many Internet customers.

SELF-STUDY PROBLEM 2

Organisational value chain

Outline how an organisational value chain encourages the breakdown of traditional organisational boundaries.

Solution to self-study problem 2

An organisational value chain focuses on the key value-creating activities within an organisation. It is less concerned with the traditional functions of organisational boundaries, instead encouraging a wider perspective to be taken by both operational managers and support areas such as accounting. From a management accounting perspective, that would mean considering the wider implications of a decision rather than just the impact at the local level. The generic value chain illustrated in figure 1.5 would be adapted to the individual needs and circumstances of a specific organisation.

Questions

1.1 Explain the value chain and list ways that value chain analysis benefits organisations.

1.2 Why do managers need to measure, monitor and motivate performance?

1.3 List three types of internal reports and explain how each is used. List three types of external reports and explain how each is used.

1.4 What types of information in addition to cost accounting are needed for management decisions?

1.5 Explain relevant information in a decision-making context.

1.6 What is a cost object?

1.7 In your own words, explain the path to higher-quality decisions.

1.8 Outline the meaning of structural cost drivers.

1.9 Identify two key influences on the nature of a management accounting system.

Exercises

1.10 **Value-added and non-value-added activities** Some activities add value to an organisation, while others do not.

REQUIRED

Determine whether each of the following activities is likely to be value-added or non-value-added, and explain your choice.

(a) Inspection activities
(b) Moving materials to workstations
(c) Manufacturing extra inventory to keep employees busy
(d) Packing to fill a customer order
(e) Product design initiatives

1.11 **Internal and external reports** Classify the following reports as internal or external.

(a) Operating budget
(b) Credit reports
(c) Financial statements
(d) Capital budget
(e) Tax returns
(f) Analysis of product mix

1.12 **Management accounting function** Differentiate between the *management accounting function* and the *management accountant*.

1.13 **Types of manager decisions** Suppose that the following are activities conducted by Microsoft Corporation.

A. Comparing the timeliness of development steps of a new release of Windows[5] with the timeline that was laid out to guide development.
B. Developing a timeline for the release of new Windows and Microsoft Office[5] products over the next year.
C. Debugging the next version of Windows.
D. Providing technical support to customers who are having problems with Microsoft Office.
E. Estimating cash expenditures for the next year.
F. Comparing budgeted costs to actual costs and discussing major differences with department managers.
G. Deciding whether to construct a new building on the Microsoft site.

Identify whether each activity is most likely part of:

(a) organisational strategies
(b) operating plans
(c) actual operations
(d) measuring, monitoring and motivating.

For each item, explain why.

Problems

1.14 Industry and organisational value chain With reference to aussieBum discussed in the scene setter at the start of this chapter, differentiate between an industry value chain and an organisational value chain.

1.15 Structural cost drivers

(a) With reference to aussieBum, demonstrate the meaning of the structural cost drivers scope, technology and experience.

(b) Classify aussieBum's likely strategy as low cost or product differentiation. Explain.

1.16 Relevant information Suppose you are responsible for ordering a replacement for your office photocopy machine. Part of your job is to decide whether to buy it or lease it.

REQUIRED

(a) Describe something that could be considered relevant information in this decision and explain why it is relevant.

(b) Describe something that could be considered irrelevant information in this decision and explain why it is irrelevant.

(c) Explain why it was important to distinguish between relevant and irrelevant information in this problem.

1.17 Uncertainties; degree of uncertainty Community Children's Hospital can invest in one of two different projects. The first project is to purchase and operate a hotel that is located two blocks from the hospital. The CEO of the hospital has no experience in operating a hotel, but the hospital does provide rooms for in-patients, and so she is familiar with cleaning requirements and managing housekeeping staff. However, the hospital does little advertising and does not have a large public relations staff. In addition, the hospital and hotel are located in a part of town that is deteriorating.

The other investment opportunity is to replace the heart monitors in the neonatal intensive care unit (critical care for newborns and infants). The new monitors would provide a range of functions, including monitoring the body temperature and blood pressure of infants, as well as monitoring heart functions. Each monitor can be used for up to four infants, with information about each infant forwarded to one computer that is monitored by a special technician. The current monitors are bedside monitors that need to be read every 10 minutes by nursing staff.

REQUIRED

(a) Prepare a list of uncertainties that the CEO faces if she buys the hotel.

(b) Prepare a list of uncertainties the CEO faces if she replaces the heart monitors.

(c) Which scenario appears to have a greater degree of uncertainty? Why?

1.18 Cost reduction; value chain analysis Budget Cupboards produces kitchen and bathroom cupboards that incorporate unusual functions, such as specialty drawers for knives and kitchen tools, and kitchen appliance holders that pop up from under the counter top. Competition in this industry has recently increased. Budget's management wants to cut costs for its basic cupboard models and then cut prices.

REQUIRED

(a) The table opposite lists potential areas for cost reduction. Two potential cost reductions are provided for the first area listed (design phase). For each of the remaining areas, identify two potential ways that Budget Cupboard's management could reduce costs.

Potential area for cost reduction	Potential cost reductions	
Design phase	Work with suppliers to reduce direct materials costs	Redesign cupboards to use fewer parts
Manufacturing process		
Administration		
Changes in quality or functionality		

(b) Budget does not currently use value chain analysis. Describe several advantages of using value chain analysis.

1.19 Quality of decisions Maria and Tracey became good friends while working at the same entity. Two years ago, they both decided to increase their savings so that they could eventually purchase homes. Each began by putting a portion of each month's salary into a savings account. At the end of the first year, they had each accumulated $4000. Because their savings accounts paid a very small interest rate, they decided to invest the savings to earn a higher rate of return. Maria and Tracey both hoped to save enough money to buy homes within five years.

Maria decided to take an investment course offered through the entity. The course taught her about different types of investments and strategies for investing. She then purchased and read an investment book to learn more. Maria learned that some investments are riskier than others, and that investors must balance risk against desired return. Higher risk leads to higher returns on average, but higher risk could also lead to low returns or even loss. She also learned that investment advisers recommend diversifying risky investments. One way to diversify is to invest in mutual funds, which invest in many different organisations. Maria decided that she was willing to assume some risk, but was not comfortable with a high level. She decided to invest her $4000 in a stockmarket mutual fund. She read client reports to learn about different mutual funds, and selected a fund that invests conservatively in fairly stable companies. However, the stockmarket did not do well in the first year. The value of her mutual fund at the end of a year was $4050.

Tracey talked with her boyfriend and other friends about how they invest. Her boyfriend's cousin recommended investing in a start-up company that sells video games. He told her that the games were very popular with teenagers and that the company would probably be acquired, resulting in big gains for investors. This opportunity sounded good to Tracey, so she decided to invest her entire $4000 in the company's shares. After 10 months, she was excited to learn that the company was being acquired. She received shares in the acquiring company in exchange for her original shares. At the end of the year, the market value of her shares was $8200.

REQUIRED

Evaluate the quality of the investment decisions made by Maria and Tracey. *Hint*: Refer to figure 1.3 (on page 10).

(a) List the information used by Maria in making her investment decision.

(b) List the information used by Tracey in making her investment decision.

(c) Did Maria appear to use high-quality information? Explain.

(d) Did Tracey appear to use high-quality information? Explain.

(e) Describe Maria's decision-making process. What did she do to explore her options? Did she appear to be biased? What were her priorities? How did she reach a conclusion?

(f) Describe Tracey's decision-making process. What did she do to explore her options? Did she appear to be biased? What were her priorities? How did she reach a conclusion?

(g) Did Maria appear to use a high-quality decision-making process? Explain.

(h) Did Tracey appear to use a high-quality decision-making process? Explain.

(i) Given your analyses of the information and decision-making processes used by Maria and Tracey, which investor made a higher-quality decision? Explain.

1.20 Relevant information; uncertainties; information for decision making Janet Baker is deciding where to live during her second year at university. During her first year, she lived in the university residence college. Recently, her friend Rachel asked her to share an off-campus flat for the upcoming school year. Janet likes the idea of living in a flat, but she is concerned about how much it will cost.

To help her decide what to do, Janet collected information about costs. She would pay $400 per month in rent. The minimum lease term on the apartment is six months. Janet estimates that her share of the utility bills will be $75 per month. She also estimates that groceries will cost $200 per month. Janet spent $350 on a new couch over the summer. If she lives in the university residence college, she will put the couch in storage at a cost of $35 per month. Janet expects to spend $7500 on university fees and $450 on books each semester. Room and board on campus would cost Janet $2900 per semester (four months). This amount includes a food plan of 20 meals per week. This cost is non-refundable if the meals are not eaten.

REQUIRED

(a) Use *only* the cost information collected by Janet for the following tasks.

   (i) List all of the costs for each option. *Note:* Some costs may be listed under both options.

   (ii) Review your lists and cross out the costs that are irrelevant to Janet's decision. Explain why these costs are irrelevant.

   (iii) Calculate and compare the total *relevant* costs of each option.

   (iv) Given the cost comparison, which living arrangement is the better choice for Janet? Explain.

(b) Identify uncertainties in the cost information collected by Janet.

   (i) Determine whether each cost is likely to be (1) known for sure, (2) estimated with little uncertainty, or (3) estimated with moderate or high uncertainty.

   (ii) For each cost that is known for sure, explain where Janet would obtain the information.

   (iii) For each cost that must be estimated, explain why the cost cannot be known.

(c) List additional information that might be relevant to Janet's decision (list as many items as you can).

   (i) Costs not identified by Janet

   (ii) Factors other than costs

(d) Explain why conducting a cost comparison is useful to Janet, even if factors other than costs are important to her decision.

(e) Consider your own preferences for this problem. Do you expect Janet's preferences to be the same as yours? How can you control for your biases as you give Janet advice?

(f) Think about what Janet's priorities might be for choosing a housing arrangement. How might different priorities lead to different choices?

(g) Describe how information that Janet gains over this next year might affect her future housing arrangements.

Suppose Janet asks for your advice.

(h) Use the information you learned from the preceding analyses to write a memo to Janet with your recommendation and a discussion of its risks. Refer in your memo to the information that would be useful to Janet.

1.21 **Relevant information; recommendation** Frank owns a caravan and loves to visit national parks with his family. However, the family only takes two one-week trips in the caravan each year. Frank's wife would rather stay in motels than the caravan. She presented him with the following itemisation of the cost per trip, hoping that he will sell the caravan and use motels instead.

	Cost per trip
Caravan:	
Cost: $20 000	
Usable for 10 seasons, two camping trips per season	$1000
Transportation expense:	
1000 km @ $0.37 per km	370
Includes:	
$0.15 per km for petrol, oil, tyres and maintenance	
$0.22 per km for depreciation and insurance	
Groceries	250
Beverages	100
Cost per trip	$ 1720
Cost per person ($1720/5 family members)	$ 344

REQUIRED

(a) What are the relevant costs for deciding whether the family should go on one more camping trip this year?

(b) What are the relevant costs for deciding whether Frank should sell the caravan? Assume the family will take the same vacations but stay in motels if the caravan is sold.

(c) What factors other than costs might influence the decision to sell the caravan? List as many as you can.

(d) Consider your own preferences for this problem. Do you expect Frank's preferences to be the same as yours? How can you control for your biases and consider this problem from Frank's point of view?

(e) Frank asks you to help him decide what to do. Do you think he should sell the caravan? Why?

1.22 Using figure 1.5 (page 12) as an example, develop an internal value chain for an airline such as VirginBlue.

REFERENCES

1 www.aussieBum.com.
2 See IMA 1983, *Statement on management accounting no. 2: management accounting terminology*, NAA, Montvale, NJ, 1 June, p. 25.

3 See Cooper, R & Slagmulder, R 1999, 'The scope of strategic cost management,' in J Edwards (ed.), *Emerging practices in cost management,* Warren, Gorham & Lamont, Boston.
4 This classification model is based on: Shank, J & Goviindarajan, V 1992, 'Strategic cost management and the value chain', *Journal of Cost Management,* pp. 5–21.
5 Registered trademarks of Microsoft Corporation.

2

Cost concepts

IN BRIEF

Managers need a basic understanding of the entity's costs if they are to react quickly to change and develop successful organisational strategies and operating plans. Managers use cost classifications and cost estimation techniques to understand and predict cost behaviour. They can then identify and estimate costs to assist with the decision-making processes.

After studying this chapter, you should be able to:

1	Understand the concept of cost behaviour.
2	Explain the different types of cost behaviour.
3	Understand cost estimation techniques.
4	Use estimation techniques to determine the cost function.
5	Utilise regression analysis in cost estimation.
6	Identify the uses and limitations of cost estimates.

Getting into the coffee business

The coffee industry has grown worldwide. From agriculture (growing) to production to retailing to consuming, participants in the coffee industry seem to be increasing all across the value chain. At the consumption end of the value chain, the Australian coffee market contains two broad channels: the retail (in-home consumption), and the food service (out-of-home consumption). Overall, per capita consumption of coffee in Australia was estimated at 2.3 kilograms in early 2006 (AustralAsian Specialty Coffee Association 2006). In the out-of-home segment of the market, BIS Shrapnel estimates that some 1.26 billion cups of coffee were served in 2005, accounting for about $3 billion in sales (Walker 2006).

Australia has three major coffee growing regions: Far North Queensland, Central and South-East Queensland, and Northern New South Wales. While Australia has not traditionally been a major participant in the coffee growing segment of the value chain, this did not stop Andrew Ford starting Mountain Top Coffee in Northern New South Wales in 1997. Mountain Top Coffee grows premium green coffee beans, predominantly for the export market. It has about 60 000 trees in production, with another 50 000 trees planned. According to Ian MacLaughlin, the owner of Skybury Coffee (one of Mountain Top Coffee's competitors), the need to develop export markets for Australian coffee beans is partly driven by the relatively higher fixed and labour costs in Australia. When starting a coffee growing business from scratch, as Andrew Ford did, an understanding of the likely costs as well as the behaviour of those costs over time and under different conditions is required. Identifying those costs that remain the same (fixed costs) and those that vary according to some key measure (variable costs) is necessary to understand the fundamentals of the business. For example, when starting a coffee growing business, common fixed costs might include land lease costs, interest on financing costs, equipment (such as a harvester) and associated costs (leasing or depreciation). Variable costs might include spraying, fertilising and harvesting costs. It is important to understand what drives these costs; for example, the volume of coffee beans produced may drive some of the variable costs.

In the production of roasted coffee beans segment of the market, a recent new entrant is DiBella Coffee, which was launched in 2002 by founder Philip DiBella. DiBella Coffee provides a variety of its coffee blends to over 600 outlets in Australia. The retail segment of the value chain in Australia is made up of a mixture of specialty coffee chains and independent coffee shops. The coffee chains include Gloria Jean's, McDonald's McCafes, Hudsons and Starbucks. Growth in this segment of the market still seems possible, with most chains planning more outlet growth. In this coffee shop segment of the market, costs would be well identified in the coffee chains and franchise segment, but independent operators would need to identify their costs and plan carefully.

Sources: AustralAsian Specialty Coffee Association 2006, *Australian coffee market key facts for 2006*, prepared by FountainHead; Australian Coffee Industry, Mountain Top Estate, www.mountaintopcoffee.com.au; Le Mesurier, K 2005, 'Tough grind pays off', *BRW*, 20 October, pp. 52–3; Walker, J 2006, 'Bottomless cups', *BRW*, 13 April, pp. 21–2; VirginBlue 2006, 'Runaway coast', *Voyeur in-flight magazine*, December.

Issues from this scene setter to look for in the chapter include:

- The importance of knowledge of cost behaviour.

- The identification and behaviour of fixed costs.

- The identification and behaviour of variable costs.

- The need for cost estimation, particularly in new ventures.

Cost behaviour

Cost behaviour at the operational level is the variation in costs relative to the variation in an organisation's activities. Accountants need to anticipate changes in costs as decisions are made about activities such as production, merchandise sales, and services. To understand cost behaviour, accountants analyse the effects of changes in their organisations' activities on costs by considering the drivers of those costs. Cost behaviour may be classified on a traditional basis using a fixed and variable cost framework, or take a more contemporary view using an activity analysis cost framework. In this chapter a more traditional view of cost is taken, and a further discussion on activity analysis can be found in chapter 4.

The ability to analyse cost behaviour requires knowledge of an organisation's economic environment and operations. Consider an airline. Its costs, such as beverage costs, vary with the number of passengers. Some costs, such as fuel and flight attendant wages, vary with the number of flights. Other costs, such as the leasing of counter space and the salaries of airport management, vary with the number of airports used by the airline. Still other costs, such as building costs and corporate headquarters salaries, do not vary with passenger, flight or airport-related volumes.

Variable, fixed and mixed costs

Total **variable costs** change proportionately with changes in activity levels. As discussed earlier, the traditional cost framework includes a consideration of variable, fixed and mixed costs. In the scene setter, we illustrated fixed and variable costs in relation to the coffee industry. In this section, we use the cycling industry to further explore these concepts. For Mount Dandenong Bikes, a bicycle manufacturer, the cost of tyres varies with the number of bicycles produced. Suppose that each tyre costs $5, the variable cost per bike is $10 and total variable cost increases by $10 for each bike produced. Figure 2.1(a) provides a graph of the variable cost of tyres. Another activity in bike production is mounting the tyres onto wheels. As the number of bikes produced increases, the labour cost to mount tyres onto wheels increases proportionately and is therefore a variable cost.

We assume that variable cost per unit remains constant, but sometimes this assumption is not true. Suppose that the managers of Mount Dandenong Bikes are able to negotiate a lower cost for tyres as their purchase quantity increases. For purchases up to 120 tyres, the variable cost per unit is constant at $10 per bike. However, the variable cost per bike drops to $6 for any additional purchases after the first 120 tyres, as illustrated in figure 2.1(b).

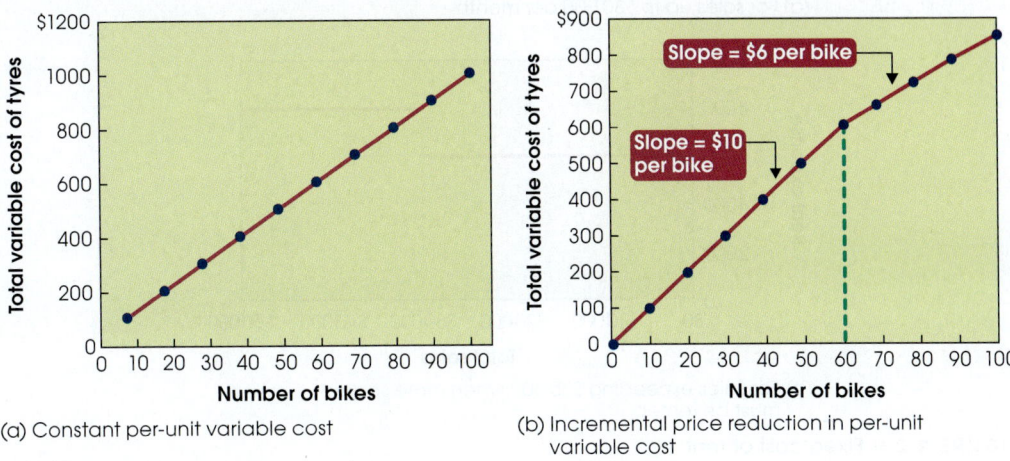

(a) Constant per-unit variable cost

(b) Incremental price reduction in per-unit variable cost

FIGURE 2.1 ■ Total variable cost of tyres for bicycle production

Total **fixed costs** do not vary with small changes in activity levels such as production, sales and services provided. Some fixed costs are easy to classify, such as rent, insurance, and property taxes. Figure 2.2(a) (on page 30) illustrates the cost of rent and sales volumes for Mount Dandenong Bikes. Within a specific range of sales ($0 to $30 000), rent cost is $6000. However, if sales are greater than $30 000, more space will be needed and total fixed cost will increase to $8000, as shown in figure 2.2(b). Fixed costs such as rent often increase in a stepwise linear manner.

Some fixed costs are more difficult to classify. For example, varying levels of bike production do not significantly change the amount of electricity used, assuming no change in hours of operation. Keep in mind that the dollar amount of a fixed cost is not necessarily 'fixed' at one value. For Mount Dandenong Bikes, the rate for a kilowatt-hour of electricity might change, the cost for heating and cooling depends on weather conditions, and the total electricity bill varies from month to month. Nevertheless, electricity is still considered a fixed cost for bike production because the cost of electricity is not significantly affected by changes in the volumes of operating activity (number of bikes produced).

In reality, many costs are **mixed costs**; they are partly fixed and partly variable. Suppose that Mount Dandenong Bikes incurs a fixed cost of $10 000 to generate a television advertisement, and then a variable cost of $500 each time the advertisement is aired on television. The total television advertising cost is a mixed cost because part is fixed and part varies with the number of times the advertisement is aired on television.

The classification of costs as fixed, variable or mixed is not always straightforward. The chapter 2 article at the end of this book provides an alternative view of the classification of marketing costs.

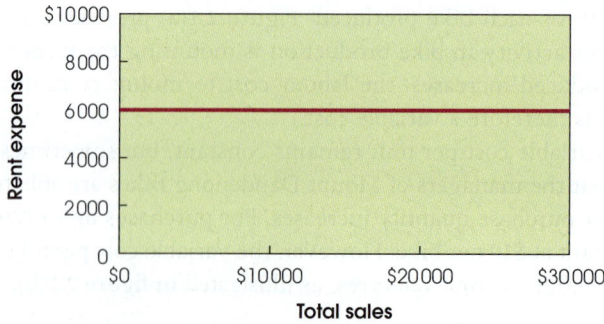

(a) For sales up to $30 000 per month

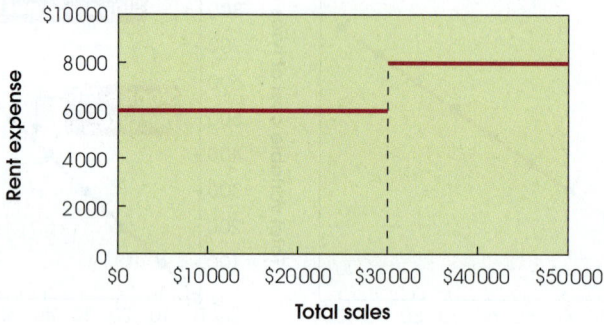

(b) For sales exceeding $30 000 when more space
must be rented

FIGURE 2.2 ■ Fixed cost of rent

Relevant range

A **relevant range** is a span of activity for a given cost object where both total fixed costs and variable costs per unit of activity remain constant. Suppose that an airline begins service to a new destination. The number of flights is estimated, gates and aircraft are leased, and employees are hired. Managers may add or drop a few flights, and the fixed costs and variable costs per flight (fuel and personnel) remain constant. However, if the new route is successful, managers may decide to add a number of new flights, in which case new gates must be leased and new employees hired. The fixed and variable costs for the original destination are no longer valid because the airline is operating within a new relevant range.

Variable cost rates can also change across relevant ranges, as was shown in figure 2.1(b). In that graph, Mount Dandenong Bikes paid $10 per bike for 0–60 bikes (120 tyres), and $6 per bike after that. Within a particular relevant range of purchases, the variable cost per tyre is constant. However, once purchase volumes move into a different relevant range, a different variable cost per bike applies. In many cases, the variable cost will be lower at a higher relevant range. But in some cases, especially when resources are limited, a higher variable cost might apply. For example, a utility company may charge customers one cost per kilowatt over a range of usage levels and then a higher amount per kilowatt for a higher level of usage. The purpose would be to encourage the conservation and efficient use of utilities.

Marginal cost is the incremental cost of an activity, such as producing a unit of goods or services. Marginal cost is often relevant for decision making. Within the relevant range, variable cost approximates marginal cost. Accordingly, accountants often use variable cost as a measure of marginal cost. Although the terms *variable cost* and *marginal cost* may be used interchangeably, they are not always the same, especially when the incremental or marginal unit moves into the next relevant range. For example, in figure 2.2(b), the first $30 000 in sales has a fixed cost of $6000 for rental of retail space. The next incremental sales (above $30 000) require an expansion of retail space, costing an additional $2000 in fixed costs. Thus, the marginal (first few) sales would increase fixed costs by $2000.

Cost functions

It is easy to assume that costs behave linearly — in other words, that fixed costs remain fixed and the variable cost per unit remains constant. However, total costs more often resemble a large S-curve, as shown in figure 2.3. Notice that within a relevant range of activity, the change in total cost as volume increases is nearly linear.

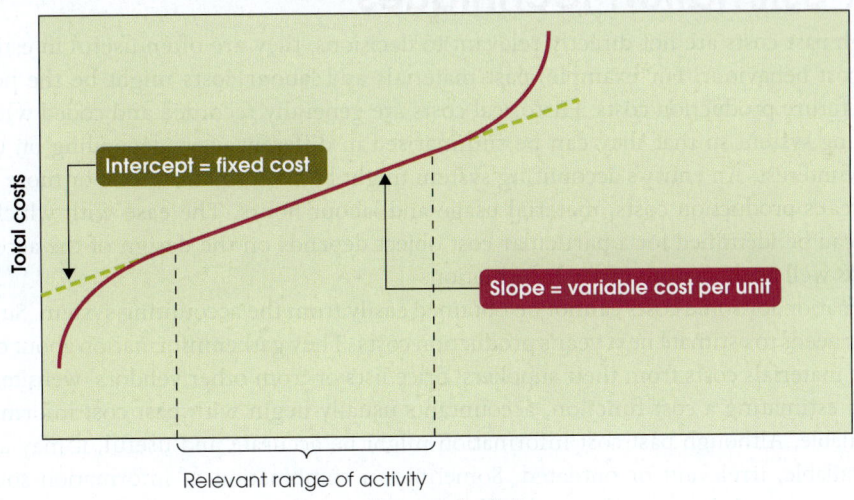

FIGURE 2.3 ■ Total costs over a wide range of activity

A **cost function** is an algebraic representation of the total cost of a cost object over a relevant range of activity. When we create a cost function, we assume that within a relevant range of activity the total fixed costs remain fixed and the variable cost per unit remains constant. Notice in figure 2.3 that when volume is very low or very high, the total cost function is non-linear. However, when volume is in the relevant range, the cost function is linear or close to linear.

Given the preceding definitions of fixed and variable costs within the relevant range, we can write the cost function algebraically as

$$TC = F + V \times Q$$

where   TC is total cost,
          F is total fixed cost,
          V is the variable cost per unit of activity, and
          Q is the volume of activity of the cost driver.

When the slope of a variable cost function changes at some point but remains linear after the change, it is called a **piecewise linear cost function**. The variable cost function in figure 2.1 (b) is piecewise linear because it involves more than one relevant range. When a fixed cost function changes at some point but remains constant after the change, it is called a **stepwise linear cost function**. The fixed cost function in figure 2.2(b) is stepwise linear because it includes more than one relevant range.

A **cost driver** is some input or activity that causes changes in total cost for a cost object. For an airline when the cost object is the entire organisation, the number of passengers is a cost driver for in-flight beverage costs. The number of flights is a cost driver for fuel and flight attendant wages. The number of airports used by the airline is a cost driver for counter space lease and airport management salaries. Cost drivers are important for a range of management accounting issues and are explored further in other parts of this text.

The same cost object might have different cost drivers in different settings. For example, when electricity is the cost object, in a retail setting the cost driver could be hours the store was open. In a manufacturing setting, the cost driver could be either machine hours or number of units manufactured, assuming that each unit requires the same number of machine hours.

Cost estimation techniques

Although past costs are not directly relevant to decisions, they are often useful in estimating future cost behaviour. For example, past materials and labour costs might be the best estimate of future production costs. Historical costs are generally recorded and coded within the accounting system so that they can be summarised in different ways depending on the cost object of interest. An entity's accounting system might be used to create one or more reports of last year's production costs, material usage and labour hours. The ease with which information can be identified for a particular cost object depends on the design of the accounting system as well as the nature of the information.

Information for some costs cannot be obtained easily from the accounting system. Suppose a manager needs to estimate next year's production costs. They gather information about changes in direct materials costs from their suppliers' price lists or from other vendors' websites.

When estimating a cost function, accountants usually begin with past cost information if it is available. Although past cost information might be accurate and useful, it may at times be unavailable, irrelevant or outdated. Sometimes a combination of information sources is the best choice and the costs obtained will require reclassification into fixed and variable cost components.

As we gather relevant information, we may have a general idea of the cost behaviour. However, we need to select one or more techniques for estimating the dollar amount of fixed and variable costs. The following techniques are used to estimate a cost function:

- engineered estimate of cost
- analysis at the account level
- graphical technique — scatter plots
- two-point method
- high-low method
- regression analysis.

Although each of these methods may be used, the choice is open-ended. No single technique is useful in all circumstances. Although some techniques are generally better than others, the best technique often depends on the circumstances for a particular decision. As we look at each technique, pay particular attention to its assumptions. Poor management decisions can result if the quality of cost estimates is not considered.

Engineered estimate of cost

One method used to estimate a cost function is the **engineered estimate of cost**. Each activity is analysed according to the amount of labour time, materials and other resources used. Costs are assigned according to these measurements. Suppose Holden begins production of a new model, such as the SS Commodore. Engineers and accountants use the new model's design specifications to estimate the cost of direct and indirect materials for a production run of Commodores. In addition, the proposed manufacturing process is analysed to determine the cost effects of any changes from the existing manufacturing processes. The accountants communicate with purchasing department personnel to determine whether the prices of inputs are likely to change. From this information, a total cost function is developed for the production of Commodores for the next period. Although engineers traditionally develop engineered estimates of cost, anyone having sufficient knowledge about activities and costs can develop a cost function using this method.

Analysis at the account level

Another way to create a cost function is to use **analysis at the account level**. Using this technique, we review the pattern of a cost over time in the accounting system and use our knowledge of operations to classify the cost as variable, fixed or mixed. Costs such as managers' salaries are usually fixed; they are often directly associated in the general ledger with a particular department or product. Costs for variable materials used in the production process are usually available in the general ledger or in production records. Costs such as manufacturing overhead are often mixed; they tend to include fixed costs such as insurance and rates for the plant, and variable costs such as indirect supplies used in manufacturing. For costs we identify as mixed, we must use another cost estimation technique such as the two-point method or regression analysis to determine the fixed and variable components. Sometimes we are uncertain about the nature of the cost function. A scatter plot provides helpful information about the relationship between a cost and potential cost driver.

Graphical technique — scatter plots

A **scatter plot** is a graphical technique in which data points for past costs are plotted against a potential cost driver. Scatter plots provide a quick way to learn more about the behaviour of a cost and to determine whether a potential cost driver is viable as Q in the cost function. We visually analyse scatter plots to improve our understanding of a cost's behaviour and to decide whether the cost might be completely fixed, completely variable or mixed.

The following data are from one of Mount Dandenong Bikes' plants. They include weekly costs for packing bikes, together with a possible cost driver, the number of bikes shipped.

Number of bikes shipped	Total packing cost
200	$729
270	$870
250	$820
210	$720
300	$950
175	$700

Figure 2.4(a) shows a scatter plot of these data (see overleaf). Notice that the data points seem to fall in a general upward linear pattern, suggesting that total packing costs increase with the number of bikes shipped. In addition, if we draw a trend line roughly through the middle of the data points as shown in figure 2.4(b) and continue the line to the vertical axis, the intercept appears to be above zero. Thus, the scatter plot suggests that the cost of packing is a mixed cost with an apparent variable component (the slope) and a fixed component (the intercept).

Two-point method

The **two-point method** uses any two sets of data points for cost and a cost driver to algebraically calculate a mixed cost function. These data points can be drawn from a scatter plot. The line should resemble the general pattern of the data and be drawn using a ruler on a printed scatter plot or using a spreadsheet's line-draw feature. Spreadsheet programs such as Excel[1] create a trend line representing the best fit for the data points.

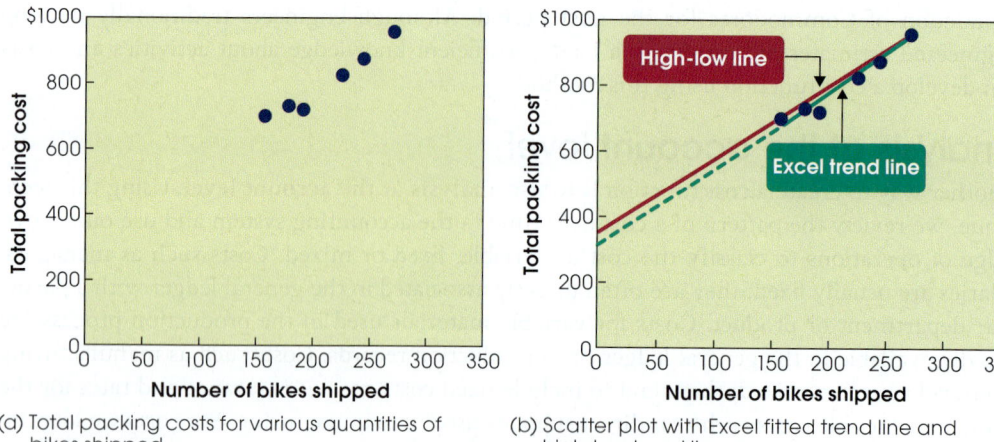

(a) Total packing costs for various quantities of bikes shipped

(b) Scatter plot with Excel fitted trend line and high-low trend line

FIGURE 2.4 ■ Scatter plot of total packing costs

We create the cost function by selecting and performing calculations with any two points on the line, even if they are not original data points. Variable cost (V) is calculated by computing the slope of the line — the change in cost compared to the change in the cost driver (Q) between the two points. Given V, the fixed cost is calculated by solving for F in the formula $TC = F + V \times Q$ for one of the two data points.

The lower trend line in figure 2.4(b) was originally generated using Excel. Two points on the trend line have values for Q of 240 and 190 bicycles on the horizontal axis. These same points have respective values for TC of $800 and $700 on the vertical axis. Using those two points, we calculate variable cost as follows:

$$\text{Change in cost} \div \text{Change in the cost driver}$$

$$= (\$800 - \$700) \div (240 - 190) \text{ bicycles}$$

$$= \$100 \div 50 \text{ bicycles} = \$2 \text{ per bicycle}$$

Thus, $V = \$2$ per bicycle. We can now calculate fixed cost using 190 bikes as follows:

$$\$700 = F + 190 \text{ bicycles} \times \$2 \text{ per bicycle}$$

$$F = \$700 - \$380 = \$320$$

The total cost function (per week) for packing bikes is estimated as

$$TC = \$320 + \$2Q$$

High-low method

The **high-low method** is a specific application of the two-point method using the highest and lowest data points of the cost driver. Although this technique is useful for illustration in classroom settings, it is inappropriate when we want to estimate an organisation's costs as accurately as possible. The problem with this method is that the highest and lowest cost driver observations are often outliers (values that might lie outside the normal range of activities). Therefore, this method frequently distorts the cost function. However, sometimes we have only two or three data points, in which case the high-low method may be our only choice.

The top trend line in figure 2.4(b) uses the highest and lowest observations for number of bicycles packed. Notice that this linear function misses most of the data points. Using the high-low method, we calculate the total cost function for Mount Dandenong Bikes' packing activities as follows:

$$\text{Change in cost} \div \text{Change in the cost driver}$$

$$= (\$950 - \$700) \div (300 - 175) \text{ bicycles}$$

$$= \$250 \div 125 \text{ bicycles} = \$2 \text{ per bicycle}$$

The variable cost V is $2 per bicycle. Fixed cost is calculated using 175 bikes as follows:

$$\$700 = F + 175 \text{ bicycles} \times \$2 \text{ per bicycle}$$

$$F = \$700 - \$350$$

$$= \$350$$

The total cost function for packing bikes, then, is

$$TC = \$350 + \$2Q$$

Estimating the cost function

Comprehensive example 1 demonstrates how to create a cost function, while figure 2.5 summarises the activities involved in estimating a cost function for a particular cost object.

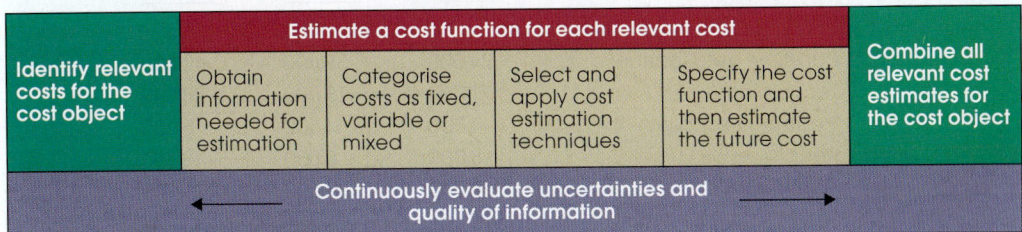

Identify relevant costs for the cost object	Estimate a cost function for each relevant cost				Combine all relevant cost estimates for the cost object
	Obtain information needed for estimation	Categorise costs as fixed, variable or mixed	Select and apply cost estimation techniques	Specify the cost function and then estimate the future cost	
	← Continuously evaluate uncertainties and quality of information →				

FIGURE 2.5 ■ Estimating relevant costs for a cost object

Comprehensive example 1

Creating a cost function using the high-low method

Small Animal Clinic is a not-for-profit clinic that provides limited veterinarian services, primarily vaccinations, for the surrounding community. The clinic has been growing each year, and its manager expects this trend to continue. The recent growth has actually been driven by an economic downturn. With rising unemployment, more people are unable to pay regular veterinarian fees. Many have turned to Small Animal Clinic, which charges a lower rate for services. A local foundation has provided Small Animal Clinic a matching grant for its services.

For example, if a pet owner pays $30 for an examination and vaccines, the foundation will match the fee with an additional $30. This support has enabled the clinic to keep its rates low.

Identify relevant costs and obtain information needed for estimation

As part of her operating plans, Lucy Brown, the manager of Small Animal Clinic, would like to create a budget of next year's revenues and costs. Lucy estimates that the clinic will provide services for 3800 visits next year. The accountant, Josh Hardy, determined that the cost object is the clinic, and the cost driver for the clinic as a whole is the number of animal visits. Then, from the accounting records, he identified five relevant costs for the clinic: part-time veterinarians, technicians, treatment supplies, rent and administration costs. He performed analysis at the account level to obtain the information needed to estimate future costs. The information for the last three years follows. Because Small Animal Clinic is a not-for-profit entity, its profit is referred to as a *surplus*.

	2006	2007	2008
Animal visits	2500	3000	3500
Veterinary fees	$ 72 500	$ 90 000	$105 000
Foundation matching grant	72 500	90 000	105 000
Total revenue	145 000	180 000	210 000
Expenses			
Part-time veterinarians	24 000	32 800	42 000
Technicians	71 000	78 000	78 049
Treatment supplies	4 000	4 600	5 200
Rent	8 000	8 500	8 750
Administration	38 000	39 600	41 200
Total expenses	145 000	163 500	175 199
Surplus	$ 0	$ 16 500	$ 34 801

Categorise costs, apply cost estimation techniques, and estimate future costs

To create individual cost functions, Josh categorises each cost as fixed, variable or mixed, and identifies potential cost drivers for the variable and mixed costs. He then selects the appropriate cost estimation technique for the mixed costs, develops the cost function, and estimates future costs for each relevant cost.

Part-time veterinarians

Josh studies the payroll records and finds a lot of variation in the cost of veterinarians. Part-time veterinarians are called in as necessary and are paid on an hourly basis. Most of their time is spent with animals, so Josh determines it is a direct cost. Therefore, he thinks that the amount of time the veterinarians spend with each animal might be a cost driver. However, the accounting system does not record the visit time per animal. Instead, records are available for the total number of animal visits. Josh considers other potential cost drivers such as number of veterinarians on call and the hours the clinic is open, but eliminates them because they seem less likely than number of animal visits to have a cause-and-effect relationship with veterinarian wages. Therefore, he categorises veterinarian fees as a variable cost and plans to use number of animal visits as the cost driver. Josh knows that although veterinarian pay is increased periodically, no increase is planned for next year. Because last year's information is the most current, he uses only last year's data to create the cost function. In 2008, this category included no fixed costs, and the variable cost per animal visit was $12 ($42 000 total cost ÷ 3500 animal visits). The cost function for veterinarians is

$$\text{TC} = \$0 + \$12 \text{ per animal visit} \times Q \text{ animal visits}$$

Josh can now estimate 2006 costs, with $Q = 3800$ animal visits.

$$\text{TC} = \$12 \text{ per animal visit} \times 3800 \text{ animal visits} = \$45\,600$$

Technicians

Josh learns from payroll records that the technical staff is permanent and paid on a salary basis. The technicians clean examination rooms, prepare supplies, fill out paperwork, handle the reception desk and assist the veterinarians with each visit. Because they work on many different tasks, Josh concludes that this cost is indirect and fixed.

Again, Josh uses the most current information in his cost function. A 2.5 per cent salary increase is expected for 2009. With no variable costs and only the fixed cost of $78 049 for 2008, the updated cost function for technicians is

$$\text{TC} = (\$78\,049 \times 1.025) + \$0Q = \$80\,000$$

Josh estimates the 2009 cost for technicians to be $80 000.

Treatment supplies

Josh believes that treatment supplies is either a variable or mixed cost. He learns from the technicians that treatment supplies include items that vary depending on the services provided, such as vaccination serum and syringes. He also learns that supplies include items such as lab coats for clinic employees that vary by number of employees rather than visits. He concludes that the cost of treatment supplies is a mixed cost, and he believes that number of animal visits has a cause-and-effect relationship for the variable portion.

Josh learns that few significant changes occurred in the cost or use of treatment supplies over the past three years. Therefore, he decides to use all three years' data to estimate the cost function. With only three data points, he uses the high-low method to separate the fixed and variable components of treatment supplies. He first identifies the highest and lowest data points for the cost driver, which is number of animal visits. The lowest number of animal visits was in 2009, and the highest number was in 2008. He calculates the variable cost per unit by dividing the change in cost ($5200 – $4000) by the change in volume (3500 – 2500) for these two data points:

$$(\$5200 - \$4000) \div (3500 - 2500) = \$1200 \div 1000 = \$1.20 \text{ per animal visit}$$

Next, Josh substitutes the variable cost rate into the cost equation for 2008 and solves for the fixed costs:

$$\text{TC} = F + V \times Q$$

$$\$5200 = F + \$1.20 \text{ per animal visit} \times 3500 \text{ animal visits}$$

$$\$5200 = F + \$4200$$

$$F = \$1000$$

Josh's cost function for treatment supplies is

$$TC = \$1000 + \$1.20 \text{ per animal visit} \times Q \text{ animal visits}$$

He can now estimate costs for treatment supplies in 2009, assuming 3800 animal visits.

$$TC = \$1000 + \$1.20 \text{ per animal visit} \times 3800 \text{ animal visits} = \$5560$$

Rent

Josh knows that rent can change annually when the lease is renewed. However, rent changes depend on local rates rather than on the level of operating activity at the clinic. Accordingly, he categorises rent as a fixed cost.

Josh uses the most recent rent amount and sets up his cost function.

$$TC = \$8750 + \$0Q$$

$$TC = \$8750$$

He does not update this figure because he learns that the property manager is not planning to increase rent for 2009. Therefore, his estimate for rent is also $8750.

Administration

Josh learns that administration includes costs to set up files for new animals and office supplies related to the paperwork for each visit. Josh reviews the general ledger entries and finds that the remainder of the administrative cost is for salaries, general office supplies, and telephone, which Josh concludes are fixed costs. Thus, he concludes that administration is a mixed cost, with animal visits as the cost driver for the variable portion.

Josh performs an account analysis of the administrative costs, separating the cost of supplies such as file folders, tabs and the forms required for each visit. From his analysis, he calculates the cost of these supplies as $8000 in 2006, $9600 in 2007 and $11 200 in 2008, or about $3.20 per animal visit. He bases his estimate of fixed administrative costs on the most recent year's data. During 2008 total administrative costs were $41 200. When he subtracts the variable cost of $11 200, this leaves $30 000 ($41 200 – $11 200) as his estimate of the fixed cost. Therefore, his cost function for administration is

$$TC = \$30\,000 + \$3.20 \text{ per animal visit} \times Q \text{ animal visits}$$

Josh now estimates administration cost for 2009.

$$TC = \$30\,000 + \$3.20 \text{ per animal visit} \times 3800 \text{ animal visits} = \$42\,160$$

Combine all relevant cost estimates

Josh creates the following summary of his cost functions and estimated costs for 2009.

Cost	Category	Fixed cost	Variable cost per visit	2009 Estimated cost for 3800 animal visits
Part-time veterinarians	Variable	$ 0	$12.00	$ 45 600
Technicians	Fixed	80 000	0.00	80 000
Treatment supplies	Mixed	1 000	1.20	5 560
Rent	Fixed	8 750	0.00	8 750
Administration	Mixed	30 000	3.20	42 160
Total		$119 750	$16.40	$182 070

The total cost function for Small Animal Clinic is

$$TC = \$119\,750 + \$16.40 \text{ per animal visit} \times Q \text{ animal visits}$$

Based on Lucy's estimate of 3800 animal visits for next year, Josh estimates that total 2009 costs will be: $\$119\,750 + \$16.40$ per animal visit × 3800 animal visits = $\$182\,070$

Estimating profit

Lucy told Josh that she did not expect any major changes from 2008 to 2009 in the types of services provided, the average fees or the matching grant. Although Josh does not know last year's average fees, he calculates it from last year's revenue information (which includes the matching grant):

Average revenue in 2008 = Total 2008 revenue ÷ Number of animal visits in 2008

= $\$210\,000$ ÷ 3500 animal visits

= $\$60$ per animal visit

Given average revenues of $60 per animal visit, budgeted revenues for next year (including the matching grant) are:

Budgeted revenues = Estimated 2009 animal visits × Average revenue rate

= 3800 animal visits × $\$60$ per animal visit

= $\$228\,000$

Using the budgeted revenues and costs as calculated, Josh tells Lucy that he expects Small Animal Clinic to earn a surplus during 2006 of $45 930 ($228 000 − $182 070).

Regression analysis

In comprehensive example 1, Josh used the high-low method to estimate the cost function for treatment supplies. This method is often not sufficiently accurate because it uses the two most extreme data points, which could distort the cost function. An alternative estimation technique is regression analysis, a statistical technique that measures the average change in a dependent variable for every unit change in one or more independent variables. Regression analysis uses all of the available data points and often improves the accuracy of a cost function.

Simple regression analysis develops a cost function by calculating values for the statistical relationship between total cost and a single cost driver. **Multiple regression analysis** develops a cost function by calculating values for the statistical relationship between total cost and two or more cost drivers.

Simple regression analysis

In figure 2.4 (on page 34) we created a scatter plot for a cost object (packing costs) and a cost driver (number of bikes). We used Excel to generate a trend line and developed a cost function using that data. Simple regression analysis is a statistical method used to find the trend line that minimises the distance from every data point to the line. The slope of the line represents the variable cost per unit, and the intercept of the line with the vertical axis represents the fixed cost. The distance between each observation and the line is called the *error term*. In locating a slope that best fits all of the available data, regression analysis minimises the squared error terms.

Simple regression analysis then estimates the following equation:

$$Y = \alpha + \beta X + \varepsilon$$

where Y is the dependent variable (total cost), α (alpha) is the intercept (fixed cost), β (beta) is the slope coefficient (variable cost per unit), X is the independent variable (the cost driver), and ε (epsilon) is the error term, also called the residual.

We usually use a computer program such as Excel or SAS to perform regression analysis. The ability of computer programs to easily perform regression analyses makes the cost of using this technique low. Thus, the cost of performing regression analysis is not likely to exceed the benefits.

Interpreting simple regression results

Regression analysis provides the best estimate of the cost function in cases with a strong positive linear relationship between the cost and the cost driver. However, the data points we use in a regression rarely fit into an absolutely straight line. Deviations from linearity may occur because the true underlying cost function is not strictly linear. Deviations may also occur because the regression data typically come from past costs and activities that might be mismeasured or include unusual events, shifts in cost behaviour over time or random fluctuations. When interpreting regression results, we need to keep in mind that we are using regression analysis *only* because we do not know the actual cost function and must estimate it. Furthermore, we might not be confident that the cost we are trying to estimate is a mixed cost. We use regression to estimate the cost function and to learn more about how the cost behaves. Figure 2.6 presents the questions that we address when using simple regression to estimate a cost function.

Question about the cost function	Relevant simple regression statistics
How confident can we be that the actual fixed cost is greater than zero (i.e. that there is a fixed component in the cost function)?	*t*-statistic and *p*-value for the alpha coefficient
How confident can we be that the actual variable cost per unit of the cost driver is greater than zero (i.e. that there is a variable component in the cost function)?	*t*-statistic and *p*-value for the beta coefficient
Overall, how well does the cost driver explain the behaviour (i.e. the variation) in the cost?	Adjusted *R*-square, as well as *t*-statistic and *p*-value for both coefficients

FIGURE 2.6 ■ Questions addressed by simple regression analysis

Figure 2.7 shows the output from regressing Mount Dandenong Bikes' packing costs on the number of bikes packed. For each coefficient (alpha and beta), the regression output includes both a *t*-statistic and a *p*-value. We examine the *t*-statistic calculated for each coefficient to evaluate whether that coefficient is significantly greater than zero. The *t*-statistic compares the coefficient with its standard error. If the coefficient is small relative to the standard error, we cannot be confident that the coefficient is different from zero. If the *t*-statistic is significantly large (above 2), we have more confidence that our estimates for fixed and variable costs are different from zero. The p-value gives the statistical significance of the t-statistic, or the probability that the coefficient is not different from zero. Acceptable p-values generally need to be less than 0.10, and preferably less than 0.05.

A low p-value for the alpha coefficient gives us confidence that the fixed cost is significantly different from zero. Similarly, a low p-value for the beta coefficient gives us confidence that the variable cost is significantly different from zero. If a p-value is too high, we conclude that the coefficient should not be used in the cost function. Sometimes only one of the coefficients is statistically greater than zero. In this case, we generally conclude that the cost is not mixed, but instead is variable or fixed (depending on which coefficient is significant).

Interpreting the output from the Mount Dandenong Bikes example (see figure 2.7), the intercept (fixed cost) is $314 and the p-value for the t-statistic is 0.002. This result means that the fixed cost has a probability of being zero about 2 in 1000 times. We are quite confident that it is different from zero. The beta coefficient ($2.07) also has a small p-value (0.0004). Using this information, our total cost function would be TC = $314 + $2.07Q, where Q is the number of bikes.

SUMMARY OUTPUT				
Regression statistics				
Multiple R	0.98203762			
R-square	0.96439789			
Adjusted R-square	0.95549736			
Standard error	20.9306335			
Observations	6			
	Coefficients	Standard error	t-statistic	p-value
Intercept	314.374297	47.2560438	6.65257335	0.00265124
X variable 1	2.06601723	0.19847861	10.409269	0.00048107

FIGURE 2.7 ■ Regression analysis results for shipping costs and number of bikes

The adjusted R-square statistic reflects an estimate of the percentage of variation in cost that is explained by the cost driver. In the Mount Dandenong Bikes example, the adjusted R-square is 0.95. This result means that the variation in number of bikes packed explains about 95 per cent of the variation in packing cost. An advantage of regression analysis when more than one potential cost driver is involved is that we can compare the adjusted R-squares from several regressions that have different cost drivers for the same cost. The cost driver that provides the highest adjusted R-square explains the largest portion of changes in cost.

We will next illustrate how to use simple regression analysis to estimate a cost function for Small Animal Clinic. The process we will use is summarised in figure 2.8 (overleaf). We will also compare the results for simple regression with the two-point and high-low methods (see comprehensive example 2 overleaf).

1. **Consider the behaviour of the cost.** Decide whether the cost is likely to be a good candidate for regression analysis. The best candidates for regression are costs that appear to be mixed.

2. **Generate a list of possible cost drivers.** The cost drivers must be economically plausible; changes in the cost driver could potentially affect cost.

3. **Gather data.** We need data for both the dependent variable (the cost being estimated) and for one or more independent variables (the cost drivers).

4. **Plot the cost for each potential cost driver.** Scatter plots that have a positive slope or a football-shaped pattern indicate a potential linear relationship between the cost and the cost driver. Eliminate any cost drivers that do not figure a positive linear relationship with cost. If no cost drivers remain, the cost should not be estimated using regression analysis.

5. **Perform the regression analysis.** For each remaining potential cost driver, perform simple regression analysis with that driver as the independent variable. If necessary, perform a series of multiple regression analyses with different combinations of cost drivers. Use a spreadsheet program such as Excel to perform the regressions.

6. **Evaluate the appropriateness of each cost driver.** Use the goodness of fit statistic (adjusted R-square) to select those cost drivers that explain a high proportion of variability in the cost.

7. **Evaluate the sign and significance of the cost function's components.** Verify that each coefficient is positive. Use the p-values for the t-statistics to determine whether the intercept coefficient reflecting fixed cost and slope coefficient reflecting variable cost are significantly different from zero.

8. **Write the cost function as TC = F + V × Q.** If significantly different from zero, use the intercept coefficient as the estimated fixed cost and the independent variable coefficient as the estimated variable cost.

FIGURE 2.8 ■ Using regression analysis to estimate a cost function

Comprehensive example 2

Estimate of cost function using the two-point method and regression analysis

When Josh shows Lucy his revenue and cost estimates, she questions him about the cost of treatment supplies. Believing his estimate to be too high, she asks him to investigate this cost further.

Revised analysis of the treatment supplies cost

When Josh originally estimated the cost function for treatment supplies, he had only three data points — the cost for each of the past three years. With so few data points, he had used the high-low method to estimate the cost function. Using quarterly data, however, would give him more data points, allowing him to use other estimation techniques that would generate a higher-quality cost function.

Josh is also concerned about the accuracy of the data for the number of animal visits, which are tracked manually at the reception desk and sometimes not recorded. He considers using the number of bills recorded in the accounting system to count the number of animal visits, but a single pet owner often brings in more than one pet and yet receives a single bill. He considers whether another cost driver would be more accurate.

Josh knows that the veterinarians use different supplies for each visit because the needs of each pet are different. For example, a puppy may get a series of vaccinations at the same time, whereas an adult dog gets only one or two vaccinations. Yet when he uses number of animal visits as the cost driver, he assumes that the same amount of supplies is used for each visit. Josh knows that the bill for each visit includes charges for supplies. Therefore, the revenue per visit varies with the number and type of supplies used. He determines that revenue might be better correlated with treatment supplies than number of animal visits. He also thinks that the data for revenue per visit are more accurate because they are recorded by the accounting system when bills are created.

Quarterly data

Although Josh believes that revenue may be better correlated with treatment supplies cost than animal visits, he decides to analyse both drivers to learn more about their behaviour. He collects the following quarterly data for his analyses.

Quarter	Treatment supplies cost	Animal visits	Revenues
2006-1	$1 000	500	$18 125
2006-2	920	725	17 400
2006-3	1 120	700	20 300
2006-4	960	575	16 675
2007-1	966	750	18 900
2007-2	1 058	960	20 700
2007-3	1 288	600	24 300
2007-4	1 288	690	26 100
2008-1	1 404	700	28 350
2008-2	1 092	595	23 100
2008-3	1 404	910	29 400
2008-4	1 300	1 295	24 150

Scatter plots

First Josh creates scatter plots of the treatment supplies cost against animal visits and against revenues. When creating the scatter plots, he wants the vertical axes on the two plots to have the same scale so that he can compare them. He visually examines the plots and fits a trend line to each plot. Josh notices that most of the cost points are relatively close to the trend line in the revenue scatter plot shown in figure 2.9(a) (overleaf), whereas many of the data points are further away from the trend line in the animal visit scatter plot in figure 2.9(b). This observation suggests that revenue is likely to provide a more accurate cost function than number of animal visits.

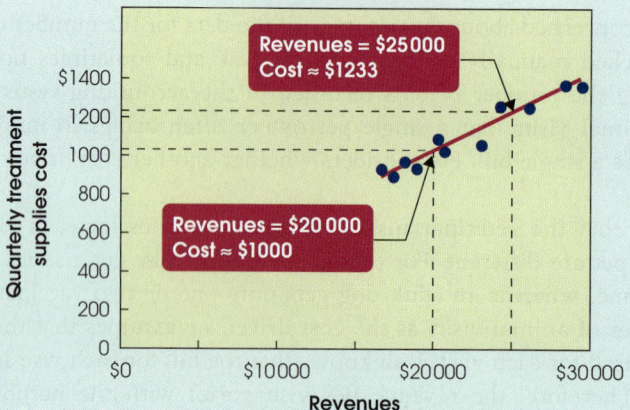

(a) Compared against quarterly revenues

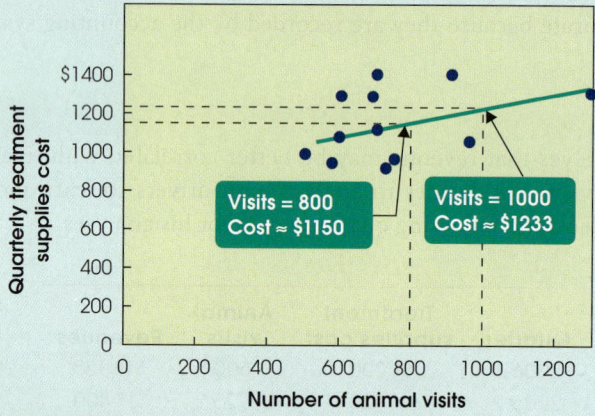

(b) Compared against quarterly animal visits

FIGURE 2.9 ■ Scatter plots for quarterly treatment supplies cost

Two-point method

First Josh decides to use the two-point method with revenue as the cost driver. He selects the points when revenues are $20 000 and $25 000, and draws a vertical line from these points on the revenue axis to the trend line, shown in figure 2.9(a). Where each vertical line intersects the trend line, he draws a horizontal line to the cost axis and visually estimates the cost for these points as $1000 and $1233 respectively. Dividing the change in cost ($1233 − $1000) by the change in revenues ($25 000 − $20 000), he estimates a variable cost of $0.047 per dollar of revenue, or 4.7 per cent of revenues. He then uses the data point for cost of $1000 to estimate the fixed cost, using the following formula for the cost function:

$$\$1000 = F + (4.7\% \times \$20\,000)$$

$$F = \$1000 - \$940 = \$60$$

Given these calculations, he estimates the cost function as

$$\text{TC} = \$60 + 4.7\% \times \text{Revenues}$$

Next Josh uses the two-point method with animal visits as the cost driver. He uses the same procedures as previously described to choose two points on the trend line, shown in figure 2.9(b). Given these two points, he estimates the cost function as shown opposite.

$$\text{TC} = \$813 + \$0.42 \times \textbf{Number of animal visits}$$

Simple regression analysis

Josh is concerned that his calculations using the two-point method may not be as accurate as he would like. He decides to perform simple regression analysis. When number of animal visits is the cost driver as in figure 2.10(a), the adjusted R-square is 0.035, which is very low. But when revenue is the cost driver as in figure 2.10(b), the adjusted R-square is quite high at 0.915, suggesting that changes in revenue explain about 91.5 per cent of the changes in supplies cost. He concludes that revenue is a much better cost driver than animal visits. However, he waits to reach a final conclusion until he analyses the rest of the regression results.

Regression statistics				
Multiple R	0.35044032			
R-square	0.12280842			
Adjusted R-square	0.03508926			
Standard error	174.643357			
Observations	12			
	Coefficients	Standard error	t-statistic	p-value
Intercept	934.164081	189.252112	4.93608271	0.00059059
Animal visits	0.28778123	0.24321795	1.18322365	0.2640863

(a) Using animal visits as the cost driver

Regression statistics				
Multiple R	0.96078362			
R-square	0.92310516			
Adjusted R-square	0.91541568			
Standard error	51.7074871			
Observations	12			
	Coefficients	Standard error	t-statistic	p-value
Intercept	258.579519	82.7169413	3.12607689	0.0107621
Revenue	0.03998896	0.00364975	10.9566301	6.8389E-07

(b) Using revenues as the cost driver

FIGURE 2.10 ■ Simple regressions for quarterly treatment supplies cost

Focusing on figure 2.10(b), Josh observes that the coefficients for both the intercept (259) and independent variable (0.040) are positive, as required to create a cost function. He notices that the *p*-value for the intercept is 0.01, suggesting only a small probability that the intercept could be zero. The *p*-value for the coefficient on revenue is even smaller at 0.000 000 68, suggesting a tiny probability that the coefficient could be zero. These results give Josh considerable confidence in the regression results. He creates a new cost function for treatment supplies as follows.

$$TC = \$259 + 4.0\% \times Revenue$$

Revised cost estimate

Josh's earlier estimate of $228 000 for 2009 revenue includes the matching grant. However, the grant, which accounts for half of all revenues, is not included in the quarterly data used to estimate the new cost function. Therefore, Josh needs to divide estimated revenues in half when using the new cost function: $228 000 ÷ 2 = $114 000. His revised estimate of the treatment supply cost for 2009 is:

$$TC = \$259 + (4.0\% \times \$114\ 000) = \$4819$$

Next, he revises his estimate of total 2009 costs. He previously estimated total costs to be $182 070, including $5560 in treatment supplies. His new estimate for total 2009 costs is $181 329 ($182 070 − $5560 + $4819). Finally, he revises his estimate of the 2009 surplus to account for changes in total costs:

$$Estimated\ surplus = \$228\ 000 - \$181\ 329 = \$46\ 671$$

Review of methods, total cost function

Josh reviews his results to gain a better understanding of how the various methods compare. A summary of his treatment supply cost estimates for 2009, for both cost drivers and for each estimation technique, follows:

		2006 Estimate
Number of animal visits (3800 estimated for 2009):		
High-low method	TC = $1000 + $1.20 per visit × Visits	$5560
Two-point method	TC = $813 + $0.42 per visit × Visits	$2409
Simple regression	TC = $934 + $0.29 per visit × Visits	$2036
Revenues ($114 000 estimated for 2009):		
Two-point method	TC = $60 + 4.7% × Revenues	$5418
Simple regression	TC = $259 + 4.0% × Revenues	$4819

Josh is glad that he is no longer using his original estimate based on the high-low method and animal visits as a cost driver. He believes that method would significantly overestimate the treatment costs. He is surprised to learn that the other two methods for animal visits as the cost driver might have significantly underestimated the cost. After comparing the two-point and regression results, he concludes that the two-point method is not very accurate. Overall, he decides that he will probably use regression analysis in the future to help with this type of estimate.

Finally, Josh revises the total cost function for the clinic. Even though revenue from pet owners is now being used as the driver for treatment supplies, other parts of the function still use the number of animal visits as the driver. He subtracts the $1.20 per animal visit that had been attributed to treatment supplies, leaving $15.20 for the other relevant variable costs. He also adjusts total fixed costs of $119 750 by subtracting $741 ($1000 old fixed cost estimate – $259 new fixed cost estimate), leaving $119 009. Thus, the revised cost function is

$$TC = \$119\,009 + (\$15.20 \times \text{Number of animal visits}) + (4.0\% \times \text{Fee revenue})$$

Josh and Lucy decide to continue budgeting average revenue per animal visit at $60 ($30 in fees plus $30 in matching grant). They can now use this cost function to analyse best-case and worst-case scenarios and will be better prepared for unexpected changes that might occur next year.

Uses and limitations of cost estimates

Uncertainties are a fact of life in the business world. Even the best available information and best decision-making processes may lead to poor outcomes. Nevertheless, managers make better decisions and obtain better average results when they use higher-quality information and decision-making processes. Because of uncertainties about future cost behaviour, we need to evaluate the quality of both our data and the various estimation techniques.

Information quality

One factor that affects the quality of past cost information is whether the accounting system is able to directly trace the costs to individual cost objects. For example, if Mount Dandenong Bikes' accounting system traces the cost of handlebars to each bicycle produced, then past handlebar costs are known with high accuracy. This information, in turn, will improve the quality of future handlebar cost estimates.

If the accounting system cannot trace a relevant cost to a cost object, the cost must instead be allocated. For example, costs such as insurance can be traced to the production facility but cannot be traced to any one bicycle. However, a portion of these costs can be allocated to each bicycle produced. Accounting systems often accumulate indirect costs into overhead cost pools that tend to include a mixture of both fixed and variable costs. Appropriate cost drivers for these cost pools are often difficult to identify. Nevertheless, past accounting data might be the best information available for estimating indirect costs.

Recall from chapter 1 that higher-quality information is more certain, complete, relevant, timely and valuable. Better accounting systems improve the quantity, relevance and timeliness of cost information. However, we may be unable to obtain higher-quality information. For example, in the Small Animal Clinic example, Josh initially lacked sufficient data to use regression analysis to separate mixed costs into fixed and variable components. This circumstance occurs frequently in the business world. Other common reasons why past cost information might be unavailable or too unreliable to use include the following:

- The organisation has operated for only a few periods.
- The organisation's operations have changed substantially.
- Inflation, deflation or other economic changes have altered the behaviour of costs.
- The organisation operates in an environment where technologies and costs change rapidly.
- The organisation's accounting system does not currently capture and report the needed information.

Under these circumstances, cost estimates based on past costs are of lower quality than cost estimates from better data. In addition, the quality of information often deteriorates over time. Accordingly, cost functions are most useful for estimating costs over short time periods, such as for the next year.

Average costs

Because financial accounting information is readily available, accountants and managers often want to rely on it for decision making. However, financial accounting measures are usually based on average costs, which are inappropriate for decision making. The **average cost (AC)** is simply computed as total costs (TC) divided by the quantity (Q) of activity or production (AC = TC/Q).

When average costs are used to estimate the cost function (TC = 0 + AC × Q), fixed costs are assumed to be variable. Therefore, future costs are either overestimated or underestimated unless future production is exactly the quantity used to calculate average cost per unit Consequently, we usually avoid using financial statement costs — or any other average costs — for decision making.

FIGURE 2.11 ■ Advantages and disadvantages of cost behaviour analysis approaches

Method and description	Advantages	Disadvantages
Engineered estimate of cost An analysis of labour time, materials and other resources used in each activity. Cost estimates are based on resources used.	■ Can use when no past data are available ■ Provides a benchmark for what future costs should be ■ Most accurate for estimating costs of repetitive activities ■ Identifies and measures some non-linear cost functions (e.g. economies of scale and learning curves)	■ Difficult to estimate some types of costs, such as overhead ■ Time-consuming ■ May not identify all costs
Analysis at the account level A review of the pattern in past costs recorded in the accounting system. Knowledge of operations is used to classify cost as variable, fixed or mixed.	■ Can be used when only one period of data is available ■ Best for costs that are fixed or variable ■ Provides information about types of costs incurred	■ Difficult to identify costs that are not strictly fixed or strictly variable ■ Relies on past costs, which might not represent future costs
Scatter plot A plot of past data points for cost against a potential cost driver. Visual analysis of the plot is used to decide whether the cost might be completely fixed, completely variable or mixed.	■ Provides information about cost behaviour in relation to potential cost drivers ■ Facilitates evaluation of whether a potential cost driver is viable	■ Does not compute a cost function ■ Relies on past costs, which might not represent future costs

FIGURE 2.11 (continued)

Method and description	Advantages	Disadvantages
Two-point method An algebraic calculation of a linear mixed cost function using any two data points of the cost and cost driver.	■ Can be used with as few as two data points ■ Computationally simple	■ Difficult to identify most representative data points for estimating future costs ■ Ignores all but two data points (inefficient use of data) ■ Mismeasures the cost function if data points come from more than one relevant range ■ Relies on past costs, which might not represent future costs
High-low method A specific application of the two-point method using the highest and lowest data points of the cost driver.	■ Same as two-point method ■ Does not require judgment for selecting data points	■ Same as two-point method ■ Highest and lowest data points are often atypical, distorting the cost function
Regression analysis A statistical technique that measures the average change in a dependent variable for every unit change in one or more independent variables. Creates a linear cost function where variable cost is the slope of the regression line and fixed cost is the intercept.	■ Increases cost function accuracy by using all available data points ■ Best for a strong positive linear relationship between the cost and cost driver ■ Easy to perform with available software ■ Provides statistics for evaluating the quality of results	■ Mismeasures the cost function if data points come from more than one relevant range ■ Inefficient for estimating a strictly fixed or strictly variable cost function ■ Relies on past costs, which might not represent future costs

Quality of estimation techniques

Figure 2.11 summarises the advantages and disadvantages of each cost behaviour analysis approach introduced in this chapter. None of the methods is best in all circumstances. For example, regression analysis is a higher-quality technique than the two-point or high-low methods for separating mixed costs into fixed and variable components. However, regression cannot be used when too few observations of past costs are available. In addition, most of the methods in figure 2.11 rely on past costs, which might need updating. The engineered estimate of cost method can be used when no past costs are available, and it also provides a benchmark that can be used to monitor the efficiency of costs in the future. Although we know that higher-quality techniques result in higher-quality information, we do not always use higher-quality techniques. Sometimes the cost exceeds the benefit; at other times we do not have adequate information required by a higher-quality technique.

Reliance on cost estimates

Concerns we have about the quality of cost information affect our reliance on the results. Managers might delay growth opportunities or alter operating decisions to avoid assuming extra risk in cases where they are less sure about their cost estimates. As managers make decisions, the quality of information affects the alternatives that they consider and the weight they place on various pieces of information.

Data limitations

The results from regression analysis are only as accurate as the data we use. The following need to be checked before data are used in regression analysis:

- The relationship between the cost and cost driver is economically plausible.
- Cost and cost driver data are matched and recorded in the appropriate period.
- Inflation and deflation have been taken into consideration.
- The relevant range reflects similar technologies across the range.
- No clerical errors occurred in the recorded data.
- Any data from periods with unusual events are eliminated.
- The activity levels for which we are predicting cost are within the relevant range; that is, we are not predicting cost for activity levels that are greater (smaller) than the largest (smallest) in our data set.

APPENDIX 2A

REGRESSION ANALYSIS — ADDITIONAL TOPICS

Multiple regression analysis

Multiple regression is used when more than one cost driver may provide the best estimate of a cost function. We use the same method to estimate the cost function as that illustrated earlier in the chapter. The only difference is that two or more independent variables (cost drivers) are used in the regression analysis.

Choosing cost drivers for multiple regression

Sometimes several cost drivers appear to be correlated with the cost we are estimating; their scatter plots show a possible linear relationship with the cost object. In these cases, we include all of the potential drivers in a multiple regression to determine the significance of each. Then we drop those drivers that have insignificant t-statistics. Remember, however, that each potential cost driver must have economic plausibility — a reason to believe that each one might drive the cost we are trying to estimate. Comprehensive example 3 demonstrates how cost drivers are used in multiple regression.

Comprehensive example 3

Using multiple regression to estimate a cost function

Print Masters Print Shop incurs overhead costs that are related to its printing machines (maintenance, depreciation, insurance etc.) and to the amount of paper printed (ink, storage and handling of paper, packing materials etc.). Figure 2A.1 summarises monthly data for overhead costs, machine hours, and reams of paper used for Print Masters Print Shop.

Month	Overhead costs	Machine hours	Reams of paper
1	$68 948	959	828 000
2	87 171	1 227	1 246 000
3	84 448	1 351	874 000
4	89 030	1 480	958 000
5	83 303	952	1 356 000
6	82 660	986	1 332 000
7	78 793	931	1 170 000
8	82 834	1 439	958 000
9	77 829	945	1 238 000
10	72 303	869	978 000
11	78 804	1 171	890 000
12	85 850	1 228	1 162 000
13	70 343	928	892 000
14	85 991	950	1 376 000
15	77 626	1 016	1 160 000
16	70 397	902	928 000
17	77 189	948	1 220 000
18	75 443	1 130	1 064 000
19	79 599	1 335	830 000
20	72 690	1 052	1 034 000
21	76 307	860	1 280 000
22	79 725	1 188	1 096 000
23	80 492	1 254	850 000
24	87 697	1 187	1 390 000
25	76 516	948	936 000
26	83 055	1 015	1 320 000
27	75 021	971	956 000
28	85 210	1 111	1 304 000
29	84 531	1 326	1 238 000
30	78 575	1 017	1 026 000

FIGURE 2A.1 ■ Data for print shop overhead costs and two potential cost drivers

Scatter plots and simple regression results

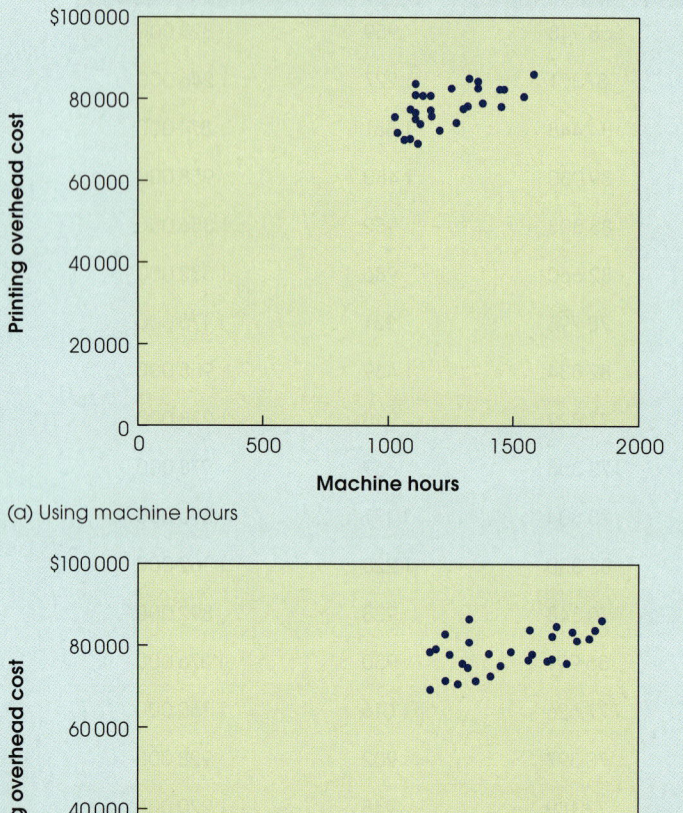

(a) Using machine hours

(b) Using reams of paper

FIGURE 2A.2 ■ Scatter plot of print shop overhead costs

A scatter plot is presented for machine hours in figure 2A.2(a) and for reams of paper in figure 2A.2(b). Each plot suggests a potential linear relationship with printing overhead costs because it appears to have an upward slope, although the slope does not appear to be very steep in either plot. Thus, based on the scatter plots, both cost drivers appear to be viable. Simple regression analysis for each potential cost driver confirms this evidence. A summary of the simple regression results is shown opposite.

As you can see from the summary opposite, the intercepts and slope coefficients for both regressions are highly significant. However, the adjusted R-square is 0.35 for machine hours and 0.22 for reams of paper. Thus, neither driver appears to be an overall good predictor of the variation in printing overhead cost.

	Machine hours	Reams of paper
Intercept coefficient	$58 800	$68 109
t-statistic (p-value)	11.43 (<0.0001)	11.63 (<0.0001)
Independent variable coefficient	$19.11	$0.02
t-statistic (p-value)	4.09 (0.0003)	3.08 (0.005)
Adjusted R-square	0.35	0.22

Multiple regression analysis

We can perform multiple regression analysis for printing overhead cost using both machine hours and reams of paper as independent variables. We will then see whether any improvement in overall explanatory ability occurs. The following excerpts come from the Excel printout for this regression:

Regression statistics	
Multiple R	0.90921678
R-square	0.82667515
Adjusted R-square	0.81383627
Standard error	2371.2674
Observations	30

	Coefficients	Standard error	t-statistic	p-value
Intercept	30338.7951	4371.83243	6.93960613	1.856E-07
Machine hours	24.3711259	2.57880204	9.45056098	4.7054E-10
Reams of paper	0.02073146	0.00247049	8.39163567	5.2945E-09

The adjusted R-square of 0.81 is much higher than for either individual cost driver. Therefore, the two drivers together appear to explain much more of the variation in printing overhead cost.

The intercept term (fixed cost) is $30 339 and is statistically significant. Both potential cost drivers — machine hours and reams of paper — are positive and significant. The total cost function is:

$$TC = \$30\,339 + (\$24.37 \times \textbf{machine hours}) + (\$0.02 \times \textbf{reams of paper})$$

If we expect that next month we will use 1000 machine hours and 1 million reams, we can predict our total cost to be

$$TC = \$30\,339 + (\$24.37)(1000) + (0.02)(1\,000\,000)$$

$$= \$30\,339 + \$24\,370 + \$20\,000$$

$$= \$74\,709$$

Regression analysis assumptions

To perform regression analysis, the number of observations must be greater than the number of independent variables. In addition, a number of assumptions are used in linear regression analysis. We investigate four of them here.

1. The dependent variable can be calculated as a linear function of a set of independent variables plus an error term. The error term is the distance from the regression trend line for each actual data point of cost versus cost driver.

2. The error terms have a normal distribution with a mean of zero. The t-statistics are based on the assumption that the errors are normally distributed. If this assumption is incorrect, we cannot know with any confidence whether the coefficients are different from zero.

3. The error terms have a constant variance for all of the observations, and they are not correlated with each other. Constant variance can be a problem with accounting data because costs from one period could be related to costs in the next period. For example, an accrual that occurs in one period is often reversed in the next period. In addition, variance often increases at higher or lower levels of activity. If error terms are correlated, the standard errors are inaccurate and therefore the t-statistics are not meaningful.

4. Relatively little correlation occurs among the independent variables. If the independent variables are highly correlated (multicollinearity), the coefficients are more likely to be inaccurate and this would create inaccuracies in our estimated cost functions. An example of correlated independent variables could be direct labour hours and machine hours, when labour is used to manage machines.

We test for the linearity assumption by examining a scatter plot to see whether the relationship between cost and the cost driver appears to have a generally linear trend. If this assumption is not met, linear regression analysis is not a useful tool. We test for normal distribution, uniform variance and uncorrelated error terms using scatter plots or other statistics methods. We plot the error terms against the independent variables. If error terms with small (large) values are associated with independent variables of small (large) values, the error terms are correlated with each other and the results from this model will not accurately reflect the underlying cost function. To determine whether independent variables are correlated, we use the correlation functions in a spreadsheet or statistical program. Independent variables that have a high correlation (above about 70 per cent) might cause problems with regression analysis. The correlated variables can be entered in a regression together and then independently to see whether the coefficient and t-statistics are affected by the correlation.

Additional regression analysis considerations

We can use regression analysis when we know that the majority of costs are likely to be only fixed or only variable, but in these cases, other techniques may be just as accurate and require less data-gathering time. Suppose we want to estimate a cost function for handlebars, which vary with production volume at Mount Dandenong Bikes. Either we ask purchasing to tell us the current per-unit cost and to check for price updates, or we divide the total cost of a recent purchase by the number of units purchased to develop an estimate of that variable cost. Similarly, to estimate a future fixed cost, we base our estimate on the fixed cost from one or more prior periods in the same manner shown for rent in comprehensive example 1.

Stepwise linear fixed costs

We learned earlier that the cost function for some fixed costs is stepwise linear. For example, in figure 2.2(b) on page 30, the cost function for rent, which increases as more space is needed due to high sales revenues, is shown opposite.

$$\text{TC} = \$6000, \text{ for } Q \leq \$30\,000 \text{ in sales}$$

$$\text{TC} = \$8000, \text{ for } Q > \$30\,000 \text{ in sales}$$

What happens if we apply regression analysis to past cost data from this stepwise linear cost function? Consider the following three possibilities:

1. If all the data points occurred when Q was below $30\,000, then rent will appear to be a fixed cost at $6000.
2. If all the data points occurred when Q was above $30\,000, then rent will appear to be a fixed cost at $8000.
3. If some data points occurred when Q was below $30\,000 and other data points occurred when Q was above $30\,000, then the regression trend line might be similar to the one shown in figure 2A.3. The simple regression results would appear to have both fixed and variable components. However, the cost estimates from the regression will be accurate only at a few points along the regression trend line.

To develop the most accurate cost function, we must define the cost according to its relevant range and reflect the appropriate limits in the cost function.

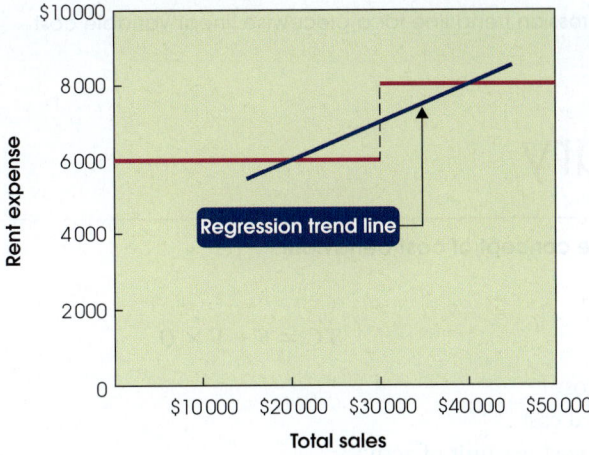

FIGURE 2A.3 ■ Regression trend line for a stepwise linear fixed cost

Piecewise linear variable costs

We learned earlier that the cost function for some variable costs is piecewise linear; the per-unit cost changes across relevant ranges of activity. For example, in figure 2.1(b) on page 29, the function for the total cost of bicycle tyres based on a volume purchase discount is

$$\text{TC} = \$10Q, \text{ for } Q \leq \text{bikes manufactured}$$

$$\text{TC} = \$600 + \$6(Q - 60), \text{ for } Q > 60 \text{ bikes manufactured}$$

What happens if we apply regression analysis to past cost data from this piecewise linear cost function? Consider the following three possibilities:

1. If all the data points occurred when Q was below 60, then the cost will appear to be variable at $10 per bike.
2. If all of the data points occurred when Q was above 60, then the cost will appear to be variable at $6 per bike.
3. If some data points occurred when Q was below 60 and other data points occurred when Q was above 60, then the regression trend line might be similar to the one shown in figure 2A.4 (overleaf). The simple regression results would underestimate per unit variable cost when Q is below 60 and overestimate it when Q is above 60.

Once again, it is important to define the cost according to its relevant range and reflect the appropriate limits in the cost function if we wish to develop the most accurate cost function.

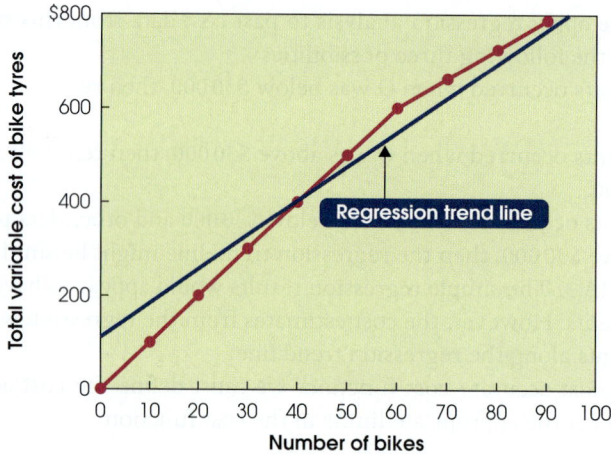

FIGURE 2A.4 ■ Regression trend line for a piecewise linear variable cost

Summary

1   **Understand the concept of cost behaviour.**

Linear cost function

$$TC = F + V \times Q$$

     TC = Total cost
     F = Total fixed cost
     V = Variable cost per unit of activity
     Q = Volume of activity (cost driver)

Assumptions
Within the relevant range, fixed costs remain fixed and the variable cost per unit remains constant.

Linear cost functions across more than one relevant range
Stepwise linear: Fixed costs change across relevant ranges.
Piecewise linear: Variable costs change across relevant ranges.

2   **Explain the different types of cost behaviour.**

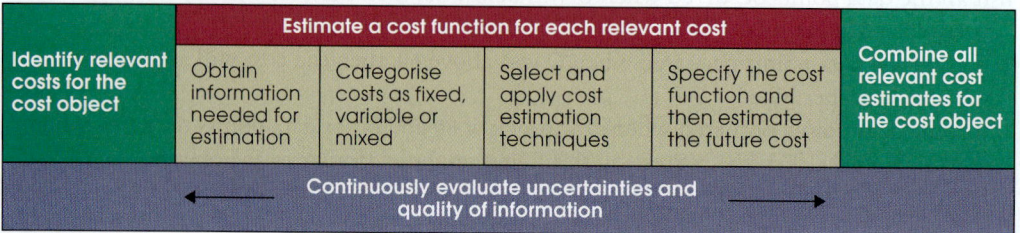

3 & 4   Understand and use estimation techniques to determine the cost function.

Engineered estimate of cost
Analyse amount of labour time, materials and other resources used in each activity. Estimate costs based on resources used.

Analysis at the account level
Review pattern in past costs recorded in the accounting system.
Use knowledge of operations to classify cost as variable, fixed or mixed.

Two-point method
Algebraically calculate a linear mixed cost function using any two data points of the cost and a cost driver. Preferably use the most representative data points.

High-low method
Apply the two-point method using the highest and lowest data points of the cost driver.

How does a scatter plot assist with categorising a cost?
Plot past data points for cost against a potential cost driver.
   Visually analyse plot to decide whether cost might be completely fixed, completely variable or mixed.

5   Utilise regression analysis in cost estimation.

Statistically measure the average change in a dependent variable for every unit change in one or more independent variables.
   Create a linear cost function where variable cost is the slope of the regression line and fixed cost is the intercept.

Simple regression
Has one independent variable.

Multiple regression (appendix 2A)
Has two or more independent variables.

6   Identify the uses and limitations of cost estimates.

Examples of reasons to estimate future costs
- Budgeting
- Planning future operations, such as setting employee work schedules, financing activities
- Making specific decisions, such as discontinuing a line of business, renting additional retail store space or hiring new employees

What do managers need to consider when using estimates of future costs?
- Uncertainties
  - Actual future costs are unknown.
  - Reliability of cost estimates is uncertain because of uncertainties about:
    - cost behaviour classification
    - cost drivers
    - changes in cost behaviour over time.
- Other considerations
  - Quality of cost information:
    - appropriateness of past costs for estimating future costs
    - accounting system information
    - information from outside the accounting system.
  - Quality of estimation techniques
  - Reasonableness of cost function assumptions

Self-study problems

Cost object; cost function estimation; opportunity cost

A computer manufacturer is deciding whether to produce a large monitor with a thin flat screen. One of the managers suggested that the incremental costs for this line of manufacturing will be primarily variable because the company currently has a lot of idle capacity.

REQUIRED

(a) What is the cost object in this decision?
(b) Is the accounting system likely to have the information needed to develop a cost function? Explain.
(c) What might be an appropriate estimation technique for this cost? Explain.
(d) What is the opportunity cost for using this idle capacity? Explain.

Solution to self-study problem 1

(a) Production of a large monitor with a thin flat screen
(b) If all of the parts for the monitor are currently used in the organisation, all of the information is likely to be contained in the accounting records. But new parts are most likely needed, since the monitor is large and probably involves different technology to achieve thin size. Thus, estimates of costs from suppliers will be needed. In addition, estimates for the amount of labour time will be needed. Although labour cost per hour can be found in the records, the amount of labour time is likely to be different for this monitor than for other monitors. If machines are used in production, an estimation of machine hours is necessary to determine whether maintenance and repair costs will increase.
(c) Estimating the cost of parts and the time involved in production is part of the engineered estimate of cost method.
(d) The opportunity cost of using idle capacity for one product is the contribution of other uses of the capacity. If another product could be manufactured and sold, that product's contribution margin is the opportunity cost. If the capacity can be rented or leased out, the rent or lease payments are the opportunity cost. If there are no other uses for the capacity, the opportunity cost is zero.

SELF-STUDY PROBLEM 2

Cost driver choice using regression

Nursery Supply manufactures wooden planter tubs for small trees. Each wooden planter requires about the same level of effort in labour and machinery. The managers of Nursery Supply want to improve the quality of their budgets. They are considering three alternative cost drivers for overhead: assembly time, labour hours and machine hours. The statistics for regressions using last year's monthly data for each of the three possible cost drivers follow:

Cost driver = Assembly time

Intercept = \$55 000 (t-statistic = 2.44, p-value = 0.08)

Slope = \$21 (t-statistic = 2.85, p-value = 0.05)

Adjusted R-square = 0.31

Cost driver = Labour hours

    Intercept = $20 000 (*t*-statistic = 2.95, *p*-value = 0.03)

    Slope = $31 (*t*-statistic = 3.00, *p*-value = 0.01)

    Adjusted *R*-square = 0.46

Cost driver = Machine hours

    Intercept = $10 000 (*t*-statistic = 1.45, *p*-value = 0.25)

    Slope = $38 (*t*-statistic = 3.19, *p*-value = 0.005)

    Adjusted *R*-square = 0.70

REQUIRED

(a) Write the cost function for each of the cost drivers.
(b) Explain the meaning of the adjusted *R*-square for the assembly time analysis.
(c) Explain the meaning of the *p*-value for the intercept in the machine hours analysis.
(d) Explain the meaning of the *p*-value for the slope in the labour hours analysis.
(e) Given only the regression results, which cost driver would you choose for overhead costs? Explain.
(f) Why do managers often use models such as a cost function to estimate future costs?

Solution to self-study problem 2

(a) Each cost function is written using the regression intercept term as the fixed cost and the slope as the variable cost.

    Cost driver = Assembly time

        TC = $55 000 + $21 × assembly time

    Cost driver = labour hours

        TC = $20 000 + $31 × labour hours

    Cost driver = Machine hours

        TC = $38 × machine hours

    (*Note:* Because the *p*-value for its *t*-statistic is 0.25, the intercept is not statistically different from zero. Therefore, the fixed cost is assumed to be zero.)

(b) The adjusted *R*-square indicates that variation in assembly time explains about 31 per cent of the variation in overhead. The remaining 69 per cent is unexplained.

(c) The *p*-value for the intercept in the regression of overhead cost against machine hours is 0.25. It means a 25 per cent probability that the intercept (fixed cost) is zero instead of $10 000.

(d) The *p*-value of the slope in the labour hours regression is 0.01, which means a 1 per cent probability that the variable cost for overhead related to labour hours could be zero instead of $31 per labour hour.

(e) First we examine the adjusted *R*-square (see figure 2.8 on page 42, items 6 and 7). At 70 per cent, machine hours appears to be the best cost driver. However, we also need to evaluate whether its coefficients are reasonable. The slope coefficient is positive and has only a small probability of being zero (*p*-value 0.005), so it is likely to be a reasonable estimate. The intercept coefficient is generally reasonable so long as it is not significantly negative. In this case, the intercept has a high p-value (0.25), so we can assume the fixed cost is zero.

(f) Managers cannot know future costs. Nevertheless, they need to estimate future costs to make decisions. A cost function based on past information helps managers estimate future costs; the function can also be updated to incorporate expected cost information so that predictions are as precise as possible. Using a model such as the cost function also helps managers be more methodical in their approach to cost estimation, improving the quality of cost estimates. Higher-quality estimation methods provide higher-quality information for decision making.

Questions

2.1 'As volume increases, total cost increases and per-unit cost decreases.' What type of linear cost function does this describe? Draw a simple graph of this type of cost function.

2.2 A motor vehicle assembly plant closes every August to retool for the next year's model. How should August's cost data be used in estimating the overhead cost function?

2.3 You have been asked to provide the managing director with an approximate cost function for the entity's activities, and it must be done by this afternoon. Some members of the board of directors want to understand why performance varies so much across store locations. They have asked for a quick analysis today and want a more detailed analysis next week. Which cost estimation technique(s) should you consider using? Explain.

2.4 At two levels of activity within the relevant range, average costs are $192 and $188 respectively. Assuming the cost function is linear, what can be said about the existence of fixed and variable costs?

2.5 You are about to start a coffee shop business. Identify the likely key costs and classify each as fixed or variable.

2.6 Explain how information from a scatter plot helps in categorising a cost as fixed, variable or mixed.

2.7 Explain the analysis at the account level approach to developing a cost function.

2.8 List two examples of non-linear cost functions and describe a method of developing a cost function for each one.

2.9 Why might some have trouble classifying costs as fixed or variable?

2.10 The trend line developed using regression analysis provides a more accurate representation of a mixed cost function than the two-point or high-low methods. Explain why.

Exercises

2.11 **Linear, stepwise linear and piecewise linear cost functions**

(a) Total fixed costs are $10 000 per week and the variable cost per unit is $8. Write the algebraic expression for the cost function and graph it. What are the assumptions of the cost function?

(b) Total fixed costs are $25 000 per week up to 2000 units a week and then jump to $35 000 per week. The variable cost per unit is $8. Write the algebraic expression for the cost function and graph it.

(c) The average cost to produce 10 000 units is $45 and the average cost to produce 12 000 units is $44. Estimate the average cost to produce 15 000 units.

(d) The total cost function for Hot Dog Days, a hot dog cart business, is TC = $5000 + 45% × total revenues. Estimate the total cost for a month when total revenues are $10 000.

2.12 Piecewise linear cost function; regression measurement error The following is the description of a cost: total fixed costs are $50 000 per month and the variable cost per unit is $10 when production is under 1000 units. The variable cost drops to $9 per unit after the first 1000 units are produced.

REQUIRED

(a) Write the algebraic expression of the cost function and graph it.

(b) Assume that the cost function just described is a reasonable representation of total costs. If the accountant performed regression analysis on weekly observations of this cost and did not realise that there were two relevant ranges, what problems would arise in the cost function that was produced? In other words, how would the cost function be mismeasured?

2.13 Cost function and assumptions Bison Sandwiches is a small restaurant that sells a variety of sandwiches and beverages. Total fixed costs are $20 000 per month. Last month total variable costs were $8000 when total sales were $32 000.

REQUIRED

(a) Write out the algebraic expression for the cost function.

(b) What assumptions do we make when we develop this cost function?

2.14 Cost function; opportunity cost; relevant costs Yummy Yoghurt sells yoghurt cones in a variety of natural flavours. Data for a recent month follow:

Revenue		$9000
Cost of ingredients	$4500	
Rent	1000	
Store attendant salary	2300	
		7800
Profit		$ 1200

REQUIRED

(a) Categorise each cost as fixed or variable.

(b) Create a cost function.

2.15 Fixed, variable and mixed costs Spencer and Church is a CPA entity engaged in local practice. Some selected items from its chart of accounts are listed below.

REQUIRED

For each account, indicate whether the account represents a fixed, variable or mixed cost for the operations of the local practice office. If mixed, indicate whether it is predominantly fixed or variable. Explain your answers.

(a) Staff wages
(b) Clerical wages
(c) Rent
(d) Licences
(e) Insurance
(f) Office supplies
(g) Professional dues
(h) Professional subscriptions
(i) Property taxes
(j) Advertising

2.16 Cost function using regression; other potential cost drivers The new cost analyst in your accounting department just received a computer-generated report that contains the results of a simple regression analysis. The analyst was estimating the costs of the marketing department using units sold as the cost driver. Summary results of the report are shown overleaf.

Variable	Coefficient	t-statistic	p-value
Intercept	12.44	1.39	0.25
Units sold	222.35	2.48	0.001
Adjusted R-square = 0.61			

REQUIRED

(a) Write an equation for the cost function based on the regression analysis.
(b) What does the adjusted R-square tell you?
(c) What other cost drivers could potentially explain marketing costs? Explain.

Problems

2.17 Cost function using high-low and regression; quality of cost estimates Following are sales and administrative cost data for Big Jack Burgers for the last four months:

	Sales	Administrative costs
September	$632 100	$43 333
October	842 500	57 770
November	1 087 900	62 800
December	1 132 100	68 333

Administrative cost is a mixed cost, and sales is a potential cost driver.

REQUIRED

(a) Using the high-low method, create a cost function for administrative costs.
(b) In your own words, explain why the high-low method might not be a good method for estimating the cost function.
(c) Create a scatter plot and add a trend line. After examining the plot, use your judgment to determine whether the cost is fixed, variable or mixed.
(d) Perform regression analysis to create a cost function for administrative costs.
(e) Can we know for certain that the cost function from part (d) provides a good estimate for next month's administrative costs? Why?
(f) Discuss whether sales are an economically plausible driver for administration costs for Big Jack Burgers.

2.18 Scatter plot; cost function using regression The following scatter plot and simple regression results used revenue as a potential cost driver for research and development costs.

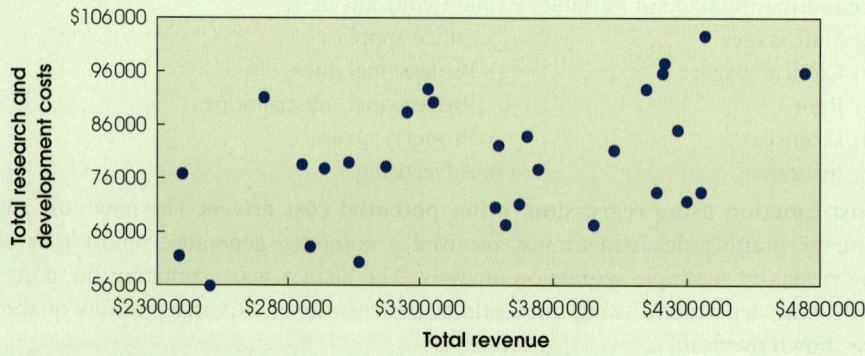

SUMMARY OUTPUT				
Regression statistics				
Multiple R	0.462332038			
R-square	0.213750914			
Adjusted R-square	0.185670589			
Standard error	10894.44062			
Observations	30			

	Coefficients	Standard error	t-statistic	p-value
Intercept	50364.97682	10834.0628	4.648761758	7.2426E-05
Revenue	0.008179276	0.002964572	2.759007802	0.01010244

REQUIRED

(a) Discuss whether the scatter plot suggests that revenue is a cost driver for research and development costs

(b) Using the regression results, write the cost function for research and development costs.

(c) Based on the regression results, discuss whether it would be appropriate to use total revenue as a cost driver for research and development costs.

(d) If you use the cost function from part (b) to estimate next month's research and development costs, what assumptions are you making? Identify at least three assumptions and discuss their reasonableness.

2.19 Cost driver; cost categories; appropriateness of regression; relevant information Susan looked at her long-distance telephone bill with dismay. After leaving her job last year to become a self-employed consultant, her long-distance charges had grown considerably. She had not changed long-distance plans for years, partly because she hated taking the time to review the range of service providers and plans. However, the size of her long-distance bill made it clear that it was time to make a change. She had recently seen numerous advertisements by telephone companies offering much lower rates than she was currently paying, but she was sure that at least some of those plans offered low rates only for night and weekend calls.

Susan called her current long-distance service provider and asked how she could obtain a lower rate. She mentioned hearing that a competitor was currently offering long distance at 5c per minute. In responding to the service representative's questions, Susan verified that most of her long-distance calls are weekday and out of state. She also agreed that her activity over the past two months — approximately 500 minutes of long distance per month — was her best estimate for future calling activity. Given this information, the service representative suggested that Susan buy the long-distance service plan with the following features:

(i) Up to 500 minutes of long distance for a flat fee of $20 per month.

(ii) No refunds would be provided for usage less than 500 minutes per month.

(iii) Any minutes over 500 per month would be billed at 10c per minute.

(iv) No service change fee or cancellation fee would apply.

REQUIRED

(a) What is the cost driver for Susan's long-distance telephone costs, assuming that the cost object is her consulting business?

(b) In the proposed service plan, which of the costs are fixed and which are variable? Explain.

(c) Would regression analysis be an appropriate tool for Susan to use in deciding whether to buy the new service plan? Why?

(d) Is the cost of Susan's current long-distance service plan relevant to this decision? Why?

(e) Explain why Susan cannot be certain whether the new service plan will reduce her long-distance costs.

(f) List additional information that might be relevant to Susan in deciding whether to buy the new service plan.

(g) Are Susan's long-distance services most likely a discretionary cost? Explain.

(h) Are Susan's long-distance services most likely a direct or indirect cost, assuming that the cost object is an individual consulting job? Explain.

(i) Describe the pros and cons of the new service plan.

2.20 Cost categories; cost function The University Lounge has been reporting losses in past months. In July, for example, the loss was $5000.

Revenue		$ 70 000
Expenses		
Purchases of prepared food	$ 21 000	
Serving personnel	30 000	
Cashier	5 500	
Administration	10 000	
University surcharge	7 000	
Utilities	1 500	75 000
Loss		$ (5 000)

The Lounge purchases prepared food directly from University Food Services. This charge varies proportionately with the number and kind of meals served. Personnel who are paid by the Lounge serve the food, tend the cash register, wait on and clean tables, and wash dishes. The staffing levels in the Lounge rarely change; the existing staff can usually handle daily fluctuations in volume. Administrative costs are primarily the salaries of the Lounge manager and her office staff. The university charges the Lounge a surcharge of 10 per cent of its revenue. Utility costs are the costs of cooling, heating and lighting the Lounge during its normal operating hours.

The university's management is considering shutting the Lounge down because it has been operating at a loss.

REQUIRED

(a) List the fixed expenses of the Lounge.

(b) List the variable expenses of the Lounge and the most likely cost driver for each expense.

(c) Write out the cost function for running the Lounge.

(d) Estimate the profit or loss for August if the revenues of the Lounge increase to $80 000.

(e) Explain why the original data show a loss but part (d) shows a profit. Be specific.

2.21 Cost behaviour; scatter plot Polar Bear Ski Wear is a shop that sells skiwear at a ski resort. Its cost accountant developed the following scatter plot for the cost of electricity for lights, heating and cooling against retail sales revenue.

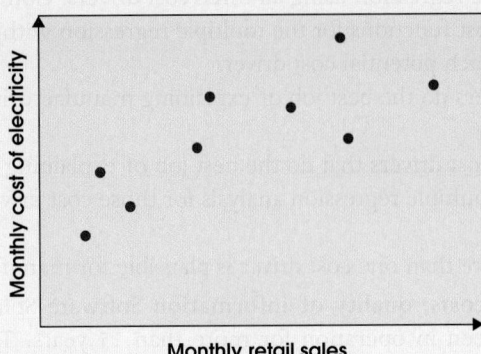

REQUIRED

(a) In a business such as retail sales, what usually causes the cost of electricity to vary?

(b) In what time of year would most skiwear be sold at a ski resort?

(c) In the scatter plot, the cost of electricity appears to be related to volume of retail sales. If this shop specialised in selling swimwear, would the scatter plot look different? Explain what would change.

(d) Identify and explain another cost that is similar in nature to the cost of electricity. When you plot the cost against a cost driver, a relationship becomes apparent. However, the cost varies with something other than the cost driver. (Think of other situations where this type of relationship might occur.)

2.22 Cost function using regression; scatter plots; three potential cost drivers Laura Mills is the controller of Peer Jets International, a manufacturer of small corporate jets. She has undertaken a project to study the behaviour of overhead cost. She has assembled factory overhead data for the last 30 months from the company's manufacturing facility. Laura has asked you to develop a model to predict the level of manufacturing overhead.

The following categories of information are available to Laura. Manufacturing overhead includes all of the overhead costs associated with the manufacturing plant. Labour hours are the number of hours manufacturing employees worked. Machine hours are the total hours that machinery was used for the period. Tons of raw materials are all of the raw materials that were used for that particular month.

Additional data for this problem is available from your instructor.

REQUIRED

(a) Create a scatter plot of manufacturing overhead for each of the potential cost drivers.

(b) Would you eliminate any of the potential cost drivers based on the scatter plots? Why?

(c) Explain why you create a scatter plot of the data before you perform regression analysis.

(d) To practise your regression analysis skills, perform a simple regression analysis of manufacturing overhead for each of the three potential cost drivers. Write the cost function from each regression.

(e) Based on the simple regression results, which cost driver does the best job of explaining manufacturing overhead costs? Explain.

(f) Do your regression results support your answer to part (b)? Explain.

2.23 **Cost function using multiple regression (appendix 2A)** Refer to the data and requirements of problem 2.22.

REQUIRED

(a) Perform multiple regression using all three cost drivers. Compare the adjusted R-squares and cost functions for the multiple regression with the results of simple regressions for each potential cost driver.

(b) Which cost drivers do the best job of explaining manufacturing overhead costs? Explain.

(c) Select only the cost drivers that do the best job of explaining manufacturing overhead costs. Perform multiple regression analysis for those cost drivers and write the cost function.

(d) Explain why more than one cost driver is plausible for manufacturing overhead costs.

2.24 **Use of prior year costs; quality of information** Software Solutions is a family-owned business that has been in operation for more than 15 years. The board of directors is comprised of mainly family members, plus a few professionals such as an accountant and lawyer. Regina is a staff accountant who has been working on the budget for the last several weeks. The chief financial officer (CFO) needs to present the budget at the next board meeting and wants a preliminary copy in two days. Regina is certain that she will not be able to finish the budget within two days. Several department heads have not turned in their preliminary figures, and two departments have budgeted large increases in fixed costs for replacing computer equipment. Regina knows she should have alerted the CFO about these budgeted increases, but she has not had time.

One of her co-workers knows that Regina is behind and suggests that she use last year's budgets for those departments that have not provided information and also for the departments that increased their budgets by large amounts. The co-worker says that the budget can be straightened out later because the board does not pay attention to the details.

REQUIRED

(a) Is this an ethical dilemma for Regina? Why?

(b) Why might it be important for the board of directors to have as much updated information as possible about the budget?

(c) What should Regina do, given that not enough time is available to gather high-quality information? Explain your thinking.

2.25 **Scatter plots; cost function using regression; two potential cost drivers** Suppose we need to predict the cost of maintenance for Brush Valley High School for the upcoming school year. From the school district records we gather weekly data about costs and volumes for two potential cost drivers: labour hours used in the maintenance department and number of enrolled students.

| | | Potential cost drivers | |
| | Total maintenance | Number of maintenance | Number of |
Week	cost	hours worked	students
1	$16 690	238	534
2	13 560	194	532
3	13 540	108	534
4	16 060	229	530
5	12 430	101	533

Week	Total maintenance cost	Number of maintenance hours worked	Number of students
6	20 860	298	537
7	18 420	244	540
8	12 310	98	540
9	13 770	108	541
10	16 990	225	538
11	20 650	289	540
12	14 770	118	539

REQUIRED

(a) Identify and explain two potential cost drivers for total maintenance cost, in addition to number of students and maintenance hours worked.

(b) Create a scatter plot, first for maintenance cost against hours worked and then maintenance cost against students.

(c) Would you eliminate either cost driver based on the plots? Explain.

(d) Perform regression analysis using each cost driver. Use your judgment to determine the most appropriate cost driver and write out the cost function for maintenance cost.

(e) Can we know for certain that the cost driver chosen in part (d) is the best cost driver? Why?

2.26 **Cost function using account analysis and high-low method** The Elder Clinic, a not-for-profit entity, provides limited medical services to low-income elderly patients. The manager's summary report for the past four months of operations is reproduced here.

	March	April	May	June	Total
Number of patient visits	849	821	778	842	3 290
Patient fees	$ 4 230	$ 4 180	$ 3 875	$ 4 260	$ 16 545
Medical staff salaries	13 254	13 256	13 254	14 115	53 879
Medical supplies used	3 182	3 077	2 934	3 175	12 368
Administrative salaries	3 197	3 198	3 197	3 412	13 004
Rent	1 000	1 000	1 000	1 100	4 100
Utilities	532	378	321	226	1 457
Other expenses	2 854	2 776	2 671	2 828	11 129
Total expenses	24 019	23 685	23 377	24 856	95 937
Operating surplus (loss)	$ (19 789)	$ (19 505)	$ (19 502)	$ (20 596)	$ (79 392)

The clinic receives an operating subsidy from the city, but unfortunately, the operating loss that has been incurred through June $(79 392) is larger than anticipated. Part of the problem is the salary increase that went into effect in June, which had been overlooked when the budget was submitted to the city last year. To compound the problem, the cold winter months traditionally bring with them an increase in cold-related health problems. Thus, the clinic is likely to experience an increase in patient visits during July.

The clinic's managers are considering an increase in patient fees to reduce losses. However, they are reluctant to raise fees because the patients have low incomes. They will raise fees only if it is necessary.

REQUIRED

(a) Use your judgment to classify costs as fixed, variable or mixed. Explain how you classified each item.

(b) Create a cost function for the Elder Clinic. Use the high-low method to estimate the function for any mixed costs.

(c) Use the cost function to estimate July expenses based on a projection of 940 patient visits.

(d) List reasons why management of the Elder Clinic cannot know with certainty what the expenses will be during July. List as many reasons as you can.

(e) Describe the pros and cons of using your cost estimate from part (c) to decide whether to raise patient fees.

(f) The managers need your July cost estimate to help them decide whether to raise patient fees. Use the information you learned from parts (a) to (e) to write a memo to the director of the Elder Clinic presenting your estimate of July costs. Provide the director with appropriate information for understanding your methodology and evaluating the reliability of your cost estimate.

2.27 Cost function judgment and methodology Suppose you have the responsibility of creating a cost function for the costs of an internet service provider's help line.

REQUIRED

(a) What is the cost object? Identify where you might obtain information about past costs for the cost object.

(b) Identify at least two potential cost drivers. Explain where you might obtain information about past volumes for each cost driver.

(c) What other information would you like to obtain before estimating the cost function? How might you obtain that information?

(d) Identify the techniques introduced in this chapter that you would be most likely to use in creating the cost function. Explain why.

2.28 Adjusting data for use with regression; outlier Smeyer Industries is a large entity with more than 40 departments, each employing 35 to 100 people. Recent experience suggests that the cost function used to estimate overhead in department IP-14 is no longer appropriate. The current function was developed three years ago. Since then, a number of changes occurred in the facilities and processes used in department IP-14. The changes happened one at a time. Each time a change was made, the cost accountant felt the change was not major enough to justify calculating a new overhead cost function. Now it is clear that the cumulative effect of the changes has been large.

You have been assigned the task to develop a new cost function for overhead in department IP-14. Initial analysis suggests that the number of direct labour hours is an appropriate cost driver. Departmental records are available for nine months. The records reveal the following information.

Month	Actual overhead	Direct labour hours
March	$68 200	8 812
April	71 250	8 538
May	68 150	8 740
June	73 500	9 176

Month	Actual overhead	Direct labour hours
July	38 310	2 123
August	70 790	9 218
September	80 350	8 943
October	68 750	8 821
November	68 200	8 794

An assistant has analysed the data for March through July and made the appropriate adjustments except for the following items (for which the assistant was unsure of the proper treatment).

(i) The semi-annual property tax bill for department IP-14 was paid on 30 June. The entire amount of $3000 was charged to overhead for June.

(ii) The costs to install a new piece of equipment with a life of 10 years in the department were charged to overhead in April. The installation costs were $4300.

(iii) Factory depreciation is allocated to department IP-14 every month. The department's share, $8000, is included in overhead.

(iv) A strike closed the plant for three weeks in July. Several non-union employees were kept on payroll during the strike. Their duties were general housekeeping and 'busy work'. These costs were charged to overhead.

You also have the details for the overhead account for the months of August and September (see following table). You were hired on 1 October and have been keeping the department accounts since then. Therefore, you know that the data for October and November are correct, except for any adjustments needed for the preceding items.

Department IP-14
Overhead control

August	Explanation	Amount
4	Miscellaneous supplies	$ 10 450
5	Payroll for indirect labour	5 500
15	Power costs: department IP-14	12 250
19	Payroll for indirect labour	6 000
19	Overtime premium	890
24	Factory depreciation	8 000
26	Miscellaneous supplies	27 700
	Total for August	$ 70 790

September	Explanation	Amount
2	Payroll for indirect labour	$ 6 000
7	Miscellaneous supplies	12 100
15	Power costs: department IP-14	11 100
15	Power costs: department IB-4	10 850
16	Payroll for indirect labour	6 500
16	Overtime premium	950
21	Miscellaneous supplies	19 350
28	Factory depreciation	8 000
30	Payroll for indirect labour	5 500
	Total for September	$ 80 350

August has 31 days and September has 30 days.

REQUIRED

(a) Using the information provided, adjust the monthly cost data to more accurately reflect the overhead costs incurred during each month.

(b) Discuss whether the data for July should be included in the estimate of future costs. Use a scatter plot to help you answer this question.

(c) Develop a cost function by regressing overhead costs in department IP-14 on direct labour hours. Discuss whether your cost function would be reasonable for estimating future overhead costs. Ignore any items you will discuss in part (d).

(d) Identify and discuss any additional adjustments that might be needed to more accurately measure overhead costs for the regression in part (c).

(e) Explain why adjustments probably need to be made to information from accounting records when estimating a cost function.

REFERENCE

1 Registered trademark of Microsoft Corporation.

A costing framework

IN BRIEF

Organisations have a range of different decisions to make using cost data. In this chapter the focus is on the determination of the full cost (or total cost) of a cost object. Managers identify one or more cost objects based on the relevant information they need for a particular decision, for budgeting and planning, or for valuing products or services. To determine the full cost requires the tracing of direct costs and the allocation of indirect costs. The cost data for this purpose may take various forms, including actual costs (found in the general ledger) or data derived from estimates of future cost.

After studying this chapter, you should be able to:

1	Understand the role of cost objects for costing purposes.
2	Differentiate between direct and indirect costs.
3	Outline the process of indirect cost allocation.
4	Identify the steps within a costing framework.
5	Apply the costing framework in a service entity setting.
6	Apply the costing framework in a support department setting.
7	Outline the limitations of cost allocation data.

The cost of providing corporate legal services in Australia

A growing issue for Australian law firms is how to compete in a global market where large corporate customers are increasingly demanding quality legal advice at highly competitive rates. Most large corporate clients now employ their own team of inhouse lawyers to manage or oversee the firm's legal activities. A significant part of the inhouse legal function is to outsource specialist legal requirements to varying external law firms. The focus for corporate clients is on obtaining unique product offerings from legal specialists who are high in quality as well as efficiently priced. This emerging environment has resulted in increasing global pricing and product competition among individual law firms striving to enhance their legal revenue growth with key corporate clients.

Their multinational corporate clients argue that for law firms to remain competitive in Australia, the firms need to properly position, price and competitively market their legal expertise. For example, the National Australia Bank (NAB) consumes more than 500 000 legal hours per year, and it expects both quality and cost efficiency in its contracted legal work. Some corporate entities such as the ANZ Bank are increasingly utilising New Zealand law firms over Australian firms because lower salaries, lower rents and a positive exchange rate can make their legal advice up to 25 per cent cheaper than that of Australian law firms (Towers et al. 2005).

For the external law firms, revenue is directly related to the time spent on an individual client project, and is often referred to as direct 'billing hours'. For a full understanding of the relationship between their revenue (total billing hours) and associated costs (costed hours), it is necessary to accurately track costs to the cost object (client project). As the majority of

their costs relate to the time spent by the salaried legal employees (for example, legal secretaries, paralegals, lawyers and senior partners), achieving the right mix of salaried hours can enhance a firm's efficiency and thus its competitiveness. The inhouse lawyer for the NAB, David Krasnostein, argues that for Australian law firms to be efficient, they need to have the bulk amount of costed hours conducted by the cheapest lawyers or paralegals, and overseen by the senior partners to maintain the expected quality of work.

In addition to the time spent by a lawyer with each client, other costs such as photocopying and telephone calls are also considered direct costs that can be traced and billed to every individual case. Indirect overhead resources — such as building, rent, equipment, insurances and utilities — are allocated to individual jobs to determine the total cost of the legal service provided. In a recent review of legal costs in New South Wales, it was found that overheads actually comprise a significant proportion of legal costs. For example, a large law firm employing more than 56 principals will have approximately 64.8 per cent overhead expenses as a percentage of its gross fee dollars. In small firms with only one lawyer, the overheads can account for as much as 73.3 per cent of gross fee dollars For firms with large overheads it is increasingly difficult to remain competitive with firms who compete on economies of scale. In these situations, it may be necessary for some firms to redesign their costing systems to better understand the relationship between their indirect overheads and the individual client jobs.

In addition to being affected by indirect overhead costs, law firms are also being called to account for their time-based billing practices. In 1958, law firms estimated their annual fee revenue to be approximately 1300 legal hours per lawyer each year. In comparison, lawyers are now expected to work more than 1800 fee-earning hours a year — an average of 12 hours a day, six days a week (Kuckes 2002). The credibility and transparency of billing practices have been questioned by corporate clients concerned with the rising costs of legal services. They are worried that time-based charging allocates all major risks to the client and rewards those who take the longest to complete work, regardless of output quality. Furthermore, with the added pressure on lawyers to increase their fee-earning targets, time-based charging can encourage lawyers to meet their firms' revenue targets by performing unnecessary work or increasing billable hours to the extent that they are too busy or tired to provide high-quality output. Time-based charging can be argued to encourage short-term efficiency outcomes to the detriment of long-term success. That is, short-term gains in efficiency can potentially compromise the overall objective of excellence and differentiation in legal service product offerings.

Sources: Information from Kuckes, N 2002, 'The hours: the short, unhappy history of how lawyers bill their clients', *Legal Affairs*, September/October; Legal Fees Review Panel Report 2005, 'Legal costs in New South Wales', December, www.lawlink.nsw.gov.au; Towers, K, Moran, S & Priest, M 2005, 'Judgement day: lawyers feel heat over costs', *Australian Financial Review*, 16 May.

Issues from this scene setter to look for in the chapter include:

- The importance of identifying cost objects.

- The role and treatment of direct and indirect costs.

- How overhead/indirect cost allocation can play an important role in a costing framework.

- The impact of different allocation bases on the determination of the cost for the cost object.

Cost objects

It is important for an entity to understand why costs are incurred — to enable the management of costs and to facilitate more informed decision making. This will require the costs in the financial records to be assigned to the specific object that caused the cost to be incurred in the first place. A **cost object** is anything for which a separate measurement of cost is desired. Examples of cost objects are products, services, customers, departments, business units or geographic regions. You should note that, even though an entity is able to view the costs through these different lenses, the total costs of the entity do not change. Figure 3.1 illustrates some of the many cost objects that cause an entity to incur the costs recorded in the accounting information system.

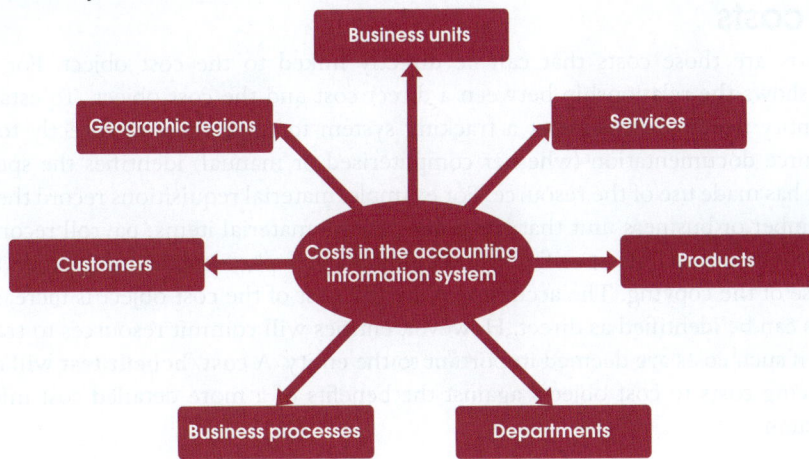

FIGURE 3.1 ■ Cost objects

Entities will use a costing system to collect and report the cost of resources used by particular cost objects. Traditionally, costing systems such as job costing and process costing have focused on the determination of the inventoriable product cost (a cost that complies with accounting standards) for external financial reporting. (Both systems are discussed in more detail in chapters 13 and 14.) These systems focus on production costs only and are typically structured on a departmental basis.

However, due to an increasingly competitive business environment coupled with an increase in the level of costs common to many cost objects, entities have had to adopt a new approach to costing systems. They have done this by trying to understand costs incurred at all stages of the value chain: from research and development to design, production, distribution and customer service. As a consequence, costing systems have been developed to support internal management rather than to merely measure the inventoriable product cost (the inventory value of manufactured products). Known as activity-based costing (ABC) systems (see chapter 4), such systems take a more contemporary approach to cost determination by enabling an entity to capture costs both pre- and post-production and to measure the cost of any cost object. The focus is on aligning costs to activities rather than departments. For example, under a conventional costing system, an entity might assign salary costs to the accounts payable department. However, the salary costs represent employees' efforts in undertaking a variety of activities such as invoice payment, cheque issuing, credit assessment and payment reconciliations against the bank account. A contemporary costing system would assign the salary costs to the activities themselves instead of to the accounts payable department.

We will now discuss how to measure the **full cost** of a cost object. In order to determine the full cost, it is necessary to identify the costs incurred by the cost object.

Direct and indirect costs

The need for cost information will determine the cost object that is the focus for cost collection. The cost information could be needed for a particular decision, for budgeting and planning, or for valuing products or services. When calculating the total cost for any cost object, it is necessary to identify those costs that have a cause-and-effect relationship with the cost object, known as direct costs, and those costs that are common to many cost objects and cannot be easily related to any specific cost object, known as indirect costs. The classification of costs as either direct or indirect depends on the particular cost object of interest; the following discussion explores how we distinguish between the two types of costs.

Direct costs

Direct costs are those costs that can be directly linked to the cost object. For example, figure 3.2 shows the relationship between a direct cost and the cost object. To establish this link, an entity needs to implement a tracking system to trace the cost directly to the cost object. Source documentation (whether computerised or manual) identifies the specific cost object that has made use of the resource. For example, material requisitions record the product, service number or business unit that has requested the material items; payroll records record employee payments against specific business units; and a photocopier might code and store the purpose of the copying. The accuracy of the full cost of the cost object is increased when more costs can be identified as direct. However, entities will commit resources to track direct costs only if such costs are deemed important to the entity. A **cost/benefit test** will assess the cost of tracing costs to cost objects against the benefits of a more detailed cost information tracing system.

FIGURE 3.2 ■ Relationship of direct cost to a single cost object

Indirect costs

Indirect costs (also referred to as **overheads**) are those costs that are used for the benefit of multiple cost objects. One cost has a relationship to many cost objects. Figure 3.3 shows the relationship between an indirect cost and the many cost objects that consume the resource. It might be possible to trace such costs directly to an individual cost object, but such an exercise would not pass the cost/benefit test. For example, what would be involved in collecting information about the number of nails used in the construction of a house or the amount of glue used to laminate office desks?

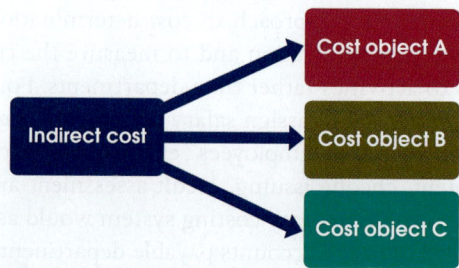

FIGURE 3.3 ■ Relationship of indirect cost to multiple cost objects

Classifying costs as direct or indirect

As explained above, the classification of a cost as either direct or indirect will depend on the specific cost object that has been identified as the focus for the cost analysis, together with a cost/benefit assessment of tracing the cost. Consider this example of how costs are identified as either direct or indirect for a specific cost object: Fabulous Diamonds is a local rock group that performs regularly at venues around the Asia–Pacific region. Costs incurred by the group during October are listed below. You will note the classification of each cost as either direct or indirect in relation to a show held at the Pony Club venue in Melbourne.

1. Rehearsal room hire to practise for the shows in October (indirect cost).
2. Petrol costs incurred to go to rehearsal and the shows in October (no record of kilometres travelled; indirect cost).
3. Wages of a sound engineer for each show (direct cost).
4. Advertising brochures for the shows during October (indirect cost).
5. Interest payment on loan for musical instruments (indirect cost).
6. Payments to band members for each show (direct cost).
7. Guitar strings — new set needed for each show (direct cost).

The cost object here is the show held at the Pony Club venue in October. Only those costs that were incurred directly for this particular show will be classified as direct costs — items 3, 6 and 7. All other costs (items 1, 2, 4 and 5) would be classified as indirect because the expenditure is for the benefit of all shows held in October.

The issue of the classification of direct and indirect costs in an industry-based setting can be explored further by reading the chapter 3 article at the end of this book.

Process of indirect cost allocation

As indirect costs are incurred for the benefit of multiple cost objects, the determination of the full cost for a particular cost object requires the assignment of indirect costs to the many cost objects that receive the benefit of the resources. **Cost allocation** refers to the allocation of indirect costs to specific cost objects.

Why would an entity allocate indirect costs? The allocation of indirect costs enables the full cost of the cost object to be determined. However, unless required by an external party, such allocation occurs at the discretion of each entity and is done to provide information for internal purposes. Entities are motivated to allocate indirect costs for many reasons:

- To determine the full cost of a specific cost object in order to undertake profitability analysis, provide a basis for pricing decisions, and assist in resource allocation decisions.
- To allocate the cost of shared services such as accounts payable, payroll and information technology. Cost assignment will remind departmental managers of the full economic impact of their decisions.
- To encourage the use of central resources. If managers are to be charged for the costs of a service (for example, legal services and training services) regardless of whether they use the service or not, then they will be encouraged to use it.
- To control costs by encouraging mutual monitoring. If a manager is to be charged for a shared service, the allocated costs will be benchmarked against external providers to ensure that the allocation is within commercial limits.
- To comply with external requirements (for example, the determination of inventoriable product costs in line with accounting standards).

Cost drivers

In order to allocate indirect costs, an appropriate cost driver (also known as an allocation base) will need to be identified to establish the link between the indirect cost and the many cost objects that make use of the resource. A **cost driver** provides a measure of activity that explains the cost object's use of the indirect cost. The accuracy of the cost allocation is increased if there is a cause-and-effect relationship between the cost driver and the cost. That is, a change in the use of the cost driver will cause a corresponding change in the amount of cost incurred. Other criteria can also be used in the selection of an appropriate cost driver. They include:

- *cause and effect* — choosing the variables that *cause* resources to be consumed (for example, allocating machine costs based on the cost object's use of machine time)
- *benefits received* — identifying the *beneficiaries* of the outputs of the cost object (for example, allocating advertising costs based on the cost object's increase in income)
- *fairness or equity* — selecting the costs that appear *reasonable* and *fair*
- *ability to bear* — allocating costs in proportion to the cost object's *ability to bear them* (for example, allocating indirect costs based on a cost object's level of profit)
- *behavioural* — selecting a cost driver *to modify behaviour* (for example, using direct labour hours to encourage a reduction in the use of labour hours).

An analysis of the above criteria shows that the cause-and-effect cost driver will be the most appropriate to use if the objective is accuracy of the full cost. All other criteria are subjective and may lead to behavioural problems. For example, if you were the manager of the department with the highest revenue, how would you react if you were burdened with the majority of the indirect costs incurred to support all departments? The benefits received by particular cost objects might be difficult to pinpoint; for example, how can an entity identify which particular department benefited from an entity-wide advertising campaign? The ability to bear criteria will burden better performing departments, while behavioural criteria are more focused on modifying behaviour than developing the most accurate full cost.

Cost drivers can be classified as either volume drivers or activity drivers. **Volume drivers** use a measure of output to assign the indirect costs; for example, labour hours, machine hours or units of output. It is assumed that indirect costs are consumed by the cost object in relation to its use of the volume driver. However, if indirect costs are caused by factors other than volume, then incorrect allocation may lead to cross-subsidisation between the cost objects. Cost objects that use more of the cost driver will be burdened with a higher proportion of indirect costs. This may lead to the entity making incorrect decisions; for example, by allocating the advertising budget to a product that is actually unprofitable.

The **activity drivers** relate to the attributes of the individual activities and recognise that factors other than volume cause indirect costs to be used by cost objects. Cross-subsidisation may be eliminated by the use of activity drivers. Accountants often use a cost hierarchy to help them identify activities, and then assign costs to these activities. ABC developers identified a number of general categories for the cost hierarchy based on different levels of operations. The classification of indirect cost according to the activity hierarchy aids in the identification of an appropriate activity cost driver. For a manufacturing entity, the hierarchy would include:

- *unit-level costs* — costs incurred for each unit of output (for example, the cost of electricity to operate machines)
- *batch-level costs* — costs incurred for the benefit of a group of products simultaneously (for example, the cost of setting up machines to manufacture batches of product)

- *product-level costs* — costs incurred for the benefit of a specific product family (for example, the cost of designing specific products)
- *facility-level costs* — costs incurred for the benefit of the whole entity (for example, the cost of running corporate headquarters).

The activity hierarchy shows that a volume driver would be appropriate only for a unit-level cost. Accountants are not restricted to these categories: others can also be used to analyse costs when organisations want to focus on different facets of their operations. For example, costs could be categorised by business segment or by strategic emphasis, such as quality or protection of the environment.

Determining the allocation rate

Indirect costs are allocated based on the usage of a chosen cost driver. The allocation process involves three steps:

1. Structure the cost allocation formula. This requires identifying the indirect costs to be allocated and selecting the cost driver that will link the indirect cost to the cost object.
2. Calculate the indirect cost rate. This is done by dividing the indirect costs by the total cost driver usage.
3. Allocate cost to the cost object. This is calculated by multiplying the indirect cost rate by the cost object's use of the cost driver.

How does an entity develop the formula to start the allocation process? The first step is to decide on the number of indirect cost pools; that is, whether there is one or many. A **cost pool** is simply a grouping of individual costs. Cost pools can be grouped on a departmental basis, an activity basis or on some other criteria. How is this grouping determined? Similar costs will be grouped together on the assumption that the same cost driver explains resource consumption for each cost by the cost object, and the number of indirect cost pools will be made via a cost/benefit test. The cost of collecting detailed data will be weighed against the cost of errors in decision making arising from having a less accurate measure of full costs. A cost allocation formula will be developed for each cost pool.

An entity may choose to measure the costs using actual costs or budgeted costs, or even further classify them according to cost behaviour (fixed or variable). This is discussed further in appendix 3A of this chapter. The determination of an actual **indirect cost rate** (the rate used to assign the cost to the cost object) will not be possible until the end of the financial period, when actual results are known. If the actual indirect cost rate is calculated on a monthly basis, it can vary from month to month due to fluctuations in the cash flow pattern. To overcome this delay in obtaining information and to smooth out fluctuations in cash flows, entities will use budgeted costs to calculate a **predetermined indirect cost rate**, which is based on budgeted costs. The use of budgeted costs will also provide a benchmark against which actual costs can be measured to assess performance and assist in pricing and budget preparation.

As the number of cost pools increases, the accuracy of the cost information also increases because each new cost pool will have a different cost driver for allocation purposes. This enables each cost pool to have an appropriate cost driver that best explains resource consumption. However, as the number of cost pools increases, the need to collect information about individual cost drivers also increases. This will lead to an overall increase in the resources needed to undertake the cost assignment.

Once the cost driver has been identified for each cost pool, the total use of the cost driver for the financial period under investigation will need to be determined. Cost driver usage will be based on either the budgeted or actual usage. By dividing the total indirect costs by the total use of the cost driver, a measure of the cost per unit of the cost driver will be calculated. The determination of this unit indirect cost rate will enable the allocation of the indirect costs to the many cost objects that have made use of the resource. Such allocation will be based on each cost object's use of the cost driver.

A costing framework

Identifying the cost pools and related cost drivers enables the full cost for the desired cost object to be determined. Figure 3.4 illustrates the process of determining the full cost (direct cost plus allocated indirect cost) for any cost object. As mentioned earlier, the level of sophistication of the costing system — that is, the number of cost pools, the classification of indirect cost pools and the cost drivers selected — will be at the discretion of each entity and determined by its information needs.

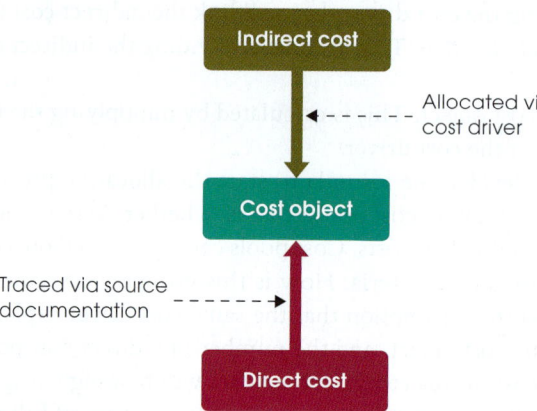

FIGURE 3.4 ■ Overview of a simple costing system to determine the full cost of a cost object

The simple costing system in figure 3.4 depicts the tracing of the direct cost via source documentation and the allocation of the indirect cost based on the cost object's use of the cost driver.

Costing systems for service entities are similar to the ones used by manufacturers (which we explore in other parts of this text). Source documents are used to trace direct costs to a specific job, and overhead costs are allocated. For example, in hospitals, physicians order treatments directly on computers at the nurses' stations. From these treatment orders, materials are requisitioned and costs and patient charges are recorded as part of each patient's stay. Charges and costs are also accumulated for resources such as the number of meals served, X-rays received and minutes spent in the operating room.

When allocating overhead, service entities often use the labour hours of their professional employees as an allocation base. For example, accountants and lawyers record professional labour hours and other direct costs to specific jobs. Overhead cost is then allocated on the basis of the professional labour hours used for each specific job.

Service entities often use information from their costing systems to facilitate cost management, productivity measurement and billing. Consulting firms and other organisations that manage large projects often track job costs in conjunction with their project management systems.

Comprehensive examples 1 and 2 demonstrate costing in a service entity.

Comprehensive example 1

Determination of full cost for operating departments

Partridge Insurance Company has three service departments — finance, personnel, and computer services — that provide services to the entity's three operating departments: home insurance, car insurance and life insurance. The following data were recorded for each department for 2007.

	Cost	Cost driver	
Finance	$ 150 000	Number of invoices	= 5000
Personnel	120 000	Number of employees =	100
Computer services	300 000	Number of computers =	60
Home insurance	500 000		
Car insurance	400 000		
Life insurance	300 000		
Total costs	$1 770 000		

The three operating departments used the service departments' activities or resources as follows:

	Invoices	Employees	Computers
Home insurance	1500	50	25
Car insurance	2000	30	25
Life insurance	1500	20	10

Partridge Insurance Company wants to determine the full cost of each operating department to assist in the pricing of insurance premiums for the various policies issued by the entity. The above information shows that each operating unit requires the three service departments to provide services such as invoice processing, personnel services and information technology support.

Step 1: Overview of cost assignment — identification of cost objects, cost pools and cost drivers

Before commencing any calculations, it is important to understand the costing system that will be used to determine the full cost. The first step is to identify the relevant cost object of interest, the number and type of cost pools, and the cost drivers to assign indirect costs. An overview of the costing system is shown in figure 3.5. The cost objects of interest are the three operating departments: home insurance, car insurance and life insurance. In order to determine the full cost for each of the operating departments, it is necessary to assign the indirect costs, which are the direct costs of each of the three service departments (that is finance, personnel, and computer services). Therefore, we have three indirect cost pools classified on a departmental basis, measuring costs on an actual basis. Figure 3.5 highlights the one-to-one relationship that exists between the direct cost and the cost objects, and the one-to-many relationship between the indirect costs and the cost objects.

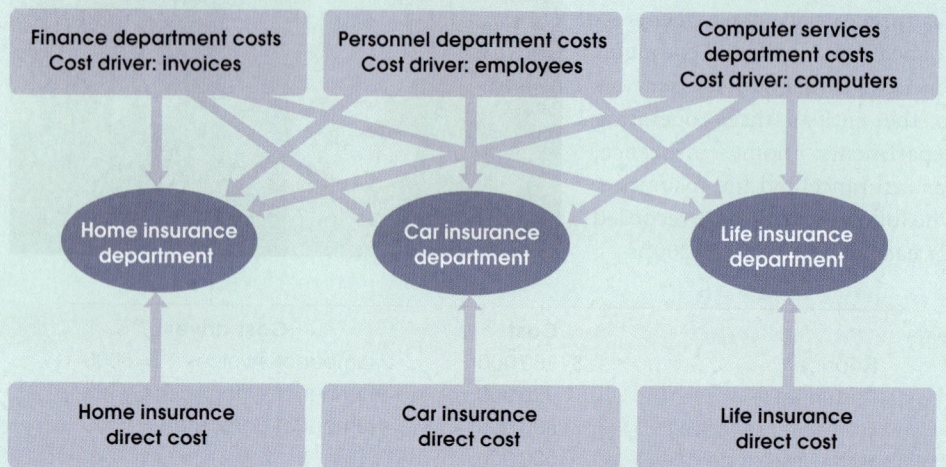

FIGURE 3.5 ■ Overview of costing system for Partridge Insurance Company

The cost drivers identified to allocate the indirect costs are the number of invoices (finance department), the number of employees (personnel department) and the number of computers (computer services department). The actual usage of the cost driver is being used for allocation purposes. Remember that the selection of an appropriate cost driver will be specific to each entity. Other cost drivers might be selected by other entities — perhaps even by different people in the same entity. For example, Partridge Insurance Company could have chosen the time taken to process the invoices rather than using the number of invoices, or the number of keystrokes per person rather than the number of computers, or salary levels rather than the number of employees. The one chosen should reflect the cause and effect link.

The next stage in the allocation process is to calculate the indirect cost rate for each service department cost pool.

Step 2: Determination of the indirect cost rates for each cost pool

In this example there will be three cost allocation formulas — one for each of the three service department cost pools. Each allocation formula will require the determination of the total cost for the accounting period and the total use of the cost driver for each service department. The indirect cost rate can then be calculated and the indirect costs allocated based upon the use of the cost driver by the individual cost objects, which in this example are the operating departments.

For the finance department the total direct costs are $150 000, with 5000 invoices being processed in the current accounting period. Each invoice paid by the finance department will lead to a $30 charge being assigned to the operating department to cover such costs as finance staff salaries, stationery and telephone costs. Using the same rationale for the personnel department costs and computer services department costs, charges of $1200 per employee and $5000 per computer will be assigned to the operating departments.

Department (Cost pool)	Allocation formula	Indirect cost rate
Finance	$150 000/5000 invoices	$30 per invoice
Personnel	$120 000/100 employees	$1200 per employee
Computer services	$300 000/60 computers	$5000 per computer

Step 3: Allocation of indirect costs to the cost objects

Now that the indirect cost rates have been determined, the allocation of the indirect costs can be undertaken by applying the indirect cost rate to the cost object's use of the cost driver. Partridge Insurance Company uses the cost object's actual use of the cost driver to allocate indirect costs. For example, the indirect cost rate for the finance department is $30 per invoice. The home insurance department raises 1500 invoices per year and will be allocated $45 000 (1500 invoices × $30) to cover its share of the costs incurred by the finance department.

	Home insurance	Car insurance	Life insurance
Finance	$45 000	$60 000	$45 000
	(1500 invoices × $30)	(2000 invoices × $30)	(1500 invoices × $30)
Personnel	$60 000	$36 000	$24 000
	(50 employees × $1200)	(30 employees × $1200)	(20 employees × $1200)
Computer services	$125 000	$125 000	$50 000
	(25 computers × $5000)	(25 computers × $5000)	(10 computers × $5000)
Indirect costs	$230 000	$221 000	$119 000

Step 4: Determination of the full cost of each cost object

The full cost for each of the cost objects can now be determined. You will notice that the total cost of $1 770 000 (refer to original information) has now been assigned to the three cost objects — the operating departments.

	Home insurance	Car insurance	Life insurance	Total costs
Indirect costs	$230 000	$221 000	$119 000	$ 570 000
Direct costs	500 000	400 000	300 000	1 200 000
Full cost	$730 000	$621 000	$419 000	$1 770 000

This illustration highlights the different lenses that have been used to view the costs — the total cost for the entity, the direct costs of the individual departments and the full cost of each operating department.

How can Partridge Insurance Company use the data from the allocation process?

- To determine the full cost of each operating unit.
- To review the current premiums on insurance policies.
- In strategic management — to make decisions about which insurance policies to offer in the future based upon individual profitability analysis of policies.
- In cost management — to pressure the service departments to lower costs if individual business managers believe that the charges are too high.

Comprehensive example 2

Costing in a law firm: costing client services

Nighthawk Law Company special-ises in copyright protection for authors. A client approached the law firm about handling his law-suit against a large film company that he believes stole the plot from one of his novels for a made-for-TV movie.

Estimated job costs and price

The law partners estimated that the case (the cost object of interest) would require 500 hours of professional labour. Nighthawk's accountant estimated the following direct costs:

Direct professional labour (500 hours)	$ 75 000
Direct support labour	20 000
Fringe benefits for direct labour	15 000
Photocopying	1 000
Telephone calls	1 000
Total direct costs	$112 000

Last year, Nighthawk's overhead totalled $450 000. The two law partners worked about 5000 professional labour hours. The accountant developed an estimated overhead allocation rate of $90 per direct labour hour ($450 000 ÷ 5000). Therefore, the estimated overhead cost for this case is $90 × 500 hours = $45 000 and the total estimated cost is $157 000 ($45 000 + $112 000). The law firm's policy is to mark up cost by 20 per cent for the estimated price. Using this mark-up, the estimated profit for the case is $31 400 ($157 000 × 20%). Using all of this information, the partners estimate the client's service price as follows:

Direct professional labour (500 hours)	$ 75 000
Direct support labour	20 000
Fringe benefits for direct labour	15 000
Photocopying	1 000
Telephone calls	1 000
Total direct costs	112 000
Overhead ($90 × 500 hours)	45 000
Total costs	157 000
Margin ($157 000 × 20%)	31 400
Total estimated service price	$ 188 400

Competitor's job costs and price

A competing law firm traces only the direct professional labour hours as a direct cost and considers all other costs to be indirect (overhead). These overhead costs are allocated at an estimated rate of $160 per professional labour hour. The accountant for this law firm estimates that this copyright case will cost $75 000 + $80 000 ($160 × 500) = $155 000. The competitor uses the same mark-up rate as Nighthawk Law Company: 20 per cent of estimated total cost, or $31 000 ($155 000 × 20%). The partner in the competitor firm estimates the client's service price as follows:

Direct professional labour (500 hours)	$ 75 000
Overhead ($160 × 500 hours)	80 000
Total costs	155 000
Margin ($155 000 × 20%)	31 000
Total estimated service price	$186 000

Monitoring job costs

The prices estimated by the two law firms are close in amount. However, the costs used to estimate the price are also used to monitor costs in each law firm. Nighthawk accounts separately for direct costs such as fringe benefits, photocopying and telephone calls. The competitor includes these costs in overhead. Each approach has its pros and cons.

Nighthawk's accounting system incurs additional costs to separately accumulate and assign fringe benefits, photocopying and telephone calls to individual jobs. Each of these costs is accumulated in a separate cost pool. Fringe benefits are allocated to jobs based on information already available about professional and support labour hours or costs. To allocate photocopying costs, the firm needs a system (such as the use of client codes) to record photocopying usage for each job. Telephone costs are traced using telephone logs. The accuracy of records for photocopying and telephone costs depends on the ability and willingness of professional and support staff to maintain good records.

The benefit of separately accumulating and assigning fringe benefits, photocopying and telephone call costs as direct costs is an improved monitoring of costs. The overhead cost pool is considerably smaller and includes fewer different types of costs. As the proportion of costs that can be directly traced to individual jobs increases, the accuracy of the costing system increases. Therefore, systems with lower proportions of overhead more accurately capture the flow of resources to individual jobs.

Applying the costing framework in a support department setting

The costing framework outlined in the previous section enables the calculation of the full cost of a cost object for different purposes and can be adapted for different settings. In order to achieve this, the costing framework is adapted to meet the specific needs of the users of the cost information. The structure is influenced by the choices relating to cost objects, cost pools and cost drivers.

Operating departments are the departments or divisions within an organisation that commonly manufacture goods or produce services for external customers or clients (for example, the home insurance, car insurance and life insurance departments of Partridge Insurance Company in comprehensive example 1). They can also be referred to as the revenue-generating departments. Support departments provide internal services to each other and to operating departments (for example, the finance, personnel and computing departments in comprehensive example 1).

As shown in figure 3.6, the process for allocating support department costs to operating departments is a further application of the costing framework discussed earlier in the chapter and demonstrated in comprehensive example 1. This section focuses on alternative ways of allocating the support department costs. The process involves the following steps:

1. Clarify the purpose of the allocation.
2. Identify support and operating department cost pools.
3. Assign costs to cost pools.
4. For each support department cost pool, choose an allocation base.
5. Choose and apply a method for allocating support department costs to operating departments.
6. If relevant, allocate support costs from the operating departments to units of goods or services.

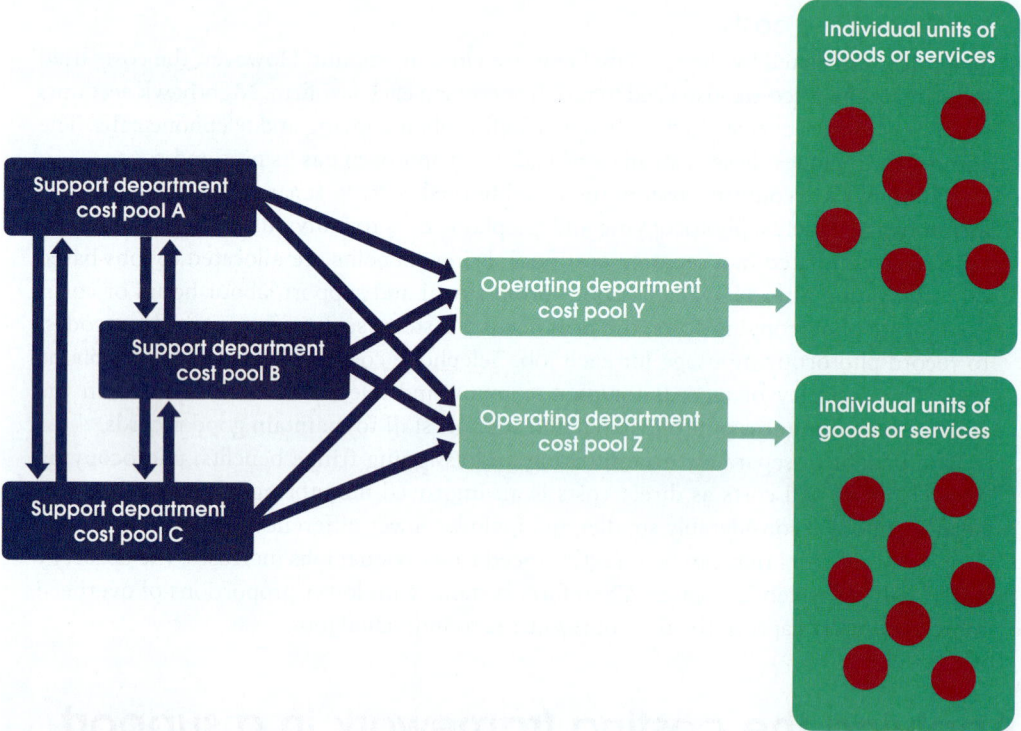

FIGURE 3.6 ■ Allocation of support department costs

Allocation methods

Three allocation methods commonly used to allocate support department costs to operating departments are:

■ direct method
■ step-down method
■ reciprocal method.

A close look at comprehensive example 1 will reveal that we used the direct method to allocate the support department costs. In the following sections we detail the three allocation methods. Each method is formally introduced and illustrated.

Direct method

The **direct method** allocates the costs of each support department only to the operating departments. Because no costs are allocated among support departments, none of the interactions among support departments are reflected under this method. *Under this method, the cost objects of interest are the operating departments.* In comprehensive example 3 we demonstrate the direct method using Middletown Children's Clinic. Suppose the accountants for the clinic have identified two support departments (housekeeping and administration) and two operating departments (medical and dental). As shown in figure 3.7, the direct method uses each support department's allocation base to allocate the costs for that department to each of the two operating departments.

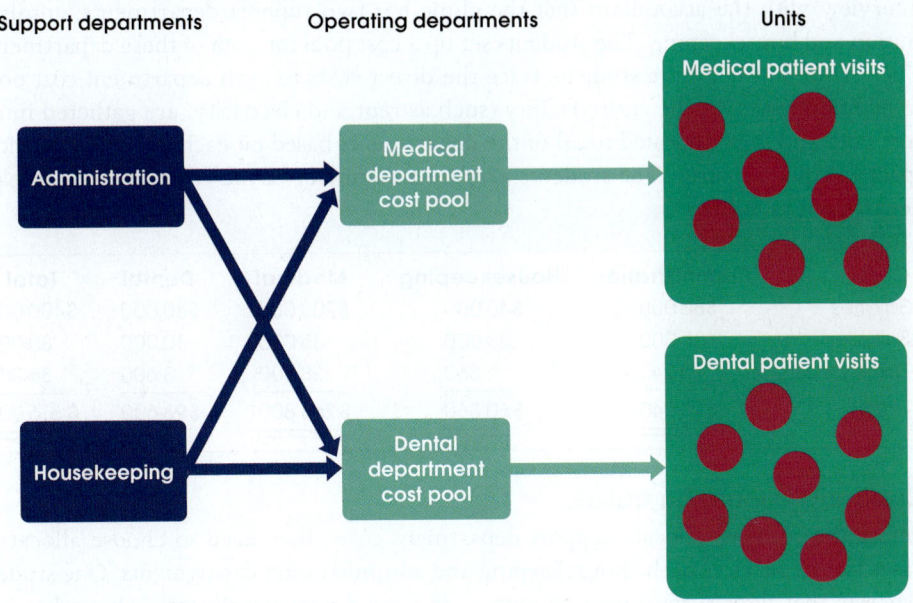

FIGURE 3.7 ■ Direct method

Comprehensive example 3

Direct method allocation

Middletown Children's Clinic, a not-for-profit organisation, operates medical and dental clinics for children of low-income families. The organisation receives private donations and state grants to help defray costs. The managers would like to set fees that are as low as possible while also covering costs.

The accounting department at the local college sponsors a work experience program, in which accounting students develop their professional skills and contribute to the community by working as volunteers for not-for-profit organisations. This

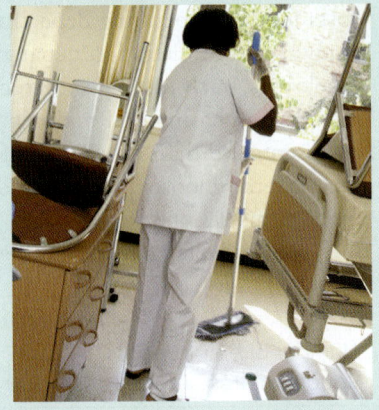

year, a team of accounting students has been assigned to the clinic. The students have been asked to help allocate all of the clinic's costs to patient visits. The clinic's managers plan to use this information to help them set fees. The students will also prepare the annual cost report for the state.

Cost object, cost pools and assigning costs

The clinic provides two different types of services: medical and dental. Because costs probably differ by the type of service provided, the students decide to treat each type of patient visit as a cost object. Therefore, they calculate costs separately for each of the two operating departments and set up a cost pool for each. They learn from an interview with the accountant that the clinic has two support departments: administration and housekeeping. The students set up a cost pool for each of these departments. The accountant helps the students trace the direct costs to each department cost pool. In addition, costs for the entire facility (such as rent and electricity) are gathered into a cost pool and then allocated to all of the departments based on each department's floor space in square metres. The students prepare a summary of the costs assigned to each department as follows.

Cost	Administration	Housekeeping	Medical	Dental	Total
Salaries	$80 000	$40 000	$200 000	$80 000	$400 000
Supplies	15 000	20 000	35 000	10 000	80 000
Facility costs	3 240	360	28 800	3 600	36 000
Total	$98 240	$60 360	$263 800	$93 600	$516 000

Choosing allocation bases

Before the students allocate support department costs, they need to choose allocation bases for the services of the housekeeping and administration departments. One student suggests that floor surface (square metres) is a good base for allocating housekeeping costs. Another student thinks that hours spent in each department would provide a better basis because the departments have different kinds of equipment and different volumes of service. They agree that hours spent is a better choice, but then learn that housekeeping does not keep records of hours by department. Therefore, they return to their alternative choice and use square metres for allocating housekeeping costs.

For the administration allocation base, the accountant suggests using either the direct costs for each operating department or the number of employees. When the students study the administration department activities, they find that many services relate to employees, such as employee recruiting, training, benefits and payroll. Other services include purchasing and maintenance. They decide that number of employees is more representative than direct costs for the overall activities in administration. Therefore, the students choose the number of employees in each department as the allocation base for administration.

The students gather the following information for the allocation bases.

	Administration	Housekeeping	Medical	Dental	Total
Number of employees	2	2	5	3	12
Square metres	900	100	8000	1000	10 000

Having calculated the total costs for each cost pool and chosen an allocation base for each support cost pool, the students are now ready to begin allocating support department costs to operating departments. The accountant tells the students that they can use any reasonable method for allocating support costs to operating departments. The students want to learn more about different methods and their effects on allocated costs.

Direct method calculations

The students begin with the direct method, which is the easiest to perform. They first draw a diagram similar to the one in figure 3.7 to clarify how they will perform calculations. They next calculate the percentage of each support department's costs allocated to each operating department. Costs for housekeeping are allocated based on square metres.

One student observes that the square metres used by administration are not relevant to the direct method because housekeeping costs are not allocated to another support department. Of the 9000 square metres used by the operating departments, the medical clinic uses 8000 square metres, or 89 per cent. Accordingly, 89 per cent of the housekeeping costs will be allocated to medical, and the remaining 11 per cent (1000 square metres ÷ 9000 square metres) will be allocated to dental.

Costs for administration are allocated based on number of employees. The medical clinic employs five of the eight employees who work for operating departments, so 62.5 per cent of the administration costs will be allocated to medical. The remaining 37.5 per cent (3 employees ÷ 8 employees) will be allocated to dental.

	Support		Production		
	Administration	Housekeeping	Medical	Dental	Total
Allocation bases					
Square metres			8000	1000	9000
			89%	11%	100%
Number of employees			5	3	8
			62.5%	37.5%	100%
Costs					
Department cost	$ 98 240	$ 60 360	$263 800	$ 93 600	$516 000
Housekeeping		(60 360)	53 720	6 640	0
Administration	(98 240)		61 400	36 840	0
Total allocated cost	$ 0	$ 0	$ 378 920	$137 080	$516 000

FIGURE 3.8 ■ Direct method cost allocation report for Middletown Children's Clinic

The students prepare a report summarising their allocations as shown in figure 3.8. The line for department cost reflects the costs that the students had previously assigned to each department. Of the $60 360 housekeeping cost, 89 per cent ($53 720) is allocated to medical and 11 per cent ($6640) is allocated to dental. Similarly, the administrative cost of $98 240 is allocated 62.5 per cent ($61 400) to medical and 37.5 per cent ($36 840) to dental. The costs allocated from the support departments are added to each operating department's costs. Thus, the total allocated costs are $378 920 for the medical clinic and $137 080 for dental. Notice that the total costs of $516 000 have not been affected by the allocation.

Step-down method

The **step-down method** allocates support department costs, one department at a time, to remaining support and operating departments in a cascading manner until all support department costs have been allocated. This method goes beyond the direct method in recognising that support departments provide support not only for the operating departments, but also for other support departments. In this method the cost objects of interest are both support and operating departments. As shown in figure 3.9, the costs for the first support department chosen are allocated to the remaining departments, both support and operating. The process continues, and costs for the remaining support departments are allocated one at a time to the remaining departments until no support department costs remain. For example, in figure 3.9 costs are allocated from administration to housekeeping, but not from housekeeping to administration.

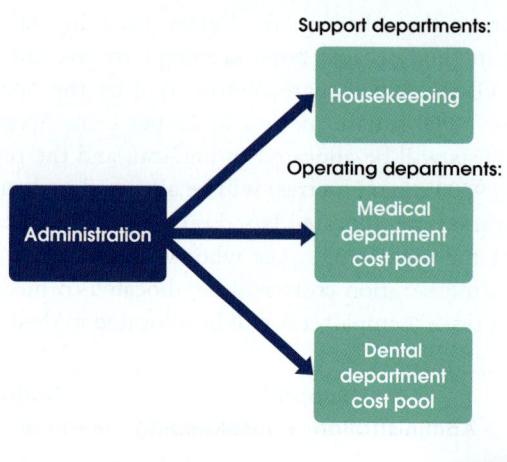

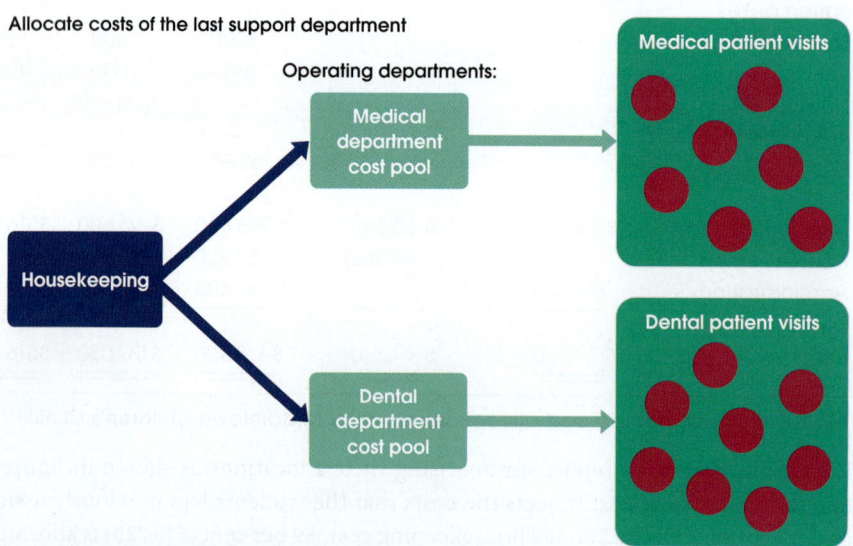

FIGURE 3.9 ■ Step-down method

The step-down method begins by ranking each support department according to the amount of service provided to other support departments. Then support department costs are allocated sequentially, beginning with the support department that provided the most service to other support departments and ending with the support department that provided the least service to other support departments. The ranking can be created using any reasonable criteria.

Sometimes a qualitative judgment is made about the degree of services. Alternatively, departments can be ranked using a quantitative measure such as the dollar amount of services provided to other support departments. Calculations for the step-down method are illustrated in comprehensive example 4.

Comprehensive example 4

Step-down method allocation

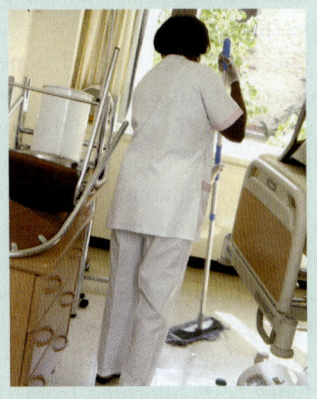

After the accounting students allocate Middletown Children's Clinic's costs using the direct method, they recalculate the allocations using the step-down method. The step-down method requires the support departments to be ranked based on the quantity of services provided to other support departments. The students decide to rank administration first because administration probably provides more support to housekeeping than vice versa. For example, administration purchases supplies and provides employee support such as payroll and benefits for the housekeeping department.

The students draw a diagram similar to the one in figure 3.9 to clarify how they will perform calculations. They first allocate administration department costs to all the remaining departments — the other support department (housekeeping) and the two operating departments. Therefore, in determining the percentage of costs for each department, they factor in the two housekeeping employees with the operating department employees. Once the administrative costs are allocated, they next allocate housekeeping costs to the two operating departments. For this allocation, they use the same percentages used for the direct method, because only the two operating departments remain. The students summarise their calculations in the report shown in figure 3.10.

In the first step, 20 per cent of the administration department's $98 240 cost goes to housekeeping ($19 648), 50 per cent to medical ($49 120) and 30 per cent to dental ($29 472). In the second step, the housekeeping costs are now $80 008 ($60 360 + $19 648) because they include an allocation from administration. Therefore, 89 per cent of $80 008 is allocated to medical ($71 207) and the remaining $8801 is allocated to dental.

| | Support | | Production | | |
	Administration	Housekeeping	Medical	Dental	Total
Allocation bases					
Number of employees		2	5	3	10
		20%	50%	30%	100%
Square metres			8000	1000	9000
			89%	11%	100%
Costs					
Total department cost	$ 98 240	$ 60 360	$263 800	$ 93 600	$516 000
Step 1: Administration	(98 240)	19 648	49 120	29 472	0
Step 2: Housekeeping	0	(80 008)	71 207	8 801	0
Total allocated cost	$ 0	$ 0	$ 384 127	$131 873	$516 000

FIGURE 3.10 ■ Step-down method cost allocation report for Middletown Children's Clinic

Reciprocal method

The **reciprocal method** simultaneously allocates costs among support departments, and then from support departments to operating departments. Because the reciprocal method allows for all of the interactions among departments, it is widely used. This method reflects support department interactions more accurately than either the direct method (which does not address the interactions at all) or the step-down method (which addresses only part of the interactions). Once again both the operating and support departments are the cost objects of interest, but this method provides a more accurate estimate of total costs in support departments.

The reciprocal method is performed in two phases. First, support department costs are allocated among each other. These interactions for Middletown Children's Clinic are shown in figure 3.11(a). To capture the cost effects of these interactions, a set of equations is created and solved simultaneously. The figure shows the simple two-department case, which can easily be performed manually. However, when more than two support departments are involved, the reciprocal method becomes mathematically complex and is more easily performed using software programs such as spreadsheet functions that solve simultaneous equations. Thus, the computations for the reciprocal method are the most complex among the three methods introduced in this section.

After solving the simultaneous equations, the allocated cost for each support department includes costs allocated from the other support departments. Next, this new total cost per support department is allocated to all of the other departments (support and operating) as shown in figure 3.11(b). The reciprocal method is illustrated in comprehensive example 5.

(a) Phase 1 — Simultaneously allocate costs among support departments

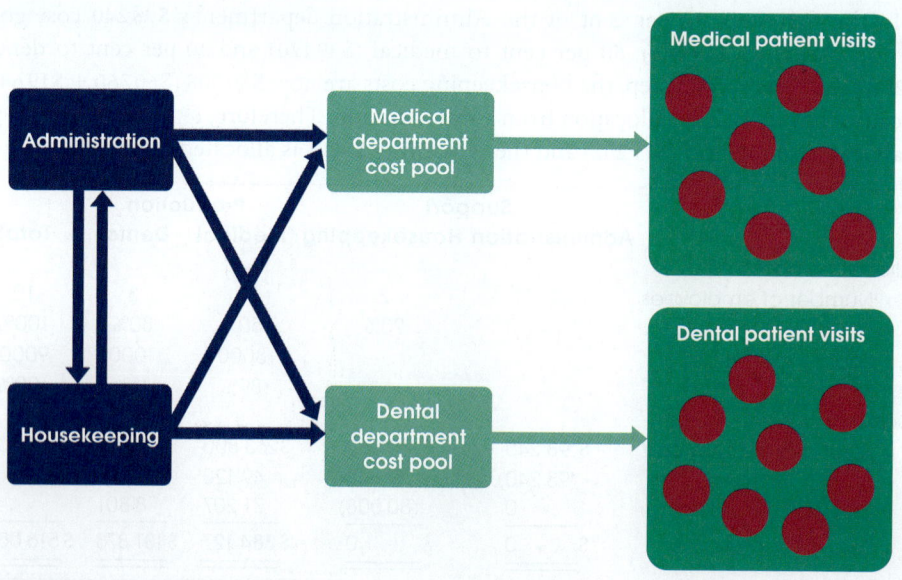

(b) Phase 2 — Allocate total costs from phase 1 to all departments

FIGURE 3.11 ■ Reciprocal method

Comprehensive example 5

Reciprocal method allocation

After completing the step-down method calculation, the accounting students are ready to apply the reciprocal method to Middletown Children's Clinic's support costs. The students adopt the same allocation bases they used previously, and they draw diagrams similar to the ones in figures 3.11(a) and 3.11(b) to clarify how they will perform calculations.

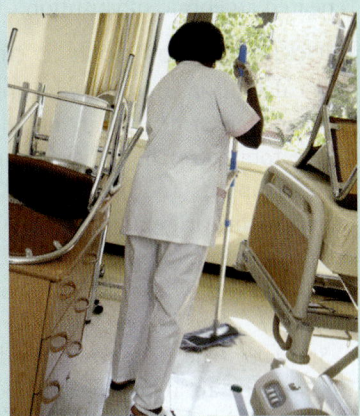

Allocate support costs among support departments

The students first allocate the support department costs to each other. To simultaneously compute costs between support departments, the students need to set up and solve simultaneous equations. The cost of each support department is written as a sum of directly assigned costs plus costs allocated from the other support department. Administration is allocated based on number of employees. The clinic has 10 employees outside of the administration department, with two of them working in housekeeping. For the purpose of allocating administration costs, housekeeping's portion of employees is 2/10, and

$$\text{Housekeeping} = \$60\,360 + 0.2\,(\text{Administration})$$

Similarly, housekeeping is allocated based on square metres. Of the 9900 square metres that are not in housekeeping, 900 square metres are in administration. Thus, for the purpose of allocating housekeeping costs, administration's portion of square metres is $900 \div 9900$, and

$$\text{Administration} = \$98\,240 + 0.09\,(\text{Housekeeping})$$

Because only two support departments are involved, only two equations need to be solved simultaneously. The students decide to use the substitution method to solve them. They substitute the administration equation into the housekeeping equation and solve for the total cost of housekeeping:

$$\text{Housekeeping} = \$60\,360 + 0.2 \times (\$98\,240 + 0.09 \times \text{Housekeeping})$$

$$\text{Housekeeping} = \$60\,360 + \$19\,648 + 0.018 \times \text{Housekeeping}$$

$$0.982 \times \text{Housekeeping} = \$80\,008$$

$$\text{Housekeeping} = \$81\,475$$

Next, they substitute the result for housekeeping into the administration equation and solve for the total cost of administration:

$$\text{Administration} = \$98\,240 + 0.09 \times \$81\,475$$

$$\text{Administration} = \$105\,573$$

When an organisation has three or more support departments, the simultaneous equations are set up in the same way. Each equation includes the total cost for the department plus a term for each of the other support departments. The simultaneous calculations become more complex, but can be easily solved with computer programs or repeated algebraic substitution.

Allocate support costs to operating departments

The calculations performed using simultaneous equations provide a total cost for each support department that includes cost allocations from other support departments. These totals are the new amount that the students next allocate to all other departments (support and operating). The new total cost for housekeeping is $81 475, which includes the original department cost of $60 360 plus an allocation of $21 115 from administration. In figure 3.12, the students allocate this new housekeeping cost based on square metres, with 9 per cent to administration, 81 per cent to medical and 10 per cent to dental.

Similarly, the new cost for administration of $105 573 includes the original cost of $98 240 plus an allocation of $7333 from housekeeping. The students allocate this new administration amount based on number of employees, with 20 per cent to housekeeping, 50 per cent to medical and 30 per cent to dental. The students create a report to summarise their allocations and to demonstrate that zero cost remains in each support department after the allocations are complete, as shown in figure 3.12.

| | Support | | Operating | | |
	Administration	Housekeeping	Medical	Dental	Total
Cost allocation bases					
Square metres	900		8 000	1 000	9 900
	9%		81%	10%	100%
Employees		2	5	3	10
		20%	50%	30%	100%
Costs					
Total department cost	$ 98 240	$ 60 360	$263 800	$ 93 600	$516 000
Housekeeping	7 333	(81 475)	65 995	8 147	
Administration	(105 573)	21 115	52 786	31 672	
Total allocated cost	$ 0	$ 0	$ 382 581	$133 419	$516 000

FIGURE 3.12 ■ Reciprocal method cost allocation report for Middletown Children's Clinic

Comparing results and choosing an allocation method

When the students finish their calculations for the three allocation methods, they create the following schedule to compare their results.

	Medical	Dental	Total
Direct method	$378 920	$137 080	$516 000
Step-down method	384 127	131 873	516 000
Reciprocal method	382 581	133 419	516 000

The managers want to know the cost for each patient visit, so the students also calculate the average allocated cost per visit. The accountant tells them that medical usually sees 12 000 patients and dental sees 10 000 patients. Dividing the total allocated costs by these volumes, the total allocated cost per visit under each method is shown opposite.

	Medical	**Dental**
Direct method	$31.58	$13.71
Step-down method	32.01	13.19
Reciprocal method	31.88	13.34

The students notice that the fully allocated costs do not vary significantly across methods. They ask their accounting lecturer whether this result is always true. She tells them that the variation depends on the data and number of departments for a given setting. With a larger number of support departments, the differences are usually greater. She also tells them that the step-down and reciprocal methods often yield similar results when only two support departments are involved. She adds that the reciprocal method is the most accurate because it takes into account all interactions.

The students discuss the effort that each method takes. They agree that the direct method requires the least amount of effort and that the reciprocal method requires the most. However, they also agree that they could easily set up a spreadsheet to calculate the clinic's allocations. After concluding that computational difficulty is not a major issue, they recommend the reciprocal method to the clinic.

Comparing the direct, step-down and reciprocal methods

As shown in the Middletown Children's Clinic example, different allocation methods result in different values. Each method has its own pros and cons. The direct method is the easiest to calculate, but computer programs reduce the importance of this issue. An advantage of the direct and step-down methods is that the calculation methods are easier to explain to managers, yet the reciprocal method most accurately considers support department interactions.

Limitations of cost allocation data

The process of allocating costs involves many uncertainties, including the following:

- identifying appropriate cost pools
- deciding whether to establish separate pools for fixed and variable costs
- choosing how to assign costs to cost pools
- identifying the most appropriate allocation bases for each cost pool
- selecting the most appropriate allocation method
- deciding whether the benefits exceed the costs of establishing a more detailed cost allocation system.

Because the process of measuring and allocating costs is uncertain and requires judgment, allocated cost information can be of low quality. The quality of allocated cost information can be improved in many ways. Accountants, managers and operational personnel can work together to identify more appropriate cost pools and allocation bases. Accounting systems can be redesigned to more accurately trace costs to activities and gather better allocation base data. In addition, accountants can adopt allocation methods to more closely match the purpose of the allocation. (In appendix 3A of this chapter, we explore one potential improvement: dual-rate allocations.) Nonetheless, the cost data used to assist in decision making still contains elements of subjectivity due to decisions taken in the costing framework. Therefore, our objective should be to enhance reliability of cost data for decision making while weighing the cost against the benefit of doing so.

Many overhead costs are fixed; they do not change with changes in the allocation base or any other measure of activity. Therefore, allocated overhead costs are not relevant information for most short-term decisions, such as special orders or the use of constrained resources. Nevertheless, managers may mistakenly assume that these allocated costs are variable, particularly when the costing system uses several cost pools and allocation bases. Another problem occurs if the allocation base used to allocate variable overhead costs is not a cost driver, which means it does not accurately reflect the use of variable cost resources.

Managers within an organisation often do not understand how costs are allocated to individual jobs. They may misinterpret cost information and rely on irrelevant information. Accountants must not only produce relevant information for each decision, but also help educate managers about appropriate uses of cost information making.

APPENDIX 3A

SINGLE- VERSUS DUAL-RATE ALLOCATIONS

The practice of using only one base to allocate both fixed and variable costs is called **single-rate allocation**. For example, at Middletown Children's Clinic, square metres were used to allocate housekeeping costs. Square metres might be appropriate for allocating housekeeping fixed costs, such as depreciation on any cleaning equipment used, but some housekeeping costs vary with the type of work required in a given area. The time housekeepers spend in each area might be a more appropriate allocation base for the variable costs. Thus, single-rate allocation probably mismeasures resources used. In addition, managers may believe that all support costs are variable, even when they include a large proportion of fixed costs.

Under **dual-rate allocation**, support costs are separated into fixed and variable cost pools, and cost drivers are identified for the variable cost pools to more accurately reflect the flow of resources. Figure 3A.1 presents the dual-rate allocation process under the reciprocal method. Compared to the single-rate allocation, the variable cost allocations reflect a more accurate estimation of the incremental costs of providing support services. Some organisations use variable costs to measure use of a department's services and assign the fixed costs as part of a department's formally adopted budget.

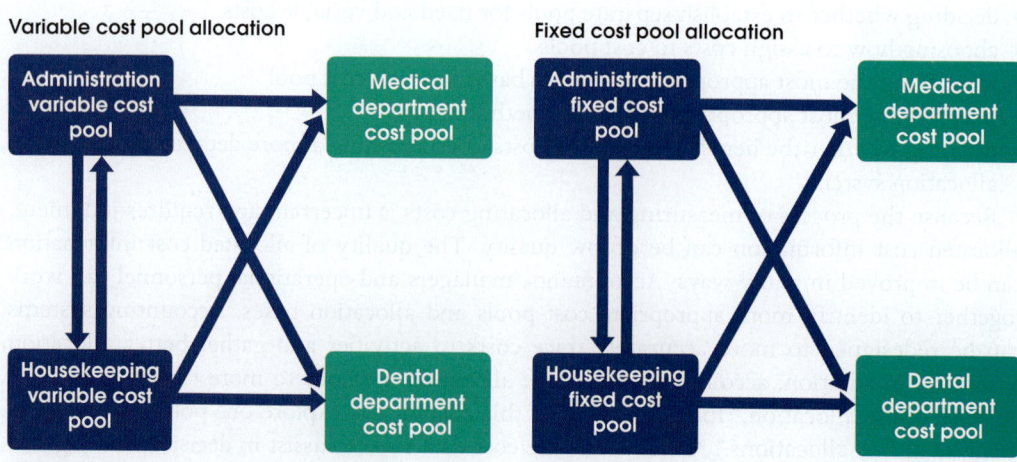

FIGURE 3A.1 ■ Dual-rate allocation

The dual-rate system also has drawbacks. It costs more to develop and maintain. Furthermore, uncertainties about how to classify costs as fixed and variable can introduce additional mismeasurement.

Comprehensive example 6 demonstrates the use of dual rates for Middletown Children's Clinic.

Comprehensive example 6

Dual rates and reciprocal method with three support departments

After the accounting students allocated administration and housekeeping costs to the operating departments, the accountant asks them whether this information could be used to charge departments for their use of other departments' services. The accountant believes that by charging for support department services, the employees in the user departments would be motivated to manage their use of the support services more cost-consciously, and some support costs might be reduced. The charges would become part of the current budgeting system in which managers are held responsible for their budgets. Managers receive performance bonuses if costs are maintained at or under budgeted levels.

Charges based on single-rate allocation

The students obtain the total allocated costs for each support department from their previous reciprocal method calculations: $105 573 for administration and $81 475 for housekeeping. Their goal is to calculate a charge representing the use of these services by other departments. Previously, they used number of employees as the allocation base for administration and square metres as the allocation base for housekeeping. They decide to use the allocation bases to calculate a charge for the use of each department's services. For administration services, other departments would be charged a cost per employee. The clinic has 12 employees, two of whom work in administration. The students calculate the charge for administration costs based on the 10 non-administration employees:

$105 573 Administration costs ÷ 10 employees = $10 557 per employee

For housekeeping services, other departments would be charged a cost per square metre. The clinic has 10 000 total square metres, of which 100 are devoted to housekeeping. The students calculate the charge for housekeeping based on the 9900 non-housekeeping square metres:

$81 475 Housekeeping costs ÷ 9900 square metres = $8.23 per square metre

The students discuss whether the charges they calculated would be reasonable. They think that the administration charge seems high. They wonder whether other departments should be charged $10 557 for administrative costs for each employee in the department. The charge might encourage managers in the clinic departments to inappropriately reduce the number of employees. For example, the managers might replace an employee with services from a temporary labour agency that would cost the clinic more overall. When the students review the housekeeping charge, they believe that an average annual charge of $8.23 per square metre is reasonable. However, one student asks whether it is reasonable for the housekeeping cost rate for administration to be the same as the cost rate for medical and dental. The clinic areas require special cleaning supplies and greater effort than the administration area. In addition, employees in other departments might feel that they have no control over a fixed charge of $8.23 per square metre. A fixed charge might reduce their motivation to keep work areas clean, increasing the time required by housekeeping.

Analysis of cost behaviour and revision of cost pools

The students had previously learned about dual rates for allocating costs, whereby fixed and variable costs are allocated separately. Some organisations use variable allocations as a charge rate for support services because the variable costs more closely represent the incremental costs that support departments incur to provide services. The students plan to analyse the behaviour of costs in the administration and housekeeping cost pools to determine whether the cost pools should be broken down into separate fixed and variable cost pools. They had previously summarised the costs, as shown here.

Cost	Administration	Housekeeping
Salaries	$80 000	$40 000
Supplies	15 000	20 000
Facility costs	3 240	360
Total	$98 240	$60 360

The students focus first on administration costs. Most of them are for salaries of the manager and the accountant. The manager is responsible for general management of the clinic. The accountant is responsible for accounting and billing functions. The accountant says she spends much more time on billing functions for the operating clinics than on general functions for the whole organisation. The billing functions include receiving information about each patient's charges from the operating departments and then billing patients or their insurance companies, receiving and depositing payments, and following up on denied insurance claims and bad debts. One student points out that the functions of the manager are different from the functions of the accountant. He argues that the costs for these two employees should not be combined in a single cost pool if other departments will be charged for the services. The other students agree that accuracy of the cost allocations will improve if they separate accounting costs from other administration costs, so they decide to establish a separate cost pool called accounting. The accountant helps the students identify the costs that should be assigned to the accounting cost pool, and she summarises the time she usually spends on activities for each department.

When the students study the housekeeping department cost records, they find that housekeeping employees are paid according to an hourly wage, and part of the department's costs vary with time spent working in each area. Therefore, the students think that the variable part of housekeeping costs could be allocated to other departments based on the time spent cleaning each area. However, housekeeping employees do not currently keep track of their time by area. The students discuss this issue with the accountant, who agrees to establish a new record-keeping system for housekeeping employees to keep track of the hours they spend in each department.

Based on their discussions with the accountant and their investigation of the types of costs in each cost pool, the students conclude that costs for all three support departments could be broken down into fixed and variable components. The students and the accountant examine past accounting records and other information to identify fixed and variable costs. The accountant estimates the cost of supplies and postage for accounting and billing activities, and the amount of her salary that should be considered a fixed cost of the accounting department. Variable costs in administration include payroll costs that vary by employee, such as fringe benefits, supplies and record keeping for employees. The costs are summarised as follows.

Department	Administration	Accounting	Housekeeping	Total
Variable costs	$ 11 052	$ 9 210	$ 30 180	$ 50 442
Fixed costs	50 348	27 630	30 180	108 158
Total cost	$61 400	$36 840	$60 360	$158 600

Charges based on variable cost allocation

The students discuss with the accountant the effects of the new support cost pool on the calculation of charges to other departments. They conclude that other departments should be charged only for variable support costs. Thus, the cost object for each support department is the variable cost of support services provided to other departments.

They next discuss the allocation bases for the variable cost pools. They plan to use the accountant's time to allocate accounting costs. They decide to continue using number of employees for administration. They want to use the time spent in various departments for housekeeping, but they lack recorded information about the amount of time spent in each area. However, the housekeepers estimate that they spend 10 per cent of their time cleaning the administration department, 5 per cent in the accounting area, 55 per cent in the medical clinic and 30 per cent in the dental clinic.

The new variable cost allocation base amounts for all departments are as follows:

	Administration	Accounting	Housekeeping	Medical	Dental	Total
Employees		1	2	5	3	11
Time spent accounting	15%		10%	50%	25%	100%
Time spent cleaning	10%	5%		55%	30%	100%

To apply the reciprocal method, the students must first calculate the total support department variable costs including interactions. They set up simultaneous equations for the interactions among administration, accounting and housekeeping. The equations are:

$$\text{Administration} = \$11\,052 + 15\% \times \text{Accounting} + 10\% \times \text{Housekeeping}$$

$$\text{Accounting} = \$9210 + (1/11) \times \text{Administration} + 5\% \times \text{Housekeeping}$$

$$\text{Housekeeping} = \$30\,180 + (2/11) \times \text{Administration} + 10\% \times \text{Accounting}$$

The students use Excel Solver to find the solutions to this set of simultaneous equations. (Instructions for using Solver are presented in appendix 3B.) The Solver results for each department's total variable cost (including interactions) to be allocated are:

Administration	$16 354
Accounting	$12 416
Housekeeping	$34 395

Given the total allocated variable cost for each support department, the students calculate the support charge per unit of allocation base. The charge for variable administration cost is based on the number of employees:

$16 345 ÷ 11 employees = $1486 per employee

The charge for accounting is based on the time spent by the accountant. The accountant works full time. Allowing four weeks of holidays and eight days of other leave, her estimated work hours per year are:

[40 hours per week × (52 − 4) weeks] − (8 days × 8 hours per day) = 1856 hours

Thus, the charge for variable accounting cost is

$12 416 ÷ 1856 hours = $6.69 (rounded) per hour

The charge for housekeeping is based on time spent cleaning. The cleaning employees work full time, or an estimated 1856 hours per year each. Based on the two housekeeping employees, the estimated total hours are 3872 per year. The charge for variable housekeeping cost is

$34 395 ÷ 3712 hours = $9.27 (rounded) per hour

The students discuss these rates with the accountant. The administration charge per employee seems low, so department managers would probably not consider these charges in making decisions about employment levels. Many administrative costs are fixed, so the variable portion is small. The accounting charges also seem low, reflecting the high proportion of fixed costs in salary for the accountant. At the same time, charging each department for variable accounting costs helps the department managers recognise that they are using accounting resources.

The housekeeping charges are similar to costs that would be paid if an outside housekeeping service were used, so the managers of the user departments are likely to think that these charges are fair. At the same time, charging the departments for housekeeping based on time spent in each department provides the managers with incentives to keep work areas clean to reduce the number of hours that housekeeping spends in them. The accountant recommends that the fixed costs be assigned to other departments as part of their annual budgets. This way all costs will be allocated, but only variable costs will be charged based on some measure of usage.

Dual-rate allocation

In addition, the accountant reminds the students that they need to allocate costs for the regulatory reports that are filed with the state. For these reports, all support costs must be allocated, not just the variable costs. The students can separately allocate the fixed support costs and then sum the fixed and variable allocations for state reporting.

The students discuss allocation bases for the fixed costs. They use number of employees as the allocation base for administration, time spent for accounting, and square metres for housekeeping. The fixed cost allocation base amounts for all departments are:

	Administration	Accounting	Housekeeping	Medical	Dental	Total
Employees		1	2	5	3	11
Accounting	15%		10%	50%	25%	100%
Square metres	600	300		8000	1000	9900

Once again, the students use Excel Solver to simultaneously allocate the costs among the support departments. (The simultaneous equations and instructions for Excel Solver are found in appendix 3B.)

The students prepare a schedule summarising the variable and fixed cost allocations and calculating the total allocated costs for operating departments, as shown in figure 3A.2. The students discuss how much they enjoyed helping the clinic and gaining experience using three different methods of allocating support department costs, including the use of Solver. They feel the experience was worthwhile. The clinic accountant is glad that the students helped her with this task. She now knows how to use Solver and can revise the allocation scheme over time as the clinic's needs and cost estimates change.

	Support departments			Operating departments		
	Administration	Accounting	Housekeeping	Medical	Dental	Total
Directly assigned costs	$ 61 400	$ 36 840	$ 60 360	$263 800	$ 93 600	$516 000
Variable cost allocation						
Administration	(16 354)	1 486	2 973	7 434	4 460	0
Accounting	1 862	(12 416)	1 242	6 208	3 104	0
Housekeeping	3 440	1 720	(34 395)	18 917	10 319	0
Fixed cost allocation						
Administration	(58 164)	5 287	10 575	26 438	15 863	0
Accounting	5 138	(34 256)	3 426	17 128	8 564	0
Housekeeping	2 678	1 339	(44 181)	35 702	4 463	0
Total allocated costs	$ 0	$ 0	$ 0	$375 627	$140 373	$516 000

FIGURE 3A.2 ■ Dual-rate support cost allocations for Middletown Children's Clinic

APPENDIX 3B

USING SOLVER TO CALCULATE SIMULTANEOUS EQUATIONS FOR THE RECIPROCAL METHOD

Solver, a tool within Excel, can be used to solve simultaneous equations. In this appendix we learn to use Solver for allocating support costs under the reciprocal method.

In comprehensive example 6 (see appendix 3A), the accounting students increased the number of support department cost pools from two to three. Therefore, they decided to use

Solver to calculate the support department allocations under the reciprocal method. Before using Solver, it is necessary to specify the simultaneous equations. For the Middletown Children's Clinic fixed cost allocation, the simultaneous equations are as follows:

$$\text{Administration} = \$50\,348 + 15\% \times \text{Accounting} + (600/9900) \times \text{Housekeeping}$$

$$\text{Accounting} = \$27\,630 + (1/11) \times \text{Administration} + (300/9900) \times \text{Housekeeping}$$

$$\text{Housekeeping} = \$30\,180 + (2/11) \times \text{Administration} + 10\% \times \text{Accounting}$$

Figures 3B.1 and 3B.2 provide results and formulas using Solver for this set of simultaneous equations. The change cells are given the names Admin, Acct, and Housekeep. Solver manipulates these cells to solve the simultaneous equations for each department's cost. The solution includes allocations from the other two support departments. The target function is the sum of the three change cells and is given the following formula:

$$=\text{Admin}+\text{Acct}+\text{Housekeep}$$

Notice in cells B15, B16, and B17 of figure 3B.1 that the simultaneous equations are listed so that they can be entered into Solver as constraints. When adding each constraint in the Solver dialogue box, set the simultaneous equation equal to (by selecting the equal sign in the pull-down menu) the change cell that represents the department for which cost you are solving. For example, the cell with the simultaneous equations for Administration should contain

$$=\text{B3}+\text{B7*Acct}+(\text{B8/G8})\text{*Housekeep}$$

Click Add next to the constraints box. The cell with this formula will be entered on the left-hand side under Cell Reference. Click on the box under Constraint and then highlight the department for the simultaneous equation in the cell reference, in this case Admin.

In the spreadsheet shown in figures 3B.1 and 3B.2, solution values from Solver feed into the bottom part of the spreadsheet that performs the allocation process. You may need to go back and forth between these two spreadsheets to understand how to set up your own spreadsheet for this problem. Notice that the values for costs and allocation bases are at the top of the

	A	B	C	D	E	F	G
1	Middletown Clinic						
2	Departments	Administration	Accounting	Housekeeping	Medical	Dental	Total
3	Costs	50348	27630	30180	263800	93600	=SUM(B3:F3)
4							
5	Allocation Bases						
6	Employees	0	1	2	5	3	=SUM(B6:F6)
7	Accounting time spent	0.15	0	0.1	.5	0.25	=SUM(B7:F7)
8	Square footage	600	300	0	8000	1000	=SUM(B8:F8)
9							
10	Change cells for solver						
11	Admin	Acct	Housekeep				
12	58164.1018577537	34256.4619090369	44180.9374373239				
13							
14	Simultaneous equations						
15	Administration	=B3+B7*Acct+(B8/G8)*Housekeep					
16	Accounting	=C3+(C6/G6)*Admin+(C8/G8)*Housekeep					
17	Housekeeping	=D3+(D6/G6)*Admin+D7*Acct					
18							
19	Target function						
20	=Admin+Acct+Housekeep						
21							
22	Allocation	Administration	Accounting	Housekeeping	Medical	Dental	Total
23	Cost	=B3	=C3	=D3	=E3	=F3	=SUM(B23:F23)
24	Administration Allocation	=-B15	=(C6/$G$6)*$B$15	=(D6/$G$6)*$B$15	=(E6/$G$6)*$B$15	=(F6/$G$6)*$B$15	=SUM(B24:F24)
25	Accounting Allocation	=B7*B16	=-B16	=D7*$B$16	=E7*$B$16	=F7*$B$16	=SUM(B25:F25)
26	Housekeep Allocation	=(B8/$G$8)*$B$17	=(C8/$G$8)*$B$17	=-B17	=(E8/$G$8)*$B$17	=(F8/$G$8)*$B$17	=SUM(B26:F26)
27	Total Allocated Cost	=SUM(B23:B26)	=SUM(C23:C26)	=SUM(D23:D26)	=SUM(E23:E26)	=SUM(F23:F26)	=SUM(G23:G26)

FIGURE 3B.1 ■ Fixed cost allocation spreadsheet for using Solver with formulas

spreadsheet. If you change any of these values, you will need to run Solver again to determine the new amounts for the three support departments.

	A	B	C	D	E	F	G
1	Middletown Clinic						
2	Departments	Administration	Accounting	Housekeeping	Medical	Dental	Total
3	Costs	$50,348	$27,630	$30,180	$263,800	$93,600	$465,558
4							
5	Allocation Bases						
6	Employees	0	1	2	5	3	11
7	Accounting time spent	15%	0%	10%	50%	25%	100%
8	Square footage	600	300	0	8,000	1,000	9,900
9							
10	Change cells for solver						
11		Admin	Acct	Housekeep			
12		$58,164	$34,256	$44,181			
13							
14	Simultaneous equations						
15	Administration	$58,164					
16	Accounting	$34,256					
17	Housekeeping	$44,181					
18							
19	Target function						
20		136601.5012					
21							
22	Allocation	Administration	Accounting	Housekeeping	Medical	Dental	Total
23	Department Cost	$50,348	$27,630	$30,180	$263,800	$93,600	$465,558
24	Administration Allocation	($58,164)	$5,287	$10,575	$26,438	$15,863	$0
25	Accounting Allocation	$5,138	($34,256)	$3,426	$17,128	$8,564	$0
26	Housekeep Allocation	$2,678	$1,339	($44,181)	$35,702	$4,463	$0
27	Total Allocated Cost	$0	$0	$0	$343,068	$122,490	$456,558

FIGURE 3B.2 ■ Fixed cost allocation spreadsheet for using Solver

Summary

1   **Understand the role of cost objects for costing purposes.**

The cost object could be anything for which a separate measurement of cost is required. Examples are products, services, departments, business units, processes, customers and activities. Cost objects represent the focus for the costing system.

2   **Differentiate between direct and indirect costs.**

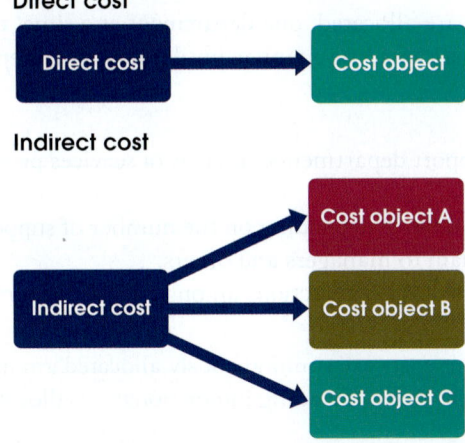

3 | Outline the process of indirect cost allocation.

1. Identify the cost object.
2. Determine indirect costs to be allocated to cost objects.
3. Select the appropriate cost driver (either volume or activity) to assign indirect costs.
4. Calculate the indirect cost rate.

4 | Identify the steps within a costing framework.

Step 1: Overview of cost assignment — identification of cost objects, cost pools and cost drivers.
Step 2: Determination of the indirect cost rates for each cost pool.
Step 3: Allocation of indirect costs to the cost objects.
Step 4: Determination of the full cost of each cost object — tracing of direct costs and allocation of indirect costs.

5 | Apply the costing framework in a service entity setting.

Provides an illustration of the application of the costing framework to a law firm — refer to comprehensive example 2 on page 84.

6 | Apply the costing framework in a support department setting.

Operating departments
Operating departments are the departments or divisions within an organisation that manufacture goods or produce services for external customers or clients.

Support departments
Support departments provide services internal to the organisation that support the operating departments.

Direct method
Each support department's cost is allocated to only the operating departments.

Pros and cons
- Easiest method computationally, but computers make this factor less important.
- Easy to explain to managers and others.
- Ignores interactions among support departments.

Step-down method
Support department costs are allocated, one department at a time, to remaining support and operating departments in a cascading manner until all support department costs have been allocated.

Pros and cons
- Requires ranking of support departments in terms of services provided to other support departments.
- Moderately easy computations, depending on the number of support departments.
- Moderately easy to explain to managers and others.
- Takes into account some of the interactions among support departments.

Reciprocal method
- First, support department costs are simultaneously allocated among support departments.
- Next, support department costs (including interactions) are allocated to operating departments.

Pros and cons
- Computationally the most complex, but computers simplify the process.
- May be difficult to explain to managers and others.
- Most accurate allocation method because it takes into account all of the interactions among support departments.

Single-rate allocation (appendix 3A)
Uses only one base to allocate both fixed and variable costs.

Dual-rate allocation (appendix 3A)
Accumulates fixed and variable costs in separate cost pools and uses different allocation bases for these cost pools.

Pros and cons
- Reduces mismeasurement of allocations.
- Reduces misunderstandings about the behaviour of support costs.
- Costs more to develop and maintain.
- May introduce additional mismeasurement from problems arising from the need to classify costs as fixed and variable.

---

7 | Outline the limitations of cost allocation data.

Uncertainties
- Identifying support and operating cost pools
- Assigning costs to cost pools
- Selecting allocation bases
- Choosing an allocation method
- Measuring the degree of services provided among support departments (step-down and reciprocal methods)

Ways to improve the quality of information
- Use dual-rate allocations
- Redesign accounting system for cost pools and allocation bases
- Make choices regarding estimated versus actual support costs and rates
- Consider perceived fairness

Self-study problems

SELF-STUDY PROBLEM 1

Direct, step-down and reciprocal methods; use of allocation information

Pet Protection is a veterinary clinic that is subsidised by the local humane society. The not-for-profit organisation was set up to encourage low-income pet owners to neuter and vaccinate their pets. The humane society would like to know the cost per animal visit to use in its fund-raising campaign literature.

The information for a recent period follows:

Costs before allocation	Support departments		Operating departments		
Direct costs	**Maintenance**	**Administration**	**Neuter**	**Vaccinations**	**Total**
Salaries	$25 000	$40 000	$100 000	$ 75 000	$240 000
Supplies	5 000	5 000	15 000	25 000	50 000

	Support departments		Operating departments		
Costs before allocation					
Direct costs	Maintenance	Administration	Neuter	Vaccinations	Total
Building-related costs	2 400	3 600	12 000	6 000	24 000
Total	$32 400	$48 600	$127 000	$106 000	$314 000
Some possible allocation bases:					
Square metres	200	300	1000	500	2000
Employees	1	1	5	3	10

REQUIRED

(a) Allocate the support department costs to the operating departments using the following:
    (i) direct method
    (ii) step-down method
    (iii) reciprocal method.
(b) Assume the neuter clinic handles 2400 pet visits and vaccinations handles 5000 pet visits. Calculate the cost per visit for each department under the three methods.
(c) A local TV station has contacted the head veterinarian at Pet Protection. The station will provide free advertising to encourage low-income pet owners to neuter their pets using Pet Protection's services. The veterinarian estimates the cost of a 10 per cent increase in business volume using the total allocated costs developed in part (a) and becomes alarmed at the large total cost. Describe the calculation of total allocated costs and explain why these costs should not be used to estimate future costs.

Solution to self-study problem 1

(a) Two assumptions are used in making these calculations: (1) the administration costs will be allocated using number of employees and maintenance costs will be allocated using square metres, and (2) the administration support department provides more services to the maintenance support department than the other way around.
    (i) Direct method allocation

	Support departments		Operating departments		
	Maintenance	Administration	Neuter	Vaccinations	Total
Allocation base percentages					
Administration					
Employees			5	3	8
Percentage			62.5%	37.5%	100%
Maintenance					
Square metres			1000	500	1500
Percentage			66.6667%	33.3333%	100%
Departmental costs	$32 400	$48 600	$127 000	$106 000	$314 000
Allocations					
Administration		(48 600)	30 375	18 225	
Maintenance	(32 400)		21 600	10 800	
Total allocated cost	$ 0	$ 0	$ 178 975	$ 135 025	$314 000

(ii) Step-down method allocation

For the step-down allocation method, administrative costs are allocated first because they are largest.

	Support departments		Operating departments		
	Maintenance	Administration	Neuter	Vaccinations	Total
Allocation base percentages					
Administration					
Employees	1		5	3	9
Percentage	11.1111%		55.5556%	33.3333%	100%
Maintenance					
Square metres			1 000	500	1 500
Percentage			66.6667%	33.3333%	100%
Departmental costs	$ 32 400	$ 48 600	$127 000	$106 000	$314 000
Allocations					
Administration	5 400	(48 600)	27 000	16 200	
Maintenance	(37 800)		25 200	12 600	
Total allocated cost	$　　0	$　　0	$179 200	$134 800	$314 000

(iii) Reciprocal method allocation

The first task in the reciprocal method is to set up and solve simultaneous equations for the interactions among the support departments. The interactions are calculated using the allocation base percentages. When only two support departments are involved, the substitution method can be used to solve the simultaneous equations.

	Support departments		Operating departments		
	Maintenance	Administration	Neuter	Vaccinations	Total
Allocation base percentages					
Administration					
Employees	1		5	3	9
Percentage	11.1111%		55.5556%	33.3333%	100%
Maintenance					
Square metres		300	1000	500	1800
Percentage		16.6667%	55.5556%	27.7777	100%

Simultaneous equations

The equation for the total costs of each support department is equal to the costs assigned to the departmental cost pool plus an allocation of the costs from the other support department:

$$\text{Cleaner} = \$32\,400 + (1/9) \times \text{Administration}$$

$$\text{Administration} = \$48\,600 + (300/1800) \times \text{Cleaner}$$

The cost for the maintenance department is calculated by substituting the administration equation into the cleaner equation:

$$\text{Cleaner} = \$32\,400 + (1/9) \times (48\,600 + (300/1800) \times \text{Cleaner})$$

$$0.981\,481\,48 \times \text{Cleaner} = \$37\,800$$

$$\text{Cleaner} = \$38\,513$$

The cost for the administration department is calculated by substituting the result for the maintenance cost into the administration equation:

$$\text{Administration} = \$48\,600 + (300/1800) \times \$38\,513$$

$$\text{Administration} = \$55\,019$$

   Next, costs are allocated from each support department to the other support departments and to the operating departments. The amounts allocated are based on the computations from the simultaneous equations. The use of simultaneous equations ensures that zero cost remains in each support department after the allocations are complete. In other words, the total cost allocated from maintenance ($38 513) is equal to the costs assigned to the maintenance cost pool ($32 400) plus the costs allocated to maintenance from administration ($6113). Similarly, the total cost allocated from administration ($55 019) is equal to the costs assigned to the administration cost pool ($48 600) plus the costs allocated to administration from maintenance ($6419).

	Support departments		Operating departments		
	Maintenance	Administration	Neuter	Vaccinations	Total
Departmental costs	$32 400	$ 48 600	$127 000	$106 000	$314 000
Allocations:					
Administration	6 113	(55 019)	30 566	18 340	0
Maintenance	(38 513)	6 419	21 396	10 698	0
Total allocated cost	$ 0	$ 0	$178 962	$135 038	$314 000

(b) The cost per visit is calculated by dividing each operating department's total direct and allocated costs by the number of pet visits per year.

	Neuter	Vaccinations
Direct method	$178 975 ÷ 2400 = $74.57 per visit	$135 025 ÷ 5000 = $27.01 per visit
Step-down method	$179 200 ÷ 2400 = $74.67 per visit	$134 800 ÷ 5000 = $26.96 per visit
Reciprocal method	$178 962 ÷ 2400 = $74.57 per visit	$135 038 ÷ 5000 = $27.01 per visit

(c) The costs per visit are calculated as follows. First, all clinic costs are assigned to departments. Some costs are traced directly to departments (salaries and supplies), and some (building-related costs) are gathered together in a general cost pool and distributed (allocated) among all of the departments. Then, the support department costs (administration and maintenance) are allocated to each other and then to the operating departments (neuter and vaccinations). Many of these costs are fixed and will not change as volumes increase (for example, salaries and building-related costs such as the lease).

   Through the allocation process, all of the fixed costs become an average cost per unit. The cost per visit is accurate only at the level of visits used in the denominator. When the veterinarian multiplies the per-visit rate times a larger number of visits, the total cost is overestimated because the per-visit cost is an average cost that includes a portion of fixed cost. These fixed costs do not increase proportionately as volumes increase, but remain constant across a relevant range. To increase the accuracy of future cost estimates, past costs need to be separated into fixed and variable categories, and a cost function needs to be developed. In addition, some of the information used in the cost function should be updated to reflect any anticipated price changes.

SELF-STUDY PROBLEM 2

Costing in the service sector

Consider the following budgeted data for a client case of Bob Crachit's accounting firm. The client wants a fixed price quotation.

Direct professional labour	$20 000
Direct support labour	10 000
Fringe benefits for direct labour	13 000
Photocopying	2 000
Telephone calls	2 000
Computer lines	6 000

Overhead is allocated at the rate of 100 per cent of direct labour cost.

REQUIRED

(a) Prepare a schedule of the budgeted total costs for the client. Show subtotals for total direct labour costs and total costs as a basis for mark-up.

(b) Assume that the partner's policy is to quote a fixed fee at 10 per cent above the total costs. What fee would be quoted?

(c) Explain why the listed estimates for costs might not be similar to the actual costs for the job. What factors could affect the accuracy of these estimates? List as many factors as you can.

Solution to self-study problem 2

(a)

Direct labour costs:	
Professional labour	$20 000
Support labour	10 000
Total	30 000
Other direct costs	23 000 (fringe benefits + copying + phone + computer*)
Allocated overhead	30 000 (100% of $30 000)
Budgeted costs	$83 000

* This assumes that computer lines and costs can be traced. If these cannot be traced, then this cost would be assigned to overhead.

(b) Fee = 110% × $83 000 = $91 300

(c) Many factors could affect these costs. Because they are estimations, any relevant factors that were left out of the estimate could influence cost. It is difficult to predict how efficient the resources will be used. It is possible that the professional labour hours required are more or less than estimated, depending on the skills of the professionals and the accuracy with which the amount of work was estimated. If something was overlooked that requires more hours, the estimate will be off. Phone costs and computer costs may be different because rates change, or the job requires more or less telephone or computer work.

Factors that could affect the actual costs: price changes for any of the resources, and unforeseen complications such as computer crashes, problems with communication systems, illness of key professional and support employees, and unforeseen problems in the actual work.

Questions

3.1 What is a cost object? Give three examples.

3.2 Explain the difference between a direct cost and indirect cost.

3.3 Discuss the importance of selecting an appropriate cost driver for cost allocation.

3.4 Explain the differences and similarities among the direct, step-down and reciprocal methods.

3.5 Explain the similarities and differences between support department costs and manufacturing overhead costs.

3.6 What should determine the choice of cost allocation method (direct, step-down and reciprocal) discussed in this chapter?

3.7 Explain how cost data is sourced in a costing framework.

3.8 Outline the key steps in a costing framework.

3.9 What factors should be considered when choosing allocation bases?

3.10 A product is started in department 1 and completed in department 2. Is department 1 a support department or an operating department? Explain.

3.11 Explain the difference between operating departments and support departments.

3.12 What are the advantages and disadvantages of using estimated support cost allocation rates?

3.13 List at least three possible allocation bases that could be used to allocate accounting department costs to other departments. Give one advantage and one disadvantage of using each allocation base.

Exercises

3.14 **Direct and indirect costs** Frida's Tax Practice has two departments, tax and audit. The tax department has two product lines, business returns and individual returns. A list of costs and three cost objects from Frida's Tax Practice follow.

REQUIRED

For each cost, identify whether it is direct or indirect for each cost object.

Cost	Cost object		
	Tax department	Personal returns	Mr Gruper's personal tax return
(a) Subscription to personal tax law updates publication			
(b) Ink supplies for tax department photocopy machine			
(c) Portion of total rent for tax department office space			
(d) Wages for tax department administrative assistant			
(e) Tax partner's salary			
(f) Charges for long-distance call to Mr Gruper about personal tax return questions			
(g) Tax partner lunch with Mr Gruper (the tax partner has lunch with each client at least once per year)			

3.15 **Direct and indirect costs; fixed, variable and mixed costs** Your sister turned her hobby into a small business called Glazed Over. She is a potter and manufactures and sells bowls that can be used for decoration or for birdbaths. She has one employee, who works 40 hours a week no matter how many bowls are made. She has asked your advice in developing a cost function for the bowls so that she can estimate costs for the next period.

REQUIRED

The following list of costs comes from your sister's general ledger. Assume the cost object is an individual unit (i.e. bowl). Categorise each cost as direct or indirect (D or I), and as fixed, variable or mixed (F, V or M).

(a) Employee wages
(b) Clay used to make bowls
(c) Depreciation on the kilns
(d) Glaze (the finish painted on the bowls)
(e) Brushes for the glaze
(f) Electricity
(g) Business licence
(h) Advertising
(i) Pottery studio maintenance (cost of weekly cleaning service)
(j) Packing materials for the bowls

3.16 Allocation rates A housekeeping support department budgets its costs at $40 000 per month plus $12 per hour. For November the following were the estimated and actual hours provided by the housekeeping support department to three operating departments.

	Estimated hours spent cleaning	Actual hours spent cleaning
Department A	1600	1500
Department B	1400	1600
Department C	2000	1800
Total	5000	4900

REQUIRED

(a) What is the support department's allocation rate if estimated activity is the allocation base?
(b) What is the support department's allocation rate if actual activity is the allocation base?
(c) List one advantage and one disadvantage for each type of allocation rate.

3.17 Allocating support costs to units A local hospital is required to account for the total cost of patient care, including support costs. Patients are assigned all direct costs. Support costs are $240 000 per month plus $90 per patient day. This 120-bed hospital averages 80 per cent occupancy.

REQUIRED

Calculate the average daily charge per patient for support costs, assuming 30 days in a month.

3.18 Direct method using estimated costs, benchmarking Devon Ltd allocates support department costs using the direct method and estimated costs. The support department costs are budgeted at $88 000 for department A, $63 000 for department B and $40 000 for department C. These costs are allocated using the proportion of total cost the firm would pay to an outside service provider.

	Support			Operating	
	Dept. A	Dept. B	Dept. C	Casting	Machine
Direct costs	$88 000	$63 000	$40 000	—	—
Labour hours				6 000	4 000
Machine hours				2 000	10 000
Costs if support services were purchased outside:					
Department A				$50 000	$60 000
Department B				$40 000	$30 000
Department C				$20 000	$30 000

REQUIRED

(a) Allocate budgeted support department costs using the direct method, first using labour hours and then with the outside cost proportions as the allocation bases.

(b) Could Devon Ltd use the cost of purchasing outside as an efficiency benchmark for the cost of both the support departments and the operating departments? List several advantages and disadvantages of this approach.

3.19 Costing for a hospital Mercy Hospital uses a costing system for all patients who have surgery. The hospital uses a budgeted overhead rate for allocating overhead to patient stays. In March, the operating room had a budgeted allocation base of 1000 operating hours. The budgeted operating room overhead costs were $66 000.

Patient Dwight Schuller was in the operating room for four hours during March. Other costs related to Schuller's four-hour surgery include:

Patient medicine	$250
Cost of nurses	3500
Cost of supplies	800

Physician cost is not included because physicians bill patients separately from the hospital billing system.

REQUIRED

(a) Determine the budgeted (i.e. estimated) overhead rate for the operating room.

(b) Determine the total costs of Schuller's four-hour surgery.

3.20 Reciprocal method The Brown and Brinkley Brokerage firm is organised into two major sales divisions: institutional clients and retail clients. The firm also has two support departments: research and administration. The research department's costs are allocated to the other departments based on a log of hours spent on tasks for each user. The administration department's costs are allocated based on the number of employees in each department.

Records are available for last period as follows.

	Support departments		Operating departments	
	Research	**Administration**	**Institutional**	**Retail**
Payroll costs	$350 000	$300 000	$400 000	$550 000
Other costs	$230 000	$150 000	$120 000	$240 000
Research hours	100	200	500	300
Number of employees	7	10	8	10

REQUIRED

Using the reciprocal method, determine the total cost of operations for each sales division. Use either simultaneous equations or Excel Solver.

3.21 Reciprocal method Paul's Valley Protection Service has three support departments (S1, S2 and S3) and three operating departments (P1, P2 and P3). The direct costs of each department are $30 000 for S1, $20 000 for S2 and $40 000 for S3. The proportions of service provided by each support department to the others are given in the following table.

	Support departments			Operating departments		
	S1	**S2**	**S3**	**P1**	**P2**	**P3**
S1	—	0.4	0.1	0.2	0.2	0.1
S2	0.1	—	0.2	0.2	—	0.5
S3	0.2	0.2	—	0.1	0.4	0.1

REQUIRED

Using the reciprocal method, allocate the support department costs to the operating departments.

3.22 Step-down, direct and reciprocal methods; accuracy of allocation Software Plus Ltd produces flight and driving simulations and games for personal computers. The company's president has a complaint about the accounting for support department costs. He points to the following table describing the use of various support departments in the company and says, 'According to this table, every department receives services from all the support departments. But I understand that only some of the support departments are bearing costs from the other support departments. Why is that?'

Support Department	Cost	Administration	Maintenance	Information systems	Games manufacturing	Simulation manufacturing
				Percentage use of services		
Administration	$40 000	0%	10%	50%	10%	30%
Maintenance	20 000	20	0	10	40	30
Information systems	50 000	35	5	0	40	20

REQUIRED

(a) What method has Software Plus Ltd been using to allocate support costs? Explain how you know.
(b) Which method would ignore all interactions among support departments? Explain.
(c) Which method would consider all interactions among support departments? Explain.
(d) Allocate the support department costs to Games and Simulations using the step-down method. Explain how you decided which department's costs to allocate first.
(e) Allocate the support department costs using the direct method.
(f) Allocate the support department costs using the reciprocal method.
(g) In your own words, explain how the step-down method improves upon the direct method.
(h) In your own words, explain how the reciprocal method improves upon the step-down method.

3.23 Direct, step-down and reciprocal methods; assign costs to departments Cost information for Lake County Library is as follows.

Direct costs	Support maintenance	Administration	Operating books	Other media	Total
Salaries	$20 000	$40 000	$50 000	$70 000	$180 000
Supplies	5 000	5 000	15 000	25 000	50 000
Allocation base volumes					
Square metres	500	500	1200	300	2500
Employees	1	1	2	1	5

In addition to directly traceable costs, the library incurred $24 000 for a building lease.

REQUIRED

(a) Allocate to departments any costs that have not been traced, and then calculate total costs assigned to each department.
(b) Allocate the support department costs to the operating departments using the direct method.

(c) Allocate the support department costs to the operating departments using the step-down method. Allocate first the costs for the support department having the largest direct costs.

(d) Allocate the support department costs to the operating departments using the reciprocal method. Use either simultaneous equations or Excel Solver.

3.24 Step-down and reciprocal methods; uncertainties; pricing Kovacik manufactures two types of piggy banks in two different departments: a kangaroo-shaped piggy bank and a platypus-shaped piggy bank. The plant is highly automated and contains only two other departments: (1) engineering and design, and (2) information systems. Kovacik allocates support department costs according to estimated service use. Estimated information for next year is as follows:

| | Support | | Operating | |
	Engineering and design	Information systems	Kangaroo bank	Platypus bank
Direct costs	$2 700	$8 000	$10 000	$20 000
Services used				
Engineering and design		10%	40%	50%
Information systems	20%		30%	50%
Production volume			8 000	4 000

Total allocated costs are assigned to individual units using the production volume.

REQUIRED

(a) Determine the estimated total allocated costs for the operating departments using the step-down method.

(b) Determine the estimated total allocated cost per unit of the kangaroo-shaped piggy bank and the platypus-shaped piggy bank under the step-down method.

(c) Explain why actual total allocated costs will turn out to be different from the estimated total allocated costs.

(d) Determine the estimated total allocated costs for the operating departments using the reciprocal method. Use either simultaneous equations or Excel Solver.

(e) Determine the estimated total allocated cost per unit of the kangaroo-shaped piggy bank and the platypus-shaped piggy bank under the reciprocal method.

Problems

3.25 Step-down and reciprocal methods; choosing methods; cost pools; uncertainties Your brother is a physician and has decided to start a home healthcare agency. The state government will reimburse treatment costs for about half of the patients under a new state-sponsored health insurance program for low-income residents. Your brother has asked you to explain the cost report that the state government requires. He tells you that he can use either the step-down or the reciprocal allocation method. He has several choices in allocation bases, but has little choice in the type of cost pools that are allowed.

REQUIRED

(a) Explain to your brother the differences in the two allocation methods. Remember that your brother is not familiar with accounting, so use language he will understand.

(b) Your brother wants to know how to choose the best allocation method and bases for his business. List some of the factors your brother should consider as he makes these decisions.

(c) One of the cost pools allowed by the state is a pool for transportation-related costs. Your brother asked colleagues at other home healthcare agencies to list the costs they include in this pool. Each organisation has some costs that are identical, such as depreciation on vehicles, gas and repairs. However, other costs in the pool are different; some agencies include facilities-related costs and others do not. Why would cost pools for the same activity include different types of cost?

3.26 Cost pools and allocation bases You are an accountant for the Department of Defence. The federal government is considering a change of rules for the allocation of research and development costs. The government is asking contractors to submit a list of potential cost pools and allocation bases for activities within research and development. The government wants contractors to separate their research and development activities into several smaller cost pools with separate allocation bases.

Your research department performs a variety of different duties, including developing new designs for products, developing and testing new materials for use in these products, designing the manufacturing processes for new products, and redesigning old products and their manufacturing processes. In addition, the research and development department creates commercial uses for new technology that has been developed under government contracts.

REQUIRED

(a) List at least four potential research and development activities that could be used as the basis for separate cost pools within the research and development department.

(b) List two or more potential cost allocation bases for each cost pool listed in part (a).

(c) List factors that you might consider in making a choice about the cost pools and the allocation bases.

3.27 Step-down method; choosing allocation order and bases Space Products manufactures commercial and military satellites. Under its government contracts, the company is permitted to allocate administrative and other costs to its military division. These costs are then reimbursed by the federal government department. Government guidelines allow administrative costs to be allocated using either the direct costs incurred in the operating divisions or the number of employees as an allocation base. Management information systems (MIS) costs can be allocated either on the basis of direct costs incurred in the operating divisions or on the basis of CPUs (a measure of computer resources used). Data concerning the company's operations appear here.

	Support departments		Operating departments	
	Administrative	MIS	Commercial	Military
Direct costs	$600 000	$200 000	$2 000 000	$4 000 000
Employees	20	10	40	50
CPUs (millions)	20	50	30	70

The MIS department is responsible for computer equipment and systems, and it maintains databases for the entire organisation.

REQUIRED

(a) Suppose Space Products uses the step-down method for allocating support department costs. Administrative costs are allocated first on the basis of the number of employees, and then MIS costs are allocated on the basis of CPUs. How much support department cost will be allocated to the military division?

(b) Space Products produced 100 military satellites in the period considered in this problem. Assuming the company uses the allocations calculated in part (a), what is the average cost per military satellite?

(c) Is the average cost that you calculated in part (b) most likely an underestimate, an overestimate or an unbiased estimate of the incremental cost of producing one more military satellite? Explain.

(d) Suppose Space Products uses the direct method of allocating support department costs. What is the maximum amount of support department cost that can be allocated to the military division under the government rules?

(e) Suppose the management of Space Products always calculates its support department cost allocations to maximise the amount of contribution received from the government. Management selects this policy because it allows the company to be more competitive in its commercial markets.

  (i) Discuss possible reasons why the government does not specify a single, unambiguous support cost allocation method.

  (ii) From a taxpayer's point of view, discuss whether you would agree with Space Product's policy.

  (iii) From a competitor's point of view, discuss whether you would agree with Space Product's policy.

3.28 **Categorisation of support costs** Suppose a charitable organisation called Food on Wheels provides meals for low-income individuals who are unable to leave their homes. To support its services, it solicits contributions from individuals and businesses. Food on Wheels needs to submit financial statements to its major sponsor. The sponsor requires expenses to be assigned to the following cost pools: administrative, fundraising and programs.

The bookkeeper for Food on Wheels is a volunteer who is taking accounting classes at the local community college. He knows that all of the costs to prepare and deliver meals should be assigned to the program. However, he is not sure how to assign some of the costs. In particular, he is concerned about the following two items.

Costs for printing and mailing a monthly newsletter The newsletter is sent out to donors and clients and asks for donations. It also describes the organisation's activities, provides information for obtaining meal services, and provides recipes for some of the meals that are served. The director of the organisation wants the cost of the newsletter to be classified as a program cost. She maintains that the program information and recipes should be considered educational material. Not-for-profit organisations typically classify educational materials as program expenses.

Director's salary and benefits The director of Food on Wheels spends much of her time raising funds, meeting with the board of directors and performing other administrative duties. She also manages the cooks and drivers, purchases food and delivery supplies, and schedules the food deliveries. The director has instructed the bookkeeper to allocate her salary and benefit costs as follows: 50 per cent to the program, 25 per cent to fundraising and 25 per cent to administration.

REQUIRED

(a) Identify and discuss uncertainties about how each of the following costs should be classified:

  (i) costs to print and mail the newsletter

  (ii) director's salary and benefits.

(b) Does this situation involve an ethical dilemma for the bookkeeper? Why?

(c) Explain why the director has a preference for costs to be assigned to program expenses.

(d) Explain how you think sponsors would prefer for the costs in part (a) to be assigned.

(e) Suppose you are reviewing cost information for another organisation. Would you expect the organisation's program costs to be biased upward, biased downward, or to be unbiased? Explain.

(f) How would you classify the costs in part (a) if you were the bookkeeper for Food on Wheels? Explain your reasoning.

3.29 **Direct, step-down and reciprocal methods using dual rates and three departments** In comprehensive example 6 (Middletown Children's Clinic), we did not perform direct or step-down methods for the dual-rate costs. Following are the allocation bases for these costs. The support cost data are on page 99.

	Administration	Accounting	Housekeeping	Medical	Dental	Total
Number of employees	1	1	2	5	3	12
Square metres	600	300	100	8000	1000	10 000
Time spent accounting	15%		10%	50%	25%	100%
Time spent cleaning	10%	5%		55%	30%	100%

REQUIRED

(a) Draw a diagram of the direct method for the Middletown Children's Clinic allocations using three support departments.

(b) Allocate the support department costs using dual rates and the direct method.

(c) Draw a diagram of the step-down method using the three support departments.

(d) Allocate the support department costs using dual rates and the step-down method.

(e) Write out the simultaneous equations for the reciprocal allocation.

(f) Set up a spreadsheet that uses Excel Solver to solve the simultaneous equations and then allocates support costs using dual rates and the reciprocal method. Check to see that your solution matches the solution in the text.

3.30 **Total cost under alternative allocation bases; special order price** Danish Hospital recently installed an RAP scanner, which is a diagnostic tool used both in suspected cancer cases and for detecting certain birth defects while the foetus is still in the womb. The scanner is leased for $5000 per month, and a full-time operator is paid $3000 per month. Data concerning use of the scanner for a typical month follow.

	Cancer detection	Birth defect detection
Revenue per scan	$600	$400
Direct costs per scan	$100	$50
Minutes required per scan	30	10
Number of scans performed	20	40

The direct costs consist primarily of supplies that are consumed in the scanning process. Currently, less than 20 per cent of the machine's capacity is used.

REQUIRED

The following questions will help you analyse the information for this problem.

(a) If the lease cost and the operator salary are allocated on the basis of minutes on the scanner, what is the total cost of a cancer scan?

(b) Suppose the cancer scans are experimental. Rather than charging $600 per scan, the hospital costs are reimbursed under a national contract. The contract will reimburse direct costs as well as an allocated share of the lease cost and operator's salary. As an allocation base, the contract allows either the number of scans or total minutes on the machine. What is the maximum reimbursable cost per cancer scan?

(c) The hospital is bidding on a state contract to supply birth defect scans to indigent pregnant women. The hospital would provide up to 14 scans a month for a fixed fee per scan. Assuming the hospital does not want to lose money on this contract, what is the minimum acceptable fee? Explain how you decided which costs are relevant.

(d) Identify uncertainties about which costs should be included in bidding for the contract described in part (c).

(e) Discuss the pros and cons of using total allocated costs, including administrative overhead, in bidding for the contract described in part (c).

(f) Suppose the hospital is bidding on the contract described in part (c). You have been asked to prepare a report of the hospital's expected costs for the contract. Write a memo to the chief accountant recommending the costs you think should be included in the expected costs. Attach to the memo a schedule showing your computations. As appropriate, refer to the schedule in the memo.

3.31 Step-down method; multiple versus single pool allocations; manager incentives The Gleason Company, an Australian division of a large international company, has prepared estimated costs for next year that can be traced to each department as follows:

Building and grounds	$ 41 010
Factory administration	78 270
Cafeteria—operating loss	4 920
Machining	104 100
Assembly	146 700
Total	$375 000

Management would like to know the estimated total allocated product cost per unit. These costs will be used as a benchmark for future period operations. The following information is available and can be used as possible allocation bases. The difference between direct labour hours and total labour hours represents hours of supervisory labour or labour hours that are used indirectly for manufacturing. The cost of these hours in machining and assembly is part of manufacturing overhead.

Department	Direct labour hours	Number of employees	Square metres	Total labour hours	Number of purchase orders
Factory administration		2	500		500
Cafeteria	1 000	2	1 000	1 000	4 000
Machining	3 000	4	500	8 000	2 000
Assembly	6 000	5	5 000	10 000	1 000
Total	12 000	14	10 000	21 000	8 000

REQUIRED

(a) Allocate the building and grounds costs to all other departments using square metres. Add the allocated costs to direct costs to arrive at the total costs assigned to each department.

(b) Explain whether each remaining department is a support or operating department.

(c) Select a reasonable allocation base for the costs of each support department. Justify your choices.

(d) Compute allocated overhead costs for each operating department. Given the allocation bases you selected in part (b), allocate support department costs to each operating department using the step-down method. Then calculate an overhead rate per direct labour hour for each operating department.

(e) Calculate overhead rates for the operating departments assuming that Gleason uses an average plant-wide factory overhead allocation rate based on direct labour hours. That is, aggregate the support department overhead costs into one cost pool, and use direct labour hours as the allocation base to determine the overhead rate per direct labour hour.

(f) What causes the difference between the rates you calculated in parts (d) and (e)?

(g) Assume that factory administration costs are allocated based on total labour hours, and that the total allocated cost is used to charge other departments for administrative services. List one advantage and one disadvantage of this charge system.

(h) Suppose that you are the manager of the machining department at Gleason. You can outsource some of your department's work. Outsourcing would reduce direct labour hours, and therefore reduce the amount of overhead allocated to your department. What factors should you consider in deciding whether to outsource?

(i) Now suppose that you are the director of finance for Gleason. The manager of the machining department has decided to outsource some tasks. When you analyse the current period results, you notice that while direct labour costs decreased in machining, outsourcing costs are slightly higher this period than the prior period's direct labour costs. When you ask the manager about these costs, he replies that the outsourcing does cost more than using direct labour but, because the amount of overhead for the department decreases, it is more profitable. What happened to the overhead that is no longer allocated to machining? Is the manager's decision beneficial to Gleason Company as a whole? Explain.

3.32 Cost allocation; behavioural issues In recent years, slow response times and frequent repairs have plagued Jetson Engineering's computer system. The cause was a substantial increase in computer-aided design work that pushed the system beyond its intended capacity. Bob Wilson, the production manager, decided that a new computer should be acquired to absorb some of the additional work. Surprisingly, six months after installing the new computer, he noticed that many of the engineers continued to use the old computer system, even though the new system had excess capacity and several features that simplified programming.

Bob discussed the situation with the supervisors of the entity's six design teams. They explained that the finance director's office allocates the cost of each computer to their work, based on the number of hours they use the computer. One responded, 'Look, the old computer didn't cost much and it's highly utilised — even the accounting department uses that machine. When the cost per hour of use is calculated, it's very low.

The new machine, on the other hand, cost a lot of money, and in the first couple of months we didn't use it much because it takes time to learn a new system. I was shocked when I saw how high my charges were for using the new machine. Because the cost is high and use is low, the cost per hour charged to my work was incredible. I'll tell you something: next month we'll probably use the new computer even less. Our job performance doesn't look very good when our jobs cost a fortune to complete because of huge allocations of computer cost.'

'What a mess,' Bob sighed. 'Even though the new computer is bought and paid for and has plenty of capacity, the engineers aren't using it. Don't they realise that most of the computer costs are fixed costs? Using the new computer for 200 hours a month doesn't really cost the company much more than using it for 20 hours a month.'

REQUIRED

Recommend a change in the allocation system at Jetson that will change the behaviour of the design teams.

3.33 **Internet activity** Go to the website of the Nokia Group (www.nokia.com). Write a brief report to the managing director advising how cost allocation can assist the entity.

3.34 **Comprehensive problem; dual versus single rates; purpose of allocation** Vines Company is a manufacturer of women's and men's swimsuits. The company uses a dual-rate system to allocate support costs. Last year's support departments' fixed and variable costs are as follows.

	Accounting	Human resources	Maintenance	Total
Variable costs	$18 420	$ 22 104	$ 60 360	$100 884
Fixed costs	55 260	100 696	60 360	216 316
Total cost	$73 680	$122 800	$120 720	$ 317 200

Allocation base amounts for all of the departments are:

	Accounting	Human resources	Maintenance	Women's	Men's	Total
Employees	2	2	4	10	6	24
Time spent for accounting	15%	10%	20%	30%	25%	100%
Time spent cleaning	5%	10%	15%	30%	40%	100%
Square metres	800	1000	1200	5000	5000	13 000
Direct costs	$73 680	$122 800	$120 720	$800 000	$500 000	$1 617 200

REQUIRED

(a) Use the following allocation bases for fixed support costs: direct costs for accounting, number of employees for human resources, and square metres for maintenance.
  (i) Allocate fixed support costs using the direct method.
  (ii) Allocate fixed support costs using the step-down method.
  (iii) Allocate fixed support costs using the reciprocal method.

(b) Use the following allocation bases for variable support costs: time spent for accounting, number of employees for human resources, and time spent for maintenance.
  (i) Allocate variable support costs using the direct method.
  (ii) Allocate variable support costs using the step-down method.
  (iii) Allocate variable support costs using the reciprocal method.

(c) Suppose support costs were not broken down into fixed and variable cost pools. What allocation base would you use to allocate the costs for each support department? Explain.

(d) Describe several possible reasons why the managers of Vines Company allocate support costs to operating departments.

(e) Discuss whether a dual-rate support cost allocation system is likely to be better for Vines Company than a single-rate system.

3.35 Costing, service sector Hawk and Eagle Co., a law firm, had the following costs last year:

Direct professional labour	$15 000 000
Overhead	21 000 000
Total costs	$36 000 000

The following costs were included in overhead:

Fringe benefits for direct professional labour	$ 5 000 000
Paralegal costs	2 700 000
Telephone call time with clients (estimated but not tabulated)	600 000
Computer time	1 800 000
Photocopying	900 000
Total overhead	$11 000 000

The firm recently improved its ability to document and trace costs to individual cases. Revised bookkeeping procedures now allow the firm to trace fringe benefit costs for direct professional labour, paralegal costs, telephone charges, computer time and photocopying costs to each case individually. The managing partner needs to decide whether additional costs other than direct professional labour should be traced directly to jobs to allow the firm to better justify billings to clients.

During the last year, more costs were traced to client engagements. Two of the case records showed the following:

	Client cases	
	875	876
Direct professional labour	$20 000	$20 000
Fringe benefits for direct labour	3 000	3 000
Secretarial costs	2 000	6 000
Telephone call time with clients	1 000	2 000
Computer time	2 000	4 000
Photocopying	1 000	2 000
Total costs	$29 000	$37 000

Three methods are being considered for allocating overhead this year:
- Method 1: Allocate overhead based on direct professional labour cost. Calculate the allocation rate using last year's direct professional labour costs of $15 million and overhead costs of $21 million.
- Method 2: Allocate overhead based on direct professional labour cost. Calculate the allocation rate using last year's direct professional labour costs of $15 million and overhead costs of $10 million ($21 million less $11 million in direct costs that are traced this year).
- Method 3: Allocate the $10 million overhead based on total direct costs. Calculate the allocation rate using last year's direct costs (professional labour of $15 million plus other direct costs of $11 million).

REQUIRED
(a) Calculate the overhead allocation rate for method 1.
(b) Calculate the overhead allocation rate for method 2.
(c) Calculate the overhead allocation rate for method 3.

(d) Using each of the three rates computed in parts (a), (b) and (c), calculate the total costs of cases 875 and 876.

(e) Explain why the total costs allocated to cases 875 and 876 are not the same under the three methods.

(f) Explain why method 1 would be inappropriate.

(g) Would method 2 or method 3 be better? Explain.

(h) Explain how job costing in a service business is different from job costing in a manufacturing business.

3.36 Allocating variable and fixed overhead in the service sector Prime Personal Trainers is a personal training service in Bankstown for people who want to work out at home. Prime offers two different types of services: Setup and Continuous Improvement. Setup services consist of several home visits by a personal trainer who specialises in determining the proper equipment for each client and helping the client set up a home gym. Continuous Improvement services provide daily, weekly or biweekly home visits by trainers.

Prime's accountant wants to create a job costing system for Setup services. She decides to use direct labour cost as the allocation base for variable overhead costs, and direct labour hours for fixed overhead cost. To estimate normal capacity, she calculates the average direct labour cost over the last several years. She estimates overhead by updating last year's overhead cost with expected increases in rent, supervisor's salaries and so on. Following are her estimates (given in euros) for the current period.

Direct labour hours (based on 250 normal hours per month)	3000
Direct labour cost	€75 000
Indirect labour cost	25 000
Variable overhead (primarily fringe benefits)	150 000
Fixed overhead (office related costs)	120 000

Inventories consist of exercise equipment and supplies that are used by Prime for new clients. The following information summarises operations during the month of October.

A number of new jobs were begun in October, but only two jobs were completed: job 20 and job 22.

Account balances on October 1:

Equipment and supplies (raw materials)	€5 000
Client contracts in process (job 20)	3 500
Client contracts in process (job 22)	1 500

Purchases of equipment and supplies:

Equipment	€54 000
Supplies	500
Total	€54 500

Equipment and supplies requisitioned for clients:

Job 20	€ 1 000
Job 21	500
Job 22	4 000
Job 23	5 000
Other jobs	40 000
Indirect supplies	500
Total	€51 000

Direct labour hours and cost:

	Hours	Cost
Job 20	10	€ 250
Job 21	18	450
Job 22	15	375
Job 23	6	150
Other clients	180	4 500
Total	229	€5 725

Labour costs:

Direct labour wages	€ 5 725
Indirect labour wages (160 hours)	1 920
Manager's salary	6 250
Total	€13 895

Office costs:

Rent	€1 000
Utilities	100
Insurance and taxes	900
Miscellaneous	1 000
Total	€3 000

REQUIRED

(a) What are the estimated allocation rates for fixed and variable overhead for the current period?

(b) What is the total overhead cost allocated to job 20 in October?

(c) What is the total cost of job 20?

(d) Calculate the amounts of fixed and variable overhead allocated to jobs in October.

(e) Why would the accountant choose to use two cost pools instead of one? Will this method make a difference in client bills when the job includes more equipment and less labour than other jobs?

Activity analysis and management

IN BRIEF

Activity-based costing (ABC) is a method that assigns costs to the specific activities performed in a manufacturing or service delivery process. ABC attempts to trace costs to cost objects through an activity lens. The costs of the various activities then become the building blocks used to compile costs for products or other cost objects. Activity-related costs are collected and cost drivers are chosen for each activity cost pool. Direct and indirect costs are then assigned to products or services using these activity-based cost pools and cost drivers. The information derived from ABC can be used with activity-based management (ABM) to improve operations and minimise activities that do not add value to the organisation.

After studying this chapter, you should be able to:

1 Explain the differences and similarities between activity-based costing (ABC) and conventional costing.

2 Understand elements of the ABC cost hierarchy.

3 Understand and work with an ABC model.

4 Describe the characteristics and use of activity-based management (ABM).

5 Outline the benefits, costs and issues related to ABC.

So, what does it actually cost?

Costing initiatives are commonly heralded for the manufacturing sector. This makes sense, as management accounting originated in that sector. Johnson and Kaplan (1987) criticised the emphasis of management accounting on manufacturing and highlighted the inability of organisations to adapt their management accounting systems to changing circumstances. Whether linked to this or not, the late 1980s saw the development of activity-based cost (ABC) systems to help improve the reliability of cost data. While initially focused on manufacturing firms, this new costing system seems to have greatly benefited organisations in the service-related sector.

With an increasing emphasis on understanding cost behaviour (especially the cost of providing specific services) and a growth in competitive tendering or outsourcing of services by organisations like local governments and universities, opportunities for the application of modern costing practices such as ABC presented themselves. A further reason that helps explain the popularity of ABC is that organisations such as local government bodies and universities found they needed more of a costing focus to better understand the costs of services that had previously received little attention. This need coincided with the emergence of ABC as a useful management accounting tool.

A number of Australian universities have embraced ABC — RMIT University, Murdoch University, Charles Sturt University and the University of Wollongong among them. They

have used ABC in a number of ways. First, as reported by accounting giant Ernst & Young (2000), universities faced with an increasingly competitive environment now demand timely, accurate and precise knowledge of all their costs. This has led to a consideration of alternative cost objects. For example, common costing and funding models focus on equivalent full-time student load as the fundamental cost object, but this may not be appropriate as the student population becomes increasingly diverse. Second, specific support service areas within universities have become ABC candidates. Common users of ABC systems within universities include areas such as *library services* to cost the cataloguing function, for example; and *information technology services* to cost specific services provided to the various university departments.

One of the interesting things about a costing focus in these areas (and in many cases in the service sector generally) is the relatively high labour content in the cost structure of the entities. As noted by Reich and Abraham (2006), the collection of staff-related activity data still remains problematic, making it difficult to be too precise and highlighting the often unstated subjective nature of even ABC cost output. Moreover, the manufacturing sector commonly provides an environment in which comparisons can be made between cost data generated under conventional costing systems and that resulting from ABC. The service sector (for example, support services within universities) does not provide the luxury of such comparisons because little if any cost data for this sector was generated under the conventional costing mode.

Sources: Information from Cleary, J, Gerdsen, T & O'Brien, L 2006, 'The activity based costing of library and information technology services in higher education', position paper, University of Newcastle; Ernst & Young 2000, 'A study to develop a costing methodology for the Australian higher education sector', final report to DETYA; Kaplan, R & Johnson, T 1987, *Relevance lost: the rise and fall of management accounting*, HBS Press; Reich, F & Abraham, A 2006, 'Activity based costing and activity data collection: a case study in the higher education sector', Faculty of Commerce papers, University of Wollongong; Wade, R & Henderson, G 2000, 'Measuring and benchmarking for libraries — a methodology and its application at the University of Wollongong and National Library of New Zealand.

Issues from this scene setter to look for in the chapter include:

■ Identification of cost objects and the use of different cost objects.

■ The suitability of activity-based costing (ABC) in both the manufacturing and service sectors.

■ The differences between conventional costing and ABC.

■ The subjectivity of cost data, however derived.

Activity-based costing (ABC) and conventional costing

A basic costing framework was illustrated in chapter 3. Cost accounting systems have adapted over time to suit changes in:

■ operational environments
■ technology
■ cost structures
■ management reporting requirements
■ organisational structures, particularly those with a new focus on the value chain.

Traditionally cost accounting systems were focused on product costing for manufacturers. More recently, cost accounting systems have evolved with a focus on activities for cost collection, thereby facilitating applications beyond the manufacturing sector. The activity view of costs has enabled an entity to extend the focus to cost objects other than products, and to take a broader view of allocation bases.

Conventional cost accounting systems

As illustrated in figure 4.1, conventional cost accounting systems trace direct costs and allocate overhead costs to each individual product. Cost allocation is a two-stage process whereby overhead costs are grouped into one or more cost pools in the first stage, and then allocated using an allocation base (such as direct labour cost or hours, machine hours or number of units) in the second stage. Labour has been a common allocation base because it was historically a significant driver of manufacturing costs. As manufacturing becomes less labour-intensive in some industries, labour-related allocation bases are increasingly viewed as arbitrary. It should be noted that labour could still be a suitable allocation base in service industries.

Allocation bases such as machine hours and number of units may also be viewed as arbitrary when they do not reflect a product's use of resources. Any poorly selected allocation base will distort product costs. Some organisations attempt to increase cost allocation relevance by using more than one overhead cost pool.

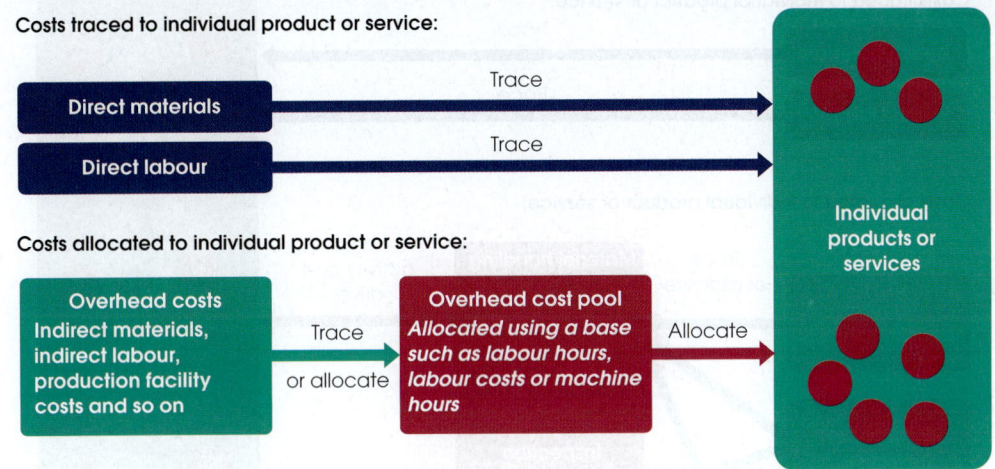

FIGURE 4.1 ■ Conventional overhead cost allocation system

Even with multiple cost pools, conventional allocation bases rarely reflect the flow of resources to products of different complexity. Suppose that a computer manufacturer uses robotic equipment to assemble custom-ordered computers. Most of the manufacturing overhead costs (for example, depreciation, insurance, general maintenance and software maintenance) are related to the robotic equipment. If the manufacturer lacks an information system that tracks time on the robotic machines or number of new set-ups required, direct labour hours are likely to be used to allocate the fixed overhead related to the machines. However, direct labour might be used only to test and package the machines for shipping, and the times needed for these tasks are the same for every machine produced. As a result, fixed overhead costs are distributed equally among all of the computers regardless of the actual time spent by the robotic machines or the number of new machine set-ups required.

In this setting, the costing system understates the cost of more complex computers that require more assembly time and machine set-ups in the robotic manufacturing process. At the same time, the system overstates the cost of simple computers requiring little robotic assembly time and few changes in set-up. If the information generated by this cost system is used for product decisions, the simple product could be de-emphasised relative to more complex products. Unfortunately, it is highly unlikely that this emphasis reflects the optimal sales mix.

Activity-based costing systems

Activity-based costing (ABC) is a system that assigns overhead costs to the specific activities performed in a manufacturing or service delivery process. It attempts to trace costs more accurately to products or other cost objects. An **activity** is a type of task or function performed in an organisation. The costs of the various activities become the building blocks used to compile total costs for products or other cost objects. The flow of costs in an ABC system is illustrated in figure 4.2. Note that this figure is an extension of the basic costing framework illustrated in figure 3.4 on page 80. Examples of the activities performed in a manufacturing setting include materials handling (moving direct materials and supplies from one part of the plant to another), engineering, inspection, customer support and information systems. Examples of activities performed in a service entity such as an insurance firm include policy preparation, development of new insurance products, client support, marketing and information technology.

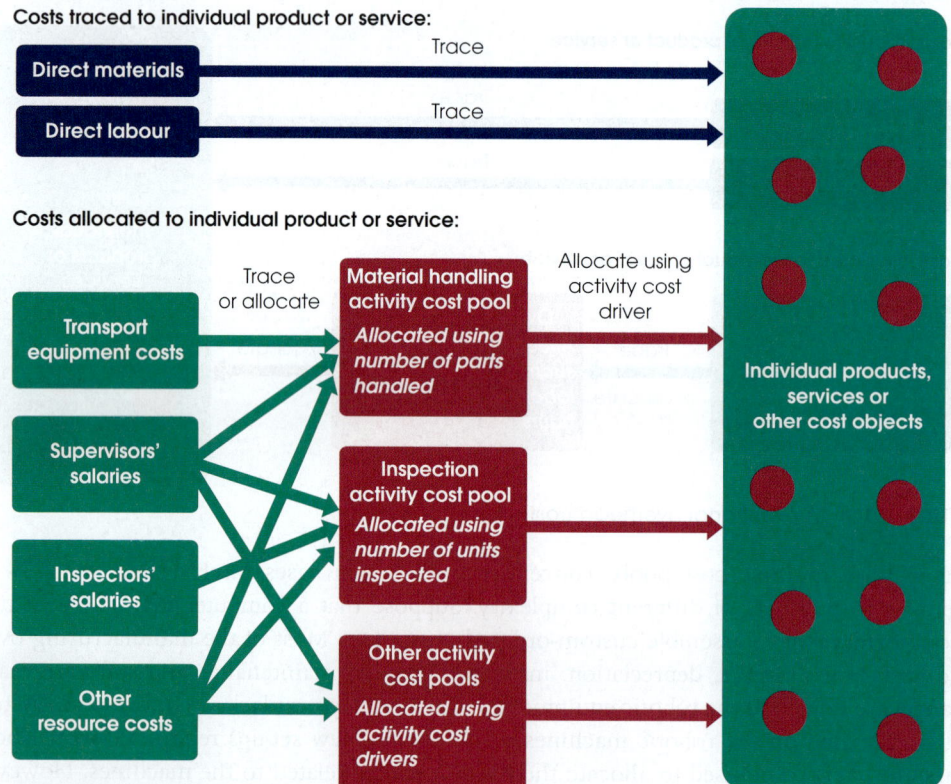

FIGURE 4.2 ■ ABC cost allocation system

Under ABC, multiple cost pools are used to reflect the various activities performed in manufacturing a product or providing a service. Accordingly, the costs of overhead resources are first assigned to activity cost pools, and then activity costs are allocated to individual products or services using cost drivers that are chosen to reflect the use of resources. Therefore, ABC focuses on activities as the fundamental characteristic driving cost pool identification and cost driver selection.

For example, if materials handling is defined as an activity, the cost of buying and maintaining equipment for materials handling (such as forklifts or conveyor belts) is traced directly to an activity cost pool for materials handling. Other costs, such as supervisors' salaries, may be allocated to a number of different activity cost pools, including materials handling. A cost driver such as number of parts handled is used to allocate materials handling costs to individual products. In this example, products that use more parts would be allocated a higher amount of materials handling costs than products that use fewer parts.

ABC cost hierarchy

Accountants often use a cost hierarchy (which we introduced in chapter 3) to help them identify activities and then assign costs to those activities. ABC developers identified a number of general categories for the cost hierarchy based on different levels of operation. These categories include the following:

- organisation-sustaining
- facility-sustaining
- customer-sustaining
- product-sustaining
- batch-level
- unit-level.

A general description of each category with examples of costs and cost drivers is provided in figure 4.3. Accountants are not restricted to these categories; other categories can be used to analyse costs when organisations want to focus on different facets of their operations. For example, costs could be categorised by business segment or by strategic emphasis, such as product/service quality or protection of the environment.

FIGURE 4.3 ■ General hierarchy of ABC costs and cost drivers

Level of activities	Examples of costs	Examples of cost drivers
Organisation-sustaining Activities are related to the overall organisation and unaffected by number or types of facilities and customers or by volumes of products, batches or units.	■ Administrative salaries ■ Headquarters housekeeping ■ Information system salaries ■ Accountant salaries and equipment	These costs might not be allocated because they do not vary with activity volumes.
Facility-sustaining Activities are related to the overall operations of a facility and unaffected by number of customers served or by quantities of products, batches or units.	■ Facility maintenance service ■ Retail store insurance and heating/cooling ■ Manufacturing plant manager's salary ■ Depreciation and liability insurance for individual hospitals in a hospital system	These costs are typically not allocated except when the organisation needs to allocate all product costs for a particular purpose.
Customer-sustaining Activities are related to individual or groups of past, current and future customers and are not driven by total sales volumes and mix.	■ Customer sales representative salaries ■ Technical support salaries and supplies ■ Customer market research ■ Special tools for a customer's order	■ Number of sales calls ■ Hours of technical support (not tied to a specific product) ■ Number of customers

(continued)

FIGURE 4.3 (*continued*)

Level of activities	Examples of costs	Examples of cost drivers
Product-sustaining Activities support the production and distribution of a single product or line of products.	■ Production line supervisor salary ■ Product advertising ■ Product design engineer salaries ■ Depreciation of equipment used to manufacture one type of product	■ Number of engineering change orders ■ Number of advertisements ■ Machine hours
Batch-level Activities are performed for each batch of product and are not related to the number of units in the batch.	■ Labour cost for new set-up at the beginning of a batch ■ Utility costs for heating a kiln for batches of pottery ■ Shipping costs for batches	■ Set-up hours ■ Number of batches ■ Weight of orders shipped
Unit-level Activities produce individual units of goods or services; resource cost is proportional to production volumes or sales volumes.	■ Materials handling wages ■ Production workers paid based on quantity produced ■ Supplies used to provide services	■ Machine hours ■ Units processed ■ Materials quantity processed

Organisation-sustaining activities

Organisation-sustaining activities are tasks or functions undertaken to oversee the entire entity. These activities occur regardless of the number of facilities operated, customers served, products sold, batches processed or units produced. For example, the activities and costs of a corporate head office would be considered organisation-sustaining because they occur regardless of customer, product line, batch or unit volumes. The salaries and office costs of the chief executive officer and chief financial officer would be considered organisation-sustaining costs. In addition, costs such as information technology services are organisation-sustaining costs if they are performed for the entire entity. Because many of these costs are fixed (for example, administrative salaries, depreciation, and rent or lease costs), usually no cause-and-effect relationships exist between organisation-sustaining costs and the activities performed at this level. Therefore, these activity costs are typically assigned to the entire organisation and might not be allocated to specific product lines, batches or units.

Facility-sustaining activities

Facility-sustaining activities are tasks or functions undertaken to provide and manage an area, location or property. These activities occur regardless of the number of customers served, products sold, batches processed or units produced. Therefore, they are assigned to the facility and not allocated to product lines, batches or units. For example an entity's manufacturing and research facilities incur costs (such as facility manager salary, building depreciation, insurance, security, car parking and telephone services) that do not vary with levels of activity in the facility. These costs would be considered facility-sustaining costs.

Occasionally managers want to know the full costs on a per-unit basis, in which case both organisation- and facility-sustaining costs are allocated. However, identifying causal links between the cost object and cost driver is problematic and can lead to unreliable cost data.

Customer-sustaining activities

Customer-sustaining activities are tasks or functions undertaken to service past, current and future customers. These costs tend to vary with the needs of individual customers or groups of customers. Training aimed at particular customers would probably be considered customer-sustaining costs. Similarly, the commissions and fees paid to sales representatives and agents would be classified as customer-sustaining.

Product-sustaining activities

Product-sustaining activities are tasks or functions undertaken to support the production and distribution of a single product or line of products. These activities are not related to units or batches, but to individual products or product lines. Some of the product-sustaining costs apply to all of the products within a particular division, while other product-sustaining costs relate to only a single product. Thus, numerous ways can be used to define product-sustaining activities at a diverse entity.

Batch-level activities

Batch-level activities are tasks or functions undertaken for a collection of goods or services that are processed as a group. They include costs such as machinery set-up costs. Batch-level costs are related to the number of batches processed, not the number of units in the batch. Thus, batch costs increase as the number of batches increases.

Unit-level activities

Unit-level activities are undertaken to produce individual units manufactured or services produced. Unit-level activities need to be performed for every unit of good or service, and therefore the cost should be proportional to the number of units produced. Unit-level costs commonly include the costs to use and maintain the equipment for filling containers, direct materials costs and (where applicable) direct labour costs.

Understanding and implementing an ABC model

Overhead costs are gathered into cost pools in the first stage and then allocated to the cost objects (such as product line, batch or units) in the second stage. ABC differs from other allocation methods in that overhead costs are assigned to a larger number of activity-based cost pools, and cost drivers are used as allocation bases. Bear in mind that the total costs are the same irrespective of the method used for allocation. The following procedures are typically followed under the ABC method.[1]

1. Identify the relevant cost object.
2. Identify activities.
3. Assign costs to activity-based cost pools.
4. For each ABC cost pool, choose a cost driver.
5. For each ABC cost pool, calculate a cost driver rate.
6. For each ABC cost pool, allocate activity costs to the cost object.

Each of these procedures is illustrated in comprehensive example 1.

Comprehensive example 1

ABC model

The Paisley Insurance Company provides a range of insurance products to a variety of residential and commercial customers. The billing department at Paisley provides account inquiry and bill printing services for the two major classes of customers — residential (60 000 accounts) and commercial (10 000 accounts). Until now, the billing department has used what could be labelled a conventional costing system. As illustrated in figure 4.4, all costs in the department are indirect and were allocated to the two classes of customer on the basis of the *number of account inquiries*.

Indirect cost pool	$
Labour — supervisors	16 800
Labour — account inquiry	59 200
Labour — billing	33 750
Building occupancy	23 500
Telecommunications	29 260
Technology/computer	89 000
Printing machines	27 500
Paper	3 660
Total indirect costs	282 670
÷ Number of inquiries	11 500
= Cost per inquiry	24.58
Cost allocation	
Cost per residential account	$3.69 per account (9000 inquiries × $24.58)/60 000 accounts
Cost per commercial account	$6.15 (2500 inquiries × $24.58)/10 000 accounts

FIGURE 4.4 ■ Billing department — conventional costing system

Due to increasing competitive forces and an expected increase in demand for Paisley's insurance services, management has questioned the cost data currently available. Moreover, a local service bureau has expressed interest in providing the functions of the billing department, giving Paisley the opportunity to outsource these services. Management requested a study to investigate the activities and costs of the billing department and so an ABC study was undertaken.

1. Identify the relevant cost object

The two relevant cost objects of Paisley's billing department are the two types of accounts: residential and commercial.

2. Identify activities

Through a series of interviews with the appropriate staff, four key activities within the billing department were identified: account inquiry, correspondence, account billing and verification. A process map (see figure 4.5) can be developed to show the linkages between activities and resources. In this step there may be less concern about actual dollar amounts and more focus on understanding the processes and activities within the billing department.

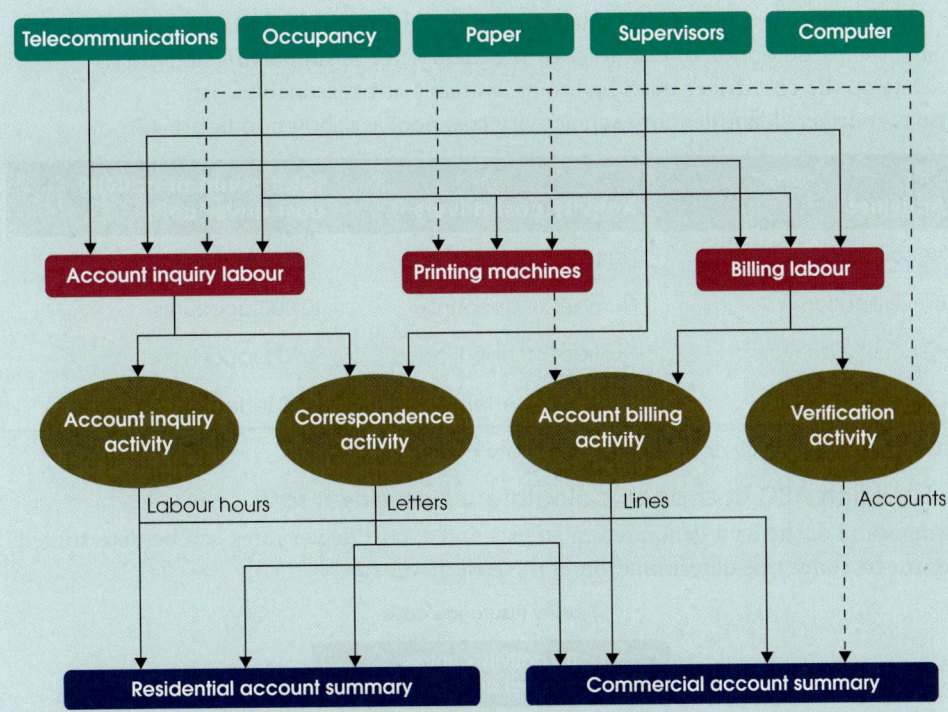

FIGURE 4.5 ■ Process map of the billing department's activities

3. Assign costs to activity-based cost pools

Using the process map in figure 4.5 as a guide, the required cost and operational data were collected to enable the costs associated with the activity cost pools to be identified. Sources of data for this exercise include the entity's accounting records, special studies and (sometimes) the best estimates of managers. Figure 4.6 contrasts the cost pools under the conventional and activity-based approaches. Note that the total costs of the billing department are still the same and it is only the cost pool structure that has changed.

Conventional view		Activity view	
Labour supervisors	$ 16 800	Account inquiry	$102 666
Labour — account inquiry	59 200	Correspondence	17 692
Labour — billing	33 750	Account billing	117 889
Building occupancy	23 500	Verification	44 423
Telecommunications	29 260	Total	$282 670
Computer	89 000		
Printing machines	27 500		
Paper	3 660		
Total	$282 670		

FIGURE 4.6 ■ Contrast of conventional and activity-based cost pools

4. For each ABC cost pool, choose a cost driver

Paisley identified cost drivers that were to be used as the allocation base, on the basis of two criteria.

- There had to be a reasonable cause-and-effect relationship between the driver unit and the consumption of resources or the incurrence of supporting activities.
- Data on the cost driver units had to be available at a reasonable cost.

The cost drivers identified for each activity cost pool are shown in figure 4.7.

Activities	Activity cost drivers	Total count of activity cost driver units
Account billing	Number of lines	1 220 000 lines
Bill verification	Number of accounts	10 000 accounts
Account inquiry	Number of labour hours	1650 labour hours
Correspondence	Number of letters	1400 letters

FIGURE 4.7 ■ Activity cost pools and activity cost drivers

5. For each ABC cost pool, calculate a cost driver rate

Using some of the data generated in steps 3 and 4, cost driver rates can be determined. Figure 4.8 shows the determination of the cost driver rates.

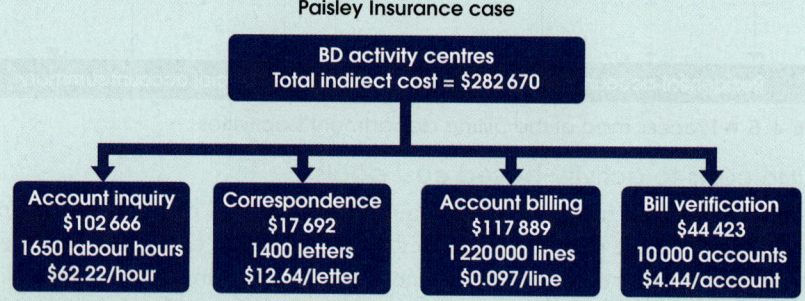

Paisley Insurance case

BD activity centres
Total indirect cost = $282 670

Account inquiry	Correspondence	Account billing	Bill verification
$102 666	$17 692	$117 889	$44 423
1650 labour hours	1400 letters	1 220 000 lines	10 000 accounts
$62.22/hour	$12.64/letter	$0.097/line	$4.44/account

FIGURE 4.8 ■ Determination of cost driver rates

6. For each ABC cost pool, allocate activity costs to the cost object

To allocate the activity cost to the two accounts, the consumption of cost driver units by each type of account are shown in figure 4.9. There is now sufficient data to allocate the activity costs to the cost objects. This is shown in figure 4.10.

Residential accounts	
Labour hours	900
Letters	900
Lines	720 000
Commercial accounts	
Labour hours	750
Letters	500
Lines	500 000

FIGURE 4.9 ■ Consumption of cost driver units by each type of account

Figure 4.11 contrasts the cost per account under the conventional and activity-based approaches. What is evident is a shift of costs from the residential accounts to the commercial account customers, suggesting the more complex nature of the commercial accounts draws more resources than were allocated under the conventional system.

	Residential	Commercial
Account inquiry	$ 55 998[a]	$ 46 665
Correspondence	11 376	6 320
Account billing	69 840	48 500
Bill verification	–	44 423
Totals	$137 214	$145 908
Accounts	60 000	10 000
Cost per account	$2.28	$14.59

[a] Being $62.22 per hour × 900 hours.

FIGURE 4.10 ■ Allocation of activity costs to each cost object

	Residential	Commercial
Conventional	$3.69	$6.15
Activity-based	$2.28	$ 14.49

FIGURE 4.11 ■ Contrast of conventional and activity-based costs for each account

Source: Adapted from Cotton, B 1998, 'Activity-based cost systems', in RS Kaplan & AA Atkinson (eds), *Advanced Management Accounting*, Prentice Hall, New Jersey, pp. 119–22.

Activity-based management (ABM)

Activity-based management (ABM) is the process of using ABC information to evaluate the costs and benefits of production and internal support activities, and to identify and implement opportunities for improvements in profitability, efficiency and quality within an entity. ABM relies on accurate ABC information. We will learn about four major uses of ABM:

- managing customer profitability
- managing product and process design
- managing environmental costs
- managing constrained resources.

Managing customer profitability

ABC can be used to identify customer-sustaining activities that cause some customers to be more costly than others. Such activities include providing sales and technical support to specific customers or groups of customers, holding inventory for just-in-time deliveries, and customising orders. Figure 4.12 describes the characteristics of customers having higher and lower costs.

FIGURE 4.12 ■ Characteristics of customers with high and low service costs

As the costs of serving specific customers are determined, managers can choose different strategies for different types of customers. For example, some customers need very little service but are quite price sensitive. Although margins for these customers are low, these customers are profitable when service costs are also kept low. Customers with high service costs are also profitable when their net margins are high enough to account for the extra service costs. Alternatively, the entity can price its extra services and let customers pick the services they are willing to pay for.

For further discussion and analysis relating to customer profitability, see the chapter 4 article at the end of this book.

Managing product and process design

An advantage of ABC is its focus on activities. As an organisation's activities are analysed more closely, managers improve their understanding of how resources are used. In turn, this analysis enables managers to improve operations and profits. They can focus resources on **value-added activities** (those which the customer/client is normally prepared to pay for), which increase the worth of an entity's goods or services to customers. Conversely, they can reduce or eliminate **non-value-added activities** (often associated with waste such as rework), which are unnecessary and therefore waste resources.

Under ABM, non-value-added activities are identified and eliminated when possible. As ABC systems are implemented, activities can be categorised as follows:
- required to produce a good or service and cannot be improved at this time
- required but the process could be improved or simplified
- not required to produce a good or service and can eventually be eliminated
- not required and can be eliminated by changing a process or procedure.

Managing environmental costs

Many managers are concerned with the effects of their organisations' manufacturing processes on the environment. In addition, many shareholders are concerned with the 'green' reputation of companies in which they invest. Federal and state regulations may require entities to reduce pollution levels. The direct costs of reducing pollution are often easily tracked, but identifying the costs and benefits of protecting the environment within conventional accounting systems is more difficult. ABC systems can be designed to identify the activities involved in environmental protection and to develop costs for those activities. Analysing overhead activities also helps managers identify opportunities for improved environmental performance.

Suppose a high-quality printing entity used inks that were detrimental to the environment. The cost of ink disposal was traditionally recorded as part of overhead cost. When management developed an ABC system, however, the disposal cost became part of an activity cost pool for the printing process that used these inks. As the activity was analysed, the high cost of disposal became more noticeable. Managers realised that they could invest in an incinerator that used high temperatures to burn the ink so thoroughly that it left little airborne or solid residual. Thus, the ABC process motivated managers to consider alternative methods to reduce the cost of pollution. Once the cost effects of pollution, waste and other environmental activities are identified, managers become more motivated to make investments that improve environmental performance. With these improvements, costs are reduced because organisations no longer incur the costs associated with pollution or waste. In addition, many non-value-added activities are eliminated, such as disposal or cleaning activities.

Although identifying the activities and costs related to environmental quality can be difficult, entities are increasingly concerned with valuing the costs and benefits of developing environmentally friendly practices. See chapter 16 for a comprehensive coverage of environmental sustainability issues.

Managing constrained resources

If an organisation faces capacity constraints, ABC can help identify each product's use of constrained resources. By analysing the activities within the constraints, efficiency improvements can be proposed and tested. Thus, ABC information can help managers identify the best way to relax constraints. ABC information can also be used in designing products and manufacturing or service delivery processes that minimise use of constrained resources.

In addition, by developing an ABC system that separates committed from flexible costs, managers would have more accurate information to determine the contribution margin per constrained resource. When products with the highest contribution margin per constrained resource are emphasised, profits are maximised.

Managing resources supplied and consumed

ABC cost models facilitate the identification of those resources that have been supplied (as reported in the financial statements) and those that have been consumed by the cost object(s). For example, if we consider the correspondence cost pool in comprehensive example 1, we note the following data:

Resources supplied	$17 692
Anticipated activity level	1400 letters
Cost per unit of activity driver	$12.64

If during the subsequent period only 1200 letters are consumed by the cost objects, then the cost of resources consumed would be $15 168 (1200 letters × $12.64). The difference between the resources supplied ($17 692) and the resources consumed ($15 168) represents unused capacity ($2524). In the longer term, Paisley's costs are going to be reduced only when the resources supplied are reduced, not necessarily when the resources consumed are reduced.

Benefits, costs and issues related to ABC

Accountants need to consider cost–benefit trade-offs when choosing activities and cost drivers for an ABC system. They must estimate the costs of alternative ABC systems and anticipate the potential benefits from alternative system designs. They also need to recognise that an ABC system might fail to meet expectations.

Benefits of ABC

ABC systems enable managers to focus on measurement at the activity level. Once activities are identified and cost drivers are chosen, employees are more aware of cause-and-effect relationships. This awareness prompts employees to search for ways to improve performance simply because they have more information about the cost effects of an activity. By more carefully analysing activity costs, the importance and materiality of some non-value-added costs becomes more apparent, and motivation to reduce those costs increases. In an ABC system, activities that do not add value to customers are more likely to be identified and eliminated from operations. Examples include holding excess levels of inventories, unnecessary transportation, waste in the set-up process, and inspection inefficiencies.

More than other costing systems, ABC systems measure the flow of resources in an entity. They reduce the arbitrariness in cost measurement by more closely matching cost allocations to the actual use of resources by operating activities. Compared to the allocation bases used in a conventional costing system, the allocation bases used in an ABC system are more likely to be cost drivers and related to costs, rather than just used to allocate cost. One of the key benefits of an ABC system would seem to be its use in special/one-off studies to assist a particular management decision. In such cases it may be unnecessary to embed ABC into the entity's system. For example, in the Paisley Insurance example earlier, ABC was used to produce more up-to-date and reliable cost data associated with residential and commercial account customers of the billing department. Having calculated the relatively more reliable costs and used them in the outsourcing decision, the objective of the ABC system implementation may have been achieved. Embedding ABC into the entity's system would be a separate and perhaps unnecessary decision.

Costs of ABC

Many costs are associated with designing and using an ABC system. They include:

- system design costs such as employee time and consulting fees
- accounting and information system modifications needed to gather and report activity and cost driver information
- employee training to use the ABC system effectively.

Sometimes the cost of developing ABC information is low, especially in cases where the activity cost is readily available and the number of times the activity is performed can be easily tracked. Suppose the activity is inspection of units. The cost consists of the salary and fringe benefits of the inspector, and all units are inspected. Identifying salary costs in an accounting system is easy, and fringe benefits costs can be estimated. The number of units produced should be readily available from production records, and the capacity of the inspection area can be easily estimated. Thus, developing an activity-based cost for inspection may be as simple as dividing the salary-related costs by a chosen measure of unit volume.

Other times, ABC information is more costly to develop. Suppose the activity is the set-up process. This process often includes labour, supplies and other resources. Because cost tracing is one of the components of cost assignment under ABC, it takes time and analysis to identify costs that can be traced and those that should be allocated. In addition, data for the cost driver (such as the number of set-ups) must be tracked.

In general, the costs of an ABC system are higher when more activities — or more complex activities — are involved. It is more difficult to accurately trace costs to activities as their complexity and number increase. In addition, increased employee training is often required. Also, the process of ABC system development bogs down if too much complexity is introduced at one time. However, a failure to sufficiently break down activities might prevent the system from providing useful information.

Accounting researchers questioned whether the costs of implementing ABC systems were worth the benefits received. They found that although ABC use was associated with higher quality and improved cycle time, for the average entity no significant association was found between ABC use and return on assets. However, ABC appeared to be related to profitability for firms using advanced manufacturing techniques that combine information technology with more flexible manufacturing practices.[2] Researchers who document successful implementations suggest that important factors include top management support, linkages to strategy, training, non-accounting ownership and performance evaluation.[3] In addition, researchers have found that for small manufacturing entities, simple ABC systems with few activities and cost drivers are best. These systems are inexpensive yet efficient, and easier for managers to understand and implement.[4]

Issues related to ABC

Limitations and uncertainties in ABC implementation

Managers use judgment to decide which activities and cost drivers to include in an ABC system because of uncertainty about the set of activities and drivers that would provide the best information. As the number of activities increases, measurement error also tends to increase because a greater number of allocations are used to assign costs to activity cost pools. In addition, it is not always possible to determine the best cost driver. Information for some cost drivers may be readily available, whereas information for a potentially superior driver might be costly to accumulate. When designing an ABC system, accountants cannot foresee all of the various ways in which the new information could be used in ABM to reduce costs or improve decision making. For example, until activities and costs are evaluated, we may not be able to identify non-value-added activities. Accordingly, the ability to identify the most valuable activities to measure and track is uncertain.

Uncertainties are also part of choosing an appropriate denominator value to determine the allocation rate. The accuracy of estimates used in the denominator affect the allocation of cost. We overstate or understate cost when the denominator estimate is too large or small. Although ABC information is more detailed, measurement errors also increase because of estimates. Thus, the additional detail does not necessarily improve the quality of information.

Accountants also face uncertainties about how an organisation's employees will respond to the design and implementation of an ABC system. In some cases, employees are afraid of major system changes, especially when their jobs might be viewed as non-value-added. As a result, some employees will fail to provide adequate information for designing the system; they might even provide misleading or incorrect information. If employees believe that their performance will be evaluated using ABC information, they may provide biased information to show better performance. Once the new system is designed, they may try to undermine implementation and training efforts. Even when employees fully embrace the new ABC system, they might misunderstand it and make inappropriate decisions. Furthermore, if an ABC system is overly complex, even the most enthusiastic employees might not be able to take full advantage of it.

Mismeasurement of costs assigned to ABC activities

As illustrated in figure 4.2 on page 128, costs must be assigned to each ABC cost pool. Errors may creep into the process of tracing or allocating individual costs, leading to mismeasurement in ABC costs. The allocation process often introduces a degree of measurement error. For example, costs such as supplies and employee benefits might be allocated to a number of activities such as set-up, maintenance and monitoring production. It is impossible to identify the exact amount of cost associated with each activity when we use allocated costs. In addition, errors are sometimes made in assigning costs directly to ABC pools.

In general, the risk of measurement error increases under the following circumstances:

- if uncertainties exist about the activity to which costs relate
- when costs are allocated instead of being traced to ABC cost pool
- when the number of ABC cost pools increases.

Recent developments in ABC: time-driven ABC[5]

Many entities have either abandoned or decided not to adopt ABC because of complexity, time and cost-related barriers to entry. Time-driven ABC is argued to be more accurate, less costly and less time-consuming than the conventional ABC discussed throughout this chapter. The purpose of this section is to explore time-driven ABC through an extension of comprehensive example 1 earlier in this chapter.

The central features of time-driven ABC are:

- a focus on capacity supplied and capacity used
- consideration of the time taken to perform each activity
- the development of a standardised cost per time unit of capacity
- the ability to adjust for flexibility of operations or specialised cost determination.

This means that for time-driven ABC, the resource demands of each cost object are directly estimated — unlike the conventional approach, where the resource costs are assigned to activities and then to the cost object.

In conventional ABC, the cost driver rate is calculated as follows:

Total assigned activity cost ÷ Total activity quantity

In time-driven ABC, the cost driver rate is calculated as follows:

Cost per time unit of capacity × Unit times of activity

Comprehensive example 2 draws on comprehensive example 1 (page 132) to highlight the differences between conventional ABC and time-driven ABC.

Comprehensive example 2

Using Paisley to compare conventional ABC and time-driven ABC

The Paisley Insurance Company employs 12 staff in its billing department (BD) operations. The time they spent performing each of the four activities was identified and is highlighted in the following table, along with the conventional ABC results from comprehensive example 1.

Activity	% of time spent	Assigned cost	Activity quantity	Cost driver rate
Account inquiry	35%	102 666	11 500 account inquiries[a]	$8.93/account inquiry
Correspondence	5%	17 692	1400 letters	$12.64/letter
Account billing	40%	117 889	1 220 000 lines	$0.097/line
Bill verification	20%	44 423	10 000 accounts	$4.44/account
	100%[b]	282 670		

[a]Recall in comprehensive example 1 that *labour hours* was identified as the suitable activity driver to reflect the cause-and-effect relationship between account inquiry costs and related account inquiry activities. In this case we use an alternative activity driver — *the number of inquiries* — which totalled 11 500 (9000 residential and 2500 commercial). This is more suitable for the time-driven ABC approach as *time* is the key capacity-related variable and so cannot be used in both parts of the following time-driven ABC cost driver equation:

Cost per time unit of capacity × Unit times of activity

[b]In conventional ABC, employees generally calculate the time spent performing each activity as a percentage of their total time. This assumes that there is no idle or unused capacity. As a result, the estimated cost driver rate will usually be overstated. In time-driven ABC, the time unit of *practical capacity* is calculated to allow for deviations from normal performance (meal breaks, machine downtime, travelling between activities etc.). As a rule-of-thumb, *practical capacity* is determined to be 80 to 85 per cent of *theoretical full capacity*.

The steps taken to determine the time-driven ABC cost driver equation follow.

Step 1: Cost per time unit of capacity at Paisley's billing department = $3.07

The cost per minute of supplying capacity is calculated as $282\,670/92\,160 = \$3.07$ where $282\,670$ is the cost of supplying capacity at Paisley (monthly overhead billing department cost) and $92\,160$ minutes is the total practical capacity provided by 12 full-time employees. Each individual works 8 hours per day; 9600 minutes per month theoretical full capacity; 80% of 9600 = 7680 practical capacity for one worker × 12 workers = 92 160 *total* minutes per month.

Step 2: Unit times of activity

This is the time it takes to carry out one unit of activity for each of the four activities identified at Paisley. Analysis of each activity identified that staff can perform an account inquiry in roughly 2.8 minutes, correspondence in 3.3 minutes, account billing in 0.03 minutes and verification in 1.8 minutes.

In the following table, the quantity of actual activity performed by Paisley in the quarter is shown. The objective of this table is to highlight both the cost driver rate calculated, and the amount of used capacity against the actual capacity available. Note that we have no unused capacity in this situation because we have applied Paisley's actual results for the month of May in this illustration.

Activity (1)	Quantity (2)	Unit time (min) (3)	Total time used (min) (4)	Cost driver rate (3) × $3.07 (5)	Total cost assigned (2) × (5) (6)
Account inquiry	11 500	2.8	32 200	8.60	98 900
Correspondence	1 400	3.3	4 620	10.13	14 182
Account billing	1 220 000	0.03	36 600	0.092	112 240
Bill verification	10 000	1.8	18 000	5.53	55 300
Total used			91 420		280 622
Total supplied			92 160		282 670
Unused capacity			0[a]		0

[a]Difference due to rounding.

For the month of June, Paisley estimated the same quantity of activity as that achieved in May. Because the actual quantities in June (column 2) differ from the estimate, we are able to identify the level of unused capacity.

Activity (1)	Quantity (2)	Unit time (min) (3)	Total time used (min) (4)	Cost driver rate (3) × $3.07 (5)	Total cost assigned (2) × (5) (6)
Account inquiry	10 000	2.8	28 000	8.60	86 000
Correspondence	1 400	3.3	4 608	10.13	14 182
Account billing	1 220 000	0.03	36 864	0.092	112 240

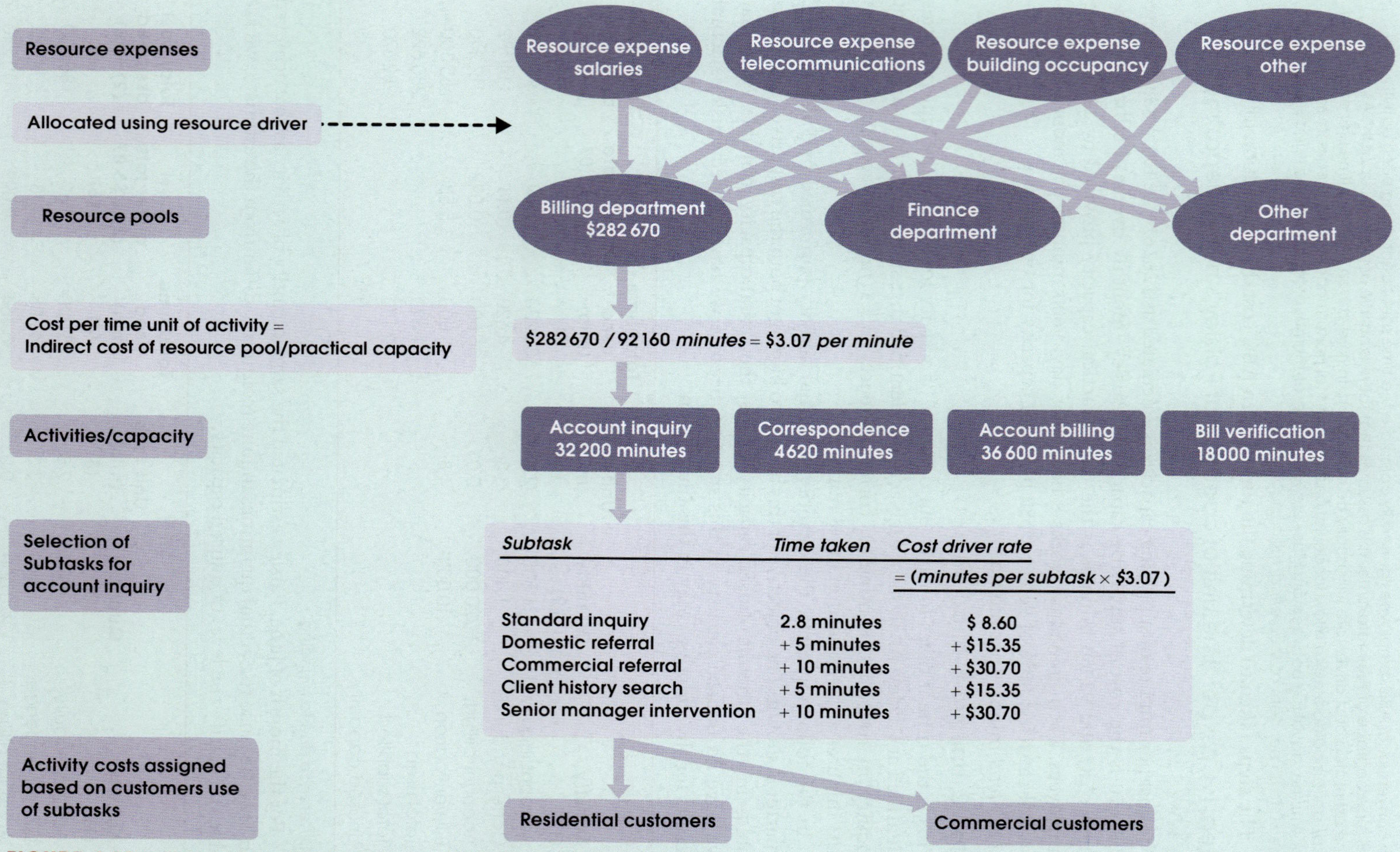

Resource expenses

Allocated using resource driver

Resource pools

Cost per time unit of activity =
Indirect cost of resource pool/practical capacity

Activities/capacity

Selection of Subtasks for account inquiry

Activity costs assigned based on customers use of subtasks

Resource expense salaries

Resource expense telecommunications

Resource expense building occupancy

Resource expense other

Finance department

Other department

Billing department
$282 670

$282 670 / 92 160 minutes = $3.07 per minute

Account inquiry
32 200 minutes

Correspondence
4620 minutes

Account billing
36 600 minutes

Bill verification
18 000 minutes

Subtask	Time taken	Cost driver rate $= (minutes\ per\ subtask \times \$3.07\ )$
Standard inquiry	2.8 minutes	$ 8.60
Domestic referral	+ 5 minutes	+ $15.35
Commercial referral	+ 10 minutes	+ $30.70
Client history search	+ 5 minutes	+ $15.35
Senior manager intervention	+ 10 minutes	+ $30.70

Residential customers

Commercial customers

FIGURE 4.13 ■ Time-driven ABC process for Paisley Insurance Company

Activity (1)	Quantity (2)	Unit time (min) (3)	Total time used (min) (4)	Cost driver rate (3) × $3.07 (5)	Total cost assigned (2) × (5) (6)
Bill verification	8000	1.8	14 400	5.53	44 240
Total used			83 872		256 662
Total supplied			92 160		282 670
Unused capacity			8 288		26 008[a]

[a]Rounding difference

Refining the model

When investigating the standard 2.8 minutes taken for an account inquiry, it was found that there were other variables contributing to the complexity of this activity. These included time spent searching client file history; senior manager referrals time; and whether the inquiry was considered a simple, average or complex account inquiry — not whether it was a domestic or commercial inquiry. This means that each variant now becomes a distinct activity, so using time-driven ABC we can adjust the 2.8 minute account inquiry to accommodate the identified variables.

The refinement is not limited to each activity. In fact, the entire four-activity approach to the billing activities of Paisley's billing department can be replaced with a single time equation.

Advantages of time-driven ABC

Time-driven ABC has the following advantages.
1. More informed decision-making in relation to the availability and best use of practical capacity:
   - the difference between time available and time required to perform activities is made more obvious
   - idle time can be quantified as input costs minus costs assigned to activities
   - more informed decisions relating to the allocation of staff to activities can be made
   - excess capacity can be eliminated or better managed.
2. Improved computer costing systems capability when using standard rates.[6]
3. Complexity of operations can be incorporated into the time-driven ABC model. For example, standard rates can be:
   - applied in real time to assign individual costs
   - used in quotations to estimate prices for new orders
   - adjusted when existing conditions change:
     - input prices change (salaries, operating expenses)
     - efficiency of the activity changes (learning curves; training programs; re-engineering processes)
     - time units change (new technology and processes).

Limitations of time-driven ABC

Time-driven ABC is relatively new and empirical evidence of benefits is minimal. Like conventional ABC, calculations are still based on subjective and rule-of-thumb estimates. This may result in key cost drivers being based on potentially inaccurate assumptions.

The standardised cost per time unit of capacity might simplify the process. However, it might not necessarily:

- capture the 'value' of time (each minute of costed time is assumed to be equal)
- differentiate the expertise (hence cost) of the employee in performing the activity
- be suitable where overhead costs lack homogeneity.

Comprehensive example 3 focuses on a detailed comparison of conventional job costing and ABC as well as exploring the application of ABC concepts.

Comprehensive example 3

Comparison of ABC and conventional job costing

Keener Doors and Windows Company produces two types of wooden doors. Regular doors are high volume and use standard parts and manufacturing processes. Premium doors are lower volume and are considered a customised, specialty item. Managers are considering the pricing policies for both doors because their major competitor recently lowered prices on regular doors. Premium doors have been selling well because they are priced lower than the competitor's specialty doors. The managers are concerned about the effects on profit margins if they reduce the price of regular doors to match the competition. Although they only consider variable costs in their pricing decisions, they would like to have more information about each product's use of overhead resources.

The cost accountant, Valerie Bradley, suggested that Keener consider implementing an ABC system to better understand the costs for all of the manufacturing activities needed to produce the doors. She believes that the regular doors use fewer overhead resources because all of the regular doors go through routine processes, whereas the premium doors require special processes. Both doors are produced in batches of 100. However, each premium door is processed further to add custom features, such as special routing effects in the wood or special window treatments. Currently, overhead is allocated based on direct labour hours but machines perform much of the work. Valerie believes that labour hours do not reflect the two products' different use of plant overhead resources.

An ABC team is assembled to analyse the manufacturing activities and costs for individual doors in both product lines. The team consists of Valerie, a product designer and several employees from the manufacturing process. They want to compare costs under the current job costing system and a new ABC system. As they consider the task, they realise that ABC allocations typically ignore facility-related costs while job costing allocations include them. For purposes of comparison, they decide to ignore facility-sustaining costs in their calculations for job costing so that the results from both systems are comparable. From the general ledger, Valerie identifies overhead costs of $18 270 000 (not including any facility costs) that were assigned to regular and premium doors last period.

Product costs using job costing

The team recreates the products' job costs using information from the general ledger. Each regular door requires $65 of direct materials and 2.5 hours of direct labour. Each premium door requires $100 of direct materials and 3 hours of direct labour. The job costing system allocates overhead using a factory-wide estimated allocation rate of $32.05 per direct labour hour based on a single cost pool for door production of $18 270 000 and direct labour hours of 570 000 for the year. The following schedule summarises the cost of each type of door:

	Regular doors	Premium doors
Direct materials:		
Regular	65.00	
Premium		$100.00
Direct labour:		
Regular ($20 × 2.5 hours)	50.00	
Premium ($20 × 3 hours)		60.00
Factory overhead:		
Regular ($32.05 × 2.5 hours)	80.13	
Premium ($32.05 × 3 hours)		96.15
Total cost	$ 195.13	$ 256.15

The team members notice that the overhead allocation for premium doors is $16.02 (or 20%) greater than for regular doors under the job costing system. However, the shop supervisor believes that premium doors use two to three times more resources than regular doors because of extra processing the premium doors receive on the most expensive equipment.

Product costs using ABC

The managers want to know whether their current pricing policy reflects any differences in resources used by regular doors compared to premium doors. Therefore, the ABC team decides that the relevant cost objects are individual doors and the activities involved in production must be analysed. When the team visits the production area, they ask about the activities performed for each type of door. They learn that the first activity is delivery of materials to workstations. They identify a materials handling cost pool for this activity.

The next steps involve work done in batches, such as the initial cutting, sanding and smoothing of doors. The team learns that two different activities are required: setting up machines for the next batch, and monitoring the machines as batches are processed. Some team members believe that these two activities could be combined into one cost pool allocated on the number of batches run. Valerie asks whether these activities differ between regular doors and premium doors. She learns that the set-up for premium door batches is more complex and takes more time than for regular doors. The batches take the same amount of time, no matter what type of door is produced. Therefore, the team identifies two activity pools — one for set-up costs and one for batch monitoring costs — because the activities in these pools are not homogeneous and cannot be allocated using a single cost driver.

After the doors are cut and sanded, they are processed through routing machines. The team discovers that premium doors require more routing machine hours because the designs are more complex. An activity pool for machining is identified. The last activity is inspection. The inspectors explain that premium doors take longer to inspect because of their greater detail. The team identifies inspection as a cost pool.

Now that the cost pools are identified, costs need to be traced or allocated to each pool. Valerie uses annual accounting records and information from employees about supplies used and the amount of time they spend performing different tasks. Materials handling costs are easy to trace because workers perform only materials handling duties, so their wages are traced directly to the cost pool. Equipment depreciation accounts are analysed, and the cost of materials handling equipment is separated. Workers estimate fuel costs and some supply costs because detailed records are not kept for these expenses. Employees who set up and monitor batches estimate the amount of time spent in each activity. The employees performing the machining estimate the time and indirect materials used on each type of door, as do the inspectors.

The team's next step is to select cost drivers. They decide to use number of parts as the cost driver for materials handling because each part is handled separately. The set-up for each batch varies with the complexity of the door design. Regular doors are processed using three simple designs. The machines automatically cut the doors to size and rout simple designs on the doors. Premium door set-up requires more time because the door designs are more complex and usually include windows. The robotic machines cut holes for and insert windows. Set-up for this process is more time-intensive. The team decides to use set-up time as the cost driver for this activity. Each batch requires about the same amount of monitoring, so the team selects number of batches as the cost driver for monitoring costs. Premium doors require more machine hours than regular doors because the routing designs are more complex, so machine hours are chosen as cost driver for machining costs. Each door requires a different amount of time to inspect, so the team selects inspection labour time as the cost driver for inspection.

Before calculating the allocation rates, the team estimates the volume for each cost driver. They have complete records for machine hours and labour hours, but are not sure about information for number of parts because that statistic is not tracked. The materials handling employees estimate the number of parts they handled last year. Records are maintained for the number of batches, so that information is readily available. Employees are asked to estimate time spent in set-up. The number of doors inspected is available, as is total time spent inspecting. However, time per regular versus premium door has not been tracked, so inspectors estimate these figures.

Next, the team gathers information about the amount of each cost driver used by regular and premium doors last month as follows.

	Regular doors	Premium doors
Number of doors per batch	100	100
Number of batches	1200	900
Number of parts per door	10	20
Machine set-up time	0.5 hours per batch	1 hour per batch
Machine hours per door	1	3
Inspection time per door	0.5 hours	1 hour

Figure 4.14 summarises the steps thus far, showing the activities, related cost drivers, overall costs, estimated volume for each cost driver and estimated allocation rates.

Machine set-up time is 0.5 hours per batch for regular doors. At $100 per hour, the cost is $50 per batch. Because each batch consists of 100 doors, the cost per regular door is $0.50. Similarly, the cost per premium door is $1.

The total ABC overhead cost for each type of door is calculated as follows:

		Regular door		Premium door
Materials handling	(10 × $1)	$10.00	(20 × $1)	$ 20.00
Machine set-up	(0.5 × $100 ÷ 100)	0.50	(1 × $100 ÷ 100)	1.00
Monitoring batches	($200 ÷ 100)	2.00	($200 ÷ 100)	2.00
Machine hours	(1 × $30)	30.00	(3 × $30)	90.00
Inspections	(0.5 × $20)	10.00	(1 × $20)	20.00
Total overhead		$52.50		$133.00

Volume	Estimated cost	Cost driver	Cost drivers: estimated volume Regular doors	Premium doors	Total	Estimated allocation rate
Number of doors			120 000	90 000	210 000	
Number of batches			1 200	900	2 100	
Activity						
Materials handling	$ 3 000 000	Number of parts	1 200 000	1 800 000	3 000 000	$1 per part
Setting up machines	150 000	Time spent	600	900	1 500	$100 per set-up hour
Monitoring batch operations	420 000	Number of batches	1 200	900	2 100	$200 per batch
Machining doors	11 700 000	Machine hours	120 000	270 000	390 000	$30 per machine hour
Inspecting doors	3 000 000	Time spent	60 000	90 000	150 000	$20 per inspection hour
Total cost	$18 270 000					

FIGURE 4.14 ■ Estimated volumes and costs developed by the ABC team at Keener Doors and Windows

Using ABC product cost information

The team believes that the calculations under ABC costing confirm their intuition that the job costing system did not accurately reflect each product's use of resources. Overhead allocated to regular doors was $80.13 under the job costing system but only $52.50 under ABC. For the premium doors, $96.15 in overhead cost was allocated by the job costing system compared to $133.00 under activity-based costing. These results suggest that the old system overstated the cost of regular doors and understated the cost of premium doors. The team believes that the ABC costs are more accurate because they better map the use of resources to each type of product.

When the team presents its results to the company's managers, they decide that the regular door price can be reduced to match competitors' prices and the premium door price can be increased. Valerie reminds the managers that this ABC information contains some allocated fixed costs (such as salaries for supervisors and equipment depreciation), and that these costs probably will not change proportionately with changes in production volumes. Therefore, these ABC costs should be used only as a guide for pricing decisions. After any pricing changes are made, the managers need to monitor sales volumes to determine the effects of price changes on demand and determine whether profitability actually improves.

Using ABM to reduce non-manufacturing costs

The managers at Keener Doors and Windows are pleased with the ABC cost information for door production and ask for additional analysis of marketing and warranty costs for doors. They feel these costs could be reduced if they better understand marketing and warranty activities and their related costs.

Because marketing and warranty service are similar for regular and premium doors, the ABC team concludes that these costs can be analysed using doors as a single product line and windows as the other product line. Thus, they plan to identify activities related to marketing and warranty costs, and then separate the costs for doors from the costs for windows. Product-sustaining marketing costs consist of advertising, marketing department employee costs, sales commissions, and marketing department supplies. The cost of advertising is relatively easy to assign because either doors or windows are featured in advertisements. Marketing department employees estimate the amount of time spent per product line, and any sales commissions are traced to each product line. Miscellaneous supplies are allocated according to employee time spent.

To analyse costs for product-sustaining warranty work, the ABC system needs to separate the costs for warranty work on doors from the warranty work on windows. Depending on the problem, sometimes doors are replaced. In these cases, detailed cost records are kept. Other times the doors are reworked. Tracking the costs of rework is difficult because employees take time from their regular tasks to rework, and they often complete rework tasks during idle times when batches are in process and do not need monitoring. Monthly rework costs rely on employee estimates of time and materials used for rework. The team concludes that the warranty work cost pool probably includes errors in cost measurement. They decide to develop a tracking system for the time and materials used for rework to get better estimates of warranty costs in the future.

The final estimates of the per-door costs for marketing and warranty follow:

Marketing	$20 per unit
Warranty work	$18 per unit

Applying activity-based management

The team members are surprised that warranty costs are nearly as large as marketing costs. They invite the product design team to meet with customer service representatives to discuss possible product changes to reduce warranty costs. The data for the last period indicate that more than half of the warranty costs — about $10 per door sold — resulted from hinge problems; the whole door must be replaced when a hinge fails. The team immediately begins to solve this problem.

The first suggestion is to reinforce the door around the hinge, but the team learns that this procedure costs $15 per door. One team member researches the newest technology in hinges and finds one that would eliminate 90 per cent of the problem at a cost of $14.50 per door, whereas the current hinges cost $12 per door. After discussing a number of other alternatives, the team recommends the new hinges. Although this increases the cost of each door by $2.50, it is likely that overall warranty costs will be reduced by $9 per door ($10 × 90%). In addition, the team believes that Keener's reputation for high quality has been hurt by the hinge problem, resulting in a loss of market share. Management accepts the team's recommendation and instructs engineering to use the new hinges to improve quality, reduce warranty work and eventually increase market share.

Summary

1   Explain the differences and similarities between activity-based costing (ABC) and conventional costing.

Conventional costing system
Few cost pools allocated using conventional allocation bases.

Activity-based costing system
Multiple cost pools reflecting activities and cost drivers for allocation bases.

Activity
Type of task or function performed in an organisation.

Activity identification
- Tracking the use of resources
- Using the cost hierarchy
- Grouping homogeneous costs

Selection of cost drivers
- Cause-and-effect relationship between cost driver and activity costs
- Judgment in choosing and evaluating potential cost drivers

2   Understand elements of the ABC cost hierarchy.

Cost hierarchy
- Organisation-sustaining activities
- Facility-sustaining activities
- Customer-sustaining activities
- Product-sustaining activities
- Batch-level activities
- Unit-level activities

3   Understand and work with an ABC model.

ABC procedures

1. Identify the relevant cost object.
2. Identify activities.
3. Assign (trace and allocate) costs to activity-based cost pools.
4. For each ABC cost pool, choose a cost driver.
5. For each ABC cost pool, calculate a cost driver rate.
6. For each ABC cost pool, allocate activity costs to the cost object.

4   Describe the characteristics and use of activity-based management (ABM).

Activity-based management

Process of using ABC information to evaluate the costs and benefits of production and internal support activities, and to identify and implement opportunities for improvements in profitability, efficiency and quality within an entity.

Applications of ABM

- Customer profitability
- Product and process design:
  - focus resources on value-added activities
  - reduce or eliminate non-value-added activities
  - target and kaizen costing.
- Environmental costs
- Constrained resources
- Resources supplied and resources consumed

5   Outline the benefits, costs and issues related to ABC.

Benefits

- Increase awareness of cause-and-effect relationships
- Promote performance improvements
- Identify non-value-added activities
- Motivate cost reduction
- Reduce arbitrariness in cost measurement
- Optimise use of constrained resources
- Resources provided versus resources consumed

Costs

- System design and capabilities if expanding activity dictionary
- Accounting system modifications
- Employee training
- Higher costs when:
  - more activities are involved
  - activities are complex
  - ABC system is complex.

Issues related to ABC

- Limitations and uncertainties in ABC implementation
- Mismeasurement of costs assigned to ABC activities
- Recent developments in ABC: time-driven ABC

Self-study problems

SELF-STUDY PROBLEM 1

Compute unit ABC costs

The Fallon Company manufactures a variety of handcrafted bed frames. The company's manufacturing activities and related data for the current year follow:

Manufacturing activity	Estimated cost	Cost driver used as allocation base	Estimated volume for cost driver
Materials handling	$400 000	Number of parts	800 000 parts
Cutting	1 200 000	Machine hours	800 000 hours
Assembly	3 000 000	Direct labour hours	150 000 hours
Wood staining	1 320 000	Number of frames stained	60 000 frames

Two styles of bed frames were produced in July: a wood frame with fewer parts, and a metal frame that required no staining activities. Direct labour is paid $25 per hour. Their quantities, direct material costs and other data follow:

	Units produced	Direct material	Machine hours	Number of parts	Direct labour hours
Wood frames	5000	$600 000	5000	100 000	6000
Metal frames	1000	200 000	500	10 000	3000

REQUIRED

(a) Compute the ABC cost allocation rates and then calculate total manufacturing costs and unit costs of the wood and metal frames.

(b) Suppose non-manufacturing activities, such as product design, were analysed and allocated to the wood frame at $10 each and the metal frame at $15 each. Moreover, similar analyses were conducted of other non-manufacturing activities, such as distribution, marketing and customer service. The support costs allocated were $50 per wood frame and $80 per metal frame. Calculate the product cost per unit including the non-manufacturing costs.

Solution to self-study problem 1

(a)

Resource or activity	Wood frames		Metal frames	
Direct materials		$ 600 000		$200 000
Direct labour	6000 × $25	150 000	3000 × $25	75 000
Materials handling	100 000 × $0.50	50 000	10 000 × $0.50	5 000
Cutting	5000 × $30	150 000	500 × $30	15 000
Assembly	6000 × $20	120 000	3000 × $20	60 000
Wood staining	5000 × $22	110 000	0 × $22	0
Total		$1 180 000		$ 355 000
Per unit	$1 180 000 ÷ 5000	$236 per unit	$355 000 ÷ 1000	$355 per unit

(b) Product cost per unit including manufacturing and non-manufacturing costs:

$$\text{Wood frame} = \$236 + \$10 + \$50 = \$296$$

$$\text{Metal frame} = \$355 + \$15 + \$80 = \$450$$

SELF-STUDY PROBLEM 2

ABC activities and cost drivers; measurement error; usefulness

You have been asked to analyse your sister's preschool operation to determine in what ways she can improve quality and reduce costs. You decide to analyse the activities provided by the preschool and use an ABC system to assign costs to the activities. The following list contains potential activities from which to choose.

- *Learning activities.* At times during the day, children are listening to stories, learning to sing simple songs, following simple directions as part of games or art activities, and playing interactively with special toys developed to enhance eye–hand coordination or understanding of spatial relations.
- *Resting.* The children rest on mats during this activity while one teacher monitors and the other teachers prepare lesson plans.
- *Snack and meal activities.* Snacks and meals are prepared by teachers and one food-service employee. Sometimes the students prepare their own snacks and practice following directions.
- *Free play activities.* While children play inside or outside, a few teachers monitor their progress while others prepare learning activities to be used later.
- *Art and craft activities.* These daily activities promote some of the same skills as the learning activities, but children are encouraged to be more creative.
- *Miscellaneous.* These activities include greeting the children, helping them with their coats, helping them use the restroom, interacting with parents and conferencing with parents.
- *Music activity.* This weekly activity encourages the children's interest in music and dance.
- *Conferencing with parents.* This quarterly activity consists of the head teacher (your sister) meeting with each child's parents for half an hour.

REQUIRED

(a) Choose several activities to use for cost pools. Explain your choices.
(b) Choose cost drivers for these pools. Explain your choices.
(c) Identify possible reasons why measurement error might exist in the ABC costs.
(d) How would you estimate the increase in future costs if your sister plans to expand her operations?

Solution to self-study problem 2

(a) First, consider the activity hierarchy. Some costs can be allocated to the organisation (for example, rent, insurance, licences). Greeting and helping children with coats may be considered part of the organisation-sustaining costs, or they may be viewed as a separate activity cost pool. This reasoning is also true for interacting with parents. However, time greeting and interacting with parents varies on a daily basis but is not necessarily dependent on the number of children or number of classes. Therefore, these activities will most likely be considered part of the facility-sustaining costs.

No product-sustaining costs are evident because the organisation has only one product.

In this entity, we can consider each class a batch when the children are all involved in a similar activity. Resting and free play could be combined into a single batch-level cost pool because no supplies are used in these activities and fewer teachers are interacting with the children. Learning, art and music activities could be combined as a second batch-level cost pool because they require similar numbers of teachers and supplies.

Snacks and meals can be considered a unit-level cost pool that varies with number of children. For this cost pool, flexible and committed costs could be tracked separately.

Parent conferences could also be a unit-level cost pool because gathering information about each child and meeting with each child's parents would require about the same amount of time per child.

Notice that the choices of activities are somewhat arbitrary. As an alternative to the preceding set of activities, a separate pool could be established for each activity described in the problem.

(b) The cost driver for resting and play could be measured in time or in days if the same times are used each day. Teacher time might be used as a cost driver for learning activities because most of the teachers are involved in these activities. Number of meals served or number of children could drive the costs of snacks and meals. Number of children would be a likely cost driver for conferencing with parents.

(c) We discuss only two possible types of measurement error in this solution; there are many other possible answers. Measurement error might occur if some of the teachers use unpaid time to prepare activities. These potential costs are not measured. The willingness to spend extra time on preparation varies among teachers. If a new teacher is hired who does not want to spend unpaid time, then labour costs could increase or the quality of the program could decrease. Another type of measurement error occurs if different groups of children require different levels of monitoring for play time and nap time. For groups that require more time, labour costs could be understated if teachers require more preparation time, or the quality of the program could suffer if no more time is spent in preparation.

(d) Because this organisation relies heavily on labour, the best predictor for expansion costs is to determine the desired ratio of children to teachers. Facility-sustaining cost changes also need to be predicted. Meal and snack costs probably contain both flexible and committed components, taking into consideration the food-service worker who is employed. The cost of raw materials, such as art supplies, would need to be separated from the activity cost pool to predict costs for more children.

Questions

4.1 Mannon Company's accountant exclaimed, 'Our cost accounting system allocates overhead based on direct labour hours, but our overhead costs appear to be more related to set-up activities than to the use of direct labour. It seems as though our costing system allocates too much cost to large batches of product and not enough cost to small batches.' Explain what she means.

4.2 Describe the ABC cost hierarchies.

4.3 The results from allocations using ABC are usually different from the results using conventional cost systems. Explain why these differences arise.

4.4 Does increasing the number of cost pools always increase the accuracy of allocations under an ABC system? Explain your answer.

4.5 Is an ABC system appropriate for every industry and every type or organisation? Explain your answer.

4.6 Should ABC be used in service industries? Why?

4.7 Does measurement error increase or decrease when ABC systems are implemented? Explain your answer.

4.8 List several costs and several benefits of implementing an ABC system.

4.9 Suppose that you are part of a student consulting team working for your university. You need to analyse accounting department activities and set up cost pools for these activities. Explain how you would identify the activities and pools.

4.10 Is ABC appropriate for an organisation that sells a wide range of customised products manufactured using flexible manufacturing systems? Why?

4.11 Explain how conventional and ABC cost systems differ.

4.12 Explain the difference between activity-based costing and activity-based management.

4.13 Outline the benefits of time-driven ABC.

4.14 Using examples, distinguish between value-added and non-value added activities.

Exercises

4.15 **Mapping costs to the cost hierarchy** Each of the costs below is incurred by Fairgood & Hernandez, a small CPA firm.

REQUIRED

Identify whether each of the following costs most likely relates to an (i) organisation-sustaining activity, (ii) customer-sustaining activity, (iii) product-sustaining activity, (iv) batch-level activity, or (v) unit-level activity. For each item, explain your choice.

(a) Receptionist salary
(b) Financial forecasting software
(c) Photocopy machine rental
(d) Cleaning service
(e) Audit manager salary
(f) Long-distance telephone charges
(g) Meal costs for entertaining clients
(h) Costs of annual employee golf party
(i) Office supplies such as paperclips and paper
(j) Annual subscription for income tax regulations

4.16 **Identifying costs using the ABC cost hierarchies** MicroBrew is a successful brewery engaged in the development and production of specialty micro brews. It uses an activity-based costing system. During the past year, it has incurred $1 250 000 of product development costs, $850 000 of materials handling costs, $2 500 000 of production line labour costs, $700 000 for production set-up costs, $500 000 in power costs for cooling beer and running equipment and $1 500 000 for manufacturing facility management.

REQUIRED

In an ABC cost hierarchy, calculate the total cost that would be classified as:

(a) facility-sustaining
(b) product-sustaining
(c) batch-level
(d) unit-level.

4.17 **ABC cost hierarchy** In ABC systems, activities are often separated into a hierarchy of six categories.

REQUIRED

In your own words, define and give examples of the following types of activities and costs in an ABC system for a national car rental company such as Hertz or Europcar.

(a) Unit-level activities and costs
(b) Batch-level activities and costs
(c) Product-sustaining activities and costs
(d) Customer-sustaining activities and costs
(e) Facility-sustaining activities and costs
(f) Organisation-sustaining activities and costs

4.18 **Cost pools and cost drivers** Following are lists of potential cost pools and cost drivers.

Cost pool	Cost driver
(a) Machining	(i) Number of employees
(b) Purchasing activities	(ii) Number of parts per unit
(c) Inspection	(iii) Kilograms of laundry processed
(d) Assembly	(iv) Number of invoices

(e) Payroll
(f) A special quick-freezing process for food
(g) Laundry in a hospital

(v) Number of batches
(vi) Number of machine hours
(vii) Number of units

REQUIRED

Match each cost driver to the most appropriate cost pool. Use each cost driver only once. Explain your choice.

4.19 **Conventional versus ABC costing** Calder Products manufactures two component parts: AJ40 and AJ60. AJ40 components are being introduced currently, and AJ60 parts have been in production for several years. For the upcoming period, 1000 units of each product are planned for manufacturing. Assume that the only relevant overhead cost is for engineering change orders (any requested changes in product design or the manufacturing process). AJ40 components are expected to require four change orders, and AJ60 only two. Each AJ40 requires 1 machine hour, and each AJ60 requires 1.5 machine hours. The cost of a change order is $300.

REQUIRED

(a) Estimate the cost of engineering change orders for AJ40 and AJ60 components if Calder uses a conventional costing method and machine hours as the allocation base.
(b) Now suppose that Calder uses an ABC system and allocates the cost of change orders using as cost driver the number of change orders. Estimate the cost for change orders for each unit of AJ40 and AJ60.
(c) Calculate the difference in overhead allocated to each product. This figure represents an amount that one product cross-subsidises the other product. Explain what that means.

4.20 **ABC costing; ABM** Applewood Electronics manufactures two large-screen television models: the Monarch, which has been produced since 2005 and sells for $900; and the Regal, a new model introduced in early 2008 that sells for $1140. Applewood's CEO, Harry Hazelwood, suggested that the company should concentrate its marketing resources on the Regal model and begin to phase out the Monarch model.

Applewood currently uses a conventional costing system. The following cost information has been used as a basis for pricing decisions over the past year.

Per-unit data	Monarch	Regal
Direct materials	$208	$584
Direct labour hours	1.5	3.5
Machine hours	8.0	4.0
Units produced	22 000	4 000

Direct labour cost is $12 per hour and the machine usage cost is $18 per hour. Manufacturing overhead costs were estimated at $4 800 000 and were allocated on the basis of machine hours. Martin Alecks, the new company controller, suggested that an activity-based costing analysis first be run to get a better picture of the true manufacturing cost. The following data were collected:

Activity centre	Cost driver	Traceable costs
Soldering	Number of solder joints	$ 942 000
Shipments	Number of shipments	860 000
Quality control	Number of inspections	1 240 000

Activity centre	Cost driver	Traceable costs
Purchase orders	Number of orders	950 400
Machining	Machine hours	57 600
Machine set-ups	Number of set-ups	750 000
Total traceable costs		$4 800 000

	Number of events		
Activity	Monarch	Regal	Total
Soldering	1 185 000	385 000	1 570 000
Shipments	16 200	3 800	20 000
Quality control	56 200	21 300	77 500
Purchase orders	80 100	109 980	190 080
Machining	176 000	16 000	192 000
Machine set-ups	16 000	14 000	30 000

Selling, general and administrative expenses per unit sold are $265 for Monarch and $244.50 for Regal.

REQUIRED

(a) Calculate the manufacturing cost per unit for Monarch and Regal under:
   (i) a conventional costing system
   (ii) the ABC system.
(b) Explain the differences in manufacturing cost per unit calculated in part (a).
(c) Calculate the operating profit per unit for Monarch and Regal under:
   (i) a conventional costing system
   (ii) the ABC system.
(d) Should Applewood concentrate its marketing efforts on Monarch or on Regal? Explain how the use of ABC affects your recommendation.

4.21 ABC costing; ABM Palmer Company uses an activity-based costing system. It has the following manufacturing activity areas, related drivers used as allocation bases and cost allocation rates:

Activity	Cost driver	Cost allocation rate
Machine set-up	Number of set-ups	$50.00
Materials handling	Number of parts	0.50
Machining	Machine hours	26.00
Assembly	Direct labour hours	22.00
Inspection	Number of finished units	12.00

During the month, 100 units were produced, requiring two set-ups. Each unit consisted of 19 parts, and used 1.5 direct labour hours and 1.25 machine hours. Direct materials cost $100 per finished unit. All other manufacturing costs are classified as conversion costs. ABC costs for research and marketing costs are $140. All other non-manufacturing ABC costs are $320 per unit.

REQUIRED

(a) Calculate the manufacturing cost per unit for the period.
(b) Calculate the total cost (manufacturing and non-manufacturing costs) per unit for the period.

4.22 ABC in job costing; ABM; non-value-added activities Kestral Manufacturing identified the following overhead costs and cost drivers for the current period. Kestral produces customised products that move through several different processes. Materials and intermediate products are moved among several different workstations. Custom features are designed by engineers.

Activity	Cost driver	Estimated cost	Estimated activity level
Machine set-up	Number of set-ups	$ 40 000	400
Materials handling	Number of times materials are moved	160 000	16 000
Product design	Design hours	100 000	2 000
Inspection	Number of inspections	260 000	13 000
Total cost		$560 000	

Information for three of the jobs completed during the period follows.

	Job 42	Job 43	Job 44
Direct materials	$ 10 000	$ 24 000	$16 000
Direct labour	$4 000	$4 000	$8 000
Units completed	200	100	400
Number of set-ups	2	4	8
Number of times materials are moved	60	20	100
Number of inspections	40	20	60
Number of design hours	20	100	20

REQUIRED

(a) If the company uses ABC, how much overhead cost should be assigned to job 42?

(b) If the company uses ABC, calculate the cost per unit for job 43.

(c) Kestral would like to reduce the cost of its overhead activities. Describe non-value-added activities and explain why reducing these specific activities might also reduce cost.

4.23 Design ABC system; calculate per-unit ABC costs; uncertainties Suppose that Elite Daycare provides two different services, full-time childcare for preschoolers, and after-school care for older children. The director would like to estimate an annual cost per child in each of the day-care programs, ignoring any facility-sustaining costs. She is considering expanding the services and wants to know whether full-time or after-school care is more profitable.

The following activities and annual costs apply to the day-care centre. Salaries and wages are $100 000. Full-time children arrive between 8 am and 9 am. Older children arrive about 3 pm. All of the children are gone by 6 pm. Employees estimate that they spend about 20 per cent of their time on meal-related activities, 20 per cent supervising naps or recreation, 10 per cent in greeting or sending children home, and the rest of the time presenting educational experiences to the children. Meals and snacks cost about $20 000. Preschoolers receive two snacks and one meal per day, and the older children receive one snack per day. On average, snacks and meals do not differ in cost. Supplies cost $10 000 for the full-time childcare program and $8000 for the after-school program.

Currently, 30 children participate in full-time care and 10 children in after-school care. Because Elite Daycare maintains a waiting list for openings in its programs, the number of children in each program remains steady.

REQUIRED

(a) Identify a cost object and then choose a set of activities and cost drivers for Elite Daycare's ABC system. Explain your choices.

(b) Using the activities you chose in part (a), estimate the annual cost per child in each program.

(c) Do uncertainties exist about the proportion of salaries and wages that should be allocated to full-time care versus after-school care? Why?

4.24 ABM; customer profitability Suppose that you are asked for suggestions about increasing profitability for a customer that purchases low-margin products and requires costly services.

REQUIRED

(a) In your own words, define activity-based management (ABM).

(b) In your own words, describe high-cost and low-cost customers.

(c) Prepare a brief paragraph suggesting methods to improve profitability for this customer.

Problems

4.25 Setting up an ABC system; uncertainties Following is a list of steps that must be performed in setting up an ABC system:

- Identify and sum the costs into activity-based cost pools.
- Choose a cost driver for each activity.
- For each ABC cost pool, allocate overhead costs to the product or service.
- Identify the relevant cost object.
- Identify the activities necessary for production or service delivery.
- For each ABC cost pool, calculate a cost allocation rate.

REQUIRED

(a) Number the steps from 1 through 6 to indicate the sequence in which they are performed.

(b) For each step, explain whether uncertainties are likely.

(c) Pick the step that you think would require the greatest use of judgment (that is, would include the most uncertainties). Explain your choice.

4.26 ABC cost hierarchy; uncertainties In ABC systems, activities are often separated into a hierarchy of categories.

REQUIRED

(a) In your own words, explain what is meant by a cost hierarchy in ABC.

(b) Explain why uncertainty is possible in classifying costs within the cost hierarchy.

(c) Explain how categorising costs into a hierarchy helps accountants determine how costs behave.

4.27 ABC versus conventional job costing; uncertainties; advantages and disadvantages Vines Ltd produces custom machine parts on a job order basis. The company has two direct product cost categories: direct materials and direct labour. In the past, indirect manufacturing costs were allocated to products using a single indirect cost pool, allocated based on direct labour hours. The indirect cost rate was $115 per direct labour hour.

The managers of Vines Ltd decided to switch from a manual system to software programs that release materials and signal machines when to begin working. Simultaneously, the company adopted an activity-based costing system. The manufacturing process has been organised into six activities, each with its own supervisor who is responsible for controlling costs. The following list indicates the activities, cost drivers and cost allocation rates.

Activity	Cost driver	Cost per unit of cost driver
Materials handling	Number of parts	$0.40
Milling	Machine hours	20.00
Grinding	Number of parts	0.80
Assembly	Hours spent in assembly	5.00
Inspection	Number of units produced	25.00
Shipping	Number of orders shipped	1500.00

The company's information system automatically collects the necessary data for these six activity areas. The data for two recent jobs follow:

	Job order 410	Job order 411
Direct materials cost	$9 700	$59 900
Direct labour cost	$750	$11 250
Number of direct labour hours	25	375
Number of parts	500	2 000
Number of machine hours	150	1 050
Number of job orders shipped	1	1
Number of units	10	200
Number of hours in assembly	2	30

REQUIRED

(a) Suppose the company had not adopted an ABC system. Calculate the manufacturing cost per unit for job orders 410 and 411 under the old, conventional costing system.

(b) Under the new ABC system, calculate the manufacturing cost per unit for job orders 410 and 411.

(c) Compare the costs per unit for job orders 410 and 411 as calculated. Explain why the cost per unit under the conventional costing system is different from cost per unit under the ABC system.

(d) Explain why uncertainties may arise about the choice of cost drivers for each activity.

(e) Identify and explain to Vine Ltd's managers the possible advantages and disadvantages of adopting the ABC system.

4.28 ABC and costing for processes Kim Mills produces three different types of fabric using two departments. In department 1, machines weave the cloth. In department 2, the cloth is dyed a variety of colours. Information for the combined use of resources in both departments for the three types of fabric follows.

Bolts are 20 yards each. All fabric is inspected during production. Robotic equipment inspects the fabric for obvious flaws as the bolts are wound up. Each bolt spends about 5 minutes in the inspection process.

	Denim	Lightweight cotton	Heavyweight cotton	Total
Monthly production in units (bolts of fabric)	1000 bolts	4000 bolts	2000 bolts	7000 bolts
Direct materials costs	$8 000	$24 000	$20 000	$52 000
Direct labour costs	$660	$1 320	$920	$2 900

	Denim	Lightweight cotton	Heavyweight cotton	Total
Direct labour hours	33 hours	66 hours	46 hours	145 hours
Machine hours	500 hours	1333.3 hours	1500 hours	3333.3 hours
Number of set-ups for dye colour changes	10 set-ups	30 set-ups	20 set-ups	60 set-ups
Inspection time	83.3 hours	333.3 hours	166.6 hours	583.2 hours

Combined overhead costs for the two departments follow:

Cost to operate and maintain machines	$40 000
Set-up costs	11 000
Inspection costs	6 996
Total	$ 57 996

Previously, Kim Mills used a costing system that focused on processes. It allocated direct materials to each product separately, but allocated direct labour and conversion costs as if they were incurred equally across the units produced. Under this costing system, the overhead cost for department 1 is $19 332 and for department 2 it is $38 664. Direct labour hours and costs in department 1 are 55 hours at $1100, and the remaining are in department 2. Direct materials for department 1 are $6000 for denim, $16 000 for lightweight and $15 000 for heavyweight. The remaining direct materials are added in department 2. No beginning or ending inventory or abnormal spoilage is recorded for Kim Mills during this period.

REQUIRED

(a) Set up a spreadsheet to perform the following calculations. Use a data input section and cell referencing.
  (i) Use conventional process costing to allocate the direct materials and conversion costs per department to total bolts produced. Develop a cost per bolt for each type of fabric. (*Hint:* You will need to first calculate the equivalent cost per bolt for conversion costs for each department.)
  (ii) Using activity-based costing, develop a cost per bolt.
(b) Compare the process costing and ABC results. Identify the products with overstated costs and those with understated costs. Explain why the costs are misstated under conventional process costing.
(c) How could managers use the ABC information to improve operations?

4.29 ABC costs; uncertainties; ABM; non-value-added activities Water Feature Company manufactures kits for fish ponds. The managers recently set up an ABC system to identify and reduce non-value-added activities. The ABC system includes the following cost pools, cost drivers and estimated costs for manufacturing activities:

Activity	Cost driver	Cost allocation rate
Materials handling	Number of parts	$1.00 per part
Forming	Moulding hours	$40.00 per hour
Moulding set-up	Number of batches	$50.00 per batch
Packing and shipping	Weight	$1.30 per kilogram
Inspection	Finished kits	$10.00 per kit
Direct labour	Finished kits	$20.00 per kit
Direct materials	Finished kits	$100.00 per kit

The company manufactures 10 kits per batch. Each kit requires 20 parts and two hours in moulding, and weighs 30 kilograms.

REQUIRED

(a) Calculate the total ABC manufacturing cost per batch.
(b) Calculate the total ABC cost per finished kit.
(c) Suppose that Water Feature's managers also want to allocate marketing costs and customer service to each product. Total marketing costs for the period were $15 000 and customer service costs were $25 000. Number of batches produced was 1000. Calculate the total ABC cost per unit and cost per kit, including the costs of marketing and customer services.
(d) Are the activities listed likely to be the only possible set of activities for Water Feature Company? Why?
(e) Describe how the managers and accountants of Water Feature Company might use this new ABC system to identify non-value-added activities.

4.30 **Uncertainties; actual versus estimated costs; practical capacity** Data Processors performs credit card services for banks. The company uses an ABC system. The following information applies to the past year:

Activity	Estimated cost	Actual cost	Cost driver
Processing transactions	$2 000 000	$2 200 000	Number of transactions
Issuing monthly statements	1 000 000	1 300 000	Number of statements
Issuing new credit cards	500 000	400 000	Number of new credit cards
Resolving billing disputes	90 000	100 000	Number of disputes
Total	$3 590 000	$4 000 000	

Cost driver	Estimated activity level	Actual activity level
Number of transactions	5 800 000	5 000 000
Number of statements	270 000	250 000
Number of new credit cards	110 000	100 000
Number of disputes	3 500	3 000

REQUIRED

(a) Are the activities listed likely to be the only possible set of activities for the ABC system? Why?
(b) Using estimated values for costs and activity, calculate an ABC allocation rate for each activity.
(c) Explain why actual costs and activity levels are likely to be different from estimated amounts.
(d) Is practical capacity likely to be higher or lower than the estimated activity levels? Explain.

4.31 **Design ABC cost system; usefulness for ABM** Shearwater Council owns and operates an animal shelter that performs three services: housing and finding homes for stray and unwanted animals, providing healthcare and neutering services for the animals, and pet training services. One facility is dedicated to housing animals waiting to be adopted. A second facility houses veterinarian services. A third facility houses the director, her staff and several dog trainers. This facility also has several large meeting rooms that are frequently used for classes given by the animal trainers. The trainers work with all of the animals to ensure that they are relatively easy to manage. They also provide dog obedience classes for adopting families.

Estimated annual costs for the animal shelter and its services are as follows:

Director and staff salaries	$60 000
Animal shelter employees' salaries	100 000
Veterinarians and technicians	150 000
Animal trainers	40 000
Food and supplies	125 000
Building-related costs	200 000

On average, 75 animals per day are housed at the facility, or about 27 375 (75 × 365) animal days in total. The number of animals housed during the year totalled 4500. In addition, the trainers offer about 125 classes during about 30 weeks throughout the year. On average, 10 families attend each class. Last year the veterinarian clinic experienced 5000 animal visits.

One of the director's staff members just graduated from an accounting program and would like to set up an ABC system for the shelter so that the director can better understand the cost for each of the shelter's services. He gathers the following information:

Square metres for each facility:	
Animal shelter	5000 square metres
Director and training	3000 square metres
Veterinarian clinic	2000 square metres
Percentage of trainer time used in classes	50%
Supplies used for veterinarian services	$75 000

REQUIRED

(a) Identify cost pools and assign costs to them, considering the three cost objects of interest.
(b) Determine a cost driver for each cost pool and explain your choice.
(c) Calculate the allocation rates for each cost pool and cost driver. Interpret the allocation rate for each cost pool (i.e. explain what it means).

4.32 Usefulness of ABC With reference to Keener Doors in comprehensive example 3 on page 144, provide answers to each of the following questions with regard to the use of ABC information for activity-based management.

(a) Why did the managers ask for additional analysis of marketing and warranty costs?
(b) When managers use ABC information to improve operations, why is it impossible to be certain that the company will achieve benefits?
(c) What benefits of ABM were illustrated? What costs did the company incur to generate these benefits?
(d) In your own words, describe how various quantitative and qualitative factors were weighed in reaching a decision about the hinge problem.

REFERENCES

1 These procedures might be combined or further separated, so the actual number of procedures in any ABC model may vary.

2 See Ittner, C, Lanen, W & Larcker, D 2002, 'The association between activity-based costing and manufacturing performance', *Journal of Accounting Research*, June.

3 See Shields, M 1995, 'An empirical analysis of firms' implementation experiences with activity-based costing', *Journal of Management Accounting Research 7*, pp. 148–66; and Foster, G & Swenson, D 1997, 'Measuring the success of activity-based cost management and its determinants,' *Journal of Management Accounting Research 7*, pp. 109–41.

4 See Needy, Nachtmann, Roztocki, Warner & Bidanda 2003, 'Implementing activity-based costing systems in small manufacturing firms: a field study', *Engineering Management Journal*, March, pp. 3–10.

5 Adapted from Kaplan, RS & Anderson, SR 2004, 'Time-driven activity-based costing', *Harvard Business Review*, November, pp. 131–8.

6 Kaplan and Anderson (2004) found that large entities require expansive activity dictionaries to reflect the complex details of their operations. A significant issue is that generic tools such as Excel and even some ABC software packages do not provide the capacity required. For example, at one company an automated ABC costing model took three days to calculate costs for 40 departments, 150 activities, 10 000 orders and 45 000 line items.

5

The strategic management of costs and revenues

IN BRIEF

Managers and accountants make decisions about long-term organisational strategies as well as short-term operating plans. These strategies and plans include mutually dependent decisions about how to control costs and price products. Managers increasingly adopt practices such as target costing and just-in-time (JIT) inventory management to help them improve efficiency and achieve profitability goals. Cost measurements help managers make these types of decisions.

After studying this chapter, you should be able to:

1 Explain the value chain activities that provide for continuous cost improvement.

2 Explain the concepts of just-in-time (JIT) manufacturing, total quality management (TQM) and the theory of constraints (TOC).

3 Understand target costing principles and techniques.

4 Explain the concept of kaizen costing and how it compares to target costing.

5 Describe the characteristics of life cycle costing.

6 Describe pricing methods and how cost-based prices and market-based prices are managed.

7 Understand the uses and limitations of cost-based and market-based pricing.

8 Explain any additional factors that might affect prices.

9 Appreciate how pricing models apply to not-for-profit and government entities.

Sony, Microsoft and Nintendo: the game console war

The computer game industry can be highly profitable for companies such as Sony, Microsoft and Nintendo, who are all battling for a share of the $30 billion a year global game market. In Australia three-quarters of all households have a device for playing console games, and $1 billion is spent annually on games. In the last decade Sony, the market leader, has sold more than 200 million PlayStation consoles globally and has held significant power over setting prices for the console game market. When Microsoft entered the market in 2001, it lost more than $2 billion on its Xbox consoles. Over time, Microsoft has reduced the prices of its Xbox consoles to remain competitive with the Sony PlayStation 2 (PS2). In 2002, analysts predicted that the Xbox would sell at a loss for three years or more. In spite of these losses, Microsoft has continued to spend more than $2 billion investing in the market and trying to draw a wider audience for its new-generation Xbox 360 console, which was released in early 2006.

Such losses represent a standard practice in the videogame console industry. Manufacturers rely on income from software sales and licensing to subsidise their hardware costs. Managers plan for losses immediately after launching a new console design but expect to generate profits over the console's life. Historically, a particular console design lasts about five years before being replaced by a new design. Thus, managers expect repeated cycles of loss followed by profit. The generation of profits is made more difficult by pricing issues, as the price companies could charge its customers for the consoles is often limited by competition.

It can be difficult for managers to decide whether to continue investing in a product that is currently unprofitable. Some readers may remember one of the first game consoles from Sega (Dreamcast). Sega's managers decided to drop this product line in 1991 after many years of losses. Alternatively, the decision to enter into the market can be just as difficult for entities to make — particularly given the anticipated early losses on hardware. Furthermore, this dynamic industry requires a significant commitment by companies to continue to make huge investments in research, product development and advertising to launch their new products.

The Nintendo Wii is the latest entrant to compete with PlayStation and Xbox consoles. Nintendo, known for its handheld GameBoy, entered the TV-based console market in December 2006 with a competitively priced product. Nintendo sold 391 901 Wii units (retail price $399.95) in the first four days of launching the product. This launch set a new record for console sales in Australia and accounted for 43 per cent of all game hardware sales in Australia. The Microsoft Xbox 360 was launched in March 2006 (retail price $649.95). It achieved sales of 30 421 units in the first four days, and over the next seven months sold 100 000 units along with more than 400 000 software games.

Prior to the Wii and Xbox 360 sales, Sony was king with its PS2, which topped 78 000 units (and 190 000 games) in its first seven months on sale. Altogether, Sony has sold over 2.1 million PS2 consoles in Australia. It spent $3 million promoting PS2 for Christmas 2006 ahead of the launch of the new generation PlayStation3 in early 2007. The price for its new PS3 is, however, set at a much higher level than the PS2, based on component price estimates (presented in table 5.1 below). Analysts argue that Sony will have to make losses on each PS3 console sold until its production costs can be reduced. Other industry analysts argue that the PS3 launch is too late and the product too expensive to compete with the Xbox.

TABLE 5.1 ■ PlayStation 3 will cost Sony a lot more to make than the Xbox 360 cost Microsoft

Component	PS3 US$	Xbox 360 US$
Processor	$150–$230	$106
Disc drive	$200–$300	$20
Graphics chip	$140	$140
Memory	$65	$65
Hard drive	$40	$40
Other doodads	$130	$130
Total	$725–$905	$501

Source: Information from Kanellos, M 2006, 'PlayStation 3 component prices: why so high?', www.news.com

TABLE 5.2 ■ Comparison of competitor products, prices and launch dates in Australia

Competitor consoles	Sony: PlayStation 3	Microsoft: Xbox 360	Nintendo: Wii
Date of launch	Originally 17 November 2006 March 2007	23 March 2006	7 December 2006
Retail price (Australia)	$829 or $999 (depending on bundle)	$649.95	$399.95

Sources: Information from Australian IT 2006, 'Fast start for Wii', 14 December, australianIT.com.au; Becker, D & Wilcox, J 2001, 'Will Xbox drain Microsoft?', CNET news, news.com.com, 6 March; Hill, J 2006, 'Xbox targets a wider audience', The Age, 23 March, www.theage.com.au; Kanellos, M 2006, 'PlayStation 3 component prices: Why so high?', CNET news, news.com.com; Moses, A 2006, 'PS3 better late than never', Sydney Morning Herald, 4 December, www.smh.com.au; Ramsay, R 2006a, '100 000 Xbox 360s sold in Oz', Gamespot, 25 October, au.gamespot.com/news; Ramsay, R 2006b, 'Wii breaks Aussie sales records', Gamespot, 13 December, au.gamespot.com/news; Tran, KTL 2002, 'Microsoft vows to spend $2 billion to restore Xbox game's momentum,' Wall Street Journal Online, 21 May.

Issues from this scene setter to look for in the chapter include:

- The techniques such as value chain analysis and just-in-time (JIT) manufacturing that might be taken by companies such as Sony, Microsoft and Nintendo to reduce their game console costs.

- How the principles of target costing can assist with the decision to invest or continue to invest in the game console market.

- How decisions in competitive markets such as the game console industry might rely on techniques such as lifecycle costing.

- How cost-based or market-based pricing might affect company profits.

- How other factors, such as the customer demand for product (for example, demand for the new Nintendo Wii), might affect the sales forecasting and produce pricing of Microsoft's and Sony's game consoles.

Value chain activities for continuous cost improvement

The link between costs and prices has become increasingly important with global competition. Managers and accountants must simultaneously manage both. Successful entities continuously improve their cost efficiency, charge competitive prices and focus on long-term organisational strategies. Over the long term, profitable organisations continuously seek ways to become more efficient, reduce costs and improve interactions with suppliers and customers. A variety of methods — such as value chain and supply chain analysis, just-in-time (JIT) production and managing quality costs — are available for analysing and improving the systems used to produce and deliver goods and services. We begin this chapter by learning several specific methods used to reduce costs, and then we explore pricing methods.

Value chain and supply chain analysis

As discussed in chapter 1, analysis of the value chain can lead to improved relationships between the entity and others in the chain, creating an extended organisation that can respond flexibly to dynamic and competitive environments. The analysis of value-added or non-value-added activities within the entity and in relation to suppliers and customers can lead to business decisions that either eliminate non-value-added activities or improve value. Value chain analysis can also lead to improved communication, as individuals in each part of the process begin to share their abilities, needs and requirements with others in the value chain.

Value chain analysis also encourages managers to consider whether they should outsource some of their value-added activities; for example, if outsourcing is less costly than performing the activity internally or if it is not a core competency of the organisation. Microsoft's managers probably decided to outsource Xbox manufacturing because the production of hardware components is not one of Microsoft's core competencies. Ultimately, the decision of whether to outsource an activity depends on both quantitative and qualitative factors.

As organisations work to increase profitability, improving their relationships with suppliers becomes a priority. Improvements can be identified through supply chain analysis. As discussed in chapter 1, the **supply chain** is the flow of resources from the initial suppliers through the delivery of goods and services to customers and clients. The initial suppliers may be inside or outside the entity. Negotiating lower costs with suppliers is a straightforward way to reduce costs. Suppliers may be willing to reduce prices, particularly for organisations willing to sign long-term purchase commitments. Occasionally, entities work with suppliers to help them reduce their costs so that the savings can be passed along.

Accountants analyse supply chains by determining inventory level requirements, starting with customer demand for products or services. Opportunities to reduce cost and improve quality are identified through tracking and analysing use patterns of raw materials, supplies, finished goods and shipped goods. Vendors are included in inventory management decisions as part of this process. With close cooperation, inventory levels can be managed to reduce the quantitative costs of insurance and storage and the qualitative costs of quality changes and timeliness of delivery.

The internet increasingly provides suppliers with access to their customers' inventory level information. Suppliers use this information to time deliveries so that their customers maintain desired inventory levels. Suppliers also use this information to improve their own production planning. Providing internet access to product or service information can be risky, however. Organisations need adequate security measures such as firewalls to protect sensitive information that might have competitive value.

Just-in-time (JIT) production

With **just-in-time (JIT) production and inventory control systems**, materials are purchased and units are produced at the time customers demand them. JIT is considered a *demand-pull system* because products and their parts are manufactured just as they are needed for each step in the manufacturing process. In JIT inventory control systems, organisations work with suppliers so that goods or materials are delivered just as they are needed for production or for sale. Suppliers make frequent deliveries of small lots of goods directly to the production floor or to sales areas in merchandising entities.

In JIT manufacturing systems, the production process is often broken into steps that are performed in *manufacturing cells*. A cell is an area where all of the equipment and labour is grouped for a particular part of the manufacturing process as shown in figure 5.1. Parts and supplies arrive just in time to be used for each specific manufacturing task. When one cell finishes its set of tasks, the product is either complete or moves to the next cell where more work is performed. Production is continuous; as soon as team members finish their production tasks on one unit, another unit is begun. The product moves through all of the cells until the manufacturing process is complete. The manufacturing sequence is organised not only to minimise handling and storage but also to minimise defect rates.

Successful implementation of JIT systems requires that entities:
- find high-quality suppliers
- choose a manageable number of suppliers

- locate suppliers with short transit times for materials being delivered
- develop efficient and reliable materials handling processes
- develop management commitment to the JIT process.

JIT systems reduce costs by maximising the use of space, reducing defect rates and increasing manufacturing flexibility. Each team member is responsible for product inspection so that defects are identified quickly and quality problems can be remedied immediately. When manufacturers produce a number of different product models under a JIT system, change-over to the next model occurs almost immediately. This approach enhances manufacturing flexibility. Experts in operations management believe that the JIT approach may be one of the most significant developments in management innovation in the last century.[1]

One drawback of JIT systems is that production halts when suppliers are unable to deliver supplies as needed. Sometimes unforeseen events interrupt the delivery schedule. For example, in 2001 the Australian company Tristar brought the automotive industry to its knees when its 350 workers went on strike for four days in protest against changes to existing work entitlements. At that time Tristar was the major supplier of power-assisted rack and pinion steering gears, ball joints, lower control arms, steering linkage components and other suspension components to four car manufacturers in Australia — Ford, Holden, Toyota and Mitsubishi. As these manufacturers work to JIT supply systems, they had only a single day's worth of components on hand and were forced to lay off thousands of workers. Toyota was the only company initially unaffected because it was manufacturing left-hand drive vehicles using components from Japan. The estimated cost of this five-day stoppage was reported to be $230 million in lost revenue with $100 million in exports disrupted. In all, 25 per cent of the Australian economy was affected in some way by this dispute.[2]

FIGURE 5.1 ■ Manufacturing process for Sony MiniDisc players

A similar situation followed in the United States shortly after the terrorist attacks of 11 September 2001, and Toyota came within 15 hours of halting production of the Sequoia SUV in its Princeton (Indiana) plant. One of Toyota's suppliers was waiting for steering sensors that were usually imported from Germany by plane, but air travel to the United States was prohibited for several days. To avoid this type of problem in the future, the supplier now ships the part by ocean rather than air, and stores enough steering sensors in the United States to provide a supply for two weeks rather than one. Although Toyota preserved its JIT system, its supplier is now required to maintain higher inventory levels than before.[3]

Total quality management (TQM): managing quality

Some organisations position themselves as high-quality producers and work towards continuous improvement in quality, while other entities seek only to match the quality of their competitors. Part of organisational strategy is the choice of product quality levels. For example, Sony has a reputation for high quality. Its potential customers might demand superior quality products and be willing to pay a premium price for a quality game console, such as the new generation Playstation 3. To improve quality, many organisations adopt a variety of business practices such as total quality management (TQM), Six Sigma,[4] lean manufacturing and kaizen costing.

Total quality management (TQM) is an organisation-wide philosophy and problem-solving methodology that focuses on systematically and continuously improving the quality of products, processes and services. Key elements of TQM include a strong customer focus, extensive employee participation and development, a well-defined and well-executed approach to process management and a strong emphasis in design quality.[5] TQM requires that an entity communicates and maintains the quality standard throughout the entire value chain.[6] As part of TQM, processes are put in place to ensure that defects and waste are eliminated from operations. In this section we focus on the quality efforts that can dramatically reduce spoilage, rework and related opportunity costs.

Activity analysis along the value chain can be used to determine the costs of quality and to help refine quality strategies. Figure 5.2 defines four categories of quality activities — prevention, appraisal, internal and external — and provides examples of activities performed within each category. These actions are taken to minimise the opportunity costs that arise when customers have problems with defective units or low-quality services. When quality failures occur, reputations suffer and market share is lost. These losses are difficult to value, and are therefore often ignored when accountants and managers consider the costs and benefits of maintaining high-quality processes.

FIGURE 5.2 ■ Quality-related activities

Definition	Examples
Prevention activities Activities performed to insure defect-free production	■ Design and process engineering ■ Routine equipment maintenance ■ Inspection of incoming raw materials ■ Quality training and meetings
Appraisal activities Activities performed to identify defective units	■ Inspection of products ■ Inspection of manufacturing process ■ Monitoring of service delivery process ■ Testing

(continued)

FIGURE 5.2 *(continued)*

Definition	Examples
Internal activities Activities undertaken in the production or rework of failed units	■ Producing spoiled units ■ Reworking spoiled units ■ Repairing machine and equipment ■ Reengineering and redesigning
External activities Activities undertaken after the product has been sold to remedy problems caused by defects and failed units	■ Product recalls (replace both good and defective units) ■ Warranty repair work ■ Replacing defective units ■ Liability lawsuits

Sometimes the costs of quality failures are extremely high, such as the loss of reputation and market share that occurs when a great deal of publicity is generated about defective goods or processes. In 1995, the reputation and profitability of South Australian smallgoods factory operator Garibaldi suffered when an *E. coli* bacterial contamination occurred that resulted in the death of a four-year old child.[7] Firestone and Ford lost market share and experienced lower sharemarket prices when news was released about an increased rollover and fatality rate in Ford Explorers that was also associated with Firestone tyres. One of Firestone's plants, in which a strike had occurred and inexperienced workers had been hired to replace the striking employees, has been implicated as a source of defective tyres.[8] The cost of quality failures such as these catastrophes is nearly impossible to value, yet is extremely important to consider in measuring the costs and benefits of proposed quality improvement initiatives.

Managers make decisions about the trade-offs of investing in different categories of quality activities. As organisations increasingly invest in prevention activities, competitors are forced to maintain equally high levels of quality. In comprehensive example 1, value chain activity analysis and activity management practices are used to reduce cost and improve quality.

Comprehensive example 1

Activity analysis and the cost of quality

Swiss Watch is a watch manufacturer in Switzerland with a reputation for producing high-quality watches. Lately, however, a competitor has advertised both quality improvements and price reductions in its line of watches. Pierre Borgeaud, the head of cost accounting at Swiss Watch, conducted a study to determine whether costs could be reduced. His initial focus was on activities related to quality. Although the managers want to maintain high quality, they also want to reduce costs and therefore prices. The study categorised quality costs into four activities: prevention, appraisal, internal and external.

Estimating the costs of quality

Using information gathered from the general ledger, last year's quality activity costs were estimated as shown overleaf (amounts in Swiss Francs).

Prevention costs (inspecting materials from suppliers)	SFr 10 000
Appraisal costs (inspection)	20 000
Internal costs (spoiled units)	5 000
External costs (warranty)	8 000
Total costs of quality	SFr 43 000

When Pierre reviewed these costs, he believed that they were too low. He decided to seek more information than provided by the general ledger accounts. He spoke with employees both individually and in their work teams and found that informal inspections occurred frequently. He asked employees to estimate time spent on quality-related activities. He learned that when defect rates begin to increase, employees respond by spending more time on quality-related activities. He estimated that it cost an additional SFr 50 000 last year in prevention costs for the informal inspections that occurred when defect rates increased. In addition, employees would spend time analysing and correcting the process to improve quality. He estimated this cost to be about SFr 2000 and categorised the cost as prevention-related. He also discovered additional internal costs of SFr 6000 incurred for rework that had not been included in the original estimates. Finally, he discovered an additional SFr 7000 in external service costs for handling returns. He summarised his revised estimate of the costs of quality as follows:

	First estimate	Additional costs	Total costs
Prevention costs	SFr 10 000	SFr 50 000 + SFr 2 000	SFr 62 000
Appraisal costs	20 000		20 000
Internal costs	5 000	6 000	11 000
External costs	8 000	7 000	15 000
Total costs of quality	SFr 43 000	SFr 65 000	SFr 108 000

Using quality cost information to better manage operations

Pierre reported his revised cost estimate to managers, who shared the information with a team of production employees. The team members were surprised at the high cost, and they discussed ways to reduce it. The team believed that the entity could reduce quality costs by identifying and removing defective units earlier in the production process. Therefore, they recommended tracking the number of defective units discovered by employees on the line versus those units found by the inspectors.

Production employees also recommend analysing the types of defects discovered by inspectors to help the employees identify and correct potential problems earlier in the production process. The team believed that some of the inspectors could be assigned to other activities, decreasing the overall costs of quality. In addition, the team recommended tracking the types of warranty problems that occur to identify changes in the design or manufacturing process that would minimise the cost of warranty work and simultaneously improve customer satisfaction.

Theory of constraints

Value chain analysis, supply chain analysis and just-in-time systems provide benefits beyond reducing non-value-added activities and costs such as inventory storage and insurance. As described above, these methods can lead to further cost reductions by focusing management attention on minimising rework, scrap and waste. In addition, managers often identify opportunities to reduce production cycle time. Sometimes the use of one method leads to another method. For example, value chain analysis might encourage accountants to analyse their supply chain and adopt JIT to reduce non-value-added activities. Value chain analysis might help accountants identify bottlenecks or other process constraints.

According to the **theory of constraints (TOC)**, an entity is viewed as a system with the main goal of making more money now as well as in the future. The system comprises a set of elements, or chain of linkages with interdependent relationships. TOC concentrates on the weakest link in the chain (the constraint) that limits the system from achieving higher performance. According to Goldratt (1990) every business system, such as a profit-making entity, must have at least one constraint.[9] The source of constraint can be diverse. The constraint might be on the *supply side*, where insufficient capacity or capabilities exist. This might be caused by a physical manufacturing or service-related constraint relating to such things as time or minutes available at the constraining factor. A supply side constraint may also be caused by a technical, policy or financial limitation. In service entities the constraining factor might be related to intangible assets such as the necessary knowledge and skills held by individuals required for the successful completion of various projects. The source of constraint might also exist on the *demand side*, where there might be insufficient demand caused by pricing, customer budgets or competition that leads to idle capacity.

Goldratt proposed a five-step focusing process for managing constraints to achieve higher performance and continuous system improvement. The five steps are:

1. *Identify* the constraint(s).
2. Decide how to *exploit* the system constraint(s). That is, how to make the best possible use of the constraint given the existing limitations.
3. *Subordinate* everything else to the constraint. That is, avoid over-utilisation of non-constraint resources and rigorously focus on what the constraint needs.
4. *Elevate* the system constraint(s). That is, offload some demand or expand capability. Take steps to minimise idle time at the constraint and consider issues such as inventory levels (JIT versus safety stock) or quality costs.
5. If in the previous steps a constraint has been broken, *go back* to step 1, but do not allow inertia to cause a system constraint.

This five-step process should continuously increase *throughput* while concurrently decreasing *inventory* and *operating expenses*.

Throughput accounting is a modified form of variable costing that measures the impact of bottlenecks and constraints on an organisation's goal achievement. It was developed in the 1980s as part of the theory of constraints.[10] Corbett argues that by focusing on throughput, inventory or investment, and operating expenses, the goals of an entity can be measured.[11] Throughput accounting is explored further in chapter 15 and in the chapter 15 article at the end of this book.

Benefits and limitations of the theory of constraints

Theory of constraints analysis can be viewed as a useful management tool to improve the system as a whole. TOC enable managers to optimise constraints while balancing the flow of production with demand. Any product mix changes generated by TOC should show immediate cash flow effects. Accountants and managers in companies using the theory of constraints method believe that throughput costing helps them make better short-term decisions. This is because virtually all costs (other than direct materials) tend to be relatively fixed in the short term.

While useful for short-term decisions, theory of constraints analysis could focus a manager's attention too much on the short-term results to the detriment of the long-term strategic goals. As a result of short-term decision making, labour and overhead costs might be unnecessarily reduced because these costs are considered to be operating costs instead of product costs. TOC will highlight these costs without indicating whether they are appropriate for the level of operations. Likewise, if costs are too high, TOC will not show how to bring them under control.

When applying theory of constraints analysis, managers should be aware of the mutually dependent relationship between their short-term operating decisions and their longer-term strategic objectives. Furthermore, other cost management literature has advocated the use of TOC with activity-based cost management (ABCM) to provide better longer-term measures of success within each area of the organisation.[12]

As we can see from this section, managers can potentially use a wide range of tools to analyse production and delivery systems, with the goal of improving cost and quality. Accountants help managers by bringing these tools to their attention and providing the analysis.

Building desired profit into decisions

Accountants use estimates of revenues and costs to provide information for a range of operating decisions. In the short term, the general rule is to sell goods or services so long as estimated revenues exceed estimated variable costs (that is, so long as a profit is expected). However, in the long term, organisations need to earn a reasonable return on investment. We will now discuss the following techniques used to plan for long-term profitability:

- target costing
- kaizen costing
- life cycle costing.

Although these methods alone do not result in increased profitability, they help accountants become more deliberate about profit planning. When costs appear to be too high, these methods also encourage accountants and managers to identify and implement cost management techniques.

Target costing

When launching a new product, managers traditionally determine the cost of the product and then use the cost to help them set a price that would achieve a desired profit margin. Managers use this information to evaluate the feasibility of the new product. An alternative decision-making approach is target costing, which uses market-based prices to determine whether products and services can be delivered at costs low enough for an acceptable profit. Competitors' products are *reverse engineered* (taken apart and put back together again) to better understand the manufacturing process and the product design. In turn, the product and manufacturing process are redesigned so that the product meets a pre-specified target cost. Organisations can then sell products at competitive prices and still earn profits.

In the late 1970s and early 1980s Komatsu, a heavy equipment company, used target costing to develop products similar in quality and functionality to those of Caterpillar. Komatsu was able to set its prices lower than Caterpillar. Prior to the mid 1980s, Caterpillar was financially stable. But in the late 1980s, the company struggled against a weak global economy and the competition from Komatsu, losing $1 billion over a three-year period. Mark Thompson, a business analysis manager with Caterpillar's wheel-loader and excavator division, recalled, 'We had to do something drastic. The viability of the company depended on it.'[13] Caterpillar's managers turned to target costing, the same method that enabled Komatsu to become so competitive. Caterpillar accountants and analysts studied publicly available financial statements to identify Komatsu's costs. They learned that Caterpillar's production costs were 30 per cent higher than Komatsu's.

Next, Caterpillar's engineers purchased, tore apart, and reverse engineered Komatsu's products to determine the processes and designs Komatsu used in manufacturing. Caterpillar managers then invested $1.8 billion in plant modernisation. They eliminated non-value-added processes, examined their procedures to purchase raw materials and supplies, moved to a just-in-time inventory system and reduced the number of parts used in Caterpillar products. Using target costing techniques, Caterpillar produced record-setting profits. Although the company's profits declined during a downturn in the heavy equipment industry during 2001 and 2002, profits rebounded with a 38 per cent increase during 2003.[14] Analysts recommended the company as an investment as of February 2004.[15]

Target costing process

As highlighted in the Caterpillar example, target costing helps organisations improve production processes and profits. **Target costing** is the process of researching consumer markets to estimate an appropriate market price, then subtracting the desired return to determine a maximum allowable cost. This target cost is the maximum cost at which the entity can produce a good or service to generate the desired profit margin. The entity then determines whether the good or service can be designed and produced to meet the target cost. This step involves managing both product design and manufacturing phases. If expected costs exceed the target, managers will choose not to provide a good or service. To date, target costing has been used primarily for products that have already been manufactured by other organisations, but it is increasingly being used for new goods and services.

The key value of target costing is that it focuses managers' attention on the design phase where most cost savings potentially occur because 70 per cent to 80 per cent of product costs are typically committed at this point. Costs that occur both when the manufacturing process is set up and during manufacturing are locked in during the design phase. For example, new equipment is chosen and direct materials are specified that will be used in production. Although the actual costs occur over a product's life cycle, the decisions made in the planning phase have the greatest influence over those costs. Under target costing, the decision to produce a good or service depends on expected costs developed in the design phase. The steps in a target costing design cycle are summarised in figure 5.3. The description of each step follows.

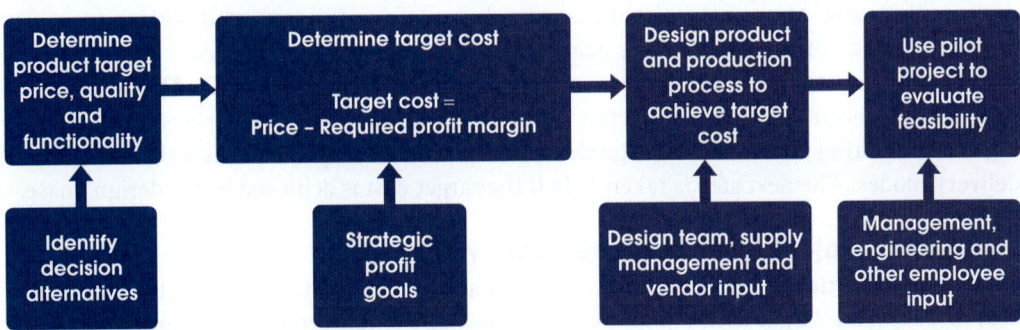

FIGURE 5.3 ■ Steps in a target costing design cycle

Determine the product target price, quality and functionality

Accountants and managers use studies such as consumer surveys, focus groups and market research of competitors' prices to determine a competitive price for a specific product. Researchers collect information about consumer preferences, including trade-offs customers are willing to make between price, quality and functionality for a product or service. A competitive price *for a given level of product quality and functionality* can then be estimated. In industries where customers are willing to pay higher prices for higher quality or more functionality, managers strategically differentiate their products and establish market positions. The same is true when customers are willing to give up a certain amount of quality or functionality to obtain lower prices.

The automobile industry provides a good example of product differentiation. Some manufacturers emphasise a low price for lower levels of quality and functionality. Other manufacturers emphasise quality and are able to charge higher prices. Some manufacturers emphasise functionality such as all-wheel-drive capability or trucks with four-door cabs. Increases in functionality are usually accompanied by increases in product prices. When cars are being designed, the marketing department analyses consumer preferences to determine the optimal levels of quality and functionality for a particular price.

Customers in some industries are unwilling to pay for higher quality or functionality. In Caterpillar's industry (heavy machinery), the products are used in construction. Purchasing decisions tend to revolve around price and only one quality factor: reliability. Extra functions such as air-conditioned cabs are unlikely to increase a product's marketability.

Determine the target cost

After a competitive price is determined for specific levels of product quality and functionality, the required profit margin is subtracted from the price to arrive at the target cost:

$$\text{Target cost} = \text{Price} - \text{Required profit margin}$$

The required profit margin is usually a function of the organisation's long-term strategic goals. Managers who use this method assume that producers cannot set the price but instead must take the market's price. Accordingly, the production decision focuses on the entity's ability to produce goods or services at the specified target cost.

Design the product and production process to achieve the target cost

A product design team is assembled from personnel in product engineering, marketing and accounting. This team designs the product at the specified levels of quality and functionality and then develops the manufacturing process. During the design phase, the team focuses on reducing the complexity of the product and manufacturing process to meet the target cost. If the team is unable to meet the target cost, the design process is reiterated with negotiations on possible trade-offs between price, quality and functionality. If the product still cannot be manufactured at the target cost after several iterations, production plans are dropped.

A similar process takes place in service industries. Teams — including professional, marketing and accounting personnel — design the type of service to be provided as well as the service delivery modes. The next step is taken only if the target cost is achieved in the design phase.

Use a pilot project to evaluate feasibility

Once the production process has been designed so that the cost to manufacture a product is at or below the target cost, a pilot project replicates a small version of the production line to determine the feasibility of the product and process design and cost. If the pilot project is successful, full production begins. If it is unsuccessful, the team returns to the design phase. Similar pilot projects are used in service entities to evaluate feasibility.

Factors that affect the success of target costing

Target costing performs best in the following situations:

- Product development and design phases are long and complex.
- The production process is complex.
- The market is willing to pay for differences in quality or function.
- The manufacturer can push some cost reductions onto suppliers and subcontractors.
- The manufacturer can influence the design of subparts.

Target costing is inappropriate in industries with simple production processes, such as food products and beverages, which are typically unable to differentiate their products based on quality and functionality. In the food industry, advertising campaigns and brand name recognition influence price the most.

Comprehensive example 2 describes the target costing process for a bike manufacturer, while the chapter 5 article at the end of this book provides examples of applications of target costing in some leading companies.

Comprehensive example 2

Target costing

Mount Dandenong Bikes (MDB) is a start-up company manufacturing high-quality mountain bikes that compete with products from companies such as Trek and Bianchi. One of MDB's employees developed a new braking system that allows bikers to descend steep slopes using a consistent braking pattern that pumps both front and back brakes at regular preset intervals, depending on the brake setting that the biker chooses. The marketing department surveyed current customers and found they would be willing to pay more for this option. Because MDB's brand name is not yet well established, prices for its bikes need to be kept below those of its major competitors. MDB's owner, Michelle Miles, wants the company to launch a line of bikes with the new braking system. Her accountant recommends that the company use target costing to develop the new product to ensure that the design is feasible.

Determine product target price, quality and functionality

After conducting customer surveys and a number of focus groups, MDB's marketing staff identify five features that are highly important to prospective customers: the weight of the bike, the bike's ability to withstand hard riding in difficult terrains for long periods of time, appearance, ease of handling, and riding comfort over rough terrain. Depending on the brand name of the bike and its components, the market price for competing models with these features ranges between $800 and $1200. The model with the highest market share in that price range is priced at $949. From the survey and focus group information gathered, Michelle believes that a bike with the new braking system and the same levels of quality and functionality as the competitors' models should be priced at $950 to achieve a 25 per cent market share. She decides to call the new model the Mountain Braker.

Determine target cost

Michelle sets a minimum profit margin of 10 per cent on new products. Given this information, Michelle's accountant sets the new product's target cost as follows:

Price	$950
Less profit margin	95
Target cost	$855

Design product and production process to achieve target cost

Michelle establishes a team to handle the product and manufacturing process design. The team consists of one person from each of the following areas: marketing, engineering, purchasing, accounting and administration.

First, the team identifies an initial cost for the Mountain Braker. The engineer alters MDB's basic bike design to incorporate the new braking system. The cost estimate of $905 is higher than the target cost of $855, so the team considers ways to reduce the cost. The team assembles information about current costs and necessary cost reductions, assuming sales of 50 000 bikes. They identify areas with the most potential for cost reduction, and then establish the following estimates for these reductions.

Cost category	Current cost per bike	Target cost	Cost reduction needed
New brake development	$ 50	$ 50	$ 0
Manufacturing	710	680	30
Total manufacturing costs	760	730	30
Selling and distribution	55	50	5
Warranty and support	35	30	5
Administration	55	45	10
Total cost	$ 905	$ 855	$ 50

Product design changes

The team decides to use value chain analysis to seek opportunities for cost reduction. They focus on the product design phase of the value chain. The engineer analyses the current design, searching for steps in the manufacturing process and components that can be eliminated. The accountant provides cost information for prospective changes. The marketing person provides information about customer reactions to proposed changes.

- *Reflectors.* The team suggests elimination of the reflectors mounted on the spokes. Because the Mountain Braker would be used primarily in very rough terrain, any reflectors are likely to break. Furthermore, the relatively few riders who use the bike on roads do not rely on reflectors but use battery-operated headlights and taillights instead. The accountant estimates that $15 per bike can be saved by eliminating both the reflectors and the process of mounting them. After sending emails to prospective customers, the marketing team member confirms that eliminating reflectors will not affect consumer demand for the product or expected price.
- *Bike seats.* When the engineer suggests a cheaper bike seat that is easier to mount, the marketing representative organises a focus group with prospective customers

to determine the effect on sales. Feedback from the focus group indicates that the price would have to be reduced if a lower-quality seat is installed, so this idea is dropped.

Supplier negotiations

The team next focuses on the direct materials purchasing function in their value chain analysis. They investigate cost reductions from current suppliers and search for similar quality components at reduced prices from new suppliers. Purchasing personnel meet with all of the components suppliers to negotiate cost reductions.

- *Handlebars.* The handlebars supplier suggests a new product with comparable quality to the current handlebars but with a cost reduction of $10 per bike. Marketing determines that the new handlebars would not affect customers' perceptions of quality.
- *Tyres.* Purchasing works with the company that supplies tyres. Buying tyres in larger lots can save the supplier delivery and storage costs, and MDB currently has storage space available. The new purchase agreement reduces costs by $5 per bike.
- *Tyre tubes.* Purchasing finds a new tyre tube vendor that can supply tubes at a cost reduction of $5 per bike.

Combined, the changes recommended by the team are expected to reduce manufacturing costs by $35 ($15 + $10 + $5 + $5), rather than the needed $30. Thus, the target cost for manufacturing costs is met. The team now focuses on the remaining costs that need to be reduced.

Non-manufacturing costs

The target costing team meets with the marketing department and the director of finance to identify reductions in selling and distribution, warranty and support, and administration costs.

- *Selling and distribution.* Marketing is concerned that reducing commissions or advertising will affect total sales and potential market share gains for MDB. Marketing wants no cost reduction on advertising or commissions for this new product. The successful introduction of the new braking system relies in part on individual sales representatives highlighting the feature and in part on an advertisement campaign featuring the braking system. However, the shipping company has agreed to a reduction in shipping costs of $5 per bike because MDB's volumes have been increasing rapidly — it is cheaper for the shipping company to ship large lots.
- *Warranty and support.* MDB's managers are concerned that reducing customer warranty and support costs — both areas in which MDB currently has a strong reputation — would be risky with a new product. If the entity reduces these costs and then is unable to provide its current level of service, a loss of reputation could result. Fortunately manufacturing costs were reduced by $5 more than originally planned. Therefore, the team decides not to reduce warranty and support costs at this time.
- *Administration.* Some administrative functions, such as payroll, have recently been outsourced. It appears that the administrative cost reduction of $10 per bike will be easily met.

Total planned cost reduction

The following summary shows the cost reduction estimates achieved by the design team.

Cost category	Reduction needed (revised)	Reduction achieved
New brake development	$ 0	$ 0
Manufacturing:	35	
Reflectors		15
Handlebars		10
Tyres		5
Tubes		5
Selling and distribution (reduced shipping charges)	5	5
Warranty and support (no reduction necessary)	0	0
Administration (outsourcing services)	10	10
Total	$50	$50

Pilot project to evaluate feasibility

Once the team reconfigures the bike, a pilot manufacturing line is set up and 100 bikes are produced. The first 50 bikes cost $780 to produce but, as the manufacturing line employees learned how to install the new braking system more quickly, the last 50 bikes cost $730 as projected.

The managers decide to begin full production of the new product. This decision turns out well for the entity; the bike sells faster and in larger numbers than anticipated.

Kaizen costing

Kaizen costing is continuous improvement in product cost, quality and functionality. It is similar to target costing in that cost targets (goals) are set based on price predictions. However, kaizen costing occurs after the product has been designed and the first production cycle is complete. Market prices tend to decrease over many products' life cycles. Under kaizen costing, accountants forecast declining prices and establish cost-reduction goals to maintain a desired level of profit margin. Therefore, the objectives of kaizen costing include not only continuous improvement but also continuous cost reduction.

Because kaizen costing relies on sales forecasts, the kaizen plan is similar to a budget, except that kaizen costing provides for explicit cost reductions. Figure 5.4 summarises the kaizen planning process for revenues and costs.

In manufacturing entities, estimated variable costs are the sum of estimates for direct material and direct labour costs, plus variable manufacturing overhead. Accountants and managers develop plans to estimate reductions for these variable costs. Estimated reductions in fixed costs are developed from human resource plans for fixed labour and service department personnel, combined with facility investment plans and the fixed expense plans (design, maintenance, advertising, sales promotions, and general and administrative expenses). These estimated costs are based on the prior period's actual costs, adjusted for any anticipated price changes.

In service entities, the estimated variable costs are developed from projections of supplies and direct labour that varies with the amount of services provided, variable overhead and any variable merchandising costs in retail industries. The estimated fixed costs are developed in the same manner used for manufacturing organisations.

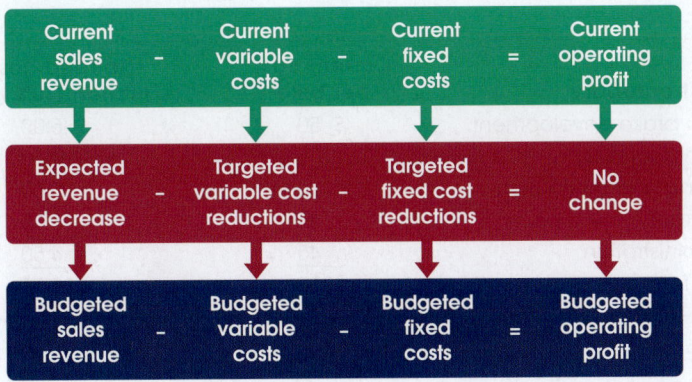

Current sales revenue	–	Current variable costs	–	Current fixed costs	=	Current operating profit
Expected revenue decrease	–	Targeted variable cost reductions	–	Targeted fixed cost reductions	=	No change
Budgeted sales revenue	–	Budgeted variable costs	–	Budgeted fixed costs	=	Budgeted operating profit

FIGURE 5.4 ■ Kaizen planning process for revenues and costs

After the targeted cost reduction goals are set, each department is assigned responsibility for specific cost reduction amounts. These goals are met in several ways. One option is to use value chain analysis to redesign the production or service process to increase overall productivity and efficiency. Meetings may be held with manufacturing or service personnel to brainstorm ideas for cost reduction. To encourage idea generation, some entities even share any initial gains in cost reduction with the employees who suggest the cost-reducing changes. Another option is to use supply chain analysis, working with suppliers and issuing target cost reductions for intermediate manufacturing parts or service supplies. Some companies work with suppliers to develop new product and process designs needed to achieve cost reductions.

Comprehensive example 3

Kaizen costing

Mount Dandenong Bikes has now been producing Mountain Brakers for two years, and sales are beginning to drop because competitors are producing similar braking systems. MDB's marketing manager believes that if the company wants sales and market share to increase, prices will have to decrease. The accountant recommends that the company use kaizen costing to reduce the price and cost of the Mountain Braker.

Cost reductions

The marketing manager estimates that the bike's price should be reduced by 10 per cent to be competitive with other manufacturers. Therefore, costs also need to be reduced by 10 per cent to maintain the same percentage margin, although the dollar value of the margin will decrease. The bike's current price is $950 with a cost of $855. The new price will be $855, and the corresponding cost reduction needed is $85.50. The current margin is $95, and the new margin will be $85.50. The summary overleaf assumes that reductions will be made proportionately across all cost categories.

Cost category	Current cost per bike	Needed cost reduction (10% goal)
New brake development	$ 50	$ 5.00
Manufacturing	675	67.50
Selling and distribution	50	5.00
Warranty and support	35	3.50
Administration	45	4.50
Total	$855	$85.50

The same team that developed the Mountain Braker at target cost in the design phase meets again to suggest further cost reduction plans. After careful analysis, they find no way to reduce costs for the new braking system at this time. Therefore, the $5 needed cost reduction for the brakes will have to come from another process or component.

Process design changes

Using value chain analysis, the team reviews both the manufacturing processes and the bike design, searching for non-value-added activities or components that can be eliminated. A new gear system has been developed by one of the vendors that eliminates two steps in the manufacturing process. As a result, the engineer estimates that one labourer could be moved to another bike production line to replace a retiring worker, reducing total labour costs. This reduction amounts to $10 per bike.

Supply chain analysis

The MDB team meets with suppliers to determine whether cost reductions or product improvements are possible from the components used in manufacturing. The wheel and spoke vendor has improved the quality of its product and dropped the price, saving $13 per bike. A new bike frame that is just as solid as the current frame has been developed from an innovative new alloy and will save MDB $35.

At the end of the last quarter, the supplier of tubes and tires asked for a small price increase. The purchasing department surveys vendor websites for tubes and tyres. After contacting several different vendors, a price reduction is negotiated with a new supplier of tyres. An additional vendor is added to supply tubes at a reduced price. These two cost savings amount to $10 per bike.

Overall, the team is able to achieve total cost reduction for manufacturing of $68 ($10 + $13 + $35 + $10). This amount is $0.50 more than is needed from manufacturing, but leaves a $4.50 required reduction because the cost of brakes could not be reduced.

Non-manufacturing costs

The team now turns its attention to achieving the remaining cost reductions. The marketing representative points out that several top mountain bike race competitors currently using the new bike generate sales efficiently. Relying on their efforts costs less than the current advertising campaign. Therefore, the team decides to reduce advertising costs by $5 per bike, which meets the selling and distribution cost target. Warranty and support costs are significantly lower than anticipated, primarily because the new braking system is so reliable. A reduction of $8 is easily attainable at this time. This amount is $4.50 ahead of target, making up for the lack of cost reduction from the brakes.

The team member from administration mentions that a new information system was installed last quarter. The department dropped some non-value-added activities, such as manual entry of production data. One staff member resigned and will not be replaced. The savings will be at least the needed $4.50 per bike.

The overall cost reduction targets and estimates are as follows:

Cost category	Kaizen cost reduction	Actual cost reduction
New brake development	$ 5.00	$ 0.00
Manufacturing:	67.50	10.00
Process change	5.00	13.00
Wheel and spoke system	3.50	35.00
Frame		10.00
Tyres and tubes		5.00
Selling and distribution		8.00
Warranty and support		
Administration (outsourcing services)	4.50	4.50
Total	$85.50	$85.50

Continuous monitoring of costs

The team reports back to the accounting department that the overall cost reduction targets can be met. Once the changes have been made, the marketing department decides to cut costs even further. However, a problem arises with the braking system. To maintain the current quality, MDB will have to pay $4 more for components because several vendors raised their prices. With these two changes, MDB is still below the kaizen cost reduction target.

Using target and kaizen costing over time

Target and kaizen costing are used together in entities facing declining prices across time. Figure 5.5 provides a generic timeline showing the use of these two methods across a product's life cycle. Some organisations may lower margins before dropping the product, but at some point the product is discontinued because cost is equal to price and no further cost reductions are possible.

Figure 5.6 (overleaf) compares target costing and kaizen costing, listing their similarities and differences, and common advantages and disadvantages.

Time			
Before production	First production period	Continuous production	Drop product
Target costing	Cost is maintained	Kaizen costing	
Product and manufacturing process design	Manufacturing at target cost	Periodic cost-reduction goals set and met	No further cost reductions available

FIGURE 5.5 ■ Target and kaizen costing over time for a product

Similarities
■ Rely on goal setting to achieve cost reduction
■ Focus on product design and the manufacturing process to find ways to reduce costs.
■ Encourage organisations to work with suppliers to reduce costs
■ Use functional teams to determine where costs can be cut
■ Encourage employees to take an active part in the cost-cutting decision-making process
■ Take advantage of the trade-offs between price, functionality and quality
■ Focus on continuous improvements in products and processes

Differences
■ Target costing occurs at beginning of the product life cycle and kaizen after that
■ Target costing sets a single goal for cost; kaizen sets cost-reduction goals

Common advantage
■ Use of goal setting encourages better performance

Common disadvantages
■ Stress of cost reduction environment can impair employee wellbeing
■ Encourages organisations to forgo some products having long-term profit potential

FIGURE 5.6 ■ Target costing compared to kaizen costing

Life cycle costing

Life cycle costing is a decision-making method that considers changes in price and costs over the entire life cycle of a good or service, from the time the product is introduced through a number of years.

Some products have high upfront costs, such as research and development; other products may incur large costs when the product is abandoned, such as environmental cleanup costs. Sometimes products cannot achieve high revenues at the beginning of their life, but generate increasing revenues over the product's life cycle. Under target costing, such products might be rejected even though they have good long-term potential. Under life cycle costing, managers consider the profitability of the product over a number of years. If forecasts predict that sales over time will cover all product costs and eventually add to profits, a life cycle budget is developed for both manufacturing and environmental costs so that decision makers can evaluate their decision and identify possible areas for cost reductions across time.

Life cycle costing is used when the initial product is produced and sold at a loss, but accountants and managers anticipate that a combination of continued sales volumes and cost reductions over time will lead to profits in the long term. It is also used to identify products that may not be profitable when the costs of decommissioning the operation are included as part of total product costs, for example, environmental cleanup costs when mines are shut down. In addition, life cycle costing is used to focus managers' attention on the high development or decommissioning costs during the product and manufacturing design phase to encourage them to manage all of these costs as they develop new products.

The opening scene setter about the Microsoft Xbox is an example of a product decision that considered the product's life cycle. Microsoft's managers decided to sell Xbox at a loss, but they expected continuing sales of games to eventually create profits for the entire product line. In addition, Microsoft probably anticipates manufacturing cost reductions for the Xbox over time. Another example of life cycle costing is the manufacture of printers and ink cartridges.

Printers are often sold at a loss, but the revenue streams from ink cartridges more than make up for these initial losses.

Price management: pricing methods

Determining appropriate prices for an organisation's products or services is an important activity because pricing decisions have both short- and long-term consequences. The Microsoft Xbox case indicates that, even in markets with few competitors, prices are often based on competitor's prices, not just production costs.

Cost-based pricing

Cost-based prices are determined by adding a mark-up to some calculation of the product's cost. To apply this method, both a cost base and a mark-up rate are selected. The cost base can be calculated in several ways. Some organisations use variable cost as the base, whereas others use an average cost that includes both variable and fixed costs. Organisations frequently rely on mark-ups they have used for many years. Such mark-ups often originate from general industry practice and may be found in trade journals. For example, clothing retailers typically price using a 100 per cent mark-up on their variable costs. If a retailer pays $10 per blouse to the wholesaler, the variable cost per blouse is $10, and the blouse would be priced at $20. Mark-up percentages are also chosen so that the organisation earns a target rate of return on investment. Given differences in calculation methods and cost structures, cost-based prices vary a great deal across organisations.

Suppose Bombardier Jets is a small company that customises Lear jets for wealthy clients. At present, the company's managers are negotiating with three potential customers for next year's sales. The company's accountants summarised cost information for each plane as follows:

| (In thousands) | Potential customer | | | Total |
	Rock star	CEO	Sports figure	
Avoidable costs				
Basic jet plane	$ 800	$ 800	$ 800	$ 2400
Production	200	1200	600	2000
Selling costs	100	200	100	400
Total avoidable costs	$ 1100	$ 2200	$ 1500	$ 4800
Unavoidable costs				
Production				$ 3000
Administration				600
Total unavoidable costs				$ 3600

The unavoidable costs are the overhead costs to customise the jets, such as facility costs (rent or depreciation etc.) and equipment-related costs. These costs are primarily fixed.

The company has a policy of calculating price by applying a 50 per cent mark-up on cost. Two potential cost-based pricing schemes follow.

Alternative A. Under this alternative, unavoidable costs are allocated to the three contracts equally ($3600 ÷ 3 jets = $1200 per jet). Then a mark-up of 50 per cent is added to total costs as shown overleaf.

(In thousands)	Potential customer			
	Rock star	CEO	Sports figure	Total
Total avoidable costs	$1 100	$2 200	$1 500	$ 4 800
Allocated unavoidable costs	1 200	1 200	1 200	3 600
Total costs	$2 300	$3 400	$2 700	$ 8 400
Price (150% of total cost)	$3 450	$5 100	$4 050	$12 600

Alternative B. Under this alternative, unavoidable costs are allocated to each contract based on its proportion of avoidable costs. For example, the rock star's allocated cost is ($1100 ÷ $4800) × $3600 = $825. A mark-up of 50 per cent is then added to total costs to arrive at the price as follows:

(In thousands)	Potential customer			
	Rock star	CEO	Sports figure	Total
Total avoidable costs	$1 100	$2 200	$1 500	$ 4 800
Allocated unavoidable costs	825	1 650	1 125	3 600
Total costs	$1 925	$3 850	$2 625	$ 8 400
Price (150% of total cost)	$2 887	$5 775	$3 938	$12 600

Which alternative would you recommend? Would you want any additional information before making this decision? As illustrated by these two price alternatives, determining product cost is not straightforward. Decision makers always face uncertainty in determining an appropriate cost base. The price differences under alternatives A and B are caused by arbitrary allocations for overhead costs that cannot be attributed directly to the product. Should such allocations influence prices? To avoid this problem, some entities use only avoidable costs in their price calculations. However, they also face uncertainty in determining an appropriate mark-up percentage. Why is the mark-up 50 per cent and not 20 per cent, 30 per cent or some other amount? What should the mark-up be if only avoidable costs are included in the calculation? Most important, what are customers willing to pay?

Market-based pricing

High quality and brand name for an entity such as Bombardier Jets are likely to be as important, if not more important, than price. Accordingly, a cost-based pricing scheme might not maximise profits. As the company's managers make pricing decisions, they need to understand competitors' prices; however, they should also consider each buyer's ability and willingness to pay for the product. To maximise profits, Bombardier Jets should charge the highest price possible, but not such a high price that the customer buys from a competitor or decides not to buy a jet.

Market-based prices are determined using some measure of customer demand. Under market-based pricing, managers strive to identify what customers are willing to pay for a good or service. As illustrated in figure 5.7, market prices are influenced by the degree of product differentiation and competition.

At one extreme, organisations face many competitors and cannot differentiate their products. In this case, the market price is the commodity price that customers would pay to any organisation offering the good or service. For example, farmers typically sell agricultural products at a quoted market price. The same is true for mining companies selling gold or silver. In such cases, managers estimate prices by referring to published rates.

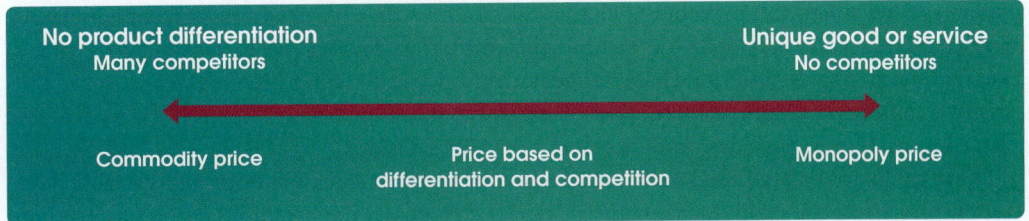

FIGURE 5.7 ■ Market prices, product differentiation and degree of competition

At the other extreme are monopolies selling unique goods or services and having no competition. Monopolies such as residential water services are often owned or regulated by the government. In these cases, the entity is not allowed to establish a free market price but must charge the regulated price. Occasionally short-term monopolies arise. For example, the only pub in town with beer after a heatwave can theoretically charge as much as the market will bear until competitors receive beer deliveries. Most goods and services fall between these two extremes. Organisations can typically differentiate their product in the market because features and brand names are important. However, these organisations are subject to competition, which must be considered when setting prices. To set prices, they estimate consumer demand for product characteristics such as quality and functionality.

Price elasticity and demand

Organisations with differentiated products can formally or informally incorporate consumer demand into their pricing policies. For example, contractors who build expensive houses often negotiate prices with individual buyers. The negotiations continue throughout the construction period when unforeseen costs arise or when the home buyer makes choices such as carpeting and wall coverings that are more expensive than anticipated. A more formal way to incorporate demand into prices is through the price elasticity of demand.

As prices increase, demand usually falls. This sensitivity of sales to price increases is called the **price elasticity of demand**. Cigarettes are an example of a product where changes in price have a substantial effect on sales; that is, demand is elastic. In contrast, customised planes such as Bombardier Jets are a product with relatively inelastic demand. Price changes have little effect on demand, and factors such as quality and the ability to customise are more important (within limits) than price.

To develop a price that maximises profit, we follow the steps shown in figure 5.8. The first step is to calculate the price elasticity of demand. To perform this calculation, data must be

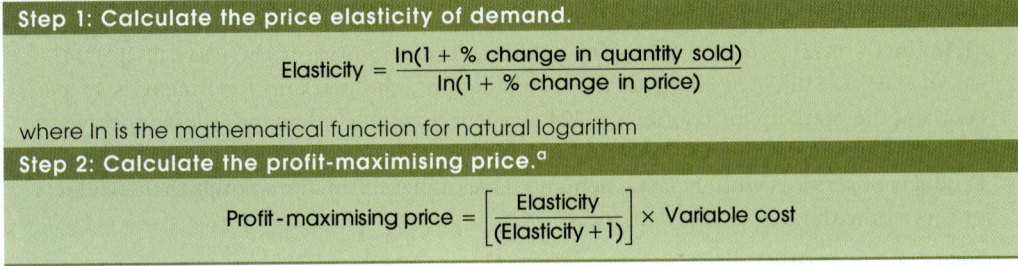

ªThe profit-maximising mark-up formula is

$$\left[\frac{\text{Elasticity}}{(\text{Elasticity}+1)}-1\right]$$

We add 1 to the mark-up before we multiply it by variable cost to determine the profit-maximising price.

FIGURE 5.8 ■ Computing the profit-maximising price

available to calculate the percentage change in quantity that occurs for a percentage change in price. The second step is to determine the profit-maximising price, a calculation that is based on the strong assumption that changes in volume result *only* from changes in price. This assumption is never completely true, however, so the mark-up amount needs to be interpreted with caution. It only provides guidance about pricing decisions.

These calculations are based on information about prices, sales volumes and variable costs. Two factors affect the profit-maximising price: (1) changes in the product's demand sensitivity to price, and (2) changes in variable costs. Information about fixed costs is irrelevant. Comprehensive example 4 shows how these calculations help an entity set prices.

Comprehensive example 4

Using price elasticity to calculate product prices

French Perfumery produces two perfumes: Breezy and Exotique. Breezy is a well-known inexpensive perfume, and its customers are sensitive to price. Several competitors market similar products, and close substitutes are available at discount chemists and department stores. Exotique is a customised perfume sold only in small boutique stores where few substitutes are available and where customers are less sensitive to price. French's accountant, Mimi, needs to develop pricing guidelines for management. She performs the following analysis.

Profit-maximising prices for Breezy and Exotique

Mimi calculates the variable cost of Breezy as $2 per mL and $10 per mL for Exotique. Based on information from historical accounting records, she believes that every 10 per cent increase in price for Breezy results in a decrease in sales of 20 per cent because customers for this product are so price sensitive. She calculates the price elasticity for Breezy as $-2.34\ [\ln(1-0.2) \div \ln(1+0.1)]$. In turn, she uses the elasticity to calculate a profit-maximising price of $3.50\ \{[-2.34 \div (-2.34 + 1)] \times \$2\}$.

Mimi estimates that for every 10 per cent increase in price, sales of Exotique would decrease only 12 per cent. She calculates the price elasticity of demand for Exotique as $-1.34\ [\ln(1-0.12) \div \ln(1+0.1)]$. The profit-maximising price is then $39.40\ \{[-1.34 \div (-1.34 + 1)] \times \$10\}$. According to these calculations, the mark-up for Breezy is 75 per cent and the mark-up for Exotique is 294 per cent. Exotique's demand is less sensitive to price changes than Breezy's, so Mimi knows that Exotique's demand is more inelastic. Products or services with inelastic demand have higher optimal mark-ups than products or services with more elastic demand.

Market price guidelines

When Mimi presents her calculations to managers, she cautions them about this information. Although the calculations seem precise, they should be interpreted only as guidelines for price setting, not absolute determinants of price. She warns them that similar to other decisions, the managers need to consider uncertainties when making pricing decisions. For example, measurement error may occur in collecting information about how price changes affect sales. She explains to the managers that these formulas are extremely sensitive to errors, and small changes in assumptions create a large effect on the calculations. Also, price elasticity can vary over time due to changes in competitor prices and customer preferences. Managers need to anticipate and monitor for changes in product demand.

Mimi also explains the following assumptions underlying her calculations:

- The price elasticity of demand is constant.
- The variable cost is constant.
- The product price has no effect on other product costs or sales.

The managers know that these assumptions may not always hold, so they decide to make small incremental changes to prices and then track profitability to determine the profit-maximising price.

Accountants use historical information to estimate the effects of price changes on sales volume. Some organisations might rely on price elasticity information published by their industries. Other organisations use optical scanners to capture historical price and volume data. The quality of this type of information improves as sales volumes increase. Companies can rapidly gather data and monitor relationships between price and volume. They can also analyse how sales behave for groups of products. For example, supermarkets often sell some products as 'loss leaders,' lowering the price on a specific product to bring customers into the store. In these cases, managers assume that increases in sales of other products will more than make up for the forgone profit from the loss leader.

The quality of product demand estimates using historical data depends in part on sales volumes. Large retailers collect large amounts of sales data and conduct price experiments to learn more about how volumes respond to price changes. Entities with lower sales volumes also collect sales and price data, but they are likely to face more error in their estimates of product demand.

Other market-based pricing methods

As illustrated with the Microsoft Xbox, companies sometimes use competitors' prices to establish their own market prices. For common products in retail settings, competitors' prices are easily observed. However, it may be difficult to learn about competitors' prices when fewer transactions occur or are made in non-retail settings.

The Internet makes it possible to learn about market prices for items that were previously difficult to value. Auction websites such as e-Bay, GraysOnline, Yahoo! and Amazon provide information on prices. Given the large range of products and prices that are readily available, these sites increase the consistency of prices, even for objects such as antiques. Because increasing numbers of organisations include product and service price information on their websites, the Internet also makes it easier for managers to monitor competitors' prices.

The Internet is likely to cause prices to become more elastic because close substitutes are more easily found and priced. The Internet also increases the global reach of many companies. Together, the Internet and global competition have forced an increasingly large number of organisations to use market-based pricing.

Cost-based versus market-based pricing

A major drawback of cost-based pricing is that it ignores customer demand. Prices are likely to be higher or lower than what customers are willing to pay for goods or services. For example, Motorola based the price of its global cellular phones on costs, rather than surveying the market for a competitive price. This decision resulted first in prices for the phone and calling rates that were higher than customers would pay, and eventually contributed to the bankruptcy of the entire project. In other situations, cost-based prices are too low and organisations forgo potential profits.

With cost-based prices, sales volumes inappropriately influence the price, causing a downward demand spiral known as the **death spiral**. If production decreases because demand has decreased, then the average product cost increases and the price based on that average cost increases. When the product has an elastic demand curve, price increases cause sales to decline even more. This decline, in turn, causes average cost to increase even further, producing more price increases and more sales deterioration. This pattern persists until the product is discontinued because it cannot cover its costs.

Despite these disadvantages, cost-based pricing is a commonly used method.[16] Surveys of manufacturers consistently report that they prefer to mark up an average cost that includes a portion of fixed cost, using a mark-up system based on desired return.[17] This preference might reflect the fact that it was difficult in the past for entity's information systems to gather the data needed to calculate profit-maximising sales prices. The major benefit of using cost-based pricing is its simplicity. Prices are calculated from readily available cost data.

Using market-based prices to estimate revenues, managers make better decisions about sales volumes or whether to sell goods or services, leading to more success in organisational strategies. The disadvantage is that estimating market demand and prices is often difficult. However, more sophisticated information systems make it easier for managers to estimate demand, marginal costs and revenues, leading to an increasing trend in the use of market-based pricing.

Other influences on price

Regardless of the general technique used, a number of other factors influence prices for individual organisations or in specific circumstances.

Some industries charge different prices at different times to reduce capacity constraints, a practice called **peak load pricing**. For example, cinemas charge less for movies shown early in the day. Telephone companies often charge less for calls made at night or on the weekend. In the airline industry, a variety of prices are offered to customers based on factors such as advanced ticket purchase, whether the customer is travelling for business or leisure, and whether the customer wants preferential seating and other services. During economic downturns, even organisations with set prices may negotiate with customers.

Price skimming occurs when a higher price is charged for a product or service when it is first introduced. The term refers to the practice of skimming the cream off the market. When new technology is introduced, such as notepads that transcribe handwriting to word processing, high prices are charged to cover the initial research and development. Prices are then reduced as competitors enter the market.

Penetration pricing is the practice of setting low prices when new products are introduced to increase market share. This practice describes Microsoft's willingness to reduce the price of Xbox to match its competition. Penetration pricing is legal if its intent is to reduce customer uncertainty about product or service value. However, if the purpose is to eliminate competition, then it could be considered predatory pricing, which is illegal in Australia.

Sometimes managers take advantage of unusual circumstances to increase prices. **Price gouging** is the practice of charging a price viewed by consumers as too high. If managers can convince consumers that prices are based on costs, they avoid being labelled as price gougers.

Transfer prices are the prices charged for transactions that take place within an entity. Prices are set for the use of support departments such as human resources and accounting. In a manufacturing setting, intermediate products are often transferred to other departments where further assembly takes place before the final product is sold to external markets. These intermediate products need to be priced so that appropriate decisions can be made about the value of selling products internally or externally. Transfer price policies also have incentive and tax effects.

Pricing in not-for-profit entities

Not-for-profit entities are concerned with many objectives other than profit maximisation. Their pricing methods tend to be more complex than those used by for-profit entities. Grants, donations and interest from endowed funds often help defray the cost of products and services. Because of these sources of funds, not-for-profits do not always expect to recover all of their costs from prices or fees they charge.

Some not-for-profit organisations charge a fee based on the client's income. This fee is called a sliding scale fee; as client income decreases, the fee decreases. Clients who can afford to pay more are charged more. Other not-for-profits charge high prices to everyone, but then provide charity services for low-income clients or discount the charges to selected clients. For example, hospitals might set prices for services high enough that revenues from insured patients cover the costs of providing services to uninsured patients. In addition, Medicare often pays for only a portion of the costs incurred by Medicare patients. Therefore, hospital managers attempt to use pricing policies to shift some of these costs to other patients. The result is that charity care and treatment of Medicare patients tend to inflate hospital prices for other patients.

Some not-for-profit entities use price-setting policies to achieve organisational goals. For example, many universities discount tuition or offer grants and scholarships to students with high entrance scores. Their goal is to improve the quality of incoming students. A stronger student body enhances these schools' reputations and may in turn increase the number of applicants.

Government regulations and pricing

Organisations are not free to establish any price they wish; some pricing practices are illegal. In Australia, illegal practices include price discrimination, predatory pricing, collusive pricing and dumping. Courts often use costs to determine whether an entity has violated laws.

Price discrimination is the practice of setting different prices for different customers. Although not-for-profit organisations charge prices according to ability to pay, Australian regulations forbid for-profit organisations from charging some customers higher prices for the same product if the intent is to lessen or prevent competition for customers. Entities can use cost differences as a defence against price discrimination charges.

It is also illegal for organisations to practice **predatory pricing**, which is the deliberate act of setting prices low to drive competitors out of the market and then raising prices. However, low prices are not considered predatory if they can be justified by cost differences.

Many governments also forbid **collusive pricing**, which occurs when two or more organisations conspire to set prices above a competitive price. Consumer welfare is harmed by such practices. In Australia, the Australian Competition and Consumer Commission (ACCC) has previously investigated allegations of petrol price fixing among rival petrol suppliers. They argue that sometimes the selling or buying prices can be set at the same level so that the price fluctuations are matched by equivalent fluctuation by competing businesses. Although this may seem like collusive behaviour, legitimate commercial reasons may include highly visible prices displayed by competitors (for example, on petrol price boards) allowing competitors to quickly adjust their prices to match price movements.[18]

Under Australian law, **dumping** occurs when a foreign-based entity sells products in Australia at prices below the market value in the country where the product is produced, and the price could harm an Australian industry. The Australian government imposes an anti-dumping tariff. The tariff is set so that the new price will be equivalent to the prices charged by Australian entities. These rules have been applied in a number of industries. Other countries enact similar laws to protect home country manufacturers from unfair competition from foreign businesses. For example, from 1999 through 2000, steel exports from India grew by 53 per cent. Because prices for Indian steel were much lower than domestic prices in the United States, Canada and Europe, these governments levied anti-dumping duties on certain steel products to protect the domestic industry.[19]

Summary

1   **Explain the value chain activities that provide for continuous cost improvement.**

Continuously improve costs over the long term by:
- enhancing efficiency
- reducing costs
- improving interactions with suppliers and customers
- identifying and eliminating non-value-added activities
- minimising rework, scrap and waste
- reducing production cycle time
- negotiating lower prices with suppliers.

2   **Explain the concepts just-in-time (JIT) manufacturing, total quality management (TQM) and the theory of constraints (TOC).**

Just-in-time manufacturing
Inventory control systems in which materials are purchased and units are produced as customers demand them.

Total quality management (TQM)
An entity-wide product, process and service quality focus comprising:
- a strong customer focus
- extensive employee participation and development
- emphasis on process management
- emphasis in design quality.

Managing quality
- Prevention activities
- Appraisal activities

- Production activities
- External activities

Theory of constraints (TOC)

Entity is viewed as a system.

- Main goal to make money now and in the future.
- Comprises a set of elements (a chain of linkages) with interdependent relationships.
- TOC concentrates on the weakest link in the chain.
- Source of constraint can be the *supply* or *demand* side of the value chain.
- Introduction to throughput accounting (chapter 15).

Five-steps of TOC

1. Identify the system's constraint(s).
2. Decide how to exploit the system's constraint(s).
3. Subordinate everything else to the above constraint(s).
4. Elevate the system's constraint(s).
5. If in the previous steps a constraint has been broken, go back to step 1, but do not allow inertia to cause a system constraint.

3 **Understand target costing principles and techniques.**

Decision-making method that considers prices as given and then determines whether products and services can be provided at costs low enough for an acceptable profit.

Target costing design cycle

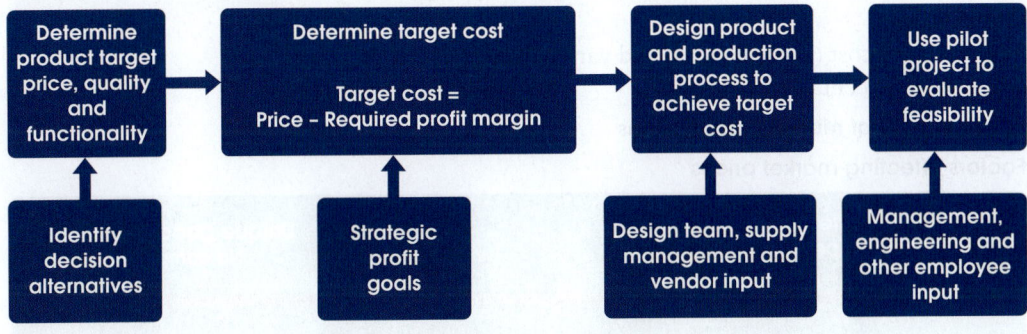

4 **Explain the concept of kaizen costing and how it compares to target costing.**

Kaizen costing

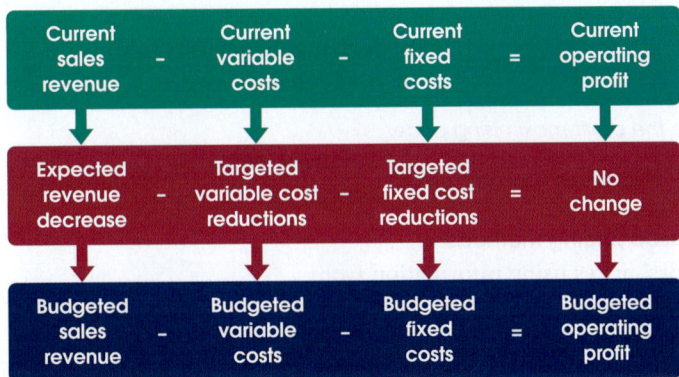

Comparison of Kaizen and target costing

Time →			
Before production	First production period	Continuous production	Drop product
Target costing	Cost is maintained	Kaizen costing	
Product and manufacturing process design	Manufacturing at target cost	Periodic cost-reduction goals set and met	No further cost reductions available

---

5 **Describe the characteristics of life cycle costing.**

Life cycle costing

Consider changes in price and costs over the entire life cycle of a good or service, from the time the product is introduced through a number of years.
- Allow initial losses or large decommissioning costs.
- Expect a combination of sales volume increases and cost reductions over time.

---

6 **Describe pricing methods and how cost-based prices and market-based prices are managed.**

Must choose:
- measure of cost (variable, fixed and variable etc.)
- mark-up percentage.

Establishment of market-based prices

Factors affecting market prices

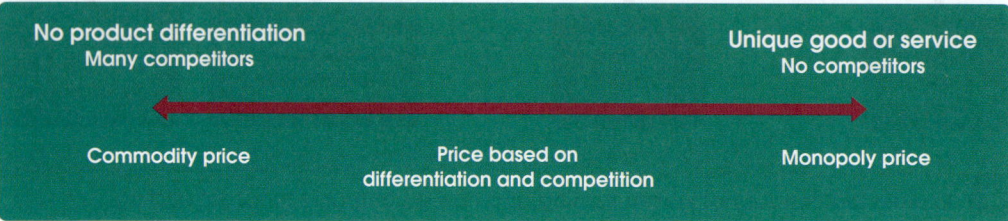

No product differentiation Many competitors		Unique good or service No competitors
Commodity price	Price based on differentiation and competition	Monopoly price

Computations for profit-maximising price

Step 1: Calculate the price elasticity of demand.

$$\text{Elasticity} = \frac{\ln(1 + \% \text{ change in quantity sold})}{\ln(1 + \% \text{ change in price})}$$

Step 2: Calculate the profit-maximising price.

$$\text{Profit-maximising price} = \left[\frac{\text{Elasticity}}{(\text{Elasticity} + 1)}\right] \times \text{Variable cost}$$

Other market-based pricing methods

Match competitors' prices using information from:
- competitor retail stores
- competitor websites
- Internet auction sites.

7 Understand the uses and limitations of cost-based and market-based pricing.

Advantages and disadvantages

	Cost-based pricing	Market-based pricing
Advantages	<ul><li>Most commonly used method</li><li>Simple</li><li>Calculated from readily available cost data</li></ul>	<ul><li>Offers better decisions about how much or whether to sell a product</li><li>Provides better success with strategies</li></ul>
Disadvantages	<ul><li>Ignores customer demand</li><li>Prices may be too high or too low</li><li>Sales volumes inappropriately influence price if fixed costs are included</li></ul>	<ul><li>Difficult to estimate market demand and prices</li><li>Method not commonly used</li></ul>

8 Explain any additional factors that might affect prices.

Other influences on price
- Peak load pricing
- Price skimming
- Penetration pricing
- Price gouging
- Transfer prices

9 Appreciate how pricing models apply to not-for-profit and government entities.

- Prices need not cover costs.
- Different prices can be set for different customers.
- Prices are often based on ability to pay.
- Organisational goals influence prices.

Governmental regulations
- Price discrimination
- Predatory pricing
- Collusive pricing
- Dumping

Self-study problems

SELF-STUDY PROBLEM 1

Target and kaizen costing

You have recently been hired as an accountant for a start-up entity in the computer peripherals industry. The owners have developed and are manufacturing several wireless devices to enhance user mobility, such as a small electronic notebook. They want to become more competitive in this market and also develop several other products. They have asked you for ideas about ways to control costs and determine whether proposed new products will be profitable.

REQUIRED
Write a memo to the owners describing how they could use target costing and kaizen costing.

Many possible approaches may be taken to write a memo on these topics. The body of one possible memo follows. Note that the memo is written to inform and help the managers of the entity make a decision.

You asked for my recommendations about ways to control costs and to determine whether proposed new products will be profitable. In this memo I briefly describe two techniques — target costing and kaizen costing — that could be implemented to achieve these goals.

Target costing. Target costing helps determine whether a proposed new product will be profitable. This technique involves the following steps:

- Estimate the market price of the proposed product.
- Given the market price, determine what the cost must be to achieve our desired profitability.
- Estimate the costs of producing the product. If the estimated cost exceeds the target cost, search for ways to reduce costs. Drop the product idea if it is not feasible to achieve the target cost.
- For potentially feasible new products, conduct pilot production projects to further evaluate estimated costs.

The biggest advantage of target costing is that it would help us focus on ways to design products and manufacturing processes to meet our profitability goals. If costs are too high, we will be forced to look for ways to reduce them, which might also lead us to make changes to the proposed features of a new product.

The target costing process would also help us involve everyone in the organisation in making product decisions and setting cost goals. This involvement would encourage employees to 'buy in' to the target costs, which will help us achieve them.

Kaizen costing. Kaizen costing helps control costs over the life of a product, taking into account the fact that selling prices decline over some product's life. The process for kaizen costing is similar to the process described for target costing. We would estimate the future selling prices of our existing products and determine the cost we need to achieve for our desired profit.

Kaizen costing would help us make decisions about products we wish to continue. If we cannot find ways to reduce costs to achieve desired profitability, then we should consider dropping it.

Risks. I believe that both of these methods would help us meet our goals. However, you should be aware of three major risks:

- Both methods involve a great deal of estimation for prices and costs. The rapid change in our industry presents a high risk of errors in our estimates that might prevent us from achieving our profitability goals.
- Teams of personnel from marketing, engineering, production and accounting would be needed for implementation. It will be critical for everyone to work toward

common goals rather than to focus only on their own work areas. Thus, the team members should be chosen carefully and would need to understand that the teams have high priority.

■ These techniques might discourage us from adopting new products or continuing existing products that have long-term value. The teams need to consider long-term as well as short-term factors in making final recommendations.

SELF-STUDY PROBLEM 2

Cost-based and market-based prices; minimum acceptable price

The Torquay Produce Suppliers packages and distributes three grades of animal feed. The material cost per tonne and estimated annual sales for each of the products are listed here:

Product	Material cost	Estimated sales
Super Premium	$16	1000 tonnes
Premium	$12	1500 tonnes
Economy	$10	2500 tonnes

The fixed cost of operating the machinery used to package all three products is $20 000 per year. In the past, prices have been set by allocating the fixed overhead to products on the basis of estimated sales in tonnes. The resulting total costs (material costs plus allocated fixed overhead) are then marked up by 100 per cent.

REQUIRED

(a) Determine the price per tonne for each grade of feed using the method described for setting prices.

(b) Does the price in part (a) take into account how much customers are willing to pay for the product? Explain.

(c) Suppose a 10 per cent increase in price would result in about a 40 per cent decrease in the amount of the economy grade feed sold. Estimate the price that would maximise profits on the economy grade feed.

(d) Explain how the price for economy grade feed calculated in part (c) should be used.

(e) Suppose a Geelong distributor would like to buy 200 tonnes of economy grade feed and has offered to pay $2400 for the special order.

  (i) What is the relevant cost to Torquay Produce Suppliers for this order?

  (ii) Considering only quantitative factors, what is the minimum acceptable price per tonne?

Solution to self-study problem 2

(a)

	Economy	Premium	Super Premium
Materials cost	$10	$12	$16
Allocated fixed overhead			
$20 000 ÷ 5000 = $4 per tonne	4	4	4
Total cost	14	16	20
Mark-up (100% of total cost)	14	16	20
Price	$28	$32	$40

(b) No. A cost-based price *assumes* that customers are willing to pay a set mark-up above cost. However, a price based on cost might be higher or lower than customers are willing to pay.

(c) The price for economy grade feed can be computed in two steps:

$$\text{Elasticity of demand} = -\ln(1 - 0.40) \div \ln(1 + 0.10) = -5.36$$

$$\text{Profit-maximising price} = [-5.36 \div (-5.36 + 1)] \times \$10 = \$12.30$$

(d) The price in part (c) is only a guideline for pricing. The elasticity formulas are sensitive to error, so the profit-maximising prices are used only as guidelines. Torquay Produce Suppliers could reduce the price of economy grade feed slowly and see how volumes and profits change.

(e) (i) The relevant cost of filling the special order is the variable cost, which in this problem is the cost of materials: $10 per tonne × 200 tonnes = $2000.

   (ii) Under the general quantitative decision rule for special orders, the minimum acceptable price is the variable cost. The minimum acceptable price would be $10 per tonne.

Questions

5.1 What is a just-in-time manufacturing system? Why would organisations choose to adopt it?

5.2 Explain the similarities and differences among target costing, kaizen costing and life cycle costing.

5.3 Identify three products for which target costing and kaizen costing could be used. Identify three products for which target costing and kaizen costing would be inappropriate.

5.4 Describe the four types of quality-related activities.

5.5 Explain the target costing cycle, and discuss the decision criteria used to determine whether a product will be manufactured using a target costing approach.

5.6 Explain cost-based pricing and give an example that shows how prices would be determined using this method.

5.7 Explain market-based pricing and explain where managers and accountants can find information that would help them set prices using this type of approach.

5.8 Supply chain analysis focuses particularly on one aspect of value chain analysis. Explain how supply chain analysis is performed and how it relates to value chain analysis.

5.9 List some common advantages and disadvantages for target and kaizen costing.

5.10 If fixed costs are included in the marked-up costs used in setting cost-based prices, a problem may occur when demand declines. Describe this problem.

5.11 Explain why not-for-profit entities do not always set prices so that their operating costs are recovered.

Exercises

5.12 **Categorising quality activities** Following is a list of quality-related activities.

QUALITY ACTIVITY
   (a) Inspection of units when they are 100 per cent complete to remove defective units
   (b) Designing a process with as few parts as possible to reduce the chance of defects
   (c) Warranty costs for defective products returned to the factory for rework
   (d) Reworking spoiled units before they leave the factory
   (e) Costs to defend the entity against lawsuits for damages caused by defective products
   (f) Tracking number of defects for each manufacturing team and posting daily defect rates on a plant-wide bulletin board

(g) Redesigning a manufacturing process to lower the rate of defects

REQUIRED

Mark each activity according to whether it pertains to the internal cost of prevention (P), appraisal (A), internal (I), or external (E) costs

5.13 Market-based price (elasticity formula) Lickety Split sells ice cream cones in a variety of flavours. Data for a recent week appear here:

Revenue (1000 cones @ $1.75 per cone)		$1750
Cost of ingredients	$640	
Rent	500	
Store attendant	600	1740
Pre-tax profit		$ 10

The manager estimates that if she were to increase the price of cones from $1.75 to $1.93 each, weekly volume would be cut to 850 cones due to competition from other nearby ice cream shops.

REQUIRED

Estimate the profit-maximising price per cone.

5.14 Market-based prices (elasticity formula) Arnie's Flowers is a small Mt Macedon florist shop. Arnie sells flowers for bouquets, and she also prepares and delivers flower arrangements.

REQUIRED

(a) Arnie is trying to decide how much to charge for a new type of rose that wholesales for $0.40 per bud. She ran a special on a similar rose last month and discovered that a 20 per cent discount on the usual price increased sales by about 35 per cent. What would you suggest as a starting price for the rose? Explain.

(b) Arnie has been wondering whether she has been charging the right prices on some of her specialty bouquets. She has been using a mark-up for all specialty items of 200 per cent (that is, she charges three times wholesale cost). Arnie estimates that a 10 per cent increase in price on such items would decrease her unit sales by about 12 per cent. Perform calculations to estimate a profit-maximising mark-up. Based on your calculation, do you think she should increase or decrease her mark-up? Explain.

5.15 JIT production Big Bertram uses the just-in-time method to manufacture golf clubs. The manufacturing schedule for the clubs is developed as customers place orders. Each club is made within a cell where five workers have production stations. The raw materials are delivered to the cell as needed. Each worker in the cell performs one step in the manufacturing process and then inspects the club before giving it to the next person. When a club is finished, it is set on a finished goods rack, which is sent to the packaging department at regular intervals.

REQUIRED

(a) What do we call a manufacturing system such as the one used by Big Bertram?

(b) Describe general advantages of this type of system.

(c) The supplier that manufactures the weights that are inserted in each club head would like to monitor Big Bertram's inventory levels through the Internet so that its new software program could release deliveries at appropriate times. List qualitative factors that might affect Big Bertram's decision about this proposal.

5.16 Quality costs using ABC versus traditional costing New-Rage Cosmetics uses a traditional cost accounting system to allocate quality control costs uniformly to all products at a rate of 14.5 per cent of direct labour cost. Monthly direct labour cost for Satin Sheen make-up is $27 500. In an attempt to more equitably distribute quality control costs, New-Rage is considering activity-based costing. The following monthly data have been gathered for Satin Sheen make-up.

Incoming material inspection:
  Cost driver — type of material
  Cost allocation rate — $11.50 per type of material
  Quantity — 12 types of material
In-process inspection:
  Cost driver — number of units
  Cost allocation rate — $0.14 per unit
  Quantity — 17 500 units
Product certification:
  Cost driver — per order
  Cost allocation rate — $77 per order
  Quantity — 25 orders

REQUIRED

(a) Calculate the amount of quality control cost assigned to each order of Satin Sheen make-up using:
   (i) activity-based costing (*Hint:* Total all the ABC costs for one month and divide by the number of orders.)
   (ii) traditional cost accounting.
(b) Explain the difference in quality control costs assigned under the two methods.

5.17 Quality costs in a lost dogs' home Suppose that the director of a lost dogs' home is concerned about an increase in number of adopted dogs returned to the home because of behaviour problems. When dogs are returned, the home incurs extra animal intake and adoption costs, in addition to extra costs for board, room and more training for the dogs. In addition, the director is concerned that adopting families may not want another dog because of their unhappy experience. The director views this as a quality problem and wants to improve quality in adoption services and reduce costs at the same time.

(a) List the four types of quality activities presented in the chapter. What type of quality problem is the lost dogs' home experiencing? Explain your answer.
(b) Will an ABC system help managers determine costs for their quality activities? Explain.
(c) List one new cost pool and cost driver that could be used to improve the director's ability to analyse quality.

5.18 Target costing Suppose that Holden used target costing to decide whether to produce a new vehicle, such as the SS Commodore.

REQUIRED

(a) Describe the steps Holden's design team would have taken.
(b) Explain why managers cannot easily predict demand for a new product such as the SS Commodore.

5.19 Market-based price (elasticity formula); uncertainties; other pricing factors Sea Breeze Sweets is a shop located at The Rocks in Sydney. It makes and sells boiled lollies in a variety of flavours. Revenue and cost data for a recent week are shown opposite.

Revenue (1500 kg @ $6 per kg)		$9000
Cost of ingredients	$2400	
Rent	800	
Wages	3200	6400
Pre-tax profit		$2600

All employees work standard shifts, regardless of how many lollies are produced or sold. Jasmine, the shop's manager, estimates that if she were to decrease the price of boiled lollies by $0.60 per kg to a new price of $5.40 per kg, weekly volume would increase by 20 per cent.

REQUIRED

(a) Calculate the price elasticity of demand.

(b) Calculate the profit-maximising price

(c) Based on the profit-maximising price, does it appear that Jasmine should drop the price of the boiled lollies? Why?

(d) List possible relevant factors that could influence Jasmine's price decision. List as many factors as you can.

5.20 Market-based (elasticity formula) and cost-based prices; special order decision Oysters Away shucks and packs oysters and sells them wholesale to fine restaurants across the country. The income statement for last year follows:

Revenue (2000 cases)		$200 000
Expenses:		
Wages for pickers, shuckers and packers	$100 000	
Packing materials	20 000	
Rent and insurance	25 000	
Administration and selling	45 000	
		190 000
Pre-tax profit		$ 10 000

Pickers, shuckers, and packers are employed on an hourly basis and can be laid off whenever necessary. Salespeople merely deliver the product, and so are paid on a salaried basis.

Linda Hanson, manager of Oysters Away, believes that a price increase of 10 per cent would result in a 15 per cent decrease in sales.

The King Krab Restaurant is providing dinner for a meeting of the Pickers, Shuckers and Packers Union in Melbourne. King Krab offered to pay Oysters Away $65 a case for 300 cases of oysters. This sale would not affect Oysters Away's regular sales.

REQUIRED

(a) Ignoring the King Krab offer, estimate the profit-maximising price for Oysters Away.

(b) Assuming Linda is not willing to lose money on the King Krab order, what is the minimum price that she should accept for the special order?

(c) What other relevant factors might Linda consider before she makes a decision about the King Krab order? List as many factors as you can.

5.21 Kaizen costing Blade Runner produces regular scooters and motorised scooters. Blade Runner scooters are considered the most reliable in the marketplace. Demand has been volatile, with huge increases in demand during the holiday season. In the past, the entity filled demand by anticipating demand increases and manufacturing inventories ahead of time.

Recently, competition in the motorised scooter line has escalated, and Blade Runner needs to reduce prices and therefore cut costs. The motorised scooter's current cost is $150. To be competitive, the marketing department says the price should be 10 per cent lower than the current price. Management currently achieves a pre-tax return of 10 per cent on sales of the scooters and wants to continue this rate of return.

The following per-unit costs for motorised scooters are based on production of 700 000 per year.

Direct materials (variable)	$ 45
Direct labour (variable)	15
Machining costs (fixed depreciation and maintenance)	10
Inspection costs (variable)	10
Engineering costs (fixed)	20
Marketing costs (fixed)	25
Administrative costs (fixed)	25
Total cost	$150

REQUIRED

(a) Calculate the price recommended by the marketing department.
(b) Given the price you calculated in part (a), calculate the new contribution margin and the target cost.
(c) Calculate the planned cost reduction for each cost category, assuming proportional cost reduction across categories.

5.22 Kaizen costing; proposed cost reductions; uncertainties Refer to the information in exercise 5.21. The following cost reduction suggestions were made by the kaizen costing team.

- *Direct materials* — suppliers agreed to cost reductions of $4.50 for direct materials.
- *Direct labour* — an engineer suggested that the scooters could be manufactured more quickly if production batches were cut in half. The engineer believes that a labour savings of $1.50 per scooter could be attained.
- *Machining costs* — the team has been unable to identify ways to reduce machining costs in the manufacturing process, but suggests that some of the machining tasks could be outsourced to suppliers so that some parts are pre-assembled, reducing the need for machine hours. This outsourcing would increase the cost of direct materials by $0.50 per unit but cut machining costs by $1.30 per unit. The supplier has been very reliable, but does not currently have the machining expertise and would have to purchase equipment and hire several workers to fill these orders.
- *Marketing* — marketing has agreed to combine advertising campaigns for both products and believes they will save $2.50 per unit without losing sales.
- *Administration and engineering* — no cost containment appears possible in administration because a new enterprise resource program was recently acquired. However, the head of engineering believes that her costs can be cut by $4 per unit. She believes that some employees are no longer needed because part of the new program was designed especially to provide information for product and manufacturing process design that had been manually collated in the past.

REQUIRED

(a) Calculate the new cost per category. Compare the total cost with the kaizen cost. Determine whether further cost-containment efforts need to be made.
(b) In your own words, describe the next step in the kaizen process.

(c) List qualitative factors that might be relevant to Blade Runner's managers as they decide on any product or process changes. List as many factors as you can.

(d) For each of the planned cost reductions, discuss uncertainties about whether the entity will achieve the planned cost reduction.

Problems

5.23 Cost reduction; JIT; value chain analysis Budget Cupboards produces kitchen and bathroom cupboards that incorporate unusual functions (such as specialty drawers for knives and kitchen tools) and kitchen appliance holders that pop up from under the countertop. Competition in this industry has recently increased. Budget's management wants to cut costs for its basic cupboard models and then cut prices.

REQUIRED

(a) The following table lists potential areas for cost reduction. Two potential cost reductions are provided for the first area listed (design phase). For each of the remaining areas, identify two potential ways that Budget Cupboard's management could reduce costs.

Potential area for cost reduction	Potential cost reductions	
	(i)	(ii)
Example: Design phase	Work with suppliers to reduce direct materials costs	Redesign cupboards to use fewer parts
Manufacturing process		
Administration		
Changes in quality or functionality		

(b) Budget Cupboards does not currently use just-in-time production or value chain analysis. Describe several advantages of using these methods when price competition increases.

5.24 Target and kaizen costing; uncertainties; manager incentives Suppose you are having a conversation with Sandy, another student in this course. Sandy is confused about the differences and similarities between target costing and kaizen costing.

Another student, Kevin, overhears your conversation with Sandy and insists that neither of these methods is beneficial. Kevin argues that some entities run into financial problems using these methods because their managers manipulated the cost estimates to appear however they wanted. If the managers wanted to launch a new product or keep an old one, they made sure their cost estimates supported their decision.

REQUIRED

(a) In your own words, explain how target costing and kaizen costing are the same and how they are different.

(b) Compare the information needed to apply the target costing and kaizen costing methods.
  (i) List the types of relevant information needed for each method.
  (ii) List the uncertainties in the relevant information for each method.

(c) Discuss ways in which managers might be able to create biased estimates under a target or kaizen costing system.

(d) Kevin argues that the types of issues you described in part (c) mean that target and kaizen costing are not beneficial. Discuss the validity of this argument.

5.25 Cost-based and market-based pricing; elasticity; uncertainties; economy effects John Gold has owned and operated Heritage Jewellery Store for a number of years. He uses the standard mark-up of 300 per cent (known as a *triple key* in this industry) and uses an average cost that includes an allocation of overhead as the cost base. Lately, jewellery sales at the store have faltered as the country faces a recession. John's son is taking a cost accounting course and suggests that his father should use a pricing formula based on the price elasticity of demand.

REQUIRED

(a) In your own words, provide a plausible explanation for John's current use of cost-based pricing.
(b) Explain elasticity to John in simple terms.
(c) In your own words, explain how price changes affect demand for products that are highly elastic.
(d) Explain why John's price elasticity of demand cannot be predicted with certainty.
(e) List possible reasons why a product's price elasticity of demand would change. List as many reasons as you can.
(f) Explain how changes in the economy affect prices. Give examples from the current business environment.

5.26 Cost-based pricing; death spiral; uncertainties; customer reaction Suppose the owner of Haywood Ceramics needs to raise prices to stay in business, but is concerned that raising prices would result in a death spiral. To avoid a decline in sales, the owner is considering sending letters to her customers explaining why the price increase is necessary. The letter would inform customers about the cost increases that necessitated the price increase, explain what the entity is doing to keep costs as low as possible, and allow customers to place orders for a given time period at the current price.

REQUIRED

(a) Describe the death spiral in your own words.
(b) Explain why the owner cannot be sure how customers will respond to a price increase.
(c) Suppose the owner decides to send letters to her customers. From a customer's point of view, discuss possible pros and cons of this strategy.
(d) Would you recommend that the owner send letters to her customers? Why?

5.27 Market-based pricing; relevant information Java Alive, a small boutique coffee shop, has asked your advice in setting pricing policies. Java has information about prices and sales over the last four years.

REQUIRED

(a) Explain how you would use the prices and sales information to suggest a possible pricing strategy.
(b) What other information would you gather before you complete your recommendation? List as many types of information as you can.

5.28 Market-based pricing; customer preferences Transrapid is a new magnetically levitated train being developed to run between major cities in Germany at a speed of 500 kilometres per hour. Engineers developed a system with trains departing every 10 minutes. Suppose Transrapid asked you to research customer preferences and to recommend a pricing policy. It costs considerably more to have trains depart as frequently as 10 minutes apart, so a cost-based pricing schedule will result in ticket prices that are considerably higher than alternative modes of transportation.

REQUIRED

(a) In addition to customer preferences, what information would you like to gather before recommending a pricing policy? Explain why each item you list is relevant.

(b) Explain why it is important to understand customer preferences before building the system.

(c) Is the need to consider customer preferences different for this organisation than for another type of entity? Why?

5.29 **Market-based price (elasticity formula); uncertainties** Hanson & Daughters produces a premium label apple juice to wholesalers at a current price of $7 per 5-litre container. Costs for a recent month, in which 100 000 5-litre containers were produced and sold, are shown below:

	Variable	Fixed
Materials	$ 10 000	$ 0
Labour	20 000	40 000
Factory overhead	10 000	80 000
Selling and administration	10 000	100 000
Total	$50 000	$ 220 000

Hanson & Daughters' customers are loyal. Recently, a 10 per cent increase in wholesale price resulted in only a 10 per cent decrease in litres sold.

REQUIRED

(a) Calculate the price elasticity of demand.

(b) Calculate the profit-maximising price.

(c) Explain why the management of Hanson & Daughters cannot be certain that another 10 per cent price increase would cause only another 10 per cent decrease in litres sold.

(d) Provide possible reasons why so many customers were willing to continue purchasing the apple juice when prices increased by 10 per cent. List as many reasons as you can.

(e) Describe the assumptions underlying the profit-maximising price you calculated in part (b). How realistic are these assumptions for Hanson & Daughters? What might occur if these assumptions are not met for Hanson & Daughters?

(f) What would you recommend to Hanson & Daughters concerning its price for apple juice? Explain your reasoning.

5.30 **Cost reduction and market-based prices at a university** Bainbridge University offers an MBA degree that is widely respected around the world. The tuition for the program has always covered the costs of the program until a recent recession increased the sensitivity of students to the cost of tuition. The business school managers decided to freeze the tuition cost for the past few years. The director of the MBA program asked a cost accounting class to act as consultants for the program and to make recommendations on possible ways to reduce costs or to increase tuition. You are part of a student team assigned to this project.

REQUIRED

(a) Is this problem open-ended? Why?

(b) List relevant types of analyses that your team might perform.

(c) Describe the steps you will take as you analyse the program, including the types of information you would like to use.

(d) Explain how you would decide on an appropriate level of tuition.

5.31 Life cycle costing Fancy Fleece developed a new outdoor wear fleece fabric that is both wind and water-resistant, but retains a soft and fuzzy feel. The research and development process was more expensive than Fancy's managers anticipated, and the materials in the fabric are also more expensive than anticipated. The managers believe that if Fancy prices the fleece to cover total costs, no one will buy it. The marketing department held several focus groups with manufacturers who produce and sell winter jackets and pants to determine an appropriate price. The marketing department also surveyed customers who recently purchased fleece jackets to determine the amount of premium they would be willing to pay for a jacket that is both wind- and water-resistant. The marketing department concluded that the new fleece fabric would sell at a price that covers variable costs, but does not cover the total costs of production and development. You have been asked to help the managers decide whether to produce the fleece and how to price it if they do produce it.

REQUIRED
(a) What kind(s) of analysis would you perform for this decision?
(b) Explain whether it would generally be better for Fancy Fleece to use cost-based or market-based pricing.
(c) Identify uncertainties about how much it will cost to produce the fleece. List as many uncertainties as you can.
(d) Explain why the managers of Fancy Fleece cannot be certain that they would be able to sell the polar fleece to cover variable costs.

5.32 Profit effect of price change The accountants at French Perfumery decided to increase the price of a scent called Breezy by 10 per cent, from $6 per bottle to $6.60. French's accountants expect the 10 per cent price increase to reduce unit sales by 20 per cent. Current sales are 200 000 bottles, and total variable costs are $800 000.

REQUIRED
(a) Estimate the pre-tax profit effect of the price change, assuming no effect on the variable cost rate, on total fixed costs or on sales of other products. (*Hint:* Calculate the contribution margin at the old and new prices and volumes.)
(b) How certain can the accountant be that volume will decline 20 per cent if the selling price increases to $6.60? What effect does this uncertainty have on the managers' decision to increase the selling price?

5.33 For-profit versus not-for-profit pricing; setting a market price Suppose the Tasmanian government decided to preserve some beautiful caves in the southwestern part of the state. To defray the cost of preservation, the Tasmanian state tourism managers decided to open the caves to guided tours. To prepare the caves for visitors, vapour locks were built so that the moisture content of the caves would remain stable. The Tasmanian government spent $10 million on the facilities. Now the managers need to decide on a price for the tours.

REQUIRED
(a) Describe how pricing policies in not-for-profit entities are different from pricing policies in for-profit entities.
(b) Use the Internet or other sources to identify current prices for other similar attractions.
(c) What additional information would you gather to evaluate the price?
(d) Do you believe that the volume of tours is likely to be sensitive to the price charged for tours? Why?
(e) The managers of the park department need your price recommendation. Use the information you learned from the preceding analyses to write a memo to the park department recommending a price for the tour. Provide appropriate information for

park department managers to understand your methodology and evaluate the risks associated with your price recommendation.

5.34 Cost-based and market-based pricing; collusion Burton Turner and Short Whittum live in a small town in northern Queensland. They both own petrol stations, and provide fuel and engine repair services for the area. The town is somewhat isolated, and during the wet months it is sometimes difficult to travel to other towns across the often-flooded river. While having coffee one morning, Turner and Whittum discuss the prices they charge for fuel and for repair services. They decide that it would be a good policy if they both set the same prices, because then customers would choose between the two businesses based on the quality of service and the brand name of the petrol.

REQUIRED

(a) What pricing alternatives are available to Turner and Whittum for setting prices? List as many alternatives as you can.
(b) Is this an open-ended problem? Why?
(c) Explore this problem from different perspectives:
    (i) Turner and Whittum
    (ii) customers
    (iii) government officials.
(d) Compare and contrast the legal and ethical issues in this situation. How are they the same? How are they different?
(e) Ignoring possible legal issues, is the proposed pricing policy of Turner and Whittum ethical? Why?
(f) Suppose you are a government official, and you receive an anonymous phone call telling you that Turner and Whittum are charging the same prices for fuel and repair services. How might you monitor the two entities to determine whether their actions are illegal?

5.35 Cost-based pricing in a not-for-profit entity Cairns Legal Services is part of a larger not-for-profit entity (Capricorn Resource Centre) that provides free legal and job placement services and houses a food bank for qualified clients. Last year's costs for 5000 visits to legal services are presented here.

Lawyer's salary	$ 90 000
Part-time secretary	12 000
Miscellaneous supplies	6 000
Paralegals' salaries	70 000
Administrative costs[a]	34 000
Rent[b]	10 000
	$222 000

[a] A portion of the administrative costs of the Cairns Council. These costs have been allocated to programs based upon the salary costs of the program.
[b] A portion of the rent for the Capricorn Resource Centre. Total rent is allocated on the basis of the space occupied by each program.

Expected grants for the next year from the federal government and the Cairns Council have been reduced due to an economic downturn. The organisation's executive director is considering dropping legal services. Eliminating the legal services program will result in a savings of about $4000 in administrative costs. The space vacated by legal services could be used by the food bank, which is presently renting quarters in another building for $8000 a year.

The director decided that individuals receiving legal services from the resource centre are to pay for their services, with exceptions based upon need determined on a case-by-case basis. It is not clear what the director means when he says that clients are to pay for their services.

REQUIRED

(a) If the director means that each person using legal services should pay for his or her own avoidable costs, what minimum fee should be charged on average for a legal service visit?

(b) If the director means that all of the people using legal services should collectively pay for the avoidable costs of the legal services program, what minimum fee should be charged on average for a visit?

(c) If the executive director wants the fee to cover the total costs of the Cairns Legal Services including avoidable and allocated costs, what minimum fee should be charged for a visit?

(d) Suppose the centre begins charging the price you calculated in part (b). What problems might arise if these fees are implemented? Consider whether the price change would affect the client's behaviour, and then how that behaviour change might affect Cairns Legal Services.

(e) Suppose the centre begins charging the price you calculated in part (c). Considering that the price is based on allocated costs, explain why this price might be viewed as arbitrary.

(f) Discuss why a Capricorn director might issue an edict about having clients pay for their services, but not provide guidance about what the edict means.

5.36 Inventory management system; data accuracy; internal controls; estimating benefits

During 2000, automobile parts company Mopar implemented a new inventory management system costing $1.5 million. Mopar, a unit of Daimler-Chrysler, distributed parts from three central and 11 regional warehouses to hundreds of parts dealers. The entity filled orders for approximately 1 million line items per week from an inventory of 280 000 parts for Chrysler, Dodge and Jeep brand vehicles.

Mopar implemented the new system to improve its management of inventory levels. The entity previously maintained inventories based on forecasted demand, but often ran out of some parts and carried inventory levels that were too high for other parts. When a customer ordered a part that was out of stock at a particular warehouse, the entity incurred extra costs to search for the part at other warehouses. If the part was not found, Mopar placed a rush order to have it shipped directly to the customer from one of its 3000 suppliers. When inventory of a part was too high, valuable warehouse space was wasted and the entity incurred unnecessary inventory carrying costs. To reduce these types of problems, the entity had manually tracked data for 100 of the highest-cost and best-selling parts. The managers used measures such as how often a part was out of stock to adjust inventory purchases.

The new inventory system included a database that would track parts at all warehouses as well as suppliers, customers and forecast levels. The system helped managers identify $3.5 million in overstocked inventory. They expected an additional $10 million in annual savings from reduced backorders and rush orders.

Sources: Information from Mopar's website at www.mopar.com; and Xenakis, J 2000, 'How to slash inventory costs,' *cfo.com*, 13 December.

REQUIRED

(a) Is Mopar's new inventory system likely to completely eliminate out-of-stock occurrences? Why?

(b) Discuss whether it would be beneficial for Mopar to institute a JIT inventory management system.

(c) Benefits from Mopar's new system depend on the accuracy of data in its inventory database. Identify possible reasons why the data may be inaccurate.

(d) Describe possible internal controls that could prevent or detect and correct inaccuracies in Mopar's inventory database.

(e) Mopar's managers expected to achieve $10 million in annual savings from reduced backorders and rush orders. Suppose you are asked to develop an estimate of these savings. How might you go about making the estimate? Why types of data would you use? What types of assumptions would you need to make?

REFERENCES

1 Schonberger, RJ 1996, *World class manufacturing: the next decade,* The Free Press, New York.

2 Source: Frost, S 2001, 'Australian auto workers halt A$17 billion industry' *ALU,* issue no. 40, July–September.

3 Ip, G 2001, 'Risky business', *Wall Street Journal,* 24 October, p. A1.

4 Six Sigma, a registered trademark of Motorola, Inc., is a system for measuring defects and improving quality.

5 As defined by the US Department of Commerce in 1994.

6 See Ittner, C & Larcker, D 1995, 'Total quality management and the choice of information and reward systems', *Journal of Accounting Research,* vol. 33, pp. 1–34.

7 Source: South Australian State Government Minister for Health 1995, media release, 1 February, Adelaide.

8 See Merrick, A 2000, 'Bridgestone tire issue clouds labor negotiations', *Wall Street Journal* (eastern edn), 1 September, p. A4.

9 Goldratt, EM 1990, *The haystack syndrome, sifting information out of the data ocean,* Croton-on-Hudson, North River Press, New York.

10 Corbett, T 1995, *'Throughput accounting',* North River Press, New York.

11 Corbett, T 1999, 'Making better decisions', *CMA Management,* November, pp. 33–7. The complete article can be found in the chapter 15 article at the end of this book.

12 Gupta, M, Baxendale, S & McMamara, K 1997, 'Integrating TOC and ABCM in a health care company', *Journal of Cost Management,* August, pp. 23–33.

13 Kroll, K 1997, 'On target', *Industry Week,* 9 June, pp. 14–22.

14 'Quarterly financial results,' news release, January 2004, available at www.caterpillar.com, click on 'Investor Information'.

15 Kahn, M 2004, 'Consumer non-cyclicals may cycle higher,' *Barron's Online,* 9 February.

16 *Survey of American manufacturers* 1992, Grant Thornton, New York; and Mochtar, K & Arditi, D 2001, 'Pricing strategy in the US construction industry,' *Construction Management and Economics,* July, pp. 405–15.

17 Shim E & Sudit, E 1995, 'How manufacturers price products,' *Management Accounting,* February.

18 Australian Competition and Consumer Commission 2001, 'ACCC calls for stronger criminal sanctions including jail sentences for price-fixing offences under Trade Practices Act', media release MR 131/01, 8 June, www.acc.gov.au.

19 Krishnan, R 2002, 'Anti-dumping action: steel industry's bane,' *Hindu Business Line* (Internet publication), 20 January.

6

Cost–volume–profit (CVP) analysis

IN BRIEF

Managers need to estimate future revenues, costs and profits to help them plan and monitor operations. They use cost–volume–profit (CVP) analysis to identify the levels of operating activity needed to avoid losses, achieve targeted profits, plan future operations and monitor organisational performance. Managers also need to analyse operational risk as they choose an appropriate cost structure.

After studying this chapter, you should be able to:

1	Understand cost–volume–profit (CVP) analysis and its use in decision making.
2	Understand the breakeven point.
3	Undertake CVP calculations for a single product.
4	Undertake CVP calculations for multiple products.
5	Outline the assumptions and limitations that managers should consider when using CVP analysis.
6	Understand the use of margin of safety and operating leverage to assess operational risk.
7	Perform CVP analysis with the use of a spreadsheet.

Telecommunications cost structure: Hutchison chases breakeven

Like some other industries, the telecommunications industry faces cost structure issues partly caused by the need for high infrastructure investment, partly caused by the changing technologies and partly caused by financing costs. A recent case in point is Hutchison Telecommunications, the owner of the 3 mobile brand. In 2003 Hutchison launched Australia's first third-generation W-CDMA network, the advanced higher-speed 3G system designed as a replacement for the ageing 2G network. It provided customers with high-speed access to a range of multimedia content including mobile TV, video calling, enhanced messaging services and high-value voice calling (Hutchison 2006). Hutchison Telecommunications' move to profitability has been delayed by about a year after it decided to subsidise the estimated $100 million cost of shifting 400 000 subscribers from its Orange network to its third-generation (3G) mobile network. Hutchison increased its accumulated losses to $2.15 billion in 2005 after recording a net loss of $547 million in the 12 months to December. Chief executive Kevin Russell said Hutchison had met its target of achieving positive earnings before interest, tax, depreciation and amortisation on a monthly basis by January 2006 but that was before the cost of internally upgrading 2G customers to its 3G network.

Analysts have estimated it will cost Hutchison about $100 million to transfer its 2G customers to 3G through subsidised handsets.

'When we set off on this path about five years ago,' Mr Russell said, 'we said we would probably need about $3 billion of funding for 3 and 3G to be break even and I think we're going to be there or thereabouts. That commitment and that number hasn't really changed.'

He said that once Hutchison moved past the break-even point, profits would improve significantly. This is more likely to occur in an environment of high relative fixed costs like infrastructure, technology, and financing costs; and when the cost linked to serving each individual customer (the variable costs) is relatively low.

Sources: Information from Boyd, T 2006, 'Break-even point remains a big call', *Australian Financial Review*, 8 March; Hogan, J 2006, 'Big interest bill worries Hutchison', *The Age*, 24 August; Hutchison 2006, www.hutchison.com.au.

Issues from this scene setter to look for in the chapter include:

- The important differences between fixed and variable costs.

- The impact of different cost structures on breakeven calculations, such as the high fixed costs experienced by Hutchison compared to an industry with lower fixed costs but higher relative variable costs.

- The importance of breakeven calculations as part of the planning process.

- The assumptions underlying breakeven calculations.

- How breakeven data can be used to assist decision making.

Cost–volume–profit (CVP) analysis

Cost–volume–profit (CVP) analysis is a technique that examines changes in profits in response to changes in sales volumes, costs and prices. Accountants often perform CVP analysis to plan future levels of operating activity and provide information about:
- which products or services to emphasise
- the volume of sales needed to achieve a targeted level of profit
- the amount of revenue required to avoid losses
- whether to increase fixed costs
- how much to budget for discretionary expenditures
- whether fixed costs expose the organisation to an unacceptable level of risk.

Profit equation and contribution margin

CVP analysis begins with the basic profit equation.

$$\textbf{Profit = Total revenue – Total costs}$$

Separating costs into variable and fixed categories (recall our discussion of fixed and variable costs in chapter 2), we can express profit as:

$$\textbf{Profit = Total revenue – (Total variable costs + Total fixed costs)}$$

or

$$\textbf{Profit = (Total revenue – Total variable costs) – Total fixed costs}$$

The **contribution margin** is total revenue minus total variable costs. Similarly, the **contribution margin per unit** is the selling price per unit minus the variable cost per unit. Both contribution margin and contribution margin per unit are valuable tools when considering the effects of volume on profit. Contribution margin per unit tells us how much revenue from each unit sold can be applied toward fixed costs. Once enough units have been sold to cover all fixed costs, then the contribution margin per unit from all remaining sales becomes profit.

If we assume that the selling price and variable cost per unit are constant, then total revenue is equal to price times quantity, and total variable cost is variable cost per unit times quantity. We then rewrite the profit equation in terms of the contribution margin per unit.

$$\textbf{Profit} = [(P - V) \times Q] - F$$

where P = Selling price per unit
        V = Variable cost per unit

$(P - V)$ = Contribution margin per unit
Q = Quantity of product sold (units of goods or services)
F = Total fixed costs

Breakeven point

Managers often want to know the level of activity required to break even (the point at which total revenue is equal to total costs) as it shows the lower limit of profit when setting prices and determining margins. A CVP analysis can be used to determine the **breakeven point**, or level of operating activity at which revenues cover all fixed and variable costs, resulting in zero profit. We can calculate the breakeven point for any CVP formula by setting profit to zero. Depending on how the formula is set up, we calculate the breakeven point in either number of units or in total revenues.

To determine the breakeven point in number of units, we restate the profit equation as follows:

Fixed costs ÷ Contribution margin per unit = Units to break even

To calculate the breakeven point in sales dollars, we must first calculate the contribution margin ratio. The **contribution margin ratio (CMR)** is the percentage by which the selling price (or revenue) per unit exceeds the variable cost per unit; alternatively, it is the contribution margin as a percentage of revenue.

Contribution margin per unit ÷ Sales price per unit = contribution margin ratio

The CVP equation is adapted to calculate the breakeven point in total revenue by dividing the fixed costs by the contribution margin ratio as follows:

Fixed costs ÷ Contribution margin ratio = Total revenue to break even

CVP analysis for a single product

To illustrate CVP analysis for a single product, let us look at an entity, Mount Dandenong Bikes. Due to the increasing popularity of cross-country cycling, the management of Mount Dandenong Bikes wants to produce a new mountain bike called Mount Dandenong Bike III. After discussions with the sales and production teams, management has forecast the following information.

Price per bike	=	$800
Variable cost per bike	=	$300
Fixed costs related to bike production	=	$5 500 000
Targeted pre-tax profit	=	$300 000
Targeted post-tax profit	=	$210 000
Tax rate	=	30%

Calculating breakeven in units and total revenue

The managers of Mount Dandenong Bikes would be interested in using the breakeven data to assess the riskiness of the venture; that is, to calculate (based on sales forecasts) how profitable the bike will be for the entity. The risk can be assessed by comparing the sales forecast to the breakeven sales. Breakeven quantity in units for Mount Dandenong Bike III is calculated as follows:

Breakeven quantity = $5 500 000 ÷ ($800 − $300) = 11 000 bikes

The breakeven point shows the managers of Mount Dandenong that the entity needs to sell 11 000 bikes to recover both the fixed and variable costs. For every bike sold, a $500 contribution margin ($800 sales price less $300 variable cost per unit) is generated to contribute towards fixed costs only, as profit is considered to be zero in this scenario. Therefore, the 11 000 bikes will generate a total contribution margin of $5 500 000 (11 000 bikes times $500) which covers the fixed costs. For Mount Dandenong Bikes to generate a profit, sales would need to exceed 11 000 bikes.

The breakeven point can also be calculated to give the total revenue required to cover both fixed and variable costs. To calculate breakeven revenues needed for the Mount Dandenong Bike III, we must first calculate the contribution margin ratio (CMR) as follows:

$$\text{CMR} = (\$800 - \$300) \div \$800 = 0.625$$

A contribution margin ratio of 0.625 means that 62.5 per cent of the revenue from each bike sold contributes first to fixed costs and then to profit after fixed costs are covered. Conversely, 37.5 cents per sales dollar contributes towards variable costs. Dividing the fixed costs by the contribution margin ratio enables the determination of breakeven sales revenue. It can be seen that revenue of $8 800 000 is required to break even:

$$\text{Sales revenue to break even} = \$5\,500\,000 \div 0.625 = \$880\,000$$

Proof:	Revenue (11 000 bikes × $800)	$8 800 000
	Variable costs (11 000 bikes × $300)	3 300 000
	Contribution margin	5 500 000
	Fixed costs	5 500 000
	Profit	$ 0

Achieving a targeted pre-tax profit

Although knowledge of the breakeven point is important to measure risk, an entity would want to earn a profit to enable funds to be available for working capital and investment. In the case of Mount Dandenong Bikes, the managers want to earn $300 000 pre-tax profit. In order to achieve this goal, Mount Dandenong Bikes would need to sell more than 11 000 bikes. Any bike sold in excess of the breakeven quantity will generate a $500 contribution margin per bike that goes straight to profit because fixed costs have already been covered at breakeven sales. We determine the quantity of Mount Dandenong Bike III needed to be sold to achieve the targeted profit by incorporating the $300 000 targeted profit into the CVP formula as follows:

$$\text{Quantity} = (\$5\,500\,000 + \$300\,000) \div (\$800 - \$300) = 11\,600 \text{ bikes}$$

Therefore, in order to generate the $300 000 pre-tax profit, Mount Dandenong Bikes will need to sell 11 600 bikes. This is 600 bikes above breakeven sales. Each bike will generate an additional $500 contribution margin, totalling $300 000 (600 bikes × $500).

The contribution margin ratio of 62.5 per cent can also be used to determine the sales revenue of the bikes needed for the targeted profit by using the contribution margin ratio as follows:

$$\text{Sales revenue} = (\$5\,500\,000 + \$300\,000) \div 0.625 = \$9\,280\,000$$

Mount Dandenong Bikes must increase sales by $480 000 (600 bikes times $800) beyond breakeven sales of $8 800 000 to generate the $300 000 pre-tax profit.

Proof:	Revenue (11 600 bikes × $800)	$9 280 000
	Variable costs (11 600 bikes × $300)	3 480 000
	Contribution margin	5 800 000
	Fixed costs	5 500 000
	Pre-tax profit	$ 300 000

With this information the managers of Mount Dandenong Bikes would now go back to their sales team to determine whether this level of sales is achievable. The managers are pleased when the sales team reports back that they have forecasted sales of 12 000 units.

Looking at after-tax profit

Sometimes, profit may be shown as an after tax amount. In order to undertake the CVP analysis, it is necessary to convert the after-tax amount to a pre-tax amount. If we want to know the amount of pre-tax profit needed to achieve a targeted level of after-tax profit, we solve the following formula for pre-tax profit:

$$\textbf{Pre-tax profit} = \frac{\textbf{After-tax profit}}{(\textbf{1} - \textbf{Tax rate})}$$

Going back to our example, Mount Dandenong Bikes plans for an after-tax profit of $210 000 and its tax rate is 30 per cent, so

$$\textbf{Pre-tax profit} = \textbf{\$210 000} \div (\textbf{1} - \textbf{0.30}) = \textbf{\$300 000}$$

The entity needs a pre-tax profit of $300 000 to earn an after-tax profit of $210 000.

Cost–volume–profit (CVP) graph

A **cost–volume–profit graph** (or **CVP graph**) shows the relationship between total revenues and total costs; it illustrates how an organisation's profits are expected to change under different volumes of activity. Figure 6.1 presents a CVP graph for Mount Dandenong Bike III.

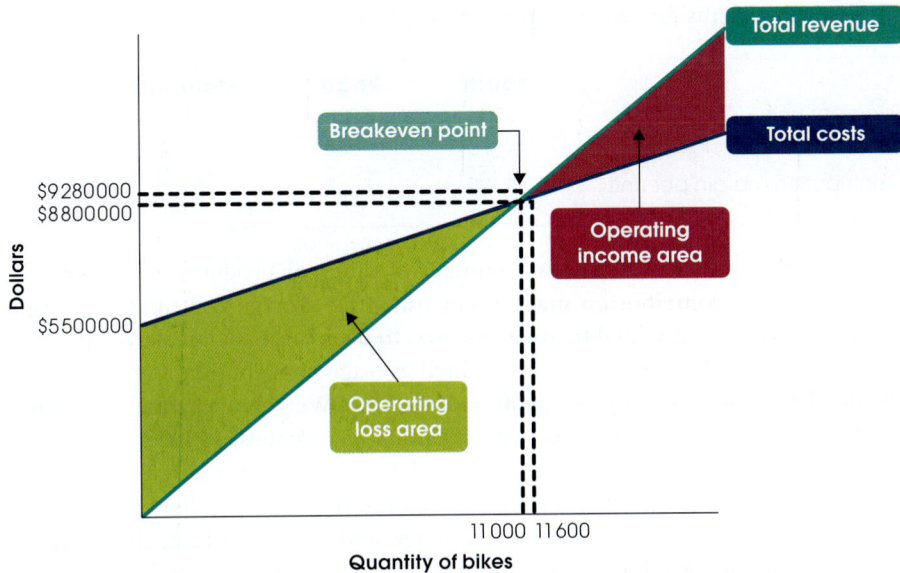

FIGURE 6.1 ■ Graph for Mount Dandenong Bike's Mount Dandenong Bike III

Notice that when no bikes are sold, fixed costs are $5 500 000, resulting in a loss of $5 500 000. As sales volume increases, the loss decreases by the contribution margin for each bike sold. The cost and revenue lines intersect at the breakeven point of 11 000, which means zero loss and zero profit. At this point total revenue and costs equal $8 800 000. Then, as sales increase beyond this breakeven point, we see an increase in profit, growing by the $500 contribution margin pre-tax and $350 contribution margin post-tax for each bike sold. Post-tax profits achieve the targeted level of $210 000 when sales volume reaches 11 600 (600 bikes above breakeven sales times $350 after tax contribution margin per bike).

CVP analysis for multiple products

Many organisations sell a combination of different products or services. The **sales mix** is the proportion of different products or services that an organisation sells. To use CVP in the case of multiple products or services, we assume a constant sales mix in addition to the other CVP assumptions that are discussed on page 218.

Let us resume our example of Mount Dandenong Bikes. In order to broaden its customer base, Mount Dandenong's design team has developed two products to complement its mountain bike range: a small road bike for children (Mount Dandenong Bike I) and a bike for youth (Mount Dandenong Bike II). The increased production will increase the total fixed costs for the entity to $14 700 000. Forecasted sales volumes for each bike are as follows. The sales mix in percentages is calculated from these volumes.

	Youth	Road	Mountain	Total
Forecasted volume (units)	10 000	18 000	12 000	40 000
Expected sales mix (units)	25%	45%	30%	100%

Because of increased competition and an economic downturn, the managers of Mount Dandenong Bikes are uncertain about the entity's ability to achieve the forecasted level of sales. They would like to know the minimum amount of sales needed for an after-tax profit of $100 000. The entity's income tax rate is 30 per cent. The expected unit selling prices, variable costs and contribution margins for each product are as follows:

	Youth	Road	Mountain
Price per unit	$200	$700	$800
Variable cost per unit	75	250	300
Contribution margin per unit	$ 125	$450	$500

When an organisation produces and sells a number of different products or services, we use the **weighted average contribution margin per unit** (the average contribution margin per unit for multiple products weighted by the sales mix) to determine the breakeven point or targeted profit in units. Similarly, we use the weighted average contribution margin ratio to determine the breakeven point or targeted profit in revenues. 'Weighted average' here refers to the expected sales mix: 10 000 youth bikes or $2 000 000 in revenues, 18 000 road bikes or $12 600 000 in revenues, and 12 000 mountain bikes or $9 600 000 in revenues. The weighted average contribution margin per unit is calculated by multiplying the individual product's contribution margin by its relative sales mix percentage and then summing the weighted contribution margin for each product. As can be seen on the following page, the weighted average contribution margin for the three bikes is $383.75.

	Youth	Road	Mountain
Contribution margin per unit	$125	$450	$500
Sales mix	25%	45%	30%
Weighted average contribution (Contribution margin × Sales mix)	$31.25	$202.50	$150
Weighted average contribution margin = $383.75			

Alternatively, the weighted average contribution margin per unit is calculated as the combined total contribution margin for all products ($15 350 000) divided by the total number of units expected to be sold (40 000), or $383.75 per unit. The **weighted average contribution margin ratio** is the combined contribution margin ($15 350 000) divided by combined revenue ($24 200 000), or 63.43 per cent; alternatively, it can be calculated by dividing the contribution margin per unit by the weighted average selling price:

Weighted average contribution margin ratio

$$= \frac{\$383.75}{(\$200 \times 0.25) + (\$700 \times 0.45) + (\$800 \times 0.30)}$$

$$= 63.43\%$$

To achieve a targeted after-tax profit of $100 000, the entity must earn a pre-tax profit of $142 857 [$100 000 ÷ (1 − 0.30)]. To compute the total number of units (bikes) that must be sold to achieve the targeted profit, we divide the fixed costs plus the targeted profit by the weighted average contribution margin per unit:

$$\text{Units needed for target profit} = Q = \frac{F + \text{Profit}}{(P - V)} = \frac{\$14\,700\,000 + \$142\,857}{\$383.75 \text{ per unit}} = 38\,678 \text{ units}$$

Therefore, Mount Dandenong Bikes needs to sell 38 678 units to achieve a targeted after-tax profit of $100 000. To determine the number of units for each product that must be sold, we multiply the total number of units (38 678) by each product's expected sales mix. For example, the entity must sell 38 678 units × 25 per cent, or 9670 youth bikes.

To calculate the amount of revenue needed to achieve the targeted after-tax profit of $100 000, we divide the fixed costs plus the targeted pre-tax profit by the weighted average contribution margin ratio:

$$\text{Revenues} = \frac{F + \text{Profit}}{\text{CMR}} = \frac{\$14\,700\,000 + \$142\,857}{63.43\%} = \$23\,400\,373$$

To determine the revenues for each product that must be sold, we multiply the total revenues ($23 400 373) by each product's expected revenue mix. For example, the entity must achieve $23 400 373 × ($2 000 000 ÷ $24 200 000), or $1 933 914 in revenues from youth bikes. Notice that the required revenue for each product is equal to the required number of units times the expected selling price. For youth bikes, 9670 units × $200 per unit = $1 934 000.

The results of calculations using units and revenues are always identical. However, in some situations per-unit information is not available. In those cases, it is necessary to perform CVP calculations using revenues.

Spreadsheets are often used for CVP computations, particularly when an organisation has multiple products. Spreadsheets simplify the basic computations and can be designed to show how changes in volumes, selling prices, costs or sales mix alter the results. The CVP analysis for Mount Dandenong Bikes products using a spreadsheet is shown in appendix 6A of this chapter.

Discretionary expenditure decision

CVP analysis also helps managers make business decisions such as whether to increase or decrease discretionary expenditures. For example, suppose the managers of Mount Dandenong Bikes want to advertise one of their products more heavily. A distributor pointed out that the road bike price was less than a competitor's price for a model with fewer features. The competitor's brand name is quite well known, but the distributor thinks that she could sell at least 10 per cent more road bikes if Mount Dandenong launched a regional advertising campaign.

The managers of Mount Dandenong estimate that an additional expenditure of $100 000 in advertising will increase road bike sales by 5 per cent, to 18 900 bikes. First, fixed costs would increase by $100 000 to $14 800 000. Second, the expected volume of road bikes sold would increase to 18 900. After-tax profits are expected to increase by $213 500, from $455 000 to $668 500. The change in sales mix affects the weighted average contribution margin; it changes from 383.75 to $385.21.

This can also be calculated by subtracting the $100 000 investment in fixed costs from the additional contribution margin of $405 000 [900 bikes × ($700 − $250)]. The resulting incremental after-tax profit is $213 500 [($405 000 − $100 000)(1 − 0.30)]. Because profits are expected to increase more than costs for this advertising campaign, the managers would be likely to make the additional investment.

Assumptions and limitations of CVP analysis

CVP analysis relies on forecasts of expected revenues and costs. CVP assumptions rule out fluctuations in revenues or costs that might be caused by common business factors such as supplier volume discounts, learning curves, changes in production efficiency or special customer discounts. In addition, many uncertainties may arise about whether CVP assumptions will be violated, such as the following:

- Can volume of operating activity be achieved?
- Will selling prices increase or decrease?
- Will sales mix remain constant?
- Will fixed or variable costs change as operations move into a new relevant range?
- Will costs change due to unforeseen causes?
- Are revenue and cost estimates biased?

All entities are subject to uncertainties, leading to the risk that they will fail to meet expectations.

Even though each organisation is subject to unique business risks, all entities face uncertainties related to the economic environment. Some organisations are subject to more uncertainty than others. For example, uncertainties are greater in industries experiencing rapid technological and market change or intense competition.

Margin of safety and degree of operating leverage

In Mount Dandenong Bikes, the managers used CVP information to help learn how much the volume of business could decline before the entity would incur a loss. CVP analysis looking at the sales mix was useful in identifying the specific products to emphasise for increased profitability. Managers are often interested in these types of questions. In addition, information from CVP analysis can be used to help manage operational risk. **Operational risk** relates to the risk of loss resulting from inadequate or failed internal processes, people and systems, or external events.

Margin of safety

The **margin of safety** is the excess of an organisation's expected future sales (in either revenue or units) above the breakeven point. The margin of safety indicates the amount by which sales could drop before profits reach the breakeven point:

$$\text{Margin of safety in units} =$$
$$\text{Actual or estimated units of activity} - \text{Units at breakeven point}$$

$$\text{Margin of safety in revenues} =$$
$$\text{Actual or estimated revenue} - \text{Revenue at breakeven point}$$

The margin of safety is computed using actual or estimated sales values, depending on the purpose. To evaluate future risk when planning, use estimated sales. To evaluate actual risk when monitoring operations, use actual sales. If the margin of safety is small, managers may put more emphasis on reducing costs and increasing sales to avoid potential losses. A larger margin of safety gives managers more confidence in making plans such as incurring additional fixed costs.

The **margin of safety percentage** is the margin of safety divided by actual or estimated sales, in either units or revenues. This percentage indicates the extent to which sales can decline before profits become zero.

$$\text{Margin of safety percentage in units} = \frac{\text{Margin of safety in units}}{\text{Actual or estimated units}}$$

$$\text{Margin of safety percentage in revenues} = \frac{\text{Margin of safety in revenue}}{\text{Actual or estimated revenue}}$$

When the original budget was created for Mount Dandenong Bikes, the breakeven point was calculated as 11 000 bikes, or $8 800 000 in revenues. However, the managers expect 12 000 mountain bikes to be sold, generating $9 600 000 in revenue. Their margin of safety in units of mountain bikes is 1000 (12 000 – 11 000) and in revenues is $800 000 ($9 600 000 – $8 800 000). Their margin of safety percentage is 8.3 per cent (being 1000 ÷ 12 000, or $800 000 ÷ $9 600 000). In other words, sales volume could drop 8.3 per cent from expected levels before the entity expects to incur a loss.

Degree of operating leverage

Managers decide how to structure the cost function for their organisations. Often, potential trade-offs are made between fixed and variable costs. For example, an entity could purchase a vehicle (a fixed cost) or it could lease a vehicle under a contract that charges a rate per kilometre driven (a variable cost). One of the major disadvantages of fixed costs is that they may be difficult to reduce quickly if activity levels fail to meet expectations, thereby increasing the organisation's risk of incurring losses.

The **degree of operating leverage** is the extent to which the cost function is made up of fixed costs. Organisations with high operating leverage incur more risk of loss when sales decline. Conversely, when operating leverage is high, an increase in sales (once fixed costs are covered) contributes quickly to profit. (The chapter 6 article at the end of this book discusses how Air Asia is to compete in the market with a low fixed-cost structure.) The formula for operating leverage can be written in terms of either contribution margin or fixed costs, as shown here.

$$\text{Degree of operating leverage in terms of contribution margin} = \frac{\text{Contribution margin}}{\text{Profit}}$$

$$= \frac{\text{Total revenue (TR)} - \text{Total variable costs (TVC)}}{\text{Profit}} = \frac{(P-V) \times Q}{\text{Profit}}$$

$$\text{Degree of operating leverage in terms of fixed costs} = \frac{F}{\text{Profit}} + 1$$

Managers use the degree of operating leverage to gauge the risk associated with their cost function and to explicitly calculate the sensitivity of profits to changes in sales (units or revenues):

% change in profit = % change in sales × Degree of operating leverage

For Mount Dandenong Bikes, the variable cost per mountain bike is $300 and the fixed costs are $5 500 000. With budgeted sales of 12 000, the managers expected to earn a pre-tax profit of $500 000 (1000 bikes × $500). The expected degree of operating leverage using the contribution margin formula is then calculated as follows:

$$\text{Degree of operating leverage} = \frac{(\$800 - \$300) \times 12\,000\,\text{bikes}}{\$500\,000} = \frac{\$6\,000\,000}{\$500\,000} = 12$$

We arrive at the same answer of 12 if we use the fixed cost formula:

$$\text{Degree of operating leverage} = \frac{\$5\,500\,000}{\$500\,000} + 1 = 11 + 1 = 12$$

The degree of operating leverage and margin of safety percentage are reciprocals.

$$\text{Margin of safety percentage} = \frac{1}{\text{Degree of operating leverage}}$$

$$\text{Degree of operating leverage} = \frac{1}{\text{Margin of safety percentage}}$$

If the margin of safety percentage is small, then the degree of operating leverage is large. In addition, the margin of safety percentage is smaller as the fixed cost portion of total cost gets larger. As the level of operating activity increases above the breakeven point, the margin of safety increases and the degree of operating leverage decreases. For Mount Dandenong Bikes, the reciprocal of the margin of safety percentage is 12 (1 ÷ 0.0833). The reciprocal of the degree of operating leverage is 0.0833 (1 ÷ 12).

Using the degree of operating leverage to plan and monitor operations

Managers need to consider the degree of operating leverage when they decide whether to incur additional fixed costs, such as purchasing new equipment or hiring new employees. They also need to consider the degree of operating leverage for potential new products and services that could increase an organisation's fixed costs relative to variable costs. If additional fixed costs cause the degree of operating leverage to reach what they consider an unacceptably high level, managers often use variable costs — such as temporary labour — rather than additional fixed costs to meet their operating needs.

For example, the managers of Mount Dandenong Bikes have been looking at restructuring their sales team — instead of employing them on a full-time basis, to subcontract them and pay commission at $50 per bike sold. This would lead to a reduction in the payroll of $200 000 per annum. The new cost function would be

TC = ($5 500 000 − $200 000) + ($300 + $50)Q = $5 300 000 + $350Q

Fixed costs would reduce by $200 000 to $5 300 000 due to the saving in salary costs, and the variable costs would increase by $50 to $350 due to the sales commission per bike. Due to the change in cost structure, the breakeven point increases considerably to 11 778 (rounded) mountain bikes [$5 300 000 ÷ ($800 − $350) per bike] or $9 422 400. Given planned sales of 12 000 mountain bikes, the pre-tax profit will be $99 900 (222 bikes × $450). Management would not be pleased with this outcome as the pre-tax profit falls from $500 000 to $99 900.

However, is this strategy more favourable at another level of sales? This can be determined by calculating the point of indifference. An **indifference point** is the level of activity at which equal cost or profit occurs across multiple alternatives. To provide the managers of Mount Dandenong Bikes with additional information as they consider changing the cost structure, the management accountant calculates the indifference point. Using the budgeted assumptions, the management accountant sets the two cost functions equal to each other and then solves for Q as follows:

$$\$5\,500\,000 + \$300Q = \$5\,300\,000 + \$350Q$$

$$\$200\,000 = \$50Q$$

$$Q = 4000$$

At the sales level of 4000, each strategy incurs the same level of expenditure of $6 700 000. When sales are fewer than 4000, Mount Dandenong Bike's profit will be greater using more variable cost. When sales exceed 4000, the entity is better off using more fixed costs. As Mount Dandenong Bike's breakeven point is considerably higher than this, the strategy to employ the sales personnel on a commission basis would not be in the entity's best interest.

To further reinforce the concepts discussed above, we will now look at comprehensive example 1, which involves the Small Animal Clinic.

Comprehensive example 1

CVP analysis

Lucy Brown, Small Animal Clinic manager, and the accountant, Josh Hardy, are completing the operating budget for 2009. Lucy estimated that the clinic will experience 3800 animal visits, and Josh estimated the cost function as follows:

$$\text{TC} = \$119\,009 + \$16.40Q$$

We can see that estimated total fixed costs are $119 009, with variable costs increasing at the rate of $16.40 per animal visit. Lucy and Josh budgeted revenue per animal visit at $60 ($30 in fees plus $30 in matching grant), giving a contribution margin of $43.60 ($60 − $16.40). Thus, they estimated that the clinic should achieve a surplus of $46 671 [($60)(3800) − $119 009 − ($16.40)(3800)] or [($43.60 × 3800) − $119 009]. The clinic is a not-for-profit entity and pays no income taxes on its surplus.

To complete the planning process for next year, Lucy asks Josh to compute the clinic's breakeven point. As manager of a not-for-profit entity, she is particularly sensitive to financial risk and wants to know how much the clinic's activity levels could drop before a loss would occur.

Compared breakeven to budget

Josh performs the following calculations to compute the breakeven point. With revenue per visit of $60 and variable cost per visit of $16.40, the contribution margin per animal visit is $43.60. Josh solves for Q with profit equal to $0 to find the breakeven point in number of animal visits:

$$Q = \frac{F + \text{Profit}}{(P - V)} = \frac{(\$119\,009 + \$0)}{\$43.60} = 2730 \text{ visits}$$

The breakeven visits for the clinic is therefore 2730. Lucy is pleased to see that the budgeted number of animal visits (3800) is significantly higher than the breakeven number. This result gives her considerable assurance that the clinic is not likely to incur a loss, even if revenues fail to achieve targeted levels or if costs exceed estimated amounts.

Potential investment in new equipment

During the first two months of 2009, Lucy learns that the number of animal visits at Small Animal Clinic is running approximately 10 per cent higher than the budget, and costs seem to be under control. Lucy thinks that the clinic might be on track for a high surplus this year.

For the past two years, Lucy has been interested in purchasing equipment costing $200 000 to provide low-cost neutering services. This year PAWS, a local charity, offered to pay for half of the equipment cost, but only after the clinic raises the other half of the funds. Currently the clinic has no excess cash because surpluses from prior years were invested in other projects. Thus, the clinic needs to raise $100 000 to receive the PAWS grant. Lucy asks Josh to calculate the number of animal visits needed to achieve a surplus of $100 000.

Calculating and analysing targeted activity level

Josh calculates the expected quantity needed to achieve $100 000 surplus as follows:

$$Q = \frac{F + \text{Profit}}{P - V} = \frac{\$119\,009 + \$100\,000}{\$60.00 - \$16.40} = \frac{\$219\,009}{\$43.60} = 5024 \text{ animal visits}$$

He then calculates the total dollar amount of revenue needed:

$$\text{Revenues} = \frac{F + \text{Profit}}{(P - V)/P} = \frac{\$119\,009 + \$100\,000}{\$43.60/\$60.00} = \$310\,389$$

Josh tells Lucy that the clinic will need to earn $301 389 in revenues or 5024 visits to achieve a surplus of $100 000. However, can the clinic achieve this level of visits?

The budgeted level of activity (3800 animal visits) is substantially higher than the level of activity needed to break even (2730 animal visits). If animal visits continue to exceed this year's budget by 10 per cent, Josh estimates that animal visits will reach 4180 (3800 × 1.10) by year-end. However, he thinks that it would be very difficult to achieve a targeted surplus of $100 000 (5024 animal visits).

CVP adjusted for change in relevant range

As Josh works on his report, he realises that the clinic's cost function might change if the number of animal visits gets very high. Lucy told him that if animal visits exceed 4000 this year, she will probably hire another technician and need to rent more space and purchase additional equipment. Therefore, Josh's cost function for 5024 visits is wrong. He develops a new cost function assuming that an additional technician, space and equipment will increase fixed costs by about $60 000 per year.

$$\text{TC} = (\$119\,009 + \$60\,000) + \$16.40Q = \$179\,009 + \$16.40Q, \text{ for } Q > 4000$$

Thus, Josh's earlier CVP analysis was incorrect when animal visits exceed 4000. The level of activity needed for a targeted surplus of $100 000 needs to be recalculated:

$$(\$179\,009 + \$100\,000) \div \$43.60 = 6400 \text{ for } Q > 4000$$

Josh notices that an activity level of 6400 animal visits is noticeably higher than the 5024 visits he first calculated. He realises how important it is to adjust for the relevant range when performing CVP analyses.

When Josh shows Lucy the new results, they agree that the clinic cannot raise the funds for new equipment by increasing the number of visits to 6400. Lucy may need to cut costs or seek other ways to pay for the neutering equipment. The additional fixed cost would also require the clinic to have a much higher volume of operations to avoid a loss.

Margin of safety

When the original budget was created for the clinic, the breakeven point was calculated as 2730 animal visits, or $163 800 in revenues. However, Lucy and Josh expected 3800 animal visits, for $228 000 in revenue. Their margin of safety in units of animal visits was 1070 (3800 – 2730) and in revenues was $64 200 ($228 000 – $163 800). Their margin of safety percentage was 28.2 per cent (1070 ÷ 3800, or $64 200 ÷ $228 000). In other words, their sales volume could drop 28.2 per cent from expected levels before they expected to incur a loss. Figure 6.2 provides a CVP graph for this information.

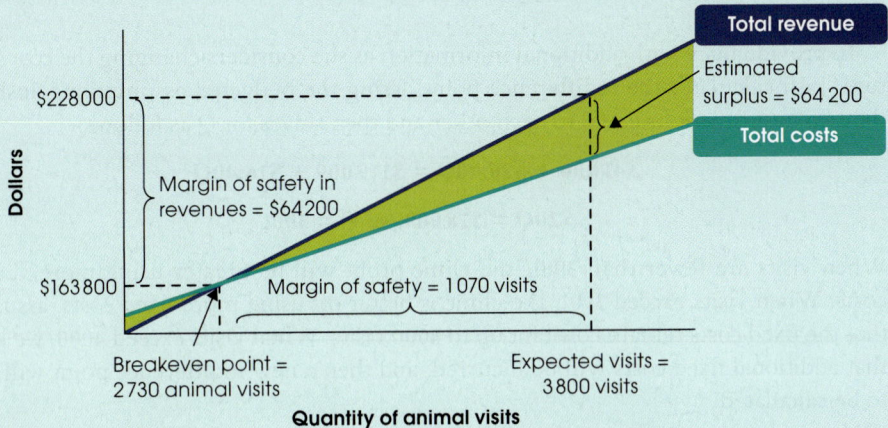

FIGURE 6.2 ■ CVP graph and margin of safety for Small Animal Clinic

Operating leverage

The variable cost per animal visit was $16.40 and the fixed costs were $119 009. With budgeted animal visits of 3800, the managers expected to earn a profit of $46 671.

The expected degree of operating leverage using the contribution margin formula is then calculated as follows:

$$\textbf{Degree of operating leverage} = \frac{(\$60 - \$16.40) \times 3800 \text{ visits}}{\$46\,671} = \frac{\$165\,680}{\$46\,671} = 3.55$$

We arrive at the same answer of 3.55 if we use the fixed cost formula:

$$\textbf{Degree of operating leverage} = \frac{\$119\,009}{\$46\,671} + 1 = 2.55 + 1 = 3.55$$

The reciprocal of the margin of safety percentage is 3.55 (1 ÷ 0.282). The reciprocal of the degree of operating leverage is 0.282 (1 ÷ 3.55).

The technicians at the Small Animal Clinic are paid a salary and work 40-hour weeks. Suppose Lucy could hire part-time technicians at $20 per hour instead of hiring full-time technicians at the current salaries of $78 009. If each visit requires about an hour of technician time, the new cost function would be TC = ($119 009 − $78 009) + ($16.40 + $20)Q = $41 000 + $36.40Q. The breakeven point decreases considerably to 1738 animal visits [$41 000 ÷ ($60 − $36.40) per animal visit] or $104 280. Profit at Q = 3800 animal visits is $48 680 [$228 000 − $41 000 − (3800 animal visits × $36.40 per animal visit)]. Operating leverage at 3800 animal visits becomes 1.84 [($41 000 ÷ $48 680) + 1], which is much lower than the 3.55 when technicians are a fixed cost. Although operating leverage improved, the cost for technicians increased from $18.75 per hour [$78 009 ÷ (2 technicians × 2080 hours per technician per year)] to $20 per hour.

The advantage of having technicians as hourly workers is that they can be scheduled only for hours when appointments are also scheduled. When business is slow fewer technician hours are needed, which means less risk of incurring losses if the number of visits drops. Figure 6.3 provides a CVP graph of the two options. Risk decreases considerably when the breakeven point is so much lower. On the other hand, it may be more difficult to hire qualified and dependable technicians unless work hours and pay can be guaranteed.

To provide Lucy with additional information as she considers changing the cost structure, Josh calculates the indifference point. Using the budgeted assumptions, Josh sets the two cost functions equal to each other and then solves for Q as follows:

$$\$41\,000 + \$36.40Q = \$119\,009 + \$16.40Q$$

$$\$20Q = \$78\,009, \text{ so } Q = 3901$$

When visits are fewer than 3901, the clinic profit will be greater using more variable costs. When visits exceed 3901, the clinic is better off using more fixed costs, assuming that the fixed costs remain constant up to 4000 visits. When visits exceed 4000, we know that additional fixed costs will be incurred, and then a new indifference point will need to be calculated.

Notice that the indifference point calculation ignores operational risk. At 3901 animal visits, the clinic is expected to earn the same profit under the two cost-function alternatives. However, the clinic's operational risk is greater for the cost function having higher fixed costs. Therefore, the clinic's manager would not necessarily be indifferent between the two cost functions if 3901 animal visits were expected.

In terms of fixed costs:

$$\text{Degree of operating leverage} = \frac{F}{\text{Profit}} + 1$$

Sensitivity of profits to changes in sales (units or revenues):

$$\text{\% change in profit} = \text{\% change in sales} \times \text{Degree of operating leverage}$$

Relationship between margin of safety and degree of operating leverage:

$$\text{Margin of safety percentage} = \frac{1}{\text{Degree of operating leverage}}$$

Higher operating leverage (lower margin of safety)

Leads to:

- greater risk of loss
- accelerated profits above the breakeven point.

---

7 **Perform CVP analysis with the use of a spreadsheet.**

- Spreadsheets are often used for CVP computations, particularly when an organisation has multiple products.
- The use of spreadsheets enables the decision maker to perform several different types of sensitivity analyses. Sensitivity analysis helps managers explore the potential impact of variations in data they consider to be particularly important or uncertain.

Self-study problems

SELF-STUDY PROBLEM 1

Cost function; targeted profit; margin of safety; operating leverage

Coffee Cart Supreme sells hot and iced coffee beverages, and small snacks. The following is last month's income statement.

Revenue		$5000
Cost of beverages and snacks	$2000	
Cost of napkins, straws etc.	500	
Cost to rent cart	500	
Employee wages	1000	4000
Pre-tax profit		1000
Tax		250
After-tax profit		$ 750

REQUIRED

(a) What is the total cost function for Coffee Cart Supreme?

(b) What is the tax rate for Coffee Cart Supreme?

(c) Calculate the amount of sales needed to reach a targeted after-tax profit of $1500.

(d) What was Coffee Cart Supreme's degree of operating leverage last month?

(e) What was Coffee Cart Supreme's margin of safety in revenue last month?

(f) What was Coffee Cart Supreme's margin of safety percentage last month?

(g) Suppose next month's actual revenues are $8000 and pre-tax profit is $2000. Would actual costs be higher or lower than expected?

(h) Coffee costs are volatile because worldwide coffee production varies from year to year. Explain how this volatility affects the quality of the cost function for Coffee Cart Supreme.

(a) To estimate the cost function, we use judgment to classify costs as fixed, variable or mixed. For a typical retail business, rent and wages are likely to be fixed. We estimate fixed costs as the sum of these two costs ($500 + $1000 = $1500). It seems reasonable that the costs of beverages and snacks ($2000) and napkins, straws etc. ($500) would vary with revenues. We use the revenues as the cost driver to estimate variable costs as $2500 ÷ $5000 = 0.50, or 50 per cent of revenues. Thus, the cost function is

$$\textbf{TC} = \textbf{\$1500} + (\textbf{50\%} \times \textbf{Revenue})$$

(b) We use income tax expense and pre-tax profit from last month to estimate the tax rate:

$$\textbf{Tax rate} = \textbf{Taxes} \div \textbf{Pre-tax profit} = \textbf{\$250} \div \textbf{\$1000} = \textbf{25\%}$$

(c) We first calculate the amount of pre-tax profit needed to achieve an after-tax profit of $1500.

$$\textbf{Targeted pre-tax profit} = \textbf{\$1500} \div (\textbf{1} - \textbf{0.25}) = \textbf{\$2000}$$

The contribution margin ratio is

$$(\textbf{5000} - \textbf{2500}) \div \textbf{5000} = \textbf{0.50 or 50\%}$$

We then perform the CVP calculation for revenues.

$$\textbf{Revenue} = (\textbf{\$1500} + \textbf{\$2000}) \div \textbf{0.50} = \textbf{\$3500} \div \textbf{0.50} = \textbf{\$7000}$$

(d) We use the results of our previous computations to calculate the contribution margin, and we then calculate the degree of operating leverage:

$$\textbf{Contribution margin} = \textbf{\$5000} - \textbf{\$2500} = \textbf{\$2500}$$

$$\textbf{Degree of operating leverage} = \textbf{Contribution margin} \div \textbf{Profit}$$

$$\textbf{Degree of operating leverage} = \textbf{\$2500} \div \textbf{\$1000} = \textbf{2.50}$$

(e) Before calculating the margin of safety, we need to calculate the breakeven point. Note that the margin of safety must be calculated in revenue dollars because we do not have unit or product mix information. The breakeven point is calculated as

$$\textbf{\$1500} \div \textbf{0.50} = \textbf{\$3000 in revenues}$$

Current revenues are $5000, so the margin of safety is calculated as

$$\textbf{Margin of safety} = \textbf{\$5000} - \textbf{\$3000} = \textbf{\$2000}$$

(f) We use the formula to calculate margin of safety percentage:

$$\textbf{Margin of safety percentage} = \textbf{\$2000} \div \textbf{\$5000} = \textbf{40\%}$$

Note that we can check our previous degree of operating leverage computation as follows:

$$\textbf{Degree of operating leverage} = \textbf{1} \div \textbf{Margin of safety percentage} = \textbf{1} \div \textbf{0.40} = \textbf{2.50}$$

(g) The expected and actual costs at $8000 revenue are

$$\textbf{Expected costs} = \textbf{\$1500} + (\textbf{50\%} \times \textbf{\$8000}) = \textbf{\$5500}$$

$$\textbf{Actual costs} = \textbf{\$8000} - \textbf{\$2000} = \textbf{\$6000}$$

Actual costs are $500 higher than expected.

(h) When any costs are volatile, predicting them is problematic. Worldwide coffee prices are uncertain for many reasons, such as weather conditions in coffee growing areas, the ability of farmers to increase crops, and coffee demand patterns. In addition, broader factors such as changes in economies and political upheaval influence costs. All of these factors reduce our ability to develop a cost function that accurately predicts future costs, which means that the quality of the cost function is diminished.

SELF-STUDY PROBLEM 2

Sensitivity analysis

REQUIRED

(a) Why is it important to be able to change the spreadsheet easily to reflect changes in assumptions?

(b) Suppose that Mount Dandenong Bikes adds a helmet to each youth bike sold. The helmets cost $25 each but incorporate new materials and an innovative design that has reduced injuries and deaths from children's bike accidents. Mount Dandenong Bike's managers believe that by advertising the new helmet as part of the youth bike package, sales will increase to 13 000. However, an advertising campaign will need to be undertaken to alert parents to the benefits of the new helmet. How much can the entity afford to spend on advertising and still expect to earn the original after-tax profit of $455 000? Assume the selling price remains at $200 per bike package.

(c) Identify CVP input factors that you believe are uncertain for this decision, and use your judgment to determine a new value for each factor. Reflect these changes in the spreadsheet to see how they affect the breakeven point and profitability. Choose a best-case and worst-case scenario to present to the managers of Mount Dandenong Bikes. Make a list of the points you would include in a memo explaining your sensitivity analysis to the managers.

Solution to self-study problem 2

(a) Accountants and managers will explore changes in more assumptions and vary the values within the spreadsheet more readily if it is easy to do. When these changes are made and the results are analysed, managers better understand how unplanned changes in future operations might affect profitability. This knowledge allows them to more readily evaluate results and adjust operating plans.

(b) Figure 6.7 provides relevant parts of the spreadsheet with the changes.

	A	B	C	D	E
1					
2	**Input section**	Youth bikes	Road bikes	Mtn. bikes	
3	Expected sales volume-units	13,000	18,000	12,000	
4	Price per unit	$200	$700	$800	
5	Variable cost per unit	$100	$250	$300	
6					
7	Fixed costs	$14,700,000			
8	Desired after-tax profit	$100,000	(enter zero for breakeven)		
9	Income tax rate	30%			
10					
11					
12	**Contribution margin**	Youth bikes	Road bikes	Mtn. bikes	Total bikes
13	Units	13,000	18,000	12,000	43,000
14	Revenue	$2,600,000	$12,600,000	$9,600,000	$24,800,000
15	Variable costs	1,300,000	4,500,000	3,600,000	9,400,000
16	Contribution margin	$1,300,000	$8,100,000	$6,000,000	$15,400,000
17					
18	Contrib. margin per unit	$100.00	$450.00	$500.00	$358.14
19	Contrib. margin ratio	50.00%	64.29%	62.50%	62.10%
20					
21	Expected sales mix in units	30.23%	41.86%	27.91%	100.00%
22	Expected sales mix in revenues	10.48%	50.81%	38.71%	100.00%
23					
24	**Expected income**				
25	Contribution margin (above)				$15,400,000
26	Fixed costs				14,700,000
27	Pre-tax income				700,000
28	Income taxes				210,000
29	After-tax income				$490,000

FIGURE 6.7 ■ Spreadsheet for Mount Dandenong Bikes youth helmet decision

With increased sales of youth bikes from 10 000 to 13 000 and an increased variable cost from $75 to $100, expected pre-tax profits increase to $700 000. Comparing $700 000 to $650 000 (figure 6.4 on page 226), Mount Dandenong Bikes can spend up to $50 000 [(490 000 − 455 000) ÷ 0.7] on advertising to maintain its current level of profitability.

(c) Many different scenarios could occur. No single answer is always correct. Your answer depends on the assumptions that you make. Following are some example assumptions for the best and worst cases. Your most likely case should be between these two values.

One best case is that the new strategy is very popular with customers. More than 13 000 of the bikes are sold. The managers discover that customers are willing to pay a higher price for the bike, so they raise the price. In addition, manufacturing efficiency improves with the greater volume, reducing variable cost per unit. Also, fixed costs are lower than expected because the managers found some costs that could be reduced.

One worst case is that the helmets fail to attract customers. In fact, sales fail to meet original expectations; fewer than 10 000 are sold. Because the entity produced extra bikes expecting an increase in demand, the managers lower the selling price to encourage additional sales. In addition, the entity hires extra workers to meet the expected demand, and other costs such as insurance and electricity are higher than expected. These changes caused both the variable and fixed costs to be higher than originally planned.

Your memo to the managers should include the following:
- explain the assumptions for the best case and worst case scenarios
- explain the reasoning behind the most likely case
- ask managers to consider beforehand how they would respond to the best- and worst-case scenarios
- make suggestions for monitoring the results for the youth bike
- encourage the managers to evaluate the advertising and product results, and make suggestions for improving the operation or dropping the new helmet, if plans are unsuccessful.

Questions

6.1 If an entity has a mixed cost function, a 10 per cent increase in sales volume should increase income by more than 10 per cent. Explain why.

6.2 Explain how to calculate a weighted average contribution margin per unit.

6.3 An organisation experiences a 20 per cent increase in pre-tax profits when revenues increase 20 per cent. Assuming linearity, what do you know about the organisation's cost function?

6.4 What is the effect on an entity's breakeven point of a lower income tax rate?

6.5 To estimate revenues, costs and profits across a range of activity, we usually assume that the cost and revenue functions are linear. What are the specific underlying assumptions for linear cost and revenue functions, and how reasonable are these assumptions?

6.6 Explain the relationship between margin of safety percentage and degree of operating leverage.

6.7 How do volume discounts from suppliers affect our assumption that the cost function is linear? Explain how we incorporate this type of cost into a CVP analysis.

6.8 Explain the term *sales mix* in your own words. How does sales mix affect the contribution margin?

6.9 How are CVP analysis and breakeven analysis related?

6.10 Can the margin of safety ever be negative? Explain your answer.

6.11 Describe three uses for CVP analysis.

6.12 Explain how CVP analysis can be used to make decisions about increases in advertising costs.

6.13 Under what circumstances will managers want sensitivity analysis results relating to a CVP analysis?

Exercises

6.14 Targeted profit; not-for-profit breakeven

(a) The variable cost per gift basket is $2, fixed costs are $5000 per month and the selling price of a basket is $7. How many baskets must be produced and sold in a month to earn a pre-tax profit of $1000?

(b) The Community Clinic (a not-for-profit medical clinic) received a lump-sum grant from the City of Sydney of $460 000 this year. The fixed costs of the clinic are expected to be $236 000. The average variable cost per patient visit is expected to be $7.64 and the average fee collected per patient visit is $4.64. What is the breakeven volume in patient visits?

6.15 CVP graph

(a) Create a CVP graph using the information in exercise 6.14, part (a). Explain the information in the graph.

(b) Create a CVP graph using the information in exercise 6.14, part (b). Explain the information in the graph.

6.16 Cost function; breakeven

(a) The average cost per unit was $234 at a volume of 1200 units and $205 at a volume of 1400 units. The profit was $24 000 at the lower volume. Estimate the variable cost per unit.

(b) Sparkle Car Wash Supplier sells a hose washer for $0.25 that it buys from the manufacturer for $0.12. Variable selling costs are $0.02 per hose washer. Breakeven is currently at a sales volume of $10 600 per month. What are the monthly fixed costs associated with the washer?

(c) Monthly fixed costs are $24 000 when volume is at or below 200 units and $36 000 when monthly volume is above 200 units. The variable cost per unit is $200 and the selling price is $300 per unit. What is the breakeven quantity?

6.17 Profit; price for targeted profit The Martell Company has recently established operations in a competitive market. Management has been aggressive in its attempt to establish a market share. The price of the product was set at $5 per unit, well below that of the entity's major competitors. Variable costs were $4.50 per unit, and total fixed costs were $600 000 during the first year.

REQUIRED

(a) Assume that the entity was able to sell 1 million units in the first year. What was the pre-tax profit (loss) for the year?

(b) Assume that the variable cost per unit and total fixed costs do not increase in the second year. Management has been successful in establishing its position in the market. What price must be set to achieve a pre-tax profit of $25 000? Assume that sales remain at 1 million units.

6.18 Cost function; breakeven Data for the most recent three months of operations for the RainBeau Salon are shown overleaf.

	March	April	May
Number of appointments	1 600	1 500	1 900
Hairdresser salaries	$14 000	$14 000	$18 000
Manicurist salaries	12 000	12 000	16 000
Supplies	900	750	950
Utilities	600	480	400
Rent	1 000	1 000	1 000
Miscellaneous	3 500	3 450	3 580
Total costs	$32 000	$31 680	$39 930

A cost-of-living salary increase occurred at the beginning of May.

REQUIRED

(a) What is the total cost function for RainBeau Salon?

(b) If the average fee per appointment is $25, estimate the appointments required in June to break even.

6.19 Breakeven; targeted profit; ROI targeted profit Madden Company projected its income before taxes for next year as shown here. Madden is subject to a 40 per cent income tax rate.

Sales (160 000 units)	$8 000 000
Cost of sales	
Variable costs	2 000 000
Fixed costs	3 000 000
Pre-tax profit	$3 000 000

REQUIRED

(a) What is Madden's breakeven point in units sold for the next year?

(b) If Madden wants $4.5 million in pre-tax profit, what is the required level of sales in dollars?

(c) If Madden's net assets are $36 million, what amount of revenue must be achieved for Madden to earn a 10 per cent after-tax return on assets?

6.20 Breakeven; targeted profit; cost changes; selling price Laraby Company produces a single product. It sold 25 000 units last year with the following results.

Sales	$625 000
Variable costs	375 000
Fixed costs	150 000
Income before taxes	100 000
Income taxes (45%)	45 000
After-tax profit	$ 55 000

In an attempt to improve its product, Laraby's managers are considering replacing a component part that costs $2.50 with a new and better part costing $4.50 per unit during the coming year. A new machine would also be needed to increase plant capacity. The machine would cost $18 000 and have a useful life of six years with no salvage value. The company uses straight-line depreciation on all plant assets.

REQUIRED

(a) What was Laraby Company's breakeven point in units last year?

(b) How many units of product would Laraby Company have had to sell in the past year to earn $77 000 in after-tax profit?

(c) If Laraby Company holds the sales price constant and makes the suggested changes, how many units of product must be sold in the coming year to break even?

(d) If Laraby Company holds the sales price constant and makes the suggested changes, how many units of product will the entity have to sell to make the same after-tax profit as last year?

(e) If Laraby Company wishes to maintain the same contribution margin ratio, what selling price per unit of product must it charge next year to cover the increased materials costs?

6.21 Targeted profit; progressive income tax rates; CVP graph Dalton Brothers pay 15 per cent in taxes on income between $1 and $40 000. All income above $40 000 is taxed at 40 per cent. The entity's variable costs as a percentage of revenues are 60 per cent. Annual fixed costs are $250 000.

REQUIRED

(a) What level of sales must the entity achieve to earn income after taxes of $150 000?

(b) Prepare a CVP graph for Dalton.

6.22 Breakeven; selling price; targeted profit with price and cost changes All-Day Lolly Company is a wholesale distributor of confectionery. The entity services grocery and convenience stores in the metropolitan area. Small but steady growth in sales has been achieved by the All-Day Lolly Company over the past few years, but confectionery prices also have been increasing. The entity is reformulating its plans for the coming fiscal year. The following data were used to project the current year's after-tax income of $100 400.

Average selling price	$4.00 per box
Average variable costs	
Cost of confectionery	$2.00 per box
Selling costs	0.40 per box
Total	$2.40 per box
Annual fixed costs	
Selling	$160 000
Administrative	280 000
Total	$440 000
Expected annual sales (390 000 boxes) = $1 560 000	
Tax rate = 40%	

Confectionery manufacturers have announced that they will increase prices of their products an average of 15 per cent in the coming year because of increases in raw material (sugar, cocoa, peanuts etc.) and labour costs. All-Day Lolly Company expects that all other costs will remain the same as during the current year.

REQUIRED

(a) What is All-Day Lolly Company's breakeven point in boxes of lollies for the current year?

(b) What average selling price per box must All-Day Lolly Company charge to cover the 15 per cent increase in the variable cost of lollies and still maintain the current contribution margin ratio?

(c) What volume of sales in dollars must the All-Day Lolly Company achieve in the coming year to maintain the same after-tax income as projected for the current year if the average selling price of lollies remains at $4 per box and the cost of confectionery increases 15 per cent?

6.23 Breakeven; operating leverage; cost function decision You are the adviser of a Junior Achievement group in a local high school. You need to help the group make a decision about fees that must be paid to sell gardening tools at the Home and Garden Show. The group sells a set of tools for $20. The manufacturing cost (all variable) is $6 per set. The Home and Garden Show coordinator allows the following three payment options for groups exhibiting and selling at the show:

A. Pay a fixed booth fee of $5600.
B. Pay a fee of $3800 plus 10 per cent of all revenue from tool sets sold at the show.
C. Pay 15 per cent of all revenue from tool sets sold at the show.

REQUIRED

(a) Calculate the breakeven number of tool sets for each option.
(b) Which payment plan has the highest degree of operating leverage?
(c) Which payment plan has the lowest risk of loss for the organisation? Explain.
(d) At what level of revenue should the group be indifferent to options (i) and (ii)?
(e) Which option should Junior Achievement choose, assuming sales are expected to be 1000 sets of tools? Explain.

6.24 ROI targeted profit; foreign exchange rates Borg Controls has a net investment in its German subsidiary of $2.68 million. The entity attempts to earn a 15 per cent pre-tax return on its investment. Variable costs for the German subsidiary are 60 per cent of revenues. Annual fixed costs are €321 000. For the current year, the manager of the German subsidiary anticipates revenues of €1.7 million. The exchange rate is expected to be €1.2 = A$1.

REQUIRED

(a) If operations meet expectations, what is the rate of return that Borg Controls will earn from its German subsidiary? (*Hint*: Calculate the rate of return by dividing pre-tax income by the net investment.)
(b) What level of revenue in euros would be required of the subsidiary for the parent to earn exactly a 15 per cent rate of return in dollars, assuming no changes in the exchange rate?

6.25 Targeted profit; margin of safety; operating leverage The following budget data apply to Newberry's Nutrition:

Sales (100 000 units)		$1 000 000
Costs		
Direct materials	$300 000	
Direct labour	200 000	
Fixed factory overhead	100 000	
Variable factory overhead	150 000	
Marketing and administration	160 000	
Total costs		910 000
Budgeted pre-tax profit		$ 90 000

Direct labour workers are paid hourly wages and go home when there is no work. The marketing and administration costs include $50 000 that varies proportionately with production volume. Assume that sales and production volumes are equal.

REQUIRED

(a) Calculate the number of units that must be sold to achieve a targeted after-tax income of $120 000, assuming the tax rate is 40 per cent.

(b) Calculate the margin of safety in both revenues and units.

(c) Calculate the degree of operating leverage.

6.26 Breakeven; targeted profit; margin of safety; operating leverage Pike Street Fudge makes and sells fudge in a variety of flavours in a shop located in the local public market. Data for a recent week are as follows:

Revenue (2000 kg @ $4.80 per kg)		$9 600
Cost of ingredients	$3 200	
Rent	800	
Wages	4 800	8 800
Pre-tax profit		800
Taxes (20%)		160
After-tax profit		$ 640

All employees work standard shifts, no matter how much fudge is produced or sold.

REQUIRED

(a) Calculate the breakeven point in units and in revenue.

(b) Calculate the number of units and the amount of revenues that would be needed for after-tax income of $3000.

(c) Calculate the margin of safety in units and the margin of safety percentage.

(d) Calculate the degree of operating leverage.

6.27 Breakeven; targeted profit; margin of safety Vines and Daughter manufactures and sells swimsuits for $40 each. The estimated income statement for 2009 is as follows:

Sales	$2 000 000
Variable costs	1 100 000
Contribution margin	900 000
Fixed costs	765 000
Pre-tax profit	$ 135 000

REQUIRED

(a) Calculate the contribution margin per swimsuit and the number of swimsuits that must be sold to break even.

(b) What is the margin of safety in the number of swimsuits?

(c) Suppose the margin of safety was 5000 swimsuits in 2008. Are operations more or less risky in 2009 as compared to 2008? Explain.

(d) Calculate the contribution margin ratio and the breakeven point in revenues.

(e) What is the margin of safety in revenues?

(f) Suppose next year's revenue estimate is $200 000 higher. What would be the estimated pre-tax profit?

(g) Assume a tax rate of 30 per cent. How many swimsuits must be sold to earn an after-tax profit of $180 000?

Problems

6.28 Cost function; breakeven; quality of information; relevant range Oysters Away picks, shucks, and packs oysters and then sells them wholesale to fine restaurants across the state. The income statement for last year is shown overleaf.

Revenue (based on sales of 2000 cases of oysters)		$200 000
Expenses:		
Wages for pickers, shuckers and packers	$100 000	
Packing materials	20 000	
Rent and insurance	25 000	
Administrative and selling	45 000	190 000
Pre-tax profit		10 000
Taxes (20%)		2 000
After-tax profit		$ 8 000

Pickers, shuckers and packers are employed on an hourly basis and can be laid off whenever necessary. Salespeople mostly deliver the product and are paid on a salaried basis.

REQUIRED

(a) Estimate the cost function for Oysters Away.

(b) What is the breakeven point in cases for Oysters Away?

(c) The manager thinks that the entity will harvest and sell 3000 cases of oysters next year. Estimate the after-tax profit.

(d) Oysters Away harvested and sold 2000 cases in each of the last several years. What does this suggest about the quality of the income information you calculated in part (c)?

(e) Describe reasons why the cost function developed for the relevant range up to 2000 cases might not hold for 2001 to 3000 cases.

6.29 Relevant information; breakeven; targeted profit; price; uncertainties Francesca would like to lease a coffee cart in Melbourne. The lease is $800 per month, and a city licence to sell food and beverages costs $20 per month. The lessor of the stand has shown Francesca records indicating that gross revenues average $32 per hour. The out-of-pocket costs for ingredients are generally about 40 per cent of gross revenues. Last year Francesca paid 25 per cent of her income in government taxes.

Francesca pays $1000 per month for her apartment. She could store the cart overnight in the apartment's garage, which is currently unused. Real estate developers in Melbourne estimate that about 20 per cent of the cost of a residential building is for the garage.

At present, Francesca is earning $2400 per month as a ski instructor for one of the big ski areas. In the summer she earns about the same income as a kayaking instructor.

REQUIRED

(a) List each piece of quantitative information in this problem. For each item, indicate whether it is relevant to Francesca's decision and explain why.

(b) If Francesca leases the cart and works 30 days in a month, how many hours will she have to work each day, on average, to be at least as well off financially as she is in her current job?

(c) If Francesca wants to work only 25 days per month, how much will revenues have to increase for her to work four hours per day and be as financially well off as she is in her current job?

(d) Can Francesca be certain that her revenues will average $32 per hour? Why?

(e) What other information might help Francesca with this decision?

6.30 Sales mix; multiple product breakeven; uncertainties; quality of information Dreamtime produces two products: regular boomerangs and premium boomerangs. Last month 1200 units of regular and 2400 units of premium boomerangs were produced and sold. Average prices and costs per unit for the month are displayed opposite.

	Regular	Premium
Selling price	$22.15	$45.30
Variable costs	4.31	6.91
Product line fixed costs	8.17	24.92
Corporate fixed costs	5.62	5.62
Operating profit	$ 4.05	$ 7.85

Product line fixed costs can be avoided if the product line is dropped. Corporate fixed costs can be avoided only if the entity goes out of business entirely. You may want to use a spreadsheet to perform calculations.

REQUIRED

(a) Assuming the sales mix remains constant, how many units of premium boomerangs will be sold each time a unit of regular boomerangs is sold?

(b) What are the total fixed product line costs for each product?

(c) What are the total corporate fixed costs?

(d) What is the overall corporate breakeven in total revenue and for each product, assuming the sales mix is the same as last month's?

(e) What is the breakeven in revenues for regular boomerangs, ignoring corporate fixed costs?

(f) Why is the breakeven for regular boomerangs different when we calculate the individual product breakeven versus the combined product breakeven?

(g) When managers monitor the profitability of regular boomerangs, are corporate fixed costs relevant? Explain.

(h) CVP analysis assumes that the sales mix will remain constant. Explain why managers generally cannot know for certain what their sales mix will be.

(i) What is the effect of uncertainty about the sales mix on the quality of the information obtained from CVP analyses?

6.31 Cost function; marginal cost; opportunity cost; usefulness of CVP A neighbour asked for your help preparing a grant for a not-for-profit after-school art program that would benefit primary school children in the neighbourhood. He wants to charge low fees for most children, but also offer some scholarships for low-income children. He needs to have one staff person for every six children to meet state regulations. He can use high school student volunteers for two of these positions, but is concerned about potential absences on their part if he relies on them for the state count. He would like the program to serve at least 30 children — more, if possible.

He wants you to help him decide on the fees to charge and also to determine how many students could receive scholarships.

REQUIRED

(a) Think about the costs involved in an after-school program. Assume that your neighbour can use the local primary school free of charge.
   (i) List costs that will be incurred for the program, and categorise them as fixed, variable or mixed.
   (ii) For each variable cost, choose a potential cost driver. Explain your choice.

(b) Do you think the cost structure would be primarily fixed or primarily variable? Explain. Remember, even though staff work only part time, they will have a regular schedule to meet the state regulations of six children per staff member.

(c) Suppose one of the staff members has only one child to help. What is the marginal cost for three scholarships?

(d) Suppose the program is fully subscribed by fee-paying children. What is the opportunity cost per scholarship?

(e) Will CVP analysis help your neighbour choose a fee that would cover at least 10 scholarships? Explain how you would set up a spreadsheet so that your neighbour could perform sensitivity analysis to make more informed decisions.

6.32 Breakeven; CVP; potential cost structure change; employee reaction Ersatz manufactures a single product. The following income statement shows two different levels of activity, which are assumed to be within Ersatz's relevant range. You may want to use a spreadsheet to perform calculations.

Ersatz Ltd Income statement		
	Activity levels	
Volume	1000 units	1500 units
Sales @ $100 each	$100 000	$150 000
Variable expenses		
Manufacturing @ $40 each	40 000	60 000
Selling @ $10 each	10 000	15 000
Administration @ $6 each	6 000	9 000
Contribution margin	44 000	66 000
Fixed expenses		
Manufacturing	10 000	10 000
Selling	11 000	11 000
Administration	20 000	20 000
Pre-tax profit	$ 3 000	$ 25 000

REQUIRED

(a) What is Ersatz's breakeven point in units?

(b) Draw a CVP chart showing the two levels of activity and the breakeven point.

(c) If Ersatz plans to sell 1300 units, what will pre-tax income be?

(d) Your boss asked you to draft an email response to Ersatz's major shareholder, who wants to know why pre-tax profit increases by more than 700 per cent when sales increase by just 50 per cent. Both your boss and the shareholder are busy people and expect short answers.

(e) Management expects that variable costs and selling prices will rise by 3 per cent, but fixed costs will not change. What will the new breakeven point be? Explain the result.

(f) Management wants to change the way that sales representatives are paid. At present, sales representatives are paid $11 000 + $10 per unit. Management will replace this formula with a payment of $20 per unit. At what level of sales will it make no difference in income which cost function is used?

(g) Add the new cost function to the preceding CVP chart.

(h) Which of the two cost functions will minimise selling expenses assuming that sales are above the indifference level calculated in part (f)?

(i) How would sales representatives be likely to respond to the new payment system?

(j) Discuss the pros and cons to the entity of changing the way sales representatives are paid.

6.33 Breakeven; avoidable fixed costs; price; CVP assumptions; operating risk Last year's income statement for King Salmon Sales is shown opposite.

Revenue (100 000 kg)		$800 000
Expenses		
Fish	$200 000	
Smoking materials	20 000	
Packaging materials	30 000	
Labour (wages)	300 000	
Administrative	150 000	
Sales commissions	10 000	
Total expenses		710 000
Income		$ 90 000

The fishing season is only three to four months long, so labour costs (wages) are for employees who are university students and work in the summer. They are hired only as needed.

REQUIRED

(a) The state government curtailed fishing because of low fish counts. Because of this restriction, King Salmon Sales can buy only 50 000 kilograms. Assume the administrative cost is incurred only if the entity sells salmon. Assuming the managers will decide to operate if the entity can at least break even, should they operate this year? (*Hint:* Calculate the breakeven quantity.) Provide calculations and explain your answer.

(b) Now assume that the administrative costs continue regardless of whether the entity sells salmon. Assuming the managers will decide to operate if the entity can at least break even, should they operate this year? Provide calculations and explain your answer.

(c) Because of the salmon shortage, suppose that retail salmon prices are increasing. What is the breakeven price for King Salmon? Assume that administrative costs continue regardless of whether the entity sells salmon.

(d) Suppose the managers rely on the preceding CVP analysis to decide whether to operate the business. What assumptions are they making?

(e) How reasonable are these CVP assumptions?

(f) Suppose the owner of King Salmon Sales asked you about the entity's cost structure. Because volumes of fish fluctuate a great deal from one year to the next, the owner is wondering if some way can be found to reduce the risk of an operating loss. Write a brief memo to explain how the proportion of fixed and variable costs affects the risk of loss when operations are close to the breakeven point.

6.34 Cost function; breakeven; targeted profit; uncertainties and bias; interpretation Joe Davies is thinking about starting a company to produce carved wooden clocks. He loves making the clocks. He sees it as an opportunity to be his own boss, making a living doing what he likes best.

Joe paid $300 for the plans for the first clock, and he has already purchased new equipment costing $2000 to manufacture the clocks. He estimates that it will cost $30 in materials (wood, clock mechanism etc.) to make each clock. If he decides to build clocks full time, he will need to rent office and manufacturing space, which he thinks would cost $2500 per month for rent plus another $300 per month for various utility bills. Joe would perform all of the manufacturing and run the office, and he would like to pay himself a salary of $3000 per month so that he would have enough money to live on. Because he does not want to take time away from manufacturing to sell the clocks, he plans to hire two salespeople at a base salary of $1000 each per month plus a commission of $7 per clock.

Joe plans to sell each clock for $225. He believes that he can produce and sell 300 clocks in December for Christmas, but he is not sure what the sales will be during the rest of the year. However, he is fairly sure that the clocks will be popular because he has been selling similar items as a sideline for several years. Overall, he is confident that he can pay all of his business costs, pay himself the monthly salary of $3000 and earn at least $4000 more than that per month. (Ignore income taxes.)

REQUIRED

(a) Perform analyses to estimate the number of clocks Joe would need to manufacture and sell each year for his business to be financially successful:
   (i) List all of the costs described and indicate whether each cost is (1) a relevant fixed cost, (2) a relevant variable cost or (3) *not* relevant to Joe's decision.
   (ii) Calculate the contribution margin per unit and the contribution margin ratio.
   (iii) Write down the total cost function for the clocks and calculate the annual breakeven point in units and in revenues.
   (iv) How many clocks would Joe need to sell annually to earn $4000 per month more than his salary?
(b) Identify uncertainties about the CVP calculations:
   (i) Explain why Joe cannot know for sure whether his actual costs will be the same dollar amounts that he estimated. In your explanation, identify as many uncertainties as you can. (*Hint:* For each of the costs Joe identified, think about reasons why the actual cost might be different than the amount he estimated.)
   (ii) Identify possible costs for Joe's business that he has not identified. List as many additional types of cost as you can.
   (iii) Explain why Joe cannot know for sure how many clocks he will sell each year. In your explanation, identify as many uncertainties as you can.
(c) Discuss whether Joe is likely to be biased in his revenue and cost estimates.
(d) Explain how uncertainties and Joe's potential biases might affect interpretation of the breakeven analysis results.
(e) Use the information you learned from the preceding analyses to write a memo to Joe with your recommendations. Attach to the memo a schedule showing relevant information. As appropriate, refer to the schedule in the memo.

6.35 CVP sensitivity analysis; bias; quality of information Jasmine Krishnan has been taking entrepreneurship courses as part of her business degree. She developed a plan to start a travel agency specialising in semester break trips for students.

She learned how to develop CVP analysis in her cost accounting class. Now she is preparing pro forma (forecasted) income statements for a brochure about her plans for the travel agency. She wants to use the information from the CVP as a basis for the statements. Her entrepreneurship professor criticised her business plan because Jasmine included too small an amount for liability insurance. However, when she included the amount suggested by her father's insurance agent, she had to set prices quite high, cut back on the amount she planned as her salary, find lower quality hotels for the students or take some combination of these actions. She thought that hotel quality and prices would affect sales volumes negatively and did not want to risk incurring losses from low revenues during her first few years. She also needed a base level of salary to at least pay for her living expenses.

She decided to ask friends and relatives to invest in her travel agency to ensure she had enough capital for the first few years. Once her reputation was well established, she assumed that higher customer volumes would cover all of her expected costs. She was confident that her planned trips would attract enough students each year to cover most of her costs. From focus groups on campus, she learned which types of trips were most appealing to other students. Now she planned to use sensitivity analysis to solve for volumes that would make the pro forma statements look attractive to investors.

REQUIRED

(a) In general, what information do we hope to gain from performing sensitivity analyses? Explain.
(b) Explain how bias might enter into Jasmine's sensitivity analyses.
(c) How might Jasmine's bias affect the quality of the investment brochure information?
(d) Identify a potential ethical problem for Jasmine.
(e) When you consider the wellbeing of Jasmine's family and friends, how would you recommend that Jasmine use sensitivity analysis for her brochure? Explain.

6.36 Small business owners; CVP research on the internet The internet provides many resources to help small business owners successfully manage their businesses. These resources include information about common techniques used for planning and managing operations.

REQUIRED

(a) Why are small business owners often unaware of common business techniques such as CVP analysis?
(b) Why might CVP analysis be even more useful to small business owners than to managers of large entities? (*Hint:* Consider whether information about the margin of safety and size of potential losses might be especially important for people who own small businesses.)
(c) Use an internet search engine to locate websites that provide information about the terms *breakeven analysis* and *cost–volume–profit analysis*. Also search for these terms on websites designed explicitly to help small business owners. Summarise what your research tells you about the uses and usefulness of breakeven and CVP analysis.
(d) Suppose you are trying to help a small business owner learn to use breakeven and CVP analysis. Write a memo to the owner explaining what you think the owner should do and include appropriate references to Internet resources that would be useful to the owner. Assume that you have already had a brief conversation with the owner about breakeven and CVP analysis, and the owner expressed an interest in learning more. Focus on communicating effectively by avoiding unnecessarily technical language and concentrating on the most important points.

6.37 Cost function; operating leverage; keeping or dropping a business The university's Student Lounge caters to students and serves sandwiches and beverages. It has been reporting losses in past months. In July, for example, the loss was $5000.

Revenue		$70 000
Expenses		
Purchases of prepared food	$21 000	
Serving personnel	30 000	
Cashiers	5 500	
Administration	10 000	
University surcharge	7 000	
Utilities	1 500	75 000
Loss		$ (5 000)

The Lounge purchases prepared food directly from University Food Services. This charge varies proportionately with the number and kind of meals served. Personnel paid by the Lounge serve the food, tend the cash register, wait on and clean tables, and wash dishes. The staffing levels rarely change; the existing staff can usually handle daily fluctuations in volume. Administrative costs are primarily the salaries of the manager and her office staff. Because the university provides support services for the Lounge (such as payroll, human resources and other administrative support), the university charges a surcharge of 10 per cent of its revenues. Utility costs are the costs of cooling, heating and lighting during the Lounge's normal operating hours.

The university's management is considering closing the Student Lounge because it has been operating at a loss.

REQUIRED

(a) What is the breakeven point for the Student Lounge from the university's perspective (including the university surcharge)? What is the breakeven point from the Student Lounge's perspective (excluding the university surcharge)?

(b) Define and calculate the degree of operating leverage for the Lounge, ignoring the university surcharge.

(c) From the perspective of university management, is the university surcharge a relevant cost in deciding whether to close the Lounge? Why?

(d) Identify possible ways that operations could be modified so that some of the fixed costs become variable costs.

(e) Given the Lounge's cost function and operating leverage, describe possible benefits of modifying operations so that some of the fixed costs become variable costs.

(f) From the perspective of university management, describe the pros and cons of closing the Student Lounge.

(g) Suppose you are the manager of the Student Lounge. Write a memo to persuade the university management to keep the club open.

6.38 **Not-for-profit breakeven price; budget alternatives** The Elder Clinic, a not-for-profit entity, provides limited medical services to low-income elderly patients. The manager's summary report for the past four months of operations is reproduced here.

	March	April	May	June	Total
Patient visits	849	821	778	842	3 290
Patient fees	$ 4 230	$ 4 180	$ 3 875	$ 4 260	$ 16 545
Medical staff salaries	13 254	13 256	13 254	14 115	53 879
Medical supplies used	3 182	3 077	2 934	3 175	12 368
Administrative salaries	3 197	3 198	3 197	3 412	13 004
Rent	1 000	1 000	1 000	1 100	4 100
Utilities	532	378	321	226	1 457
Other expenses	2 854	2 776	2 671	2 828	11 129
Total expenses	24 019	23 685	23 377	24 856	95 937
Operating surplus (loss)	$(19 789)	$(19 505)	$(19 502)	$(20 596)	$(79 392)

The clinic receives an operating subsidy from the state government, but unfortunately the operating loss incurred through June ($79 392) is larger than anticipated. Part of the problem is the salary increase that went into effect in June, which had been over-looked when the budget was submitted to the state government last year. To compound the problem, the cold winter months traditionally bring with them an increase in cold-weather-related health problems. Thus, the clinic is likely to experience an increase in patient visits during July.

The accountant made the following assumptions in developing the cost function:

- Salaries are fixed, and June values are used.
- Medical supplies vary with patient visits.
- Rent and utilities are fixed, and last period's costs are used.
- Other expenses are mixed and using regression, fixed cost is $702 and variable cost is $2.53 per patient visit.

Clinic management is considering an increase in patient fees to reduce losses.

REQUIRED

(a) Develop a cost function for this data (refer to chapter 2). Use the cost function you developed to solve for the average patient fee necessary to break even, assuming there are 940 patient visits. Compare this new fee with the average patient fee charged during March through June.
(b) Suppose the clinic raises its patient fees to break even. What problems do you see from the elderly patients' perspective if the fee is raised?
(c) In this setting, would an increase in fees be likely to affect patient volume? What problems do you see from the clinic's perspective if the fee is raised?
(d) Other than raising the fee, what ideas might the clinic consider to balance the budget?

6.39 **Cost function; targeted profit; operating leverage; CVP graph; owner goals** Trang Nguyen owns Trang's Stained Glass in Sydney. The business produces and sells three different types of stained glass windows: small, medium and large. Trang has two full-time employees who work regular schedules to cut glass and assemble the windows. She borrowed money from the bank to start the business and pay living expenses. She is concerned that her cash flows might not be high enough either to pay herself or to repay the bank loan. She would like to generate approximately $10 000 in pre-tax profit each month to cover her living expenses and repay the loan.

The following revenue and cost information covers the past four months.

	June	July	August	September
Revenues	$9 050	$10 531	$12 946	$16 116
Raw materials and supplies	1 745	2 433	3 074	4 029
Labour	3 880	4 041	4 246	4 282
Rent	2 000	2 000	2 000	2 200
Miscellaneous	525	701	747	793
Profit	$ 900	$ 1 356	$ 2 879	$ 4 812

REQUIRED

(a) Develop a cost function for Trang's Stained Glass.
(b) Determine the level of revenue Trang's Stained Glass must generate to achieve the targeted profit of $10 000 per month.
(c) Calculate Trang's degree of operating leverage for September.
(d) Interpret Trang's degree of operating leverage.
(e) Create a CVP graph showing the breakeven point, targeted profit and margin of safety.
(f) Write a memo to Trang with recommendations about ways she might achieve her goals.

6.40 **Building and using a CVP financial model** Toddler Toy Company sells baby dolls, teddy bears and toy cars. The managers established a preliminary budget using the following assumptions. They would now like to evaluate the sensitivity of budgeted results to different sets of assumptions.

Toddler Toy Company
Assumptions for coming year

	Baby dolls	Teddy bears	Toy cars
Volume	200 000	125 000	225 000
Price	$3.50	$2.75	$3.15
Variable costs	$2.05	$1.75	$2.45
Fixed costs	$65 000	$125 000	$35 000
Targeted pre-tax profit	= $0		
Investment	= $2 million		
Capacity	= 1 million units		

REQUIRED

(a) Create a spreadsheet that the managers can use for sensitivity analysis. Modify input data in the spreadsheet to answer the following parts of this problem. You may wish to add cell references for percentage changes in prices, volumes and costs.

(b) Assume that the volume of dolls sold increases to 225 000 units with no change in fixed or variable costs. What is the new pre-tax profit? Does the number produced by your financial model appear to be reasonable? (Manually estimate the increase in pre-tax profit if volume increases and fixed costs remain constant. Compare this figure to your spreadsheet result.)

(c) Based on the original assumptions, what is the effect on pre-tax profit if variable costs increase by 5 per cent for each of the three product lines? Assume that nothing else changes.

(d) Return to the original assumptions. Assume that a sales manager proposed a new advertising campaign to boost sales volume. The campaign would cost $30 000 and is estimated to increase the volume of each product as follows:
- Baby doll sales increase by 20 000 units.
- Teddy bear sales increase by 7500 units.
- Toy car sales increase by 30 000 units.

What would be the effect on pre-tax profit if this plan were adopted?

(e) Return to the original assumptions. Now assume that due to competition, Toddler Toys must cut prices on each of its three products by 20 per cent. In addition, a new advertising campaign costing $45 000 must be instituted to counteract bad publicity. Given these assumptions, what is the new breakeven point?

(f) Return to the original assumptions. What would be the pre-tax profit if Toddler Toys increases the price of all three products by 10 per cent and the volume of each product line decreases by 5 per cent?

(g) Given the same assumptions as in part (f), how many units must Toddler Toys sell to earn a targeted pre-tax profit of $100 000? A targeted pre-tax profit of $150 000? A pre-tax return on investment (ROI) of 10 per cent? (*Hint:* To determine the targeted pre-tax profit, multiply 10 per cent by the amount invested.)

(h) Spreadsheets for financial modelling allow sensitivity analysis of revenues, costs and quantities such as estimated product volumes.
   (i) Explain why it is not possible to perfectly estimate revenues, costs and quantities.
   (ii) Explain how sensitivity analysis can help managers evaluate the pros and cons of alternatives.

(iii) Explain how manager bias might influence estimates of revenues, costs and quantities.

6.41 Building and using a CVP financial model The following information for Pet Palace, a large retail store that sells pet-related merchandise, was recorded for the first quarter. The store tracks merchandise according to product type. The category 'Other' includes accessories such as dog beds, leashes, kitty litter boxes, bird cages and so on. The entity is considering several different strategies to improve operations for the next quarter.

Input data	Food	Toys	Pets	Other	Total
Revenue	$500 000	$150 000	$75 000	$200 000	$925 000
Variable costs	200 000	50 000	60 000	50 000	360 000
Fixed costs					550 000
Tax rate					25%

REQUIRED

(a) Create a spreadsheet that Pet Palace managers can use for sensitivity analysis. Modify information in the data input section and answer the questions in the following parts.

(b) What is Pet Palace's breakeven point? What total revenue is necessary for a targeted after-tax profit of $100 000?

(c) Pet Palace managers are considering their advertising campaign for the next period. They believe they could spend an additional $10 000 on advertising for a product line and increase sales by 10 per cent. One manager wants to increase advertising on pets because that product line is currently the smallest. Another manager believes the advertisements should promote the most profitable products, but he is not sure which products those would be. What is the after-tax profit if pets are promoted? What is the most profitable product? What is the after-tax profit if that product is promoted?

(d) What factors, other than the quantitative results, might influence managers' decisions to increase advertising?

Budgeting

IN BRIEF

An entity's long-term strategies are communicated and advanced through short-term and long-term budgets. In addition, budgets provide a mechanism for monitoring an organisation's progress toward its goals. Comparisons of actual to budgeted revenues and costs help managers evaluate performance, leading to improved operations and more accurate planning. Some entities provide employee incentives for meeting or exceeding budget-based benchmarks. Accordingly, budgets are used in planning, monitoring and motivating performance.

After studying this chapter, you should be able to:

1   Understand the role of budgets in developing both short- and long-term plans.

2   Understand the role of the master budget and its preparation.

3   Develop a cash budget.

4   Understand the use of budget targets as performance benchmarks.

5   Describe how budgets are used to monitor and motivate performance.

6   Outline other approaches to budgeting.

Budgets for the healthcare sector

Budgeting for healthcare provision in Australia is major exercise that requires budgeting by different levels of management for a diverse range of activities performed in both public and private settings. In Australia, total health expenditure as a share of GDP is around 9.2 per cent (OECD 2006). Of this, 67.5 per cent of total health expenditure is funded by public sources. Funding arrangements between federal and state governments allow taxpayer dollars to be targeted to specific areas to ensure that world-class health standards are available to the Australian community both now and in the future. For example, in the 2006–07 federal health budget, funds were allocated to promoting good health, prevention and early intervention, and health and medical research. This is in addition to the regular funding the federal government gives hospitals for public healthcare provision to the Australian community.

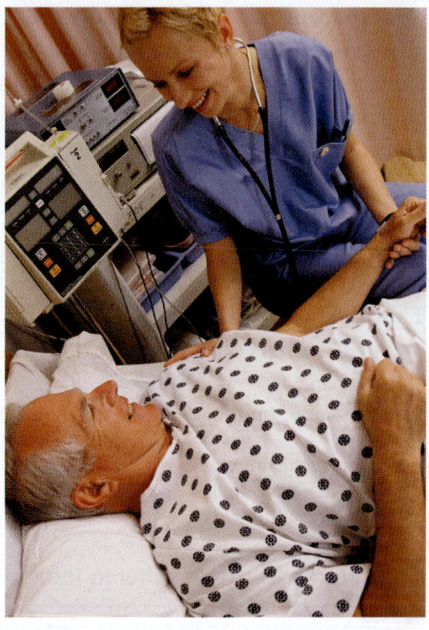

Public hospitals have individual boards of management that manage overall hospital operations. Hospital revenue is negotiated with the government and is referred to as *case-mix funding*. Case-mix ensures that a predetermined mix of services is provided by every individual public hospital relative to its asset base, skills and expertise. For example, some hospitals may specialise in children's health. Other hospitals may provide maternity services, heart–lung transplants, major trauma, orthopaedic surgery, oncology services etc. Most patient medical and surgical treatments are allocated a code (a diagnosis-related group or DRG) with an associated standard cost weight that is based on an average patient receiving an average standard of care in an average hospital. It is the job of the management accountant to monitor how well the hospital is managing its case-mix funding targets (a 'bucket' of funds), which is annually capped by governments at a predetermined level. If hospitals over-supply services, they will run into budget deficit. If they under-provide services, they can be penalised by the government and have their future funding budget reduced. They will also be penalised if they do not get the mix of patient treatments right, particularly if patients do not get access to the varying treatments they require in a reasonable time. Hence, it is very important that every public hospital monitor its budgets and the associated activities very closely.

More recently, Australian private hospital companies such as Ramsay Health are becoming involved in work previously only performed by public hospitals. Ramsay Health Care, the largest private hospital company in Australia, announced that it would allocate more than $400 million of its capital expenditure budget to convert its largest hospitals into major teaching and research institutions (Lyall 2006). It currently has 65 hospitals and more than 7200 beds, and surgery performed in them accounts for 56 per cent of all surgery undertaken in Australia by private hospitals. This includes major surgery. Ramsay recently reported an annual tripling of its net profit to $87.6 million and EPS growth of 15 to 20 per cent this financial year. However, its share price fell 1 cent to $11.11 after the $400 million budget announcement (Lyall 2006). Thus, budgeting in private hospitals is as critical as that in public hospitals, particularly when shareholders are monitoring the entities' bottom-line performance.

At operational level within individual hospitals, the production departments might commonly include areas such as the operating theatres, emergency department, intensive care unit, medical and surgical wards, radiology and pathology. The support departments of hospitals might commonly include administration, supply department, health and research, clinical teaching, patient services, laundry and catering. Budgeting is now integral to a clinician's management function. For example, a head surgeon in a public hospital may be required to be actively involved in the achievement of case-mix targets. Further, budgeting activities conducted by a nurse manager in the operating department will be concentrated around costs such as staff (the surgical team required for each operating list), the use of disposable surgical equipment, anaesthetic drugs, painkillers, antibiotics, intravenous fluids and non-disposable assets such as anaesthetic, sterilising and packaging equipment. They, like many other non-accounting managers in varying industries, closely liaise with the management accountant to ensure monthly and annual budget targets are achieved and are achievable.

Sources: Information from Department of Health and Ageing, Canberra, *Federal health budget 2006–2007*, www.health.gov.au/budget2006; Department of Human Resources, Victoria, *Casemix funding*, www.health.vic.gov.au; Lyall, K 2006, 'Ramsay to splash out on teaching', *The Australian*, 23 November; OECD 2006, Health data statistics and indicators for 30 countries, www.oecd.org.

Issues from this scene setter to look for in the chapter include:

- The importance of setting and monitoring budgets at all levels within the entity.

- The role that non-accountants might play in setting, monitoring and using budgets.

- How management accountants fit in a team environment such as a hospital.

- The stakeholders that might be interested in budget setting and related hospital performance.

Budgeting — a tool for short- and long-term planning

University students routinely anticipate both school-related expenditures (such as fees and books) and living expenses (such as rent and food). Before each semester begins, they may develop financial plans. These plans consider expenses and also potential incoming funds such as scholarships, loans and wages.

At the end of each month or semester, students might compare their actual expenditures to those they had planned. They can then use these comparisons to adjust their plans for future spending or financing. For example, if expenses are outpacing revenues, students have several choices. They can lower their living expenses. They might transfer to a less expensive university, switch from full-time to part-time status or take fewer subjects. They might also increase funds by applying for more scholarships or loans, or by increasing their work hours.

Every organisation faces the same budgetary problems that students face. In the upcoming fiscal period, plans must be developed to anticipate revenues, expenses and cash flows. At the end of the period, actual results are compared to the plan to identify gaps, or variances, from the plan. A **budget** is a formalised financial plan for operations of an entity for a specified future period. This plan helps the organisation coordinate the activities needed to carry out the plan. A budget is an entity's financial roadmap; it reflects management's forecast of the financial effects of an entity's plans for one or more future time periods. (The chapter 7 article at the end of this book reinforces the relevance of budgeting to organisations.) Several objectives are met through the use of budgets, as summarised in figure 7.1.

- Developing and communicating organisational strategies and goals for the entire entity as well as for each segment, division or department

- Assigning decision rights (authority to spend, and responsibility for decision outcomes)

- Motivating managers to plan in advance

- Coordinating operating activities such as sales and production

- Establishing prices for the internal transfer of goods and services

- Measuring and comparing expected and actual outcomes

- Monitoring actual performance and investigating variances when necessary

- Motivating managers to provide appropriate estimates, meet expectations and use resources efficiently

- Re-evaluating and revising strategies and operating plans as conditions change

FIGURE 7.1 ■ Budget objectives

In preparing budgets, managers forecast a number of events such as the volume of goods or services they will sell. Using these estimates, plans are developed to determine the resources an organisation needs, including employees, raw materials and supplies, cash and anything else necessary to the future operations.

Budgets also provide a mechanism for defining the responsibilities and financial decision-making authority, or **decision rights**, of individual managers. For example, separate budgets are often developed for each department within an organisation. The manager of each department is then given authority to spend the organisation's resources in accordance with the budget, and is also responsible for meeting budgeted goals.

Budget cycle

A **budget cycle** is a series of steps that entities follow to develop and use budgets, as summarised in figure 7.2 (overleaf). Managers typically begin the process by revisiting and possibly revising the organisational vision and core competencies. The rest of this chapter addresses the other steps in the budget cycle. We first learn to translate operating plans into a master budget and then learn how managers monitor actual results, investigate differences between actual and budget, and evaluate and reward performance.

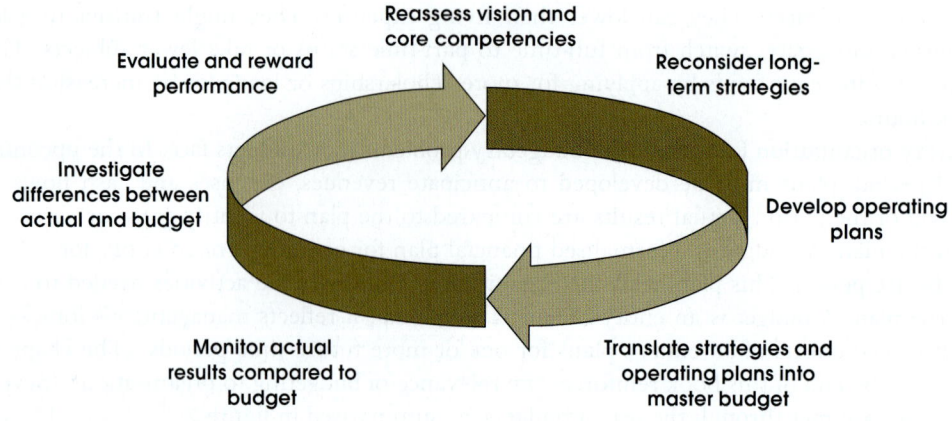

FIGURE 7.2 ■ Budget cycle

The role of the master budget

A **master budget** is a comprehensive plan for an upcoming financial period, usually a year. Master budgets reflect an entity's future operating and financing decisions, and are often summarised in a set of **budgeted financial statements**. These statements are forecasts of the future income statement, balance sheet and cash flows, given an organisation's sales forecasts and expenditure plans for the next period.

Figure 7.3 shows the development of a master budget in a manufacturing organisation. The master budget includes an **operating budget** — management's plan for revenues, production and operating costs. Preparation of the operating budget begins with the organisation's strategies, which in turn lead to a sales forecast and the revenue budget. The volume of production is next forecast using beginning inventory levels, sales forecasts and desired ending inventory levels. The production budget leads to budgets for direct materials, direct labour and manufacturing overhead. These budgets are used to create budgets for ending inventory and cost of goods sold. The operating budget also includes budgets for individual support department costs. All of the components of the operating budget are combined with any non-operating items and income taxes in a budgeted income statement. Non-operating items might include interest expenses, gains or losses on the sale of fixed assets, or earnings from investments.

The master budget also includes **financial budgets** — or management's plans for capital expenditures, long-term financing and cash flows — leading to a budgeted balance sheet and budgeted statement of cash flows. The cash budget is part of the financial budgets. A **cash budget** reflects the effects of management's plans on cash, and summarises the information that accountants gather about the expected amounts and timing of cash receipts and disbursements. The cash budget is addressed later in the chapter. The capital budget reflects long-term investment. The long-term financing budget, budgeted balance sheet and budgeted statement of cash flows are beyond the scope of this textbook.

Developing a master budget

Accountants develop a master budget in consultation with top management and every departmental manager within an entity. The master budget is developed using a set of **budget assumptions**, which are plans and predictions about next period's operating activities. Revenues are budgeted assuming a particular forecast of sales volumes and prices, or assuming an estimated percentage change from the prior year. Individual costs are budgeted assuming a fixed amount to be spent — as a percentage of revenues, as a percentage change from the prior year or on some other basis. Accountants assist managers in the process of developing budget assumptions. They may analyse past revenue and cost trends and behaviour, gather information about possible cost changes and obtain estimates from engineers about the effects of planned production changes.

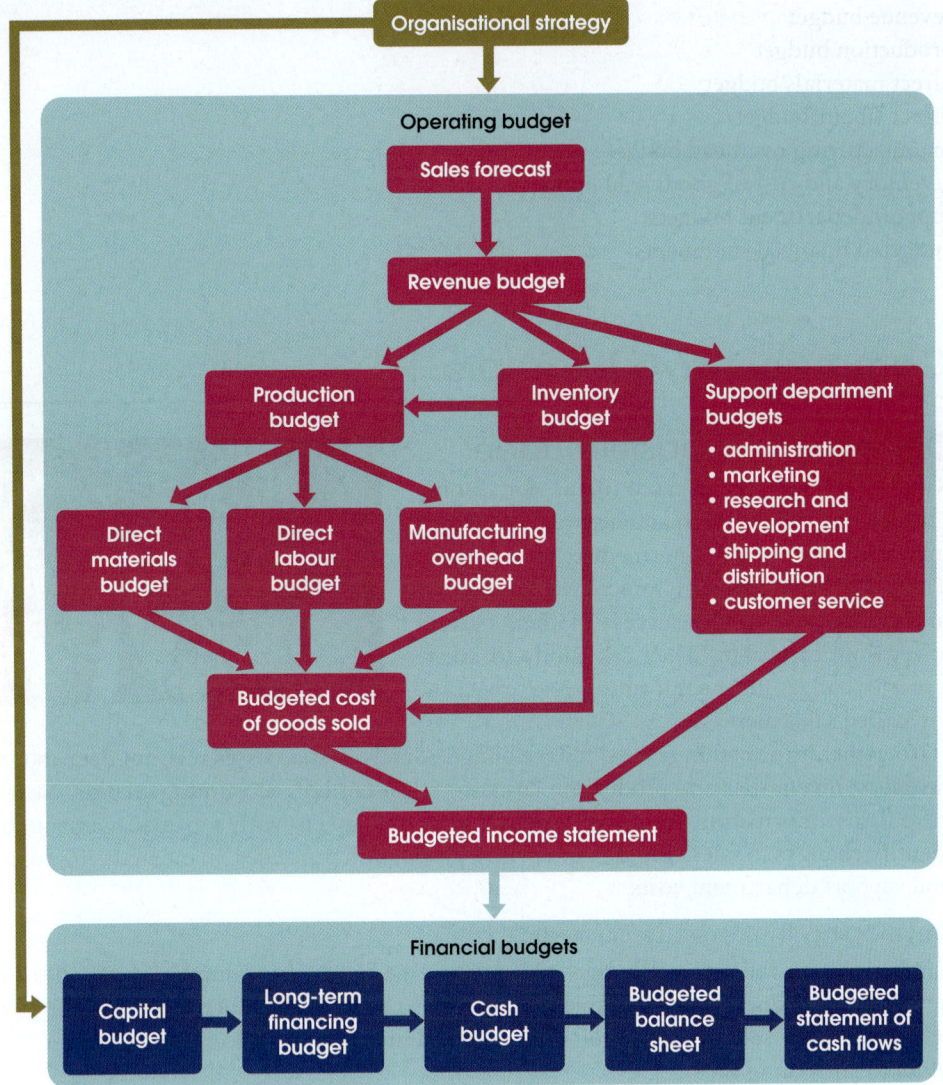

FIGURE 7.3 ■ Developing a manufacturer's master budget

The master budget is usually developed in the sequence shown in figure 7.3 for a manufacturing entity. Given the organisation's strategy, the first step is to forecast sales volumes and revenues. However, some organisations develop the production and support department budgets simultaneously with the revenue budget. Also, some parts of the production and support department budgets might be developed independently of the revenue budget.

The process of developing a master budget becomes increasingly complex as entities become larger. It is often more complex for international organisations. Communication can be more time-consuming because international business segments participate in the budgeting process. Cultural and legal differences influence both internal and external operations and need to be considered. The economies of different countries rarely move in tandem and forecasting sales is more difficult. In addition, currency translations and differences in inflation and deflation rates greatly increase uncertainty in the planning and budgeting process.

In comprehensive example 1, we revisit Mount Dandenong Bikes to show how the accountant develops a master budget by creating individual budgets in the following order:

- revenue budget
- production budget
- direct materials budget
- direct labour budget
- manufacturing overhead budget
- inventory and cost of goods sold budget
- support department budgets
- budgeted financial statements.

Comprehensive example 1

Developing a master budget

Sandy McEwan is an accountant for Mount Dandenong Bikes, a manufacturer of sturdy mountain bikes for intermediate-level bikers. The entity's managers are forecasting an increase in sales because of the success of their current advertising campaign. They ask Sandy to create a master budget for the upcoming year, given the forecasted sales increase.

To gather information needed for the budget, Sandy first accesses relevant data about revenues, inventories and production costs from last period's accounting records. Next, he obtains information from every department and meets with top management to identify changes in sales volumes and prices, production processes, manufacturing costs and support department costs.

Developing the revenue budget

Sandy prepares the revenue budget first because he needs the volume of bike sales to develop the production and variable cost budgets. The managers forecasted that 100 000 bikes would be sold at a price of $800 each. Sandy develops the revenue budget for Mount Dandenong Bikes.

Revenue budget			
	Selling price	Units sold	Total revenues
Bikes	$800	100 000	$80 000 000

Developing the production budget

Sandy next develops the production budget. According to prior accounting records, beginning finished goods inventory consists of 2500 bikes at a cost per unit of $454.75, or $1 136 875 total. Given the anticipated increase in sales volume, the managers want to increase finished goods inventory to 3500 units. Sandy calculates the number of bikes that will be manufactured this period, factoring in the sales forecast and both beginning and targeted ending inventory levels.

Production budget (units)	
Sales	100 000
Targeted ending inventory	3 500
Total finished units needed	103 500
Less beginning inventory	(2 500)
Production	101 000

Developing the direct materials budget

Now Sandy can determine the amount of direct materials that must be purchased. The beginning inventory consists of:

Beginning direct material inventories:	
Wheels and tyres	$ 20 000
Components	70 000
Frames	50 000
Total	$ 140 000

The cost per unit of direct materials is expected to be:

Direct materials (cost per unit):	
Wheels and tyres	$20
Components	70
Frame	50

The managers want ending inventories to be:

Targeted ending direct material inventories:	
Wheels and tyres	$ 25 000
Components	87 500
Frames	62 500
Total	$175 000

Given these assumptions, Sandy prepares the following direct materials budget.

Direct materials budget	
Production of 101 000 bikes:	
Wheels (101 000 × $20)	$ 2 020 000
Components (101 000 × $70)	7 070 000
Frames (101 000 × $50)	5 050 000
Total direct materials used	14 140 000
Targeted ending inventory	175 000
Less beginning inventory	(140 000)
Total purchases	$ 14 175 000

Developing the direct labour budget

The quantity and cost of direct labour per unit is expected to be:

Direct labour	Hours	Cost per hour
Assembly	1.5	$25
Testing	0.15	15

Sandy prepares the direct labour budget, which forecasts the number of labour hours and the total direct labour costs for producing 101 000 bikes.

Direct labour budget	
Labour hours budget:	
Assembly (101 000 units × 1.5 hours)	151 500 hours
Testing (101 000 units × 0.15 hours)	15 150 hours
Total labour hours	166 650 hours
Labour cost budget:	
Assembly (151 500 × $25)	$3 787 500
Testing (15 150 × $15)	227 250
Total labour cost	$ 4 014 750

Developing the manufacturing overhead budget

In addition to the direct costs of production, overhead costs need to be included in the budgeting process. Sandy uses information that he collected from last year's operations and updates it with current prices. The cost per unit of variable manufacturing overhead is expected to be as follows:

Variable overhead (cost per unit):	
Supplies	$20.00
Indirect labour	37.50
Maintenance	10.00
Miscellaneous	7.50
Total	$75.00

Sandy expects $20 200 000 to be spent on fixed manufacturing overhead costs.

He calculates the fixed overhead allocation rate by dividing budgeted fixed overhead costs by the budgeted volume of production:

$$\$20\,200\,000 \div 101\,000 \text{ units} = \$200 \text{ per unit}$$

Sandy prepares the manufacturing overhead budget for producing 101 000 bikes.

Manufacturing overhead budget	
Variable manufacturing overhead costs:	
Supplies (101 000 units × $20)	$2 020 000
Indirect labour (101 000 units × $37.50)	3 787 500
Maintenance (101 000 units × $10)	1 010 000
Miscellaneous (101 000 units × $7.50)	757 500
Total variable overhead (101 000 units × $75)	7 575 000

Fixed manufacturing overhead costs:	
Depreciation	4 040 000
Property taxes	1 010 000
Insurance	1 414 000
Plant supervision	5 050 000
Fringe benefits	7 070 000
Miscellaneous	1 616 000
Total fixed overhead	20 200 000
Total overhead	$ 27 775 000
Manufacturing overhead allocation rates (cost per unit):	
Variable	$75
Fixed	$200

Developing the inventory and cost of goods sold budgets

To prepare budgeted cost of goods sold, Sandy needs forecasted costs for ending inventories. Using the fixed and variable production costs, he prepares the ending inventories budget, summarised as follows.

Ending inventories budget	
Direct materials (cost per unit):	
Frame	$ 50.00
Components	70.00
Wheels	20.00
Total direct materials	140.00
Direct labour:	
Assembly (1.5 hours × $25)	37.50
Testing (0.15 hours × $15)	2.25
Total direct labour	39.75
Manufacturing overhead	
Variable	75.00
Fixed	200.00
Total overhead	275.00
Total cost per unit	$454.75
Budgeted cost of ending inventory:	
3500 units × $454.75 per unit	$1 591 625

Using information from the preceding budgets, Sandy prepares the cost of goods sold budget for the forecasted sale of 100 000 units.

Cost of goods sold budget		
Beginning finished goods		$ 1 136 875
Direct materials used	$ 14 140 000	
Direct labour	4 014 750	
Manufacturing overhead	27 775 000	

Cost of goods manufactured	45 929 750
Total available	47 066 625
Ending finished goods	(1 591 625)
Cost of goods sold	$ 45 475 000

Developing the support department budgets

Having completed the production cost budgets, Sandy next estimates other operating costs, that is, the budgeted costs for all of the support departments. In this illustration, the support costs are all fixed. In other situations, support costs could contain a mixture of fixed and variable costs.

Support department information is gathered from each department manager. The support department budget is summarised as follows.

Support department budget	
Department	**Fixed costs**
Administration	$ 16 478 215
Marketing	9 886 929
Distribution	4 943 465
Customer service	1 647 821
Total	$32 956 430

Developing the budgeted income statement

Finally, Sandy combines the information from all of the individual operating budgets to prepare the budgeted income statement. The entity's managers do not anticipate any non-operating income statement items, so no additional items must be included in the budgeted income statement except for income taxes at the expected rate of 30 per cent.

Budgeted income statement		
Revenues (revenue budget)		$80 000 000
Cost of goods sold (cost of goods sold budget)		45 475 000
Gross margin		34 525 000
Operating costs (support department budgets):		
Administration	$16 478 215	
Marketing	9 886 929	
Distribution	4 943 465	
Customer service	1 647 821	
Total operating costs		32 956 430
Operating income		1 568 570
Income taxes ($1 568 570 × 30%)		470 571
Net income		$ 1 097 999

Sandy reviews the budgeted income statement information with the entity's controller. The budgets are then presented at a meeting with the CEO and the various department heads.

Budgeting in non-manufacturing entities

The individual budgets shown in figure 7.3 on page 255 are for a manufacturing entity. The specific types of budgets that comprise a master budget depend on the nature of an organisation's goods or services and its accounting system. For example, some service entities do not carry inventory; the direct costs of producing services are recognised as a period cost in the income statement. Thus, budgets for these organisations generally would not include inventory computations and might not include direct materials. Other service industries, such as retailers, would carry inventory. The categories chosen for individual budgets are based on the categories that managers use to plan and monitor operations.

In the not-for-profit sector, budgets are often a primary source of information about the operations of the entity. Although donors request financial statements, budgets provide much of the operating information used by managers. In governmental entities, budgets must often be legally adopted, placing restrictions on spending authority.

Developing a cash budget

The cash budget reflects the effects of management's plans on cash and summarises information that accountants gather about the expected amounts and timing of cash receipts and disbursements. Cash budgets may be prepared quarterly, monthly, weekly or even daily to help management plan the entity's short-term borrowing or investing.

Operating cash receipts and disbursements

Operating cash receipts are estimated from budgeted revenues, taking into account the nature of customer transactions. For example, if sales are made on account, then forecasts must be made for bad debts and for the timing of customer payments. Comprehensive example 2 on Mount Dandenong Bikes includes a simple timing difference for accounts receivables. Several problems at the end of this chapter feature more variation in the timing of receivables and discounts, and the effects of bad debts on the cash budget.

Operating cash disbursements are estimated from the budgets for direct materials, direct labour, manufacturing overhead and support departments. The timing of cash disbursements for these items depends on the payment terms with employees and vendors. For example, the organisation might pay employees on the 15th and last day of each month. Payments to vendors might be made in the month after the purchase of goods or services. Some expenses, such as depreciation, do not require a cash payment.

Other planned cash flows

In addition to operating cash flows, organisations have many other types of cash flows, including the following:
- purchasing or selling property, plant and equipment
- borrowing or repaying long-term debt
- paying interest on debt
- issuing or redeeming capital stock
- paying dividends to shareholders.

Although the purchase or sale of property, plant and equipment is planned in the capital budget, the cash effects of borrowing and repaying are reflected in annual cash budgets. Similarly, cash flows related to long-term debt and capital stock are planned in the long-term financing budget, but the changes in annual cash flows need to be reflected in the cash budget.

Short-term borrowing or investing

Managers typically use short-term loans or investments to balance the cash budget, taking into account the desired cash balance. Short-term loans may be pre-arranged as a line of credit with a financial institution; the organisation can borrow up to a specified amount as needed to cover cash shortages. Entities often use excess cash to repay short-term debt, with any remainder placed in liquid investments.

The purpose of the cash budget is to ensure adequate levels of cash for day-to-day operations. If an organisation lacks the necessary cash to fund its operations at any given moment, then it is insolvent. Successful new, fast-growing entities, especially franchise companies or companies growing by acquisition, sometimes fail because their assets are not liquid and they cannot pay their employees. To prepare a cash budget, three types of cash transactions are planned:

1. cash receipts
2. cash disbursements
3. short-term borrowings or investments.

Comprehensive example 2 demonstrates the preparation of a cash budget for Mount Dandenong Bikes.

Comprehensive example 2

Developing a cash budget

The managers tell Sandy that they plan to invest $8 million in new equipment during the second quarter. This expenditure means that the entity may not have enough cash and short-term investments to cover operating cash requirements. Sandy decides to prepare a quarterly cash budget to estimate the entity's borrowing needs.

Cash receipts

To develop the cash receipts portion of the budget, Sandy creates a quarterly schedule showing the timing of cash receipts expected from customers during the year. Because the entity sells merchandise to its customers on account, he needs to forecast the time it will take customers to pay their accounts. He analyses prior accounting records to estimate the sales and collection patterns. He then asks the marketing and credit managers whether they anticipate any changes in sales or collection patterns.

Sandy learns that about half of the entity's $80 million sales occur in the fourth quarter because of holiday sales. Sales are fairly even throughout the other three quarters. Given this information, Sandy forecasts sales revenues as follows:

First quarter (50% × $80 000 000 ÷ 3 quarters)	$ 13 333 333
Second quarter	13 333 333
Third quarter	13 333 334
Fourth quarter (50% × $80 000 000)	40 000 000
Total budgeted revenue	$ 80 000 000

Customers usually pay in 30 days and sales are uniform within each quarter, so Sandy forecasts that two-thirds of each quarter's sales will be received in cash during the quarter and one-third in the next quarter. Therefore, first-quarter receipts will include collection of accounts receivable from the prior year. Fourth-quarter revenues from the prior year were expected to be $30 million, so first-quarter receipts should include $10 million (1/3 × $30 000 000). Mount Dandenong sells to the same bicycle dealers every year and has eliminated those who do not pay on time. Therefore, bad debts are usually immaterial; he assumes that all accounts receivable will be collected. The managers do not anticipate any other receipts, such as new long-term borrowings, during the year. Sandy's forecast of cash receipts is presented in figure 7.4. The total estimated amount received from customers ($76 666 667) is less than the budgeted amount of revenues ($80 000 000) because accounts receivable at the end of the year ($40 000 000 − $26 666 667 = $13 333 333) are greater than accounts receivable at the beginning of the year ($10 000 000).

| | Quarter | | | | |
	First	Second	Third	Fourth	Total
Beginning accounts receivable	$10 000 000				$10 000 000
First-quarter sales	8 888 889	$ 4 444 444			13 333 333
Second-quarter sales		8 888 889	$ 4 444 444		13 333 333
Third-quarter sales			8 888 889	$ 4 444 445	13 333 334
Fourth-quarter sales				26 666 667	26 666 667
Total receipts	$ 18 888 889	$13 333 333	$13 333 333	$ 31 111 112	$ 76 666 667

FIGURE 7.4 ■ Cash receipts from customers at Mount Dandenong Bikes

Cash disbursements

Next, Sandy analyses prior accounting records and supplier contracts to identify the normal timing of cash payments to vendors, employees and others. He also asks the production and other department managers whether they anticipate any changes in purchasing or payment patterns.

Sandy forecasts that half of the production will take place during the fourth quarter, to match the pattern of sales. Therefore, half of the direct material purchases will occur during the fourth quarter, with the other half occurring during the first three quarters. Assuming that production is uniform across the first three quarters, Sandy forecasts purchases as follows:

First quarter (50% × $14 175 000 ÷ 3 quarters)	$ 2 362 500
Second quarter	2 362 500
Third quarter	2 362 500
Fourth quarter (50% × $14 175 000)	7 087 500
Total budgeted purchases	$14 175 000

Payments for direct materials are made a month after purchase. As a result, two-thirds of the purchases are paid during each quarter and one-third is paid during the following quarter. Fourth-quarter purchases for the prior year were expected to be $6 million, so payments for these purchases of $2 million (1/3 × $6 000 000) are expected in the first quarter. He uses this information to prepare the quarterly schedule for direct material disbursements in figure 7.5. The total amount paid ($13 812 500) is less than the budgeted amount of direct material purchases ($14 175 000) because accounts payable at the end of the year ($7 087 500 − $4 725 000 = $2 362 500) are greater than accounts payable at the beginning of the year ($2 000 000).

| | Quarter | | | | |
	First	Second	Third	Fourth	Total
Beginning accounts payable	$2 000 000				$ 2 000 000
First-quarter purchases	1 575 000	$ 787 500			2 362 500
Second-quarter purchases		1 575 000	$ 787 500		2 362 500
Third-quarter purchases			1 575 000	$ 787 500	2 362 500
Fourth-quarter purchases				4 725 000	4 725 000
Total disbursements	$ 3 575 000	$2 362 500	$2 362 500	$5 512 500	$13 812 500

FIGURE 7.5 ■ Disbursements for direct materials purchases at Mount Dandenong Bikes

Sandy forecasts that the remaining variable costs are incurred in the same pattern as direct material purchases — half over the first three quarters and half during the fourth quarter. He learns that property taxes are due in the second and fourth quarters and insurance payments are due in the first and third quarters. He also knows that depreciation will not be paid because it is a non-cash expense, so he removes it from the list of expenses. Sandy forecasts that the remaining fixed costs are incurred uniformly across the four quarters. He assumes that all costs other than direct material purchases are paid in the quarter in which they are incurred. In addition, he learns from management that the entity will spend $8 million on new equipment during the second quarter. Given these forecasts and assumptions, Sandy completes the cash disbursements section of the cash budget in figure 7.6.

Short-term investments and borrowings

Sandy expects cash and short-term investments at the beginning of the period to total $9 million. The managers wish to maintain a minimum cash balance of $200 000. Any cash deficiencies are financed with the entity's line of credit and require quarterly interest payments at an annual rate of 6 per cent. The entity's policy is to budget zero earnings on short-term investments.

Sandy uses this information to complete the short-term financing portion of the cash budget. He realises that the entity will need to liquidate its short-term investments during the second quarter. It will also have to borrow $1 336 742 in the second quarter and an additional $3 360 951 in the third quarter. These short-term borrowings, totalling $4 697 693 can then be repaid during the fourth quarter when sales increase. Total interest costs on the line of credit are estimated to be $90 516. A summary of the short-term financing budget is shown in figure 7.7.

	Quarter				
	First	**Second**	**Third**	**Fourth**	**Total**
Cash receipts:					
Revenues (figure 7.4)	$18 888 889	$ 13 333 333	$13 333 333	$ 31 111 112	$76 666 667
Cash disbursements:					
Direct materials purchases (figure 7.5)	3 575 000	2 362 500	2 362 500	5 512 500	13 812 500
Direct labour costs	669 125	669 125	669 125	2 007 375	4 014 750
Variable overhead costs:					
Supplies	336 666	336 667	336 667	1 010 000	2 020 000
Indirect labour	631 250	631 250	631 250	1 893 750	3 787 500
Maintenance	168 333	168 333	168 334	505 000	1 010 000
Miscellaneous	126 250	126 250	126 250	378 750	757 500
Fixed overhead costs:					
Property taxes		505 000		505 000	1 010 000
Insurance	707 000		707 000		1 414 000
Plant supervision	1 262 500	1 262 500	1 262 500	1 262 500	5 050 000
Fringe benefits	1 767 500	1 767 500	1 767 500	1 767 500	7 070 000
Miscellaneous	404 000	404 000	404 000	404 000	1 616 000
Support department costs	8 239 107	8 239 108	8 239 107	8 239 108	32 956 430
Purchase of equipment		8 000 000			8 000 000
Total disbursements	17 886 731	24 472 233	16 674 233	23 485 483	82 518 680
Excess receipts (disbursements)	$ 1 002 158	$(11 138 900)	$(3 340 900)	$ 7 625 629	$ (5 852 013)

FIGURE 7.6 ■ Summary of cash receipts and disbursements for Mount Dandenong Bikes

	Quarter			
	First	**Second**	**Third**	**Fourth**
Beginning balance, cash and short-term investments	$ 9 000 000	$10 002 158	$200 000	$ 200 000
Excess receipts (disbursements)	1 002 158	(11 138 900)	(3 340 900)	7 625 629
Line of credit:				
Borrowings		1 336 742	3 360 951	
Interest on borrowings			(20 051)	(70 465)
Repayments				(4 697 693)
Ending balance, cash and short-term investments	$10 002 158	$ 200 000	$200 000	$3 057 471

FIGURE 7.7 ■ Short-term financing budget for Mount Dandenong Bikes

Budgets as performance benchmarks

Managers and accountants use budgets to monitor operations by comparing actual results to the original budget forecasts. These comparisons serve as benchmarks for performance and help them evaluate whether strategies and operations are meeting expectations. For example, managers learn whether desired sales volumes are achieved or whether costs are under control. In addition, accountants monitor budgets to improve the quality of the budgeting process over time.

Budget variances and uncertainties

Differences between budgeted and actual results are called **budget variances**. If actual revenues are larger than the budget, or actual costs are lower than the budget, the variance is categorised as a **favourable variance**. Conversely, an **unfavourable variance** occurs when actual costs are greater than budgeted or actual revenues are less than budgeted.

Determining the underlying reasons for a variance is sometimes complicated. Suppose an entity experiences a favourable cost variance. This variance might be obtained by efficient use of overhead items. However, it could also occur because managers failed to follow budgeted plans and engaged in less activity than expected.

Because budgets are based on forecasts about the future, it is impossible to prevent variances by exactly achieving budgeted revenues and costs. The degree of forecast uncertainty varies across entities and across time. For example, Splashdown, a Melbourne Porta-loo company, experienced a 25 per cent increase in sales revenue after the release of the cult movie *Kenny* in 2006. Some entities have fairly predictable revenues and costs, especially those that purchase and sell under fixed price, long-term contracts. Other organisations have volatile or unpredictable revenues and costs. Budgets are likely to be less accurate — significant variances are more likely to occur — in highly competitive industries, when selling newly developed goods and services, or when subject to fluctuating raw material costs such as petroleum prices.

Static and flexible budgets

The interpretation of budget variances is complicated by deviations from budgeted volume levels. Many costs are variable; they are expected to change proportionately with changes in production levels. Thus, we would expect total variable costs to deviate from budget if sales volumes — and therefore production volumes — deviate from budget. However, a **static budget** is based on forecasts of specific volumes of production or services. All variable costs are calculated for a specific volume of operations. If a static budget is compared to results for a different level of volume, budgeted variable costs are overstated when fewer units or services are produced than budgeted. Similarly, budgeted variable costs are understated if more units or services are produced. These volume effects hide any variances due to operational efficiencies or inefficiencies.

A budget that reflects a range of operations is called a **flexible budget**. Cost–volume–profit analysis is a simple version of a flexible budget. Flexible budgets separate fixed and variable costs to more accurately reflect the effects of activity levels on cost. For planning purposes, flexible budgets are used to study the sensitivity of budgeted revenues and costs to different volume levels. A number of software packages for flexible budgeting are available for large entities. For small entities, Excel and other spreadsheets provide similar analysis. These software packages and spreadsheets allow financial modelling of budgets under many different circumstances.

When evaluating actual results at the end of a period, the flexible budget is set at the actual sales or production volume and used as a benchmark for analysing variances. Organisations that use a static budget transform it into a benchmark by adjusting its variable costs to reflect actual volume. However, because fixed costs are not expected to vary with volume, they are not adjusted for any differences between budgeted and actual volumes. Therefore, the flexible budget uses actual volume for variable costs and the budgeted fixed costs. Comprehensive example 3 on Mount Dandenong Bikes illustrates variances for static and flexible budgets.

Comprehensive example 3

Static versus flexible budget variances

At the end of the budget cycle, Sandy compares actual results for the period to the budget. He plans to create a budget variance report for management.

Static budget variances

Sandy creates the summary in figure 7.8, comparing revenues and costs under the static budget with the actual income statement. He uses the budgeted variable costs for this period. Variable costs per bike include:

Direct materials:	
Wheels/tyres	$ 20.00
Components	70.00
Frame	50.00
Total direct materials	140.00
Direct labour	39.75
Variable overhead	75.00
Total cost per bike	$254.75

	Static budget	Actual	Variance	
Bikes sold	100 000	113 500	13 500	Favourable
Revenue	$80 000 000	$90 500 000	$10 500 000	Favourable
Production costs:				
Variable	25 475 000[a]	29 492 408	(4 017 408)	Unfavourable
Fixed overhead	20 200 000	19 400 000	800 000	Favourable
Support department costs	32 956 430	37 565 337	(4 608 907)	Unfavourable
Income	$ 1 368 570[b]	$ 4 042 255		
Total variance			$ 2 673 685	Favourable

[a]Budgeted variable costs × 100 000 = $254.75 × 100 000 = $25 475 000.
[b]Differs from budgeted income statement total by $200 000 because some overhead costs are allocated to inventory on the budgeted balance sheet. An increase of 1000 units in inventories was budgeted this period (beginning inventories = 2500 and ending inventories = 3500). These additional units give rise to a $200 000 (1000 × $200 per unit overhead allocation) increase in income because this amount of fixed overhead is not included on the income statement.

FIGURE 7.8 ■ Static budget variances at Mount Dandenong Bikes

Sandy includes the budgeted fixed costs for manufacturing overhead ($20 200 000) and the budgeted support department costs ($32 956 430). He calculates variances for sales volume, revenue and each of the cost categories. When Sandy compares the actual results to the budget, he is pleased with the organisation's performance during the period. The overall variance was favourable by nearly $2.7 million, and the revenue variance was positive and large — $10.5 million. However, he is concerned about the large unfavourable cost variances.

As Sandy thinks more about the cost variances, he realises that he would expect to see unfavourable variable production cost variances because the sales volume was higher than planned. Because he used a static budget in his schedule, the cost variances did not reflect the actual volume of sales. Therefore, the schedule gave him poor quality information for analysing last period's costs.

Flexible budget variances

Sandy decides to create a new budget variance analysis that reflects the actual volume of sales. He first transforms the static budget into a flexible budget by recalculating budgeted revenues using actual sales volumes (113 500) and budgeted selling price ($800). He then recalculates budgeted variable production costs by multiplying the actual sales volume (113 500) times the budgeted variable cost per unit of $254.75. Because fixed costs are not expected to vary with changes in volume, no adjustments are made to either budgeted fixed production costs or support costs. Finally, Sandy recalculates the variances. Figure 7.9 summarises his revised variance schedule.

Based on the new schedule, Sandy realises that the entity's performance was worse than he previously thought. After accounting for the higher sales volume, the total flexible budget variance is unfavourable by more than $4.6 million. These variances indicate the following:

- The average selling price per bike was lower than the budget.
- The average variable production cost per bike was higher than the budget.
- Total fixed production costs were lower than the budget.
- Total fixed support costs were significantly higher than the budget.

	Flexible budget	Actual	Variance	
Bikes sold	113 500	113 500		
Revenue	$90 800 000[a]	$90 500 000	$ (300 000)	Unfavourable
Production costs:				
Variable	28 914 125[b]	29 492 408	(578 283)	Unfavourable
Fixed overhead	20 200 000	19 400 000	800 000	Favourable
Support department costs	32 956 430	37 565 337	(4 608 907)	Unfavourable
Income	$ 8 729 445	$ 4 042 255		
Total variance			$ (4 687 190)	Unfavourable

[a]Actual quantity sold times budgeted selling price per bike of $800.
[b]Actual quantity sold times this period's budgeted variable cost per unit of $254.75.
FIGURE 7.9 ■ Flexible budget variances at Mount Dandenong Bikes

Sandy plans to investigate the reasons for the large unfavourable fixed support cost variance. However, he is unsure whether the other variances are significant enough to justify spending time investigating them. He decides to meet with the controller to discuss how to proceed. This discussion is presented later in the chapter, in comprehensive example 4 on Mount Dandenong Bikes.

budgets reflect the most recent results and also incorporate significant changes in business strategy, operating plans and the economy. With current information at hand, the managers can quickly increase or decrease costs and inventory levels during economic upturns or downturns. In turn, production can probably be resumed or expanded quickly when the economy picks up.

Cisco Systems is a provider of hardware, software and consulting services. It uses a budgeting system that combines traditional budgeting with a rolling budget that includes information from an Internet-based ordering system. The system provides real-time volume data to update forecasts. As a result, Cisco's managers can make quick changes in operations during downturns. Each year an annual plan is established based on a combination of top-down management guidance and bottom-up input from operational managers. This budget is then updated quarterly, and any changes are translated into budget targets for future periods.[1]

Activity-based budgets

Traditional budget models are developed around a few cost drivers that are primarily output-based. For example, in the Mount Dandenong Bikes example, production costs were separated into direct materials, direct labour and variable and fixed overhead. **Activity-based budgeting** uses activity cost pools and their related cost drivers to anticipate the costs for individual activities. A budget is developed for each activity in an entity's activity-based system.

Suppose that Mount Dandenong Bikes used activity-based budgeting. Its key production cost drivers might then include frame assembly, wheel attachment, painting, accessory attachment, inspection and packaging. In addition, activities would be developed for the support departments. For example, the marketing department might include personal customer contacts and website customer maintenance as well as other activities. The costs for each activity would be budgeted separately, as shown in figure 7.12.

Activity	Budgeted cost	Cost driver	Budgeted volume	Budgeted cost per unit of cost driver
Customer-related costs:				
Personal customer contacts	$ 48 000	Number of contacts	2400 contacts	$20 per customer contact
Website customer maintenance	30 000	Web service hours	2000 hours	$15 per hour
Other activities	9 808 929			
Total marketing activities	$9 886 929			

FIGURE 7.12 ■ ABC budgeting for marketing department at Mount Dandenong Bikes

Kaizen budgets

Kaizen costing is a system developed in Japan and used for products that tend to have decreasing prices or increasing quality across time, such as home entertainment centres, mobile phones and computers. **Kaizen budgets** set targeted cost reductions across time, anticipating market price reductions across the life of a product. In addition to cost reductions, quality improvements are also targeted. When kaizen budgeting is performed, cost reduction and quality improvement goals are explicitly embedded in the budgets. For example, Mount Dandenong Bikes could budget for cost reductions of 15 per cent for direct labour and 10 per cent in assembly time to meet cost and production targets in anticipation of competitors' price decreases. In addition, the entity could budget an increase in the quality of components. If the costs of quality improvements are less than the savings from reduced labour and cycle time, overall costs are reduced. Therefore, Mount Dandenong Bike's kaizen budget would reduce the cost of each bike while improving quality.

Summary

1   **Understand the role of budgets in developing both short- and long-term plans.**

Budget objectives

- Developing and communicating organisational strategies and goals for the entire entity as well as for each segment, division or department
- Assigning decision rights (authority to spend, and responsibility for decision outcomes)
- Motivating managers to plan in advance
- Coordinating operating activities such as sales and production
- Establishing prices for the internal transfer of goods and services
- Measuring and comparing expected and actual outcomes
- Monitoring actual performance and investigating variances when necessary
- Motivating managers to provide appropriate estimates, meet expectations and use resources efficiently
- Re-evaluating and revising strategies and operating plans as conditions change

Budget cycle

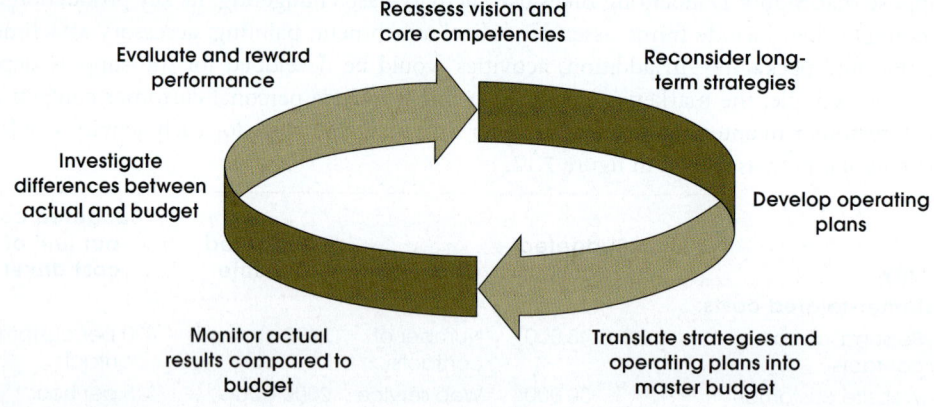

2   **Understand the role of the master budget and its preparation.**

Master budget overview

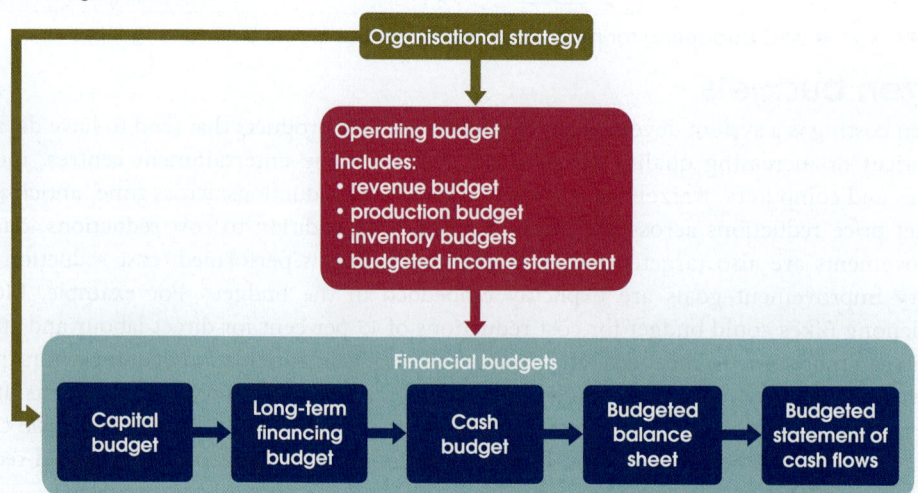

Production and inventory budgets

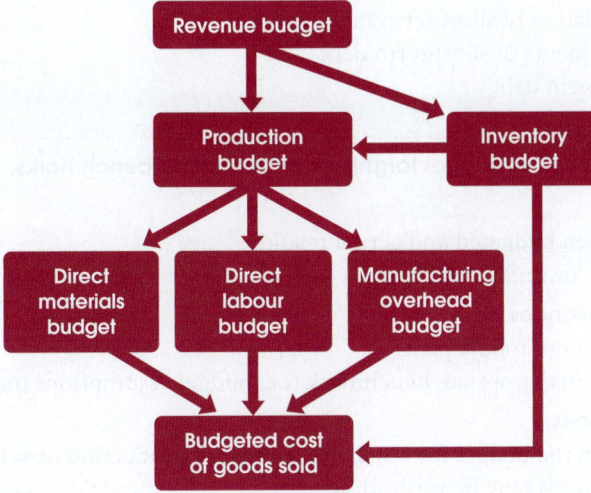

Budgeted income statement

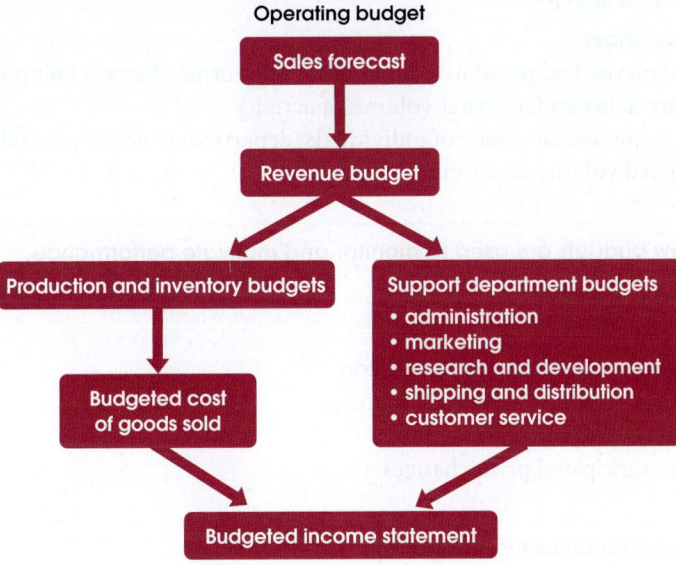

---

3 **Develop a cash budget.**

Operating cash receipts and disbursements
- Forecast timing of cash receipts from customers
- Forecast timing of cash payments for direct materials, direct labour, variable and fixed overhead, and support department costs

Other planned cash flows
- Purchase or sale of property, plant and equipment
- Proceeds or repayments of long-term debt
- Proceeds or redemption of capital stock
- Dividends to shareholders

Balancing the cash budget
- Desired cash balance
- Purchase or liquidation of short-term investments
- Proceeds or repayments of short-term debt
- Interest on short-term debt

4 Understand the use of budget targets as performance benchmarks.

Budget variances
- Differences between budgeted and actual results
- May be favourable or unfavourable

Major reasons for variances
- Actual activities do not follow plans
- Budget may be an inappropriate benchmark (i.e. budget assumptions may be incorrect)

Static budget variances
- Variances based on the budget for a specific volume of production or services
- Variable cost variances may be misleading
- Useful for measuring performance of individuals/departments responsible for achieving budgeted volume of activity

Flexible budget variances
- Variances based on the budget adjusted for actual sales or production volume
- Variable costs are adjusted for actual volume of activity
- Useful for measuring performance of individuals/departments *not* responsible for achieving budgeted volume of activity

5 Describe how budgets are used to monitor and motivate performance.

- As benchmarks
- To reward performance

Budget adjustments for performance evaluation
- Use flexible budget to adjust for actual volumes
- Remove costs not under managers' control
- Update costs for anticipated price changes

6 Outline other approaches to budgeting.

- Long-term budgets
- Rolling budgets
- Activity-based budgets
- Kaizen budgets
- Extreme programming

Self-study problems

SELF-STUDY PROBLEM 1

Constructing a master budget

Summer Select Patio Furniture is a manufacturer of patio furniture. The patio table department produces table sets. Each table set consists of four chairs, a table and an umbrella. The accountant at Summer Select gathered the following information from all of the departments in the organisation so that she can prepare next year's budget. No change occurred in costs from last period to this period. Support department costs are allocated between two separate production departments. Following is information about costs for the patio table department.

Manufacturing costs

Direct materials	Chairs	$75
	Table	$42
	Umbrella	$20
Direct labour:		
Hours	Assembly	2
	Packing	0.2
Cost per hour	Assembly	$20.00
	Packing	$10.00
Cost per unit	Assembly	$40.00
	Packing	$2.00

Inventories

	Beginning	Targeted ending
Direct materials:		
Chairs	$15 000	$20 000
Tables	$10 000	$12 000
Umbrellas	$5 000	$7 000
Finished goods	1000 units at $304 per unit	1200 units

Revenue assumptions

Selling price	$500
Table sets sold	50 000

Estimated variable manufacturing overhead costs

Supplies	$ 422 000
Indirect labour	627 500
Maintenance	80 000
Miscellaneous	125 500
Total	$1 255 000

Estimated fixed manufacturing overhead costs

Depreciation	$1 004 000
Property taxes	251 000
Insurance	351 400
Plant supervision	1 255 000
Fringe benefits	1 757 000
Miscellaneous	401 600
Total	$5 020 000

Estimated support department costs

Department	Fixed costs
Administration	$4 819 200
Marketing	2 891 520
Distribution	1 445 760
Customer service	481 920
Total	$9 638 400

REQUIRED

Prepare the following budgets: revenue, production, direct materials, direct manufacturing labour, manufacturing overhead, ending inventory, cost of goods sold and support department costs. Then prepare a budgeted income statement, assuming an income tax rate of 35 per cent.

Solution to self-study problem 1

Revenue budget

The revenue budget calculates forecasted revenues, given forecasted sales volume and price.

	Selling price	Units sold	Total revenues
Table sets	$500	50 000	$25 000 000

Production budget (units)

The production budget calculates the number of units that need to be produced, given current and targeted ending inventory levels and budgeted sales.

	Table sets
Sales	50 000
Targeted ending inventory	1 200
Total finished units needed	51 200
Less beginning inventory	1 000
Production	50 200

Direct materials budget

The direct materials budget calculates the budget for purchases of raw materials, given the beginning and targeted ending inventory levels and budgeted production volume.

Budgeted usage:	
Chairs (50 200 sets × $75 per set)	$3 765 000
Tables (50 200 sets × $42 per set)	2 108 400
Umbrellas (50 200 sets × $20 per set)	1 004 000
Total direct materials used	6 877 400
Add targeted ending inventory	39 000
Deduct beginning inventory	(30 000)
Total purchases	$6 886 400

Direct manufacturing labour budget

The direct manufacturing labour budget calculates the amount of direct labour hours needed for budgeted production and then determines the cost.

Labour hours budget:

Assembly (50 200 sets × 2 hours)	100 400
Packing (50 200 sets × 0.2 hours)	10 040
Total labour hours	110 440

Labour cost budget:

Assembly (100 400 hours × $20 per hour)	$2 008 000
Packing (10 040 hours × $10 per hour)	100 400
Total labour cost	$2 108 400

Manufacturing overhead budget

The manufacturing overhead budget summarises the expected fixed and variable overhead costs.

Variable manufacturing overhead costs:	
Supplies	$ 422 000
Indirect labour	627 500
Maintenance	80 000
Miscellaneous	125 500
Total variable overhead	1 255 000
Fixed manufacturing overhead costs	
Depreciation	1 004 000
Property taxes	251 000
Insurance	351 400
Plant supervision	1 255 000
Fringe benefits	1 757 000
Miscellaneous	401 600
Total fixed overhead	5 020 000
Total overhead	$6 275 000
Manufacturing overhead allocation rates	Cost per set
Variable ($1 255 000 ÷ 50 200 sets)	$25
Fixed ($5 020 000 ÷ 50 200 sets)	$100

Ending inventories budget

The ending inventories budget determines the unit costs and then forecasts the cost of ending inventory units.

Unit costs (cost per table set):	
Direct materials:	Cost per unit
Chairs	$ 75.00
Table	42.00
Umbrella	20.00
Total direct material	137.00
Direct labour:	
Assembly	40.00
Packaging	2.00
Total direct labour	42.00
Overhead:	
Variable	25.00
Fixed	100.00
Total overhead	125.00
Total unit cost	$304.00

Cost of goods sold budget

The cost of goods sold budget calculates the cost of inventory available for sale during the period and the cost of goods sold.

Beginning finished goods (1000 sets × $304 per set)		$ 304 000
Cost of goods manufactured:		
Direct materials	$ 6 877 400	
Direct labour	2 108 400	
Manufacturing overhead	6 275 000	
Total cost of goods manufactured		15 260 800
Total goods available for sale		15 564 800
Less ending finished goods (1200 sets × $304 per set)		(364 800)
Cost of goods sold		$15 200 000

Support department costs budget

The support department costs budget forecasts the total non-manufacturing-related costs for the period.

Department	Fixed costs
Administration	$ 4 819 200
Marketing	2 891 520
Distribution	1 445 760
Customer service	481 920
Total	$9 638 400

Budgeted income statement

Once all of the budget schedules have been prepared, the budgeted income statement is created. Revenue is drawn from the revenue budget, and cost of goods sold from the cost of goods sold budget. Then the operating costs from the support department costs budget are subtracted to determine operating income.

Revenues		$25 000 000
Cost of goods sold		15 200 000
Gross margin		9 800 000
Operating costs:		
Administration	$ 4 819 200	
Marketing	2 891 520	
Distribution	1 445 760	
Customer service	481 920	9 638 400
Operating income		161 600
Income tax expense ($161 600 × 35%)		56 560
Net income		$ 105 040

SELF-STUDY PROBLEM 2

Comparing actual results to a flexible budget

Suppose that the manager of Summer Select Patio Furniture is evaluated based on budgeted expectations. She is responsible for both sales and production costs. This period the entity produced and sold more units than budgeted, and she expects to get a bonus. Refer to self-study problem 1 for Summer Select Patio Furniture's static budget. The entity's actual results for the period are shown opposite.

Sales volume				54 000 table sets
Sales revenue				$25 500 000
Variable production costs				10 980 000
Fixed production costs				5 000 000
Fixed support department costs				9 415 300

REQUIRED

(a) Prepare a flexible budget based on actual sales volumes, and then calculate the flexible budget revenue and cost variances.

(b) Review the variances from part (a). For each variance, briefly describe the types of operating or budgeting problems that might have caused these variances.

(c) Compose at least three questions the accountant could ask the manager to better understand how the largest variances arose.

Solution to self-study problem 2

(a) To create a flexible budget for evaluating the department manager's performance, we modify the static budget to reflect the actual volume of sales, and remove any costs not under the manager's control. It requires a recalculation of budgeted variable costs to reflect actual volume. Because fixed costs remain fixed within a relevant range, we assume that they will not change with the changes in volume. However, we remove the support department costs because they are allocated and not under control of the manager.

	Static budget	Flexible budget	Actual	Variance F = Favourable U = Unfavourable
Sales volume	50 000	54 000	54 000	
Revenue	$25 000 000	$27 000 000[a]	$25 500 000	$1 500 000 U
Variable production costs	10 200 000[b]	11 016 000[c]	10 980 000	36 000 F
Fixed production costs	5 020 000[d]	5 020 000	5 000 000	20 000 F
Fixed support costs	9 638 400	Not applicable	Not applicable	Not applicable
Forecasted operating income	$ 141 600	$10 964 000	$ 9 520 000	$1 444 000 U

[a]54 000 × $500.
[b]50 000 × ($137 + $42 + $25).
[c]54 000 × ($137 + $42 + $25).
[d]Total budgeted fixed costs.

(b) Following are possible explanations for each of the variances; you may think of others:

- The revenue variance is the biggest problem for Summer Select. Instead of selling the furniture for $500 a set, the average revenue was $472.22 ($25 500 000 ÷ 54 000). It is possible that weather or economic factors reduced demand, and so the furniture was discounted during the season. It is also possible that sales volumes were better than expected because of the discounted price. The volume is larger than budgeted, but with the reduced selling price, a large unfavourable revenue variance occurred.
- Variable production costs might be lower than the flexible budget because prices for direct materials, direct labour or variable overhead costs were lower than budget. Or, the use of materials or labour might have been more efficient than in the budget.

For example, less scrap might have occurred or employees might have been more productive than anticipated. Other types of variable production costs might also have been lower than budget. For example, machinery might have required fewer repairs than expected. Also economies of scale may have been introduced, such as fewer set-up costs because production runs were longer, or direct materials costs may have been lower because of volume discounts. However, the favourable variance could possibly signal a reduction in quality, which could create a problem with future sales.

■ Fixed production costs were slightly less than expected. The $20 000 variance is a small percentage of the budgeted fixed production costs, so it might be a random variation in cost.

■ Fixed support costs might have been lower than the budget for many different reasons: unexpected decreases in the costs of fixed items such as computer software, better purchase prices for office supplies, or outsourcing of services.

It is important to keep in mind that the variances in part (a) are net amounts. Most likely, each cost category includes some favourable and some unfavourable variances. A relatively small net variance could consist of two or more large offsetting items.

(c) The following list contains possible questions; you may think of others.

 (i) Why were prices discounted, and will the new price carry over to next period?

 (ii) Is the favourable variance in variable production costs due to changes in the quality of materials? How did the savings arise?

 (iii) Were any fixed production costs either much larger or much smaller than expected?

Questions

7.1 Explain how the following budgets relate to each other: the revenue budget, the production budget and the direct materials budget.

7.2 How can budgeting assist an entity to efficiently use its human resources?

7.3 What are the objectives of participative budgeting?

7.4 What distinguishes zero-based budgeting from other types of budgeting?

7.5 How are the master budget and flexible budget related?

7.6 What methods do organisations use to minimise budgetary slack?

7.7 What adjustments should be made to static budgets before they are used for management performance evaluation?

7.8 What are some of the challenges that organisations face when allocating budget authority and responsibility?

7.9 Blowervacs produces and sells leaf blowers. Production levels are high in the summer and beginning of autumn and then taper off through the winter. Sales are high in the autumn and early winter and then taper off in the spring. Explain why preparing a cash budget might be particularly important for Blowervacs.

7.10 Describe the types of information that managers use to develop budgets.

7.11 Discuss the similarities and differences between annual budgets and rolling budgets.

7.12 How are budgets related to organisational strategies?

Exercises

7.13 **Production, direct materials and direct labour budgets** Seer Manufacturing has projected sales of its product for the next six months as shown opposite.

January	40 units
February	90 units
March	100 units
April	80 units
May	30 units
June	70 units

The product sells for $100, variable expenses are $70 per unit and fixed expenses are $1500 per month. The finished product requires 3 units of raw material and 10 hours of direct labour. The entity tries to maintain an ending inventory of finished goods equal to the next two months of sales and an ending inventory of raw materials equal to half of the current month's usage.

REQUIRED

(a) Prepare a production budget for February, March and April.
(b) Prepare a forecast of the units of direct materials required for February, March and April.
(c) Prepare a direct labour hours budget for February, March and April.

7.14 **Production, labour, materials and sales budgets** Bullen & Company makes and sells up-market carry bags for laptop computers. John Crane, controller, is responsible for preparing Bullen's master budget and has assembled the data below for 2008.

The direct labour rate includes wages, all employee-related benefits and the employer's share of payroll tax. Labour-saving machinery will be fully operational by March. Also, as of 1 March, the entity's enterprise agreement calls for an increase in direct labour wages that is included in the direct labour rate.

Bullen expects to have 10 000 bags in inventory at 31 December 2007, and has a policy of carrying 50 per cent of the following month's projected sales in inventory.

	2008			
	January	**February**	**March**	**April**
Estimated unit sales	20 000	24 000	16 000	18 000
Sales price per unit	$80	$80	$75	$75
Direct labour hours per unit	4.0	4.0	3.5	3.5
Direct labour hourly rate	$15	$15	$16	$16
Direct materials cost per unit	$10	$10	$10	$10

REQUIRED

(a) Prepare the following budgets for Bullen & Company for the first quarter of 2008. Be sure to show supporting calculations:
  (i) production budget in units
  (ii) direct labour budget in hours
  (iii) direct materials budget
  (iv) sales budget.
(b) Calculate the total budgeted contribution margin for Bullen & Company for the first quarter of 2008. Be sure to show supporting calculations.
(c) Discuss at least three behavioural considerations in the profit-planning and budgeting process.

7.15 **Flexible budget variances; profit effect of market share decline** Data for the Stove Division of Appliances Now, which produces and sells a complete line of kitchen stoves, are shown overleaf.

(In thousands)	Budget	Actual
Revenue	$16 491	$17 480
Variable production costs	5 892	6 451
Fixed manufacturing costs	1 977	2 032
Variable selling expenses	456	550
Fixed selling expenses	1 275	1 268
Administrative expenses	4 773	5 550
Operating income	$ 2 118	$ 1 629

The budget, set at the beginning of the year, was based upon estimates of sales and costs. Administrative expenses include charges by corporate headquarters for providing strategic guidance. These fixed costs are allocated to divisions using revenues as the allocation base.

REQUIRED

(a) Assume that a different volume of stoves was sold than was budgeted and prepare a flexible budget using the change in revenue to adjust the variable costs. Calculate budget variances.

(b) Due to a booming economy, the division's unit sales were higher than anticipated, even though the division's share of the home refrigerator market fell from 22 per cent to 20 per cent during the year. Using information from the flexible budget, estimate the impact on profits of the decline in market share. (*Hint:* First estimate what the total sales should have been.)

7.16 Purchases, cost of goods sold and cash collection budgets The Zel Company operates at local flea markets. It has budgeted the following sales for the indicated months.

	June	July	August
Sales on account	$1 500 000	$1 600 000	$1 700 000
Cash sales	200 000	210 000	220 000
Total sales	$1 700 000	$1 810 000	$1 920 000

Zel's success in this specialty market is due in large part to the extension of credit terms and the budgeting techniques implemented by the entity's owner, Barbara Zel. Ms Zel is a recycler; that is, she collects her merchandise daily at neighbourhood garage sales and sells the merchandise weekly at regional flea markets. All merchandise is marked up to sell at its invoice cost (as purchased at garage sales) plus 25 per cent. Stated differently, cost is 80 per cent of selling price. Merchandise inventories at the beginning of each month are 30 per cent of that month's forecasted cost of goods sold. With respect to sales on account, 40 per cent of receivables are collected in the month of sale, 50 per cent are collected in the month following sale and 10 per cent are never collected.

REQUIRED

(a) What is the anticipated cost of goods sold for June?
(b) What is the beginning inventory for July expected to be?
(c) What are the July purchases expected to be?
(d) What are the forecasted July cash collections?

7.17 Direct materials budgeted payments New Ventures intends to start business on the first of January. Production plans for the first four months of operations are shown opposite.

January	20 000 units
February	50 000 units
March	70 000 units
April	70 000 units

Each unit requires 2 kilograms of material. The entity would like to end each month with enough raw material inventory on hand to cover 25 per cent of the following month's production needs. The material costs $7 per kilogram. The managers anticipate being able to pay for 40 per cent of purchases in the month of purchase. They will receive a 10 per cent discount for these early payments. They anticipate having to defer payment to the next month on 60 per cent of their purchases. No discount will be taken on these late payments. The business starts with no inventories on 1 January.

REQUIRED

Determine the budgeted payments for purchases of materials for each of the first three months of operations.

7.18 **Cash budget for revenues and expenses** Myrna Manufacturing is located in France and has projected sales in units for four months of operations as follows:

January	€25 000
February	€30 000
March	€32 000
April	€35 000

The product sells for €18 per unit. Twenty-five percent of the customers are expected to pay in the month of sale and take a 3 per cent discount; 70 per cent are expected to pay in the month following sale. The remaining 5 per cent will never pay.

It takes 2 kilograms of materials to produce a unit of product. The materials cost €0.75 per kilogram. In January no raw materials are in beginning inventories, but managers want to end each month with enough materials for 20 per cent of the next month's production. The entity pays for 60 per cent of its materials purchases in the month of purchase and 40 per cent in the following month.

It takes 0.5 hours of labour to produce each unit. Labour is paid €15 per hour and is paid in the same month as worked. Overhead is estimated to be €2 per unit plus €25 000 per month (including depreciation of €12 000). Overhead costs are paid as incurred.

Myrna will begin January with no finished goods or work in process inventory. The managers wish to end each month with 25 per cent of the following month's sales in finished goods inventory. They will end each month with no work in process.

REQUIRED

Prepare a cash budget listing cash receipts and disbursements for February. The entity will begin February with a cash balance of €80 000.

7.19 **Flexible budget and variances; performance measurement; reasons for variances** Play Time Toys is organised into two major divisions: marketing and production. The production division is further divided into three departments: puzzles, dolls and video games. Each production department has its own manager.

The entity's management believes that all costs must be covered by sales of the three product lines. Therefore, a portion of headquarters, marketing and the production division costs are allocated to each product line.

The entity's accountant prepared the performance report overleaf for the manager of the dolls production department.

Performance report dolls production department (Volumes and total dollar amounts are in thousands.)	Cost forecasts	Budget	Actual	Variance
Sales volume	1 000	1 000	1 100	100 F
Revenue	$12.00/unit	$12 000	$12 400	$ 400 F
Direct materials	2.00/unit	2 000	2 100	(100) U
Direct labour	1.00/unit	1 000	1 225	(225) U
Variable factory overhead	1.00/unit	1 000	1 100	(100) U
Fixed factory overhead	0.80/unit	800	1 020	(220) U
Production division overhead	0.10/unit	100	105	(5) U
Headquarters	0.20/unit	200	220	(20) U
Marketing	0.50/unit	500	550	(50) U
Operating income	$ 6.40/unit	$ 6 400	$ 6 080	$(320) U

REQUIRED

(a) Is Play Time using a static budget or a flexible budget to calculate variances? Explain. Do you agree with this approach? Why?

(b) Develop an appropriate benchmark for evaluating the performance of the dolls production department. Decide whether to include or exclude each cost category, and explain your decisions.

(c) Use the benchmark you created in part (b) to calculate variances.

(d) Review the variances from part (c). Briefly describe the types of operating or budgeting problems that might have caused these variances.

7.20 Prepare cash budget A college student, Brad Worth, plans to sell atomic alarm clocks with CD players over the Internet and by mail order to help pay his expenses during the summer semester. He buys the clocks for $32 and sells them for $50. If payment by cheque accompanies the mail orders (estimated to be 40 per cent of sales), he gives a 10 per cent discount. If customers include a credit card number for either Internet or mail order sales (30 per cent of sales), customers receive a 5 per cent discount. The remaining collections are estimated to be:

One month following	15%
Two months following	6%
Three months following	4%
Uncollectible	5%

Sales forecasts are as follows:

September	120 units
October	220 units
November	320 units
December	400 units
January	out of the business

Brad plans to pay his supplier 50 per cent in the month of purchase and 50 per cent in the following month. A 6 per cent discount is granted on payments made in the month of purchase; however, he will not be able to take any discounts on September purchases because of cash flow constraints. All September purchases will be paid for in October.

He has 50 clocks on hand (purchased in August, to be paid for in September) and plans to maintain enough end-of-month inventory to meet 70 per cent of the next month's sales.

(a) Prepare schedules for monthly budgeted cash receipts and cash disbursements for this venture. During which months will Brad need to finance purchases?

(b) Brad planned simply to write off the uncollectibles. However, his accounting professor suggested he turn them over to a collection agency. How much could Brad let the collection agency keep so that he would be no worse off?

Problems

7.21 Time budget; uncertainties; performance evaluation; priorities Patricia sighed and briefly closed her eyes. She was frustrated with the reconciliation she was working on. She was sure that she was missing something, but could not determine what it was. And she felt the clock ticking, Patricia knew that the time budget for this assignment was only three hours, and she had already worked on it for two hours.

Patricia started with a CPA entity after graduation, three months ago. Her first few assignments had been stressful. She had been a good student in school, and she expected to do well at work, too. But she often felt inadequate here, as though she was supposed to know more than she did. Her supervisor, Ron, told her not to worry too much. He said that her job was to learn and that she would be performing well soon. 'All new-hires are slow to begin with,' he told her, 'Just let me know if you have any questions.' However, Patricia felt that she had pestered him with enough questions. Most of the time, the answers to her questions seemed so obvious … after Ron had answered them.

She looked at the reconciliation again.

REQUIRED

(a) Explain why it might be difficult to establish accurate time budgets for accounting tasks.

(b) Provide possible reasons why Patricia's time on this assignment could exceed the budget.

(c) Explain why Patricia is reluctant to seek Ron's help on this assignment.

(d) Describe how Ron might evaluate Patricia's performance assuming:
   (i) She seeks his help and completes the assignment in four hours.
   (ii) She does not seek his help and completes the assignment in eight hours.

(e) Suppose Patricia does not seek Ron's help and completes the assignment in eight hours.
   (i) What priorities has Patricia used in making this choice?
   (ii) Has Patricia behaved ethically? Why?

(f) What could Patricia learn from this experience that will improve her performance in the future?

(g) Suppose Patricia asked for your advice.
   (i) Use the information you learned from the preceding analyses to write a memo to Patricia with your recommendation. Refer in your memo to the information that would be useful to Patricia.
   (ii) Write one or two paragraphs explaining how you decided what information to include in your memo.

7.22 Budgeting for next semester; assumptions; monitoring Suppose a friend asks you to help her prepare a budget for the next semester.

REQUIRED

(a) Assuming you followed a process similar to that presented in this chapter, which budgets would you help her prepare? Explain your choices.

(b) Create a list of information needed to complete the various budgets. Identify which pieces of information need to be estimated.

(c) Create a list of the assumptions your friend will need to make for estimating the necessary information.

(d) How should your friend monitor her budget performance throughout the semester? Write an explanation that your friend, who is not familiar with accounting, will understand.

7.23 Performance benchmarks; variances and analysis Central Coast Public Clinic is a free outpatient clinic for public assistance patients. Among other services, the clinic provides visiting nurses for elderly patients in their homes. A homemaker who cleans and performs other household tasks accompanies each nurse. When the nurses are not visiting clients, they work at the office preparing for visits. When the homemakers complete their visits, they go home.

Each year, the clinic receives a budget allotment from the state government. The government does not allow the clinic to spend more than this allotment. The clinic, in turn, allocates its budget among its various programs. The visiting nurse program was authorised (and spent) $250 396 in 2007 and $279 476 in 2008 as follows.

	2007	2008
Nurses	$ 135 378	$ 145 019
Homemakers	60 046	71 500
Medical supplies	18 197	21 402
Cleaning supplies	6 894	9 216
Transportation	9 068	11 144
Clinic general overhead	20 813	21 195
Total expenditures	$250 396	$279 476
Home visits	4 312	5 101
Average cost per home visit	$58.07	$54.79

The nursing staff received a 5 per cent increase in salary one-third of the way through 2008. The homemakers did not receive an increase in wages in 2007 or in 2008. The prices of medical supplies increased about 2 per cent during 2008 compared to 2007. The prices of cleaning supplies were relatively constant across the two years.

Transportation is provided by the nurses, who are reimbursed $0.20 per kilometre. The clinic's general overhead is allocated to programs on the basis of budgeted program salaries.

REQUIRED

(a) In this problem you are not given a budget for 2008. If you want to evaluate performance of the 2008 clinic, what can you use as the basis of a flexible budget to develop a benchmark?

(b) Prepare a schedule to evaluate the performance of this program in 2008 using the benchmark suggested in part (a).

(c) If you were the general manager of the clinic, what would you like to discuss with the head of the visiting nurse program concerning the 2008 results? Explain.

(d) How many patients should have been served in 2008 for $279 476 if costs had been under control?

7.24 Comprehensive manufacturing master budget problem The accountant at Fighting Kites has always prepared a budget that is calculated using only one estimated volume of sales. He has asked you to help him set up a spreadsheet that can be used for sensitivity analysis in the budgeting process. This year it appears that the entity may not meet expectations, which could result in a loss. He is concerned that the entity will incur a loss again next year, and wants to develop a budget that will easily reflect changes in the assumptions. After gathering information about next year's operations, he will provide information using a what-if sensitivity analysis.

PART 1: SPREADSHEET WITH INPUT BOX, REVENUE AND PRODUCTION BUDGETS

Following are the assumptions regarding revenues, direct materials and labour costs, and inventory levels.

Direct materials per kite:

Nylon	$10
Ribs	$5
String	$2

Direct labour:

Hours	Assembly	0.5
	Packing	0.1
Cost per hour	Assembly	$30.00
	Packing	$15.00
Cost per kite	Assembly	$15.00
	Packing	$1.50

Inventory information:

	Beginning	Targeted ending
Direct materials:		
Nylon	$5 000	$7 000
Ribs	$3 000	$3 200
String	$1 000	$1 200
Finished goods (units)	2 000 kites	2 200 kites
Finished goods (cost)	$97 850	

Revenue assumptions:

Selling price	$75
Volume of kite sales	80 000

REQUIRED

(a) Create a spreadsheet with a data input box at the top. Into this box put all of the relevant assumption data. This box should be formatted with a border to separate the input data from the cell-referenced data. Set up each schedule with cell references to information in the data input box. Any changes made to information in this box should be reflected through all of the schedules that you set up. As you proceed through parts 2 and 3 of this problem, more information will be given that needs to be located in the assumptions box, such as next year's estimated variable and fixed manufacturing overhead, and support department costs. You will need to leave space in the data input box for this information, or add more rows as you develop the spreadsheet.

(b) Prepare a revenue budget.

(c) Prepare a production budget in units.

(d) Prepare the direct materials usage budget and a direct materials purchases budget.

(e) Prepare a direct labour budget (in hours and cost).

PART 2: OVERHEAD, ENDING INVENTORY AND COST OF GOODS SOLD BUDGETS

Refer to the information for part 1. Following are estimated manufacturing overhead costs. Both fixed and variable overhead will be allocated based on the number of kites produced.

Estimated variable manufacturing overhead costs:

Supplies	$ 160 250
Indirect labour	200 650
Maintenance	80 200
Miscellaneous	40 100
Total variable overhead costs	$ 481 200

Estimated fixed manufacturing overhead costs:

Depreciation	$ 211 728
Property taxes	28 872
Insurance	67 368
Plant management	240 600
Fringe benefits	336 840
Miscellaneous	76 992
Total fixed overhead costs	$ 962 400

REQUIRED

(f) Prepare a manufacturing overhead budget and determine variable and fixed overhead allocation rates by dividing the budgeted overhead by budgeted labour hours for the fixed overhead and units for the variable overhead.

(g) Prepare a schedule that calculates the unit costs of ending inventory in finished goods, and then prepare the ending inventories budget.

(h) Prepare a cost of goods sold budget.

PART 3: BUDGETED INCOME STATEMENT

Refer to the information for parts 1 and 2. Following is the information that the accountant collected about support department costs.

Support department:	Fixed costs
Administration	$ 1 034 580
Marketing	620 748
Distribution	310 374
Customer service	103 458
Total support department costs	$ 2 069 160

REQUIRED

(i) Prepare a support department costs budget.

(j) Prepare a budgeted income statement. Assume an income tax rate of 25 per cent.

PART 4: CASH BUDGET WITH BAD DEBTS AND BORROWING

Refer to the information for parts 1, 2 and 3. The entity's managers budget cash flows on a quarterly basis so that they can plan short-term investments and borrowings.

Kite sales are highest during the spring and summer. Sales are fairly even within each quarter, but sales vary across quarters as follows:

January–March	10%
April–June	50%
July–September	30%
October–December	10%

Accounts receivable at the end of the prior year, consisting of sales made during December, totalled $90 000. Payments from customers are usually received as follows:

Pay during the month goods are received	50%
Pay the next month	47%
Bad debts	3%

The managers plan to maintain beginning inventory quantities during January and February, but to increase inventories to the targeted levels by the end of March and maintain those levels throughout the rest of the year. The entity pays its vendors 10 days after raw materials are received, so approximately two-thirds of all purchases are paid in the month of production and one-third are paid the following month. Accounts payable at the end of the prior year totalled $13 000. Employee wages and other production costs are paid during the month incurred. Property taxes are paid in two equal instalments on 31 March and 30 September, and insurance is paid annually on 30 June. Support costs are paid evenly throughout the year. Estimated income tax payments are made at the end of each quarter based on 25 per cent of total estimated taxes for the year.

In addition to customer receipts, the entity expects to receive $10 000 in proceeds from the sale of equipment during January. It also plans to purchase and pay for new equipment costing $50 000 during January.

The entity finances its short-term operations with a line of credit from the bank, which had a balance of $150 000 at the end of the previous year. The line of credit agreement requires the entity to maintain a minimum cash balance of $100 000 (non-interest-bearing). The entity's line of credit requires quarterly interest payments at an annual rate of 5.5 per cent. (For simplicity, assume that all borrowings and repayments occur on the last day of each quarter.)

REQUIRED

(k) Prepare quarterly budgets for cash receipts, cash disbursements and short-term financing.

7.25 Budget planning sensitivity analysis Refer to the information from problem 7.24, parts 1, 2 and 3. The budget indicates that the entity is likely to incur a loss during the next period. The accountant asks you to assist him in developing sensitivity analyses that will help the manager identify possible ways to avoid a loss. To perform sensitivity analysis, you will alter volume of production, volume of sales, selling prices, direct material prices, wage rates and overhead and support department costs.

REQUIRED

(a) Identify the assumptions that are relevant for sensitivity analysis. Relevant assumptions are ones that the manager could potentially influence by changing the entity's operating plans.

(b) Identify possible changes in budget assumptions that might eliminate the forecasted loss (that is, those, that would lead to a breakeven situation).

(c) Perform sensitivity analysis using the input section of your spreadsheet to determine a set of assumption changes that would cause budgeted income to break even. Explain your choices.

(d) Describe uncertainties and their effects on the assumptions you made in part (a).

7.26 Comprehensive restaurant master budget problem You are the accountant for Wok and Egg Roll Express. Following are assumptions about sales for the coming month. Wok offers three basic meals: noodle bowls, egg rolls and rice bowls. Each meal can be prepared with several different meats or with vegetables only. Costs and prices are similar for all varieties of each meal. Prices for noodles bowls are $4 each, egg rolls are $3 each and rice bowls are $3.50 each. Estimated sales for the next month are 200 noodle bowls, 100 egg roll meals and 500 rice bowls per day.

PART 1: REVENUES BUDGET; UNCERTAINTIES; REVENUE STRATEGIES

REQUIRED

(a) Prepare a revenue budget for the next month assuming it is 30 days long.

(b) Discuss factors that affect the budgeted volumes of meals.

(c) Identify possible ways the owner could increase total revenues. Discuss the pros and cons for each of your ideas.

PART 2: DIRECT MATERIALS BUDGET; UNCERTAINTIES; COST CONTROL STRATEGIES

The owner of Wok and Egg Roll Express studied the cost of direct materials for each type of meal. He estimates that noodle bowls use about $1 in direct materials, egg rolls use about $0.75 and rice bowls use about $0.90. Food is purchased daily to ensure high quality. Beginning and ending inventory amounts are minimal.

REQUIRED

(d) Explain why you would not need to prepare a production budget for Wok and Egg Roll Express.

(e) Prepare a direct materials usage budget and a direct materials purchases budget.

(f) Discuss reasons why actual costs might be different from budgeted costs in part (e).

(g) Suppose the prices of food ingredients increase. Identify possible ways the owner could keep food costs within the budget. Discuss drawbacks for each of your ideas.

PART 3: DIRECT LABOUR BUDGET; UNCERTAINTIES; COST CONTROL STRATEGIES

The owner of Wok and Egg Roll Express employs cooks and cashiers. The cashiers take orders and collect payment, transfer food from the cooks to customers, and clean tables. Cooks are paid $10 per hour, and cashiers are paid $8 per hour. Wok operates four shifts: 10 to 2, 11 to 2, 2 to 10, and 5 to 8. Weekdays and weekends are staffed similarly. Following are the shifts and required workers.

Shift	Cooks	Cashiers
10 am to 2 pm	2	2
11 am to 2 pm	3	3
2 pm to 10 pm	2	2
5 pm to 8 pm	3	3

REQUIRED

(h) Prepare a labour budget showing hours and costs for a month. (Assume 30 days per month.)

(i) Discuss reasons why actual labour costs might turn out to be different from budgeted costs in part (h).

(j) Identify possible ways the owner could reduce labour costs. Discuss possible drawbacks for each of your ideas.

PART 4: OVERHEAD BUDGET; UNCERTAINTIES; COST CONTROL STRATEGIES

Wok and Egg Roll Express does not separately account for production versus general overhead. Fixed overhead includes production overhead as well as support services and general administration. Variable overhead includes labour-related costs such as payroll taxes and employee benefits. Wok has estimated variable overhead costs as $2.50 per direct labour hour. Following are the estimated fixed overhead costs for one month:

Fixed overhead costs:	
Utilities	$ 1 300
Manager	5 000
Lease	2 000
Miscellaneous	2 500
Total	$10 800

REQUIRED

(k) Prepare an overhead costs budget for one month.

(l) Discuss reasons why actual overhead costs might turn out to be different from budgeted costs in part (k).

(m) Identify possible ways the owner could reduce overhead costs. Discuss possible drawbacks for each of your ideas.

PART 5: BUDGETED INCOME STATEMENT; UNCERTAINTIES; PROFIT STRATEGIES

Refer to the information from the preceding budgets. The income statement for Wok and Egg Roll Express consists of revenues less direct costs (direct materials and direct labour) to determine the gross margin. Then the overhead costs are deducted to determine operating income.

REQUIRED

(n) Prepare a budgeted income statement ignoring income taxes.

(o) What are the major uncertainties in Wok's budget? Explain.

(p) Wok's owner would like to increase profits from the store. Suggest several possible ways to accomplish this goal. Explain your reasoning.

7.27 **Prepare cash budget from financial statements** The Red Bean Company processes and distributes beans. The beans are packed in 500-gram plastic bags and sold to grocery chains for $0.50 each in boxes of 100 bags. During March the entity anticipates selling 16 000 boxes (sales in February were 14 000 boxes). Typically, 80 per cent of the entity's customers pay within the month of sale, 18 per cent pay the month after, and 2 per cent of sales are never collected.

The entity buys beans from local farmers. The farmers are paid $0.20 per 500 grams, cash. Most of the processing is done automatically. Consequently, most ($80 000) of the entity's factory overhead is depreciation expense.

The entity advertises heavily. For March managers expect to publish $75 000 worth of advertisements in popular magazines. This amount is up from February's $60 000 of advertisements. The entity pays for 10 per cent of its advertising in the month the advertisements are run and 90 per cent in the following month. March's budgeted income statement and statement of cost of goods manufactured and sold follow. All costs and expenses are paid for as incurred unless specifically indicated otherwise. The entity will begin March with a cash balance of $25 000, and pays a monthly dividend of $15 000 to the owners.

Income statement

Sales	$800 000
Cost of goods sold	540 000
Gross margin	260 000
Administrative salaries	80 000
Sales commissions	69 000
Advertising	75 000
Bad debts expense	16 000
Operating income	$ 20 000

Statement of cost of goods manufactured and sold

Beginning balance direct materials	$ 20 000
Direct materials purchases	330 000
Materials available for use	350 000
Ending balance direct materials	30 000
Direct materials used	320 000
Labour costs incurred	90 000
Overhead costs	115 000
Cost of good manufactured	525 000
Beginning finished goods balance	45 000
Goods available for sale	570 000
Ending finished goods balance	30 000
Cost of good sold	$540 000

REQUIRED

From the information provided, prepare a cash budget for March.

7.28 Organisational resources; uncertainties; performance; government budget responsibility

REQUIRED

(a) (i) Explain how the budgeting process helps top managers articulate decisions about the use of resources.

(ii) Explain how a budget identifies the resources available to individual departments within an organisation.

(b) (i) Explain why the cost of resources such as labour and direct materials is uncertain. Include the effects of market forces in your discussion.

(ii) Explain how changes in the price of resources such as labour and direct materials might cause managers to change the way those resources are used.

(iii) Explain how the issues you discussed in parts (i) and (ii) can result in budget variances.

(c) (i) Explain how budgets can be used to measure organisational performance.
 (ii) Explain how each of the following budget adjustments improves measurement of variances when evaluating the performance for individual managers within an organisation:
    (I) using flexible budgets to adjust for actual volumes
    (II) removing allocated costs
    (III) updating costs for anticipated price changes.
 (iii) How can the analysis of budget variances lead to continuous improvement in an organisation?

REFERENCE

1 See Myers, R 2001, 'Budgets on a roll', *Journal of Accountancy*, December, pp. 41–6.

8

Relevant costs for decision making

IN BRIEF

Managers make a variety of non-routine operating decisions that include special orders, outsourcing, keeping or dropping a product line, and constrained resources. Decisions are also made about when to sell joint products and/or when to further process. Costs are an important part of making these decisions. However, qualitative factors are also important, sometimes overriding cost considerations. Managers weigh a variety of quantitative and qualitative factors in choosing the best course of action.

After studying this chapter, you should be able to:

1	Be aware of the process for making non-routine operating decisions.
2	Understand the decision-making process to accept, reject and price special orders.
3	Appreciate the decision-making process to keep or drop products, segments or whole businesses.
4	Understand the decision-making process to insource or outsource an activity (make or buy).
5	Explain the decision-making process for product emphasis and constrained resources.
6	Identify the qualitative factors important to non-routine operating decisions.
7	Identify the limitations and uncertainties that should be considered when making non-routine operating decisions.
8	Demonstrate an understanding of joint costing issues.

Flexible manufacturing at Golden Circle

Ask most Australians and they would probably associate the company Golden Circle with pineapples. This Australian-owned entity began operations in 1947, and processes more than 80 per cent of the pineapples grown in Australia by 200 growers. This equates to 120 000 tonnes of fresh pineapples each year. Today, the company manufactures over 500 fruit and vegetable products, with pineapple now accounting for only 20 per cent of its product range. In addition to packaged fruit and vegetables, the product range also includes cordials, softdrinks, jams, conserves and baby food. The nature of the industry and product range demonstrates that a number of different products (joint products) may come from the same input of raw product or fruit.

Due to the diversity of potential products supplied within the fruit and vegetable processing industry, key operators such as Golden Circle have the ability to operate in several key markets and offer upstream and downstream products within these industry value chains. For example, table 8.1 highlights the industries where Golden Circle is a key player. It also lists the recognised industry code and the major competitors.

TABLE 8.1 ■ The industry where Golden Circle operates as a key player

Industry in Australia	Industry code	Golden Circle's competitors
Fruit juice drink manufacturing	C2187	Cadbury Schweppes Coca-Cola Amatil
Fruit and vegetable processing	C2130	Coca-Cola Amatil Simplot Australia
Softdrink, cordial and syrup manufacturing	C2181	Cadbury Schweppes Coca-Cola Amatil San Miguel Australia

Source: Data compiled from IBISWorld Australia, www.ibisworld.com.au.

Rather than outsource certain activities, such as product packaging, Golden Circle has invested in inhouse operations such as a can supply system, a Tetra Pak plant (which produces 40 million litres of fruit drinks annually) and a robotic blow-moulding facility capable of producing 50 million plastic cordial and beverage bottles annually. In 1990 it also incorporated a sugar refinery within its 16.5 hectare site. One of the major reasons behind these investments and decision not to outsource these activities relates to the quality of the final product offered to consumers.

For instance, Golden Circle claims that because the farms are close to the factory, beetroot picked in the morning, 80 kilometres away, will be in the can by nightfall. The situation is similar with pineapples. When the pineapples arrive at the plant, they are inspected, washed and graded. They are then peeled and cored, and the waste (a by-product) is used in animal feed. If the pineapples are to be canned, they are placed onto automated pine lines for slicing and canning. Alternatively, the peeled and cored pineapples could be transferred to a different department depending on the final product required.

Given the seasonal nature of fresh fruit and vegetables, manufacturing companies like Golden Circle must have relatively flexible manufacturing capabilities. For example, they must make decisions about whether to commit the production process to a certain product line as and when the produce comes into season (ripens). Sometimes, decisions regarding special production runs might need to be made if fruit or vegetables ripen earlier or later than anticipated, or if customers request special production runs of a particular product. This is particularly important because the industry thrives on the quality and freshness of its output. Further, like many Australian entities, Golden Circle might be confronted with the need to consider outsourcing some activities (buying in rather than making or performing the service inhouse). This might apply to support services or even core activities like production. Of course, in all these kinds of decisions, there are both quantitative and qualitative factors to consider.

Sources: Information from Golden Circle, www.goldencircle.com.au; IBISWorld, *Fruit and vegetable processing in Australia*, www.ibisworld.com.au.

Issues from this scene setter to look for in the chapter include:

■ The process of decision making for a range of different types of operating decisions.

■ The different types of (non-routine) operating decisions.

■ Issues associated with outsourcing decisions.

■ Issues associated with special order decisions.

■ Costing issues associated with joint products.

■ The need to consider both quantitative and qualitative factors in such decisions.

Non-routine operating decisions

Many management decisions are unique, making it impossible to create a 'cookbook' to memorise and use. This chapter focuses on non-routine operating decisions. These types of decisions arise when we re-evaluate operations because we want to improve processes, or because resource shortages occur or a customer wants special treatment. Some examples of non-routine decisions include:

■ whether to commit resources for a special order
■ whether to use internal resources or to outsource some activities
■ whether to discontinue a product line or business subunit or segment
■ how to manage limited resources.

Most of these decisions require the use of relevant costs/revenues and other qualitative information that must (1) arise in the future, and (2) vary with the action taken. Figure 8.1 provides a decision process capable of being used for non-routine operating decisions.

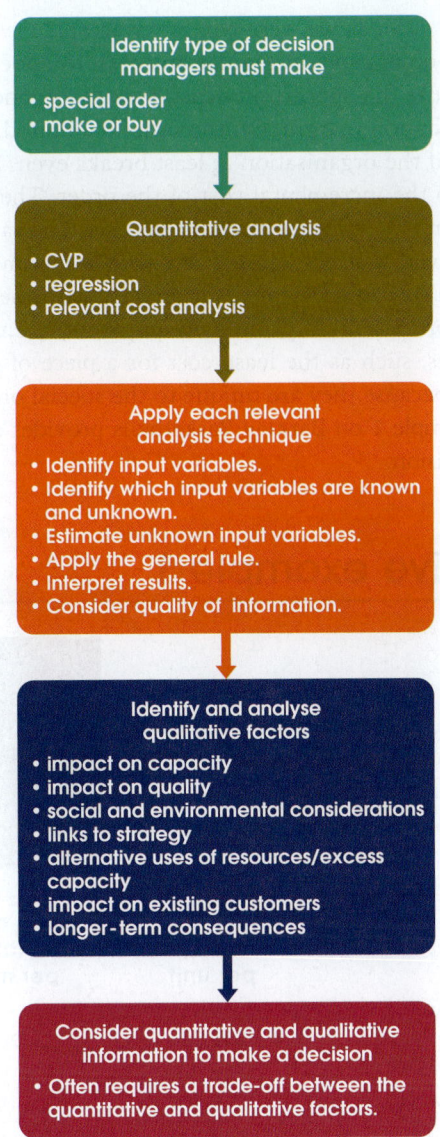

FIGURE 8.1 ■ Process for addressing non-routine operating decisions

Special orders

Managers need to determine whether to accept a customer's special order, one that is not part of the entity's normal operations. A special order occurs when an existing or new customer places a one-off request for a product or services which may or not be part of the normal operations. The characteristics of a special order may include reduced price, personalisation, non-standard order size or special delivery characteristics. Moreover, the entity may be willing to accept a special order to use idle capacity in order to increase short-term profits or the entity may have a strategic intent to secure business.

General rule for special order decisions

Each non-routine operating decision introduced in this chapter employs a guideline — a general rule — to make a decision. The general rule for special orders is that we want to be as well off after accepting the order as we were before we accepted it. To make this decision, we need to know whether the order replaces regular business. If it does, the price should be at or above the usual price, because the opportunity cost (benefit forgone) of accepting this order is the loss of the usual contribution margin. On the other hand, if idle capacity is available, the special order is acceptable if the organisation at least breaks even. In this case, the minimum acceptable price is equal to the incremental cost of the order. The incremental cost includes most of the variable costs and incremental direct fixed costs. The variable manufacturing costs are usually relevant. However, variable selling costs such as commissions are often irrelevant if the entity requesting the special order places it directly with the manufacturer. Most fixed costs (such as rent and depreciation on plant and equipment) are unavoidable, making them irrelevant. Some fixed costs, such as the lease cost for a piece of equipment needed for the special order, are relevant because they are unique to the special order.

The comprehensive example 1 on Barkley Basketballs provides an opportunity to practise making a special order decision.

Comprehensive example 1

Special orders

Barkley Basketballs Ltd manufactures high-quality basketballs at its plant, which has a production capacity of 50000 basketballs per month. Current production is 35000 per month. The manufacturing costs of $24 per basketball are categorised as follows:

	Variable cost per unit	Fixed cost per unit (at 35000 per month)	Total cost per unit
Manufacturing costs:			
Direct materials	$12.00	$0.00	$12.00
Direct labour	2.00	0.00	2.00
Manufacturing overhead	0.50	9.50	10.00
Total cost to manufacture	$14.50	$9.50	$24.00
Sales commission	$ 1.00	$0.00	$ 1.00

Jack O'Neil operates not-for-profit basketball camps for disadvantaged youths. Jack asks Billie Walton, CFO at Barkley Basketballs, to sell him 5000 basketballs at $23 per ball, or $115000 for the entire order.

Billie speaks to the cost accountant and then goes to the production floor to speak to several supervisors to gather information for this decision. She determines that the direct labour cost is variable. Workers are paid an hourly wage and are sent home when there are no balls to manufacture. These workers have no guaranteed salary, but demand is stable so they always work at least half-time, and often 40 hours a week.

Billie asks about the manufacturing overhead and finds that it consists of variable and fixed costs incurred to run the plant where the basketballs are manufactured. Overhead includes insurance, property taxes, depreciation, utilities and various other plant-related costs. She finds that all of the fixed costs are related to a capacity level of 50 000 and will not change if she uses part of the idle capacity of 15 000 units. The supervisor warns her, however, that once production exceeds 40 000 basketballs, bottlenecks occur and the production process will slow down and cause inventory levels to congest the plant, sometimes causing overtime to be paid.

Quantitative analysis

With the 5000 basketballs produced for Jack, total production for the month would be 40 000 basketballs. Bottlenecks and slowdowns do not occur until production exceeds 40 000. Therefore, the special order is within the relevant range of production; the fixed costs should remain fixed. The relevant revenues and costs per basketball are as follows:

Selling price	$23.00
Variable costs (materials, labour and overhead)	$14.50

In deciding whether to accept this special order, fixed costs are irrelevant because they are unavoidable. They will be incurred whether 35 000 or 40 000 basketballs are produced. The variable cost of $1 sales commission per ball is also irrelevant because no sales representatives are involved in this particular transaction. Therefore, the contribution margin for each special order basketball would be $23 − $14.50 = $8.50. For 5000 basketballs, the total contribution margin would be $42 500.

Qualitative factors

Based on the preceding quantitative analysis, Billie wants to accept the order. However, she first needs to consider the qualitative aspects of the decision. If she sells the basketballs at this lower price, other customers might demand lower prices too, causing Barkley Basketballs to get into a pricing war with itself. However, Jack's entity is not-for-profit; Billie doubts that other customers would object to giving it a discount.

Billie also believes that the company could enhance its reputation if Jack publicises Barkley Basketballs' support of the basketball camps. To evaluate the value of such publicity, she meets with the marketing manager, Mark Jordan. Mark cannot quantify the value, but he suggests that the publicity would definitely help promote the Barkley Basketballs brand name. In addition, the company has funded basketball camps in the past, in keeping with its policy of supporting the community.

Making the decision

After considering all of these factors, Billie discusses the special order with Jack. She offers to lower the price even further than $23. Jack is pleasantly surprised and offers to publicise Barkley Basketballs' generosity. Billie and Jack settle on a price of $20 per ball. The contribution margin of the special order is reduced from $42 500 to $27 500 (5000 balls at $20 − $14.50).

In this situation, Billie is willing to reduce the price of the special order even further for several reasons. In the past, the company donated money to not-for-profit basketball camps, so providing basketballs at a discount fits with management's desire to act in a socially responsible manner. She also believes the company will benefit from additional publicity. And, the company will still earn a profit from the special order. Although Billie has agreed to a lower price than usual, the special order meets the general rule: ample capacity is available, and the price is greater than the relevant costs (variable production costs).

Evaluating the decision process

Later that week, Billie reviews the decision to sell Jack O'Neil basketballs at $20 each. She visits Mark Jordan, who insists that the value of the publicity exceeds the reduction of $15 000 in contribution margin. Billie concludes that the decision to sell the balls at a discount was appropriate.

Note the process used to make this decision. Billie first identified the type of decision (special order). She knew that she needed to know the relevant costs to make this decision. She categorised costs as fixed and variable to help her identify relevant information. Next, she determined which costs were relevant and irrelevant to the special order. In this case, all of the variable production costs and none of the fixed costs or sales commissions were relevant. In manufacturing settings such as this one, where the same product is made repeatedly, manufacturing costs can be estimated with high accuracy. Billie had good reason to be confident in her quantitative analysis. She then weighed the quantitative factors and qualitative factors and decided that, overall, it was best for Barkley Basketballs to offer the special order at a price of $20 per ball.

Billie categorised costs and factors as shown in figure 8.2.

	Fixed costs	Variable costs	Qualitative
Relevant	May increase if $Q > 40 000$ per month (beyond the relevant range)	Direct material + direct labour + variable overhead = $12 + $2 + $0.50 as long as $Q < 40 000$ per month	Potential publicity for selling ball at a discount
Irrelevant	Manufacturing overhead	Sales commission per ball (not paid on this special order)	Price concerns of other customers

FIGURE 8.2 ■ Relevant costs and qualitative factors for Barkley Basketballs

Product line and business segment (keep or drop) decisions

When organisations provide multiple products (goods or services), they periodically review operating results for each product, group of products (product line) or business segment and decide whether to keep or drop the product or segment. If financial statement data are used in these calculations, average costs are often mistakenly included as relevant information. However, managers need to separate relevant and irrelevant cash flows. Therefore, they may need to develop distinct cost functions for each product, product line or segment.

General rule for keep or drop decisions

The general rule is that we discontinue a product, service or business segment when its total contribution margin does not cover avoidable fixed costs (fixed costs that are eliminated if the product is dropped). We first separate costs into fixed and variable. The variable costs are usually relevant. To identify relevant fixed costs, we consider how fixed costs would change if we drop the product, service or segment. Thus, we categorise fixed costs as avoidable or unavoidable. To identify and estimate avoidable fixed costs, we analyse the nature of the fixed cost and its relation to the two alternatives (keep or drop). For example, dropping a product might mean that an employee in accounting or marketing could be laid off. The labour costs and fringe benefits for that employee are relevant to the keep or drop decision. They are fixed costs that can be directly associated with the product and are avoidable if the product is dropped. Alternatively, the lease cost for a manufacturing facility that produces a number of products is unavoidable if only one product is dropped. Therefore, the lease cost is irrelevant.

Comprehensive example 2 on Home Aide Services provides an opportunity to practise making a keep or drop decision.

Comprehensive example 2

Keep or drop

Home Aide Services is a not-for-profit entity that provides a variety of services for people who would prefer to live at home but need assistance. The organisation has several lines of service, including housekeeping, meals, and shopping and transportation services. Lately the organisation has suffered a decline in surplus. The manager, Justin Bean, wants to drop one of the services to increase profitability. Following are the monthly cash flows for each service.

Cash flow	Housekeeping	Meals	Shopping	Total
Revenues	$30 000	$15 000	$10 000	$55 000
Variable costs	15 000	3 000	1 000	19 000
Contribution margin	15 000	12 000	9 000	36 000
Fixed costs	20 000	6 000	5 000	31 000
Surplus (deficit)	$ (5 000)	$ 6 000	$ 4 000	$ 5 000

Quantitative analysis

When Justin tells Elizabeth Klein, the accountant, that housekeeping services should be dropped to save the organisation $5000, Elizabeth says she needs to analyse costs further. The next day she reports to Justin that instead of having an overall surplus of $5000, Home Aide Services would incur a deficit of $2000 if housekeeping were dropped. She presents the following information about the remaining product lines if housekeeping were discontinued:

Cash flow	Meals	Shopping	Total
Revenues	$15 000	$10 000	$25 000
Variable costs	3 000	1 000	4 000
Contribution margin	12 000	9 000	21 000
Fixed costs	13 000	10 000	23 000
Surplus (deficit)	$ (1 000)	$ (1 000)	$ (2 000)

Justin asks how this could be. Elizabeth explains that when she analysed the costs in more detail, she found that the fixed costs for housekeeping included benefits for the housekeepers. The cost of benefits would be avoided if housekeeping were dropped. These costs are $8000. Total fixed costs are now $23 000 ($31 000 – $8000). These fixed costs are unavoidable and are allocated to the remaining departments. They include the cost of depreciation on cars as well as administrative costs for the entire entity that had been allocated to housekeeping.

Labour costs are a small part of the meal department's total cost. Only $1000 of fixed costs would be avoided if meals were dropped; the employees who prepare meals also help with administrative work. Shopping and transportation includes $4000 in avoidable fixed costs. This amount represents salary and benefits costs for drivers who are available all hours that the service is open.

Cash flow	Housekeeping	Meals	Shopping	Total
Revenues	$30 000	$15 000	$10 000	$55 000
Variable costs	15 000	3 000	1 000	19 000
Contribution margin	15 000	12 000	9 000	36 000
Avoidable fixed costs	8 000	1 000	4 000	13 000
Department surplus	$ 7 000	$11 000	$ 5 000	23 000
Unavoidable fixed costs				18 000
Overall surplus				$ 5 000

Elizabeth prepares the following report for Justin.

Relevant benefits and costs	Housekeeping	Meals	Shopping
Revenue forgone	$(30 000)	$(15 000)	$(10 000)
Savings in labour and overhead	23 000	4 000	5 000
Net benefit (cost)	$ (7 000)	$(11 000)	$ (5 000)

With this new information, Justin analyses the costs again. He realises that all of the services are contributing to the unavoidable fixed costs and should be continued.

Qualitative factors

Elizabeth observes that competitors provide all three services. Therefore, dropping housekeeping could affect demand for the other services. Clients might not want to deal with two separate entities when one could provide all the different services they need. Even if housekeeping were just breaking even, it should not be eliminated if dropping it would alienate current customers and cause demand for the other services to decrease. In addition, employee morale could suffer if a number of workers were laid off.

Making the decision

Given this new cost analysis and the qualitative factors, Justin decides to retain all of the current services. However, he decides to investigate alternative ways that the entity could improve its surplus. First he considers any opportunity costs. If housekeeping were dropped, could Home Aide add nursing or other services instead? Would the surplus added from nursing be higher than housekeeping?

Insource or outsource (make or buy) decisions

Outsourcing, finding outside vendors to supply products and services, has become an increasingly common practice. **Insourcing** is the practice of providing the good or service from internal resources. For manufacturers, outsourcing decisions are often called **make or buy** decisions: Does the entity make the product or provide the service internally, or buy it from an outside supplier? Potential cost savings as well as organisational strategies drive such decisions. Some managers outsource any activity they view as unrelated to the organisation's core competencies.

General rule for make or buy decisions

The general rule for make or buy decisions is to choose the option with the lowest relevant cost. Managers compare the outsourcing costs with the incremental costs for insourcing. Existing fixed costs are relevant only if they can be avoided through outsourcing. The costs for insourcing also include opportunity costs. Sometimes extra space or capacity from outsourcing can be converted to other uses. Another product could be manufactured or the space rented out. The forgone benefits (contribution margin from the new product or rent payments) are an opportunity cost for insourcing.

Comprehensive example 3 on Wombat Publishers provides an opportunity to practise making an outsourcing decision. Further information on outsourcing can be found in the chapter 8 article at the end of this book.

Comprehensive example 3

Insource or outsource

Wombat Publishers produces the bookcovers for its hardbound books. Recently, Marliss Book Binders purchased new robotic equipment that cuts, trims and prints bookcovers in one process. Marliss offered to provide bookcovers for Wombat at $2 per book. Mark Bonaray, the cost accountant for Wombat Publishers, analyses the cost information for internally producing hardbound bookcovers as follows:

	Total costs for 100 000 bookcovers	Cost per unit
Direct materials	$ 75 000	$ 0.75
Direct labour	50 000	0.50
Manufacturing overhead	100 000	1.00
Supervisor's salary	50 000	0.50
Total cost	$275 000	$ 2.75

After summarising the costs for producing the bookcovers inhouse, Mark needs to identify costs that are relevant and irrelevant to the decision. First, he gathers more information. He learns from the production manager that the supervisor could be laid off if the bookcovers are outsourced. As a cost accountant, Mark already knows that manufacturing overhead is an indirect cost. In this case, it is allocated to books based on the number of direct labour hours used in each production process. Overhead costs will be incurred even if the bookcovers are outsourced. However, after examining past utility bills, Mark estimates that closing off the part of the plant where bookcovers are produced would save about $30 000, or $0.30 per bookcover.

Quantitative analysis

Although outsourcing would save $30 000 of the manufacturing overhead, the remaining $70 000 (or $0.70 per bookcover) will be incurred under each alternative and is therefore irrelevant to the decision. The relevant production and outsourcing costs for this decision are as follows:

	Cost per unit		Total cost for 100 000 bookcovers	
Relevant costs	Make	Buy	Make	Buy
Purchase bookcovers		$2.00		$200 000
Direct materials	$0.75		$ 75 000	
Direct labour	0.50		50 000	
Manufacturing overhead	0.30		30 000	
Supervisor's salary	0.50		50 000	
Total relevant costs	$2.05	$2.00	$205 000	$200 000

Based only on the preceding cost information, Wombat would save $5000 by outsourcing the bookcovers. However, Mark has not yet considered potential opportunity costs of continuing to produce the bookcovers inhouse. If Wombat Books has an alternative use for the space that houses the bookcover operations, the contribution margin from the use of that space would be relevant to the decision. For simplicity, we assume that Wombat's management has no alternative use for the space and therefore no opportunity costs to consider for this decision.

Qualitative factors

Another factor Mark considers is the quality of the bookcovers, which is emphasised in Wombat's book production process. Wombat's sales managers believe that high-quality covers are important to sales. The quality of Marliss's sample covers appears to be high, possibly even higher than Wombat's current level of quality.

Mark is also concerned about the timeliness of delivery. He speaks with Wombat's bookcover supervisor, who explains that the department is able to respond to changes in production volumes if given lead time. It has been relatively easy to have Wombat's employees work overtime or to hire part-time employees when a book appears to be a best seller, causing production levels to rise. When Mark asks Marliss about its ability to manage a very large order caused by unanticipated demand, the sales representative cannot guarantee that such an order could be produced quickly. This concerns Mark, who is aware that when books are best sellers, large volumes must be produced quickly.

Making the decision

When Mark summarises the relevant information for the decision, he concludes that the savings from outsourcing and the quality differences are relatively small. In addition, he decides that being able to meet demand is worth the additional cost. Based on his analysis, he recommends that the entity continue producing its own bookcovers.

Constrained resources

When no capacity constraints apply or alternative uses of fixed resources are available, the products with the highest contribution margin per unit are emphasised. However, sometimes managers face limits in capacity, materials or labour. When these limits restrict an entity's ability to provide enough products (goods or services) to satisfy demand, the organisation faces a **constraint**. For example, in comprehensive example 3, Wombat Publishers needs cardboard to make bookcovers. In the case of a shortage of cardboard, the entity faces a shortage of direct materials, or a direct materials constraint. A shortage of labour to run machines or to load books into packing crates would be a labour constraint. Similarly, a shortage of machines to bind the covers onto the books would be a capacity constraint.

When faced with one or more constrained resources, managers have several options. One option is to maximise the contribution margin within the constraint; that is, emphasise the product that contributes the most in light of the constraint. A second option is to incur additional costs to relax the constraint. Two options are available to relax constraints.

1. Purchase goods or services from an outside supplier.
2. Add internal capacity or redesign products and processes to use existing capacity more efficiently.

Managers can also try both options, maximising profit while simultaneously relaxing the constraint.

General rule for choosing the product mix when resources are constrained

When resources are constrained, we need to emphasise products and services that maximise the contribution margin per unit of constrained resource. For example, Fabulous Furniture produces teak tables and chairs for outdoor use. Normally the entity sells about 100 tables and 800 chairs a month. Because of industrial action at the local shipyards, it is unable to purchase enough timber locally to meet current demand.

The sales manager wants to know which product to emphasise — the tables or the chairs — to maximise profits. The accountant calculates the contribution margin per board metre for tables and chairs to make this decision. The contribution margin per table is $400, and the contribution margin per chair is $150. Tables require 4 board metres of teak and chairs require 2 board metres. The contribution margin per board metre for tables is $100 ($400 ÷ 4 board metres), and for chairs is $75 ($150 ÷ 2 board metres). To maximise the contribution margin, the sales manager should emphasise tables and sell as many as possible. If the demand for tables is filled, then the sales manager should emphasise chairs.

General rule for relaxing constraints for one or two products

The general rule for relaxing a short-term constraint for direct materials, direct labour or capacity is that managers would be willing to pay not only what they are already paying, but also some or the entire contribution margin per unit of constrained resource. Their goal would be to acquire added capacity, thereby eliminating the constraint.

In the furniture example, Fabulous Furniture is currently paying $50 per board metre for teak. Once the entity has manufactured as many tables and chairs as possible with the limited supply of teak, it will still experience demand for chairs. Customers will buy elsewhere if they cannot purchase chairs from Fabulous. Fabulous forgoes $75 in contribution margin per board metre on each chair customers would have purchased had teak been available. Consequently, Fabulous can afford to pay what it currently pays ($50), plus up to the entire contribution margin per board metre ($75) to buy more teak. If Fabulous can find a source of teak for $125 ($50 + $75) or less per board metre, it can meet customer demand for chairs.

As the variable cost per unit (including the new cost of materials or labour) approaches the selling price of the product or service, managers become indifferent to purchasing more of the constrained resource for continued production. This general rule is valid under the following assumptions:

- The organisation will forgo sales if the resource constraint is not relaxed.
- Fixed costs are unaffected by short-term decisions made to relax constraints.
- The managers want to maximise profits in the short term.
- Sales of one product do not affect sales of other products.

Capacity constraints are time constraints; that is, we have limited time available for processing products because one or more bottlenecks slow production. Any process, part or machine that limits overall capacity is a **bottleneck**. To maximise use of bottleneck resources, we emphasise products that have the highest contribution margin per bottleneck hour. We calculate the relevant contribution margin in terms of time needed at the bottleneck resource.

For example, suppose Fabulous has only one three-axis milling machine (a computerised piece of equipment that cuts and routs unusual shapes). The milling machine processes all of the tables and chairs, but it can process only four tables per hour or 12 chairs per hour. The contribution margin per machine hour for tables is $1600 (4 × $400) and for chairs is $1800 ($150 × 12). Chairs should be emphasised because they have the highest contribution per hour at the bottleneck resource.

In comprehensive example 4, we revisit Wombat Publishers to practise making a constrained resource decision.

Comprehensive example 4

Constrained resource

Suppose the managers of Wombat Publishers decide that the entity should continue to make its own bookcovers. In performing his analysis, Mark assumes ample capacity and materials are available. However, one of Wombat's children's books, *Barry Plotter, mathematical wizard*, sells many more copies than expected. This increase in demand leads to a shortage of the special cardboard

needed for the bookcovers. In turn, Wombat is unable to publish enough books to meet current demand. Customers — both children and their parents — are becoming quite frustrated with Wombat.

Qualitative factors

Mark discusses the cardboard shortage with the sales manager, Dina Wilkinson, who thinks the entity will in all likelihood forgo sales if demand cannot be met in a timely manner. In addition, the sales manager believes Wombat must continue to build positive brand name recognition for the Barry Plotter series, so that further books in the series will be well received. Given this information, Mark would like to find some way to produce enough books to meet customer demand.

Quantitative analysis

The books that have already been produced and sold covered all of the entity's fixed costs related to developing, editing and designing the books and their covers. The wholesale price of the books is $10 each. The direct materials ($0.75) and direct labour ($0.50) costs for the covers total $1.25. The remaining variable costs for each book are $1.50 for paper and $1.50 royalty to the author. Therefore, total variable costs per book are $4.25, and the contribution margin per book is $5.75.

At Mark's request, the purchasing agent, Bruce Maxwell, researches alternative cardboard suppliers. Although Bruce locates a supplier, he is concerned because the lowest-cost supplier is demanding a price of $4 per cover for timely delivery.

Making the decision

Mark decides that, in the short run, he is willing to give up some of the contribution margin for this title to build long-term customer satisfaction. Therefore, he is willing to pay as much as the original cost of the cardboard ($0.75 per book) and the original contribution margin ($5.75 per book), or $6.50 per book. He recommends that Bruce purchase additional cardboard at the asking price of $4 per book. The variable costs for this additional printing now include $4 (bookcover materials), $0.50 (bookcover labour), $1.50 (paper) and $1.50 (royalty), for a total of $7.50 per book. Thus, the contribution margin from each additional book that Wombat produces and sells will be $2.50 ($10 − $7.50). Even though this amount is lower than the original contribution margin of $5.75, Wombat continues to earn at least some contribution margin through its effort to relax the constrained resource of the bookcover cardboard.

Uncertainties and limitations for non-routine operating decisions

Figure 8.3 (overleaf) summarises the relevant information commonly used for making non-routine operating decisions, as illustrated in this chapter.

Managers make higher-quality decisions when they use higher-quality information and higher-quality decision processes. It is not sufficient for managers to identify relevant information when making non-routine operating decisions. They must also consider the quality of information, and they must evaluate alternatives objectively and thoroughly.

Type of decision

Information	Special order	Product line and business segment (keep or drop)	Insource or outsource (make or buy)	Product emphasis (under constraints)	Relax constrained resource
General decision rule	Accept if price is greater than or equal to the sum of variable cost, relevant fixed costs and opportunity cost	Drop if contribution margin is less than the sum of relevant fixed costs and opportunity cost	Outsource if buy cost is less than or equal to the sum of variable cost and relevant fixed costs minus opportunity cost	Emphasise product with highest CM per unit unless resources are constrained, then emphasise product with highest CM per unit of constrained resource	Incur cost to relax constraint if cost is less than or equal to the sum of CM per unit of constrained resource and the current variable cost of the resource
Relevant fixed costs	Only new fixed costs associated with the special order	Only fixed costs that can be avoided if drop	Only fixed costs that can be avoided if buy		Only new fixed costs to relax the constraint
Opportunity cost	Contribution margin of any regular business replaced	Benefits from using released capacity for other purposes	Benefits from using released capacity for other purposes		
Examples of qualitative factors	■ Will regular customers expect lower prices? ■ Will this order lead to improved brand name recognition? ■ Can we deliver without disrupting current schedules?	■ Will dropping one product affect sales of other products? ■ Will lay-offs affect worker morale?	■ Is it easier to ensure high quality via insourcing or outsourcing? ■ Will delivery be timely? ■ Are there uncertainties about the supplier's ability to meet contractual obligations? ■ Is this activity a core competency?	■ Does the product emphasis agree with strategic plans? ■ Are sales of one product likely to affect sales of other products?	■ Are there other ways to relax the constraint? ■ How would brand recognition be affected by delivery delays? ■ Will the decision affect future supply costs?
Examples of major uncertainties	■ How accurate are the cost estimates? ■ Are we operating in the relevant range? ■ Will fixed costs increase at higher capacity levels?	■ How accurate are the revenue and cost estimates? ■ How will customers respond to the dropped product?	■ How accurate are the cost estimates? ■ Is our measure of quality appropriate? ■ How reliable is the vendor or resource supplier?	■ How accurate are the contribution margin estimates? ■ How reliable are the product demand forecasts?	■ How accurate are the contribution margin estimates? ■ How accurate are the constraint use estimates?

FIGURE 8.3 ■ Summary of information used in non-routine operating decisions

Quality of information

Three major factors affect the quality of information for non-routine operating decisions: uncertainties, timeliness, and analysis technique assumptions.

- Uncertainties. Many uncertainties are involved in non-routine operating decisions, as illustrated in the last row of figure 8.3. Uncertainties about future revenues and costs affect all of these decisions. Future revenues and costs can vary depending on changes in the economic environment, customer demand, competition, government regulation, vendor quality, technology and many other factors. However, the degree of uncertainty varies from decision to decision. For example, fewer uncertainties come with a special order from a long-time customer than from a new customer. Similarly, fewer uncertainties accompany outsourcing with a nearby entity than with an entity on another continent. In addition, decisions having a shorter time horizon, such as a special order that can be completed within one week, are less uncertain than decisions having a longer impact, such as dropping a product.
- *Information timeliness.* Many non-routine operating decisions must be made quickly and rely on up-to-date information. For example, a customer might require a prompt reply to a special order request, or managers may need to change production plans to emphasise different products as circumstances change. Access to timely information is particularly important in industries such as computer manufacturing, where technology, demand and prices change rapidly. Cost information that is only one month old may be irrelevant. Thus, the accessibility and currency of the information system affect the quality of decisions.
- *Analysis technique assumptions.* The reasonableness of assumptions affects the quality of information generated from an analysis technique. For example, regression analysis is useful for estimating costs only within a relevant range of activity. CVP analysis assumes that the revenue and cost functions are linear and that operations remain in a relevant range of activity. Although the validity of assumptions cannot be known with certainty, the validity of assumptions in a rapidly changing business environment is more uncertain than in a stable environment.

The general decision rules we learn in this chapter assume that the entity's goal is to maximise short-term profits. This assumption ignores qualitative factors that might be more important than short-term profits for some decisions.

Quality of decision process

Three major aspects of the decision-making process affect the quality of non-routine operating decisions: decision-maker bias, sensitivity analysis and prioritisation.

- *Decision-maker bias.* Sometimes decision makers are biased, which reduces their ability to objectively and thoroughly analyse relevant information. Another type of bias involves a preference for either quantitative or qualitative information. Some people tend to rely primarily on quantitative analyses because they are more comfortable with what they view as precise answers. Others, recognising the uncertainties in quantitative analyses, prefer to rely on qualitative factors to make decisions. The best approach is to weigh carefully both quantitative and qualitative factors, taking into account the strengths and weaknesses of information for a particular decision.
- *Sensitivity analysis.* One way to improve decisions in light of low information quality and potential biases is to perform one or more sensitivity analyses. Sensitivity analysis helps managers evaluate how quantitative results would change with changes in various pieces of information. For example, estimates of incremental costs or of cost savings could be

increased to evaluate risk. Sometimes the degree of risk in the quantitative estimates for one option might make that option less desirable than another option having less risk.

- *Prioritisation*. Operating plans are designed to help achieve an entity's long-term strategies. In turn, the strategies depend on an entity's vision and core competencies. When addressing any non-routine operating decision, managers should consider whether each option is consistent with the organisation's strategies, vision and core competencies. Entities such as Toyota have established a market position based on high product reliability, making that characteristic an important strategic issue. Some entities, such as Woolworths, place strategic importance on low costs and prices. Samsung Electronics' strategy includes protecting the environment. By considering these types of qualitative issues, managers avoid taking actions that conflict with the entity's long-term interests.

Joint products and costs

Some industries simultaneously produce a group of products through a single process. Consider a fish farm where products include fresh fish, frozen fish, frozen fish entrees and fish fertiliser. In the process of making one product, one or more other products or services are created, called **joint products**. As another example, the waste management process of an environmental management firm or a local council can generate revenue from a product, biogas, as well as from the collection of food residuals. Other examples of joint products are readily found in many industries such as oil and gas, chemicals and foods.

Joint products fall into two categories: main product and by-products. A main product has high sales value compared to other joint products. At the fish farm, fresh fish, frozen fish and fish entrees are main products. A by-product has low sales value compared to the other joint products. Fish fertiliser is an example of a by-product. Table 8.2 presents a list of industries that manufacture joint products and gives examples of main products and by-products.

TABLE 8.2 ■ Examples of industries that manufacture joint products

Industry	Main products	By-products	Example entity
Petroleum (crude oil)	Petrol, diesel, jet fuel	Asphalt	Shell Oil
Copper mining	Copper, silver, lead, zinc	Malachite, azurite	BHP Mining
Cheese production	Fresh cheese, butter	Buttermilk	Bega Cheese
Timber	Timber, veneer, plywood	Bark dust, sawdust	Black Forest Timber
Beef production	Cuts of meat, leather	Dog bones, bonemeal for gardens	Herds

Joint costs are all of the costs incurred to jointly produce a group of goods. These costs are common to all of the joint products and are incurred prior to the split-off point, the point at which individual products are identified. At the fish farm, the split-off point is the point at which the fish are caught and cleaned. The joint costs include the costs to maintain the fish ponds such as labour, fish food, insurance and property taxes, plus all of the costs to clean fish and prepare them for further processing.

Separable costs are the costs incurred after the split-off point. These incremental costs can be easily traced to each specific product. At the fish farm, separable costs are incurred for packaging fresh fish, freezing fish, preparing entrees, and pulverising and emulsifying the waste and bottling it for fertiliser. Figure 8.4 shows the common and separable activities involved in raising fish and lists several of the costs for these activities.

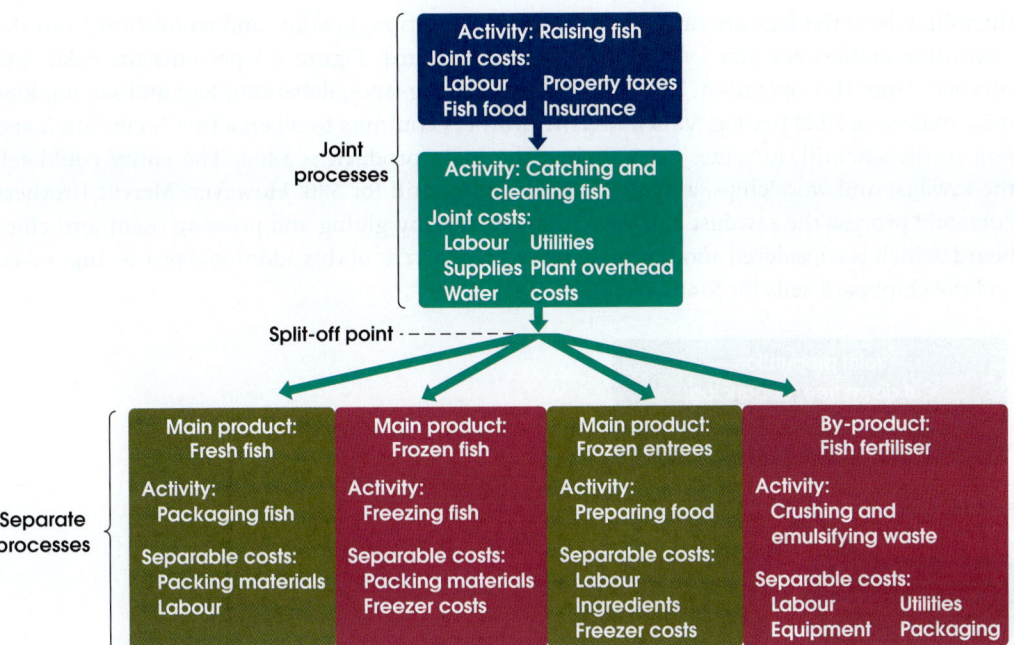

FIGURE 8.4 ■ Raising and processing fish at a fish farm

Allocating joint costs

An entity commits to joint costs when managers decide to produce joint products. Joint costs must be allocated to each product for reporting inventory and cost of goods sold on financial statements, income tax returns and other types of reports. Joint costs must also be allocated for government regulatory reports when entities that sell to both government agencies and commercial organisations seek reimbursement of costs on government-funded projects. Occasionally legal processes scrutinise joint cost allocations, such as when an organisation must support the transfer price used between divisions located in high-tax and low-tax countries. A tax audit by a government or corporate body, or government litigation, may also require joint cost allocation information. In addition, joint costs are sometimes used internally for evaluating division or segment performance.

For the waste management of an environmental management firm or local council, joint costs might be allocated between the collection of food residuals and the production of biogas and biosolids. The allocation of joint costs assists in matching revenues and costs. Therefore, the allocated costs of biogas would be expensed in the accounting period when biogas is sold, and the allocated costs of any unsold biogas would be included in inventory on the balance sheet. Similarly, the allocated cost of collecting food residuals would be recorded on the income statement in the same period in which the revenues are recorded.

Several different methods are used to allocate joint costs to main products. In the following sections we learn about these methods:

- physical output method
- market-based methods:
  - sales value at split-off point
  - net realisable value (NRV)
  - constant gross margin NRV.

To illustrate these methods, we use a sawmill example. Merritt Brothers owns and operates a sawmill in northern Victoria. The entity hires loggers who cut timber and bring it to the mill, where the logs are sawed into timber. In addition, sawdust and woodchips from the sawmill operation are glued and pressed into chipboard. Figure 8.5 presents the costs and revenues from this operation. The joint costs of cutting trees, debarking logs and sawing logs into timber are $220 per log, which Merritt Brothers commits to when a tree is cut down and sent to the sawmill. Revenue from timber, the main product, is $400. The entity could sell the sawdust and woodchips, a by-product, to a pulp mill for $40. However, Merritt Brothers currently process the sawdust and woodchips further by gluing and pressing them into chipboard, which is considered another main product. The cost of this additional processing is $46, and the chipboard sells for $146.

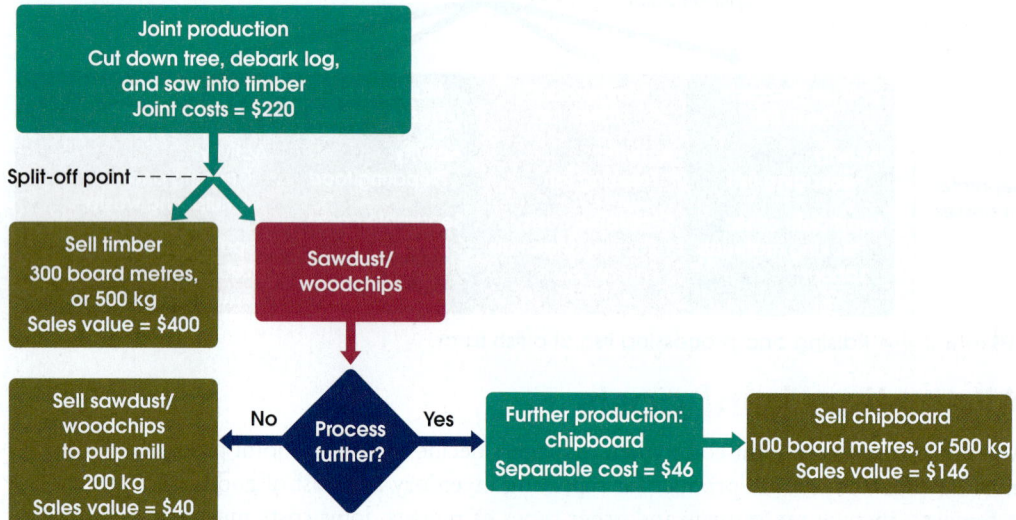

FIGURE 8.5 ■ Merritt Brothers' revenues and costs for processing one log

Physical output method

The **physical output method** allocates joint costs using the relative proportion of physical output for each main product. This method is only used when output for all main products can be expressed using the same physical measure, such as metres, kilograms or litres. Each main product is allocated a proportion of joint costs based on that product's physical output divided by the total physical output of all main products.

For Merritt Brothers, either kilograms or board metres could be used as an allocation base. Suppose the entity uses kilograms of final product as the physical volume allocation base. Each log processed results in 500 kilograms of chipboard and 500 kilograms of timber. Thus, the relative weight of chipboard is 500 kilograms/1000 kilograms. The joint costs of $220 are multiplied by this proportion to calculate the amount of joint costs allocated to chipboard:

$$(500 \text{ kg}/1000 \text{ kg}) \times \$220 = \$110$$

A similar set of calculations leads to allocation of $110 of joint costs to timber as follows:

	Main products		
	Chipboard	Timber	Total
Base (kilograms of final product)	500 kg	500 kg	1000 kg
Proportion	500 kg/1000 kg	500 kg/1000 kg	
Allocated joint costs	$110	$110	$220

Suppose Merritt Brothers instead uses the number of board metres of final product as the allocation base. For each log processed, the entity produces 100 board metres of chipboard and 300 board metres of timber. In this case, the amount of joint costs allocated to each main product is calculated as follows:

| | Main products | | |
	Chipboard	Timber	Total
Base (board metres of final product)	100 metres	300 metres	400 metres
Proportion	100 metres/400 metres	100 metres/400 metres	
Allocated joint costs	$55	$165	$220

Sales value at split-off point method

Market-based methods use some proportion of the profit contribution for each main product to determine the joint cost allocation rate. Under the **sales value at split-off point method**, joint costs are allocated based on the relative sales value of main products at the point where joint production ends. For Merritt Brothers, joint production of a log creates timber that can be sold for $400, and sawdust and woodchips that can be sold without further processing for $40. The relative proportions of sales values at the split-off point are used to allocate the joint costs of each main product as follows:

| | Main products | | |
	Chipboard	Timber	Total
Base (sales value at split-off point)	$40	$400	$440
Proportion	$40/$440	$400/$440	
Allocated joint costs	$20	$200	$220

Net realisable value method

The **net realisable value (NRV) method** allocates joint costs using the relative value of main products, taking into account both the additional sales value that is created and costs that are incurred after joint production ends. NRV for each main product is calculated as the final selling price minus separable costs. For Merritt Brothers, timber is not processed further, so its net realisable value is equal to its sales value at the split-off point, or $400. The NRV for chipboard is expected to be $100 ($146 – $46) after further processing. The joint cost allocation calculations are as follows:

| | Main products | | |
	Chipboard	Timber	Total
Base (net realisable value)	$100	$400	$500
Proportion	$100/$500	$400/$500	
Allocated joint costs	$44	$176	$220

Constant gross margin NRV method

The **constant gross margin NRV method** allocates joint costs so that the gross margin percentage for each main product is identical. This method involves two sets of computations. First, the combined gross margin percentage for main products is calculated. Second, joint costs are allocated to each main product to achieve a constant gross margin.

1. Calculate the combined gross margin percentage. To calculate the combined gross margin, create an income statement for the main products. The gross margin is determined by subtracting the joint and separable costs from the sales. Then the gross margin is divided by sales to determine the gross margin percentage. Continuing with the Merritt Brothers example,

Determine sales:		
Sales: Timber		$400
Chipboard		146
Combined sales		546
Determine costs:		
Joint costs	$ 220	
Separable costs: Timber	0	
Chipboard	46	
Combined product costs		266
Combined gross margin		$280
Combined gross margin percentage ($280 ÷ $546)		51.3%

2. Allocate joint costs to achieve a constant gross margin. The desired gross margin, based on the preceding calculation, is first subtracted from the sales value to determine the desired amount of total product cost for each main product. Next, separable costs are subtracted from total product costs to determine the amount of joint costs to be allocated to each main product.

	Main products		
	Chipboard	Timber	Total
Sales	$146	$400	$546
Less gross margin (51.3% × sales)	75	205	280
Total product costs	71	195	266
Less separable costs	46	0	46
Allocated joint costs	$ 25	$ 195	$220

Choosing an appropriate joint cost allocation method

Although each of these joint cost allocation methods is logical, the allocation process itself is arbitrary. We cannot trace joint costs to each product because we always incur all of the joint costs to produce any one product. Therefore, no method for allocating joint costs develops a true cost per product.

Each method of joint cost allocation simply assigns a different proportion of cost to product, and therefore results in a different allocated cost per product. In turn, different allocation methods result in different measures of profitability for each product. Consider the comparison of the gross margin for Merritt Brothers under different allocation methods for each log processed and sold (shown opposite).

Main product	Physical output (weight)	Sales value at split-off point	Net realisable value	Constant gross margin NRV
Timber:				
Sales value	$ 400	$400	$ 400	$ 400
Allocated joint costs	(110)	(200)	(176)	(195)
Separable costs	(0)	(0)	(0)	(0)
Product gross margin	**290**	**200**	**224**	**205**
Chipboard:				
Sales value	146	146	146	146
Allocated joint costs	(110)	(20)	(44)	(25)
Separable costs	(46)	(46)	(46)	(46)
Product gross margin	**(10)**	**80**	**56**	**75**
Total gross margin	$ 280	$280	$ 280	$ 280

Notice that the total gross margin per log is not affected by the joint cost allocation method. The cost allocation affects only the relative gross margins for the individual products. Accordingly, the joint cost allocation method used by an entity affects the apparent profitability of different products. Sometimes a product can give the appearance that it is sold at a loss, when in fact the entity profits from producing the joint product.

Pros and cons of alternative allocation methods

An allocation method should be chosen to avoid giving the mistaken impression that one or more products are sold at a loss. Under the physical output method, such distortions are likely to occur when the incremental contribution (incremental revenues less incremental costs) of some products is relatively high compared to other products. For example, if Merritt Brothers uses the physical output method using weight as the allocation base, the gross margin for chipboard is negative. If the managers make product-related decisions with this information, they might decide to quit producing chipboard. However, chipboard's incremental revenues exceed its incremental costs. If the entity were to sell the sawdust and woodchips for $40 (the sales value at split-off point), it would forgo the $100 incremental contribution from producing and selling chipboard ($146 revenue less $46 in separable costs). Thus, if chipboard is dropped, profit drops by $60 per log ($100 – $40). To avoid this problem, market value methods are generally superior to the physical output method.

Nevertheless, the physical volume method is commonly used in some industries because all units are similar in size and have comparable net realisable values. Suppose an entity grows tomatoes and then manufactures different products such as tomato sauce and salsa. The entity incurs joint costs of raising, picking, cleaning and chopping tomatoes. Possible physical output measures include weight, volume or number of same-sized bottles. If the incremental contributions of the different products are similar, a physical output measure would provide approximately the same cost allocation as the other methods. In addition, the physical output method is the easiest to calculate.

If most or all products are sold at the split-off point, then the sales value at split-off point method is generally most appropriate. This method avoids the physical output method problem of negative contribution for some products. As long as the total gross margin at the split-off point is positive, expected revenues always exceed allocated costs under the sales value at split-off point method. However, some products may need further processing before they can be sold and have no value at the split-off point, or the net realisable value of each joint product may change greatly after further processing. In these cases, this method could distort the relative profitability of products. For example, at Merritt Brothers the net realisable value of the chipboard increases from $40 at the split-off point to $100 ($146 − $46) after processing.

The two NRV methods are generally preferred because they are based on the ability of each product to 'pay' for its allocated cost. Using these methods, products appear profitable as long as their revenues are greater than their separable costs. Because the constant gross margin NRV method is more complicated, the NRV method is often chosen. However, the constant gross margin NRV method allocates joint costs so that all joint products appear to have equal profitability. This approach best reflects the inseparability of the joint production process.

Each of these allocation methods is illustrated in comprehensive example 5.

Comprehensive example 5

Choosing an appropriate joint cost allocation method

Tim Nakamura, an accounting major at the local university, is working part-time as an accountant for Merritt Brothers. When Tim prepares financial statements for the entity, he needs to choose an allocation base for assigning joint costs to products. First he examines the differences in the allocations and margins for chipboard under the different methods. The following table summarises his findings:

Allocation method	Joint cost allocated to chipboard	Chipboard gross margin
Physical output (using weight)	$110	$(10)
Sales value at split-off point	20	80
Net realisable value	44	56
Constant gross margin NRV	25	75

Tim wants to find the simplest method that most fairly values the contribution of chipboard, since it is the joint product with least value. First, he eliminates the physical output method using weight as the allocation base. Weight distorts the profitability of chipboard because the allocated amount is higher than its revenue. With this allocation method, Merritt appears to lose money on each sale. Tim knows that the sale of chipboard contributes to overall profitability. Next he eliminates the constant gross margin NRV method because he thinks the calculations would be more difficult to explain to the mill owners and managers. Because the sales value at split-off point method does not reflect the increased value of separately producing chipboard, Tim decides that the NRV method would be the best choice. This method takes into account information about revenues and separable costs for the chipboard.

REQUIRED

Set up the target function (contribution margin function) and the constraints for this problem. Enter these constraints and the target function into Excel Solver[1] or another linear programming package and print out a formula sheet and all of the reports.

(a) What is the optimal product mix?

(b) What is the total contribution margin for that product mix?

(c) Following the general decision rule, what would the managers of Mrs Meadows be willing to pay to relax each constraint?

(d) Which constraints are binding?

(e) By how much could the contribution margin for Soft Chunk increase before the optimal product mix changes?

8.25 Keep or drop and constrained resource The income statement for King Salmon Sales, which produces smoked salmon, follows:

Revenue (100 000 kg)		$800 000
Expenses		
Fish	$200 000	
Smoking materials	20 000	
Packaging materials	30 000	
Labour (wages)	300 000	
Administration	150 000	
Sales commissions	10 000	
Total expenses		710 000
Pre-tax income		$ 90 000

Assume that the administrative costs are fixed and that all of the other costs are variable.

REQUIRED

(a) Suppose the state government curtails fishing because of low fish counts. As a result, King Salmon Sales can buy only 50 000 kilograms of salmon this year. Assume that the selling price, fixed costs and variable costs remain the same as last year. Using only quantitative information, should King Salmon operate this year? Explain your answer, using calculations. (*Hint:* Before you begin, identify the type of non-routine operating decision, the decision options and the relevant information for this decision.)

(b) Assume King Salmon can buy up to 70 000 kilograms of fish at $2 per kilogram and that the remainder of the fixed and variable costs remain the same as last year. Also assume that the selling price remains the same as last year and that the market will purchase at least another 30 000 kilograms of fish. If the managers of King Salmon wish to sell more salmon, what should they be willing to pay to purchase more fish? (*Hint:* This type of decision is different from part (a). Before you begin, identify the type of non-routine decision, the decision options, and the relevant information.)

8.26 Product emphasis and constrained resource Emily developed an innovative computer game, called Home By Myself (HBM). It was so successful that she quickly followed up with two sequels: Home By Myself II (HBM2) and Home By Myself III (HBM3). The costs of developing the games were $95 000 for HBM, $10 000 for HBM2 and $15 000 for HBM3.

The production process consists of copying the games to blank DVDs using her computer and then packing them with printed instructions in a display box. It takes longer to copy the original game than the sequels. In one hour Emily can produce (ready for shipping) about 20 copies of HBM, 30 copies of HBM2 or 45 copies of HBM3.

	HBM	HBM2	HBM3
Selling price	$49.00	$29.00	$29.00
Costs			
Blank DVD	1.00	0.50	0.50
Instructions and packaging	4.00	2.00	2.00
Pro rata development costs[a]	19.00	1.00	3.00
Margin	$25.00	$25.50	$23.50
Daily demand	120 games	120 games	90 games

[a]The pro rata development costs were determined for each game by dividing the game's development costs by 5000, the estimated minimum total demand for each game.

REQUIRED

(a) What is the contribution margin per hour of Emily's time for each game?
(b) In what order should Emily produce the games?
(c) Using the general decision rule for constrained capacity, what is the most Emily should be willing to pay per hour for a worker to duplicate and pack DVDs after her normal working hours? (Assume that the worker would work at the same pace as Emily.)

8.27 **Multiple products and resource constraints; sensitivity analysis** Wildlife Foods prepares wild birdseed mixes and sells them to local pet stores, grocery stores and wild bird stores. Two types of mixes have been most successful: Flight Fancy and Multigrain. Flight Fancy generates a contribution margin of $12 per 100-kilogram bag and Multigrain contributes $9 per 100 kilograms. Because Wildlife Foods has been very thorough in its sterilisation process, the birdseed never germinates and grows. Therefore, it is a top seller and the entity can sell all of the birdseed it produces.

The seed is processed in three stages: mixing, sterilisation and packaging. The time requirements for each batch of 100 bags of Flight Fancy and 10 000 kilograms of Multigrain (which is sold in bulk rather than bags) follow.

	Minutes required		
	Mixing	Sterilisation	Packaging
Flight Fancy	200	200	100
Multigrain	100	300	0 (sold in bulk)
Minutes available	6 000	12 000	4 500

REQUIRED

(a) Using a spreadsheet program such as Excel Solver, find the optimal product mix given the current constraints and contribution margins.
(b) Which constraints are binding?
(c) What happens if minutes available for mixing are doubled? Does another constraint become binding? What is the optimal product mix now?

8.28 **Special order** The Cone Head House sells ice cream cones in a variety of flavours. Data for a recent week are shown opposite.

Revenue (1000 cones @ $1.50)	$1 500
Cost of ingredients	530
Rent	300
Store attendant	600
Income	$ 70

The Cone Head's manager received a call from a university student club requesting a bid on 100 cones to be picked up in three days. The cones could be produced in advance by the store attendant during slack periods and then stored in the freezer. Each cone requires a special plastic cover that costs $0.05.

REQUIRED

(a) What are the manager's decision options?

(b) What quantitative information is relevant for this decision?

(c) Using the general decision rule, what is the minimum acceptable price per cone for this special order?

(d) Explain why the Cone Head's manager might be willing to sell cones at the price you calculated in part (c).

8.29 Special order; qualitative factors Beautiful Biscuits (BB) sells biscuits, brownies and beverages to small local shops. the selling price per brownie is $1.25, the variable cost is $0.75 and the average cost is $1. the principal of a primary school asked bb to provide 10 dozen brownies for its spring picnic. the principal wants to buy the brownies at BB's cost. Unlike regular sales, each special order brownie must be delivered in a plastic container to protect it from dust. The containers cost $0.05 each. The brownies can be prepared ahead of time when workers are not busy.

REQUIRED

(a) Under the general decision rule for special orders, what is the minimum price per brownie that BB's management should accept?

(b) If the principal can pay no more than $0.80 per brownie, should BB take the order? Why?

(c) List several qualitative factors that could affect BB's decision if the special order price for brownies is $0.80.

8.30 Outsourcing computations; uncertainties Saguaro Systems produces and sells speakers and CD players. The following information has been collected about the costs related to the systems:

Selling price per unit	$70
Production costs per unit	
Direct materials	$22
Direct labour	$16
Variable overhead	$2
Total fixed overhead	$360 000

Saguaro normally produces 25 000 of these systems per year.

The managers have recently received an offer from a Chinese entity to produce these systems for $48 each. The managers estimate that $260 000 of Saguaro's fixed costs could be eliminated if they accept the offer.

REQUIRED

(a) Which type of non-routine operating decision is involved here? What are the managers' decision options? What quantitative information is relevant to the decision?

(b) Perform a quantitative analysis for the decision, and present your results in a schedule.

(c) Under the general decision rule for this type of decision, what production level is required for Saguaro's managers to be indifferent?

(d) List as many uncertainties as you can for this decision.

8.31 Special order computations; qualitative factors The Feed Barn packages and distributes three grades of animal feed. The material cost per tonne and estimated annual sales for each of the products are listed.

Product	Material cost	Estimated sales
Super Premium	$10.00	2 000 tonnes
Premium	8.00	3 000 tonnes
Economy	7.00	5 000 tonnes

The fixed cost of operating the machinery used to package all three products is $10 000 per year. In the past, prices have been set by allocating the fixed operating cost to products on the basis of estimated sales in tons. The resulting full costs (material costs plus allocated fixed operating cost) are then marked up 100 per cent. The Feed Barn has received an offer from a foreign entity for 1000 tonnes of the premium grade feed. Sales to the foreign entity would not affect domestic sales but would require an increase in fixed production costs of $2000.

REQUIRED

(a) Which type of non-routine operating decision is involved here? What are the managers' decision options?

(b) What relevant quantitative information is required for this type of decision?

(c) Using only quantitative information, what is the minimum price that the Feed Barn's managers should be willing to accept from the foreign entity?

(d) What types of qualitative factors would the Feed Barn's managers typically consider before agreeing to the sale? Explain.

8.32 Keep or drop; multiple product breakeven; qualitative factors Horton and Associates produces two products named the Big Winner and the Loser. Last month 1000 units of the Loser and 4000 units of the Big Winner were produced and sold. Average prices and costs for the two products for last month follow:

	Loser	Big Winner
Selling price	$95	$225
Direct materials	40	95
Direct labour	5	25
Variable overhead	5	15
Product line fixed costs	10	40
Corporate fixed costs	25	25
Average margin per unit	$10	$25

The production lines for both products are highly automated, so large changes in production cause very little change in total direct labour costs. Workers who are classified as direct labour monitor the production line and are permanent employees who regularly work 40 hours per week.

All costs other than corporate fixed costs listed under each product line could be avoided if the product line were dropped. Corporate fixed costs totalled $125 000, and the total sales amounted to 5000 units, producing the average cost per unit of $25. About $10 000 of the corporate fixed costs could be avoided if the Loser were dropped, and about $15 000 of the corporate fixed costs could be avoided if the Big Winner were dropped. The remaining $100 000 could be avoided only by going out of business entirely.

REQUIRED

(a) What is the overall corporate breakeven in total sales revenue, assuming the sales mix is the same as last month's?

(b) What is the breakeven sales volume (in units produced and sold) for the Loser? (In other words, what is the sales volume at which Horton should be financially indifferent between dropping and retaining the Loser?)

(c) List at least two qualitative factors that would affect the decision to keep or drop the Loser.

8.33 Product emphasis and keep or drop; product breakeven; relevant information The income statement information for Kallapur and Trombley Cotton Growers follows:

	Premium	Regular	Fancy	Total
Sales units	100 bales	100 bales	100 bales	300 bales
Sales	$2 200	$1 600	$1 800	$5 600
Variable costs	1 400	1 000	1 080	3 480
Contribution margin	800	600	720	2 120
	Premium	**Regular**	**Fancy**	**Total**
Production line fixed costs[a]	640	725	520	1 885
Corporate costs (allocated)[b]	90	80	105	275
Total fixed costs	730	805	625	2 160
Operating income (loss)	$ 70	$ (205)	$ 95	$ (40)

[a]If the entity drops the product, these costs are no longer incurred.
[b]None of these corporate costs is expected to change if a product line is dropped.

REQUIRED

(a) Using the general decision rule, which product should the entity emphasise? Support your answer with calculations.

(b) Using the general decision rule, should the entity drop Regular (assuming no changes in demand for other products)? Support your answer with calculations. Show how operating income would change if Regular were dropped.

(c) At what point (in bales) would the managers be indifferent to dropping Regular? In other words, what is the breakeven point for Regular?

(d) What other information would you want before you make a decision about whether to drop Regular?

Problems

8.34 Identifying joint costs; choice of allocation method Roses to Go is a flower farm that specialises in fragrant roses for florist shops.

REQUIRED

(a) List five joint costs that are likely to be incurred by Roses to Go in raising roses.

(b) The roses are sold by the dozen, with no difference in price for any of the bouquets. Which joint cost allocation method would be most appropriate? Explain your choice.

(c) Now assume that Roses to Go raises two different types of roses: fragrant roses and regular roses. The growing requirements for the two types of roses do not differ. However, fragrant roses sell for twice as much as regular roses. Which joint cost allocation method would be most appropriate? Explain your choice.

8.35 Separable and joint costs; NRV; operating income; by-product Doe Ltd grows, processes, cans and sells three main pineapple products: sliced pineapple, crushed pineapple and pineapple juice. The outside skin, which is removed in the cutting department and processed as animal feed, is treated as a by-product.

Doe's production process is as follows: Pineapples are first processed in the cutting department. The pineapples are washed and the outside skin is cut away. Then the pineapples are cored and trimmed for slicing. The three main products (sliced, crushed, juice) and the by-product (animal feed) are recognisable after processing in the cutting department. Each product is then transferred to a separate department for final processing.

The trimmed pineapples are forwarded to the slicing department, where they are sliced and canned. Any juice generated during the slicing operation is packed in the cans with the slices. The pieces of pineapple trimmed from the fruit are diced and canned in the crushing department. Again, the juice generated during this operation is packed in the can with the crushed pineapple. The core and surplus pineapple generated from the cutting department are pulverised into a liquid in the juicing department. An evaporation loss equal to 8 per cent of the weight of the good output produced in this department occurs as the juices are heated. The outside skin is chopped into animal feed in the feed department.

Doe Ltd uses the net realisable value method to assign costs of the joint process to its main products. The by-product is inventoried at its net realisable value. The NRV of the by-product reduces the joint costs of the main products.

A total of 270 000 kilograms entered the cutting department in May. The schedule shows the costs incurred in each department, the proportion by weight transferred to the four final processing departments, and the selling price of each product.

	May processing data and costs		
Department	Costs incurred	Proportion of product by weight transferred to departments	Selling price per kg of final product
Cutting	$60 000	—	None
Slicing	4 700	35%	$0.60
Crushing	10 580	28	0.55
Juicing	3 250	27	0.30
Animal feed	700	10	0.10
Total	$79 230	100%	

REQUIRED

(a) How many kilograms of pineapple result as output for pineapple slices, crushed pineapple, pineapple juice and animal feed?
(b) What is the net realisable value of each of the main products?
(c) What is the amount of the cost of the cutting department (joint costs) assigned to each of the main products and the by-product using Doe's allocation method?
(d) What is the gross margin for each of the three main products?
(e) How valuable is the gross margin information for evaluating the profitability of each main product?

(f) If no market exists for the outside skin as animal feed and, instead, it must be disposed of at a cost of $800, what effect will this cost have on the costs allocated to the main products?

8.36 Special order capacity constraint; relevant information; qualitative factors Rightway Printers, a book printing shop, is operating at 95 per cent capacity. The entity has been offered a special order for book printing at $8.50 per book; the order requires 10 per cent of capacity. No other use for the remaining 5 per cent idle capacity can be found. The average cost per book is $8 and the contribution margin per book for regular sales is $1.50.

REQUIRED

(a) Which type of non-routine operating decision is involved here? What are the managers' decision options?
(b) What information is relevant for this decision? Does the problem give you all of the information the managers need to make a decision? What other information is needed?
(c) Using the general decision rule, what premium are the managers willing to pay (per book) to relax the constrained capacity, assuming no qualitative factors are relevant?
(d) Explain how capacity affects the quantitative analysis for this decision.
(e) What qualitative factors could affect this decision?

8.37 Make or buy; qualitative factors Vernom Ltd produces and sells to wholesalers a highly successful line of summer lotion and insect repellents. Vernom has decided to diversify to stabilise sales throughout the year. A natural area for the entity to consider is the production of winter lotions and creams to prevent dry and chapped skin.

After considerable research, a winter products line has been developed. However, because of the conservative nature of the entity's managers, Vernom's CEO has decided to introduce only one of the new products for this coming winter. If the product is a success, further expansion in future years will be initiated.

The product selected is a lip balm to be sold in a lipstick-type tube. The product will be sold to wholesalers in boxes of 24 tubes for $8 per box. Because of available capacity, no additional fixed charges will be incurred to produce the product. However, a $200 000 fixed charge will be assigned to allocate a fair share of the entity's fixed costs to the new product. The remaining overhead costs are variable.

Using estimated sales and production of 100 000 boxes of lip balm as the standard volume, the accounting department has developed the following costs per box of 24 tubes.

Direct labour	$ 4
Direct materials	6
Total overhead	3
Total	$13

Vernom approached a cosmetics manufacturer to discuss the possibility of purchasing the tubes for the new product. The purchase price of the empty tubes from the cosmetics manufacturer would be $1.80 per 24 tubes. If Vernom accepts the purchase proposal, it is estimated that direct labour and variable overhead costs would be reduced by 10 per cent and direct materials costs would be reduced by 20 per cent.

REQUIRED

(a) Should Vernom Ltd make or buy the tubes? Show calculations to support your answer.
(b) What would be the maximum purchase price acceptable to Vernom for the tubes? Explain.

(c) Instead of sales of 100 000 boxes, revised estimates show sales volume at 125 000 boxes. At this new volume, additional equipment at an annual rental of $20 000 must be acquired to manufacture the tubes. However, this incremental cost would be the only additional fixed cost required, even if sales increased to 300 000 boxes. (The 300 000 level is the goal for the third year of production.) Under these circumstances, should Vernom make or buy the tubes? Show calculations to support your answer.

(d) The entity has the option of making and buying at the same time. What is your answer to part (c) if this alternative is considered? Show calculations to support your answer.

(e) What qualitative factors should Vernom managers consider in determining whether they should make or buy the lipstick tubes?

8.38 Special order; qualitative factors; uncertainties; sensitivity Jazzy Cases manufactures several different styles of jewellery cases. Management estimates that during the first quarter of this year the entity will operate at about 80 per cent of normal capacity. Two special orders have been received, and management is making a decision about whether to accept either or both orders.

The first order is from Penny-Wise Department Stores. The manager would like to market a jewellery case similar to one of Jazzy's current models. Penny-Wise wants its own label on the cases and is willing to pay $5.75 per case for 20 000 cases to be shipped by 1 April. The cost data for Jazzy's case, which is similar to the requested case, follow:

Selling price per unit	$ 9.00
Cost per unit	
Raw materials	$ 2.50
Direct labour (0.25 hours × $12)	3.00
Overhead (0.25 machine hours × $4)	1.00
Total cost per unit	$ 6.50

According to the specifications supplied by Penny-Wise, the special order case requires less expensive raw materials. Therefore, the raw materials for the special order will cost $2.25 per case. Management believes that the remaining costs, labour time and machine time will remain the same as for Jazzy's case.

The second order is from the Star-Mart Company. Its managers want 8000 cases for $7.50 per case. These jewellery cases, to be marketed under the Star-Mart label, would also need to be shipped by 1 April. However, these cases are somewhat different from any cases currently manufactured by Jazzy. Following are the estimated unit costs:

Cost per unit	
Raw materials	$3.25
Direct labour (0.25 hours × $12)	3.00
Overhead (0.5 machine hours × $4)	2.00
Total cost per unit	$8.25

In addition to these per-unit costs, Jazzy would incur $1500 in set-up costs and would need to purchase $2500 in special equipment to manufacture these cases. Currently, Jazzy would have no other use for the equipment once this order was filled.

Jazzy's capacity constraint is total machine hours available. The plant capacity under normal operations is 90 000 machine hours per year, or 7500 hours per month. Fixed manufacturing overhead costs are allocated to production on the basis of machine hours at $4 per hour and are budgeted at $360 000 per year.

Jazzy can work on the special orders throughout the entire first quarter, in addition to performing its normal production. Jazzy's managers do not expect any repeat sales to be generated from either special order.

REQUIRED

(a) What is the excess capacity of machine hours available in the first quarter? Explain how machine hour capacity affects the special order decision.

(b) Ignore the Star-Mart order. Using the general decision rule, what is the minimum acceptable price for the Penny-Wise order?

(c) Ignore the Penny-Wise order. What is the contribution margin per case for the Star-Mart order? What would be the total expected profit (loss) incurred by accepting this order?

(d) Using only quantitative information, decide which special orders Jazzy should accept.

(e) What qualitative factors are likely to be important to this decision?

(f) Identify and explain uncertainties that affect Jazzy's decision.

(g) What might happen to costs if Jazzy's production exceeds 95 per cent of its capacity? Discuss how increased use of capacity from a special order might affect the entity's costs. (*Hint*: Think about whether bottlenecks could arise and how they might affect costs.)

(h) Suppose you are the cost accountant for Jazzy.

   (i) Write a memo to Jazzy's management recommending whether the entity should accept each of the special orders. Attach to the memo a schedule showing your computations. As appropriate, refer to the schedule in the memo.

   (ii) Write one or two paragraphs explaining how you decided what information to include in your memo.

8.39 Special order computations and decision George Jackson operates a small machine shop. He manufactures one standard product available from many other similar businesses, and he also manufactures custom-ordered products. His accountant prepared the following annual income statement.

	Custom sales	Standard sales	Total
Sales	$50 000	$25 000	$75 000
Costs			
Materials	10 000	8 000	18 000
Labour	20 000	9 000	29 000
Depreciation	6 300	3 600	9 900
Power	700	400	1 100
Rent	6 000	1 000	7 000
Heat and light	600	100	700
Other	400	900	1 300
Total costs	44 000	23 000	67 000
Income	$ 6 000	$ 2 000	$ 8 000

The depreciation charges are for machines used in the respective product lines. The power charge is apportioned on an estimate of power consumed. The rent is for the building space, which has been leased for 10 years at $7000 per year. The rent and the heat and lights are apportioned to the product lines based on the amount of floor space occupied. All other costs are current expenses identified with the product line causing them.

A valued custom-parts customer has asked Jackson if he would manufacture 5000 special units for her. Jackson is working at capacity and would have to give up some other business to take this order. He cannot renege on custom orders already agreed to, but he would have to reduce the output of his standard product by about one-half for a year while producing the specially requested customer part. The customer is willing to pay $7 for each part. The material cost will be about $2 per unit and the labour will be $3.60 per unit. Jackson will have to spend $2000 for a special device that will be discarded when the job is done.

REQUIRED

(a) Calculate and present the following costs related to the 5000-unit custom order.
   (i) The incremental cost of the order
  (ii) The full cost of the order (incremental plus allocated fixed costs such as depreciation, rent etc.)
 (iii) The opportunity cost of taking the order
 (iv) The sunk costs related to the order
(b) Should Jackson take the order? Explain your answer.

8.40 Foreign versus domestic production and comparative advantage Scott Mills was originally a producer of fabrics, but several years ago intense foreign competition led management to restructure the entity as a vertically integrated cotton garment manufacturer. Scott purchased spinning organisations that produce raw yarn and fabricators that produce the final garment. The entity has both domestic and international operations.

The domestic spinning and knitting operations are highly automated and use the latest technology. The domestic operations are able to produce cotton fabric for $1.52 per kilogram. The domestic fabricating operations are located exclusively in rural areas. Their locations keep total average labour costs to $16.40 per hour (including fringe benefits). The cost to ship products to the entity's distribution centre is $0.10 per kilogram.

The entity's foreign subsidiary is a fabricating operation located in the Maldives, a group of islands near India. The average wage rate there is $0.70 per hour. The subsidiary purchases cotton fabric locally for $1.60 per kilogram. The finished products are shipped to Scott Mills' distribution centre in New South Wales at a cost of $1.80 per kilogram. Both the domestic and foreign subsidiary use the same amount of fabric per product. Scott Mills has been producing three products for the private label market: sweatshirts, dress shirts and lightweight jackets. In the past the entity processed a new order at whichever fabricating plant had the next available capacity. However, projections for the next few years indicate that orders will far exceed capacity. Management wants each plant to specialise in one of the products.

The plants are constrained by the amount of sewing time available in each. The domestic plant has 8000 hours of sewing machine time available per week, while the foreign subsidiary has 10 000 hours available per week. The domestic plant's variable overhead is charged to products at $4 per machine hour, while the subsidiary's variable overhead averages $1 per machine hour.

The windcheaters require 1 kilogram of cotton fabric to produce, the dress shirts use 400 grams of fabric and the jackets require 1 kilogram of fabric. The domestic plant has special-purpose equipment that allows workers to sew a sweatshirt in 6 minutes, a shirt in 15 minutes and a jacket in one hour. The foreign plant's equipment constrains production to five sweatshirts per hour, three dress shirts per hour or two jackets per hour. The wholesale prices are $8.76 each for the sweatshirts, $7.50 for the dress shirts and $37 for the jackets.

REQUIRED

(a) Using only quantitative information, should the entity close its domestic operations and expand the foreign subsidiary?

(b) Assuming that wages in the domestic operations remain constant, at what level of wages in the foreign subsidiary would the managers be indifferent between producing sweatshirts at one location versus the other?

(c) Discuss qualitative factors, including ethical issues, that might influence the decision in part (a).

(d) Discuss whether production quality is likely to be a bigger concern for products produced at the foreign subsidiary versus products produced in the domestic operation.

(e) If demand for each product exceeds capacity, in which product should each plant specialise?

(f) Management insists on manufacturing all three products to maintain good customer relations. If demand for each product exceeds capacity, management would prefer to specialise according to your answer to part (e). At which plant should management produce the third product?

8.41 Outsource; relevant costs; qualitative factors; uncertainties; biases Falco Services processes mortgage loan applications. The cost of home appraisals is included in its service fee, but Falco uses an outside appraisal service. The cost of appraisals has been increasing rapidly over the last several years, reaching $180 per appraisal last year. Falco's CFO asked one of the accountants to estimate the cost of doing the appraisals inhouse. Several of Falco's mortgage brokers worked previously as real estate agents and have performed informal appraisals; however, none have professional appraisal experience. The accountant's son-in-law owns the entity that currently performs most of the appraisals.

The accountant prepares a report for the CFO that includes the following estimates for 1000 appraisals. Appraisers would have to be hired, but no additional computer equipment, space or supervision would be needed. The report states that the total costs for 1000 appraisals would be $195 000 or $195 per appraisal. The current appraisal price is $180, so the report recommends that Falco continue to outsource the appraisal services.

Costs:	
Supplies and paper	$ 5 000
Professional labour	100 000
Overhead	90 000
Total costs	$ 195 000
Cost per appraisal	$ 195

Professional labour is the cost to hire two appraisers. Overhead consists of fixed overhead, which is allocated at 50 per cent of the cost of professional labour, and variable overhead (mostly fringe benefits), which is 40 per cent of the cost of professional labour. Falco's CFO has to decide whether to continue to use the appraisal service or to hire appraisers and provide the service inhouse.

REQUIRED

(a) Which type of non-routine operating decision is involved here? What are the managers' decision options?

(b) What is the expected total incremental cost for 1000 appraisals?

(c) Which costs in the accountant's report are not relevant? Prepare a revised report that includes only relevant costs.

(d) Using the general decision rule, should Falco outsource appraisal services or provide this service itself?

(e) List uncertainties about Falco's ability to begin a new appraisal service at or below the cost calculated. List as many uncertainties as you can.

(f) List possible qualitative factors that Falco's CFO should consider in making this decision. List as many as you can.

(g) Explain why the accountant might have been biased, and explain what effects that might have on the cost report.

(h) What are the costs to Falco of relying on the accountant's report for this decision? What are the costs to the accountant of admitting that she might be biased in preparing information for this decision?

8.42 Keep or drop uncertainties; relevant information; qualitative factors Gourmet Fast Foods produces and sells many products in each of its 35 different product lines. Occasionally a product or an entire product line is dropped because it ceases to be profitable. The entity does not have a formalised program for reviewing its products on a regular basis to identify products that should be eliminated.

At a recent meeting of Gourmet's top management, the head of operations stated that several products or possibly an entire product line were currently unprofitable. After considerable discussion, management decided that Gourmet should establish a formalised product discontinuance program. The purpose of the program would be to review the entity's individual products and product lines on a regular and ongoing basis to identify problem areas.

The CFO proposed that a person be assigned to the program on a full-time basis. This person would work closely with the marketing and accounting departments to determine the factors that indicate when a product's importance is declining, and to gather the information that would be required to evaluate whether a product or product line should be discontinued.

REQUIRED

(a) Explain why the managers of Gourmet Fast Foods cannot know for sure when a product or product line should be discontinued.

(b) What factors might indicate the diminishing importance of a product or product line? List as many factors as you can.

(c) If you were assigned to this position, what information would you want from the accounting system?

(d) If you were assigned to this position, would you want any information other than that produced by the accounting system? If so, what type of information would be useful, and where would you be likely to obtain it?

(e) List several benefits of assigning an employee full-time responsibility for a product discontinuance program.

(f) If you were assigned to this position, describe the steps you would take as you analyse a given product.

8.43 Outsource computations; qualitative factors; cost of quality Mills and Vines just received a bid from a supplier for 6000 motors per year used in the manufacture of electric lawn-mowers. The supplier offered to sell the motors for $88 each. Mills and Vines' estimated costs of producing the motor follow on the next page.

Direct materials	$40
Direct labour	20
Variable overhead	20
Fixed overhead	64

Prior to making a decision, the entity's CEO commissioned a special study to see whether any decreases were possible in fixed overhead costs. The entity would avoid two set-ups, which would reduce total spending by $10 000 per set-up. One inspector would be laid off at a savings of $28 000. A person in materials handling could also be laid off at a savings of $20 000. Engineering work would be reduced by 500 hours at $15 per hour. Although the work decreases by 500 hours, the engineer assigned to the motor line also spends time on other products.

REQUIRED

(a) Ignore the information from the special study. Using the general decision rule, determine whether the motor should be produced internally or purchased from the supplier.
(b) Repeat the analysis, using the information from the special study.
(c) Identify and discuss any qualitative factors that would affect the decision, including strategic implications.
(d) After reviewing the special study, the controller made the following remark: 'This study ignores the additional activity demands that purchasing the motor would cause. For example, although the part would no longer be inspected on the production floor, we will need to inspect the incoming parts in the receiving area. Will we actually save any inspection costs?' Discuss whether you agree with the controller. Identify and explain other costs that might increase if the part is outsourced.

8.44 **Product emphasis with constrained resource; cost function; uncertainties** Riteway currently produces and sells five different products. Total demand for the products exceeds the entity's capacity to produce all of them. The constraint on production is the time available on a special machine. Data on the products and time required on the special machine are summarised in the following chart.

	Product				
	A	B	C	D	E
Selling price	$12	$15	$18	$24	$32
Variable manufacturing cost	$8	$9	$11	$12	$18
Variable marketing cost	$1	$1	$3	$2	$6
Machine hours needed per unit	0.2	0.3	0.25	0.5	0.4
Maximum unit demand per period	10 000	7 500	20 000	1 500	2 000

The entity has only 5500 hours of time available on the special machine per period. Fixed costs are $110 000 per period.

REQUIRED

(a) How many units of each product should the entity produce and sell to maximise income?
(b) On further analysis, it was determined that while fixed costs do not vary as production volumes change, they do vary based on the number of different product lines. If only two types of products are produced, these costs are $60 000, but if all five types of products are produced, these costs will be $135 000.

Using the two-point method, determine a linear cost function for the cost of product lines.

(c) Describe possible business reasons for the cost behaviour described in part (b).

(d) Using the results from part (a) and the cost function you developed for part (b), prepare an income statement for the entity by product line and by total products.

(e) Review the results in part (d). Prepare a new product line income statement that reflects any changes that should be made in the production plans to maximise income.

(f) Identify reasons why the managers cannot be certain that they have accurately estimated the following for each product: selling price, variable costs, machine hours needed per unit and maximum unit demand per period.

(g) Discuss how the uncertainties in part (f) might affect the managers' production decisions.

8.45 Comprehensive problem Elder Services is a not-for-profit entity that has three departments in three separate locations, in addition to the headquarters. The entity provides services for elderly clients who are still living at home. One department provides meals, one department provides cleaning services and one department provides healthcare services. Elderly Services relies on client fees and a small grant from the state government to provide services. Following are the results from last year's operations.

Departments	Meals	Cleaning	Health	Total
Visits	10 000	10 000	10 000	30 000
Revenues	$ 50 000	$100 000	$ 150 000	$300 000
Variable cost (labour and supplies)	30 000	50 000	120 000	200 000
Fixed overhead costs	4 000	8 000	10 000	22 000
Transportation				
($4000 fixed + $5000 variable)	9 000			9 000
($10 000 fixed + $2000 variable)		12 000		12 000
$5000 variable[a]			5 000	5 000
Headquarter costs allocated (based on revenues)	10 000	20 000	30 000	60 000
Total expenses	53 000	90 000	165 000	308 000
Surplus (deficit)	$ (3 000)	$ 10 000	$ (15 000)	$ (8 000)

[a]Nurses use their own cars.

In the past, the government provided small grants each year to cover losses for Elder Services. However, due to an economic downturn and decreased tax funds in the current year, the government will not be able to provide any support next year. In light of these changes, the managers of Elder Services are trying to decide how to balance the budget.

REQUIRED

(a) What is the contribution margin per visit for each department?
Consider the next three situations independently.

(b) To eliminate losses, the director of Elder Services would like to close the department that provides health services for clients. Assume no alternative uses are planned for the health services building and no change would occur in headquarters costs. Estimate the surplus (deficit) if the health services department is closed.

(c) What would the estimated total surplus (deficit) be if cleaning services increase by 2000 clients, assuming no changes in fixed costs?

(d) What would the estimated total surplus (deficit) be if Elder closes the meals division and that space is leased to another entity for $2000 per month?

Suppose you are hired to help Elder's managers decide what to do about the lack of funding from the government this year. Ignore parts (b), (c) and (d) and answer the following questions as part of your analysis.

(e) Which type of non-routine operating decision does Elder Services need to make? What are the managers' decision options?

(f) Perform quantitative analyses to help you decide whether one or more of the options listed in parts (b), (c) and (d) would be beneficial to the finances of Elder Services.

(g) Now assume that the options in parts (b), (c) and (d) above are available. List uncertainties about Elder Services' ability to achieve the quantitative results for each option: (b), (c) and (d). List as many uncertainties as you can.

(h) List qualitative factors that the managers of Elder Services need to consider in making this decision. List as many factors as you can.

(i) As a consultant to Elder Services, how might you go about acquiring qualitative information?

(j) Suppose you decide to interview Elder Services employees to help you gather qualitative information. Identify possible reasons that information you obtain from employees might be biased. List as many reasons as you can.

(k) Describe possible trade-offs the managers of Elder Services might need to make in deciding what to do.

REFERENCE

1 Registered trademark of Microsoft Corporation.

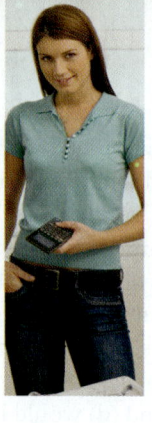

Investment decisions

IN BRIEF

Managers periodically make decisions about long-term investments for new projects or replacement of old assets. These decisions focus on creating long-term value consistent with organisational strategies. The outcomes from these decisions are generally more uncertain than shorter-term decisions because we forecast further into the future. In addition, the time value of money also becomes important.

After studying this chapter, you should be able to:

1	Understand investment decisions.
2	Identify relevant cash flows for strategic investment decisions.
3	Perform and interpret net present value (NPV) analysis.
4	Understand the uncertainties of NPV analysis.
5	Understand alternative methods (IRR, payback, accrual accounting rate of return) used for investment decisions.
6	Identify additional issues to be considered for strategic investment decisions.
7	Understand how income taxes affect strategic investment decision cash flows.
8	Understand how real and nominal methods are used to address inflation in an NPV analysis.

Capital budgeting for nuclear power in Australia

Energy plays an important role in improving people's lifestyles. In Australia, our energy consumption is growing and is forecasted to increase by 50 per cent over the next 15 years. The available power resources in Australia (currently 80 per cent coal-fuelled) will not cope with the increasing demands. Further investment opportunities are required for long-term power supply, and options are currently being investigated by government. Due to Australia's high greenhouse gas emissions from the current coal-fired power plants, nuclear energy has been advocated as the optimal 'clean' power alternative. In 2005, Australia exported around 12 000 tonnes of uranium (enough to supply more than twice its annual electricity needs) but has not yet used uranium to fuel its own energy industry. Recently, the Prime Minister of Australia, John Howard, claimed that nuclear power was 'inevitable' in Australia. In a recent policy review commissioned by the federal government, it was suggested that Australia could quadruple its 2005 revenue from exporting uranium oxide if it first enriched and fabricated the fuel. This could be achieved if the Australian government invested in nuclear reactors, with a recommended 25 reactors to be installed by 2050. Furthermore, greenhouse gases could be reduced by one-fifth, and electricity could be supplied to a third of the country. Nevertheless, the decision to invest in nuclear power is deemed politically sensitive and requires adopting world's best practice to prevent unsafe reactor designs and minimise environmental risks, and to reassure the community that the power will not be diverted to make bombs.

According to a recent study (see www.nuclearinfo.net), accurate capital budgeting and subsequent cost control is a major factor in determining the successful provision of environmentally clean and cheap electricity in Australia. This report details the history of costing issues faced by nuclear power plant investors around the world. The most significant implementation

problems relate to design flaws and licensing delays (for example, the Shoreham plant in Long Island, New York State, cost $5 billion to build and was never allowed to operate). Subsequent operational costing issues highlighted in the report were as a result of inadequate operator training and non-uniform designs that prevented the achievement of economies of scale in output volume.

The study provides a breakdown of the history of costs relating to nuclear power plant employment. In general, the costs consist of the:

- construction costs of building a plant with 1 GW capacity (approximately $1000 per kW)
- operating costs of running the plant and generating energy (approximately 1.3 cents per kW-hour)
- cost of waste disposal from the plant (approximately 0.2 cents per kW-hour)
- cost of decommissioning the plant (approximately 10 per cent of construction costs).

According to the report, construction costs are difficult to quantify but estimates provided have been based on worldwide examples. Construction timeframes were estimated to be around three years to completion and commencement of operations. Part of the operating cost estimates includes the raw material (uranium ore) costs, which are approximately 0.05 cents per kW-hour. The costs provided were based on a 40-year plant lifetime with discount interest rates of around 5 per cent. If the proposed capital budgeting scenario lives up to its promises, the study concludes that nuclear power will provide cheaper electricity than any other fossil-fuel-based generating facility in Australia. While the investment analysis might suggest nuclear power is a financially worthwhile investment for Australia, it is important to note that the final decision to invest in a project such as this one will depend on many other qualitative factors, including stakeholder acceptance.

Sources: Information from Australian Bureau of Agriculture and Resource Economics (ABARE) 2003, *Australian energy; national and state projections to 2019–20*, report for the Ministerial Council on Energy, June; *The Economist* 2006, 'Nuclear power: the ghostly flickers of a new dawn', 23 November, p. 77; Howard, J (Prime Minister) 2006, transcript of address to the Committee for Economic Development of Australia, Sydney Convention and Exhibition Centre, 18 July, www.pm.gov.au; *Nuclear power education*, www.nuclearinfo.net, accessed 3 July 2007.

Issues from this scene setter to look for in the chapter include:

The importance of understanding the underlying factors of how and why investment decisions are made.

The inherent difficulties for decision makers when determining the relevant cash flows for investment decisions.

The methods used to determine the potential future success of investment projects.

The uncertainties and limitations of investment decisions.

Investment decisions

Compared to operating decisions that primarily affect short-term activities, strategic decisions have long-term effects. As we learned in chapter 1, managers develop strategies from the entity's vision and core competencies. These strategies are aimed at the organisation's overall purpose, which usually includes long-term profitability. The chapter 9 article at the end of this book explores the link between strategic planning and capital budgeting.

Capital budgeting

Capital budgeting is a process that managers use when they choose among investment opportunities that have cash flows occurring over a number of years. These opportunities commonly fall into three categories:

1. *Operational capital investment decisions*, which affect only part of an entity's operations, have easily predictable lives and represent relatively small capital outlays for an entity.
2. *Strategic capital investment decisions*, which affect all or a considerable part of an entity's operations, have uncertain lives and require large investments.
3. *Investment decisions to comply with regulatory, safety, health and environmental requirements*, which are acquisitions that cannot be deferred or rejected without incurring potentially huge penalties in the future.

The objective of capital budgeting is to increase the long-term value of the organisation. Figure 9.1 summarises the steps in the capital budgeting process. The process is similar to that for non-routine operating decisions (chapter 8). The major difference is that capital budgeting decisions affect cash flows in future years. Therefore, the **time value of money**, which refers to the idea that a dollar received today is worth more than a dollar received in the future, is an important factor. Because of its importance, we will learn analysis techniques that allow managers to account for the time value of money when evaluating capital budget decisions.

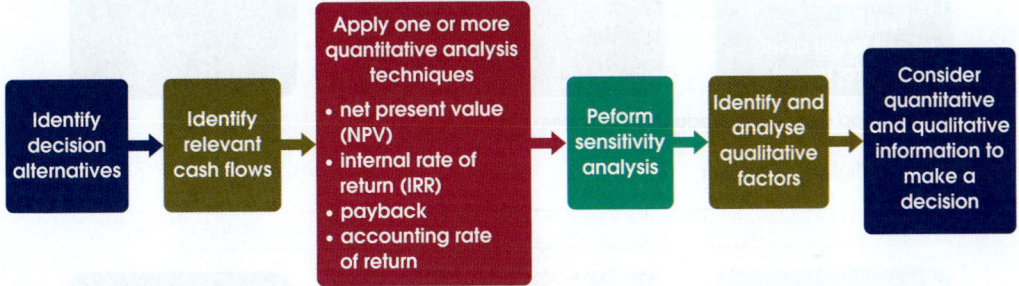

FIGURE 9.1 ■ Process for addressing capital budgeting decisions

Decision alternatives

Entities identify new projects, products and services through a variety of methods. Individuals, teams and whole departments are responsible for identifying future investment opportunities. Organisational strategies are reflected in long-term decisions about products, services and acquisitions of new business segments. For example, organisations that maintain reputations for low-cost, high-quality products want to invest in new technology to improve quality while reducing cost.

Sometimes organisational strategy requires consideration of new product lines or business segments to expand the organisational scope. For example, Motorola managers identified a need for a global cellular phone service. The managers at Wendy's, consistent with their strategy to sustain high levels of growth, established a 2003 capital budget of US$200–220 million for capital spending on new restaurant development. Similarly, DuPont revised its strategy to focus anew on developing new products. Once projects that align with the entity's strategies are identified, capital budgeting analysis is performed to determine their financial viability.

When deciding whether to accept or reject proposals, managers analyse capital budgeting projects as if they were stand-alone projects. However, they may face capital constraints so that accepting one project would eliminate another. In these cases, alternative investments are commonly analysed simultaneously so that they can be compared.

Relevant cash flows

The process of identifying relevant cash flows for capital budgeting decisions is similar to the process for any other type of decision. Relevant cash flows must arise in the future, and differ among decision alternatives (possible courses of action).

Figure 9.2 presents timelines and lists of common types of cash flows for two different types of capital budgeting decisions: new product or process development, and asset replacement decisions. Cash flows must be estimated for all future periods affected by the potential investment. We usually begin by creating a timeline to help us think about the nature and timing of relevant cash flows.

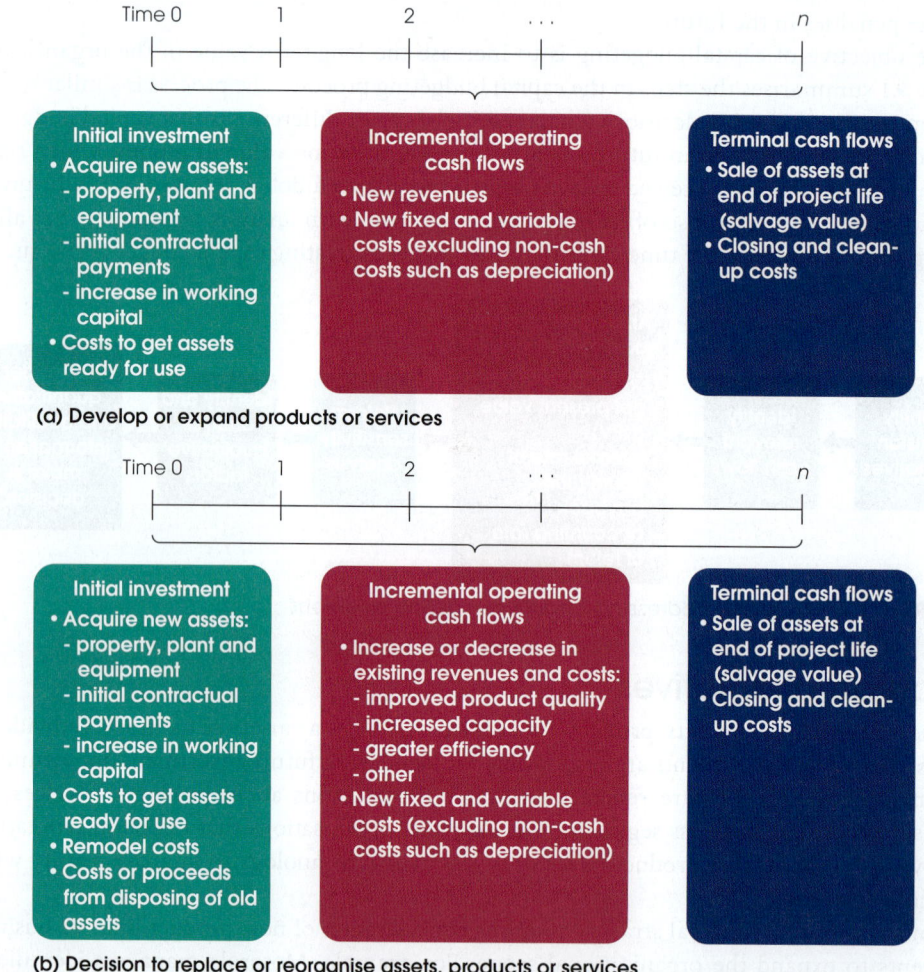

(a) Develop or expand products or services

(b) Decision to replace or reorganise assets, products or services

FIGURE 9.2 ■ Common cash flows for long-term decisions

At the beginning of the project, time 0, the entity faces initial cash outflows such as the purchase of new property, plant, equipment and other costs required to get assets ready for use in operations. Sometimes these outflows include initial contractual payments (such as signing bonuses) or additions to working capital (such as inventories). Initial cash inflows or outflows may also come from the disposal of old assets at the beginning of a project.

During years 1 through the life of the project (*n* years), the project has annual incremental operating cash flows. For a new or expanded product or service, these cash flows may include new revenues as well as new fixed and variable costs. When replacing or reorganising assets, revenues and costs may increase or decrease because of improved product quality, increased capacity or greater efficiency.

Any terminal cash flows appear at the end of the project's life (time n). Terminal cash flows typically include proceeds from the sale of assets at the end of the project (the salvage value). However, assets such as equipment may be obsolete and have zero salvage value. Some projects require terminal cash outflows, such as the costs to reinstate the quality of land (called land reclamation) at the end of a mining operation.

In this chapter, we learn the four methods listed in figure 9.1 for quantitatively analysing potential investment projects. The first two methods — net present value (NPV) and internal rate of return (IRR) — explicitly take into account the time value of money, making them preferred methods. However, many managers still use the other less-preferred methods — payback, and accrual accounting rate of return. Therefore, we introduce all of these methods and present advantages and disadvantages of each.

Net present value (NPV) method

In business, we need to value a project today but the associated cash flows occur in the future. Therefore, we discount the future dollars to determine their value in today's dollars. In appendix 9B of this chapter you will find tables with factors that you multiply by cash flows to determine either a **future value** (the amount received in the future for a given number of years at a given interest rate) for a given investment today, or a **present value** (the value in today's dollars of a sum received in the future).

Suppose you want to buy a $20 000 sports car two years from now. Assume you can invest money today and earn a rate of return of 10 per cent per year. How much would you have to invest today so that in two years you will have $20 000? In other words, what present value is needed to create a future value of $20 000 at an annual interest rate of 10 per cent? To calculate the present value, we multiply the future value ($20 000) by the present value factor for 10 per cent and two time periods. Using table 9B.1 for present value of $1 (see appendix 9B, page 373), locate the *10%* column and go down to the row representing *2* periods. The factor is 0.826. Multiply this factor by the future value of $20 000. You need $16 520 today to have enough money in two years to buy the car.

Present value of a series of cash flows

Managers are often involved in evaluating projects with different time horizons. One project might end in 5 years and another in 10 years. The future values of such projects are not strictly comparable, because a dollar received 5 years from now is not worth the same as a dollar received 10 years from now. For this and other reasons, the cash flows for projects are generally converted to their present values. The projects can then be compared on a common basis.

The **net present value method (NPV)** determines whether an organisation would be better off investing in a project based on the net amount of discounted cash flows for the project. The net present value of a project is calculated as:

$$\text{NPV} = \sum_{t=0}^{n} \frac{\textbf{Expected cash flow}_t}{(1+r)^t}$$

where t = time period (year)
$\quad n$ = life of the project
$\quad r$ = discount rate

The expected cash flows include the initial investment, incremental operating cash flows and terminal cash flows. If the NPV is positive, the project is generally considered acceptable because it is expected to increase the entity's value. If investment resources are limited, invest in the project(s) having the highest NPV. Following is an example of the NPV method.

Suppose Gordon wants to convert a motel of 30 000 square metres into apartments that he will rent to university students. The initial investment is $1 400 000. Gordon expects to rent the apartments for $1 per square metre per month, and to pay a management company fees representing 15 per cent of rents. He forecasts that property taxes and insurance will be about $30 000 per year. Therefore, the incremental cash flows are $276 000 = [$1 per m^2 × 30 000 m^2 × 12 months) × (1 − 0.15)] − $30 000. Gordon expects to be able to sell the building at the end of 10 years for $400 000. (We will ignore income taxes for these calculations.) Gordon's discount rate is 14 per cent. The cash flows for this project are shown in figure 9.3. The total discounted cash flow after the initial investment is the sum of individual present values, as follows:

Period	Interest rate	Present value factor (PVF)	Cash flow	Discounted cash flow
1	14%	0.877	$276 000	$ 242 052
2	14	0.769	276 000	212 244
3	14	0.675	276 000	186 300
4	14	0.592	276 000	163 392
5	14	0.519	276 000	143 244
6	14	0.456	276 000	125 856
7	14	0.400	276 000	110 400
8	14	0.351	276 000	96 876
9	14	0.308	276 000	85 008
10	14	0.270	276 000	74 520
10	14	0.270	400 000	108 000
		Total discounted cash flows		$1 547 892

Notice that the incremental operating cash flows during years 1 through 10 are identical. In other words, Gordon expects to receive an annual annuity of $276 000 per year for 10 years, and in year 10 he also receives the terminal value of $400 000.

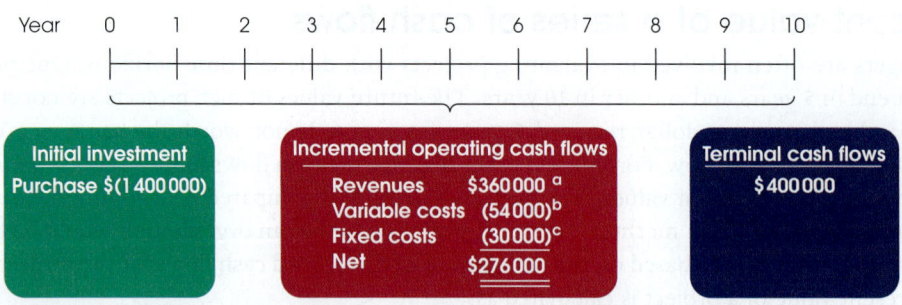

^{a}Revenue = 30000 sq m × $1 per sq m × 12 months per year = $360000 per year
^{b}Management fee = $360000 × 15% = $54000
^{c}Property tax and insurance

FIGURE 9.3 ■ Timeline for Gordon's apartment building project

In the case of an annuity (that is, equal net cash flows each year), we can simplify the present value calculation using the present value of an ordinary annuity (PVFA) of $1 factor from table 9B.2 in appendix 9B (on page 374) as shown opposite.

$$PV = \$276\,000 \times (\text{PVFA 10 years, 14\%}) + \$400\,000 \times (\text{PVF 10 years, 14\%})$$

$$= \$276\,000 \times 5.216 + \$400\,000 \times 0.270$$

$$= \$1\,439\,616 + \$108\,000$$

$$= \$1\,547\,616$$

Notice that we obtain the same present value for the project cash flows (the difference between $1 547 892 and $1 547 616 is due to rounding) regardless of the method we use. However, if we are performing these calculations manually, we can often save time by using the annuity table.

Net present value of a project

Once we calculate the present value of a series of cash flows for Gordon's project, we can compare the net present value to the investment amount because both amounts are now valued in today's dollars. We use the following formula to calculate NPV for Gordon's project:

$$\text{NPV} = \text{Initial investment cash outflow} + \text{PV of cash inflows}$$

$$= -\$1\,400\,000 + \$1\,574\,616$$

$$= \$174\,616$$

At the end of 10 years, we estimate that Gordon will have realised $174 616 in today's dollars. Because this net present value amount is greater than zero, the general rule is that Gordon would want to invest in this project.

If Gordon were considering more than one investment, he could calculate the profitability index for each project. The **profitability index** is the ratio of the present value of the cash inflows to the present value of the investment cash outflows. The decision rule for a solitary investment is that the investment should be undertaken if the index is equal to or greater than 1. For example, Gordon's profitability index would be:

$$\text{Profitability index} = \frac{\text{Present value of cash inflows}}{\text{Present value of investment cash outflows}} = \frac{\$1\,574\,616}{\$1\,400\,000} = 1.125$$

If Gordon were comparing a number of different projects and could not undertake all of them, he would consider both today's dollar amount and the profitability index. The profitability index and the NPV method always accept and reject the same project, but the index allows managers to rank projects according to their profitability. It provides a simple way to identify which projects are expected to earn a higher return.

Identifying a reasonable discount rate

A discount rate, r, must be selected to apply the NPV formula. The **discount rate** is the interest rate that is used across time to reduce the value of future dollars to today's dollars. Many decision makers simply set the discount rate at the entity's **weighted average cost of capital**, which is the weighted average rate for the costs of the various sources of financing such as debt and equity. However, this method ignores variations in risk among projects. If a project involves little risk, then a lower discount rate might be appropriate. Conversely, a higher discount rate is appropriate for projects having higher risk.

Judgment is required to incorporate an estimate of project risk. One way to think about project risk is to consider the return on other investment opportunities that appear to be of similar risk. For example, the sharemarket has returned, on average, about 11 per cent across time. We can think about how the risk of a particular project compares with the risk of investing long term in the sharemarket. If the project seems more (less) risky than investing in the market, a discount rate greater (less) than 11 per cent might be appropriate.

Uncertainties and sensitivity analysis

When we perform NPV analysis, the general rule is to accept the project if NPV is greater than zero. Many assumptions are built into this general rule. For example, we assume that we know each of the following:

- cost of initial investment
- timing and dollar amounts of incremental revenues and costs
- terminal values
- project life
- appropriate discount rate.

However, we cannot know any of these factors with absolute certainty. Also, uncertainties grow with the number of years being forecast; a 15-year project has more uncertainties than one completed in five years.

Cash flow uncertainties

The preceding illustration for Gordon's apartment building decision includes little uncertainty about the initial investment cash flows. Gordon knows for certain the purchase price of the motel, and negotiates a final bid with a building contractor for converting the motel into apartments. Some uncertainty may be involved in the cost of renovation. So long as the specific nature of the renovations are known and can be completed fairly quickly before costs change, the cost estimate from the contractor should be reasonably close to the final cost. However, renovation of Gordon's motel could rise dramatically if contractors discover unforseen problems, such as asbestos that must be removed.

We always encounter uncertainty when estimating future revenues, costs and terminal values. However, our ability to accurately estimate cash flows decreases as we forecast further into the future. Long timeframes reduce our ability to anticipate customer tastes, changes in technology, productivity, competition, availability of resources and changes in regulation. For example, certain entities (such as healthcare providers that provide services covered by Medicare) rely heavily on reimbursement from the government. Changes in reimbursement rates or changes in the basis of reimbursement greatly affect the expected revenues of these organisations. As another example, unexpected spikes in petrol and diesel prices affect transportation entities and the organisations that use them, such as freight distributors and grocery stores.

Estimating cash flows for projects involving new products or services is more difficult than for projects involving changes or expansions of existing products and services. Revenues must sometimes be based on a market that does not currently exist. It is nearly impossible to anticipate all potential costs. Substantial errors are likely in these types of predictions.

Project life and discount rate uncertainties

The expected life of a project is also uncertain. Difficulties in estimating the life of a project are often related to difficulties in estimating revenues and costs. Managers are likely to continue a project if it is profitable. The reverse is true if the project is unprofitable. Managers may also change how they define an organisation's core competencies. Such changes increase or decrease the strategic importance of a project, leading to an extension or cancellation of the project.

Several factors affect the discount rate for NPV analysis including interest rates, inflation and the riskiness of the project. However, none of these factors are known, and the length of time for capital projects increases the uncertainty.

Estimation bias

Because of the many uncertainties involved, managers use considerable judgment in making capital project estimates. However, those responsible for forming the estimates are often the ones who originated the idea for the project. Intentionally or not, these managers are likely to form estimates that favour adoption of the project. In addition, they are more likely to fail to identify all possible project costs than to anticipate costs that will not occur — another estimation bias that favours project adoption.

Sensitivity analysis

Sensitivity analysis helps managers evaluate how their NPV results would change with variations in the input data. Spreadsheets enable the discount rate, cash flows and any other underlying assumptions to be easily varied to consider alternate outcomes. Decision makers can then consider the results of alternative scenarios under different sets of assumptions (see comprehensive example 1). For example, what is the change in NPV if we reduce our revenue estimates by 10 per cent? What if we increase the discount rate by 1 per cent? What if the terminal value is zero? The sensitivity of results to variations in assumptions helps managers evaluate the risk of investments.

Comprehensive example 1

Net present value and sensitivity analysis

Gordon has a basement space in the building that would not be suitable for units because it has no windows. A friend offered to rent the space from Gordon for $60 000 per year, with an increase of $2000 after three years. She will use the space to house an upscale health spa for women. However, Gordon would like to open a health club to serve the students at his building, people living in the neighbourhood and people who work nearby.

Relevant cash flows and timeline

Gordon hires a consultant to gather information about the project and to recommend a plan of action. The fee for this service is $5000. The following list includes the relevant information the consulting entity estimates for the project.

1. The cost of renovation and new equipment that will be purchased is $650 000. The terminal value is estimated at $100 000 after five years.
2. Promotion costs to advertise the club will be $120 000 for the first year and $50 000 per year thereafter.
3. The revenues for the health club are estimated as $300 000 in the first year, $400 000 in the second, and $500 000 in the third through fifth years.
4. The operating costs for the health club are estimated as $200 000 for the first year and $130 000 for each of the following years.

Gordon sets up a timeline, shown in figure 9.4 (overleaf). Notice that he ignores sunk costs (the fee paid to the consulting entity) and includes opportunity costs (forgone rent).

NPV analysis

Gordon sets up a spreadsheet as shown in figure 9.5. He organises the spreadsheet with an input section so that any of the assumptions made for the NPV analysis can be easily varied in performing a sensitivity analysis, and uses a 10 per cent discount rate. He includes a cell reference (B13) for changes in revenues. Based on these NPV calculations, Gordon expects to realise $1851 in today's dollars, over and above the investment amount of $650 000, if he invests in the health club.

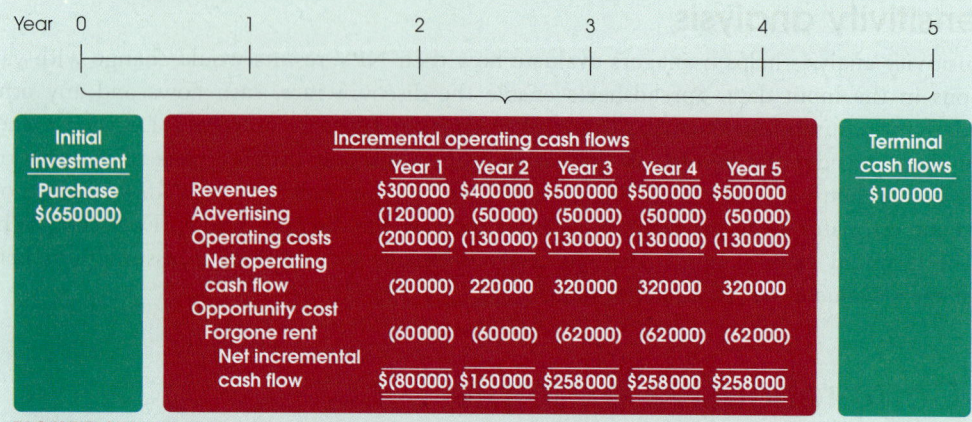

FIGURE 9.4 ■ Timeline for Gordon's health club project

	A	B	C	D	E
1	Gordon's Health Club Project				
2	Assumptions				
3	Discount rate	10%		Teminal value	$100,000
4	Initial investment	$650,000			
5	Cash flows				
6	Period	Revenues	Operating costs	Advertising	Forgone rent
7	1	$300,000	$200,000	$120,000	$60,000
8	2	$400,000	$130,000	$50,000	$50,000
9	3	$500,000	$130,000	$50,000	$62,000
10	4	$500,000	$130,000	$50,000	$62,000
11	5	$500,000	$130,000	$50,000	$62,000
12	Change to assumptions for sensitivity analysis:				
13	Change revenues	0%			
14					
15					
16	PV calculations				
17		Net cash flows	Discounted		
18	1	($80,000)	($72,727)		
19	2	$160,000	$132,231		
20	3	$258,000	$193,839		
21	4	$258,000	$176,217		
22	5	$258,000	$160,198		
23	Total discounted operating CF		$589,759		
24	Terminal value				
25	5	$100,000	$62,092		
26					
27	NPV				
28	Operating CF	$589,759			
29	Terminal value	$62,092			
30	Less				
31	Investment	($650,000)			
32	NPV	$1,851			

Examples of Excel formulas:
  Net cash flow in cell B18: =(1+$B$13)*B7–(C7+D7+E7)
  Discounted cash flow in cell C18: =–PV($B$3,A18,,B18)

FIGURE 9.5 ■ NPV calculations for Gordon's health club

When Gordon reviews his spreadsheet calculations with the consultants, they indicate some uncertainty about the assumptions. The consulting team is concerned that the revenue estimates might be too high. The building is located in an older part of town, and people might not want to walk in the neighbourhood at night to get to the club. They suggest that Gordon reduce the revenues by 5 per cent for sensitivity analysis. He enters –5% in the appropriate input cell. With this drop in revenues, he would incur a $79 696 loss over the five-year life of the project. Gordon decides to develop a series of spreadsheets varying all of the assumptions to reflect possible changes in future economic conditions. He will then discuss this decision further with the consulting team.

Internal rate of return

The **internal rate of return (IRR)** method determines the discount rate necessary for the present value of the discounted cash flows to be equal to the investment. Therefore, the IRR represents the investment's 'own' rate of return as opposed to the NPV, which is determined by the cash flows being benchmarked against at set return. In other words, the method solves for the discount rate at which a project's NPV equals zero. The calculation of IRR is similar to NPV analysis in that it is based on discounted cash flows. In the NPV analysis, we assumed a discount rate and solved for the NPV. In the case of IRR, we search for the discount rate that results in an NPV of zero. This discount rate is the internal rate of return.

IRR calculations

Earlier in the chapter, Gordon analysed a decision to invest in the apartment building for students. Suppose he is now trying to decide whether to install coin-operated vending machines in the apartment building. He knows that students eat a lot of snack foods, but the closest 24-hour convenience store is eight blocks away. Gordon thinks that the students will purchase beverages and food from vending machines if he installs them. The equipment will cost $5000 and have a useful life of five years. He expects to net $1500 in annual cash flows from operating the machines (revenues minus food and maintenance costs). The equipment will have no terminal value at the end of five years. Gordon thinks it could be a good investment but he would like to know what his expected rate of return would be. The cash flows for this project are shown in figure 9.6 (overleaf).

Gordon wants to find the discount rate at which the NPV equals zero. Recall that the NPV is calculated by subtracting the initial investment from the NPV of cash inflows. Because the cash inflows are uniform across time, Gordon can use the present value of an ordinary annuity of $1 table (see table 9B.2 in appendix 9B). Then, the IRR is the interest rate ($X\%$) at which:

$$\textbf{Initial investment = NPV of cash inflows}$$

$$\$5000 = \$1500 \times (\textbf{PVFA 5 years, } X\%)$$

Solving for the present value of an annuity factor:

$$(\textbf{PVFA 5 years, } X\%) = \$5000 \div \$1500 = 3.333$$

Gordon uses the table to locate the interest rate ($X\%$) at which the present value of an annuity factor is approximately equal to 3.333 for a time period of five years. Finding the row for five time periods, he sees that the factor for 15 per cent is 3.352. This factor is very close to 3.333, so he concludes that the IRR is close to 15 per cent. This return is higher than the discount rate he used to calculate the net present value of the apartment complex, and this project is probably less risky, so Gordon decides it is a worthwhile investment.

The approach using the present value of an ordinary annuity of $1 table can be applied only when the cash flows from a project are uniform over time. For uneven cash inflows, such as for Gordon's apartment building project, a trial-and-error approach may be used along with the present value table. We first try a discount rate and calculate the NPV of the project using that discount rate. If the NPV is greater than zero, we try a larger discount rate; if it is less than zero, we decrease the discount rate.

We can easily calculate a more precise IRR using a spreadsheet. Using Excel's[1] IRR function (see figure 9.7), Gordon learns that the IRR for his coin-operated machine project is 15.24 per cent. When he calculates the NPV using the IRR as the discount rate, the NPV is zero.

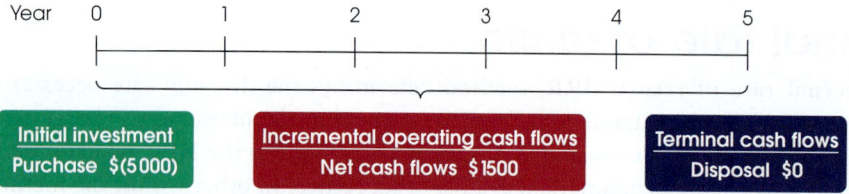

FIGURE 9.6 ■ Timeline for Gordon's coin-operated equipment project

	A	B
1	Net cash flows:	
2	Time 0	($5,000)
3	Year 1	$1,500
4	Year 2	$1,500
5	Year 3	$1,500
6	Year 4	$1,500
7	Year 5	$1,500
8		
9	IRR	15.24%
10	NPV	$0

Excel formula to calculate internal rate of return in cell B9: =IRR(B2:B7)
Excel formula to calculate net present value in cell B10: =B2+NPV(B9,B3:B7)

FIGURE 9.7 ■ IRR for Gordon's coin-operated equipment project

Comparison of NPV and IRR methods

Certainly without spreadsheets, the net present value method is computationally simpler than the internal rate of return method. Determining IRR can be time-consuming, particularly for projects returning uneven cash flows. The use of a spreadsheet reduces the effort considerably. However, if several projects are being analysed, their NPVs can be summed to determine the NPV for that group or portfolio of projects, whereas IRR can be neither summed nor averaged.

An important difference between the two methods is that the IRR method assumes cash inflows can be reinvested to earn the same return that the project would generate. However, it may be difficult for an entity to identify other opportunities that could achieve the same rate when IRR is high. In contrast, the NPV method assumes that cash inflows can be reinvested and earn the discount rate — a more realistic assumption. If the discount rate is set equal to the organisation's cost of capital, then alternative uses of cash would include paying off creditors or buying back shares. For the preceding reasons, the NPV method is preferable.

Both methods are used widely in business. One reason for the continued use of IRR is that many people find it intuitively easier to understand than NPV. In addition, managers may want to compare the IRR on prior projects to current project return rates as they consider new investment. For example, Gordon could compare the IRR for the health club with any new projects and decide whether to accept a project with a lower IRR.

Payback method

The **payback method** measures the amount of time required to recover the initial investment. Assuming that cash flows from the project are constant over future years, the payback period can be calculated by dividing the initial investment cash flow by the annual incremental operating cash flows. Consider Gordon's decision to install vending machines:

$$\text{Number of years to pay back the investment} = \frac{\text{Initial investment}}{\text{Annual incremental operating cash flow}} = \frac{\$5000}{\$1500} = 3.33$$

Thus, the payback period for this example is 3.33 years. If incremental annual cash flows are uneven, then the payback period can be found by calculating the cumulative incremental operating cash flows until the initial investment amount has been fully covered. The number of years needed to cover the initial investment is the payback period.

Future cash flows can be discounted to reflect the opportunity cost of using funds for other projects; this is referred to as **discounted payback**. A key disadvantage of payback is that it does not value the cash flows that are received after the investment has been recovered. However, the payback method is used extensively as a screening tool, and sometimes used with NPV or IRR when meaningful estimates of relevant cash flows are lacking because the project or product is so new that it provides no historical data for reference. Longer payback periods reflect higher risk; therefore, projects with shorter payback periods are preferable because cash is not committed over long periods.

Accrual accounting rate of return method

The **accrual accounting rate of return** is the expected increase in average annual operating income as a percentage of the initial increase in required investment. In Gordon's vending machine decision, the net increase in income needs to be adjusted so that it reflects accrual accounting income. For financial statements, suppose that Gordon uses straight-line depreciation. With a five-year life and no terminal value, annual financial statement depreciation is $1000 per year ($5000 ÷ 5 years). Assuming depreciation is the only difference between cash flows and financial statement income, accrual accounting income is $500 ($1500 − $1000). The accrual accounting rate of return of 10 per cent is the expected incremental accounting income from the project divided by the initial investment ($500 ÷ $5000).

This method presents several problems. First, it ignores the time value of money. In addition, depreciation is deducted from the numerator but the full investment amount is the denominator, so the investment amount is essentially double counted. This method is frequently used to evaluate division or department performance because the financial information is readily available, but it is not an appropriate method for evaluating long-term investment decisions.

Other considerations for investment decisions

Managers consider qualitative factors as well as quantitative analyses when making an investment decision. In this section, we learn about a variety of factors that affect the final capital budgeting decision. We also discuss long-term monitoring of results.

Strategic investments — qualitative factors

Qualitative factors often influence investment decisions. Sometimes these factors cannot be quantified, and other times numerical estimates would be so uncertain that decision makers find them useless.

Estimating the future cash flows from implementing an enterprise-wide system such as those sold by Oracle, PeopleSoft or SAP involves high uncertainty. The benefits of such systems include increased timeliness of information and increased availability of new information. Therefore, many organisations make these types of decisions based on the experience of other organisations as well as the information they receive from the enterprise-wide system developers and sales representatives.

The need for a timely decision sometimes overrides the use of a formal capital budgeting process such as NPV. Timeliness can be particularly important when new opportunities arise suddenly and an organisation needs to take action before its competitors. Another related consideration is the ability of an organisation to envision new products and services. Entities often stumble when they concentrate solely on the improvement of existing products and services because they fail to recognise changes in customer preferences, technology or other factors that call for shifts in products and services. Innovative organisations typically focus on combining formal quantitative analysis with exploration of future trends.

Moving baseline

One of the issues often ignored in capital budgeting decisions is a concept commonly referred to as the *moving baseline*. The moving baseline concept challenges conventional comparisons, which are usually between what might be (the financial effect of adopting the project) and the status quo (things remaining as they are). The moving baseline suggests that if the project is not adopted, the 'status quo' may not remain; performance may deteriorate. For example, the adoption of an upgraded voice and data network may result in strong additional cash flows through better customer service and speedy processing. However, the decision to not adopt the upgrade may result in the loss of customers due to lower-levels of customer service (relative to competitors) and slower processing time. A consideration of the moving baseline commonly results in increasing the attraction of the proposed project. In effect, investments may need to be made simply to maintain current operating performance and avoid a performance decline.

Reputation, environment, quality and community

If a proposed capital project would affect the environment in a negative way, the project might harm an organisation's reputation. Projects adversely affect the environment in a number of ways such as producing hazardous waste, emitting chemicals into the air, or polluting lakes streams or landfills. Sometimes the cost of environmental impact creates direct cash flow effects that are included in NPV analyses, such as permit fees for air emissions. However, many environmental costs are not borne by the emitting entity but by society as a whole. For example, real estate developers are not assessed for the degradation in neighbourhood noise levels that result from increased traffic to a new shopping centre. To encourage entities to adopt environmentally friendly policies, several organisations index entities according to their pollution-control practices. In addition, some mutual funds are comprised strictly of 'green' investments.

Because reputation effects are difficult to value, managers typically incorporate these concerns qualitatively. An increasing number of entities are developing environmental policy statements to help guide their strategic decisions, and they may make environmental investments without formal quantitative analysis. To attract customers and investors who are concerned about the environment, some organisations advertise their 'green' practices.

Many organisations invest a great deal of time and money to improve product or service quality. These decisions are often made without formal quantitative consideration of the long-term costs and benefits. For some entities, quality requirements from markets such as the European Union must be met to sell products or services. Other entities hold high-quality standards as a part of their competitive strategies. Because measuring and predicting the costs and benefits of total quality management (TQM) practices are difficult, organisations typically implement them without performing NPV analysis.

In some cases, an investment under consideration would result in a potentially negative impact on employees. If new equipment or manufacturing processes replace employees, the impact needs to be evaluated for displaced employees and also for the morale of remaining employees. If job responsibilities or perceptions of job stability change as a result of the project, the remaining employees may be negatively affected. Sometimes organisations forgo or modify projects to reduce negative impacts on employees.

Some projects result in a large impact on the community. Bringing a large new facility into a small community can change the dynamics of the entire community. Closing a plant or service upon which a community relies can result in a negative reputation for an organisation. A negative corporate image can have far-reaching effects on the entity as a whole, including loss of market share and morale problems with employees and management.

Making and monitoring investment decisions

Managers consider a number of factors when making the final decision about a proposed capital budgeting project. The results of any quantitative analyses as well as the qualitative issues already discussed are taken into account. Accountants often prepare analyses of projects that align with organisations' strategic plans. Managers use these analyses to examine financial outcomes under a number of different scenarios. They often have a better grasp than accountants of certain business factors, such as competitors' product development and prices. In addition, managers may use their own informal estimates to determine an NPV.

After a project has been accepted, accountants and managers monitor its progress and compare actual performance to the capital budget expectations. Some projects are relatively simple to implement and require little monitoring (for example, the replacement of equipment in a coin-operated laundry). Other projects are more complex, such as Gordon's new line of business through the health club. More complex projects that take longer to implement need more monitoring to reduce the probability of budget overruns.

Because these projects are long-lived, outcomes are almost always different from expectations. A **post-investment audit** provides feedback about whether operations are meeting expectations. When results are below expectations, processes are investigated and improvements can be implemented. In addition, the process of re-evaluating past decisions usually improves future decision making. The more we learn about factors that affect the accuracy of our forecasts and investigate unanticipated problems or benefits, the better we can predict these occurrences in future projects.

Income taxes and the net present value method

Income taxes affect an organisation's cash flows and, in turn, capital budgeting decisions. Because individual states and countries have different income tax rules, the specific tax effects on a proposed project depend on the tax jurisdictions of the organisation and the project. Taxes become even more complex as an entity grows and expands internationally. In addition, income tax laws change periodically, and capital budgeting requires current knowledge of tax laws. Before developing NPV analyses in a complex entity, accountants consult tax experts so that their analyses reflect the cash flows that would actually take place. Importantly, the tax effects of an investment decision may be a key driver of a decision to proceed with an investment.

Most cash flows associated with capital budgeting projects either increase or decrease income taxes in the year of the cash flow. However, the initial investment generally cannot be deducted immediately from taxable income. Instead, depreciation can be deducted in future years for investments such as buildings, land improvements, equipment and furnishings. This depreciation deduction is often referred to as a **tax shield**; the depreciation shields part of operating income from the payment of income taxes. In addition, operating cash flows and gains or losses on assets' terminal values affect the amount of income tax paid.

Calculating incremental tax cash flows

Once we forecast depreciation for the life of the project, we can calculate the incremental tax cash flow, which is the amount that will be paid or saved on taxes each year of the project. We combine the operating cash flow for each year with that year's depreciation, and then multiply the total by the marginal income tax rate.

We also need to calculate the tax cash flow based on the terminal value of the project. This calculation requires the following steps. First, find the total amount of tax depreciation that accumulated from the time of the initial investment to its disposal. Subtract the total depreciation from the initial investment; the remainder is the tax basis. In turn, subtract this amount from the disposal value. The remainder is a taxable gain or loss. Multiply this amount by the marginal income tax rate to find the incremental tax cash flow at the end of the project.

For Gordon's apartment building decision (figure 9.3 on page 360), the initial investment is $1 400 000 with estimated cash flows of $276 000 annually. Gordon expects to be able to sell the building at the end of 10 years for $400 000. Suppose that for tax purposes Gordon uses straight-line depreciation with an annual deduction of $100 000 and has a 30 per cent marginal income tax rate. His income tax expense each year will be $52 800 [($276 000 − $100 000) × 30%]. His incremental cash flow becomes $223 200 ($276 000 − $52 800). We discount these cash flows to compare them with the initial investment as follows:

$$PV = \$223\,200 \times (PVFA\ 10\ years,\ 14\%) + \$400\,000 \times (PVF\ 10\ years,\ 14\%)$$

$$= \$223\,200 \times 5.216 + \$400\,000 \times 0.270$$

$$= \$1\,164\,211 + \$108\,000$$

$$= \$1\,272\,211$$

and the NPV = $1 272 211 − $1 400 000 = −$127 789. Before considering income taxes, our previous calculations resulted in an NPV of $174 616 ($1 574 616 − $1 400 000). When income taxes are factored in, the NPV becomes negative.

APPENDIX 9A

INFLATION AND THE NET PRESENT VALUE METHOD

The NPV calculations in the chapter did not take into account the fact that many revenues and costs tend to inflate or deflate over time. When these changes occur, it is inappropriate to use today's revenue and cost values when forecasting future cash flows, particularly for projects spanning many years. Sometimes costs such as transportation fuel increase rapidly. Wages or supplies might increase at a slower rate over time. Still other costs, such as new technology, might actually decrease over time. Cash flows from projects in other countries sometimes have different inflation rates from those in Australia. Managers need to incorporate these types of expected differences in their NPV analyses.

Inflation is the decline in the general purchasing power of the monetary unit, meaning that more monetary units (such as dollars) are needed to purchase goods or services. **Deflation** is the opposite, or an increase in the general purchasing power of the monetary unit. Because either can distort an NPV analysis, cash flows should be adjusted for anticipated levels of inflation or deflation.

Real and nominal methods for NPV analysis

Two types of interest rates need to be considered when analysing inflation, as shown in figure 9A.1. The first type, the **real rate of interest**, is the rate of return required on investments when no inflation is a factor. It is calculated as the sum of the risk-free rate and a risk premium. The **risk-free rate** is the 'pure' rate of interest paid on short-term government bonds (without considering inflation). The **risk premium** is an element above the risk-free rate that entities demand for undertaking risks. The second type, the **nominal rate of interest**, is the rate of return required on investments when inflation is present. It is calculated by increasing the real rate of interest by the expected rate of inflation.

Cash flows and the discount rate should be measured using a consistent approach. In the **real method**, cash inflows and outflows are forecast in real dollars (no inflation) and discounted using a real rate. The examples we have used so far in the chapter used real cash flows.

In the **nominal method**, cash inflows and outflows are forecast in nominal dollars (inflated) and discounted using a nominal discount rate. Real cash flows can be converted to nominal cash flows using the following formula:

$$\textbf{Nominal cash flow} = \textbf{Real cash flow} \times (1 + i)^t$$

where i = rate of inflation

t = number of time periods in the future

Suppose Gordon hires an accountant at $35 000 per year to help with his new businesses. If the accountant's salary is valued in a NPV analysis using the real method over a five-year period, the cash flows will be uniform across time. But if the salary inflates at 2 per cent per year, the cash flows will increase across time. Figure 9A.2 compares the real and nominal cash flows.

Real rate of interest = Risk-free rate + Risk premium
Nominal rate of interest = (1 + Real rate) × (1 + Inflation rate) − 1

FIGURE 9A.1 ■ Real and nominal interest rates

In some cases, the depreciation expense that can be deducted on an income tax return does not change over time. However, under inflation, the real amount of annual depreciation tax savings decreases over time. Nominal cash flows can be converted to real cash flows as follows:

$$\textbf{Real cash flow} = \frac{\textbf{Nominal cash flow}}{(1 + i)^t}$$

FIGURE 9A.2 ■ Real versus nominal wages

Period	Real cash flows	Nominal cash flows
1	$35 000	$35 000 × 1.02 = $35 700
2	$35 000	$35 000 × 1.02^2 = $36 414

(continued)

Period	Real cash flows	Nominal cash flows
3	$35 000	$35 000 × 1.02^3 = $37 142
4	$35 000	$35 000 × 1.02^4 = $37 885
5	$35 000	$35 000 × 1.02^5 = $38 643

Internal consistency in NPV analysis

If cash inflows and outflows are valued in real terms and then discounted using a nominal rate, or vice versa, the approach is internally inconsistent. Because nominal rates include inflation, they tend to be higher than real rates. Discounting real cash flows using a nominal rate creates a bias against the adoption of many worthwhile capital investment projects because the discounted present value of cash inflows is understated. Discounting nominal cash flows using a real rate overstates discounted cash flows and creates a bias toward accepting projects that may have a negative NPV.

When we expect relevant cash flows to be influenced by inflation or deflation, we must select a method (real or nominal) and then use that method consistently for all calculations. We perform the NPV analysis as before. The only differences are as follows:

- Cash flows must be adjusted so that they are internally consistent with the method used.
- Only a real discount rate should be used under the real method, and only a nominal discount rate should be used under the nominal method.

Figure 9A.3 summarises the types of adjustments to cash flows that are required under the real and nominal methods.

Cash flow	Adjustments for real method	Adjustments for nominal method
Initial investment	No adjustment	No adjustment
Depreciation tax shield	Adjust from a nominal to a real amount for each year (deflate)	No adjustment
Remaining cash flow: ■ Incremental operating cash flows ■ Income taxes on incremental cash flows ■ Terminal cash flows ■ Income taxes on terminal gain or loss	If original cash flow estimates include inflation, then the cash flows must be adjusted from nominal to real amounts for each year; the tax cash flows must then be recalculated	If original cash flow estimates do not include inflation, then the cash flows must be adjusted from real to nominal amounts for each year; the tax cash flows must then be recalculated

Adjustment formulas:

$$\text{Nominal cash flow} = \text{Real cash flow} \times (1 + i)^t$$

$$\text{Real cash flow} = \frac{\text{Nominal cash flow}}{(1 + i)^t}$$

where i = rate of inflation

t = number of time periods in the future

FIGURE 9A.3 ■ Cash flow adjustments required under the real and nominal methods

APPENDIX 9B Present and future value tables

TABLE 9B.1 ■ Present value of $1

Periods	4%	5%	6%	7%	8%	9%	10%	11%	12%	13%	14%	15%	16%	17%	18%
1	0.962	0.952	0.943	0.935	0.926	0.917	0.909	0.901	0.893	0.885	0.877	0.870	0.862	0.855	0.847
2	0.925	0.907	0.890	0.873	0.857	0.842	0.826	0.812	0.797	0.783	0.769	0.756	0.743	0.731	0.718
3	0.889	0.864	0.840	0.816	0.794	0.772	0.751	0.731	0.712	0.693	0.675	0.658	0.641	0.624	0.609
4	0.855	0.823	0.792	0.763	0.735	0.708	0.683	0.659	0.636	0.613	0.592	0.572	0.552	0.534	0.516
5	0.822	0.784	0.747	0.713	0.681	0.650	0.621	0.593	0.567	0.543	0.519	0.497	0.476	0.456	0.437
6	0.790	0.746	0.705	0.666	0.630	0.596	0.564	0.535	0.507	0.480	0.456	0.432	0.410	0.390	0.370
7	0.760	0.711	0.665	0.623	0.583	0.547	0.513	0.482	0.452	0.425	0.400	0.376	0.354	0.333	0.314
8	0.731	0.677	0.627	0.582	0.540	0.502	0.467	0.434	0.404	0.376	0.351	0.327	0.305	0.285	0.266
9	0.703	0.645	0.592	0.544	0.500	0.460	0.424	0.391	0.361	0.333	0.308	0.284	0.263	0.243	0.225
10	0.676	0.614	0.558	0.508	0.463	0.422	0.386	0.352	0.322	0.295	0.270	0.247	0.227	0.208	0.191
11	0.650	0.585	0.527	0.475	0.429	0.388	0.350	0.317	0.287	0.261	0.237	0.215	0.195	0.178	0.162
12	0.625	0.557	0.497	0.444	0.397	0.356	0.319	0.286	0.257	0.231	0.208	0.187	0.168	0.152	0.137
13	0.601	0.530	0.469	0.415	0.368	0.326	0.290	0.258	0.229	0.204	0.182	0.163	0.145	0.130	0.116
14	0.577	0.505	0.442	0.388	0.340	0.299	0.263	0.232	0.205	0.181	0.160	0.141	0.125	0.111	0.099
15	0.555	0.481	0.417	0.362	0.315	0.275	0.239	0.209	0.183	0.160	0.140	0.123	0.108	0.095	0.084
16	0.534	0.458	0.394	0.339	0.292	0.252	0.218	0.188	0.163	0.141	0.123	0.107	0.093	0.081	0.071
17	0.513	0.436	0.371	0.317	0.270	0.231	0.198	0.170	0.146	0.125	0.108	0.093	0.080	0.069	0.060
18	0.494	0.416	0.350	0.296	0.250	0.212	0.180	0.153	0.130	0.111	0.095	0.081	0.069	0.059	0.051
19	0.475	0.396	0.331	0.277	0.232	0.194	0.164	0.138	0.116	0.098	0.083	0.070	0.060	0.051	0.043
20	0.456	0.377	0.312	0.258	0.215	0.178	0.149	0.124	0.104	0.087	0.073	0.061	0.051	0.043	0.037
21	0.439	0.359	0.294	0.242	0.199	0.164	0.135	0.112	0.093	0.077	0.064	0.053	0.044	0.037	0.031
22	0.422	0.342	0.278	0.226	0.184	0.150	0.123	0.101	0.083	0.068	0.056	0.046	0.038	0.032	0.026
23	0.406	0.326	0.262	0.211	0.170	0.138	0.112	0.091	0.074	0.060	0.049	0.040	0.033	0.027	0.022
24	0.390	0.310	0.247	0.197	0.158	0.126	0.102	0.082	0.066	0.053	0.043	0.035	0.028	0.023	0.019
25	0.375	0.295	0.233	0.184	0.146	0.116	0.092	0.074	0.059	0.047	0.038	0.030	0.024	0.020	0.016
26	0.361	0.281	0.220	0.172	0.135	0.106	0.084	0.066	0.053	0.042	0.033	0.026	0.021	0.017	0.014
27	0.347	0.268	0.207	0.161	0.125	0.098	0.076	0.060	0.047	0.037	0.029	0.023	0.018	0.014	0.011
28	0.333	0.255	0.196	0.150	0.116	0.090	0.069	0.054	0.042	0.033	0.026	0.020	0.016	0.012	0.010
29	0.321	0.243	0.185	0.141	0.107	0.082	0.063	0.048	0.037	0.029	0.022	0.017	0.014	0.011	0.008
30	0.308	0.231	0.174	0.131	0.099	0.075	0.057	0.044	0.033	0.026	0.020	0.015	0.012	0.009	0.007

TABLE 9B.2 ■ Present value of an ordinary annuity of $1

Periods	4%	5%	6%	7%	8%	9%	10%	11%	12%	13%	14%	15%	16%	17%	18%
1	0.962	0.952	0.943	0.935	0.926	0.917	0.909	0.901	0.893	0.885	0.877	0.870	0.862	0.855	0.847
2	1.886	1.859	1.833	1.808	1.783	1.759	1.736	1.713	1.690	1.668	1.647	1.626	1.605	1.585	1.566
3	2.775	2.723	2.673	2.624	2.577	2.531	2.487	2.444	2.402	2.361	2.322	2.283	2.246	2.210	2.174
4	3.630	3.546	3.465	3.387	3.312	3.240	3.170	3.102	3.037	2.974	2.914	2.855	2.798	2.743	2.690
5	4.452	4.329	4.212	4.100	3.993	3.890	3.791	3.696	3.605	3.517	3.433	3.352	3.274	3.199	3.127
6	5.242	5.076	4.917	4.767	4.623	4.486	4.355	4.231	4.111	3.998	3.889	3.784	3.685	3.589	3.498
7	6.002	5.786	5.582	5.389	5.206	5.033	4.868	4.712	4.564	4.423	4.288	4.160	4.039	3.922	3.812
8	6.733	6.463	6.210	5.971	5.747	5.535	5.335	5.146	4.968	4.799	4.639	4.487	4.344	4.207	4.078
9	7.435	7.108	6.802	6.515	6.247	5.995	5.759	5.537	5.328	5.132	4.946	4.772	4.607	4.451	4.303
10	8.111	7.722	7.360	7.024	6.710	6.418	6.145	5.889	5.650	5.426	5.216	5.019	4.833	4.659	4.494
11	8.760	8.306	7.887	7.499	7.139	6.805	6.495	6.207	5.938	5.687	5.453	5.234	5.029	4.836	4.656
12	9.385	8.863	8.384	7.943	7.536	7.161	6.814	6.492	6.194	5.918	5.660	5.421	5.197	4.988	4.793
13	9.986	9.394	8.853	8.358	7.904	7.487	7.103	6.750	6.424	6.122	5.842	5.583	5.342	5.118	4.910
14	10.563	9.899	9.295	8.745	8.244	7.786	7.367	6.982	6.628	6.302	6.002	5.724	5.468	5.229	5.008
15	11.118	10.380	9.712	9.108	8.559	8.061	7.606	7.191	6.811	6.462	6.142	5.847	5.575	5.324	5.092
16	11.652	10.838	10.106	9.447	8.851	8.313	7.824	7.379	6.974	6.604	6.265	5.954	5.668	5.405	5.162
17	12.166	11.274	10.477	9.763	9.122	8.544	8.022	7.549	7.120	6.729	6.373	6.047	5.749	5.475	5.222
18	12.659	11.690	10.828	10.059	9.372	8.756	8.201	7.702	7.250	6.840	6.467	6.128	5.818	5.534	5.273
19	13.134	12.085	11.158	10.336	9.604	8.950	8.365	7.839	7.366	6.938	6.550	6.198	5.877	5.584	5.316
20	13.590	12.462	11.470	10.594	9.818	9.129	8.514	7.963	7.469	7.025	6.623	6.259	5.929	5.628	5.353
21	14.029	12.821	11.764	10.836	10.017	9.292	8.649	8.075	7.562	7.102	6.687	6.312	5.973	5.665	5.384
22	14.451	13.163	12.042	11.061	10.201	9.442	8.772	8.176	7.645	7.170	6.743	6.359	6.011	5.696	5.410
23	14.857	13.489	12.303	11.272	10.371	9.580	8.883	8.266	7.718	7.230	6.792	6.399	6.044	5.723	5.432
24	15.247	13.799	12.550	11.469	10.529	9.707	8.985	8.348	7.784	7.283	6.835	6.434	6.073	5.746	5.451
25	15.622	14.094	12.783	11.654	10.675	9.823	9.077	8.422	7.843	7.330	6.873	6.464	6.097	5.766	5.467
26	15.983	14.375	13.003	11.826	10.810	9.929	9.161	8.488	7.896	7.372	6.906	6.491	6.118	5.783	5.480
27	16.330	14.643	13.211	11.987	10.935	10.027	9.237	8.548	7.943	7.409	6.935	6.514	6.136	5.798	5.492
28	16.663	14.898	13.406	12.137	11.051	10.116	9.307	8.602	7.984	7.441	6.961	6.534	6.152	5.810	5.502
29	16.984	15.141	13.591	12.278	11.158	10.198	9.370	8.650	8.022	7.470	6.983	6.551	6.166	5.820	5.510
30	17.292	15.372	13.765	12.409	11.258	10.274	9.427	8.694	8.055	7.496	7.003	6.566	6.177	5.829	5.517

TABLE 9B.3 ■ Future value of $1

Periods	4%	5%	6%	7%	8%	9%	10%	11%	12%	13%	14%	15%	16%	17%	18%
1	1.040	1.050	1.060	1.070	1.080	1.090	1.100	1.110	1.120	1.130	1.140	1.150	1.160	1.170	1.180
2	1.082	1.103	1.124	1.145	1.166	1.188	1.210	1.232	1.254	1.277	1.300	1.323	1.346	1.369	1.392
3	1.125	1.158	1.191	1.225	1.260	1.295	1.331	1.368	1.405	1.443	1.482	1.521	1.561	1.602	1.643
4	1.170	1.216	1.262	1.311	1.360	1.412	1.464	1.518	1.574	1.630	1.689	1.749	1.811	1.874	1.939
5	1.217	1.276	1.338	1.403	1.469	1.539	1.611	1.685	1.762	1.842	1.925	2.011	2.100	2.192	2.288
6	1.265	1.340	1.419	1.501	1.587	1.677	1.772	1.870	1.974	2.082	2.195	2.313	2.436	2.565	2.700
7	1.316	1.407	1.504	1.606	1.714	1.828	1.949	2.076	2.211	2.353	2.502	2.660	2.826	3.001	3.185
8	1.369	1.477	1.594	1.718	1.851	1.993	2.144	2.305	2.476	2.658	2.853	3.059	3.278	3.511	3.759
9	1.423	1.551	1.689	1.838	1.999	2.172	2.358	2.558	2.773	3.004	3.252	3.518	3.803	4.108	4.435
10	1.480	1.629	1.791	1.967	2.159	2.367	2.594	2.839	3.106	3.395	3.707	4.046	4.411	4.807	5.234
11	1.539	1.710	1.898	2.105	2.332	2.580	2.853	3.152	3.479	3.836	4.226	4.652	5.117	5.624	6.176
12	1.601	1.796	2.012	2.252	2.518	2.813	3.138	3.498	3.896	4.335	4.818	5.350	5.936	6.580	7.288
13	1.665	1.886	2.133	2.410	2.720	3.066	3.452	3.883	4.363	4.898	5.492	6.153	6.886	7.699	8.599
14	1.732	1.980	2.261	2.579	2.937	3.342	3.797	4.310	4.887	5.535	6.261	7.076	7.988	9.007	10.147
15	1.801	2.079	2.397	2.759	3.172	3.642	4.177	4.785	5.474	6.254	7.138	8.137	9.266	10.539	11.974
16	1.873	2.183	2.540	2.952	3.426	3.970	4.595	5.311	6.130	7.067	8.137	9.358	10.748	12.330	14.129
17	1.948	2.292	2.693	3.159	3.700	4.328	5.054	5.895	6.866	7.986	9.276	10.761	12.468	14.426	16.672
18	2.026	2.407	2.854	3.380	3.996	4.717	5.560	6.544	7.690	9.024	10.575	12.375	14.463	16.879	19.673
19	2.107	2.527	3.026	3.617	4.316	5.142	6.116	7.263	8.613	10.197	12.056	14.232	16.777	19.748	23.214
20	2.191	2.653	3.207	3.870	4.661	5.604	6.727	8.062	9.646	11.523	13.743	16.367	19.461	23.106	27.393
21	2.279	2.786	3.400	4.141	5.034	6.109	7.400	8.949	10.804	13.021	15.668	18.822	22.574	27.034	32.324
22	2.370	2.925	3.604	4.430	5.437	6.659	8.140	9.934	12.100	14.714	17.861	21.645	26.186	31.629	38.142
23	2.465	3.072	3.820	4.741	5.871	7.258	8.954	11.026	13.552	16.627	20.362	24.891	30.376	37.006	45.008
24	2.563	3.225	4.049	5.072	6.341	7.911	9.850	12.239	15.179	18.788	23.212	28.625	35.236	43.297	53.109
25	2.666	3.386	4.292	5.427	6.848	8.623	10.835	13.585	17.000	21.231	26.462	32.919	40.874	50.658	62.669
26	2.772	3.556	4.549	5.807	7.396	9.399	11.918	15.080	19.040	23.991	30.167	37.857	47.414	59.270	73.949
27	2.883	3.733	4.822	6.214	7.988	10.245	13.110	16.739	21.325	27.109	34.390	43.535	55.000	69.345	87.260
28	2.999	3.920	5.112	6.649	8.627	11.167	14.421	18.580	23.884	30.633	39.204	50.066	63.800	81.134	102.967
29	3.119	4.116	5.418	7.114	9.317	12.172	15.863	20.624	26.750	34.616	44.693	57.575	74.009	94.927	121.501
30	3.243	4.322	5.743	7.612	10.063	13.268	17.449	22.892	29.960	39.116	50.950	66.212	85.850	111.065	143.371

TABLE 9B.4 ■ Future value of an ordinary annuity of $1

Periods	4%	5%	6%	7%	8%	9%	10%	11%	12%	13%	14%	15%	16%	17%	18%
1	1.000	1.000	1.000	1.000	1.000	1.000	1.000	1.000	1.000	1.000	1.000	1.000	1.000	1.000	1.000
2	2.040	2.050	2.060	2.070	2.080	2.090	2.100	2.110	2.120	2.130	2.140	2.150	2.160	2.170	2.180
3	3.122	3.153	3.184	3.215	3.246	3.278	3.310	3.342	3.374	3.407	3.440	3.473	3.506	3.539	3.572
4	4.246	4.310	4.375	4.440	4.506	4.573	4.641	4.710	4.779	4.850	4.921	4.993	5.066	5.141	5.215
5	5.416	5.526	5.637	5.751	5.867	5.985	6.105	6.228	6.353	6.480	6.610	6.742	6.877	7.014	7.154
6	6.633	6.802	6.975	7.153	7.336	7.523	7.716	7.913	8.115	8.323	8.536	8.754	8.977	9.207	9.442
7	7.898	8.142	8.394	8.654	8.923	9.200	9.487	9.783	10.089	10.405	10.730	11.067	11.414	11.772	12.142
8	9.214	9.549	9.897	10.260	10.637	11.028	11.436	11.859	12.300	12.757	13.233	13.727	14.240	14.773	15.327
9	10.583	11.027	11.491	11.978	12.488	13.021	13.579	14.164	14.776	15.416	16.085	16.786	17.519	18.285	19.086
10	12.006	12.578	13.181	13.816	14.487	15.193	15.937	16.722	17.549	18.420	19.337	20.304	21.321	22.393	23.521
11	13.486	14.207	14.972	15.784	16.645	17.560	18.531	19.561	20.655	21.814	23.045	24.349	25.733	27.200	28.755
12	15.026	15.917	16.870	17.888	18.977	20.141	21.384	22.713	24.133	25.650	27.271	29.002	30.850	32.824	34.931
13	16.627	17.713	18.882	20.141	21.495	22.953	24.523	26.212	28.029	29.985	32.089	34.352	36.786	39.404	42.219
14	18.292	19.599	21.015	22.550	24.215	26.019	27.975	30.095	32.393	34.883	37.581	40.505	43.672	47.103	50.818
15	20.024	21.579	23.276	25.129	27.152	29.361	31.772	34.405	37.280	40.417	43.842	47.580	51.660	56.110	60.965
16	21.825	23.657	25.673	27.888	30.324	33.003	35.950	39.190	42.753	46.672	50.980	55.717	60.925	66.649	72.939
17	23.698	25.840	28.213	30.840	33.750	36.974	40.545	44.501	48.884	53.739	59.118	65.075	71.763	78.979	87.068
18	25.645	28.132	30.906	33.999	37.450	41.301	45.599	50.396	55.750	61.725	68.394	75.836	84.141	93.406	103.740
19	27.671	30.539	33.760	37.379	41.446	46.018	51.159	56.939	63.440	70.749	78.969	88.212	98.603	110.285	123.414
20	29.778	33.066	36.786	40.995	45.762	51.160	57.275	64.203	72.052	80.947	91.025	102.444	115.380	130.033	146.628
21	31.969	35.719	39.993	44.865	50.423	56.765	64.002	72.265	81.699	92.470	104.768	118.810	134.841	153.139	174.021
22	34.248	38.505	43.392	49.006	55.457	62.873	71.403	81.214	92.503	105.491	120.436	137.632	157.415	180.172	206.345
23	36.618	41.430	46.996	53.436	60.893	69.532	79.543	91.148	104.603	120.205	138.297	159.276	183.601	211.801	244.487
24	39.083	44.502	50.816	58.177	66.765	76.790	88.497	102.174	118.155	136.831	158.659	184.168	213.978	248.808	289.494
25	41.646	47.727	54.865	63.249	73.106	84.701	98.347	114.413	133.334	155.620	181.871	212.793	249.214	292.105	342.603
26	44.312	51.113	59.156	68.676	79.954	93.324	109.182	127.999	150.334	176.850	208.333	245.712	290.088	342.763	405.272
27	47.084	54.669	63.706	74.484	87.351	102.723	121.100	143.079	169.374	200.841	238.499	283.569	337.502	402.032	479.221
28	49.968	58.403	68.528	80.698	95.339	112.968	134.210	159.817	190.699	227.889	272.889	327.104	392.503	471.378	566.481
29	52.966	62.323	73.640	87.347	103.966	124.135	148.631	178.397	214.583	258.583	312.094	377.170	456.303	552.512	669.447
30	56.085	66.439	79.058	94.461	113.283	136.308	164.494	199.021	241.333	293.199	356.787	434.745	530.312	647.439	790.948

Summary

1 Understand investment decisions.

Capital budgeting process

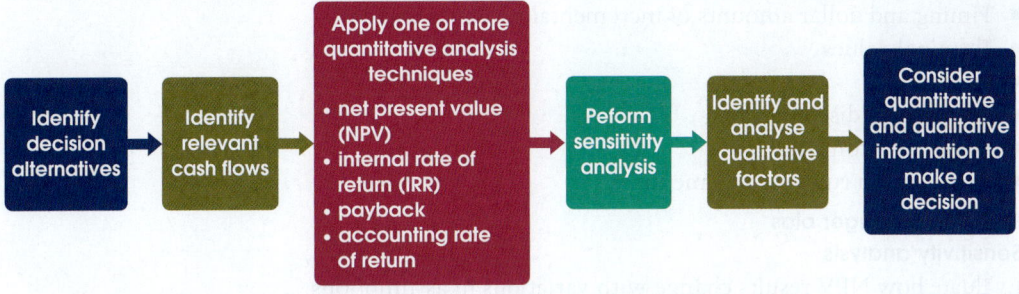

Types of long-term investment decisions

- Operational
- Strategic
- Compliance

2 Identify relevant cash flows for strategic investment decisions.

Common types of relevant cash flows

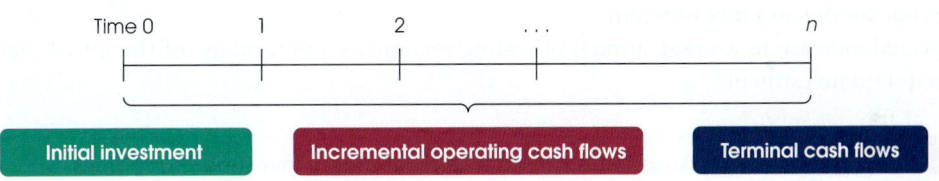

3 Perform and interpret net present value (NPV) analysis.

Calculation of net present value

$$\text{NPV} = \sum_{t=0}^{n} \frac{\text{Expected cash flow}_t}{(1+r)^t}$$

$$= \sum_{t=0}^{n} \text{Expected cash flow}_t \times \text{PVF}_{r,t}$$

Potential discount rates

- Weighted average cost of capital
- Rate reflecting project risk

General decision rules

- Projects with a positive NPV are generally acceptable.
- If investment resources are limited, invest in the project(s) having the highest NPV.

- If profitability index is greater than 1, accept project.
- Projects can be ranked on a profitability index.

4 **Understand the uncertainties of NPV analysis.**

Major assumptions and uncertainties
- Cost of initial investment
- Timing and dollar amounts of incremental revenues and costs
- Terminal values
- Project life
- Appropriate discount rate
- Marginal income tax rate
- Depreciation rules for income taxes

Potential manager bias
Sensitivity analysis
Evaluate how NPV results change with variations in assumptions.

5 **Understand alternative methods (IRR, payback, accrual accounting rate of return) used for strategic investment decisions.**

Internal rate of return (IRR)
Discount rate necessary for the present value of the discounted cash flows to be equal to the investment.

Payback
Measures the amount of time required to recover the initial investment.

Accrual accounting rate of return
Expected increase in average annual operating income as a percentage of the initial increase in required investment.

6 **Identify additional issues to be considered for strategic investment decisions.**

Qualitative issues
- Difficulty in estimating cash flows for new information technology
- Need for speedy decisions
- Encouraging innovation in new products and services
- Reputation
- Environmental effects
- Quality of product or service
- Employees
- Community

Post-investment audit
Improve implementation, results and accuracy of future capital budgets.

7 **Understand how income taxes affect strategic investment decision cash flows.**

Income tax cash flows
- Tax on incremental operating cash flows
- Tax on terminal gain or loss
- Depreciation tax shield

8 Understand how real and nominal methods are used to address inflation in an NPV analysis.

Real method

Discount real cash flows at the real rate of interest.

$$\text{Real rate of interest} = \text{Risk-free rate} + \text{Risk premium}$$

Nominal method

Discount nominal cash flows at the nominal rate of interest.

$$\text{Nominal rate of interest} = (1 + \text{Real rate}) \times (1 + \text{Inflation rate}) - 1$$

Internal consistency in NPV analysis

Cash flows and interest rate must be calculated using the same method (real or nominal). Cannot use real method if different cash flows are subject to different rates of inflation (or deflation).

Self-study problems

SELF-STUDY PROBLEM 1

Capital budgeting cash flows; NPV; IRR; payback; sensitivity analysis

Newberry and Mills Company is considering the purchase of new robotic manufacturing equipment. The purchase price is $85 000. The cost for shipping the machine to the plant is $2000. Another $3000 will be spent to remodel the area in which the machine is to be installed. The purchase price includes installation costs. The entity has already spent $1500 in travel costs and employee time on the search for this equipment. The machine is expected to save $30 000 a year in labour and insurance expenses over the next four years, and is expected to be obsolete in four years. Newberry and Mills uses a 10 per cent discount rate as the required rate of return on capital budgeting projects. Ignore income taxes.

REQUIRED

(a) Calculate the net present value.
(b) Calculate the profitability index.
(c) Calculate the internal rate of return.
(d) Calculate the payback period.
(e) List factors that you would vary to perform sensitivity analysis and explain why you would vary them.

Solution to self-study problem 1

(a) First we summarise the cash flows across time. Notice that the $1500 in travel and employee costs is a sunk cost and does not affect the NPV calculation. Also, no terminal cash flows occur for this project.

Time 0		Years 1–4
Investment		$30 000 savings
$85 000	purchase	
2 000	shipping	
3 000	remodel	
$90 000		

Because cash flows are equal across time, we can treat the incremental cash flows in years 1 through 4 as an annuity to calculate NPV:

$$NPV = -\$90\,000 + \$30\,000 \times (PVFA\ 4\ years,\ 10\%)$$

$$= -\$90\,000 + \$30\,000 \times 3.170 = -\$90\,000 + \$95\,100$$

$$= \$5100$$

(b) Profitability index = $95 100 ÷ $90 000 = 1.057
(c) IRR (calculated using the IRR function in an Excel spreadsheet) = 12.59%
(d) Payback = $90 000 ÷ $30 000 = three years
(e) Factors that could be varied for sensitivity analysis include all of the assumptions such as the initial investment amount, the labour and insurance savings, and the discount rate. Because we cannot know future economic conditions, and we cannot know whether technology developments will improve models more rapidly than we expect, we need to perform sensitivity analysis for all of the assumptions we make. Even the initial investment could change if remodelling is more substantial than expected.

SELF-STUDY PROBLEM 2

NPV; IRR; payback with inflation and income taxes (appendix 9A)

Kestrel and Sons drills residential and commercial wells. The entity is in the process of analysing the purchase of a new drill that would cost $80 000 and have an expected useful life of six years. Several employees have spent $5000 in travel expenses to locate the best drill. Operating the drill would increase revenue by $60 000 per year, but cost an additional $39 000 for labour, maintenance and other related costs. The managers estimate the salvage value of the drill to be $8000. Kestrel's marginal income tax rate is 25 per cent. Government regulations require that each well be registered and that the location of the well meets certain health require-ments, such as being at least 100 metres away from septic and sewage systems. An ongoing controversy over the last 15 years centres around whether individual homeowners should be allowed to drill wells, but so far no regulation has been proposed.

REQUIRED

(a) Using a five-year depreciation, an inflation rate of 4 per cent, a risk-free rate of 5 per cent and a risk premium of 8 per cent, calculate the net present value for the purchase of the drill using the nominal method.
(b) Calculate the internal rate of return.
(c) Calculate the payback period using nominal cash flows.
(d) What regulatory issues would Kestrel consider as qualitative factors?
(e) How would the issues you identified in part (d) affect your assessment of the project risk?

Solution to self-study problem 2

(a) Figure 9.8 provides a spreadsheet with the NPV calculation using the nominal method for Kestrel and Sons. This spreadsheet demonstrates a different format than shown in the chapter examples.
(b) Figure 9.9 (page 382) provides a spreadsheet with the IRR calculation for Kestrel and Sons.
(c) Because the net cash flows in this problem are not uniform (that is, they are not identical) across time, the payback period must be calculated by manually determining the years it takes to recover the investment. Payback does not include the time value of money, so we analyse the cash flows before they are discounted.

	Net nominal cash flow	Balance to recover
Time 0		$80 000
Year 1	$16 380 + $4000 = $20 380	$80 000 – $20 380 = $59 620
Year 2	$17 035 + $6400 = $23 435	$59 620 – $23 435 = $36 185
Year 3	$17 717 + $3840 = $21 557	$36 185 – $21 557 = $14 628
Year 4	$18 425 + $2304 = $20 729	$14 628 – $14 628 = 0

The initial investment is expected to be fully recovered in more than three years, but less than four. We can estimate the proportion of the fourth year needed to complete the payback as:

$$\$14\,628 \div \$20\,729 = 0.7 \text{ of year 4}$$

Thus, the payback period is estimated as 3.7 years.

	A	B	C	D	E
1	Cash flows:				
2	Increase in revenue	$60,000	Discount rate information:		
3	Increase in labour	($39,000)	Risk-free	5.00%	
4	Total	$21,000	Project risk	8.00%	
5	Terminal value	$8,000	Inflation	4.00%	
6	Investment:				
7	Purchase equipment	($80,000)	Tax rate	25.00%	
8					
9	Nominal discount rate	17.52%			
10					
11	Incremental cash flows:				
12	Period	Incremental CF	Inflated	Less tax	Discounted
13	1	$21,000	$21,840	$16,380	$13,938
14	2	$21,000	$22,714	$17,035	$12,335
15	3	$21,000	$23,622	$17,717	$10,916
16	4	$21,000	$24,567	$18,425	$9,660
17	5	$21,000	$25,550	$19,162	$8,548
18	6	$21,000	$26,572	$19,929	$7,565
19	Total PV of incremental cash flow				$62,961
20					
21	Depreciation tax savings:				
22	Period	MACRS	Depreciation	Tax savings	Discounted
23	1	20.00%	$16,000	$4,000	$3,404
24	2	32.00%	$25,600	$6,400	$4,634
25	3	19.20%	$15,360	$3,840	$2,366
26	4	11.52%	$9,216	$2,304	$1,208
27	5	11.52%	$9,216	$2,304	$1,028
28	6	5.76%	$4,608	$1,152	$437
29	Total PV of tax savings				$13,077
30					
31		Today's dollars	Inflated	After tax	Discounted
32	Terminal value	$8,000	$10,123	$7,592	$2,882
33					
34	Net present value:				
35	Incremental CF	$62,961			
36	Tax savings	$13,077			
37	Terminal value	$2,882			
38	Less investment	($80,000)			
39	NPV	($1,080)			

Examples of Excel formulas:
Nominal discount rate in cell B9: =(1+D3+D4)*(1+D5)–1
Inflated incremental cash flow in cell C15: =–FV($D$5,A15,,B15)
After-tax incremental cash flow in cell D15: =C15*(1–$D$7)
Present value of incremental cash flow in cell E15: =–PV($B$9,A15,,D15)

FIGURE 9.8 ■ NPV calculation for self-study problem 2(a)

	A	B	C	D	E	F
41	Combined cash flows:					
42	Period	Investment	Incremental CF	Tax savings	Terminal	Total
43	0	($80,000)				($80,000)
44	1		$16,380	$4,000		$20,380
45	2		$17,035	$6,400		$23,435
46	3		$17,717	$3,840		$21,557
47	4		$18,425	$2,304		$20,729
48	5		$19,162	$2,304		$21,466
49	6		$19,929	$1,152	$10,123	$31,203
50						
51	Internal rate of return	17.46%				

Excel formula to calculate internal rate of return in cell B51: =IRR(F43:F49)

FIGURE 9.9 ■ IRR calculation for self-study problem 2(b)

(d) Kestrel would have to consider the possible upcoming change in regulation making it impossible for homeowners to drill wells. The percentage of wells drilled that are residential would decrease greatly. If this percentage is high, Kestrel may not be able to bring in the predicted revenue.

(e) The risk premium should probably be increased if residential drilling is a large (say, greater than about 30 per cent) proportion of Kestrel's business. Sensitivity analysis can be done around the discount rate by varying the risk premium to determine the risk rate that brings the net present value to zero.

Questions

9.1 Forecasting the terminal value of equipment 20 years from now is difficult to do accurately, but errors in estimation probably have a small effect on the NPV. Explain.

9.2 Suppose an entity has five different capital budgeting projects from which to choose, but has constrained funds and cannot implement all of the projects. Explain why comparing the projects' NPVs is better than comparing their IRRs.

9.3 Describe the pros and cons of each of the capital budgeting methods learned in this chapter:
(a) net present value
(b) internal rate of return
(c) payback
(d) accrual accounting rate of return.

9.4 When projects have longer lives, it is more difficult to accurately estimate the cash flows and discount rates over the life of the project. Explain why this statement is true.

9.5 (Appendix 9A) The present value of a given cash flow gets smaller as the number of periods gets larger, regardless of whether cash flow is discounted with a real rate or nominal rate. Explain why this relationship happens and what it means from an economic perspective.

9.6 (Appendix 9A) Two methods can be used to incorporate the effects of inflation or deflation into an NPV analysis. In your own words, explain how a nominal discount rate is different from a real discount rate. Why are analyses using the nominal approach potentially more accurate than those using the real approach?

9.7 (Appendix 9A) How might inflation influence a decision to acquire an asset now rather than later?

9.8 If an entity has unlimited funds, what criterion should be used to determine which projects to invest in?

9.9 An international entity requires a rate of return of 15 per cent domestically and in developed countries, but 25 per cent in less-developed countries. Does this requirement mean that the entity is exploiting the less-developed countries?

9.10 When we covered cost–volume–profit (CVP) analysis in chapter 6, we calculated the amount of pre-tax profit needed to achieve a given level of after-tax profit. We could calculate a pre-tax rate of return given an after-tax rate of return. Why would it be inappropriate to use a pre-tax discount rate in capital budgeting? (For example, if an entity requires an after-tax return of 10 per cent and has a marginal income tax rate of 50 per cent, why not use a 20 per cent pre-tax rate of return and ignore the separate income tax calculations?)

9.11 A community health clinic operates as a not-for-profit entity. Typical capital expenditure decisions involve acquiring equipment that will perform medical tests beyond those currently possible at the clinic (hence, adding revenues) and/or perform tests more efficiently than currently (hence, decreasing expenses). To evaluate such expenditures, the clinic uses a discount rate equal to the return on its investment trust portfolio. Briefly explain why it does this.

Exercises

9.12 Time value of money
   (a) What is the present value of $8000 received in seven years at 8 per cent interest?
   (b) Bonnie Lee buys a savings bond for $125. The bond pays 6 per cent and matures in 10 years. What amount will Bonnie receive when she redeems the bond?
   (c) Erik Peterson needs to have $10 000 at the end of five years to purchase a second car. His investment returns 6 per cent. How much does he need to invest now?
   (d) Conan Bardwell will receive $1000 in six years from an investment that returns 12 per cent. How much did he invest?

9.13 Capital budgeting process Put the following six steps for capital budgeting in the most likely order, numbering the first activity as number 1, the second as 2 and so on.
   ■ Perform sensitivity analysis
   ■ Identify decision alternatives
   ■ Analyse qualitative factors
   ■ Identify relevant cash flows
   ■ Apply the relevant quantitative analysis technique
   ■ Consider quantitative and qualitative information to make a decision

9.14 NPV calculations with taxes Overnight Laundry is considering the purchase of a new pressing machine that would cost $96 000 and produce incremental operating cash flows of $25 000 annually for 10 years. The machine has a terminal value of $6000 and is depreciated for income tax purposes using straight-line depreciation over a 10-year life. Overnight Laundry's marginal tax rate is 33.3 per cent. The entity uses a discount rate of 18 per cent.

REQUIRED

What is the net present value of the project?

9.15 NPV and IRR calculations Axel Ltd is planning to buy a new machine with the expectation that this investment should earn a rate of return of at least 15 per cent. This machine, which costs $150 000, would yield an estimated net cash flow of $30 000 a year for 10 years.

REQUIRED

(a) What is the net present value for this proposal?
(b) What is the internal rate of return for this proposal?

9.16 **NPV, IRR, ARR and payback methods** Amaro Hospital, a not-for-profit entity that is not subject to income taxes, is considering the purchase of new equipment costing $20 000 to achieve cash savings of $5000 per year in operating costs. The estimated useful life is 10 years, with no salvage value. Amaro's minimum expected return is 14 per cent.

REQUIRED

(a) What is the net present value of this investment?
(b) What is the internal rate of return?
(c) What is the accrual accounting rate of return based on the initial investment?
(d) What is the payback period?

9.17 **Present value and future value calculations** Crown Ltd agreed to sell some used equipment to one of its employees. Alternative financing arrangements for the sale have been discussed, and the present and future values of each alternative have been determined.

REQUIRED

(a) Crown offered to accept a $1000 down payment and set up a note receivable that calls for four $1000 payments at the end of each of the next four years. What is the net present value of this note if it is discounted at 6 per cent?
(b) The employee agrees to the down payment but would like the note for $4000 to be payable in full at the end of the fourth year. Because of the increased risk associated with the terms of this note, Crown would apply an 8 per cent discount rate. What is the true selling price of the equipment?
(c) Suppose the employee borrows the $5000 at 8 per cent interest for four years from a bank so that he can pay Crown the full price of the equipment immediately. Also, suppose that Crown could invest the $5000 for three years at 7 per cent. What is the selling price of the equipment? What would be the future value of Crown's investment?

9.18 **Relevant cash flows; NPV analysis with taxes and inflation (appendix 9A)** Clearwater Bottling Company sells bottled spring water for $12 per case, with variable costs of $7 per case. The company has been selling 200 000 cases per year, and expects to continue at that rate unless it accepts a special order from Blue Danube Restaurant. Blue Danube has offered to buy 20 000 cases per year at $9 per case. Clearwater must agree to make the sales for a five-year period. Blue Danube will not take fewer than 20 000 cases but is willing to take more.

Clearwater's current capacity is 210 000 cases per year. Capacity could be increased to 260 000 per year if new equipment costing $100 000 were purchased. The equipment would have a useful life of five years and no salvage value. Maintenance on the new equipment would increase fixed costs by $20 000 each year. Variable costs per unit would be unchanged. Clearwater has a marginal income tax rate of 25 per cent. Inflation is estimated to be 4 per cent over each of the next five years. The risk-free rate is estimated to be 5 per cent. Clearwater can earn a rate of 12 per cent if it invests in an alternative investment having similar risk.

REQUIRED

(a) Create a timeline showing the relevant cash flows for this problem.
(b) Ignoring inflation, using straight-line depreciation over five years and using a 12 per cent discount rate, determine the NPV if 20 000 cases are sold.
(c) Ignoring inflation, using straight-line depreciation over five years and using a 12 per cent discount rate, determine the number of cases Blue Danube would need to purchase to bring the NPV to zero.

9.19 NPV analysis Government supervisors in a remote area of Queensland are considering the purchase of a small used plane to save on travel costs. The plane will cost $400 000 and can be sold in five years for 20 per cent of the original cost.

REQUIRED

If 10 per cent is the required rate of return, what minimum annual savings in transportation costs are needed for this plane to be a good investment? Ignore income taxes.

9.20 NPV and payback with taxes Equipment with a cost of $60 000 will, if acquired, generate annual savings of $30 000 for six years, at which time it will have no further use or value. The entity has a marginal tax rate of 40 per cent and requires a 10 per cent rate of return. It uses straight-line depreciation. Ignore inflation.

REQUIRED

(a) What is the after-tax cash flow for each year?
(b) What is the NPV of this investment?
(c) What is the payback period?

9.21 IRR Ferris Industries has $50 000 available to invest in new equipment. Management is considering four different equipment investments, each of which requires $50 000. The expected after-tax cash flow for each project has been estimated as follows:

	Year					
	1	2	3	4	5	6
Project 1	$10 000	$12 000	$14 000	$16 000	$16 000	$16 000
Project 2	40 000	5 000	(3 000)	40 000	5 000	1 000
Project 3	18 000	(16 000)	50 000	50 000	3 000	3 000
Project 4	30 000	-	-	30 000	30 000	30 000

REQUIRED

(a) Rank the projects in terms of desirability using the internal rate of return for each project as the criterion. Use Excel or a similar spreadsheet to calculate the IRRs.
(b) What other factors should be considered in making the decision of which investment to choose?

9.22 Alternative technologies and capital budgeting with taxes Lymbo Company must install safety devices throughout its plant or it will lose its insurance coverage. Two alternatives are acceptable to the insurer. The first costs $100 000 to install and $20 000 to maintain annually. The second costs $150 000 to install and $10 000 to maintain annually. Each has a five-year income tax life and a 15-year useful life. Lymbo's discount rate is 12 per cent, its marginal tax rate is 30 per cent and it uses straight-line depreciation.

REQUIRED

(a) Which system should be installed? Why?
(b) If Lymbo were a not-for-profit entity that does not pay income taxes on its operations, which system would be installed?

9.23 Equipment replacement; NPV; IRR; payback Garco is considering replacing an old machine that is currently being used. The old machine is fully depreciated, but it can be used for another five years, at which time it would have no terminal value. Garco can sell the old machine for $60 000 on the date that the new machine is purchased.

If the purchase occurs, the new machine will be acquired for a cash payment of $1 million. Because of the increased efficiency of the new machine, estimated annual cash savings of $300 000 would be generated during its useful life of five years. The new machine is not expected to have any terminal value.

REQUIRED

(a) Garco requires investments to earn a 12 per cent return. What is the net present value for replacing the old machine with the new machine?

(b) What is the internal rate of return to replace the old machine?

(c) What is the payback period for the new machine?

Problems

9.24 Capital budgeting methods; sensitivity analysis; spreadsheet development; uncertainties Your brother Jack was laid off from his job with a large and famous software company. He would like to sell his shares in the company and use the proceeds to start a restaurant. The shares are currently valued at $500 000. He received a job offer from a competitor that will pay $90 000 per year plus benefits. He asked you to help him decide the best course of action.

REQUIRED

(a) What are the alternatives that Jack faces?

(b) Choose the most appropriate analysis technique and explain your choice.

(c) If your brother chooses to open a restaurant, what are his opportunity costs?

(d) List the steps you would take to develop a spreadsheet that your brother could manipulate to help with the quantitative aspects of this decision. Assume that you have time only to set up a template and that your brother will fill in the specific information. However, you need to tell him the general categories of information he will need to gather.

(e) List uncertainties about whether taking the job offer would turn out well for your brother. List as many uncertainties as you can.

(f) List uncertainties about whether opening a restaurant would turn out well for your brother. List as many uncertainties as you can.

(g) Explain why it is possible for your brother to make a good decision even though he cannot know for sure how well his alternatives would work out.

9.25 IRR; developing a discount rate; evaluating risk The local homeless shelter received a large donation from a wealthy benefactor and asked you to review its decision-making process for the proposed investment choice. The shelter's financial adviser suggested using the internal rate of return (IRR) to evaluate three different projects:

- a hotel that offers rooms based on the renter's ability to pay
- an apartment complex for elderly who receive rent subsidisation from a federal government agency
- a small cardboard-box manufacturing entity that will serve as a job training facility for homeless clients.

REQUIRED

(a) In your own words, describe the advantages and disadvantages of using IRR for this decision.

(b) This not-for-profit entity uses an IRR hurdle rate of 15 per cent for most projects. Is it a good idea for an organisation to use the same hurdle rate for most projects? Why?

(c) List information that might help you develop a hurdle rate for each project.

(d) Which alternative do you believe is most financially risky for the homeless shelter? Explain your thinking.

9.26 Real interest rates; uncertainties; effects of time (appendix 9A) Managers often use the real interest rate to help them decide whether to take on a new project.

REQUIRED

(a) What two factors are included in the real interest rate?

(b) What economic factors could affect the two aspects you identified in part (a)? List as many factors as you can.

(c) Discuss how certain you can be that interest rates will remain constant over the life of a project.

(d) Does the time length of a project affect your answer to part (c)? Why?

9.27 Choice of method; uncertainties; addressing company policy Green Jade Resorts, a Singapore company that owns and operates golf resorts, has hired you to analyse its investment opportunities in Australia. The entity's managers have always used the payback method and have asked you to prepare an analysis comparing three different resorts: one on the Gold Coast, another on the Sunshine Coast and a third golf resort in the Northern Territory.

REQUIRED

(a) List four methods that could be used to analyse this long-term decision. Describe each method in your own words.

(b) In your own words, describe the advantages and disadvantages of each method you identified in part (a).

(c) Explain why it is not possible to perfectly predict a project's cash flows.

(d) In using quantitative results for decision making, would you place equal reliance on the results of all four analysis techniques? Explain.

(e) Discuss how the managers of the Singapore company might respond to your advice if you recommend an analysis method other than the payback method.

(f) Write a brief memo to the CEO of the Singapore company recommending your choice of analysis method, and explaining the most important issues for the CEO to consider when choosing an analysis method.

9.28 Timeline; relevant costs; NPV; payback; uncertainties Irrigation Supply is negotiating with a major hardware chain to supply heavy-duty sprinkler heads at $18 000 each year for five years. Irrigation Supply would need to retool at a cost of $20 000 to fill this order. Incremental costs associated with the order (in addition to the retooling costs) would be $12 000 per year. In addition, existing fixed overhead costs would be reallocated among Irrigation Supply's products, which would result in a $1000 overhead charge against the special order. For income taxes, the retooling costs would be depreciated using the straight-line method with no terminal value, ignoring the half-year convention. Irrigation Supply's marginal income tax rate is 25 per cent. Assume that all cash flows (except the initial retooling costs) occur at year-end. The entity's discount rate is 16 per cent.

REQUIRED

(a) Create a timeline showing the relevant cash flows for this problem.

(b) What is the net present value of the special order?

(c) What is the payback period for this project?

(d) For this problem, what do you learn from the NPV analysis and what do you learn from the payback period?

(e) The managers of the hardware store (the customers in this problem) believe that demand will ensure their ability to purchase sprinkler heads from Irrigation Supply. Explain why the hardware chain's managers cannot be certain about the future demand for sprinkler heads.

(f) Discuss how uncertainties for the hardware store could lead to uncertainties for Irrigation Supply.

9.29 **NPV with and without inflation; tax effects (appendix 9A)** Cy Keener, CEO of the Brisbane Architectural Design Group, is considering an investment to upgrade his current computer-aided design equipment. The new equipment would cost $110 000, and have a five-year useful life and a zero terminal value. The new equipment would generate annual cash operating savings of $36 000. The entity's required rate of return is 18 per cent each year.

REQUIRED

(a) Calculate the net present value of the project. Assume a 25 per cent marginal tax rate and straight-line depreciation, ignoring the half-year convention.

(b) Keener is wondering whether the method in part (a) provides a correct analysis of the effects of inflation. The 18 per cent required rate of return incorporates an element attributable to anticipated inflation. For purposes of his analysis, Keener assumes that the existing rate of inflation, 5 per cent annually, will persist over the next five years. Recalculate the NPV, adjusting the cash flows as appropriate for the 5 per cent inflation rate.

(c) Compare the quantitative results for parts (a) and (b). In general, how does inflation affect capital budgeting quantitative results?

(d) Explain why managers cannot predict future inflation rates with total accuracy.

(e) In your own words, explain how failure to consider the effects of inflation might bias managers' capital budgeting decisions.

9.30 **NPV with taxes and inflation; uncertainties; sensitivity analyses and interpretation (appendix 9A)** Kelly Black is manager of the customer service division of a retail computer store, Quik Computers. Kelly would like to buy computer diagnostic equipment that costs $10 000. The equipment will last five years. Kelly estimates that the incremental operating cash savings from using the equipment will be $3000 annually, measured at current prices. For income tax purposes, she will depreciate the equipment using the straight-line method and ignoring the half-year convention. Kelly requires a 10 per cent real rate of return. The annual inflation rate is 5 per cent, and the marginal income tax rate is 30 per cent.

REQUIRED

(a) Create a spreadsheet schedule showing the net present value calculations for the equipment.

(b) Identify factors in your calculations that are uncertain, and explain why.

(c) Explain how changes in technology might influence the risk involved in this project.

(d) Decide which of the factors you identified in part (b) would likely have a significant impact on the net present value calculation. Use your spreadsheet to vary each of these factors, performing sensitivity analyses.

(e) Use the quantitative results and your judgment to interpret your sensitivity analyses. Which factors seem to have the largest and smallest effects on the NPV results?

(f) Describe the pros and cons of investing in the equipment.

(g) Suppose you are the cost accountant for Quik Computers. Use the information you learned from the preceding analyses to write a memo to Kelly with your recommendation about whether to accept or reject this project. Refer in your memo to one or more attachments of spreadsheet schedules that would be useful to Kelly. In your memo, address the most important factors that Kelly should consider in making the decision.

9.31 **Timeline; maximum payment for zero NPV; qualitative factors; uncertainties** The Hotshots are a professional basketball team with a long tradition of winning. However, over the last three years the team has not won a major championship, and attendance at games has dropped considerably. A large basketball manufacturer is the team's major corporate sponsor. Carl Cliff, president of the basketball company, is also the president of the Hotshots. Cliff proposes that the team purchase the services of a star player, Bob Jackson. Jackson would create great excitement for Hotshots fans and sponsors.

Jackson's agent notifies Cliff that terms for the superstar's signing with the Hotshots are a signing bonus of $8 million payable now and a house in a Sydney beachside suburb at a cost of $5 million. The annual salary and cost of living adjustments are under negotiation.

Cliff's initial reaction is one of shock. However, he decides to examine the cash inflows expected if Jackson is signed for a four-year contract. Net gate receipts would most likely increase by $2 million a year, corporate sponsorships would increase $2.5 million per year, television royalties would increase $0.5 million per year and merchandise income (net of costs) would increase $1 million per year. Cliff believes that a 12 per cent discount rate is appropriate for this investment. The Hotshots' marginal tax rate is 20 per cent. The signing bonus can be amortised (depreciated) over the four-year period for income tax purposes, providing an annual tax deduction of $2 million.

REQUIRED

(a) Create a timeline showing the relevant cash flows for this problem.
(b) Assuming that he is not willing to lose money on the contract, what is the maximum amount per year that Cliff would be willing to pay Jackson? You will need to set up a spreadsheet for this calculation and through trial and error find an amount that brings the NPV to zero, or use an algebraic approach and annuity factors.
(c) Identify possible additional factors that Cliff should consider when deciding whether to sign Jackson to the four-year contract. List as many factors as you can.
(d) For each of the relevant cash flows in this problem, discuss why Cliff cannot be certain about the dollar amount of the cash flow.

9.32 **NPV with taxes and inflation; qualitative factors; sensitivity analysis (appendix 9A)**
Wildcat Welders manufactures new and repairs old irrigation sprinkler systems in Western Australia. The entity has been plagued with industrial accidents involving its old welding technology. A new (safer) welding robot has been developed that will reduce labour costs, worker's compensation costs and direct materials costs. The investment would be $10 million. The annual cash savings would be $7 million but it would cost $2 million a year to operate the machine.

The robots have an eight-year useful life with a terminal value of $1 million. The robots qualify for a government depreciation schedule that allows for faster depreciation of some capital assets. The schedule is as follows:

Year	1	2	3	4	5	6	7	8
Depreciation rate	14.29%	24.49%	17.49%	12.49%	8.93%	8.92%	8.93%	4.46%

Inflation is estimated to be 5 per cent per year. The risk-free rate is estimated to be 4 per cent, and the entity's managers require a minimum risk premium of 6 per cent. Wildcat's marginal income tax rate is 25 per cent.

REQUIRED

(a) Develop a spreadsheet to calculate the NPV of this project, using the nominal rate method. Be sure to include a data input box at the top of the spreadsheet to allow for sensitivity analysis.

(b) Identify a qualitative factor that could potentially override a negative NPV in making the decision to buy this equipment. Explain.

(c) Alter the risk premium to perform sensitivity analyses, and answer the following questions:

   (i) Explain how you decided which values of the risk premium were reasonable to investigate.

   (ii) Describe how changing the risk premium affects the net present value for this project.

   (iii) The new equipment would most likely lower Wildcat's risk of future lawsuits because of the reduced accident rate. Explain how this factor affects your assessment of the appropriateness of the risk premium.

(d) Because Wildcat is uncertain about whether the annual cash savings from the equipment would be $7 million, alter the cash savings to perform sensitivity analyses and answer the following questions:

   (i) Explain how you decided which values of the cash savings were reasonable to investigate.

   (ii) Describe how changing the cash savings affects the net present value for this project.

   (iii) Identify the level of cash savings that results in a NPV of zero.

(e) Suppose that current inflation is 2 per cent. Given this information, how reasonable is the inflation rate used by Wildcat? Perform sensitivity analysis around the inflation rate by changing the rate and observing the effects of the change on NPV. Explain how you made your choices.

REFERENCE

1 Registered trademark of Microsoft Corporation.

- 2 Prepare a flexible budget and explain its uses
- 3 Record direct cost variances
- 4 Identify and explain direct variance information using analysis and use it
- 5 Record overhead costs and the overhead variances
- 6 Understand how overhead variance information is analysed and used
- 7 Use variance information to evaluate the efficiency of a process
- 8 Explain the potential benefits and concerns of standard costing

10

Standard costs and variance analysis

IN BRIEF

Accountants produce information that managers use to monitor operations. Standard costs and variances from budgets are an important part of that information. Variances are calculated by comparing standard revenues and costs with actual revenues and costs. Through the analysis of these variances, managers identify operating processes that need investigation and possible improvements. They also learn whether planned improvements in operations have been achieved. Variance information helps managers create more accurate plans for future operations. In addition, variance analysis provides information for evaluating employee performance.

After studying this chapter, you should be able to:

1 Understand how standard costs are established.

2 Describe how variances are formed.

3 Calculate direct cost variances.

4 Understand how direct cost variance information is analysed and used.

5 Calculate variable and fixed overhead variances.

6 Understand how overhead variance information is analysed and used.

7 Close off manufacturing cost variances at the end of the period.

8 Explain which profit-related variances are commonly analysed.

Standard labour costs: Australian icon 'Blundstone' moves manufacturing offshore

The Australian footwear industry has two major iconic products that have become well-known functional products as well as high-end fashion products around the world. One is the 'Ugg' boots (sheepskin boots) and the other the Blundstone boots (tough cowhide, elastic-sided work boots).

Ugg boots have been popular in Australian households for many years now. In the 1960s Australian surfers would put on Ugg boots to warm their feet after coming in from riding the waves. UGG® Australia (now owned by Deckers, a US company) markets its Ugg boots as high-end luxury fashion footwear. They have been made famous by celebrities Pamela Anderson, Sarah Jessica Parker and Paris Hilton, with their ultimate rise in popularity occurring in 2000 when talk show host Oprah Winfrey was sent a pair of Ugg boots. She loved them so much that she purchased 350 pairs for her entire staff and has featured them several times since on her well-known 'Oprah's favourite things' segment.

Blundstone began making rural work boots in Hobart in the 1870s. Sales in 2006 amounted to more than 1.25 million pairs of boots annually. In the past, Blundstone footwear had been largely self-sufficient with its own tannery, component manufacturing processes, inhouse technicians, designers and research and development division. However, the entity announced in 2007 that it could not afford to keep manufacturing Blundstone boots in Australia and was moving its manufacturing operations offshore. Like UGG Australia, the product remains synonymous with Australia but manufacturing in Australia is no longer deemed to be a viable option.

As most of their products would be 'standard', Blundstone and Ugg probably plan and monitor production through carefully developed standards relating to the production inputs. For example, they would know the exact amount of leather (cowhide or kangaroo) or sheepskin required for each boot, and would evaluate the quality of these materials purchased; the amount of labour per boot in the production process, along with overhead consumed, would be much the same for each style of boot. Careful attention would also be given to the amount of leather or skin wastage that is standard for each boot. Detailed analysis of the usage and cost of inputs would help in maintaining profit margins. Even so, this has not saved Blundstone's Australian manufacturing plant in Tasmania, with the entity deciding in 2007 to move production offshore. The main reason behind this decision was the cost of labour. Blundstone's managing director argued that even superior machinery and manufacturing technology in Australia could not make up for the low direct labour hour per boot achieved by producers in low-cost locations.

Sources: Information from Khadem, N 2007, 'Bootmaker took money before it took a walk', *The Age*, 17 January, p. 5; www.blundstone.com; www.UGGAustralia.com.

■ The environment where standards for production or service activity are suitable.

■ The use of direct materials standards to plan and monitor production.

■ The use of direct labour and standards to plan and monitor production.

■ The use of overhead standards to plan and monitor production.

■ The use of standard cost information.

Monitoring and motivating performance

When managers create operating plans for the next period, they prepare a budget for revenues and costs. These plans include expectations about employee productivity and other factors that affect revenues and costs. Managers then monitor actual operations to determine whether operating targets are met. By studying differences between budgeted and actual results, managers also identify ways to improve future operations and to establish more realistic future budgets. In this chapter we learn the process that managers use to establish expectations and to analyse variances for major categories of revenues and costs.

Standard costs

To improve the ability of managers to plan operations and monitor performance, organisations often establish a set of standards for expected costs. A **standard cost** is the cost managers expect to incur to produce goods or services under operating plan assumptions. Key assumptions include:

■ volume of production activity
■ production processes and efficiency
■ prices and quality of inputs.

As shown in figure 10.1, the total standard cost for a unit of output is the sum of standard costs for the resources used in production. Typical resources include direct materials, direct labour, fixed overhead and variable overhead. Standards are also established for the cost of each resource. For example, the standards for direct costs include the price of the direct costs and the expected quantity of input for each unit of output. Suppose that Benny's, a wholesale gourmet ice cream manufacturer, uses a standard cost system. Frozen blackberries are *one* of the direct materials used in Benny's Purple Madness ice cream. The entity's managers determine that one kilogram of frozen blackberries should be included in each bucket of ice cream. They forecast that frozen blackberries this year will cost $1 per kilogram. We can describe the standard cost of frozen blackberries for every bucket of ice cream as follows:

Standard price per unit of input:

$1 per kg

Standard quantity of input per unit of output:

1 kg of blackberries per bucket of ice cream

Standard cost of blackberries per unit of output:

**1 kg of blackberries per bucket of ice cream × $1 per kg of blackberries
= $1 per bucket of ice cream**

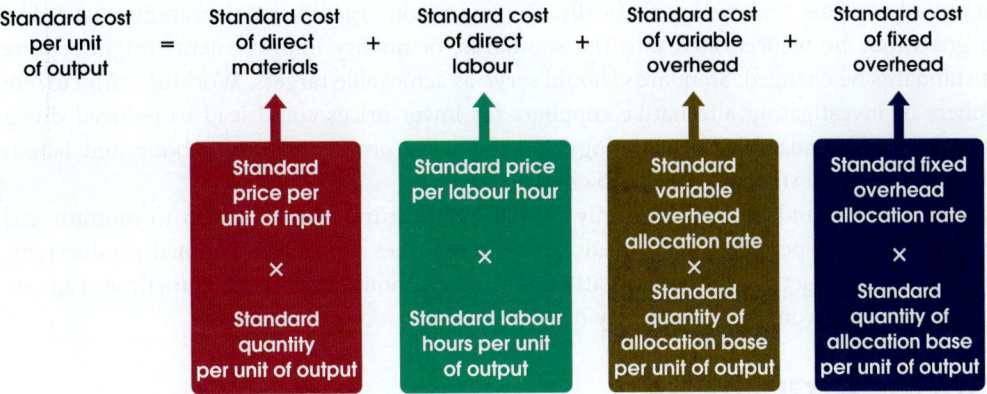

FIGURE 10.1 ■ Typical cost standards for production

Standard cost categories

In this chapter, we focus on measuring and monitoring the standard costs for direct materials, direct labour, fixed overhead and variable overhead. These cost categories are traditionally the ones used for manufactured goods. The cost categories that are measured and monitored in a given entity depend on the following:

- nature of goods or services
- cost accounting system used
- costs that managers consider important
- cost/benefit trade-off for monitoring individual costs.

For example, consider the cost of a clothing item sold by a retail store. The managers of the store might consider it unimportant to allocate and monitor labour and overhead costs for individual pieces of clothing sold. They might instead choose to focus only on the direct cost of the clothing. Professional service organisations, such as accounting entities, might track primarily direct labour costs. Organisations that use activity-based costing monitor overhead costs for individual activities.

In practice, many variations of specific costs are measured and monitored by accountants and managers. Although we focus in this chapter on traditional cost categories, the methods introduced here can be adapted to many different settings. The chapter 10 article at the end of this book highlights the use of a standard costing system at a world-class manufacturer of fittings and hoses.

Developing standard costs

Standards are set for the price of direct materials, as well as for the amount of direct materials that should be used to produce each unit. Similarly, standards are set for the price per direct labour hour and for the amount of hours needed per unit of output. In addition, standards are set for overhead costs. No exact rules are prescribed for developing these standard costs. Sometimes managers simply use the most recent year's data, while at other times they evaluate and incorporate historical trends. To set a standard for the next period, they update historical data for expected changes in costs or processes. For new products, standards are often set with the assistance of industrial engineers, who estimate quantities and costs for direct materials, direct labour and production overhead. Managers might also seek the periodic assistance of industrial engineers to find ways to improve efficiency, modify output quality or identify cost reduction opportunities for existing products. Production plans include expected efficiency and quality, which means that the normal cost of waste and defects is included in standard costs.

Standard costs are reviewed periodically. Depending on organisational strategy, cost reduction goals may be incorporated into the standards, or quality improvements might require that standards be changed. Standards should serve as achievable targets. Working with current suppliers or investigating alternative suppliers for lower prices could lead to reduced direct materials price standards. As technology improves the productivity of robotic and labour processes, efficiency standards will also change.

Managers use standard costs not only to help plan future costs, but also to monitor and motivate employee performance. To encourage employees to achieve planned productivity, standards are often set at a level that is attainable, but without much slack. Sometimes tightening standards can promote productivity improvements.

Variance analysis

Variances are calculated for two purposes: monitoring and bookkeeping. Variances calculated for bookkeeping purposes do not need to be analysed, but variances used to monitor performance need to be analysed. **Variance analysis** is the process of calculating variances and then investigating the reasons they occurred. This information is then used to improve future operating plans, as shown in figure 10.2. We learned in chapter 7 that a budget variance is a difference between budgeted and actual results. Similarly, a **standard cost variance** is a difference between a standard cost and an actual cost. Variance analysis can be used whether or not an organisation uses a standard costing system. The process requires only the ability to compare actual results with some type of benchmark, which might be standard costs, budgeted costs or some other measure of expectations. When entities have a standard cost system in place, the standard costs are used in budgeting to develop flexible budgets.

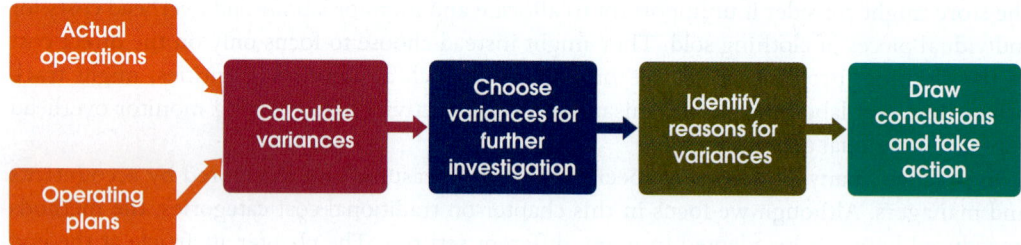

FIGURE 10.2 ■ Variance analysis

Deciding which variances to investigate

Simply calculating the dollar amount of a variance is not useful for decision making. The value of variance investigation is in identifying the reasons for a variance and then using that information to improve future decision making. However, variance investigation and decision making is time-consuming. Therefore, managers perform detailed investigation only for variances they consider important. This process is commonly referred to as management by exception.

Importance is decided in two ways. First, the variances that will be calculated and monitored need to be chosen. Managers may decide that a variance is important only if it is larger than a given dollar amount or a given percentage of the budget. Other factors also justify variance investigation. When variance trends are increasing, managers may want to know what causes the trend so that it can be eliminated if possible.

Suppose an unfavourable variance of $3000 occurred last year in the cost of Benny's Purple Madness ice cream — actual cost exceeded standard cost by $3000. Was it caused by an unanticipated increase in the cost of direct materials? Was labour less efficient than expected?

If so, did an equipment failure create unexpected employee downtime? Was employee turnover higher than usual, reducing average worker productivity? Did total production levels decline, causing actual fixed overhead cost per unit to be higher than expected? Managers must evaluate these types of questions before deciding what actions to take, if any. Accountants assist in this process, acting as detectives who discover the reasons for cost variances.

Manager conclusions and actions

Once managers identify the reasons for variances, they draw conclusions about what has occurred and consider whether some type of corrective action is needed. Suppose the managers of Benny's find that the unfavourable variance was caused primarily by an unanticipated rise in the cost of ingredients. The managers would next want to know whether the cost increase was temporary or was expected to continue. If the higher cost is expected to continue, they might decide to bring costs back into control by switching to less expensive ingredients. Or, they might decide that their standard cost is no longer appropriate and should be increased to reflect the new cost. If the cost increase was temporary, they might decide that no action should be taken. Sometimes a variance investigation uncovers an error in the accounting records, causing the appearance of a variance when none exists. In this case, managers might take action to correct the accounting system to avoid similar future errors. Figure 10.3 provides a summary of the general conclusions about variances and related management actions.

General conclusion about variance	General management action
Operations are out of control.	Take action to correct operations.
Operations are better than expected.	Monitor quality to ensure it is maintained.
Operations are better than expected and quality is maintained.	Modify future operating plans to take advantage of gains.
Benchmark is inappropriate.	Revise benchmark to improve the accuracy of future plans.
Error made is in accounting records.	Take action to correct accounting system.
Variance is random or is not expected to recur.	Do nothing.

FIGURE 10.3 ■ General conclusions about variances and management actions

Separating variances into components

Identifying the reasons for variances can be time-consuming. However, by using categories in the accounting system to separate variances into component parts, the process becomes easier and the most useful information is produced.

Suppose the unfavourable variance for Benny's Purple Madness ice cream is separated into the following categories used in its standard costing system: direct materials, direct labour, fixed overhead and variable overhead. This type of breakdown helps managers identify the sources of variances and also highlights possible offsetting of favourable (F) and unfavourable (U) variances between components. The aggregation of favourable and unfavourable variances could hide production problems that need to be investigated. In addition, this breakdown helps managers identify variances that are sufficiently large to justify further investigation. We will now explore how such variances can be further analysed to provide more insight into the costs of producing the ice cream.

Direct cost variances

Recall from figure 10.1 that standard costs for direct materials and direct labour consist of a standard price times a standard quantity for each of the direct resources that should be used in production. As a result, as shown in figure 10.4, the total variance for direct costs can be broken down into the following two components:

- price variance
- efficiency variance.

The following discussion uses Benny's to demonstrate the calculation of the direct cost variance (summarised at the end of this section in figure 10.5).

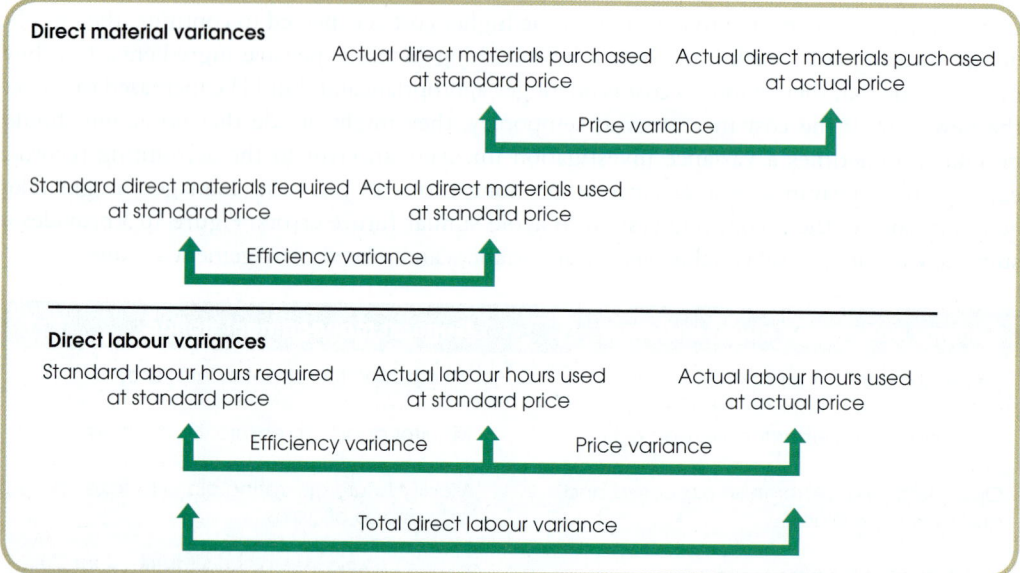

FIGURE 10.4 ■ Direct cost variances

Price variances

A **price variance** is the difference between standard and actual prices paid for resources purchased and used in the production of goods or services. We informally calculate price variances frequently in our daily lives. For example, we may compare the advertised prices of groceries with a standard price (the price we usually pay), and then decide to purchase certain items. Suppose softdrink usually costs $5 for a 12-pack, but is on sale at $2.50. After comparing the sale price to the $5 standard, we may decide to purchase more than the usual amount. Our standard price for two 12-packs of softdrink would have been $10 ($5 per pack × 2 packs), and our actual cost would be $5 ($2.50 per pack × 2 packs). By taking advantage of the sale, we achieve a favourable price variance of $5 ($10 − $5).

This example illustrates several limitations of a price variance. The price variance does not take into account whether sufficient cash flows, storage space or usage requirements justify and accommodate purchasing resources in larger quantities. Perhaps our kitchen lacks sufficient space to store extra groceries if we purchase more than our weekly usage. If we purchase large quantities of perishable foods, they may spoil before they are needed. Also, the price variance does not reflect possible quality differences between resources purchased at higher or lower prices. Suppose the brand of softdrink that is on sale is not the brand we prefer. We may be willing to pay a higher price for our preferred brand. In a business entity, it might be inefficient to use lower-quality direct materials even when they are cheaper.

Direct materials price variance

A **direct materials price variance** compares the standard price for direct materials to the actual price for the amount of direct materials purchased. Direct materials price variances are calculated using the following formula:

$$\text{Direct materials} \atop \text{price variance} = \left(\text{Standard} \atop \text{price} - \text{Actual} \atop \text{price}\right) \times \text{Quantity} \atop \text{purchased}$$

Suppose that Benny's had purchased 110 kilograms of blackberries (one of the direct material inputs to Benny's Purple Madness ice cream) at $1.25 per kilogram. The standard cost is $1 per kilogram. Therefore, the price variance for these berries is

$$(\$1 \text{ per kg} - \$1.25 \text{ per kg}) \times 110 \text{ kg} = \$27.50 \text{ U}$$

This variance is unfavourable because the actual price paid for frozen blackberries is higher than the standard price. Similar calculations would be made for *each* of the direct materials used to produce Purple Madness ice cream.

The direct materials price variance is usually calculated at the time direct materials are purchased. Therefore, direct materials are recorded in raw material inventory at the standard cost rather than actual cost. Two advantages come with this practice. First, it reduces book-keeping complexity. Because all units of direct material are recorded at the same standard cost, the actual cost of individual batches of direct material purchases need not be tracked. Second, this approach allows managers to identify the price variance during the period in which the variance occurred — at the time direct materials are purchased. Purchasing department personnel are often held accountable for price variances, so it is more appropriate to measure the variance at the time of purchase rather than at the time the direct materials are used. Depending on how quickly inventory is used, a delay in recognition could prevent managers from rapidly taking any needed action.

Direct labour price variance

A **direct labour price variance** compares the standard price with the actual price for labour. Direct labour price variances are calculated using the following formula:

$$\text{Direct labour} \atop \text{price variance} = \left(\text{Standard labour} \atop \text{price per hour} - \text{Actual labour} \atop \text{price per hour}\right) \times \text{Actual} \atop \text{hours used}$$

Suppose that Benny's paid $9 per hour for 9.5 hours of work in *packing* 100 buckets of Purple Madness ice cream. The standard labour rate is $8 per hour. The direct labour price variance is calculated as

$$(\$8 \text{ per hour} - \$9 \text{ per hour}) \times 9.5 \text{ hours} = \$9.50 \text{ U}$$

This variance is unfavourable because Benny's paid more for labour per hour than the standard called for. Similar calculations would be made for other types of direct labour used to produce Purple Madness ice cream.

Efficiency variances

An **efficiency variance** provides information about how economically direct resources such as materials and labour were used. We informally assess our own efficiency frequently in our daily lives. For example, when we plan a bicycle ride on the weekend, we may believe that it will take two hours to ride 30 kilometres. Once we finish the ride, we compare the actual length of time to our estimate. We might use this information to gauge our effort on the ride or to change our estimate for future trips. The variance calculation does not consider any factors that might have affected efficiency; these factors must instead be considered by managers when investigating the variance. For example, suppose one of the tyres on the bicycle is faulty and becomes flat during the ride. The time needed to fix the tyre would cause us to take longer than expected to complete the trip.

Direct materials efficiency variance

The **direct materials efficiency variance** compares the standard amount of materials that should have been used to the amount of materials actually used. This difference is valued at the standard price. The formula follows:

$$\text{Direct materials efficiency variance} = \left(\begin{array}{c} \text{Standard quantity} \\ \text{for actual output} \end{array} - \begin{array}{c} \text{Actual quantity} \\ \text{for actual output} \end{array} \right) \times \begin{array}{c} \text{Standard} \\ \text{price} \end{array}$$

Assume Benny's produced a batch of 100 buckets of Purple Madness ice cream using 90 kilograms of blackberries (recall the standard quantity is 1 kilogram per bucket). Here are calculations for the variance:

$$[(1 \text{ kg per bucket} \times 100 \text{ buckets}) - 90 \text{ kg}] \times \$1 \text{ per kg}$$

$$= (100 \text{ kg} - 90 \text{ kg}) \times \$1 \text{ per kg} = \$10 \text{ F}$$

This variance is favourable because fewer direct materials were used than called for at standard. Although we call this variance favourable, using fewer blackberries likely affects the quality of Benny's ice cream, so this variance may be investigated. Similar efficiency variance calculations would be performed for each of the direct materials used to produce Purple Madness ice cream.

Direct labour efficiency variance

The **direct labour efficiency variance** compares the standard amount of labour hours that should have been used to the amount actually used; it values this difference at the standard labour price per hour.

$$\text{Direct labour efficiency variance} = \left(\begin{array}{c} \text{Standard hours} \\ \text{for actual output} \end{array} - \begin{array}{c} \text{Actual hours for} \\ \text{actual output} \end{array} \right) \times \begin{array}{c} \text{Standard} \\ \text{price} \end{array}$$

Suppose one group of employees at Benny's is responsible for hand-packing ice cream into 1-bucket containers. The standard amount of time to pack 1 bucket of ice cream is 0.1 hour, and 9.5 hours were used to pack 100 buckets. The direct labour efficiency variance is calculated as

$$[(100 \text{ buckets} \times 0.1 \text{ hour per bucket}) - 9.5 \text{ hours}] \times \$8 \text{ per hour}$$

$$= (10 \text{ hours} - 9.5 \text{ hours}) \times \$8 \text{ per hour} = \$4 \text{ F}$$

This variance is favourable because actual hours were less than standard hours. Similar calculations would be performed for other types of direct labour used to produce Purple Madness ice cream.

Journal entries for direct costs and variances

In a standard cost system for a manufacturer, inventory accounting entries are recorded using standard costs. Differences between actual and standard costs are recorded in variance accounts. Later in the chapter, we learn to close variance accounts at the end of an accounting period. Figure 10.5 summarises the variances and journal entries used by Benny's for the frozen blackberries direct material and the direct labour for packing 100 buckets of Purple Madness ice cream.

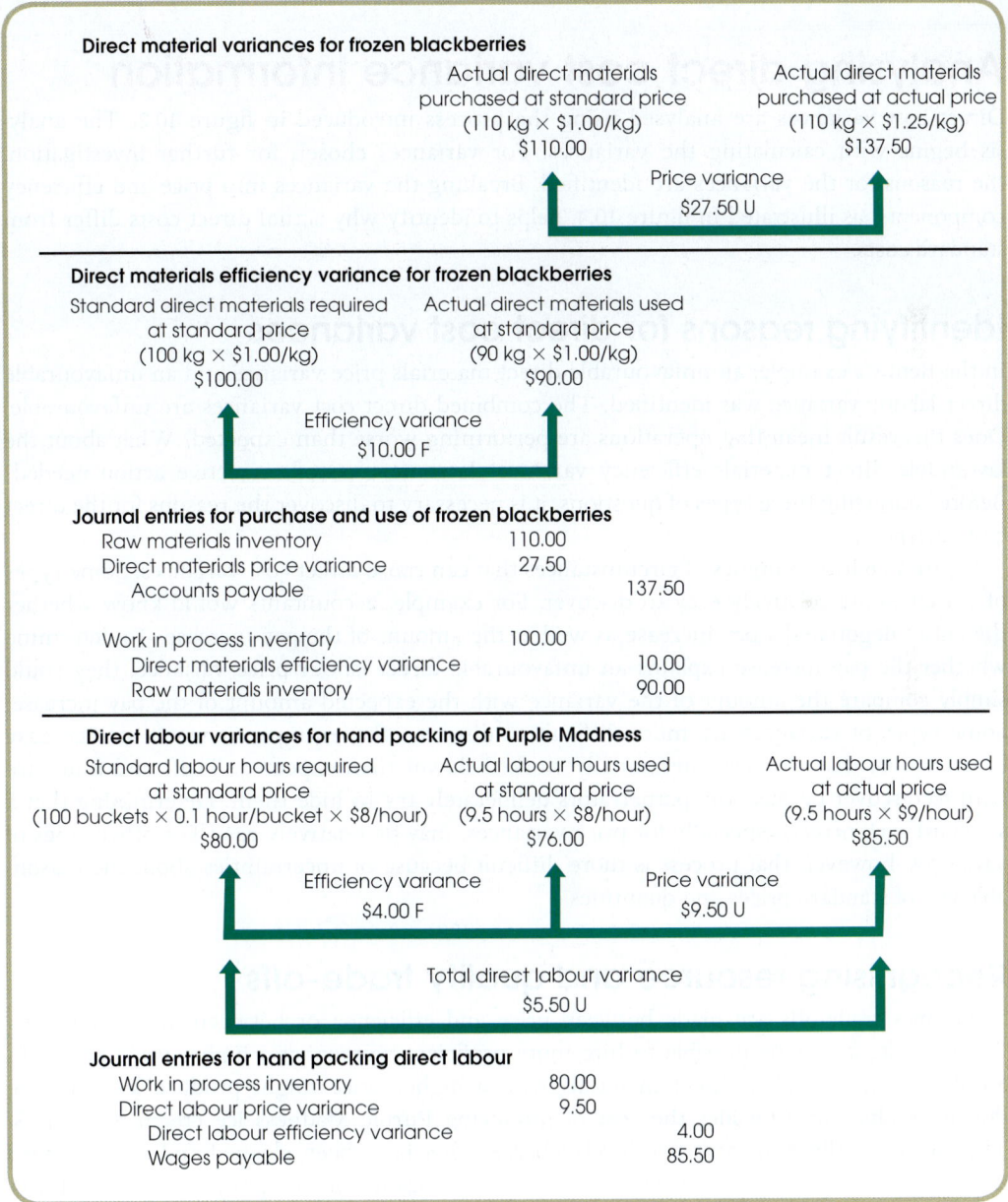

FIGURE 10.5 ■ Direct cost variances for Benny's Purple Madness ice cream

Figure 10.5 contains the journal entries recording the purchase and use of the frozen blackberries. It shows that when 110 kilograms of frozen blackberries are purchased, they are recorded in raw material inventory at standard cost ($110) and the price variance is recorded ($27.50 U). Then 90 kilograms are removed from raw materials inventory at standard cost ($90). The direct materials price and efficiency variances account for the difference between actual and standard costs.

The labour journal entry is also presented in figure 10.5. The entry for work in process inventory is made at the standard quantity and standard cost. Wages payable is credited for the actual wages owed to employees. The direct labour price and efficiency variances account for the difference between actual and standard costs.

Analysing direct cost variance information

Direct cost variances are analysed using the process introduced in figure 10.2. The analysis begins with calculating the variances. For variances chosen for further investigation, the reasons for the variances are identified. Breaking the variances into price and efficiency components, as illustrated in figure 10.4, helps to identify why actual direct costs differ from standard costs.

Identifying reasons for direct cost variances

In the Benny's example, an unfavourable direct materials price variance and an unfavourable direct labour variance was identified. The combined direct cost variances are unfavourable. Does this result mean that operations are performing worse than expected? What about the favourable direct materials efficiency variance? Is some type of corrective action needed? Before addressing these types of questions, it is necessary to discover the reasons for the direct cost variances.

Figure 10.6 lists examples of circumstances that can cause direct cost variances. Some types of variances are relatively easy to discover. For example, accountants would know whether the entity negotiated a pay increase as well as the amount of the pay increase. To determine whether the pay increase explains an unfavourable direct labour price variance, they could simply compare the amount of the variance with the expected amount of the pay increase. Some types of variances are more difficult to discover. For example, it would not be easy to determine that workers intentionally worked slower than expected. Theft and fraud are hard to discover because the perpetrators deliberately try to hide them. Determining that a standard is incorrect, especially for price variances, may be relatively easy. For other types of variances, however, that process is more difficult because of uncertainties about the reasonableness of standard prices and quantities.

Recognising resource and quality trade-offs

Sometimes trade-offs are made between price and efficiency or between different inputs. For example, it may be possible to hire more proficient workers at a higher wage per hour. Similarly, higher-quality direct materials with a higher price might produce less spoilage during production. Consider the cost of producing Purple Madness ice cream at Benny's. The entity usually purchases frozen blackberries that have been cleaned and can be added directly to the ice cream. During fresh blackberry season, the company could pay a lower price for fresh blackberries that have not been cleaned. However, it would incur greater direct labour time for cleaning the berries. Thus, the trade-off is made between the price paid for the blackberries and the labour time required. Quality differences also affect this decision. Suppose managers believe that fresh blackberries have a better flavour than frozen blackberries. They may purchase fresh blackberries to achieve better flavour even if they cost more overall.

Direct materials variances	Direct labour variances
Price:	**Price:**
■ Change in price paid for materials caused by:	■ Change in average wages paid to employees caused by:
– a change in the quality of materials purchased	– a new union contract or enterprise agreement
– a change in quantity purchased, leading to a change in purchase discount	– a change in average experience or training of workers
– a new supplier contract	– a change in the government-mandated minimum wage
■ Unreasonable materials price standard	■ Unanticipated overtime hours
■ Error in the accounting records for the actual price of materials	■ Unreasonable labour price standard
	■ Error in the accounting records for the actual price of direct labour
Efficiency:	**Efficiency:**
■ Normal fluctuation in materials usage	■ Normal fluctuation in labour hours
■ Change in production processes, causing a change in the quantity of materials used	■ Change in average labour time caused by:
■ Change in proportion of materials spoiled caused by:	– a change in equipment, technology or other aspect of production processes
– a change in quality of materials	– a change in average worker experience or training caused by:
– a change in equipment, technology or other aspect of production processes	■ improved performance from effective training programs
– equipment malfunction	■ change in employee turnover
– intentional worker damage	– intentional work slowdown
■ Theft of raw materials	■ Intentional or unintentional over- or under-reporting of labour hours
■ Unreasonable materials quantity standard	■ Unreasonable labour hours standard
■ Error in the accounting records for the quantity of materials used	■ Error in the accounting records for the quantity of labour hours

FIGURE 10.6 ■ Examples of reasons for direct cost variances

When analysing variances, it is necessary to consider possible trade-offs. A favourable variance in one area might be partially or completely offset by an unfavourable variance in another area. For example, say Benny's managers eliminate monitoring of labour efficiency and focus instead on spoilage rates to increase quality. As a result, labour efficiency could decline and product defect rates improve. However, what if the variance caused by the decline in labour efficiency was larger than the gain from improved quality (that is, lower product defect rates). This may prompt the managers to resume monitoring practices to bring labour efficiency back into control.

Analysing interactions between incentives and variances

Some entities reward employees for meeting or exceeding benchmarks set as standard costs. However, such rewards create a new set of problems. Suppose employees in the cutting department of a clothing manufacturer are rewarded based on how quickly they cut fabric. The cut fabric is then transferred to the sewing department. If employees in the cutting department become less precise as they increase output, the sewing department could face a decrease in efficiency. That decrease could ripple through the rest of the production process. Or, the sewing department might pass along the quality problem into finished goods, contributing further to a long-term quality problem for the entity. If the sewing department is also rewarded based on meeting efficiency standards, employees in that department would be penalised for fixing a problem created by the cutting department. Only when variances are analysed can managers identify whether the incentives are working as expected to promote overall organisational success.

Overhead variances

Organisations use standard cost systems to monitor overhead costs in addition to direct costs. To monitor overhead costs, a **standard overhead allocation rate** is created at the beginning of each period. Overhead is typically allocated using an allocation base such as production units, direct labour costs, direct labour hours or machine hours. Separate allocation bases and rates are often used for fixed and variable overhead costs.

The **standard variable overhead allocation rate** is determined by estimating the variable amount of overhead cost per unit of an allocation base as follows:

$$\text{Standard variable overhead allocation rate} = \frac{\text{Estimated variable overhead cost}}{\text{Estimated volume of an allocation base}}$$

For example, the accountant at Benny's estimated the variable overhead cost as $150000 and the labour hours as 75000, so the cost function for variable overhead costs is $2 per direct labour hour.

Accountants choose allocation bases for variable overhead that reflect the use of variable resources. Indirect labour costs, such as maintenance wages, might be related to direct labour costs; as the number of employees providing direct labour increases, the number of maintenance worker hours increases. When the proportion of labour-related costs in the variable overhead cost pool is high, direct labour hours or direct labour cost are appropriate allocation bases. Alternatively, indirect materials cost such as paint, plastic stripping and decals applied to toy cars could be a large proportion of the variable overhead cost pool. In this case, the estimated volume of units would be the most appropriate allocation base.

Although fixed costs do not vary with volume, we need to develop an allocation rate to assign these costs to inventory and cost of goods sold.

The **standard fixed overhead allocation rate** is determined as follows:

$$\text{Standard fixed overhead allocation rate} = \frac{\text{Estimated fixed overhead cost}}{\text{Estimated volume of an allocation base}}$$

For example, if the estimated fixed overhead cost for Benny's is $200000 and the entity allocates fixed overhead based on units produced using a normal volume of 500000 buckets of ice cream during the year, the standard fixed overhead allocation rate is $200000 ÷ 500000 buckets, or $0.40 per bucket. Therefore, standard fixed overhead of $0.40 will be allocated to the cost of each bucket of ice cream.

At the end of the period, variances between standard allocated overhead costs and actual costs are analysed. The **variable overhead budget variance** is the difference between allocated variable overhead cost and actual variable overhead cost. The **fixed overhead budget variance** is the difference between allocated fixed overhead cost and actual fixed overhead cost. As shown in figure 10.7, the overhead variances can be broken down into the following components:

- variable overhead budget variance:
  - spending variance
  - efficiency variance
- fixed overhead budget variance:
  - spending variance
  - volume variance.

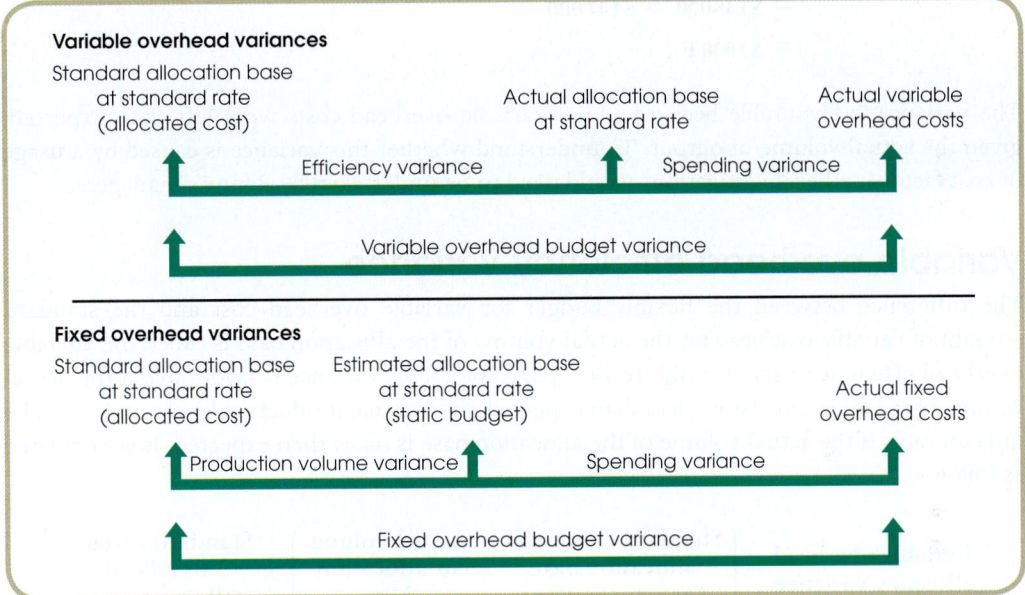

FIGURE 10.7 ■ Overhead cost variances

Variable overhead spending variance

The **variable overhead spending variance** is the difference between the total expected variable overhead costs for the actual output and the actual variable overhead costs for that level of output. We can break this down into more detail to show the comparison.

Actual variable overhead cost for actual use of allocation base

= Actual use of variable overhead resources × Cost paid for resources consumed

compared to

Expected variable overhead cost for actual use of allocation base

= Expected use of variable overhead resources

× Expected cost for resources consumed

The variable overhead spending variance helps managers monitor whether the organisation spent the planned amount on overhead. Because variable overhead costs are expected to vary with activity, the calculation for the spending variance takes into account the actual volume of activity. We can see from the breakdown above that the spending variance can be influenced not only by the amount paid for variable overhead resources, but also by the amount used of the resource for the given level of activity of the allocation base.

For Benny's, the allocation base for variable overhead is direct labour hours. The normal volume of direct labour hours is 500 000 buckets × 0.15 hours per bucket, or 75 000 hours. The standard variable overhead allocation rate is $2 per direct labour hour. Suppose actual variable overhead costs total $147 000 and actual labour hours are 74 000. The variable overhead spending variance is calculated as:

$$\begin{array}{l} \text{Variable overhead} \\ \text{spending variance} \end{array} = \left(\begin{array}{c} \text{Standard variable} \\ \text{overhead allocation rate} \end{array} \times \begin{array}{c} \text{Actual volume of} \\ \text{allocation base} \end{array} \right) - \begin{array}{c} \text{Actual variable} \\ \text{overhead cost} \end{array}$$

$$= (\$2.00 \text{ per hour} \times 74\,000 \text{ hours}) - \$147\,000$$

$$= \$148\,000 - \$147\,000$$

$$= \$1000 \text{ F}$$

The variance is favourable because actual variable overhead costs were less than expected, given the actual volume of output. To understand whether this variance is caused by a usage or cost factor further investigations would need to be undertaken by Benny's managers.

Variable overhead efficiency variance

The difference between the flexible budget for variable overhead cost and the standard amount of variable overhead for the actual volume of the allocation base is called the **variable overhead efficiency variance** (figure 10.8, page 408). This variance is favourable if the actual volume of the allocation base is less than expected given actual production levels, and it will be unfavourable if the actual volume of the allocation base is more than expected. It is calculated as follows:

$$\begin{array}{l} \text{Variable overhead} \\ \text{efficency variance} \end{array} = \left(\begin{array}{c} \text{Standard volume of} \\ \text{allocation base} \\ \text{for actual output} \end{array} - \begin{array}{c} \text{Actual volume} \\ \text{of allocation} \\ \text{base} \end{array} \right) \times \begin{array}{c} \text{Standard variable} \\ \text{overhead} \\ \text{allocation rate} \end{array}$$

For Benny's, assume that 498 000 buckets of ice cream were produced. The standard number of direct labour hours for actual production is 74 700 hours (498 000 buckets × 0.15 hours per bucket) and 74 000 actual hours were used. The standard variable overhead allocation rate is $2 per direct labour hour. Therefore the variable overhead efficiency variance calculation is:

$$(74\,700 \text{ hours} - 74\,000 \text{ hours}) \times \$2 \text{ per hour} = \$1400 \text{ F}$$

The variance is favourable because actual direct labour hours are less than expected, given actual production of 498 000 kilograms of ice cream.

Fixed overhead spending variance

The **fixed overhead spending variance** is the difference between estimated fixed overhead costs and actual fixed overhead costs. Fixed overhead costs are not expected to fluctuate with levels of activity. Thus, the spending variance is not affected by the volume of activity; it reflects the amount by which the actual spending on fixed overhead differs from the estimated fixed overhead (the static budget), as shown in figure 10.8 (overleaf). The spending variance helps managers monitor whether the entity spent the planned amount on overhead. We use the following formula:

$$\text{Fixed overhead spending variance} = \text{Estimated fixed overhead costs} - \text{Actual fixed overhead costs}$$

The fixed overhead budget at Benny's was $200 000 and actual costs were $203 000. The fixed overhead spending variance is calculated as

$$\$200\,000 - \$203\,000 = \$3000\text{ U}$$

The variance is unfavourable because more was spent of fixed overhead than was estimated.

Production volume variance

The difference between the standard amount of fixed overhead cost allocated to products and the estimated fixed overhead costs is called the **production volume variance** (figure 10.8). If actual volumes of the allocation base exceed normal (that is, estimated) volumes, fixed overhead will be overapplied and the variance will be favourable. Conversely, if actual volumes of the allocation base are less than normal volumes, fixed overhead will be underapplied and the variance will be unfavourable. The production volume variance is calculated only for fixed overhead. This variance is used for bookkeeping purposes. The actual overhead costs need to be allocated to inventory each period. This variance is used to adjust balances at the end of the period so that the total costs recorded in the financial statements are equal to the actual costs incurred. The variance is calculated as follows:

$$\text{Production volume variance} = \left(\begin{array}{c} \text{Standard volume of} \\ \text{allocation base} \\ \text{for actual output} \end{array} - \begin{array}{c} \text{Estimated} \\ \text{volume of} \\ \text{allocation base} \end{array} \right) \times \begin{array}{c} \text{Standard fixed} \\ \text{overhead} \\ \text{allocation rate} \end{array}$$

For Benny's, suppose estimated fixed overhead was $200 000 and the estimated volume of the allocation base was 500 000 buckets (normal production). The standard allocation rate is $200 000 ÷ 500 000 buckets = $0.40 per bucket. Actual production was 498 000 buckets. The production volume variance is calculated as

$$(498\,000\text{ buckets} - 500\,000\text{ buckets}) \times \$0.40\text{ per bucket} = \$800\text{ U}$$

Because actual production was less than normal, Benny's fixed overhead is underapplied, causing an unfavourable variance.

Journal entries for overhead costs and variances

Organisations often use an overhead cost control account to keep track of actual and allocated overhead costs. As actual overhead costs are incurred, they are debited to the account. The account is then credited for the standard amount of overhead costs allocated to inventory. The remaining balance in the overhead cost control account is the total variance. This balance for fixed overhead costs is closed to separate spending and volume variance accounts, while the balance for variable overhead costs is closed to separate spending and efficiency variance accounts. The journal entries for Benny's are shown in figure 10.8 together with a summary of overhead variances.

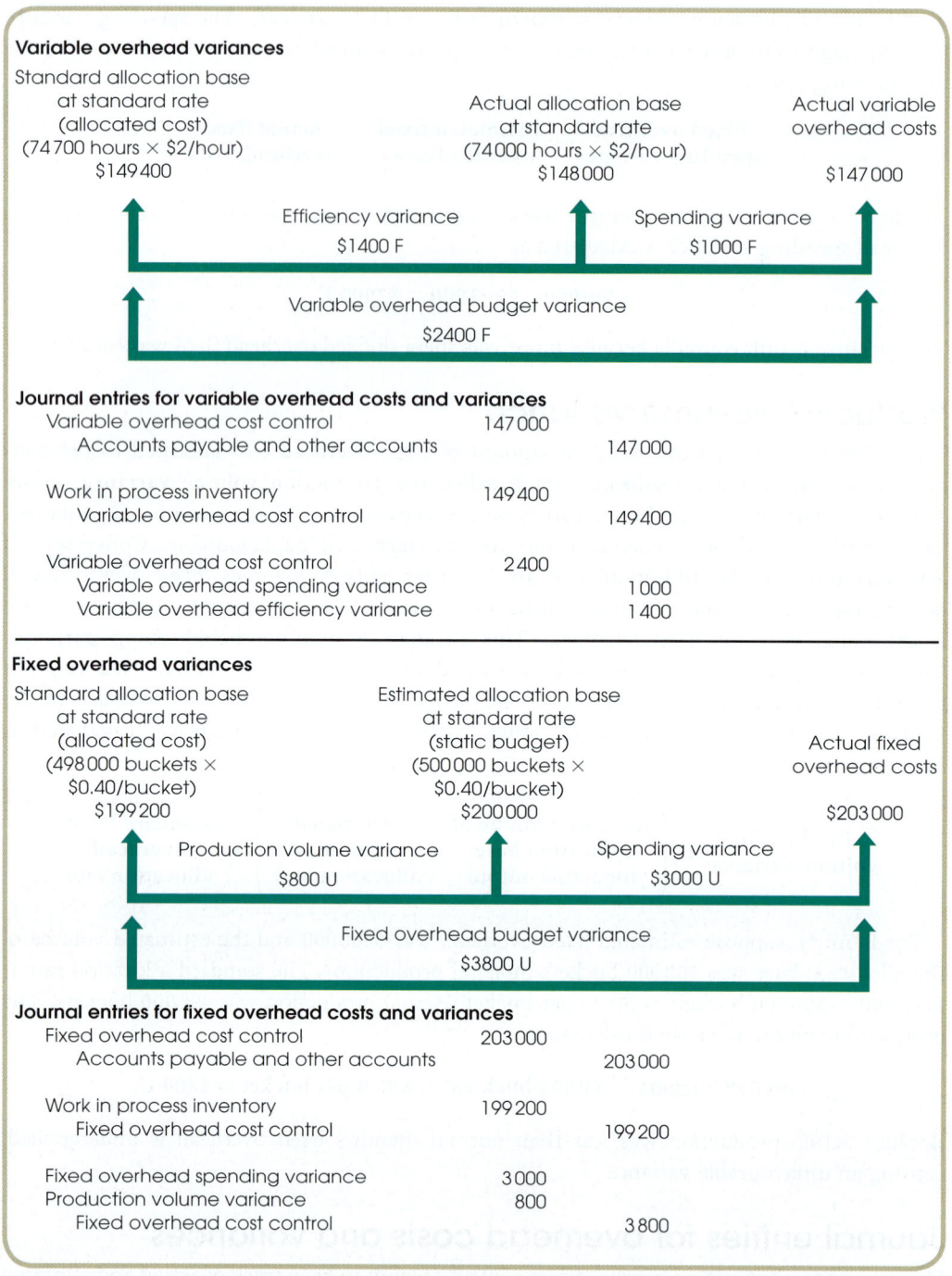

Variable overhead variances

Standard allocation base at standard rate (allocated cost) (74 700 hours × $2/hour) $149 400		Actual allocation base at standard rate (74 000 hours × $2/hour) $148 000		Actual variable overhead costs $147 000
	Efficiency variance $1400 F		Spending variance $1000 F	
	Variable overhead budget variance $2400 F			

Journal entries for variable overhead costs and variances

Variable overhead cost control	147 000	
Accounts payable and other accounts		147 000
Work in process inventory	149 400	
Variable overhead cost control		149 400
Variable overhead cost control	2 400	
Variable overhead spending variance		1 000
Variable overhead efficiency variance		1 400

Fixed overhead variances

Standard allocation base at standard rate (allocated cost) (498 000 buckets × $0.40/bucket) $199 200		Estimated allocation base at standard rate (static budget) (500 000 buckets × $0.40/bucket) $200 000		Actual fixed overhead costs $203 000
	Production volume variance $800 U		Spending variance $3000 U	
	Fixed overhead budget variance $3800 U			

Journal entries for fixed overhead costs and variances

Fixed overhead cost control	203 000	
Accounts payable and other accounts		203 000
Work in process inventory	199 200	
Fixed overhead cost control		199 200
Fixed overhead spending variance	3 000	
Production volume variance	800	
Fixed overhead cost control		3 800

FIGURE 10.8 ■ Overhead variances for Benny's

Analysing overhead variance information

The process of analysing overhead variance information is similar to the process for direct cost variances. The analysis begins with calculating and then identifying the reasons for variances. Breaking the variances into spending, volume and efficiency components (illustrated in figure 10.8) helps to identify why actual overhead costs differ from standard costs.

Analysing overhead spending variances

Accountants investigate spending variances to pinpoint the specific fixed and variable overhead costs that differ from expectations. Usually the investigation includes analysing the spending variances for individual overhead costs such as supplies, depreciation, property taxes, insurance and supervision salaries. Similar to direct costs, many reasons potentially explain why overhead costs differ from expectations. Figure 10.9 provides examples of possible reasons for fixed and variable overhead spending variances. Sometimes unanticipated changes occur in costs. For example, an unfavourable spending variance might arise because an additional supervisor had to be hired when an increase in demand required increased production. Sometimes spending is out of control. For example, the staff may include too many maintenance employees. Once the reasons for variances are identified, managers decide what action to take, if any (see figure 10.3).

Variable overhead variances	Fixed overhead variances
Spending:	**Spending:**
■ Unanticipated change in prices paid for variable overhead resources caused by:	■ Unanticipated change in prices for fixed overhead resources caused by:
– variation in prices for supplies or indirect labour	– change in estimate asset life for depreciation
– new supplier or labour contract	– change in electricity, other utility, insurance or property tax rates
■ Out of control or improved efficiency in variable overhead cost spending	■ Out-of-control or improved efficiency in fixed overhead cost spending
■ Change in type or extent of variable overhead resources used, for example:	■ Change in activity level to a new relevant range, requiring change in fixed resources such as:
– change from inhouse to outsourced equipment maintenance services	– hire or lay off a supervisor
– increase or decrease in normal spoilage, rework or scrap	– increase or decrease fixed hours of maintenance staff
■ Unreasonable standard variable overhead allocation rate caused by:	– depreciation change from purchase or disposal of property, plant and equipment
– inappropriate allocation base	■ Unreasonable estimate for fixed overhead costs
– poor estimate of variable overhead costs	■ Error in the accounting records for actual fixed overhead costs
– poor estimate of allocation base volume	
■ Error in the accounting records for actual variable overhead costs	
Efficiency:	**Production volume:**
■ Fluctuation in efficiency of the allocation base (e.g. labour hours, labour costs, machine hours, units produced)	■ Normal fluctuation in volume of allocation base (usually caused by changes in demand)
	■ Improved production processes
	■ Unreasonable estimate of volume of the allocation base
	■ Error in the accounting records for actual output

FIGURE 10.9 ■ Examples of reasons for overhead variances

Interpreting the variable overhead efficiency variance

Variable overhead costs are allocated to production based on an estimated volume of an allocation base. The allocation base used for variable costs is typically some type of resource input (such as labour hours, labour costs or machine hours) or the volume of output. Because the direct cost efficiency variances already provide information about the efficiency of inputs and outputs, overhead efficiency variances provide no new information.

For example, consider the Benny's illustration. Recall that direct labour hours were used to calculate the standard variable overhead allocation rate. The variable overhead efficiency variance was favourable because actual labour hours exceeded standard labour hours. However, the inefficient use of labour hours was already reflected in the favourable direct labour efficiency variance (refer to figure 10.5). Thus, the variable overhead efficiency variance provides no new information; for monitoring purposes it is meaningless. However, this variance must be calculated for bookkeeping reasons; it helps to explain why variable overhead costs allocated are different from actual variable overhead costs.

Interpreting the production volume variance

By definition, fixed overhead costs are not expected to vary with volume of production. However, a production volume variance exists because fixed overhead costs are allocated to production based on an estimated level of an allocation base. In turn, the estimated level of the allocation base depends on the estimated level of production. We usually produce more or less than estimated, and so we allocate more or less of our estimated fixed cost than we expected. At the end of each accounting period, we adjust the accounting records for this difference. Figure 10.8 shows the adjusting journal entries for Benny's.

As shown in figure 10.9, actual production volume (and volume of the allocation base) may differ from estimated volume because of normal fluctuations, production problems, improved production processes, unreasonable estimates or accounting errors. Managers need to analyse the reasons for actual production volume differing from estimated volume to determine what type of action (if any) is needed. In general, we would expect production volume to vary with sales levels. Thus, the investigation of production volume variances tends to focus on the deviation between actual and estimated sales. Although managers want to know why production volume deviates from the budget, the dollar amount of the production volume variance does not require investigation. The production volume variance also provides information about capacity utilisation. Therefore, it may be monitored to achieve long-term goals of operating at optimal capacity levels. The relationship between capacity and demand may be monitored to find those optimum capacity levels where throughput (the rate at which products are manufactured) is equal to demand.

Cost variance adjustments

When all of the production entries and variances are recorded for an accounting period, an additional entry is made to eliminate the variance accounts. If the total variance is favourable, fewer resources were used than estimated, so we need to decrease the costs in inventory and cost of goods sold. If the total variance is unfavourable, more resources were used than estimated, so the costs in inventory and cost of goods sold need to be increased.

The type of adjustment made typically depends on whether variances are material, a decision that is a matter of judgment. Amounts are generally viewed as material if their treatment would affect the decisions of people who rely on reported values. If the net amount of variances is deemed immaterial, the adjustment is usually made only to cost of goods sold. However, the existence of material variances means that the standard costs assigned to product units do not fairly represent the actual cost of the units. Thus, if the net amount of variances is material, a more accurate adjustment procedure is needed. A proportionate share of the variance should be allocated to work in process, finished goods inventory and cost of goods sold.

The following comprehensive examples demonstrate the entire standard costing process. Example 1 focuses on the development of standard costs. Example 2 focuses on the determination of the direct cost variances. Example 3 focuses on the analysis of the direct cost variances. Example 4 focuses on overhead variance analysis. Example 5 concludes with the cost variance adjustments.

Comprehensive example 1

Setting standard costs

Concrete Transformation manufactures concrete blocks at its plant in Mildura. When Karen Matthews, the company's new accountant, started work last month, she learned that the entity had never used standard costs. She decided to implement a standard cost system to help the managers monitor operating performance.

Karen toured the production facilities with Jordan, the labour supervisor. She learned that workers combine cement mix, sand and water; then they pour the mixture into block forms. The blocks are turned out of the forms and allowed to dry in the sun. Once the blocks are dry, they are stacked on pallets and loaded on trucks for shipment to customers. Workers can be sent home if no work is scheduled; therefore, direct labour cost is variable.

Relevant cash flows and timeline

Because the entity had not previously used standard costs, Karen decided to set next month's standards based on past experience, adjusted for expected changes in activities or costs. To gather information for creating cost standards, Karen first studied the accounting and production records for the past year. Then she reviewed the next month's production schedule, which showed a planned volume of 90 000 blocks. After conducting interviews to learn about next month's production activities and costs, she did not expect any changes from prior costs.

Karen identified the following potential direct costs for producing the blocks: cement mix, sand, water and direct labour. Sand and water are readily available on the entity's land, so it does not incur any costs for them. (In reality, some costs would most likely be incurred for these resources but this example avoids complications by assuming no cost.) Therefore, the only direct materials cost is the cement mix. Based on past accounting and production records, Karen set a standard cost for cement mix of $10 per kilogram. She also estimated that it should take about 1 kilogram of cement mix per block. In addition, Karen set the direct labour cost standard at $10 per hour, and the standard for quantity of labour at 100 blocks per labour hour.

Karen next turned to the production overhead costs and determined that some costs were variable and others were fixed. Variable costs consisted of the cost of supervisors; as the number of direct labour hours increases, the number of supervisor hours also increases. Karen set the variable overhead standard at $2 per labour hour. She then classified all remaining overhead costs as fixed, and estimated next month's spending at $180 000. After considering several allocation bases for the fixed overhead costs, Karen decided that volume of production would be appropriate. With planned production of 90 000 blocks, she set the standard fixed overhead allocation rate at $2 ($180 000 ÷ 90 000 blocks) per block.

Following is a summary of the standards Karen established for the next month:

Direct materials:	
Cost of cement mix	$10 per kg
Quantity of cement mix	1 kg per block
Standard cost per block ($10 per kg × 1 kg per block)	$10
Direct labour:	
Labour pay rate	$10 per hour
Quantity of direct labour	100 blocks per labour hour
Standard cost per block ($10 per hour × 1 hour per 100 blocks)	$0.10
Fixed overhead:	
Planned spending	$180 000
Volume of allocation base (blocks produced)	90 000 blocks
Standard cost per block ($180 000 ÷ 90 000 blocks)	$2
Variable overhead:	
Spending per labour hour	$2
Standard cost per block ($2 ÷ 100 blocks)	$0.02
Total standard cost per block (10 + 0.10 + 2 + 0.02)	$12.12

Based on these standards and the expected production volume of 90 000 blocks, Karen created the following budget for next month's production costs:

Direct materials (90 000 blocks × $10 per block)	$ 900 000
Direct labour (90 000 blocks × $0.10 per block)	9 000
Fixed overhead	180 000
Variable overhead (90 000 blocks × $0.02 per block)	1 800
Total standard production costs (90 000 blocks × $12.12 per block)	$1 090 800

Comprehensive example 2

Variances for direct materials and direct labour

At the end of the first month of operations after Karen developed the cost standards, she collected the following data needed to perform a direct cost variance analysis:

- 100 000 cement blocks were produced.
- The entity purchased 130 000 kg of cement mix for $975 000.
- 120 000 kg of cement mix were used.
- Direct labour employees were paid $16 500 and worked 1100 hours.

Direct materials price variance

Karen first calculates the direct materials price variance. The purchase price last month for the cement mix was $975 000 for 130 000 kilograms, or $7.5 per kilogram. The standard cost is $10 per kilogram. She calculates the direct materials price variance as follows:

$$\textbf{(Standard price – Actual price)} \times \textbf{Quantity purchased}$$
$$= (\$10 - \$7.50) \times 130\,000 \text{ kg}$$
$$= \$325\,000 \text{ F}$$

Because the price per kilogram that Concrete Transformation paid last month is less than expected, the direct materials price variance is favourable.

Direct labour price variance

Next, Karen calculates the direct labour price variance. During the month, Concrete Transformation paid its employees $16 500 for 1100 hours of work. Thus, the actual price for labour was $15 per hour ($16 500 ÷ 1100 hours). The standard cost is $10 per hour, so $11 000 should have been paid for 1100 hours of work. Therefore, the direct labour price variance is

$$\textbf{(Standard labour price per hour – Actual labour price per hour)}$$
$$\times \textbf{Amount of labour hours used}$$
$$= (\$10 - \$15) \times 1100 \text{ hours}$$
$$= \$5500 \text{ U}$$

Because the entity paid more than the standard labour wage, the direct labour price variance is unfavourable.

Direct materials efficiency variance

After completing the direct cost price variances, Karen calculates the direct cost efficiency variances. Efficiency variances are calculated based on actual production volume (that is, the quantity of concrete blocks produced). During the last month, the entity produced 100 000 blocks using 120 000 kilograms of cement mix. The standard quantity of direct materials is 1 kilogram per block for a total of 100 000 kilograms of cement mix. Karen calculated the direct materials efficiency variance as follows:

$$\textbf{(Standard quantity for actual output – Actual quantity for actual output)}$$
$$\times \textbf{Standard price}$$
$$= [(1 \text{ kg per block} \times 100\,000 \text{ blocks}) - 120\,000 \text{ kg}] \times \$10 \text{ per kg}$$
$$= (100\,000 \text{ kg} - 120\,000 \text{ kg}) \times \$10 \text{ per kg} = \$200\,000 \text{ U}$$

The materials efficiency variance is unfavourable because more materials than the standard quantity were used.

Direct labour efficiency variance

To calculate the direct labour efficiency variance, Karen first determines the amount of labour that should have been used to produce 100 000 blocks and then compares it to the amount of labour actually used, which was 1100 direct labour hours. The standard quantity of labour is 100 blocks per hour. The direct labour efficiency variance is calculated as follows:

$$\textbf{(Standard hours for actual output – Actual hours for actual output)}$$
$$\times \textbf{Standard price}$$
$$= [(\textbf{100 000 blocks} \times \textbf{1 hour per 100 blocks}) - \textbf{1100 hours}] \times \textbf{\$10 per hour}$$
$$= (\textbf{1000 hours} - \textbf{1100 hours}) \times \textbf{\$10 per hour} = \textbf{\$1000 U}$$

Because actual hours exceeded standard hours, the direct labour efficiency variance is unfavourable.

Summary of direct cost variances

After calculating the individual direct cost variances, Karen creates a summary showing all of the variances, as shown in figure 10.10.

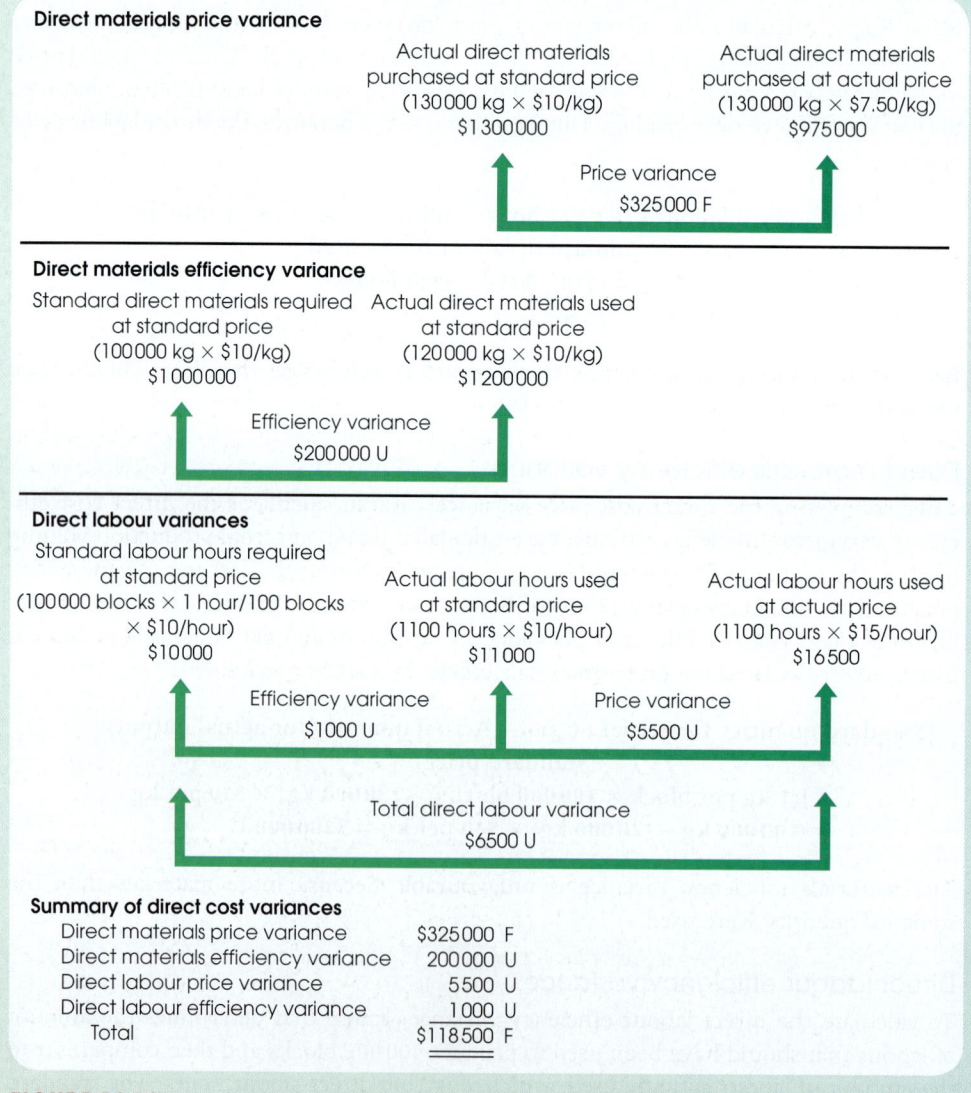

Direct materials price variance

Actual direct materials purchased at standard price (130 000 kg × $10/kg) $1 300 000

Actual direct materials purchased at actual price (130 000 kg × $7.50/kg) $975 000

Price variance $325 000 F

Direct materials efficiency variance

Standard direct materials required at standard price (100 000 kg × $10/kg) $1 000 000

Actual direct materials used at standard price (120 000 kg × $10/kg) $1 200 000

Efficiency variance $200 000 U

Direct labour variances

Standard labour hours required at standard price (100 000 blocks × 1 hour/100 blocks × $10/hour) $10 000

Actual labour hours used at standard price (1100 hours × $10/hour) $11 000

Actual labour hours used at actual price (1100 hours × $15/hour) $16 500

Efficiency variance $1000 U

Price variance $5500 U

Total direct labour variance $6500 U

Summary of direct cost variances

Direct materials price variance	$325 000	F
Direct materials efficiency variance	200 000	U
Direct labour price variance	5 500	U
Direct labour efficiency variance	1 000	U
Total	$118 500	F

FIGURE 10.10 ■ Direct cost variances for Concrete Transformation

Comprehensive example 3

Analysing direct cost variance information

Karen examines the total favourable variance of $118 500 (figure 10.10). In some cases, an overall favourable variance means that the organisation has no problems — operations performed better than expected. However, Karen is concerned about the large unfavourable efficiency variance for cement mix, and she is puzzled by its large favourable price variance. In addition, the unfavourable direct labour price variance seems high relative to total labour costs. However, Karen decides to focus her attention on only the two largest variances because these explain most of the total direct cost variance.

First, Karen considers the favourable price variance for cement mix. She speaks with Ricardo, who purchases direct materials. He has found a new supplier with better prices. Because he receives a bonus based on reducing the entity's costs, he is looking forward to a sizeable bonus. Karen tentatively thinks that the future standard cost for cement mix should be reduced to reflect the new lower price.

Next, Karen investigates the unfavourable efficiency variance for cement mix. She speaks with Jordan, the labour supervisor. He is very upset about a decrease in the quality of the cement mix from the new supplier; the mix contains inadequate quantities of an ingredient that prevents the blocks from slumping, or losing shape, when they are turned out of the forms. Although 120 000 blocks were produced, 20 000 of them were rejected because of the slumping problem. In addition, more labour hours were needed, leading to overtime payments. These factors explain the unfavourable direct labour price variance. Jordan is concerned that some of the blocks shipped to customers are not the correct shape. Some customers might become dissatisfied and no longer purchase cement blocks from the entity.

Karen plans to recommend to management that the entity pay a higher price (the original standard) for the higher-quality cement mix. Although it appeared that the entity saved money overall last month from the lower-priced mix, most of the savings were offset by unfavourable variances elsewhere caused by the lower quality. Furthermore, she believes that just the risk of lost sales in the future outweighs the cost savings. Karen also plans to work with management to design a better reward system that avoids any further adverse effects that result from the purchasing agent's bonus plan.

Comprehensive example 4

Overhead variances

Karen had previously established the following standard costs for fixed and variable overhead:

Variable overhead (allocated based on direct labour hours):

Standard cost per direct labour hour	$2
Standard quantity of allocation base per block (1 hour per 100 blocks)	0.01 hours
Standard cost per block (0.01 hours per block × $2 per hour)	$0.02

Fixed overhead (allocated based on units):

Estimated cost	$180 000
Estimated volume of allocation base (blocks produced)	90 000 blocks
Standard cost per block ($180 000 ÷ 90 000 blocks)	$2

At the end of the month, Karen determines that actual fixed overhead costs were $175 000. Actual variable overhead costs were $2500 and 1100 actual labour hours were used.

Variable overhead spending and efficiency variances

Karen analyses variable overhead costs, which are allocated based on direct labour hours. Actual variable overhead costs were $2500 and actual direct labour hours were 1100. She calculates the variable overhead spending variance as follows:

$$\left(\begin{array}{c} \textbf{Standard variable} \\ \textbf{overhead} \\ \textbf{allocation rate} \end{array} \times \begin{array}{c} \textbf{Actual} \\ \textbf{volume of} \\ \textbf{allocation base} \end{array} \right) - \begin{array}{c} \textbf{Actual} \\ \textbf{variable} \\ \textbf{overhead cost} \end{array}$$

$$= (\$2 \text{ per labour hour} \times 1100 \text{ hours}) - \$2500$$

$$= \$2200 - \$2500$$

$$= \$300 \text{ U}$$

The variable overhead spending variance is unfavourable because more was actually spent than should have been spent, given actual labour hours.

Next she calculates the variable overhead efficiency variance. Based on actual production of 100 000 blocks, the standard volume of the allocation base is 1000 direct labour hours (100 000 blocks × 0.01 hour per block). Given the standard cost of $2 per hour, the variable overhead efficiency variance is calculated as follows:

$$\left(\begin{array}{c} \textbf{Standard volume of} \\ \textbf{allocation base for} \\ \textbf{actual output} \end{array} - \begin{array}{c} \textbf{Actual} \\ \textbf{volume of} \\ \textbf{allocation base} \end{array} \right) \times \begin{array}{c} \textbf{Standard} \\ \textbf{variable overhead} \\ \textbf{allocation rate} \end{array}$$

$$= (1000 \text{ labour hours} - 1100 \text{ labour hours}) \times \$2 \text{ per hour}$$

$$= \$2000 - \$2200$$

$$= \$200 \text{ U}$$

The variance is unfavourable because actual labour hours used in production exceeded the standard number of labour hours (see figure 10.11).

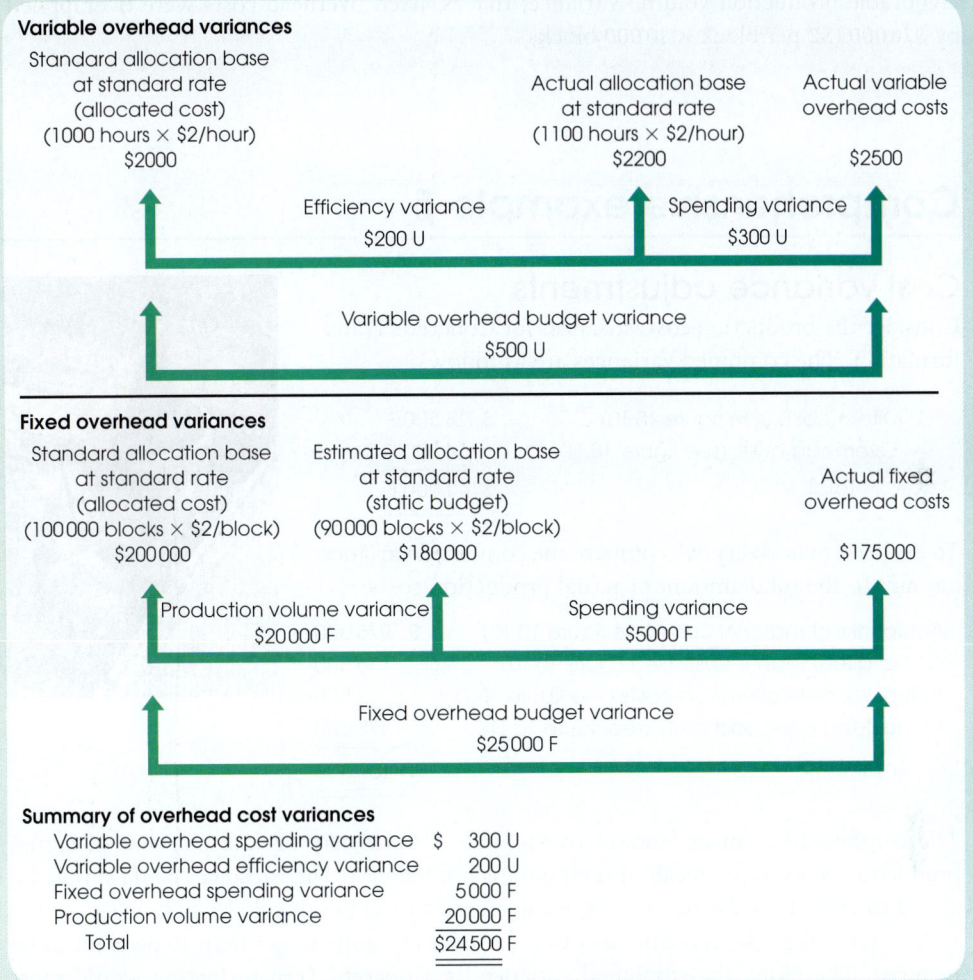

Variable overhead variances

Standard allocation base
at standard rate
(allocated cost)
(1000 hours × $2/hour)
$2000

Actual allocation base
at standard rate
(1100 hours × $2/hour)
$2200

Actual variable
overhead costs

$2500

Efficiency variance
$200 U

Spending variance
$300 U

Variable overhead budget variance
$500 U

Fixed overhead variances

Standard allocation base
at standard rate
(allocated cost)
(100 000 blocks × $2/block)
$200 000

Estimated allocation base
at standard rate
(static budget)
(90 000 blocks × $2/block)
$180 000

Actual fixed
overhead costs

$175 000

Production volume variance
$20 000 F

Spending variance
$5000 F

Fixed overhead budget variance
$25 000 F

Summary of overhead cost variances

Variable overhead spending variance	$ 300 U
Variable overhead efficiency variance	200 U
Fixed overhead spending variance	5000 F
Production volume variance	20 000 F
Total	$24 500 F

FIGURE 10.11 ■ Overhead variances for Concrete Transformation

Fixed overhead spending and production volume variances

First, Karen calculates the fixed overhead spending variance as follows:

Estimated fixed overhead costs – Actual fixed overhead costs
= **$180 000 – $175 000 = $5000 F**

The fixed overhead spending variance is favourable because less was spent than expected (see figure 10.11).

Next, Karen calculates the production volume variance as follows:

$$\left(\begin{array}{c} \textbf{Standard volume} \\ \textbf{of allocation base} \\ \textbf{for actual output} \end{array} - \begin{array}{c} \textbf{Estimated} \\ \textbf{volume of} \\ \textbf{allocation base} \end{array} \right) \times \begin{array}{c} \textbf{Standard fixed} \\ \textbf{overhead} \\ \textbf{allocation rate} \end{array}$$

= **(100 000 blocks − 90 000 blocks) × $2 per block**

= **$20 000 F**

Estimated production volume was 90 000 blocks, but 100 000 blocks were actually produced. Therefore, 10 000 more blocks were produced than expected, resulting in a favourable production volume variance; that is, fixed overhead costs were overapplied by $20 000 ($2 per block × 10 000 blocks).

Comprehensive example 5

Cost variance adjustments

Consider the production cost variances for Concrete Transformation. The combined variances are as follows:

Direct costs (see figure 10.10)	$ 118 500 F
Overhead costs (see figure 10.11)	24 500 F
Total	$143 000 F

To evaluate materiality, we compare the combined variance amount to the total amount of actual production costs:

Actual direct material costs (see figure 10.10)	$ 975 000
Actual direct labour costs (see figure 10.10)	16 500
Actual variable overhead costs (see figure 10.11)	2 500
Actual fixed overhead costs (see figure 10.11)	175 000
Total	$1 169 000

The combined variances amount to $143 000 ÷ $1 169 000, or 12.2 per cent of actual production costs. If we decide this amount is not material, the variances could simply be closed to cost of goods sold; that is, we decrease cost of goods sold by $143 000.

As a general guide, accountants often consider amounts larger than 10 per cent to be material. Therefore, the combined variance for Concrete Transformation would most likely be considered material. In this case, the variances would be closed to the general ledger accounts that contain the current period's standard production costs. For Concrete Transformation, standard costs allocated to production during the period totalled 100 000 blocks × $12.12 standard cost per block, or $1 212 000. Assume that these costs are included in the following general ledger accounts at the end of the accounting period:

	$	%
Work in process inventory	0	0
Finished goods inventory (5000 blocks × $12.12 per block)	60 600	5
Cost of goods sold (95 000 blocks × $12.12 per block)	1 151 400	95
Total	1 212 000	100

Of the standard costs allocated during the accounting period, 5 per cent remain in finished goods inventory and 95 per cent is recognised in cost of goods sold. Therefore, we decrease each of these accounts; finished goods by $7150 (5 per cent of $143 000), and cost of goods sold by $135 850 (95 per cent of $143 000). The journal entry to record the adjustment is:

Direct materials price variance	$325 000^a	
Fixed overhead spending variance	$5 000	
Production volume variance	$20 000	
Direct materials efficiency variance		$200 000
Direct labour price variance		$5 500
Direct labour efficiency variance		$1 000
Variable overhead spending variance		$300
Variable overhead efficiency variance		$200
Finished goods inventory		$7 150
Cost of goods sold		$135 850

^a This example is a simplified version of the adjustment for the direct materials price variance. Technically, if the variance were material, it would be apportioned on a pro rata basis to direct materials and production, with the production amount added to the other production variances and closed in aggregate as shown in the full entry.

After making this adjustment, the actual production costs are recorded in the inventory and cost of goods sold accounts, as required by generally accepted accounting principles for financial reporting.

APPENDIX 10A

PROFIT-RELATED VARIANCES

This appendix introduces the analysis of variances that are used to monitor revenues and contribution margins. These variances help managers monitor factors other than cost that affect profitability.

Revenue variances

Before managers estimate revenues for the next period, they assess market conditions, develop marketing strategies and establish the type and quality of goods or services they wish to sell. Given assumptions and plans for these factors, they set the following standards for operating revenue performance:

$$\begin{matrix} \text{Standard (or budgeted)} \\ \text{revenues} \end{matrix} = \begin{matrix} \text{Standard (or budgeted)} \\ \text{selling price} \end{matrix} \times \begin{matrix} \text{Standard (or budgeted)} \\ \text{sales volume} \end{matrix}$$

When actual revenues are compared to standard revenues, the difference is called a **revenue budget variance**. Revenue variances are caused by a number of different factors such as changes in demand, sales price or discounting practices. In addition, because total revenue is based on a projected sales mix among products, changes in the mix cause changes in revenues. Managers are often concerned about variances between planned and actual revenues, so accountants produce and analyse several variances that reflect the success of marketing efforts.

Sales price and revenue sales quantity variances

As shown in figure 10A.1, the revenue budget variance can be broken down into two types of variances. The **sales price variance** reflects the difference between standard and actual selling prices for the volume of units actually sold. The sales price variance is calculated using the formula shown overleaf.

Sales price variance = (Actual price – Standard price) × Actual volume sold

This variance is favourable if the actual selling price exceeds the standard price. It is unfavourable if the reverse is true. When an entity sells more than one product or service, the combined variance is calculated as the sum of sales price variances for all products and services.

The **revenue sales quantity variance** reflects the difference between the standard and actual quantity of units sold at the standard selling price. The revenue sales quantity variance is calculated using the following formula:

Revenue sales quantity variance = (Actual volume sold – Standard volume sold) × Standard price

This variance is favourable when actual sales quantities exceed standard quantities, and it is unfavourable otherwise. When an entity sells more than one product or service, the combined variance is calculated as the sum of revenue sales quantity variances for all products and services.

Suppose that Benny's sells both blackberry and French vanilla ice cream. Following is information about the standard and actual sales for the period.

Product	Standard price	Standard volume	Actual price	Actual volume
Blackberry	$7 per bucket	1000 buckets	$6.50 per bucket	1500 buckets
French vanilla	$6 per bucket	2000 buckets	$5.75 per bucket	1700 buckets

Total standard revenues are $19 000: $7000 (1000 buckets × $7 per bucket) for blackberry ice cream and $12 000 (2000 buckets × $6 per bucket) for French vanilla ice cream. Actual revenues are $19 525: $9750 (1500 buckets × $6.50 per bucket) for blackberry ice cream and $9775 (1700 buckets × $5.75 per bucket) for French vanilla ice cream.

As shown in figure 10A.2, the revenue budget variance is calculated as follows:

$$[(\textbf{1000 buckets} \times \$7 \textbf{ per bucket}) + (\textbf{2000 buckets} \times \$6 \textbf{ per bucket})]$$
$$- [(\textbf{1500 buckets} \times \$6.50 \textbf{ per bucket}) + (\textbf{1700 buckets} \times \$5.75 \textbf{ per bucket})]$$
$$= \$19\,000 - \$19\,525$$
$$= \$525 \textbf{ F}$$

This variance is favourable because revenues are higher than standard. However, sales prices for both products were less than expected. Benny's managers want to understand the influence of the price changes separately from the volume changes, so their accountant breaks this variance into the sales price variance and the revenue sales quantity variance.

The sales price variance for blackberry ice cream is $750 U [($6.50 per bucket – $7 per bucket) × 1500 buckets], and the sales price variance for vanilla is $425 U [($5.75 per bucket – $6.00 per bucket) × 1700 buckets]. The total sales price variance of $1175 ($750 U + $425 U) is unfavourable because both prices were lower than standard.

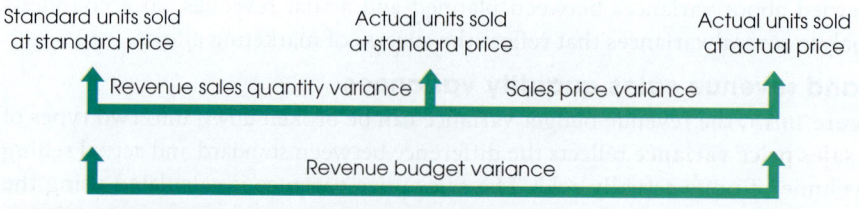

FIGURE 10A.1 ■ Revenue budget variances

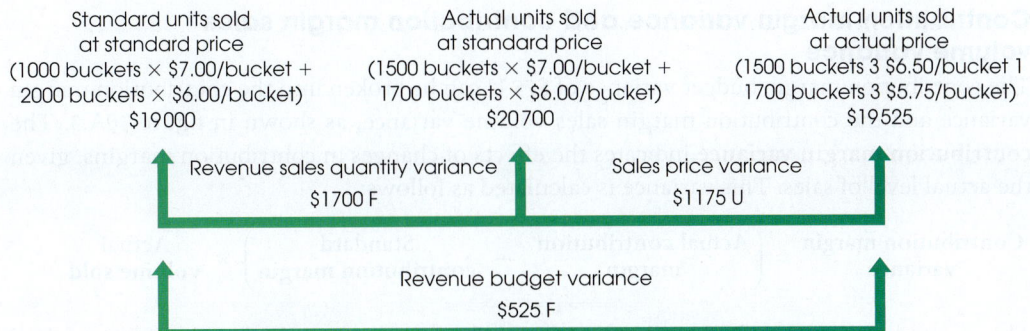

Standard units sold at standard price (1000 buckets × $7.00/bucket + 2000 buckets × $6.00/bucket) $19 000		Actual units sold at standard price (1500 buckets × $7.00/bucket + 1700 buckets × $6.00/bucket) $20 700		Actual units sold at actual price (1500 buckets 3 $6.50/bucket 1 1700 buckets 3 $5.75/bucket) $19 525

Revenue sales quantity variance
$1700 F

Sales price variance
$1175 U

Revenue budget variance
$525 F

FIGURE 10A.2 ■ Revenue budget variances for Benny's (two products)

The revenue sales quantity variance for blackberry of $3500 [(1500 buckets – 1000 buckets) × $7 per bucket] is favourable because Benny's sold more than standard. The variance for vanilla of $1800 [(2000 buckets – 1700 buckets) × $6 per bucket] is unfavourable because Benny's sold less than standard. The total variance of $1700 F ($3500 F – $1800 U) is favourable because the largest variance ($3500) was favourable. The combined sales price and revenue sales quantity variance is $525 F ($1700 F – $1175 U), the same value as the revenue budget variance that we calculated earlier.

Contribution margin-related variances

For organisations that sell more than one product, analysis of the total contribution margin is often useful, especially when an entity's products are substitutes for each other. The **contribution margin budget variance** reflects the difference between standard and actual contribution margins. At Benny's, some ice cream flavours are more expensive than others because of the cost of special ingredients. For customers who are price sensitive, a cheaper flavour is probably a good substitute for a more expensive flavour. When the economy is down, Benny's probably sells more of the cheaper ice cream. When the economy recovers, expensive ice creams sell better. Because the contribution margin of each flavour affects profitability, plans are made for a specific sales mix with specific contribution margins. At the end of a period, managers analyse the contribution margin budget variance. This analysis helps them know which products to advertise and provides guidance for future budgeting tasks.

Suppose that Benny's has standard contribution margins for blackberry and vanilla ice cream as follows:

	Standard contribution margin	Actual contribution margin
Blackberry	$1.00 per bucket	$1.15 bucket
French vanilla	$1.25 per bucket	$1.00 bucket

The standard contribution margin is $3500 [(1000 buckets × $1 per bucket) + (2000 buckets × $1.25 per bucket)]. However, actual sales were 1500 buckets of blackberry at a contribution margin of $1.15 each and 1700 buckets of vanilla at a contribution margin of $1 each. The actual contribution margin for this sales mix and contribution margin per product is $3425 (1500 buckets × $1.15 per bucket + 1700 buckets × $1 per bucket). The contribution margin budget variance is $75 ($3500 – $3425), which is unfavourable because the total actual contribution margin is lower than the total standard contribution margin.

Contribution margin variance and contribution margin sales volume variance

The contribution margin budget variance of $75 U can be broken into the contribution margin variance and the contribution margin sales volume variance, as shown in figure 10A.3. The **contribution margin variance** indicates the effects of changes in contribution margins, given the actual level of sales. This variance is calculated as follows:

$$\text{Contribution margin variance} = \left(\text{Actual contribution margin} - \text{Standard contribution margin} \right) \times \text{Actual volume sold}$$

This variance is favourable when the actual contribution margin is higher than the standard contribution margin, and it is unfavourable otherwise. When an entity sells more than one product or service, the combined variance is calculated as the sum of contribution margin variances for all products and services.

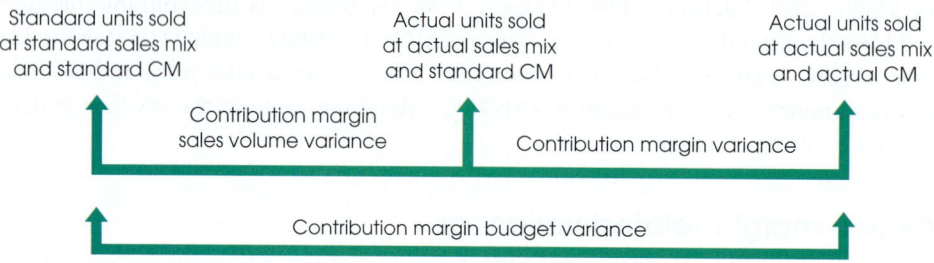

FIGURE 10A.3 ■ Contribution margin (CM) budget variances

The **contribution margin sales volume variance** indicates the effects of changes in units sold, given the standard contribution margins. The variance is calculated as follows:

$$\text{Contribution margin sales volume variance} = \left(\text{Actual volume sold} - \text{Standard volume sold} \right) \times \text{Standard contribution margin}$$

This variance is favourable when actual sales quantities exceed standard quantities, and it is unfavourable otherwise. When an entity sells more than one product or service, the combined variance is calculated as the sum of contribution margin volume variances for all products and services.

For Benny's, the contribution margin variance for blackberry is $225 F [1500 × ($1 − $1.15)] and for French vanilla is $425 U [1700 × ($1 − $1.25)]. The total contribution margin variance is $200 U ($425 − $225), as shown in figure 10A.4. In other words, the entity achieved a lower average contribution margin per bucket than standard. Although the actual contribution margin per bucket for blackberry ice cream was higher than standard, it was more than offset by the reduction in contribution margin on French vanilla ice cream. The contribution margin sales variance for blackberry is $500 F [(1500 buckets − 1000 buckets) × $1 per bucket] and for French vanilla is $375 U [(1700 buckets − 2000 buckets) × $1.25 per bucket].

The total contribution margin sales volume variance is $125 F ($500 F + $375 U). Benny's sold more total units of ice cream than planned, resulting in a favourable contribution margin sales volume variance. The sum of the contribution margin variance of $200 U and the contribution margin sales volume variance of $125 F reflects the contribution margin budget variance of $75 U.

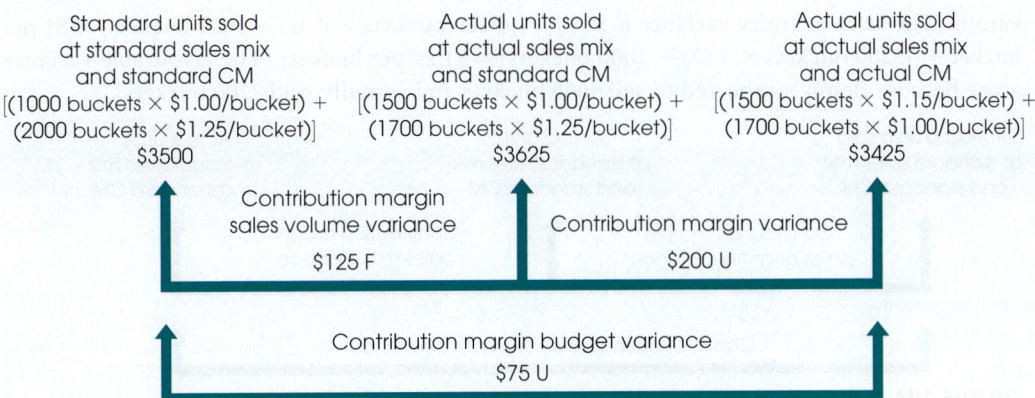

FIGURE 10A.4 ■ Contribution margin (CM) budget variances for Benny's (two products)

Contribution margin sales mix variance and contribution margin sales quantity variance

When an entity sells more than one product or service, the contribution margin sales volume variance can be broken into two more variances: the contribution margin sales mix variance and the contribution margin sales quantity variance, as shown in figure 10A.5. The **contribution margin sales mix variance** examines the effects of changes in the sales mix, given the standard contribution margin and actual quantity of units sold. The variance is calculated as follows, where total actual sales volume is the combined actual volume for all products:

$$
\begin{array}{l}
\text{Contribution} \\
\text{margin sales} \\
\text{mix variance}
\end{array}
=
\begin{array}{l}
\text{Sum} \\
\text{for all} \\
\text{products of}
\end{array}
\left\{ \left[
\begin{array}{l}
\text{Actual} \\
\text{sales} \\
\text{volume}
\end{array}
-
\left(
\begin{array}{l}
\text{Total} \\
\text{actual sales} \\
\text{volume}
\end{array}
\times
\begin{array}{l}
\text{Standard} \\
\text{sales mix} \\
\text{percentage}
\end{array}
\right)
\right]
\times
\begin{array}{l}
\text{Standard} \\
\text{contribution} \\
\text{margin}
\end{array}
\right\}
$$

The standard sales mix percentage is the standard number of units for the product as a percentage of the total standard number of units for all products. This variance is favourable when a shift occurs in sales mix toward products having a higher standard contribution margin.

The **contribution margin sales quantity variance** examines the effects of changes in quantities sold, given the standard contribution margins and standard sales mix. The variance is calculated as:

$$
\begin{array}{l}
\text{Contribution} \\
\text{margin sales} \\
\text{quantity variance}
\end{array}
=
\begin{array}{l}
\text{Sum} \\
\text{for all} \\
\text{products of}
\end{array}
\left\{ \left[
\left(
\begin{array}{l}
\text{Total actual} \\
\text{sales} \\
\text{volume}
\end{array}
\times
\begin{array}{l}
\text{Standard} \\
\text{sales mix} \\
\text{percentage}
\end{array}
\right)
-
\begin{array}{l}
\text{Standard} \\
\text{sales} \\
\text{volume}
\end{array}
\right]
\times
\begin{array}{l}
\text{Standard} \\
\text{contribution} \\
\text{margin}
\end{array}
\right\}
$$

The standard sales mix percentage is the standard number of units for the product as a percentage of the total standard number of units for all products. This variance is favourable if the total actual sales volume for the organisation is greater than standard.

The calculations of these variances for Benny's are presented in figure 10A.6. The standard proportion (that is, sales mix) of buckets sold for blackberry is 33 per cent [1000 buckets ÷ (1000 buckets + 2000 buckets)], while the standard proportion for French vanilla is the remaining 67 per cent. The contribution margin sales volume variance ($125 F) is broken into two other contribution margin variances. The contribution margin sales mix variance is $111 U{[1500 buckets − (3200 buckets × 0.33)] × $1 per bucket + [1700 buckets − (3200 buckets × 0.67)] × $1.25 per bucket}. The variance is unfavourable because a larger proportion of blackberry was sold than expected, and blackberry has a lower standard contribution margin than French vanilla. The sales quantity variance is $236 F {[(3200 buckets × 0.33) − 1000 buckets] × $1 per bucket + [(3200 buckets × 0.67) − 2000 buckets] × $1.25 per bucket}. The favourable variance arose because Benny's expected to sell 3000 buckets and actually sold 3200 buckets.

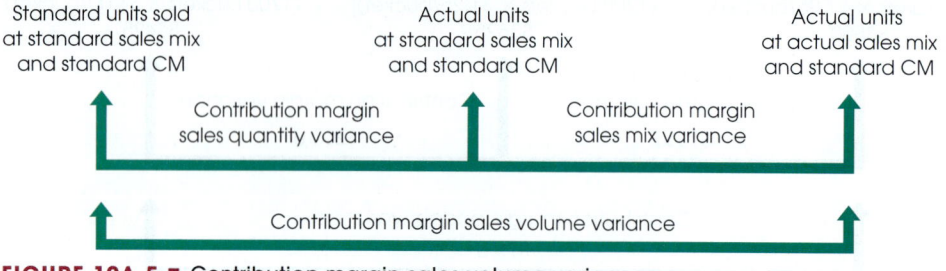

FIGURE 10A.5 ■ Contribution margin sales volume variances

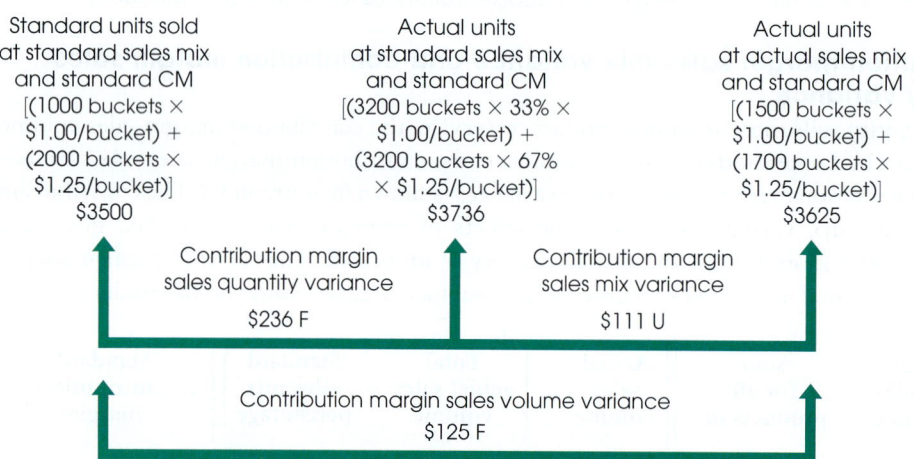

FIGURE 10A.6 ■ Contribution margin (CM) sales volume variances for Benny's (two products)

Analysing revenue and contribution margin variance information

The process of analysing these variances is similar to the process used for cost variances. Once variances have been computed, the reasons for variances are investigated. For example, after analysing the variances in figures 10A.2, 10A.4 and 10A.6, Benny's managers might investigate the following questions.

■ Why were ice cream selling prices different from standard prices? For example, does the price fluctuate from day to day based on the cost of cream or other ingredients? Are discounts sometimes offered?

■ Why was the proportion of blackberry ice cream larger than standard? Did advertising emphasise the higher-priced blackberry ice cream?

■ Why was the overall volume of sales higher than expected? Is this part of a trend? Are particular customers ordering more ice cream than usual? Is this event related to weather? Is the trend expected to continue?

■ Will the increased contribution margin for blackberry ice cream continue? It appears that costs were reduced, because prices decreased and contribution margin increased. Will the cost reduction continue into the next period?

■ Can cost reductions be found for French vanilla to compensate for the reduced price?

■ Should advertising emphasise blackberry even more because it now has the largest contribution margin?

- What do the answers to all of the preceding questions suggest about ways to increase profits for Benny's?

After considering these types of questions, the managers would decide what action, if any, to take.

Summary

1   Understand how standard costs are established.

Establishing standard costs
- Information used:
  - historical costs and trends
  - expected changes in costs or processes
  - estimates from industrial engineers.
- Key assumptions:
  - volume of production activity
  - production processes and efficiency, including expected waste and defects
  - prices and quality of inputs.
- Attainability:
  - to motivate performance, set standards with little slack.

Standard costs for manufactured products

$$\text{Standard cost per unit of output} = \text{Standard cost of direct materials} + \text{Standard cost of direct labour}$$
$$+ \text{Standard cost of variable overhead} + \text{Standard cost of fixed overhead}$$

2   Describe how variances are formed.

A *standard cost* variance is a difference between a standard cost and an actual cost.

Variance analysis process

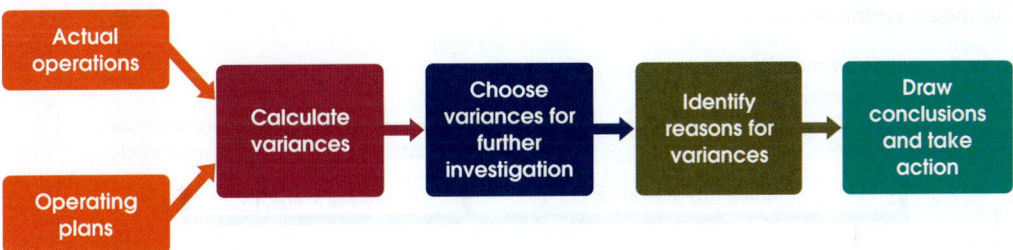

Factors influencing the choice of variances to monitor
- Nature of goods or services
- Cost accounting system used
- Costs that managers consider important
- Cost/benefit trade-off for monitoring individual costs

Factors influencing further investigation of variances
- Size of variance
- Trends in variances

Management conclusions and actions

See figure 10.3 (page 397).

Calculate direct cost variances.

Direct cost variances

Direct material variances

	Actual direct materials purchased at standard price	Actual direct materials purchased at actual price
	← Price variance →	

Standard direct materials required at standard price	Actual direct materials used at standard price
← Efficiency variance →	

Direct labour variances

Standard labour hours required at standard price	Actual labour hours used at standard price	Actual labour hours used at actual price
← Efficiency variance →	← Price variance →	
← Total direct labour variance →		

---

4 **Understand how direct cost variance information is analysed and used.**

For general process, see point 2.

For examples of reasons for direct cost variances, see figure 10.6 (page 403).

Resource and quality trade-offs reflected in direct cost variances

- Price and efficiency
- Different inputs

---

5 **Calculate variable and fixed overhead variances.**

Overhead variances

Variable overhead variances

Standard allocation base at standard rate (allocated cost)	Actual allocation base at standard rate	Actual variable overhead costs
← Efficiency variance →	← Spending variance →	
← Variable overhead budget variance →		

Fixed overhead variances

Standard allocation base at standard rate (allocated cost)	Estimated allocation base at standard rate (static budget)	Actual fixed overhead costs
← Production volume variance →	← Spending variance →	
← Fixed overhead budget variance →		

6   Understand how overhead variance information is analysed and used.

For the general process, see point 2.

For examples of reasons for overhead variances, see figure 10.9.

7   Close off manufacturing cost variances at the end of the period.

Immaterial variances

- Close to cost of goods sold

Material variances

- Standard costs do not fairly represent the actual cost of the units
- Distribute proportionately among:
  - work in process
  - finished goods
  - cost of goods sold.

8   Explain which profit-related variances are commonly analysed.

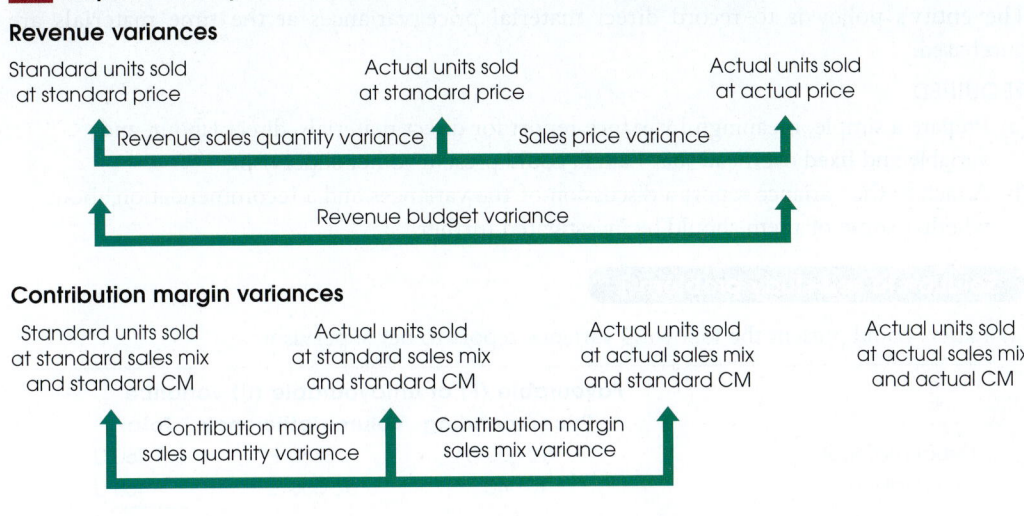

Revenue variances

Contribution margin variances

Self-study problems

SELF-STUDY PROBLEM 1

Direct cost and overhead variances, variance analysis

Latiefa is the cost accountant at Hallet and Sons, manufacturer of exquisite glass serving bowls. The materials used for the bowls are inexpensive but the process is labour intensive. The supervisor decided to use cheaper labour this period to see whether costs could be reduced.

Latiefa needs to prepare a report for her supervisor about how effective operations had been during the month of January. She had set the following standards.

		Cost per unit
Direct materials	3 kg @ $2.50	$7.50
Direct labour	5 h @ $150	75.00
Factory overhead:		
Variable	$3 per direct labour hour	15.00
Fixed	$20 per unit	20.00

Variable overhead is allocated by labour hours, and fixed overhead is allocated by unit. Estimated production per month is 40 000 standard direct labour hours.

Records for January based on production of 7800 units indicated the following:

Direct materials purchased	25 000 kg @ $2.60
Direct materials used	23 100 kg
Direct labour	40 100 hours @ $14.60
Variable overhead	$119 000
Fixed overhead	$180 000

The entity's policy is to record direct material price variances at the time materials are purchased.

REQUIRED

(a) Prepare a simple, meaningful variance report for direct materials, direct labour, and variable and fixed overhead that Latiefa could present to her supervisor.

(b) Attach to the variance report a discussion of the variances and a recommendation about whether some of them should be investigated further.

Solution to self-study problem 1

(a) Latiefa could present the following variance report to her supervisor:

	Favourable (F) or unfavourable (U) variance		
	Price/spending	Volume/efficiency	Total
Direct materials	$2 500 U	$750 F	$ 1 750 U
Direct labour	16 040 F	16 500 U	460 U
Total direct cost variance			2 210 U
Variable overhead	1 300 F	3 300 U	2 000 U
Fixed overhead	20 000 U	4 000 U	24 000 U
Total overhead cost variance			26 000 U
Total variance			$28 210 U

Calculation check:

Standard costs allocated based on actual production	
[7800 units × ($7.50 + $75 + $20 + $15)]	$916 500
Less actual costs:	
Direct materials:	
Materials used at standard cost	
(23 100 kg × $2.50)	$57 750
Unfavourable price variance for material purchases [25 000 kg × ($2.60 – $2.50)]	2 500
Total direct material cost	60 250

Direct labour (40 100 h × $14.60)		585 460
Variable overhead		119 000
Fixed overhead		180 000
Total actual costs		944 710
Total variance		$ 28 210 U

Details of the calculations are shown in figure 10.12.

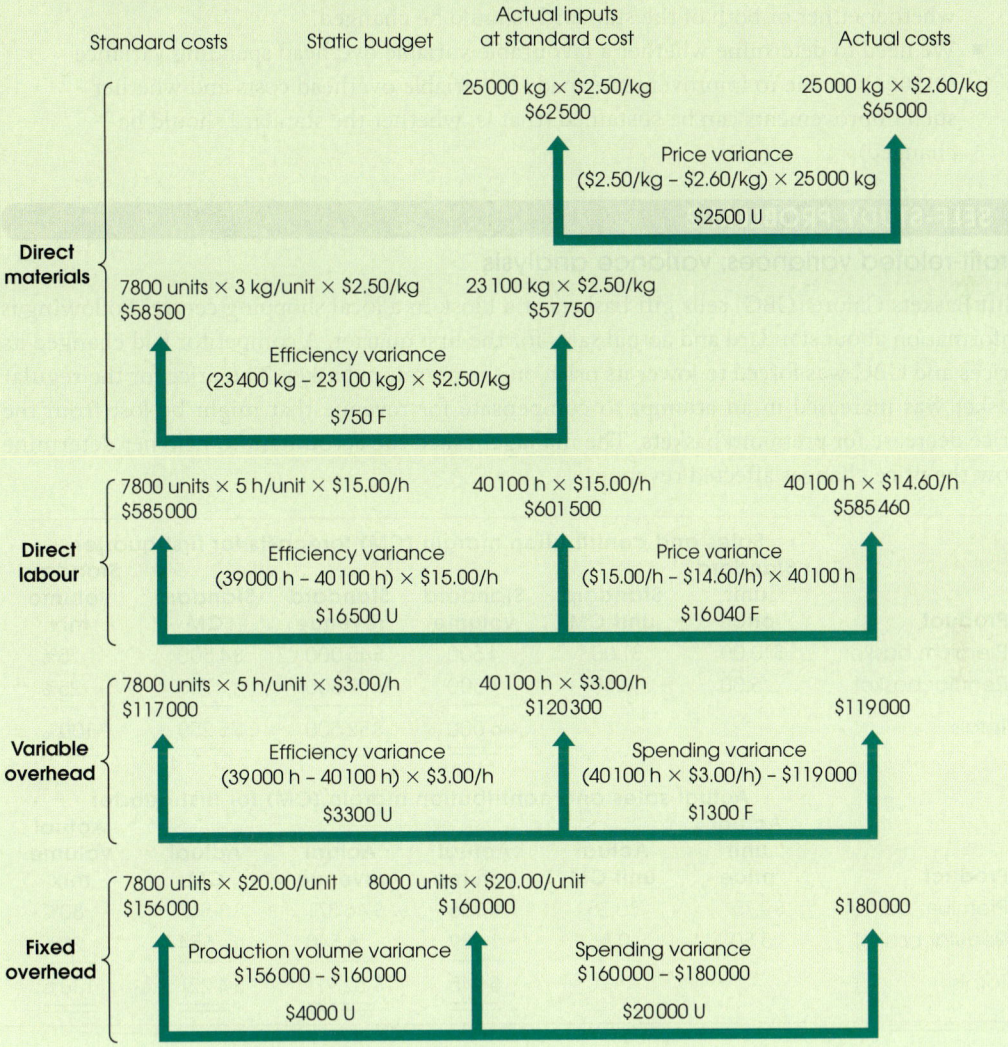

FIGURE 10.12 ■ Calculations for self-study problem 1

(b) Discussion of most significant variances:

■ Because the supervisor hired less-expensive labour this month, it is not surprising that the direct labour price variance is large and favourable ($16 040). However, this positive variance is more than offset by a large unfavourable direct labour efficiency variance ($16 500). It appears that more hours were required to compensate for less-skilled labour. This variance should be investigated to verify the conjectures.

- If less-skilled labour has a negative effect on quality, sales could be lost. Any potential change in the quality of output needs to be investigated.
- The fixed overhead spending variance was very large and unfavourable ($20 000). These costs might be out of control and need to be investigated.

Discussion of less-significant variances:
- Given the unfavourable direct materials price variance ($2500) and the favourable direct materials efficiency variance ($750), it is possible that the quality purchased this period has improved because less was used than expected. However, a price increase is also a possible explanation. These variances should be investigated to determine whether either or both of the standards should be changed.
- We need to determine whether a favourable variable overhead spending variance ($1300) was due to improvements made in variable overhead costs and whether such improvements can be sustained (that is, whether the standard should be changed).

SELF-STUDY PROBLEM 2

Profit-related variances; variance analysis

Gift Baskets Galore (GBG) sells gift baskets at a kiosk in a local shopping centre. Following is information about standard and actual sales for the first quarter. A competitor had changed its prices and GBG was forced to lower its price on the premium basket. The price for the regular basket was increased in an attempt to compensate for revenue that might be lost from the price decrease for premium baskets. The manager asked the accountant to help her determine how the price changes affected revenues.

	Sales and contribution margin (CM) forecasts for first quarter					
Product	Standard unit price	Standard unit CM	Standard volume	Standard revenue	Standard CM	Standard volume mix
Premium basket	$10.00	$1.00	4 500	$45 000	$4 500	75%
Regular basket	5.00	0.50	1 500	7 500	750	25%
Totals			6 000	$52 500	$5 250	100%

	Actual sales and contribution margin (CM) for first quarter					
Product	Actual unit price	Actual unit CM	Actual volume	Actual revenue	Actual CM	Actual volume mix
Premium basket	$9.75	$0.75	4 756	$46 371	$3 567	80%
Regular basket	5.50	0.55	1 189	6 540	654	20%
Totals			5 945	$52 911	$4 221	100%

REQUIRED

(a) For the premium basket, calculate the two revenue budget variances: sales price variance and the revenue sales quantity variance.

(b) Calculate all of the contribution margin variances: the contribution margin budget variance comprised of the contribution margin variance and contribution margin sales volume variance. Then break down the contribution margin sales volume variance into the contribution margin sales mix variance and the contribution margin sales quantity variance.

(c) Write a paragraph discussing these variances. Examine the current pricing policy and explain any changes you think the manager should consider.

Solution to self-study problem 2

(a) See figure 10.13.

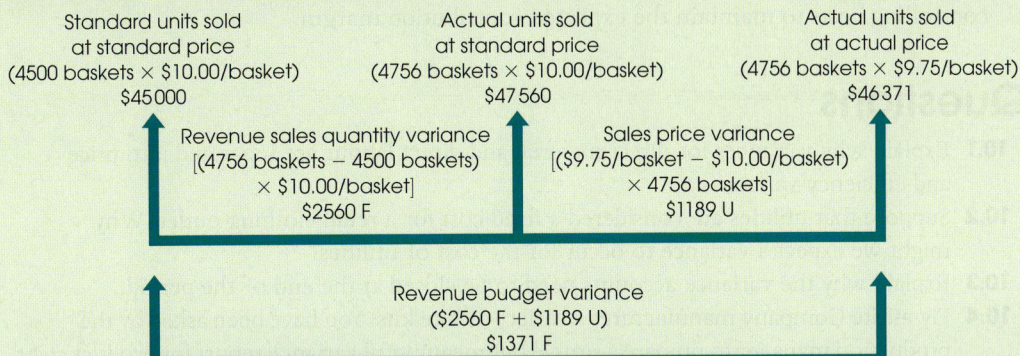

FIGURE 10.13 ■ Calculation of premium gift basket revenue variances

(b) See figure 10.14.

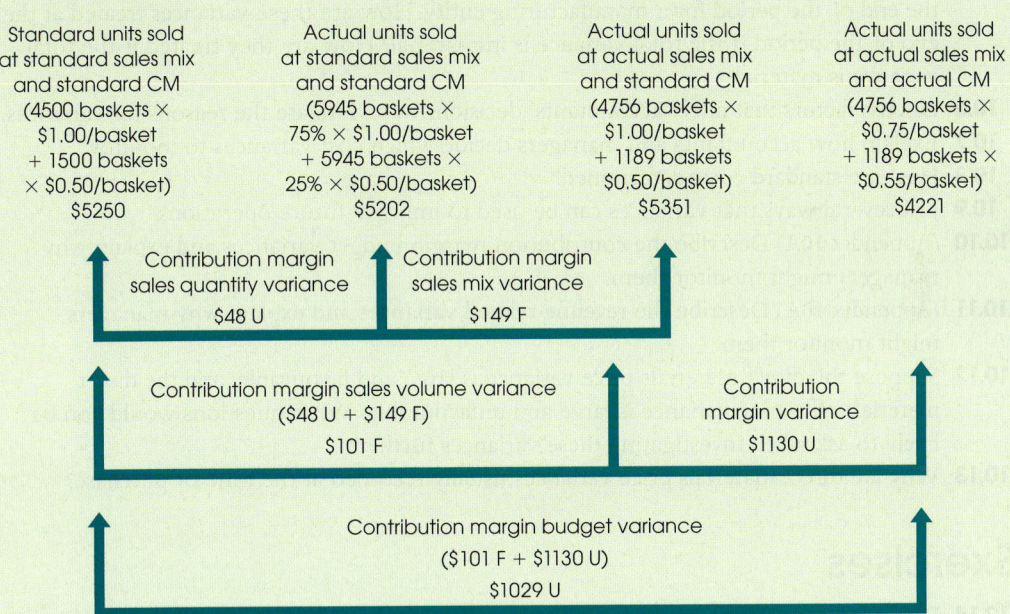

FIGURE 10.14 ■ Calculation of Gift Baskets Galore contribution margin variances

(c) For the premium baskets, the price decrease is reflected in the unfavourable sales price variance ($1189). However, the price variance is more than offset by a favourable revenue sales quantity variance ($2560). The contribution margin budget variance for Gift Baskets Galore is $1029 U. This variance is comprised of the contribution margin variance of $1130 U (reflecting only the effect of the changes in contribution margin for each product) and the contribution margin sales volume variance of $101 F (reflecting the effects of the changes in number of units sold). The contribution margin sales volume variance ($101 F) can be broken into the contribution margin sales mix variance of $149 F (reflecting the effects of the change in sales mix on contribution margin) and the contribution margin sales quantity variance of $48 F (reflecting the effects of the changes in units sold).

More premium baskets were sold, and this variance favourably affected the revenue sales quantity variance. However, the contribution margin on premium baskets was lower than expected, resulting in an unfavourable contribution margin variance. Managers will want to investigate reasons for the price decrease of premium baskets and consider controlling costs to maintain the expected contribution margin.

Questions

10.1 Explain why variances for direct material and direct labour are separated into price and efficiency variances.

10.2 Suppose that utilities are considered a fixed cost for a retail clothing outlet. Why might we expect a variance to occur for the cost of utilities?

10.3 Explain why the variance accounts need to be closed at the end of the period.

10.4 Fly-a-Kite Company manufactures a variety of kite kits. You have been asked by the production manager to prepare a simple but meaningful variance report for product costs so that she can identify areas in need of improved cost control. List all of the variances you would present in the variance report for production costs and explain why each is useful.

10.5 Identify the common variances that are needed to reconcile the accounting records at the end of the period for a manufacturing entity. How are these variances treated at the end of the period if the total variance is immaterial? How are they treated if the total variance is material?

10.6 Discuss factors that affect accountants' decisions to investigate the reasons for variances.

10.7 Explain how accountants and managers decide which cost variances to monitor.

10.8 How are standard costs determined?

10.9 List several ways that variances can be used to improve future operations.

10.10 (Appendix 10A) Describe the contribution margin budget variances and explain why managers might monitor them.

10.11 (Appendix 10A) Describe the revenue-related variances and explain why managers might monitor them.

10.12 Suppose the direct materials price variance is large and favourable, and the direct materials efficiency variance is large and unfavourable. What questions would you be likely to ask when investigating these variances further?

10.13 Why are direct materials price variances usually recorded at the time of purchase?

Exercises

10.14 **Direct labour variances and overhead spending variance** The following data for Kitchen Tile Company relates to the production of 18 000 tiles during the past month. The entity allocates fixed overhead costs at a standard rate of $19 per direct labour hour.

> Direct labour:
>   Standard cost is 6 tiles per hour at $24 per hour
> Actual cost per hour was $24.50
>   Labour efficiency variance was $6720 F
> Fixed overhead costs:
>   Estimated = $60 000
>   Actual = $58 720

(a) How many actual labour hours were worked to produce the 18 000 tiles?
(b) What is the price variance for direct labour?
(c) What is the budget variance for fixed costs?

10.15 **Direct materials and labour variances; variances to investigate** The managers of Nakatani Enterprises established the following standards for Model 535:

	Quantity standard	Price standard
Direct materials	0.8 kg per unit	$2 per kg
Direct labour	0.2 hours per unit	$17 per hour

Last month, 15 342 units of Model 535 were produced at a cost of $26 870 for direct materials and $47 000 for direct labour. A total of 13 252 kilograms of direct materials was used. Total direct labour hours amounted to 2730 hours. During the same period, 11 000 kilograms of direct material were purchased for $21 730. The entity's policy is to record materials price variances at the time materials are purchased.

REQUIRED

(a) What is the total standard cost for direct materials and direct labour for the output this period?
(b) What was the direct materials price variance?
(c) What was the direct materials efficiency variance?
(d) What was the direct labour price variance?
(e) What was the direct labour efficiency variance?
(f) Identify any variances that are material (greater than 10 per cent of total direct cost at standard). Discuss whether you would investigate these variances.

10.16 **Direct materials and direct labour variances; journal entries** The following information pertains to Nell Company's production of one unit of its manufactured product during the month of June. The entity recognises the materials price variance when materials are purchased.

Standard quantity of materials	5 kg
Standard cost per kilogram	$0.20
Standard direct labour hours	0.4
Standard wage rate per hour	$7.00
Direct materials purchased	100 000 kg
Cost of direct materials purchased per kilogram	$0.17
Direct materials consumed for manufacture of 10 000 units	60 000 kg
Actual direct labour hours required for 10 000 units	3900
Actual direct labour cost per hour	$7.20

REQUIRED

(a) Calculate the price and efficiency (quantity) variances for materials and labour.
(b) Record the journal entries for purchase and use of direct materials and the journal entries for direct labour.

10.17 **Variable and fixed overhead variances; journal entries** Derf Company allocates overhead on the basis of direct labour hours. Two direct labour hours are required for each unit of product. Planned production for the period was set at 9000 units. Manufacturing overhead is estimated at $135 000 for the period (20 per cent of this cost is fixed). The 17 200 hours worked during the period resulted in the production of

8500 units. Variable manufacturing overhead cost incurred was $108 500 and the fixed manufacturing overhead cost was $28 000.

REQUIRED

(a) Determine the variable overhead spending variance.
(b) Determine the variable overhead efficiency (quantity) variance.
(c) Determine the fixed overhead spending (budget) variance.
(d) Determine the production volume (fixed overhead volume or denominator) variance.
(e) Prepare journal entries to close these variances at the end of the period.

10.18 Profit-related variances (appendix 10A) Following is information for the Mitchellville Products Company for the month of July.

	Master budget	Actual
Units	4000	3800
Sales revenue	$60 000	$53 200
Variable manufacturing costs	$16 000	$19 000
Fixed manufacturing costs	$15 000	$16 000
Variable selling and administrative expense	$8 000	$7 600
Fixed selling and administrative expense	$9 000	$10 000

REQUIRED

(a) Determine the revenue budget variance.
(b) Determine the sales price variance.
(c) Determine the revenue sales quantity variance.
(d) Determine the contribution margin sales quantity variance.

10.19 Contribution margin variances; analysis (appendix 10A) Metropolitan Motors is a car retailer. Salespeople have the authority to negotiate with customers for price, but are given target profits. The entity classifies the cars it sells into one of three broad groups: economy, family or luxury. Target sales and average expected contribution margins per unit for March were estimated as follows:

Class	Unit sales	Average contribution margin
Economy	10	$400
Family	20	$800
Luxury	5	$1300

During March the car manufacturer ran a special promotion to reduce an overstock of economy cars. The manufacturer offered to pay directly to the salespeople a bonus of $75 for each economy car sold. Actual sales and total contribution margin earned by Metropolitan Motors for March turned out to be as follows:

Class	Unit sales	Total contribution margin earned
Economy	25	$5625
Family	10	$7500
Luxury	3	$4200

REQUIRED

(a) Calculate the contribution margin budget variance.
(b) Calculate the contribution margin variance and contribution margin sales volume variance.

(c) Calculate the contribution margin sales mix variance and the contribution margin sales quantity variance.

(d) Should the management of Metropolitan Motors be pleased or upset with the manufacturer for running the special promotion? Why?

10.20 Direct cost and overhead variances; decision to automate Plush pet toys are produced in a largely automated factory in standard lots of 100 toys each. A standard cost system is used to control costs and to assign cost to inventory.

	Price standard	Quantity standard
Plush fabric	$2 per metre	15 metres per lot
Direct labour	$10 per hour	2 hours per lot

Variable overhead, estimated at $5 per lot, consists of miscellaneous items such as thread, a variety of plastic squeakers, and paints that are applied to create features such as eyes and whiskers. Fixed overhead, estimated at $24 000 per month, consists largely of depreciation on the automated machinery and rent for the building. Variable overhead is allocated based on lots produced. The standard fixed overhead allocation rate is based on the estimated output of 1000 lots per month.

Actual data for last month follow.

Production	2400 lots
Sales	1600 lots
Plush fabric purchased	30 000 metres
Cost of fabric purchased	$62 000
Fabric used	34 000 metres
Direct labour	4200 hours
Direct labour cost	$39 000
Variable overhead	$12 000
Fixed overhead	$24 920

The entity's policy is to record materials price variances at the time materials are purchased.

REQUIRED

(a) Calculate the commonly used direct cost and overhead variances.

(b) Management is considering further automation in the factory. Robot-controlled forklifts could reduce the standard direct labour per lot to 1.5 hours.

  (i) Estimate the savings per lot that would be realised from this additional automation.

  (ii) Assume the entity would be able to generate the savings as calculated. Considering only quantitative factors, calculate the maximum price the managers would be willing to pay for the robot-controlled forklifts. Assume the entity's management requires equipment costs to be recovered in five years, ignoring the time value of money.

10.21 Journal entries for closing variances Following are the variances for Fine Products Manufacturing Company for the month of March. Assume that the price variance for direct materials is calculated at the time of purchase and that the amount of direct materials purchased is equal to the amount of direct materials used, with no beginning or ending inventories for direct materials.

Direct materials price variance	$2000 U
Direct materials efficiency variance	1500 F
Labour price variance	5000 U
Labour efficiency variance	2000 U
Fixed overhead spending variance	200 U
Variable overhead spending variance	1000 F
Variable overhead efficiency variance	1200 U

Fine Products considers anything greater than $5000 as a material variance. Following are end of period inventory balances.

Work in process	$ 2 000
Finished goods	6 000
COGS	24 000

REQUIRED

(a) Determine whether the total variance amount is material.

(b) Prepare a journal entry to close the variances at the end of March.

10.22 Profit-related variances (appendix 10A) Pet Toys Ltd expected to sell one plush toy for each two footballs sold. Planned sales and variable costs for 2008 were as follows:

	Footballs	Plush toys	Total
Sales (100 000 footballs)	$300 000	$150 000	$ 450 000
Variable costs	175 000	50 000	225 000
Contribution margin	$125 000	$100 000	$ 225 000

During 2008 a competitor came out with a similar plush toy at a lower price. Management reacted by dropping its selling price for plush toys, but the results were disappointing. Actual sales were as follows:

Footballs (95 000 @ $3.30)	$313 500
Plush toys (40 000 @ $2.40)	96 000
Total sales	$409 500

REQUIRED

(a) Determine the revenue budget variance, the sales price variance and the revenue sales quantity variance.

(b) Determine the contribution margin budget variance, the contribution margin variance and the contribution margin sales volume variance.

(c) Determine the contribution margin sales mix variance and the contribution margin sales quantity variance.

Problems

10.23 Cost variances; variance analysis; employee motivation Raging Sage Coffee is a franchise that sells cups of coffee from a cart in shopping centres. A computerised standard costing system is provided as a part of the franchise package. A portion of the standard cost data follows.

	Price	Quantity
Coffee beans	$6 per kg	0.04 kg per cup
Clerk/brewer	$10 per hour	0.05 hours per cup

In its first month of operation, the Launceston franchise recorded the following data:

Coffee sold	8260 cups
Coffee beans used	224 kg
Coffee beans purchased	240 kg
Cost of coffee beans purchased	$1800
Clerk/brewers' total hours	600 hours
Clerk/brewers' total wages	$6000

The entity's policy is to record materials price variances at the time materials are purchased.

REQUIRED

(a) Are direct labour hours for the cart most likely fixed or variable? Explain.
(b) Given your answer to part (a), should a direct labour efficiency variance be calculated? Why?
(c) Calculate the direct materials price and efficiency variances.
(d) How many cups of coffee did the franchise owners expect to sell this period? Compare this estimate to the amount actually sold.
(e) Provide possible explanations for the drop in sales.
(f) Suppose the clerks/brewers currently receive a bonus based on their ability to control costs as measured using cost variances. Recommend a bonus system that might help the owners contain costs but also increase sales.

10.24 Cost standards; cost variances; improving cost variance information Sunglass Guys produces two types of wraparound sunglasses on one assembly line. The monthly fixed overhead is estimated at $235 707, and the variable overhead is estimated at $8.15 per Regular Wrap and $12.32 per Deluxe Wrap.

The entity set up a standard costing system and follows the common practice of basing the overhead rate on the total standard direct labour hours required to produce the estimated volume. The company uses only one overhead rate for fixed and variable overhead costs. Data concerning these two products appear here:

	Regular	Deluxe
Estimated monthly volume	4300 units	1400 units
Standard direct labour	0.2 hours per unit	0.3 hours per unit

Last month, actual production volume was 4500 units of the Regular Wraps and 1300 units of the Deluxe Wraps. Actual variable overhead was $54 238 and actual fixed overhead was $237 859. The nine full-time employees who are classified as direct labour worked regular schedules for a total of 1564 hours.

REQUIRED

(a) Calculate the standard overhead rate per direct labour hour.
(b) Explain why the entity's overhead cost variances would provide poor information for monitoring and controlling costs.
(c) Using the information available to you in this problem, suggest a method of allocating overhead costs that would provide better variance information. Using this method, calculate relevant variances for monitoring and controlling overhead costs.
(d) For bookkeeping purposes, Sunglass Guys needs to calculate a production volume variance and a variable overhead efficiency variance. Calculate these variances, assuming that overhead costs are allocated using the method in part (c).

(e) Because employees work regular schedules, direct labour costs tend to be fixed. Also, variable overhead consists primarily of indirect materials and facility-level costs (such as building rent, assembly line equipment and utilities). These costs do not differ between Regular Wraps and Deluxe Wraps. Given this information, recommend a better cost allocation base for variable overhead. Explain your choice.

10.25 **Developing direct cost standards; cost variances; use of variance analysis** The Mighty Morphs produces two popular games, Powerful Puffs and Mini-Mite Morphs. Following are standard costs:

	Powerful Puffs		Mini-Mite Morphs	
	Standard quantity	Standard price	Standard quantity	Standard price
DVDs	1.08 DVD/unit	$0.35/DVD	1.08 DVD/unit	$0.35/DVD
Documentation	1.03 book/unit	$3/book	1.03 book/unit	$5/book
Assembly labour	0.01 hour/unit	$15/hour	0.03 hour/unit	$15/hour

The standards call for more than one disk and documentation book per unit because of normal waste due to faulty DVDs and poor binding.

Actual costs for last week follow:

DVDs purchased (@ $0.39)	$780
Number of DVDs used	2025
Number of Powerful Puffs games produced	1000
Powerful Puffs documentation printed (@ $2.95)	$4425
Number of Powerful Puffs documentation used	1005
Number of Mini-Mite Morphs games produced	800
Mini-Mite Morphs documentation printed (@ $4.75)	$4750
Number of Mini-Mite Morphs documentation used	825
Assembly labour cost (55 hours)	$795

Management decided that it would require too much effort to keep track of how many DVDs and hours are used for each of the games separately. Accordingly, the DVD materials and labour variances are combined rather than computed separately for each game. The price variances are recorded at the time of purchase.

REQUIRED
(a) What is the documentation price variance for Mini-Mite Morphs?
(b) What is the efficiency variance for DVDs?
(c) What is the sum of all variances for assembly labour for both games?
(d) Calculate last week's estimated cost of waste for DVDs and documentation.
(e) Discuss the pros and cons of building waste into the standards.

10.26 **Cost variance analysis; use of variance information** Baker Street Animal Clinic uses a particular serum routinely in its vaccination program. Veterinarian technicians give the injections. The standard dose is 10cc per injection, and the cost has been $100 per 1000cc. According to records, 2000 injections were administered last month at a serum cost of $2270. The veterinarian noted that the serum for the injections should have cost $2000 [($0.10 per cc) × (10cc per injection) × (2000 injections)]. Moreover, she noted some carelessness in handling the serum that could easily lead to unnecessary waste. When this issue was brought to the attention of the technicians, together with the $270 discrepancy in costs, they claimed that the $270 excess costs must be due to the inflated prices charged by the veterinarian supply company. Purchasing records reveal that the price for the serum used last month had indeed increased to $105 per 1000cc.

REQUIRED

(a) Provide variance calculations to help you evaluate the technicians' argument.

(b) Discuss whether a significant waste of serum occurred last month. Include quantitative and qualitative information in your discussion.

(c) If you were the manager for the Baker Street Animal Clinic, how would you use the results of your analyses in parts (a) and (b)? Explain.

10.27 **Normal and abnormal waste; adjustment of variances** Damson Products prepares monthly financial statements. It closes its variance accounts at that time. For the month of May the entity's accounting records reveal the following variances (the comments were supplied by appropriate operating personnel).

Variance	Amount	Percentage of standard	Comment
Direct material price	$658 U	0.04%	Normal fluctuation
Direct material efficiency	12 600 U	11.38%	$13 000 lost in spring flood
Direct labour price	376 F	0.11%	Normal fluctuation
Direct labour efficiency	9 700 U	9.62%	$9000 for days plant was closed during flood
Variable overhead spending	507 F	0.21%	Normal fluctuation
Variable overhead efficiency	412 U	0.18%	Normal fluctuation
Fixed overhead spending	782 F	0.07%	Normal fluctuation
Production volume	10 400 U	11.29%	$10 200 due to time lost in flood; the rest represents normal decreased spring operations

The entity uses a standard fixed overhead allocation rate based on annual operations. The entity was closed several days when a nearby stream flooded after heavy rains. The entity does not have flood insurance, and the lost material and labour costs were charged to production. At the end of the month, the entity has no raw material and no work in process inventories. The standard cost of finished goods inventory is $34 000, and the standard cost of goods sold is $305 000.

REQUIRED

(a) For each variance, explain whether the total amount of the variance should all be closed as a production variance or whether part of the amount should be closed to a separate flood loss account.

(b) Prepare journal entries to close out the variances.

(c) What is the cost of finished goods and cost of goods sold after the variance accounts are closed?

10.28 **ABC costing; single versus dual rate spending variances; performance evaluation** Data Processors Ltd performs credit card services for banks. The entity uses an ABC system. Following is information for the past year:

Activity	Estimated cost	Actual cost	Cost driver
Processing transactions	$2 000 000	$2 200 000	Number of transactions
Issuing monthly statements	1 000 000	1 300 000	Number of statements
Issuing new credit cards	500 000	400 000	Number of new credit cards
Resolving billing disputes	90 000	100 000	Number of disputes
Total	$ 3 590 000	$4 000 000	

Cost driver	Estimated activity level	Actual activity level
Number of transactions	5 000 000	5 800 000
Number of statements	250 000	270 000
Number of new credit cards	100 000	110 000
Number of disputes	3 000	3 500

(a) Using standard values for costs and activity, calculate an ABC allocation rate for each activity.

(b) Prepare an operating cost statement for Data Processors Ltd that compares the static budget, the flexible budget and actual costs.

(c) Calculate the spending variance for the cost of processing transactions. (*Hint*: Treat this activity the same way you would treat variable overhead costs.)

(d) Suppose the costs for processing transactions include some fixed and some variable costs, as shown:

	Estimated cost	Actual cost
Fixed costs	$1 000 000	$1 300 000
Variable costs	1 000 000	900 000
Total	$2 000 000	$2 200 000

Given this new information, calculate spending variances for the cost of processing transactions.

(e) Discuss possible reasons for the variances calculated in part (d).

The CEO and CFO of Data Processors want your opinion about whether and how ABC variance information should be used in departmental manager performance evaluations.

(f) Use the information you learned from the preceding analyses to write a memo to the CEO and CFO presenting your evaluation of (i) whether the use of ABC cost variances in departmental manager performance evaluations would likely improve organisational performance, and (ii) which spending variance — the one from part (c) or part (d) — would provide better information for evaluating the credit card transaction processing manager's ability to control costs. As you write the memo, consider what information the CEO and CFO will need from you to help them make a final decision.

10.29 **Reconcile standard to actual income; performance evaluation; budget (appendix 10A)**
The Software Development Company produces computer programs on DVDs for home computers. This business is highly automated, causing fixed costs to be very high, but variable costs are minimal. The entity is organised along three product lines: games, business programs and educational programs. The average standard selling prices for each are $16 for games, $55 for business programs and $20 for educational programs. The standard variable cost consists solely of one DVD per program at $2 per DVD, without regard to the type of program. Fixed costs for the period were estimated at $535 000. For the current period, standard sales are 40 000 games, 2000 business programs and 10 000 educational programs. Actual results are as follows.

Sales:		
Games	(35 000 DVDs)	$616 000
Business	(4000 DVDs)	198 000
Educational	(11 000 DVDs)	220 000
Total sales		1 034 000

Variable costs	(50 750 DVDs)	106 575
Fixed costs		533 500
Pre-tax income		$393 925

REQUIRED

(a) Calculate standard pre-tax income and then reconcile it to actual pre-tax income by calculating the contribution margin sales mix variance, revenue sales quantity variance, sales price variance, materials price and quantity variances, and the fixed cost spending variance.

(b) A new marketing manager was hired during the period. The manager changed prices and redirected sales efforts.

   (i) Discuss whether one or more of the preceding variances are relevant to evaluating the performance of the new marketing manager.

   (ii) What do the variances suggest about the new manager's performance? Explain.

(c) An analysis reveals that the entity will have to pay $1.80 per DVD next period. Prepare next period's master budget. Assume a standard of one disk per program, total unit sales of 55 000, and the actual sales mix and sales prices from this period.

(d) Discuss possible reasons why the entity might not meet its budget for next period.

10.30 Evaluate grading scheme; professional responsibilities Variance analysis reflects information about actual performance relative to a standard. Variance analysis reports provide managers with information about the performance of employees, from direct labour to supervisors and managers. Grades provide similar information for recruiters who want to hire graduating students. Following is information about Professor Grader's performance measurement system.

Professor Grader is popular; almost all of his students receive As. This phenomenon is widely attributed to Professor Grader's superior teaching skills. Grades for this professor's courses are determined as follows:

Item	Points
Mid semester exam	200
Attendance	200
Major assignment	200
Final exam	400

A student needs 700 points for an A, 600 points for a B, 500 for a C and 400 for a D. From the 200 points given for perfect attendance, a student loses 5 points for every class missed (out of 40 class meetings); however, attendance is seldom taken.

If the major assignment paper is 20 pages or longer, 200 points are earned; 10 points are lost for each page less than 20 (thus, a 12-page paper is worth 120 points).

Professor Grader has given the same mid semester exam for the past 20 years. To reduce the number of exam copies in students' files, Professor Grader does not return the exams; grades are simply reported to individual students. A student group obtained a copy of the exam 15 years ago. They have chosen not to share the exam with any person not a member of the group; thus Professor Grader usually observes that grades on this exam are nearly normally distributed.

The final exam is a take-home exam that the students have two weeks to complete.

REQUIRED

(a) Is it possible to develop a perfect system for measuring student performance in a course? Why?

(b) How much variation is likely in student performance for each of the four graded items? Explain.

(c) Describe the weaknesses in Professor Grader's grading system as a performance measurement system.

(d) What are Professor Grader's professional responsibilities to various stakeholders in this situation?

(e) Discuss whether Professor Grader has acted ethically in this situation. Describe the ethical values you use to draw your conclusions.

(f) Is it ethical for students in this situation to access a copy of the prior mid-semester exam or to seek assistance in completing take-home assignments? Does Professor Grader's system affect the students' responsibilities? Describe the ethical values you use to draw your conclusions.

10.31 Evaluating a proposal for measuring performance Benerux Industries has been in business for 30 years. The entity's major product is a control unit for elevators. The entity has a reputation for manufacturing products of exceptionally high quality, resulting in higher prices for its units than competitors charge. Higher prices, in turn, have meant that the entity has been comfortably profitable. A major reason for the high product quality is a loyal and conscientious workforce. Production employees have been with the entity for an average of 18 years.

Recently the entity hired a cost accountant from the local university. After a few months at Benerux, the new accountant proposed a performance measurement report consisting of two parts. The first part will report the actual number of units started during each month, the target number of units that should have been started and a variance. The second part will calculate an actual cost per good unit completed during each month, the target cost per unit and a variance.

The new accountant provided the following additional information concerning the performance report: The first part of the report concentrates on units started because many units are scrapped in the manufacturing process (to maintain high quality). Therefore, the best measure of effort expended is the number of units on which work was begun. The target number of units to be begun in a month is the number of units started in the corresponding month last year plus 5 per cent. In the second part of the report, actual costs per unit will be calculated by dividing total production cost incurred during the month by the number of good units completed during the month.

The target cost per unit is the average cost for manufacturing this kind of product as determined from industry newsletters.

The proposal concluded with the following comments: 'This report should be prepared and distributed quarterly. For maximum benefit I suggest that a bonus be awarded whenever units started exceeds target and costs are below target. This system will result in substantially improved profits for the entity. It should be implemented immediately.'

REQUIRED

(a) Is it possible to develop a perfect system for monitoring and motivating worker performance? Why?

(b) Explain what the managers might learn by monitoring each of the variances in the proposed performance measurement system.

(c) Discuss possible reasons why the entity did not previously use a variance system to monitor and motivate worker performance.

(d) Describe weaknesses in the proposed performance measurement system.

(e) If you were the CFO of Benerux Industries, how would you respond to the new cost accountant's proposal? Discuss whether you agree with the proposal and explain how you would communicate your response.

10.32 Direct and overhead cost variance analysis; closing accounts at end of period
Jennifer has just been promoted to manager of the piston division of Car Parts Co. The division, which manufactures pistons for hydraulic drives, uses a standard cost system and calculates the standard cost of a completed piston as $85, as follows:

	Quantity	Price	Cost per piston
Piston shaft	1	$35/piston shaft	$35
Shaft housing	1	$20/housing	20
Direct labour	0.4 hours	$15/hour	6
Variable factory overhead	0.4 hours	$10/hour	4
Fixed factory overhead	0.4 hours	$50/hour	20
Total standard cost			$85

The fixed overhead rate is based on an estimated 1000 units per month. Direct labour is nearly a fixed cost in this division. Selling and administrative costs are $50 000 per month plus $10 per piston sold.

The following information is for production during April:

Number of pistons manufactured	950
Purchase of 1000 piston shafts	$34 950
Number of piston shafts used	954
Purchase of 1000 shaft housings	$20 000
Number of shaft housings used	950
Direct labour costs (397 hours)	$6 120
Variable factory overhead costs	$3 677
Fixed factory overhead costs	$18 325
Selling and administrative costs	$59 101

The entity's policy is to record materials price variances at the time materials are purchased. You may want to use a spreadsheet to perform calculations.

REQUIRED
(a) Prepare a flexible cost budget for the month of April.
(b) Calculate all of the common direct cost variances. (*Note*: There are no variances for shaft housings.)
(c) Calculate all common factory overhead variances.
(d) Calculate a total variance for the selling and administrative costs.
(e) Prepare a complete, yet concise, report that would be useful in evaluating control of production costs for April.
(f) Prepare a report that sums all the variances necessary to prepare the reconciling journal entry at the end of the period. Explain how you would close the total variance; that is, identify the account or accounts that would be affected, and whether expenses in the accounts will be increased or decreased to adjust the records for the total variance.
(g) Suppose you are manager of the piston division and you are reviewing the report prepared in part (e). Use information in the report to identify questions you might have about April's production costs.

10.33 Cost–volume–profit pricing and standard cost variances Bramlett Company has several divisions, and has just built a new plant with a capacity of 20 000 units of a new product. A standard costing system has been introduced to aid in evaluating managers' performance and for establishing a selling price for the new product. Bramlett currently faces no competitors in this product market. Managers price the product at standard variable and fixed manufacturing cost, plus a 60 per cent mark-up. Managers hope this price will be maintained for several years.

During the first year of operations, 1000 units per month will be produced. During the second year of operations, production is estimated to be 1500 units per month. In the first month of operations, employees were learning the processes, so direct labour hours were estimated to be 20 per cent greater than the standard hours allowed per unit. In subsequent months, employees were expected to meet the direct labour hours standards.

Experience in other plants and with similar products led managers to believe that variable manufacturing costs would vary in proportion to actual direct labour dollars. For the first several years, only one product will be manufactured in the new plant. Fixed overhead costs of the new plant per year are expected to be $1 920 000 incurred evenly throughout the year.

The standard variable manufacturing cost (after the break-in period) per unit of product has been set as follows:

Direct materials (4 pieces @ $20 per piece)	$ 80
Direct labour (10 hours @ $25 per hour)	250
Variable overhead (50% of direct labour cost)	125
Total	$455

At the end of the first month of operations, the actual costs incurred to make 950 units of product were as follows:

Direct materials (3850 pieces @ $19.80)	$76 230
Direct labour (12 000 hours @ $26)	312 000
Variable overhead	160 250
Fixed overhead	172 220

Bramlett managers want to compare actual costs to standard to analyse and investigate variances and take any corrective action.

REQUIRED

(a) What selling price should Bramlett set for the new product according to the new pricing policy? Explain.

(b) Using long-term standard costs, calculate all direct labour and manufacturing overhead variances.

(c) Is it reasonable to use long-term standard costs to calculate variances for the first month of operations? Why?

(d) Revise the variance calculations in part (b), using the expected costs during the first month of operations as the standard costs.

(e) Provide at least two possible explanations for each of the following variances:
   (i) direct labour price variance
  (ii) direct labour efficiency variance
 (iii) variable overhead spending variance
 (iv) fixed overhead spending variance.

(f) As shown in figure 10.2 (page 396), the reasons for variances must be identified before conclusions and actions are decided upon. For two of the variance explanations you provided in part (e), explain what action(s) managers would most likely take.

(g) Would it most likely be easier or more difficult to analyse the variances at the new plant compared to Bramlett's other plants? Explain.

10.34 Auditor evaluation of variances for error and fraud; accounting principles for variances Auditors must plan and perform an audit to obtain reasonable assurance about whether the financial statements are free of material misstatements, which may be caused by either error or fraud. Errors are unintentional misstatements caused by factors such as mistakes in processing accounting data, misinterpretation of facts and confusion about accounting principles. Fraudulent financial reporting and misappropriation of assets are the only two types of financial statement fraud. Fraudulent financial reporting consists of intentional misstatements caused by factors such as manipulation of accounting data, misrepresentation of facts and intentional misapplication of accounting principles. Misappropriation of assets includes stealing assets such as inventory and causing an entity to pay for goods or services that were not received.

Auditors perform a variety of procedures to gather and evaluate information that will help them identify possible material misstatement. One potential audit procedure is to analyse a company's cost variances, which might be caused by error or fraud.

REQUIRED

(a) For each of the following variances, describe *in detail* a possible error that could cause a variance even when no variance actually exists.
   (i) Direct materials price
   (ii) Direct materials efficiency
   (iii) Direct labour price
   (iv) Direct labour efficiency
   (v) Variable overhead spending
   (vi) Variable overhead efficiency
   (vii) Fixed overhead budget
   (viii) Production volume

(b) Suppose a material amount of raw materials inventory theft took place during the past year. Which of the variances in part (a) would most likely reflect this fraud? Explain.

(c) Discuss possible reasons why variance analysis might not uncover the theft described in part (b).

(d) Suppose a production manager fraudulently entered a fictitious employee into the payroll system during the past year. The fictitious employee's salaries are deposited directly into a bank account that is then accessed by the production manager. Which of the variances in part (a) would most likely reflect this fraud? Explain.

(e) During the current year, suppose an accountant accidentally records a large equipment repair as an addition to property, plant, and equipment. Assume that equipment repairs and equipment depreciation are both recorded in variable overhead costs. Which of the variances in part (a) would most likely reflect this accounting error? Discuss how this error would affect the variance during the current year. Discuss how this error would affect the variance during the next year.

(f) Suppose an entity's managers want to report higher earnings on the income statement. Describe in detail a possible way that the managers could improve reported earnings by intentionally misapplying accounting principles for variances.

Performance evaluation and compensation

IN BRIEF

Owners commonly use accounting information to measure performance, monitor managers' actions and motivate decisions that are in the owners' interest. Similarly, managers use accounting information to measure, monitor and motivate the actions of employees. Before managers or employees can be held accountable for the results of their decisions and actions, their rights and responsibilities need to be defined. Then return on investment, residual income, economic value added or other measures can be used to gauge and reward performance. In large entities, resources may be transferred internally from one department to another. When prices for these transfers are set appropriately, goal congruence is strengthened and may increase the value of the organisation. However, transfer prices can encourage suboptimal decisions that may be beneficial at the divisional level, but not at the organisational level.

After studying this chapter, you should be able to:

1. Explain agency theory.

2. Explain how decision-making responsibility and authority relate to performance evaluation.

3. Explain how responsibility centres are used to measure, monitor and motivate performance.

4. Outline the uses and limitations of return on investment, residual income and economic value added for monitoring performance.

5. Outline how compensation is used to motivate performance.

6. State alternative prices used for transferring goods and services within an entity.

7. Calculate transfer prices and outline the issues associated with transfer pricing.

Performance and pay at a leading telco

The pursuit by Western governments around the world to privatise previously government-operated entities tends to attract much interest from the financial press and community at large. In Australia, the telecommunications giant Telstra is one such entity. For a number of years it has operated as a partially privatised entity; until late 2006 the government held 51 per cent of the equity in the telco. More than 50 per cent of these shares were sold to private investors in the most recent sell-down of government-owned shares in 2006. With privatisation came the deregulation of the telecommunications market, leaving Telstra to face competition in some of its key businesses for the first time.

At the end of each financial year attention is focused on the compensation paid to senior executives of companies, and Telstra is no exception. There are increasing calls for compensation paid to senior executives, with particular emphasis on payments to the chief executive officer (CEO) to be linked to company performance. As one of Australia's largest companies, Telstra's annual reports are studied each year to assess the levels and structure of the compensation. Consequently, the $8.7 million paid to Telstra CEO Sol Trujillo in the 2005–06 financial year attracted much attention. It is not so much the amount that the critics attacked but rather the $1.5 million short-term cash bonus paid for the successful delivery of the new business strategy and transformation plan for the entity. Moreover, Telstra paid out $54 million to consultants to develop the plan. But the criticisms go further to question some of the fundamentals of the pay structure.

When speaking of performance measures, Australian treasurer Peter Costello said: 'Quite frequently, what companies do is have a bonus for a chief executive who outperforms the market … they don't have a bonus for just increasing share price' (Sainsbury 2006). With respect to the nature and structure of short-term incentives paid wholly in cash for the first time, telecommunications analyst Gary Pinge suggested that 'there is a risk of management making short-term decisions in order to get maximum short-term incentive payouts' (Sainsbury & Maiden 2006).

Nevertheless, the chairman of Telstra defended the pay packet, claiming: 'Mr Trujillo's incentive payment for 2005–06 recognised that he led a detailed review of the company's problems; developed a comprehensive multi-year plan for the most rapid and dramatic ever transformation of a telecommunications company worldwide; assembled the resources including executive talent to execute the plan and achieved major milestones in the first year' (Sainsbury 2006).

It was not just the CEO's pay that attracted criticism. Despite a drop in profitability, Telstra executives received more than 70 per cent of the maximum possible short-term incentive. The company's remuneration report suggests that the short-term incentives are based on company EBIT (earnings before interest and tax), cost savings, the number of sites equipped with 3G technology, the share of the broadband market and individual accountabilities. With an array of both financial and non-financial measures combined with time lags for specific decisions, it is not always likely that the apparent reward will match the visible performance.

Sources: Information from Sainsbury, M 2006, 'Trujillo spends big for bonus — Telstra chief's $1.5m reward after paying $54m for report', *The Australian*, 28 September; Sainsbury, M & Maiden, S 2006, 'Trujillo's $8.7m bonanza queried', *The Australian*, 27 September; Uren, D 2006, 'Bonus buffer for Telstra elite', *The Australian*, 11 September.

Issues from this scene setter to look for in the chapter include:

- Issues associated with the selection of appropriate performance measures to evaluate performance at all levels within an entity.

- The structure of reward systems.

- The role of agency theory in reward systems.

- How longer-term incentives are developed.

- How pay to senior executives and divisional managers is linked to performance.

- The behavioural influence of performance measures.

Decision-making authority and responsibility

As entities grow in size, top managers have an increasingly difficult time maintaining control over decision making. On the positive side, many entities benefit from the wide range of expertise among employees. However, as decision making is dispersed, mechanisms must be established for measuring, monitoring and motivating decisions throughout the organisation.

Agency theory

Agency theory is an analytical framework that examines these potential conflicts between owners and managers, and between managers and employees; Within agency theory, the two types of information consumers are principals and agents. **Principals** hire agents to make

for both their effort and the quality of their decisions. Employees carry out tasks that result from these decisions and are held responsible for their effort and compliance with top-down decisions. Therefore, individual and team efforts require close monitoring to determine their contributions toward success. Managers use variance and productivity reports to gauge employee (individual and team) efforts.

In decentralised entities, decision making occurs throughout management levels and in the field. Employees in lower levels are held responsible for their efforts and the quality of their decisions. Therefore, accounting systems are used to provide decision-making information for all levels, from management to front-line employees. Broader accounting measures related to overall financial performance are then used to measure and monitor performance.

Responsibility accounting is the process of assigning authority and responsibility to managers of subunits, and then measuring and evaluating their performance. Under responsibility accounting, managers are held responsible only for factors over which they have control. **Responsibility centres** are subunits (segments, divisions, departments) in which managers are accountable for specific types of operating activities. Four common types of responsibility centres are cost centres, revenue centres, profit centres and investment centres. Figure 11.4 provides specific examples of each responsibility centre and examples of performance measures that are likely to be used in these centres. It is important to note that regardless of the type of responsibility centre, the performance measure(s) selected to evaluate performance need to reflect the organisational goals and strategic directions of the entity and the responsibility centre. Performance measures influence behaviour and decision making. Poorly selected performance measures may encourage poor decision making by managers of responsibility centres.

Responsibility centres	Examples	Performance measures used
Cost centres	■ Manufacturing departments ■ Service production departments, such as road maintenance for a city ■ Support departments, such as accounting and billing departments in a hospital ■ Discretionary cost centres, such as marketing and research and development	■ Cost budgets and variances ■ Comparisons to benchmark cost per unit or service ■ Efficiency measures (days to close, number of new products) ■ Industry benchmarks (e.g. R&D as a percentage of sales)
Revenue centres	■ Travel agencies ■ Sales departments for manufacturers	■ Revenue budgets and variances ■ Growth in revenues ■ Customer satisfaction
Profit centres	■ Retail sales outlets for clothing, books or restaurants ■ Corporate divisions and departments responsible for revenues and costs	■ Revenue and cost budgets and variances ■ Accounting earnings such as operating income or earnings before or after taxes
Investment centres	■ Corporate divisions and business segments responsible for investment decisions	■ Return on investment (ROI) ■ Residual income ■ Economic value added (EVA)

FIGURE 11.4 ■ Examples of responsibility centres and performance measures

Cost centres

In **cost centres**, managers are held responsible only for the costs under their control. Some cost centres provide support services that are relatively easy to monitor because their outputs are measurable. Cost centres are also used for subunits that produce goods or services eventually sold by others. Managers in these cost centres are responsible for producing their goods or services efficiently.

Cost centre managers are expected either to minimise costs for a certain level of output or to maximise output for a certain level of cost. Cost centre performance is measured and monitored several ways. Some organisations rely on cost budgets and variances. Measures of other factors such as quality and timeliness of delivery are also relevant.

Revenue centres

In **revenue centres**, managers are held responsible for the revenues under their control. Revenue centres frequently sell products from manufacturing subunits. Managers are expected to maximise sales. If the manager in a revenue centre is responsible for setting prices, gross revenues can be used as a performance measure. If corporate headquarters rather than the manager sets prices, then managers' performance can be evaluated using a combination of sales volumes measured in units and sales mix. Many organisations treat their sales departments as revenue centres, and reward employees based on sales generated. In not-for-profit entities, fundraising activities might be treated as a revenue centre.

Profit centres

Managers in **profit centres** are held responsible for both revenues and costs under their control. Profit centres produce and sell goods or services, and may include one or several cost centres. Profit centre managers are responsible for decisions about inputs, product mix, pricing, and the volume of goods or services produced. Because profit centres include both revenues and costs, performance is typically measured using some combination of revenue and cost measures. Not-for-profit entities tend to use revenue and cost budgets and variances as performance measures, although some focus managers' attention on operating margins when performance is poor. For-profit entities use some measure of profits such as accounting earnings.

Investment centres

Managers of **investment centres** are held responsible for the revenues, costs and investments under their control. Investments include any assets related to the investment centre, such as fixed assets, inventory, intangible assets and accounts receivable. Investment centres resemble profit centres, where profitability is related to the assets used to generate the profits.

Because investment centres include revenues, costs and investment, performance measures need to address all of these factors. We will shortly learn about three commonly used measures: return on investment (ROI), residual income and economic value added (EVA).

Responsibility centres and suboptimal decision making

Top managers use judgment to decide the best types of responsibility centres for the entity. The choices depend on the size of the organisation, the nature of operations and the organisational structure. Ideally, responsibility centres should reduce agency costs by holding managers responsible for decisions over which they have authority. For example, accounting departments are often viewed as cost centres because their managers have authority primarily for the expenditure of resources. Similarly, business segments are generally treated as investment centres because segment managers have authority over revenues, costs and investment.

Nevertheless, responsibility centre accounting sometimes leads to suboptimal decision making. Too often managers make decisions that are in the best interests of their own responsibility centres, but suboptimal for the entity as a whole. Each type of responsibility centre has a specific set of agency problems. Managers in cost centres focus on minimising costs and maximising efficiency, which can lead to declines in quality and delivery time-liness. In turn, sales could drop and the overall entity suffers. Similarly, revenue centre managers, who are typically rewarded for increasing revenues, may fail to consider product contribution margins and inappropriately emphasise less-profitable products. These managers have incentives to offer discounts and generous payment terms that reduce overall profit-ability. In profit centres, managers are encouraged to stress short-run profits by cutting costs — such as maintenance, advertising, and research and development — that benefit long-term performance. Similarly in investment centres, managers may reduce investment to increase short-term results. Or, they may invest in projects that are more or less risky than is appropri-ate for the entity. To address these agency problems, appropriate performance measures and reward systems need to be implemented. The impact of using different financial performance measures on management decision making will be illustrated the following section using investment centres.

Income-based performance evaluation

Investment centres are common in large decentralised organisations, and provide a useful vehicle to demonstrate the behaviour-influencing focus of alternative performance measures. Because managers are responsible for costs and revenues, as well as for investments, the measures used for monitoring and motivating purposes typically include the return and the size of investment. Three measures commonly used to evaluate investment centre performance are:

- return on investment
- residual income
- economic value added (EVA).

Return on investment

Return on investment (ROI) is the ratio of operating income to average operating assets. Operating income is calculated as earnings before interest and taxes (EBIT). Operating assets include all assets used in the production of goods or services, such as cash, accounts receiv-able, inventory, and plant and equipment. Non-operating assets (such as investments in other entities, or property and equipment currently rented to other entities) may be excluded from this calculation. When evaluating the entire entity's performance, all assets would be included because owners want to evaluate their return based on the entire investment. But when evalu-ating the performance of a subunit, judgment is used to determine which assets should be included. Any assets included should be under the control of the managers being evaluated. The average of beginning and ending operating assets is calculated for this component for two main reasons. First, the measure is intended to capture operations over a period of time, not just at the end of the time period. Second, the measure could be manipulated by temporarily decreasing investment at the time performance is measured.

ROI is used to evaluate investment centre performance. It can be compared across subunits within a single organisation, among a group of entities within an industry, and within a single organisation across time. In addition, ROI can be decomposed into two components that provide additional information about performance. ROI is decomposed by multiplying both the numerator and denominator by revenue and then rearranging terms:

$$\textbf{ROI = Operating income} \div \textbf{Average operating assets}$$
$$= (\textbf{Operating income} \div \textbf{Average operating assets}) \times (\textbf{Revenue} \div \textbf{Revenue})$$
$$= (\textbf{Revenue} \div \textbf{Average operating assets}) \times (\textbf{Operating income} \div \textbf{Revenue})$$

Because revenue divided by average operating assets represents investment turnover, and operating income divided by revenue represents the return on sales, we can now rewrite the ROI formula as:

$$\textbf{ROI = Investment turnover} \times \textbf{Return on sales}$$

The decomposition of ROI into investment turnover and return on sales is often referred to as *DuPont analysis*. The method originated at the global science company DuPont Company in the early 1900s so that results from a wider range of business activities could be compared. Investment turnover is a measure of the sales generated by each dollar invested in operating assets. Return on sales measures managers' abilities to control the operating expenses related to sales during a period. This decomposition focuses attention on the role that assets play in generating revenues and the role that increased revenues and decreased costs play in generating profits. Improvement in ROI occurs when sales increase and costs do not increase proportionately (some cost is fixed), when costs are reduced for a given level of sales, or when investment decreases for a given level of income. In this manner, ROI provides managers guidance about factors that improve performance (see comprehensive example 1).

Comprehensive example 1

Return on investment

Computer Wizards is an Australian company that produces and sells computer monitors nationally and internationally. Jason Black is responsible for New Zealand operations and Cecilia Earnhart manages the Australian division. Following is information about two divisions.

	New Zealand division	Australian division
Average operating assets	$2 000 000	$200 000
Operating income	$500 000	$60 000

The top managers of Computer Wizards measure the performance of its divisions using ROI. Following are the calculations for each division.

$$\textbf{New Zealand's ROI = \$500 000} \div \textbf{\$2 000 000 = 25\%}$$

$$\textbf{Australian ROI = \$60 000} \div \textbf{\$200 000 = 30\%}$$

Jason was recently hired from outside the company to improve operations in the New Zealand division. One of his objectives is to achieve an ROI at least as high as the

Australian division. Given the New Zealand division's sales of $5 000 000, Jason decomposes the ROI as follows.

$$\text{Return on sales} = \$500\,000 \div \$5\,000\,000 = 10\%$$

$$\text{Investment turnover} = \$5\,000\,000 \div \$2\,000\,000 = 2.5 \text{ times}$$

$$\text{ROI} = 10\% \times 2.5 = 25\%$$

This decomposition highlights three general ways he can increase ROI: increase sales, decrease costs or decrease investment in operating assets. Jason decides to investigate these alternatives.

Increasing ROI

One alternative is to focus primarily on increased sales. The New Zealand division currently has idle capacity, and Jason would like to emphasise a new group of products. He believes that current capacity can support an increase in sales of $600 000 without requiring additional investment. The increased sales would increase operating income by $116 000. The expected return on sales would then be

$$\$616\,000 \div \$5\,600\,000 = 11\%$$

and investment turnover would be

$$\$5\,600\,000 \div \$2\,000\,000 = 2.8 \text{ times}$$

leading to an improved ROI slightly higher than that of the Australian division:

$$\$616\,000 \div \$2\,000\,000 = 30.8\% = 11\% \times 2.8$$

Alternatively, Jason could focus on reducing expenses. He believes that manufacturing costs could be reduced by as much as $100 000. He would implement this plan using kaizen costing; that is, by organising a team with members from marketing, accounting and engineering to analyse production activities and identify non-value-added activities that could be eliminated. Also, the products and manufacturing processes could be redesigned to reduce the number of parts or processes. If the team is successful and expenses are reduced by $100 000, operating income would be $600 000 instead of $500 000. This plan alone could increase return on sales to

$$\$600\,000 \div \$5\,000\,000 = 12\%$$

and ROI would equal that of the Australian division:

$$12\% \times 2.5 = 30\%$$

Jason considers one more approach to increase ROI. He can reduce the New Zealand division's investment in operating assets. He knows that internal processes are inefficient; inventory and work in process are built up throughout different manufacturing areas. He would like to implement cellular production and just-in-time inventory practices. These modifications would allow the division to sell a small building currently in use. He believes that these actions would reduce operating assets to $1 667 000. The investment turnover would then be

$$\$5\,000\,000 \div \$1\,667\,000 = 3 \text{ times}$$

and ROI would be

$$10\% \times 3 = 30\%$$

Jason knows that increasing sales, reducing costs and changing production processes are all worthy long-term goals, but it will take a year or more to see the results of any of these plans. He would prefer to increase ROI within a shorter timeframe. Recently a competitor made an offer to sell the New Zealand division a component that is currently manufactured inhouse. If Jason purchases the component, operating earnings would decrease, but he could easily sell the small building because most of it houses the production facility for the component. Investment turnover would still be three times, but return on sales would drop to 9 per cent ($450 000 ÷ $5 000 000) and thereby increase ROI to 27 per cent.

Choosing a plan of action

Jason decides to discuss his options with Renee Forsyth, the chief financial officer for Computer Wizards. All of the plans he is considering require a great deal of time and effort. He believes that the strategies are sound but is uncertain whether his expectations can be met. An increase in sales depends in part on the continuing upswing of the economy. Cost reductions take time and concentrated effort on the part of employees. Changing the manufacturing process could take several years because a new floor plan would have to be laid out, teams would have to be established and work would be disrupted while implementing the new lines. Furthermore, the employees might need several months to work efficiently under the new system. The easiest choice is to outsource, and Jason knows that outsourcing would improve his ROI in the short run. However, he believes that focusing on inhouse manufacturing cost reductions would be a better strategy for Computer Wizards in the long run. The company's use of ROI to measure performance discourages this type of strategy, so Jason wonders whether a different performance measure could be adopted that would better reward behaviour to benefit the overall entity.

Advantages and disadvantages of ROI

A division's ROI is easily compared with internal and external benchmarks and with other divisions' returns on investment. Holding managers responsible for some level of ROI reduces the tendency of managers to overinvest in projects. Another advantage of ROI is that its components motivate managers to increase sales, decrease costs and minimise asset investments.

However, ROI also discourages managers from investing in projects that reduce the division's ROI, even though they might improve the ROI for the overall entity or have only a short-term negative effect on a division's ROI. Suppose Jason had an opportunity to invest $1 750 000 in a project that would generate sales of $2 500 000 and a return on sales of 10 per cent (same as the original assumptions), or $250 000 operating income per year. The division's ROI including this investment would be

$$\text{Investment turnover} = \$7\,500\,000 \div 3\,750\,000 = 2 \text{ times}$$

$$\text{ROI} = 10\% \times 2 = 20\%$$

Even though the investment reduces the division's ROI, Computer Wizards forgoes $250 000 if the project is not undertaken. If the level of risk and the return are comparable to projects from other divisions, Computer Wizards would prefer the benefits from this investment.

Another disadvantage of ROI is that it does not incorporate measures of risk. Managers may increase ROI by investing in riskier projects, which often have higher returns than less-risky projects. If they are rewarded solely for increasing ROI, managers may undertake risky projects without considering the added risk to the entity. This problem arises more often when managers' time horizons are short; for example, when they are planning to retire or change jobs. In such cases, managers often prefer immediate improvements in performance measures.

Furthermore, when managers with short-time horizons evaluate projects based on ROI, they might inappropriately cut costs that provide long-term benefit for the entity. For example, they might cut research and development, maintenance or employee training; or forgo an investment project because of its short-term impact on divisional ROI.

ROI is typically calculated using financial accounting assets and income. Under financial accounting rules, assets are recorded at their original cost, and some intangible assets (such as brand name) are not recognised. These rules cause the investment in assets to be understated, particularly when the value of assets (such as property) has increased or when an entity has significant intangible assets. Understatements in assets cause ROI and investment turnover to be overstated. In addition, financial accounting rules measure revenues and costs in ways that can distort ROI. For example, overhead or support department costs might be allocated to a division using a method that does not reflect the division's use of resources. If the division's costs are understated or overstated, ROI will be distorted.

Residual income

Because of the disadvantages of ROI just described, some organisations prefer to use residual income to measure performance of subunits. **Residual income** measures the dollar amount of profits in excess of a required rate of return (commonly referred to as a capital charge). It is calculated as follows:

$$\frac{\text{Residual}}{\text{income}} = \frac{\text{Operating}}{\text{income}} - \left(\frac{\text{Required rate}}{\text{of return}} \times \frac{\text{Average}}{\text{operating assets}} \right)$$

Many entities set a minimum return expectation for operations and new investments. Residual income takes this expectation into consideration; it is the difference between actual operating income and the required income, given the entity's investment in operating assets and its required rate of return. The size of investment affects residual income less than ROI because it is used only to value the dollar amount of expected return, not as a denominator. Compared to ROI, residual income is less influenced by changes in investment. Comprehensive example 2 demonstrates the calculation of residual income.

Comprehensive example 2

Residual income

Jason consults with Renee, and they decide to investigate other performance measures. The first option they consider is residual income. The required rate of return for the company is 10 per cent. Given the investment in operating assets, the required dollar amount of return for each division is as follows:

	New Zealand	Australia
Average operating assets	$2 000 000	$200 000
Required rate of return	10%	10%
Required return	$ 200 000	$ 20 000

Residual income is calculated as follows:

	New Zealand	Australia
Operating income	$500 000	$60 000
Required return (capital charge)	200 000	20 000
Residual income	$300 000	$40 000

Renee explains that the New Zealand division provides Computer Wizards with $300 000 in income above and beyond the required return. However, as they discuss the value of residual income as a performance measure, Jason suggests that it has some of the same problems as ROI because it is still based on operating income. In addition, Renee cannot compare results in the New Zealand division to Australia's because of the size difference in the two divisions. Therefore, they decide to consider other alternatives.

Advantages and disadvantages of residual income

The use of residual income does not penalise investment in projects with lower returns than current project returns. Suppose the New Zealand division invests $1 750 000 in new assets that generate annual sales of $2 500 000 and operating income of 10 per cent ($250 000). If this project is undertaken, the New Zealand division residual income will be

Operating income ($500 000 + $250 000)	$750 000
Required return [($2 000 000 + $1 750 000) × 10%]	375 000
Residual income	$375 000

Because the project is expected to increase residual income by $75 000 ($375 000 − $300 000), managers would be motivated to invest in it. In general, when residual income is used as a performance measure, managers are willing to invest in any projects with returns equal to or greater than the required rate of return.

However, residual income has its own problems. Because it is an absolute dollar value, larger subunits are more likely to have larger residual incomes. For Computer Wizards, the New Zealand division's residual income is much greater than that of the Australian division. As a result, managers find it difficult to compare performance across units.

A disadvantage it shares with ROI is that residual income increases as investment and costs decrease (holding sales constant). Therefore, managers may cut costs such as research and development, maintenance, or employee training that likely have long-term benefits for the entity.

Another problem with residual income occurs if senior managers from each subunit estimate their own required rate of return; they have incentives to set a required rate of return that is too low. In turn, a low required rate of return encourages managers to invest in less-profitable projects. They may also invest in less-risky projects and forgo riskier projects that would be profitable for the overall entity. Because operating income is measured using financial accounting information, residual income suffers from the same earnings-related problems as ROI.

Economic value added

Economic value added (EVA®) is a type of residual income that incorporates a number of adjustments to reduce the disadvantages produced by residual income.[1] Many different entities use EVA, including Telstra and Coca-Cola. The basic EVA calculation follows.

$$\text{EVA} = \frac{\text{Adjusted after-tax}}{\text{operating income}} - \left[\binom{\text{Weighted average}}{\text{cost of capital}} \times \left(\frac{\text{Adjusted}}{\text{total assets}} - \frac{\text{Current}}{\text{liabilities}} \right) \right]$$

The weighted average cost of capital (WACC) is calculated by analysing all sources of invested funds, including both debt and equity financing (valued as the opportunity cost to investors). It is the after-tax cost of all long-term financing for the entity or division. With EVA, each division can use its actual cost of capital, taking into consideration the industry and risk characteristics.

The adjustments made to develop the EVA calculation include substituting after-tax operating income for EBIT, which is consistent with using the (after-tax) weighted average cost of capital and also gives managers incentives to reduce taxes. Analysts and consultants recommend that organisations choose among 160 other adjustments to provide managers with incentives specific to the entity. One purpose of adjusting financial accounting income and assets is to minimise suboptimal decision making.

Measures used for internal purposes need not follow accounting standards or **generally accepted accounting principles (GAAP)**, which are a set of accounting methods and disclosures typically used to prepare financial statements for external parties. Instead, the measures are created to reflect economic costs and benefits over time. For example, research and development costs, which must be recognised immediately as an expense under GAAP, are often capitalised for EVA calculations. This adjustment encourages managers to invest in research and development projects that have long-term value for the entity. Similarly, long-term leases accounted for as operating leases under GAAP are often treated as capital leases for EVA calculations. This adjustment reduces managers' incentives to use operating leases to artificially understate the entity's investment in assets. They are then encouraged to make long-term asset acquisition decisions based on the best alternative for the organisation, rather than on their financial accounting treatment. The calculation of EVA is demonstrated in comprehensive example 3.

Comprehensive example 3

Economic value added

Jason and Renee next consider the use of EVA at Computer Wizards, and calculate EVA for each division. Jason develops the following information:

	New Zealand	Australia
Total assets	$2 000 000	$200 000
Operating income	$500 000	$60 000
Weighted average cost of capital	7.2%	10%
Current liabilities	$20 000	$5 000
After-tax operating income	$300 000	$40 000
Tax rate	40%	33.33%

Jason and Renee first calculate EVA without any adjustments beyond income taxes:

$$EVA = \frac{\text{Adjusted after-tax}}{\text{operating income}} - \left[\frac{\text{Weighted average}}{\text{cost of capital}} \times \left(\frac{\text{Total}}{\text{assets}} \times \frac{\text{Current}}{\text{liabilities}} \right) \right]$$

EVA New Zealand:

After-tax operating income	$300 000
WACC × (Total assets – Current liabilities)	
[7.2% × ($2 000 000 – $20 000)]	142 560
	$ 157 440

EVA Australia:

After-tax operating income	$40 000
WACC × (Total assets – Current liabilities)	
[10% × ($200 000 – $5 000)]	19 500
	$20 500

Because EVA incorporates income taxes, incentive is provided to minimise taxes paid. In addition, the weighted average cost of capital is a more realistic capital charge than managers' subjective choices of required rates of return. The Australian division operates in a riskier business environment than the New Zealand division, which is reflected in its higher WACC.

Comparison of ROI, residual income and EVA

After completing these computations, Jason and Renee decide to examine the rankings of the two divisions using these three measures. Under ROI, the Australian division (30 per cent) appears to perform better than the New Zealand division (25 per cent). But under residual income and EVA, the New Zealand division outperforms the Australian division. They recognise that size has an effect on both residual income and EVA. Renee decides to use both ROI and EVA as performance measures. Jason suggests that Renee also consider the use of non-financial performance measures. He believes that increasing customer satisfaction should increase financial performance because repeat and new customers will increase revenues. Renee agrees that by focusing on customer satisfaction, any potential customer-related problems are likely to be discovered sooner, and agrees to give the measure further consideration.

Advantages and disadvantages of EVA

Several advantages of EVA result from the various adjustments made to personalise the measure to each entity. These adjustments provide specific incentives that align the goals of managers with owners. However, some disadvantages need to be considered as well. For example, the appropriateness of the specific cost of capital for a division or entity is a matter of judgment, as is the level of risk that has been incorporated. The adjustments are also a matter of judgment. We do not know how to perfectly measure economic revenues, costs or assets, and a variety of acceptable ways provide different incentives. Because EVA is so complex, consulting entities often must be used to determine the appropriate adjustments. This process can be expensive and time-consuming.

Motivating performance with compensation

To reduce agency costs, organisations use compensation contracts that provide incentives for agents to increase the value of the entity. These contracts commonly include cash-based bonuses, and equity-based awards such as shares and share options. Earnings and growth targets are often set as goals in these compensation packages. The compensation package for senior executives in companies (such as the CEO) is commonly set by the board of directors under advice from the company's remuneration committee. These packages are commonly structured to include components that are both fixed (such as base pay) and variable (such as incentives in the forms of cash or equity based on performance).

Bonus system incentives

As entities increase in size, more sophisticated incentive packages are required to align the goals of employees and owners. Compensation contracts can be based on accounting earnings; other financial measures such as ROI, residual income and EVA; and non-financial measures such as customer satisfaction or market share. Examples of financial performance measures are shown in figure 11.5, along with examples of benchmarks or targets and the rewards that could be used to motivate behaviour. A number of key variables of interest exist to ultimately determine the compensation received by a senior executive. These include: the level of base pay, the measure(s) used to set the target performance, the specific targets set, and the form of reward (such as cash or equity-based). Equity-based rewards commonly include shares or share options. Share options give the holder the right to buy shares at some time in the future at a predetermined price. In recent years, the use of share options in executive compensation contracts has attracted criticism essentially due to the use of low targets, the size of the option reward, and the alleged abuse of some of the practices associated with options (such as back-dating the predetermined price).

Financial measure	Example of benchmark or target	Example of reward
ROI	A set percentage	Cash bonus or equity-related reward
EVA	Dollar target or percentage change	Cash bonus or equity-related reward
Operating income or growth in income	Dollar target or percentage growth target	Cash bonus or profit sharing
Cost savings	Cost reduction of a set percentage (e.g. 5 per cent)	Gain sharing — employees receive a percentage of the savings
Revenue growth	A set percentage	Cash bonus plus paid family vacation to award ceremony at resort destination

FIGURE 11.5 ■ Financial performance measures and examples of targets and rewards

Compensation contracts often include a base salary and bonuses. In the largest Australian companies, bonuses typically make up 40 per cent or more of the total compensation for top executives. Bonuses may be a combination of cash, shares, share options and deferred compensation (salary or bonuses paid in the future, often after retirement). CEO compensation attracts controversial press coverage, particularly when CEOs achieve pay increases at a time of declining or stagnant company performance. While a wide variation exists in compensation packages among executives, a recent study in Australia suggests that for the preceding five years, CEO base salaries increased 73 per cent while total shareholder returns increased 42 per cent.[2]

Long-term versus short-term incentives

For many years, compensation practices were criticised because they were based on accounting earnings. In addition to the problems already described, managers could also reduce the level of investment in assets such as equipment, thereby reducing depreciation expense and in turn increasing accounting earnings. However, the reduced investment negatively affects future earnings if sales are forgone because of limited capacity or increases in maintenance and downtime costs for old equipment that should have been replaced. In addition, manufacturers sometimes increase revenues by forcing their customers to carry large inventories. These types of actions may increase short-term earnings but often have negative effects on long-term earnings potential.

There have been attempts to focus the attention of executives on the long-term performance of the entity. This can be achieved in a number of ways, although equity-based rewards have been common vehicles. Whether the compensation is partly structured to focus on the long-term depends on two key factors:

1. *The time horizon relating to the target measure.* For example, if a reward is contingent on meeting a ROI target or an earnings per share target based on a one-year performance, then the focus is more short term. On the other hand, if the same measures are based on a three- or five-year average, then there is more focus on longer-term outcomes in the use of the measure itself.

2. *The 'lasting' nature of the reward itself.* For example, compared to cash, equity-based rewards such as shares and share options are viewed as having a more lasting effect. Executives holding shares or share options are therefore more likely to take actions that will (where possible) enhance the share price.

To focus managers more on the long term, many companies increased the use of equity-based compensation. Share options, in particular, became popular during the 1980s and 1990s. Compensation tied to the value of equity was viewed as a way to encourage managers and other employees to focus on increasing the long-term value of the company and addressing the agency problem discussed earlier. It was assumed that giving executives the opportunity to become substantial shareholders in the company would motivate them to act in the best interests of that company. Entities around the globe have followed this practice of incorporating significant levels of equity-based rewards into compensation contracts. More recently, however, there has been some backlash against this practice, predominantly caused by the high-profile corporate collapses where questionable corporate behaviour has been in part linked to the large equity holdings of executives. The link is based on the temptation of executives to mask problems through creative accounting practices, resulting in the reporting of inflated profits with the expectation of maintaining or increasing share price values.

As already mentioned, practices across companies are varied but most have compensation structures in line with shareholder and market expectations. Nevertheless, each year there are usually some controversial practices that attract the attention of the financial press. For example, the decision by the Coles Myer board to adjust downwards the original targets relating to earnings per share in the 2005–06 financial year attracted criticism from some of its own key shareholders.[3] Shareholders at Lend Lease were critical of the decision of the company's board to pay a $2.2 million bonus to the CEO despite the performance target — that Lend Lease's total returns outstrip the ASX average for the previous three years — not being met.[4]

Transfer pricing

When one business unit relies on other units within an entity for goods or services, a problem arises that affects the measurement of financial performance. Suppose Porcelain & More, a kitchen and bath fixtures manufacturer, operates with three profit centres: fixtures, sinks and tubs. Sinks and tubs are sold as kits that include fixtures. In their kits, the sink and tub profit centres use the taps and handles produced by the fixture profit centre. Thus, these fixtures are transferred from one department to the other two departments, and the fixtures need to be priced appropriately. A **transfer price** is the price used to record revenue and cost when goods or services are transferred between responsibility centres in an entity.

Transfer prices and conflicts among managers

When compensation is tied to the financial performance of subunits, managers tend to overlook their contribution to the entire organisation and focus instead on how decisions affect their subunit's financial performance. Conflicts arise among managers, leading to suboptimal operating decisions.

Suppose that the fixtures department at Porcelain & More sells fixtures for a market price of $20 to external customers. When sold externally, the fixtures department receives credit in its operating income for the entire contribution margin. How should the fixtures be priced when fixtures are transferred internally to the sink and tub departments? The manager of the fixtures department would like to recognise the same revenue that is recorded for external sales. However, managers from the sink and tub departments would like to record in their books only the variable cost for the fixtures that are internally transferred. They have legitimate claims, because their departments are responsible for selling kits that include fixtures. The managers from the three departments are in conflict with each other. All of them would prefer to show high profits and therefore would prefer to recognise most of the contribution for each product sold.

The following chart shows prices and sales for last year. Assume that the fixtures department has plenty of capacity and sells 37 000 sets of fixtures. Of these, 20 000 sets go to the external market, 12 000 to the sinks department and 5000 to the tubs department.

	Fixtures	Sinks	Tubs	Total
Units sold	37 000	12 000	5000	54 000
Market price	$20	$75	$150	
Variable cost	$10	$30	$75	

Each department's contribution margin, assuming that fixtures are transferred at market price, is summarised as follows:

	Fixtures	Sinks	Tubs	Total
External revenue	$ 400 000	$ 900 000	$ 750 000	$ 2 050 000
Transfer price	340 000	(240 000)	(100 000)	0
Other variable costs	(370 000)	(360 000)	(375 000)	(1 105 000)
Contribution margin	$ 370 000	$ 300 000	$ 275 000	$ 945 000

The external market demand is for only 20 000 sets of fixtures. Suppose the sink and tub department managers insist on using the variable cost of $10 for the transfer price. The following calculations summarise each department's contribution margin if all departments record variable cost as the transfer price for fixtures.

	Fixtures	Sinks	Tubs	Total
Revenue	$400 000	$900 000	$750 000	$2 050 000
Transfer price	170 000	(120 000)	(50 000)	0
Other variable costs	(370 000)	(360 000)	(375 000)	(1 105 000)
Contribution margin	$200 000	$420 000	$325 000	$ 945 000

Notice that the total contribution margin to Porcelain & More does not change under either alternative — it is $945 000 regardless of the transfer price policy. If the fixtures department always has excess capacity, its managers may be willing to sell at variable cost because they have no other outlets for their fixtures. However, they would prefer a transfer price that includes some portion of fixed costs, because fixture production requires the use of resources such as equipment and supervisor time. If the fixtures department has no excess capacity (that is, if every set of fixtures produced can be sold on the open market), its managers will be unwilling to sell internally when the transfer price is below market price.

Now assume that the transfer price is set at the market price of $20. The fixtures department has excess capacity, but sinks and tubs can buy fixtures from a supplier who sells them for $18 a set, although the quality is slightly lower than those manufactured by the fixtures department. The fixtures department continues to sell 20 000 units externally. Sinks and tubs purchase from the outside supplier. Following is the contribution margin for each department.

	Fixtures	Sinks	Tubs	Total
Revenue	$400 000	$900 000	$750 000	$2 050 000
Fixtures purchase cost	0	(216 000)	(90 000)	306 000
Other variable costs	(200 000)	(360 000)	(375 000)	(935 000)
Contribution margin	$200 000	$324 000	$285 000	$ 809 000

Compared to the results with fixtures transferred internally, the overall contribution margin for Porcelain & More is lower by $136 000 ($945 000 − $809 000). The difference is equal to the incremental cost to the entity of purchasing the fixtures externally versus manufacturing them internally: 17 000 units × ($18 − $10) = $136 000. In addition, the sinks and tubs are sold with lower-quality fixtures. Yet, when fixtures are purchased externally, managers in both the sink and tub departments appear to be better off when they are evaluated on the performance of their individual departments. A transfer price policy based on market price encourages the managers to make suboptimal decisions for the entity as a whole.

Setting an appropriate transfer price

The perfect transfer price would be the opportunity cost of transferring goods and services internally. If external demand is zero and the selling division has excess capacity, the transfer price would be the variable cost. This price is the minimum price the selling division would typically be willing to accept from an outside buyer when it has excess capacity. However, if capacity is limited and goods or services can be sold externally, then the opportunity cost would be the market price (commonly calculated as the variable cost plus any forgone contribution margin). To sell internally, the department forgoes an external sale and so should charge the market price.

Although the opportunity cost is the best transfer price policy, it is rarely used because the price would vary with capacity. Most managers prefer stable transfer prices across time. In addition, selling managers may regard a price equal to variable cost as unfair when excess capacity exists, because the purchasing department receives credit for the entire contribution margin for products that are essentially manufactured by both departments. Therefore, other transfer price polices are typically used.

The following methods are often used for setting transfer price policies in manufacturing and service organisations:

- cost based
- activity based
- dual rate
- negotiated
- market based.

Cost-based transfer prices

Cost-based transfer prices are based on the cost of the good or service transferred. Cost can be computed in different ways, ranging from variable costs to fully allocated costs. If a product has no external market because it is a subcomponent of another product, some type of cost-based transfer price is commonly used.

Suppose that the fixtures department of Porcelain & More usually produces about 40 000 sets of fixtures and incurs about $200 000 in manufacturing overhead cost during an accounting period. The average fixed cost per unit would be $5 ($200 000 ÷ 40 000 units). Under a full production cost transfer price policy, Porcelain & More could set a transfer price of $15 ($10 variable cost + $5 fixed cost). This transfer price allows each department to split the contribution margin that arises when fixtures are sold as part of sink and tub kits.

Cost-based transfer prices present several disadvantages. When products have an external market and departments are profit centres, the transfer price affects decisions about transferring internally or purchasing externally. This situation can lead to suboptimal decisions, such as the purchase of units from external providers shown in the earlier Porcelain & More example. In addition, when transfer prices include allocated fixed costs, managers in selling departments do not have as much incentive to reduce fixed costs. They can pass the responsibility for allocated fixed costs to another department through the transfer pricing policy.

Activity-based transfer prices

A variation of cost-based transfer prices is the use of **activity-based transfer prices**. Here, the purchasing unit is charged for the unit-level, batch-level and possibly some product-level costs for products transferred, plus an annual fixed fee that is a portion of the facility-level costs. Suppose the tubs department at Porcelain & More plans to buy enough fixtures internally so that it uses 20 per cent of fixture's capacity. Under activity-based transfer pricing, the tubs department could pay for the unit and batch costs of each fixture and also pay 20 per cent of the fixtures department facility-level costs. By making this lump sum payment, the tubs department essentially reserves some of the fixture department's capacity for units it will purchase internally.

An advantage of activity-based transfer pricing is that the purchasing department has an incentive to accurately project the number of units it will purchase internally. This accuracy enhances an entity's planning abilities. Suppose managers in the fixtures department believe that external sales will be forgone by selling 20 per cent of their fixtures to the tub department. Because they receive a fixed price from the tub department, they know ahead of time that they need to increase capacity to accommodate external sales. They can more easily plan for these changes.

However, because of uncertainty in demand, organisations may sometimes need to reallocate capacity to attain the highest contribution. In a changing business environment, departments should be allowed to subcontract with each other so that the departments with the best opportunities are using most of the capacity.

Market-based transfer prices

Market-based transfer prices are based on competitors' prices or on the supply-and-demand relationship. They are appropriate under a restrictive set of conditions. These conditions include the presence of a highly competitive market for the intermediate product so that the selling department can sell as much as it wants to outside customers and the purchasing department can buy as much as it wants from outside suppliers, all without affecting the price. These conditions are rarely met. However, when they are, the market price provides an objective value for intermediate products. The problem with market-based transfer prices is that information about underlying costs is not revealed, and this lack of information encourages suboptimal decision making, as illustrated in the Porcelain and More example.

Dual-rate transfer prices

Dual-rate transfer prices allow the selling department to be credited for the market price, and the purchasing department to be charged the variable cost. When financial statements are consolidated at the end of the accounting period, adjustments are made so that overall organisational profit is accurately reported. This method provides appropriate information and incentives when the selling department has excess capacity. Also, it is most similar to a policy that uses an opportunity cost for the transfer price. A disadvantage of the method is that it overstates profitability at the subunit level, and managers may believe that the entity as a whole is more profitable than it actually is.

Negotiated transfer prices

Negotiated transfer prices are based on an agreement reached between the managers of the selling and purchasing departments. This method ensures that both managers have full information about costs and market prices, and that the transfer price provides appropriate incentives. A disadvantage of this method is that it usually requires more time because both managers prefer more contribution margin. Managers' time is valuable to the organisation for other responsibilities, and negotiation time may not be a high priority for the organisation as a whole. Comprehensive example 4 demonstrates the application of negotiated transfer prices.

Comprehensive example 4

Negotiated transfer prices

The New Zealand division of Computer Wizards produces computer monitors. These monitors are sold on the open market for $110 each or the Australian division uses them as part of a complete computer package. When the monitor is transferred internally, the entire computer package gives the entity a contribution margin of $415 each. The entity currently uses market price plus shipping as a

transfer price. Jason is happy with this transfer price, but Cecelia has asked Renee to consider changing the policy, because her division shows lower earnings than it should. She would prefer to purchase monitors from Jason, but often purchases less-expensive and lower-quality monitors from an external vendor to improve her division's earnings.

The New Zealand division can produce 10 000 monitors per month and usually operates at 70 per cent capacity. The following data pertain to production at this level.

	Average cost
Direct materials	$25
Direct labour	15
Supplies	5
Total variable cost per monitor	45
Allocated fixed costs	50
Total average cost per monitor	$95

If a monitor is sold on the open market, the customer pays the shipping cost. The cost of shipping a monitor from New Zealand to Australia is about $10 each.

The New Zealand division is currently operating at 50 per cent of its capacity, substantially below normal. Jason would like to sell more monitors internally to help cover fixed costs. Both managers contact Renee, who tells them to negotiate a policy that is fair to both divisions. Jason would like to set a transfer price that is below the market price but above the variable cost, so that some of the fixed costs are covered by internal transfers. Cecelia would prefer to pay only the variable cost plus the shipping charge because the New Zealand division's fixed costs will not change if production increases, and workers would be idle part of the time without the internal transfers.

After negotiating for several weeks, the two managers go back to Renee for help. Renee has laid out the following information based on a selling price for the computer package of $950.

	Average cost
Direct materials	$240
Direct labour	75
Supplies	175
Total variable cost per monitor	490
Cost of monitor	110
Allocated fixed costs	$200
Total average cost per computer package	$800

Renee explains that, from Computer Wizard's perspective, the contribution margin on monitors sold externally is $65 ($110 − $45). When the monitor is transferred internally, the relevant cost to Computer Wizards is $45, the variable cost. The relevant contribution margin for the computer package is $415 ($950 − $490 − $45). When Cecelia purchases a monitor externally for $110, the contribution margin is $350 ($950 − $490 − $110). Therefore, corporate headquarters would prefer internal transfers over purchases from outside vendors.

Renee suggests that Cecelia pay Jason a flat amount to help cover fixed costs and also pay the variable cost for each monitor transferred. Jason agrees to this policy as long as the division operates with excess capacity. However, he points out that when the division lacks enough capacity to fill both external and internal orders, he will sell externally and forgo internal transfers to increase profits for the New Zealand division.

Renee calculates the difference in the entity-wide contribution margin when transferring monitors internally versus purchasing them externally at $65 ($415 − $350). This difference happens to be the same as the contribution margin for the New Zealand division when monitors are sold externally. Therefore, Jason and Cecelia are indifferent to whether sales take place internally or externally *when the New Zealand division is at capacity*. Meanwhile, both managers agree that developing a transfer price policy that suits not only both divisions but also the overall entity is more difficult than it first appeared.

Additional transfer price considerations

The preceding section addressed the incentives of managers for transfer prices between operating units. The following additional factors affect the choice of transfer prices.

International income taxes

For entities that do business internationally, the taxable location of profit is affected by transfer price policies. An organisation with subsidiaries located in high-tax and low-tax countries could potentially charge a high transfer price in the low-tax countries so that most of the contribution margin arises where taxes are lowest. To restrict entities' abilities to shift income in this manner, income tax regulations typically stipulate the use of market-based transfer prices. The details of international tax regulation are complex and beyond the scope of this textbook.

Transfer prices for support services

Many organisations set transfer prices for support services. Their objective is to motivate efficient use and cost-effective production of internal support services such as accounting, printing, human resources and purchasing. When support departments provide services without charge to user departments, the user departments tend to use the support services inefficiently. In turn, inefficient use tends to encourage support departments to grow unnecessarily large. Transfer prices can encourage more efficient use of support services.

Transfer prices are often based on fully allocated costs and therefore include allocations of fixed support department costs and allocations from other support departments. As a result, the transfer prices can be high. High transfer prices can encourage user departments to outsource the support services. As we learned in the Porcelain & More example, outsourcing is not always beneficial to the entity as a whole. Outsourcing can cause internal services to be duplicated, resulting in excess capacity and inefficient use of resources.

Setting transfer prices for internal services

Because top managers prefer to have support services used efficiently, they want to set transfer prices that motivate this behaviour. The best transfer price policy is an opportunity cost approach. Each department is charged an amount that reflects the value of any opportunities forgone by not using the service for its next best alternative use.

Suppose that Computer Wizards' production and assembly equipment needs routine maintenance to prevent downtime during regular hours of operation. The maintenance department schedules its repair and maintenance time during lunch hours and at the end of each production shift. Currently, the maintenance department is operating close to capacity. Other departments need to schedule non-routine tasks, such as painting walls and repairing damaged flooring, well in advance. If a department wants maintenance personnel to hang pictures in an office, the value of the opportunity forgone might be the cost of hiring a contractor to provide routine maintenance on equipment or to paint walls. However, if the maintenance department has extra capacity and workers are idle part of the time, the opportunity cost of hanging pictures would be zero.

Implementing a transfer price policy based on opportunity costs is problematic because opportunities change over time with changes in demand and capacity. In addition, finding and valuing alternative uses for some services can be difficult. Therefore, organisations use transfer price policies for internal services similar to those used for transferring goods. Cost-based transfer prices range from variable costs to fully allocated costs. Market-based transfer prices are set at amounts that would be paid if the service were outsourced.

Some entities establish a price per job for each task, keep prices low on jobs they want to have performed internally, and set prices high on jobs that are considered unnecessary or inappropriate. Suppose the managers of Computer Wizards believe that the maintenance personnel should not be hanging pictures. They could set the transfer price for hanging pictures high enough to discourage other departments from asking the maintenance department to perform this service.

Transfer of corporate overhead costs

Another type of transfer price occurs when corporate overhead costs are allocated to other responsibility centres. Managerial performance rewards based on accounting profits can stimulate much discussion between corporate headquarters and profit centre managers about whether allocating overhead costs is appropriate, and whether the allocation plan and allocation bases are appropriate. Under responsibility accounting, managers should be held accountable only for costs that they control. Because they have little or no control over corporate costs, they should not be held responsible for those costs in performance evaluations.

Many organisations do allocate corporate headquarters costs, however. Sometimes these are considered a corporate tax and are allocated based on revenues or profitability. In this manner, subunits operating under optimal circumstances absorb more overhead than subunits with poor results because of economic or industry conditions that are not under managers' control.

Summary

 Explain agency theory.

Principals and agents
Principals hire agents to make decisions for them and to act on their behalf.

Agency costs
Costs that arise when agents fail to act in the interest of principals:
- losses from poor decisions
- losses from incongruent goals
- monitoring costs

- goal alignment costs
- contracting costs.

Reducing agency costs

To measure, monitor and motivate performance:

- Assign responsibility for decision making.
- Link decision-making authority to performance measurement.
- Use income-based measures to assess performance.
- Motivate performance with compensation schemes.
- Establish prices for the transfer of goods and services within an organisation.

2 Explain how decision-making responsibility and authority relate to performance evaluation.

Centralised and decentralised entities

Advantages and disadvantages: see figure 11.3 on page 452.

General versus specific knowledge

Decision authority is related to the type of knowledge within an entity.

3 Explain how responsibility centres are used to measure, monitor and motivate performance.

Types of responsibility centres

- Cost centres
  - Discretionary cost centres
- Revenue centres
- Profit centres
- Investment centres

Issues

Reduce agency costs by holding managers responsible for the decisions over which they have authority. Measuring performance at the responsibility centre level can lead to suboptimal decisions.

4 Outline the uses and limitations of return on investment, residual income and economic value added for monitoring performance.

Return on investment (ROI)

$$\text{ROI} = \frac{\text{Operating income}}{\text{Average operating assets}}$$

DuPont analysis:

$$\text{ROI} = \left(\frac{\text{Sales}}{\text{Average operating assets}} \right) \times \left(\frac{\text{Operating income}}{\text{Sales}} \right)$$

$$\text{ROI} = \text{Investment turnover} \times \text{Return on sales}$$

Residual income

$$\frac{\text{Residual}}{\text{income}} = \frac{\text{Operating}}{\text{income}} - \left(\frac{\text{Required rate}}{\text{of return}} \times \frac{\text{Average}}{\text{operating assets}} \right)$$

Economic value added (EVA)

$$EVA = \frac{\text{Adjusted after-tax}}{\text{operating income}} - \left[\frac{\text{Weighted average}}{\text{cost of capital}} \times \left(\frac{\text{Adjusted}}{\text{total assets}} - \frac{\text{Current}}{\text{liabilities}} \right) \right]$$

Advantages and disadvantages

ROI is easier to compare across subunits, but motivates suboptimal decisions, both in long-term investment and short-term cost cutting.

Residual income provides more appropriate investment incentives than ROI but is not comparable across subunits.

EVA minimises suboptimal decision-making incentives but is complex to calculate and not comparable across subunits.

---

5   Outline how compensation is used to motivate performance.

Bonus system incentives

Examples of performance measures:

- ROI
- residual income
- EVA
- operating income or growth in income
- cost savings
- revenue growth.

Motivating long-term versus short-term performance

- Equity-based rewards

---

6   State alternative prices used for transferring goods and services within an entity.

Ideal transfer price

- Opportunity cost

Alternatives

- Cost-based transfer price
- Activity-based transfer price
- Market-based transfer price
- Dual-rate transfer price
- Negotiated transfer price

---

7   Calculate transfer prices and outline the issues associated with transfer pricing.

Uses

- Assign cost to goods and services transferred internally for financial reporting and income taxes.
- Motivate efficient use of support services.
- Allocate corporate overhead costs.

Incentive issues

- Conflicts among managers
- Suboptimal decision making
- Managers should not be held responsible for costs over which they have no control
- International income taxes

Self-study problems

ROI; residual income; EVA

Outdoor Express is a large manufacturer of recreational equipment. Performance of the camping division is measured as an investment centre because the managers make all the decisions about investments in operating equipment and space. Following is financial information for the camping division:

Average operating assets	$2 000 000
Current liabilities	500 000
Operating income	300 000

Camping division's required rate of return is 12 per cent, but Outdoor Express's weighted average cost of capital is 9 per cent, and the tax rate is 30 per cent.

REQUIRED

(a) Calculate return on investment for the camping division.
(b) Calculate residual income for the camping division.
(c) Calculate EVA for the camping division.
(d) Briefly discuss the advantages and disadvantages of each method.

Solution to self-study problem 1

(a)

$$ROI = \frac{\text{Net operating income}}{\text{Average operating assets}} = \frac{\$300\,000}{\$2\,000\,000} = 15\%$$

(b) Residual income = Net operating income – (Required rate of return × Investment)

$$= \$300\,000 - (12\% \times \$2\,000\,000) = \$300\,000 - \$240\,000 = \$60\,000$$

(c) EVA = After-tax operating income – [Weighted average cost of capital × (Total assets – Current liabilities)]

$$= [\$300\,000 \times (1 - 0.30)] - [9\% \times (\$2\,000\,000 - \$500\,000)]$$

$$= \$210\,000 - \$135\,000 = \$75\,000$$

(d) ROI and residual income motivate managers to reduce costs and investment, whereas EVA provides incentives to invest as long as the return is equal to or greater than the required rate of return. In addition, ROI and residual income do not include taxes, so no incentive is provided for managers to minimise taxes. EVA can be adjusted for intangibles such as leases and R&D spending. Therefore, it can be designed to minimise managers' abilities to artificially improve the performance measure.

Transfer price; excess versus full capacity; outsourcing

The Perth division of Aeronautic Controls (AC) produces a digital thermometer. The thermometer can be sold on the open market for $180 each, or it can be used by the Brisbane division in the production of a temperature control gauge that has a unit contribution margin of $140 (given that the digital thermometer is transferred at variable cost plus shipping).

The Perth division is currently operating at 70 per cent of its capacity of 2000 digital thermometers per month. Following are average costs per unit at this level of capacity:

	Average cost
Direct materials	$ 50
Variable supplies	10
Fixed costs	100
Total average cost per thermometer	$160

If a digital thermometer is sold on the open market, the customer pays the shipping cost. The cost of shipping a digital thermometer from Perth to Brisbane is $15.

REQUIRED

(a) What is the best transfer price for AC overall if a digital thermometer is transferred to Brisbane and the Perth division is operating at 70 per cent of capacity?
(b) What is the best transfer price for AC overall if a digital thermometer is transferred to Brisbane, but the Perth division is operating at full capacity and the digital thermometer could have been sold on the open market?
(c) Suppose the Brisbane division can purchase a substitute for the digital thermometer from an outside supplier for $100 (including shipping costs). Under ordinary circumstances, what single transfer price would motivate the managers of both divisions to act in AC's interests at either excess or full capacity?
(d) What are the potential problems with the transfer price identified in part (c)? Explain.

Solution to self-study problem 2

(a) When the Perth division has excess capacity (30 per cent in this case), the transfer price should be the variable cost of $75 (direct materials of $50 plus supplies of $10 and shipping of $15).
(b) If the Perth division could sell all of its thermometers on the open market, the transfer price should be the market price of $180 plus $15 shipping = $195.
(c) First consider the contribution margin for each division from the perspective of the entire entity. Selling the temperature control gauge results in a contribution margin of $140 per unit. Selling the digital thermometers results in a contribution margin of $105 ($180 – $75 thermometer variable cost). When Perth has excess capacity, the total contribution margin is $245 ($140 + $105).

For each unit produced with a digital thermometer from an outside supplier, the Brisbane division's contribution margin is reduced by $25 ($100 – $75) from $140 to $115. However, from the perspective of the entire entity, the contribution margin is $115 from Brisbane plus $105 from Perth, or $220 in total. If the internal transfer takes place, the contribution margin is only $140. Therefore, transfers should take place only when Perth has excess capacity. To motivate this behaviour, the transfer price should be equal to or greater than $75 and equal to or less than $100. Setting the transfer price at $90 + $10 shipping would give Brisbane incentive to purchase inside if Perth had capacity, but purchase outside if Perth had no capacity because the transfer price would be the same with either purchase. In addition, Perth would have incentive to sell to the external market when possible because the contribution margin of $105 on external sales is greater than the $35 ($90 – $65) contribution margin for internal sales.
(d) The Brisbane division might find an external vendor that could produce the digital thermometer at a cost less than the transfer price, but that would decrease AC's overall

contribution margin. In addition, the Brisbane division could forgo special orders that would have a positive contribution margin for AC if the division uses the internal transfer price to determine whether to accept the order.

Questions

11.1 Explain how return on investment (ROI) is calculated and how it can be decomposed into two financial measures.

11.2 Explain how and why the use of ROI for performance evaluation can cause managers to make decisions that could be harmful to an entity in the long run.

11.3 Explain how residual income is calculated, and define required rate of return in your own words.

11.4 Explain why the use of residual income for performance evaluation provides better incentives in some ways than ROI, but still causes managers to make some decisions that could be harmful to an entity in the long run.

11.5 Explain the differences between general and specific knowledge. Give an example of an industry where knowledge is quite general and an example of an industry that requires specific knowledge.

11.6 Explain why organisational form may vary if specific knowledge versus general knowledge is needed for decision making.

11.7 Describe agency costs and give several examples of them.

11.8 Explain how EVA differs from residual income.

11.9 Identify the four different types of responsibility centres and explain the general objectives of each.

11.10 An organisation's plant in Queensland manufactures a product that is shipped to a branch in Tasmania for sale. Does it make any difference which branch (each is a profit centre) is charged for the cost of transportation? Explain.

11.11 A national company, Fast Print, decided to expand into several developing countries. The company has been managed under a centralised organisational form, but is considering changing to a decentralised form. List the advantages and disadvantages of making this change.

11.12 Suppose transfer prices are set at market prices and a manager who previously purchased internally begins to purchase externally. Explain what it means to say that the outsourcing decision might have been suboptimal.

11.13 Describe as many different methods for setting transfer prices as you can.

Exercises

11.14 **Responsibility centres; agency theory; performance measures** Your brother recently bought a small business with several coffee carts located around the city. Two workers share responsibility for each cart. All beverages are prepared using identical recipes and ingredients, but the baked goods and other items sold by each cart are chosen by the employees who operate the carts each day. Your brother asked your advice in determining how best to compensate the employees. He thinks he should give them bonuses when costs are contained, and pay them a flat salary otherwise.

REQUIRED

(a) What type of responsibility centre is each cart?

(b) Explain how agency theory relates to your brother's situation.

(c) List several financial performance measures that might be relevant for measuring employee performance.

(d) List one non-financial measure that might be important to the success of this business.

11.15 Residual income; ROI; EVA The following selected data pertain to Brannard Company's Construction Division for last year.

Sales	$2 000 000
Variable costs	$1 200 000
Traceable fixed costs	$200 000
Average invested capital (assets)	$3 000 000
Current liabilities	$200 000
Required rate of return	15%
Marginal tax rate	36%
Weighted average cost of capital	12%

REQUIRED

(a) Calculate the residual income.

(b) Calculate the return on investment.

(c) Calculate the economic value added.

11.16 ROI; residual income; breakeven point; contribution margin Mersey Company's industrial photo-finishing division, Vale, incurred the following costs and expenses in the last period.

	Variable	Fixed
Direct materials	$200 000	
Direct labour	150 000	
Factory overhead	70 000	$42 000
General, selling and administrative	30 000	48 000
Totals	$450 000	$90 000

During the period, Vale produced 300 000 units of industrial photo prints, which were sold for $2 each. Mersey's investment in Vale was $500 000 and $700 000 at the beginning and ending of the year respectively. Vale's weighted average cost of capital is 15 per cent.

REQUIRED

(a) Determine Vale's return on investment for the year.

(b) Calculate Vale's residual income (loss) for the year.

(c) How many industrial photo print units did Vale have to sell during the year to break even?

(d) What was Vale's contribution margin for the year?

11.17 EVA for segments Following is information for the Fulcrum Company's three business segments located in Europe.

	Segment A	Segment B	Segment C
Pre-tax operating income	$8 000 000	$4 000 000	$6 000 000
Current assets	8 000 000	6 000 000	8 000 000
Long-term assets	32 000 000	26 000 000	16 000 000
Current liabilities	4 000 000	2 000 000	3 000 000

Fulcrum's applicable tax rate for the segments is 30 per cent, and its weighted average cost of capital for each segment is 10 per cent.

REQUIRED

Determine the segment with the highest EVA.

11.18 **ROI; transfer prices; taxes; employee motivation** Fowler Electronics produces colour plasma screens in its Windsor plant in Vietnam. The screens are then shipped to the entity's plant in Sturt, where they are incorporated into finished televisions. Although the Windsor plant never sells plasma screens to any other assembler, the market for them is competitive. The market price is $750 per screen.

Variable costs to manufacture the screens are $350. Fixed costs at the Windsor plant are $2 000 000 per period. The plant typically manufactures and ships 10 000 screens per period to the Sturt plant. Taxes in Vietnam amount to 30 per cent of pre-tax income. The Windsor plant has total assets of $20 000 000.

The Sturt plant incurs variable costs to complete the televisions of $110 per set (in addition to the cost of the screens). The Sturt plant's fixed costs amount to $4 000 000 per period. The 10 000 sets produced each period are sold for an average of $2500 each. For Sturt, the tax rate is 45 per cent of pre-tax income. The Sturt plant has total assets of $30 000 000.

REQUIRED

(a) Determine the return on investment for each plant if the screens are transferred at variable cost.

(b) Determine the return on investment for each plant if the screens are transferred at market price.

(c) To reduce taxes, will Fowler prefer a transfer price based on cost or market price? Explain.

(d) Will the top managers in each plant prefer to use cost or market price as the transfer price? Explain.

(e) How would you resolve potential conflict over the transfer price policy?

11.19 **Choice of transfer price** The following information relates to a new computer chip that Hand Held has developed for its new mobile phone that contains a personal organiser:

Chip division	
Market price of finished chip to outsiders	$24
Variable cost per unit	12
Contribution margin	$12
Total contribution for 30 000 units	$360 000
Mobile phone division	
Market price of finished products	$128
Variable costs:	
From chip division	12
Other direct materials	50
Mobile phone division	
Assembly	38
Packaging	20
Contribution margin	$ 8
Total contribution for 20 000 units	$ 160 000

The variable costs of the mobile phone division will be incurred whether it buys from the chip division or from an outside supplier.

REQUIRED

(a) What is the highest price that the managers of the mobile phone division would want to pay the chip division for the chip? Explain.

(b) If the chip division is working at full capacity and cannot produce additional units, what transfer price for the chip would be best for the entity as a whole? Explain.

(c) If the chip division is not operating at capacity and has no prospect of reaching capacity, what is the lowest price its managers would typically be willing to sell chips to the mobile phone division?

11.20 Choice of transfer price; fairness to managers Prem International has two large subsidiaries: Oil and Chemical. Oil is an oil-refining entity, and its main product is petrol. Chemical produces and sells a variety of chemical products. Chemical owns a polystyrene processing plant next to Oil's refinery. The polystyrene plant was built at the same time that Oil built a benzene plant at the refinery. Benzene is the raw material needed by Chemical to produce polystyrene. Chemical's managers believe they can sell 100 million kilograms of measure of polystyrene per year, which is less than full capacity. Following are Chemical's expected revenues and costs for the polystyrene plant (volume is measured in weight because weight is not affected by temperature):

	Per kg
Selling price	$0.30
Costs: Benzene (to be purchased from Oil)	$?
Variable production costs	0.03
Fixed production costs	0.05

Oil can operate at full capacity and sell all of the petrol it produces. Following are Oil's expected revenues and costs for the production of petrol:

	Per kg
Selling price	$ 0.16
Costs: Crude oil	$0.06
Variable production costs	0.02
Fixed production costs	0.07

For every kilogram of benzene that Oil produces, it will forgo selling a kilogram of petrol. However, 100 million kilograms per year would be only a small portion of total volume at the refinery. Following are Oil's expected revenues and costs for the production of benzene (these costs include the costs of refining the crude oil):

	Per kg
Selling price (to Chemical)	$?
Costs: Crude oil	$0.06
Variable production costs	0.04
Fixed production costs	0.09

REQUIRED

(a) On an entity-wide basis, should Prem International produce polystyrene this year? Why?

(b) Using the usual quantitative rules for short-term decisions, what is the maximum price that Chemical's managers would be willing to pay for benzene?

(c) Would Chemical's managers be willing to pay the maximum transfer price calculated in part (b)? Why?

(d) Using the usual quantitative rules for short-term decisions, what is the minimum price that Oil's managers would be willing to receive for benzene?

(e) Would Oil's managers be willing to receive the minimum transfer price calculated in part (d)? Why?

(f) What transfer price might be fair to the managers of both subsidiaries? Explain.

11.21 Transfer price; sale to outside versus inside customer Ajax division of Carlyle Company produces electric motors, 20 per cent of which are sold to the Bradley division of Carlyle and the remainder to outside customers. Carlyle treats its divisions as profit centres and allows division managers to choose their sources of sale and supply. Corporate policy requires that all interdivisional sales and purchases be recorded at variable cost as transfer price. Ajax division's estimated sales and standard cost data for 2008, based on its full capacity of 100 000 units are as follows:

	Bradley	Outsiders
Sales	$ 900 000	$ 8 000 000
Variable costs	(900 000)	(3 600 000)
Fixed costs	(300 000)	(1 200 000)
Gross margin	$(300 000)	$ 3 200 000
Unit sales	20 000	80 000

Ajax has an opportunity to sell the 20 000 units to an outside customer at a price of $75 per unit on a continuing basis. Bradley can purchase its requirements from an outside supplier for $85 per unit.

REQUIRED

Assuming that Ajax division desires to maximise its gross margin, should Ajax accept the new customer and drop its sales to Bradley for 2008? Why?

Problems

11.22 ROI; residual income; explaining the better measure The following financial data are for the evaluation of performance for Kimberley Mining:

Average operating assets	$500 000
Net operating income	$65 000
Minimum required rate of return	10%

Kimberley Mining currently uses return on investment to evaluate investment centre managers. An accounting student from the local university suggested to the controller that residual income could be a better performance measure.

REQUIRED

(a) Calculate ROI for Kimberley Mining.

(b) Calculate residual income for Kimberley Mining.

(c) Write a brief memo to the controller explaining why residual income is a better performance measure.

11.23 **Lease versus buy decision; ROI; residual income; EVA; manager incentives** Refer to the information in problem 11.22. The manager of Kimberley Mining is considering a new project. She can buy or lease equipment that will reprocess tailings from old mines to remove any traces of gold left behind by the original separating processes. The purchase price of the equipment is $150 000. The cost to lease is $2000 per month. She estimates the return (incremental revenues minus incremental expenses, including lease cost) to be $40 000 per year. She knows that purchasing the equipment will increase the value of average operating assets. If she leases the equipment, expenses will increase, but not assets. (In other words, the lease will be accounted for as an operating lease.) Although it is more cost effective to purchase the equipment, she has decided to lease it.

REQUIRED
(a) Calculate the new ROI if the equipment is (i) purchased, or (ii) leased.
(b) Calculate the new residual income if the equipment is (i) purchased, or (ii) leased.
(c) One of the adjustments that can be made using EVA is to treat all operating lease costs as if they were purchases — in other words, to capitalise the lease. If Kimberley Mining used EVA with this adjustment, how might the manager's incentives and behaviour change? Explain.

11.24 **Transfer price; entity versus division profit; idle capacity** The furniture division of International Woodworking purchases timber and makes tables, chairs and other wood furniture. Most of the timber is purchased from the Port Angeles Mill, also a division of International Woodworking. The furniture division and the Port Angeles Mill are profit centres. The furniture division manager proposed a new Danish-designed chair that will sell for $150. The manager wants to purchase the timber from the Port Angeles Mill. Production of 800 chairs is planned using capacity in the furniture division that is currently idle. The furniture division can purchase the timber for each chair from an outside supplier for $60. International Woodworkers has a policy that internal transfers are priced at variable cost plus allocated fixed costs. Assume the following costs for the production of one chair:

Port Angeles Mill		Furniture division	
Variable cost	$40	Variable costs:	
Allocated fixed cost	30	Timber: Port Angeles Mill	$ 70
Fully absorbed cost	$70	Furniture division variable costs:	
		Manufacturing	75
		Selling	10
		Total variable cost	$155

REQUIRED
(a) Assume that the Port Angeles Mill has idle capacity and would incur no additional fixed costs to produce the required timber. Would the furniture division manager buy the timber for the chair from the Port Angeles Mill, given the existing transfer price policy? Why?
(b) Calculate the contribution margin for the entity as a whole if the manager decides to buy from the Port Angeles Mill and is able to sell 800 chairs.
(c) What transfer price policy would you recommend if the Port Angeles Mill always has idle (excess) capacity? Explain why this transfer price policy provides incentives for the managers to act in the best interests of the entity as a whole.
(d) Explain how the idle capacity affects the recommendation in part (c).

11.25 Transfer price; incentives for internal services Avra Valley Services has two divisions, Computer Services and Management Advisory Services. Both divisions work for external customers and, in addition, work for each other. Fees earned by Computer Services from external customers were $400 000 in 2008. Fees earned by Management Advisory Services from external customers were $700 000 in 2008. Computer Services worked 3000 hours for Management Advisory Services last year, and Management Advisory Services worked 1200 hours for Computer Services. The total costs of external services performed by Computer Services were $220 000, and for Management Advisory Services costs were $480 000.

REQUIRED

(a) Determine the operating income for each division and for the entity as a whole if the transfer price from Computer Services to Management Advisory Services is $50 per hour, and the transfer price from Management Advisory Services to Computer Services is $60 per hour.

(b) The manager of Computer Services has found another entity willing to provide the same services as Management Advisory Services at $50 per hour. All of the employees in both units are guaranteed 40-hour working weeks. Currently, Management Advisory Services has idle capacity because of an economic downturn. Calculate the change in operating income for the entity as a whole if Computer Services uses outsourced services instead of using Management Advisory Services.

(c) Recommend a transfer price policy that would provide incentives to use the internal services. Explain your recommendation.

(d) Discuss possible qualitative factors that might affect the attractiveness of the outsourcing option.

11.26 ROI; residual income; EVA; effect on investment decision; performance evaluation Strong Welding Equipment Company produces and sells welding equipment nationally and internationally. Following is information about two divisions.

	Brazil	US
Invested capital (total assets)	$4 000 000	$400 000
Net operating income	$1 000 000	$120 000
Required rate of return	10%	10%
Weighted average cost of capital	9%	9%
Current liabilities	$80 000	$10 000
After-tax income	$600 000	$80 000

REQUIRED

(a) Calculate each division's ROI.

(b) Calculate each division's residual income.

(c) Calculate each division's EVA.

(d) Suppose the Brazilian division had an opportunity to invest $3 500 000 in a project that would generate sales of $5 000 000 and return on sales of 10 per cent, or $500 000. Would the division manager be likely to undertake this project if he or she is evaluated using ROI? Explain.

(e) Recommend a performance evaluation measure that would increase the managers' incentives to make decisions that would be in the best interests of the owners.

11.27 **Choosing type of responsibility centre; support cost allocation; ROI** The ATCO Company purchased the Dexter Company three years ago. Prior to the acquisition, Dexter manufactured and sold plastic products to a wide variety of customers. Since becoming a division of ATCO, Dexter only manufactures plastic components for products made by ATCO's Macon division. Macon sells its products to hardware wholesalers.

ATCO's corporate management gives the Dexter division management a considerable amount of authority in running the division's operation. However, corporate management retains the authority for decisions regarding capital investments, price setting of all products, and the quantity of each product to be produced by the Dexter division.

ATCO has a formal performance evaluation program for the management of all of its divisions. The performance evaluation program relies heavily on each division's return on investment. The accompanying income statement of Dexter division provides the basis for the evaluation of Dexter's divisional management.

The corporate accounting staff prepare all of the divisions' financial statements. The corporate general services costs are allocated on the basis of sales dollars, and the computer department's actual costs are apportioned among the divisions on the basis of use. The net division investment includes division fixed assets at net book value (cost less depreciation), division inventory, and corporate working capital apportioned to the division on the basis of sales dollars.

Dexter division of ATCO Company
Income statement for the year ended 31 October 2008
(in thousands of dollars)

Sales		$4 000
Costs and expenses:		
Direct materials	$500	
Direct labour	1 100	
Factory overhead	1 300	
Total	2 900	
Less: Increase in inventory	350	
Cost of goods sold		2 550
Engineering and research		120
Shipping and receiving		240
Division administration:		
Manager's office	210	
Cost accounting	40	
Personnel	82	
Total division administration		332
Corporate headquarters costs:		
Computer	48	
General services	230	
Total corporate headquarter costs		278
Total costs and expenses		3 520
Divisional operating income		$ 480
Net plant investment		$1 600
Return on investment		30%

REQUIRED

(a) Discuss the financial reporting and performance evaluation program of ATCO Company as it relates to the responsibilities of the Dexter division.

(b) Based upon your response to part (a), recommend appropriate revisions of the financial information and reports used to evaluate the performance of Dexter's divisional management. If you conclude that revisions are not necessary, explain why they are not needed.

REFERENCES

1 EVA is a registered trademark of Stern Stewart & Co. More information can be found at www.sternstewart.com.
2 See Durie, J 2006, 'Reporting the results of a study by Australian Council of Superannuation Investors', *Australian Financial Review*, 15 November.
3 Information from an article by Blair Speedy in *The Australian*, 3 November 2006, p. 19.
4 Information from article by Anthony Klan in *The Australian*, 17 November 2006, p. 21.

Strategy and the balanced scorecard

IN BRIEF

Successful entities adopt a strategic decision-making process to ensure that strategies and operating activities are aligned with the organisation's vision and core competencies. They also engage in continuous improvement by monitoring and learning from the results of their strategies and operations. Accountants develop and track a variety of financial and non-financial measures to monitor results. The balanced scorecard is a formal approach for identifying and measuring an entity's performance from four perspectives: financial, customer, internal business process, and learning and growth. Approaches such as the balanced scorecard motivate individuals and units throughout an organisation to work towards a common vision and improve strategic and operating success.

After studying this chapter, you should be able to:

1 Outline the role of strategic decision making.

2 Understand how financial and non-financial measures are used to evaluate organisational performance.

3 Explain the balanced scorecard.

4 Outline the role of strategy maps.

5 Explain how a balanced scorecard is implemented.

6 Identify the strengths and weaknesses of the balanced scorecard.

Measuring up at Hunter Health

Hunter Health operates in the Hunter and Newcastle regions of New South Wales, providing health services to over 520 000 people. The health services provided include public health, health promotion, community health, acute hospital, aged, mental health, rehabilitation and palliative care services. It is one of the largest employers in the Hunter region, employing over 9600 staff. Hunter Health (1992a) uses the balanced scorecard to 'implement its core strategies for improving the health of Hunter communities'.

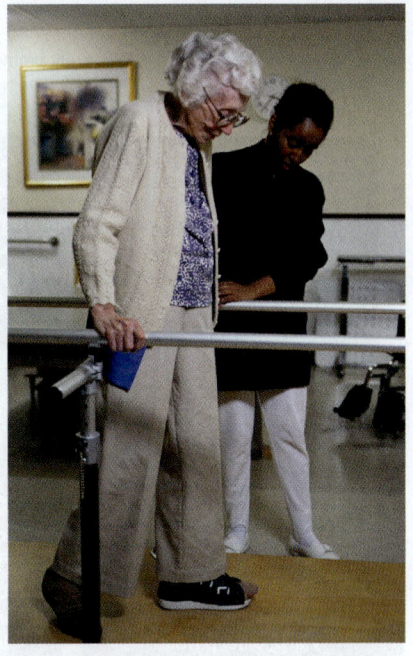

The balanced scorecard was first trumpeted by Kaplan and Norton in 1992. It has gone through a series of developments since then. Initially, it was used by entities to introduce non-financial measures of performance into the formal performance-measurement system, so that non-financial measures could sit alongside financial measures in providing indicators of success. These measures were commonly classified in four key areas: financial, customer, internal processes, and innovation and learning. Since its initial introduction in the early 1990s, key developments in the balanced scorecard have included its increasing role as a key strategic tool, and the use of strategy maps to reinforce the causal links between the measures used in the scorecard.

Hunter Health has tried to use its balanced scorecard to capture these two key uses. Its use as a strategic tool is highlighted in the quote from Hunter Health in the first paragraph above. Hunter Health has also used a strategy map to create links between each of its measures. The strategy map used by Hunter Health is provided below. Most organisations will develop the balanced scorecard and strategy maps to suit their own purpose, but we can better understand the general role of strategy maps by considering Hunter Health's (1992b) own description of its strategy map:

> To understand the logic of the strategy map, you start from the top focus area (Community and Patients) by asking, to achieve our vision what are the key outcomes we must deliver for our community and patients?

> It then moves down to the critical Partnership, Integration and internal Processes and Resource objectives necessary to achieve these outcomes, and finally to the long-term drivers of change and improvement, the People, Learning and Innovation perspective.

> Because of the linkages between the objectives in the different focus areas, improvements in performance of one objective in a lower focus area should result in an improvement in performance for some objectives in a focus area.

The use of the balanced scorecard in the health sector is growing, with some states now mandating that hospitals and service providers incorporate the tool into their reporting framework.

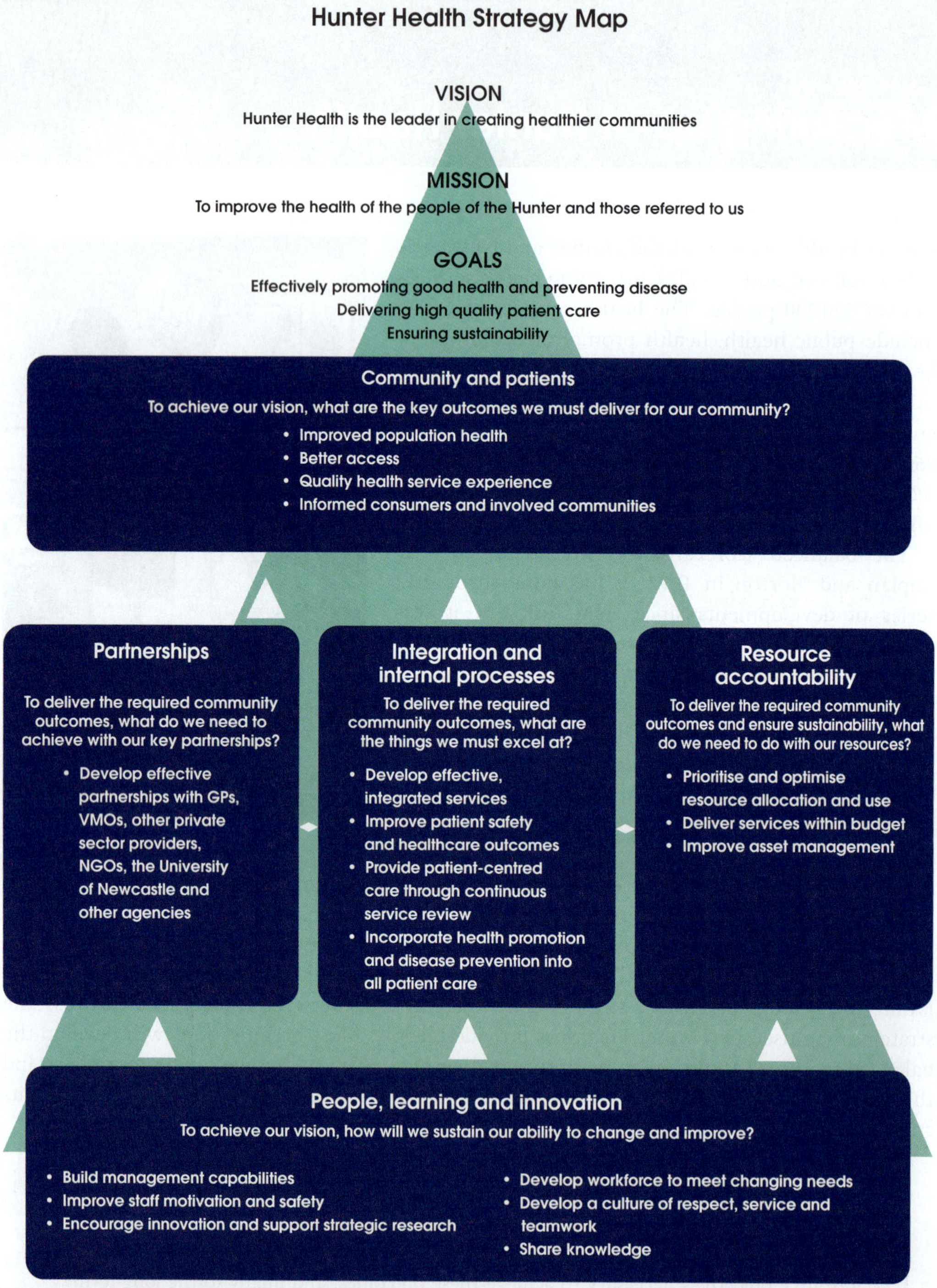

Hunter Health Strategy Map

VISION
Hunter Health is the leader in creating healthier communities

MISSION
To improve the health of the people of the Hunter and those referred to us

GOALS
Effectively promoting good health and preventing disease
Delivering high quality patient care
Ensuring sustainability

Community and patients
To achieve our vision, what are the key outcomes we must deliver for our community?

- Improved population health
- Better access
- Quality health service experience
- Informed consumers and involved communities

Partnerships
To deliver the required community outcomes, what do we need to achieve with our key partnerships?

- Develop effective partnerships with GPs, VMOs, other private sector providers, NGOs, the University of Newcastle and other agencies

Integration and internal processes
To deliver the required community outcomes, what are the things we must excel at?

- Develop effective, integrated services
- Improve patient safety and healthcare outcomes
- Provide patient-centred care through continuous service review
- Incorporate health promotion and disease prevention into all patient care

Resource accountability
To deliver the required community outcomes and ensure sustainability, what do we need to do with our resources?

- Prioritise and optimise resource allocation and use
- Deliver services within budget
- Improve asset management

People, learning and innovation
To achieve our vision, how will we sustain our ability to change and improve?

- Build management capabilities
- Improve staff motivation and safety
- Encourage innovation and support strategic research
- Develop workforce to meet changing needs
- Develop a culture of respect, service and teamwork
- Share knowledge

FIGURE 12.1 ■ Hunter Health strategy map

Sources: Information from Hunter New England Area Health Service (a) 'About Hunter Health' and (b) 'Balanced Scorecard strategy map', www.hunter.health.nsw.gov.au; Kaplan, R & Norton, D 1992, 'The balanced scorecard: measures that drive performance', *Harvard Business Review*, September–October, pp. 134–42.

■ The links between strategy and performance measurement.

■ The components of a balanced scorecard and its key uses.

■ The role of strategy maps in performance measurement.

Strategic decision making

Managers make decisions in a strategic way to clarify the entity's vision and core competencies. (An overview of management decision making is provided in figure 12.2.) The vision is the core purpose and ideology of the entity (many organisations choose to keep the vision fairly broad), while the core competencies are the entity's strengths relative to competitors. Strategies are the tactics managers use to take advantage of core competencies while working towards the organisation's vision. Strategies guide long-term decisions such as the types of goods and services offered and the long-term methods of competition. Commonly, we speak of generic strategies as being either those aimed at achieving low-cost products/services or product/service differentiation, although the line between the two has become blurred with

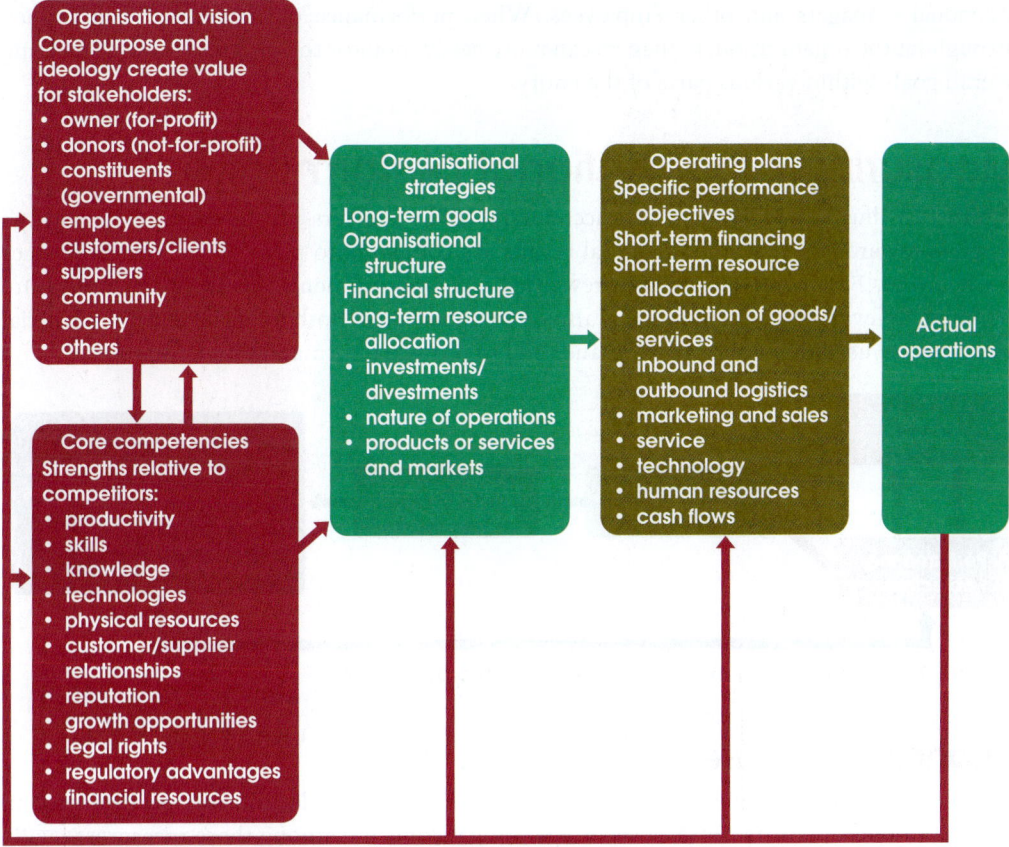

Measure performance, monitor progress and motivate employees

FIGURE 12.2 ■ Overview of management decision making

increasing demands on organisations for high quality at lower cost. Strategies also lead to operating plans, including an annual budget. In turn, operating plans guide short-term decisions such as launching advertising campaigns, hiring employees or purchasing inventory. As entities' actual operations unfold, results are measured and monitored against both short-term operating plans and long-term strategies. The feedback loops in figure 12.2 lead to revisions at any of the levels of management decision making.

The nature of the organisation's strategies and operating plans influences the types of performance objectives that are used. **Performance objectives** — the specific goals that managers choose to measure and monitor — help motivate employees to carry out strategies and plans. For example, being the market leader for a specific product might be a long-term goal. This goal could be tied to the performance objective of achieving a 35 per cent market share within a five-year time horizon.

Successful entities communicate to all employees their organisational vision, strategies, goals and objectives. This communication helps align employee goals with organisational goals. Accountants develop and track financial and non-financial performance measures to evaluate the efforts of individual employees, teams, departments, divisions and subunits. When performance measures are monitored throughout the entity, progress towards the vision is more easily evaluated and rewarded.

Even when no statements of organisational vision, mission and core values are established, managers often establish performance objectives for individual divisions, product lines and departments. These objectives help entities assign decision authority and responsibilities to individual managers and other employees. When performance objectives are well aligned throughout the organisation, managers can more easily monitor the progress towards meeting overall goals within various parts of the entity.

Measuring organisational performance

Figure 12.3 illustrates a process that accountants and managers use to evaluate the entity's progress towards its vision. First, actual results are compared to plans. Then any differences are analysed. Finally, employees are rewarded and improvements are identified for future planning. Re-evaluation of the vision is also often undertaken. Both financial and non-financial measures are used to monitor performance and to provide information for this process.

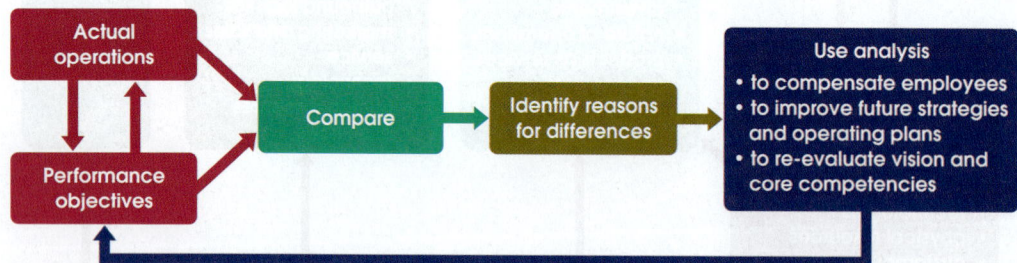

FIGURE 12.3 ■ Monitoring measurable performance objectives

Financial measures

Managers traditionally relied on **financial measures** that provide information measured in dollars or ratios of dollars. Sales, costs or operating income are among those measures usually obtained from the financial accounting system, which is designed to report financial measures for the overall organisation, divisions, product lines and departments. Financial measures also compare budget to actual results. We explore the use of financial measures for evaluating responsibility centre performance in chapter 11.

Non-financial measures

Non-financial measures provide performance information that cannot be measured in dollars. Defect rates, throughput time and employee retention are among the non-financial measures used more frequently in recent years to reflect performance that promotes long-term financial success. One important issue relating to non-financial measures is that they still need to be quantified in some way. For example, customer satisfaction is not a measure in itself but an important dimension we might like to measure. Many entities do this by developing a customer satisfaction index based on formal feedback mechanisms from customers. Non-financial measures are commonly classified as *lead indicators*; if the operations to which the lead indicators refer are managed well, then this will lead to enhanced performance as reported in the financial measures, which are commonly classified as *lag indicators*.

Using a combination of measures

A combination of measures is often used to monitor and motivate performance within an organisation. No single measure provides a complete picture of performance. In addition, a combination of financial and non-financial measures is usually more consistent with an entity's long-term goals than financial measures alone. This combination of financial and non-financial measures is an appropriate starting point for our next section: the balanced scorecard.

Balanced scorecard

Traditionally, entities focused on financial outcomes such as sales and profits. When evaluating business processes, they tended to focus on ways to maintain control over product costs. Although financial outcomes are important, this limited focus does not automatically provide guidance in achieving desired results. Nor does it encourage improvements when current financial results are satisfactory. Some organisations focused on long-term strategies, but their approaches were often informal and piecemeal. For example, entities collect data about customer satisfaction but then use the data only to find areas that need immediate improvement, not as part of an overall strategic approach.

In the early 1990s, Harvard University professor Robert Kaplan and consultant David Norton developed the **balanced scorecard**, a formal method to incorporate both financial and non-financial performance measures into organisational management systems. The aim of the balanced scorecard is to translate organisational visions and strategies into performance objectives and related measures that can be monitored over time. The balanced scorecard approach helps managers more fully integrate strategies throughout the entity, anticipate and prevent possible future problems, and identify and take advantage of opportunities.

At the heart of the balanced scorecard is a continuous, strategic analysis of the organisation from multiple perspectives. The most common approach is to use the four perspectives shown in figure 12.4 (overleaf): financial, customer, internal business process, and learning and growth. Within each perspective, managers and other employees study the entity and identify linkages with other perspectives. For example, if employees are better trained (under learning and growth), they are more likely to make suggestions that improve customer-related business processes, such as reducing the time between receipt of a customer order and product delivery. As customer satisfaction increases, financial performance is also more likely to increase. These analyses help accountants and managers identify the most important performance objectives — the aspects of operations that must be successful for the organisation to achieve its vision. Measures are then developed for the performance objectives within each perspective to help managers and employees monitor and work towards long-term goals.

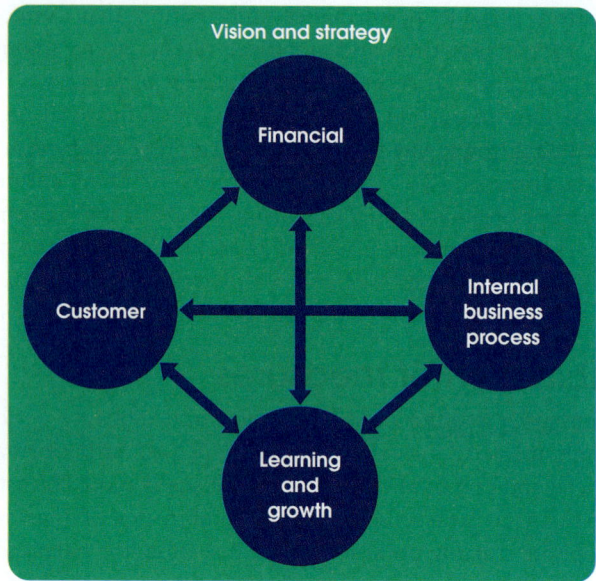

FIGURE 12.4 ■ Four perspectives in a balanced scorecard

Financial perspective and related measures

When accountants and managers analyse their entities from a **financial perspective**, they identify desired financial results, given the organisation's vision. For-profit entities usually have goals of providing owners with some level of return on investment. Not-for-profit entities typically have financial goals of maintaining a certain level of financial liquidity and stability, accumulating sufficient resources for some long-term purpose, or gaining maximum efficiency from resources. Financial goals and objectives encourage managers to evaluate the effectiveness of their strategies and operating plans based on the economic wellbeing of the organisation. They also help employees relate the activities they perform to the entity's financial outcomes.

Financial perspective measures are designed to determine an organisation's progress towards desired financial results. In for-profit entities, these measures are usually related to profitability, growth and owner value. Common measures include operating income, return on investment, residual income and economic value-added. In not-for-profit entities, financial measures often include operating income, cost per service provided, and variances from budgets.

Customer perspective and related measures

When accountants and managers analyse the entity from a **customer perspective**, they are concerned with identifying the customers that they want, and developing strategies to get and keep them. The analysis includes identifying the targeted customers, markets and products that are most consistent with the organisation's vision and core competencies. Entities that better meet customer needs — creating value for customers — are also more likely to generate desired financial results. Thus, this link connects the financial and customer perspectives.

In assessing customer needs, managers consider their organisational strategies, and examine the nature of products or services compared to consumer views about trade-offs among price, quality and functionality.

The customer's perspective is usually evaluated using outcome measures such as market share and customer satisfaction. The performance measures used in for-profit and not-for-profit entities are often similar. These measures include customer retention and profitability, new customer acquisition, and market share in a targeted market segment or geographical region. Customers are often surveyed to gather information on their perceptions about and interactions with the entity. Market surveys and focus groups are also used to measure image and reputation.

Internal business process perspective and related measures

When accountants and managers analyse the organisation from an **internal business process perspective**, they are concerned with the methods and practices used inside the entity to produce and deliver goods and services. One goal of this analysis is to improve processes that will increase customer satisfaction. Another goal is to improve the efficiency of operations, which contributes directly to the organisation's financial results. Internal business processes can be analysed using a value chain approach. A value chain is the sequence of business processes through which value is added to goods and services. Analysis of the value chain leads to the identification of processes that are critical to the organisation's success. Often, customer-related processes are emphasised in balanced scorecards because these processes have the greatest impact on customer satisfaction and financial success. Figure 12.5 presents a generic customer-oriented value chain including three principal internal business processes: the innovation cycle, the operations cycle and the post-sales service cycle.

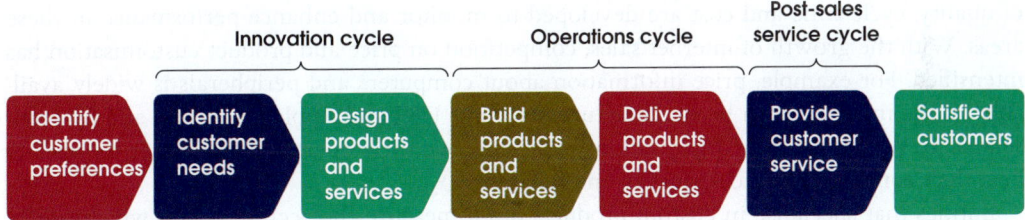

FIGURE 12.5 ■ Customer-oriented value chain analysis

Source: Copyright 1996, by The Regents of the University of California. Reprinted from the *California Management Review,* vol. 39, no. 1. By permission of The Regents.

An alternative to the value chain approach is an operational audit conducted by internal auditors. An operational audit is an objective and systematic examination of evidence to provide an independent assessment of the performance of an entity, program, activity or function. Operational audits provide information to improve accountability and to facilitate decision making.

Innovation cycle and related measures

The first step in the value chain, the **innovation cycle**, is concerned with processes to identify customer needs and to design goods and services that meet those needs. Many entities mistakenly focus their efforts primarily on more efficient production of existing products. Yet goods and services must meet customer needs. The balanced scorecard encourages managers to establish internal processes that identify customer preferences for quality, functionality and price, and also predict the potential market size. Organisations often use market and customer research to identify and nurture new markets, new customers and new needs of current customers. Managers brainstorm completely new products, and also develop new opportunities and markets for existing products.

The innovation process also ensures that proposed goods and services are produced efficiently, given the organisation's core competencies. For example, entities use target costing and kaizen costing to reduce product prices and improve quality.

Operations cycle and related measures

The second step in the value chain, the **operations cycle**, is concerned with production and delivery of goods or services that are identified and designed in the innovation cycle. The operations cycle addresses the short-term wellbeing of the entity. It begins with the systems used to accept and process customer orders, and is complete with delivery of the good or service. Quality, efficiency, consistency and on-time delivery are emphasised in this part of the value chain.

Historically, many entities focused on the operations process. Cost containment goals and cost monitoring methods were often in place at the commencement of operations. Traditional financial measures such as standard costs, budgets and variances were often used to monitor operational performance. This focus sometimes led to suboptimal behaviour. For example, efficiency measures create incentives to build inventories so that labour and machines are kept busy. Quality is sacrificed to increase efficiency. Excessive inventory levels and poor quality are costly to organisations over time. As a result, traditional measures of operations may be only a small part of a balanced scorecard approach.

Over the last several decades, entities have increasingly competed on quality and timely delivery, in addition to price. For example, Dell Computers advertises the quality and reliability of its systems as well as its ability to deliver computers within days of an order. Measurements of quality, cycle time and cost are developed to monitor and enhance performance in these areas. With the growth of internet sales, competition on price and product customisation has intensified. For example, price information about computers and peripherals is widely available on the internet, both by manufacturers such as Dell and Apple Computer and by retail sellers. To be competitive, organisations must improve their operations processes to meet or beat their competitors' prices, quality and reliability.

Entities that specialise in custom products often measure the accuracy with which orders are completed and speed of delivery. The specific operating characteristics identified and monitored as performance objectives depend on the organisation's vision, core competencies and strategies. Managers choose performance measures to monitor organisational progress, rewarding positive trends in areas that lead to customer satisfaction and financial success.

Post-sales service cycle and related measures

The final step in the value chain, the **post-sales service cycle**, considers the service provided to customers after product delivery. Post-sales services include providing warranty work, handling returns, correcting defects and collecting and processing payments. In addition, when products are highly sophisticated, entities often train the employees who will be using them. Another aspect of the post-sales service cycle is the safe disposal of hazardous wastes and by-products.

For some organisations, post-sales service is part of a product differentiation strategy. Hospitals have recently focused on the billing and collection processes of post-sales service. By emphasising accurate coding on patient bills, hospitals have fewer claims denied by insurers and increase their operating revenues. To achieve greater accuracy in coding, many hospitals provide in-depth employee training and hire better-educated employees in their billing and collections departments.

Performance measures for customer-related post-sales service could include aspects of the billing and collections cycle, such as the dollar amount of bad debts and days in accounts receivable. In addition, costs for warranty work and rework can be measured, or the number of defective products returned or reworked can be tracked. Measures for waste and by-product disposal could include number of kilograms of waste and clean-up costs.

Traditional versus balanced scorecard approaches to internal business processes

Traditionally, internal operations were monitored to improve existing operations. With the balanced scorecard approach, the emphasis is on identifying *new* processes and eliminating non-value-added processes. In addition, the balanced scorecard approach strives to incorporate innovative processes into operations, whereas traditional measurement systems emphasise delivery of today's products to current customers.

Learning and growth perspective and related measures

When accountants and managers analyse an entity from a **learning and growth perspective**, they are concerned with achieving future success by discovering new and better strategies. They also want to improve customer satisfaction and internal business processes, ensure that employees have sufficient knowledge and expertise, and check that internal processes support existing strategies. The learning and growth perspective is naturally linked to the internal business process perspective. As managers focus on improving internal business processes, they also identify opportunities for enhancing the capabilities of employees, information systems and operating procedures. To take advantage of these opportunities, employee training and education is emphasised, as is the development of information technology and systems. By analysing and improving procedures, entities also work towards aligning the goals and objectives of all stakeholders, including employees, suppliers, customers and shareholders. Implementation of a balanced scorecard system is an example of this type of process; it is a formal method for engaging in learning and growth throughout an entity.

Employee learning and growth measures include satisfaction, retention, training and skill development. These measures are tailored for the type of organisation and industry. To assist in decision making, information systems must produce timely, reliable and accurate information about customers, competitors and operations. Measures of information timeliness and accuracy include number of days to close (the amount of time that elapses before financial statements are available to managers) and errors per report. Over time, company policies become outdated. Periodically, these policies need to be analysed to determine whether they are current or should be changed in response to new knowledge or technologies. A performance measure could be the number of times that policies and procedures are reviewed over a five-year period. To monitor learning and growth measures, current performance of operations is usually used as a baseline and improvements are evaluated over time.

Clearly, any balanced scorecard developed must be structured to meet the needs of the entity to which it relates. Figure 12.6 (a) and (b) (overleaf) demonstrates the different types of balanced scorecards that might evolve to meet organisational needs. In chapter 16 we explore the balanced scorecard further, particularly as it relates to issues of sustainability management accounting.

FIGURE 12.6 ■ Sample balanced scorecards

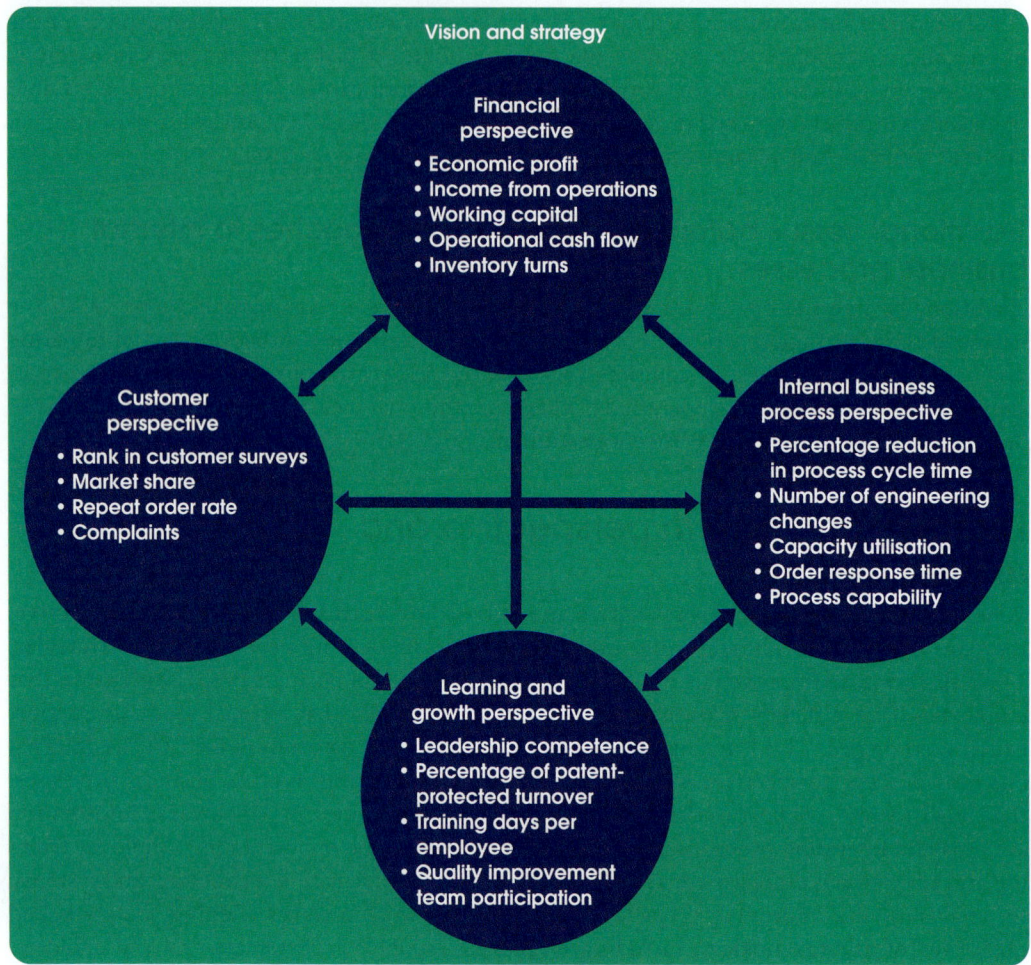

(a) Balanced scorecard measures at Royal Philips Electronics

Source: Copyright 2002, *Strategic Finance,* published by the Institute of Management Accountants (IMA) 2002, Montvale, NJ, www.imanet.org. Used with permission.

Balanced scorecard perspectives from 2000–01 to 2003–04				
	2000–01 Actual %	2001–02 Actual %	2002–03 Actual %	2003–04 Target
Customer perspective				
Community satisfaction	92	90	93	90% or better
Medical practitioner satisfaction	71	72	75	80% or better
Pharmacist satisfation	90	92	91	90% or better
Prompt processing	93	93	93	90% or better

(continued)

FIGURE 12.6 *(continued)*

Balanced scorecard perspectives from 2000–01 to 2003–04	2000–01 Actual %	2001–02 Actual %	2002–03 Actual %	2003–04 Target
Internal business processes perspective				
Claim processing accuracy	93	98	98	99%
Medicare transactions online*	49	50	50	N/A[†]
General practices online	86	86	90	N/A[††]
Growth and development perspective				
Staff satisfaction	66	73	72	Improvement reflected in 2004 survey

* Includes Mediclaims and internet electronic transactions.
[†] To be calculated differently from 2002.
[††] Currently no target set although practices are being encouraged to move online.

(b) Balanced scorecard measures at the Health Insurance Commission (HIC)

Source: Medicare Australia Health Insurance Commission Annual Report, 2002–03, p. 10.

Strategy maps

Strategy maps came to prominence in 2004 when Kaplan and Norton (2004) published their book *Strategy maps*, which focused on the use of linking organisational strategy to the measures developed for the balanced scorecard. In some ways, strategy maps became the link between strategy and the balanced scorecard. In Kaplan and Norton's own words:

> A strategy map provides a visual representation of the strategy … It provides a single-page view of how objectives in the four perspectives integrate and combine to guide the strategy … the strategy map shows how the multiple measures on a properly constructed Balanced Scorecard provide the instrumentation for a single strategy … It illustrates the cause-and-effect relationships that link desired outcomes in the customer and financial perspectives to outstanding performance in critical internal processes — operations, management, customer management, innovation and regulatory/social processes.[1]

The focus of the strategy map should be to illustrate the links between the perspectives and the measures within each perspective. For example, if it is too difficult to identify the cause-and-effect links, then it is most likely that the wrong measures have been selected. In this way, the strategy map is a good check on the usefulness of the balanced scorecard measures.

The strategy map for Hunter Health in figure 12.1 (page 488) provides one example of what a strategy map could look like for a not-for-profit entity. The Hunter Health strategy map could be further developed with more specific links between measures. Organisations are likely to adapt the strategy map to meet their specific needs, so not all strategy maps will look the same. For example, figure 12.7 (overleaf) shows the strategy map of the Campus Life Services division at the University of California, San Francisco, which looks a little different from the Hunter Health example. Nevertheless, the same outcome is being sought — a demonstration of the links between the measures and perspectives.

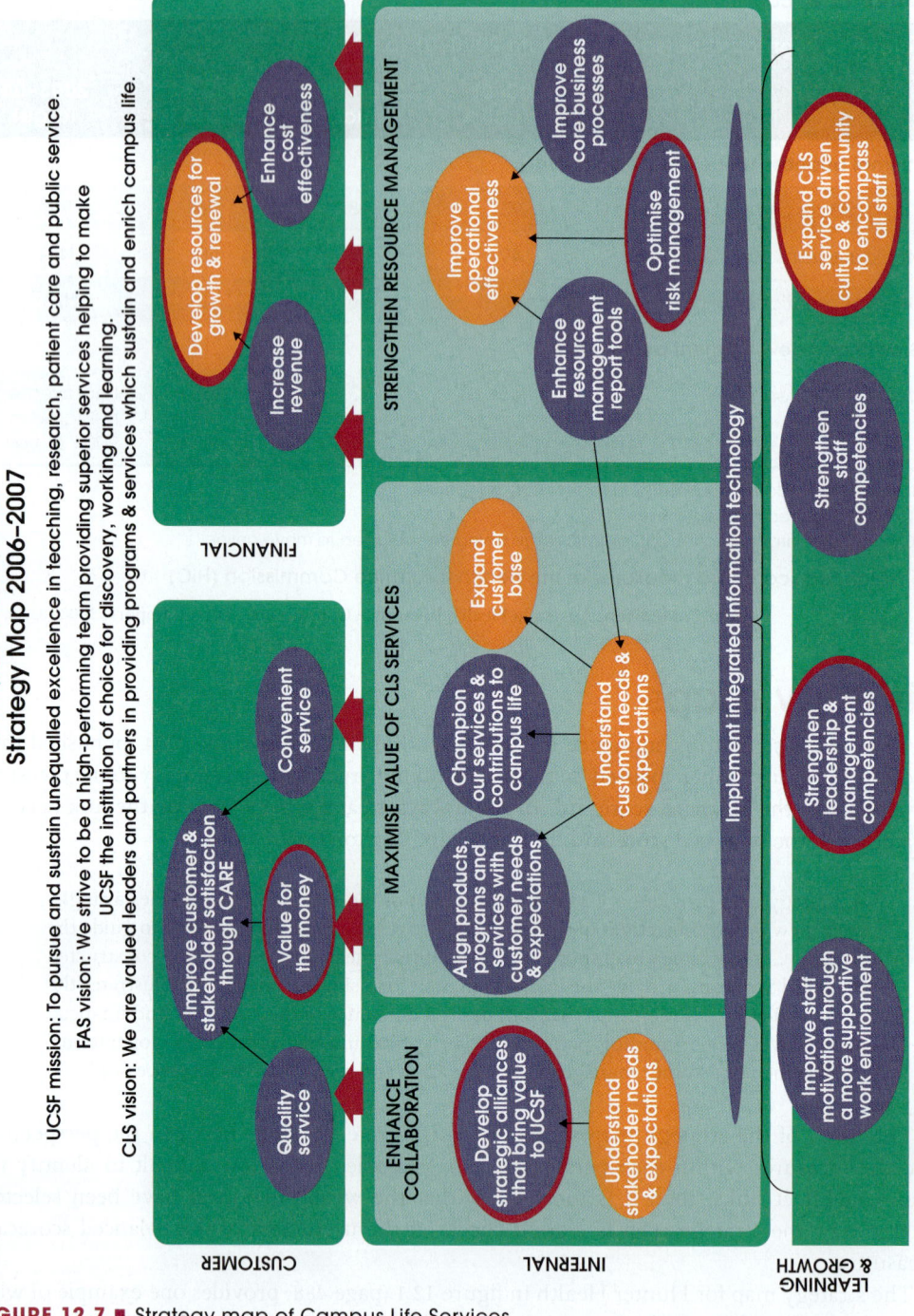

Campus *Life* Services
Strategy Map 2006–2007

UCSF mission: To pursue and sustain unequalled excellence in teaching, research, patient care and public service.

FAS vision: We strive to be a high-performing team providing superior services helping to make UCSF the institution of choice for discovery, working and learning.

CLS vision: We are valued leaders and partners in providing programs & services which sustain and enrich campus life.

FINANCIAL
- Develop resources for growth & renewal
- Enhance cost effectiveness
- Increase revenue

CUSTOMER
- Improve customer & stakeholder satisfaction through CARE
- Convenient service
- Value for the money
- Quality service

INTERNAL

STRENGTHEN RESOURCE MANAGEMENT
- Improve core business processes
- Improve operational effectiveness
- Optimise risk management
- Enhance resource management report tools

MAXIMISE VALUE OF CLS SERVICES
- Expand customer base
- Champion our services & contributions to campus life
- Understand customer needs & expectations
- Align products, programs and services with customer needs & expectations

ENHANCE COLLABORATION
- Develop strategic alliances that bring value to UCSF
- Understand stakeholder needs & expectations

Implement integrated information technology

LEARNING & GROWTH
- Expand CLS service driven culture & community to encompass all staff
- Strengthen staff competencies
- Strengthen leadership & management competencies
- Improve staff motivation through a more supportive work environment

BLUE = FAS aligned objective   ORANGE = CLS specific objective   RED OUTLINE = CLS priority

FIGURE 12.7 ■ Strategy map of Campus Life Services

Source: Campus Life Services, University of California, San Francisco,
http://cas.ucsf.edu/cls.

Steps in implementing a balanced scorecard

The process of implementing a balanced scorecard is summarised in figure 12.8. These general steps are customised for each entity. Note that these steps focus on the technical aspects of implementation. A range of behavioural aspects will also influence the success or otherwise of the implementation. These include:

- top management support
- achieving a management buy-in
- use of multiple champions
- adequate communication throughout the implementation process
- use of implementation feedback protocols
- organisation-wide participation.

FIGURE 12.8 ■ Steps in implementing a balanced scorecard

Clarify vision, core competencies and strategies

Clarifying the entity's vision, core competencies and strategies is central to the balanced scorecard approach. The vision provides an overall direction for the organisation. The core competencies and strategies provide guidance for achieving the organisational vision over the long term. To clarify the vision, statements are developed at the organisational level and for divisions, product lines or departments. This process leads to discussion and consensus, which further clarify an entity's purpose. Similarly, the process of clarifying core competencies and strategies helps others understand how to achieve the organisation's vision.

Analyse perspectives to develop performance objectives and measures

The next step is to analyse the organisation from the four perspectives. This step translates the organisation's vision and strategies into a set of performance objectives within each perspective. The analyses identify what the organisation must do well to attain its vision, focusing on the linkages between perspectives. The performance objectives should be limited to factors that achieve the organisation's vision and strategies.

The four perspectives introduced earlier are most commonly used for balanced scorecards. However, different entities define their perspectives differently. These perspectives differ by ownership type (for-profit versus not-for-profit), by industry, by organisation, and by subunit within organisations.

For each performance objective, one or more measures are identified to monitor the organisation's progress. Corrective action is then taken, as needed. The measures are financial and non-financial, covering both quantitative and qualitative data. Accountants are often more comfortable with quantitative measures, such as the average time to complete a customer's order or the number of new customers obtained. However, qualitative data, such as the results of customer and employee satisfaction surveys, are useful for some performance objectives.

Input measures capture activity or effort whereas outcome measures capture results. Balanced scorecards focus on these types of expected links. Overall, balanced scorecards usually contain a range of measures, with four to seven performance measures used for each of the perspectives.

Construct a strategy map to reinforce links between measures

As outlined earlier, the use of strategy maps in a balanced scorecard framework is a more recent development. Organisations are able to confirm the usefulness of their measures through construction of a one-page diagrammatic representation of the links between the measures in each of the perspectives. This can occur at a relatively broad level like the strategy map of Hunter Health in figure 12.1 (page 488), or it might be more specific, showing links between most of the measures.

Communicate, link throughout the organisation and refine

The balanced scorecard is usually presented as a top-down plan. High-level executives define the vision, core competencies and strategies of the organisation, then communicate them to divisions and departments. Yet success of the balanced scorecard approach depends on the efforts of individuals throughout the entity. To succeed, the balanced scorecard must be communicated both up and down the organisation. Links must be developed between organisational, divisional, departmental and individual objectives. Aligning goals increases the likelihood that all employees work together.

Sometimes the results of multiple units are formally combined with the results of another unit. For example, the results of individual departments might be combined into the results of a division. Part of this balanced scorecard combines data for all offices within the physical plant department. For instance, the safety office is responsible for all lost time from work-related injuries and for ensuring that all physical plant employees receive peer review safety training. Similarly, the human resources office is responsible for hiring employees within a desired timeframe.

Sometimes a common set of balanced scorecard measures is used across departments. These measures are common because some of the performance objectives are the same. Common measures help ensure consensus throughout the entity, minimising the need to develop separate systems for data collection. Measures that differ across offices relate to operating activities that are unique to individual offices/departments/divisions.

Organisation-wide implementation of a balanced scorecard requires significant amounts of communication and time. The process often begins with pilot projects, then expands across the entity as experience is gained and more sectors of the entity participate in the process. Refinements are often made to the original balanced scorecard after organisations have implemented it at the lowest levels.

Establish performance targets and action plans

It is not sufficient for an entity to create a balanced scorecard to measure progress towards its long-term vision and strategies. The organisation must also establish specific performance targets and related action plans, all of which are usually tied directly to each performance objective in the balanced scorecard. Performance targets are set for three- to five-year periods with interim milestones, increasing the organisation's focus on long-term results. Some entities formally reward individuals or groups of employees for attaining performance targets. The action plans give employees specific guidance about their efforts towards targets.

When the balanced scorecard is used to compensate employees, different weights may be placed on various measures in employee bonus packages. For example, if customer satisfaction ratings are inadequate, bonuses are made more dependent on improved satisfaction ratings. However, finding the optimal weighting among measures is difficult. If too much weight is put on customer satisfaction and not enough on financial measures, employees may spend a great deal of time in activities that increase satisfaction but do not improve profits.

Collect and analyse scorecard data to monitor performance

Balanced scorecard measures are captured periodically — monthly, quarterly, annually or other timeframes. Scorecard data are collected and analysed for different measures using different timeframes. Before calculations and comparisons to targets can be performed, systems for data collection must be established. In some cases, accounting systems are developed to capture relevant data. Non-financial measurement instruments may need to be developed. Survey instruments are either acquired or developed. Methods then need to be established for collecting samples and summarising results. Trends in balanced scorecard measures are analysed.

Investigate variances and reward employees

Actual results are compared to performance targets to determine whether the results are better or worse than desired. Then significant variances are analysed to identify their causes, leading to modifications in future plans. If the balanced scorecard is also used for employee compensation, rewards are computed and distributed.

Provide feedback and refine the balanced scorecard

An important part of the balanced scorecard method is the feedback loop that uses results and experience to refine the process. Managers use their analysis of balanced scorecard results to evaluate the success of their strategies and operating plans. This evaluation leads to revisions in organisations' visions, core competencies, strategies and operating plans. The effectiveness of the balanced scorecard is also gauged. Accountants and managers modify the set of measures to adapt to changes in the entity and to provide better information over time. Some measures may be dropped or changed, and new measures may be added.

Comprehensive example 1 demonstrates the implementation of a balanced scorecard in a hospital setting.

Comprehensive example 1

Implementing a balanced scorecard

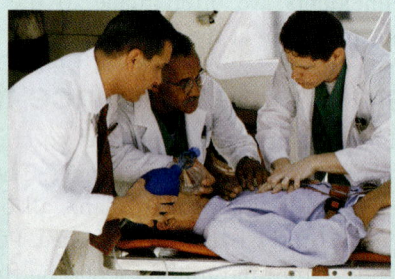

Two hospitals in a large regional area have trauma centres, but neither trauma centre is financially successful. Because the region needs at least one trauma centre, the state and local governments meet with hospital officials to determine the best course of action. Both hospitals had spent considerable time reviewing their visions, core competencies and current business strategies. They agree that only the teaching hospital should continue operating a trauma centre. The teaching hospital's mission is to provide both high-quality patient care and a learning centre for medical students. The teaching hospital needs a trauma centre so that medical students can prepare more thoroughly for careers as GPs and specialists. Teaching hospitals also have a mission to provide care to patients who are unable to pay, and the trauma centre provides treatment for a large number of low-income patients every year. Therefore, the decision to continue treating patients at the trauma centre fits well with the teaching hospital's mission.

Top managers at the teaching hospital decide to institute a balanced scorecard. They focus first on service in the trauma centre, because many more patients will be admitted when the other hospital closes its trauma centre. These managers believe that new measures of efficiency could help ease the transition.

The managers are also concerned about the current losses incurred by the trauma centre. Care is provided for a number of patients who are unable to pay, including aged pensioners and the unemployed. Victims of car accidents and physical assaults also require care. Clinical processes in the trauma centre need to be both cost effective and high quality to maintain the hospital's reputation.

Clarify vision, core competencies and strategies

A team of hospital administrators and trauma centre employees meet to discuss the balanced scorecard implementation. The team decides that the hospital's vision, core competencies and strategies also apply to the trauma centre. The hospital and trauma centre's patient care goals are to provide high-quality care in a timely manner and at a low cost for all patients, and also to provide care for those patients unable to pay. The hospital and trauma centre's teaching goals are to provide a high-quality education for medical students, focusing on technological developments and innovative patient care treatment.

Analyse perspectives to develop performance objectives and measures

The team decides that the standard four perspectives (financial, customer, internal business process, and learning and growth) are appropriate for analysing the trauma centre strategies and operations.

From a financial perspective, the hospital needs to at least break even to guarantee ongoing operations. The controller analyses historical records for the department and finds that it has always operated at a loss. Until last year, research grants and government subsidies were usually enough so that the centre broke even. The financial perspective is important because the centre needs financial resources to continuously update the equipment and technology needed to provide high-quality patient care. After discussing performance measures, three are chosen that are identical to those used by the hospital as a whole (see figure 12.9 overleaf). Two of the measures are profit margin ratios, which address the trauma centre's ability to control costs relative to revenues. The operating margin ratio includes only operating costs and revenues, while the excess income margin ratio includes non-operating revenue in the form of donations and grants, which typically supply the needed funds for expansion or new technology. The third measure addresses reimbursement levels for the trauma centre.

Next, the team analyses the customer perspective. The hospital outsources patient satisfaction surveying, and it monitors average satisfaction by department to focus on patients' perceived quality of care. However, the survey results are only available quarterly. The department wants measures that predict patient satisfaction and that can be monitored daily. With timely feedback, problems will be identified and corrected quickly, before too many patients are unhappy with some aspect of service. The team decides that most patients would care about the average time they wait for a nurse to respond to their call buttons. In addition, several quality-of-care measures could be monitored, such as the error rate in medication delivery and patient satisfaction with meals. The final list is included in figure 12.9.

The team then analyses the internal business process perspective. The hospital's long-term goals include managing patient care and clinical processes efficiently to maintain high quality and contain costs. The team decides that four aspects of internal business processes are critical to the trauma centre's success. It then focuses on identifying measures for those four aspects.

For innovation processes, the team would like to motivate improvements in routine care such as delivering medications, changing wound dressings and answering call buttons. Process improvements include innovative ways to streamline daily routines and to increase patient comfort. The number of process improvements in routine care will be tracked.

Clinical processes involve the technical aspects of care giving, such as setting up monitoring equipment and then using the information provided. The team decides to focus on the readmission rate as a performance measure for clinical processes. Sometimes patients are readmitted because complications arise at home. Some insurance entities may not pay for readmissions, and patients are unhappy to be readmitted. In addition to focusing on the decision to discharge patients at an appropriate time, tracking this measure will also encourage nurses to focus on the discharge process. The team believes that time spent on discharge instructions is linked to the readmission rate. For example, patients are sometimes readmitted because they become dehydrated at home.

Some medications require patients to drink extra amounts of water; if this requirement is not carefully explained during the discharge instruction process, patients do not recover as quickly and may require readmission. The team considered using length of stay as a measure, but this factor varies a great deal with patients' severity of illness and is not under the nurses' control.

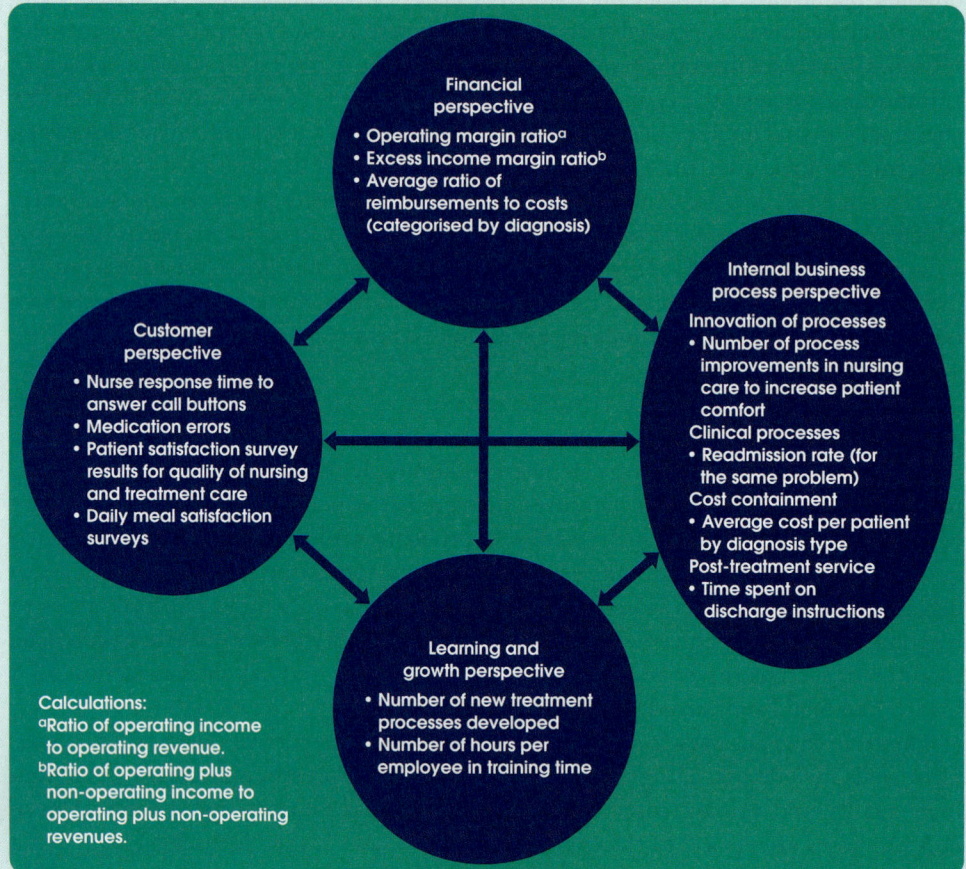

FIGURE 12.9 ■ Balanced scorecard measures for the teaching hospital's trauma centre

The team considers several possible ways to measure cost containment, but decides to focus initially on a general measure of cost — the average cost per patient by diagnosis type. This measure can be monitored as frequently as desired, allowing trauma centre managers to quickly identify any adverse trends in cost. It also provides a way for managers to monitor cost effects when new procedures are implemented.

The trauma centre's managers consider post-treatment service to be very important. Service after a patient leaves the centre contributes to the quality of the patient's care. The team decides to measure this aspect using the time spent on discharge instructions. With more time spent on discharge instructions, patients should receive better home care, reducing the probability that they will be readmitted. The team considers measuring the number of telephone calls made and emails sent with follow-up questions about patient home care, but decides that it is more important to focus on instructions before the patient goes home.

Finally the team focuses on the learning and growth perspective. To maintain and improve the trauma centre's reputation for innovative patient treatment, the team decides to track the number of new treatment processes developed. Because new technologies and care-giving practices are developed continually, the hospital provides a variety of medical education classes for nurses and other department staff. To encourage employees to take advantage of these classes, the team chooses number of hours of training per employee as performance measure.

Communicate, link throughout the organisation and refine

Once the team develops a tentative balanced scorecard for the trauma centre, the plan is presented to top hospital administrators and to employees in the centre. The administrators consider whether the trauma centre objectives align with the overall hospital mission, strategies and objectives. They believe that this scorecard appropriately addresses the hospital mission and praises the team. Employees and medical students also feel that the scorecard helps them understand how the trauma centre's objectives should be carried out.

Establish performance targets and action plans

The balanced scorecard team believes that the measures in figure 12.9 are appropriate for analysis. They ask the accounting department to collect information about last year's operations so they will have baseline information for comparison with future results. The team recommends that management and employees review the trends each month. After three months, the usefulness of this list of performance measures will be reassessed and the balanced scorecard can be changed accordingly.

Figure 12.10 (overleaf) summarises the information developed by the accounting department for last year's operations. The hospital's accounting system tracks patient charges for supplies and services by department; however, reimbursement is tracked at the hospital level because different payers pay different portions of charges, and some patients do not pay. Therefore, the patient revenue is assigned to the trauma centre based on its average mix of care for non-paying, Medicare, privately insured and other patients. As a result, revenue is measured with error, and the information may not be of quality high enough for a performance measure.

The cost data about patient care in the trauma centre is quite accurate, although patient costs include fixed cost allocations. Any change in the allocation bases or methods reduces comparability of patient cost information over time. Patient survey information is gathered by the quality and utilisation department. Although the team would like daily information about customer satisfaction measures, surveys about meals and nurse response time to call buttons are given randomly to 20 per cent of the trauma centre patients during the first three days of each month. The survey response information is forwarded to the accounting department on the third day. The accounting department does not have time to track this measure more frequently. Employees estimate their time in training each month. Because they do not always fill out the reports, they are contacted by accounting each month to update any missing estimates. Time spent on discharge instructions for each patient will be reported by discharge nurses using a new form developed by the accounting department. Once a month, accountants will meet with physicians and nurses to determine the number and type of improvements and innovations in treatment and care-giving processes.

Overall department financial information:	
Patient revenue	$5 040 000
Operating costs (cost of patient care)	6 300 000
Non-operating revenues	1 500 000
Non-operating costs	300 000
Information on trauma centre operations	
Number of patient admissions	252
Total nurse response time to call button (200 patient calls)	1000 minutes
Number of medication errors	10
Patient satisfaction survey results for quality of nursing and treatment care	
Number surveyed	130
Average satisfaction rating (1 to 5 = very satisfied)	3.8
Other patient-related data	
Average satisfaction rating on daily meal satisfaction surveys (1 to 5 = very satisfied)	2.9
Total patient days	2142
Readmissions	5
Minutes spent on discharge instructions	5040
Employee-related information	
Total time spent in training (hours)	875
Number of employees	35
Process improvement	
Number of process improvements in nursing care	3
Number of process improvements in treatment	2

FIGURE 12.10 ■ Balanced scorecard data for the teaching hospital's trauma centre

The balanced scorecard team uses the information in figure 12.10 to calculate last year's performance as shown in figure 12.11. Team members review this information and then meet with personnel at the other hospital to collect information about its trauma centre. They then determine appropriate benchmarks and action plans for the trauma centre during the transition period.

FIGURE 12.11 ■ Baseline balanced scorecard results for the teaching hospital's trauma centre

Financial perspective performance measures

Operating margin ratio:

$$\frac{\text{Operating margin}}{\text{Patient revenue}} = \frac{5\,040\,000 - 6\,300\,000}{5\,040\,000} \qquad (25)\%$$

Excess income margin ratio:

$$\frac{\text{Operating plus non-operating income}}{\text{Operating plus non-operating revenue}} = \frac{\$(60\,000)}{\$6\,540\,000} \qquad (1)\%$$

Ratio of reimbursement to cost

$$\frac{\text{Patient revenue}}{\text{Operating costs}} = \frac{\$5\,040\,000}{\$6\,300\,000} \qquad 0.8$$

(continued)

FIGURE 12.11 (*continued*)

Customer perspective performance measures	
Average nurse response time to answer call buttons (in minutes)	5
Medication errors	10
Average satisfaction with quality of nursing and treatment care	3.8
Average satisfaction with daily meals	2.9
Internal business process perspective	
Innovation of processes	
Number of process improvements in routine care	3
Clinical processes	
Readmission rate (Readmissions ÷ Total admissions)	2%
Cost containment	
Average cost per patient (Operating costs ÷ No. of admissions)	$25 000
Post-treatment service	
Time spent on discharge instructions (minutes)	20
Learning and growth perspective	
Number of new treatment processes developed	2
Average training hours per employee	25

Because measures for the combined trauma centres are likely to be different from the current centre, a transition period will be needed to determine appropriate benchmarks. During the transition time, trauma centre staff hired from the other hospital will be introduced to the scorecard. Within several months, targets can be set for every performance measure, and monitoring will begin. Information from the scorecard will be evaluated to determine areas in need of improvement. In addition, the current balanced scorecard will be re-evaluated and changed as appropriate.

Strengths and weaknesses of the balanced scorecard

Similar to other new accounting techniques, the balanced scorecard has both strengths and weaknesses.

Strengths

Entities are under increasing pressure to meet customer needs, use resources efficiently, compete effectively under changing conditions, employ new technologies and operating methods, and provide a good return to shareholders. These demands require more effective implementation of vision and strategies. The proponents of the balanced scorecard method argue that it improves performance by helping organisations integrate their visions and strategies into operations more completely. Many of the advantages of this approach, already described, are summarised in figure 12.12 (overleaf).

Weaknesses

Any method designed to help entities improve management decision making involves weaknesses because the process of management decision making is inherently uncertain. No perfect solutions have yet been discovered. Major weaknesses of the balanced scorecard are summarised in figure 12.12. First, the balanced scorecard faces questions about its costs and benefits.

Considerable time and effort are needed to develop and use the balanced scorecard. Outside consultants are often employed, and the time involved for key managers can be considerable.

Strengths	Weaknesses
Communication and linkages ■ Encourages clarification and updating of vision and strategies ■ Improves communication and consensus throughout the entity ■ Links short-term and long-term performance objectives to the vision and strategies	Implementation is expensive and time-consuming Uncertainties ■ Appropriateness of vision and strategies ■ Accuracy of identified core competencies ■ Best set of performance objectives and measures ■ Reliability of scorecard data ■ Reasonableness of targets ■ Doubt about links among perspectives
Guidance for improvements ■ Enables periodic performance reviews of progress towards vision and strategies ■ Leads to improved financial performance ■ Helps managers use operational data for decision making	Mistakes in implementation ■ Ambiguous or generally defined objectives ■ Information systems not integrated ■ Insufficient resources ■ Lack of senior management support ■ Focusing on inappropriate objectives
Motivation ■ Aligns unit and individual goals with the organisational vision and strategies ■ Motivates employee effort ■ Reduces optimisation of subunits at the expense of the entity as a whole ■ Promotes action towards achieving strategies	Biases ■ Manager selection of familiar or easily attainable objectives and measures ■ Resistance from units and individuals ■ Process viewed as a temporary fad
	May be inappropriate for compensation
	Vision may not adequately capture core values including relations with regulators, approach towards the environment etc.

FIGURE 12.12 ■ Strengths and weaknesses of a balanced scorecard

Uncertainties

Uncertainty is part of any balanced scorecard. The underlying assumptions are that the vision and core competencies have been properly identified and that implementation of the organisation's strategies leads to success. However, the best choices for a vision and set of strategies are ambiguous; managers might incorrectly identify the entity's strengths relative to competitors. Furthermore, the process of identifying appropriate performance objectives and measures is not straightforward. The balanced scorecard methodology requires managers to identify the most important aspects of operations, yet they cannot be known with certainty. Once performance objectives are selected, additional uncertainty about the best set of measures arises. Some measures are more reliable than others, although less-reliable measures can at times address a more relevant aspect of operations.

Uncertainties about choices of information for a balanced scorecard challenge managers and accountants. For example, potential customer satisfaction measures include market share, number of return customers, number of new customers, and ratings on satisfaction surveys. Although the number of return customers and number of new customers can be measured with a high degree of accuracy, this information may not be as relevant for gauging customer satisfaction as other measures. Market share may or may not be reliable, depending on the accuracy of information about total industry sales. Many factors influence the reliability of survey ratings, including the survey design, methods for collecting samples and the types of customers surveyed. To decide on the best measure, managers and accountants need to weigh the quality and relevance of information across potential measures.

Another uncertainty is the best choice for performance targets, including how quickly an entity should be able to achieve its performance objectives. Low targets may fail to motivate sufficient effort. High targets discourage performance when employees perceive them as unrealistic.

The balanced scorecard also assumes specific linkages among the four perspectives. In particular, it assumes that improved performance in internal business processes and in learning and growth lead to improved customer-related measures. In turn, improved customer-related measures are assumed to lead to improved financial performance. These assumptions, however, might not hold because of uncertainties about the measures and about the inter-relationships among aspects of an organisation's activities. Researchers found cause-and-effect relationships only between the customer perspective measures and financial performance measures. Although research studies do not prove the absence of links, they raise doubts about the linkage that managers and accountants need to consider.

Mistakes in implementation

Analysts and consultants point out a number of areas where mistakes are often made in balanced scorecard implementations, leading to poor results. Sometimes performance objectives are ambiguous or defined too generally, reducing the balanced scorecard's effectiveness in communicating the actions needed to achieve the entity's vision and strategies. Sometimes the organisation's information systems are not designed adequately to capture information needed. The balanced scorecard can be expensive to implement, and may face inadequate resources for designing, implementing, communicating, following through on results and refining the methodology over time. Although senior managers are generally involved in the initial adoption of a balanced scorecard, they may give the process inadequate support.

Another mistake relates to the selection of inappropriate objectives and related measures. Author Jim Collins argues that many entities focus on the wrong financial measures. His research suggests that managers of the best-performing companies often succeed because they adopt more insightful measures to monitor their businesses. For example, Gillette shifted its focus from profit per division to profit per customer. This shift helped Gillette recognise the importance of repeatable purchases of high-margin products such as Mach3 razor cartridges. Companies where managers failed to adopt similarly insightful measures were not as successful.[2]

Biases

Several types of biases reduce the effectiveness of a balanced scorecard. Recent research suggests that managers select performance measures with which they are most familiar — measures that may not induce behaviour that leads to financial success.[3] In addition, managers have incentives to choose performance objectives and measures that highlight areas that are strengths instead of areas that need improvement. Any organisational change is likely to encounter resistance. For example, employees may view the balanced scorecard as a temporary management whim that does not deserve their attention. These types of resistance can prevent the entity-wide commitment and effort required for balanced scorecard success.

Other factors

Some questions surround whether or how the balanced scorecard should be used to compensate employees. Because of the uncertainties already discussed, many employees perceive balanced scorecard measures to be unfair for use in compensation calculations. In addition, weights or other formulaic approaches for using balanced scorecard results lead to game-playing and suboptimisation, contrary to the purpose of a balanced scorecard.

Another criticism of the balanced scorecard approach is that it does not adequately capture core values, including relations with regulators or approaches towards the environment. An entity's core values are theoretically embedded in its vision and strategies. However, current literature on the balanced scorecard places little emphasis on values.

How valuable is the balanced scorecard?

Given these perceived weaknesses in the balanced scorecard, some people are inclined to dismiss this methodology; they want greater certainty about benefits. However, any method that managers use to help them develop and implement business strategies is subject to significant uncertainty. We learned in chapter 1 about the path to higher-quality management decisions, presented again in figure 12.13. Higher-quality decisions occur from use of the following:

- higher-quality information
- higher-quality reports
- higher-quality decision-making processes.

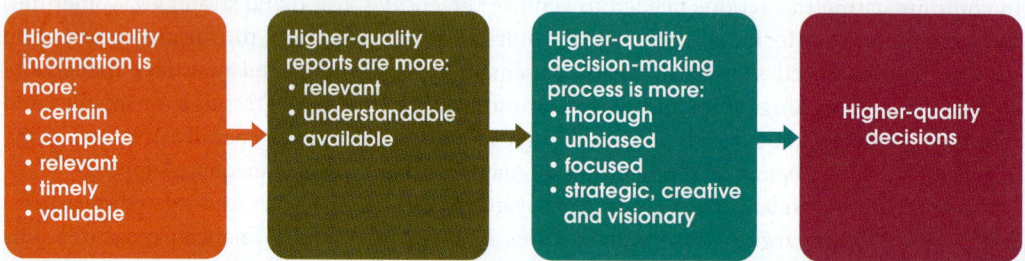

FIGURE 12.13 ■ Path to higher-quality management decisions

The best questions to ask about the balanced scorecard methodology are whether it helps managers and employees throughout the entity make higher-quality decisions, and whether the benefits from improved decision making exceed the costs of implementing and maintaining a balanced scorecard. Is the information in a balanced scorecard of higher quality than the information managers previously used? Are balanced scorecard reports more relevant, understandable and available on a timely basis? Does use of the balanced scorecard encourage managers and other employees to be more thorough, less biased, more focused, and more strategic, creative and visionary? Proponents of the balanced scorecard methodology argue that the answer to each of these questions is 'yes.' They also point out that the balanced scorecard should not be viewed as a static formulaic approach. Instead, it must be re-evaluated and refined periodically to provide better information for monitoring and motivating performance. Periodic re-evaluation allows managers to eliminate or alter measures that do not fit well and to identify potential new measures that offset unintended negative effects. As the entity learns, it can do a better job of designing and using a balanced scorecard. Organisations that fail to engage in continuous improvement are less likely to achieve high-quality results.

Summary

---

1 **Outline the role of strategic decision making.**

Overview of management decision making

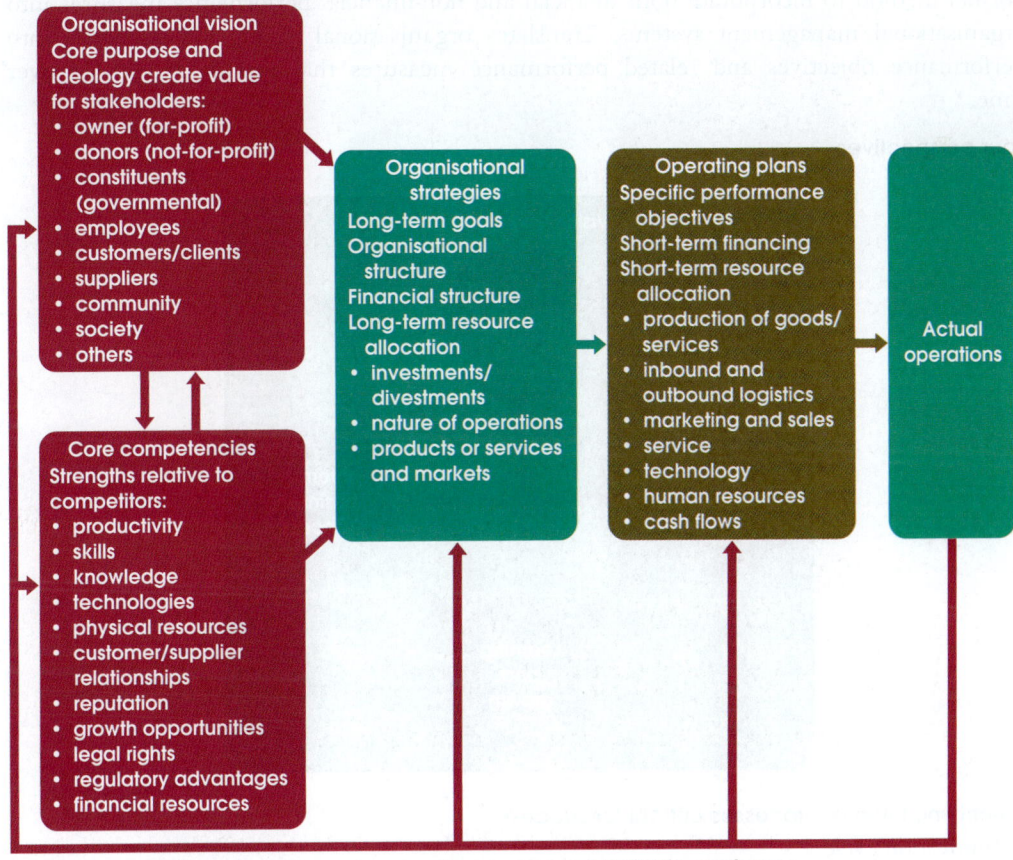

Measure performance, monitor progress and motivate employees

---

2 **Understand how financial and non-financial measures are used to evaluate organisational performance.**

Financial measures
Information measured in dollars or ratios of dollars

Non-financial measures
Information that cannot be measured in dollars

Monitoring measurable performance objectives

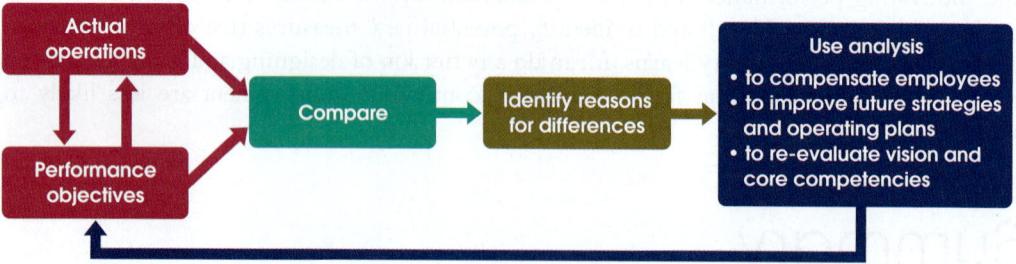

3 **Explain the balanced scorecard.**

Balanced scorecard

Formal method to incorporate both financial and non-financial performance measures into organisational management systems. Translates organisational vision and strategies into performance objectives and related performance measures that can be monitored over time.

Four perspectives

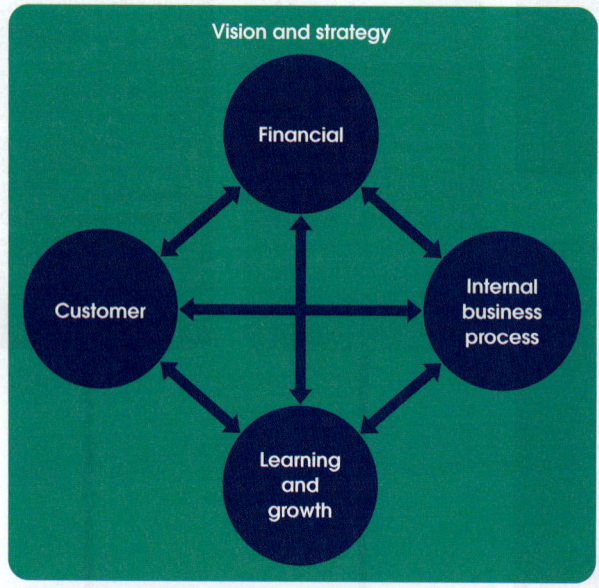

Identifying internal processes critical for success

- Innovation cycle
- Operations cycle
- Post-sales service cycle

4 **Outline the role of strategy maps.**

Strategy maps provide the links between the entity's strategy and the perspectives and measures used in the balanced scorecard. The objective is to outline the cause-and-effect links between the measures in each of the perspectives. Ideally, this would be represented diagrammatically on a one-page document.

5   Explain how a balanced scorecard is implemented.

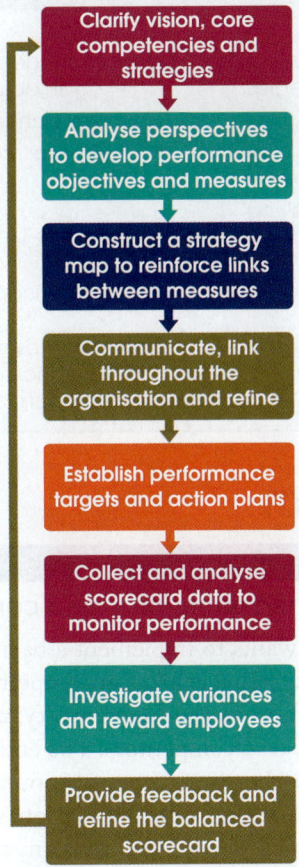

6   Identify the strengths and weaknesses of the balanced scorecard.

Strengths	Weaknesses
Communication and linkages ■ Encourages clarification and updating of vision and strategies ■ Improves communication and consensus throughout the entity ■ Links short-term and long-term performance objectives to the vision and strategies	**Implementation is expensive and time-consuming** **Uncertainties** ■ Appropriateness of vision and strategies ■ Accuracy of identified core competencies ■ Best set of performance objectives and measures ■ Reliability of scorecard data ■ Reasonableness of targets ■ Doubt about links among perspectives
Guidance for improvements ■ Enables periodic performance reviews of progress towards vision and strategies ■ Leads to improved financial performance ■ Helps managers use operational data for decision making	**Mistakes in implementation** ■ Ambiguous or generally defined objectives ■ Information systems not integrated ■ Insufficient resources ■ Lack of senior management support ■ Focusing on inappropriate objectives

Strengths	Weaknesses
Motivation	Biases
■ Aligns unit and individual goals with the organisational vision and strategies	■ Manager selection of familiar or easily attainable objectives and measures
■ Motivates employee effort	■ Resistance from units and individuals
■ Reduces optimisation of subunits at the expense of the entity as a whole	■ Process viewed as a temporary fad
■ Promotes action towards achieving strategies	
	May be inappropriate for compensation
	Vision may not adequately capture core values including relations with regulators, approach towards the environment etc.

Self-study problem

SELF-STUDY PROBLEM 1

Balanced scorecard implementation; pros and cons

Mount Dandenong Bikes (MDB) wants to implement a balanced scorecard. Its mission statement reads, 'We build high-quality, reliable bikes at competitive prices.' The entity's competitive strategy is to continuously improve the functionality, reliability and quality of its bikes while holding prices at levels similar to competitors. The entity operates three subunits organised around the product lines for the three types of mountain bikes it currently produces. A fourth bike line in development includes a finished design, with engineers currently working on the plans for the manufacturing process. MDB sells directly to bike shops and operates an Internet site that allows bike shops to place orders for customised products.

REQUIRED

(a) Describe the implementation cycle for the balanced scorecard at MDB.
(b) Describe the four perspectives of the balanced scorecard, and list one or more performance objectives for each perspective that are likely to be important for MDB.
(c) Pick one performance objective for each perspective in part (b) and identify two or more potential measures. Explain how each measure would link to improved financial performance.
(d) Describe the pros and cons of implementing a balanced scorecard for MDB.

Solution to self-study problem 1

(a) Steps for implementing a balanced scorecard for MDB (see figure 12.8 on page 499):
   1. *Clarify vision, core competencies and strategies.* MDB already developed its mission statement. The entity's managers should also consider writing a vision statement and core values statement. In addition, the managers need to clarify MDB's core competencies. Even though the entity already specified its strategies, the managers should review them and revise them as necessary.
   2. *Analyse perspectives to develop performance objectives and measures.* The managers need to analyse the entity's vision and strategies from each of the four perspectives for the balanced scorecard: financial, customer, internal business process, and learning and growth. Within each perspective, they need to identify performance objectives and

related measures. To identify performance objectives, the managers must determine the critical actions that the organisation must take to achieve its strategies. They need to define what they mean by high quality from a customer's perspective. They also need to analyse competitors' prices and quality to determine the amount of cost containment and levels of quality needed.

3. *Construct a strategy map to reinforce links between measures.* The managers will use the perspectives and related measures identified in step 2 to illustrate the links between each of the measures. This will be shown diagrammatically in a strategy map, which also serves as a useful vehicle to test the adequacy of the measures. If cause-and-effect links cannot be demonstrated, then a reassessment of the measures will be necessary.

4. *Communicate, link throughout the organisation and refine.* The managers will develop a communication plan and obtain assistance from personnel throughout the organisation in clarifying and refining the decisions made in steps 1 and 2. The managers would then decide whether the different subunits should develop their own balanced scorecards. The final set of performance objectives and measures must be communicated effectively to align employee efforts with the entity's objectives.

5. *Establish performance targets and action plans.* Through discussions among management and employees at different levels in the entity and analysis of previous results, performance targets and action plans are developed for each performance objective. The managers must also decide whether to use the balanced scorecard data for employee compensation. For employees whose compensation depends on the results, managers need to prioritise the objectives that relate to that employee's performance and establish a weighting scheme for linking rewards to performance. For example, production line employees could receive bonuses when production quantity and quality reach target levels.

6. *Collect and analyse scorecard data to monitor performance.* The managers need to ensure that information systems are in place to collect and report scorecard data. Trends can be noted. As data are collected, actual results can be compared to targets.

7. *Investigate variances and reward employees.* The managers need to analyse reasons for variance from targets. They also need to consider what the results mean for future strategies, operating plans and performance objectives.

8. *Provide feedback and refine the balanced scorecard.* The managers need to establish a feedback loop so that the information they learn is used to make adjustments as they go through the balanced scorecard process in the future. It means a re-evaluation of the process, beginning at step 1, as necessary.

(b) Four perspectives and possible performance objectives:

- The *financial perspective* analyses the economic consequences of MDB's operations and decisions. A possible performance objective is a profitability level that is in the top quartile within the industry.
- The *customer perspective* analyses the role of customers in MDB's success. Possible performance objectives are:
  - provision of goods and services that satisfy customers so that they remain loyal
  - an increase in the size of the loyal customer base.
- The *internal business process perspective* analyses the role of the entity's internal methods and practices in MDB's success. Possible performance objectives are:
  - continuous improvements in functionality and quality that are important to customers (innovation cycle)
  - production of each bike as cost effectively as possible in a timely manner (operations cycle)

- reliable products, with few returns and little warranty work (operations and post-sales service cycle)
- customer satisfaction with interactions that occur after purchase (post-sales service cycle).

■ The *learning and growth perspective* analyses the role of continuous improvement efforts in MDB's success. Possible performance objectives are:
- productive and well-trained employees
- systems that support operations in a cost-effective manner.

(c)

Performance objective	Measures and links to financial performance
Financial perspective A profitability level in top quartile within the industry	■ Operating margin. A higher operating margin leads to higher profits, which is a common indicator of financial success. ■ Economic value-added. EVA takes into account the level of profits as well as the cost of capital. ■ Average price per bike. The average price feeds into both operating margin and EVA. As prices go up, if costs and volumes are held constant, operating margins and EVA should increase.
Customer perspective Provision of goods and services that satisfy customers so that they remain loyal	■ Customer satisfaction ratings (with emphasis on quality and price satisfaction). If customer satisfaction ratings are high, MDB is likely to keep its current customers and add new ones, which would lead to higher market share, higher sales volumes, better operating margins and higher EVA. ■ Market share. Higher market share would lead to higher sales volumes, better operating margins and higher EVA. ■ Number of return customers and number of new customers. If the number of return and new customers increases, then sales volumes should also increase, leading to better operating margins and higher EVA.
Internal business process perspective Reliable products with few returns and little warranty work	■ Number of bikes returned. If return rates and warranty work are low, customers are more satisfied and sales increase, leading to higher profits. In addition, MDB spends less on post-sales service, which also increases profits. ■ Dollar value of warranty work. Same as above.
Learning and growth perspective Productive and well-trained employees	■ Employee retention. Satisfied and well-trained employees are less likely to leave the entity. They also will monitor quality and efficiency of the production lines and make suggestions for improvements, leading to better cost-efficiency and higher-quality products, in turn leading to higher profits. More satisfied employees are also more likely to have positive interactions with customers, leading to improved sales and higher profitability. ■ Employee hours of training. Better training improves performance of work and interactions with customers, leading to higher sales and lower costs, increasing profits.

(d) **Pros:** MDB begins the process of clarifying and updating its vision. Communication improves throughout the organisation as the vision and strategies are refined. Long-term and short-term performance objectives are linked to the vision and strategies. This linkage enables employees to understand their contribution to the overall entity and aligns employee goals with those of MDB. Individual employees use their scorecards to guide their efforts towards reaching MDB's goals and objectives. MDB managers will periodically review their vision and core competencies, and their progress towards achieving them. Managers also have better information for decision making. These actions should lead to improved financial performance.

Cons: Implementing a balanced scorecard is expensive and time-consuming. If MDB is already operating efficiently, the benefits from implementing the scoreboard may not be as large as the costs. If the vision or understanding of core competencies is inappropriate or inadequate, goals and objectives in the balanced scorecard may not relate to improved financial performance. If targets are unreasonably high or low, employees have no motivation to meet them. If the objectives are not well thought-out and communicated clearly, employees may not understand the objectives or how they relate to overall organisational performance. Measures could be chosen for which no data are available, or the data available are measured incorrectly or with error. Managers may choose performance measures that represent their strengths, rather than making unbiased choices.

Questions

12.1 Explain the differences between financial and non-financial performance measures and give two examples of each.

12.2 Identify four potential perspectives for a balanced scorecard and explain how they are related.

12.3 Allied Trucking moves produce from farms to markets. Its managers decided to implement a balanced scorecard around the entity's vision statement: 'We aim to be the industry leader in cost-effective and timely delivery of produce.' Provide two potential performance measures for each of the four perspectives for the balanced scorecard for Allied Trucking.

12.4 Explain what core competencies are. How do they relate to organisational strategies?

12.5 Suppose that a car dealership decided it would no longer compensate employees with sales commissions, but instead pay a salary with a bonus for high customer satisfaction ratings. What problems would you foresee from the dealership's financial perspective?

12.6 Describe the implementation process for the balanced scorecard.

12.7 What is strategic decision making? What role does it play in the balanced scorecard?

12.8 Outline the purpose of strategy maps.

12.9 (a) Pick two public companies, go to their websites and identify their major strategies.
(b) Pick one of the companies from part (a) and go to the website of a competitor in the same industry. (For example, if you chose Coles, you might go to the website of Woolworths.) Now compare the strategies of both companies and list any similarities and differences.

12.10 Explain why demand might increase for relevant and useful information in the future. What professional skills will help you meet that need?

12.11 Explain why you will need to continuously learn new accounting techniques, as well as develop in-depth knowledge about industries within which you work.

Exercises

12.12 Balanced scorecard measures for financial perspective Following is financial information for the last period about China Express, a regional entity with a number of fast-food stores:

Revenue from operations	$10 450 200
Operating costs	$9 927 690
After-tax profits	$391 883
Cost of capital	12%
Required rate of return	15%
Average assets	$4 180 080

REQUIRED

Describe and calculate several measures that could be used for the financial perspective.

12.13 Financial and non-financial measures Managers increasingly use a mixture of financial and non-financial measures for organisational performance.

REQUIRED

In the following list of performance measures, identify those that are financial (F) and those that are non-financial (N).

(a) Customer satisfaction ratings
(b) Market share
(c) Operating margin
(d) Return on sales
(e) Annual average purchase amount per customer
(f) Defect rate
(g) Normal spoilage
(h) Labour efficiency variance
(i) Number of new products developed annually
(j) Revenues from new products introduced this year

12.14 Balanced scorecard measures for customer perspective Flowing Wells High School is in the process of developing a balanced scorecard. The administrators decided that their customers are parents and future employers of their students. They believe the students are their products.

REQUIRED

Discuss whether each of the following potential measures would be useful for the customer perspective in the balanced scorecard.

(a) Parent ratings of satisfaction with the high school curriculum
(b) Graduation rate
(c) Percentage of students employed during the summer after graduation
(d) Employer satisfaction ratings for Flowing Wells High School graduates
(e) Monthly earnings of graduates
(f) Number of graduates attending classes beyond high school
(g) Cost per student per year
(h) Number of classes per student per semester
(i) Average number of college credit hours completed per teacher

12.15 Learning and growth perspective Suppose Markman Ltd, a large pharmaceutical company, is concerned about the ability of its research and development department to develop profitable new prescription drugs. Once a drug has been developed and patented, it takes 9 to 12 years to meet all of the regulatory requirements. The company can then market the drug for about 11.5 years, on average, before the patent expires. Then competitors produce generic drugs. Employees currently participate in profit-sharing plans, but the company wants to give additional bonuses to improve performance. Markman decided to implement a balanced scorecard approach.

REQUIRED

(a) Explain why monitoring and rewarding non-financial performance might be particularly important for Markman.

(b) List one objective for Markman's learning and growth perspective.

(c) List two performance measures for the objective you picked in part (b).

12.16 Balanced scorecard measures for four perspectives Part of the process for developing a balanced scorecard is to identify one or more measures for each perspective.

REQUIRED

Categorise each of the following potential balanced scorecard measures according to the following perspectives:

    F Financial
    C Customer
    I   Internal business process
    L Learning and growth

(a) Percentage of customer orders delivered on time

(b) Ratio of research and development cost to number of new products developed

(c) Economic value added (EVA)

(d) Number of hours of employee training

(e) Direct labour price variance

(f) Market share

(g) Percentage of customer orders delivered without error

(h) Days in accounts receivables

(i) Throughput time

(j) Direct materials efficiency variance

(k) Asset turnover

(l) Employee retention rate

(m) Percentage of bad debts collected

(n) Customer satisfaction ratings

(o) Number of degrees and certificates held per employee or department

(p) Percentage of purchase orders that are error free

12.17 Strategic plans; balanced scorecard measures for not-for-profit entity Suppose you have been invited by a classmate to help found a new not-for-profit entity named Students Care. The organisation's purpose is to provide scholarship money for children in Africa who have become orphans because of the AIDS epidemic. The organisation will operate only on campus, and the target donors are students. Suppose a wealthy businesswoman has offered to coordinate distribution of the scholarship funds to needy students, but wants to see a business plan for the organisation that describes the organisational vision and lists the core competencies, strategies and operating plans.

REQUIRED

(a) Explain what each item on the businesswoman's list means. For each item, provide a possible example for Students Care.

(b) Consider the perspective of internal business processes. Your classmate wants to measure the number of hours per week that volunteers spend collecting donations but you believe it should be dollars collected per volunteer hour spent in collection, measured on a weekly basis. Give one advantage and one disadvantage for each measure.

(c) You have had difficulty determining a measure of learning and growth, but a campus association recently organised a series of short workshops on improving student fundraising activities, as well as other aspects of governing student entities. Discuss the advantages and disadvantages of using the number of Students Care volunteers attending workshops as a measure for this perspective.

12.18 Balanced scorecard perspectives, performance objectives and measures Perspectives, performance objectives and potential performance measures for the balanced scorecard at Holiday Resorts are as follows:

Perspectives
- (i) Financial
- (ii) Customer
- (iii) Internal business
- (iv) Learning and growth

Performance objectives
- A. Reduce housekeeping costs
- B. Improve the quality of and results from advertising campaigns
- C. Decrease vacancy rate during the off-season
- D. Increase number of return customers
- E. Increase overall profits
- F. Increase the use of internet-based reservations
- G. Retain high-quality employees
- H. Increase the number of activities available to customers
- I. Improve the quality of stay for holiday makers
- J. Provide employee training in quality customer service
- K. Reduce error rate in reservations

Potential performance measures
1. Operating margin
2. Customer complaint rate
3. Survey customers at check-in about how they first heard about the resorts
4. Housekeeping cost per room
5. Number of employee hours spent in training
6. Error rate in reservation process
7. Percentage of reservations made using the website
8. Customer surveys about satisfaction and quality
9. Employee turnover rates
10. Number of activities per resort that are available to customers
11. Percentage and number of return customers
12. Number of hours of employee training offered
13. Vacancy rates
14. Customer focus groups inquiring about quality and potential success of advertising
15. Number of suggestions that improve quality of service

REQUIRED

(a) For each perspective (i–iv), identify at least one appropriate performance objective (A–K).

(b) For each performance objective (A–K), identify at least one appropriate performance measure (1–15).

(c) Explain the links between the measures.

12.19 Future direction of accounting information Think about the type of work you will perform in your future career.

REQUIRED

(a) Give examples of the types of financial and non-financial information you will probably use in your work.
(b) List several methods you could use to produce information that will help predict future operations for your employer or for clients.
(c) What types of continuous learning do you foresee in your career?
(d) Explain why you may need to use creative or innovative ideas in your career.

Problems

12.20 Balanced scorecard; strategy map and implementation Mark Moreland, a dentist, decided to join a small group of dentists so that he no longer has to be on call every night. Practice members share the responsibility of emergencies with other members of the group. In the past, Mark differentiated his practice by specialising in the treatment of families with children. None of the other dentists specialise in families but all of them treat some children. Mark's son just finished an accounting degree and recommended that the dental group consider implementing a balanced scorecard as they develop the policies and practices for the new group.

REQUIRED

(a) Explain what each of the four perspectives of the balanced scorecard mean in the context of a dental group.
(b) Recommend several methods the group could use to assess a performance objective of patient satisfaction.
(c) Recommend two measures for each of the four perspectives for the dental group. Explain your recommendations.
(d) Construct a strategy map to reflect the links between the measures selected. Briefly discuss the links.

12.21 Balanced scorecard; financial and non-financial measures Dyggur Equipment manufactures and sells heavy equipment used in construction and mining. Customers are contractors who want reliable equipment at a low cost. The entity's strategy is to provide reliable products at a price lower than its competitors. Management wants to emphasise quick delivery and quick turnaround when equipment needs repair or service so that contractors are not without their equipment often or for long. Dyggur is considering the performance measures shown below for use in its balanced scorecard.

REQUIRED

Categorise each of the following potential balanced scorecard measures as follows:

    F Financial
    C Customer
    I Internal business process
    L Learning and growth

(a) Manufacturing cycle time per product
(b) Market share
(c) Average ratings on customer satisfaction surveys
(d) Average cost per unit
(e) Economic value added
(f) Percentage of receivables collected

(g) Dollar value of warranty work

(h) Time between order and delivery

(i) Time it takes to repair returned equipment

(j) Number of focus groups for new products

(k) Number of new uses for current products

(l) Number of times new technology is applied to current products

(m) Number of product change suggestions from sales

(n) Number of engineering change orders to improve manufacturing cycle

(o) Revenue growth

(p) Employee training hours

(q) Number of quality improvement suggestions from employees

(r) Number of new customers

(s) Number of repeat customers

(t) Employee turnover rate

(u) Defect rates for manufacturing production

(v) Percentage of error-free rates in:
   (i) purchasing
   (ii) billing
   (iii) customer record keeping

12.22 Strategy; balanced scorecard measures and process Refer to the information in problem 12.21. Dyggur Equipment wants to offer weekend servicing of heavy equipment. None of its competitors offer this service, and management believes this service will bring in new business and help retain current customers.

REQUIRED

(a) List several advantages and disadvantages of this strategy.

(b) List one financial and two non-financial performance measures that could be used to monitor the success of this plan.

(c) Suppose the managers decide to launch this new service. At the end of the first year of operating weekend service, performance is evaluated by gathering and analysing measures such as those identified in part (b). How can this information be used to improve performance for the next period?

12.23 Mission statement; strategy; balanced scorecard implementation Squeezers Juice and Tea Company manufactures organic juices and chai teas that are sold at wholefoods stores. Several of its products have been featured in movies because the company's products are popular with celebrities. The owners and employees value organic products and innovative combinations of juices and teas with outstanding taste. Several employees have found sources of unusual ingredients from organic farmers around the world. The ingredients are more expensive than those used by other juice manufacturers. Although Squeezers cannot set unrealistically high prices, it focuses on high quality. Demand for the entity's products is stable even though it sets the highest prices for juices in its market.

Recently, the costs of several unusual ingredients increased because of weather conditions. The owner is concerned that increasing prices any more could reduce demand. She has taken a business workshop and learned about the balanced scorecard. She wants to incorporate a balanced scorecard at Squeezers.

REQUIRED

(a) Draft a potential mission statement for Squeezers. Explain how you decided what should be included in the statement and how it should be worded.

(b) Explain the entity's business strategy and core competencies.

(c) Identify several performance objectives for each of the four perspectives.

(d) Select two performance objectives for each of the four perspectives, and identify a potential performance measure for each. Explain your choices.

(e) Describe possible methods to collect the data needed for each of the performance measures in part (d). For example, what existing information might be available? What new record keeping might be required? Would the company need to develop surveys?

12.24 Balanced scorecard measures China Express owns a number of stores that sell fast food. As part of its compensation packages, China Express provides employees with bonuses based on customer satisfaction surveys. Recent analysis of the data shows a positive correlation between survey ratings and sales; that is, as customer satisfaction increases, sales increase. However, at a certain point in this trend, sales plateau even though the ratings continue to increase. In addition, increasing customer satisfaction causes costs to also increase because more time is spent with each customer, and more employees are on hand to help with food preparation and cashiering to reduce the time that customers wait for their food to be prepared. Other factors that appear to affect customer satisfaction are the general cleanliness of the store and the attitudes of the cashiers as they provide customer service. A factor that strongly affects sales at each store is its health rating from the local council. These ratings are published in the local daily newspaper. When a store has a low rating, sales at that outlet drop off until publication of an improved rating occurs. The owner wants to add one or more financial performance measures to the bonus package so that employees will earn more money when customer satisfaction increases at the same time that financial performance is also increasing.

REQUIRED

(a) Describe advantages and disadvantages of using a combination of performance measures reflecting the customer and financial perspectives.

(b) Management would like to add other customer-related measures and is considering replacing survey satisfaction with some other measure. List one potential measure and list at least one advantage and one disadvantage for it.

(c) List one additional performance measure that could be included in the compensation package. Explain what it is and what it would contribute.

12.25 Participative strategic planning process and benefits; manager behaviour (Assumes knowledge from management classes) Quantum Computers produces and sells laptop computers. The entity is currently deciding whether to continue concentrating on the laptop computer market or to expand by entering the highly competitive computer desktop workstation market.

Most of the management staff has been with Quantum for a long time. Michael Mitchem, Quantum's president, wants his management staff to assist him in Quantum's strategic planning process. Mitchem has scheduled a three-day offsite meeting for the management staff to join together for the entity's strategic planning process.

REQUIRED

(a) What functional areas should be discussed during the strategic planning process?

(b) Identify at least six factors to be considered in a thorough strategic planning process that will move a company such as Quantum to another level of product development.

(c) Identify at least three benefits that Quantum can derive from a participatory strategic planning process.

(d) Discuss the expected behaviour of the managers at Quantum who participate in the three-day offsite strategic planning meeting.

12.26 Balanced scorecard; strengths and weaknesses Brewster House is a not-for-profit shelter for the homeless. Lately funding has decreased, but the demand for overnight shelter has increased. In cold weather, clients are turned away because the shelter is full. The director believes that the current capacity could be used more efficiently. No one has taken time to analyse the physical layout of the shelter and current use of space. Several rooms are used for storage that could probably be used for temporary housing. The stored boxes need to be sorted and moved. Volunteers currently assign beds and manage overnight housing, because the director is busy with fundraising. Volunteers work just a few shifts each week, so no one has taken responsibility for coordinating improvements in the services offered. The director is considering whether to implement a balanced scorecard to focus the attention of all volunteers on areas that need improvement.

Brewster receives funds from several sources, including a set annual budget from the local council and direct donations from supporters. The director develops a budget each year based on expected funding but she cannot precisely predict donations. The budget is used primarily to justify funding requests submitted to the council.

The director has asked a group of accounting students from the local university to evaluate operations and recommend whether the entity should develop a balanced scorecard. She cannot give bonuses based on the measures, but she wonders whether developing and monitoring performance measures would encourage the volunteers to increase the use of capacity. She also wonders whether some information from the balanced scorecard could be used to show donors the effectiveness of operations.

REQUIRED

(a) Describe several potential costs and benefits of the balanced scorecard for this organisation.
(b) Describe one potential measure for each scorecard perspective appropriate for Brewster House. Explain how information for each measure will be collected.
(c) Prepare a memo to the director that recommends whether Brewster House should adopt a balanced scorecard. In writing the memo, consider what information the director needs from you to help her make a decision.

12.27 Strategies and balanced scorecard measures for a country Brian Henshall, foundation emeritus professor of management at the University of Auckland, suggests a number of potential performance measures that could be used to monitor performance for the country of New Zealand. Henshall recommends that the country publish measures monthly to gauge progress. He also argues that a discussion of potential performance measures would help citizens define what they want. Ultimately, the measures could be used to monitor the performance of elected officials. Following are some of Henshall's suggestions.[4]

Tangible wealth:

- gross domestic product (GDP) percentage change as a measure of growth
- the ratio of government wealth creation to business wealth creation as a measure of government economic performance
- GDP per person employed and per total number of people in New Zealand as efficiency measures
- New Zealand dollar exchange rate (percentage change for last quarter or last year) as a measure of economic stability
- number of bankrupt firms to all trading entities as a measure of business stability.

Environmental intangible wealth:

- a pollution index that measures degradation of the environment from pollution
- a ratio of protected land relative to total government-owned land
- a ratio of alternative energy resources relative to total energy produced.

Physical and social infrastructure:

- educational expense as a percentage of GDP
- healthcare expense as a percentage of GDP
- accidents index
- serious crimes index.

Demographics:

- changes in population growth, year to year
- growth in education levels
- a demographic index that monitors innovations by diversity of peoples
- unemployment rates.

REQUIRED

(a) Suppose government officials developed an objective to increase the number of university graduates because they believe increased education will lead to increased GDP. Brainstorm and identify several ideas for action plans to carry out this strategy.

(b) Pick one of your ideas from part (a) and discuss its pros and cons.

(c) Brainstorm ideas for action plans to increase the number of high school graduates.

(d) Pick one of your ideas from part (c) and discuss its pros and cons.

12.28 Strategy, balanced scorecard for organisation and employee Mark Hopper owns Dane Champions, a dog kennel that raises champion Great Danes for showing and breeding. His vision is to be the best-known breeder of Great Danes globally. His strategy is to breed and sell dogs from outstanding lineage from the standpoint of both physical health and good-natured temperaments. Following is information about operations over the last year.

Number of breedings	10
Number of puppies	45
Number of puppies sold	40
Number of puppies returned	2
Revenue from puppies	$24 000
Kennel operating costs (not including Mark's salary)	$35 000
Travel expenditures	$55 000
Number of trips to dog shows	20
Winnings from dog shows	$110 000
Number of championships	17
Number of dogs shown	4
Puppy owners' average satisfaction rating on a scale of 1 to 5, with 5 as most satisfied	4.5
Training time to prepare puppies for new homes (total hours)	14
Training time to prepare dogs for shows (hours per week per dog)	2

REQUIRED

(a) Is the entity's strategy one of cost leadership or product differentiation? Explain.

(b) (i) Prepare a simple balanced scorecard with one performance measure for each of the four perspectives for Dane Champions using only the data presented. Explain your choices.

(ii) Explain how these measures are linked.

(c) Kennel operating costs include the cost of a local high school student who cleans out the kennels every afternoon after school. Mark is considering whether to set up an individual scorecard for the student. He only pays minimum wage, and although the student is fairly slow, the kennels are kept reasonably clean. Mark wonders whether the student would resent being monitored more closely. Describe one reason for using a scorecard with the student and one reason against using it.

12.29 Balanced scorecard variances A large hardware store has used a balanced scorecard for several years. The store's vision is to provide customers with low-cost goods and a high-quality shopping experience. The entity's strategy has been to focus on reducing waiting time for help on the floor and at the checkout counter. Information for the last two years follows.

	2007	2008
Average sale (Total revenue/Total invoices)	$15	$12
Average variable cost per sale	$7	$7
Average customer wait time at counter	1.5 minutes	1.5 minutes
Average customer waiting time for help on the sales floor	3 minutes	2 minutes
Shipping cost per order	$18	$15
Total returns	$57 000	$60 000
Total revenue	$800 000	$748 000
Total labour cost	$200 000	$220 000
Utilities cost (electricity and phone)	$2 100	$2 400
Number of items out of stock	120	180
Employee turnover	2	3

REQUIRED

(a) Classify each performance measure according to one of the four balanced scorecard perspectives.
(b) Analyse the change in each performance measure from 2007 to 2008. Give one possible reason for the change.
(c) Which performance measures need further investigation? Explain.
(d) What do the balanced scorecard results suggest about the success of the entity's strategy to reduce waiting time? Explain.
(e) When an organisation focuses on one strategy, problems sometimes arise in other areas. Do the balanced scorecard results provide evidence of possible deterioration in any operational areas? Explain.

12.30 Evaluate balanced scorecard design Frieda's Fizz brews specialty softdrinks, including ginger beer and other flavours. Its vision is 'To proudly produce and sell extraordinarily smooth, rich and delicious softdrinks to satisfy kids of all ages.' The entity has a reputation for high quality and unique flavour, enabling it to sell softdrinks at a premium price to gourmet grocery stores in the local area. The entity's managers plan to expand the business to other geographic regions, but they want to ensure that they maintain high quality as the entity grows. They have decided to implement a balanced scorecard, and they have chosen the following balanced scorecard measures:

Financial perspective
1. Breakdown of manufacturing cost per case: ingredients, direct labour, packaging materials and overhead

2. Operating profit per case

3. Return on investment

Customer perspective

4. Number of customer complaints relating to taste, freshness, package integrity, appearance and foreign objects

5. Quality index (an internal measure of manufacturing quality, including microbiology and chemistry)

6. Percentage sales growth

Internal business process perspective

7. Ratio of plant production hours to total available time

8. Throughput (number of cases packaged)

9. Waste and scrap as a percent of total production cost

Learning and growth perspective

10. Number of work-related injuries

11. Number of training hours per employee

12. Number of community volunteer hours per employee

REQUIRED

(a) Explain why uncertainties exist about the best balanced scorecard measures for Frieda's Fizz. (Do **not** discuss any of the measures already listed. Instead, focus on why any set of measures might not provide ideal information and on why the managers cannot know with certainty which set of measures is best.)

(b) For the balanced scorecard perspective:
   (i) Describe the strengths and weaknesses of the measures chosen for that category.
   (ii) Reach a conclusion about the reasonableness of the set of balanced scorecard measures for that category.

(c) What are the pros and cons of implementing a balanced scorecard?

(d) How valuable do you think the balanced scorecard will be in helping the managers of Frieda's Fizz meet its vision? Explain.

(e) The managers of Frieda's Fizz want your evaluation of their proposed balanced scorecard. Use the information you learned from the preceding analyses to write a memo to the managers presenting your evaluation of
   (i) whether they should adopt a balanced scorecard
   (ii) the proposed balanced scorecard design.

12.31 Strategic planning; SWOT analysis; continuous improvement

REQUIRED

(a) Refer to figure 12.2 on page 489. Explain the purpose of each of the steps in the management decision process.

(b) (i) Explain why uncertainties about an entity's strengths, weaknesses, opportunities and threats lead to uncertainties about the its core competencies and strategies.
   (ii) Explain the role of strategic information in:
       I. identifying an organisation's core competencies
       II. choosing strategies
       III. choosing measures for a balanced scorecard.

(c) Explain why the use of both financial and non-financial measures is important for evaluating an entity's performance.

(d) Explain why the process of developing a balanced scorecard is never complete.

REFERENCES

1 From Kaplan, R & Norton, D 2004, 'How strategy maps frame an organisation's objectives', *Strategic Finance*, March/April, p. 45.

2 See Collins, J 2001, *Good to great: why some companies make the leap … and others don't*, HarperBusiness, New York, pp. 106–07.

3 See Lipe, M & Salterio, S 2000, 'The balanced scorecard: judgmental effects of common and unique performance measures', *The Accounting Review,* July, pp. 283–96.

4 Information from Henshall, BD 2002, 'Kiwi Scorecard,' *New Zealand Management*, July 2002, pp. 15 ff.

13

Job costing for financial reporting

IN BRIEF

Custom products, which are produced singly or in small batches, need to be valued for financial reporting. Job costing is an accounting method used to assign product costs to custom products in order to determine the inventoriable product cost. In job costing, direct costs are traced and overhead costs are allocated to individual jobs.

After studying this chapter, you should be able to:

1 Understand the flow of costs through the manufacturing process.

2 Calculate the inventoriable product cost for customised products.

3 Understand the issues related to the allocation of overhead to individual jobs.

4 Differentiate between actual costing and normal costing.

5 Understand the issues associated with spoilage, rework and scrap handled in job costing.

6 Identify the uses and limitations of job costing for financial reporting.

Incat: the importance of calculating job costs for financial reporting

Incat Pty Ltd is a privately owned Tasmanian manufacturer of large-scale commercial and military high-speed catamarans. They currently employ around 500 staff and export wave-piercing and k-class catamarans to Europe, Asia and the Americas. The vessels are tailor-made to suit individual customer and route requirements.

Incat began operations in 1977 with its first vessel (hull number 001), an 18-metre catamaran called *Derwent Explorer* that was built for Sullivans Cove Ferry operators. It wasn't long before Incat's reputation for innovative strategies in catamaran design and manufacture spread globally. It built its first high-speed car-carrying catamaran (a 74-metre vessel) for an English company called Sea Containers in 1990. For Robert Clifford, the founder and chairperson of Incat, this new catamaran proved to be the culmination of his previous years of experience and innovation in ship building: 'In all imaginable ways the ship was a journey into the future. Never before had a ship of this size been built of aluminium. Never before had a ship carried cars at 40 knots' (quoted in Wickham 2005, p. 92). The new owners were so impressed with the vessel, called *Hover Speed Great Britain*, that they entered it in a competition to win the Blue Riband Hales Trophy for the fastest commercial ship crossing of the Atlantic Ocean. To win the trophy, *Hover Speed Great Britain* would have to cross the Atlantic in less than three days, ten hours and 40 minutes. It managed to cross the finish line with an average speed exceeding the previous record by 1.1 knots per hour.

Many orders followed as a result of this success, and Incat recruited staff with diverse skills necessary to build ships to varying customer requirements and specifications. Between 1996 and 1999, Incat directly employed over 1000 people and contributed approximately 25 per cent of Tasmania's export earnings. However, this whirlwind of success was not to last. Increasing

competition and economic downturn meant that a number of ships built by the company (without customer orders) remained unsold for about three years. With the money tied up in the unsold vessels and no major catamaran orders in the pipeline, Incat's management responded with cost-cutting exercises. As direct labour contributes significantly to the cost of every job, staff cutbacks followed. Trade unions were called in and strikes followed. Eventually, in 2001, the receivers were called in.

At the height of Incat's economic downturn, the costs of goods sold represented nearly 80 per cent of total revenue before depreciation and tax. Luckily for Incat, its future was turned around after winning a major US defence contract for 'tactical response' water vehicles in 2002. The entity is slowly regaining the position held in the late 1990s, with more orders on its books (hull numbers 063, 064 and 065 are currently under construction). Job numbers 064 and 065 are an order from Japanese company Libera Ltd for two 112-metre car/passenger ferries to operate within Japan. The first will be the world's largest diesel-powered ship capable of travelling at over 40 knots. It has the following specifications: a carrying capacity of 1500 tonnes; capacity for over 800 lane metres for trucks and other heavy vehicles plus 150 cars (or if trucks are not carried, for over 400 cars); a passenger capacity up to 1000 persons; and restaurants and bar areas and other facilities.

Sources: Information from Incat website, www.incat.com.au; Wickham, M 2005, 'Entrepreneurship and the management of innovation in the global marketplace: the Incat story', *The Management Case Study Journal*, vol. 5, iss. 2, November, pp. 83–93.

Issues from this scene setter to look for in the chapter include:

- The importance of assigning direct costs to individual jobs.

- The allocation of manufacturing overhead to individual jobs.

- The process of determining an inventoriable product cost.

- An understanding that the inventoriable product cost may not adequately provide managers with detailed information for decisions relating to outsourcing or re-engineering value chain activities in production.

Understand the flow of costs through the manufacturing process

Customised products pose special problems because the nature and levels of costs vary from product to product. Therefore, the accounting systems must be designed to capture costs for individual units or batches of goods as the manufacturing process unfolds.

In this chapter, we focus on measuring and monitoring the product cost of customised goods for financial reporting purposes. Such product costs are known as inventoriable product costs. **Inventoriable product costs** are the direct and indirect costs of producing goods, and comprise costs incurred in the manufacturing process only. For the production of an Incat catamaran, for example, direct costs include materials such as aluminium, wiring, and cabinetry, as well as labour directly involved in the production of an individual catamaran. In addition to direct materials and direct labour costs, product costs also include overhead costs related to production. At Incat, production overhead includes costs related to the manufacturing facility, such as depreciation of equipment and insurance costs. The inventoriable product cost excludes the cost of operating activities that are not directly related to production, such as selling and administration. Remember that for costs recorded in the general ledger, the entity is required to comply with the rules and regulations governing financial accounting, and Australian Accounting Standard AASB 102 *Inventories* excludes the inclusion of non-manufacturing costs as part of the inventoriable product cost.

When a customer with specific product requirements places an order, we call the order a job. For example, the order from Liberia Ltd for two car ferries would be considered individual jobs by Incat, and this is reflected in the two job numbers, 064 and 065, to separately identify the two vessels. This will allow Incat's management accountant to differentiate the costs between different jobs. Orders are also placed for batches of product, such as a batch of a particular style and size of men's running shoes sold under the brand name of a retail shoe store. The shoe manufacturer would consider this order a job.

Job costing is the process of assigning costs to custom products. The cost objects are the individual jobs. Direct materials and direct labour are traced to individual jobs, and manufacturing overhead is allocated. Manufacturers that use job costing include aircraft builders, custom motorcycle and motor vehicle manufacturers, and custom design jewellers among others.

When goods are customised, many costs are easily traced to individual products due to source documents such as material requisitions and labour time records. **Source documents** are manual or electronic records created to capture and provide information about transactions or events. For example, the vessels manufactured by Incat are customised to suit each customer. Costs of direct materials such as aluminium can easily be traced to an individual vessel. It is also easy to trace the cost of direct labour to construct the vessels. Other production costs, such as the production supervisor's salary or building insurance, are indirect and are therefore allocated as part of overhead to an individual vessel.

One of the purposes of measuring current and past product costs is to provide information for financial statements. Under generally accepted accounting principles (GAAP), product costs must be assigned to inventory. Such costs are classified as *work in process* while the products are in production, and then reclassified as *finished goods* once the production process is complete and the goods are sent to the warehouse. When the products are sold, the cost is transferred to *cost of goods sold*. This practice allows inventory to be reported at cost on the balance sheet, and cost of goods sold to be matched against revenues on the income statement. Thus, job costing in a manufacturing entity assigns costs first to inventory and then to cost of goods sold when jobs are completed and sold, as shown in figure 13.1.

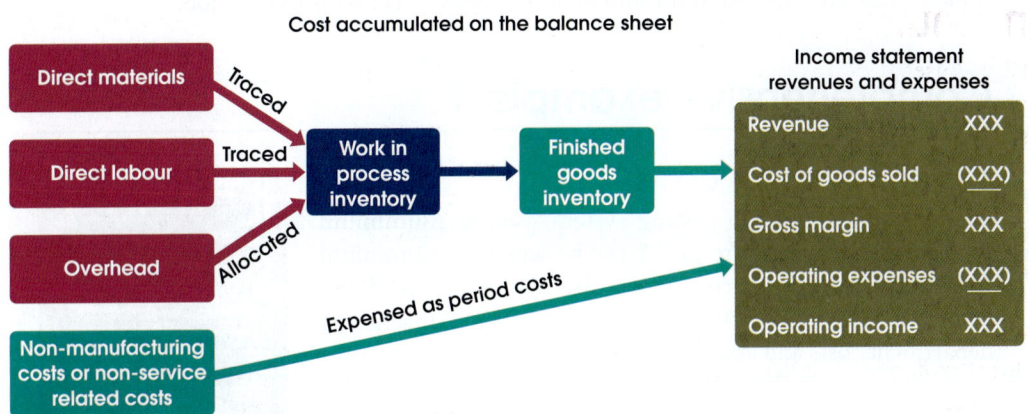

FIGURE 13.1 ■ Cost flows in a manufacturing job costing system

To measure the cost of individual jobs, job costing systems typically include a subsidiary ledger. As shown in figure 13.2, direct costs are traced and manufacturing overhead costs are allocated to each job. Total work in process (WIP) is equal to the sum of the accumulated costs for all jobs in the subsidiary ledger. The use of a subsidiary ledger allows the costs of individual jobs to be tracked, and provides the information to move costs for individual jobs through the ledgers as they move through the production process.

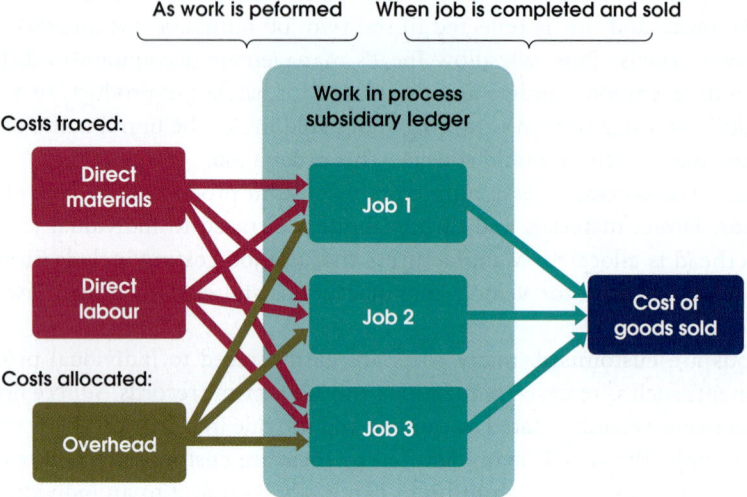

FIGURE 13.2 ■ Tracing and allocating product costs to jobs

Job costing is also frequently used in service industry organisations such as hospitals, accounting entities and repair shops. However, as there is no requirement to integrate the system into the financial reporting system, such entities are not the focus of this chapter.

Calculating the inventoriable product cost for customised products

To understand how an inventoriable product cost is calculated, we will work through an example using an entity that produces aluminium vents for heating and cooling systems, and works with contractors on large commercial jobs. Job costing is an appropriate method as each customer order requires different styles and lengths of vents and joints. Comprehensive example 1 illustrates how Aluminium Benders assigns direct costs to each job.

Comprehensive example 1

Assigning direct costs

An overview of the job costing system used at Aluminium Benders is shown in figure 13.3. It can be seen that Aluminium Benders has two direct cost pools (direct material and direct labour) and two manufacturing overhead cost pools (machining department costs and assembly department costs).

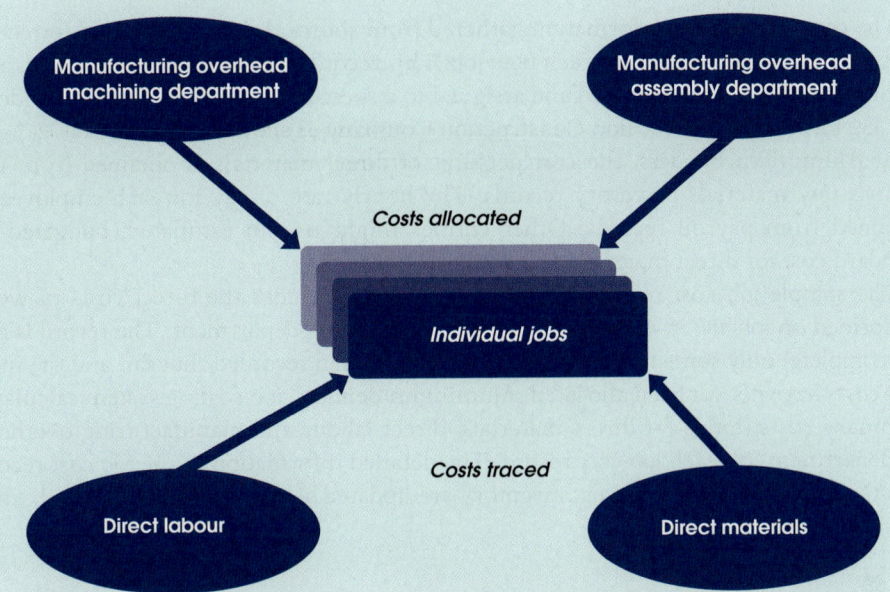

FIGURE 13.3 ■ Overview of the job costing system at Aluminium Benders

Assigning direct costs

Accounting records are used to trace the costs of direct materials and direct labour to each job. The direct labour employees at Aluminium Benders create daily time reports that show the time they spend on individual jobs. The accounting department uses the time reports to calculate employee pay and to trace direct labour hours to individual jobs. As shown in figure 13.4, each time report may include several different jobs. (We focus on job 482 for Aluminium Bender's customer, Fallon Construction Company.) Similarly, when materials such as sheet metal or metal joints are requisitioned for each job, they are tracked in the accounting system using the materials requisition form shown in figure 13.4.

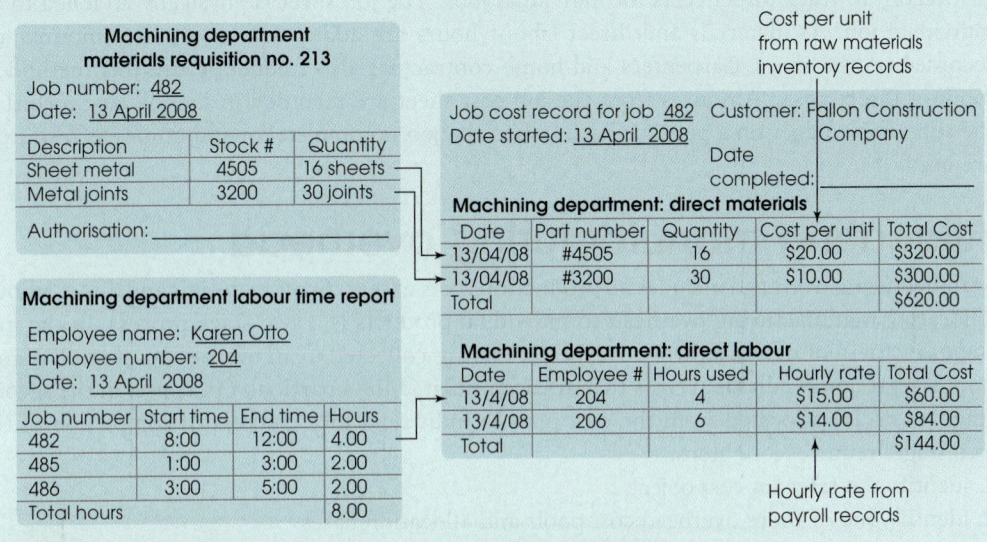

FIGURE 13.4 ■ Partial job cost record for Aluminium Benders

The cost and activity information gathered from source documents is used to record costs in a subsidiary ledger for each new job. This record is called a **job cost record**, and it contains all of the costs traced and assigned to a specific job. For Aluminium Benders, job 482 for its customer, Fallon Construction Company, is shown in figure 13.4.

At Aluminium Benders, the cost per unit of direct materials is obtained from the entity's raw materials inventory records. The hourly rate of pay for each employee is obtained from payroll records. Other entities might use an estimated, budgeted or standard cost for direct materials and direct labour.

The sample job cost record shown in figure 13.4 includes the direct costs of work performed on job 482 in Aluminium Benders' machining department. The record is not yet complete; only some materials and labour have been recorded thus far, and the indirect costs have not yet been allocated. Aluminium Benders' job costing system calculates summary costs (totals for direct materials, direct labour and manufacturing overhead by department) on each job cost record. The detailed information in the job cost record and the totals in work in process inventory are updated as new costs are incurred, until the job is completed.

Computerised and manual job costing systems

Maintaining the detailed job cost records shown in figure 13.4 can be time-consuming and prone to clerical error. Therefore, job cost records are often part of a software package. Direct labour and direct material data are entered into electronic source documents (online time records and material requisitions). From there, the data are automatically posted into the job cost record and the general ledger system. This approach allows managers to immediately view job costs even before the job is completed. Specialised software packages are most likely to be used in large organisations or in entities where jobs are complex or require many resources.

In small businesses, job cost records may be tied less formally to the general ledger system. Instead of using source documents to track direct costs, such entities might use a manual job cost record to track direct costs for individual jobs. The job sheet is physically attached to an individual job. As materials and direct labour hours are added to the job, the amounts are recorded on the sheet. Carpenters and home contractors also frequently use this method to monitor direct costs. Amounts from the job cost sheet are recorded in the job cost record in the subsidiary ledger on a periodic basis, when the job is complete, or sometimes as resources are used.

Allocating manufacturing overhead

Manufacturing overhead includes all production costs except direct materials and direct labour. Allocating manufacturing overhead to individual products is a two-stage process. In the first stage, a variety of manufacturing overhead costs are collected in an overhead cost pool. A **cost pool** is a group of individual costs that are accumulated for a particular purpose. In the second stage, costs are allocated from the cost pool to individual jobs. Successful completion of the two stages requires four steps.

1. Identify the relevant cost object.
2. Identify one or more overhead cost pools and allocation bases.
3. For each overhead cost pool, calculate an overhead allocation rate.
4. For each overhead cost pool, allocate costs to the cost object.

1. Identify the relevant cost object

In a job costing system, the cost object is a job. Sometimes a job consists of an individual product, and sometimes it consists of a batch of products. In our example at Aluminium Benders, the cost object of interest is job 482, which is for the manufacture of a large number of aluminium vents required for a specific building by customer Fallon Construction.

2. Identify one or more overhead cost pools and allocation bases

Manufacturing overhead costs are accumulated in one or more cost pools. Some organisations use a single entity-wide or plant-wide cost pool for all fixed and variable overhead costs. Other organisations use separate cost pools for fixed and variable overhead costs. Fixed overhead includes costs such as production management salaries and space rental. Variable overhead includes any cost that varies with activity levels, such as supplies and (sometimes) electricity. If work is performed in separate departments or work areas, separate overhead cost pools may be designated for each department or activity. Accountants use judgment in choosing the number and type of overhead cost pools for a given entity.

The choice of overhead cost pools depends on the organisation of production, the nature of overhead costs and the usefulness of different types of overhead information to management. For example, Aluminium Benders has two production departments: machining and assembly. Each work area might be under the supervision of a different manager who is responsible for controlling costs. The use of separate overhead cost pools for each area would help top management monitor the performance of area managers. Alternatively, a single manager might oversee multiple work areas. Organisations are also more likely to use different overhead cost pools for different types of work activities. For example, machining the aluminium vents and joints is a different type of activity from assembling parts into the finished product. It is appropriate to use different cost pools when the nature or level of overhead costs differs across activities.

For each overhead cost pool, an allocation base is chosen to assign overhead costs to cost objects. An **allocation base** is a measure of activity, preferably a cost driver, used to allocate costs to a cost object. If some portion of an overhead cost pool varies with a cost driver, it can be used as the allocation base. For example, the cost of some employee benefits varies with labour hours and labour costs. Indirect costs such as supplies in the machining department may vary with machine use. For cost pools that consist only of variable costs or a mixture of fixed and variable costs, accountants use allocation bases that are likely to affect at least a portion of the costs. For a fixed overhead cost pool, accountants choose an allocation base that is related to activities even though fixed costs are not expected to vary with the allocation base. Manufacturing job costing systems frequently allocate overhead using one of the following bases:

- direct labour hours
- direct labour costs
- machine hours.

Whichever allocation base is selected, it will be necessary for the entity to maintain records of its use. In our example, the financial controller of Aluminium Benders, Sean Hardy, met with the supervisor of each production department to discuss the best allocation bases to use. After discussions it was determined that, in the machining department, overhead is to be allocated to production jobs using machine hours as the allocation base. In the assembly department, direct labour cost is to be used as the allocation base.

In machining, Sean learns the machines require little direct labour. A large portion of cost in the overhead pool relates to operating the machines, such as depreciation, maintenance and replacement parts. Thus, Sean concludes that machine hours are a reasonable allocation base.

The assembly department has few machines, but labour is used heavily. The labour mix is varied, with both skilled and unskilled workers. Sean agrees that direct labour cost is a reasonable allocation base because some overhead expenses, such as holiday and sick leave pay, vary with labour cost.

However, if Sean had found that the same cost driver/allocation base could be used for both production departments, then only one overhead cost pool would have been used to allocate overhead.

3. For each overhead cost pool, calculate an overhead allocation rate

The **allocation rate** is the dollar amount per unit of allocation base used to allocate overhead to each cost object. (Remember, in a job costing system, each job is a cost object.) If we know the total amount of overhead cost and the total quantity of the allocation base, the **actual overhead allocation rate** is calculated as follows:

$$\text{Actual allocation rate} = \frac{\text{Actual overhead cost}}{\text{Actual quantity of allocation base}}$$

Alternatively, overhead may be allocated using an **estimated allocation rate**. To calculate an estimated rate for the next period, we estimate total overhead costs and the total quantity of the allocation base, and then calculate the rate as follows:

$$\text{Estimated allocation rate} = \frac{\text{Estimated overhead cost}}{\text{Estimated quantity of allocation base}}$$

To understand which allocation rate is more appropriate, it is necessary to understand the differences in the use of actual and normal costing to measure costs in the job costing system.

Actual and normal costing

Under **actual costing**, overhead is allocated using the actual volume of the allocation base times the actual allocation rate. Because managers often need cost information before total actual cost and resource use information is available at the end of the period, estimates are typically used to allocate overhead. When the estimated allocation rate and actual quantity of the allocation base are used to allocate overhead, the method is called normal costing. Information from normal costing systems is used to prepare interim income statements, to manage costs and to estimate costs for bids throughout a period. Figure 13.5 compares actual costing and normal costing. Under both methods, actual direct materials and direct labour are traced to each job.

	Actual costing	Normal costing
Direct costs recorded	Actual cost of direct materials and direct labour	Actual cost of direct materials and direct labour
Overhead cost allocation rate	$\dfrac{\text{Actual overhead cost}}{\text{Actual quantity of allocation base}}$	$\dfrac{\text{Estimated overhead cost}}{\text{Estimated quantity of allocation base}}$
Overhead allocation	Actual allocation rate × Actual quantity of allocation base	Estimated allocation rate × Actual quantity of allocation base

FIGURE 13.5 ■ Similarities and differences between actual and normal costing

4. For each overhead cost pool, allocate costs to the cost object

Aluminium Benders uses a normal costing method to allocate an estimated overhead rate to each job. Separate overhead cost pools are used for each department, but fixed and variable costs are combined in each pool. The following estimates were developed by Sean for all manufacturing during 2008:

	Machining	Assembly
Production overhead	$1 400 000	$2 400 000
Direct labour cost	$700 000	$1 000 000
Direct labour hours	35 000	100 000
Machine hours	25 000	10 000

Using normal costing the estimated overhead allocation rate for each department is:

Machining: $1 400 000 ÷ 25 000 machine hours = $56 per machine hour

Assembly: $2 400 000 ÷ $1 000 000 direct labour cost

= 240% of direct labour cost (or $2.40 for every $1 of labour incurred)

The assignment of overhead to individual jobs requires information about each job's use of the allocation base. Sean Hardy has created an online system so that the machine operator records the machine hours used for each job. For job 482, three machine hours are recorded for April 2008 and the overhead is allocated based on an estimated allocation rate of $56 per machine hour. This results in an allocation of $168 ($56 by 3 hours) to job 482 in the machining department, as shown in figure 13.6.

Job cost record for job 482			Customer: Fallon Construction Company	
Date started: 13 April 2008			Date completed: _____	

Machining department: overhead

Date	Allocation base	Hours used	Allocation rate per hour	Allocated overhead
13/4/08	Machine hours	3	$56.00	$168.00
Total				$168.00

FIGURE 13.6 ■ Partial job cost record showing overhead allocation for Aluminium Benders for job 482

Overapplied and underapplied overhead

Under normal costing, periodic adjustments need to be made to reconcile the actual overhead cost with the amount of overhead that has been allocated to jobs. When we determine the overhead allocation rate, we estimate both the cost of overhead (numerator) and the volume of the allocation base (denominator). At the end of the period, the amounts of overhead in the inventory accounts (work in process, finished goods, cost of goods sold) are either too little or too much, and so adjustments need to be made. **Overapplied overhead** occurs when actual costs are less than the total amount of overhead allocated to inventory accounts. In contrast, **underapplied overhead** occurs when actual costs are more than the amount of overhead allocated.

To correct for overapplied or underapplied overhead, we first compare the amount of overhead allocated to actual overhead cost:

Overapplied (underapplied) overhead = Allocated overhead – Actual overhead

Suppose it is the end of the fiscal year at Aluminium Benders and the balances in the accounts represent all transactions for the period. Balances in the overhead cost control accounts for the machining department and assembly department cost pools are shown in figure 13.7. Machining department overhead costs incurred totalled $1 600 000, while costs allocated to jobs totalled $1 120 000 (20 000 machine hours × $56) giving rise to a underapplied overhead of $480 000. Assembly department overhead costs incurred totalled $2 700 000, while costs allocated to jobs totalled $2 880 000 ($1 200 000 direct labour cost × 240%) with an overapplied overhead of $180 000. The combined amount of underapplied overhead is therefore $300 000 (being $480 000 machining underapplied overhead – $180 000 assembly overapplied overhead). The total amount of overhead incurred must then be recorded as a product cost for the period. This is done by an adjusting entry, which is shown later in this chapter.

Machining department overhead cost control account		Assembly department overhead cost control account	
Total costs incurred 1 600 000	Total costs 1 120 000 allocated	Total costs incurred 2 700 000	Total costs 2 880 000 allocated
Underapplied overhead 480 000			Overapplied 180 000 overhead

(a) Before adjustment

Machining department overhead cost control account		Assembly department overhead cost control account	
Total costs incurred 1 600 000	Total costs 1 120 000 allocated	Total costs incurred 2 700 000	Total costs 2 880 000 allocated
	480 000 Adjustment	Adjustment 180 000	
Balance 0			0 Balance

(b) After adjustment

FIGURE 13.7 ■ Overhead cost control accounts for Aluminium Benders

Comprehensive example 2

Costing a specific job

Sean Hardy, financial controller of Aluminium Benders, wants to be sure that he understands how Aluminium Benders' job costing system allocates overhead, so he recalculates the allocations for job 482. This job was completed this week and shipped to a large office building construction site. The information opposite was recorded on the job cost record for job 482.

	Machining	Assembly
Direct materials requisitioned	$40 000	$70 000
Direct labour cost	$28 000	$10 000
Direct labour hours	200	1 000
Machine hours	100	500

Using the allocation rates computed previously, Sean recalculates the amount of overhead for job 482 as follows:

Machining: 100 machine hours × $56 per machine hour = $5600

Assembly: $10 000 direct labour cost × 240% of direct labour cost = $24 000

Next, Sean creates a report for management of the total costs for job 482 as follows:

	Machining	Assembly	Total
Direct materials requisitioned	$40 000	$ 70 000	$110 000
Direct labour cost	28 000	10 000	38 000
Overhead allocated	5 600	24 000	29 600
Total cost	$ 73 600	$104 000	$177 600

Gross profit for job 482 can be calculated by deducting the costs from the revenue generated from the sale. At the end of the period, the $177 600 will be transferred to the cost of goods sold account.

Recording transactions in the financial accounting system

The general ledger in a manufacturer's job costing system typically includes separate inventory accounts for raw materials, work in process and finished goods, and represents the flow of costs through the production process (refer back to figure 13.1, page 533). For Aluminium Benders, the general journal entries (figure 13.8) and the general ledger entries (figure 13.9) are shown to record the costs for job 482, from the issue of raw material to the revenue received from the customer. Notice that the ledger entries are referenced back to the journal entries.

FIGURE 13.8 ■ Journal entries for job 482

1 Work in process (job 482)		DR	$40 000	
Raw materials inventory		CR		$40 000
To record direct materials requisitioned for job 482 in machining				
2 Work in process (job 482)		DR	$28 000	
Wages payable		CR		$28 000
To record direct labour used for job 482 in machining				
3 Work in process (job 482)		DR	$5 600	
Machining department overhead cost control		CR		$5 600
To record overhead allocated to job 482 in machining				
4 Work in process (job 482)		DR	$70 000	
Raw materials inventory		CR		$70 000
To record direct materials requisitioned for job 482 in assembly				

(continued)

FIGURE 13.8 (continued)

5	Work in process (job 482)		DR	$10 000	
	Wages payable		CR		$10 000
	To record direct labour used for job 482 in assembly				
6	Work in process (job 482)		DR	$24 000	
	Assembly department overhead cost control		CR		$24 000
	To record overhead allocated to job 482 in assembly				
7	Finished goods inventory (job 482)		DR	$177 600	
	Work in process (job 482)		CR		$177 600
	To record completion of job 482				
8	Cost of goods sold		DR	$177 600	
	Finished goods inventory (job 482)		CR		$177 600
	To record the delivery of job 482				

Raw materials inventory

| | | $40 000 | 1 |
| | | $70 000 | 4 |

Job 482 Work in process inventory

1	$40 000		
2	$28 000		
3	$5 600		
4	$70 000		
5	$10 000		
6	$24 000	$177 600	7
	$0		

Finished goods inventory

| 7 | $177 600 | $177 600 | 8 |

Cost of goods sold

| 8 | $177 600 | |

Wages payable

| | | $28 000 | 2 |
| | | $10 000 | 5 |

Machining department overhead cost control

| | | $5 600 | 3 |

Assembly department overhead cost control

| | | $24 000 | 6 |

FIGURE 13.9 ■ T-accounts for job 482

Purchases of raw materials (not illustrated) are recorded in the raw materials inventory account. As direct materials are traced to a job, the cost of the materials is transferred to work in process inventory (entries 1 and 4). Some types of direct materials, such as supplies, are not traced to individual jobs when they are used; such costs are transferred into an overhead cost pool. However, this situation is not illustrated. As direct labour employees report their work time, the cost of their wages is debited to the jobs they work on and wages payable is credited for the wages earned (entries 2 and 5).

Many organisations use overhead cost control accounts to monitor the costs for each overhead cost pool. As actual overhead costs are incurred, they are debited to the control account. For example, the assembly department supervisor's salary would be debited to the assembly department overhead cost control and credited to wages payable. Overhead allocated to individual jobs is debited to work in process and credited to the control account (entries 3 and 6).

When a job is complete, the work in process account includes all of the direct material, direct labour and overhead costs that have been assigned to the job. The total cost can then be transferred to finished goods inventory (entry 7). Finally, when revenue for the job is earned, the total cost is transferred from finished goods to cost of goods sold (entry 8).

Refer back to figure 13.7, which shows the ledger accounts for the individual manufacturing department overhead control accounts. We have already calculated a net underapplied overhead of $300 000 as follows:

	Overapplied or (underapplied) overhead
Machining	$ (480 000)
Assembly	180 000
Net underapplied overhead	$(300 000)

Now we must record an adjusting entry so that the total actual amount of overhead incurred is recorded as a product cost for the period. The balance of overapplied or underapplied overhead must be removed through an adjustment at the end of the accounting period. If the amount of the adjustment is material, it is allocated on a pro rata basis among work in process, finished goods (if any) and cost of goods sold. This pro rata allocation is prescribed by GAAP, which requires inventory to be recorded at actual cost. If the amount is immaterial, however, it is simply assigned to cost of goods sold.

Because the method of adjusting for overapplied or underapplied overhead depends on materiality, we need to decide whether the $300 000 amount for Aluminium Benders is material. One way to evaluate materiality is to calculate the net overapplied or underapplied overhead as a percentage of actual overhead costs. For Aluminium Benders, this calculation is:

$$\$300\,000 \div (\$1\,600\,000 + \$2\,700\,000) = 7\%$$

Many accountants view amounts smaller than 10 per cent to be immaterial. If we decide that the adjustment for Aluminium Benders is immaterial, we adjust the cost of goods sold total. Because overhead was underapplied, cost of goods sold would be increased as follows:

Cost of goods sold	DR	$300 000
Assembly department overhead cost control	DR	$180 000
Machining department overhead cost control	CR	$480 000

If we decide that the adjustment for Aluminium Benders is material, it must be allocated on a pro rata basis among work in process, finished goods and cost of goods sold. Suppose the balances in these accounts before the adjustment are:

Ending work in process	$ 100 000
Finished goods	20 000
Cost of goods sold	10 000 000
Total	$ 10 120 000

The adjustment of $300 000 would be allocated on a pro rata basis among these accounts based on each account's proportion of the total. The adjusting journal entry is shown overleaf.

Ending work in process ($100 000 ÷ $10 120 000 × $300 000)	DR	$2 964	
Finished goods ($20 000 ÷ $10 120 000 × $300 000)	DR	$593	
Cost of goods sold ($10 000 000 ÷ $10 120 000 × $300 000)	DR	$296 443	
Assembly department overhead cost control	DR	$180 000	
Machining department overhead cost control	CR		$480 000

The balances before and after the adjustment would be:

	Before adjustment	Adjustment	After adjustment
Ending work in process	$ 100 000	$ 2 964	$ 102 964
Finished goods	20 000	593	20 593
Cost of goods sold	10 000 000	296 443	10 296 443
Total	$10 120 000	$300 000	$10 420 000

Whether the adjustment is considered material or immaterial, zero balances are left in both overhead cost control accounts after the adjustment, as shown in figure 13.7.

Spoilage, rework and scrap in job costing

No matter how carefully goods are manufactured, occasionally some units do not meet quality standards; they are spoiled. **Spoilage** refers to units of product that are unacceptable and are discarded, reworked or sold at a reduced price. Examples of spoilage in job costing include:

- units in batches of clothing that have flaws in the material or sewing
- several valves in a batch that do not function properly when tested at the end of production
- a custom-ordered birdhouse that has an off-centre round hole.

Different types of spoiled products are handled in different ways. For example, if the material flaws are not too noticeable, the clothing can be sold as irregular. Perhaps the birdhouse can be sold at a discount, but the valves probably cannot be sold and must be discarded or reworked.

Spoilage is typically identified through some type of inspection process. Sometimes inspection occurs at the end of the production process immediately before units are moved to finished goods inventory. Other times, inspection occurs at one or more intermediate stages during production. Inspection can also occur at the beginning of the process. For example, denim fabric can be checked for flaws before it is introduced into the production process for manufacturing jeans. Other practices, such as conducting preventive maintenance on equipment rather than waiting for machinery problems to develop, help minimise spoilage.

To calculate the cost of a partially complete spoiled unit, we add up all direct materials and labour costs used and allocate overhead according to the amount of work completed before the unit was removed from production. The way spoilage cost is handled depends on whether the spoilage is considered normal or abnormal.

Normal and abnormal spoilage

Normal spoilage consists of defective units that arise as part of regular operations. If normal spoilage arises from the requirements of a specific job, the cost of the spoiled units is charged to the job. For example, suppose one of Aluminium Benders' customers wants vents in an irregular shape. If the sheet metal is more difficult to bend into such shapes and materials are consequently spoiled in the machining process, then the cost of the spoilage would be charged to that job.

Normal spoilage also occurs periodically as a regular part of all jobs. For example, suppose that in the machining department at Aluminium Benders the cutting device periodically cuts off centre, no matter how much care is taken by the machine operators. This loss has nothing to do with any specific order; instead, it is a normal part of operations. The cost of normal spoilage common to all jobs is charged to overhead and is allocated with other overhead costs to all jobs.

Abnormal spoilage is spoilage that is not part of everyday operations. It occurs for reasons such as the following:

- out-of-control manufacturing processes
- unusual machine breakdowns
- unexpected electrical outages that result in a number of spoiled units.

Some abnormal spoilage is considered avoidable; that is, if managers monitor processes and maintain machinery appropriately, little spoilage will occur. To highlight these types of problems so that they can be monitored, abnormal spoilage is recorded in a loss from abnormal spoilage account in the general ledger and is not included in the job costing inventory accounts (work in process, finished goods, cost of goods sold). Comprehensive example 3 demonstrates normal and abnormal spoilage for Aluminium Benders for jobs 512 and 489.

External stakeholders such as shareholders typically do not have access to explicit information about an entity's spoilage rates or costs. Although abnormal spoilage is recorded in a separate loss account in the general ledger, it is typically combined with other financial statement items. Thus, spoilage rarely appears as a line item on published financial statements. Exceptions tend to be large catastrophes, such as damage caused by an earthquake, that are publicly known before financial statements are issued. Therefore, external stakeholders must use indirect ways to analyse the quality of an organisation's production processes. An entity with a high spoilage rate might have a lower than average gross profit margin, higher than average warranty liabilities or a poor reputation for product quality.

Comprehensive example 3

Assigning spoilage costs

When job 512 was being processed in the machining department, a piece of sheet metal was off centre in the bending machine and two vents were spoiled. This problem occurs periodically, is considered normal spoilage and is recorded as an overhead cost. Because this step comes first in the procedure for making the vents, the only costs incurred were for direct materials ($25). The following journal entry records normal spoilage as an overhead cost, assuming the sheet metal cannot be sold at a discount and its cost has been recorded in work in process inventory.

Overhead cost control (normal spoilage)	DR	$25
Work in process inventory (cost of spoiled sheet metal)	CR	$25

If these costs had been abnormal spoilage, they would have been recorded to a loss from abnormal spoilage account instead of the overhead cost control account.

Job 489 required an especially thin sheet metal to reduce the weight of the vents. When two of the vents were being assembled, they were spoiled because the metal twisted and could not be joined properly. Because the thin metal was a specific requirement for this job, the costs for the spoiled units were recorded as a cost for job 489. Direct materials cost $100 and direct labour cost $150 for the vents up to the time they were spoiled. The metal can be sold to a recycler at a discounted price of $50. The journal entries for the use of direct materials and labour are the same as if the direct materials and labour were not spoiled, because these are additional costs for this specific job. However, the following journal entries record the value of the sheet metal at the time it is spoiled and the subsequent sale of the metal.

Raw material inventory (metal to be sold to recycler) DR	$50	
Work in process inventory (job 489) CR		$50
Cash DR	$50	
Raw material inventory CR		$50

Rework

Rework consists of spoiled units that are repaired and sold as if they were originally produced correctly. For example, electronic equipment that is specially ordered, such as computers or batches of mobile phones, are reworked when defects are discovered during the manufacturing process or through inspection at the end of the process. If the cost of rework is tracked, it is recorded in the same manner as spoilage; normal rework is charged to overhead or to a specific job, and abnormal rework is recorded as a line item loss. Rework costs are often not tracked, however.

Units are sometimes reworked and then sold at a regular price through regular marketing channels. Other times, reworked units remain flawed and must be sold at a reduced price. Costs and benefits are analysed to decide whether to rework a spoiled unit. Suppose a clothing manufacturer discovers several jeans with back pockets sewn on upside down. If the pockets are carefully removed and then sewn on correctly, it might be difficult to tell that there was ever a problem. However, additional cost is added for the labour time to fix the pockets. Furthermore, the pockets might rip more easily because the material has been weakened. The managers need to evaluate whether the costs of reworking the pockets outweigh the benefits.

Scrap

Scrap consists of the bits of direct material left over from normal manufacturing processes. Sometimes it has value and can be sold, and sometimes it is discarded. New technology affects whether something is considered scrap. For example, for many years timber mills burned sawdust, for which they had no alternative uses, in tepee-shaped silos that glowed red at night. As trees became a scarce resource, sawdust became more valuable. With improved glues and new manufacturing processes, products such as specialty logs for fireplaces and chipboard were developed. A process was developed to turn sawdust into pulp for paper mills. Sawdust is no longer scrap but has become an important by-product of milling timber.

Some manufacturers track scrap to measure whether resources are being used efficiently. Scrap is also tracked if it has value and could be stolen. Often it is recorded in physical terms. For example, gold scraps from jewellery manufacture are weighed, the weight is recorded and the scraps are stored in a safe.

From an accounting standpoint, we need to plan for and sometimes guard scrap by setting up control systems. We also need to determine the effect of the value of scrap on inventory costing and the income statement. If scrap can be sold, the revenue is recorded either at the time it is produced or at the time it is sold. When the value of scrap is immaterial, it is simply recorded as part of other revenues in the income statement.

In job costing, scrap sometimes arises as part of specific jobs. If we can trace it to individual jobs, revenue from the scrap is credited to the specific job in work in process. Scrap revenue reduces the cost of the job with which it is associated. If scrap is common to all jobs, or if it is not worth tracing to individual jobs, the scrap revenue offsets overhead cost for the period. This entry reduces overhead cost for all jobs produced.

If scrap is held for a period of time before it is reused as direct material or sold, we need to estimate its net realisable value so that the value of the scrap can be used to offset overhead costs in the same period in which the overhead costs and associated revenues are recognised. When the price of scrap is volatile, such as gold scraps from jewellery manufacture, estimating its value is more difficult. Some entities develop creative ways to use scrap to benefit employees and others. For example, print shops sometimes bind scrap paper into scratch pads and give them to employees, customers or public schools.

Spoilage opportunity costs

We have learned about methods used to account for the direct costs of spoilage, rework and scrap. Although the direct costs can be significant, managers need to consider several other issues related to the quality of their production processes. One of these is the opportunity costs of spoilage and rework, which can be large. Opportunity costs include the following:

- forgone profit
- loss of reputation and market share.

An entity forgoes the normal profit from resources that are used to produce spoiled units. Forgone profit is a bigger problem when capacity limits are involved, because the organisation forgoes the profit on resources employed as well as the contribution margin from good units that might have been produced. In addition, some proportion of spoiled units is likely to mistakenly pass inspection. As the number of spoiled units increases, a larger number of spoiled units will inevitably be sold to customers. The sale of these defective units leads to loss of market share because consumers switch brands. The entity eventually loses its reputation for quality products. This leads to further erosion of market share, including customers who never had direct quality problems. These opportunity costs, which are often much greater than the cost of the spoiled units, are not tracked by the accounting system.

Uses and limitations of job cost information

Job costing systems measure the cost of products, primarily for customised goods and services. The information from a job costing system can be used for several purposes, including the following:

- reporting inventory and cost of goods sold values on financial statements and income tax returns
- developing cost estimates to assist in bidding on potential future jobs
- measuring actual costs to compare to estimated costs
- developing cost estimates for short-term or long-term decisions.

Because a job costing system accumulates and reports costs for individual jobs, the tendency is to mistakenly believe that job costs are measured accurately and that the costs assigned to a job are incremental, that is, would not be incurred if the job were not undertaken. However, job costing systems are subject to uncertainties and require judgment.

Uncertainties in measuring job costs

Little uncertainty tends to surround the direct costs assigned to a job, because those costs are traced to each job. However, judgment is used to decide which direct costs will be traced. Occasionally direct costs are quite small, and the cost of creating a system to track them is greater than the benefit achieved. (The chapter 13 article at the end of this book provides a snapshot of likely developments in technology in this area.) In these cases, costs that might potentially be traced are instead included with indirect costs in a pool of overhead costs. However, changes in technology sometimes allow accountants to trace costs that were previously too costly to trace. For example, most large photocopiers today include security systems that track the number of copies made to specific account codes. These systems minimise the cost of tracing photocopy costs to individual jobs. Without such a system, the cost of tracking individual copies could be overly expensive. Tracking the use of software and internet services for networked computers or monitoring small supplies such as nails and tape during manufacturing is more difficult. These costs are treated as indirect costs and become part of overhead.

Accountants also choose the type and number of cost pools to use for overhead. For example, overhead costs were pooled at the department level in Aluminium Benders. However, overhead could have been pooled at the plant level. Alternatively, the overhead costs in each department could have been separated into fixed and variable pools. Accountants consider several factors when they choose the number and kind of cost pools to use. From a management control perspective, if costs are tracked to a department or a process, the managers of that department or process can be held responsible for controlling costs. When overhead costs from many departments are pooled, managers and employees within each department have little incentive to control costs. In addition, different departments usually perform different tasks, so their costs may be quite different. If costs are allocated on a department level and these costs more accurately reflect the flow of resources, products can be designed to spend less time in costly departments. When deciding whether to use department or plant-wide cost pools, the benefit gained from gathering information about department costs and the use of department resources by other departments must be worth the cost of tracking them.

Ideally, we would prefer that the overhead allocation process reflect the flow of overhead resources to each product. Thus, an ideal overhead allocation base would be a cost driver. However, fixed overhead is not expected to vary with any allocation base, and it is not always possible to identify or to accurately measure a cost driver for variable overhead. Thus, allocated overhead generally does not accurately measure the overhead resources used by a job.

Uncertainties in estimating future job costs

Managers use job cost estimates to establish a bid for a job, decide whether to accept a job, or make other types of decisions. Managers then monitor operations by comparing actual job costs to the original estimate. Whenever we estimate future events, we face uncertainties about whether the estimates will be accurate. Thus, actual job costs will almost certainly be different from estimated job costs. Managers analyse the differences to evaluate the efficiency of operations and to improve future job cost estimates.

Under normal costing, overhead is allocated to jobs using an estimated overhead allocation rate. The estimated rate is based on estimates of the total overhead cost and the total volume of the allocation base. Actual costs and activity levels are affected by many unforeseen events. These include unanticipated cost inflation or deflation, or an economic downturn that causes business activities to fall short of expectations. Actual costs also differ from expectations because of unexpected improvements or deterioration in production efficiency.

Differences between estimates and actual amounts cause overhead to be overapplied or underapplied, and then adjustments are required at the end of an accounting period. However, judgment is necessary in the way that adjustments are made.

Summary

Understand the flow of costs through the manufacturing process.

Cost flows in manufacturing job costing

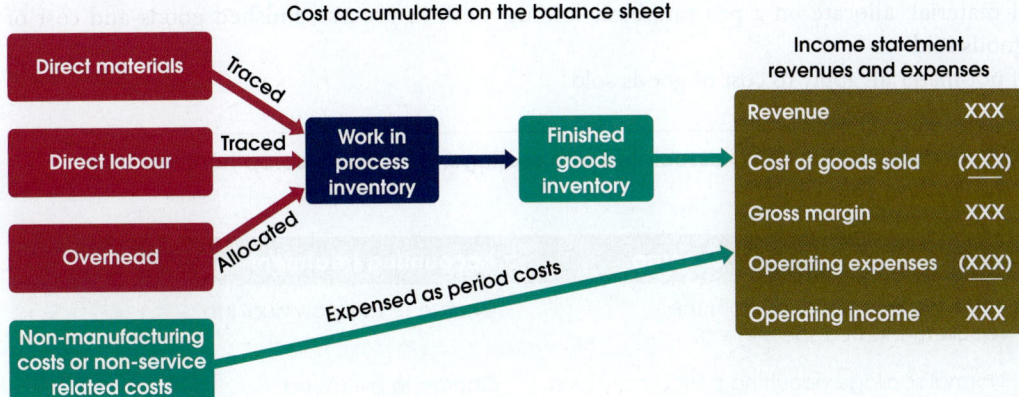

Accounting system
- Source documents (e.g. employee time reports and material requisitions)
- Job cost record
- Job cost software

2 **Calculate the inventoriable product cost for customised products.**

Inventoriable product cost is used for financial reporting and includes manufacturing costs only.
Direct costs (material and labour) are traced with source documentation.
Indirect costs are allocated using an allocation base. It is appropriate to use different cost pools when the nature or level of overhead costs differs across activities.

3 **Understand the issues related to the allocation of overhead to individual jobs.**

Procedures for allocating overhead costs to jobs:
1. Identify the relevant cost object.
2. Identify one or more overhead cost pools and allocation bases.
3. For each overhead cost pool, calculate an overhead allocation rate.
4. For each overhead cost pool, allocate costs to the cost object.

Types of overhead cost pools
- Entity-wide
- Plant-wide
- Separate departments
- Separate activities or processes
- Separate fixed and variable overhead costs

4 Differentiate between actual costing and normal costing.

Actual costing

$$\text{Actual allocation rate} \times \text{Actual quantity of allocation base for job}$$

Normal costing

$$\text{Estimated allocation rate} \times \text{Actual quantity of allocation base for job}$$

Adjustment for overapplied or underapplied overhead

$$\text{Overapplied (underapplied) overhead} = \text{Allocated overhead} - \text{Actual overhead}$$

If material: allocate on a pro rata basis among work in process, finished goods and cost of goods sold.

If not material: apply to cost of goods sold.

5 Understand the issues associated with spoilage, rework and scrap handled in job costing.

Type of spoilage, rework or scrap	Accounting treatment
Normal spoilage arising from the requirements of a specific job	Charge to the individual job
Normal spoilage occurring periodically as a regular part of all jobs	Charge to overhead
Abnormal spoilage	Charge to separate loss account
Opportunity costs of spoilage	Not measured
Rework for defects arising from the requirements of a specific job	Charge to individual job
Rework for defects occurring periodically during normal production	Charge to overhead
Rework for abnormal defects	Charge to separate loss account
Sale of scrap	Record at time of production or at time sold. If not material: record as other income
Scrap traced to individual jobs	Credit to individual job
Scrap common to all jobs or difficult to trace to jobs	Credit to overhead

6 Identify the uses and limitations of job costing for financial reporting.

Uses of job cost information

- Assign costs to work in process, finished goods and cost of goods sold for financial statement and income tax returns
- Provide information to help managers:
  - monitor operating costs
  - develop job bids
  - make short-term or long-term decisions.

Allocation of overhead costs
- Required for financial and tax accounting of manufactured goods
- Optional otherwise
- Fixed overhead allocation generally not relevant for short-term decisions

Uncertainties
- Which estimated job costs are relevant for decision making
- Whether and how to trace direct costs
- Choice of overhead cost pools
- Choice of allocation bases
- Estimated overhead allocation rate (under normal costing)
- Method for adjusting overapplied or underapplied overhead (under normal costing)

Self-study problems

SELF-STUDY PROBLEM 1

Normal costing with two overhead cost pools

William Felix & Sons uses an estimated overhead rate for allocating production overhead to job orders. The rate is on a machine hour basis for the machining department and on a direct labour cost basis for the finishing department. The entity estimated the following for 2008:

	Machining	Finishing
Production overhead cost	$10 000 000	$8 000 000
Machine hours	200 000	33 000
Direct labour hours	30 000	160 000
Direct labour cost	$900 000	$4 000 000

During January, the cost record for job order no. 806 shows the following:

	Machining	Finishing
Direct materials requisitioned	$14 000	$3 000
Direct labour cost	$600	$1 250
Direct labour hours	30	50
Machine hours	130	10

Total costs and machine hours were as follows for 2008:

	Machining	Finishing
Production overhead incurred	$10 200 000	$7 900 000
Direct labour cost	$950 000	$3 900 000
Machine hours	220 000	32 000

REQUIRED
(a) What is the estimated overhead rate that should be used in the:
   (i) machining department?
   (ii) finishing department?
(b) What is the total overhead allocated to job 806?
(c) Assuming that job 806 manufactured 200 units of product, what is the unit cost of job 806?

(d) What is the total amount of over- or underapplied overhead in each department at the end of 2008?

(e) Provide reasons why Felix uses two different overhead application bases. Also discuss why Felix might use machine hours and labour costs to allocate overhead costs.

Solution to self-study problem 1

(a) Overhead rates should be calculated using estimated costs and allocation bases:
   (i) Machining: $10 000 000 ÷ 200 000 = $50 per machine hour
   (ii) Finishing: $8 000 000 ÷ $4 000 000 = 200% of direct labour cost

(b) Using the overhead rates from part (a), the total overhead allocated to job 806 should be as follows:

Machining department: $50 × 130 machine hours	$6 500
Finishing department: 200% × $1250 direct labour cost	2 500
Total overhead allocated to job 806	$9 000

(c) To calculate per-unit costs, first calculate the total cost for the batch and then divide by the number of units:

	Machining	Finishing
Direct materials	$14 000	$3 000
Direct labour	600	1 250
Overhead allocated	6 500	2 500
Total	$ 21 100	$6 750

Total costs: $21 100 + $6 750 = $27 850
Cost per unit: $27 850 ÷ 200 units = $139.25 per unit

(d)

Machining department overhead allocated (220 000 × $50)	$ 11 000 000
Actual overhead in machining	10 200 000
Overapplied overhead	$ 800 000
Finishing department overhead allocated ($3 900 000 × 200%)	$ 7 800 000
Actual overhead in finishing	7 900 000
Underapplied overhead	$ 100 000

(e) Felix must believe that the overhead costs in each department are related to different allocation bases. Machining is likely to have more overhead expense for buying, maintaining and using machines. Therefore, machine hours are likely to reflect the activities involved in running machines. In the finishing department, more labour-related costs are incurred. Therefore, it is logical to use labour dollars as an allocation base. Although accountants attempt to pick allocation bases that are related to the activities in a cost centre, the allocations are still arbitrary. Changes in volumes do not result in proportionate changes in costs. A portion of the costs are often fixed and unaffected by changes in the level of the allocation bases. In other words, allocation bases are not necessarily cost drivers. Instead, they are simply measures of activity used to allocate costs logically.

SELF-STUDY PROBLEM 2

Normal and abnormal spoilage

Flockhart Company produces custom-made garden sheds using recycled materials. Currently two jobs are in process: numbers 689 and 690. During production of job 689, lightning hit the factory and caused an electricity surge followed by an outage. Lightning strikes are relatively unusual in the region where the factory is located. At the time of the strike, wood was being sawed to fit job 689. The saw malfunctioned and ruined a large piece of timber that originally cost $175. During production of job 690, two pieces of timber had sawing errors and were scrapped. These pieces of timber originally cost $80 and $75; they could be sold as scrap for $20 and $30. Sawing errors occur for many different jobs on a regular basis.

REQUIRED

(a) Consider the spoilage for job 689. Should it be categorised as normal or abnormal spoilage? Explain.
(b) Consider the spoilage for job 690. Should it be categorised as normal or abnormal spoilage? Explain.
(c) Prepare journal entries for the spoilage on both jobs. Assume that the scrap timber has not yet been sold.
(d) Describe the actual and opportunity costs of spoilage.

Solution to self-study problem 2

(a) The spoilage for job 689 is abnormal spoilage because it occurred from an unusual force of nature. Abnormal spoilage is not part of normal operations and occurs because systems are out of control or an unusual event occurs, such as loss of electricity from an unusual storm. Abnormal spoilage is recorded as a loss for the period.
(b) The spoilage for job 690 is normal spoilage because it arises as a part of ongoing operations. If it occurs because of the requirements of a specific job, it is recorded as a cost for that job. If it occurs as part of operations, it is recorded as an overhead cost.
(c) Journal entry for abnormal spoilage (assuming the requisition of raw material was not recorded as a job cost):

Loss from abnormal spoilage	DR	$ 175
Work in process inventory	CR	$175
Abnormal spoilage of timber (job 689 — spoiled timber at cost)		

Overhead cost control	DR	$105
Raw material inventory (scrap timber)	DR	$ 50
Work in process inventory	CR	$155
Normal spoilage of timber (job 690 — spoiled timber at cost)		

(d) The actual costs of spoilage include the dollar amounts for direct materials, direct labour and overhead that have been incurred up to the point that the spoiled units are removed from production. The opportunity costs of spoilage include warranty and return costs, and potential loss of reputation and market share. It is difficult to estimate these costs but they can be considerable.

Questions

13.1 List three examples of job cost records you would receive if you were building a new home. (*Hint:* Itemised bills made out to you are usually job cost records.)

13.2 Will underapplied and overapplied overhead arise under both actual and normal costing? Explain your answer.

13.3 Within the area where you live, work or attend school, name three businesses that would probably use job costing.

13.4 How does the point of inspection (and therefore completion) affect the cost of spoilage?

13.5 Part of a contract between a union and a company guarantees that all manufacturing employees earn five hours of overtime each week. In the company's job costing system, should overtime be treated as a direct or indirect cost?

13.6 Compare actual and normal cost systems. Discuss the ways in which they are similar and the ways they differ.

13.7 Exquisite Furniture designs and manufactures custom furniture from exotic materials. Explain why spoilage is sometimes recorded as a cost for a specific job and other times as overhead for this entity.

13.8 Explain how manufacturing overhead cost pools and cost allocation are related.

13.9 Describe the procedures used in job costing.

13.10 List the most common allocation bases used in job costing and explain under what circumstances each base would be most appropriate.

13.11 List several different sources of information used in job costing, and explain why this information is required.

Exercises

13.12 **Job costing; determination of manufacturing overhead rates** Sheldon Manufacturing estimates the following activity for 2008:

Expected production	10 000 units
Expected direct labour hours	10 000 hours
Expected manufacturing overhead	$100 000
Manufacturing overhead is allocated on the basis of direct labour hours.	

At the end of the financial period the following information was collected:

Direct labour hours	9000 hours
Manufacturing overhead	$120 000

REQUIRED

(a) What was the predetermined manufacturing overhead rate calculated at the beginning of 2008?

(b) What was the actual manufacturing overhead rate for 2008?

(c) Explain the difference between the rates calculated in (a) and (b) above.

13.13 **Job costing over- and underapplied overhead; journal entries** Shane's Shovels produces small custom-made earth-moving equipment for landscaping companies. Manufacturing overhead is allocated to work in process using an estimated overhead rate. During April, transactions for Shane's Shovels included the following:

Direct materials issued to production	$180 000
Indirect materials issued to production	30 000

Other manufacturing overhead incurred	250 000
Overhead allocated	225 000
Direct labour costs	75 000

Beginning and ending work in process were both zero.

REQUIRED

(a) What was the cost of jobs completed in April?

(b) Was manufacturing overhead underapplied or overapplied? By how much?

(c) Write out the journal entries for these transactions, including the adjustment.

13.14 Normal and abnormal spoilage Franklin Fabrication produces custom-made security doors and gates. Currently two jobs are in process: 359 and 360. During production of job 359, the supervisor was on holidays and the employees made several errors in cutting the metal pieces for the two doors in the order. The spoiled metal pieces cost $20 each and had zero scrap value. In addition, an order of five gates that had been manufactured for job 360 required a fine wire mesh that sometimes tore as it was being mounted. Because a similar wire could be used that was much easier to install, the customer had been warned that costs could run over the bid if any difficulty was encountered in installing the wire. One of the gates was spoiled during the process of installing the wire. The cost of the materials and direct labour for the gate was $150. The gate and metal were hauled to the dump and discarded.

REQUIRED

(a) Should the spoilage for job 359 be categorised as normal or abnormal spoilage? Explain.

(b) Should the spoilage for job 360 be categorised as normal or abnormal spoilage? Explain.

(c) Prepare spoilage journal entries for both jobs.

13.15 Direct costs and overhead Job 87M had direct material costs of $400 and a total cost of $2100. Overhead is allocated at the rate of 75 per cent of prime cost (direct material and direct labour).

REQUIRED

(a) How much direct labour was used?

(b) How much overhead was allocated?

13.16 Analysis of WIP T-account Jasper Company uses a job costing system. Overhead is allocated based on 120 per cent of direct labour cost. Last month's transactions in the work in process account are shown here:

Work in process			
Beginning balance	48 000		
Direct materials	160 000	To finished goods	442 000
Direct labour	120 000		
Factory overhead	150 000		

Only one job, number 850, was still in process at the end of the month. Job 850 was charged with $9000 in overhead for the month.

REQUIRED

(a) What is the ending balance in the WIP account?

(b) How much direct labour cost was used for job 850?

(c) What is the amount of direct materials used for job 850?

13.17 Journal entries Langley uses a job costing system. At the beginning of June, two orders were in process as follows:

	Order 88	Order 105
Direct materials	$1000	$900
Direct labour	1200	200
Overhead allocated	1800	300

There was no inventory in finished goods on 1 June. During June, orders numbered 106 to 120 were put into process.

Direct materials requirements amounted to $13 000, direct labour costs for the month were $20 000 and actual manufacturing overhead recorded during the month amounted to $28 000.

The only order in process at the end of June was order 120, and the costs incurred for this order were $1150 of direct materials and $1000 of direct labour. In addition, order 118, which was 100 per cent complete, was still on hand as of 30 June. Total costs for this order were $3300. The entity's overhead allocation rate in June was the same as that used in May and is based on labour cost.

REQUIRED

(a) Prepare journal entries (with supporting calculations) to record the cost of goods manufactured, the cost of goods sold and the closing of the overapplied or underapplied overhead to cost of goods sold.

(b) Describe the two different approaches to closing overapplied or underapplied overhead at the end of the period. How do you choose an appropriate method?

13.18 Cost of goods sold schedule Rebecca Ltd is a manufacturer of machines made to customer specifications. All production costs are accumulated by means of a job order costing system. The following information is available at the beginning of October 2008.

Raw materials inventory, 1 October	$16 200
Work in process, 1 October	5 100

A review of the job order cost sheets revealed the composition of the work in process inventory on 1 October as follows:

Direct materials (assuming no indirect materials this month)	$1320
Direct labour (300 hours)	3000
Factory overhead allocated	780
	$5100

Activity during October was as follows:

Raw materials costing $20 000 were purchased.
Direct labour for job orders totalled 3300 hours at $10 per hour.
Factory overhead was allocated to production at the rate of $2.60 per direct labour hour.

On 31 October, inventories consisted of the following:

Raw materials inventory	$17 000
Work in process:	
Direct materials	4 320
Direct labour (500 hours)	5 000
Factory overhead allocated	1 300

REQUIRED

Prepare a detailed schedule showing the cost of goods manufactured for October.

13.19 Job costing journal entries Vern's Van Service customises light trucks according to customers' orders. This month the entity worked on five jobs, numbered 207 to 211. Materials requisitions for the month were as follows:

Ticket	Carpet	Paint	Electronics	Other	Total
207	$ 40	$ 350	$ 580	—	$ 970
208	75	200	375	—	650
209	200	400	200	—	800
210	30	150	770	—	950
211	60	—	50	—	110
Indirect	—	—	—	$750	750
Total costs					$4230

An analysis of the payroll records revealed the following distribution for labour costs:

	Job						
	207	208	209	210	211	Other	Total
Direct labour	$1400	$1200	$800	$1700	$400	—	$5500
Indirect labour	—	—	—	—	—	$2200	2200
Total costs							$7700

Other overhead costs (consisting of rent, depreciation, taxes, insurance, utilities etc.) amounted to $3600. At the beginning of the period, management anticipated that overhead cost would be $6400 and total direct labour would amount to $5000. Overhead is allocated on the basis of direct labour dollars.

Jobs 207 to 210 were finished during the month; job 211 is still in process. Jobs 207 to 209 were picked up and paid for by customers. Job 210 is still on the lot waiting to be picked up.

REQUIRED

(a) Prepare the journal entries to reflect the incurrence of materials, labour and overhead costs; the allocation of overhead; and the transfer of units to finished goods and cost of goods sold.

(b) Close overapplied or underapplied overhead to cost of goods sold.

13.20 Allocating overhead; over- and underapplied overhead; spoilage The Futons for You Company sells batches of custom-made futons to customers and uses predetermined rates for fixed overhead, based on machine hours. The following data are available for last year:

Budgeted and actual fixed factory overhead cost	$160 000
Budgeted machine hours	100 000
Actual machine hours used	110 000

	Machine hours used
Job 20	11 000
Job 21	16 000
Job 22	14 000
Job 23	9 000

REQUIRED

(a) Calculate the estimated overhead allocation rate to be used for the year.

(b) Determine the overhead to be allocated to job 21.

(c) Determine total overapplied or underapplied overhead at the end of the year.

(d) Should cost of goods sold be increased or decreased at the end of the year? Why?

(e) If the amount of overapplied or underapplied overhead is material, how is it assigned?

(f) Suppose Job 21 required a special fabric cover for the futon pads. This type of fabric dulled the blades of the cutting machine, and a number of fabric covers were unusable. Should this spoilage be recorded for job 21 or for all jobs processed this period? Explain your answer.

13.21 Journal entries for job costing At the beginning of the accounting period, the accountant for ABC Industries estimated that total overhead would be $80 000. Overhead is allocated to jobs on the basis of direct labour cost. Direct labour was budgeted to cost $200 000 this period. During the period, only three jobs were worked on. The following summarises the direct materials and labour costs for each:

	Job 1231	Job 1232	Job 1233
Direct materials	$45 000	$70 000	$30 000
Direct labour	70 000	90 000	50 000

Job 1231 was finished and sold, job 1232 was finished but is waiting to be sold, and job 1233 is still in process. Actual overhead for the period was $82 000.

REQUIRED

Prepare the following journal entries.

(a) Cost recorded during production

(b) Cost of jobs completed

(c) Cost of goods sold

(d) Allocation of overapplied or underapplied overhead allocated on a pro rata basis to the ending balances in work in process, finished goods and cost of goods sold

13.22 Spoilage journal entries Jones Company manufactures custom doors. When job 186 (a batch of 14 custom doors) was being processed in the machining department, one of the wood panels on a door split. This problem occurs periodically and is considered normal spoilage. Direct materials and labour for the door, to the point of spoilage, were $35. In addition, a storm caused a surge in electricity and a routing machine punctured the wood for job 238. This incident occurred at the beginning of production, so spoilage amounted to only the cost of wood, at $200.

REQUIRED

(a) Prepare the journal entries for normal and abnormal spoilage.

(b) Now suppose that the wood from abnormal spoilage can be sold for $25. Record the journal entries for the disposal value.

(c) Jones Company is considering hiring someone to inspect all wood after it arrives at the plant but prior to production. Discuss the pros and cons of hiring an inspector.

Problems

13.23 Collecting overhead cost information A family member asked you to review the accounting system used for Hanna's, a custom stained-glass manufacturing business. The owner currently uses a software package to keep track of her bank account but does not produce financial statements. The owner seeks your help in setting up a costing system so that financial statements can be produced on a monthly basis.

REQUIRED

(a) What kind of costing system is needed for this setting?

(b) You plan to categorise the banking data for entry into the financial statement records. List the categories you might use for these entries. List only broad categories here [see parts (c), (d) and (e) for more details].

(c) List several costs that might be included in a fixed overhead category.

(d) List several costs that might be included in a variable overhead category.

(e) List several costs that might be included in direct materials.

(f) Write a memo to the owner discussing the alternative choices for the costing system. Include an explanation of the type of information that would need to be captured to support the costing system.

13.24 Cost of rework; control of scrap; accounting for scrap Dapper Dan Draperies manufactures and installs custom-ordered draperies.

REQUIRED

(a) For all drapes, occasionally the sewing equipment malfunctions and the drape must be reworked. Explain how to account for the cost of rework when it is needed.

(b) Explain how to account for the cost of rework when customers choose a fabric that is known to require rework.

(c) Explain why scrap will always arise in this entity.

(d) Dapper Dan can sell scraps to quilting groups or just throw them away. List several factors that could affect this decision.

(e) If Dapper Dan decides to sell scraps, explain the accounting choices for recording the sales value.

13.25 Accounting for scrap You are helping a friend, Jonah, set up a new accounting system for a small start-up construction entity. He specialises in custom-made energy efficient homes that are built on a cost-plus basis. Cost-plus means that his customers pay a fixed percentage above the sum of direct and overhead costs.

As he goes through the accounts, Jonah asks why you set up a separate account for scrap. He does not believe that scrap should be recorded anywhere in his accounting system because it is worth little, and theft is no problem. He makes weekly trips to a recycling plant where he receives a small sum for the scrap. Most of the time Jonah works on only one house, and the scrap is only for that house. However, once in a while he works on several houses, and the scrap for all of the houses is recycled at once.

REQUIRED

(a) Explain the two ways that scrap can be recorded in a job costing system.

(b) Choose the appropriate method for Jonah and explain your choice.

(c) Suppose you are a prospective homeowner. Explain to Jonah why you believe the revenue from scrap associated with your home should be recorded as a reduction in your costs rather than his overall costs.

(d) Write a brief (and diplomatic) paragraph to convince Jonah that he needs to account for the revenues from scrap.

13.26 Job costing; overhead rates The Eastern Seaboard Company uses an estimated rate for allocating factory overhead to job orders based on machine hours for the machining department, and on a direct labour cost basis for the finishing department.

The company budgeted the following for last year:

	Machining	Finishing
Factory overhead	$5 000 000	$ 3 000 000
Machine hours	250 000	14 000
Direct labour hours	15 000	16 000
Direct labour cost	$225 000	$ 2 400 000

During December, the cost record for job 602 shows the following:

	Machining	Finishing
Direct materials requisitioned	$7 000	$2 000
Direct labour cost	$300	$6 750
Direct labour hours	20	300
Machine hours	35	5

REQUIRED

(a) What is the estimated overhead allocation rate that should be used in the machining department? In the finishing department?

(b) What is the total overhead allocated to job 602?

(c) Assuming that job 602 consisted of 200 units of product, what is the unit cost for this job?

(d) What factors affect the volume of production in a period? Can we know all of the factors before the period begins? Why?

(e) Explain why the company would use two different overhead allocation bases.

13.27 Plant-wide versus production cost pools Flexible Manufacturers produces small batches of customised products. The accounting system is set up to allocate plant overhead to each job using the following production cost pools and overhead allocation rates

Labour-paced assembly	$25 per direct labour hour
Machine-paced assembly	$18 per machine hour
Quality testing	$2 per unit

Actual resources used for job 75:

Direct labour hours	3 hours
Machine hours	1.25 hours
Number of units	36 units

The factory accountant wants to simplify the cost accounting system and use a plant-wide rate. If the preceding costs were grouped into a single cost pool and allocated based on labour hours, the rate would be $35 per direct labour hour.

REQUIRED

(a) What cost should be allocated to job 75 using the plant-wide overhead rate?

(b) What cost should be allocated to job 75 using the production cost pool overhead rates?

(c) Why do the allocated amounts in parts (a) and (b) differ?

(d) Which method would you recommend? Explain your choice.

13.28 Effects of robotic equipment on overhead rates 'Our costs are out of control, our accounting system is screwed up, or both!' exclaimed the sales manager. 'We are simply non-competitive on a great many of the jobs we bid on. Just last week we lost a customer when a competitor underbid us by 25 per cent! And I bid the job at cost because the customer has been with us for years but has been complaining about our prices.'

This problem, raised at the weekly management meeting, has been getting worse over the years. The Johnson Tool Company produces parts for specific customer orders. When the entity first became successful, it employed nearly 500 skilled machinists. Over the years the entity has become increasingly automated and now uses a number of different robotic machines. It currently employs only 75 production workers but output has quadrupled.

The problems raised by the sales manager can be seen in the portions of two bid sheets brought to the meeting (as reproduced below). The bids are from the cutting department, but the relative size of these three types of manufacturing costs is similar for other departments.

The cutting department charges overhead to products based on direct labour hours. For the current period, the department expects to use 4000 direct labour hours. Departmental overhead, consisting mostly of depreciation on the robotic equipment, is expected to be $1 480 000.

An employee can typically set up any job on the appropriate equipment in approximately 15 minutes. Once machines are operating, an employee oversees five to eight machines simultaneously. All that is required is to load or unload materials and monitor calibrations. The department's robotic machines will log a total of 25 000 hours of run time in the current period.

For bid 74683, the entity was substantially underbid by a competitor. The company did get the job for bid 74687, but the larger jobs are harder to find. Small jobs arise frequently, but the entity is rarely successful in obtaining them.

Cutting department	
Bid # 74683	Machine run time: 3 hours
Materials	
Steel sheeting	$280.25
Direct labour	
Equipment set-up (0.25 hours @ $12.50)	3.13
Equipment tending (1 hour @ $12.50)	12.50
Overhead (1.25 hours @ $370)	462.50
Total costs	$758.38

Cutting department	
Bid # 74687	Machine run time: 11 hours
Materials	
Steel sheeting	$2 440.50
Direct labour	
Equipment set-up (0.25 hours @ $12.50)	3.13
Equipment tending (1.25 hours @ $12.50)	15.63
Overhead (1.5 hours @ $370)	555.00
Total costs	$ 3 014.26

REQUIRED

(a) Critique the cost allocation method used within the current cost accounting system.
(b) Suggest a better approach for allocating overhead. Allocate costs using your approach and compare the costs of both jobs under the two systems.
(c) Discuss the pros and cons of using job costs to determine the price for a job order.

13.29 Classification of rework costs; uncertainties; critique of rework and scrap policy Fran Markus is in the cost accounting group at Boats Galore, a large manufacturing company that produces customised boats and yachts. The company sometimes experiences quality problems with its fibreglass raw material, causing flawed areas in boat hulls. The problem is often fixed by reworking the flawed areas. Other times the hull is scrapped because it is too flawed, and a new hull is fabricated. The spoilage policy at Boats Galore is to charge the cost of rework and spoilage to overhead unless it arises because a hull design is particularly complicated. In those cases, the cost is assigned to the job.

Two boats currently under construction require triple the amount of materials and labour time to enhance boat security. The customer wants each hull to be able to withstand the explosion of a small bomb. It is the company's first order with this hull construction. Because of the new design and fibreglass process, the customer has agreed to a cost-plus contract and will pay cost plus a fixed percentage of cost. This contract assures that Boats Galore does not incur a loss from developing the enhanced security hull. This week, the third layer on one of the boat hulls had a flaw in the fibreglass. The area was reworked, after which it met the security requirements.

Fran receives weekly data on labour and materials for each boat under construction. For regular production, workers estimate the time and materials used to rework flawed fibreglass areas, and Fran adds those costs to overhead instead of recording them as a cost of the particular job. Now she needs to decide how to record the cost of rework for the enhanced security hulls. The production people are not sure whether the flaw was due to poor quality fibreglass or to the triple hull design. If Fran adds the cost to the job order, the customer will pay for the labour and supplies as part of the cost-plus price. If she adds the cost to overhead, the cost will be spread across all jobs and only part of it will be allocated to the job having the enhanced security hulls.

(a) Critique the company's accounting policy for rework and scrap.

(b) Describe uncertainties about the accounting treatment for the rework costs on the enhanced security hull job.

(c) Discuss the pros and cons of alternative accounting treatments for the rework costs on this job.

(d) Suppose you are an accounting work-experience student at Boats Galore. Fran asks you to recommend an accounting treatment for the rework costs on the enhanced security hull job.

  (i) Write a memo to Fran with your recommendation. As you write the memo, consider what information Fran will need from you to help her make a final decision.

  (ii) Write one or two paragraphs explaining how you decided what information to include in your memo.

14

Process costing for financial reporting

IN BRIEF

Some products are mass-produced, making it impractical to trace costs to individual units. Process costing provides a way to overcome this challenge by assigning costs to production departments and then allocating the costs from the department to individual units. The practice of process costing is complicated by the fact that some physical units are likely to be partially complete at the beginning and end of the accounting period. Furthermore, entities typically produce some proportion of defective or spoiled units. To assign costs appropriately to all of the units processed (completed, partially complete or spoiled), accountants must understand both the production process and the various methods for applying process costing.

After studying this chapter, you should be able to:

1	Assign costs to mass-produced products.
2	Understand the concept of equivalent units and how they relate to the production process.
3	Calculate product costs using the weighted average method.
4	Calculate product costs using the FIFO method.
5	Calculate product costs in a process where there are multiple production departments.
6	Handle spoilage costs in process costing.
7	Identify the uses and limitations of process cost information.

Changing times in the Australian steel production industry

Current annual steel production in Australia is around 8 million tonnes, which represents a turnover in excess of $21 billion per annum (ASI 2006). Over the past few years, the global steel market has undergone major peaks and troughs. A slump in the Australian steel industry forced BHP to close its Newcastle steelworks in 1999. Since then, a turn of events stimulated by the economic boom in China has reinvigorated the global steel manufacturing industry. As a result, the fortunes of the key players in the Australian steel market have been affected by the strong demand for steel from Chinese factories. Steel prices have increased threefold, with steel manufacturers reporting strong profit margins. Nevertheless, the boom is expected to be short lived because China is now shifting from being a major customer to a global competitor (Long 2006). As a result of recent substantial growth in China's mass steel production capacity, the prices of raw materials have increased while the global commodity prices of cast steel and rolled steel have declined. The Chinese steel industry is now 50 times larger than Australia's and is continuing to grow (ASI 2006). A global steel glut is forecast.

The major steel companies in Australia (BlueScope, OneSteel and Smorgon Steel) have reacted to the competition with a rationalisation of their operations and significant restructuring. Recently, Smorgon Steel closed its pipe and tube mill operations in Melbourne, and Blue-Scope Steel ceased downstream tin milling operations at its Port Kembla facility. The CEO of Smorgon Steel, Ray Horsburgh, considers the trend in Australia will be towards distribution rather than trying to compete in a commodity market. BlueScope Steel CEO, Kirby Adams, says declining manufacturing in Australia, particularly in the automotive and white goods industries, has led to a significant reduction in domestic steel consumption. BlueScope Steel aims to increase its market share through steel product innovations, and has recently invested heavily in manufacturing operations in China and Vietnam to fulfil its strategic objectives (BlueScope Steel website).

The production of steel comprises three major processing stages. Initially, the raw material (iron ore) is blended with coal and limestone, then placed in a blast furnace to make iron. In the BlueScope Steel facility at Port Kembla (near Wollongong), the two blast furnaces operate in a continuous process, 24 hours a day, to make iron. The molten iron with recycled scrap iron (one-fifth of the total volume) is transferred to the steel making department. In this second stage, the iron is converted to steel by blasting the molten iron with oxygen, and injecting carbon and other additives into the steel making vessels. In the third stage, the liquid steel is transferred to the casting department where slabs of cast steel are produced. BlueScope Steel has three continuous slab casters in operation at its Port Kembla operations. The cast slab is either sold as cast steel or processed further into rolled steel and other steel products in the entity's downstream facilities.

In a mass production environment such as this, the average cost of cast or rolled steel is driven by both cost levels and production volumes. Because average costs can be reduced by spreading fixed costs over a larger number of units, production capacity and volumes are closely monitored by Australian steel manufacturers such as BlueScope Steel. Furthermore, continuous monitoring of the average cost of steel is also important in an environment where profits are only made if the product selling price is higher than the average cost of local production.

Sources: Information from Australian Steel Institute (ASI) 2006, submission to the 'Inquiry into the state of Australia's manufactured export and import competing base now and beyond the resource boom', submission 9, House of Representatives Standing Committee on Economics, Finance and Public Administration, Parliament House, Canberra; BlueScope Steel website, www.bluescopesteel.com; Long, S 2006, 'Nerves of steel needed as metallic bubble bursts', ABC Online, Inside Business, 26 February, www.abc.net.au/insidebusiness.

Issues from this scene setter to look for in the chapter include:

- Understanding how the average costs of steel production are used in monitoring broad-level product profitability.

- How costs might be assigned to mass-produced products such as cast or rolled steel.

- How, in continuous production such as that found in steel manufacturing operations, the determination of 'equivalent units' of completed product is necessary for cost allocation and financial reporting purposes.

- How the process costing techniques learned in this chapter can be useful for measuring and monitoring processes for financial reporting purposes.

- Understanding that the averaging techniques inherent in process costing might not adequately provide Australian steel manufacturing managers with detailed information for decisions relating to outsourcing or re-engineering value chain activities in steel production.

Accounting for the cost of mass-produced goods

The accounting approach for assigning product costs to mass-produced products is called **process costing**. The purpose of process costing is to assign costs to each unit of a good. However, it is time-consuming and costly to trace costs directly to individual units when products are identical and mass-produced. Thus, production costs are traced to cost pools reflecting the production process (usually departments) and then allocated to individual units in a two-stage process. Examples of products for which process costing is used include beverages, food, chemicals, petroleum, plastic products and pharmaceuticals. Some industries that have traditionally been in the business of mass production have sought ways of moving away from this environment. The chapter 14 article at the end of this book explores issues associated with the move from mass production to mass customisation.

In many entities, the production process consists of work performed in a sequence of departments. Thus, costs are assigned to each production department and then allocated to all units that pass through the department. Consider the flow of work and costs for a cherry processor. Fresh cherries are received and washed in the first department. At this point in the process, some of the cherries are sold on the market as fresh cherries. Other cherries will be processed further. In the second department, the cherries are placed in vats and then covered with a syrup solution, brought to a boil and then prepared for canning or drying. Most of the cherries are canned in the second department, but some are transferred to a third department where the syrup is drained before the cherries are dried and packaged. Notice that each department incurs a variety of costs. Costs in the first department include the purchase price of the cherries, labour, equipment depreciation and maintenance, water, electricity and supplies. It would be impossible to directly measure the cost of water used to clean each kilogram of cherries. However, costs such as water are allocated to each kilogram of cherries by dividing the total cost of water by the total kilograms of cherries processed.

Assigning direct materials and conversion costs

Similar to job costing, costs in a process costing system are assigned to products using a two-stage process. However, in process costing, all costs are first assigned to departments. Costs are then allocated from departments to individual product units, as shown in figure 14.1(a).

In a conventional process costing system, the two categories of product cost are direct materials and conversion costs. **Conversion costs** are direct labour and production overhead costs. Direct materials and conversion costs are allocated separately because they are usually incurred at different points in the production process. Figure 14.1(b) shows the cost flow within a department. Some costs, such as indirect materials and indirect labour, are traced to departments through materials and payroll records. However, a number of costs are allocated to departments, such as the cost of rent and insurance for a shared production facility.

FIGURE 14.1 ■ A conventional process costing system

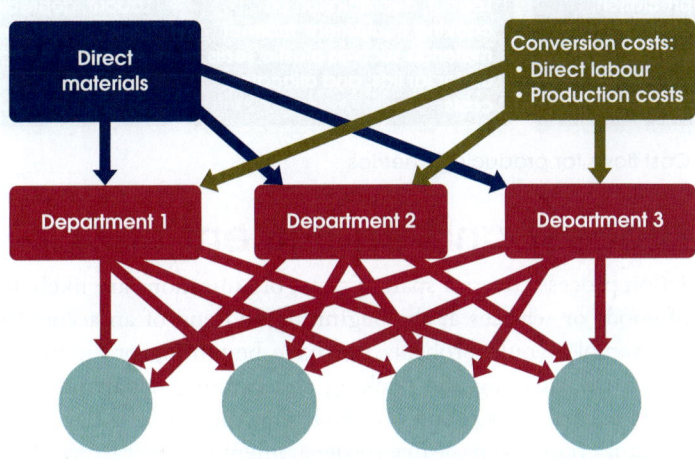

(a) Product cost flows

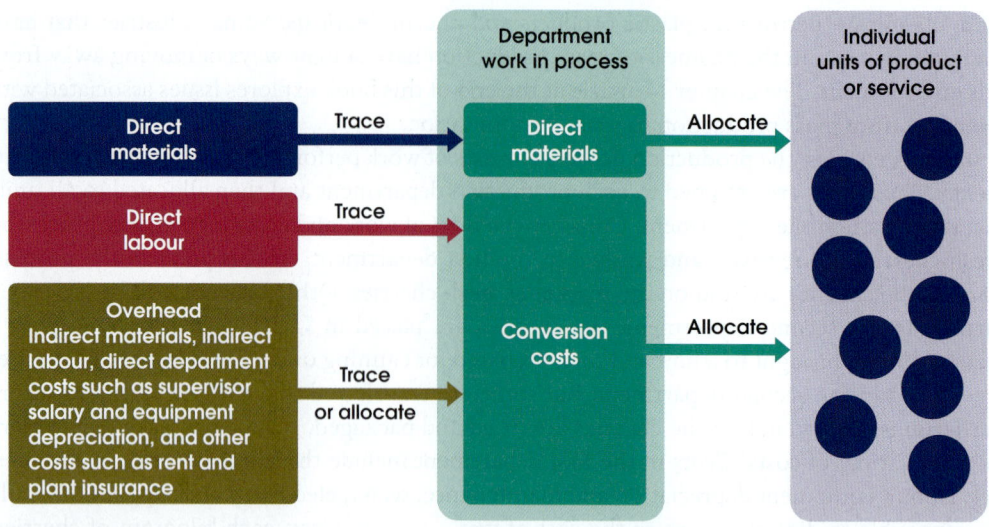

(b) Departmental cost flows

Figure 14.2 illustrates how costs are incurred for the cherry production process. In the cleaning department, the direct materials (cherries) are added at the beginning of the process. In the cooking and canning department, some direct materials (water and syrup) are added at the beginning of the process, and others (jars and lids) are added at the end of the process. In the drying department, packaging materials are used at the end of the process. The conversion costs are added throughout processing in all three departments.

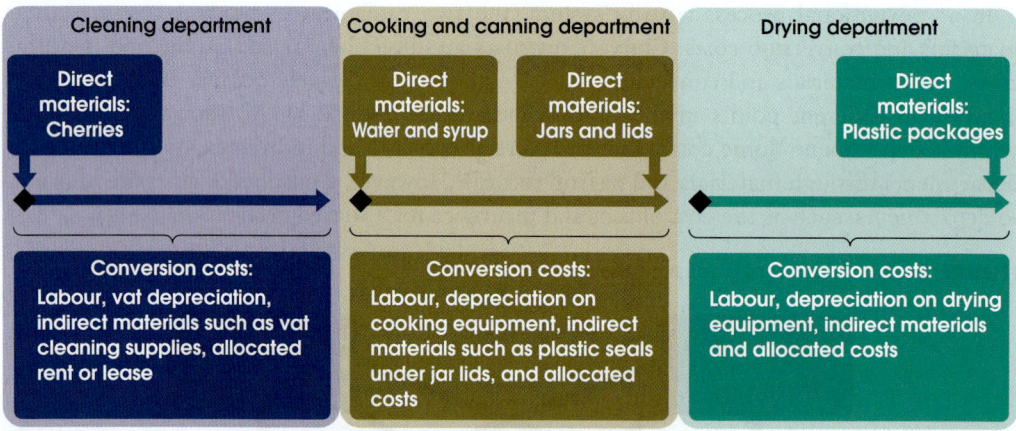

FIGURE 14.2 ■ Cost flows for producing cherries

Work in process and equivalent units

When the production process covers a span of time, organisations are likely to have partially complete units of goods or services at the beginning and end of an accounting period. The cherry processing example would probably not have beginning or ending work in process (WIP) inventories for the cleaning and cooking and canning departments. The processing in these departments occurs quickly and is complete at the end of a day's operating activity. However, WIP inventory remains in the drying department for several days. Suppose at the end of an accounting period cherries in the drying department are in various stages of completion. Some are completely dried and waiting to be packaged. Others were just put into the drying equipment and will need to remain there for several days. We know the number of kilograms the department is currently processing, and we know that we have cherries at many different stages of completion. We estimate the amount of completion for the entire volume of cherries in the department. For example, if a large amount of cherries (relative to all of the cherries in the department) has just begun the drying process, we might estimate that the cherries are 20 per cent complete on average. However, if most of the cherries are waiting to be packaged, we might estimate that the cherries are 80 per cent complete on average.

To calculate the cost allocation for partially complete units, we take the percentage of completion into account. **Equivalent units** measure the resources used in partially completed units relative to the resources needed to complete the units. For work in process inventory, equivalent units are the number of units that could have been completed if all resources had gone to complete whole units instead of to partially complete units. Suppose WIP in the drying department consists of 1000 kilograms of cherries estimated to be 20 per cent complete. The conversion cost allocated to these cherries is equivalent to the cost needed to fully compete 200 kilograms of cherries (1000 kg × 20%). Thus, we estimate that ending WIP consists of 200 equivalent kilograms with respect to conversion costs.

Hybrid costing systems and operation costing

As manufacturing systems incorporate more technology, entities become more flexible in meeting the diverse needs of their customers. Products that were once mass-produced are now customised. Although most of the manufacturing process might be performed identically for all units, at some point individual units are customised. For example, Harley Davidson customises its motorcycles with special accessories and colours. Flexible manufacturing systems are used in many industries such as computers, cars and bicycles. Customers order these products with specific features. The manufacturing process is a combination of mass-produced components, but during assembly the products are customised. **Hybrid costing** is the accounting approach used to assign product costs by applying a combination of both job and process costing. Often, process costing is used to the point of customisation, after which the direct costs are traced to each specific job.

Operation costing is a particular type of hybrid method used when similar batches of identical products are manufactured. Units in each batch are identical, but the processing of each batch is different and may not include the same steps. For example, consider the production of notebook computers having different configurations. Some batches go through the same processes but differ based on type of memory chip or size of hard drive installed. Some batches go through fewer processes than others. For example, some notebook computers are sold with only one installed battery, while others have both an installed battery and an extra battery.

Operation costing systems track costs using work orders for each batch. These work orders include detailed information about the direct materials required and the steps needed in the manufacturing operation. Direct materials are traced to each batch through the work orders and then allocated to units. In addition, all units within a batch are allocated uniform amounts of overhead. Unlike conventional process costing, operation costing usually includes more than two types of cost pools. The cost pools are designed to match the separate processes that may be allocated to batches of products. This matching of processes and cost pools improves the accuracy of cost assignment to individual products. Managers are better able to focus on the control of physical processes within a given production system because their financial information more accurately matches the flow of resources through specific processes. The focus in this chapter will be on process costing.

Process costing methods

Several methods are used to measure the costs that are allocated for process costing. In this chapter, we will discuss the first-in, first-out (FIFO) and weighted average methods.

Under the **first-in, first-out (FIFO) method**, the current period's costs are used to allocate cost to work performed this period. In the **weighted average method**, costs from beginning WIP (performed last period) are averaged with costs incurred during the current period, and then allocated to units completed and ending WIP.

Suppose a company called Premier Plastics mass-produces plastic products and small appliances designed by a famous Australian architect. One manufacturing facility is dedicated to the production of a premier line of CD/DVD storage units. The plant has two production departments: the moulding department and the assembly department.

In the moulding department, plastic liquid is prepared and poured into moulds. As shown in figure 14.3, plastic mix ingredients are added at the beginning of the process. Conversion costs include direct labour, facility and equipment depreciation, cleaner's wages, electricity, building insurance, supervisor salaries and many other overhead costs. Although the conversion costs are incurred throughout the moulding process, they are not incurred evenly. For example, the machines are periodically shut down for cleaning and maintenance. More labour is required to monitor certain parts of the process, such as when plastic mix ingredients are added. Nevertheless, we simplify the accounting by assuming that conversion costs are incurred evenly throughout the process. When the moulding process is complete, the outer shells are transferred to the assembly department.

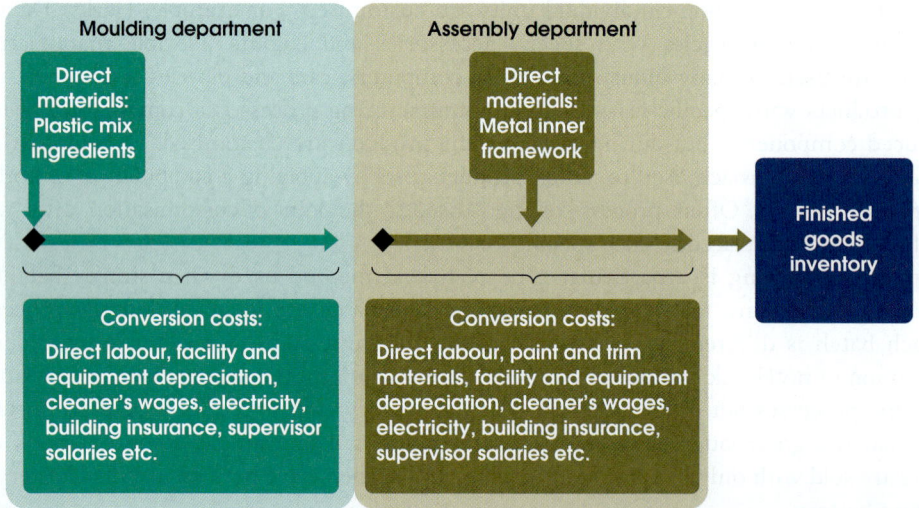

FIGURE 14.3 ■ Cost flows for producing plastic CD/DVD storage units

In the assembly department, machines remove any rough edges and then smooth the outer and inner surfaces. Next, a metal inner framework for holding CDs and DVDs is inserted. Thus, direct materials are added partway through this process. Finally, details are painted on each unit. Because the cost for paint and trim for each storage unit is small, those costs are considered indirect and included in conversion costs. The completed units are transferred to finished goods inventory. As orders are processed, the units are transferred to the shipping department for packing and delivery.

Premier Plastics commenced operations in March. Nancy Redhouse, the cost accountant for Premier Plastics, wants to help the managers monitor operational costs, so she is considering which is the best method to use for process cost reports. The moulding department head also wants to use cost information to motivate employees operating the new machines to identify potential process improvements that could further reduce cost or increase quality.

It was first thought that the process cost reports would be prepared using the weighted average method. However, Nancy is concerned that this method might not provide managers with the most current cost information. The FIFO method provides more current cost information. Nancy decides to prepare process cost reports for the first three months using both methods so that she can discuss the results with the managers and obtain feedback for the final decision. She uses a four-step process to prepare the process cost report under each method.

1. Summarise total costs to account for.
2. Summarise physical and equivalent units.
3. Calculate the cost per equivalent unit.
4. Account for cost of units completed and cost of ending WIP, thereby preparing the process cost reports.

The following calculations focus on process costing for the moulding department over the first three months of production activities. The first month portrays the simplest scenario, with no beginning or ending work in process. During the second month, the computations become slightly more complex with the addition of ending WIP. The third month includes both beginning and ending WIP. For each month, we prepare cost reports to summarise and compare the results for the FIFO and weighted average methods.

Process cost reports without beginning or ending WIP — first month (March)

During March, 10 000 units are started by the moulding department of Premier Plastics, completed and transferred to the assembly department. When no work in process is involved, the equivalent unit cost is the average cost per unit for the period, calculated by dividing total cost for direct materials and conversion by the total units produced. Therefore, the cost per equivalent unit is the same under both the FIFO and weighted average methods.

At the end of March, interim financial reports will need to be prepared and it will be necessary to value finished goods. The valuation process for this month is simplified because all goods started were completed. However, as there are no subsidiary ledgers when using a process costing system, it is necessary to undertake calculations outside the ledger; this is achieved through the preparation of a production cost report. Comprehensive example 1 develops the production cost report for the month of March, comparing the valuation under a FIFO methodology and a weighted average methodology for valuation purposes.

Comprehensive example 1

Process cost reports without beginning or ending WIP

Step 1 Summarise total costs to account for

For March, the moulding department of Premier Plastics incurred costs of $100 000. The cost of direct materials used during March is $30 000, and conversion costs incurred are $70 000.

Step 2 Summarise physical and equivalent units

	Beginning WIP	Complete beginning WIP	Work this period Start and complete	Start ending WIP	Total work performed this period	Total units to account for
Physical units	0	0	10 000	0	10 000	10 000
Equivalent units:						**Total work**
Direct materials	0	0	10 000	0	10 000	10 000
Conversion costs	0	0	10 000	0	10 000	10 000

Step 2 illustrates the calculation of the physical flow of units and enables the determination of how many units need to be valued for reporting purposes. As all units are both started and completed in the same period, the calculation of total product cost is simply the total of all costs incurred and recorded in WIP for the month. Obviously, the number of total equivalent units is equal to 10 000.

Step 3 Calculate the cost per equivalent unit

The cost per equivalent unit is determined by dividing the cost to be allocated by the equivalent units calculated in step 2 for each cost pool. An average cost is then calculated for each cost pool.

FIFO

Direct materials:

$$\frac{\text{Direct materials cost}}{\text{Equivalent units for total work performed this period}} = \frac{\$30\,000}{10\,000} = \$3$$

Conversion costs:

$$\frac{\text{Conversion costs}}{\text{Equivalent units for total work performed this period}} = \frac{\$70\,000}{10\,000} = \underline{7}$$

Total cost per equivalent unit: $\underline{\underline{\$10}}$

Weighted average. Calculations are the same as for FIFO because there is no beginning WIP.

Step 4 Prepare the process cost reports for moulding department: March

	FIFO Calculation	Units	Costs	Weighted average Calculation	Units	Costs
New units started, completed and transferred out	10 000 × $10	10 000	$100 000			
Total units completed and transferred out		10 000	100 000	10 000 × $10	10 000	$100 000
Total accounted for		10 000	$100 000		10 000	$100 000

As shown in step 2, the summary of physical units and equivalent units manufactured during March is simple. Because no beginning or ending WIP needs to be accounted for, the number of physical units is equal to the number of equivalent units for both direct materials and conversion costs.

Comparison of weighted average and FIFO. Because no beginning WIP is involved, the costs per unit are the same under both the FIFO and weighted average methods. These methods differ only when beginning WIP must be taken into account. As shown in step 3, the direct materials cost is $3 per unit and conversion costs are $7 per unit. Total cost per unit is $10. Thus, the cost for the 10 000 units produced is $100 000, which is equal to the total costs to account for.

Process cost reports with ending WIP — second month (April)

For the month of April, the moulding department has ending WIP but no beginning WIP. During April, 12 000 units are started. At the end of the month, 10 000 are completed and transferred out to the assembly department and 2000 units started are only 30 per cent complete (see comprehensive example 2).

Comprehensive example 2

Process cost reports with ending WIP in second month

Step 1 Summarise total costs to account for
The cost of direct materials used during April is $36 000, and conversion costs are $74 200. Therefore, $110 200 needs to be assigned to inventory.

Step 2 Summarise physical and equivalent units

				Work this period		
	Beginning WIP	Complete beginning WIP	Start and complete	Start ending WIP (30%)	Total work performed this period	Total units to account for
Physical units	0	0	10 000	2 000	12 000	12 000
Equivalent units:						**Total work**
Direct materials	0	0	10 000	2 000	12 000	12 000
Conversion costs	0	0	10 000	600	10 600	10 600

The total work performed during April is the sum of the units that were started, completed and transferred out and the equivalent units in ending WIP. Direct materials in the moulding department are added at the beginning of production, so the 2000 units in ending WIP are 100 per cent complete with respect to direct materials, and equivalent units for direct materials equal 2000. The total amount of work performed during April for direct materials is 12 000 equivalent units. However, we assume that conversion costs in the moulding department are incurred evenly throughout production. Therefore, the 2000 physical units in ending WIP are counted as 600 equivalent units (2000 units × 30%) for conversion costs. The total amount of work performed during April for conversion costs is 10 600 equivalent units.

Equivalent units need to be calculated for the ending WIP because the units still have further processing in the moulding department.

Step 3 Calculate the cost per equivalent unit

FIFO

Direct materials:

$$\frac{\text{Direct materials cost}}{\text{Equivalent units for total work performed this period}} = \frac{\$36\,000}{12\,000} = \$3$$

Conversion costs:

$$\frac{\text{Conversion costs}}{\text{Equivalent units for total work performed this period}} = \frac{\$74\,200}{10\,600} = 7$$

Total cost per equivalent unit: $10

Weighted average. Calculations are the same as for FIFO because there is no beginning WIP.

Comparison of weighted average and FIFO. Because Premier Plastics began April with no beginning WIP, the costs per unit are again the same under the FIFO and weighted average methods. However, because we have ending WIP that is partially complete, we now use equivalent units rather than actual units to calculate the per-unit cost.

The inventory valuation process begins by determining the equivalent number of units that will have costs assigned. Remember, at the end of the period the moulding department WIP account will need to be balanced by transferring the cost of completed goods to the assembly department WIP account, with the balance of costs for incomplete units staying in the moulding department WIP account.

Step 4 Process cost reports for moulding department: April

	FIFO			Weighted average		
	Calculation	Units	Costs	Calculation	Units	Costs
New units started, completed and transferred out	10 000 × $10	10 000	$100 000			
Total units completed and transferred out		10 000	100 000	10 000 × $10	10 000	$100 000
Ending WIP:		2 000			2 000	
Direct materials	2 000 × $3		6 000	2 000 × $3		6 000
Conversion costs	600 × $7		4 200	600 × $7		4 200
Total ending WIP cost			10 200			10 200
Total accounted for		**12 000**	**$ 110 200**		**12 000**	**$ 110 200**

As the direct materials cost remains $3 per unit and conversion costs are $7 per unit, the total equivalent unit cost remains $10. Thus, the cost allocated to the 10 000 units completed is $100 000. For ending WIP, the cost of direct materials is $6000 and conversion costs are $4200. We can double-check our calculations by verifying that the sum of costs accounted for ($110 200) is equal to the sum of beginning WIP plus the costs incurred during April ($0 + $36 000 + $74 200 = $110 200).

Comparison of weighted average and FIFO. As before, with no beginning WIP, there are no cost difference between the FIFO and weighted average methods. The reason for this is that all costs were incurred in the current period.

Process cost reports with beginning and ending WIP — third month (May)

For May, there is beginning WIP as well as ending WIP. Beginning WIP includes 2000 units (closing WIP for April with an inventory value of $110 200); 9000 units are started, completed and transferred to the assembly department; and another 1000 units are started and 40 per cent complete in ending WIP. The cost of direct materials used during May is $30 500, and conversion costs incurred are $76 680 (see comprehensive example 3).

Comprehensive example 3

Process cost reports with beginning and ending WIP

Step 1 Summarise total costs to account for

For May, we have to account not only for the current costs incurred, but also for the costs assigned to the ending WIP for April. The cost breakdown is as follows:

	Direct material	Conversion costs
Ending WIP — April	$6 000	$4 200
Current costs — May	$30 500	$76 680
Total costs to account for = $117 380	$36 500	$80 880

Step 2 Summarise physical and equivalent units

			Work this period			
	Beginning WIP (30%)	Complete beginning WIP (70%)	Start and complete	Start ending WIP (40%)	Total work performed this period	Total units to account for
Physical units	2 000	0	9 000	1 000	10 000	12 000
Equivalent units:						**Total work**
Direct materials	2 000	0	9 000	1 000	10 000	12 000
Conversion costs	600	1 400	9 000	400	10 800	11 400

The total units to account for during May (12 000) include both beginning WIP and the units started during the month. The total work performed during the month is the sum of work performed to complete beginning WIP units, the units both started and completed, and the work performed on units started but not yet completed. Because direct materials are added at the beginning of the process, no additional direct materials were needed to complete beginning WIP, meaning the units were 100 per cent complete with respect to direct materials.

Conversion costs are added throughout the process, so part of the conversion costs for beginning WIP was incurred last period and part was incurred this period. The beginning WIP consisted of 2000 units that were 30 per cent complete, or 600 equivalent units with respect to conversion costs. Conversion work performed during May consisted of completing the beginning WIP of 1400 [2000 units × (1 − 30%)] equivalent units, plus the 9000 units started and completed, plus 400 equivalent units in ending WIP (1000 units × 40%), for a total of 10 800 units.

Step 3 Calculate the cost per equivalent unit

FIFO:

Direct materials:

$$\frac{\text{Direct materials cost}}{\text{Equivalent units for total work performed this period}} = \frac{\$30\,500}{10\,000} = \$3.05$$

Conversion costs:

$$\frac{\text{Conversion cost}}{\text{Equivalent units for total work performed this period}} = \frac{\$76\,680}{10\,800} = \underline{7.10}$$

Total cost per equivalent unit: $\underline{\underline{\$10.15}}$

FIFO costs. To determine the equivalent unit cost under FIFO, current period costs are divided by the number of equivalent units for total work performed this period. During May, equivalent unit costs are calculated as shown above: $3.05 for direct materials and $7.10 for conversion costs. These costs are allocated to the work performed to complete beginning WIP, to the units started and completed, and to the equivalent units in ending WIP. We can double-check our calculations by verifying that the sum of costs accounted for ($117 380) is equal to the sum of beginning WIP plus costs incurred during May ($10 200 + $30 500 + $76 680 = $117 380).

Weighted average:

Direct materials:

$$\frac{\text{Beginning WIP} + \text{Direct materials cost}}{\text{Equivalent units for total work}} = \frac{\$6\,000 + \$30\,500}{12\,000} = \$\,3.0417$$

Conversion costs: $\dfrac{\text{Beginning WIP} + \text{Conversion cost}}{\text{Equivalent units for total work}} = \dfrac{\$4\,200 + \$76\,680}{11\,400} = \underline{7.0947}$

Total cost per equivalent unit: $\underline{\underline{\$10.1364}}$

Weighted average costs. Under the weighted average method, the costs from beginning WIP are averaged with the costs incurred during the period. Average costs — rather than current period costs alone — are then allocated to the units completed and in ending WIP. As shown above, the weighted average cost per equivalent unit is $3.0417 for direct materials and $7.0947 for conversion costs. Because beginning WIP and current period costs are averaged under the weighted average method, average cost per unit is simply allocated to the total units completed and transferred out and to the equivalent units in ending WIP.

Comparison of weighted average and FIFO. During May, the per-unit costs differ between FIFO and weighted average. FIFO reflects only the current period costs ($3.05 for direct materials and $7.10 for conversion), while weighted average blends last period's and this period's costs ($3.0417 for direct materials and $7.0947 for conversion). Most entities experience at least some fluctuation in costs between accounting periods, leading to differences in the per-unit costs calculated under weighted average and FIFO. The costs per unit under weighted average are lower than the FIFO costs, indicating that costs increased in May.

Step 4 Process cost reports for moulding department: May

	FIFO			Weighted average		
	Calculation	Units	Costs	Calculation	Units	Costs
Beginning WIP	(from April cost report)	2 000	$ 10 200			
Costs to complete beginning WIP:						
Direct materials	0 × $3.05		0			
Conversion costs	1 400 × $7.10		9 940			
Total costs added this period			9 940			
Total cost of beginning WIP transferred out		2 000	20 140			
New units started, completed and transferred out	9 000 × $10.15	9 000	91 350			
Total units completed and transferred out		11 000	111 490	(2 000 + 9 000) × $10.1364	11 000	$111 500
Ending WIP:		1 000			1 000	
Direct materials	1 000 × $3.05		3 050	1 000 × $3.0417		3 042
Conversion costs	400 × $7.10		2 840	400 × $7.0947		2 838
Total ending WIP cost			5 890			5 880
Total accounted for		**12 000**	**$117 380**		**12 000**	**$117 380**

FIFO costs. The cost per equivalent unit calculated in step 3 is allocated to the work performed to complete beginning WIP, to the units started and completed, and to the equivalent units in ending WIP. We can double-check our calculations by verifying that the sum of costs accounted for ($117 380) is equal to the sum of beginning WIP plus costs incurred during May ($10 200 + $30 500 + $76 680 = $117 380).

Weighted average costs. As shown in step 3, weighted average cost per equivalent unit is $3.0417 for direct materials and $7.0947 for conversion costs. Because beginning WIP and current period costs are averaged under the weighted average method, average cost per unit is simply allocated to the total units completed and transferred out to the equivalent units in ending WIP.

Comparison of weighted average and FIFO. As Nancy reviews her work, she notices that the weighted average method requires fewer calculations. However, she thinks the extra work for FIFO is not a problem because she plans to use a spreadsheet to create future reports. From a management perspective, she thinks that FIFO is probably a better method because it provides more precise information about any changes in per-unit cost between periods. During May, the difference in per-unit cost between weighted average and FIFO was small ($10.1364 versus $10.15). However, she believes it is large enough that managers will prefer the more current data provided by FIFO. When Nancy discusses the two methods with the managers, they agree that the FIFO method provides them with the best information for monitoring monthly costs.

General ledger accounts for process costing

In process costing, separate WIP accounts are maintained for each production department. Pools of product costs are accumulated in WIP and are then allocated to the individual units. In a conventional system, two cost pools are used for costs incurred within a department: direct materials and conversion costs. As units are completed in the first department, their costs are transferred to WIP for the second department. The costs for these transferred-in units are pooled separately from other costs in the second department. Then additional direct materials (if any) and conversion costs are added. At the end of production in the second department, the three categories of cost (transferred-in costs, direct materials and conversion costs) are assigned to units and the costs are transferred out. This process continues for each department until the products are transferred into finished goods.

Figure 14.4 shows the general ledger accounts and inventory cost flows for the two production departments at Premier Plastics. First, direct materials move from raw material inventory to the moulding department. Conversion costs are accumulated in the WIP account for each department. The costs for the completed units in the moulding department are transferred to the assembly department WIP account. In the assembly department, additional direct material and conversion costs are added. When assembly work is completed, costs are transferred from the assembly department WIP to finished goods inventory.

Journal entries for process costing are similar to those for job costing. The main difference is that materials, labour and overhead costs are assigned to departments rather than to specific jobs. The costs are then allocated from each department to individual units. Figure 14.5 provides the ledger and general journal entries for FIFO process costing for the moulding department of Premier Plastics during May.

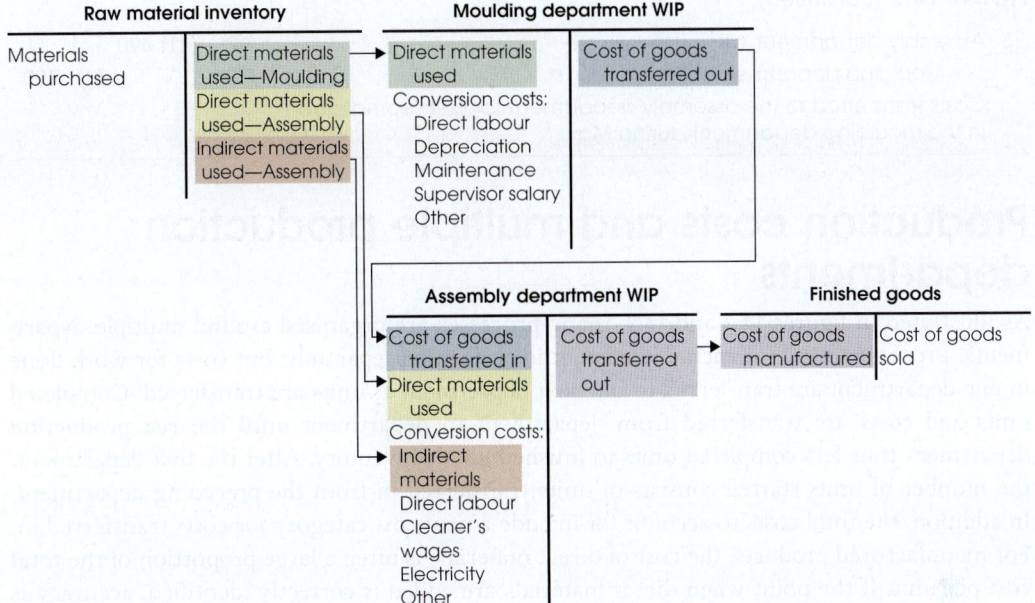

FIGURE 14.4 ■ Process costing general ledger accounts for producing plastic CD/DVD storage units

Ledger entries:

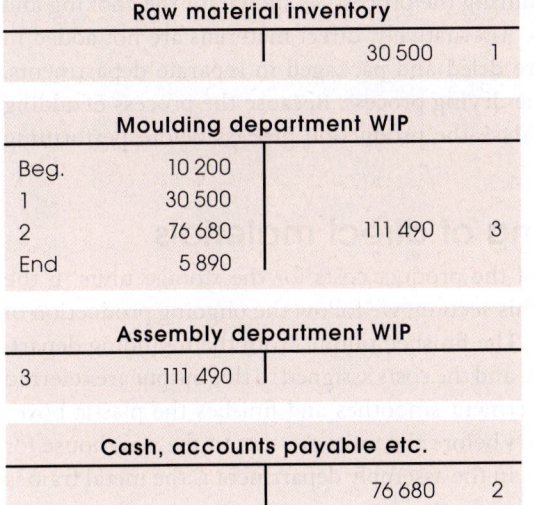

FIGURE 14.5 ■ FIFO process costing — ledger and journal entries for the moulding department for May

Raw material inventory

		30 500	1

Moulding department WIP

Beg.	10 200		
1	30 500		
2	76 680	111 490	3
End	5 890		

Assembly department WIP

3	111 490		

Cash, accounts payable etc.

		76 680	2

Journal entries:

1	Moulding department WIP — direct materials	DR	$ 30 500	
	Raw material inventory	CR		$ 30 500
	Direct materials used in the moulding department during May			
2	Moulding department WIP — conversion costs	DR	$ 76 680	
	Cash, accounts payable etc.	CR		$ 76 680
	Conversion costs incurred in the moulding department during May			

(continued)

FIGURE 14.5 (continued)

| 3 | Assembly department WIP | | DR | $111 490 | |
| | Moulding department WIP | | CR | | $111 490 |

Costs transferred to the assembly department for units completed in the moulding department during May

Production costs and multiple production departments

As illustrated in figures 14.2 and 14.3, many processes are organised around multiple departments. Process costing for each department is performed separately, but costs for work done in one department are transferred to the next department as units are transferred. Completed units and costs are transferred from department to department until the last production department transfers completed units to finished goods inventory. After the first department, the number of units started consists of units transferred in from the preceding department. In addition, the total costs to account for include a new cost category for costs transferred in. For manufactured products, the cost of direct materials is often a large proportion of the total cost per unit. If the point when direct materials are added is correctly identified, accuracy is increased in the equivalent unit calculations and cost for WIP inventories.

In many processes, direct materials are added at the beginning and WIP is always 100 per cent complete with respect to direct materials. However, direct materials are sometimes added later in the process, as shown in the assembly department in figure 14.3 (page 570). Direct materials may also be added more than once during the process, as shown for the cooking and canning department in figure 14.2 (page 568). Alternatively, direct materials are not added in some processes. For example, if cherries were dried and packaged in separate departments, no direct materials would be added during the drying process. Because the process of adding direct materials varies, accountants must analyse the production process before performing process costing calculations.

Transferred-in costs and timing of direct materials

Previously we focused on the development of the product costs for the storage units in the moulding department of Premier Plastics. In this section, we follow the ongoing production of the storage units in the assembly department. The finished output from the moulding department is transferred to the assembly department, and the costs assigned to this output are referred to as transferred-in costs. The assembly department smoothes and finishes the plastic boxes and adds a metal framework for the CDs/DVDs before the units are sent to the warehouse for delivery to customers. The major cost incurred in the assembly department is the metal frames (direct material) that are added when the storage units are about 50 per cent complete; it is assumed that conversion costs are added evenly throughout the assembly process.

After hearing that the managers in the moulding department were pleased with their new FIFO process cost report, the managers in the assembly department asked Nancy to prepare a similar report for their department for June. The following illustrations show both FIFO and weighted average methods to enable the managers in the assembly department to compare the methods.

Nancy followed the same four steps she used for the moulding department to create a cost report for the assembly department. The procedures to prepare the process cost reports for the assembly department are similar to those performed previously for the moulding department except for the transferred-in costs and timing for the addition of direct materials (see comprehensive example 4).

Comprehensive example 4

Transferred-in costs and timing of direct materials

Step 1 Summarise total costs to account for

Nancy first refers to the cost flows she previously developed for the assembly department (shown in figure 14.3) and gathers information about June's operations. She determines that beginning WIP inventory (1000 units) are 20 per cent complete. The cost of beginning WIP includes the costs transferred in from the moulding department in May under FIFO ($10.15 per unit) and weighted average ($10.1364 per unit). Added to these units during May in the assembly department were conversion costs of $10 per unit under FIFO (total cost of $10 × 200 = $2000) and $9.95 per unit under weighted average (total cost of $9.95 × 200 = $1990).

FIFO:

	Transferred in	Direct materials	Conversion costs	Total cost
Beginning WIP	$ 10 150	$ 0	$ 2 000	$ 12 150
Current period costs	95 890	22 000	98 000	215 890
Total costs to account for	$106 040	$22 000	$100 000	$228 040

Weighted average:

	Transferred in	Direct materials	Conversion costs	Total cost
Beginning WIP	$ 10 136	$ 0	$1 990	$ 12 126
Current period costs	95 806	22 000	98 000	215 806
Total costs to account for	$ 105 942	$22 000	$99 990	$227 932

During June, 10 000 units were transferred in from the moulding department. The total cost of units transferred in under weighted average was $9.5806 per unit, or $95 806 total. Nancy calculates that the cost would have been $95 890 total under FIFO, or an average of $9.589 per unit. During June the assembly department incurred direct material costs of $22 000 and conversion cots of $98 000.

Step 2 Summarise physical and equivalent units

	Beginning WIP (20%)	Complete beginning WIP (80%)	Start and complete	Start ending WIP (60%)	Total work performed this period	Total units to account for
Work this period						
Physical units	1 000	0	8 000	2 000	10 000	11 000
Equivalent units:						**Total work**
Transferred in	1 000	0	8 000	2 000	10 000	11 000
Direct materials	0	1 000	8 000	2 000	11 000	11 000
Conversion costs	200	800	8 000	1 200	10 000	10 200

Nancy determined that beginning WIP inventory (1000 units) was 20 per cent complete. Of the 10 000 units transferred in, 8000 units were completed and transferred out to finished goods inventory. The remaining 2000 units in ending WIP inventory were 60 per cent complete.

Transferred-in costs are treated as a third category of cost, similar to the treatment of direct materials and conversion costs. However, as units are transferred from moulding to assembly, they are always 100 per cent complete.

Because direct materials are added when units are 50 per cent complete and beginning WIP was only 20 per cent complete, none of the units in beginning WIP included direct materials. Then, 100 per cent of the direct materials were added to beginning WIP during June. Ending WIP was 60 per cent complete, so 100 per cent of the direct materials to those units were added during June.

Step 3 Calculate the cost per equivalent unit

In order to calculate the cost per equivalent unit, the costs incurred need to be assigned to each cost pool. This is necessary because costs have been added at different stages of the process, and not all items of inventory have consumed all costs. After finishing the cost breakdown as shown in step 1, Nancy compares the equivalent cost per unit in the assembly department using weighted average and FIFO. The weighted average equivalent unit cost is $21.434 and the FIFO cost is $21.389.

FIFO:

Transferred in:

$$\frac{\text{Transferred-in costs}}{\text{Equivalent units for total work performed this period}} = \frac{\$95\,890}{10\,000} = \$9.589$$

Direct materials:

$$\frac{\text{Direct materials cost}}{\text{Equivalent units for total work performed this period}} = \frac{\$22\,000}{11\,000} = 2.000$$

Conversion costs:

$$\frac{\text{Conversion cost}}{\text{Equivalent units for total work performed this period}} = \frac{\$98\,000}{10\,000} = 9.800$$

Total cost per equivalent unit: $21.389

Weighted average:

$$\text{Transferred in:} \quad \frac{\text{Beginning WIP} + \text{Transferred-in costs}}{\text{Equivalent units for total work}} = \frac{\$105\,942}{11\,000} = \$9.6311$$

$$\text{Direct materials:} \quad \frac{\text{Beginning WIP} + \text{Direct materials costs}}{\text{Equivalent units for total work}} = \frac{\$22\,000}{11\,000} = 2.000$$

$$\text{Conversion costs:} \quad \frac{\text{Beginning WIP} + \text{Conversion costs}}{\text{Equivalent units for total work}} = \frac{\$99\,990}{10\,200} = 9.8029$$

Total cost per equivalent unit: $21.4340

Step 4 Process cost reports for assembly department: June

	FIFO			Weighted average		
	Calculation	Units	Costs	Calculation	Units	Costs
Beginning WIP	(from May cost report)	1 000	$ 12 150			
Costs to complete beginning WIP:						
Direct materials	1 000 × $2		2 000			
Conversion costs	800 × $9.8		7 840			
Total costs added this period			9 840			
Total cost of beginning WIP transferred out		1 000	21 990			
New units started, completed, and transferred out	8 000 × $21.389	8 000	171 112			
Total units completed and transferred out		9 000	193 102	(1 000 + 8 000) × $21.434	9 000	$192 906
Ending WIP:		2 000			2 000	
Transferred in	2 000 × $9.589		19 178	2 000 × $9.6311		19 262
Direct materials	2 000 × $2		4 000	2 000 × $2		4 000
Conversion costs	1 200 × $9.8		11 760	1 200 × $9.8029		11 764
Total ending WIP cost			34 938			35 026
Total accounted for		**11 000**	**$228 040**		**11 000**	**$227 932**

To complete the production cost report, Nancy multiplies the equivalent units determined in step 2 for each cost pool by the cost per equivalent unit calculated in step 3 in order to determine inventory values.

Nancy notices that the cost per equivalent unit that is added in the assembly department is similar under both methods, which means that costs during June were similar to May's costs. She asks the managers whether costs in the assembly department fluctuate much from month to month. The managers tell her that a long-term contract with suppliers guarantees prices for at least a one-year period and labour contracts are negotiated annually, so the costs do not fluctuate much from month to month. In addition, volumes do not fluctuate a great deal.

Because costs in the department rarely fluctuate and volumes are reasonably stable, the costs added will be similar under both methods, so either method would be appropriate. However, because the moulding department is now using FIFO, units are transferred in at FIFO cost. To be consistent, Nancy decides that the assembly department should also use FIFO.

Accounting for spoilage in process costing

Production processes often create **spoilage**, which are units of product that are unacceptable and are either discarded or sold at a reduced price. Sometimes spoiled units are reworked (that is, repaired) and sold as if they were originally produced correctly. The costs of spoilage include the resources that are wasted due to spoilage, including the full amount of product costs for units that are discarded and the rework costs for units that are repaired. From an accounting perspective, decisions must be made about how to record the costs of spoilage. Should they be included in the product cost of all good units sold, or should they be recognised as a separate loss? The accounting treatment depends on whether the spoilage is a normal part of the production process.

Recall from chapter 13 that **normal spoilage** consists of defective units that arise as part of regular operations. Because normal spoilage is considered an ordinary and inherent part of operations, the cost of normal spoilage is included in the costs of all good units produced. The cost of normal spoilage is considered necessary for producing good units. For example, if Premier Plastics finds that one out of every 1000 storage units is faulty when inspected at the end of production, then that proportion of spoilage will be treated as normal. If the managers modify operations to reduce product failures, then a new lower rate of spoilage will become normal.

Recall also from chapter 13 that **abnormal spoilage** is spoilage that is not part of everyday operations. Because abnormal spoilage is considered unusual and is not an inherent part of operations, the cost of abnormal spoilage is excluded from product costs and is recorded as a separate loss. Abnormal spoilage occurs because of events such as strikes and natural disasters, or it occurs because operations are out of control. For example, at Premier Plastics an equipment malfunction that ruins a large number of storage units would be considered abnormal spoilage.

To properly account for spoilage in a process costing system, accountants need to identify the point in the production process where spoiled units are removed. Different entities establish different procedures for inspection and removal of spoiled units. Spoilage caused by poor-quality raw materials can sometimes be identified before materials are added to production. Inspection could also occur in the middle of production, at the end of the process in one department, or when processing in all departments is complete. If spoiled units are removed before they are 100 per cent complete, the costs of direct materials and conversion need to be estimated at the point the units are removed from production.

The costs of spoilage are accounted for in a two-step process. First, all product costs are accumulated in the departmental WIP account as usual. The computation of cost per equivalent unit includes all work performed, regardless of whether the units are spoiled. If spoiled units are 100 per cent complete at the time they are removed from production, they are treated the same as any other unit. If they are less than 100 per cent complete, the calculation of equivalent units depends upon their completion percentage, similar to ending WIP. Second, the costs of normal spoilage are allocated to the good units produced, and the costs of abnormal spoilage are written off as a loss for the accounting period. Therefore, the cost of each good unit includes an allocation for the cost of normal spoilage. The cost per good unit transferred out is calculated as follows:

Cost per good unit transferred out

$$= \frac{\text{Total cost of good units transferred out} + \text{Cost of normal spoilage}}{\text{Total good units transferred out}}$$

Comprehensive example 5 illustrates spoilage using the FIFO method.

Comprehensive example 5

FIFO cost report with normal and abnormal spoilage

While collecting information to prepare the moulding department process cost report for July, Nancy learns that 1000 units were spoiled and discarded. The previous month there was no spoilage. She is puzzled by the high quantity of spoilage during July.

Nancy discusses the spoilage with the moulding department manager. He tells her that 300 units were spoiled because of a problem that occurs three or four times a year with the quality of the plastic raw material. The problem causes a slight discoloration in a number of units. In addition, a new employee accidentally programmed the moulding machine incorrectly, spoiling 700 units during July. All spoilage is discovered when units are turned out of the moulds, at the end of the moulding processing (when they are 100 per cent complete).

After further discussion with the moulding department manager, Nancy learns that approximately 2 per cent of units throughout the year are spoiled because of discoloration. Thus, she decides that for the raw material problem, up to 2 per cent of units produced should be accounted for as normal spoilage. She decides that the spoilage caused by the incorrect equipment setting should be accounted for as abnormal spoilage because in a department with little employee turnover, the manager tells her, this problem rarely occurs.

Nancy finds that during July, 3000 units in beginning WIP were completed, and 9000 units were started and completed. Ending WIP consisted of 1200 units that were 70 per cent complete. Total costs added this period are $28560 in direct materials and $86184 in conversion costs.

Step 1 Summarise total costs to account for

Before the cost per equivalent unit can be calculated, Nancy had to separate the costs into the two costs pools and then assign the costs to the time period in which they were incurred; that is, either last month and/or the current period. She obtains the beginning WIP cost from the June FIFO cost report: $18525 ($8400 direct materials and $10125 conversion costs) and adds the current costs incurred in production.

FIFO:	Direct materials	Conversion costs	Total cost
Beginning WIP	$ 8 400	$10 125	$ 18 525
Current period costs	28 560	86 184	114 744
Total costs to account for	$36 960	$96 309	$133 269

Step 2 Summarise physical and equivalent units

	Beginning WIP (50%)	Complete beginning WIP (50%)	Start and complete	Start ending WIP (70%)	Total work performed this period	Total units to account for	Spoiled units (100%)
				Work this period			
Physical units	3 000	0	9 000	1 200	10 200	13 200	(1 000)
Equivalent units:						**Total work**	
Direct materials	3 000	0	9 000	1 200	10 200	13 200	(1 000)
Conversion costs	1 500	1 500	9 000	840	11 340	12 840	(1 000)
Total spoilage							1 000
Less: Normal spoilage		(3 000 + 9 000) × 2%					240
Abnormal spoilage							760

Nancy summarises the work performed in terms of physical and equivalent units, and then adds a column showing the 1000 spoiled units. Because spoiled units were identified and removed when they were 100 per cent complete, they represent 1000 equivalent units for both direct materials and conversion costs. Nancy next separates the spoilage between normal and abnormal. She calculates the maximum normal spoilage for July as 240 units (12 000 units completed during July × 2%), which is less than the 300 units spoiled due to discoloration. Therefore, she considers 240 units as normal spoilage. She classifies the remaining 60 discoloured units plus the 700 units spoiled from the incorrect machine setting as abnormal spoilage (total 760 units).

Step 3 Calculate the cost per equivalent unit

FIFO:

Direct materials:

$$\frac{\text{Direct materials cost}}{\text{Equivalent units for total work performed this period}} = \frac{\$28\,560}{10\,200} = \$\,2.80$$

Conversion costs:

$$\frac{\text{Conversion costs}}{\text{Equivalent units for total work performed this period}} = \frac{\$86\,184}{11\,340} = \underline{7.60}$$

Total cost per equivalent unit: $\underline{\underline{\$10.40}}$

Step 4 Process cost report for moulding department: July

	FIFO		
	Calculation	Units	Cost
Beginning WIP	(from June cost report)	3 000	$ 18 525
Costs to complete beginning WIP:			
Direct materials	0 × $2.80		0
Conversion costs	1 500 × $7.60		11 400
Total costs added this period			11 400

	FIFO		
	Calculation	Units	Cost
Total cost of beginning WIP transferred out		3 000	29 925
New units started, completed and transferred out	(9 000 − 1 000) × $10.40	8 000	83 200
Normal spoilage	240 × $10.40		2 496
Total units completed and transferred out		11 000	115 621
Abnormal spoilage	760 × $10.40		7 904
Ending WIP:		1 200	
Direct materials	1 200 × $2.80		3 360
Conversion costs	840 × $7.60		6 384
Total ending WIP cost			9 744
Total good units accounted for	13 200 − 1 000	**12 200**	
Total costs accounted for			**$133 269**

When Nancy prepares the cost report, she calculates the cost of good units started, completed and transferred out. She then adds the cost of normal spoilage to arrive at the total cost transferred to the assembly department ($115 621). Abnormal spoilage is added below this subtotal to reconcile the total cost.

Using spoilage cost information

Nancy is concerned about the total costs for spoilage this period. The 1000 spoiled units cost $10 400 ($2496 + $7904). However, she is even more concerned about other problems that arise when spoilage is high. Sometimes inspectors miss some spoiled units, which are then sold as good units. When defective storage units are sold, return costs increase and customers are less satisfied. The designer storage units are expensive, and Premier Plastic's reputation suffers when units are less than perfect. Nancy knows that Japanese competitors have zero defect tolerance policies, so their customers rarely receive flawed storage units. She decides to meet with the plastics department manager to emphasise the need for lower levels of spoilage.

Uses and limitations of process costing information

Process costing systems measure the cost of products, primarily for mass-produced goods. The product costs are used to value inventory and cost of goods sold for external reports such as financial statements and income tax returns. They are also used by managers to monitor operations and develop estimates of future costs for decision making. When managers use process costing information, they need to be aware that it measures the costs of processes, which are then allocated to individual units. Thus, process costing is useful for measuring and monitoring processes. However, process costing is also subject to a number of limitations.

Monitoring process quality and costs

An entity's profitability and long-term success often depend on the ability of managers to control processes and costs. Organisations frequently compete both on product quality and cost. Managers use process cost information to help them evaluate whether production processes are operating as expected. They compare actual process costs to budgets, standards or prior periods to identify potential production problems. For example, in Premier Plastics, units were spoiled during July when an employee improperly programmed the moulding equipment. This type of event causes actual costs to be higher than expected. If the managers had not already been aware of this production problem, the calculation of process costs at the end of the month would have alerted them to it.

Managers do not rely on process costing systems alone to monitor quality and cost. They also implement quality control systems, and they separately monitor resource use such as direct materials and direct labour. Quality systems can include inspection to identify spoiled units. Information about normal and abnormal spoilage can then be integrated into the process costing system to help managers measure and monitor the cost of resources wasted due to spoilage.

Process costing information and decision making

Product costs developed in a process costing system are average costs and might not adequately represent relevant costs for many types of decisions such as product pricing, outsourcing, product emphasis or special orders. Sometimes process costing systems can be modified to do a better job of providing managers with estimates of relevant information, such as marginal (or incremental) cost per unit. For example, conversion costs could be divided into fixed and variable cost pools. Managers could then estimate marginal cost using the direct material cost per unit plus the variable conversion cost per unit. Production costing systems often include multiple cost pools representing different activities in the production process. More precise categorisations of cost improve managers' ability to monitor operations as well as to estimate information for decisions.

Uncertainties and mismeasurement of cost flows

It is rarely possible to determine exactly how costs are incurred during process costing. For example, in the moulding department at Premier Plastics, more labour might be used during the beginning of the process when plastic ingredients are added and at the end of the process when units are turned out of the moulds. Equipment and electricity use might be greater during the middle of the processing. However, it is difficult to exactly measure how and when costs such as labour, equipment depreciation, maintenance and utilities are incurred. Accordingly, at least some mismeasurement typically occurs in the allocation of costs in a process costing system.

Also, mismeasurement occurs when accounting for spoilage. Normal spoilage is based on an estimate. Any errors in identifying normal spoilage quantities automatically cause mismeasurement in abnormal spoilage. Therefore, abnormal spoilage costs may be overestimated or underestimated, with an opposite mismeasurement in the cost of good units.

Mismeasurement is likely to be greatest in entities that have little experience producing a product. Over time, greater knowledge is gained about production processes, and the cost allocations become more accurate. However, little benefit may come from developing an accounting system to more accurately allocate process costs. Often, the simple assumptions used throughout this chapter provide sufficiently accurate costs.

Work in process units at different stages of completion

At the end of each period, the percentage of completion for work in process needs to be estimated. Depending on the process, all of the units in work in process inventories might be at different stages of completion. For example, in the assembly department at Premier Plastics, some units of WIP will have the rough edges removed but still be awaiting smoothing. Some will have been smoothed but await the next step within assembly. Others will have the metal framework added but await final paint and trim work.

When work is at many different stages of completion, estimating the average percentage of completion for ending inventories involves some guesswork. However, these estimates affect the equivalent unit costs for both the current and next period. If the percentage of completion is overestimated in this period, the number of units in the denominator is too large, causing cost per equivalent unit to be too low in this period. Because ending WIP is completed during the next period, an overestimate in this period will cause an underestimate of the work performed in the next period. If ending inventories are a small part of the total costs allocated in this period, inaccurate estimates are less of a problem. But if ending inventories are relatively large, inaccurate estimates could distort process cost reports in this period and the next period.

APPENDIX 14A

STANDARD COSTING USE IN MASS PRODUCTION

A **standard cost** is the cost managers expect to incur for production of goods or services under operating plan assumptions. Under a standard costing system, accounting entries for direct materials, conversion costs and transferred-in costs are recorded at standard (or expected) rather than actual costs. Actual costs are accumulated in a control account, and then costs are allocated to WIP using a standard rate per equivalent unit. At the end of the period, adjustments are made for the differences between actual and standard costs.

Standard costs are used for a variety of reasons. For example, they simplify the process of making accounting entries during the period; actual costs need not be compiled for product costs to be recorded. Standards also provide a benchmark against which actual costs can be compared. Managers and operating employees can then be rewarded based on whether the standards are achieved or exceeded. These rewards provide motivation for monitoring operations and maintaining higher productivity levels.

Standard costs are allocated to units in a manner similar to FIFO process costing. The difference is that no equivalent cost per unit is calculated. Instead, a standard cost is used to allocate costs to inventory. Comprehensive example 6 revisits the Premier Plastics moulding department in May.

Comprehensive example 6

Incorporating standards into process costing

Step 1 Summarise total costs to account for

The standard costs to account for are based on the investigations undertaken by the engineering department. Engineering staff have reviewed the production process and developed standards costs for the CD/DVD storage units. The standards costs are direct materials $3 and conversion costs $7. The total costs to account for will be determined by the equivalent units for

each cost pool multiplied by the standard cost. To do this, we will need to calculate the equivalent units.

Step 2 Summarise physical and equivalent units

			Work this period			
	Beginning WIP (30%)	Complete beginning WIP (70%)	Start and complete	Start ending WIP (40%)	Total work performed this period	Total units to account for
Physical units	2000	0	9000	1000	10 000	12 000
Equivalent units:						**Total work**
Direct materials	2000	0	9000	1000	10 000	12 000
Conversion costs	600	1400	9000	400	10 800	11 400

For May, there is beginning WIP as well as ending WIP. Beginning WIP includes 2000 units; 9000 units are started, completed and transferred to the assembly department; and another 1000 units are started and 40 per cent complete in ending WIP.

Step 3 Calculate the cost per equivalent unit

As standard costs are used to value inventory, there is no need to calculate a cost per equivalent unit.

Step 4 Process cost report for moulding department: May

	Standard cost		
	Calculation	Units	Cost
Beginning WIP	(from April cost report)	2 000	$ 10 200
Costs to complete beginning WIP:			
Direct materials	0 × $3		0
Conversion costs	1 400 × $7		9 800
Total costs added this period			20 000
Total cost of beginning WIP transferred out		2 000	20 000
New units started, completed and transferred out	9 000 × $10	9 000	90 000
Total units completed and transferred out		11 000	110 000
Ending WIP:		1 000	
Direct materials	1 000 × $3		3 000
Conversion costs	400 × $7		2 800
Total ending WIP cost			5 800
Total accounted for		**12 000**	**$115 800**

Assuming no change from the prior month in the standard costs, the cost of beginning WIP is carried over from the previous month at the cost per equivalent unit. Therefore, beginning WIP includes direct materials cost of $6000 (2000 × $3) and conversion costs of $4200 (600 × $7), for a total of $10 200. During May, standard costs are first allocated to the equivalent units of work performed to complete beginning WIP: $0 for direct materials and $9800 for conversion costs. Next, standard costs of $90 000 ($10 × 9000 units) are allocated to the units started, completed and transferred out. Finally, standard costs of $3000 for direct materials and $2800 for conversion costs are allocated to ending WIP. The total amount of standard cost to account for (beginning WIP plus costs allocated during May) is $115 800.

When standard costs are used as benchmarks, they are compared to actual costs calculated using either weighted average or FIFO. In this example for Premier Plastics, Nancy could compare the standard cost of $10 per unit with the actual weighted average cost per equivalent unit in May of $10.1364 or to the FIFO cost of $10.15. From these comparisons, it appears that actual costs are higher than standard. When actual costs are higher than standard costs, managers investigate the causes and analyse ways to improve operations. If actual costs are lower, the causes may also be analysed so that managers better understand the improvements that have taken place.

Summary

1   Assign costs to mass-produced products.

Cost flow in process costing
Steps for preparing a process cost report
1. Summarise total costs to account for.
2. Summarise total physical and equivalent units.
3. Calculate the cost per equivalent unit.
4. Account for cost of units completed and cost of ending WIP.

2   Understand the concept of equivalent units and how they relate to the production process.

Equivalent units
Measure of the resources used in partially completed units relative to the resources needed to complete the units.

Equivalent units and pattern of cost flow
Direct materials
- Added at the beginning of the process
- Added during the process
Conversion costs
- Incurred evenly throughout the process
- Incurred unevenly
Identification of spoiled units
- Inspection at the end of the process
- Inspection during the process

3 Calculate product costs using the weighted average method.

Weighted average method

Costs from beginning WIP (performed last period) are averaged with costs incurred during the current period and then allocated to units completed and ending WIP.

Calculation of cost per equivalent unit

$$\frac{\text{Beginning WIP} + \text{Current period costs}}{\text{Equivalent units for total work}}$$

4 Calculate product costs using the FIFO method.

First-in, first-out (FIFO) method

The current period's costs are used to allocate cost to work performed this period.

Calculation of cost per equivalent unit

$$\frac{\text{Current period costs}}{\text{Equivalent units for work performed this period}}$$

5 Calculate product costs in a process where there are multiple production departments.

Transferred-in costs

Costs of processing performed in a previous department.
Transferred-in costs are pooled separately from other costs.

6 Handle spoilage costs in process costing.

Normal spoilage

Definition: defective units that arise as part of regular operations.
Accounting: cost of normal spoilage is allocated to good units produced.

Abnormal spoilage

Definition: spoilage that is not part of everyday operations.
Accounting: cost of abnormal spoilage is recorded as a loss for the period.

7 Identify the uses and limitations of process cost information.

Uses of process cost information

- Measure costs of mass-produced products.
- Assign costs to inventory and cost of goods sold for financial statements and income tax returns.
- Monitor operations and costs.
- Develop estimates of future costs for decision making.
- Analyse the costs and benefits of quality improvements.
- Identify potential areas for process improvements.

Uncertainties and mismeasurement in process costing

- Actual cost flows might not be known.
  - When are direct materials added?
  - When are conversion costs incurred?
  - How complete are the units in ending work in process?
- What amount of spoilage is normal?
- How achievable are standard costs?

APPENDIX SUMMARY

Standard costing use in mass production

Standard costing

The cost managers expect to show for production of goods or services under operating plan assumptions.

Self-study problems

SELF-STUDY PROBLEM 1

Weighted average and FIFO process cost reports

Evergreen Kit Company produces kits for plastic aeroplanes and car models. The company uses process costing to assign costs to its inventory. The company always used the weighted average method but Jussi, the company's new accountant, is thinking about recommending a change to the first-in, first-out (FIFO) method. He plans to prepare inventory cost reports for March using both methods so that he can compare the results.

The company has only one production department. Direct materials are introduced at the beginning of the process, and conversion costs are incurred evenly throughout the manufacturing process. Once each unit is completed, it is transferred to finished goods inventory. Jussi collected the following data for the month of March:

Beginning inventory:	
Work in process (40% complete)	10 000 units
Costs:	
Direct material	$ 8 000
Conversion costs	2 220
Total cost of beginning WIP	$ 10 220
Units completed and transferred out during March	48 000 units
Units started during March	40 000 units
Ending WIP inventory (50% complete)	2 000 units
Direct material cost used during March	$44 000
Conversion costs incurred during March	$36 000

REQUIRED

(a) Using the weighted average method:
   (i) Summarise total costs to account for.
   (ii) Summarise total physical units and equivalent units.
   (iii) Calculate costs per equivalent unit.
   (iv) Prepare a process cost report.
(b) Following the same procedures, prepare a process cost report using the FIFO method.
(c) Prepare a table to compare the total costs and cost per equivalent unit under weighted average and FIFO. Provide possible explanations for the difference between FIFO and weighted average costs.

Solution to self-study problem 1

(a) **Weighted average**
   (i) Summarise total costs to account for.

	Direct materials	Conversion costs	Total cost
Beginning WIP	$ 8 000	$ 2 220	$10 220
Current period costs	44 000	36 000	80 000
Total costs to account for	$52 000	$38 220	$90 220

(ii) Summarise total physical units and equivalent units.

Because direct materials are added at the beginning of the process, all 2000 WIP units are 100 per cent complete with respect to direct materials. However, these 2000 units are only 50 per cent complete with respect to conversion costs, which translates to 1000 equivalent units in ending WIP for conversion costs (50% × 2000).

		Work this period				
	Beginning WIP (40%)	Complete beginning WIP (60%)	Start and complete	Start ending WIP (50%)	Total work performed	Total to account for
Physical units	10 000	0	38 000	2 000	40 000	50 000
Equivalent units:						Total work
Direct materials	10 000	0	38 000	2 000	40 000	50 000
Conversion costs	4 000	6 000	38 000	1 000	45 000	49 000

(iii) Calculate costs per equivalent unit.

$$\text{Weighted average:} \quad \frac{\text{Beginning WIP} + \text{Current period costs}}{\text{Equivalent units for total work}}$$

Direct materials	$52 000 ÷ 50 000	$1.04
Conversion costs	$38 220 ÷ 49 000	0.78
Total cost per equivalent unit		$1.82

(iv) Prepare a process cost report (i.e. account for cost of units completed and cost of ending WIP).

	Calculations	Units	Costs
Completed and transferred out	(10 000 + 38 000) × $1.82	48 000	$87 360
Ending WIP		2 000	
Direct materials	2000 × $1.04		2 080
Conversion costs	1000 × $0.78		780
Total ending WIP			2 860
Total accounted for		50 000	$90 220

(b) **FIFO**

Steps 1 and 2 are identical to the schedules presented in part (a). Because the problem did not provide separate beginning WIP costs for weighted average and FIFO, we use the same beginning WIP values for parts (a) and (b).

(iii) Calculate cost per equivalent unit

$$\frac{\text{Current period costs}}{\text{Equivalent units for work performed this period}}$$

Direct materials	$44 000 ÷ 40 000	**$1.10**
Conversion costs	$36 000 ÷ 45 000	0.80
Total cost per equivalent unit		**$1.90**

(iv) Prepare a FIFO cost report (i.e. account for cost of units completed and cost of ending WIP)

	FIFO		
	Calculation	Units	Costs
Beginning WIP		10 000	$ 10 220
Costs to complete beginning WIP:			
Direct materials	0 × $1.10		0
Conversion costs	6 000 × $0.80		4 800
Total costs added this period			4 800
Total cost of beginning WIP transferred out		10 000	15 020
New units started, completed and transferred out	38 000 × $1.90	38 000	72 200
Total units completed and transferred out		48 000	87 220
Ending WIP:		2 000	
Direct materials	2 000 × $1.10		2 200
Conversion costs	1 000 × $0.80		800
Total ending WIP cost			3 000
Total accounted for		**50 000**	**$90 220**

(c) **Compare weighted average and FIFO**

The following table compares total costs and equivalent unit costs under weighted average and FIFO. Remember, the total costs accounted for are equal in this problem *only* because we used the same beginning WIP costs for both methods.

	Weighted average	FIFO
Costs transferred out	$87 360	$ 87 220
Ending WIP	2 860	3 000
Total costs accounted for	$90 220	$90 220
Costs per equivalent unit:		
Direct materials	$ 1.04	$ 1.10
Conversion costs	0.78	0.80
Total	$ 1.82	$ 1.90

The weighted average costs include both current period and prior period costs, while the FIFO costs include only current period costs. Because the costs per unit for FIFO are higher than for weighted average, average production costs during March were higher than during the previous month. An increase occurred in both direct materials and conversion costs. These increases might have been caused by inflation in the cost of resources, a decline in production volume, production inefficiencies or other factors.

Questions

14.1 Under what conditions will weighted average and FIFO process costing consistently produce similar equivalent unit costs?

14.2 Under what conditions could a process complete more units during the period than it started?

14.3 'We treat spoiled units as fully completed regardless of when the spoiled units are detected. This method makes unit costing much simpler.' What is wrong with this approach?

14.4 In a continuous processing situation (such as an oil refinery), the beginning and ending WIP inventories are frequently the same. How does this simplify determination of equivalent units completed?

14.5 Although process costing appears to use precise measurements, it requires several estimates. Discuss where judgment is needed in collecting information for process costing.

14.6 Suppose the percent completion of ending WIP is overestimated at the end of year 1. How does this measurement error affect the process costing results in year 1 and year 2?

14.7 Explain the difference between the weighted average and FIFO methods for process costing. Explain why an entity might choose one method over the other.

14.8 Describe the differences between mass production and custom production of goods and services. Explain how these differences influence the costing method.

14.9 A department within a processing operation has some finished units physically on hand. Should they be counted as completed units or as ending inventory in the department? Explain.

14.10 In processes involving pipeline operations or assembly line operations, if the pipeline or assembly line is always full, then beginning and ending WIP inventories are always 50 per cent complete with regard to conversion costs. Explain.

14.11 When units are transferred from one department to another, how are normal spoilage costs recorded?

14.12 An entity has one machine through which is drawn a standard type of wire to make nails. With minor adjustments, different sized nails are produced with different sized wire. Would you recommend that the entity employ job or process costing methods?

14.13 List two factors that could affect managers' choices for the number of times and points in processing to inspect units.

14.14 List three factors that managers might consider in deciding whether to expend resources to reduce spoilage.

Exercises

14.15 **Equivalent units under weighted average and FIFO** Francisco's mass-produces folding chairs in Port Sorrell. All direct materials are added at the beginning of production, and conversion costs are incurred evenly throughout production. The following production information is for the month of May:

	Physical units
Beginning WIP (40% complete)	9 000
Started in May	50 000
Completed in May	47 000
Ending WIP (30% complete)	12 000

REQUIRED

(a) Calculate the equivalent units used to calculate cost per unit under the weighted average method.

(b) Calculate the equivalent units used to calculate cost per unit under the FIFO method.

14.16 Equivalent unit cost under weighted average and FIFO Fine Fans mass-produces small electric fans in Hawley Beach for home use. All direct materials are added at the beginning of production, and conversion costs are incurred evenly throughout production. The following production information is for the month of October:

	Physical units
Started in October	100 000
Completed in October	94 000
Ending WIP (60% complete)	15 000
Beginning WIP (20% complete)	9 000
	Costs
Beginning work in process costs:	
Direct materials	$18 000
Conversion costs	36 000
Costs added this period:	
Direct materials	100 000
Conversion costs	200 000

REQUIRED

(a) Calculate the equivalent cost per unit using the weighted average method.

(b) Calculate the equivalent cost per unit using the FIFO method.

14.17 Cost per equivalent unit under weighted average Felix and Sons is a toy maker that produces Flying Flingbats, a soft foam rubber weapon. All direct materials are added at the beginning of production, and conversion costs are incurred evenly throughout production. Conversion was 75 per cent complete for the 8000 units in WIP on 1 December and 50 per cent complete for the 6000 units in WIP on 31 December. During the month, 12 000 Flingbats were completed and transferred out as finished goods. Following is a summary of the costs for the period:

	Direct materials	Conversion costs
Work in process, 1 December	$19 200	$ 7 200
Costs added in December	31 200	21 600

REQUIRED

Using the weighted average method, prepare a schedule calculating the total cost per equivalent unit for December.

14.18 Account for costs under weighted average Refer to the information in exercise 14.17.

REQUIRED

Prepare a process cost report under the weighted average method.

14.19 Cost per equivalent unit under FIFO Refer to the information in exercise 14.17.

REQUIRED

Using the FIFO method, prepare a schedule calculating the cost per equivalent unit for April.

14.20 **Account for costs under FIFO** Refer to the information presented in exercise 14.17.

REQUIRED

Prepare a process cost report under the FIFO method.

14.21 **Costs and journal entries under weighted average and FIFO** Humphrey Manufacturing produces car parts and batteries. All direct materials are added at the beginning of production, and conversion costs are incurred evenly throughout production. The following production information is for the month of April:

Units:	
Work in process, 31 March: 6000 units (40% complete)	
Units started in April: 42 000	
Units completed during April: 40 000	
Work in process 30 April: 8000 units (25% complete)	
Costs in beginning WIP:	
Direct materials	$ 7 500
Conversion costs	2 125
Total	$ 9 625
Costs added this period:	
Direct materials added in April	$ 70 000
Conversion costs added in April	42 500
Total	$ 112 500

REQUIRED

(a) Using the weighted average method, assign costs to production for this period.
(b) Using the FIFO method, assign costs to production for this period.
(c) Write out the journal entries for either the weighted average or FIFO methods.

Problems

14.22 **FIFO process costing; transferred-in costs; direct materials added during process** Benton Industries began the year with 15 000 units in department 3 as beginning WIP. These units were one-third complete, with $40 470 transferred-in costs for prior departments' work and $14 322 for department 3 conversion costs. During the year, 93 000 additional units were transferred into department 3 from department 2 at a cost of $224 130. Department 3 incurred materials costs of $166 840 and conversion costs of $315 228 during the year. Department 3 ended the year with 11 000 units in WIP ending. These units were 40 per cent complete.

REQUIRED

Determine the cost of goods completed and the cost of ending WIP in department 3 using FIFO process costing. Assume that conversion costs are incurred evenly and materials are added in department 3 when units are 60 per cent complete.

14.23 **Process costing under weighted average; spoilage; journal entries** Victoria's Closet mass-produces luxurious sleepwear for women. Consider the following data for the flannel nightgown department for the month of January. All direct materials are added at the beginning of production in the department, and conversion costs are incurred evenly throughout production. Inspection occurs when production is 100 per cent complete. Normal spoilage is 6600 units for the month.

	Physical units
Beginning WIP (25% complete)	11 000
Started during January	74 000
Total units to account for	85 000
Good units completed and transferred out during current period:	
From beginning work in process	11 000
Started and completed	50 000
Spoiled units	8 000
Ending WIP (75% complete)	16 000
Total units accounted for	85 000
	Costs
Beginning WIP:	
Direct materials	$ 220 000
Conversion costs	30 000
Total beginning WIP	250 000
Costs added during current period:	
Direct materials	1 480 000
Conversion costs	942 000
Costs to account for	$ 2 672 000

REQUIRED

Prepare a process cost report using the weighted average method.

14.24 Process costing under FIFO; spoilage; standard costing Refer to the information provided in problem 14.23.

REQUIRED

(a) Prepare a process cost report using the FIFO method.

(b) Explain how a standard cost report would differ from the FIFO report you just produced.

(c) Under what circumstances would a standard cost report be preferable to a FIFO cost report? Explain your answer.

14.25 Abnormal spoilage; quality savings; opportunity costs Kim Mills produces material for knitwear. The knit cloth is sold by the bolt. November data for its milling process follow. Beginning WIP was 20 000 units. Good units completed and transferred out during the current period totalled 90 000. Ending WIP was 17 000 units. Inspection occurs at the 100 per cent stage of completion regarding conversion costs, which are incurred evenly throughout the process. Total spoilage is 7000 units. Normal spoilage is 3600 units. Direct materials are added at the beginning of the process.

REQUIRED

(a) Calculate abnormal spoilage in units.

(b) Assume that the manufacturing cost of a spoiled unit is $1000. Calculate the amount of potential savings if all spoilage were eliminated, assuming that all other costs would be unaffected.

(c) Discuss the opportunity costs of spoilage and why it might be important to require low defect rates in a manufacturing process.

14.26 Spoilage with inspection point other than 100 per cent Use the information for Kim Mills from problem 14.25. Now, assume that inspection occurs when units are 40 per cent complete.

REQUIRED
(a) Calculate total spoilage for conversion cost calculations.
(b) If normal spoilage is 1800 units instead of 3600, what is abnormal spoilage this period for conversion costs?
(c) List several costs and benefits from moving inspection to an earlier position in the manufacturing process.

14.27 Process costing under weighted average and FIFO; choice of method Red Dog Products manufactures toys for dogs and cats. The most popular toy is a small ball that dispenses tiny treats and is placed within a larger ball. To get the treats, dogs must roll the balls around until the treats fall out. These balls are mass-produced from plastic. Direct materials are introduced at the beginning of the process, and conversion costs are incurred evenly throughout the manufacturing process. Once each unit is completed, it is transferred to finished goods. Data for the month of March are as follows:

Beginning WIP (30% complete):	
Direct material	$25 000
Conversion costs	3 000
Total	$28 000
Units started during March	80 000 units
Units completed and transferred out during March	88 000 units
Ending WIP inventory (50% complete)	12 000 units
Direct material cost added during March	$220 000
Conversion costs added during March	$74 000

REQUIRED
(a) Prepare a process cost report using the weighted average method.
(b) Prepare a process cost report using the FIFO method.
(c) What factors might affect the cost accountant's choice of process costing method? Explain.

14.28 Normal and abnormal spoilage; quality improvements Empire Forging produces small plumbing valves. January data for its valve-making process follow. Beginning WIP was 60 000 units. Good units completed and transferred out during the current period totalled 420 000. Ending WIP was 68 000 units. Inspection occurs at the 100 per cent stage of completion with respect to conversion costs, which are incurred evenly throughout the process. Total spoilage is 36 000 units. Normal spoilage is 12 600 units. Direct materials are added at the beginning of the process.

REQUIRED
(a) Calculate abnormal spoilage in units for January.
(b) Calculate the number of units started in January.
(c) Calculate the percentage of units produced that is considered normal spoilage, and calculate the total percentage of units spoiled this period. List several potential business risks when spoilage rates increase dramatically.
(d) Provide arguments for the manager of the valve department about the trade-offs between investing in quality improvements and incurring the costs of undetected spoiled units.

14.29 Process costing under weighted average and FIFO; spoilage The Rally Company operates under a process cost system using the weighted average method. All direct materials are added at the beginning of production in the department, and conversion costs are incurred evenly throughout production. Inspection occurs when production is 100 per cent completed.

Following are data for July. All unfinished work at the end of July is 25 per cent completed. The beginning inventory is 80 per cent completed.

Beginning inventories	
Direct materials	$4 000
Conversion costs	$3 200
Costs added during current period	
Direct materials	$36 000
Conversion costs	$32 000
Physical units	
Units in beginning inventory	2 000
Units started this month	18 000
Total units completed and transferred out	14 800
Normal spoilage	1 000
Abnormal spoilage	1 000

REQUIRED

(a) Prepare a spreadsheet that uses a data input box and calculates information necessary for a weighted average process cost report and presents the cost report in an easily understood format.

(b) Copy the spreadsheet into a new range or new worksheet. If you use a new worksheet, highlight the tab and rename the worksheet 'FIFO.' Now alter the weighted average calculations so that the spreadsheet uses data from the input box to calculate the information necessary for a FIFO process cost report and presents the cost report in an easily understood format.

(c) Describe factors that would affect an accountant's choice of process costing method, and make a recommendation for a process costing method for Rally. Explain your choice.

14.30 Choice of costing method; process cost report; transferred-in units; spoilage Toddler Toys produces toy construction vehicles for young children. Plastic pieces are moulded in the plastics department. These pieces are transferred to the assembly department, where direct materials are added after some assembly has been done. For example, plastic pieces of road graders are put together, then the blades and wheel assemblies are added, and finally some details are painted on the sides and back. The direct materials are added in the assembly department when the process is 75 per cent complete. Beginning inventory is 80 per cent complete and ending inventory is 25 per cent complete. Following are data for August.

Beginning inventory costs for the assembly department:	
Transferred in	$ 4 000
Direct materials	2 000
Conversion costs	1 600
Total cost	$ 7 600

Costs incurred in the assembly department during current period:	
Transferred in	$36 000
Direct materials	18 000
Conversion costs	16 000
Total cost	$70 000
Physical units in the assembly department:	
Units in beginning inventory	2 000
Units started this month	18 000
Total units completed and transferred out	14 800
Normal spoilage	1 000 (100% complete)
Abnormal spoilage	1 000 (100% complete)

REQUIRED

(a) Choose a process costing method for the assembly department. Explain your choice and describe its pros and cons.

(b) Prepare a cost report using the method you chose in part (a).

14.31 Process costing under weighted average and FIFO; spoilage; rework The accountant at Cellular Advantage needs to close the books at the end of January using the following information. Direct materials are added at the start of production. Conversion costs are incurred evenly throughout production. Inspection occurs when production is 75 per cent completed. Normal spoilage is 13 200 units per month.

Physical units	
Work in process, beginning (30% complete)	22 000
Started during the month	148 000
Total units to account for	170 000
Good units completed and transferred out during current period:	
From beginning work in process	22 000
Started and completed	100 000
Total good units completed	122 000
Spoiled units	16 000
Work in process, ending (60% complete)	32 000
Total units accounted for	170 000
Costs	
Beginning inventory:	
Direct materials	$ 440 000
Conversion costs	60 000
Total beginning inventory	500 000
Costs added during current period:	
Direct materials	2 960 000
Conversion costs	1 884 000
Total costs to account for	$5 344 000

REQUIRED

(a) Prepare a process cost report using the weighted average method.

(b) Prepare a process cost report using the FIFO method.

(c) Explain why an entity might specify limits for normal spoilage, after which spoilage is considered abnormal.

(d) To reduce spoilage, units are sometimes reworked. How are rework costs recorded?

14.32 Two departments; two periods; FIFO and weighted average; estimate accuracy Rausher Industries began a new product line this year. Management wants a cost report for the current year and a budget for next year. The product requires processing in two departments. Materials are added at the beginning of the process in department 1. Department 2 finishes the product but adds no direct materials.

During the year work was begun on 12 000 units in department 1, and 9000 of these units were transferred to department 2. The remaining 3000 units were 60 per cent complete with regard to conversion costs in department 1, which incurred $36 000 in material costs and $14 040 in conversion costs.

Department 2 completed and sent 7000 units to the finished goods warehouse. It ended the period with 2000 units 40 per cent complete with regard to department 2's conversion costs, which were $32 760 for the period.

The plan for next year is to begin an additional 15 000 units in department 1. Management expects to finish the year with 5000 units one-half converted in department 1. Department 2 is expected to complete 14 000 units, and its ending inventory is expected to be 70 per cent complete. Materials are expected to be $48 600, and conversion costs for departments 1 and 2 are expected to be $14 545 and $59 075 respectively.

REQUIRED

(a) Prepare cost reports for the current year and a budgeted cost report for next year assuming the entity uses the following:
   (i) FIFO process costing
   (ii) weighted average process costing.

(b) The employee responsible for estimating the percentage completion had experience estimating completion percentages for one of Rausher's other product lines. However, she is wondering whether she could improve the accuracy of her estimates. A colleague in another department suggested that she consider using techniques such as timing one unit through each department and identifying points in the production process where units appear to be 25 per cent complete, 50 per cent complete and so on.
   (i) Comment on whether the suggested method is likely to provide an accurate estimate of work in process.
   (ii) List two advantages of improving the accuracy of the estimate. What might be a disadvantage?

14.33 Comparison of actual to standard processing costs; use in bonus decisions Tiffany Campbell is the cost accountant in a small manufacturing entity, Computer Components (CC). CC produces components for one of the large computer manufacturers. Its strategy is to provide highly reliable components at the lowest possible price. To help maintain cost competitiveness, Tiffany produces two process cost reports each month, one based on the FIFO method and the other based on the standard cost method. When the reports are complete, costs from the two systems are compared. If actual costs are under control (that is, within the standard costs) for a particular division, the manager receives a small bonus. If costs have been under control throughout the year, a larger bonus is given at the end of December.

This month Tiffany investigated the results for Kevin Meledrez's division. Actual direct material costs were higher than standard cost, so the equivalent unit cost was higher than the standard. When she spoke to Kevin about the direct material costs in his division, he argued that the standard cost needs to be changed because the current supplier increased the cost of a particular part. Kevin believes that he should not be held responsible for costs that are not under his control; when prices change, the standard should also change.

Tiffany asked Kevin whether he had investigated other vendors who sell the same part to see whether the price change was across the board for all vendors. Kevin says that he has used this vendor for a number of years and is satisfied with the quality and timeliness of delivery. He does not believe that another vendor would provide the same quality and service, so he does not want to consider changing suppliers at this time.

REQUIRED

(a) Identify a variety of reasons why actual costs are likely to be different from standard costs for Computer Components.

(b) Discuss whether Kevin would be likely to make the same argument about changing the standard if the supplier's price had decreased.

(c) Describe the pros and cons of changing vendors.

(d) Explain the benefit to the entity of giving managers bonuses based on comparisons of actual to standard costs.

(e) Discuss the advantages and disadvantages of adopting a policy of adjusting the standard cost for changes in vendor prices.

(f) Suppose Tiffany asks for your advice. Use the information you learned from the preceding analyses to write a memo to Tiffany with your recommendation. As you write the memo, consider information that Tiffany needs from you to help her make a final decision.

14.34 Techtra makes electronic components used by other entities in a wide variety of end products. Initially Techtra bid for any type of electronic assembly work that became available (mostly subcontract work from other entities experiencing temporary capacity problems). But over the years the entity narrowed its focus. It now produces essentially three products, although minor variations within each product line yield a large number of different models.

Each of the products goes through three separate operating departments: assembly, soldering and testing. When an order is received, it goes to production scheduling. Personnel there schedule time in each of the three departments. The availability of parts usually determines when a job can be started in the assembly department. If parts are not in stock, they are usually received from suppliers within a week. On the appropriate day, the computerised scheduling program places the job on the assembly department's job list. Simultaneously, an electronic materials requisition goes to the stores department. Materials handling people then deliver the parts to the assembly department. The assembly operation is semiautomatic. When the department is ready to begin a new job, a worker inserts the appropriate guides into the equipment and adjusts the various settings. Parts are then loaded into the machines, which do the actual assembly. Because a worker keeps several machines running simultaneously, each order is processed using several (sometimes all) of the machines available in the department. Once the units for an order are assembled, an assembly department worker enters its completion in the computerised production system. The system then adds the job to the soldering department's job list. Materials handling personnel load assembled product onto racks and take them to the soldering department.

Soldering processes the jobs on a first-in, first-out basis unless production scheduling asks for priority treatment for a particular job. For each job the soldering machines must be set up for the appropriate product, but thereafter the operation is totally automatic. Once a job is completed, an entry is made in the production system, which adds it to the testing department's job list. The products are then reloaded onto racks and transported to the testing department.

By the time the products get to the testing department, many of the jobs are near or past their promised delivery date. Thus, the production scheduling system directs the testing department to work on jobs in the order of promised delivery date. Normally the entity expects 3 per cent to 5 per cent of the products to be defective, and plans its lot size for each order accordingly. However, from time to time an entire order must be scrapped due to faulty assembly or soldering on every unit. When an order is scrapped, it is noted in the production system and a rush replacement order is sent to the assembly department. Completed jobs that pass testing are immediately shipped to customers.

Workers in the assembly, soldering and testing departments each enter information in the production system detailing the amount of time spent working on specific jobs. This information, plus the materials requisitions, is used by the cost accounting system to track the cost of each job. The cost accounting system allocates departmental overhead to each job using overhead allocation rates based on budgeted overhead costs and budgeted hours for each department. General factory overhead — which includes production scheduling, materials handling, property taxes and so on — is charged to each job based on total materials costs. Within each of the three product types, the average cost per unit varies primarily with the size of each job order because of set-up costs. The cost data are used to update the entity's pricing sheets and to determine the efficiency with which each order was produced.

The managers are considering a change in the organisation of the plant. They propose that the plant floor, instead of being arranged in functional departments, could consist of manufacturing 'cells' for each product; that is, they would establish clusters of assembly machines, soldering machines and test equipment. Each cluster would be dedicated to making only one type of product. Under this arrangement, when an order is processed, individual units would proceed one by one through the assembly, soldering and test equipment in the appropriate cell. Most jobs would be completed within a day, but large jobs would sometimes take up to a week. The managers are also considering a change in the way parts are ordered from suppliers. The entity would place orders for each job, requesting delivery of parts on the day production is scheduled to begin.

REQUIRED

(a) Describe how the proposed changes would likely affect each of the following.
  (i) Size of work in process and raw materials inventories
  (ii) Material handling and machine set-up costs
  (iii) Cost of defective units
  (iv) Ratio of units produced to units ordered
  (v) Production scheduling costs and machine utilisation rates
  (vi) Average cost per unit of product
  (vii) Ability to fulfil a customer's rush order
(b) Assuming the managers adopt the proposed manufacturing changes.
  (i) What would be the advantages of adopting a process costing system?
  (ii) The entity would no longer carry significant inventories. How would this change affect the cost accounting?

15

Absorption, variable and throughput costing

IN BRIEF

Accountants use absorption costing for inventory and cost of goods sold when preparing financial statements according to generally accepted accounting principles (GAAP). Under absorption costing, all manufacturing costs (fixed and variable), including allocated overhead, are assigned to units manufactured. This accounting method provides useful information by matching manufacturing costs against revenues. As an alternative to absorption costing, variable costing (variable costs only) and throughput costing (direct material costs only) are two methods that accountants use to provide managers with incremental cost information.

After studying this chapter, you should be able to:

1 Understand the difference between absorption costing and variable costing, and prepare income statements under each method.

2 Calculate absorption costs using normal costing.

3 Understand throughput costing and construct an income statement using this method.

4 Identify the uses and limitations of absorption, variable and throughput costing income statements.

Harley-Davidson: scarcity or abundance?

As of February 2002, Harley-Davidson's sales had grown steadily for several years; its share price was up 31 per cent over the previous 12 months. However, the company's dealers reported that they were now carrying inventories, whereas they had previously waited one to two years to fill customer orders. These reports led analysts to conclude that sales for Harley-Davidson's motorcycles were slowing. The analysts argued that the company was trying to hide the slow-down by engaging in channel stuffing — pushing dealers to buy bikes they did not need.

The analysts' arguments seemed plausible because channel stuffing had been used by managers of other companies to artificially boost sales and profits during sales downturns. This tactic works best in situations such as Harley-Davidson's; dealers are willing to buy excess inventories because their future allocations of new models depend on past purchases. Further-more, the company's financing arm provides loans to finance dealer purchases. Harley-Davidson recognises revenue from its dealers even if the dealers have not yet sold the bikes to their customers.

Harley-Davidson's managers stated that demand for the company's products had not slowed down. They argued instead that they had boosted inventories to meet customer demand. For a number of years prior to 2002, manufacturing had increased by 15 per cent annually. Harley's managers said that they wanted to keep frustrated biker 'wannabes' from buying competing brands instead of waiting for a backordered Harley. They also claimed that they had increased inventories of bikes and accessories in anticipation of the company's 100-year anniversary in 2003.

Under generally accepted accounting principles (GAAP), inventories and cost of goods sold must be accounted for using full absorption costing in which both variable and fixed manufacturing costs are assigned to all units produced. When manufacturing increases, as it did for Harley-Davidson, the cost per unit usually decreases because the fixed cost per unit generally decreases. Lower per-unit costs then result in a higher gross margin for each unit sold, leading to the appearance of higher profitability on the income statement. In addition, under absorption costing, when inventory levels increase during a time period, the cost of goods sold (COGS) *expense* on the income statement is smaller than the manufacturing *costs* incurred because some units (and their allocated fixed costs) are held in inventory.

These effects of full absorption accounting are not a problem, so long as sales levels do not decline. However, if sales slow and inventory from prior periods is sold, COGS expense will be higher than the manufacturing costs incurred during the period. In this case, declining sales have an especially negative effect on profits because of both declining revenue and higher COGS.

Harley-Davidson's financial statements may not have resolved investors' concerns when evaluating the arguments made by analysts and by company managers. If sales were artificially high, then absorption costing would delay recognition of costs on the income statement. The main question was whether Harley's sales would continue to grow. As long as sales increased each year and its variable and fixed costs did not increase, profits would continue to increase. However, if sales were to drop off, then the company's financial performance would deteriorate rapidly.

Fortunately for Harley-Davidson, its sales continued to increase during 2002. Although the US economy suffered, sales in some sectors increased. Americans began purchasing expensive toys such as all-terrain vehicles and motorcycles, even though they were cutting back on other expensive items such as costly dinners and clothing.

Sources: Information from Brown, K 2002, 'Heard on the street,' *The Wall Street Journal,* 12 February, p. C1; and Hallinan, J 2002, 'Serious fun,' *The Wall Street Journal,* 27 August, p. A1.

Issues from this scene setter to look for in the chapter include:

- How the use of absorption costing can artificially increase profits when production is greater than sales.

- When using absorption costing, how the calculation of profit influences choices made in relation to the fixed overhead allocation rate.

- Problems with the use of absorption costing for internal decision making.

- How variable costing and throughput costing may provide more appropriate information for some decision making.

Absorption costing and variable costing

With computerised accounting systems, accountants can easily calculate costs in a variety of ways; reports for outside distribution can be different from reports for inside management. In this section we compare absorption costing, which is intended for outside distribution, with variable costing, which is often used for managerial decision making.

Different measures of cost for different purposes

No single measure of inventory and cost of goods sold is best for all situations. Financial statement reporting requires average costs, but short-term internal decision making requires only incremental costs. Managers use both variable and fixed cost information for monitoring operations. Meanwhile, GAAP determines how costs should be measured for reporting to external parties such as investors. As we learn in this chapter, different types of information are useful in different settings.

Absorption costing

When accountants prepare financial statements according to GAAP, they use absorption costing. Under **absorption costing**, all manufacturing costs are recorded on the balance sheet as part of the cost of inventory and are then expensed as part of the cost of goods sold (COGS) when units are sold (figure 15.1). Both fixed and variable manufacturing costs are assumed to have future value to the entity, and are accordingly treated as **product costs**. They include direct materials, direct labour and manufacturing overhead.

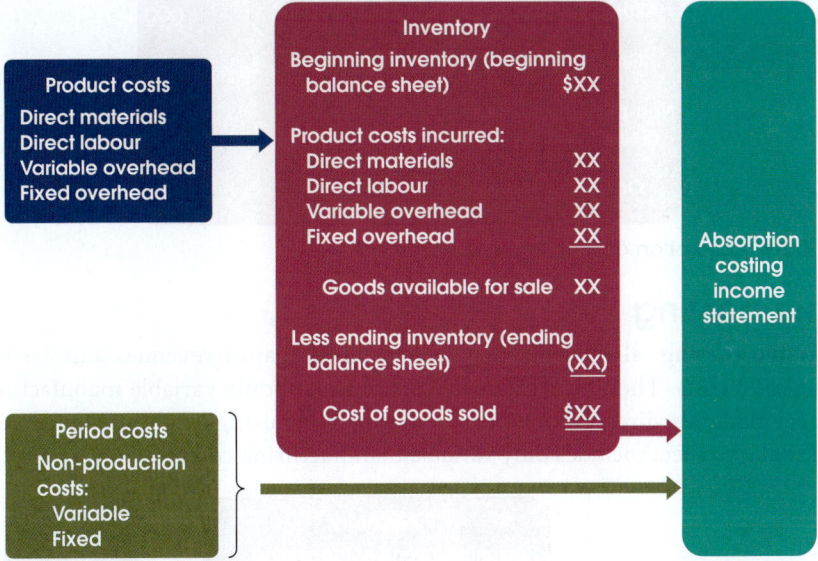

FIGURE 15.1 ■ Absorption costing

Under absorption costing, direct costs are traced to products and manufacturing overhead is allocated to products. Fixed overhead may be allocated to units using either an actual or budgeted allocation rate. If manufacturing volume is used as the allocation base, fixed overhead cost can be allocated to units using either an actual or an estimated allocation rate as follows:

$$\text{Actual fixed overhead allocation rate} = \frac{\text{Actual fixed overhead cost}}{\text{Actual production volume}}$$

$$\text{Estimated fixed overhead allocation rate} = \frac{\text{Estimated fixed overhead cost}}{\text{Estimated production volume}}$$

When using an estimated fixed overhead allocation rate, several alternative choices are available for the estimated manufacturing volume; we learn about these later in the chapter.

Given the treatment of fixed overhead costs under absorption costing, both manufacturing and sales volumes affect the timing of when fixed overhead is recognised as an expense. If units are produced and sold in this period, overhead costs incurred to produce these units are expensed in this period. If units from the last period are sold, some overhead costs from the last period are expensed in this period. If units produced in this period are not yet sold, the overhead allocated to those units will not be expensed until a future date when the units are sold. The overhead cost associated with those units is included in inventory on the balance sheet.

The absorption costing income statement (figure 15.2) reflects the focus in GAAP on distinguishing between manufacturing and non-manufacturing costs. All manufacturing costs are expensed as COGS to match them against revenues when units are sold. Non-manufacturing costs such as administration, marketing and distribution are treated as period costs. **Period costs** are all costs other than production costs that are assigned to the cost of inventory. GAAP requires that period costs be expensed when incurred because these costs are assumed to have no future benefit.

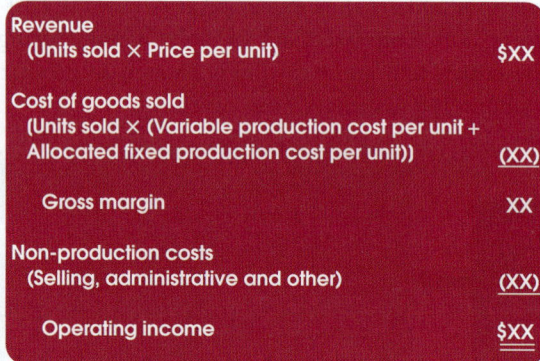

FIGURE 15.2 ■ Absorption costing income statement

Variable costing

Under **variable costing**, all variable costs are matched against revenues and fixed costs are treated as period costs. Therefore, product costs consist of only variable manufacturing costs such as direct materials, direct labour and variable manufacturing overhead (figure 15.3). Inventory on the balance sheet includes only variable manufacturing costs under variable costing.

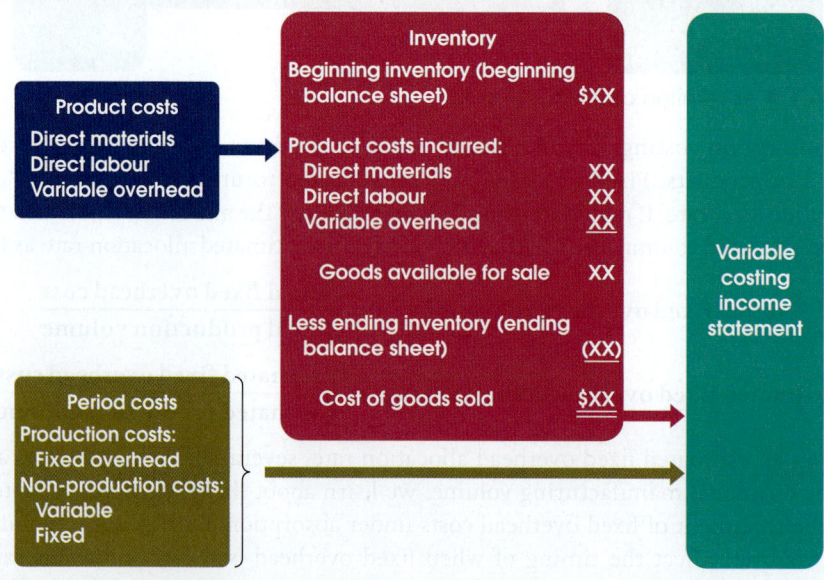

FIGURE 15.3 ■ Variable costing

Expenses in a variable costing income statement are organised differently from an absorption costing income statement. In a variable costing income statement, all costs are separated into variable and fixed categories (figure 15.4); variable manufacturing costs are reported separately from fixed manufacturing costs. Similarly, variable non-manufacturing costs, such as sales commissions, are reported separately from fixed non-manufacturing costs. All variable costs, manufacturing and non-manufacturing, are subtracted from revenues to arrive at the contribution margin. Then all fixed costs, manufacturing and non-manufacturing, are subtracted to determine operating income. This presentation improves the ability of managers to identify cash flows relevant to a product or service for internal decision making.

Revenue	
(Units sold × Price per unit)	$XX
Variable costs:	
Production (Units sold × Variable production cost per unit)	(XX)
Non-production (Units sold × Variable non-production cost per unit, such as sales commissions)	(XX)
Contribution margin	XX
Fixed costs:	
Fixed production costs	(XX)
Fixed non-production costs	(XX)
Operating Income	$XX

FIGURE 15.4 ■ Variable costing income statement

Absorption costing compared to variable costing

Managers and other employees regularly make decisions about short-term resource allocations within an entity. To do so, they estimate the effects of alternative decisions on cash flows (incremental revenues and costs). Because fixed costs are constant within a relevant range of activity, total fixed costs generally do not change under alternative short-term decisions. Thus, income statements based on absorption costing do not provide managers or other users with the relevant information needed for short-term operating decisions because they factor in costs that are not relevant to those decisions. Therefore, variable costing income statements are often preferred for internal reporting.

Although the use of variable costing for internal reports has numerous advantages, many organisations use absorption costing for both internal and external reporting. Often, managers traditionally used absorption costing because it was expensive and inconvenient to use two different reporting formats. Also, advocates of absorption costing for internal reporting believe that matching revenue and costs provides better information about opportunity costs for the entity. They believe that fixed costs are essentially capacity costs, so absorption costs reflect different products' use of capacity.

Comprehensive example 1 (overleaf) compares income statements across time under absorption costing and variable costing.

Comprehensive example 1

Absorption costing and variable costing income statements

Boats Afloat Yacht Company recently started to manufacture recreational yachts. The accountant, Joan Ardmore, prepared the second quarter income statements using absorption costing as follows.

Boats Afloat Yacht Company Second quarter income statement				
	April	May	June	Quarter total
Revenue @ $100 000 per unit	$100 000	$100 000	$300 000	$500 000
Cost of goods sold	100 000	70 000	210 000	380 000
Gross margin	0	30 000	90 000	120 000
Administrative and selling expenses	20 000	20 000	40 000	80 000
Operating income (loss)	$ (20 000)	$ 10 000	$ 50 000	$ 40 000

The sales manager, Stephanie Reynolds, analyses these results and asks Joan to explain why a loss was posted in April but not in May, given that one boat was sold each month. The income statement was prepared using absorption costing, with fixed overhead allocated based on actual costs and actual manufacturing volumes. Joan decides to prepare variable costing income statements for the same period so that she can more easily explain the absorption costing income statement to Stephanie. Joan first reviews the information she gathered and her calculations for the absorption income statement. The selling price per yacht is $100 000, and the entity incurred the following costs.

Variable costs per yacht			
Direct materials			$20 000
Direct labour			$15 000
Variable manufacturing overhead			$5 000
Variable selling			$10 000
Fixed costs per month			
Fixed manufacturing overhead			$60 000
Fixed administrative and selling			$10 000
Manufacturing and sales quantities			
	April	May	June
Manufacturing	1	2	2
Sales	1	1	3

Absorption costing

When absorption costing is used, all manufacturing overhead (fixed as well as variable) is allocated to inventory. When the entity produces only one product, fixed manufacturing overhead costs can be easily allocated on a pro rata basis among the actual units produced. The absorption cost per unit is the sum of the variable manufacturing cost per unit plus the actual fixed overhead allocation rate per unit.

	Absorption cost per unit		
	April	May	June
Fixed manufacturing overhead	$ 60 000	$60 000	$60 000
Divided by number of units produced	1	2	2
Actual fixed overhead per unit	60 000	30 000	30 000
Variable manufacturing costs per unit:			
Direct materials	20 000	20 000	20 000
Direct labour	15 000	15 000	15 000
Variable manufacturing overhead	5 000	5 000	5 000
Total variable cost per unit	40 000	40 000	40 000
Total absorption cost per unit	$100 000	$70 000	$70 000

	Absorption cost of goods sold		
	April	May	June
Number of units sold	1	1	3
Absorption cost of unit(s) sold:			
Produced during April	$100 000		
Produced during May		$70 000	$ 70 000
Produced during June			
(2 @ $70 000 each)			140 000
Total cost of goods sold	$100 000	$70 000	$210 000

In April, Boats Afloat produced and sold the same quantity of yachts, resulting in no ending inventory. In May, however, Boats Afloat produced two units and sold only one. Thus, one unit remained in inventory at a cost of $70 000. Then in June, two units were produced and three were sold. June's cost of goods sold reflected sales of three units; two produced in June and one drawn from inventory. Inventory at the end of June was zero.

Variable costing

Joan now separates administrative and selling expenses into variable and fixed categories and prepares variable costing income statements. Notice that under variable costing, income for the months when one boat was sold (April and May) is the same.

	Administrative and selling costs		
	April	May	June
Variable selling cost per unit	$ 10 000	$ 10 000	$ 10 000
Times number of units sold	1	1	3
Total variable selling cost	10 000	10 000	30 000
Fixed administrative and selling expenses	10 000	10 000	10 000
Total administrative and selling expenses	$ 20 000	$ 20 000	$ 40 000

	Variable costing income statements			
	April	May	June	Quarter total
Revenue @ $100 000 per unit	$100 000	$100 000	$300 000	$500 000
Variable manufacturing expenses (for units sold)	40 000	40 000	120 000	200 000
Variable selling expenses	10 000	10 000	30 000	50 000
Contribution margin	50 000	50 000	150 000	250 000
Fixed manufacturing expenses	60 000	60 000	60 000	180 000
Fixed administrative and selling expenses	10 000	10 000	10 000	30 000
Operating income (loss)	$ (20 000)	$ (20 000)	$ 80 000	$ 40 000

Reconciling absorption and variable costing incomes

Notice in comprehensive example 1 that when manufacturing levels are the same as sales levels, income is the same under absorption and variable costing. When manufacturing is greater than sales, absorption income is greater than variable income. In turn, when manufacturing is less than sales, absorption income is less than variable income. Reconciling the two incomes involves calculating the difference in overhead cost that is either added to or subtracted from inventory because sales volumes do not equal manufacturing volumes. Figure 15.5 presents reconciliation calculations that are then illustrated using comprehensive example 2 on Boats Afloat.

Absorption versus variable costing			
	Operating income	Inventory on the balance sheet	Reconciliation calculations
Manufacturing = Sales	Absorption costing income = Variable costing income	No change in inventory quantity on the balance sheet	No reconciliation needed because no difference in income
Manufacturing > Sales	Absorption costing income > Variable costing income	Inventory quantities on the balance sheet increase	Difference in income is equal to: 1. increase in absorption costing inventory minus increase in variable costing inventory 2. fixed overhead allocated during the current period to units added to inventory
Manufacturing < Sales	Absorption costing income < Variable costing income	Inventory quantities on the balance sheet decrease	Difference in income is equal to: 1. decrease in absorption costing inventory minus decrease in variable costing inventory 2. fixed overhead allocated to units in prior period to units removed from inventory

FIGURE 15.5 ■ Reconciling absorption and variable costing

Comprehensive example 2

Reconciling absorption costing and variable costing income statements

Working from the two income statements, Joan prepares the following reconciliation report. Next she shows Stephanie the two income statements, explaining the preparation of each one. When Stephanie observes that the quarterly incomes under the two methods are the same, Joan points out that this occurred because the quarter had no beginning or ending inventories. Joan then shows Stephanie the reconciliation report and explains her calculations.

	April	May	June
Difference in income:			
Absorption costing income (loss)	$ (20 000)	$ 10 000	$ 50 000
Variable costing income (loss)	(20 000)	(20 000)	80 000
Difference	$ 0	$ 30 000	$ (30 000)
Difference in change in inventory:			
Absorption costing:			
Ending inventory	$ 0	$ 70 000	$ 0
Beginning inventory	0	0	70 000
Increase (decrease)	0	70 000	(70 000)
Variable costing:			
Ending inventory	$ 0	$ 40 000	$ 0
Beginning inventory	0	0	40 000
Increase (decrease)	0	40 000	(40 000)
Difference	$ 0	$ 30 000	$ (30 000)

The only difference in inventory cost between absorption costing and variable costing is the amount of fixed overhead allocated to inventory under absorption costing. Therefore, the change in inventory difference can be presented by calculating the change in fixed costs included in absorption costing inventory. Ending inventory in May consists of one unit produced during May, when $30 000 in fixed overhead was allocated to each unit. This unit was then sold during June. The difference in operating income between absorption and variable costing is summarised as follows:

	April	May	June
Change in fixed costs included in absorption costing inventory:			
Fixed costs in ending inventory	$0	$ 30 000	$ 0
Fixed costs in beginning inventory	0	0	30 000
Increase (decrease)	$0	$ 30 000	$ (30 000)

After examining the two different income statements and the reconciling report, Stephanie decides she wants to receive monthly income statements using both methods. She wants the same financial statement information that is shared with banks and other external stakeholders, in case someone calls and has questions about the entity's financial performance measured under GAAP. She also wants to use the variable costing income statement to analyse the operating performance of the organisation and its managers.

Stephanie also wants to set up a profit-sharing plan for all employees, rewarding employees when the amounts received from sales cover the costs for the period. She realises that the variable costing income statement provides this information by more accurately measuring substantive economic changes across time.

Incentives to build up inventories

In comprehensive example 2, absorption costing operating income for Boats Afloat is higher than variable costing operating income in periods when the inventory quantities increase. Under absorption costing, part of an entity's fixed overhead cost is recorded as inventory on the balance sheet. As inventory quantity increases, the amount of fixed cost included in inventory increases. Because that portion of fixed cost is not expensed until later, operating income also increases. As a result, managers using absorption costing have incentives to inappropriately build up inventory quantities, especially when sales during the current period decrease. Managers may be motivated by many factors:

- Managers' reputations often increase as a result of increases in reported operating income.
- Managers frequently receive bonus payments based on their ability to meet or exceed targeted operating income levels.
- Managers may be biased in their sales forecasts, preventing them from promptly recognising a decline in sales.

Disincentives to build up inventories

Managers might avoid inventory build-ups for several reasons. If managers become aware of a sales decline, they could be unwilling to use an inventory build-up that, while strengthening short-term earnings, would negatively affect future earnings when those units are either sold or written off. If bonuses are based on variable costing income, managers will not be rewarded for inventory build-ups. The Harley-Davidson case that opened this chapter shows another disincentive; analysts routinely monitor companies' inventory levels. Excessive inventory levels are often viewed as evidence of poor management or deteriorating sales. In addition, some entities use just-in-time (JIT) inventory management. Under JIT, the potential build-up of inventory is unlikely; so income differences under absorption and variable costing are small.

Uncertainties about desirable inventory levels

In the Harley-Davidson case, managers stated that they intentionally wanted dealers to carry higher inventories to better meet customer demand. Analysts responded that sales were in decline and that dealer inventory increases signalled a forthcoming decline in the company's financial health. Because of uncertainties about factors influencing future sales, it was not possible for outsiders such as investors to determine whether Harley-Davidson's inventories were too high. These uncertainties included the following:

- the extent to which long wait times would cause customers to buy from competitors
- the increase in sales to individuals who would not have waited

- whether an increase in inventories and corresponding decrease in customer wait times would reduce the mystique of the Harley-Davidson brand, causing a decrease in future product demand
- the most desirable manufacturing and inventory levels.

To further complicate matters, outsiders could not know whether the managers were completely candid in explaining their manufacturing policies or whether their manufacturing decisions were biased.

A closer look at absorption costing using normal costing

Under absorption costing in comprehensive example 1, fixed production overhead for Boats Afloat was allocated to each yacht based on the actual cost incurred and the actual number of yachts produced each month. An alternative method under absorption costing is to allocate fixed overhead costs using normal costing. Normal costing uses actual direct costs and actual production volumes with an estimated fixed overhead allocation rate.

Suppose the accountant for Boats Afloat calculates an estimated fixed overhead allocation rate based on annual budget data. Assuming that budgeted fixed overhead is $720 000 and annual production is budgeted to be 24 units, the rate used for allocation would be estimated as follows:

$$\text{Estimated fixed overhead allocation rate} = \text{Estimated fixed overhead cost} \div \text{Estimated production volume}$$

$$= \$720\,000 \div 24 \text{ units}$$

$$= \$30\,000 \text{ per unit}$$

The fixed overhead allocation for the month of April would be:

$$\text{Fixed overhead allocation} = \text{Actual units produced} \times \text{Estimated fixed overhead allocation rate}$$

$$= 1 \text{ unit} \times \$30\,000 \text{ per unit}$$

$$= \$30\,000$$

Motivation for normal costing

Using an estimated fixed overhead allocation rate is often preferred to the use of rates based on actual costs for three reasons: denominator, numerator and information timeliness.

Actual production volumes fluctuate (denominator reason). If overhead is allocated based on actual volume, then the fixed cost per unit could be artificially high or low in different time periods. In the Boats Afloat example, total cost per yacht varied from $70 000 to $100 000 because of differences in fixed production overhead per unit. These differences were caused by variations in production volume across individual months. If production volumes fluctuate randomly or seasonally, then an estimated fixed production overhead rate could be used to avoid distorting costs for individual units.

Fixed production overhead costs fluctuate (numerator reason). Fixed overhead costs often fluctuate throughout a time period. Suppose an entity is located in a region with cold winters. Utility costs for production facilities might be high during winter months and low during summer months. If fixed overhead is allocated based on actual costs incurred each month, units produced during the winter would be allocated higher overhead costs than units produced during summer months. When an estimated fixed production overhead rate is used, this type of per-unit cost distortion would be avoided.

Actual volume and fixed overhead costs are not known until after accounting for the period is completed (information timeliness). Normal costing allows managers to assign costs to inventory when the accounting cycle has not been completed. Managers often need to cost inventory during each month or shortly after a month's end. It might not be possible to gather and report complete cost and volume data quickly enough to use actual costs for fixed overhead allocation. So long as normal costs are reasonable estimates, they can be used for faster-paced valuations.

Allocation rate denominator considerations

When calculating an estimated fixed overhead allocation rate, accountants choose the allocation base to use as the denominator. Allocation bases such as direct labour hours, direct labour costs, machine hours or number of units are often used. In this chapter we focus on allocating fixed overhead based on production volumes or different measures of capacity to present the most general case. Capacity is a measure of the constraints within an entity. It can be measured in a number of ways.

Four different levels of capacity could be used as the estimated volume of production under absorption costing. Two of these measures are *supply-based capacity levels*; they measure the amount of capacity that is available for production:

- **Theoretical capacity** is the upper capacity limit; it assumes continuous, uninterrupted production 365 days per year. Theoretical capacity is the maximum volume of goods or services that an entity could hypothetically produce.
- **Practical capacity** is the upper capacity limit that takes into account the organisation's regularly scheduled times for production. Practical capacity excludes potential production that could take place during anticipated and scheduled maintenance downtimes, holidays or other times in which production would normally be interrupted. In other words, practical capacity is theoretical capacity reduced for expected downtimes. Practical capacity is estimated using engineering studies and labour use patterns.

Two additional measures are *demand-based capacity levels*; they measure the amount of capacity needed to meet sales volumes:

- **Normal capacity** is an average use of capacity over time. Normal capacity is the typical volume of goods or services an entity produces to meet customer demand.
- **Budgeted or expected capacity** is the anticipated use of capacity over the next period. Budgeted or expected capacity is based on management's planned operations in which customer demand is forecast.

Volume variance with normal costing

The **volume variance** is the difference between the amount of estimated fixed overhead costs used to calculate the allocation rate and the amount of fixed overhead costs actually allocated to inventory during the period. If allocated volume is greater than estimated volume, then too much fixed overhead is allocated to inventory and the inventory amounts need to be reduced by the variance amount. If allocated volume is less than estimated volume; too little fixed overhead cost is allocated to inventory and inventory values need to be increased by the variance amount. For example, suppose Boats Afloat estimates that fixed overhead costs will be $60 000 per month and fixed overhead is allocated to units using normal capacity of two units per month, or $30 000 per unit. In a month when only one yacht is produced, the volume variance would be:

Volume variance = Expected fixed overhead cost – Allocated fixed overhead cost

$$= \$60\,000 - \$30\,000$$
$$= \$30\,000$$

In this example, allocated overhead was less than estimated overhead, so inventory accounts on the financial statements need to be increased by $30 000 to ensure that the expense recorded this period is equal to estimated fixed overhead.

When preparing financial statements under GAAP, this variance would be closed to cost of goods sold if it were immaterial. If material, it would be allocated on a pro rata basis among cost of goods sold, finished goods and work in process (if any). In this example, the volume variance would be considered material because it is large compared to estimated fixed overhead costs, so cost of goods sold, finished goods and work in process would all be increased.

Evaluating denominator choices

Because volume variances must be adjusted at the end of an accounting period, the inventory and cost of goods sold values on the financial statements are not affected by the choice of denominator when calculating the estimated fixed overhead allocation rate. Therefore, no income effects need to be considered when choosing the denominator value.

However, managers sometimes use information from the normal costing system for pricing and product emphasis decisions. In addition, the denominator choice often affects budgets. To provide the highest-quality cost information for planning and decision making, inventory values should reflect realistic estimates of the use of resources. The quality of information for decision making and planning decreases when absorption cost information is based on unrealistic capacity levels.

Another factor to consider in choosing the denominator is how the choice affects the management of an organisation's capacity. The largest costs in fixed production overhead are often related to capacity, such as building rent, depreciation, utilities and maintenance. Thus, we can think of the estimated fixed overhead allocation rate as an estimated cost of capacity per unit that could be used to motivate managers to use capacity efficiently. The best choice would allocate a cost to each unit produced, not only to emphasise the need to cover fixed costs but also to provide information about the opportunity cost of unused capacity.

If theoretical capacity is used as the allocation base, the fixed overhead allocation rate is unrealistically small. Therefore, theoretical capacity is rarely used in practice. If normal or budgeted capacity is used, inventory values simply reflect the current use of capacity, which may not be the most efficient use of capacity. In contrast, practical capacity reflects an attainable target for production. When practical capacity is used in the denominator, the fixed overhead allocation rate reflects the cost of supplying capacity. Internal reports can be developed to highlight the capacity available versus the capacity used. These reports focus managers' attention on unused capacity. Thus, the use of practical capacity motivates managers to find new ways to use available capacity. They may be encouraged to increase demand, develop new products, or consider leasing out or eliminating unused capacity.

Throughput costing

Throughput costing is a modified form of variable costing that treats direct labour and variable overhead as period expenses. Developed in the 1980s as part of the theory of constraints (also see chapter 5), throughput costing has become popular for internal reporting purposes.

It was developed when some managers realised that product costs under both absorption and variable costing are excessive because they include more than direct materials. The chapter 15 article at the end of this book illustrates further the usefulness of throughput costing for business decision making.

In many entities, conversion costs such as direct labour and overhead do not vary proportionately with volume of manufacturing. Under throughput costing, inventory is valued using only direct material costs (figure 15.6). All other costs are treated as period costs.

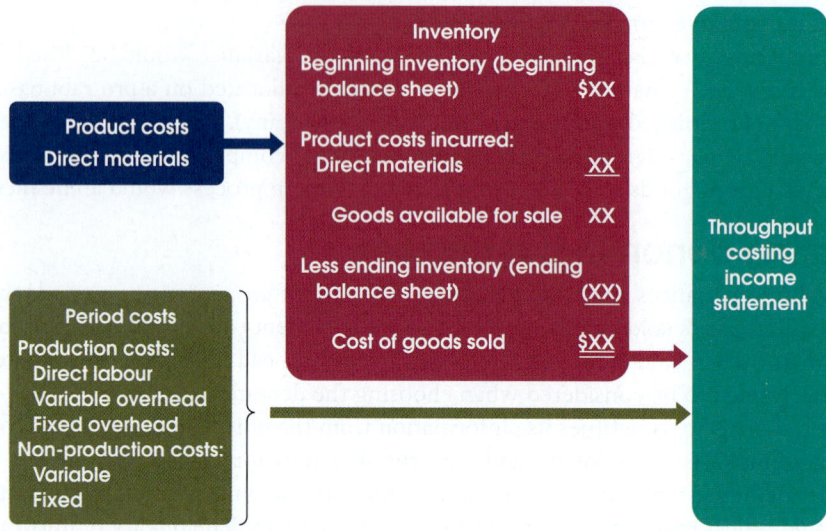

FIGURE 15.6 ■ Throughput costing

The throughput contribution is defined as revenue less direct materials costs for the units sold. Accountants and managers in companies using theory of constraints methods believe that throughput costing helps them make better short-term decisions because costs other than direct materials tend to be relatively fixed in the short run. For example, direct labour may be a fixed cost if workers are guaranteed a work schedule such as a 40-hour week. When direct labour is fixed and little or no variable overhead cost is involved, the variable income statement is similar to the throughput costing income statement. Figure 15.7 shows an income statement format for throughput costing.

Revenue
(Units sold × Price per unit) $XX

Direct material costs:
  Production (Units sold × Direct materials
  unit cost)   (XX)

      Throughput contribution   XX

Other costs:
  Production (Direct labour + Fixed and
  variable overhead)   (XX)
  Non-production costs (Fixed and variable
  selling and administration)   (XX)

      Operating income $XX

FIGURE 15.7 ■ Throughput costing income statement

Following is a throughput income statement for Boats Afloat for the quarter April to June.

Revenue (5 units × $100 000 per unit)		$500 000
Direct materials (5 units × $20 0000 per unit)		100 000
Throughput contribution		400 000
Other costs:		
Operating expenses:		
Other variable productions costs	$100 000	
Fixed overhead costs	180 000	
Variable selling costs	50 000	
Fixed administrative and selling costs	30 000	360 000
Throughput costing operating income		$ 40 000

Throughput contribution is revenue less the cost of direct materials for the units sold. The operating expenses of $360 000 include the costs of direct labour and variable overhead for the entire period (5 units × $20 000 per unit = $100 000), variable administrative and selling costs (5 units × $10 000 = $50 000), fixed manufacturing cost (3 months × $60 000 = $180 000) and fixed selling costs (3 months × $10 000 = $30 000). As an alternative format, totals for manufacturing- and non-manufacturing-related costs may also be presented separately.

Advantages of throughput costing

Throughput costing can be thought of as an extreme version of variable costing. Only direct material costs are assigned to inventory and cost of goods sold. When costs such as direct labour and manufacturing overhead are categorised and treated as operating costs rather than product costs (inventory), managers' attitudes about these costs tend to change. They are encouraged to reduce operating costs when needed, such as when sales decline. Under throughput costing, managers are more likely to consider reducing costs such as direct labour. Conversely, under absorption costing, many manufacturing costs are initially categorised as assets (inventory) until goods are sold. As a result, managers may perceive less need to reduce direct labour and overhead cost. Compared to absorption and variable costing, throughput costing also reduces the incentives for managers to build up inventory to inappropriate levels.

Comparison of absorption, variable and throughput costing

Figure 15.8 (overleaf) compares the assumptions used in absorption costing, variable costing and throughput costing. These accounting methods differ based on the costs that are considered product costs. Under absorption costing, all manufacturing costs are product costs. Under variable costing, only variable manufacturing costs are product costs. Under throughput costing, only direct materials costs are product costs. These methods affect how quickly manufacturing overhead and other costs are expensed on the income statement. Because managers monitor operating income, these methods affect how quickly they are motivated to consider changing manufacturing plans related to these costs.

Absorption costing	Variable costing	Throughput costing
GAAP	Not GAAP	Not GAAP
Useful for external reporting purposes	Useful for performance evaluation and internal decision making	Useful for short-term capacity decision making, focuses managers attention on reducing labour and overhead costs because they are considered operating costs instead of product costs (inventory)
Direct material and direct labour are inventory costs	Direct material and direct labour are inventory costs	Only direct materials are inventory costs
Fixed and variable manufacturing overhead allocated to inventory	Fixed manufacturing overhead expensed as a period cost. Variable manufacturing overhead allocated to inventory	Direct labour, fixed and variable overhead, and all other costs expensed as operational expense, a period cost
Administrative and selling costs (both fixed and variable) expensed as period costs	Administrative and selling costs separated into fixed and variable costs and expensed as period costs	Administrative and selling costs expensed as operational expense, a period cost
Inventory costs (including per-unit fixed and variable manufacturing costs) not expensed until the units are sold	Inventory costs (only manufacturing variable costs) not expensed until the units are sold	Inventory costs (only direct materials) not expensed until the units are sold

FIGURE 15.8 ■ Comparison of absorption, variable and throughput costing

Before technology made it relatively easy to draw many different reports from one database, most entities established an accounting system designed primarily to meet financial and tax accounting requirements. Because absorption costing is required by GAAP and income tax rules, it tended to be the only method used. With improved technology, organisations are now able to produce information reports for many different purposes.

Absorption costing income statements focus on matching manufacturing costs to revenues on the income statement. This information is important for external users, such as investors, who monitor the trends in product costs for an entity over time and for comparison with competitors. Variable costing income statements are often used to evaluate the performance of a division or manager, or as a source for information for decision making. Throughput costing statements help managers determine the most efficient use of resources in the short term.

Comprehensive example 3 further demonstrates the differences between absorption and variable costing approaches.

Comprehensive example 3

Absorption costing and variable costing

Ski Doodle is a small family-owned business that manufactures snowmobiles. Abel, the co-owner's son, has performed the entity's accounting functions for several years. He always prepares variable costing income statements because the family makes product-related decisions on a regular basis and prefers using incremental costs for those decisions. Recently, the family decided to apply for a loan to expand operations. The bank asked for this month's financial statements and wants them to conform to GAAP.

Variable costing

The information for the current period reports along with Ski Doodle's variable costing income statement follow.

Ordinarily, Ski Doodle's prices and costs are:	
Price	$10 000 per snowmobile
Variable manufacturing costs:	
Raw materials	$2 000 per snowmobile
Direct labour and variable overhead	$2 000 per snowmobile
Fixed manufacturing costs	$60 000 per month
Selling and administrative costs:	
Variable	$500 per snowmobile
Fixed	$30 000 per month

Beginning finished goods inventory for the year was zero. Average manufacturing is about 12 snowmobiles per month. Sales are seasonal, so in some months no snowmobiles are produced or sold, while manufacturing and sales are high in other months.

This month beginning inventory was zero, 20 snowmobiles were manufactured and 18 snowmobiles were sold.

Variable costing income statement		
Revenue (18 × $10 000)		$180 000
Variable costs		
Manufacturing (18 × $4000)	$72 000	
Selling (18 × $500)	9 000	81 000
Contribution margin		99 000
Fixed costs		
Manufacturing	$60 000	
Administrative and selling	30 000	90 000
Operating Income		$ 9 000

Ending inventory is valued at $8000 (2 units × $4000 variable manufacturing cost per unit).

Absorption costing with actual volume

When Abel develops the absorption costing income statement, he realises that he needs to choose either actual volume or some estimate of volume to calculate the fixed overhead allocation rate. He decides to produce this month's statement both ways to see how they differ from each other and from the variable costing income statement information with which he is familiar.

First Abel produces an absorption costing income statement using actual manufacturing levels. The actual fixed overhead allocation rate is $60 000 ÷ 20 units = $3000 per unit. Accordingly, the absorption cost per unit is $7000 ($4000 variable cost plus $3000 allocated fixed overhead), and COGS is $126 000 (18 units sold × $7000 per unit).

Absorption costing income statement (actual volume)	
Revenue (18 $10 000)	$ 180 000
Cost of goods sold (18 × $7000)	126 000
Gross margin	54 000
Administrative and selling [$30 000 + (18 × $500)]	39 000
Operating income	$ 15 000

Ending inventory is valued at $14 000 [2 units × ($4000 + $3000)].

The difference in incomes between variable costing and absorption costing arises because allocated fixed overhead costs increase the value of the absorption costing inventory on the balance sheet. With no beginning inventory, the change in this illustration equals the fixed overhead costs that are included in ending inventory. The two units in ending inventory were each allocated $3000 in fixed overhead. Therefore, total fixed overhead in ending inventory is $6000. Abel prepares a formal reconciliation of the two incomes as follows:

Variable costing income	$ 9 000
Increase in fixed overhead costs in absorption inventory ($6000 ending – $0 beginning)	6 000
Absorption costing income	$15 000

Another way to reconcile the two incomes is to calculate the difference in the change in inventory cost between the two costing methods:

Increase in absorption costing inventory ($14 000 ending – $0 beginning)	$14 000
Increase in variable costing inventory ($8000 ending – $0 beginning)	8 000
Difference	$ 6 000

Absorption costing with normal capacity

Next, Abel allocates fixed overhead using an estimated allocation rate based on a normal capacity level of 12 snowmobiles per month. In this case, the estimated fixed overhead allocation rate is $5000 per unit ($60 000 ÷ 12 units). The cost of each unit produced under absorption costing is now $9000 ($4000 variable cost + $5000 allocated fixed overhead).

Absorption costing income statement (normal capacity)	
Revenue (18 × $10 000)	$180 000
Cost of goods sold (18 × $9000)	162 000
Gross margin	18 000
Administrative and selling [$30 000 + (18 × $500)]	39 000
Operating income (loss)	$ (21 000)

Choice of fixed overhead allocation rate denominator and volume variance adjustment

After he completes the preceding calculations, Abel realises that his choice of denominator level for the fixed overhead allocation rate affects the operating income, which in turn affects the bank's appraisal of Ski Doodle's creditworthiness. Based on his analyses, he thinks the bank will view the entity more favourably if fixed overhead is allocated using the actual manufacturing level. Income for the current period appears higher than when using normal capacity.

Although Abel does accounting for the family business, he is not formally trained as an accountant. Therefore, he is unsure whether his calculations and conclusions are accurate. He suspects that too much overhead has been allocated under the normal capacity version of the absorption costing income statement. He decides to meet with Matt Goodings, the company's CPA.

Matt tells Abel, 'I'm very impressed with what you've done here. I have only one comment about your calculations. When using an estimated volume to allocate fixed costs, there is always a volume variance — the difference between estimated and allocated fixed overhead cost. You estimated a normal capacity of 12 units per month, but said that sales increased more than expected this year. You now expect that manufacturing will average more than 12 units per month. You estimated fixed overhead costs to be $60 000. However, under your estimated normal capacity, $100 000 (20 units × $5000) of fixed overhead costs is allocated to units produced last month. Thus, you have a volume variance of $40 000 — you allocated more overhead to snowmobiles than the estimated cost. Generally accepted accounting principles require you to make an adjustment for this variance in your calculations to insure that only actual costs are recorded in inventory and cost of goods sold. I'll show you how.' Matt shows Abel the following calculations.

$$\text{Volume variance} = \text{Estimated fixed overhead} - \text{Allocated fixed overhead}$$

$$= \$60\ 000 - (20\ \text{units} \times \$5000\ \text{per unit})$$

$$= \$40\ 000$$

The volume variance of $40 000 is far more than 10 per cent of the estimated fixed overhead cost of $60 000. Matt concludes that the variance is material and should be allocated on a pro rata basis among the 20 units produced that are in cost of goods sold and ending inventory. The adjustment is $2000 per unit ($40 000 ÷ 20 units):

Adjustment for the volume variance:	
Cost of goods sold ($2000 × 18 units)	$36 000
Ending inventory ($2000 × 2 units)	4 000
Total volume variance	$40 000

Because more fixed overhead was allocated than estimated, the absorption cost per unit should be reduced by $2000 per unit. Abel recasts the income statement with the volume variance adjustment as follows.

Absorption costing income statement (normal capacity with volume variance adjustment)		
Revenue (18 × $10 000)		$ 180 000
Cost of goods sold:		
Normal costing (18 × $9000)	$ (162 000)	
Volume variance (18 × $2000)	36 000	(126 000)
Gross margin		54 000
Administrative and selling [$30 000 + (18 × $500)]		(39 000)
Operating income (loss)		$ 15 000

Abel observes that the operating income using normal capacity with the volume variance adjustment is now identical to the operating income when actual volume was used to allocate fixed overhead. Therefore, the financial statements are not affected by the choice of denominator used for the estimated fixed overhead allocation rate.

Summary

1   **Understand the difference between absorption costing and variable costing, and prepare income statements under each method.**

Absorption costing

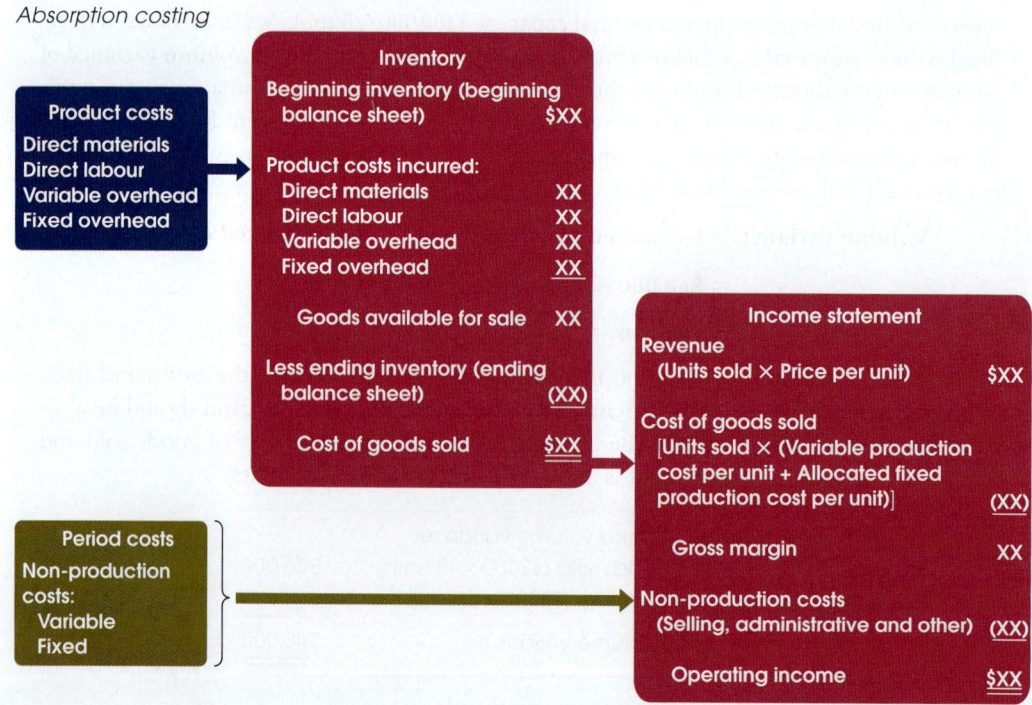

Variable costing

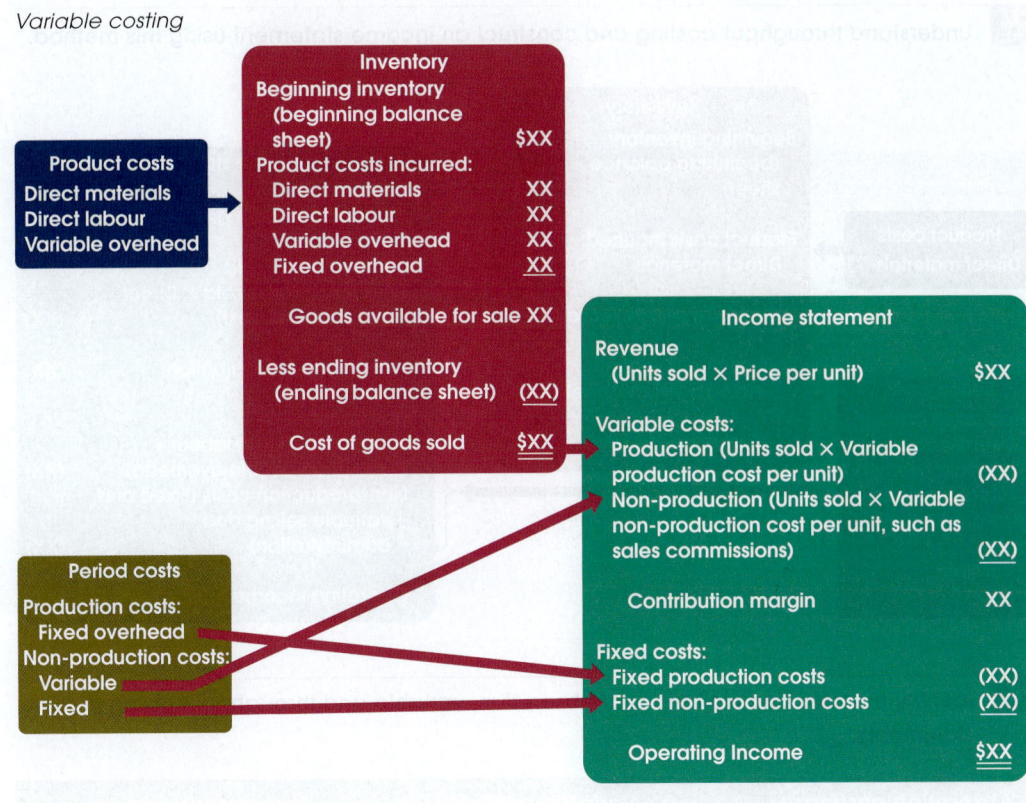

---

2   **Calculate absorption costs using normal costing.**

Normal costing

$$\text{Estimated fixed overhead allocation rate} = \frac{\text{Estimated fixed overhead cost}}{\text{Estimated production volume}}$$

Alternative measures of manufacturing volume for normal costing

- Theoretical capacity
- Practical capacity
- Normal capacity
- Budgeted or expected capacity

Volume variance under normal costing

$$\text{Volume variance} = \text{Expected fixed overhead cost} - \text{Allocated fixed overhead cost}$$

If material: allocate on a pro rata basis among all manufacturing during the period (units in work in process, finished goods and cost of goods sold).

If immaterial: allocate to cost of goods sold.

3 Understand throughput costing and construct an income statement using this method.

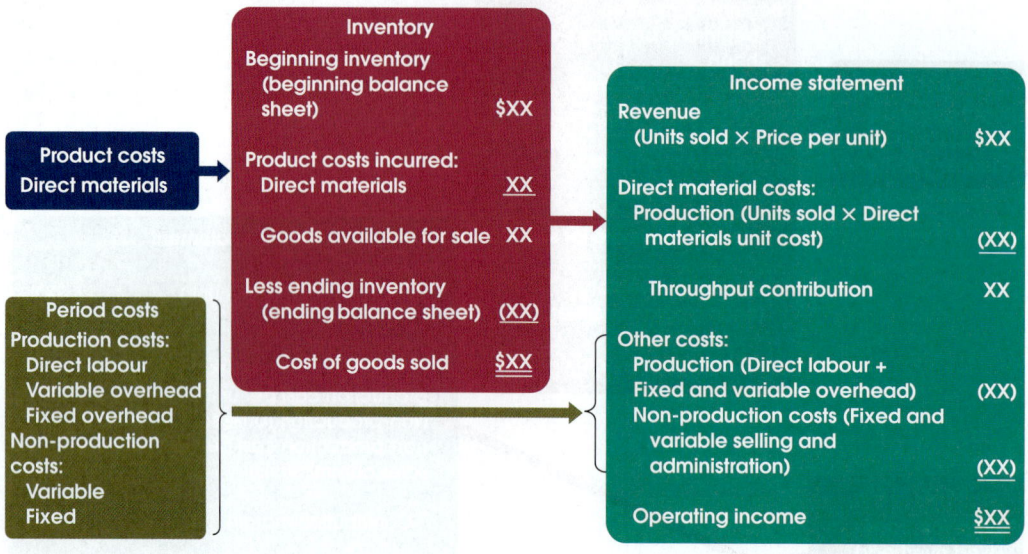

4 Identify the uses and limitations of absorption, variable and throughput costing income statements.

Absorption costing	Variable costing	Throughput costing
GAAP	Not GAAP	Not GAAP
Useful for external reporting purposes	Useful for performance evaluation and internal decision making	Useful for short-term capacity decision making, focuses managers attention on reducing labour and overhead costs because they are considered operating costs instead of product costs (inventory)
Direct material and direct labour are inventory costs	Direct material and direct labour are inventory costs	Only direct materials are inventory costs
Fixed and variable manufacturing overhead allocated to inventory	Fixed manufacturing overhead expensed as a period cost. Variable manufacturing overhead allocated to inventory	Direct labour, fixed and variable overhead, and all other costs expensed as operational expense, a period cost
Administrative and selling costs (both fixed and variable) expensed as period costs	Administrative and selling costs separated into fixed and variable costs and expensed as period costs	Administrative and selling costs expensed as operational expense, a period cost
Inventory costs (including per-unit fixed and variable manufacturing costs) not expensed until the units are sold	Inventory costs (only manufacturing variable costs) not expensed until the units are sold	Inventory costs (only direct materials) not expensed until the units are sold

Self-study problem

Absorption, variable and throughput costing

During its second year of operations, Grilling Machines, an entity that manufactures and sells electric tabletop grills, produced 275 000 units and sold 250 000 units at $60 per unit. The beginning inventory balance was 5000 units. No changes in fixed or variable costs occurred in the second year. The managers expected to sell 220 000 units, the same volume of manufacturing as last year. They set that amount as the normal capacity for allocating fixed overhead costs during the second year. For simplicity, assume that the budgeted fixed manufacturing overhead cost equals the actual cost this period. Also, assume that the entity uses the FIFO cost flow assumption. The following costs were incurred during the year:

Variable cost per unit:	
Direct materials	$15.00
Direct labour	$10.00
Manufacturing overhead	$12.50
Selling and administrative	$2.50
Total fixed costs:	
Manufacturing overhead	$2 200 000
Selling and administrative	$ 1 375 000

REQUIRED

(a) Prepare income statements using absorption costing, variable costing and throughput costing. Provide the details of your calculations in a schedule for each income statement.

(b) Reconcile the difference between operating incomes based on absorption costing and variable costing. Create a schedule to show your work.

(c) Reconcile the difference between operating incomes based on variable costing and throughput costing. Create a schedule to show your work.

(d) Suppose the accountant for Grilling Machines used an actual fixed overhead allocation rate rather than an estimated rate. Using this method, calculate the cost of goods sold and ending inventory under absorption costing. Compare the results to those calculated in part (a).

(e) If the volume variance is not material, how is it closed at the end of the period? Explain the reasoning behind this treatment.

Solution to self-study problem 1

(a) Calculations for the absorption costing income statement.
Before calculating the product cost per unit, it is necessary to calculate the fixed overhead cost allocation and the volume variance adjustment. The entity's policy is to allocate fixed overhead using normal capacity, which was estimated at 220 000 units.

$$\text{Estimated fixed overhead allocation rate} = \$2\,200\,000 \text{ Estimated fixed overhead}$$
$$\div\ 220\,000 \text{ Normal volume of units}$$
$$= \$10 \text{ per unit}$$

At the end of the year, the entity must make an adjustment for its volume variance, which is the difference between total fixed overhead allocated to manufacturing and the original estimate of fixed overhead costs.

Estimated fixed overhead ($10 per unit × 220 000 units)	$2 200 000
Allocated overhead ($10 per unit × 275 000 units)	2 750 000
Volume variance	$ 550 000

The volume variance is considered material because it is greater than 10 per cent of the estimated fixed overhead cost.

$$\$550\,000 \div \$2\,200\,000 = 25\%$$

Material volume variances are adjusted to all units produced. For this problem, 250 000 of the units are in cost of goods sold, and 25 000 units are added to inventory. Because more fixed overhead cost was allocated than estimated, the absorption cost per unit must be reduced by the volume variance.

$$\text{Volume variance per unit produced} = \$550\,000 \div 275\,000 \text{ units}$$

$$= \$2 \text{ per unit}$$

Given the preceding calculations, the absorption product cost per unit is:

Direct materials	$15.00
Direct labour	10.00
Variable overhead	12.50
Fixed overhead allocation rate	10.00
Subtotal before volume variance adjustment	47.50
Volume variance adjustment per unit	(2.00)
Total absorption cost per unit	$45.50

We can now calculate the value of ending inventory: 275 000 units were produced this year and 250 000 were sold, causing inventory to increase by 25 000 units. Beginning inventory was 5000 units, so ending inventory is 30 000 units. Also, recall that the costs in year 1 were the same as the costs in year 2. Because actual volume during year 1 was 220 000 units (rather than 275 000), no volume variance adjustment was needed in year 1. Therefore, beginning inventory was valued at an absorption cost of $47.50 per unit. Under the FIFO cost flow assumption, the beginning inventory was the first units sold and all the units added to inventory are valued at $45.50 per unit.

Units added to inventory (30 000 units × $45.50 per unit)	$1 365 000
Ending inventory	$1 365 000

Because inventory increased during year 2, cost of goods sold under FIFO is calculated taking into consideration that the first units sold were the opening balance of 5000 units and the remaining sales of 245 000 were from the current period's production:

Cost of goods sold	
5 000 units × $47.50 per unit	$ 237 500
245 000 units × $45.50 per unit	11 147 500
	$ 11 385 000

Figure 15.9 shows the three income statements.

ABSORPTION COSTING
Income statement

Revenue ($60 × 250 000)	$15 000 000
Cost of goods sold	(11 385 000)
Gross margin	3 615 000
Selling and administrative	(2 000 000)
Operating income	$ 1 615 000

Reconciliation of product costs

Beginning inventory		$ 237 500
Product costs incurred:		
Direct materials	4 125 000	
Direct labour	2 750 000	
Variable overhead	3 437 500	
Fixed overhead allocated	2 750 000	
Volume variance adjustment	(550 000)	
Goods available for sale		12 750 000
Less ending inventory		(1 365 000)
Cost of goods sold		$ 11 385 000

VARIABLE COSTING
Income statement

Revenue ($60 × 250 000)		$15 000 000
Variable costs:		
Cost of goods sold		(9 375 000)
Selling and administrative		(625 000)
Contribution margin		5 000 000
Fixed costs:		
Fixed manufacturing overhead	(2 200 000)	
Fixed selling and administrative	(1 375 000)	
Operating income		$ 1 425 000

Reconciliation of product costs

Beginning inventory		$ 187 500
Product costs incurred:		
Direct materials	4 125 000	
Direct labour	2 750 000	
Variable overhead	3 437 500	
Goods available for sale		10 500 000
Less ending inventory		(1 125 000)
Cost of goods sold		$ 9 375 000

THROUGHPUT COSTING
Income statement

Revenue ($60 × 250 000)	$15 000 000
Cost of goods sold	(3 750 000)
Throughput contribution	11 250 000
Other costs:	
Manufacturing conversion costs	(8 387 500)
Selling and administrative	(2 000 000)
Operating income	$ 862 500

Reconciliation of product costs

Beginning inventory		$ 75 000
Produce costs incurred:		
Direct materials	4 125 000	
Goods available for sale		4 200 000
Less ending inventory		(450 000)
Cost of goods sold		$ 3 750 000

FIGURE 15.9 ■ Absorption, variable and throughput costing income statements for grilling machines

To prepare the reconciliation of total product costs in figure 15.9, calculate the total amounts for each of the variable manufacturing costs based on actual manufacturing of 275 000 units:

Direct materials (275 000 units produced × $15 per unit)	$ 4 125 000
Direct labour (275 000 units produced × $10 per unit)	2 750 000
Variable overhead (275 000 units produced × $12.50 per unit)	3 437 500
Total variable manufacturing costs	$ 10 312 500

This reconciliation of product costs provides a double-check on the accuracy of the cost of goods sold and inventory calculations.

Fixed and variable selling and administrative costs are combined on the absorption costing income statement:

Fixed selling and administrative	$ 1 375 000
Variable selling and administrative (250 000 units sold × $2.50)	625 000
Total selling and administrative	$ 2 000 000

Calculations for the variable costing income statement

The calculations for the variable costing income statement are similar to those for the absorption costing income statement, except fixed overhead is not allocated as a product cost. Therefore, the variable manufacturing cost per unit used in calculating cost of goods sold and inventory is:

Direct materials	$15.00
Direct labour	10.00
Variable overhead	12.50
Total variable cost per unit	$37.50

Because last year's variable cost per unit is the same as this year's, the units in beginning inventory and the units added to inventory are each valued at $37.50 per unit:

Beginning inventory (5000 units × $37.50 per unit)	$ 187 500
Units added to inventory (25 000 units × $37.50 per unit)	937 500
Ending inventory	$1 125 000

Cost of goods sold is also valued at $37.50 per unit:

Cost of goods sold (250 000 units × $37.50 per unit)	$ 9 375 000

The reconciliation of product costs shown in figure 15.9 provides a double-check on the accuracy of the cost of goods sold and inventory calculations.

When preparing the income statement, variable selling and administrative costs are separated from fixed selling and administrative costs.

Calculations for the throughput costing income statement

The calculations for the throughput costing income statement are similar to those for the variable costing income statement, except that the only product cost is direct materials.

Therefore, the cost per unit used in calculating cost of goods sold and inventory is:

Direct materials	$15

Because last year's direct material cost per unit is the same as this year's direct material cost per unit, the units in beginning inventory and the units added to inventory are each valued at $15 per unit:

Beginning inventory (5000 units × $15 per unit)	$ 75 000
Units added to inventory (25 000 units × $15 per unit)	375 000
Ending inventory	$ 450 000

Cost of goods sold is also valued at $15 per unit:

Cost of goods sold (250 000 units × $15 per unit)	$ 3 750 000

The reconciliation of product costs shown in figure 15.9 provides a double-check on the accuracy of the cost of goods sold and inventory calculations.

All of the manufacturing conversion costs are combined into a single line item on the throughput costing income statement:

Direct labour (275 000 units produced × $10 per unit)	$ 2 750 000
Variable overhead (275 000 units produced × $12.50 per unit)	3 437 500
Fixed overhead	2 200 000
Total conversion costs	$ 8 387 500

The fixed and variable selling and administrative costs are combined as previously calculated for the absorption costing income statement.

(b) Reconciliation of absorption costing and variable costing income:

Variable costing income	$ 1 425 000
Increase in fixed overhead costs in absorption inventory[a]	$ 190 000
Absorption costing income	$ 1 615 000

[a]Units added to inventory × Fixed overhead cost per unit.

[30 000 units × ($10 per unit − $2 per unit)]	$ 240 000
Less 5000 units × $10	(50 000)
Increase in fixed overhead expenses	$ 190 000

Under absorption costing, $200 000 of this year's fixed overhead cost is held as ending inventory. Therefore, absorption costing income is $200 000 higher than variable costing income.

The difference in income also could have been calculated using the difference between costing methods in the change in inventory during the year:

Change in absorption costing inventory:		
Ending inventory	$ 1 365 000	
Beginning inventory	237 500	
Change		$ 1 127 500

Change in variable costing inventory:		
Ending inventory	$ 1 125 000	
Beginning inventory	187 500	
Change		937 500
Difference between methods		$ 190 000

(c) Reconciliation of variable and throughput costing income:

Throughput costing income	$ 862 500
Increase in variable conversion costs in absorption inventory:	
Units added to inventory × Variable conversion cost per unit	
[25 000 units × ($10 + $12.50)]	562 500
Variable costing income	$1 425 000

Under variable costing, the direct labour of $10 per unit and the variable manufacturing costs of $12.50 per unit are held as ending inventory. Therefore, variable costing income is $562 500 higher than throughput costing income.

The difference in income also could have been calculated using the difference between costing methods in the change in inventory during the year:

Change in variable costing inventory:		
Ending inventory	$1 125 000	
Beginning inventory	187 500	
Change		$ 937 500
Change in throughput costing inventory:		
Ending inventory	$ 450 000	
Beginning inventory	75 000	
Change		375 000
Difference between methods		$ 562 500

(d) Using actual fixed overhead costs and actual manufacturing, the fixed overhead allocation rate would have been:

$$\$2\,200\,000 \div 275\,000 \text{ units produced} = \$8 \text{ per unit}$$

This rate is equal to the net amount allocated in part (a) under the normal costing method:

Estimated fixed overhead allocation rate	$ 10
Volume variance adjustment per unit	(2)
Net fixed overhead allocation	$ 8

This calculation demonstrates that it does not matter which volume measure is used to allocate fixed overhead during the year. Under absorption costing, any material volume variance is adjusted to all units produced, so that actual fixed overhead cost is reflected on the financial statements.

(e) When the volume variance is not material, accountants simplify the adjustment by allocating the entire amount to cost of goods sold. This simplification eliminates the need to revalue units in inventory. Although revaluing the inventory was not difficult for this self-study problem, the computations and accounting entries can become cumbersome when an entity has many products. By definition, an immaterial volume variance would not affect the decisions of people who rely on the financial statements. Therefore, it does not matter how the volume variance is adjusted. It is simpler to allocate the entire amount to cost of goods sold.

Questions

15.1 Explain the similarities and differences among absorption, variable and throughput costing.

15.2 Explain how variable costing income statements can be reconciled to absorption costing income statements.

15.3 Explain how income could fall even though the unit sales level rises.

15.4 The volume of manufacturing in a period has an effect on income calculated using absorption costing but has no effect on income calculated using variable costing. Explain.

15.5 The basic issue in variable and absorption costing could be said to be one of timing rather than amount. Explain.

15.6 What is the difference between a cost that is variable and variable costing?

15.7 Explain how the breakeven point would be affected under both absorption and variable costing.

15.8 If inventory physically increases during the period, income under absorption costing will be higher than income using variable costing. Explain.

15.9 Why does GAAP require absorption costing?

15.10 An entity uses variable costing for internal reports. It must convert the variable costing results to absorption costing results for external reports. How can this conversion be accomplished?

15.11 How can the use of absorption costing lead managers to make dysfunctional decisions for the entity?

Exercises

15.12 Absorption and variable income Famous Desk Company manufactures desks for office use. The variable cost of 100 units in beginning inventory is $80 each. The absorption cost is $146.67 per unit. Following is information about this period's manufacturing.

Selling price	$300 per desk
Variable manufacturing cost	$80 per desk
Fixed manufacturing costs	$10 000 per month
Variable selling and administrative	$30 per desk
Fixed selling and administrative	$6 000 per month

REQUIRED

(a) Estimate operating income for a month in which 200 desks are manufactured and 220 are sold if the company uses variable costing.

(b) Estimate operating income for a month in which 200 desks are manufactured and 220 are sold if the entity uses absorption costing and allocates fixed manufacturing costs to inventory using a rate based on normal capacity of 150 desks per month.

15.13 Absorption and variable income; reconcile incomes Rock Crusher Ltd produces two grades of sand (A100 and A300) used in the manufacture of industrial abrasives. The results of operations last year were as follows:

	A100	A300	Total
Manufacturing	4 000 tonnes	6 000 tonnes	10 000 tonnes
Sales	3 000 tonnes	4 000 tonnes	7 000 tonnes
Revenue	$90 000	$150 000	$240 000
Variable manufacturing costs	$20 000	$15 000	$35 000
Variable selling costs	$15 000	$20 000	$35 000

Fixed manufacturing costs were $100 000 and fixed selling and administrative costs were $60 000. The entity held no beginning inventories.

REQUIRED

Prepare a spreadsheet that can be used to answer all of the following questions.
(a) If Rock Crusher uses a variable costing system, what was the operating income?
(b) If Rock Crusher uses absorption costing and allocates actual fixed manufacturing costs to inventory on the basis of actual tonnes produced, what was the operating income?
(c) Reconcile and explain the difference between your answers to parts (a) and (b).

15.14 Absorption and variable inventory and income Plains Irrigation uses absorption costing for its external reports and variable costing for its internal reports. Data concerning inventories appear here:

Valuation basis	September	October	November
Absorption cost	$1346	$2598	$2136
Variable cost	$854	$1647	$1329

REQUIRED

(a) Why is the value of inventory for Plains Irrigation higher when absorption costing is used than when variable costing is used? Is this result always the case? Why?
(b) What is the relationship between absorption costing and variable costing operating income in October? (State which valuation basis will yield the higher operating income and by how much the two operating incomes will differ.)

15.15 Absorption, variable and throughput inventory and income Asian Iron began last year with no inventories. During the year, 10 500 units were produced of which 9400 were sold. Data concerning last year's operations appear here:

Revenue	$ 32 900
Variable direct materials costs	2 300
Variable direct labour costs	3 300
Variable manufacturing overhead	2 800
Variable selling	940
Fixed manufacturing overhead	8 250
Fixed selling and administrative costs	14 560

Variable manufacturing costs reflect the variable cost to produce the number of units manufactured. However, variable selling costs are not incurred until the units are sold, so they reflect the cost for the number of units sold. Asian Iron allocates actual manufacturing overhead costs to inventory based on actual units produced.

REQUIRED

(a) Calculate the value of ending inventory on the balance sheet under the following methods:
- (i) variable costing
- (ii) absorption costing
- (iii) throughput costing.

(b) Calculate operating income under each of the following methods:
- (i) variable costing
- (ii) absorption costing
- (iii) throughput costing.

(c) Estimate the variable costing operating income if 12 110 units were produced and sold in a year.

15.16 Absorption and variable inventory and income; reconcile incomes Wild Bird Feeders produces deluxe bird feeders for distribution to catalogue companies and wild bird stores. The entity uses an absorption costing system for internal reporting purposes but is considering using variable costing. Data regarding Wild Bird's planned and actual operations for 2008 are presented here.

Beginning finished goods inventory in units		30 000
	Planned activity	**Actual activity**
Sales in units	140 000	125 000
Manufacturing in units	140 000	130 000

The planned per-unit cost figures shown in the schedule were based on the manufacturing and sale of 140 000 units in 2008. Wild Bird uses an estimated manufacturing overhead rate for allocating manufacturing overhead to its product. Thus, a combined manufacturing overhead rate of $9 per unit was employed for absorption costing purposes in 2008. Any overapplied or underapplied manufacturing overhead is closed to cost of goods sold at the end of the reporting year.

	Planned costs		Incurred
	Per unit	**Total**	**costs**
Direct materials	$24	$ 3 360 000	$ 3 120 000
Direct labour	18	2 520 000	2 340 000
Variable manufacturing overhead	4	560 000	520 000
Fixed manufacturing overhead	5	700 000	710 000
Variable selling expenses	14	1 960 000	1 750 000
Fixed selling expenses	7	980 000	980 000
Variable administrative expenses	1	140 000	125 000
Fixed administrative expenses	6	840 000	850 000
Total	$79	$11 060 000	$10 395 000

The 2008 beginning finished goods inventory for absorption costing purposes was valued at the 2007 planned unit manufacturing cost, which was the same as the 2008 planned unit manufacturing cost. No work in process inventories were recorded either at the beginning or end of the year. The planned and actual unit selling price was $99 per unit for 2008. You may want to use a spreadsheet to perform calculations.

REQUIRED

(a) What was the value of Wild Bird's actual ending finished goods inventory on the absorption costing basis?

(b) What was the 2008 actual ending finished goods inventory on the variable costing basis?

(c) What were the manufacturing contribution margin and the total contribution margin under variable costing for Wild Bird's actual results for 2008?

(d) Under absorption costing, what were the total fixed costs on the income statement?
  (i) What were the fixed selling and administrative costs?
  (ii) What was the amount of overhead allocated to COGS at standard cost?
  (iii) Do we need to consider sales of units from last period?
  (iv) What was the amount of underapplied or overapplied overhead closed to COGS?
  (v) Sum these amounts for the total fixed costs.

(e) What was the total variable cost expensed in 2008 on the variable costing income statement?

(f) Was absorption costing income higher or lower than variable costing income for 2008? Why?

(g) What is the amount of difference in income using absorption costing versus variable costing? How did it arise?

15.17 Absorption, variable and throughput income; reconcile incomes The following price and operating cost information applies to Happy Bikers Motorcycle Company.

Price	$10 000 per motorcycle
Variable manufacturing costs:	
Raw materials	$2 000 per motorcycle
Direct labour and variable overhead	$1 000 per motorcycle
Fixed manufacturing costs	$40 000 per month
Variable selling and administrative	$250 per motorcycle
Fixed selling and administrative	$40 000 per month

No beginning balance in finished goods is evident because the beginning inventory account on the balance sheet is zero. Average manufacturing is 10 motorcycles per month. Sales are seasonal, so in some months no motorcycles are produced while in other months manufacturing is high.

During the most recent month, the entity produced 18 motorcycles and sold 15.

REQUIRED

(a) Prepare an income statement for the most recent month using the variable costing method.

(b) Prepare an income statement for the most recent month using the absorption costing method and choose a denominator level that represents 'normal' capacity.

(c) Prepare an income statement for the most recent month using the throughput costing method.

(d) Prepare a schedule that reconciles the incomes among the three income statements.

Problems

15.18 Differences in income; choice of absorption and variable costing King Island Lobster Company is a privately held company that buys lobsters from local fishermen and then delivers them to restaurants in several of Australia's larger cities. The owners use variable costing income statements, but one owner's daughter, who just started taking university accounting classes, suggested that absorption income statements meet GAAP and so should be used.

REQUIRED

(a) Explain the difference between absorption and variable income statements.

(b) Provide possible reasons why the company uses variable costing income statements.

(c) Provide possible benefits to the company from using an absorption costing income statement.

(d) What type of statement would you recommend for King Island Lobster Company? Why?

(e) What additional information about King Island Lobster Company would you like to have to improve your recommendation in part (d)?

15.19 Absorption, variable and throughput income; normal capacity; choice of denominator Giant Jets is a French company that produces jet aeroplanes for commercial cargo companies. The selling price per jet is €1 000 000. Currently the company uses actual volumes to allocate fixed manufacturing overhead to units. However, Giant Jets' accountant is considering the use of standard costs to produce the absorption income statements. The company anticipates the following.

Variable costs per jet:			
Direct materials			€200 000
Direct labour			150 000
Variable manufacturing overhead			50 000
Variable selling			100 000
Fixed costs per month:			
Fixed manufacturing overhead			€600 000
Fixed administrative and selling			100 000
Sales and manufacturing quantities:			
	2008	**2009**	**2010**
Manufacturing	10	6	8
Sales	10	4	10

REQUIRED

(a) Prepare income statements using the variable costing method.

(b) Prepare income statements using the throughput costing method.

(c) Prepare income statements using the absorption costing method. Allocate fixed overhead using actual units produced in the denominator.

(d) In your own words, define 'normal capacity'.

(e) Prepare an income statement using the absorption cost method and choose a denominator level that represents normal capacity. Explain your choice for normal capacity.

(f) Prepare a brief summary that reconciles the incomes among the three income statements for each year.

15.20 Absorption, variable and throughput income and inventory; method for manager bonus Fighting Kites produces several different kite kits. Last year, it produced 20 000 kits and sold all but 2000 kits. The kits sell for $30 each. Costs incurred are listed here.

Materials purchased	$50 000
Materials used	40 000
Other variable manufacturing costs	60 000
Fixed manufacturing costs	100 000
Variable selling costs	18 000
Fixed selling and administrative costs	100 000

Beginning inventory last year held 2000 kits. Assume that under variable costing, the value of this inventory would have been $10 000. Assume that under absorption costing, the value of this inventory would have been $15 000.

REQUIRED

(a) If Fighting Kites uses variable costing, what was its operating income? What was the ending balance in finished goods inventory?

(b) If Fighting Kites uses throughput costing, what was its operating income? What was the ending balance in finished goods inventory?

(c) If Fighting Kites uses absorption costing and a denominator level of 25 000, what was its operating income?

(d) If you were asked to make a recommendation for the absorption costing denominator level for next period's operations, what would you suggest? Explain your choice.

(e) If the manager of Fighting Kites is given a bonus based on income, which type of income statement would you recommend to evaluate manager performance? Explain your choice.

15.21 **Absorption and variable income and uses; reconcile incomes** Security Vehicles converts Hummers into luxury, high-security vehicles by adding a computerised alarm and radar system and various luxury components. The finished vehicles are sold for $100 000 each. Variable manufacturing costs (including the cost of the basic Hummer) are about $60 000 per vehicle. Fixed manufacturing costs are $60 000 per month. The fixed costs for administrative and selling expenses are $20 000 per month plus $5000 per vehicle sold.

At the beginning of last year, Security had no inventories of finished vehicles. In January it produced four vehicles and sold three. In February it produced five and sold six.

REQUIRED

(a) What is the operating income for January if Security uses a variable costing system?

(b) What is the operating income for January if Security uses an absorption costing system?

(c) Reconcile the difference between the absorption and variable costing operating incomes in February.

(d) Explain why Security Vehicles might produce both variable and absorption income statements for the same time period.

15.22 **Over/underapplied overhead; units versus machine hours as allocation base** Northcoast Manufacturing Company, a small manufacturer of parts used in appliances, just completed its first year of operations. The company's controller, Vic Trainor, has been reviewing the actual results for the year and is concerned about the allocation of manufacturing overhead. Trainor uses the following information to assess operations.

- Northcoast's equipment consists of several machines with a combined cost of $2 200 000 and no residual value. Each machine has an output of five units of product per hour and a useful life of 20 000 hours.
- Selected actual data of Northcoast's operations for the year just ended are presented here.

Product manufactured	500 000 units
Machine utilisation	130 000 hours
Direct labour usage	35 000 hours
Labour rate	$15 per hour

Total manufacturing overhead	$1 130 000
Cost of goods sold	$1 720 960
Finished goods inventory (at year-end)	$430 240
Work in process inventory (at year-end)	$0

- Total manufacturing overhead is allocated to each unit using an estimated plant-wide rate.
- The budgeted activity for the year included 20 employees, each working 1800 productive hours per year to produce 540 000 units of product. The machines are highly automated, and each employee can operate two to four machines simultaneously. Normal activity is for each employee to operate three machines. Machine operators are paid $15 per hour.
- Budgeted manufacturing overhead costs for the past year for various levels of activity are shown here.

Units of product	360 000	540 000	720 000
Labour hours	30 000	36 000	42 000
Machine hours	72 000	108 000	144 000
Manufacturing overhead costs:			
Plant supervision	$ 70 000	$ 70 000	$ 70 000
Plant rent	40 000	40 000	40 000
Equipment depreciation	288 000	432 000	576 000
Maintenance	42 000	51 000	60 000
Utilities	144 600	216 600	288 600
Indirect material	90 000	135 000	180 000
Other costs	11 200	16 600	22 000
Total	$ 685 800	$ 961 200	$ 1 236 600

You may want to use a spreadsheet to perform calculations.

REQUIRED

(a) Choose the budgeted level of activity (in units) closest to actual activity for the period and determine the dollar amount of total over/underapplied manufacturing overhead. Explain why this amount is material.

(b) Vic Trainor believes that Northcoast Manufacturing Company should be using machine hours to allocate manufacturing overhead. Using the data given, determine the amount of total over/underapplied manufacturing overhead if machine hours had been used as the allocation base.

(c) Explain why machine hours might be a more appropriate allocation base than number of units.

(d) Explain why using units as denominator volume might cause managers to build up inventories under absorption costing in periods when sales were slumping.

15.23 Recommend income format Your brother started a small business, GameZ, that produces a software game he developed. It is his first year in business, and he kept detailed records. However, his business records consist primarily of entries in his chequebook plus information using a simple method of adding and subtracting cash on a spreadsheet.

Your brother has asked your advice about the kind of financial statements that would be helpful to his business. He would like you to prepare information for two different uses. First, he needs a small bank loan to provide cash during the low season in August.

Most of his sales are made in December. He has a steady, low volume of sales for most of the rest of the year. He wants to approach his bank about a line of credit upon which he could draw in August and then pay off in January. In addition, he would like to be able to analyse information from his operations to make decisions about whether to develop a new game, what price to set and how much he could devote to advertising. He also recently hired an assistant to whom he assigned a great deal of responsibility for general operations. He would like to be able to monitor and reward her performance in some way.

REQUIRED

Write a memo to your brother in response to his request. Include the following aspects in your memo.

(a) Outline his possible choices for income statement formats.

(b) List the advantages and disadvantages of each format.

(c) Recommend and explain which type of statement should be used for each of his desired purposes.

15.24 Bonuses and manufacturing decisions; profit variances; income statement format
Palm Producers is expecting sales growth, and so it built nearly identical automated plants in Sandy Beach, Queensland, and in Singapore to produce its new Palm Powerhouse.

Each plant manager is responsible for producing adequate inventories to meet sales orders and for maintaining quality while producing the Palm Powerhouse at the lowest possible cost. Under PP's decentralised organisation, each plant maintains its own accounting records. Quarterly reports are filed with the corporate controller's office and are then reviewed by corporate management. The following reports were filed for the third and fourth quarter by the two plants.

Sandy Beach plant
Income statement for third and fourth quarters
(in thousands of dollars)

	Third quarter	Fourth quarter
Revenue	$97 452	$110 951
Cost of goods sold	77 165	74 613
Selling and administration expenses	12 378	12 632
Interest expense	4 312	4 251
Tax expense	1 259	6 809
Net income	$ 2 338	$ 12 646

Sandy Beach plant
Statement of financial position for third and fourth quarters
(in thousands of dollars)

	Third quarter	Fourth quarter
Assets		
Cash	$ 2 346	$ 322
Inventory	12 872	30 972
Plant (net of depreciation)	152 456	148 635
Total assets	$ 167 674	$179 929

	Third quarter	Fourth quarter
Liabilities and owners' equity (OE)		
Accounts payable	$ 214	$ 1 782
Construction bond payable	140 385	138 426
Owners' equity	27 075	39 721
Total liabilities & OE	$ 167 674	$179 929

Singapore plant
Income statement for third and fourth quarters
(translated to A$, in thousands of dollars)

	Third quarter	Fourth quarter
Revenue	$ 101 832	$ 111 085
Cost of goods sold	82 127	87 990
Selling and administration expenses	10 943	10 453
Interest expense	3 854	3 733
Tax expense	1 718	3 118
Net income	$ 3 190	$ 5 791

Singapore plant
Statement of financial position for third and fourth quarters
(translated to A$, in thousands of dollars)

	Third quarter	Fourth quarter
Assets		
Cash	$ 1 564	$ 3 642
Inventory	11 324	13 832
Plant (net of depreciation)	142 342	138 580
Total assets	$155 230	$ 156 054
Liabilities and owners' equity (OE)		
Accounts payable	$ 347	$ 221
Bond payable	135 762	130 921
Owners' equity	19 121	24 912
Total liabilities & OE	$155 230	$ 156 054

REQUIRED

(a) Suppose each plant manager receives a bonus based on absorption costing operating income that is 5 per cent of operating income. Calculate the bonus for each manager. Explain how this bonus plan might affect the managers' manufacturing decisions.

(b) Examine changes in sales relative to cost of goods sold between the two quarters. What are two possible explanations for Sandy Beach plant's profit increase during the fourth quarter?

(c) Assume that variable costs in this industry are an immaterial part of cost of goods sold. Recast the financial statements using the variable costing approach.

(d) What would you conclude about the relative performances of the two plant managers in the fourth quarter?

(e) Suppose you are the cost accountant for Palm Producers. Write a memo to the CFO recommending the type of income statement that would be best for monitoring divisional performance. Attach to the memo a schedule showing any calculations that might be useful to the CFO. As appropriate, refer to the schedule in the memo.

16

Sustainability management accounting

IN BRIEF

The relationship between management accounting control systems and organisational goals and culture is a key consideration for managers wishing to pursue sustainability management practices in their individual businesses. Sustainability management is a process undertaken by entities striving for a simultaneous improvement of their *economic*, *environmental* and *social* goals. Sustainability management accounting is the tool used by organisations to achieve their sustainability management goals. Sustainability management decision making is optimised when supported by management accounting tools that are aligned with sustainability management strategies.

After studying this chapter, you should be able to:

1 Understand the concepts of sustainability, sustainability management and sustainability management accounting.

2 Explain why it is essential for management accountants to have an understanding of external sustainability reporting requirements.

3 Explain the role that ethical decision making plays in a sustainability management framework.

4 Understand the scope and benefits resulting from sustainability management accounting practices.

5 Demonstrate an understanding of key sustainability management accounting tools. In particular, explain how cost allocation, life cycle costing, capital budgeting and performance measurement are treated under a sustainability lens.

6 Describe the issues faced by managers when trying to implement sustainability change processes within their entities.

Visy Industries

Visy Industries was established in Melbourne in 1948. Owned by the Pratt family, it has grown to become one of the world's largest privately owned packaging and recycling companies. Visy has operations in Australia, New Zealand and the United States, and employs more than 8000 people. In 2005, its total manufacturing revenues exceeded $2.8 billion, with total manufacturing assets exceeding $3 billion. In addition, the Pratt Foundation is one of the largest private sources of philanthropy in Australia, donating more than $10 million a year.

Visy is committed to recycling and other environmentally friendly practices. Its corporate philosophy is 'we make it, we take it . . . and we make it again', and its business mission is 'to make our customers more profitable and more environmentally sustainable'. Visy began operations as the manufacturer of corrugated cardboard boxes almost 60 years ago. In 1979, in an effort to improve environmental sustainability, the entity built its first paper recycling mill to supply its own packaging paper needs. It now boasts a recycling rate of 125 per cent: it is producing 1.1 million tonnes of packaging while recovering and recycling 1.4 million tonnes of used packaging. Now, the majority of its products are recyclable or made from recycled content.

Visy was voted Australia's leading company for environmental performance over four consecutive years by the *Sydney Morning Herald* and *Age* newspapers' annual corporate reputation index, and continues to demonstrate its commitment to sustainability in both private and societal ways. For example, Pratt Water was established to promote and pursue a national vision for water management by focusing on the need for:

- new investment in water saving infrastructure
- the development and deployment of water recycling technologies

- the provision of sustainable long-term benefits to the environment, economy and communities through better water management.

Visy's sustainability philosophy is disseminated throughout its operational activities, which consist of six major operating divisions:

- Visy Recycling — collects, sorts and reprocesses recyclable materials from more than 2.3 million households, 35 000 businesses and about 3000 schools every week.
- Visy Pulp and Paper — seven paper recycling mills produce 715 tonnes of 100 per cent recycled content paper and 250 000 tonnes of unbleached craft paper made from sawmill residues, softwood plantation and wastepaper.
- Visy Board — is Australia's largest manufacturer of corrugated boxes. It also provides a wide range of cost-effective technology, automation and packaging systems.
- Visy Specialties — produces high-impact point-of-sale displays and specialty cartons.
- VisyPak Beverage and VisyPak Food — provides steel cans, paperboard and plastic packaging.
- Visy Industrial Packaging — creates high-quality steel, tinplate and plastic packaging.

Visy also has six service-based activities.

To pursue its vision and its strategic objectives of linking organisational growth to the environment, Visy requires a diverse range of management accounting tools operating at both strategic level and operational level — and along the entire value chain. A major difficulty faced by many entities, such as Visy, is how to identify and link sustainability revenues and related costs to the entities' current and future operations. For example, how are sustainability costs allocated to products *and* how are they communicated throughout the organisation? The steps Visy would need to undertake are first to identify the sustainability opportunities at an organisational as well as societal level. This might lead to initial strategies relating to revenue, cost flow determination and capital budgeting relating to the potential sustainability opportunity. Second, realisation of the identified opportunities would be based on management decisions being made at different stages throughout both organisational and industry value chains. Third, Visy's suite of sustainability management accounting tools should be able to measure and monitor the outcomes of its operations and their success in aligning the economic, environmental and social dimensions with Visy's business strategy.

Source: Information from the Visy website, www.visy.com.au.

Issues from this scene setter to look for in the chapter include:

- Strategies for determining a suitable approach to sustainability management.

- The evolutionary path towards sustainable production and innovations within entities.

- The impact of value chain sustainability activities, and lifecycle analysis and costing, on management accounting control systems.

- The importance of organisational culture on sustainability change processes.

- The strategies that enable organisations such as Visy to successfully manage their economic, social and environmental dimensions in unison.

- The factors required for successful sustainability practices within organisations.

- The impact of legislation and changing societal demands on the scope of sustainability management practices undertaken by entities.

Sustainability and management accounting

As we have outlined throughout this book, cost (or management) accounting constitutes the central tool for internal decision making and primarily focuses on satisfying the information needs of internal management. As you will recall, the generally accepted management accounting practices are *not* regulated by law as they are in financial accounting. Thus, managers will adopt the specific management accounting practices and associated tools that will satisfy their individual organisational goals and culture.

In the last decade there has been a growing awareness of, and concern for, social and environmental welfare issues. Increasingly, entities around the world are being called to account for their social and environmental practices. While many organisations have implemented specific environmental or social management systems for financial, regulatory, ethical or other purposes, the issue for management accountants is how to integrate these systems with the general management of the entity. An emerging strategy for many organisations, like Visy Industries, is to incorporate *sustainability* in their management control practices. For sustainability culture and related practices to develop within entities, *sustainability management* strategies should be aligned with *sustainability management accounting* systems.

Sustainability

In 1983, the United Nations set up the World Commission on Environment and Development (WCED) to promote quality of life for the present as well as future generations. At a broad level, the UN defines *sustainability* as the 'development that meets the need of the present without compromising the ability of future generations to meet their own needs'.[1] The key goals relating to sustainability and sustainable development are to:

- live within our environmental resource limits
- achieve social justice
- foster economic and social progress.

Environmental factors and the impact on global economies is receiving strong political attention around the world. For example, the Stern Review, the most comprehensive review ever carried out on the economics of climate change, estimates that the risks of unabated climate change could be equivalent to 20 per cent of global GDP.[2] Political and societal pressures are being reflected in changing organisational practices. Within global corporate environments, achieving sustainability outcomes is an often complex process that requires substantive change. The notion of sustainability is highly complex and as a worldwide concept it is often open to different interpretations, mainly because of the multiple cultures and interest groups that make up our global societies.

For organisations to encompass the notion of sustainability within their business practices, several key sustainability management factors need to be considered. For example, a change in corporate culture requires critical thinking, reflection and education focusing on long-term organisational learning and widespread knowledge acquisition. Change is more likely to be achieved by the work of multidisciplinary, cross-departmental teams rather than individual champions promoting sustainability. Thus, participation and collaboration from multiple stakeholders along the value chain — from the suppliers to the organisational employees through to the customers — is a key factor for successful sustainability management outcomes.

Sustainability management

The process of implementing sustainability into an organisation is not a well known path. It is not something we can follow from a text book or copy from another organisation. Each place is unique and requires us to do new things, reflect and adjust ...[3]

As this quote suggests, the process of implementing sustainability is unique to every entity. The path taken might depend on the industry in which the organisation operates (for example, mining, industrial, service, government), with outcomes reflected in the entity's underlying mission, the image it wishes to portray to stakeholders and the strategic goals it wants to accomplish.

Sustainability management is the measuring, monitoring and simultaneous control of three important dimensions — the *economic*, *environmental* and *social* dimensions. These dimensions are often in conflict, and the role of sustainability management is to improve all three dimensions in unison — to maximise corporate profits while reducing environmental and social impact.

The process of sustainability management can be considered as a broad entity-wide process that contributes strategically towards the simultaneous improvement of the economic, environmental and social dimensions. Together, the three dimensions present a broad scope for analysing information that is both financial and non-financial in nature. Most importantly, sustainability management should encompass both private as well as societal impacts.[4] The **private impacts** are those that are internal or have a direct impact on the organisational value chain. **Societal impacts** are often considered 'externalities', or those costs and benefits that are not generally accounted for in an entity's conventional accounting system. For example, a negative externality might be the pollution that is emitted from dirty production process that affects the health of surrounding residents. An example of a positive externality is an improvement in the health and productivity of people in a locality or region because of investment by businesses.

For most organisations, sustainability management is a continuous cycle as highlighted in figure 16.1. The cycle commences with the identification of sustainability opportunities, followed by the process of realising the sustainability opportunities, which are measured and monitored as part of an entity's management control system. This cycle allows for management to reflect on the actions taken and to develop and direct future sustainability practices. Sustainability opportunities are continuously enabled through technological advances, knowledge acquisition and changes to societal expectations.

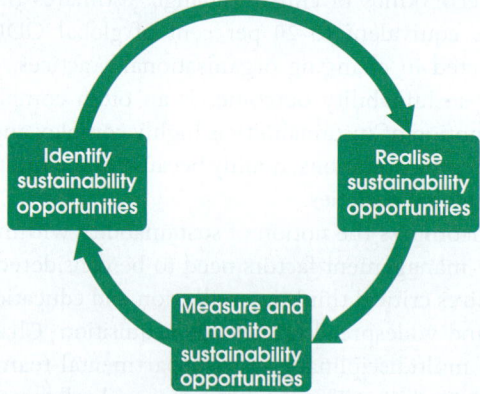

FIGURE 16.1 ■ Sustainability management cycle

Sustainability opportunities can focus on minimising costs by improving current use of resources, or they might present as innovative ways of bringing fresh revenue into the entity. Sometimes, the requirement for sustainability can take a contingency perspective, where sustainability management opportunities emerge through the requirement to comply with tightening legislative requirements and other external factors such as political and societal pressure. Generally, sustainability opportunities arise in situations where organisations consider, or are required to consider, the impact that their current operations might have on environmental and social performance. A crucial aspect of sustainability management is that the economic, environmental and social dimensions are continually managed in unison.

Comprehensive example 1 examines a carbon trading system to combat Australia's greenhouse gas emissions and illustrates sustainability opportunities that will potentially influence the direction of Australia's future energy production and utilisation by organisations. Given that the global market for carbon trading is set to be one of the largest global futures trading schemes, the requirement for carbon trading accounting by organisations will become an important aspect of management accounting control systems.

When you read the example, consider the opportunities that might arise for Australian industries if carbon trading is introduced at a national or international level. Carbon credits represent a new class of asset. Industries that are heavy emitters of carbon dioxide will be faced with potential financial rewards or liabilities, so carbon trading has the potential to motivate educational, behavioural and cultural responses within organisations and individuals. The amount and type of energy consumed will become a larger focus for entities. For example, alternative renewable energy resources such as that provided by solar power or wind farms provide additional opportunities for organisations to reduce greenhouse gas emissions and enhance profits through carbon credits. A 2007 report released by the Ernst & Young Renewable Energy Group anticipated that global investment in renewable energy could reach US$750 billion within a decade.[5]

Comprehensive example 1

Greenhouse gas emissions and carbon trading

Greenhouse gas emissions are part of a naturally occurring cycle called the 'greenhouse effect', where radiation is trapped within the earth's atmosphere to keep the planet warm enough for habitation. Greenhouse gases consist of water vapour, carbon dioxide, methane, nitrous oxide and chlorofluorocarbons (CFCs). Excess greenhouse gas emissions are created by human activities such as burning fossil fuels (coal, petroleum and natural gas) to provide energy for industrial processes, transportation, agriculture, heating, lighting and so on; clearing land and burning forests; farming and intensive agriculture practices; decomposing waste in landfill rubbish tips; and industrial atmospheric pollutants. This human action has increased atmospheric carbon dioxide levels by 30 per cent, thereby trapping radiation and contributing to a changing climate (or global warming). The concentration of carbon dioxide is rising at a faster rate than can be absorbed by the plants, soils and oceans of the world, causing an increase in the frequency of extreme weather events such as floods, droughts and cyclones; rises in sea levels; changing rainfall patterns; and decreasing sea ice and melting glaciers.

Australia's human-induced emissions of greenhouse gases are among the highest per capita in the world. Australian emissions — around 27 tonnes per person per year — are comparable to those of North America and New Zealand, but higher than those of Europe. Under the Kyoto Protocol, developed countries as a whole are required to reduce their greenhouse gas emissions by at least 5 per cent by 2008–12.[6] Australia's expected commitment to the Kyoto Protocol is to limit the growth of its greenhouse gas emissions in the commitment period (2008–12) to 8 per cent above 1990 levels; that is, the level of emissions should be no more than 8 per cent higher than the levels in the 1990. Australia is allowed this increase because many of the country's exports are greenhouse gas intensive (for example, the supply of aluminium, steel and agricultural products). In addition, the opportunity to switch to forms of energy that emit lower greenhouse gases is somewhat limited. Other factors such as population growth (with a concomitant growth in energy demand) and changing patterns of land use have also contributed towards the target determination. Given these factors, Australia's target is equivalent to targets faced by other developed nations, and equates to a reduction in emissions of about 30 per cent per capita.

More recently, carbon trading systems have developed around the world to combat global warming. It is anticipated that the varying global emissions trading systems will be linked using a pool of credits created under the Kyoto Protocol, creating a carbon credit price.[7] In 2005, the European Union (EU) set up the largest carbon trading system; it is based on EUAs (European emissions allowances). The number of EUAs created by each 25 EU member state equates to that state's Kyoto Protocol commitment. That is, one EUA represents the right to emit one tonne of carbon dioxide equivalent. The EU entities that are the largest emitters are imposed with annual carbon dioxide emission targets based on their national EUA. (Generally, the largest emitters are power utilities, oil refineries, building products manufacturers and other heavy industry entities such as iron and steel producers, the pulp and paper industry, and producers of cement, glass, lime, brick and ceramics.) If these entities emit more than their allowance, they must pay a fine of €40 per tonne for each tonne over the agreed target, and offset their emissions by buying EUAs on the open market. The key sustainability factor to the carbon trading scheme is that entities can sell their surplus EUAs if they emit less greenhouse gases. This creates an enormous incentive for organisations to lower their emissions output.

The first phase of the global carbon trading market relates to the 2005–07 period. The second phase, which is due to coincide with the Kyoto Protocol's first commitment period (2008–12), requires entities to pay a €100 per tonne fine as well as purchase an emissions allowance if they exceed their emissions targets. Currently, EUAs are commonly traded as forward contracts (that is, EUAs for delivery at a future date). In 2005, the trading volume reached €5.5 billion. Carbon trading has the potential to become one of the world's largest commodities markets. During the second phase, more installations will be added to the emissions trading scheme, which may be extended to include airlines and car manufacturers. It is anticipated that there will be insufficient emission allowances to meet demand (Borod & Tan 2006). The market currently operates through brokers, and EUAs are electronically traded on a daily basis as carbon financial instruments (CFIs) on the European Climate Exchange (ECX).

There is a direct link between the cost of energy and the price of the EUA. For example, increased demand for power in the EU leads to greater demand for EUAs needed to offset the higher emissions from the fossil fuels burned to increase power supply. As power generated from burning gas produces half the greenhouse gas emissions from burning coal, a strategy available to organisations is to switch/convert their operations from coal to gas. Thus, the price spread between coal and gas is closely monitored.

If Australia joins the European Union trading system, a financial incentive for reduced carbon dioxide emissions is created for high-energy emitters. While Australia has not ratified the Kyoto Protocol, under a plan proposed in 2006 by Australia's states and territories, electricity entities would have to hold tradeable permits to emit greenhouse gases starting in 2010. The government would spend $60 million dollars on 42 clean energy projects as part of the Asia–Pacific climate partnership, as well as considering using nuclear power to further reduce greenhouse emissions.

Sources: Information from 'Australia studies a carbon-trading system to cut emissions', Bloomberg News, 7 February 2007, www.greenhouse.crc.org.au; Borod, RS & Tan, M 2006, 'Carbon: is it just hot or is it a new asset class', *International Securitization & Finance Report,* 15 February; Cooperative Research Centre for Greenhouse Accounting, supported by the Australian National University; 'How are EU Emissions bought and sold?' Carbon News and Info, 01/11/06, www.carbonpositive.net; *Strategic Plan for the National Carbon Accounting System for Land Based Sources and Sinks 1999–2001,* Australian Government Department of the Environment and Water Resources, Australian Greenhouse Office, www.greenhouse.crc.org.au.

Sustainability accounting

The environmental or 'sustainability accounting package' includes financial accounting, auditing or assurance services as well as the application of management accounting techniques that suit a sustainability management framework. Sustainability management will produce the most benefits when it becomes an integrated practice with the tools of sustainability accounting. The sustainability accounting package should be viewed in unison and integrated with other social and environmental guidelines provided by such organisations as the United Nations and the International Organization of Standardization.[8]

For financial accountants, the focus is on reporting environmental liability costs to external parties such as shareholders and financial institutions. Sustainability audits and assurance services are designed to improve the quality and context of information provided, and generally to monitor and verify corporate disclosures. In some countries, audited environmental or sustainable reporting is a mandatory process. In Australia, however, these services are generally voluntary and unregulated — but are increasingly being used by organisations to promote their image and reporting credibility with their stakeholders.[9] The information required for external financial reporting purposes is far narrower than that required for internal management accounting purposes. As highlighted in figure 16.2 (overleaf), there is a vast array of information that flows internally, but it is condensed to fit external regulatory requirements or management disclosure choices.

For management accountants, the focus is on internal reporting for sustainability management purposes. Sustainability management accounting uses techniques similar to the conventional and contemporary management accounting techniques covered in the earlier chapters of this text, but does so through a sustainability lens. As highlighted in figure 16.2, sustainability management accounting is the management accounting arm of the wider sustainability or environmental accounting package.[10] **Sustainability management accounting** is the tool that is used to attain the organisation's (or specific business unit's) sustainability goals. It simultaneously integrates the economic, environmental and social performance of an entity with strategic management.

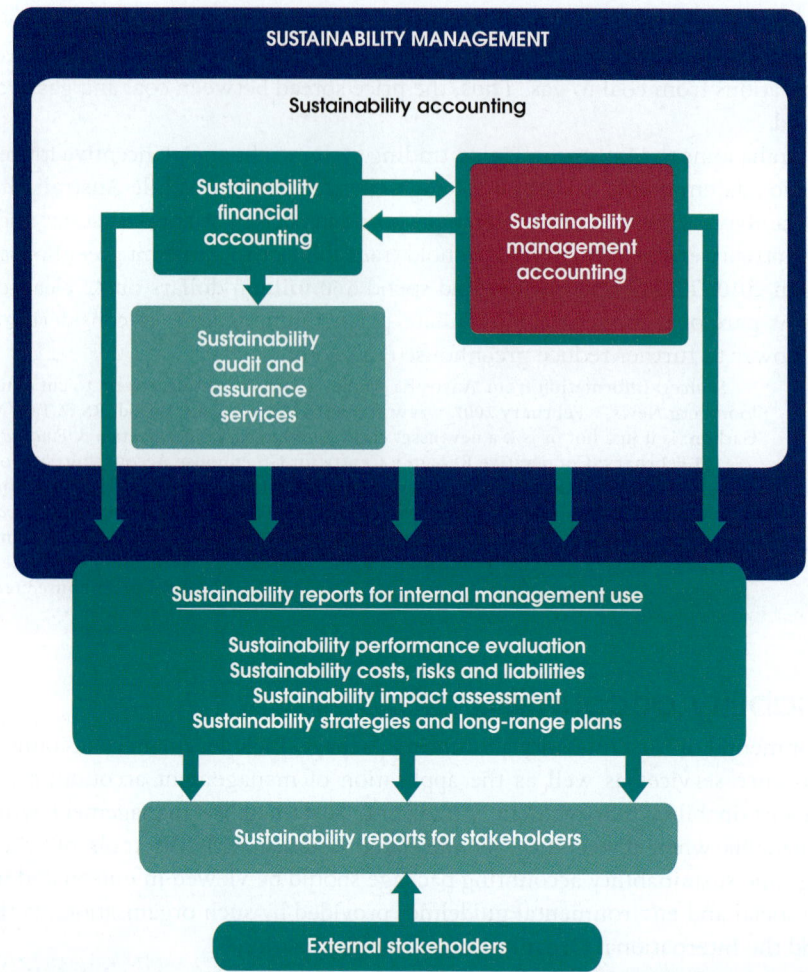

FIGURE 16.2 ■ The context of sustainability accounting as part of sustainability management

Source: Adapted from Pohjola, T 2005, 'Application of an environmental modelling system', in PM Rikhardsson et al. (eds), *Implementing management accounting,* pp. 169–92.

Ideally, management accountants working in environments that encourage sustainability accounting should have a thorough understanding of the drivers (reputation, regulation, revenue enhancement, cost control etc.) behind a sustainability culture as well as the relationship between external reporting and internal management practices. It is desirable that management accountants should be able to apply internal sustainability management accounting control practices to the information being disclosed in external reports and likewise match the information being disclosed externally to internal management accounting control systems. The sustainability management accountant's role is to provide information for both sustainability decision making and financial sustainability reporting. Some recent developments in sustainability reporting are highlighted in the next section.

Sustainability accounting and external reporting

The media is placing greater emphasis on a number of issues relating to greenhouse gas emissions, including water consumption and wastage by organisations and clean versus dirty energy production using resources such as coal, uranium, water, wind and solar power. Supermarkets promote recyclable green bags for groceries as an alternative to environmentally hazardous plastic bags. Governments are promoting energy-saving products by offering rebates and concessions. Sustainability management is an emerging and growing trend for many organisations, and even television programs (such as Carbon cops) are promoting 'green-living' for Australians.

Particular products are sought after by consumers because they have an environmentally friendly image and/or are supplied by an entity that is recognised for its sustainability and philanthropic efforts (for example, Visy products). Organisations such as BHP Billiton, National Australia Bank and Santos are looking to promote their image through corporate disclosures and by investment in sustainability management practices within their organisations.[11] Increasingly, companies are faced with significant economic considerations that might relate to their current and future sustainability management practices. Legislative requirements for corporate reports and disclosures relating to their social and environmental practices are increasing. In general, there is growing societal pressure for sustainability management practices to be enacted upon by companies.

Corporate disclosures and sustainability reporting in Australia is generally voluntary. However, in countries such as France, Germany and Norway, legislation is driving the increase in social and environmental reporting.[12] Table 16.1 provides an overview of the factors that account for the increasing number of entities reporting their corporate social performance.

TABLE 16.1 ■ Factors to explain increased corporate social reporting

Factors	%
Economic considerations	74
Ethical considerations	53
Innovation and learning	53
Employee motivation	47
Risk management or risk reduction	47
Access to capital or increased shareholder value	39
Reputation or brand	27
Market position (market share) improvement	27
Strengthened supplier relationships	21
Cost savings	9
Improved relationships with government authorities	9
Other	11

Source: Chua, WF 2006, 'Extended performance reporting: a review of empirical studies', Institute of Chartered Accountants in Australia, 2006, p. 10.

Until recently, research in this area has tended to be the domain of financial accounting researchers. However, it is now acknowledged that there is a growing need for research on how management accounting tools may assist in the translation of entities' sustainability disclosures to their internal management practices.[13] Thus, the conversion of external reports to internal sustainability management practices and control systems (and vice versa) is a developing domain for future management accountants and management accounting researchers.

Recent initiatives relating to sustainability reporting

Companies are increasingly using the balanced scorecard and triple bottom line reports (financial, social, environmental) as accounting tools to present their disclosures externally.[14] Ethical investors are increasing in numbers and also demanding greater information about the entity's internal sustainability performance. Potential investors are often sceptical about the extent to which organisations might legitimise their activities with sustainability disclosures, suspecting them of using disclosure merely as a form of 'impression management'.[15] There is a view among certain ethical investors that the voluntary nature of disclosure can increase the potential for reporting bias. This scepticism is compounded by non-uniform information that makes it difficult for stakeholders to compare businesses. To alleviate stakeholder scepticism, initiatives are emerging to improve the reliability of reports. Such initiatives also have an impact on the internal dynamics of management control systems and organisational teams and structures. The most widely reported initiatives have been:

1. Australian Securities Exchange (ASX) Principles of Good Corporate Governance and Best Practice Recommendations, which provide a practical guide for companies listed on the ASX.
2. Increased reporting of sustainability practices by directors in annual reports and other special reports that promote the social and environmental role their entities undertake.
3. Company constitutions that provide for corporate social responsibility.
4. The Global Reporting Initiative (GRI), which is a globally accepted reporting framework that entities may follow.

ASX Principles of Good Corporate Governance and Best Practice Recommendations

The ASX Principles of Good Corporate Governance and Best Practice Recommendations were the result of the formation of the ASX Corporate Governance Council in 2002. Its overriding mission was to:

> develop and deliver an industry-wide, supportable and supported framework for corporate governance which could provide a practical guide for listed companies, their investors, the wider market and the Australian community.[16]

Companies must disclose in their annual reports the extent to which they follow the ASX best practice recommendations. If they do not elect to follow any of the recommendations, they must explain their decision. Figure 16.3 presents the 10 principles provided as guidelines for listed entities to follow. The principles directly and indirectly affect sustainability management practices within organisations through sustainability risk identification, performance measurement and reward systems.

Principle 10 relates directly to social accountability by corporations. It recommends that companies demonstrate their responsibility to both the community and to the individual:

> Aside from the need to effectively manage risk and support compliance with the company's legal obligations, there is the broader issue of enhancement of corporate reputation. In this context, consultation with the governments and communities in whose territory business is conducted is important.

> Public or social accountability by corporations is generally based on 'notions of legitimacy, fairness and ethics. The board has a responsibility to set the tone and standards of the company and to oversee adherence to these' (recommendation 10.1, p. 59).

This sets the trend for increased reporting of sustainability practices by Australian companies. As well as using their annual reports to disclose how well they have met these 10 principles,

A company should:
1. **Lay solid foundations for management and oversight** Recognise and publish the respective roles and responsibilities of board and management.
2. **Structure the board to add value** Have a board of an effective composition, size and commitment to adequately discharge its responsibilities and duties.
3. **Promote ethical and responsible decision-making** Actively promote ethical and responsible decision-making.
4. **Safeguard integrity in financial reporting** Have a structure to independently verify and safeguard the integrity of the company's financial reporting.
5. **Make timely and balanced disclosure** Promote timely and balanced disclosures of all material matters concerning the company.
6. **Respect the rights of shareholders** Respect the rights of shareholders and facilitate the effective exercise of those rights.
7. **Recognise and manage risk** Establish a sound system of risk oversight and management and internal control.
8. **Encourage enhanced performance** Fairly review and actively encourage enhanced board and management effectiveness.
9. **Remunerate fairly and responsibly** Ensure that the level and composition of remuneration is sufficient and reasonable and that its relationship to corporate and individual performance is defined.
10. **Recognise the legitimate interests of stakeholders** Recognise legal and other obligations to all legitimate stakeholders.

FIGURE 16.3 ■ The ASX 10 essential corporate governance principles

Source: ASX Corporate Governance Council 2003, *Principles of good corporate governance and best practice recommendations.*

companies are also preparing many special sustainability reports. Such reports typically promote the organisation's general sustainability practices or its other specific environmental or social practices considered to be in the interests of their stakeholders. The reports and companies are analysed closely by ethical investment groups to develop sustainability measures for benchmarking purposes.

Increased provision for corporate sustainability reporting by companies

Due to the increasing evaluation of an organisation's sustainability activities by potential investors and other stakeholders, a market for benchmarking sustainability is developing. For example, the Global 100 Most Sustainable Corporations in the World project analyses the sustainability practices of around 1800 companies to derive the top Global 100 publicly listed entities. At the World Economic Forum in January 2007, Australian companies listed in the Global 100 for their intangible value assessment included Westpac, Investa and IAG (Insurance Australia Group).[17] In Australia, the Australian SAM Sustainability Index (AuSSI) is used to evaluate the sustainability performance of companies listed on the ASX; index values are published daily in *The Australian*.[18] The Dow Jones Sustainability Index (DJSI), in partnership with the Sustainable Asset Management (SAM) Group, provides a framework for evaluating entities on their corporate economic, environmental and social performance. The SAM group reviews more than 1200 global companies annually, focusing on policies and practices relating to corporate governance, risk management, branding, climate change, labour practices and supply chain standards. As a result of the reviews, 250 companies worldwide are listed on the DJSI — 12 of them are Australian listed companies.

Eighteen companies were identified as DJSI global sustainability 'supersector leaders' in 2006 (see table 16.2) Among them are Australian companies Westpac (banking) and Investa Property Group (financial services). Westpac uses its DJSI result as a promotional vehicle. The banking corporation claims that its image has been enhanced by the sustainability practices it has adopted, and by being designated (for five consecutive years) as the world's most sustainable bank by the Global 100 and the DJSI.[19]

TABLE 16.2 ■ DJSI World — supersector leaders (2006–07)

Name	Market sector	Country
BMW	Automobiles & parts	Germany
Westpac Banking Corp.	Banks	Australia
Norsk Hydro	Basic resources	Norway
DSM NV	Chemicals	Netherlands
Holcim	Construction & materials	Switzerland
Sodexho Alliance SA	Travel & leisure	France
Statoil	Oil & gas	Norway
Investa Property Group	Financial services	Australia
Unilever	Food & beverage	Netherlands
Novartis	Healthcare	Switzerland
3M Company	Industrial goods & services	USA
Allianz	Insurance	Germany
ITV Plc	Media	UK
Procter & Gamble Co.	Personal & household goods	USA
Kesko	Retail	Finland
Intel Corp.	Technology	USA
BT Group Plc	Telecommunications	UK
Veolia Environment	Utilities	France

Source: Dow Jones Sustainability Indexes, Supersector leaders 2006–07, www.sustainability-indexes.com.

In order to remain on the Global 100 and DJSI (or any other sustainability benchmarking list), a company must continually meet the stringent social and environmental requirements of that list. This requires sustainability management to become an integral part of the entity's culture. It also requires that these efforts be captured by sustainability management accounting tools, particularly in strategic and operational performance evaluation. For example,

Investa argues that: 'sustainability means adopting business strategies and practices that meet the needs of the Group and its stakeholders today while protecting the human and natural resources that will be needed into the future'.[20] Reporting frameworks, such as the GRI framework, can help align the benchmarked guidelines set by the DJSI or Global 100 with an entity's internal management control systems.

GRI and sustainability reporting framework

The Global Reporting Initiative (GRI) framework is the global sustainability reporting framework most commonly used by reporting entities around the world. The GRI vision is that 'reporting on economic, environmental and social performance will become as routine and comparable as financial reporting'.21 Many organisations around the world have become GRI members and follow its sustainability reporting guidelines. The latest version of performance indicators (released in October 2006) comprises 49 core indicators, provided in figure 16.4. In Australia, about 30 companies are organisational stakeholders of the GRI: ANZ, NAB, Westpac, Lend Lease and BHP Billiton among others. Comprehensive example 2 explains the reason an Australian mining company became a GRI organisational stakeholder.

Comprehensive example 2

GRI and BHP Billiton

Australia's largest mining company, BHP Billiton, gave the following reason for deciding to become an organisational stakeholder of the GRI:

> BHP Billiton is the world's largest diversified resources company. The long-term, stable nature of our business affords a number of advantages. Within the sustainability arena, this stability translates into a capacity to plan for the longer term. Central to our business, as our Charter states, is our 'overriding commitment to health, safety, environmental responsibility and sustainable development.' Supporting this, among other things, our Health, Safety, Environment and Community Policy recognises that to be successful we need to 'build relationships based on honesty, openness, mutual trust and involvement.' It is this commitment, which is key to why we fully endorse the intent of the GRI. We chose to become an Organisational Stakeholder of the GRI as we strongly support the mission of the GRI to develop globally accepted sustainability reporting guidelines through global multi-stakeholder processes. We recognise, that sustainability reporting is an important management tool to facilitate the integration of sustainable development concepts within traditional business thinking. By providing a common basis from which sustainability reports can be prepared, utilisation of the GRI enhances the credibility, consistency, and comparability of our reporting. Thus, through our commitment to GRI, we are able to enhance the transparency of our organisation, contribute to improved stakeholder relationships and thereby create business value. A further demonstration of our commitment to the GRI has been our reporting 'in accordance' with the GRI 2002 Sustainability Reporting Guidelines since 2002. The full content of our reports can be viewed at www.bhpbilliton.com.

> *Source:* BHP Billiton 2004, 'Reason for joining as an OS', Global Reporting Initiative, May, www.globalreporting.org.

FIGURE 16.4 ■ GRI core indicators

Global Reporting Initiative™ (GRI) indicators
Economic

Economic performance

EC1	Economic value generated and distributed, including revenues, operating costs, employee compensation, donations and other community investments, retained earnings, and payment to captial providers and governments. (Core)
EC2	Financial implications and other risks and opportunities for the organization's activities due to climate change. (Core)
EC3	Coverage of the organization's defined benefit plan obligations. (Core)
EC4	Significant financial assistance received from government. (Core)

Market presence

EC6	Policy, practices, and proportion of spending on locally-based suppliers at significant locations of operation. (Core)
EC7	Procedures for local hiring and proportion of senior management hired from the local community at significant locations of operation. (Core)

Indirect economic impacts

EC8	Development and impact of infrastructure investments and services provided primarily for public benefit through commercial, in-kind, or pro bono engagement. (Core)

Environmental

Materials

EN1	Materials used by weights or volume. (Core)
EN2	Percentage of materials used that are recycled input materials. (Core)

Energy

EN3	Direct energy consumption by primary energy source. (Core)
EN4	Indirect energy consumption by primary source. (Core)

Water

EN8	Total water withdrawal by source. (Core)

Biodiversity

EN11	Location and size of land owned, leased, managed in, or adjacent to, protected areas and areas of high biodiversity value outside protected areas. (Core)
EN12	Description of significant impacts of activities, products, and services on biodiversity in protected areas and areas of high biodiversity value outside protected areas. (Core)

Emissions, effluents, and waste

EN16	Total direct and indirect greenhouse gas emissions by weight. (Core)
EN17	Other relevant indirect greenhouse gas emissions by weight. (Core)
EN19	Emissions of ozone-depleting substances by weight. (Core)
EN20	NO_x, SO_x, and other significant air emissions by type and weight. (Core)
EN21	Total water discharge by quality and destination. (Core)

(continued)

FIGURE 16.4 (*continued*)

Global Reporting Initiative™ (GRI) indicators

EN22	Total weight of waste by type and disposal method. (Core)
EN23	Total number and volume of significant spills. (Core)

Products and services

EN26	Initiatives to mitigate environmental impacts of products and services, and extent of impact mitigation. (Core)
EN27	Percentage of products sold and their packaging materials that are reclaimed by category. (Core)

Compliance

EN28	Monetary value of significant fines and total number of non-monetary sanctions for non-compliance with environmental laws and regulations. (Core)

Social performance: labor practices & decent work

Employment

LA1	Total workforce by employment type, employment contract, and region. (Core)
LA2	Total number and rate of employee turnover by age group, gender, and region. (Core)

Labor/management relations

LA4	Percentage of employees covered by collective bargaining agreements. (Core)
LA5	Minimum notice period(s) regarding significant operational changes, including whether it is specified in collective agreements. (Core)

Occupational health and safety

LA7	Rates of injury, occupational diseases, lost days, and absenteeism, and number of work-related fatalities by region. (Core)
LA8	Education, training, counseling, prevention, and risk-control programs in place to assist workforce members, their families, or community members regarding serious diseases. (Core)

Training and education

LA10	Average hours of training per year per employee by employee category. (Core)

Diversity and equal opportunity

LA13	Composition of governance bodies and breakdown of employees per category according to gender, age group, minority group membership, and other indicators of diversity. (Core)
LA14	Ratio of basic salary of men to women by employee category. (Core)

Social performance: human rights

Investment and procurement practices

HR1	Percentage and total number of significant investment agreements that include human rights clauses or that have undergone human rights screening. (Core)

(*continued*)

FIGURE 16.4 (*continued*)

Global Reporting Initiative™ (GRI) indicators

HR2	Percentage of significant suppliers and contractors that have undergone screening on human rights and actions taken. (Core)

Non-discrimination

HR4	Total number of incidents of discrimination and actions taken. (Core)

Freedom of association and collective bargaining

HR5	Operations identified in which the right to exercise freedom of association and collective bargaining may be at significant risk, and actions taken to support these rights. (Core)

Child labor

HR6	Operations identified as having significant risk for incidents of child labor, and measures taken to contribute to the elimination of child labor. (Core)

Forced and compulsory labor

HR7	Operations identified as having significant risk for incidents of forced or compulsory labor. and measures to contribute to the elimination of forced or compulsory labor. (Core)

Social performance: society

Community

SO1	Nature, scope, and effectiveness of any programs and practices that assess and manage the impacts of operations on communities, including entering, operating, and exiting. (Core)

Corruption

SO2	Percentage and total number of business units analyzed for risks related to corruption. (Core)
SO3	Percentage of employees trained in organization's anti-corruption policies and procedures. (Core)
SO4	Actions taken in response to incidents of corruption. (Core)

Public policy

SO5	Public policy positions and participation on public policy development and lobbying. (Core)

compliance

SO8	Monetary value of significant fines and total number of non-monetary sanctions for non-compliance with laws and regulations. (Core)

Social performance: product responsibility

Customer health and safety

PR1	Life cycle stages in which health and safety impacts of products and services are assessed for improvement, and percentage of significant products and services categories subject to such procedures. (Core)

(*continued*)

FIGURE 16.4 (*continued*)

Global Reporting Initiative™ (GRI) indicators
Products and service labeling
PR3   Type of product and service information required by procedures, and percentage of significant products and services subject to such information requirements. (Core)
Marketing communications
PR6   Programs for adherence to laws, standards, and voluntary codes related to marketing communications, including advertising, promotion, and sponsorship. (Core)
Compliance
PR9   Monetary value of significant fines for non-compliance with laws and regulations concerning the provision and use of products and services. (Core)

Source: Global Reporting Initiative 2006, Core indicators, www.globalreporting.org.

A recent review of sustainability disclosures of the top 100 ASX listed companies revealed that the majority did not report according to the GRI indicators.[22] In this study, conducted by the University of Sydney for CPA Australia, one point was awarded to a company for each of the 40 GRI indicators that it reported against. The points total for a company became its Sustainability Disclosure Index, or SDI. BHP Billiton reported against the widest range of indicators, achieving an SDI of 31. However, the median SDI was 5 and the average SDI was 6, with one company recording an SDI of zero. This research indicates that there is still scope for improved sustainability reporting by many Australian entities.

Most importantly for the management accountant, these indicators are not only useful for corporate disclosures but they also provide a realistic sustainability platform on which to base the development of an internal management control system. The indicators may be useful for senior or operational manager evaluation when part of operational budgeting activities, performance evaluation and/or reward structures.

Ethical considerations

As indicated earlier, ethical considerations are one of the key reasons for the increased social and environmental reporting by organisations. For example, the KPMG research found that ethical considerations represented 53 per cent of the reasons for increased corporate social reporting (see table 16.1, page 655). Ethical considerations are built into the ASX Principles of Good Corporate Governance, particularly principle 10 (see figure 16.3, page 657). Furthermore, ethical considerations were overriding many of the core GRI indicators (see figure 16.4, page 660). Ethics plays an important role in sustainability management because of its strategic relevance to overall organisational performance.

Ethical behaviour is the responsibility of every employee within an entity. The unethical behaviour of a few accountants and managers can greatly affect investor beliefs and the value of the sharemarket. When investors lose faith in information produced by organisations, they are less likely to invest in those organisations and market downturns occur. These events happen because accountants and managers fail to use ethical decision making. The steps in ethical decision making are presented in figure 16.5 (overleaf).

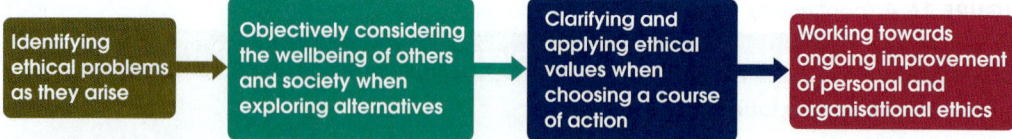

| Identifying ethical problems as they arise | → | Objectively considering the wellbeing of others and society when exploring alternatives | → | Clarifying and applying ethical values when choosing a course of action | → | Working towards ongoing improvement of personal and organisational ethics |

FIGURE 16.5 ■ Steps in ethical decision making

When following these steps in developing management control systems — particularly performance evaluation systems — the constructs relating to ethics and ethical decision making are often difficult for managers to classify, quantify, measure and monitor. One of the main reasons is the social and cultural diversity of individual entities.[23] The ASX 10 essential corporate governance principles and the GRI indicators provide broad, generally accepted guidelines that can be accommodated by most entities. However, more is required of the entity. The unique preferences, values and social claims of those potentially affected by organisational practices should be considered in greater detail within every sustainability management accounting framework.

Comprehensive example 3 illustrates the current social issues faced by Indonesian well operator Lapindo Brantas. Santos has an 18 per cent ownership stake in the Indonesian entity. Consider the potential social exposure for both direct and indirect stakeholders of these organisations. What do you think some of the stakeholder social issues and claims might be? How might an entity protect itself from these risks? The comprehensive example also highlights the risks and liabilities that can arise for larger companies that have certain minority interests. Just because investments are not directly under parent company control does not mean that sustainability responsibilities and liabilities are waived. The scope and benefits relating to sustainability management accounting are discussed in greater detail in the next section.

Comprehensive example 3

Santos pays for clean-up operation

In early 2006 a town called Sigaorjo in East Java, Indonesia, was swamped by 13 metres of mud. Some 15 000 villagers were displaced. The catastrophe also forced the permanent relocation of the cross-Java toll road, a rail link, a gas pipeline and other infrastructure. The massive cleanup and rebuilding costs were estimated at up to $1 billion. Blame for the mudflow was initially attributed to incorrect drilling practices at an exploration well owned by Lapindo Brantas, in which Santos has an 18 per cent ownership stake. Given the enormity of the disaster, though, geologists have argued that it was more likely to be an 'act of God' — the result of a mud volcano. The mud continues to flow out of the ground at 200 000 cubic metres a day, and experts say that the flow may continue for a further 30 years.

Nine months after the disaster, the liability for payment of the costs was decided. The national government will pay $570 million to rebuild the infrastructure. The family who controls Lapindo Brantas stated that, because of 'Indonesian values', the family would pay for houses, factories, other businesses and rice paddies now under mud, totalling $350 million. Santos believes that it will now have to pay only about $32 million (that is, 18 per cent of $180 million for civil works and emergency relief). Although the losses to Santos are much lower than initially feared, it paid a high price over the nine months of confusion. Until recently, it had been unable to inform the Australian Securities Exchange or investors of its total exposure to liability. Thus, market speculation over potential losses for Santos resulted in a significant share price decline (from $12.50 in April 2006 to $9.20 in early 2007), which wiped about $1 billion of Santos's market capitalisation.

Source: Information from Mellish, M 2007, 'Santos clean-up bill lower than feared', *Australian Financial Review*, 8 February, p. 19.

Scope and benefits of sustainability management accounting

Traditional as well as contemporary management accounting techniques can be used in sustainability management control practices to:

- plan and direct management attention to sustainability issues
- inform sustainability management decisions
- control and motivate behaviour towards sustainable outcomes.

Sustainability management accounting is a two-way process of reporting information for decision-making.

1. It can generate information about how the use of resources with sustainability-related impacts can affect the financial performance of the entity.
2. It can be used to consider how organisational operations might affect environmental and social performance.

For organisations to develop a sustainability culture with knowledge of sustainability management accounting applications, the scope of sustainability management accounting practice should be communicated to all employees. Once the sustainability boundaries are defined, specific management accounting tools can be developed to optimise management decisions.

Sustainability scope considerations

The *scope* of sustainability management accounting undertaken by organisations relates to the process of identifying and measuring costs and revenues associated with sustainability management. This is done by identifying the easiest internal costs and revenues through to the more difficult costs and revenues. The greatest difficulty is often associated with societal costs and revenues, or those that are external to the entity — the 'externalities', previously considered beyond the scope of sustainability accounting because they do not affect the balance sheet. For strategic management purposes, externalities should not be ignored. Efforts by governments and lobby groups are increasingly aimed at creating new legislative and reporting requirements to make organisations more liable for their externalities. This requires that the previously ignored costs (and even revenues) be included in the financial statements and performance reports of the entity that created the externality. Thus, an astute business manager would insist that all information relating to the identification and measurement of externalities — whether they are currently in existence or potentially created through incorrect or non-sustainable management decisions — be included in the reports.

Refer back to comprehensive example 1 on page 651; 'carbon accounting' might be interpreted as the most recent vehicle for internalising previously ignored externalities.

If carbon credits are vehicles of income or liabilities for entities, then carbon accounting has the potential to dramatically alter decision-making processes relating to the allocation of entity resources. Because carbon accounting involves measuring production efficiencies in relation to greenhouse gas emissions, the management accountant will be required to track and report monthly/annual emission targets as if they were potential revenue or liabilities for the organisation. The process of carbon accounting will therefore affect processes along the entire value chain — from the choice of raw materials and suppliers, design or re-engineering requirements, type of energy used in production processes, methods of waste management adopted, inhouse or outsourced production, and packaging and transportation options, as well as the image and culture to be presented to suppliers, staff, and potential and existing customers.

Figure 16.6 outlines the scope for sustainability management accounting practices in organisations. The scope (in ascending order of difficulty) begins with the easier to measure factors at level 1 through to the more difficult societal impacts at level 5. The sum of levels 1 to 4 is generally referred to as 'private costs'. That is, the costs that directly affect entities' reported profits. Note that while level 5 externalities might previously have been ignored by organisations, sustainability management is optimised when all current (or potential future) externalities are identified and internalised and (where possible) included in sustainability management accounting control systems.

	Scope	Description
Private costs	Level 1	**Conventional costs** Includes the costs of direct raw materials, utilities, labour, supplies, structures, capital equipment and related depreciation
	Level 2	**Hidden costs** Includes upfront environmental costs such as search costs relating to finding environmentally conscious suppliers, initial design costs of environmentally preferable products, regulatory costs that are often obscured in overhead costs, and future decommissioning or remediation costs
	Level 3	**Contingent costs** Defined in probabilistic terms and includes fines for breaching environmental requirements, cleanup costs, lawsuits relating to unsound products or service provision
	Level 4	**Image and relationship costs** Are difficult to determine and would seldom be separately identified within an accounting system. However, they could be expected to have some influence on the value of some intangible assets such as goodwill, brand names and so forth.
Societal costs	Level 5	**Societal costs** Are often referred to as externalities, and represent costs that an entity imposes upon others as a result of its operations but which the entity typically ignores. These costs include environmental damage caused by the organisation for which it is not held accountable, or adverse health effects caused by organisation-generated emissions for which the organisation is not held responsible. It is difficult and sometimes controversial to put a cost on these effects and, with the exception of a few organisations worldwide, most entities ignore such costs when calculating profits. However, physical measures can be developed and related key performance indicators (KPIs) can be used to assess performance.

FIGURE 16.6 ■ Scope for sustainability management accounting practices

Source: Information from United States Environmental Protection Agency 1995, *An introduction to environmental accounting as a business management tool: key concepts and terms*, Washington, June.

Management decisions benefiting from sustainability management accounting

Several types of management decisions benefit from sustainability management accounting information. They are listed in figure 16.7.

Product design	Capital investments
Process design	Cost control
Facility siting	Waste management
Purchasing	Cost allocation
Operational	Product retention and mix
Risk management	Product pricing
Sustainability compliance strategies	Performance evaluations

FIGURE 16.7 ■ Types of management decisions benefiting from sustainability management accounting information

Source: Information from United States Environmental Protection Agency 1995, *An introduction to environmental accounting as a business management tool: key concepts and terms,* Washington, June, p. 6.

Specific management accounting tools may assist with decision making as a result of identifying and measuring revenues and the direct and indirect costs associated with sustainability management practices. Cost accounting techniques may be used to measure sustainability cost flows. Capital budgeting projects relating to long-term sustainability management might be used as a vehicle to communicate sustainability strategies throughout the entity, as well as promoting wider-level discussions on the opportunity costs related to sustainability projects. Product costing and pricing techniques that encourage sustainability-related overhead costs to be directly allocated to department and products could enhance management decisions.

Strategic sustainability practices for the improved use of resources might include industry- or entity-wide strategic tools (such as value chain analysis) to identify the value-adding opportunities throughout the entire value chain. The flow of raw materials along the value chain can be evaluated for compliance with the entity's sustainability standards. Likewise, the sustainability costs related to waste from general production processes (solids, effluent, emissions) or material losses (scrap, rejects, dumping of dead and excess stock) should be accounted for in materials flow analysis.

Sustainability management accounting will also inform make or buy decisions. Life cycle assessment is useful in encompassing all organisational functions relating to sustainability opportunities over an extended period of time. Of growing importance is the need to determine the opportunity costs and risk assessment of forgoing sustainability opportunities and investment. For example, the choice of energy resources and the potential impact on carbon emissions is a growing concern for global entities, and needs to be considered in calculations for internal decision-making purposes.

The balanced scorecard (see chapter 12) is considered a useful tool for sustainability performance evaluation as well as a strategy communication tool — particularly once it is adapted to become a sustainability balanced scorecard. As mentioned earlier, a growing number of Australian companies are using management accounting tools such as the balanced scorecard as a combination tool for corporate sustainability disclosure and internal management control.

Sustainability management accounting tools

We will now look at some of the more widely used tools in sustainability management practices. The scope and strategies relating to sustainability are typically reflected in operational routines and practices, and are managed and communicated within the management accounting control framework. For improved decision making, sustainability-related income and sustainability-related costs in particular are traced to sustainability-related pools. The drivers of sustainability income and costs can be managed using a holistic value chain approach and life cycle analysis. The process of capital budgeting for sustainability can be better managed when sustainability costs, income and associated drivers are readily identifiable by managers with detailed sustainability knowledge.

Sustainability cost allocation

In many organisations, sustainability costs tend not to be treated as separate costs within the accounting system. They are generally treated as overheads, without their own related cost driver(s), and allocated equally to the cost objects. In some circumstances, sustainability costs might also be accounted for as period costs. The identification and classification of sustainability boundaries, costs and cost objects requires entity-wide involvement. The tracking and tracing of sustainability costs, and the determination of cost pools and related cost drivers, is crucial for sustainability management accounting purposes. Before sustainability costs can be allocated to the cost object, consensus among the key managers is vital. For example, the cost object might be individual business units, production departments, costs centres, production lines, specific equipment, or the individual job, product or service. Input from department managers is important, particularly where the performance of that unit or manager is based on sustainability cost consumption. In comprehensive example 4, a common situation is presented where sustainability costs can be lost in incorrect or general overhead cost pools.

Comprehensive example 4

Sustainability costs and product prices

An Australian chemical company, ChemAus, has five different business units that operate in various sectors and provide chemical products for the paint and building industries as well as for the food and pharmaceutical industries.

On one production site, a processing plant provides top-up production services for the different business units at various stages throughout the year when the units have no idle capacity of their own. During the months of July and August, this top-up plant operated two different processes simultaneously for two of the five business units. One process (for the pharmaceutical business unit) is considered to be relatively clean and the other process (for the industrial chemical department) is 'dirty' and consumes substantial environmental costs.

Each of the business units supplies its own raw materials, and the top-up production plant manager factors in a direct labour cost per production hour. The manager also calculates the overhead charged to each business unit at an hourly rate based on production hours utilised by the business unit. The top-up production plant also receives charges from other cost centres throughout the 25-hectare manufacturing site. For example, it is charged for its annual use of facilities provided by other costs centres that are owned by ChemAus. The production plant is charged an annual fee for its continual use of the wastewater treatment plant (contaminated water from the production plant is treated by the plant before clean water is pumped into a nearby river). Another cost department provides specialised energy supplies that can be high in carbon dioxide emissions. Certain processes emit solid waste that needs to be stored in drums and collected by a chemical waste contractor. This contractor provides a weekly waste pick-up service for the entire site, and the top-up plant is charged an annual disposal fee based on the average number of waste drums collected from the plant throughout the year. There are other environmental costs relating to legal fees, fines and permits that are absorbed by corporate head office and charged in corporate overheads to the production plant.

The manager of the top-up plant consolidates all these costs into one production overhead cost pool, and uses the total costs to determine the transfer price charged for every production hour provided to the individual business units. How should the organisation account for its sustainability production costs?

For an organisation like ChemAus to fully understand the impact of sustainability costs on product pricing, it is important that these specific environmental cost centres and environmentally driven costs are differentiated from the other traditional overhead basket of costs. The final determination of product cost will depend on how the environmental costs are allocated. In figure 16.8, the problem of environmental costs being allocated equally among processes and products is highlighted. Accounting for sustainability, in figure 16.8 and comprehensive example 4, might require the isolation and tracking of sustainability costs to the cost object (that is, the 'dirty' production process). This will enable the cross-subsidised 'dirty' products to be sold at a higher price that reflects the environmental harm caused by their production. Alternatively, it allows the more environmentally friendly product the opportunity to maintain market share at a less expensive price. In this situation, it could be difficult to make comparisons between two entirely different products in different sectors. Nevertheless, by isolating the environmental costs, managers are provided with greater insights into alternative or improved sustainability production processes.

	'Clean' process A	'Dirty' process B
Revenues	$200	$200
Production costs	100	100
Environmental costs	0	50
True profit	100	50
If environmental costs are overhead	25	25
Then the book profit is	$ 75	$ 75
Which is incorrect by	−25%	+33%

FIGURE 16.8 ■ Sustainability costs and overhead cost allocation

Source: Schategger, S & Burritt, R 2000, *Contemporary environmental accounting: issues, concepts and practice*, Greenleaf Publications, Sheffield, UK.

Activity-based costing (ABC) enhances the understanding of business processes associated with each product by allocating sustainability costs on the basis of the activities that caused the cost. As discussed in chapter 4, ABC aims to direct the indirect costs more accurately to the cost object. ABC will reveal where sustainability value is added and where it is lost. Thus, in sustainability management accounting, activity analysis can help to improve the economic consequences of sustainability management by preventing the distortion of product or service provision as well as providing more accurate information for investment decisions.

In the ChemAus example, certain sustainability allocation bases might provide greater insight for costing in the top-up processing plant. For example, what if the water treatment plant installed a meter on every input line and charged on volume of emissions or waste treated per line. Likewise, it might be more appropriate to monitor toxicity levels rather than volume. Certain processes might emit large volumes of relatively clean water compared to others with far greater toxicity levels but lower volume output. As all water must enter the river at safe levels, dirtier production output waste will absorb higher treatment costs and potentially greater business risks relating to spills and litigation. Alternatively, the relative costs of treating different kinds of waste emissions might also be a more suitable allocation base for the water treatment plant. Every situation requires individual assessment for the correct choice of allocation base.

Sustainability life cycle costing

Life cycle analysis is a technique that evaluates all the activities involved in the design, development, production, sale, transportation and disposal of a product or service (see figure 16.9). The life cycle of a product or a service is often referred to as 'cradle to grave'.

Life cycle costing involves summing the costs of these activities throughout the internal and industry value chains — whether they are part of an entity's activities or not. Life cycle analysis is integral to sustainability management, and is about making more informed decisions in relation to the inputs and outputs generated through organisational activities.

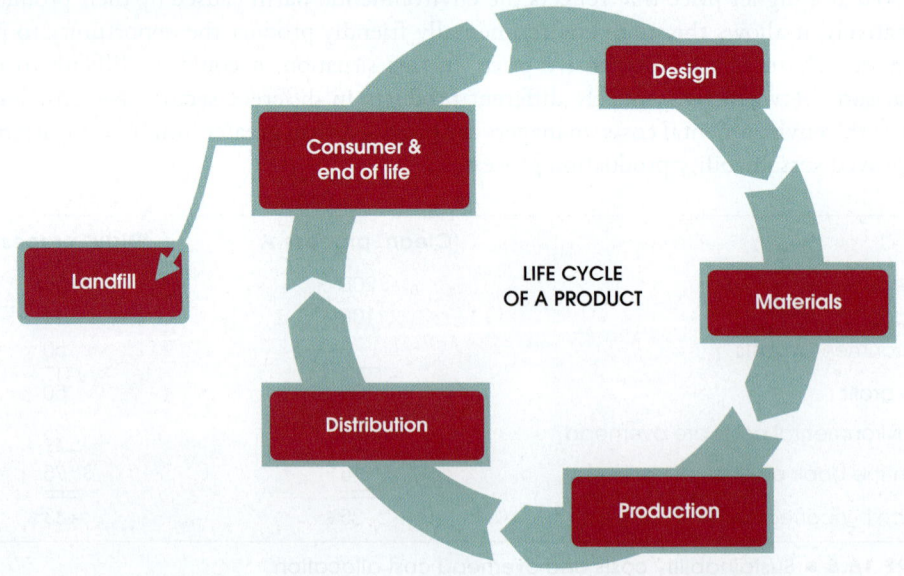

FIGURE 16.9 ■ Life cycle of a product

Source: Environmental Protection Agency, Victoria, www.epa.vic.gov.au.

Activity analysis can provide information relating to the life cycle costs of value chain activities pertaining to:

- the products manufactured (decisions may be made to drop or outsource)
- the preferred sustainability suppliers
- re-engineering the design of product or service
- re-engineering operating processes to accommodate changes in
  - energy sources
  - waste disposal
  - packaging and recycling.

When taking a life cycle approach, both private and societal sustainability activities and costs can be included.

A sustainable operation is based on the principle that 'what goes in must come out'. In most cases, *non-productive output* occurs as a result of operations. The non-productive output (different forms of waste) must be stored or disposed of — resulting in additional sustainability costs for the entity. Figure 16.10 provides an example of a general input–output chart of accounts that could form the basis for sustainability reporting and decision making. The items are measured in physical units of mass or energy. If the general input–output chart of accounts is used by senior managers for sustainability decision-making purposes, they can provide valuable insights for managing life cycles and evaluating the impact of resource (in)efficiencies on the bottom line. These insights might not be revealed with traditional cost management tools.

Input in kg/kWh	Output in kg
Raw materials	Product
Auxiliary materials	Main product
Packaging	By-products
Operating materials	Waste
Merchandise	Municipal waste
Energy	Recycled waste
Gas	Hazardous waste
Coal	Waste water
Other fuels	Heavy metals
Externally produced electricity	Carbon dioxide
Internally produced electricity	Carbon monoxide
Water	Nitrogen oxide

FIGURE 16.10 ■ General input–output chart of accounts

Source: Adapted from Jasch, C 2003, 'The use of environmental management accounting (EMA) for identifying environmental costs', *Journal of Cleaner Production*, vol. 11, p. 674.

Waste disposal is a growing issue among entities. In Victoria, a resource efficiency program in 12 participant companies found $23 million per annum of lost value through non-productive resource flows.[24] The chapter 16 article at the end of this book explains how companies have traditionally focused on cost savings through standard inputs relating to materials or labour rather than evaluating their resource efficiency. In general, entities have not traditionally measured the bottom-line impact of their non-productive output.

Comprehensive example 5 on creative thinking at the Original Juice Company relates to non-productive resource flows. This example highlights how organisations can utilise input–output resource flow analysis to search for better ways to manage their resources and waste. In this situation, the Original juice Company managed to turn its non-productive output (waste citrus peel) into an asset.

Comprehensive example 5

Non-productive resource flows

In the early 1990s, an orange juice manufacturer in Victoria had a waste problem with orange peel. The Original Juice Company squeezed up to 90 000 tonnes of fresh citrus fruit each year — that's a lot of oranges, and a lot of peel left over.

In a dry form, the peel could be sold as a high protein stock feed, but to achieve the necessary degree of dryness it needed pressing. This generated up to 4 million litres a month of effluent — liquid waste high in citrus oil and sugars. Discharged into a nearby water-way, the waste created environmental problems. Of particular concern was biochemical oxygen demand.

But with some creative thinking, the orange-peel problem was turned into an asset. The company realised that citrus oil and sugar were potentially marketable products. By investing in equipment worth just over $1 million, it now saves about $450 000 each year in waste disposal costs and earns $250 000 a year in citrus oil and molasses sales. The company profit has increased, and the pollution load on the environment has decreased.

As the Original Juice Company found, life cycle analysis with input–output resource flows can highlight potential areas for investment in sustainable practices. Sustainability investment requires capital budgeting projects are viewed with a sustainability lens for the true benefits, or otherwise, to be realised.

Source: Extract from Nova 1998, 'Cleaner production — a solution to pollution?', Australian Academy of Science, November, www.science.org.au.

Sustainability and capital budgeting

Capital budgeting for sustainability can be a difficult project requiring 'soft' often-intangible data to be evaluated in conjunction with quantitative data that is based on the best possible estimates of future costs and liabilities. Recall that capital budgeting involves economic variables relating to:

- initial investment costs
- discounted operating costs and earnings
- profit generated
- net present value, return on investment and payback.

In general terms, if the investment is more profitable than gaining interest on a bank deposit, then the project is considered to be worthwhile.

All capital budgeting projects relating to sustainability should consider the conventional costs associated with the project *but* should also focus on the contingent and image-related costs that represent the true profitability and riskiness of the project. Sustainability capital budgeting should reflect the varying scope, levels and categories highlighted in figure 16.6 (page 666). The different sustainability categories for decision-makers to consider should consist of:

- conventional costs (raw materials, utilities, labour)
- administration costs (monitoring, reporting and training)
- contingency costs (potential cleanup, accidents, compensations, fine)
- image benefits and costs (often referred to as 'intangible' costs, or goodwill)
- external costs (potentially internalised at a later stage though regulation, taxes, fees, fines).

Figure 16.11 provides an outline of a sustainability capital budgeting calculation sheet recommended by the United Nations Division for Sustainable Development. The UN suggests that this calculation sheet be used to highlight the sustainable costs and benefits of a single project. It can also be used as a basis for direct comparisons between alternative projects. When inputting data into the format provided in figure 16.11, it is important to recognise that, as with most capital budgeting projects, the inputs and outputs for the initial years should be reasonably quantifiable, accurate and reflect the true position. However, the later years of the capital budgeting calculations often require 'guesstimates', which should be sufficient.

FIGURE 16.11 ■ Sustainability capital budgeting sheet

Calculation sheet Environmental/social cost/expenditure categories	Initial investment	Year 1	Year 2	Year 3	Year 4	Future liability	Soft factors
1. **Waste and emission treatment**							
1.1 Depreciation for related equipment							
1.2 Maintenance, operating materials, services							
1.3 Personnel							
1.4 Fees, taxes, charges							
1.5 Fines and penalties							
1.6 Insurance and environmental liabilities							
1.7 Provisions for cleanup costs, remediation							
2. **Prevention and environmental management**							
2.1 External services for environmental management							
2.2 Personnel for general environmental management activities							
2.3 Research and development							
2.4 Extra expenditure for integrated technologies							
2.5 Other environmental management costs							
3. **Material purchase value of non-product output**							
3.1 Raw materials							
3.2 Packaging							
3.3 Auxiliary materials							

(continued)

FIGURE 16.11 (*continued*)

3.4	Operating materials							
3.5	Energy							
3.6	Water							
4.	**Processing costs of non-product output**							
Σ	**Environmental expenditure**							
5.	**Environmental revenues**							
5.1	Subsidiaries, awards							
5.2	Other earnings							
Σ	**Environmental revenues**							
6.	**Soft factors**							
6.1	Increased turnover, customer satisfaction, new markets, differentiation from competitors, improved customer relationships							
6.2	Improved corporate image							
6.3	Improved contacts with authorities and agencies, reduced legal compliance costs							
6.4	Reduced risks for accidents, liabilities and contaminated land							
6.5	Increased creditworthiness, better ratings by investment companies							
6.6	Better community relations							
6.7	Increased employee motivation and morale, less worker illness and absenteeism							
Σ	**Total benefit**							

Source: United Nations Division for Sustainable Development 2001, 'Environmental management accounting procedures and principles', prepared for the Expert Working Group on 'Improving the role of government in the promotion of environmental management accounting', New York, p. 108.

The main aim of this calculation process is to highlight costs and not ignore potential savings from sustainability projects. Furthermore, sustainability capital budgeting contributes to ensuring that the so-called soft or intangible factors at least are recognised and become some sort of rough estimates. The benefits of sustainability are highlighted in the following savings potential:

- benefits from reducing waste emissions and disposal costs — carbon emission credits, internal and eternal disposal costs, related equipment, transport, insurance and liability, production permits and sustainability reporting costs
- reduction in worker health costs, reduced risks of accidents and worker absenteeism because of dangerous materials and reduced motivation, external stakeholder liabilities and contingencies
- savings in energy, water, materials, packaging and scrap
- potential earnings from emerging/new by-products
- improved relations with authorities, which may shorten waiting times for permits and regulated procedures
- savings in remediation costs, which can be extremely high in non-renewable energy production facilities.[25]

Recognising and quantifying sustainability costs and benefits is invaluable for organisations in two ways. Firstly, it is essential for calculating the profitability of existing sustainability investments; and second, this knowledge is essential for understating the potentially hidden or contingent costs relating to long-term operations and future projections. In addition to savings, positive outcomes relating to improved employee morale, shareholder, community and customer satisfaction, and image and relationship enhancement can also flow to the entity.

Capital budgeting for sustainability should be done with maximum knowledge, specialist input and appropriate timelines to ensure that all possible quantitative and qualitative factors are included in the model. Tangible cash flows relating to the impact of changes in input prices and other matters, such as those relating to the regulatory environment (that is, future fees, fines and penalties), must be taken into account. It is also essential that the less tangible aspects are included in the management accounting information.

Different sustainability scenarios should be raised, costed and made available to decision makers. Recall the chapter 9 scene setter on capital budgeting for nuclear power operations. For optimum sustainable decisions, other capital investment scenarios must be evaluated. The alternative scenarios presented could range from capital investment to improve traditional coal-powered operations right through to other sustainable and renewable power sources relating to solar, wind or water-generated power.

Sustainability balanced scorecard

The balanced scorecard is a performance measurement system that links key performance measures with business strategy in four main ways: financial, customer, internal processes, and innovation and learning (refer to chapter 12). The key to balanced scorecard success is the focus on the cause-and-effect relationships between the performance measures that ultimately lead to successful operations as measured by shareholder wealth (the score) in the financial perspective. The balanced scorecard was originally intended to be the *shareholder* scorecard.[26] Kaplan and Norton did not consider it to be a *stakeholder* card despite introducing key measures relating to staff and customers. Over time, the balanced scorecard has been adapted for use in the not-for-profit and public sectors where financial outcomes are not necessarily the goals. It has also begun to be popular with organisations as a tool for monitoring sustainability.

A sustainability balanced scorecard can be developed in three different ways.[27]
1. The environmental and social aspects can be integrated within the four standard perspectives.
2. An additional 'sustainability' perspective can be added.
3. A separate sustainability balanced scorecard can be developed.

If the sustainability measures are captured within the existing scorecard, this ensures that cause-and-effect relationships are developed between the measures and perspectives so that sustainability becomes entwined within the entity's overall vision and strategic objectives. Sustainability actions can thereby be captured in organisational 'innovation and learning' perspectives and become integral to the value chain activities ('internal processes') undertaken by the organisation. Successful sustainability practices will be rewarded by the 'customer' who purchases the entity's products or services. Sustainability success should then be reflected in the 'financial' perspective. This should demonstrate that the social, environmental and financial dimensions are managed in unison. One concern with this first style of integrated scorecard is that for 'successful' sustainability operations, entities might focus solely on their private measures (financial success) to the exclusion of societal measures. Depending on how the measures are integrated into the balanced scorecard, there is a risk that the organisation might ignore the externalities to focus on the bottom line.

The second development relates to an additional sustainability perspective being added. This reinforces the fact that sustainability is central to the organisation's mission and strategies. An additional quadrant also provides scope for approximately four to six more key sustainability measures to be included in the balanced scorecard (recall that a traditional scorecard has about 22 to 24 measures in total). The importance placed on achieving these measures will depend on the weighting given to these measures in comparison to the others. A problem that has been previously identified with balanced scorecard use is that too much emphasis tends to be placed on the financial quadrant in comparison to others.[28] This is a risk with the sustainability measures, particularly when including an additional quadrant and related measures. In this situation, the weighting of measures has the potential to be diluted in comparison to the financial measures and so receive less attention by managers and subordinates who are being evaluated.

A separately 'derived' sustainability balanced scorecard is considered to be the most useful of the three approaches.[29] First, it enables sustainability teams or departments to more closely monitor the social, environmental and financial dimensions. Secondly, it does not consist of individual sustainability measures that are 'tacked onto' existing operational measures. All measures on this scorecard have been derived from operations where sustainability is the fundamental building block. For optimal outcomes, the individually derived sustainability balanced scorecard should not be viewed independently from other performance measurement systems but considered as an *extension* of the other alternatives.[30] In this way, the derived scorecard should be developed in conjunction with an existing balanced scorecard to ensure that the sustainability measures are given strategic relevance and position in the management accounting framework. Thus, the difference between the first two scorecard alternatives and the derived balanced scorecard is that the derived scorecard measures emerge from a core balanced scorecard in which sustainability becomes the fundamental driver.

The scope of sustainability accounting encourages the inclusion of items previously treated as externalities or societal costs. A further extension to the 'derived' sustainability balanced scorecard can be made by adding an additional 'societal' perspective.[31] This means that the purpose of the derived scorecard can both fulfil the private interests of the firm and shareholder, and also draws managers' attention to the strategically relevant societal interest to be captured in the additional perspective. Figure 16.12 presents an overview of the process of formulating a sustainability balanced scorecard.

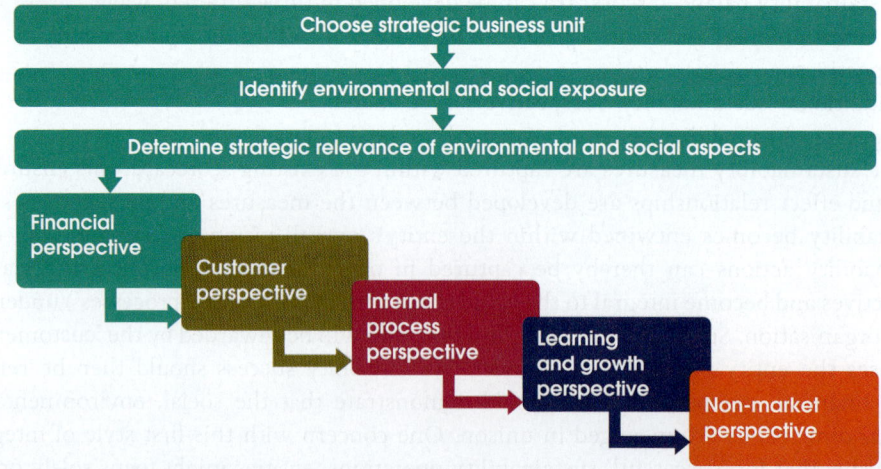

FIGURE 16.12 ■ Process of formulating a sustainability balanced scorecard

Source: Figge, F, Hahn, T, Schaltegger S & Wagner, M 2002, 'The sustainability balanced scorecard — linking sustainability management to business strategy', *Business Strategy and the Environment,* Wiley InterScience, www.interscience.wiley.com.

The measures should be tailored to the specific business unit and fit with the entity's corporate vision and strategies. The environmental measures might relate to emissions, waste, materials, energy or other factors that can directly affect the environment. The social aspects relate to any factor/exposure of a business unit, and the additional societal (or non-market) perspective measures might relate to freedom of action, legitimacy or legality.[32] Success in fully realising opportunities for cost savings or revenue generation through sustainability accounting requires that both technical and human factors work together.

Sustainability management accounting — issues relating to successful integration

For sustainability management practices to be integrated into an entity's culture (and for the sustainability opportunities management cycle to function), several key technical and behavioural issues must be considered.[33] The technical issues, as highlighted in figure 16.13, relate to strategic development being supported by appropriate management accounting systems. A broad view of sustainability costs and benefits is necessary to capture associated externalities. Costing systems should enable sustainability costs and benefits to be directly allocated to the associated operations of the entity rather than being accumulated within overhead accounts, treated as period costs or allocated to wrong revenue or costing categories.

Technical issues	Behavioural issues
■ Defining sustainability costs	■ Senior management support
■ Suitable objectives in line with sustainability strategies	■ Multiple advocates
■ Identification of suitable social and environmental measures for performance evaluation	■ Creating ownership of the project of participants
■ Setting challenging but achievable targets	■ Not conducting other initiatives that could conflict with sustainability management protocols
■ Positioning of sustainability performance within the organisational performance measurement system	■ Perceptions of management accounting within the company
■ Able to demonstrate sustainability links to operations via strategy map	■ Suitable communication and feedback mechanisms
■ Issues associated with regularity of reporting, timeliness of feedback and format of reports	
■ Use of a pilot test	
■ Use of external consultant or not	

FIGURE 16.13 ■ Sustainability management accounting: technical and behavioural issues

If suitable management accounting tools are in place with appropriate feedback mechanisms, the behavioural issues relating to performance evaluation and rewards (discussed in chapter 11) should be minimised. To optimise organisational change towards sustainability, other factors such as top management support and the adoption of a team-based approach in preference to a single sustainability 'champion' to promote sustainability throughout the organisation should be considered. For example, by using a multidiscipline team (or cross-departmental teams), sustainability management ownership is created across the entity and the potential for change to corporate culture is increased.

For management accountants, an opportunity to play a key role in the sustainability management change process — as a change agent (where high consideration is given to many non-financial factors) — may be provided. A note of caution: if 'accounting' is viewed as a purely financial function by other organisational members, then a change in the way accounting is viewed within the entity might be required. It is essential that there is adequate communication between all business units and support departments.

Progress towards sustainability may also be thwarted if other initiatives conflict with sustainability management practices. For example, if an entity is undergoing a downsizing program, then issues relating to the social setting and employee morale must be managed if the remaining employees are to support the sustainability program. In such situations, it is essential for managers to recognise that sustainability management practices that are economically sound should continue to be practised in times of crisis and not only when operations are successful.[34]

Some of the issues outlined in figure 16.13 have also been recognised as key factors affecting sustainability change in recent research conducted for the Australian Government Department of the Environment and Heritage (ARIES). An outline of this project's findings (see comprehensive example 6) provides useful insights for sustainability development in Australian entities.

Comprehensive example 6

Shifting towards sustainability

A research project was conducted by the Australian Research Institute in Education for Sustainability (ARIES) to understand more deeply how sustainability practices might evolve within organisations (Hunting & Tilbury 2006). Action research involving 10 major corporate and government entities in Australia yielded six major insights into optimising a shift towards sustainability among corporations. (Note that action research is research that aims to innovate, not just improve practice.) Entities that participated in the sustainability project included Amcor Australasia, BHP Billiton, Australian Government Department of the Environment and Heritage, National Australia Bank, Parramatta City Council, Toyota Australia, Visy Industries, Wesley Mission (Sydney), Westpac Banking Corporation and Yarra Valley Water.

The six major insights into successful organisational change for sustainability that emerged from this research are:

1. Adopt a clear, shared vision for the future.
2. Build teams, not just champions.

3. Use critical thinking and reflection.
4. Go beyond stakeholder engagement.
5. Adopt a systematic approach.
6. Move beyond expecting a linear path to change.

These insights are a strategic tool for managers to use when implementing sustainability management practices within their organisations. We will now examine some of the case study examples of the six insights provided by the companies involved in the sustainability research project.

Amcor's vision was reflected in the development of a cross-department stakeholder team (network of champions) who translated the vision into a project where positive performance indicators (PPIs) for health, safety and the environment were built into a web-based balanced scorecard and tested at pilot sites. A final set of sustainability balanced scorecard measures was universally implemented at Amcor in May 2006.

At Yarra Valley Water, a 'sustainability circle' was established to promote the integration of sustainability management within the entity. Its members comprised executive team members and specific internal and external knowledge experts. They identified the need for increased support for knowledge sharing. Teams across functional workgroups were given change projects. As a result of knowledge sharing, strategies for managing greenhouse gas emissions and alternative ways of providing more sustainable water and sewerage services were devised.

Westpac had developed a comprehensive supply chain management system aimed at helping staff build sustainability performance improvements into supplier contracts. However, the system was under-utilised as a result of a belief that the system was under-resourced. Critical thinking and reflection revealed the need for a top-down management approach. The staff redefined the vision for sustainable supply chain management. They then developed implementation strategies based on clear drivers that aimed to identify the risks and provide a more targeted and efficient process for sustainability performance improvement.

As an alternative to generalised staff training programs on sustainability, Toyota Australia entered into a partnership with Yarra Valley Water to develop measures that related to the level of staff awareness of sustainability issues. The two entities continued to combine their forces to understand more deeply the drivers for staff awareness and to develop practical measures for assessing and tracking staff awareness levels. Learning needs were identified and tailored programs, such as ways of reducing greenhouse gas emissions, were subsequently provided.

During the project, both National Australia Bank (NAB) and Westpac managers found common interests in wanting to link sustainability strategies with supply chain management (procurement policies and procedures). This subsequently evolved to a supply chain working party (also involving ANZ) under the auspices of the Australasian Group of the United Nations Environment Program Finance Initiative.

BHP Billiton aimed to implement non-traditional value measurements relating to risk mitigation strategies and avoidance activities in supplier agreements. A cross-functional team was formed to identify the existing value measurements both internal and external to the organisation and link them with the newly identified non-traditional values of measurement. Subsequently, a new measurement method was derived from a systems thinking approach taken by the team. It was tested in a pilot project before being rolled out across the entity.

Visy Industries' goal was to implement staff training to build internal capacity and action for sustainability. Initially, a training package that addressed the perceived gap in sustainability knowledge was developed, but the entity's corporate environment department determined it not adequately targeted for the desired goals to be achieved. A revised package built on engaging key internal stakeholders resulted in opening up lines of communication, leading to a deeper understanding of site needs and identification of levers for change. With external assistance, a 12-month tailored staff training package resulted.

Sources: Information from Hunting, SA. & Tilbury, D 2006, 'Shifting towards sustainability: six insights into successful organisational change for sustainability', Australian Research Institute in Education for Sustainability (ARIES) for the Australian Government Department of the Environment and Water Resources, Sydney, www.aries.mq.edu.au and www.deh.gov.au.

Summary

1 **Understand the concepts of sustainability, sustainability management and sustainability management accounting.**

Sustainability

The development that meets the need of the present without compromising the ability of future generations to meet their own needs.

Sustainability management

The process of measuring, monitoring and simultaneous control of the economic, environmental and social dimensions of an entity.

Sustainability management accounting

The tool that simultaneously integrates the economic, environmental and social performance of an entity with strategic management

2 **Explain why it is essential for management accountants to have an understanding of external sustainability reporting requirements.**

Sustainability management accounting provides internal sustainability management reports for translation to external disclosures.

Sustainability management accounting translates external sustainability reporting guidelines into strategic sustainability management practices and affects internal reporting frameworks.

3 **Explain the role that ethical decision making plays in a sustainability management framework.**

Ethics as part of external management disclosure:

- ASX corporate governance principles
- GRI indicators
- translation to internal management control systems.

Ethics as part of the internal management decision-making process:

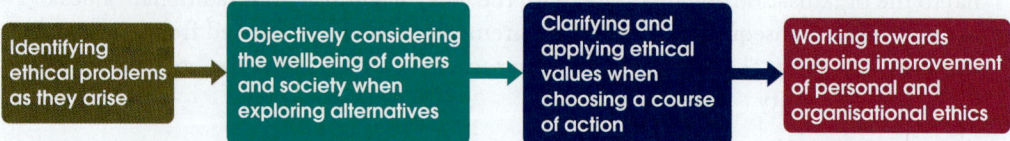

Identifying ethical problems as they arise → Objectively considering the wellbeing of others and society when exploring alternatives → Clarifying and applying ethical values when choosing a course of action → Working towards ongoing improvement of personal and organisational ethics

4 Understand the scope and benefits resulting from sustainability management accounting practices.

Scope

■ Conventional costs	Private
■ Hidden costs	
■ Contingent costs	
■ Image and relationship costs	
■ Societal	Societal

Benefits

Product design	Capital investments
Process design	Cost control
Facility siting	Waste management
Purchasing	Cost allocation
Operational	Product retention and mix
Risk management	Product pricing
Sustainability compliance strategies	Performance evaluations

5 Demonstrate an understanding of key sustainability management accounting tools. In particular, explain how cost allocation, life cycle costing, capital budgeting and performance measurement are treated under a sustainability lens.

Cost allocation
- Sustainability costs isolated from other overhead costs pools
- Sustainability costs should be traced to the cost object

Life cycle costing
- The sum of the 'cradle to grave' costs throughout industry and internal value chains
- Should include both private and societal costs

Capital budgeting
- Includes conventional cash flows associated with the project
- Adapt conventional model to include contingent, image and external benefits and costs

Performance measurement
- Sustainability balanced scorecard
- Social and environmental aspects integrated within the four perspectives
- An additional sustainability perspective
- A separate sustainability balanced scorecard

6 Describe the issues faced by managers when trying to implement sustainability change processes within their entities.

Technical issues	Behavioural issues
■ Defining sustainability costs	■ Senior management support
■ Suitable objectives in line with sustainability strategies	■ Multiple advocates
■ Identification of suitable social and environmental measures for performance evaluation	■ Creating ownership of the project of participants
■ Setting challenging but achievable targets	■ Not conducting other initiatives that could conflict with sustainability management protocols
■ Positioning of sustainability performance within the organisational performance measurement system	■ Perceptions of management accounting within the company
■ Able to demonstrate sustainability links to operations via strategy map	■ Suitable communication and feedback mechanisms
■ Issues associated with regularity of reporting, timeliness of feedback and format of reports	
■ Use of a pilot test	
■ Use of external consultant or not	

Self-study problems

SELF-STUDY PROBLEM 1

Sustainability balanced scorecard

ChemAus owns a petrochemical plant that refines and produces paints and resins for the building industry. The plant uses a large amount of water in its production processes. The water is treated in an onsite water treatment plant before clean water is emitted into the adjoining river system. The heavy metal waste is stored in drums and collected by contractors on a weekly basis. The petrochemical plant has had previous environmental issues with the EPA regarding toxic spills in the adjoining river and complaints about its excessive greenhouse gas emissions. ChemAus is a subsidiary company of ChemWide Ltd, a large multinational group based in Denmark. Senior managers from ChemWide Ltd were concerned about their sustainability rating with shareholders and called a meeting with the Australian managers to discuss opportunities for improving their image and stakeholder relationships.

REQUIRED

Outline some of the quantitative and qualitative factors about its sustainability performance that ChemWide Ltd might discuss in its meeting. How could a sustainability balanced scorecard be used by ChemAus?

ChemWide Ltd could use a number of strategies to guide its discussion at the meeting. Figure 16.4 (GRI core environmental and social indicators) provides a useful framework for evaluating sustainability performance by providing a range of indicators against which the entity could benchmark its performance. For an Australian perspective, ChemWide Ltd could make us of the Australian SAM (AuSSI) sustainability index as a guide for discussion.

ChemAus could develop a balanced scorecard based around key measures from the GRI and SAM sustainability indices. For example, measures that relate to activities within a chemical industry might include staff awareness and training, energy consumption (amount and type), waste (greenhouse gas emissions, other waste), number/type of workplace accidents, water consumption/treatment and environmental litigation costs.

SELF-STUDY PROBLEM 2

Ethical decision making: the right thing to do[35]

In the past, drug makers have been reluctant to invest in cures for diseases in developing countries such as Africa and South America. Most people in these countries cannot afford to pay for treatments, and managers have typically invested in other long-term projects having higher returns. However, a few pharmaceutical companies have chosen to invest in neglected diseases, including tuberculosis, malaria and other tropical diseases. As an example, Glaxo-SmithKline formed a joint venture with the World Health Organization to develop a malaria drug that costs less than 50 cents for a three-day treatment.

This type of investment has several goals. From a reputation perspective, managers accused of keeping drug prices artificially high may believe that providing low-cost cures will alleviate pressure from regulators and consumers to lower prices for drugs sold in the United States and other developed countries. Furthermore, people from some less-developed countries will eventually have the ability to pay for cures. Finally, 'it is the right thing to do,' according to journalist Robert Langreth. Novartis chairman Daniel Vasella says, 'If you only look at maximizing short-term profit, you may not survive in the long term'.

REQUIRED

Using figure 16.5 on page 664, address the following question for this ethical dilemma to improve your skills in making ethical decisions. Think about your answers to these questions and discuss them with others.

Does an ethical problem arise if pharmaceutical companies charge lower prices for drugs in developing countries than in developed countries? Why?

GlaxoSmithKline and other large pharmaceutical companies are often criticised for failing to develop drugs that are needed in developing countries or for not selling drugs in those countries at low prices. Partnership with an entity such as the World Health Organization (WHO) is a highly visible way of addressing this type of criticism. In addition, WHO has existing supply chain relationships in developing countries that would make it easier for GlaxoSmithKline to distribute drugs in those countries.

Questions

16.1 Define the terms 'sustainability', 'sustainability management' and 'sustainability management accounting'.

16.2 Is sustainability achievable in all entities regardless of their operating activities?

16.3 Why should the economic, environmental and cultural dimensions be managed in unison?

16.4 Will organisational efforts towards sustainability result in reduced organisational profits?

16.5 Outline the relationship between sustainability reporting and sustainability management accounting.

16.6 What types of management decisions can benefit through using sustainability cost information?

16.7 Discuss the importance of ethical decision making in a sustainability management accounting framework.

16.8 What are the potential benefits from developing an input–output chart of accounts?

16.9 What key measures should be included in a sustainability balanced scorecard?

16.10 What are some of the factors that managers should consider when implementing sustainability practices in their organisations?

Exercises

16.11 Capital budgeting and sustainability Read the chapter 9 scene setter on capital budgeting for a nuclear power plant (page 355).

REQUIRED

Comment on the quantitative and qualitative factors that would be considered by managers when contemplating a capital budgeting project such as a nuclear power plant.

16.12 **Sustainability threats and opportunities** The World Coal Institute claims that coal provides over 23 per cent of global primary energy needs and generates over 38 per cent of the world's electricity. Coal is one of the cheapest forms of fuel available on the planet. However, burning fuel produces carbon dioxide, which contributes to excessive greenhouse gas emissions and global warming. Rather than change energy sources, Clean Coal Technologies (CCTs) have been promoted as a means of reducing emissions, reducing waste as well as increasing the efficiency (or amount of energy) gained from coal.[36]

REQUIRED

Referring to the information in this problem and drawing on comprehensive example 1 (page 651), discuss some of the sustainability management threats and opportunities for the future of Australian coal producers.

16.13 **Carbon trading**

REQUIRED

(a) Explain how carbon trading might reduce greenhouse gas emissions.

(b) How might the existence of carbon trading schemes affect the management accounting system within organisations?

16.14 **GRI indicators** Comment on how the GRI core environmental and social indicators (see figure 16.4, page 660) might help drive the social and environmental components of internal reporting frameworks.

16.15 **Contingent costs** List some costs that could be considered to be 'contingent' sustainability-related costs for the mining industry.

16.16 **Externalities and sustainability** Read the scene setter at the beginning of this chapter. Using Visy Industries as an example, list some of the positive externalities that might be achieved as a result of Visy's operations. What are some of the negative externalities that Visy has attempted to overcome with its sustainability operations?

16.17 Sustainability cost classification Using the following table, classify each sustainability cost according to its appropriate category (levels 1–5).

Category level 1–5	Sustainability cost
Contingent costs	Cleanup costs from a chemical accident
Conventional costs	Community relations program
Image and relationship costs	Costs associated with prolonged licensing permits
Potentially hidden costs	Costs associated with stricter monitoring
Societal costs	Decommissioning of site
	Disposal of waste
	Environmental labelling
	Feasibility studies
	Future compliance costs
	Goodwill/impairment related costs
	Habitat and wetland protection
	Landscaping around site
	New capital equipment costs
	Personal injury
	Petroleum
	Raw materials
	Remediation costs
	Site studies
	Staff training
	Sustainability legal expenses
	Sustainability reports

16.18 Sustainability disclosures; management accounting tools Search the newspapers/ internet to find examples of Australian companies disclosing their sustainability practices using management accounting information or tools such as the balanced scorecard. Provide a report on your findings.

Problems

16.19 Sustainable management practices In a recent Environmental Victoria audit, it was found that Australian supermarkets could save $41.6 million annually if 'green bags' were universally adopted.[37] This audit was conducted at Leo's Fine Foods in Kew, Victoria. It was conducted as a timed experiment; that is, clocking a checkout operator on the time taken to fill reusable green or single-use plastic shopping bags. The results are highlighted in the table shown overleaf.

No. of items	Average time (seconds)		
	Single-use bags	Reusable bags	Difference
4	5.35	5.30	–0.05
8	14.23	13.15	–1.08
16	31.98	32.75	+0.77
32	73.73 (1.13.73)	79.28 (1.19.28)	+5.55
48	124.97 (2.04.97)	114.22 (1.54.22)	–10.75

The results show that there was little difference in transaction times for single-use bags compared with reusable bags. As a result of this experiment, Henty strongly suggests that governments introduce a levy on single-use plastic bags to encourage further use of green bags.[38]

REQUIRED

(a) If you were designing/conducting this experimental process, what concerns might you might have about the results being considered representative of the true situation being investigated?

(b) What other sustainable management practices might supermarkets employ to decrease waste?

16.20 Sustainability; outsourcing; monitoring measures To reduce costs and focus on core competencies, many entities are increasingly outsourcing manufacturing activities to vendors in countries having low labour costs such as China, India, Thailand, Indonesia and Mexico. Certain activists claim that this practice is socially irresponsible. They claim that numerous factory problems in low-cost countries include excessive work hours, poverty wages, toxic gas releases and harassment of union organisers.[39] Such conditions have prompted individuals and organisations to reconsider their purchasing habits and policies.

Activist groups sometimes target individual companies to publicise the working conditions of outsource staff. Since 1995, Nike has been criticised for human rights abuses, labour exploitation and environmental damage by companies that manufacture its athletic shoes and apparel. Nike outsources its manufacturing to more than 900 factories in over 50 countries, but most of its manufacturing is done in a handful of low-cost countries. Several groups recommended that consumers should boycott Nike products until its outsource factories meet acceptable standards.

Nike has actively worked to address concerns about worker conditions in its outsource factories. Its manufacturing code of conduct has been in place since 1992, and the following mission statement for its workers and factories is posted on its website:

Mission: To make responsible sourcing* a business reality that enhances workers' lives.

*Through compliance, partnerships and outreach

Nike established a set of goals to improve working conditions and instituted monitoring practices to evaluate factory compliance. It now considers compliance issues before placing production orders, and it includes compliance monitoring costs in its purchasing decision process. Nike conducts audits of the manufacturing facilities and implements action plans to resolve issues related to health and safety, pay and benefits, terms of work and management–worker relations.[40]

During 2004, controversy remained about whether Nike had done enough to improve worker conditions. Nike's managers asserted that they had resolved problems with conditions in outsource factories. However, activists contended that the problems persisted. Nike had been targeted by these groups partly because it operated in an industry that had widespread labour abuse, was the largest sportswear maker in the world and had high profits. They argued that Nike could afford to pay more to its outsource partners to improve worker pay and factory conditions. They hoped that Nike would change its policies, placing greater pressure on other companies to take similar actions.[41]

On the other hand, some people argued that boycotts against companies such as Nike caused more harm than good; workers who were already poor often lost their jobs, and unionisation efforts and other improvements were hindered.[42] It was also difficult for companies to adequately monitor working conditions at outsource locations. Workers were often afraid to talk to inspectors, and they sometimes provided inaccurate information. For example, they sometimes erroneously said that they were not paid overtime because they did not understand how their pay was calculated.[43]

REQUIRED

(a) Describe whether and how sustainability management practices (i.e. business practices related to human rights, labour standards and the environment) affect your decisions as a consumer.

(b) Is it possible for you to know the conditions under which the products you purchase are produced? Why?

(c) Is it possible for managers of companies such as Nike to know with certainty that their outsource partners comply with agreed-upon working conditions? Why?

(d) What does it mean for Nike to include compliance monitoring costs in its purchasing decision process?

(e) Identify and explain four measures that a company such as Nike could use to monitor worker conditions in outsource factories. For each measure, describe how the company might collect reliable data.

(f) How should entities such as Nike weigh corporate social responsibility and profits when deciding whether or how to outsource manufacturing? Describe the values you use in drawing your conclusions.

16.21 Ethical decision making — promoting inappropriate uses of ABC When ABC was first developed, consultants sometimes promoted it for inappropriate uses. Many consulting services focused on using ABC information for short-term decisions, such as pricing and product emphasis. Yet in the early stages of ABC and ABM development, both flexible and committed costs were included in ABC cost pools and were not tracked separately. As a result, ABC unit costs included both fixed and variable costs, even when the fixed costs were irrelevant for decision making. ABC promoters suggested that all costs were variable in the long run, and they ignored criticism of their methods.

If ABC cost rates include fixed costs, their unquestioned use in setting prices is detrimental to operations. If demand falls then production volumes might fall too, causing costs per unit to increase followed by increases in prices. This type of pricing policy can lead to a death spiral, in which prices increase inappropriately as volumes decline.

After ABC was developed, it was quickly added to cost accounting curriculums at many different universities. However, a few academics were highly critical of ABC and eventually provided evidence that overhead costs included a large portion of fixed costs, even in the long run.[44] As research evidence accumulated, ABC consultants advised entities not to allocate facility-level costs and to categorise costs within each activity cost pool as flexible and committed. Then total costs could be used to analyse processes and improve operations, but flexible cost information could be retrieved for decision making.

Currently, 'incremental ABC cost analysis' services are being promoted. These services are sometimes called predictive accounting. Because consulting services can be expensive and judging the outcome of new ideas difficult, managers need to incorporate healthy scepticism when considering the potential costs and benefits of products and services promoted by consultants.[45]

REQUIRED

What ethical problems might arise for managers when considering the use of consultants to develop ABC techniques for sustainability opportunities? Your answers should relate to the promotion of ABC for pricing, other short-term decisions, and incremental ABC or predictive accounting relating to sustainability opportunities. You should also consider the potential for consultant bias and whether the technique will benefit the client, particularly when the consulting service might have uncertain outcomes.

16.22 Sustainability and job costing in a service sector Green and Greener Co., a law firm specialising in environmental litigation, had the following costs last year:

Direct professional labour	$15 000 000
Overhead	21 000 000
Total costs	$36 000 000

The following costs were included in overhead:

Fringe benefits for direct professional labour	$ 5 000 000
Paralegal costs	2 700 000
Telephone call time with clients (estimated but not tabulated)	600 000
Computer time	1 800 000
Photocopying	900 000
Total overhead	$11 000 000

The entity recently improved its ability to document and trace costs to individual cases. Revised bookkeeping procedures now allow it to trace fringe benefit costs for direct professional labour, paralegal costs, telephone charges, computer time and photo-copying costs to each case individually. The managing partner needs to decide whether more costs other than just direct professional labour should be traced directly to jobs to allow the entity to better justify billings to clients.

During the last year, more costs were traced to client engagements. Two of the case records showed the following:

	Client cases	
	875	876
Direct professional labour	$20 000	$20 000
Fringe benefits for direct labour	3 000	3 000
Secretarial costs	2 000	6 000
Computer time	2 000	4 000
Photocopying	1 000	2 000
Total costs	$29 000	$37 000

Three methods are being considered for allocating overhead this year:

- Method 1: Allocate overhead based on direct professional labour cost. Calculate the allocation rate using last year's direct professional labour costs of $15 million and overhead costs of $21 million.
- Method 2: Allocate overhead based on direct professional labour cost. Calculate the allocation rate using last year's direct professional labour costs of $15 million and overhead costs of $10 million ($21 million less $11 million in direct costs that are traced this year).
- Method 3: Allocate the $10 million overhead based on total direct costs. Calculate the allocation rate using last year's direct costs (professional labour of $15 million plus other direct costs of $11 million).

REQUIRED

(a) Calculate the overhead allocation rate for method 1.
(b) Calculate the overhead allocation rate for method 2.
(c) Calculate the overhead allocation rate for method 3.
(d) Using each of the three rates calculated in parts (a), (b) and (c), calculate the total costs of cases 875 and 876.
(e) Explain why the total costs allocated to cases 875 and 876 are not the same under the three methods.
(f) Explain why method 1 would be inappropriate.
(g) Would method 2 or method 3 be better? Explain.
(h) Explain how professional service entities (like law firms) might engage in sustainability practices.

16.23 Ethical decision making — inappropriate allocation of underapplied overhead[46] The Australian government has contracted with alternative energy industry organisations to develop new energy technologies. These contracts are sometimes based on cost. Because these organisations are also developing technologies for non-government entities, incentives exist to shift overhead costs to the government so that commercial operations become more competitive. Because cost allocations are private information, research provides only indirect evidence that this cost shifting occurs. The following vignette is fictional, but it illustrates potential ethical problems that arise when governments use cost-based contracts for product development.

Deep Water Hydro is a hydroelectricity energy company that focuses on innovative research and development solutions for alternative energy supply for both commercial and government agencies. Because one of its commercial contracts fell through last year, the entity had fewer jobs than anticipated. Consequently, the company's overhead costs were underapplied at the end of the year, so an adjustment was made to increase cost of goods sold.

Deep Water's policy is to allocate production overhead as a percentage of direct labour costs for each contract. One of the government contracts completed last year was to develop a hydroelectricity generator that would supply energy from seawater entering Port Philip Bay in Melbourne. The job contract was based on cost-plus-fixed-fee for a total cost of $245 million. The hydroelectricity project was Deep Water's only government contract last year. Commercial business completed was $105 million, so cost of goods sold (COGS) totalled $350 million.

Disagreement about underapplied overhead adjustment

The government official in charge of the contract complained to the federal contract auditor that Deep Water's underapplied overhead should not have been closed to COGS.

Instead, he argued that it should have been allocated on a pro rata basis among the contracts in progress, finished goods and COGS. The auditor asked to see the cost accounting records and financial statements for the period. Following is an analysis of the direct costs and cost allocations (in millions):

	Contracts in progress	Finished goods inventory	Cost of goods sold	Total work on jobs this period
Direct materials used	$250	$50	$100	$400
Direct labour	92	8	50	150
Overhead allocated	184	16	100	300
Total before adjustment	526	74	250	850
Add: Underapplied overhead	0	0	100	100
Total after adjustment	$526	$74	$350	$950

The $350 million in COGS included $245 million for the government contract. When the underapplied overhead ($100 million) was closed to COGS, the government portion of underapplied overhead was $70 million [$100 × ($245 ÷ $350)]. Because the contract specified that the government would pay costs plus a fixed amount, the overhead adjustment effectively increased the revenue under the contract by $70 million.

Actual direct labour costs were $150 million, and the pre-adjustment allocated overhead was $300 million. Therefore, the original allocation rate was 200 per cent ($300 ÷ $150) of direct labour cost. Total actual overhead turned out to be $400 million (the $300 million plus the $100 million underapplied). If Deep Water accountants could have perfectly estimated overhead at $400 million and direct labour cost at $150 million, they would have used 267 per cent ($400 ÷ $150) as the allocation rate.

The underapplied overhead amount was material ($100 million out of $400 million, or 25 per cent). Therefore, the government auditor decided that it should have been allocated on a pro rata basis among the three accounts that reflected work done this period: contracts in progress, finished goods and cost of goods sold. Had this method been used, the adjustment would have been allocated as follows:

	(millions)
Contracts in progress ($526 million ÷ $850 million) × $100 million	$ 61.9
Finished goods ($74 million ÷ $850 million) × $100 million	8.7
Cost of goods sold ($250 million ÷ $850 million) × $100 million	29.4
Total adjustment	$100.0

The government's share of the COGS adjustment would be ($245 ÷ $350) × $29.4 million = $20.6 million. When the auditor compared this to the original adjustment of $70 million, she knew the government had been overcharged.

Alternative methods for allocating overapplied or underapplied overhead
The auditor offered Deep Water three alternatives for allocating the overhead adjustment. Under governmental contracts, underapplied overhead could be allocated based on direct materials cost, direct labour cost or total direct costs. If Deep Water uses

direct materials, COGS is increased by $25 million, of which the government portion is $17.5 million. If direct labour cost is used, COGS is increased by $33.3 million, of which the government portion is $23.3 million. If total direct cost is used, COGS is increased by $27.3 million, of which the government portion is $19.1 million.

The government and Deep Water must now negotiate to determine the most appropriate proration method.

REQUIRED

(a) Is allocating proportionately more cost to government contracts an ethical problem for Deep Water? Why?

(b) When the government pays more than commercial customers pay for work done, does this situation pose a business problem, a social problem or both? Explain.

(c) Discuss the preferences of various stakeholders for this problem, including:
- Deep Water managers
- Deep Water shareholders
- Deep Water commercial customers
- Deep Water governmental customers
- Deep Water competitors
- Australian taxpayers.

(d) Is it fair for the government to pay more for products and services than commercial customers pay? Is it fair for taxes to subsidise the overhead costs for a private business?

(e) How can an entity monitor whether its accounting practices are ethical?

16.24 **Ethical decision making; timely reporting of sustainability budget problems**
A dilemma that individuals face is whether to be truthful when it appears that a project is over budget. Being over budget typically means that actual costs exceed budgeted costs or that a planned timeline will not be met. People often delay reporting an over-budget condition either because they believe they can catch up later or because they wish to delay negative repercussions. Unfortunately, information delays prevent managers from responding rapidly and decisively to delays in project timing and cost overruns, leading to additional dissatisfaction and inefficiencies.

Suppose an energy company establishes a budget of professional hours for a particular sustainability audit job. The hours are broken down by audit area, with one area being the valuation of 'clean energy' inventory and cost of goods sold. During the last year, the audit client adopted new procedures for assigning product costs to individual units. The audit budget includes extra hours for the estimated time needed to document and assess the reasonableness of the new method.

Many factors could cause this part of the audit to be over budget. Consider the following two scenarios:

1. The client failed to establish appropriate records needed to easily audit the new method, and this part of the audit will require more than the budgeted time to complete.

2. The auditor assigned to this part of the audit is inexperienced and is unable to complete the work in the budgeted time.

Regardless of the reason for the overage, managers in charge of the audit need to be notified as soon as possible so that they can consider possible ways to realign staff and complete the total job on time. In addition, in the first scenario the audit entity might be able to bill the client for the extra work involved if the audit contract includes a provision for such price adjustments. However, this scenario would most likely require the client to be notified promptly, while the work is still being performed. In the second scenario, the overage may result in a poor performance evaluation, especially if the auditor has similar problems in other audit areas. Yet the overage might be considered reasonable in light of the auditor's inexperience. Even so, the auditor should be able to accomplish the following:

- develop alternative estimates of time and resource requirements for a project
- effectively facilitate and control the project process and take corrective action as needed.

Therefore, the auditor must quickly recognise an impending overage and formulate appropriate strategies for completing the task as efficiently as possible. The auditor also needs to keep her supervisor apprised of the situation and seek help, when needed.

REQUIRED

(a) Have you ever failed to meet a deadline on a group project? If so, what were the reasons for the delay? When and how did you report the delay to your team members? Has someone you know failed to meet a deadline? Does a failure to meet an agreed-upon deadline create an ethical problem? Why?

(b) Explore the responsibilities, expectations, assumptions, incentives and consequences for this problem from different perspectives, including:

- the team member who is late
- other team members
- the team's client.

(c) Draft a policy statement that you could adopt with future team members to handle project delays. How might this policy lead to improved team performance?

(d) Think about your future career. How can you work towards developing your professional responsibility as a member of a work team?

16.25 Ethical decision-making — wasted soup[47] While she was watching operations at a food processing plant, a consultant noticed a large amount of soup on the floor under a filling machine. An operator washed this soup away each day. When asked about the loss of soup, the production manager replied that no losses occurred. In this manager's view, no problem existed because the production line operating costs were below budgeted costs. Later, a productivity team analysed the amount of soup wasted over a given time period. The team estimated the cost of the leak to be $750 000 a year. To correct the problem, the plant installed a set of valves costing $50 000. The new valves eliminated the loss of soup.

Instead of measuring performance against expected budget levels, managers could compare actual profits to ideal profits that could be earned if operations were to run at their true potential. By focusing on the gap between ideal and actual profits, managers are encouraged to identify lost profit potential and to reconsider critical processes. Once gaps are identified, managers rank them according to their value to the organisation and correct them in priority order.

REQUIRED

(a) Is it an ethical problem when employees observe inefficiencies in the workplace, such as the loss of soup in this case? Why?

(b) Why is it common for employees to do nothing when they observe inefficiencies? Compare the responsibility of operation workers to the responsibility of the operating manager with respect to identifying and correcting inefficiencies. In what ways are the responsibilities the same? In what ways are they different?

(c) Is it ethical for employees to ignore inefficiencies? Why? What values did you use to arrive at the conclusion?

(d) People do not always seek to achieve their best performance. For example, students sometimes apply minimum effort to achieve a targeted grade. What does it mean for individuals to seek continuous improvement?

16.26 **Environmental accounting reports; ABC and ABM for environmental costs** Many countries provide motivation for entities to produce environmental accounting reports. For example, 12 countries — United Kingdom, Denmark, Netherlands, Belgium, France and Germany among others — participate in the European Environmental Reporting Awards program. In Japan, the Global Environmental Forum and the National Association for the Promotion of Environmental Conservation have given Environmental Report Awards since 1997. In addition, Tokyo Keizai and the Green Reporting Forum have given a Green Reporting Award since 1998. These awards encourage organisations to take responsibility for environmental conditions that affect the wellbeing of society as a whole. Visy Industries in Australia (refer to the scene setter at the beginning of this chapter) has also been recognised by similar Australian sustainability awards programs.

You are required to conduct research about corporate environmental disclosures. Choose one company located in Japan and a competitor located in Australia. Go to each company's website and search for information about its environmental policies and procedures. Two possible companies are Canon (www.canon.com) and Kodak (www. kodak.com).

Also conduct research to find governmental guidelines for environmental accounting. Go to the website of the Environmental Protection Authority in your state or territory (for example, www.epa.vic.gov.au; www.epa.sa.gov.au) and search for information about environmental or sustainability accounting. Now perform a similar search on the website of Japan's Ministry of the Environment (www.env.go.jp/en). Skim through the information that you find on each website.

In its Environmental Accounting Guidelines of 2002, Japan's Ministry of the Environment identified the following environmental conservation cost categories:

Content	Category
Business area cost	Environmental conservation cost to control environmental impacts resulting from key business operations within the business area
Upstream/downstream cost	Environmental conservation cost to control environmental impacts resulting from key business operations upstream or downstream
Administration cost	Environmental conservation cost stemming from administrative activities
R&D cost	Environmental conservation cost stemming from R&D activities
Social activity cost	Environmental conservation cost stemming from social activities
Environmental remediation cost	Cost incurred for dealing with environmental degradation
Other costs	Other costs related to environmental conservation

(a) Is environmental accounting an ethical issue? Why?

(b) Which company provides the easiest-to-find and most understandable information about environmental policies and procedures? Explain.

(c) Discuss a company's responsibilities for reporting environmental information to various stakeholders including shareholders, managers, employees, other companies, government regulators, product customers and the general public.

(d) If one company provides better reporting than a competitor of its environmental behaviour, policies and procedures, does this mean that the company is more environmentally responsible than its competitor? Why?

(e) What factors are likely to affect an entity's willingness to publish an environmental accounting report?

(f) Discuss possible reasons why the governments of different countries place different degrees of emphasis on environmental accounting reports.

(g) Discuss ways in which ABC systems could be used to capture information for environmental accounting reports.

(h) Discuss ways in which the process of preparing and publishing an environmental accounting report is likely to help a company reduce its environmental costs.

(i) Should all governments require companies to publish environmental accounting reports? What values did you use to arrive at your conclusion?

16.27 **Performance evaluation and sustainability balanced scorecard** BHP Billiton has a 100 per cent ownership interest in Olympic Dam, one of Australia's largest underground mines. Olympic Dam mines about 10 million tonnes of ore to produce copper, uranium, gold and silver. In 2006, BHP Billiton began preparing an environmental impact statement (EIS) for the state and federal governments relating to a proposed major expansion at this site. In early 2007, the EIS was published in draft form for public and government comment. If approvals are received, the proposed expansion will begin in 2009. Construction and commissioning is expected to take about four years.

According to the BHP Billiton report:

> the principal components of the proposed expansion to be addressed by the EIS will include:
> - increasing the amount of ore mined from 10 million tonnes per annum to about 40 million tones per annum (at the time of writing, technical studies indicate that the preferred option would be an open pit in the undeveloped southern portion of the ore body)
> - establishing a new plant for processing the ore
> - sourcing and supplying additional water, possibly from a coastal desalination plant
> - sourcing and supplying additional energy
> - constructing, relocating or upgrading transport infrastructure
> - providing additional infrastructure and services associated with an increased workforce, including expansion of the local Roxby Downs township.[48]

Olympic Dam is situated in South Australia near Roxby Downs and Andamooka (550 km from Adelaide). It sources its water from the Great Artesian Basin. BHP Billiton is proactive in its sustainability activities and is regularly monitored by worldwide sustainability indexes such as the SAM Sustainability Index (see the SAM performance report opposite). BHP Billiton also reports in accordance with the GRI.

Corporate Sustainability Assessment Results

Explanations:

The scores reflect the company's performance across economic, environmental and social criteria compared to its industry average, best and worst performing company in the DJSI World and DJS STOXX in the company's industry. The values for the total score, the dimension and the criteria scores are on a scale from 0 to 100%. Their weighting in the total score is shown in the last column. The DJSI Guidebooks on www.sustainability-index.com contain further information on the assessment methodology.

	Company score (%)	Average score (%)	Best score (%)	Lowest score DJSI World (%)	Lowest score DJSI STOXX (%)	Lowest score DJSI North America (%)	Weighting of dimension or criteria in total score (%)
Explanations	is the actual score of the company	is the industry group's average score	is the highest score reached by a company in the specific industry	is the lowest score of a DJSI World Compnent in the specific industry	is the lowest score of a DJSI STOXX component in the specific industry	is the lowest score of a DJSI North America component in the specific industry	is the weighting of the dimension respectively criteria to calculate the total score

Total scores:

	Company score (%)	Average score (%)	Best score (%)	Lowest score DJSI World (%)	Lowest score DJSI STOXX (%)	Lowest score DJSI North America (%)
Total score	86	57	86	72	84	59

Dimension scores:

	Company score (%)	Average score (%)	Best score (%)	Lowest score DJSI World (%)	Lowest score DJSI STOXX (%)	Lowest score DJSI North America (%)	Weighting in total score (%)
Economic dimension	91	66	92	78	87	58	22.5
Environmental dimension	93	53	93	70	84	61	33.5
Social dimension	79	55	84	71	78	58	44

(continued)

Criteria scores:

Economic dimension

Criteria	Company score (%)	Average score (%)	Best score (%)	Lowest score DJSI World (%)	Lowest score DJSI STOXX (%)	Lowest score DJSI North America (%)	Weighting in total score (%)
Corporate governance	88	70	88	71	71	83	6
Risk & crisis management	82	53	96	59	79	45	6
Codes of conduct compliance/ corruption & bribery	97	68	100	78	93	69	5.5
Transparency (IS)	100	66	100	100	100	30	5

Environmental dimension

Criteria	Company score (%)	Average score (%)	Best score (%)	Lowest score DJSI World (%)	Lowest score DJSI STOXX (%)	Lowest score DJSI North America (%)	Weighting in total score (%)
Environmental performance (eco-efficiency)	100	46	100	55	85	70	7
Environmental reporting	100	83	100	100	100	95	3
Environmental policy/management system (IS)	98	64	98	72	90	62	5
Advanced environmental performance (IS)	100	48	100	100	100	100	2
Climate strategy (IS)	83	29	83	45	66	30	6
Biodiversity (IS)	93	55	93	76	76	51	4.5
Mineral waste management (IS)	83	59	92	78	78	38	4

Social dimension

Criteria	Company score (%)	Average score (%)	Best score (%)	Lowest score DJSI World (%)	Lowest score DJSI STOXX (%)	Lowest score DJSI North America (%)	Weighting in total score (%)
Labor practice indicators	95	66	95	66	66	78	5
Human capital development	41	27	100	41	41	14	5.5
Talent attraction & retention	66	41	74	60	60	60	5.5
Corporate citizenship/philanthropy	70	39	100	70	70	26	3.5
Social reporting	89	69	98	89	89	87	3
Stakeholder engagement (IS)	96	57	96	82	82	50	3.5
Social impacts on communities (IS)	100	61	100	86	86	63	3.5
Mine closure (IS)	100	63	100	62	82	83	4
Occupational health & safety (IS)	85	63	94	70	76	69	7.5
Standards for suppliers (IS)	64	50	97	43	64	56	3

* Criteria assessed based on publicly available information only. ** Not sufficient significant information available.
(IS) Industry specific criteria (does not apply for all industries)

Source: Information from BHP Billiton website, http://hsecreport.bhpbilliton.com.

REQUIRED

Refer to the information in this problem on the proposed expansion of Olympic Dam and the BHP Billiton Sustainability report of 2006.

(a) Prepare a report highlighting some of the management accounting techniques/tools that will be useful for BHP Billiton in its sustainability decision making processes. You may refer to the management accounting techniques discussed in this chapter as well as drawing on other chapters throughout the textbook for your report. As a minimum, this report should include techniques and issues relating to product costing; investment decisions and performance evaluation.

(b) Develop a suitable sustainability balanced scorecard for the senior manager of the Olympic Dam.

REFERENCES

1 United Nations Division for Sustainable Development, www.un.org/esa/sustdev.

2 The Stern Report, www.sternreview.org.uk.

3 Hunting, SA & Tilbury, D 2006, 'Shifting towards sustainability: six insights into successful organisational change for sustainability', Australian Research Institute in Education for Sustainability (ARIES) for the Australian Government Department of the Environment and Water Resources, Sydney, www.aries.mq.edu.au and www.deh.gov.au. Further discussion on this research can be found towards the end of this chapter.

4 Figge, F, Hahn, T, Schaltegger S & Wagner, M 2002, 'The sustainability balanced scorecard — linking sustainability management to business strategy', *Business Strategy and the Environment,* Wiley InterScience, www.interscience.wiley.com.

5 See Renewable Energy Group 2007, *Renewable energy country attractiveness indices, Q2 2007,* Ernst & Young, www.ey.com.

6 As a result of international concerns over global warming, several countries joined an international treaty called the United Nations Framework Convention on Climate Change (UNFCCC) in 1992 and approved the Kyoto Protocol, which has more powerful and legally binding measures. The Kyoto Protocol entered into force on 16 February 2005. Many countries have signed and ratified the Kyoto protocol. Australia signed the Kyoto Protocol on 29 April 1998 but has not ratified the agreement because of concerns for employment, particularly within the coal industry (www.unfccc.int/Kyoto_protocol).

7 See the Stern Report.

8 'ISO (International Organization of Standardization) is an international body of technical standards for various industries. The precise guidelines of ISO provide a long-term economic benefit for businesses that chose to implement them. In manufacturing, ISO 9000 quality standards are universally accepted and the newer ISO 14000 standards for the environmental are now catching on' (www.isostandardsguide.com). ISO 14001 was first released in 1996 and specifies the actual requirements for an entity's environmental management system in which it can be expected to have an influence.

9 Chua, WF 2006, 'Extended performance reporting: a review of empirical studies', Institute of Chartered Accountants in Australia.

10 We will use the term 'sustainability' management accounting' to refer to both social and environmental management accounting. Many earlier texts refer only to 'environmental accounting' concepts. While these terms tend to be used interchangeably by some authors, note that in this book we consider the scope of sustainability management accounting to include both the 'private' as well as the 'societal' impact. Earlier environmental management accounting books tend to consider only the 'private' costs and benefits —those that are traditionally accounted for within the entity's accounting system. More recent trends (driven in part by external reporting requirements)

are towards including social and environmental, private and societal sustainability management.

11 These companies are just a few of the growing number of entities that produce special social, environmental, sustainability or triple bottom line reports to promote their activities to their shareholders and the wider community.

12 For further discussion of corporate social responsibility reporting trends in Australia, see Chua, WF 2006.

13 For example, refer to publications from the Environmental and Sustainability Management Accounting Network, www.eman-eu.net.

14 Chua, WF 2006.

15 See Gray, RH 2000, 'Current development and trends in social and environmental auditing, reporting and attestation: a review and comment', *International Journal of Auditing*, vol 4, pp. 247–68; Deegan, C 2002, 'The legitimising effect of social and environmental disclosures — a theoretical foundation', *Accounting, Auditing & Accountability Journal*, vol. 15, no. 3, pp. 282–311; O'Donovan, G 2002, 'Environmental disclosures in the annual report: extending the applicability and predictive power of legitimacy theory', *Accounting, Auditing & Accountability Journal*, vol. 15, no. 3, pp. 344–71; Nue, D, Warsame, H & Pedwell, K 1998, 'Managing public impressions: environmental disclosures in annual reports', *Accounting, Organisations and Society*, vol. 23, no 3, pp. 265–82.

16 ASX Corporate Governance Council 2003, *Principles of Good Corporate Governance and Best Practice Recommendations*.

17 Cambridge Sustainability Research Digest 2007, University of Cambridge, January, www3.cpi.cam.ac.uk.

18 The AuSSI was launched in 2005 and is published by SAM Indexes (a wholly-owned subsidiary of SAM Group). The Dow Jones Indexes takes responsibility for the index calculation. In 2006, the DJSI-based investment assets amounted to over US$5 billion, representing an increase of 30 per cent over the last 12 months (www.aussi.net.au).

19 Westpac website, www.everygeneration.com.au.

20 Investa website, 'Sustainability policy', www.investa.com.au.

21 From 'What we do', www.globalreporting.org.

22 Refer to the CPA Australia website for Mark Coughlin's address to the Sustainability Summit, www.cpaaustralia.com.au.

23 Figge et al. (2002), p. 278.

24 Clay, S, & Peyton, A 2006, 'Resource efficiency audit: the baseline versus the bottom line', *WME magazine*, September, pp. 27–30. (The entire chapter 16 article is reproduced at the end of this book.)

25 This information has been adapted from United Nations Division for Sustainable Development 2001, 'Environmental management accounting procedures and principles', prepared for the Expert Working Group on 'Improving the role of government in the promotion of environmental management accounting', New York.

26 Refer to the introduction of Kaplan and Norton's 1996 text: Kaplan, R & Norton, D 1996, *The balanced scorecard*, Harvard Business School Press; also Kaplan & Norton 2001, *The strategy-focused organisation*, Harvard Business School Press.

27 See Figge et al. (2002) for further discussion on the sustainability balanced scorecard.

28 Lipe, M & Salterio, S 2000, 'The balanced scorecard: judgemental effects of common and unique performance measures', *The Accounting Review*, vol. 75, no. 3, pp. 283–98.

29 Figge et al. (2002).

30 ibid.

31 ibid.

32 ibid, p. 279.

33 In the past, successful implementation of management accounting innovations has been commonly divided into 'technical' and 'behavioural' issues (see Chenhall &

Langfield-Smith 1998; Young 1998; Shields 1998). This book takes a similar approach when considering the change towards sustainability practices within entities.

34 See Figge et al. (2002), p. 273.

35 Based on Langreth R 2002, 'A cure for neglect', *Forbes,* 18 March.

36 See www.wci-coal.com.

37 Henty, J 2007, 'Supermarket bag packing: a comparative time trial', Environment Victoria, February, www.envict.org.au.

38 ibid.

39 See Connor (2001); The NikeWatch Campaign.

40 Nike website, www.nike.com/nikebiz.

41 'Just stop it,' the NikeWatch Campaign, available at the Oxfam Australia website, www.caa.org.au/campaigns/nike.

42 Connor, T 2001, 'Still waiting for Nike to respect the right to organize,' *Global Exchange,* 28 June, available at www.corpwatch.org.

43 'Sweatshop wars,' *Economist.com,* 25 February 1999.

44 Pownall, G 1986, 'An empirical analysis of the regulation of the defense contracting industry: the Cost Accounting Standards Board,' *Journal of Accounting Research*, vol. 24, no. 2, pp. 291–316.

45 Noreen E & Soderstrom, N 1994, 'Are overhead costs strictly proportional to activity? Evidence from hospital service departments,' *Journal of Accounting & Economics,* January, pp. 255–279.

46 Adapted from Pownall 1986.

47 Thompson and C. Rosen 2003, 'Accounting for higher profits,' *Optimize,* January, pp. 29–34.

48 Information from the BHP Billiton website, http://sustainability.bhpbilliton.com.

Articles

CHAPTER 1

Slave to the supply chain

Conflicting supply chain models are exerting an undue influence on some business sectors.

Just when business thinks it's got it all worked out, markets go and change. The supply chain initiatives of the past decade, which used information technology and managerial techniques to transform, or re-engineer, companies are being re-thought. Changes at the customer end are making distribution strategies more problematic.

Except, perhaps, in Australia. Of the country's two big supermarket chains, Woolworths' imitation of United States retail giant Wal-Mart has proven more successful than Coles Myer's strategy, which is more an emulation of British retailers. But their supply chain strategies have not only determined their companies' fates, they have also made the environment for suppliers onerous. Most suppliers are being asked to deliver with greater frequency, in effect taking on the retailers' inventory costs. They have little control over volumes, and are being asked to adhere to strict protocols. No negotiations are available.

This produces a heavy emphasis on taking costs from existing practices, rather than system-wide innovation. Associate professor Bryan Lukas, head of the marketing and management department at the University of Melbourne, says the main retailers have been 'tightening the screws' on their suppliers. This, he says, is the opposite philosophy to that applied by car manufacturer Toyota, widely accepted as the best exponent of production efficiency and innovation in the world.

'Toyota offers land to suppliers on favourable conditions. The suppliers see Toyota as an extension of their livelihood, and are willing to give ideas and suggestions [about improving the system]. In Australia, the relationships are short-term and hard-nosed. If you have a good idea, why would you give it to them when you are going to be screwed anyway?'

The cost savings can be sizeable. According to John Lydon, a principal and supply chain specialist for consultants McKinsey & Co, consumer products companies have taken about 20 per cent of costs out of their supply chains in the past five years. By contrast, the mining and energy sectors have made few gains, despite having about a third of their cost base in the supply chain. '[The mining companies] are not involved in shipping and that has led to great supply inefficiencies,' he says.

But a supply chain battle based on squeezing suppliers is likely to be an endeavour with declining utility. Savings inevitably become more difficult to achieve unless there is innovation across the whole system. One response is to move into other industries. Mark Reynolds, senior practice manager for consulting firm Accenture, says Woolworths is becoming a de facto trucking company for suppliers, doing frequent deliveries from the factory gate.

Coles Myer takes another approach, sending one truck a week with one load. 'Coles Myer is doing a milk run. It is wildly successful. It is taking a bottom-up approach, and Woolworths, a top-down approach. They are simply managing the fleet. The big trend is to go to the factory gate, but only Coles and Woolworths have the scale to do that.'

Australia is well behind what is happening internationally, mainly because of the heavy concentration of the industry base. Greg Cudahy, Accenture's global head of supply chain practice, says companies are using multiple supply chains more often, depending on the customer. In some instances, even deliberate scarcity is created. Cudahy cites the example of a Streets ice cream that was deliberately released in volumes fixed so it would run out. 'You have "stock outs" with intent. There is a scarcity benefit to only having a limited number.'

The problem is increased complexity in customer behaviour. Lukas says the supply chain 'is the last frontier of marketing, without a doubt'. John Gattorna, author of Living Supply Chains and an academic at the Macquarie Graduate School of Management, says markets are fragmenting. 'It is causing some confusion among suppliers that now have to think deeply about which combination of products, sales channels, pricing and physical fulfilment to use. Some companies are going in the opposite direction and trying to make their businesses easier to manage by seeking to standardise processes, technology and channels. All of which just leads eventually to more exceptions, and therefore, higher costs-to-serve.'

The solution is to segment the market for a product or service along 'behavioural lines', Gattorna says. 'Human behaviour is not as chaotic as first thought. There are never more than three or four really dominant types of buying behaviour in the market for any product or service category. There might be up to 16 or so variants, but never more than three or four at a time.'

Gattorna says one type of behaviour, 'continuous replenishment', is where the customer seeks a trusting relationship. Price is not as important as being predictable and regular. The main requirement is to stay close to the customer and to share forecasts. Margins are usually high and customer retention paramount.

A second type, 'lean supply', where the emphasis is on consistent lowest-price products delivered regularly to schedule, are something different. There is no consideration of brand or a relationship. The imperative is to make accurate forecasts of demand that bring the benefits of scale, and other synergies.

Agile supply chains are a third type. 'We are being besieged by a new breed of very demanding customer who turns up unannounced and wants the world, and very quickly,' Gattorna says. 'They don't have any loyalties other than to themselves because they want instant gratification, and they put a lot of pressure on the supplier to get their way. These customers can be managed, but you can't let them intimidate you.'

He says in this case it is necessary to build in additional capacity which may at times be standing idle, an additional cost. 'You therefore have to charge more to get a fair return on investment and maintain margins. Fashion fits very well into this type of supply chain.'

The fourth type of supply chain is the 'fully flexible' system. 'This is where customers find themselves with major problems of a pressing nature, and they look to the supplier to lead with innovative solutions. Price is not an issue.'

Gattorna says designing and operating all four supply chains requires developing four combinations of 'organisational structures, processes, key performance indicators, internal communications, training programs, and, above all, the same number of leadership styles.' He says some of the sub-cultures have difficulty co-existing because they are opposites.

'Therein lies the challenge. It all boils down to the ability of companies to mirror on the inside of the company what they see on the outside in the marketplace — the biggest rewards going to those finding practical ways to do this. Only a few have achieved this to date: Zara, the Spanish fashion retailer and manufacturer; Li & Fung, the Hong Kong supply chain management company; and the Foster's Group, which is starting to implement this type of strategy.'

Source: James, D 2006, *BRW*, 5 October, p. 52.

CHAPTER 2

Tell bean counters your variable is fixed

It's early summer, and it's just about time to devise your strategy for the annual marketing budget ritual. That means planning for next year and perhaps struggling to find spending givebacks this year so the corporate brass can make their third- and fourth-quarter numbers.

Budgeting is a numbing numbers game, with long hours squinting at a monitor tweaking spreadsheets building in hidden fat you can give back later without hurting your program. But you can spice things up this year: Just tell the bean counters that your advertising and sales promotion expenses are fixed, not variable, costs. Your logic will rest on solid ground, and that will drive budget-slashers right up the wall.

At many companies, the finance-driven view of corporate operations still treats marketing expenses — particularly advertising and sales promotion — as variable costs tied to volume. When unit sales projections head south, they reason, any variable cost that isn't nailed down is fair game for budget liposuction. What they do not realize is that advertising and promotion expenses actually are investments. Advertising and sales promotion create the real assets that build and maintain businesses: market presence, competitive parity (if not advantage), sales leads and a loyal customer base.

Market presence is the ability to have a company, its products and brands, and the value they deliver recognized in the marketplace. Robust marcom is essential for drawing prospects to your Web site and for maintaining competitive strength within business-to-business portals. Marcom fuels the steady flow of sales leads that represent future business.

Finally, the very asset that is the business — a loyal customer base — depends on constant marketing maintenance. Given a slowdown in unit volume, would the bean counters cut payments on the factory mortgage? Probably not, even if they could. But customers are more the core of a business than its bricks-and-mortar.

So in the real world, advertising and sales promotion are less a variable, discretionary cost metered by ups and downs of unit volume and are more a fixed cost of doing business. Without incurring advertising and sales promotion expenses, marketing momentum slows like a flywheel with its motor shut off. Marketplace presence erodes, and new prospects do not appear in the future when they're needed to replenish an attrited account base. Getting the flywheel started again — refilling the lead pipeline and recovering from the nonstatus of an out-of-sight, out-of-mind producer — takes tremendous effort, or you go out of business.

Marketing reasoning does not stop many a company from demanding marketing budget givebacks, however. It's far easier to make 'temporary' cuts in the advertising and sales promotion plan compared with reengineering manufacturing operations or refinancing mortgages. And the effects of cutting advertising and sales promotion aren't as noticeable to financially oriented managers calling the shots. The reason is that accountants have done a poor job in measuring the value of advertising and promotion-generated assets. The problems start with the way traditional cost accounting strives to assign costs to revenue streams as precisely and contemporaneously as possible. So the stereotypical accountant links the cost of making a product to the receipts from selling it, and by extension, the cost of selling a unit of product is part of that unit's overall cost.

Given that logic, traditional planners predict selling costs at budget time according to the unit sales forecast. It's a neat and clean allocation of expenses to the revenue they produce, with little of the messy year-to-year carryover of costs with inexactly measured values.

Ironically, marketing vigor alone seemed until recently to become a new standard for driving stock values, particularly for dot-com firms, the pendulum of thought about marketing spending having swung too far in the other direction. But this year's burst in the stock speculation bubble is putting value investors — with some of them fixated on the instant gratitude of quarterly earnings — back in the driver's seat. They see their money gobbled up at one end of the corporate cow and expect something better to come out the other end in the way of immediate revenue and profit growth.

This summer, politely test how adamantly you can challenge the budget-cutters. Tell them that the cost of keeping customers is fixed, that the cost of lavish furnishings in the CEO's suite is variable, and see if they understand the business well enough to get the point.

Source: Donath, B 2000, *Marketing News*, 19 June, p. 14.

Distinguishing between direct and indirect costs is crucial for Internet companies

Cost management is an important aspect of running a corporation successfully. A crucial part of cost management is the proper allocation of costs to various products and services. Indeed, the way costs are allocated plays a key role in determining the reported profitability of individual products and/or services. In addition, product-line decisions and pricing decisions (of both an internal and external nature) often are affected by cost allocation decisions.

At the heart of cost allocation decisions is the dichotomy between direct and indirect costs. Because a given cost can be direct with respect to one cost objective and indirect with respect to another cost objective, determining the appropriate cost objective is fundamental. This fact notwithstanding, there seems to be a growing concern, if not confusion, on the importance of the distinction between direct and indirect costs for Internet-based businesses. We argue that the distinction between direct and indirect costs is as important for Internet-based companies as it is for other companies. The e-commerce revolution, however, requires many companies to make a fundamental change in the way they consider the notion of a cost objective and, in turn, cost management. In particular, Internet-based companies need to view the *customer* as a primary cost objective for purposes of allocating costs.

Direct vs. indirect costs: a traditional view

Direct costs can easily be traced to the cost objective and can be assigned to the cost objective in a straightforward manner. In contrast, *indirect costs* cannot be easily traced to the cost objective.[1] They need some sort of allocation scheme. Thus, the choice of cost objective is critical to the determination of whether a cost is considered direct or indirect.

A *cost objective* is the purpose for which a cost is being measured. Further, it is quite common for a given cost to be measured for multiple purposes. Thus, a given cost may be direct with respect to one cost objective and indirect with respect to another cost objective.[2] Traditionally, products, services, and departments have served as key cost objectives in managing the operations of a firm. In manufacturing firms, the primary cost objective is traditionally assumed to be the physical products being produced. A computer manufacturer, for example, would usually consider the need to determine the cost of producing a computer as the primary purpose for which costs (at least manufacturing costs) are being measured. As such, the costs of materials and labor that can easily be traced to the production of individual computers would be considered direct costs. Costs of materials and labor that cannot be directly related to the production of individual computers would be considered indirect costs. In a similar vein, the costs associated with depreciating machinery, utilities, and accident insurance would be additional indirect costs in most manufacturing firms.

Knowing the costs of manufacturing a product is important in determining the product's profitability, even where prices are market driven,[3] because in these markets the costs will determine the desirability of being in the market. In markets where prices are driven more by costs, knowing the cost of producing a product is all that more important. Further, many new cost management techniques, such as target costing, are focused on controlling product costs. Assessing the contribution of one subunit versus another subunit within a given company also requires a financial manager to determine product costs for transfer pricing purposes. Accordingly, choosing products as the primary cost objective seems quite logical for most manufacturing firms.

Whereas tangible products are logical choices for primary cost objectives in most manufacturing firms, services are logical choices for primary cost objectives in other firms. For example, in the banking industry, the distinction between a direct and an indirect cost is usually considered in terms of whether the cost can or cannot be directly related to a particular service (e.g. processing a loan). Choosing departments as the primary cost objective seems to make sense in other firms. For example, in a retail department store, the distinction between direct and indirect costs is often thought of in terms of whether the cost can or cannot be related to a specific department (e.g. men's clothing). As with measuring the cost of products, measuring the cost of services and departments will facilitate profitability analysis as well as pricing decisions.[4]

Yet a fundamental change in the way many companies do business has taken place over the past five years. This change falls under the rubric of e-commerce (i.e. electronic commerce) and is largely the result of the Internet. E-commerce has changed the way companies interact with their suppliers and, even more important, the way they interact with their customers. In fact, Internet commerce has changed the very essence of the way many companies do business. Now, many companies generate a large portion of their revenues via the Internet, and a growing number generate the *majority* of their revenues that way. We refer to these companies as Internet-based because they epitomize the essence of the new Information Economy.[5]

To date, most companies still consider costs as being direct or indirect in terms of products, services, or departments. This is true even for many Internet-based firms. Though the basic nature of doing business has changed for a large segment of our economy, the essence of cost management has not changed. In particular, many Internet-based firms have not abandoned the old way of thinking about cost objectives. Yet the important distinction between direct and indirect costs is becoming fuzzy. Some people even argue that distinguishing between direct and indirect costs is no longer a valid way to look at costs for a company operating in an e-commerce environment where intangible assets (e.g. intellectual capital) are so prevalent. For example, in the popular book *The Blur*, Davis and Myer argue that 'direct costs are dead, and diminishing marginal returns died with them, a victim of intangibles.' We disagree!

In our opinion, the need to differentiate between direct and indirect costs is as valid today in an e-commerce environment as it is in a traditional (brick-and-mortar) environment. Profitability analysis, product-line decisions, and pricing decisions are still significantly affected by the way costs are classified in terms of direct and indirect. The thing that is often no longer valid, however, is the focus on the old notion of cost objectives for firms that operate in an e-commerce environment. We believe companies actively involved in e-commerce need to view customers, as well as products, services, and departments, as key cost objectives. Nowhere is this need more important than in Internet-based firms.

Direct vs. indirect costs in Internet-based firms

The number of firms that derive the majority of their sales over the Internet has grown at a rapid rate. The U.S. Bureau of Census conservatively estimated that $5.3 billion (0.64%) of retail sales in the fourth quarter of 1999 was conducted using the Internet.[6] Furthermore, this estimate excludes the huge number of Internet sales from business to business. Clearly, the growth of the Internet is changing all facets of commerce. Understanding the impact of these changes on corporate cost management systems is vital.

The distinguishing feature of an e-commerce environment is that business transactions are handled electronically. The hallmark of such an environment has become the way firms interact with customers via the Internet. A logical way to decide whether to classify a firm as being dominated by an e-commerce environment is to use the percentage of the firm's sales generated from the Internet. For a firm to be eligible for the Dow Jones Internet Composite Index (which is further subdivided into the Dow Jones Internet Commerce Index and the Dow Jones Internet Service Index), the company must generate at least half of its sales via the Internet.[7]

Internet customers, be they households, businesses, or government agencies, can and do conduct quick and inexpensive shopping comparisons. These comparisons take place in a nanosecond, with the click of a mouse. Hence companies are required to continually adjust prices to respond to price changes initiated by competitors. At the same time, their competitors are making similar price adjustments. As a result, companies are required to expend continuous real-time efforts at attracting and tracking customers.

In the e-commerce environment, where information search costs approach zero and competitors match price cuts almost instantaneously, competing only in price is not likely to be the means to attracting and maintaining a loyal customer base. Pricing over the Internet has pushed firms to operate in highly competitive, if not purely competitive, economic markets. Businesses are quickly learning that a comparative advantage in the cyber marketplace (or, as some have called it, the marketspace) can be secured only by competing effectively in quality customer service to the point of becoming customer-centric. Understanding and managing such services requires the allocation of these costs among customers. The proper allocation, in this regard, requires that customers become a key, if not the primary, cost objective for the purposes of distinguishing between direct and indirect costs.

Most Internet-based firms use business models that are classified as business-to-business (B2B) or business-to-consumer (B2C). As the names of these models indicate, B2B means that the firm is using the Internet to generate sales of goods and services to other businesses, while B2C means that the firm uses the Internet to generate sales directly to consumers (i.e. retail sales). In addition, the business models used by some Internet-based firms would be classified as business-to-government (B2G) or consumer-to-consumer (C2C). B2G means that the firm sells its products and services primarily to government agencies. C2C means that the firm (for example, eBay) facilitates direct trades among consumers by providing a central marketplace in cyberspace. A firm using a C2C business model typically generates revenues from fees and commissions paid by consumers for participating in the electronic marketplace. Of course, many major corporations use more than one of the above business models.

Security analysts and the general investing public commonly use the B2B designation to refer to companies (e.g. Ariba and i2 Technologies) that produce products and services (e.g. software and consulting) to facilitate B2B transactions among businesses via the Internet. The products and services produced by such B2B firms use the Internet to help match sellers of inputs of production with the buyers of these inputs in an efficient manner so firms secure the right inputs at the right time at minimum cost. Such supply chain management benefits sellers by expanding their geographical market to the entire globe and benefits buyers by facilitating the search for low-cost suppliers, reducing the processing costs associated with materials acquisition, and reducing their inventory holding costs.

While the companies designated in the media as B2B firms have often been associated with generating high growth in revenues and profits, the larger effects of the B2B revolution are seen outside the firms given the B2B designation. The larger impact on the economy comes from the rapidly expanding number of firms that have embraced B2B for their supply chain management and for sales of their products to other businesses. Irrespective of whether a firm uses the Internet to sell its products and/or services to other businesses, to consumers, or to government agencies, the environment of electronic commerce requires successful firms to focus data collection on customers or customer classes. Because selling via the Internet empowers customers by reducing their information search costs and their costs of switching from one vendor to another, firms selling via the Internet have stronger motivation to treat customers as key cost objectives than do firms that sell through non-Internet sources.

Whether using e-commerce for retail sales or business-to-business sales, companies must devote substantial resources to providing their customers with a user friendly, secure, and hassle-free shopping experience. The development, maintenance, and enhancement of software that keeps track of customer preferences is essential for ensuring such an experience. In essence, Internet-based firms rely much less on traditional infrastructure assets, such as buildings, and more on computers, specialized software, and intellectual capital that cater to customers in cyberspace.

When comparing one seller with another, customers cannot compare the service level that would be provided as easily as they can compare quoted prices. Nevertheless, with the wealth of information on the Web, including the seller's website, websites of consumer groups, bulletin boards, and message boards, customers can gather information about the quality of service at a fraction of the cost of a decade earlier. These comparisons result in diminishing customer loyalty. Moreover, with venture capitalists funding start-up companies on a regular basis and with more brick-and-mortar companies adding e-commerce divisions, new competition is constantly coming to the marketplace. Thus, companies face a dynamic, increasingly competitive environment.

In this new environment, companies that are going to be competitive need to devote substantial resources to attracting customers through advertising on the Internet as well as in traditional media (e.g. newspapers, magazines, and television) that direct customers to the firm's Internet sales site. During the actual sales, it is easier for competitive Internet-based firms than traditional firms to customize the physical product (e.g. specifications of a machine being purchased by one firm from another) or service (e.g. loan agreement) being sold. Internet-based sales provide an easy mechanism for direct and instantaneous contact with customers so companies can quickly modify products to new specifications (e.g. the addition or deletion of a clause in a loan agreement). It is also incumbent upon e-commerce firms to provide a high level of post-sale services to customers because such services are often carried out in an easy, quick, and inexpensive manner. Tracking delivery from the time of sale is a good example of the type of post-sale service easily provided in an e-commerce environment.

For all the reasons we have noted, tracing costs to individual customers and/or customer classes is an essential competitive strategy for Internet-based companies. In other words, the customer must be a primary cost objective for them. Furthermore, tracing costs to customers cannot be considered a one-time or even periodic investment. Instead, tracing costs to customers must be done on a continuous basis and requires a real-time cost system. For many Internet-based companies, this requires a major change from the way they accumulate costs.[8] In fact, Internet-based firms that fail to treat customers as a primary cost objective face the danger of being outsmarted by the competition and left with the least profitable customers in the marketplace.[9]

For an Internet-based retailer, the costs of products a customer buys would be classified as direct costs for the customer. For an Internet-based manufacturing firm, the manufacturing cost of products would represent an intermediate cost objective, and the total cost (including costs which are indirect with respect to products) would be traced directly to the customers. Because software can identify the specific Internet advertising that routes a particular customer to the firm's e-store, the cost of this advertising can also be allocated to customers in [a] logical manner. It may even be possible to trace specific software-related costs to particular customers in an e-commerce environment, thereby treating these costs as direct costs in terms of customers.[10] In essence, many of the costs of pre- and post-sale services, as well as the costs for services incurred during the actual sale, could be traced to individual customers and/or customer classes and treated as direct costs for e-commerce firms.[11] Costs that cannot be traced directly to individual customers and/or customer classes, such as the costs associated with computer hardware, would be treated as indirect costs.

By treating the customer as a primary cost objective, effective resource allocation decisions will be enhanced. In addition, effective customer profitability analysis, pricing decisions, and marketing decisions will be greatly facilitated. Finally, and of no small consequence, the use of customers as a primary cost objective will facilitate the very essence of being an Internet-based firm (i.e. an Internet-based cost management system will facilitate e-commerce business).

It is well known, and accepted, that focusing on the needs and desires of customers is fundamental to running a successful business. This is true whether the business is Internet-based or brick-and-mortar. Yet a fundamental cost objective for Internet-based firms needs to be the customer. In other words, in accumulating and allocating costs, Internet-based firms need to adopt a customer focus. Once they recognize this fact, it becomes clear that the distinction between direct and indirect costs is as important for them as it is for other firms.

Of course, the fact that Internet-based firms need to adopt a customer focus in allocating costs in no way mitigates the potential importance of knowing the costs of individual products (or services) as well as departments. Thus, Internet-based firms may well consider other cost objectives in differentiating between direct and indirect costs. To the extent that this is the case, the argument that distinguishing between direct and indirect costs is a relevant and important activity for Internet-based firms is only strengthened.

Use management accounting techniques properly

Cost allocations are fundamental to effective cost management, and, as we have emphasized, a key aspect of cost allocations is the distinction between direct and indirect costs. Nevertheless, the claim that this distinction is not relevant to Internet-based companies has been promulgated lately. We disagree with this claim, for the reasons given above. A fundamental aspect of our argument is the need for Internet-based firms to trace costs to customers. Hence, Internet-based firms need to treat the customer as a primary cost objective in differentiating between direct and indirect costs.

The new Information Economy has important implications for the field of management accounting. Direct vs. indirect costs is only one such implication. Other implications include the way companies need to consider performance measures, profit planning, and the use of cost information for pricing decisions. While the sum of these implications represents a fundamental shift in the management accounting paradigm, it does not represent the demise of management accounting. Indeed, the proper use of management accounting techniques is more relevant to the survival of firms in today's dynamic information economy than ever before in the history of commerce.

---

1. Indirect costs are often referred to as overhead costs. Because the term overhead is misleading, we will use indirect to refer to such costs.

2. For examples illustrating this point, see Chapter 3 of Gordon, *Managerial Accounting: Concepts and Empirical Evidence*, in Further Reading section.

3. In the extreme case of prices being set by the marketplace, we have what economists refer to as a purely competitive market. In a purely competitive market, firms essentially take the market price as given and need to focus on cost management techniques to earn a desirable level of profit.

4. Of course, firms are interested in many cost objectives. Hence, the designation of one cost objective as primary does not preclude the use of other cost objectives.

5. Our definition of what constitutes an Internet-based firm is consistent with the way Dow Jones derives its list of such firms (i.e. for more information, see http://indexes.dowjones.com./djii/djiiabout.html)

6. The U.S. Department of Commerce reports (*Digital Economy 2000*, June 2000, p.9), 'private estimates for consumer e-commerce in the fourth quarter of 1999 ranged from approximately $4 billion to $14 billion.'

7. Clearly, the trend is for all firms to increase their Internet-based sales. Accordingly, the distinction between Internet-based firms and non-Internet-based firms is one of degree rather that absoluteness. Over time, it seems logical to expect more and more firms to become Internet-based.

8. Although not the focus of this article, it is equally important for Internet-based firms to identify the revenues of individual customers and/or customer classes.

9. The growing emphasis on linking customers to the production process in the emerging literature on supply chain management is consistent with this argument. For an interesting discussion on the use of 'customer-product maps,' in the context of supply chain management, see Cloud in the Further Reading section.

10. In a non-e-commerce environment, computer-related costs are traditionally considered to be indirect with respect to a firm's products and services. Given that these assets are an important aspect of an e-commerce firm's assets, this reclassification has nontrivial implications.

11. Recent work in database design has centered on customer-focused data models. This work has particular relevance to the arguments presented in this section.

FURTHER READING

R. J. Cloud, 'Supply Chain Management: New Role for Finance Professionals,' *Strategic Finance*, August 2000, pp. 28–32.

S. Davis and C. Myer, *Blur: The Speed of Change in the Connected Economy*, Addison Wesley, 1998.

Dow Jones Internet Indexes, Dow Jones Company, 2000, http://indexes.dowjones.com./djii/djiiabout.html.

L. A. Gordon, *Managerial Accounting: Concepts and Empirical Evidence*, 5th Edition, McGraw-Hill, 2000.

United States Commerce Dept., *Digital Economy 2000*, June 2000, http://www.esa.doc.gov/de2000.pdf.

Source: Gordon, LA & Loeb, MP 2001, *Management Accounting Quarterly*, summer, pp. 13–17.

CHAPTER 4

Using activity-based costing to assess channel/customer profitability

Better understanding of your customers' profitability picture is imperative for survival in today's competitive environment. Here the CFO of an employment services company used ABC to analyze the company's prortability picture at the customer channel- and individual customer-level.

'With better information and accounting systems, firms are beginning to disaggregate revenues and costs to customer or account level. This analysis often reveals previously hidden subsidies across customers, products, and markets.'[1]

Most firms are well aware of the 80/20 rule in which a small fraction of customers accounts for a large share of revenues and most of a firm's profits. As the above quote states, that small fraction of profitable customers subsidizes the firm's other unprofitable or, at best, breakeven customers. Instead of accepting the 80/20 rule, firms should strive to identify those subsidized customers and work with them in either altering the servicing of those customers (including pricing) to a more equitable arrangement or outsourcing the servicing of those customers altogether.

Temp Employment Company, Inc. (TEC), a firm in the employment services industry, used Activity-Based Costing (ABC) in assessing the profitability picture in order to better understand which customers were profitable and which were subsidized. This article describes the journey of TEC's chief financial officer through the ABC implementation and subsequent analysis. (Note: The name of the actual company has been changed and the financial data altered to protect the company's confidentiality.)

ABC and the firm

TEC is a multi-office employment services firm offering temporary employment and permanent placements. The temporary employment division represents over 70% of TEC's business and is the focus of this article. Before covering how TEC used ABC information to assess its profitability picture, TEC's ABC implementation will be briefly discussed. Table 1 summarizes the four-step process TEC completed in transforming its cost management system.

TABLE 1 ■ Four steps in developing an ABC system

1. Develop the activity dictionary.
2. Determine how much the organization is spending on each of its activities.
3. Identify the organization's products, services, and customers.
4. Select activity cost drivers that link activity costs to the organization's products, services, and customers.
R. S. Kaplan and R. Cooper, Cost & Effect: Using integrated Cost Systems to Drive Profitability and Performance, *Harvard Business School Press, Boston, Mass., 1998.*

Step 1. Develop the activity dictionary.

In the first step, TEC was divided into activities. It would have been possible to divide TEC into several activities, but it was important to develop a simple, yet meaningful, system. Three activities were defined as relevant to the operations of the firm: 1) filling work orders, 2) hiring temporary employees, and 3) processing payroll/billing.

The *filling work orders* activity begins once an order is received from a customer and ends when the customer is provided with the name(s) of the temporary employee(s) assigned to work for them. The *hiring temporary employees* activity involves the process of hiring employees for temporary assignments. This activity begins when an application is completed and ends once the employee is debriefed on company polices and entered in the system. The last activity, *processing payroll/billing*, involves the weekly payroll and customer billing process.

Step 2. Determine how much the organization is spending on each of its activities.

Once the activities were identified, the CFO assigned the direct costs associated with each one. Any resource that could not be directly traced to an activity was initially assigned to a general overhead account. Once the directly traceable resources were assigned to each activity, the general overhead was allocated. Table 2 summarizes the results of assigning the costs to the three activities of TEC. The general overhead was allocated to each activity on the basis of the directly traceable costs of each activity to total directly traceable costs.

TABLE 2 ■ Temp Employment Company, Inc. — Activity-rate calculations

Account name	Total	Filling work orders	Hiring temporaries	Processing payroll	General overhead	Total allocated
Salaries & wages	$125 638	$ 57 501	$ 16 197	$12 308	$39.632	$125 638
Payroll taxes	11 192	5 118	1 442	1 095	3 537	11 192
Advertising	55 896	25 494	30 402	---	---	55 896
Automotive	15 718	7 722	---	---	7 996	15 718
Telephone	11 746	7 048	2 349	2 349	---	11 746
Rent	9 600	2 400	2 400	4 800	---	9 600
Other operating expenses	91 144	10 760	1 961	4 305	74 118	91 144
Total operating expenses	$320 934	$116 043	$54 751	$24 857	$125 283	$320 934
Allocation of general overhead		74 307	35 059	15 917	(125 283)	$ ---
	$320 934	$190 350	$89 810	$40 774	$ ---	$320 934
Cost drivers						
# of temporaries ordered		3 946				
# of applicants			3 380			
# of hours worked				246 370		
Activity rates		$48.239	$26.571	$0.1655		

Step 3. Identify the organization's products, services, and customers.

As mentioned earlier, TEC offers two services, temporary employment and permanent placements. Within each service offering, TEC's customers are separated between two channels, industrial and clerical, depending upon the job classification of the position they are seeking to fill. Industrial customers hire temporary employees to fill touch-labor positions (such as assembly, machine operator). On the other hand, clerical customers seek to hire office positions (such as receptionist or secretarial).

Step 4. Select activity cost drivers that link activity costs to the organization's products, services, and customers.

The goal of identifying a cost driver for an activity is to determine the source that causes the consumption of that activity — what drives the activity. The cost driver identified must be quantifiable and reasonably accessible. The three activities and the related cost drivers are discussed next.

Filling work orders

The first activity identified was 'filling work orders'. As stated earlier, customer service coordinators begin to fill work orders once a customer calls in a request for a temporary employee. If a customer does not call in an order, there is no work order to fill. It makes sense then that the cost driver for the 'filling work orders' activity is the number of temporaries ordered by customers.

This is used as the cost driver instead of the number of orders generated because an individual order can be for more than one temporary employee. The more temporaries on an order, the more servicing of the account is required. Thus, the number of temporaries ordered is a better indicator of resources consumed by the activity than the number of orders.

Hiring temporary employees

The company cannot hire temporaries unless someone comes in seeking employment. The cost driver used for 'hiring temporary employees' is the number of applicants seeking employment. Each person seeking employment at TEC requires significant resources and time before he/she is eligible for a job assignment.

Processing payroll/billing

Processing a paycheck for each employee and generating an invoice for each customer is performed weekly and is based on the number of hours worked. Because each hour worked requires this activity, the number of hours worked during the period in question appears to be the best cost driver for the 'processing payroll/billing' activity.

Step 5. Calculate activity rates for each activity identified.

TEC added another step, which was to calculate the activity rate for each activity identified. The following activity rates were calculated (see table 2):

Filling work orders	$48.2390
Hiring temporary employees	$26.5710
Processing payroll/billing	$0.1655

The information collected from these five steps was used to assess TEC's profitability at the customer level. Customer profitability analysis was conducted in three stages. The first stage assessed customer-channel profitability (industrial and clerical channels). In the second stage, the information obtained from the first stage was used to assess classes of customers within each channel. Finally, the third stage involved assessing the profitability of individual customers.

Channel profitability

Table 3 displays the profitability picture by customer channel. When the gross margins are examined, major differences between the channels become apparent. TEC's margin in the industrial channel is significantly less than its margin in the clerical channel. The industrial customers demand lower rates for temporary employees, but the tight labor market prevents TEC from lowering wage rates. Also, industrial customers have significantly higher workers' compensation rates than clerical customers, which we will discuss later. Customers in the clerical channel demand quality over price, so a higher bill-to-pay rate is permissible.

TABLE 3 ■ Temp Employment Company, Inc. — Profitability analysis by customer channels

	Clerical	%	Industrial	%	Total	%
Sales	$294 714	100.0%	$1 859 852	100.0%	$2 154 566	100.0%
Cost of sales						
Wages — temporary employees	200 377	68.0%	1 323 827	71.2%	1 524 204	70.7%
Payroll taxes & fees	28 629	9.7%	251 879	13.5%	280 508	13.0%
Total cost of sales	229 006	77.7%	1 575 706	84.7%	1 804 712	83.8%
Gross margin	65 708	22.3%	284 146	15.3%	349 854	16.2%
OVERHEAD ALLOCATIONS						
Filling work orders:						
Number of temporaries ordered	508		3 438		3 946	
× Activity rate	$48.239		$48.239		$48.239	
	24 505	8.3%	165 846	8.9%	190 351	8.8%
Hiring temporary employees:						
Number of applicants	3 380		3 380		3 380	
× % of orders to total	12.9%		87.1%		100%	
Applicants by channel	436		2 944		3 380	
× Activity rate	$26.571		$26.571		$26.571	
	11 585	3.9%	78 225	4.2%	89 810	4.2%
Processing payroll/billing:						
Hours worked	32 890		213 480		246 370	
× Activity rate	$0.1655		$0.1655		$0.1655	
	5 443	1.8%	35 331	1.9%	40 774	1.9%
Total overhead allocation	41 534	14.1%	279 402	15.0%	320 936	14.9%
Net profit	$24 174	8.2%	$4 744	0.3%	$28 918	1.3%

In allocating activity cost between channels for the 'hiring temporary employees' activity, the CFO discovered there was no easily accessible procedure for determining if an applicant applied for clerical or industrial employment. That information is documented only if the applicant is hired by TEC. For the initial analysis, the CFO decided to use the ratio of the number of temporaries ordered by channel to total temporaries ordered across both channels. Multiplying this ratio by the total number of applicants provided the number of applicants for each channel.

There is some logic with the formula. The number of temporaries ordered determines the types of temporaries needed; this, in turn, forces the firm to focus its energies on hiring those types of temporaries. In other words, there is a close relationship between the number of temporaries ordered and the type of individuals applying for employment at TEC. Procedures were instituted to capture the relevant information during the application process to assign 'hiring temporary employees' costs more accurately to the appropriate channel in the future.

As shown in table 3, the industrial channel comprises only 16% of total company profits, while its sales are over 86% of total company sales. The channel's net profit is only 0.3% of sales. In sharp contrast, the clerical side shows profits of 8.2% of sales. From the initial analysis of table 3, the CFO began to see potential signs of trouble. TEC's largest customer channel is on the verge of going into the red. The clerical channel does not have enough sales to support the entire company for any length of time. Conclusion: The industrial channel must be an income producer for the overall success of the company. The initial analysis shows overall signs of weakness, but the CFO decided to analyze the industrial channel in more detail by applying ABC to the three classes of customers in the industrial channel to identify problems better.

Industrial class profitability

By examining the composition of the industrial channel, the CFO discovered it was possible to divide the channel into three classifications by workers' compensation (WC) rates. As previously stated, the industrial customers are charged a much higher workers' compensation rate than clerical customers. In addition, there is a wide range of rates charged within the industrial channel. The industrial customers are divided into three classes by workers' compensation rates: Low WC class (WC rates under $5/$1000 of wages paid), Average WC class (WC rates $5 to $8.99/$1000 of wages paid), and High WC class (WC rates $9 and over/$1000 of wages paid). Table 4 displays the cost allocation of the industrial channel by workers' compensation rates.

Low WC class

The Low WC rate class is 20% of the total industrial channel, but it is responsible for over 400% of the industrial channel profits. An obvious conclusion is that the company is incurring losses elsewhere (i.e. the Low WC rate class is subsidizing other unprofitable customers). TEC budgeted an 18% gross margin for the industrial channel; the Low WC class's gross margin is in line with the budget. From this analysis, the Low WC class appears to be contributing to the overall success and profits of the company. The goal of TEC should be to maintain the current pricing arrangements for these customers, The company also should look into targeting industries that would fall into this class to increase the sales volume and, in turn, the net profits of the company.

High WC class

As expected, the gross margin is lower in the High WC class than in the other classes due to the large increase in the WC rate. What is surprising, however, is that the wages paid to the temporary employees are over 73% of sales as compared to just over 70% for Low WC class employees. Ideally, higher rates should be charged to those customers with higher variable costs, but the company is unable to do so because of the competitive nature of the industry. The low gross margin is partly attributable to one customer who accounts for nearly 70% of the total sales generated in this class. The customer, a trailer manufacturer, is a consistent user of long-term temporaries. TEC conceded a price break to the customer due to the high-volume use of temporaries.

The High WC class generates a net profit even with the low gross margin. The overhead allocation is significantly less than with the other two classes because of the long-term nature of the assignments of the temporary employees in this class. Only 165 temporaries were

TABLE 4 ■ Temp Employment Company, Inc. — Profitability analysis by industrial channel classes

	Low WC rates	%	Average WC rates	%	High WC rates	%	Total	%
Sales	$369 911	100.0%	$1 280 184	100.0%	$ 209 757	100.0%	$1 859 852	100.0%
Cost of sales								
Wages — temporary employees	260 019	70.3%	909 247	71.0%	154 561	73.7%	1 323 827	71.2%
Payroll taxes & fees	43 284	11.7%	174 037	13.6%	34 558	16.5%	251 879	13.5%
Total cost of sales	303 303	82.0%	1 083 284	84.6%	189 119	90.2%	1 575 706	84.7%
Gross margin	$66 608	18.0%	$ 196 900	15.4%	$ 20 638	9.8%	$ 284 146	15.3%
OVERHEAD ALLOCATIONS								
Filling work orders:								
Number of temporaries ordered	554		2 719		165		3 438	
× Activity rate	$48.239		$48.239		$48.239		$48.239	
	26 724	7.2%	131 162	10.2%	7959	3.8%	165 846	8.9%
Hiring temporary employees:								
Number of applicants	2 944		2 944		2 944		2 944	
× % of orders to total	16.1%		79.1%		4.8%		100%	
Applicants by channel	474		2 329		141		2 944	
× Activity rate	$26.571		$ 26.571		$ 26.571		$ 26.571	
	12 594	3.4%	61 876	4.8%	3 755	1.8%	78 225	4.2%
Processing payroll/billing:								
Hours worked	45 140		146 023		22 317		213 480	
× Activity rate	$0.1655		$0.1655		$0.1655		$ 0.1655	
	7 471	2.0%	24 167	1.9%	3 693	1.8%	35 331	1.9%
Total overhead allocation	46 789	12.6%	217 205	17.0%	15 408	7.3%	279 402	15.0%
Net profit	$ 19 819	5.4%	$(20 305)	–1.6%	$5 230	2.5%	$4 744	0.3%

ordered during the period of analysis. The low number of temporaries ordered (the cost driver for the 'filling work orders' activity) results in the class being allocated less cost for the 'filling work orders' activity.

Average WC class

The last class in the industrial channel to examine, the Average WC class, is suffering from a net loss. The largest class in relation to total sales volume, it is also allocated over 77% of the overhead costs based on the activity analysis and is responsible for only 69% of the industrial sales. Is the Average WC class being penalized with excessive overhead allocation? No. The customers in the Average WC class consume considerable time and effort to service.

The typical job assignments within this class vary from one day to several weeks. Customers order from one to more than 20 temporaries for these assignments, and customer service coordinators are continually searching for temporaries to fill these jobs. The firm's classified advertisements heavily recruit for employees in this class, and the heavy recruitment means more individuals apply for employment. The Average WC class should be allocated a large portion of overhead. The activity analysis accomplishes that task.

Examining the net profits shown in table 4 demonstrates the classic whale-curve effect. The Low WC class generates over 400% of total profits while the Average WC class loses over 400% of total profits. This leaves the profits generated by the High WC class comprising nearly 100% of the industrial channel profits. Even at this second stage of analysis, areas that need further investigation are revealed.

Customer profitability

Table 5 summarizes the activity analysis of the four largest customers of TEC according to sales volume. The four customers account for almost 42% of the total sales volume of the company and over 48% of the industrial channel sales. Using activity-based costing, an analysis of these four customers was undertaken to uncover problem areas with them.

Chemical company

TEC supplies 100% of the chemical company's production and supervisory personnel. Initial results indicate a net profit of 9.8%, much higher than even the electrical channel net-profit percentage. One reason for this is the low overhead allocation to this customer. For example, under the 'filling work orders' activity, only 86 temporaries were ordered, a relatively low number. One of the reasons for this is the long-term nature of the assignments. Another reason is the hiring practices of the company. The chemical company has one person on-site to recruit employees. Once the chemical company hires a recruit, TEC is notified about the new employee, and the application is sent to him or her. For these two reasons, the over-head consumed by the chemical company is minimal as compared to other customers. As long as the company continues the use of an on-site coordinator to recruit, it should continue to generate profits for TEC.

Trailer manufacturer

Similar to the chemical company, the trailer manufacturer requests long-term employees. Orders for the trailer manufacturer are for normal turnover and peak periods of production. For the period under examination, only 56 temporaries were ordered, normal for the time of year. The gross margin for the customer is uncomfortably low due to the billing arrangement with the customer and the high WC rates incurred. Because the customer does not consume a large portion of the activities identified, however, it is not burdened with a high overhead allocation and is generating just over 3% net profit. As long as the trailer manufacturer maintains the low consumption of activities, TEC should be able to maintain the current profit level.

TABLE 5 ■ Temp Employment Company, Inc. — Profitability analysis by selected customers

	Chemical company	%	Trailer manufacturer	%	Newspaper publisher	%	Food processor	%
Sales	$466 733	100.0%	$145 764	100.0%	$122 604	100.0%	$ 167 327	100.0%
Cost of sales								
Wages — temporary employees	341 620	73.2%	110 473	75.8%	92 205	75.2%	120 451	72.0%
Payroll taxes & fees	65 366	14.0%	24 350	16.7%	18 621	15.2%	23 411	14.0%
Total cost of sales	406 986	87.2%	134 823	92.5%	110 826	90.4%	143 862	86.0%
Gross margin	$ 59 747	12.8%	$10 941	7.5%	$ 11 778	9.5%	$ 23 465	14.0%
OVERHEAD ALLOCATIONS **Filling work orders:**								
Number of temporaries ordered	86		56		928		332	
× Activity rate	$48.239		$48.239		$48.239		$48.239	
	4 149	0.9%	2 701	1.9%	44 766	36.5%	16 015	9.6%
Hiring temporary employees:								
Number of applicants	2944		2944		2944		2944	
× % of orders to total	2.5%		1.6%		27.0%		9.7%	
Applicants by channel	74		47		794		285	
× Activity rate	$26.571		$26.571		$26.571		$26.571	
	1 954	0.4%	1 250	0.9%	21 099	17.2%	7 580	4.5%
Processing payroll/billing:								
Hours worked	47 371		15 113		13 000		22 762	
× Activity rate	$0.1655		$0.1655		$ 0.1655		$ 0.1655	

(continued)

TABLE 5 (*continued*)

	Chemical company	%	Trailer manufacturer	%	Newspaper publisher	%	Food processor	%
	7 840	1.7%	2 501	1.7%	2 152	1.8%	3 767	2.3%
Total overhead allocation	13 942	3.0%	6 453	4.4%	68 017	55.5%	27 363	16.4%
Net profit	$45 805	9.8%	$4 488	3.1%	$(56 239)	−45.9%	$(3 898)	−2.3%

Newspaper publisher

The newspaper company is a good example of the typical customer in the average WC class. It manages its temporary employment needs differently from the other two customers discussed. The customer calls daily to order the number of temporaries needed that night, usually ranging from 10 to 40 individuals. Customer service coordinators are constantly searching for temporaries to fill the needs of this customer. The newspaper publisher consumes a significantly higher proportion of activities than the other two customers.

One of the peculiar situations regarding this company is the standing request by a few of the temporary employees themselves to work at the newspaper publisher. As a result, the customer service coordinators only have to call the temporaries and ask what shift they want to work. Even though the company requested 928 temporaries during the time period investigated, some of those requests were filled rather easily. How was the situation handled by the activity-based costing model? Basically, the situation was ignored. The newspaper company was allocated the same rate no matter how easy or difficult it was for TEC to fill the orders. This was one of the deficiencies of the activity analysis performed by the CFO.

Table 5 illustrates some startling results for the newspaper publisher, the first being the low gross margin. The culprit is the low ratio of bill-to-pay rates. TEC was required to lower its rates to retain the customer. The low bill rates along with the high overhead allocation result in a large net-loss situation. The company is allocated 27% of the 'filling work orders' activity while accounting for just over 6% of the industrial channel's revenue. A similar pattern holds true for the 'hiring temporaries' activity. Some tough decisions must be addressed regarding the future of servicing the newspaper publisher.

Food processing company

The company uses temporary employees for its production line on a consistent basis throughout the year, with a mix of long- and short-term assignments. As displayed in table 5, the company generated higher sales than the newspaper publisher, but it only had requests for 332 temporaries as compared to 928. The gross margin for the food processor is the highest among the customers examined, but the high gross margin does not offset the activities consumed by the customer. The bottom-line result is a net loss. As with the newspaper publisher, TEC must address the net-loss situation.

Final analysis

The activity analysis conducted by the CFO generated some startling results. It reaffirmed some beliefs and destroyed others held by TEC's management. The company held to the notion that the sales composition of the company was 60% industrial and 40% clerical. Table 3 clearly indicates the composition as 85% industrial and 15% clerical. This is one explanation for the overall weak profit. As explained earlier, the industrial customers traditionally generate lower profits. Driving the analysis to the industrial channel class provides a richer description of TEC's profitability picture.

Table 4 shows that the largest industrial class, the Average WC class, is generating significant losses. In other words, almost 70% of the company's business is generating losses. What can be done to reverse this situation? An immediate response might be to attempt to increase the bill rates charged, but the industrial temporary employment industry is very elastic, and any attempt at increasing rates will produce an immediate decrease in demand. Another area of concern is the pay rates. TEC has been forced to increase the pay rates due to the low unemployment rate. The pool of temporary employees is small, so they demand a higher rate. Because the company cannot raise billing rates or lower pay rates, the only area available for improvement is overhead reduction.

Some revealing results are encountered in table 5. TEC's first problem is with the newspaper publisher. The bill rates and pay rates are fixed, so can the overhead allocated to this customer be lowered? One way is to change the way the customer requests and uses temporaries. As mentioned earlier, the customer calls daily with an order for temporaries and is unconcerned whether the temporaries are new or repeats. A preferred method would have the customer call, or be called, once a week with an order for the entire week. The temporaries could be assigned on a weekly basis. Also, an analysis of the number of temporaries usually ordered would be helpful to determine if a small core of long-term assignments could be employed. This method would reduce the consumption of activities by the customer and turn it into a profitable venture for TEC.

A key point: A reduction in the overhead allocated to a customer will not, in and of itself, reduce the overhead incurred by the company, Activity-based costing does not reduce costs — it only reallocates them based on the consumption of activities identified. As a result, a customer who begins to consume fewer activities without the simultaneous reduction in overhead by the company will only result in a shifting of overhead allocation to another customer, creating a possible death spiral effect. Once a customer consumes fewer activities, the company must either permanently remove the associated overhead to benefit from the reduction in costs consumed by the customer or utilize the freed capacity to generate additional revenue.

Overall, the activity analysis described here has shown that activity-based costing can be used as a strategic tool. It produced useful information to provide management with direction for costing and marketing strategies. The ABC model used will allow for better-informed decision making at TEC. Traditionally, TEC used gross margin analysis to set prices and develop budgets. Now it can use ABC for setting prices and developing budgets. This case study also demonstrates that ABC information can be used for more than just costing products and services: It can be used to develop a firm's profitability picture.

Developing strategic initiatives designed to transform TEC's unprofitable customers into profitable customers is the CFO's next challenge. In addition, the activity analysis will assist in bidding for contracts in the future. Before the ABC analysis, a bid was prepared without understanding the true cost of servicing the contract. As a result, the company was awarded contracts in the past that did not generate profits. By Using ABC, the company can better understand the costs associated with servicing a contract and provide a competitive bid that, if won, will be profitably serviced.

---

1. J. N. Sheth, R. S. Sisodia, and A. Sharma, 'The Antecedents and Consequences of Customer-Centric Marketing', *Journal of the Academy of Marketing Science*, Vol. 28, No. 1, 2000, pp. 55–66.

Source: Searcy, DL 2004, *Management Accounting Quarterly*, winter, pp. 51–60.

CHAPTER 5

Best practices in target costing

The Consortium for Advanced Manufacturing — International (CAM-I), the American Institute of CPAs, and the University of Akron recently sponsored a major study to benchmark best practices in target costing. This study examined the ways in which target costing has been applied in a variety of industries, the level of success and measurable improvements achieved, and the factors that influenced the success of these applications.

The study began with a survey to collect information about target costing practices throughout the United States. After analyzing the survey results, conducting telephone interviews, and reviewing secondary research, the research team selected four companies as having best practices in target costing. The team then conducted site visits at each of the 'best practice' companies, namely The Boeing Company, Caterpillar, DaimlerChrysler, and Continental Teves (a supplier of automotive brake systems). The results of the study are discussed here.

Target-costing principles

Target costing can best be described as a systematic process of cost management and profit planning. The six key principles of target costing are:[1]

1. **Price-led costing.** Market prices are used to determine allowable — or target — costs. Target costs are calculated using a formula similar to the following:
   market price – required profit margin = target cost.
2. **Focus on customers.** Customer requirements for quality, cost, and time are simultaneously incorporated in product and process decisions and guide cost analysis. The value (to the customer) of any features and functionality built into the product must be greater than the cost of providing those features and functionality.
3. **Focus on design.** Cost control is emphasized at the product and process design stage. Therefore, engineering changes must occur before production begins, resulting in lower costs and reduced 'time-to-market' for new products.
4. **Cross-functional involvement.** Cross-functional product and process teams are responsible for the entire product from initial concept through final production.
5. **Value-chain involvement.** All members of the value chain — e.g. suppliers, distributors, service providers, and customers — are included in the target costing process.
6. **A life-cycle orientation.** Total life-cycle costs are minimized for both the producer and the customer. Life-cycle costs include purchase price, operating costs, maintenance, and distribution costs.

The target costing process

Essentially, companies use target costing to establish concrete and highly visible cost targets for their new products. To maximize cost control and enhance profit improvement, most companies set relatively aggressive targets. The process begins when top management establishes a target cost for a new product, for example, a Chrysler Neon or a Caterpillar Excavator. A cost estimating group will then decompose the target cost for the product as a whole into cost targets for subassemblies and individual component parts — engine, transmission, seats, and so on.

Frequently 'gap' exists between the target cost and cost projections for the new product based on current designs and manufacturing capabilities. Closing the gap through cost reduction is central to the target costing process. This is accomplished through cross-functional target costing teams, which analyze the product's design, raw material requirements, and manufacturing processes to search for cost savings opportunities. The cross-functional teams employ a variety of management tools and initiatives to help them achieve their objectives.

The following section describes some of these tools and initiatives and other characteristics of successful target costing companies.

Target costing enablers

The best practice companies demonstrated certain commonalities in their operations and the way in which they supported the target costing process. They all had very effective organizational structures, responded to the 'voice of the customer', streamlined their product development process, and actively engaged their supply chain to achieve target costing objectives. To better understand these practices, we visited the four companies that had achieved the most success in each area. Our objective was to document 'best practices' in deploying these key elements of target costing.

At each best practice company, target costing is supported by a matrix organizational structure where a vertical, functional organization combines with horizontal, cross-functional teams. For example, U.S. Operations for DaimlerChrysler has five platform teams that cover large cars, small cars, mini-vans, trucks, and jeeps. Each team is cross-functional and includes members from design engineering, manufacturing engineering, purchasing, production, and finance. The target costing system determines cost objectives and performance goals for each platform team, and meeting these goals is an important component of team members' annual performance reviews.

The target costing system at DaimlerChrysler makes use of a 'toolbox' of management initiatives to improve productivity and reduce costs. The toolbox includes value engineering/value analysis, design for manufacturing assembly, paper kaizen, and lean manufacturing. Each initiative is implemented through workshops composed of multifunctional teams. The teams vary from five to 30 individuals and meet anywhere from one to five days. The workshops are 'working' sessions where participants brainstorm, troubleshoot, and generally try to solve problems and improve operations.

- **Value engineering/analysis** is used to increase the value of DaimlerChrysler's products to consumers through improved designs. Changing a part's design can be quite expensive because it generally requires new tooling. Therefore, the benefits of the new design to the consumer must more than offset the cost of the new tooling.
- **Design for manufacturing assembly** (DFMA) occurs throughout product design but before the first pilot vehicle is built. Essentially, DFMA evaluates the effectiveness of the design with regard to assembly operations. One benchmark is to minimize the number of vehicle components and to simplify the assembly processes. The result is fewer assembly errors and improved reliability and serviceability of the vehicles.
- **Paper kaizen** is the term used to promote the concept of continuous improvement. It is most effective immediately after a new part is designed but before the manufacturing process begins. During this stage in a product's life cycle, workstation setups, assembly steps, and process flows are simulated and optimized on paper before expenses are incurred.
- **Lean manufacturing** occurs after product launch and extends beyond DaimlerChrysler to include its supply chain. Benefits from this 'hands on' workshop include improved material flow and the elimination of unnecessary inventory movement, reduced setup times, and a general optimization of the workforce.

Voice of the customer

The best practice companies actively solicit input from the customer on design issues. While this practice is no different from those of many other companies, these companies take it a step further — they examine whether or not their customers are willing to *pay* for the design innovations. If the cost of the innovation is greater than its value to the customer, the innovation should be abandoned. We found numerous examples of 'value analysis' during the site visits. For example:

- One of Boeing's customers requested heated floors. Before target costing. The Boeing Company was inclined to provide almost whatever the customer wanted without regard to cost. The company now prices airplane options separately. When this particular customer learned that the price for heated floors was more than $1 million, it reconsidered its request.
- DaimlerChrysler used value analysis to evaluate many of the options that are available for its vehicles. After considering the tradeoff between cost and customer value for several lighting options, one of the platform teams decided to provide lighting for interior controls but forgo under-the-hood lighting.
- Continental Teves went beyond its direct customers to learn from the automobile consumer. It discovered that once vehicle purchasers were educated on the use of anti-lock brake systems (ABS) and the resulting safety benefits, they were more interested in purchasing ABS as an option for their vehicle. To leverage this discovery, Continental built a trailer that serves as a 'mobile exhibit' to teach the public about ABS. One section of the trailer has a foot pedal simulator that allows the consumer to feel the 'pulsating' motion of the pedal when he or she applies ABS brakes.

Product development

The product development process at The Boeing Company has changed markedly in recent years. The characteristics of new airplanes are dependent upon the size of the market (potential sales volume), the number of seats required, and customer choices with regard to technological requirements. Before target costing was introduced, engineers tended to design 'engineering marvels' with little regard to cost. These airplanes had hundreds of customer-specific product features, most of which were not transferable from one customer to the next. Boeing now tries to minimize unique customer requirements and incorporate changes that will provide value to a large customer base.

Through target costing, the costs associated with adding new components or changing aircraft configurations, such as moving kitchen galleys to new locations on the airplane, are much more visible. Any changes that are incorporated into a new airplane must satisfy a life-cycle-based business case. In other words, customers must be willing to pay for the incremental, nonrecurring costs of the change. Furthermore, many of the technological advancements are expensive to implement on a 'piecemeal' basis. Therefore, as technology improves, some strategic advancements are incorporated into existing models, and others are held 'in a drawer' until a new family of airplanes is developed (such as the new Boeing 777). For example, the product development team recently learned that a competitor had developed a common cockpit design for its airplanes. This new design will be evaluated using the above criteria, as it is expected to save money for both the manufacturer (fewer new cockpit components to design and manufacture) and the customer (lower training costs and fewer component parts to inventory).

Supply chain

In addition to internal operations, each of the best practice companies relies on cost savings opportunities from its supply chain to meet cost targets. At both DaimlerChrysler and Continental Teves, approximately 75% of the value of their products comes from purchased raw materials and components. In this environment, target-costing goals would be almost impossible to achieve without the participation of their suppliers. In fact, both companies view their supply chains as part of an 'extended enterprise' where they share design information, cost information, and establish inter-company teams to meet cost reduction goals.

TABLE 1 ■ Modification of current product: known adjustments

	Current costs	Projected savings	Adjusted costs	Explanation of known adjustments
Assembly	5.4%	1.5%	3.9%	Efficiency improvements due to redesigning sheet metal, as documented on current production models.
Cab	7.9	.8	7.1	Replace current cab with the 'Classy Cab'. PF quote already received.
Engine	8.6	.7	7.9	Cost estimate from engineering for switching to different configuration.
Hydraulics	19.1	1.6	17.5	New pump design.
Power train	12.0	0	12.0	
Structures	20.0	0	20.0	
Linkage	18.0	0	18.0	
Other	9.0	0	9.0	
Total	**100.0%**	**4.6%**	**95.4%**	

To encourage process improvements among its suppliers, DaimlerChrysler rates the performance of each supplier on a yearly basis. A major component of the rating system is the 'SCORE' (Supplier COst Reduction Effort) program. Each supplier is asked to achieve the equivalent of a 5% annual cost reduction based on its total annual sales to DaimlerChrysler. This cost reduction goal includes any supplier suggestions that result in lower costs for DaimlerChrysler. For example, one supplier suggested changing a vehicle's front rail system from several pieces to one unit. While the new design did not reduce the supplier's cost, it did improve the unit's quality and reduce DaimlerChrysler's assembly costs. Under Daimler-Chrysler's SCORE system, the supplier received credit for this innovation.

Continental Teves has developed a cost-modeling tool to determine target costs for the components it outsources. The cost targets are based on material costs, cycle times, labor rates, overhead, and other characteristics. The model is sophisticated, and it adjusts wage and occupancy rates to correspond with the appropriate rates for the region of the country in which the supplier operates. Furthermore, the model's overhead allocation rates differ based on the type of supplier. Full-service suppliers, responsible for product research and design, are allowed higher overhead allocation rates than suppliers that simply 'build to print'. If a supplier is unable to meet its target costs, Continental might ask to send a team there to view its operations. Continental will then analyze the supplier's manufacturing processes, tolerances, and material content and generally verify the assumptions in its cost-modeling tool. After negotiations, however, if Continental still believes the supplier's costs are too high, it might consider bids from other suppliers.

Target costing steps at Caterpillar

Once companies have the tools and systems in place to support target costing, they often develop a standardized approach for achieving their target costing objectives. Caterpillar offers a good illustration to highlight the target costing process for one of its new products. For this particular vehicle, management set the target cost at 94.6% of a comparable model, creating an initial gap of 5.4%. The cost of the comparable model is based on current manufacturing capabilities. Therefore, to achieve the target, costs must be reduced by 5.4%.

A cost improvement team is then assembled from product design, manufacturing engineering, production, marketing, and purchasing to determine how to close the gap. Initially, the group evaluates component part substitutions that would reduce costs but still provide the product features and benefits necessary to satisfy customer requirements. The group also

TABLE 2 ■ Modification of current product: sample questionnaire[*]

	Assembly	Cab	Engine	Hydraulics	Power train	Structures	Linkage	Other	TOTAL
1. Are there more than five suppliers from whom you can purchase materials?	0	0	0	1	1	1	1	0	
2. Are you more costly than best-in-class supplier (either Caterpillar or non-Caterpillar)?	0	0	0	1	0	0	0	0	
3. Do you plan to survey your supplier cost breakdown?	0	0	0	1	0	0	1	0	
4. Is the current manufacturing process younger than two years?	0	0	0	1	0	0	0	0	
5. Does labor represent more than 40% of your total cost?	0	0	1	1	0	0	1	0	
6. Is your 'unit setup cost/total unit cost' ratio greater than 5%?	0	0	1	1	0	0	0	0	
7. Do you see potential for material specification changes?	0	0	0	1	0	0	0	0	
8. Do you see potential for tolerance loosening?	0	0	0	1	0	0	1	0	
9. Does the current family of parts contain nonapproved parts?	0	0	0	1	0	1	1	0	
10. Can the current design or manufacturing processes be subjected to emerging innovative technologies?	0	0	0	1	0	0	0	0	
Total	0	0	2	10	1	2	5	0	20
Relative proportions	0%	0%	10%	50%	5%	10%	25%	0%	100%
Distribution of .8 in cost reduction	.0%	.0%	.08%	.40%	.04%	.08%	.20%	.0%	.80%

[*]Yes = 1; No = 0

Current costs for a comparable model	100.0%
Target cost for new product	94.6%
Cost gap	5.4%

considers opportunities to reduce costs through efficiency improvements. Table 1 shows that the cost improvement team identified 4.6% in 'known' savings through an initial evaluation of cost savings opportunities.

Having reduced the gap by 4.6%, the team must find an additional 0.8% in savings to achieve the 5.4% cost reduction target. At this stage, the cost improvement team surveys the operational groups to identify potential cost savings opportunities. The responses to the questionnaire do not recommend specific solutions, but they do identify where improvement opportunities are more likely to be successful (see table 2). Each 'yes' response on the questionnaire indicates an opportunity for cost reduction, and the component part category (cab, engine, hydraulics, etc.) that has the largest number of positive responses is viewed as having the greatest potential for saving money. Table 2 highlights a sample questionnaire, and a tally of the responses indicates the extent to which each part category will be targeted for cost reduction. In this case, hydraulics will be responsible for achieving the highest percentage (50%) of the cost savings that are needed. Therefore, the cost of hydraulics must be reduced by .4% (.50 × .08).

Table 3 illustrates the final step in the process. It takes the adjusted costs column from Table 1 and subtracts the additional savings that are required for each component part category. The right-hand column in table 3 illustrates the target cost for the new vehicle, broken down to the component level. To recap, Caterpillar began with current costs for a comparable product (100%) and, after deducting known savings based on existing technology (table 1) and potential savings based on an analysis of the questionnaire (table 2), established cost targets for each component of the new vehicle.

TABLE 3 ■ Modification of current product: final target cost assignments

	Adjusted costs	Distribution of .8% in cost reduction	Target cost for new product
Assembly	3.9%	0.00%	3.90%
Cab	7.1	0.00	7.10
Engine	7.9	.08	7.82
Hydraulics	17.5	.40	17.10
Power train	12.0	.04	11.96
Structures	20.0	.08	19.92
Linkage	18.0	.20	17.80
Other	9.0	0.00	9.00
Total	**95.4%**	**.80%**	**94.60%**

Best practice companies consistent in approach

Target costing is still relatively new to U.S. companies. Nevertheless, it is being adopted in some key industries, namely the transportation and heavy equipment industries. Intensive competition, extensive supply chains, and relatively long product development cycles characterize these industries.

The best practice companies were relatively consistent in the way in which they applied target costing. The other companies follow a similar approach to the target costing steps at Caterpillar that were highlighted in the last section. All of the best practice companies employ a cross-functional organizational structure, listen to the 'voice of the customer', emphasize cost reduction during the new product development cycle, and are very effective at removing costs throughout the supply chain. For these companies, target costing has proven to be a very effective means of cost control and profit enhancement.

1. These principles are adopted from S. Ansari, J. Bell, and the CAM-I Target Cost Core Group, *Target Costing, The Next Frontier in Strategic Cost Management*, Irwin, Chicago, 1997.

Source: Swenson, D, Ansari, S, Bell, P & IL-Woon, K 2003, *Management Accounting Quarterly*, winter, pp. 12–17.

CHAPTER 6

Low cost, high hopes

Fed up with 34 years of red ink on the domestic routes of state-owned Malaysia Airlines, the government has turned to low-cost carrier Air Asia to bail it out. Starting in August, Air Asia will take over 96 of the airline's 118 domestic routes, only four of which have been profitable.

Now it falls to Tony Fernandes, the 42-year-old founder and CEO of Air Asia, to prove that his low-cost model can work where Malaysia Airlines failed. Fernandes, a former Warner Music executive, says his lower cost structure — at 2.1 cents per seat per kilometre, the lowest in the world — means he needs to fill only 56% of his seats to break even, compared with 70% for Malaysia Airlines. With nearly two-thirds of its passengers booking their flights online and no-frills service, Air Asia either breaks even or makes a profit on all 53 routes it serves within Malaysia and to destinations such as Thailand, Indonesia, and Macau, Fernandes says. His company reported a pretax profit of $24 million for the nine months ended March 2006 on revenue of $168 million.

'For four years I have been griping that we've been competing against a state-owned and subsidised airline,' Fernandes says. 'This will be significant to our earnings.' Terms of the deal weren't revealed, but the government agreed to pay Malaysia Airlines $236 million to compensate it for giving up domestic routes. Air Asia also got a number of unspecified incentives, including what some say is a $5 million subsidy to service some rural routes.

'Who can blame Fernandes for being confident of making headway where Malaysia Airlines couldn't manage its domestic routes profitably?' says Wee Kim Hong, head of research at M&A Securities in Kuala Lumpur. 'He had already made Air Asia profitable, even when Malaysia Airlines was subsidized.' Citigroup aviation analyst Corrine Png predicts Air Asia's annual passenger load could increase from 3.5 million to 8.5 million as a result, contributing as much as $211 million a year in additional revenue.

Fernandes and Air Asia chairman Pahamin Rajab bought the company in 2001 for 27 cents. At the time it was a money-losing air-charter service with $13 million in debt owned by a Malaysian conglomerate. After turning Air Asia into a highflying success, Fernandes started lobbying for a level playing field in the domestic sector. The government had reportedly been compensating Malaysia Airlines $135 million a year to maintain air service on its domestic routes and to provide fuel subsidies.

Even with those subsidies the airline reported a pretax loss of $416 million on revenue of $3.3 billion for the 12 months ended in March. But while Malaysia Airlines CEO Idris Jala shook hands with Fernandes on the government's plan to create two national champions in the aviation sector — one full-service, the other low-cost — it was clear his own rescue plan for the airline, announced in February, had been thwarted. Malaysia Airlines officials declined to comment.

Although Jala's plan didn't take off — save for manpower reductions of about 6000, currently underway, analysts say it is crucial for the airline to overhaul its international routes, some of which were inaugurated for political rather than commercial reasons by former Prime Minister Mahathir Mohamed and continue to lose money. It also needs to focus on destinations like

London and Vienna, usually profitable for Asian carriers, where it is said to be operating at a loss. 'International flights produce a higher yield by nature,' says Joe Laughlin, a vice president at OAG Data, a London aviation-research firm. 'So it makes sense from a financial standpoint to focus on premium international travel.'

It might also make sense, says Wee of M&A Securities, for Malaysia Airlines to take a stake in Air Asia, similar to what Singapore Airways has done with low-cost carriers Tiger Airlines and Valuair. 'The next logical step for Malaysia Airlines,' says Wee, 'is to consider the realities and make the most of the collaboration.'

Neither Fernandes nor Malaysia Airlines would comment on future plans. But the next few months will make it clear whether one of Malaysia's best entrepreneurs can take a losing business off the government's hands and spin a profit.

Source: **Sakran, TS 2006,** *Fortune Magazine,* **8 July, pp. 14–15.**

CHAPTER 7

Who needs budgets? You do.

Budgets aren't just about the numbers. They're about communicating vital information within the organization. And in the very near future, the budgeting function in your organization may be called on to serve as a role model for communicating information in business-to-business (B2B) collaborative planning processes.

Budget bashing has become a popular topic and has even led to the suggestion that budgets are outdated and no longer needed, but don't be too hasty in advocating that your organization dump its budgeting process. Although such a position might make you popular with some colleagues, it isn't in your organization's best interests. The reason? The most important aspect of your budgeting process soon may be as a communication model for reducing information asymmetries and uncertainties between your organization and its B2B partners. The communication procedures that your organization has developed for its strategic and operational budgeting process may provide the best blueprint for effective, efficient interorganizational communication.

Keep your budgets

Talk regarding the budgeting process frequently revolves around target revenues and costs and how these targets are set, used — and misused. But rather than suggest dumping the budget, a much better approach is to determine why problems exist and fix them. If your process promotes a command-and-control environment, then incorporate more participation. If your incentive system is too restrictive or if it invites managers to create slack, then revise it. If the financial targets are no longer appropriate for your evolving organization, then expand or change the targets. Many companies have successfully implemented and used balanced scorecards and other methods to identify targets, and, even before balanced scorecards, they used performance evaluation based on world-class benchmarks.

Any revisions to your budgeting procedures should recognize that the biggest benefit of the current process is probably in enhancing interdepartmental communication throughout your organization in order to coordinate efforts and attain strategic and operational goals. The budgeting process allows upper-level operating and financial managers to communicate information about the strategic and operational goals of the organization. These executives have access to business intelligence efforts and to the tools to assess the competitive environment. They need to communicate many aspects of the big picture (the organization and the environment) and how these aspects impact each part of the organization.

The budgeting process also allows lower-level operating and financial managers and front-line employees to have their fingers on the pulse of the organization. They understand the business processes and procedures. Because they often have valuable information that can impact both short- and long-term goals and priorities, they need to have a process for communicating both internal and external perspectives on their assigned tasks.

This communication is critical because information asymmetries exist among departments and levels within the organization. Also, a company needs to recognize and deal with uncertainties in its environment, such as the changing nature of competition.

B2B collaboration

As business-to-business partnerships flourish, many organizations are developing closer ties than ever before. These relationships involve interorganizational coordination, communication, and information sharing at an unprecedented level. If your budgeting process has been done correctly, it has already identified the information that needs to flow from one unit to another within your organization, so it should provide a good baseline for communicating with your B2B partners. In both intra- and interorganizational planning, the type and amount of information, as well as the level of communication, depend on the situation, the interdependence and interactions between units, and whether those interactions are product or process focused.

Table 1 shows several types of information that will need to be communicated for the different levels of interdependencies — low, medium, high, and very high. Some software packages address many technical and procedural difficulties involved in communication between organizations. For larger organizations, MySAP.com Business Suite has applications that link global buyers, sellers, logistics providers, financial institutions, and even customs and trade authorities. It also offers a range of business functions including analysis, forecasting, and collaborative planning. For smaller organizations, Net-Suite offers applications that include partner relationship management, purchasing and vendor management, and shipping integration with FedEx and UPS.

Let's take a look at what's involved in each type of B2B relationship.

TABLE 1 ■ Types of information in B2B collaboration

Level of interdependence and information sharing	Situation	Product-focused relationships (exchange and supply chain relationships)	Process-focused relationships (outsourcing of technology, service, or support functions)
Low	Standardized goods or services with multiple providers and customers	Price Quantity Quality Lead-time Delivery options	Price Volume Processing or turnaround time
Medium	Specialized goods or services with few providers and customers Some supply chain relationships	Specification assurance Quality assurance Cost data and price constraints Projected demand and supply	Description of procedures Interoperability issues Auditability Required input and output data Costing and pricing procedures

(continued)

TABLE 1 (*continued*)

Level of interdependence and information sharing	Situation	Product-focused relationships (exchange and supply chain relationships)	Process-focused relationships (outsourcing of technology, service, or support functions)
High	Supply chain alliances Project joint ventures	Open information on cost data Production capacity Profit/loss fairness Target costing Business intelligence Going-concern assurance	Processing capacity Profit/loss fairness Target costing Business intelligence Going-concern assurance
Very high	Strategic alliances or networks Collaborative business ventures for primary or important products or services	Goal setting for market niche Risk preferences Risk behavior Profit/loss sharing	Goal congruence Risk preferences Risk behavior Profit/loss sharing

Low level of interdependence

At the lowest level of interdependence, B2B relationships arise from occasional or recurring transactions that involve exchanging relatively standardized goods or services. In these situations, multiple providers and customers exist in the market. Coordination between organizations is low to nonexistent, and collaborative planning rarely needs to take place. But, similar to internal budgeting and control processes, information about the trading partner may be accumulated and evaluated.

Information such as price and delivery options is usually available on the supplier's website, and suppliers also may operate online marketplaces. Dell Computers and Staples, for instance, offer goods to both businesses and consumers. Staples Online Marketplace offers more than office supplies — it also offers services like copying and photo developing, among others.

Third parties may operate portals where buyers and providers can place and respond to bids for goods and services via auctions or reverse auctions.

ChemConnect.com helps buyers and sellers of chemicals, plastics, and related products find trading partners. They offer three marketplaces: one where prequalified members buy and sell commodities in real time; one for sellers to find new customers, which includes electronic catalogs and forward auctions, where buyers bid on products or services and the bidding price increases over time during the bidding period; and one for buyers to purchase items via requests for quotes and reverse auctions, where sellers are invited to bid on fulfilling an order for products or services and the bidding price decreases during the bidding periods.

The information exchanged between organizations through online marketplaces may not be proprietary and may have been used for the make-or-buy or do-or-outsource decision. If the information is proprietary, portals like ChemConnect offer the opportunity for completely anonymous trades. In an internal budgeting situation, the analyses leading to the cost and quantity data would be communicated as part of the operational budgeting process. To allow for informed transactions, ChemConnect offers chemical market information and e-mail alerts for completed deals.

Medium level of interdependence

Interdependence and information sharing increase when goods or services have special characteristics, when systematic sourcing (a longer-term relationship) is desired, and/or when there are only a few providers or customers. For this type of relationship, some coordination between each organization's activities and processes is needed to attain both operational and strategic goals.

For this level of interdependence, companies need to communicate price and cost constraints, product specifications, and other proprietary data so negotiations similar to internal budget negotiations can take place. Companies may also share or jointly establish supply-and-demand forecasts and production schedules. Take, for example, Boeing's relationships with aircraft engine suppliers, such as General Electric and Rolls Royce. General Electric worked for two years to develop engines for the 777-200 and 777-300 models in Boeing's 777 commercial airplane family. For Boeing's 7E7 Dreamliner, GE and Rolls Royce developed commercial jet engines that had the same standard interface, allowing either engine to be fitted to the 7E7.

For process outsourcing, companies may need to resolve interoperability issues concerning systems, processes, and data. Budget information previously used only internally for business process management may need to be shared for successful business process integration. Amazon.com, for example, provides a comprehensive set of technology services, order fulfillment, and customer service for Target at Amazon.com and Target's online sites — Target.com, MarshallFields.com, and Meryyns.com. Amazon.com also cobranded with Toys 'R' Us to provide an efficient Internet distribution system for the toy store.

In some alliances, the members are actually competitors who cooperate to purchase materials and supplies, transport goods, share warehouses, or share technology-based services. Marriot and Hyatt, although competitors, own a procurement consortium for the hotel industry. And Borders, a mall bookseller, dropped its money-losing Web venture and teamed with online competitor Amazon.com for services similar to those Amazon provides for its other alliances.

For control purposes, the user may require the same level of auditability of the provider's process as is needed for its own processes. For example, Dell Computers' supply chain management system requires that suppliers have the ISO 14001 certification, a standard for environmental management systems, and the OHSAS 18001 certification, a standard for workplace health and safety management systems. Dell provides training for suppliers on what it expects of them, asks key suppliers to conduct self-audits, and holds regular reviews with key suppliers to attain that control.

High level of interdependence

Interdependence and information sharing increase even further in strong supply chain alliances and project joint ventures. Collaborative planning and coordination take place at both the operational and strategic levels. These networks operate almost as if they're members of a single organization, with electronic data interchange (EDI) communications and electronic funds transfer (EFT) transactions taking place between the systems and people from each organization.

A common problem in supply chains is the bullwhip effect, where erratic shifts in orders up and down the chain cause production and inventory problems. In some industries, this problem has been solved by multiple organizations along the supply chain setting up networks that share demand information. Consider Wal-Mart. The world's largest retailer is known for its supply chain alliances and continuous improvement efforts in the handling, moving, and tracking of inventory. One of its most notable examples of information sharing is with Procter & Gamble, a supplier that has access to information on every P&G item Wal-Mart sells.

By monitoring inventory levels at the stores, P&G uses knowledge of Wal-Mart's desired thresholds to electronically manage its inventory replenishment for Wal-Mart.

In some cases, the term 'dependence' is more appropriate than interdependence. For example, Wal-Mart and the U.S. Department of Defense have mandated that many of their suppliers not use bar codes and instead use RFID (radio frequency identification), a wireless form of product identification. It allows noncontact reading of data through tags that emit a radio signal and that contain more information, such as product expiration dates, than traditional bar codes.

Many budgeting and control issues arise between organizations that arise within vertically integrated organizations. Some of the following issues may require iterative negotiations involving simulations and revised calculations:

- How to distribute profits or losses and cost savings in a fair manner to all those involved;
- How to allocate overhead and support services costs;
- How to best acquire, distribute, and use business intelligence; and
- How to set and achieve target-costing goals.

For some longer-term alliances and project joint ventures, enough information must also be communicated to assure partners that each one is truly a going concern. Some enterprise risk management techniques used for strategic and tactical planning may reduce financial, operational, and technological uncertainties by identifying, measuring, and monitoring risks in those areas. Much communication in supply chain alliances is intended to reduce the information asymmetries between the organizations and the uncertainties in the environment.

Very high level of interdependence

Strategic alliances and collaborative business ventures involve the highest amount of interdependence and communication. Companies may need to collaborate to shape and determine the venture's strategic direction and assure goal congruence between or among the organizations. Communication may become more interactive and iterative, with negotiations possibly involving research, development, and substantial investments. Companies may also need to align risk preferences and limit risky behavior of alliance members.

Hewlett-Packard and Disney, for example, have been strategic partners for many years, with HP engineers and Disney imagineers collaborating on ventures such as Epcot Center's new attraction called Mission: SPACE. HP has also partnered with SAP AG to deliver integrated solutions for customers, such as P&G. Former HP Chairman and CEO Carly Fiorina stated at SAPPHIRE 2003, SAP's annual event, that she believed HP and SAP 'share a common vision' and used 'SAP's NetWeaver, which allows companies to create and improve business processes across their value chain without changing out all the underlying technology foundation' as an example.

Another example is the alliance between SAP and Microsoft known as Project Mendocino. This alliance's strategic objective was to jointly develop a software application that used the familiar Microsoft Office environment to access selected SAP business processes and data, including financial reporting. The result? The release of Duet Software, which SAP and Microsoft jointly market, sell, and support.

Communication is key to B2B collaborations

Be aware that the same problems that arise in the internal budgeting process can arise in B2B relationships. If one partner has more power than the other, the powerful partner may need to take steps to incorporate the less powerful partner in the decision-making process. Agreements and contracts need to be prepared carefully to avoid incentives to create slack and untruthful reporting. Targets and performance evaluations should be based on a balanced scorecard.

But always keep in mind that communication is a key ingredient in successful relationships. Just as communication is critical to reducing information asymmetries that exist among departments and levels within an organization and to reducing uncertainties that exist in the organization's environment, communication is imperative to reducing information asymmetries and uncertainties that exist in B2B relationships. The best role model for B2B collaborations that require effective, efficient interorganizational communication should be your internal budgeting process.

Source: Greenberg, PS & Greenberg, RH 2006, *Strategic Finance*, August, pp. 41–5.

CHAPTER 8

Outsourcing? At your own risk

Before outsourcing any process or function, it's essential to assess the risks enterprise-wide.

Outsourcing some of your business processes and information technology (IT) functions to entities overseas may appear to cut costs and maximize profitability. But it can also cause other, significant risks if it isn't managed effectively. In other words, outsourcing may ultimately increase, rather than decrease, the total risk for your organization. So before you decide to outsource, we suggest analyzing it from the perspective of enterprise risk management (ERM).

Ubiquity of outsourcing

ERM analysis of outsourcing is so important because more companies are outsourcing a greater number of functions than ever before.

Business process outsourcing is expected to grow from $38.9 billion in 2003 to $1.2 trillion by 2006, according to data from the Gartner Group and IDC Consulting, Inc. A June 2003 Deloitte Consulting report, *The Offshoring Imperative*, predicted that two million financial services jobs, such as brokerage transaction processing clerks, and $356 billion in core financial transaction operations will be outsourced by 2008.

It used to be that only large companies outsourced business functions, and even those were limited to information technology (IT) and payroll. But since the mid-1990s, small-sized and mid-tier companies have also been doing it because prices have come down and more companies are able to afford it.

Outsourcing began transcending IT and payroll to include software applications through the 'application service provider model' and a 'managed service provider' system whereby vendors host and maintain a company's software on the vendor's off-site system or manage company networks of hardware and software at the company's site. By the late 1990s, the rise of the Internet had enabled companies to outsource entire business processes and professional staff that traditionally were internal. Internal auditors and financial reporting and tax professionals, for example, are now candidates for outsourcing. Also ripe for outsourcing are critical business processes, such as customer support, cash management, tax preparation, accounts receivable, and accounts payable.

In fact, our analysis of public announcements of outsourcing decisions by more than 300 U.S. companies in the period of 1997 to 2003 shows that all types of business processes are potential outsource candidates. Topping our list is supply chain management by 28% of the companies we looked at, with insurance claims processing at 16% and financial services also at 16% of business processes shifted to third-party providers, as shown in figure 1. Investment securities transaction processing by brokerage firms and banks and human resources/payroll functions are also frequently outsourced, at 15% and 13%, respectively.

Among IT functions, our research shows hardware/software/help desk support representing 26% of IT functions outsourced, followed by network management at 18%, application development and programming at 16%, e-commerce at 15%, and data centers at 13%, as shown in figure 2.

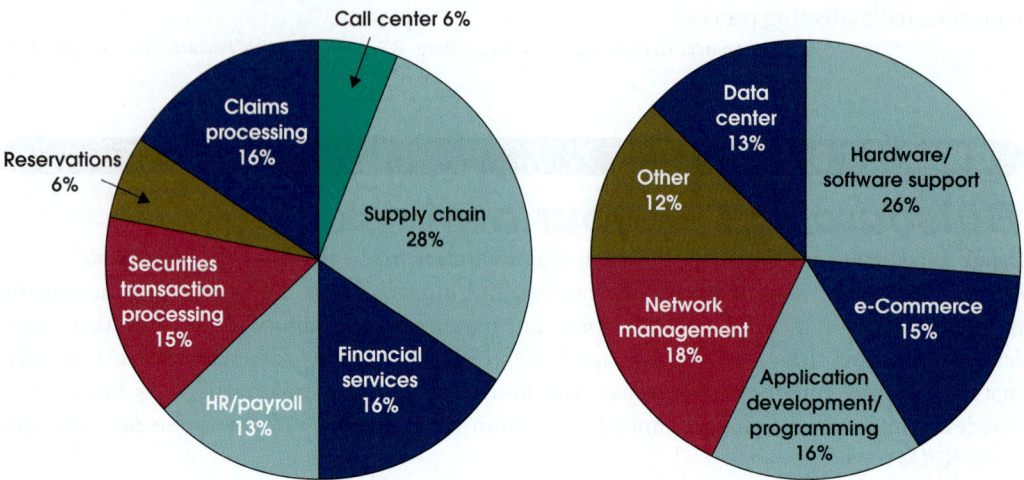

FIGURE 1 ■ Business processes outsourced.   **FIGURE 2** ■ IT functions outsourced.

Nor is outsourcing unique to any particular industry. Outsourcing among the 300 companies we examined spans numerous industries but is dominated by sellers of services, led by finance and insurance at 22%, as illustrated in figure 3.

Why are we seeing these outsourcing trends? One of the primary rationales is either cost containment or cost reduction.

With growing frequency, outsourcing decisions are spurred by opportunities to capture huge labor cost savings by shifting core business processes to highly capable overseas providers whose labor rates are dramatically lower than comparable ones in the U.S. IBM Corporation, for example, is shifting programming and project management work from the U.S. to China, where labor costs are estimated to be less than $25 per hour compared to $80 in the U.S. Others are doing so for the same reasons, making global outsourcing of services a pervasive part of U.S. corporate strategy. We should also mention that these jobs are not only going to Chinese or Indian companies — they're also going to companies in Malaysia, Pakistan, Singapore, South Africa and Australia.

Executives claim they aren't compromising on expertise to obtain these costs savings. In fact, the most frequent reason cited for outsourcing, showing up in 24% of the decisions announced, is for external expertise that's either equivalent to that available in the U.S. or unique. It even exceeds cost savings, which were cited in 20% of the decisions (see figure 4). Outsourcing announcements by the 300 companies we studied also shows outsourcing would help them focus on core competencies by shifting noncore activities off-site and improve customer service.

Opponents of outsourcing, however, scoff at any reason other than cost savings, arguing that anything but cost savings is merely a public relations tactic to shift the debate over labor costs.

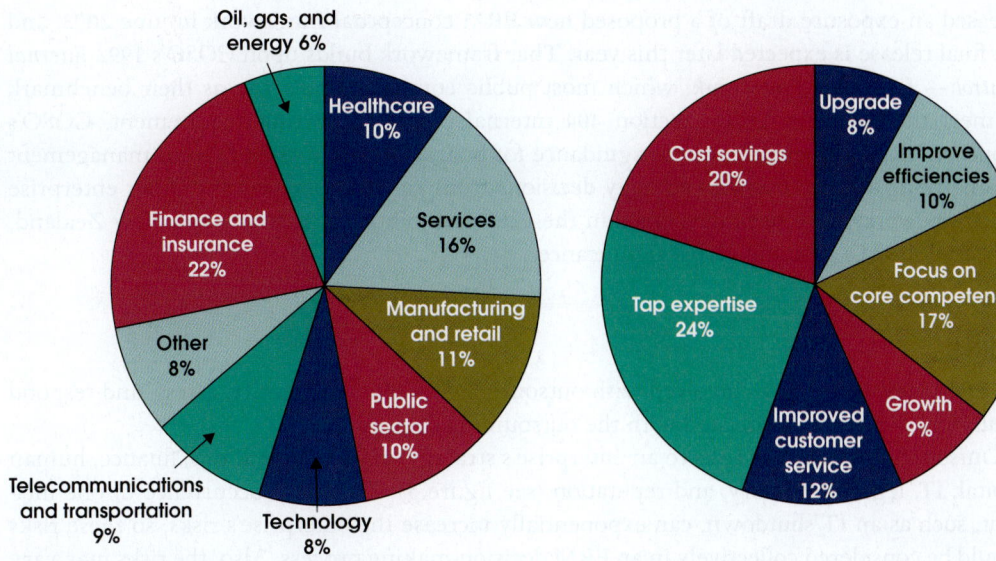

FIGURE 3 ■ Outsourcing by industry

FIGURE 4 ■ Reasons for outsourcing

Enter ERM

The strategic decision to outsource activities to an external provider can be an effective response to managing key risks. As companies face the financial risks of increasing labor and other process costs, management's decision to outsource portions of labor-intensive activities to lower-cost markets may be an effective risk-reduction strategy. But if management makes the decision to reduce these financial risks on a 'silo basis,' it fails to control for the presence of other risks created by the outsourcing decision. Thus, the total portfolio of risks facing the enterprise may exceed the risk reductions sought, and the outsourcing decision may have increased the enterprise's risk profile beyond levels that stakeholders would tolerate.

It's critical for management and the board of directors to take an objective, comprehensive view of all the risks associated with any outsourcing decision. Merely focusing on potential cost savings without looking at the new risks associated with the outsourcing decision may result in a naive denial of significant risks threatening the company's survivability. Some of those risks can be significant alone, while others may not be significant individually but can be catastrophic when they interact with other risks.

Again, before outsourcing, evaluate and monitor it from an enterprise risk management perspective.

Enterprise risk management is a growing business paradigm in the U.S. and abroad. The recent corporate scandals in the U.S. and Europe only further pressed the importance of ERM on senior executives and boards of directors because of their ultimate responsibility to effectively manage risks across the entire organization. Moreover, U.S. think tanks have been advocating that management design and implement enterprise risk management guidelines and processes. These are needed to ensure that key risks affecting the enterprise are identified and measured and that effective responses are implemented to monitor and control risk exposures — at least within a level acceptable to the entity's stakeholders, such as investors, creditors, and regulators.

The Committee of Sponsoring Organizations of the Treadway Commission (COSO) is helping management and the board of directors implement effective ERM processes. COSO released an exposure draft of a proposed new ERM conceptual framework in June 2003, and the final release is expected later this year. That framework builds upon COSO's 1992 *Internal Control — Integrated Framework*, which most public companies now use as their benchmark to meet the Sarbanes–Oxley Section 404 internal control reporting requirement, COSO's proposed ERM framework provides guidance for boards of directors and senior management for analyzing all core business strategy decisions from an ERM perspective. Other enterprise risk frameworks have been developed in the U.K. and jointly in Australia and New Zealand, indicating ERM's growing global significance.

Risks

An ERM view of the risks involved with outsourcing attempts to identify, assess, and respond to *all* significant risks associated with the outsourcing decision.

Outsourcing can create risks to an enterprise's strategy/market, operations, finance, human capital, IT, legal/regulatory, and reputation (see figure 5). The mere occurrence of one incident, such as an IT shutdown, can exponentially increase the enterprise's risks, so these risks should be considered collectively in an ERM decision-making process. Also, the risks may vary across organizations, so the board of directors and management should identify which ones their outsourcing decision may affect.

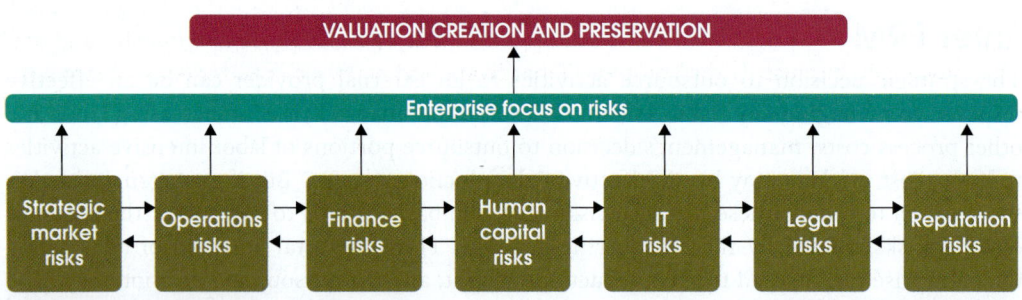

FIGURE 5 ■ ERM brings together all risks

Next we elaborate on how outsourcing can affect different aspects of enterprise risk.

Strategic/market risks. In outsourcing, management typically wants to shift processes related to core strategy and market position — such as customer call centers, help lines, reservation centers, or complaint response — to off-shore providers. But when outsourcing core business processes begins to involve outsourcer interaction with customers and other vital business partners, any breaches in the effectiveness of product or service delivery and maintenance can directly hinder a company's ability to accomplish its strategic objectives. Poor training and suboptimal delivery of customer services may affect the company's ability to maintain and expand its customer base, and communication breakdowns due to cultural differences can result in providers failing to interpret customer needs and concerns accurately. Thus, in an effort to save on labor costs, the organization may threaten its strategic/market position.

Another strategic risk of outsourcing is revealing confidential information, and bringing an outsourcing partner into a company's core business processes inherently reveals part of a company's strategy. A breach in confidential strategic and competitive market information can come from differences between the two companies' corporate culture, ethics, and governance and can threaten the outsourcer's competitive advantage and heighten strategic/market risks if they're not managed effectively.

Operational risks. Outsourcing business processes can lead to operational cost savings involving labor, supply chain management, and infrastructure. But outsourcing parts of the operations, such as supply chain management, requires investments in infrastructure.

Moreover, selecting the wrong vendor can significantly affect operational risk, which often increases as the transition of processing from internal to external operations begins. Vendors need to be capable of learning complex operational processes, and you may need to invest in training and education for them. Also, thorough investigation of a vendor's reputation and capabilities is critical to ensure core business operations are maintained at desired production and quality levels. In addition, basic processing needs must be addressed, such as technology and IT personnel, to ensure that the transfer of operations goes smoothly.

Additionally, the risk of not achieving core operational objectives in an outsourcing arrangement can adversely affect the enterprise's strategic/market risks. A breakdown in production or service delivery quality, for example, may not only halt operations temporarily but also make customers frustrated because of delays and back orders. This, in turn, would threaten the company's strategic/market position.

Financial risks. To a company's finance professionals, outsourcing can increase cash flow and financial reporting risks. While outsourcing is designed to increase net cash flows, many hidden costs may actually decrease cash flows if the costs aren't managed effectively. There can be extensive, unpredictable costs involved in performing vendor due diligence, including travel and other investigation costs to avoid surprises when the relationship gets under way. Costs of developing infrastructure to support off-site operations can be extensive and not fully anticipated because of the complex IT hardware and software requirements. There also are ongoing costs that can't be ignored or completely predicted, such as monitoring contract performance of availability, security, and quality metrics. Finally, there may be unanticipated costs, such as employee layoffs in U.S. operations or other restructurings in both U.S. and overseas operations, that can impact the total cost of outsourcing.

Financial reporting of outsourcing arrangements can add significantly to your reporting process and risk. U.S. public companies are rushing to comply with the multitude of requirements for the Sarbanes–Oxley Act of 2002, particularly the new Section 404 requirements for management reporting on internal control effectiveness. As companies begin to outsource key business processes — including finance and accounting — there will be more risk concerned with supporting, maintaining, and monitoring the effectiveness of internal controls. Creating a uniform control environment is more difficult when operations are spread across cultures around the globe. As more financial data reside on offshore servers, controlling the backup and recovery of that data becomes more important. Outsourcing may make documenting, testing, and evaluating the operating effectiveness of those offshore controls more difficult. All of this creates a risk that the board of directors and management must address. In addition to management's ability to assess outsourced controls, external auditors will need to evaluate those controls as well.

Human capital risks. Of course, outsourcing jobs also has inherent risk. Labor cost savings through outsourcing typically come from laying off U.S.-based employees. As the outsourcing trend continues, employee groups, including labor unions, are paying closer attention to the relationship between outsourcing and unemployment. In many cases, employee groups are becoming more vocal, often taking their concerns to state and federal politicians in an attempt to encourage legislative initiatives to curb the growth of offshore outsourcing arrangements.

Anger among American workers is building as outsourcing is predicted to grow. Grassroots efforts in New Jersey and California, for example, have prompted protectionist legislation.

In fact, the New Jersey Senate is considering a bill (Senate No. 494) to outlaw offshoring of state jobs. The bill, which is being evaluated at the Senate Committee level, would restrict outsourcing of state government work by forcing government contractors to pay American wages regardless of where the work is being done. That, in effect, would take away a major incentive for state government agencies and state government contractors to outsource.

This backlash to outsourcing jobs, particularly from unionized labor, could lead to significant new costs for companies. For example, if a class action suit were brought against a company, the company would have to mount a legal defense. In addition, companies often need laid-off workers during the transition period to help train their overseas counterparts. So not only must these workers be paid severance but also retention bonuses. All of these costs could ultimately threaten the labor cost-savings potential that motivated the outsourcing decision in the first place.

In-house survivors of outsourcing can also become demoralized. If their sentiments aren't addressed properly, employee turnover, operational slowdowns, or even employee strikes can ensue. These threats not only affect the organization's human capital, but they interact with key operational and strategic risks discussed earlier. For example, employee work stoppages halt operational processes that delay production and complicate other supply-chain relationships. The resulting lack of timely delivery of goods or services leads to customer frustration and ultimate loss of strategic market share for the company.

So there's clearly a crying need to evaluate the potential effect of outsourcing on human resources and across the entire enterprise.

IT risks. Because many outsourcing arrangements depend on information technology, IT is a particularly risky area.

Traditionally, outsourcing has shifted portions of a company's IT infrastructure to third-party providers. Many people say IT outsourcing will continue to lead the overseas exodus, with the Internet enabling its growth. The speed and availability of the Internet to capture, share, and transfer information globally has enabled companies to shift functions to any location around the world that has Internet access. Accompanying this, however, are the inherent risks associated with Internet activity. Computer viruses, denial-of-service attacks, privacy issues, and electronic data transfer concerns are all IT risks that must be managed with constantly updated technologies, such as firewalls, encryption, digital signatures, and other security prevention techniques.

In addition, transferring key IT operations from the U.S. to overseas markets takes more than flipping a switch from servers in the U.S. to those overseas. Vendors need technology specifications and other infrastructure requirements before they can deliver services in overseas IT centers, and there may be struggles to communicate IT specs to vendors. What used to be accomplished internally, informally, and face-to-face may now need to be more formal. Once IT operations are developed off-site, they must be tested and documented to ensure they're fully functional at desired performance levels. You should also expect long lead times in hardware acquisitions and software development, which can threaten perceived cost savings in many outsourcing arrangements.

Still further shifting of an enterprise's IT 'backbone' to offshore locations makes it more important than ever to assess the continuity of operations and disaster recovery controls. Also, geopolitical risks, such as threats of terrorism and war, are obviously real in numerous areas around the globe. Any shutdown of an IT operations center or the IT backbone failing to operate for prolonged periods may threaten the IT investment and significantly increase other risks, including operations risks and strategic/market risks. In addition, you should address the costs and time to bring outsourced IT operations back in-house if that becomes necessary.

We believe all of these IT risks should be viewed from an enterprise basis to ensure that individual and interactive risk exposures are monitored effectively and managed to a level acceptable to stakeholders.

Legal regulatory risks. In addition to emerging legislation designed to slow down the shift of U.S. jobs overseas, numerous other legal/regulatory risks must be considered in any outsourcing decision. Legal issues related to the privacy, confidentiality, and security of business transactions may increase legal risks for the enterprise if they aren't managed effectively. When customers, suppliers, and other business partners suffer damages from unsecured transactions, legal and regulatory actions can ensue.

Companies also must monitor regulations to make sure outsourcing decisions don't lead to violations. For example, banking industry regulators have their own guidelines and bulletins aimed at clarifying a bank's duties for managing risk in outsourcing relationships. Companies and their outsourcing partners must stay informed about evolving regulations that could affect any aspect of their operations.

Enterprises should also stay abreast of legal and regulatory requirements of the country hosting the offshore operations. Those countries may have different tax and labor laws than the U.S., and those laws may affect how an entity conducts business there. Acceptable ways of transacting business in the U.S. may not comply with legal provisions in the host country.

Reputation risks. Of all the risks, one of the hardest to measure — but often the most crucial — is threats to a company's reputation. Enterprises are wise to invest in efforts to maintain and enhance their external image so they can retain and attract vital business partners and market share and protect and increase the price of their securities in the capital markets.

As outsourcing trends continue to catch the attention of the American public, negative perceptions can create huge reputation risks. Fear of job loss, particularly in slow economic times, can profoundly impact the local or national reputation of any enterprise considering offshore outsourcing Negative publicity regarding outsourcing to overseas markets has led to protests and demonstrations across the country that have attacked the image of some companies. These demonstrations have attracted media attention because they have been well organized and widely publicized. If American public opinion suddenly swings toward intense opposition to offshoring, enterprises already in outsourced arrangements may be in situations they never anticipated when they made the outsourcing decision, such as being directly targeted by negative ads, boycotts, or other protests highlighting the company's outsourcing contracts. Customers and business partners may avoid doing business with companies that transfer jobs from U.S. citizens to foreign workers, which harms their reputations and threatens the enterprise's strategic/market position.

Managing outsourcing risk

There are numerous opportunities to outsource many different types of business and IT processes, including those not traditionally outsourced. While these opportunities have generated benefits for many companies, particularly labor cost savings, numerous risks can arise that affect multiple aspects of the organization. Not only should these risk exposures be evaluated and monitored across the enterprise, but their interactive or cumulative effect must also be managed on a portfolio basis. Failure to evaluate and manage outsourcing risks from an enterprise risk management perspective can lead to an accumulation of risks far greater than the risk savings offered by the outsourcing arrangement, thereby exposing key stakeholders to greater amounts of risk than they desire. An enterprise risk management approach to outsourcing can help management and the board of directors live up to expectations related to effective risk management for the organization.

Source: Beasley, M, Bradford, M & Pagach, D 2004, *Strategic Finance*, July, pp. 23–9.

CHAPTER 9

Tie your capital budget to your strategic plan

Otherwise, you might be spending money for the wrong projects.

At a recent board of directors meeting for a local company, the group was about to approve an expenditure for upgraded equipment. During the discussion, one of them asked, 'How does this proposed equipment fit into our strategic plan?' What followed was disconcerting. No one knew the answer. Further, several members of the board didn't understand the importance of the question. These directors — who were conscious of their responsibilities as stewards of corporate assets, their responsibilities for internal control, and their responsibilities to third parties, particularly investors and creditors — hadn't considered the relationship of capital acquisitions to the strategic plan. They hadn't considered what might happen if they upgraded equipment to support a product that was in the mature stage of its life cycle, possibly approaching a point where it would be phased out.

As corporate financial professionals, you need to recognize that capital asset decisions are the most irrevocable long-range activities because they:

- involve significant corporate funding;
- are the least flexible in terms of changing the strategic direction of the business;
- are the least flexible for conversion into more liquid assets;
- may geographically impact the long-term raw material supply capabilities of the business (for example, newer manufacturing facilities are located near deep-water ports to accept raw materials arriving from around the world);
- may geographically impact the business's long-term customer access (for example, a company would place a new plant near existing product delivery points or concentrations of potential customers); and
- involve decisions about assets that are unique to the company.

Since the unique features of capital assets represent the source of a company's product individuality and position in the marketplace, capital decisions must support the company's strategic plans. The irony is, this decision process has become one of management's most mechanical activities, reduced to the 'best set of numbers' or an extension of the sales forecast rather than the assurance that acquisitions support the corporate vision expressed in the strategic plan and mission statement.

Defining the strategic plan

The strategic plan must be a living document that:

- managers keep on their desks and refer to frequently, perhaps even daily.
- is updated when events occur, not because time periods expire.
- requires management explanations when its projections aren't met. Everyone has to understand any significant variations from the planned activities so adjustments can be made to the plan.
- represents management's philosophy of managing with a planning process. Here it's both a product and a process The product is the plan — the written document. The process is the interaction that takes place among the employees and management to develop the plan.
- reflects the corporate leadership's visions of the company's future.
- must be shared with all corporate stakeholders, employees, and even customers and vendors so they can embrace it as their own.

- is supported with individual functional plans developed by the corporate units. It uses marketing's sales projections, manufacturing's production projections, human resources' training objectives, and similar plans from the rest of the divisions.
- uses a systems approach to show how the functional plans interact with the overall strategic plan. It considers how each corporate function influences the other organisational activities, recognizing that all parts (subsystems) of a company must operate together toward a common purpose as stated in the corporate mission statement.
- is recognized in the company's financial reporting system as a way to measure the company's progress in implementing the strategic plan. (The financial reporting system is a universally recognized measurement mechanism.)
- contains objectives — specific measurable results that outline exactly what should be accomplished in a given timeframe.
- identifies the strategies — the how, where, and when of resource commitment to achieve objectives.

The strategic plan should focus first on the customers' needs, then on the business's capabilities to meet those needs with its products and services. Operating managers are the ones who'll make the plan happen (sales, production). Staff managers are supporting observers who add their definitive, focused expertise (financial, legal, human resources) when and where it's required.

Building the plan

The strategic plan begins with a corporate mission statement defining the company's purpose and where the business wants to be in the future, including how it plans to get there. It identifies guidelines for targeting the corporate market, such as:
- customer needs in that market,
- customers' level of education and income,
- customers' consumption habits,
- potential mix of products and services, and
- customers of today and tomorrow.

It also identifies the corporate organisational features, such as:
- its projected size and potential for growth,
- its resources and capabilities,
- an analysis of its physical plant capabilities,
- an analysis of its technology developments,
- a review of the staff support requirements in the planning period, and
- use of these resources in achieving corporate goals.

Managing the assets

As you develop the strategic plan, you'll need to look at your fixed-asset base — the permanent physical base the company uses to produce its product. Managing capital assets must be a prime consideration.

The stages of asset management are the acquisition, maintenance, and disposition of plant and equipment.

1. Companies acquire new physical assets when operating management determines the plant facilities are inadequate to support corporate needs for growth or corporate citizenship, such as environmental concerns and safety.

Acquisitions include:

- equipment replacement expenditures to replace the older machinery and reduce maintenance and operating costs;
- expansion investments that enlarge manufacturing or other company facilities, including those to expand current markets or invade new markets;
- investments to support strategic improvements in existing products and the addition of new products that offset or replace deteriorating markets and protect the company's revenue position; and
- combinations of the above

2. Maintenance is the second stage of capital asset management. Management usually is concerned with just the level of expense and its immediate effect on net income rather than the long-term economic viability of the asset. 'If it's not broke, don't fix it' is the old adage here. But they should be concerned about the potential for piecemeal maintenance programs for older facilities.

   If a strategic view says the facilities have a long-term value, delaying asset replacement programs unnecessarily drains the company's resources. This is the wrong way to save money or improve profits.

   If a strategic view says the facilities have no long-term value, then get rid of the assets. There's no advantage to maintaining nonviable assets.

3. Disposition of assets rarely gets proper attention. A prevailing management attitude seems to be, 'We already own it, so let's use it.' If an asset doesn't have a long-term strategic fit, get rid of it while it is still has value. Even though the asset may not have value for your company, it may still have value for another company. If another company can acquire the asset and use it profitably without degrading its own long-term strategy, both companies will benefit from the transaction.

The goal here is to ensure the assets will be fully utilized and support management's strategic vision.

Is the program effective?

Once you've defined your asset management program, identify the key measurements that will keep the program viable and effective:

Periodically review all capital asset acquisition projects to make sure you still need them. If the product sales and production requirement projections supporting the acquisition are no longer valid, then you need to determine if customers still want the product. You may have to make minor modifications or maybe even abandon the project. Do the same for your entire asset base.

After you've completed an acquisition, review the project to see if the initial planning projections were on target. If they weren't, then you need to take steps to improve the process for making future projections.

Continuously review all capital acquisition expenditures, large and small, to make sure that all assets are being acquired according to the strategic plan rather than in a piecemeal fashion. Many companies give top executives the individual authority to acquire equipment up to specified dollar amounts. Over time, this can generate a formidable asset base that may not support the current corporate strategic direction.

The capital budget

Remember, the capital budget is the portion of the strategic plan that selects which assets you should acquire and that allocates available resources among the proposed ideas, projects, and products based on quantitative and qualitative evaluations to determine the best investment for the company's future. It's the most dynamic aspect of the corporate decision-making process and has four interdependent steps:

1. Defining and communicating a firm's long-range and strategic plans and goals;
2. Developing a system that permits the orderly gathering and ranking of investment proposals;
3. Determining the accuracy of the estimates that will be used in the estimated rate of return calculations; and
4. Determining and assigning levels of risk probabilities to each investment proposal.

Only after considering all these steps as an integrated whole can you make a valid 'go' or 'no go' capital budgeting decision.

Since capital expenditures are long-term commitments, you should consider only strategically defined, thoroughly thought-out, qualitative and quantitative capital budgeting proposals. The classical concept of capital budgeting decisions says a company will accept investment proposals up to that point where marginal costs equal revenues. But since you can't accept all capital investment proposals, you need to rank them based on some mathematical standard and keep going until you reach the point where funds aren't available or the project's return falls below the company's hurdle rate. You'll make these choices after you accept the mandatory and nonfinancial operating necessity proposals, such as pollution devices, safety programs, or employee benefits.

Effective implementation is key

The driving force of any strategic plan is its effective implementation — allocating scarce corporate resources in a way that ensures you'll continuously achieve corporate long-term objectives. Once you've developed the corporate strategic plan assumptions, the next step is to merge this information into the various functional plans and link all short-term and long-term plans. After the functional plans for marketing, production, human resources, finance, and other support units are developed, the data is consolidated into the corporate plan.

The capital budgeting program provides a foundation for the overall strategic operating plan with its view of future economic benefits. The prime decision-making factors of the capital program should be:

- the time value of money,
- the cost of capital, and
- the inherent risk of each project/proposal.

Fixed assets are long-term present-dollar commitments that will be used over a long period of time in the normal course of business. Capital budgeting decisions are more than far-reaching — they are future-defining. Every capital budget expenditure must provide assets that have the highest priority in the strategic plan.

Source: Migliore, HR & McCracken, DE 2001, 'Tie your capital budget to your strategic plan', *Strategic Finance*, June, p. 38.

CHAPTER 10

Standard costing *is alive and well* at Parker Brass

Many people have condemned standard costing, saying it is irrelevant to the current just-in-time-based, fast-paced business environment. Yet surveys consistently show that most industrial companies in the United States and abroad still use it. Apparently, these companies have successfully adapted their standard costing systems to their particular business environments. In addition, many academics have contributed ideas on how the standard costing system could be and has been made more responsive to the needs of companies operating in this new economy.

The Brass Products Division at Parker Hannifin Corporation (hereafter, Parker Brass), a world-class manufacturer of tube and brass fittings, valves, hose, and hose fittings, is one of the standard costing success stories. It operates a well-functioning standard costing system of which we will show you some highlights.

What's special about the standard costing system at Parker Brass?

Parker Brass uses its standard costing system and variance analyses as important business tools to target problem areas so it can develop solutions for continuous improvement. Here are some examples of these standard costing-related tools:

- **Disaggregated product line information.** Parker Brass has been divided into Focus Business Units (FBUs) along product lines. Earnings statements are developed for each FBU, and variances are shown as a percentage of sales. If production variances exceed 5% of sales, the FBU managers are required to provide an explanation for the variances and to put together a plan of action to correct the detected problems. To help the process, a plant accountant has been assigned to each FBU. As a result of these steps, each unit is able to take a much more proactive approach to variance analysis.

- **Timely product cost information.** In the past, variances were reported only at month-end, but often a particular job already would have been off the shop floor for three or more weeks. Hence, when management questioned the variances, it was too late to review the job. Now, exception reports are generated the day after a job is closed (in other words, the day after the last part has been manufactured). Any jobs with variances greater than $1000 are displayed on this report. These reports are distributed to the managers, planners or schedulers, and plant accountants, which permits people to ask questions while the job is still fresh in everyone's mind.

- **Timely corrective action.** Because each job is costed (in other words, transferred out of Work-in-Process and into Finished Goods) 10 days after the job has closed, there is adequate time for necessary corrective action. For example, investigating a large material quantity variance might reveal that certain defective finished parts were not included in the final tally of finished parts. Such timely information would allow management to decide whether to rework these parts or to increase the size of the next job. This kind of corrective action was not possible when variances were provided at the end of each month

- **An effective control system.** Summary reports are run weekly, beginning the second week of each month, to show each variance in total dollars as well as each variance by product line and each batch within the product line. In addition, at the end of each month, the database is updated with all variance-related information. As a result, FBU managers can review variances by part number, by job, or by high dollar volume.

- **Employee training and empowerment.** Meetings are held with the hourly employees to explain variances and earnings statements for their FBU, thereby creating a more positive atmosphere in which the FBU team can work. These meetings help employees understand that management decisions are based on the numbers discussed and that if erroneous data are put into the system, then erroneous decisions may be made. For example, a machine may not be running efficiently. An operator may clock off of the job so that his or her efficiency does not look bad. Because the machine's efficiency is not adversely impacted, no maintenance is done to that machine, and the inefficiency continues. In addition, because the operator is not charging his/her cost to a job, the cost is being included in indirect labor, and manufacturing costs increase. If the operator had reported the hours correctly, management would have questioned the problem, and the machine would have been fixed or replaced based on how severe the problems were.

What new variances has Parker Brass designed?

In addition to the aforementioned innovations that Parker Brass has made to adapt its standard costing system to its particular business environment, the company has created the following new variances:

- The standard run quantity variance to explain situations where the size of a lot is less than the optimal batch quantity.
- The material substitution variance to evaluate the feasibility of alternative raw materials.
- The method variance to assess situations where different machines can be used for the same job.

The standard run quantity variance

The standard run quantity variance (SRQV) represents the amount of setup cost that was not recovered because the batch size was smaller than the earlier determined optimal batch size. Because setup costs are included in the standard labor hours for a batch, producing a smaller quantity per batch than the standard batch quantity is likely to create an unfavorable labor efficiency variance (LEV). Unless, however, the impact of actual production inefficiencies is separated from setup-related inefficiencies, the LEV reflects the combined impact of these two causes of inefficiencies and is not really useful for taking the necessary corrective action.

FIGURE 1

Panel A: the facts	
Standard production in 1 hour (units)	50
Standard batch quantity (units)	2000
Standard hours needed for 2000 units	40
Standard time needed for 1 setup (hours)	4
Standard labor rate per hour	$10
Actual quantity produced (units)	1200
Actual setup hours for 1 setup	4
Actual productive labor hours to make 1200 units	24
Actual labor cost for 28 hours at $10 per hour	$280

Panel B: workings			
	Setups	Production	Total
Standard time per unit:			
Standard setup time (hours)	4		
Standard production time (hours)		40	
Standard batch size (units)	2000	2000	
Hence, standard time per unit (hours)	0.002	0.020	0.022
Standard time charged\ for 1200 units:			
Standard time per unit (hours)	0.002	0.020	0.022
# of units actually produced	1200	1200	1200
Standard time charged (hours)	2.40	24.00	26.40

(continued)

FIGURE 1 (*continued*)

Panel C: solution		
If SRQV is determined, the journal entry would be:		
Work in process [(26.40)($10)]	$264	
SRQV [(4.00 − 2.40)($10)]	$16	
Accrued payroll		$280
If SRQV is <u>not</u> determined, the journal entry would be:		
Work in process [(26.40)($10)]	$264	
LEV [{28.00 − (1200)(0.022} {$10}]	$16	
Accrued payroll		$280

See figure 1 for an illustration of this issue. Panel A shows that standard batch quantity is 2000 units, the standard production during one hour is 50 units, and, hence, 40 standard hours are needed to produce 2000 units. In addition, it takes four standard and actual hours to set up one batch. Panel B reveals that standard hours for setup and production labor are 0.002 and 0.020 per unit, respectively, for a total of 0.022 per unit. In addition, because actual quantity produced is 1200 units, the total standard hours chargeable to these 1200 units is 26.40 [(0.002 + 0.020)(1200)].

Finally, panel C shows the recommended journal entry whereby an SRQV is created. This SRQV represents the unrecovered setup costs because 1200 units were manufactured instead of the standard batch quantity of 2000 units. Thus, because the company expected to spend $40 [(4 hours) ($10 per hour)] on each setup, the setup cost relating to the 800 (2000 − 1200) units not produced, or $16 U, is considered an unfavorable SRQV or the cost of producing small lots. On the other hand, using traditional standard costing, this amount of $16 U would most likely have been categorized as an LEV. Yet there really is no LEV and the variance of $16 U attributed to labor efficiency is merely the unabsorbed portion of the setup cost attributable to the 800 units that were not produced.

The advantages of extracting the standard run quantity variance are many. First, the SRQV ordinarily would be included in the LEV and could provide a misleading impression of labor's efficiency. Second, because just-in-time practices recommend smaller lots and minimal finished goods inventory, the SRQV is essentially the cost of adopting JIT. Third, to the extent that setup cost and the cost of carrying inventory are competing undesirables, a determination of the cost of small lots could be used in the trade-off analysis against the cost of holding and carrying inventories. Finally, to the extent that this variance can be separated for each customer, it would reveal how much of a loss was suffered by allowing that customer to purchase in small lots. Such information could be used in future bids. If a customer's schedule required a smaller lot, then that customer's job cost could be enhanced appropriately.

The material substitution variance

The material substitution variance (MSV) assumes perfect or near perfect substitutability of raw materials and measures the loss or gain in material costs when a different raw material is substituted for the material designated in the job sheet. Substitutions may be made for many reasons. For example, the designated material may not be available or may not be available in small-enough quantities, or the company may want to use up material it purchased for a product that it has since discontinued.

The usefulness of MSV is discussed in figure 2. Panel A shows that both materials. M1 and M2, can be used to manufacture a product, and it is assumed that two pounds is the standard input per unit for both materials. Material M1 is the material designated in the job sheet, but material

M2 can be substituted for M1. The standard cost of M2 ($11 per lb.) is higher than that for M1 ($10 per lb.), and M2 is used because M1 is currently not available and a valued customer needs a rush job. Panel B reveals that the standard quantity needed to manufacture 2000 units is 40 lbs.

Panel A: the facts	
Standard price per pound of material M1	$10
Standard price per pound of material M2	$11
Standard material quantity (M1 & M2) to make 100 units (lbs.)	2
Actual quantity produced (units)	2000
Actual pounds of M2 purchased and used	43
Panel B: workings	
Standard quantity to produce 2000 units:	
Standard material quantity to make 100 units (lbs.)	2
Actual quantity produced (units)	2000
Hence, standard quantity to produce 2000 units	40
Panel C: solution	
If MSV is determined, the journal entry would be:	
Work in process [(40.00)($10)]	$400
MEV [(43.00 – 40.00)($11)]	$33
MSV [(40.00)($11 – $10)]	$40
Material — M2 [(43.00)($11)]	$473
If MSV is not determined, the journal entry might be:	
Work in process [(40.00)($11)]	$440
MEV [(43.00 – 40.00)($11)]	$33
Material — M2 [(43.00)($11)]	$473

FIGURE 2

For the purposes of this illustration, we assume that material price variance (MPV) is detected when material is purchased (in other words, the material account is maintained at standard cost). Hence, panel C reveals the recommended journal entry whereby MSV is created. The MSV represents the benefit obtained by substituting a more expensive material (M2) for the less expensive material (M1) and hence represents the loss through substitution. The MSV is $40 U because (1) 40 lbs. is the standard quantity of M1 and M2 needed to manufacture 2000 units, and (2) M2 costs $1 more per lb. than M1. In addition, the material efficiency variance (MEV) is $33 U because 43 lbs. instead of the standard quantity of 40 lbs. were used to manufacture 2000 units.

In contrast, the traditional standard costing system might ignore the substitution, and the job might be charged with the standard cost of using 40 lbs. of M2. In that scenario, the job would cost $40 more and could have an impact on customer profitability analysis even though the customer did not request the substitution.

Now Parker Brass is evaluating an extension that would be to relax the simplifying assumption that both materials require the same standard input. See figure 3. It adopts the facts from figure 2 except that 1.9 lbs. of material M2 are required for 100 units instead of 2 lbs. for both materials in figure 2. In this situation, we have two MSVs, one for the price impact called 'MSV-Price' and the other for the efficiency impact, called 'MSV-Efficiency'.

Panel C shows the recommended journal entry whereby two MSV variances are created. First, MSV-Price is unfavorable because M2, a more expensive material, is being substituted for M1. As a result, MSV-Price is $40 U as material M2 costs $1 more per lb. than material M1. On the other hand, as you might expect, the MSV-Efficiency is favorable because only 1.9 lbs. of M2 are required to make 100 units as compared to 2 lbs. required for M1. Thus, MSV-Efficiency is $22 F because each batch of 100 units requires 38 lbs. of M2 against 40 lbs. of M1. The net result of the MSV variances is $18 U [(38 lbs.)($11) − (40 lbs.)($10)], suggesting that, barring any other complications, the substitution of M2 for M1 is not likely to be profitable under existing circumstances.

Finally, the MEV using material M2 is $55 U, reflecting the fact that 43 lbs. of material M2 actually were used whereas only 38 lbs. of material M2 should have been used. This variance could have been caused because M2 was a new material and required initial learning and other nonrecurring costs. In such a case, the standard quantity of 38 lbs. for 2000 units may not need to be changed. On the other hand, the MEV variance may have been caused because of the inherent difficulty in working with material M2. In such a case, the standard of 38 lbs. for 2000 units may need to be amended. In contrast, as was shown in panel C of figure 2, the journal entry that is likely to be made using traditional standard costing would completely ignore the impact of material substitution and would likely inflate the cost of this particular job.

Panel A: the facts		
Standard price per pound of material M1		$10
Standard price per pound of material M2		$11
Standard material quantity of M1 to make 100 units (lbs.)		2
Standard material quantity of M2 to make 100 units (lbs.)		1.9
Actual quantity produced (units)		2000
Actual pounds of M2 used		43
Panel B: workings		
	Material M1	Material M2
Standard quantity to produce 2000 units:		
Standard material quantity for 100 units (lbs.)	2	1.9
Actual quantity produced (units)	2000	2000
Hence, standard quantity to produce 2000 units	40	38
Panel C: solution		
If MSV is determined, the journal entry would be:		
Work in process [(40.00)($10)]	$400	
MEV [(43.00 − 38.00)($11))]	$55	
MSV-Price [(40.00)($11 − $10)]	$40	
MSV-Efficiency [(40.00 − 38.00)($11)]		$22
Material — M2 [(43.00)($11)]		$473
If MSV is not determined, the journal entry might be:		
Work in process [(38.00)($11)]	$418	
MEV [(43.00 − 38.00)($11)]	$55	
Material — M2 [(43.00)($11)]		$473

FIGURE 3

The advantages of extracting the MSV are as follows. First, determining MSV lets the company assign the MSV cost to a customer whose rush job may have required using a more expensive material like M2. On the other hand, the MSV could be written off if the substitution were made to benefit the company. Also, creating an MSV and breaking it up into its price and efficiency components allows the company to evaluate whether the substitution of M2 for M1 is a profitable one. While all these calculations can also be performed off the accounting system, creating the MSV makes the process a part of the system so a history of such evaluations is available for future reference.

Method variance

A method variance occurs when more than one machine can be used to manufacture a product. For example, a plant may have newer machines that it normally would expect to use to manufacture a product, so its standards would be based on such new machines. Yet the same plant may also keep, as backups, older and less efficient machines that also could manufacture the same product but would require more inputs in the form of machine and/or labor hours. For this example, we assume that labor hours and machine hours have a 1:1 relationship. As a result, the method variance becomes pertinent because the traditional LEV from operating the older machines could potentially include the following two impacts. First, an older machine may need additional labor hours to perform the same task, and the additional hours would be reflected in the LEV. Second, the LEV would include the workers' efficiency or lack thereof on the older machine.

We evaluate the usefulness of the method variance in figure 4. Panel A shows that both machines, A and B, can be used to manufacture a product. Machine A is the more efficient machine and the one used for setting the standard time. Machine B is the backup. Panel B shows that the standard machine hours needed to produce 1800 units are 30 on machine A and 36 on machine B, which can be compared to the 35 hours actually used to manufacture 1800 units on machine B.

Panel C of figure 4 reveals the recommended journal entry whereby a method variance is created. This method variance represents the loss incurred by substituting the backup machine B for machine A. Because machine B's standard of 36 labor hours is greater than machine A's standard of 30 hours, there is an unfavorable method variance of $120. On the other hand, because machine B took 35 hours to manufacture 1800 units instead of its standard of 36 machine hours, there is a favorable LEV of $20. As you can see, while there was a loss incurred by using machine B instead of machine A, the actual usage of machine B was efficient. In contrast, assuming the traditional costing system recognizes that machine B was used, it is likely to charge the job $720 [(36 hours) ($20 per hour)] instead of the $600 [(30 hours)($20 per hour)] that would have been charged if machine A had been used.

Here are the advantages of extracting the method variance. First, the impact of the method variance ordinarily would be included in the LEV and would provide a misleading impression of labor's productivity. Second, the method variance could be used to isolate the additional cost that was incurred during the year by operating machine M2. This could permit a trade-off between purchasing a new machine and continuing to maintain the older machine, especially if tight delivery schedules are not the norm. Finally, the product cost would still be based on the standards for the more efficient new machine, and the job would not be charged a higher cost merely because a less efficient machine was used. That means a job that was completed on the older machine would not be penalized.

Panel A: the facts	
Machine A: standard time needed for one unit (minutes)	1.0
Machine B: standard time needed for one unit (minutes)	1.2
Labor rate per hour	$20
Actual quantity produced (units)	1800
Actual labor hours used to make 1800 units using machine B	35
Actual labor cost	$700

Panel B: workings	Machine A	Machine B
Standard hours needed for 1800 units on:		
Standard time needed for one unit (minutes)	1.0	1.2
Actual quantity produced (units)	1800	1800
Hence, the standard hours needed	30	36

Panel C: solution		
If method variance is determined, the journal entry would be:		
Work in process [(30.00)($20)]	$600	
Method variance [(36.00 – 30.00)($20)]	$120	
LEV [(36.00 – 35.00)($20)]		$20
Accrued payroll		$700
If method variance is not determined, the journal entry might be:		
Work in process [(36.00)($20)]	$720	
LEV [(36.00 – 35.00)($20)]		$20
Accrued payroll		$700

FIGURE 4

Relevant, not irrelevant

As you can see from the Parker Brass examples, standard costing has not become irrelevant in the new, rapid-paced business environment Parker Brass not only has managed to modify its standard costing system to achieve disaggregated and timely cost information for timely corrective action, but it has also designed additional variances to determine how setup time relating to small batches should be absorbed, whether an alternative raw material is economically feasible, and how a product's cost might reflect the use of alternate production facilities.

Source: Johnson, D & Sopariwala, P 2000, *Management Accounting Quarterly*, winter, pp. 1–9.

CHAPTER 11

Everyone gets a share

Employee share plans are becoming popular, but they are not always the best way to motivate employees and cultivate loyalty.

The chief executive officer of the thriving last-minute hotel accommodation web site Wotif, Graeme Wood, is planning an initial public offering (IPO) of his six-year-old company for the first half of 2006. From the outset Wood was keen for each employee to own shares in the company, along the lines of the web company Google, which has created three billionaires so far.

For Wood, one of the advantages of employee share ownership is that it will motivate staff to control costs for the sake of profits, 'so that they'll think twice before they order a new bit of stationery'. At Woolworths, this extends to signs at head office alerting staff to today's share price, reminding them that tomorrow's price is 'up to you'.

Employee share plans are firmly entrenched in large Australian public companies, from Qantas to Coles Myer. Overseas companies such as Intel, Microsoft and Home Depot have used share options to attract all levels of employees to the business. At Intel, for example, about 90% of employees have shares in the company.

But the trend for all staff to be involved in equity plans is shifting, particularly in the United States, due to a change in accounting practices that declares employee stock options to be a compensation expense, and so they must be a part of a company's profit-and-loss statement. As a result, in December last year, Intel announced it would limit share options to senior staff. Berkshire Hathaway's chairman, Warren Buffett, has publicly championed this legislative change. Buffett argues that having to report these costs should not hurt the bottom line of the business because companies should only be granting these bonuses and options if they bring value to the company and its shareholders.

Graeme Wood is designing an employee share plan that he hopes will appeal to all staff, not just the senior executives who will be locked into short and long-term incentive programmes. Long-term incentive (LTI) programmes have been lucrative for senior managers in Australian companies recently. According to a 2005 Mercer survey on executive pay, the median three-year return among the top 100 companies on the Australian Stock Exchange is 33%. Companies at the 75th percentile, such as the National Australia Bank, Suncorp-Metway and Tabcorp Holdings, had an average 22% compound annual return, which means healthy bonuses for senior executives on LTIs.

Wood believes there is value in all staff having a stake in the business. But this sense of ownership has to be weighed against the risks and volatility of the stockmarket. 'It is a brave man who says your share price will never go backwards,' says Wood, who does not like to contemplate walking through the office when the share price is underperforming. That would be a 'double whammy' for morale. An underperforming company is demoralising enough without the thought that employees' personal wealth is also at stake. Under the new company structure, Wood will retain 35% of the company, and 40% will be under offer. The IPO is estimated to be worth about $100 million.

Wood also needs to consider the fact that people have different appetites for risk. Share plans are not always appealing, and many employees do not really understand how share ownership works. Like most companies, Wotif will hold seminars and provide written information about how the share plans will work, but staff do not always pay attention. Plans for Wotif's employee share plans will be finalised in February, and Wood expects all staff to be able to benefit from the IPO. The senior tier of managers will have a share component in their salary packages.

Liquidity and transparency

The executive chairman of recruiter Ambition Group, Nick Waterworth, was never interested in all staff becoming share owners when his business had its IPO in November 1999. He wanted a 'sexy staff share plan' that would tie in important staff. Rather than looking for private equity, Waterworth wanted a business model that offered liquidity and transparency. 'People can look in the paper and see what their shares are worth,' he says. Only 15 of the company's 130 staff are on LTI plans.

Ambition Group's share plans have broadened to three types. About 20% of staff are involved in a tax-exempt plan, in which staff can invest $1000 of their pre-tax salary each year. There is a deferred plan, in which staff can defer income into purchasing fixed amounts of shares. Tax is paid only when the employee sells the shares. This can be done only after 10 years of ownership or if the employee leaves the company. Waterworth is not convinced that shares are necessary for all his staff; he believes that people are motivated by different things at different stages of their careers.

The third share ownership plan at Ambition centres on senior staff. Shares, rather than options, are used, and annual grants are made to key staff. There are three to four-year vesting periods, with hurdles based on earnings per share performance. If the company has performed well, an executive could be eligible for about five times his salary in long-term incentive payments. Waterworth is confident that the combination of short-term and long-term incentive schemes is an effective way to attract senior talent. In 2005, the company's share price increased by more than 27%.

Performance hurdles

Throughout the 2005 annual general meeting season, a common agenda item was the approval of share options for senior management. Clearly, Australian companies are working on the premise that senior management is motivated by share option plans.

Commonwealth Bank shareholders were asked to approve a $12-million LTI plan for its new chief executive, Ralph Norris. BHP Billiton's chairman, Don Argus, outlined a new package for chief executive Chip Goodyear — an extra 600 000 shares if Goodyear reaches performance targets over the next five years. National Australia Bank's chief executive John Stewart's new contract includes an LTI plan with 140 000 performance rights and 500 000 performance options, subject to shareholder approval.

All of these contracts are closely tied to performance hurdles. Argus explained to shareholders that for Goodyear to receive all those shares in 2010, the total shareholder return must exceed the return of a comparable group of companies by 5.5% each year.

The idea of offering share incentives to senior executives is not always championed. The late management author and political economist Peter Drucker said: 'Stock option plans reward the executive for doing the wrong thing. Instead of asking 'Are we making the right decision? He asks, 'How did we close today?' It is encouragement to loot the corporation.'

The trends

Pay

According to a 2005 Mercer survey of the chief-executive salary packages of more than 100 of Australia's largest companies, chief executives are on about twice the salary and more than twice the bonus of those reporting to them, and their long-term incentive programmes are worth about three times as much.

Performance

Senior executives can expect demanding performance hurdles as part of their long-term incentive programmes.

Motivation

Boards and remuneration committees need to consider how tougher incentive programmes will affect the motivation of executives.

Source: Ross, E 2006, 'Everyone gets a share', *BRW*, 19 January, p. 86.

CHAPTER 12

The balanced scorecard at Philips Electronics

It's used to align company vision, focus employees on how they fit into the big picture, and educate them on what drives the business.

When a management tool becomes popular, it's only logical to question whether it's a fad or the future. One performance measurement tool — the balanced scorecard (BSC) — has broad appeal. Approximately 50% of *Fortune 1000* companies in North America and about 40% in Europe use a version of the BSC, according to a recent survey by Bain & Co. The number of software and consulting firms currently providing BSC-related products and services supports these statistics. But do companies think the BSC is here to stay? Philips Electronics does. This worldwide conglomerate has gathered its more than 250 000 employees in 150 countries around the card because it sees this tool as the future — not a trendy tool. The key benefit for Philips: Management can streamline the complicated process of running a complex international company with diverse product lines and divisions. Here's how it cascades throughout the organization.

The drive to implement the balanced scorecard at Philips Electronics came from the top down — as a directive from the Board of Management in Europe to all Philips divisions and companies worldwide. The directive went to each of the companies and their quality departments, with the effort in the medical division headed by the Quality Steering Committee that reports to the president of Philips Medical Systems. (Later we'll look specifically at the experiences of the Philips Medical Systems North America (PMSNA).)

Philips Electronics has used the balanced scorecard to align company vision, focus employees on how they fit into the big picture, and educate them on what drives the business. An essential aid to communicating the business strategy, the BSC works as a vehicle to take key financial indicators and create a quantitative expression of the business strategy. In fact, Philips Electronics' management team uses it to guide the quarterly business reviews worldwide in order to promote organizational learning and continuous improvement.

The road to implementation

Philips' underlying belief in creating their balanced scorecard is that understanding what drives present performance is the basis for determining how to achieve future results. With this understanding in mind, Philips designed the scorecard to provide a shared understanding of the organization's strategic policies and vision of the future. Their operating principle in the design was to determine factors that were critical for achieving the company's strategic goals.

The tool has helped Philips Electronics focus on factors critical for their business success and align hundreds of indicators that measure their markets, operations, and laboratories. The business variables crucial for creating value, which are known as the four critical success factors (CSFs) on the Philips Electronics BSC, are:

Competence (knowledge, technology, leadership, and teamwork),
Processes (drivers for performance),
Customers (value propositions), and
Financial (value, growth, and productivity).

Here's how these critical success factors came to life at the company.

Top-level scorecard criteria are the driving determinant for lower-level scorecard criteria. Philips wanted to make implicit assumptions about the way the business creates value explicitly through CSFs. In other words, the goal was to translate assumed relationships such as customer satisfaction and product sales into critical success factors to measure performance. To do so, they identified which financial and customer CSFs give a competitive edge, and then they determined the process CSFs that have the greatest impact on the financial and customer CSFs giving the company that edge. Competence CSFs deliver required process, customer, and financial results.

To express the strategy in measurable objectives, the team established a performance management system that measures progress toward the corporate vision. This system links short-term actions with long-term strategy so employees understand how their day-to-day activities help achieve the company's stated goals.

In order to focus employees on the few vital goals and business priorities, the BSC cascades down throughout the organization. Top management initially deployed the BSC by setting annual operational targets, which were brought down through organizational layers as goals for the divisions worldwide and objectives at the business unit level. By deploying top-level CSFs throughout the organization, goals can be clearly linked to the business strategy as well as to all employees.

The Philips Electronics balanced scorecard has three levels. The highest is the strategy review card, next is the operations review card, and the third is the business unit card. In addition, the plan is to implement another level of the card — the individual employee card — in 2003.

The corporate quality department created specific guidelines for metric linkage for the entire company. These guidelines state that all top-level scorecard critical success factors for which the department is responsible must link metrically to lower-level cards. Three criteria were established to accomplish this. The first is inclusion: Top-level CSFs must be addressed by lower-level CSFs to achieve top-level metric goals. The second is continuity: Critical success factors must be connected through all levels, and lower-level measurements shouldn't have longer cycle times than higher-level measurements. The third criterion is robustness: Meeting lower-level CSF goals must assure that higher-level CSF goals will be met or surpassed. Goals in all card levels align with goals in the next level above, and goals become fewer and less complex as you drill down through the organization.

The BSC at work in the business units

At the business unit level, critical success factors were developed for each of the four perspectives of the card — competence, processes, customers, and financial. They established guidelines for the deployment of CSFs at lower levels in the company, stating that departments must select CSFs for which the department has a major control responsibility. These CSFs — key BSC indicators — monitor the implementation of the business strategy.

The management team of each business unit reached consensus on which CSFs distinguish the business unit from the competition. They used a value map to derive customer critical success factors by analyzing customer survey data that reflected perceived performance relative to the price for competing products. Process CSFs were derived by determining how process improvements can deliver customer requirements. Competence CSFs were identified by determining what human resources and competencies were required to deliver the other three perspectives of the card. Standard financial reporting metrics were used as financial CSFs.

The next step was for each business unit to determine key indicators at the business unit level that measure critical success factors. Assumptions about relationships between processes and results were quantified and performance drivers determined. Targets were then set based on the gap between present performance and desired performance for the current year plus two and four years in the future. The criteria: Targets must be specific, measurable, ambitious, realistic, and timephased. Targets are derived from an analysis of market size, customer base, brand equity, innovation capability, and world-class performance.

Examples of indicators at the business unit level include:

Financial	**Processes**
Economic profit realized	Percentage reduction in process cycle time
Income from operations	Number of engineering changes
Working capital	Capacity utilization
Operational cash flow	Order response time
Inventory turns	Process capability
Customers	**Competence**
Rank in customer survey	Leadership competence
Market share	Percentage of patent-protected turnover
Repeat order rate	Training days per employee
Complaints	Quality improvement team participation
Brand index	

In cascading the card down from the organizational level to the business unit level, six key indicators consistently came to the forefront for all business units:

- Profitable revenue growth,
- Customer delight,
- Employee satisfaction,
- Drive to operational excellence,
- Organizational development,
- IT support.

These six key drivers relate to each other as well as to the balanced scorecard's four critical success factors. Organizational development and IT support drive the competence perspective; customer delight and employee satisfaction drive the customer perspective; operational excellence drives the process perspective; and profitable revenue growth drives the financial perspective. And each quarter the BSC metrics are used as the reporting format for the review of each business unit's performance.

Successes and challenges

Although there are many successful implementations at the Philips companies, let's look at the implementation of the balanced scorecard at Philips Medical Systems North America (PMSNA). It served as an alignment tool to focus on their strategic intent to become a $1 billion company by the year 2001.

It simultaneously guided a cultural change effort to increase accountability for results. Eventually the BSC is expected to replace the monthly accountability calls to the field office where sales are reported against forecasted numbers. Another success for the card within this division is the creation of an operational scorecard for action planning and tracking results in real-time: Data are automatically transferred from internal reporting systems and fed into the online BSC report, which is immediately accessible and contains the new results. An upcoming enhancement to customer service and satisfaction reporting will be the automatic feed of data gathered by the Gallup Organization into the online BSC report in a similar fashion.

Finally, implementing the card responded to common questions raised in the annual employee motivation survey, such as 'How does what I do every day fit into the bigger picture of the company?' The balanced scorecard enables employees to understand exactly what they need to do on a daily basis in order to impact results.

Chris Farr, former vice president of quality and regulatory at PMSNA and who was responsible for the BSC, says that companies must get buy-in to the metrics and share measures quarterly with all employees in order to succeed. 'Management must give full access to their employees,' Farr says. 'The metrics must be shared and visible.'

To share the metrics with employees, Philips Electronics uses traffic-light reporting to indicate how the actual performance compares with the target. Green indicates meeting target, yellow indicates in-line performance, and red warns that performance is below target. The visibility of results using a traffic-light model means ease-of-use with quick, easily recognizable metrics. Philips Medical Systems employs Lotus Notes-based online reporting using a system they call Business Balanced Scorecard On-Line (BBS ON-Line).

Farr said the balanced scorecard's primary strength is gaining the commitment and participation of management and employees regarding company objectives. 'Employees have helped to create measures that are meaningful to customers and to the business,' he says. 'In this process, employees have analyzed what makes the business successful and gained a greater understanding of the business enterprise.'

Other strengths include:

- The BSC promotes the sharing of best practices and creates a communication system worldwide. Each element of the card has an owner whom employees can contact to share success strategies and product fixes. BSC fosters communication, collaboration, and problem solving.
- The BSC supports a company's cultural change to a learning organization by creating a common knowledge base. If a metric is in the red zone, the employee can quickly access how to fix potential problems and avoid repeating others' mistakes, saving time and money in problem solving.
- The BSC represents an enhancement to the current 'Yellow Pages' in use at Philips. Out of a total workforce of more than 250 000, roughly 22 000 employees have chosen to share project knowledge and interests on a voluntary basis using the Philips Yellow Pages. Employees working on similar projects can communicate successes and pitfalls using the Yellow Pages on the employee intranet. The BSC takes the concept further with a defined owner accountable for each element on the card.

Other lessons Philips Electronics learned include:

- Software for use in capturing and transferring data to a BSC in real time should be selected carefully and researched fully prior to implementing the balanced scorecard. Many commercial products are available, and Philips Electronics uses a Lotus Notes-based reporting system they call Business Balanced Scorecard On-Line for Web-based reporting.
- A balance must be reached to maintain visibility for employee access while maintaining confidentiality of company results that are sensitive and proprietary.
- In trying to determine employee-level performance indicators, the team learned that many critical success factors can't be directly impacted by employees.

Fad or future?

The use of a balanced scorecard as a strategic tool represents an opportunity for an executive team to align their company to the strategic intent. Since the BSC represents a fundamental change in how an organization is measured and held accountable for results, it also poses threats to an established corporate culture and has potential weaknesses if it isn't executed properly. Yet the balanced scorecard is a powerful strategic tool — not the latest management fad — for strategic planning, goal setting, goal alignment, and measurement. No other tool provides the ability to balance all aspects crucial to business performance in 2002 and beyond.

Source: Gumbus, A and Lyons, B 2002, *Strategic Finance*, November, pp. 45–9.

CHAPTER 13

RFID: the changes it will bring

The year is 2054. A fugitive walks into the Gap to buy some clothes for his companion. A retinal scanner reads his eyes upon entry, and a nearby holographic image says: 'Hello, Mr Yakimoto. Welcome back to the Gap. How'd those assorted tank tops work out for you?' This is a scene from *Minority Report* starring Tom Cruise. It's science fiction. Or is it?

Radio Frequency Identification (RFID) promises to make this scenario more science than fiction — and sooner than you might think. As RFID moves into the mainstream, technologies similar to consumer identification will become a reality. RFID will also have a major impact on companies, large and small, as well as the accountants working for them. The technology will affect inventory management, contingent liabilities, depreciation, supplychain management, and even customer interaction.

What is RFID?

Like bar coding, RFID is a technology that enables scanning for tracking purposes, but that's where the similarities end. Bar codes use the Universal Product Code (UPC) system that identifies the manufacturer code and the product code of the item. RFID goes much further. Scanning an item equipped with RFID can return a variety of data including the manufacturer, item information, which supplier shipped it, the specific cost associated with the item, the path it took to get to the store, and almost any other kind of relevant data you could want.

And there are other fundamental differences between bar codes and RFID (see table 1 for more information). Bar codes require a 'line of sight', and the scanner usually must be within a foot of the actual product. If an inventory manager has a case of various items, he or she must unload the case, scan each item, and then repackage the case. This interaction can result in increased labor costs and the possibility of damage to items.

A typical RFID system consists of transceivers, tags, and a computer system to process the information. There are two types of tags: active and passive. Active tags have an internal battery that permits tags to be read from a greater distance. These tags also constantly transmit data. Passive tags don't have a battery and only transmit data when a transceiver activates them by coming within range. Although active tags are larger and more expensive, they have many more potential applications.

Transceivers read and transmit data from the tags to the computer system. An individual with a hand transceiver can simply move the unit within range of the items to be counted, and the transceiver will capture all the information the tags contain. This process requires no product handling and may be completed in seconds. The lack of human interaction with the products avoids damage to the inventory, and very few miscounts are likely to occur.

Corporate effects

The impact that RFID will have on businesses will reach into a number of areas from counting to costs and revenues to warranties.

Inventory costing and inventory management

There are two types of inventory systems: the perpetual system and the periodic system. The perpetual system allows managers to know with a great deal of precision what items are in stock at any given time. In contrast, the periodic system usually entails a full count of inventory once per period. The costs associated with doing a full count more than once per period can be significant. An organization that uses a periodic system must typically keep a close eye on shelf levels to determine when items need to be reordered and/or shelves restocked. RFID can support a perpetual inventory system.

Another potential benefit with RFID is related to assigning costs correctly. Both the periodic and perpetual systems use inventory-costing systems like first-in, first-out (FIFO) and last-in, first-out (LIFO) to assign costs to items. These systems assign costs to outgoing products based on previous invoice prices. A FIFO system assigns the cost of the first items received, whereas LIFO would start from the latest invoice. The result is that the real cost of an item is never recorded, and aging and obsolescence are rarely taken into account. Overall, although the perpetual system does a better job of keeping the books updated to the minute, it's just as flawed as the periodic system when it comes to assigning appropriate costs to specific items.

The best way to assign the proper costs to items sold is the Specific Identification Method (SIM). SIM is a way to track inventory when each item can be identified. Specific identification is usually used for large, easily traceable items. This method is often reserved for low-volume, high-priced products because it can be a very costly system for companies that have large inventories and numerous transactions. It requires each individual item to be tracked and to have an assigned cost. But since bar codes only identify the manufacturer's code and product code, it's impossible for a retailer to know, for example, which shipment a particular can of tomatoes came from and the unit price associated with that shipment.

With an RFID system, units can be tracked on an individual basis. Each item can have a tag, and each tag can transmit manufacturer codes, product codes, exact associated costs, date manufactured, length of time on the shelf, and other useful information. Since exact costs are available at any time over the course of the year, a snapshot of the company's inventory can be taken. Precise inventory levels, cost of goods sold, and a more accurate net income can be obtained at any time.

Boeing Co. has recently started preparing its suppliers for the push to RFID, although no mandate has been put in place at this time. Over time, Boeing expects that RFID will lower receiving costs, improve the ability to track parts, and reduce the risk that unapproved components will find their way into the planes. They expect their suppliers to benefit through lower inventory costs, improved configuration control, and more detailed repair histories.

Labor costs

Saving money on salaries is another major benefit of RFID. Considerable time can be saved by not having to count individual items. Picture, for example, a stock boy sorting through every item in a store and scanning the bar code or manually writing down counts of items vs. any store employee standing in the middle of the stockroom and collecting all the information with one push of a button.

With an active system where item movement is constantly tracked, a perpetual count of inventory will be updated the instant there's a change. If a retail outlet has transceivers placed strategically throughout the store, inventory management personnel can be notified about stock deficiencies. Fewer personnel will be needed because companies will no longer use staff to track inventory and determine restocking.

It's important to note that while this technology is extremely powerful, no system is infallible. It would be in a company's best interests to employ auditors to make sure that tags and transceivers are working properly. While this will offset some of the labor savings, the benefits will outweigh the costs.

Depreciation

In the fast-paced technology sector, today's newest item or component can be obsolete tomorrow. This rapid movement through the product life cycle presents a challenge for companies and their accountants. Intel, for example, produces millions of chips and other products annually. To keep its manufacturing facilities stocked with necessary supplies, there are components in transit constantly. James Kellso, manager of Intel's Supply Network Research, determined that management of his inventory in transit had major implications on the company because the items depreciate as much as 5% per week. By implementing active RFID tags with global positioning capabilities (GPS), Intel was able to reduce inventory by 82%.

For manufacturing companies with large inventories, RFID provides distinct advantages. ES3 LLC, a supplychain services firm that co-locates inventories of multiple manufacturers, uses RFID to keep track of its inventory located throughout a 230-acre facility. The technology gives the company instant tracking and data for all 1900 trailer-slots in its yard. Geoff Davis, executive vice president of ES3, estimates that he saves 33% of his normal labor requirement with this information and avoids the risk of spoiled cargo, late departures, lost trailers, and excessive detention.

Revenue creation

While there are many cost-saving benefits associated with RFID technology, there are also revenue-creating ones. For example, retailers can be notified immediately and stocking staff automatically prompted for replenishment if shelf quantities dip below desired levels. This benefit can't be overemphasized. The costs associated with raising brand awareness, inciting purchase intentions, and actually getting the customer to the store are very high. It's a huge waste of money when a customer is ready to buy but the sale can't be consummated because the shelf is bare.

Extra Future Store, a supermarket in Rheinbert, Germany, has already taken this capability to the next level. Extra has its entire inventory outfitted with RFID tags and its shelves and shopping carts equipped with transceivers. Store employees are always aware of inventory levels. And the shopping carts are equipped with monitors that inform customers of sales promotions as well as items in an upcoming aisle that they may have an interest in based on the current contents of their cart.

Warranty/service benefits

The automobile manufacturing process, for instance, involves many parts and long labor hours. When a defective part is discovered, all cars assembled using that particular part must be identified and fixed before leaving the plant. This process may require stopping the manufacturing line, closing the auto yard, or calling back cars that have already made it off the premises. All of these fixes are time-consuming, labor-intensive, and can increase the direct labor costs per car and decrease net income.

With RFID, many of these difficulties can be avoided. If all parts have tags, the plant manager can easily identify the location of all the parts that need to be replaced or called back. RFID also can improve asset utilization, reducing warranty and scrap inventory.

By reducing expected warranties, a company can also reduce its contingent liabilities. If a company operates in a business environment where warranty expenses are probable and can be estimated reasonably, then the benefit of RFID's ability to reduce warranty expenditures will have an immediate impact on the income statement since assigning an estimated liability for warranties occurs concurrently with a warranty expense.

Costs and drawbacks

A major drawback of RFID is that there is no standard system currently in place. Two basic architectures that are jockeying for position are EPC Global, which can connect to the Internet, and ISO/IEC, which is being used by the International Organization for Standardization.

Another drawback is the large investment required to implement an RFID system. Today each tag costs approximately $0.30. At this price, wholesalers, manufacturers, and large ticket retailers are the only ones who can afford RFID. For the high-volume retailer, $0.30 can be prohibitive. On the other hand, as more companies embrace the technology, the price of RFID tags is expected to come down to around $0.05 due to economies of scale. In addition, the costs of training, computer system upgrades, and changes to business processes add to the difficulties of implementing an RFID system.

A third drawback involves supply-chain integration. This difficulty should be diminished as the larger retailers demand that their suppliers implement the RFID system. Leading the push to RFID are Wal-Mart and the U. S. Department of Defense (DOD). Both organizations have mandated that their suppliers comply with their RFID guidelines.

Wal-Mart, already known for its innovative inventory and supply-chain management, continues to take a leading position in the implementation of RFID. Rollin Ford, recently appointed Wal-Mart CIO, has indicated that the company has no plans to slow down its RFID initiatives and that it even planned to stop accepting Genl (first generation RFID) shipments from its suppliers.

The DOD contends with multiple layers of bureaucracy and red tape in nearly everything it does. The Department would like to counteract some of the delays and cut waste from its supply chain with RFID. According to Alan Estevez, assistant deputy undersecretary of defense for Supply Chain Integration, the Army lost $1.2 billion in materials that weren't received in the field. Interestingly, many calls for supplies start with handwritten orders from the field. The DOD now requires suppliers to begin implementing RFID systems and expects the new system can shave about 27 days (from 33 days to five days) off the time it takes to get needed supplies to troops.

Company performance and the accountant's role

While initiating a move toward RFID will involve substantial investment, the cost savings and revenue creation will more than cover the costs over time. Savings can be achieved in many ways. In the technology industry, where depreciation rates can be very large, good inventory management is essential to maximizing profits. With an RFID system in place, a supplier can track inventory sent out to its customers. A supplier can also keep a continuous count of the inventory levels of its customers and automatically send replenishments as needed, in effect creating a just-in-time system.

There are many new challenges that the accounting industry will face as a result of RFID. With respect to inventory-costing methods, specific identification hasn't really been feasible for most companies until now. Use of the FIFO and LIFO systems cause inherent inaccuracies in ending inventory calculations as well as cost-of-goods-sold estimates. These inaccuracies present a direct challenge to one of the most fundamental principles of accounting: to portray the company's financial position accurately. While the deviation from this principle has been accepted due to the associated costs of using a specific identification inventory system, RFID will soon make it possible to achieve more accurate costs.

What is happening now?

RFID is becoming more and more popular. A study released recently by trade organization Computing Technology Industry Association (CompTIA) at RFID World 2006 in Dallas, Texas, suggests that about 59% of responders have tried the technology. About 15% of the companies have actually implemented RFID projects.

RFID also is being used in more and more industries. GlaxoSmithKline (GSK) announced that it will begin putting RFID tags on bottles of Trizivir, an HIV medicine. Working with IBM to develop this RFID system, GSK chose Trizivir for the pilot program because the FDA has identified it as one of 32 drugs most susceptible to counterfeiting and diversion. RFID has been used to tag poultry in Taiwan to combat the Avian Flu epidemic and in Canada to tag cattle. RFID is being used by NASCAR, libraries, and many other businesses.

It seems there are two significant hurdles that need to be overcome for RFID to be more successful. The first is the shortage of skilled professionals, and the second involves potential privacy concerns. The CompTIA survey reported that about 50% of the companies expect problems in finding educated and trained professionals to implement new RFID projects.

Regarding privacy, many people and organizations are concerned about the capability of RFID to remain active and unnoticed after sale. In fact, the chips are so small that when they're placed within an item of clothing it's possible for the consumer to not even realize they are there. Many are concerned that companies will use this technology to track consumers' shopping or travel habits. While it's possible to disable tags, the paranoia of shoppers could cause a consumer backlash against the technology. Many privacy advocates have called on companies to state their intended use of the technology. Currently, there is no regulation, so many states are trying to fill this void in standards by introducing RFID bills. For example, a New Hampshire bill suggests that a label be included to warn people about the potential fallouts over the information. Though the FCC regulates the frequencies that are used in RFID, and some ISOs have been published for the RFID industry, there is still concern regarding the covert scanning of RFIDs and the possible misuse of information.

Whatever the final decisions of the regulators might turn out to be, RFID is finding its place as a valuable tool in business.

Source: Markelevich, A & Bell, R 2006, *Strategic Finance*, August, p. 46.

CHAPTER 14

From mass production to mass customization: postponement of inventory differentiation

Customers are demanding. They want customized products and services, and they want their orders filled more quickly than before. To cope, companies often struggle to predict customer demand while remaining both efficient and flexible. As this article explains, one strategy for addressing a demanding marketplace is postponement, *which refers to organizing operations so that, at the point of differentiation, work-in-process can be made into multiple versions of the product as close as possible to the point when demand is known. Postponement involves delaying the movement or assembly of mass-produced product until after a customer order is received*.

This article introduces the concept of *postponement* as it relates to inventory levels of highly customized products that face high demand uncertainty. Postponement is the process of organizing the operations function so that at the point of differentiation the work-in-process can be made into multiple versions of the product as close as possible to the point when demand is known. Postponement involves delaying the movement or assembly of mass-produced product until after a customer order is received.

Successful implementations of postponement improve customer service levels and reduce inventory costs. With postponement, configurable generic products are forecast in aggregate, which is more accurate than forecasts for individual finished products. Specific product forecasts are needed close to the time that a customer order is received, when demand is known with greater accuracy. In general, there are two types of postponement — time and form. *Time postponement* refers to delaying the differentiation tasks to as late as possible in the process. *Form postponement* involves delaying the completion of the final product configuration until after the customer requirements are known. *Partial* postponement involves postponing only those final products that face uncertain demand. Finished products whose demands are predictable are produced without postponement.

Forecast and inventory

Customer expectations of suppliers are rising. They increasingly demand customized products and services and that their orders be filled more quickly than before. Companies struggle to find ways to remain efficient and flexible enough to respond to an increasingly diverse marketplace. Even without trying to customize their products, many companies find it difficult to fulfill orders swiftly and at an acceptable cost. The number of products available for customer choice has increased dramatically. Most products are offered with multiple variations tailored to meet the needs of specific market segments. Supporting a large number of offerings leads to high overhead and administrative costs. Higher product complexity leads to higher manufacturing costs because of specialized processes, more setups, and quality assurance.

Customer demand for a diverse product line can be difficult, if not impossible, to predict. The presence of product variety creates difficulties in forecasting and problems related to inventory and customer service. Demand must be forecast for every possible combination of size, color, and finish. Increased product variation increases the forecast error and, consequently, errors in product shipment and product imbalances. Overforecasting results in excess inventory. Underforecasting results in shortages and poor customer service. These two situations are often addressed by transfers between stores or price reductions, both of which erode profit margins.

Some managers choose simply to stock as much finished goods as they can, risking the write-off of perhaps millions of dollars. These inventories are believed to provide protection from stockouts caused by the uncertainty of demand. The cost of holding inventory, extensive product proliferation, and the risk of obsolescence, especially in rapidly changing markets, make the expense of holding large inventories of finished goods prohibitive. High-demand items naturally have safety stock assigned to them, but in many organizations there are so many very-low-demand items that keeping any stock in these items is prohibitively expensive. Companies must now provide good service while maintaining minimal inventories.

EXHIBIT 1 ■ Tradeoff curves for inventory level and customer service level

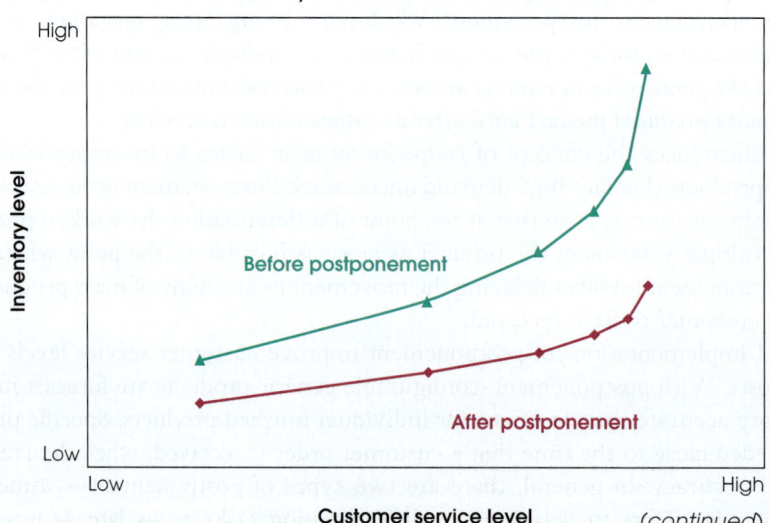

(continued)

EXHIBIT 1 (*continued*)

Customer service level	Inventory level	
	Before postponement	After postponement
0.800	1997.89	1610.94
0.900	2492.89	1854.78
0.950	2902.35	2026.68
0.975	3255.58	2161.49
0.990	3663.05	2306.82
0.999	4500.66	2584.80

A traditional view of operations of companies in the goods-producing sector is that their operations fall somewhere on a spectrum ranging from make-to-stock (MTS) to make-to-order (MTO). The make-to-stock environment is characterized by highly standardized products produced in low variety and at high volume. Operations exhibit low flexibility, require high capitalization in specialized equipment, and benefit from low operating costs. The make-to-order environment is characterized by providing high-variety, high levels of customization at relatively low volumes. Operations are flexible, require low capitalization, and usually have high operating costs. Pressured by customers with increasingly discriminating tastes, manufacturers struggle to provide the variety of MTO with the volume benefits of MTS.

Postponement defined

One approach available to manufacturers to quickly provide customized products in substantial volume is to change from *mass production* to *mass customization*. Mass customization is the ability to customize a large volume of products and deliver them at close to mass-production prices. Mass customization takes the approach of creating variety and customization through flexibility and quick response. The importance of individual products decreases, as the same process can be used to produce many products and product families.

EXHIBIT 2 ■ Tradeoff curve for inventory level and forecast accuracy

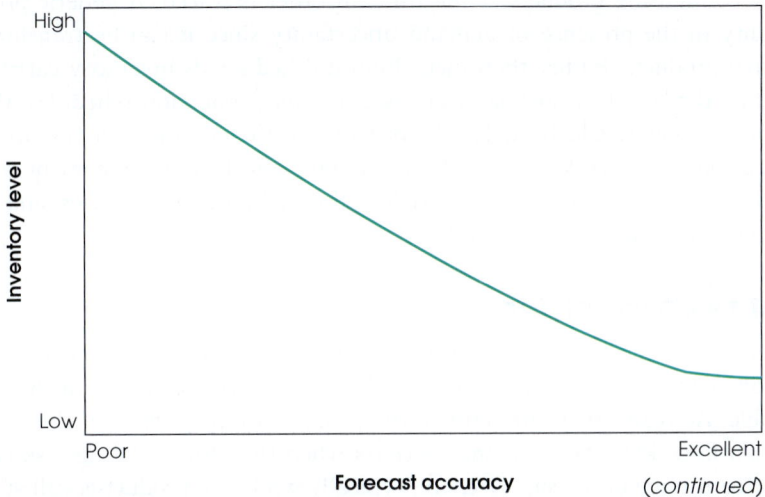

(*continued*)

EXHIBIT 2 *(continued)*

Forecast accuracy (Std. dev. of forecast error)	Inventory level
400	2917
385	2867
369	2817
354	2767
338	2717
322	2667
306	2617
289	2567
273	2517
256	2467
238	2417
221	2367
202	2317
184	2267
164	2217
144	2167
122	2117
99	2067
73	2017
39	1967
0	1950

One innovative way of achieving mass customization is to postpone the final configuration of standardized semifinished products into a wide variety of end products. Postponement holds that a product is processed to the point where it remains generic, and that final processing to customize the product is delayed until demand is realized. A firm can offer tremendous variety and fill orders quickly without having to stock a large amount of finished inventory by configuring products at the time an order is placed. A generic product offers more flexibility in the presence of demand uncertainty since it can be transformed into a variety of final products. Rather than incur high finished-goods inventory carrying costs or incur stockouts that result in lost sales or disrupt plant production schedules, the customization of the product would be delayed until the customer order arrives. In addition to improving customer service levels, the direct tangible effect of postponement is to increase semifinished, work-in-process inventories, reduce finished-goods inventories, and at the same time lower the aggregate inventory level.

Types of postponement

Postponement can be classified into two major categories — time and form postponement. Time postponement involves delaying the product differentiation stages of the operation as late as possible. Activities that differentiate the product are performed at the latest point in the production flow. Early postponement occurs when the differentiating task is performed at some upstream stage of the supply chain, typically while the product is still at the factory.

Late postponement occurs when the point of differentiation occurs at some downstream point in the supply chain, perhaps in a distribution center. House paint is a classic example of time postponement. The unique color selected by the customer at the point of sale is produced by adding the necessary pigment while the customer is present and can be performed in a length of time that is acceptable to the customer.

Form postponement is characterized by standardizing the upstream stages as much as possible so that the product remains generic longer. Standardization of components effectively delays the point of product differentiation through increasing component commonality and modularization. As the level of form postponement is increased, we are effectively moving from early postponement to late postponement.

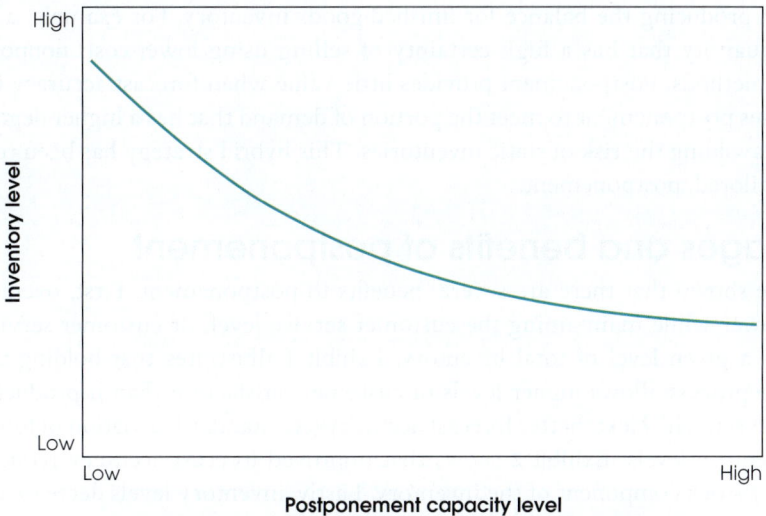

Postponement capacity level	Inventory level
0	2917
60	2867
124	2817
196	2767
281	2717
386	2667
536	2617
844	2567
1000	2557

EXHIBIT 3 ■ Tradeoff curve for inventory level and postponement capacity level

Form postponement can occur at different stages of production. Manufacturing/assembly postponement consists of shipping semifinished product to a distribution center for assembly after customer orders are received. Packaging postponement can address the proliferation resulting from marketing product in different package sizes. The bulk product is shipped to a distribution center and packaged based on customer orders. Labeling postponement results from identifying the same product with different brand names and labeling the product as such after the order is received. A Dell computer is characterized by extensive form postponement. The unique, specifically configured computer that the customer orders is assembled when the customer order is received from standard components, modules, and subassemblies.

Full versus partial postponement

Recent studies suggest that any amount of postponement is beneficial from the perspectives of improved customer service level and/or reduced inventory investment. There is, however, a cost associated with postponement because production costs with postponement are typically higher than without it. This raises the question of whether or not it is necessary to postpone all of a product. A substantial part of the benefits can be realized by postponing some of the product and producing the balance for finished-goods inventory. For example, a firm would produce a quantity that has a high certainty of selling using lower-cost, nonpostponement production methods. Postponement provides little value when forecast accuracy is high. The firm then uses postponement to meet the portion of demand that has a higher degree of uncertainty, thus avoiding the risk of static inventories. This hybrid strategy has been referred to as partial, or tailored, postponement.

Advantages and benefits of postponement

Studies have shown that there are several benefits to postponement. First, overall inventory levels are lower while maintaining the customer service level, or customer service level can improve for a given level of total inventory. Exhibit 1 illustrates that holding undifferentiated work-in-process allows higher levels of customer satisfaction than if products had to be started 'from scratch'. Next, better forecast accuracy (the standard deviation of forecast errors) reduces inventory levels. Exhibit 2 shows that improved forecast accuracy reduces the need for the safety stock component of the inventory. Lastly, inventory levels decrease as more of a product is postponed. Exhibit 3 illustrates that as we postpone more products (increasing postponement capacity), the undifferentiated work-in-process and the finished inventory become smaller.

With postponement, the distribution system becomes less dependent on demand forecasting for finished goods and does a better job of matching supply with demand. Smaller batches may cost more to produce, but these costs are offset by reduced inventory holding costs. The much larger separate inventories that would otherwise be needed to stock each combination of product variety can be avoided, thus creating a lower cost of obsolescence. A postponement strategy would be beneficial if the benefits exceed the costs.

Firms facing high distribution costs would benefit primarily from packaging and time postponement. Form postponement would have the greatest impact on high-value products. Products facing high demand uncertainty would benefit from as much time postponement as possible. Postponement may be of marginal benefit when there is little demand uncertainty, low value of short time to market, low product proliferation, or low inventory value.

Other advantages include increased sales due to fewer stockouts and the ability to operate with a reduced forecasting window and its associated reduced forecast error. However, delivery times may increase, as it takes time to perform the postponed, differentiating stages of the operation. Postponing the final stages to another country can create a global manufacturing presence in other countries, address protectionism and local content laws, enhance marketing efforts of locally produced goods, and create an attraction to products manufactured locally.

Bibliography

Feitzinger, E., & Lee, H. L. (1997, January/February). Mass customization at Hewlett-Packard: The power of postponement. Harvard Business Review, pp. 116–121.

Graman, G. A., & Magazine, M. J. (2002). A numerical analysis of capacitated postponement. Production and Operations Management, 11(3), 340–357.

Lee, H. L., & Billington, C. (1994). Designing products and processes for postponement. In S. Dasu & C. Eastman (Eds.), Management of design: Engineering and management perspectives (pp. 105–122). Norwell, MA: Kluwer Academic Publishers.

Zinn, W. (1990). Should you assemble products before an order is received? Business Horizons, 33(2), 70–73.

Zinn, W., & Bowersox, D. J. (1988). Planning physical distribution with the principle of postponement. Journal of Business Logistics, 9(2), 117–136.

Source: Graman, GA & Bukovinsky, DM 2005, *Journal of Corporate Accounting and Finance*, November/December, pp. 61–5.

CHAPTER 15

Making better decisions

Traditional cost accounting has suffered severe criticisms in past years. It seems that everyone agrees that it is obsolete. Two questions summarize most of the discussions about this:

1. Can cost methods change so that they can give us good information?

2. Do costs need to be allocated to products to make good decisions?

Those that believe that the problem with the prevailing management accounting system is that it does not allocate costs well to products tend to advocate activity-based costing (ABC) as the solution. ABC tries to better allocate the costs to products. These people would answer 'yes' to both questions above.

But there are some people who believe that you should not allocate any costs to products. Throughput accounting (TA) is based on this. It does not allocate any costs to products. It does not calculate the cost of products. These people would answer 'no' to both questions. They believe that allocation is not able to give us good information any more, because it is based on erroneous assumptions.

You can talk about how allocation can be improved or how allocation cannot be improved. Or you can talk about if you need allocation or not. This article concentrates on the second question. Even if more complicated allocation methods can solve the problem of traditional cost accounting, do you need them? Is there a simpler way to make good decisions? If that simpler way exists, then, even if allocation methods give good information, you would not need them.

Any organization needs an information system that will tell its managers if what they are doing is taking the organization toward its goal. You can use a compass as an analogy to management accounting. The compass shows us the direction you are going and you can then certify ourselves if you are in the right course or if you need to make some corrections in our course.

The owners determine the North of an organization (its goal). In the case of the organizations that you will talk about here, suppose that the goal is to make money now and in the future. The performance measurements used to verify if the company is going towards its goal are net profit (NP) and return on investment (ROI). These two measurements give the position of the company in relation to its goal, but they are not very useful to make day-to-day decisions.

For the managers' day-to-day decisions it is necessary to have a bridge between their decisions and actions and the profitability of the company. Today most companies use traditional cost accounting as this bridge.

The theory of constraints (TOC) TA is based on TOC, so you first need to understand the basic concepts behind TOC. TOC sees any company as a system; that is, a set of elements between which there is a relationship of interdependence. Each element depends on the others in some way, and the global performance of the system depends on the joint efforts of all the elements of the system. One of the most fundamental concepts is the recognition of the important role that the system's constraint has.

Eliyahu Goldratt, in *'What is this thing called the Theory of Constraints, and how should it be implemented?'* (Croton-on-Hudson, North River Press, 1990) says, 'Every action taken by any organization — any part of the organization — should be judged by its impact on the overall purpose. This immediately implies that, before you can deal with the improvement of any section of a system, you must first define the system's global goal; and determine the measurements that will enable us to judge the impact of any subsystem and any local decision, on this global goal… A system's constraint is nothing more than what you feel to be expressed by these words: anything that limits a system from achieving higher performance versus its goal… In our reality any system has very few constraints… and at the same time any system in reality must have at least one constraint.'

Following this reasoning Goldratt created TOC's process of ongoing improvement, always focusing the efforts towards the system's goal. This process has five steps:

1. Identify the system's constraint(s).
2. Decide how to exploit the system's constraint(s).
3. Subordinate everything else to the above decision.
4. Elevate the system's constraint(s).
5. If in the previous steps a constraint has been broken, go back to step 1. But do not allow inertia to cause a system constraint.

TA's performance measurements To judge if a company is moving towards its goal, it is necessary to answer three simple questions: How much money is generated by your company? How much money is captured by your company? And how much money do you have to spend to operate it? The measurements are intuitively obvious. What is needed is to turn these questions into formal definitions. Below you have the formal definitions.

If the system generates money by earning interest at a bank, it is definitely throughput, or the rate at which the system generates money. Most production managers think that if they have produced something, it deserves to be called throughput. Throughput should not be associated with shuffling money internally. Throughput means to bring fresh money from the outside, thus the additional words-through sales.

Throughput is fresh money that has two sides, revenue and the totally variable costs (TVC). The use of the words variable and cost may be confusing with the measures used in cost accounting. The fundamental element here, without any doubt, is the word totally, or totally variable in relation to the units sold.

A TVC is that amount incurred when one more product is sold. You have product and company's throughput. A product's throughput is its price minus its totally variable cost (TVC). A product's contribution to the company's throughput is its throughput multiplied by the number of units sold. Consequently, a company's throughput is the summation of all the products' total throughput. Throughput is the only of the three measurements to identify with individual products.

Inventory: all the money the system invests in purchasing things the system intends to sell. This measure and the conventional accounting measure assets might be mistaken, but differ drastically when referring to work in process and finished goods inventory. In TOC there is no added value to the product. Goldratt says, 'Added value. To what? To the product. But our concern is not the product, but rather the company. So what you actually ask ourselves is, "When is the only point in time that you add value to the company?" Only when you sell, not a minute before. The whole concept of adding value to a product is a distorted local optimum.'

Operating expense: all the money the system spends in turning inventory into throughput. 'Taking added value out of inventory does not mean that you do not have these outlays of money,' says Goldratt. 'Operating expense (OE) is understood as all the money you have to pour into the machine on an ongoing basis to turn the machine's wheels?'

TOC does not classify them as fixed, variable, indirect, direct, etc. OE is simply all other accounts that did not go into Throughput or into Inventory. The increases or decreases in OE are analyzed on a case-by-case basis, where its impact on the bottom line is taken into account. The most common error is to think TOC tags OE as fixed. TOC does not classify the expenses as fixed or semi-variable, what really matters is if it is totally variable or not totally variable.

TOC says that these three measurements are sufficient to make the bridge between NP and ROI and the managers' daily actions. These are the formulas that show this bridge:

$$NP = T - OE$$

$$ROI = (T - OE)/I$$

With these three measurements (T, I and OE) you can know the impact a decision has on the company's bottom line. Any decision that has a positive impact on ROI is a decision that takes the company towards its goal. You do not need to calculate the NP for all the company, neither the ROI. You can calculate the incremental NP and ROI. If they are positive and if the ROI is equal to or greater than a predetermined ROI, then it is a good decision.

'In evaluating any action, you must remember that you have three measurements, not just one. Otherwise extremely devastating actions will be taken. This means that the final judge is not the measurements themselves, but the relationships between these measurements,' says Goldratt. This is exactly what TA tries to do and that is why TA does not allocate costs to products. To measure the impact of a decision on the company's NP and ROI you do not need to calculate the cost of products.

A fourth measurement Now, to be able to calculate the impact on the three measurements, especially throughput, you need to understand the relationship between the system's capacity constraint and the company's products. When a company does not have enough capacity to deliver what the market wants, the company has to decide what it will sell and what it will not sell.

In this case, to increase throughput the company needs to squeeze the maximum it can from its available capacity. As Goldratt has shown, a production process is much like a chain, it has one weak link. The capacity of the production processes is dictated by one weak link, the bottleneck. If the company wants to increase its throughput it has to explore this resource.

Let us suppose that our company has a bottleneck. The available time on this resource is limited. Different products use the constraint's time differently. One product might need five minutes on the constraint while another needs half an hour. It is obvious that the one that uses less time should have a preference.

You also want to increase the company's throughput. Different products have different throughput. A product that has a throughput of US$100 should have preference over another product whose throughput is US$40.

As you can see, you want to give preference to products that have a bigger throughput and at the same time, give preference to products that use the least time on the constraint. You will have a problem when, comparing two products, one has a greater throughput, while the other uses less time on the constraint. To solve this problem you need to have a relative measurement that takes into account that you want to maximize throughput and at the same time minimize the time spent on the constraint.

To decide which one most contributes to the company's bottom line you need to divide the product's throughput by the time it uses on the constraint, finding the product's throughput per time of the constraint.

To better understand this measurement all you need to do is think as if the company is selling its most scarce resource, the time of the constraint. The products that better pay for the time they use are the ones that most contribute to the company's bottom line.

When you use this measurement the assumption is that the market demands more than the company can produce. But this is not always the case. When the company has more capacity than the market demands, the criteria of comparison between products should be the throughput per unit, because there is no resource limiting the company's performance. Any product sale that increases the company's throughput and that doesn't increase OE (or at least does not increase it more than it increased throughput), contributes for the increase of the bottom line.

TOC doesn't make any correlation between production volume, or other system's variables, with OE. The assumption is that the person making the decision is able to quantify the impact it will have on OE, and therefore there is no need to try to discover any kind of relationship between OE and some variable of the system.

Any way, throughput/time of the constraint or throughput/unit should not be considered alone when evaluating a decision. Whatever the decision, it is necessary to quantify its impact on the three basic measurements so that you can know the impact the decision will have on the company's NP and ROI.

Basic difference between throughput accounting and cost accounting methodologies
The basic difference is that TA does not trace costs to products as do the cost accounting methodologies. TA does not calculate the cost of a product, to make decisions it uses the throughput per unit of product, the time each product uses of the CCR and the company's operating expenses.

This difference is due to a basic difference in viewing improvement. One assumption behind cost accounting methodologies is that high local efficiencies will lead to high global efficiency.

What this means is that cost accounting is based on the assumption that maximizing the use of all the activities (high local efficiencies) will lead to a better profitability. Because of this assumption it gathers data on the use of all resources/activities. It wants to make sure that all resources/activities are being efficiently used. The concept of the cost of a product is a result of this search for high local efficiencies.

As seen, TA's basic assumption is the complete opposite of cost accounting's assumption. TA is based on the assumption that a company has very few constraints and that if you increase the efficiency of non-constraint resources you will not be improving the company's performance (as a matter of fact you might actually be decreasing it's performance). It argues that if you view a company as a system you will not want to maximize the use of every resource and activity because you know that in a system there are constraint and non-constraint resources/activities. The only place where you want high local efficiencies is on the constraints.

This bask difference will lead managers to act very differently. In a cost accounting environment managers will be induced to focus their efforts in increasing efficiencies anywhere, as this will reduce the cost of products. In a throughput accounting environment managers will be induced to focus their efforts in increasing the efficiency of the constraint.

Throughput accounting statements Now you will see how you can turn these concepts into useful tools for management. You will see what throughput accounting statements are trying to do, and help managers answer the three questions: What is the impact of the decision on throughput? What is the impact of the decision on operating expense? What is the impact of the decision on inventory?

Table 1 shows the statement for the company's operating expense. Table 2 shows the data on all the company's products. To build this statement the company needs to have the data on its products' price, TVC and time on the constraint, the other columns of throughput per unit and throughput/time on the constraint are a result of these data. The products are presented in a decreasing manner according to their throughput/time on the constraint.

TABLE 1 ■ Operating expense

Month xx

Item	US$
Wages	550000
Sales and marketing	250000
Rent	55000
Transport	18000
Financial expenses	11000
Depreciation	10000
Others	20000
Total	914000

TABLE 2 ■ Data base of the products

Month xx

A	B	C	D (B–C)	E	F (D/E)
Product	Price	TVC	Throughput per unit	Time on constraint	Throughput/ time on CCR
Red	125	51	74	4	18.50
Blue	237	83	154	10	15.40
Yellow	82	30	52	4	13.00
Green	155	75	80	8	10.00
Orange	60	27	33	4	8.25

In column E you have the time on the constraint. Here you need to add up the times that all the parts that compose the final product use of the constraint. This is the only process time that this methodology requires. You only need to have trustworthy data on the constraint.

In this statement you can manipulate the selling price, the TVC and the product's time on the constraint to evaluate the impact of decisions on the company's profitability. With this statement ready, the company may then do the forecast of its financial performance according to the sales mix or even may do various simulations to see the impact of a decision on the company's bottom line. The statement to do these forecasts and/or simulations is the one shown on table 3.

In this statement you enter the sales forecast for each product and you accumulate the utilization of the constraint and the total throughput per product. If there is an internal constraint

TABLE 3 ■ Maximum profit mix/sales mix

Month xx

Capacity of constraint = 70 000 minutes   Demand/capacity of constraint = 154%

G	H	I	J	K		L	
Product	Demand (forecast)	Max. thr. mix	Sales mix	Acum. utiliz of constraint %		Total throughput per product	
Red	5 000	5 000	5 000	28.6	28.6	370 000	370 000
Blue	1 500	1 500	400	50	34.3	231 000	61 600
Yellow	7 200	7 200	7 200	91.1	75.4	374 400	374 400
Green	1 500	775	150	100	77.1	62 000	12 000
Orange	8 000	0	4 000	100	100	0	132 000

Total throughput	1 037 400	950 000
OE	914 000	914 000
Net profit	123 400	36 000
Inventory	5 500 000	5 500 000
ROI (annual)	26.9%	7.5%

the demand/capacity of the constraint will be greater than 100%. In the example the company has a capacity constraint, its demand/capacity of the constraint is 154%, which means it would need over 50% more capacity to deliver all the demand.

After the demand column you have the columns for maximum throughput mix and sales mix. The maximum throughput mix is generated automatically by allocating the available capacity from top down. In other words, you assume you will produce and sell only the most profitable products until there is no capacity left. In the example the maximum throughput mix is 5000 reds + 1500 blues + 7200 yellows + 775 greens. You do not have any capacity left to produce the remaining demand for Green and Orange.

With this you have calculated the maximum profit the company can generate in the period being analyzed (US$123 400.) In the majority of the cases the companies cannot impose a product mix to the market. What happens is that many products, even when not very profitable for the company, need to be sold to satisfy the market and guarantee the company's future.

Therefore, it is necessary to find a sales mix, starting from the demand. In column J of table 3, the company should enter its sales mix. Here the quantity to be produced and sold shall never exceed the demand quantity of column H. If you have an internal capacity constraint you need to decide what products you are not going to supply part of the demand, or even all of it. Here there is no way out and in this statement the accumulated utilization (column K) cannot go over 100%. This compels the company to make a decision about what clients and products are more important, always taking into account the financial aspects and the marketing aspects.

In the example, the company decided that for marketing reasons, it should sell 50% of the demand for product Orange, even though it is the least profitable product. To be able to do this the company has to decide where it will free capacity. In other words, what product(s) it will stop producing to be able to produce product orange? This company decided to sell only 400 blues and 150 greens.

In the columns 'Accumulated utilization of the constraint' and 'Total throughput per product' you always have two divisions. The first one shows the results for the mix of maximum profit and the second one shows the sales mix results. At the end of the statement you calculate the company's total throughput, then subtract the OE from it and find the company's NP. Right after that you have the company's investment and its ROI.

If the company has no capacity constraint, there will be no difference between the maximum profit mix and the sales mix columns. With these statements ready, the company can start analyzing the impact of decisions on the company's profitability.

Making decisions When making a decision you should estimate the impact it would have on the company's throughput, inventory and operating expense. Again here, you see the importance of the constraint. The variation in OE and inventory are easier to estimate and they are entered directly on these statements.

Using the example above, suppose that you want to know what the impact on profitability would be if you decreased a part's time on the constraint, offloading it to another resource in the company. This change in process will increase the part's TVC by US$5 and will require the hiring of another worker. This worker will cost the company US$1000 a month.

This raw material is part of product yellow, which means that its TVC will increase by US$5, going to US$35. With this the company will be able to reduce this product's time on the constraint by one minute, from four to three minutes.

The OE statement would now be like table 4. As yellow's TVC and time on the constraint also changed, you have to introduce these changes, in the products' database, table 5. Product yellow's throughput/time on the constraint increased from 13 to 15.67, making it go from the third to second most profitable product. You now have to estimate the impact on the company's throughput.

TABLE 4 ■ Operating expense
Month xx

Item	US$
Wages	551 000
Sales and marketing	250 000
Rent	55 000
Transport	18 000
Interest	11 000
Depreciation	10 000
Others	20 000
Total	**915 000**

TABLE 5 ■ Data base of the products
Month xx

A	B	C	D (B–C)	E	F (D/E)
Product	Price	TVC	Throughput per unit	Time on constraint	Throughput/time on constraint
Red	125	51	74	4	18.50
Yellow	82	35	47	3	15.67
Blue	237	83	154	10	15.40
Green	155	75	80	8	10.00
Orange	60	27	33	4	8.25

To estimate this impact the company first has to make the decision of how to use the capacity freed by this process. As now every Yellow will use only three minutes of the constraint instead of four the company still has 7200 minutes of available capacity.

Depending on which product it decides to produce and sell, its total throughput will increase more or less. In this case the company decided to use these 7200 minutes to make product green, as shown on table 6. As each green uses eight minutes of the constraint the company can make an extra 900 units. This will make green's total throughput increase by US$72 000 (900 units × US$80). Yellow's total throughput, on the other hand, will decrease US$36 000 due to the US$5 increase in its TVC (7200 units × US$5). Therefore, the company's total throughput will increase US$36 000. As OE increased US$1000, the net profit increased US$35 000.

In this case, where there was no variation in Inventory, it is enough to measure the impact on NP. As long as NP increases (as long as T increases more than OE) it is a decision that will increase the company's profitability. When there is an increase in Inventory you have to verify if the increase in NP (if there is an increase in NP) is enough to pay for the increase in Inventory.

TABLE 6 ■ Maximum profit mix/sales mix

Month xx

Capacity of constraint = 70000 minutes   Demand/capacity of constraint = 143.7%

G	H	I	J	K		L	
Product	Demand (forecast)	Max. thr. mix	Sales mix	Acum. utiliz of constraint %		Total throughput per product	
Red	5 000	5 000	5 000	28.6	28.6	370 000	370 000
Yellow	7 200	7 200	7 200	59.4	59.4	338 400	338 400
Blue	1 500	1 500	400	80.9	65.1	231 000	61 600
Green	1 500	1 675	1 050	100	77.1	134 000	84 000
Orange	8 000	0	4 000	100	100	0	132 000

Total throughput	1 073 400	985 000
OE	915 000	915 000
Net profit	158 400	71 000
Inventory	5 500 000	5 500 000

These statements allow for forecasts and simulations. In a very short time managers can simulate some improvement suggestions, appropriation requests, clients' proposals, etc. The decision process becomes much more transparent and accessible.

These statements on their own are not sufficient for managers to make decisions, but they are necessary for them to do so. Without such statements managers are making decisions without knowing the impact of these on the company's profitability.

Conclusion You have seen a method that allows you to make decisions without the need to allocate costs to products. It is a simple and logical method. It also supplies trustworthy information fast, enabling managers to make good decisions fast. These are the qualities a management information system should have and that today no other system has.

However, throughput accounting concepts will conflict with many existing measurements and mental models in the company. These conflicts stem from a basic assumption behind TOC: that local optimizations do not lead to global optimization. Many measurements being used today are based on the exact opposite of this assumption: local efficiencies lead to global efficiency. If these conflicts are not properly dealt with the company will not be able to enjoy all the benefits that this new methodology can offer.

What throughput accounting does is calculate the impact a decision will have on the company's overall performance. It does this without allocating costs to products. The only basic assumption behind this method is, as Goldratt says, 'In the goal only one assumption is postulated. The assumption that you can measure the goal of an organization by throughput inventory and operating expenses. Everything else is derived logically from that assumption.'

If you agree that using these three global measurements you can measure the impact any decision will have on the company's overall performance, then why allocate costs to products?

Source: Corbett, T 1999, *CMA Management*, November, pp. 33–7.

CHAPTER 16

Resource efficiency audit: the baseline vs the bottom line

Resource efficiency schemes can not only help manufacturers get more bang for their buck, but also carve a way forward for continuous innovation and improvement.

Businesses, particularly in the manufacturing sector, are continually striving for ways to maintain global competitiveness and increase profitability. One common drive is cost reductions, with the main response being to focus on labour costs and efficiencies. An alternate focus on resource costs and efficiencies can also contribute significant cost reductions. Improving the efficiency with which materials, water and energy are used will also help businesses respond to the increasing pressure to reduce their environmental footprint.

In manufacturing, the costs associated with purchasing resources are often higher than the costs of labour. A study in 2000 by the Victorian Department of Innovation, Industry and Regional Development, *Environmental Best Practice Benchmarking Report,* showed waste disposal costs in food companies were typically about 0.5 per cent of total manufacturing costs, where resource costs are more typically 50–60 per cent.

These data are consistent with Australian Bureau of Statistics reports across 10 industry sectors that show the cost of material inputs as a percentage of turnover ranged from 29–51 per cent, with an average of 42 per cent. Data from the manufacturing sector in Germany indicate a similar contribution (see figure 1).

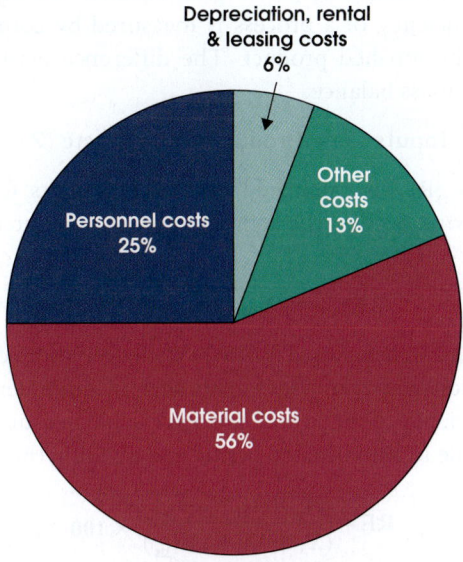

FIGURE 1 ■ Typical cost structure in German manufacturing

Sustainability Victoria's work with businesses suggests the main reason for the focus on labour rather than resource efficiency is because they do not see the bottom line impact of non-productive resource flows, largely due to accounting deficiencies or because they don't measure resource efficiencies in a transparent manner. Better information on resource efficiency can clearly identify and quantify opportunities to strip out costs, with companies usually then having the knowledge and resources to drive innovation and continuous improvement.

The 12 companies that participated in Sustainability Victoria's resource efficiency program in 2004/05 identified more than $23 million per annum of lost value through non-productive resource flows. This was associated with 12 500 tonnes of waste that cost them $950 000 in disposal fees, a ratio of lost resource value to disposal costs of 23:1.

This article presents a methodology for implementing a resource efficiency scheme, indicating how existing systems provide the basis for its success and presents examples of successful outcomes. A comparison to Six Sigma is included to show how resource efficiency is an extension of this popular business improvement model.

Defining resource efficiency

Resource efficiency can be considered as both a business performance measure and an improvement strategy.

As a measure, a resource efficiency program can indicate how efficiently raw materials are being converted into finished goods. A review of a soft drink filling operation showed 99.8 per cent of PET bottles were being successfully filled, a very high resource efficiency for PET containers. In contrast, a steel foundry found the efficiency of steel usage was only 51 per cent and a fabrics manufacturer had a resource efficiency of 85 per cent for one product and 77 per cent for another. Efficiencies will obviously range across different sectors, but the key is to use this measure as a baseline for ongoing improvements.

Where resource efficiency is adopted as an improvement strategy, the program will use the measured baseline data, identify priority areas for improvement and set targets and actions to improve the efficiency year after year.

Measuring resource efficiency

Resource efficiency can be measured for the overall business, a single process or a single raw material. The resource efficiency of a process is measured by comparing the weight of the inputs to the weight of the finished product. The difference between these weights is the waste, which provides the mass balance.

$$\text{Inputs (X)} = \text{Products (Y)} + \text{Waste (Z)}$$

The resource efficiency (RE) is calculated using the weights for each measure. For the example of the PET soft drink bottles, the approach focused on one input weight (kg) and one output weight (kg).

$$RE_{PET} = (Y_{PET}/X_{PET}) \times 100$$

This type of measure is straightforward for PET bottles but more complex for a process such as peanut butter production which includes a number of ingredients combined in the final product. The resource efficiency of the overall process can be measured by summing the weight of the finished product made in a nominated period and dividing this by the sum of all inputs.

$$RE = \frac{(Y_1 + Y_2 + ... Y_n)}{(X_1 + X_2 + ... X_m)} \times 100$$

Linking resource efficiency to lean manufacturing FACT FILE

INC Corporation is a medium-size supplier of high-performance engineered materials for automotive manufacturers, with products such as acoustic materials, automotive trim, thermal insulation and textile laminates and coatings. A significant driver for its pursuit of resource efficiency has been the increasing contribution of material cost to total sales (see figure 2).

INC includes all material inputs in its Bill of Materials (BOM), including raw (and auxillary) materials, consumables and packaging. An allowance is made in the BOM for a degree of intrinsic waste, including cut-outs, perimeter waste from moulds and yield from a bulk quantity, such as the length of a roll. But it does not allow for poor quality (rejects), testing, Inventory and distribution losses. A major objective of its lean manufacturing program is to identify and eliminate these wastes to increase materials and labour efficiency.

Using financial data, INC quantified its overall materials efficiency as 85 per cent for the 2005 financial year. Further evaluation of individual products identified which products and processes contributed to the overall loss of incoming raw materials. This was done by comparing BOM requirements with actual usage over a defined period. The wastage was calculated by:

$$W = M.(P - Q.V - \Delta R - \Delta F.Q) \text{ kg}$$

where
M = mass of raw material
P = purchase quantity received
Q = allowed quantity from bill of materials
V = volume sold
ΔR = difference between opening and closing stock of raw materials
ΔF = difference between opening and closing stock of finished goods

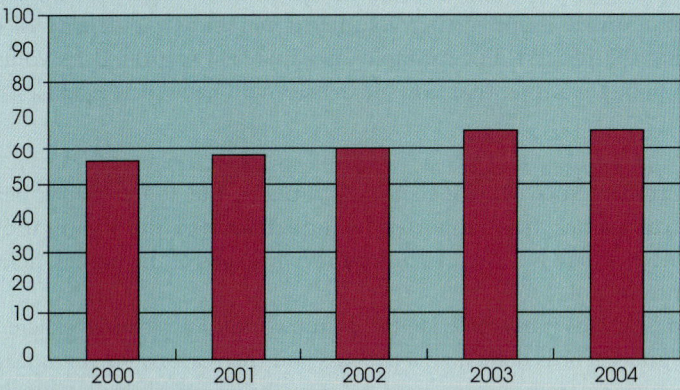

FIGURE 2 ■ Material costs are up as a proportion of total sales

Where the quantity (weight) received could not be obtained, the formula was adjusted to use the actual purchase costs divided by the unit raw material cost to calculate quantity received. INC found just four materials contributed significantly to the non-productive material flows, with annual loss of value of about $1.4 million, and even higher when system costs including wasted labour, energy, waste disposal and capital were included. A further analysis of the BOM revealed on-costs such as packaging, logistics and quality costs were under-recovered. Through a series of measures, INC increased overall materials efficiency to 93 per cent, reducing the cost of non-productive flows by $750 000 pa. The measurement technique also highlighted a range of unprofitable products, prompting INC to exit them which improved materials efficiency another 5 per cent and reduced the total cost of materials to sales by almost 20 per cent.

Stock levels at the start and end of the period may need to be considered. For example, existing stock may have been consumed and therefore the use of purchase data would underestimate the actual inputs. However, if the nominated period is long enough and there is reasonable regularity with purchases and sales, an assumption that the stock levels remain the same could be valid.

Sourcing data

To measure the resource efficiency of a business or process, data can be obtained in a number of ways, including:
- physical measurement of resource flows;
- examination of purchasing and sales records;
- examination of quality control records;
- interrogation of company production management systems, such as bills of materials (BOM), materials requirement planning (MRP) and enterprise resource planning (ERP) systems; and
- evaluation of finance reports.

It is important to gather data in a form that can be aggregated. Weight is generally used as it can be applied to most resources. Some data conversion may be needed to calculate the weight of inputs and finished goods. This could come from sales data that identifies numbers of units or financial numbers only (conversion: weigh a single unit), sheets of material [determine weight as kg/m^2], volumes of water or other liquid inputs (calculate density as kg/l) and yield data that reports production rates or time-based efficiencies (if unit weights are known).

One area where errors can be made is converting volume to weight as the density of the material may be altered during the process. For example, as a material is ground its volume will decrease but its weight will be the same, therefore its density will have increased.

Beyond Six Sigma

Six Sigma is a quality measurement tool developed by Motorola in the 1990s that is being adopted by many Australian companies. It is supported by a methodology for organisational improvement, known as DMAIC, which is an acronym for the five stages of the model: define, measure, analyse, improve and control.

DMAIC is further explored below as it can provide the framework for a resource efficiency improvement program. Six Sigma records defects in a process and the reasons for them. More particularly, it focuses on variations from an accepted position by examining the standard deviation. A highly variable process will report a lower Six Sigma measurement, indicating a lower quality.

Production processes adopting Six Sigma will use defects to measure quality performance. However, this measure alone does not address the loss of material as by-products or other wastes generated during production. A resource efficiency program can therefore extend a Six Sigma program to account for all losses in a process, which can deliver greater benefits than by using Six Sigma alone (see fact file).

The DMAIC framework

As described above, DMAIC can help realise a range of business opportunities, including increased customer satisfaction, reduced defects and increased resource efficiency.

DMAIC needs to be implemented as a formal project within the business, with appropriate levels of resources and management commitment. Without this support the program is unlikely to be fully completed, meaning the full potential will not be realised.

Inside Six Sigma

FACT FILE

A manufacturer uses 350 kg of raw materials to produce 1000 chocolate bars with a target weight of 300 g/bar.

Quality control criteria are set for the products that define whether a finished good is too light or too heavy, in other words, defective. The upper control limit (UCL) and lower control limit (LCL) are presented in figure 3 along with a histogram presenting the weights of the 1000 bars produced. It shows 80 bars outside the weight criteria, so the yield of the produced bars is therefore 92 per cent.

The number of defective opportunities (reasons) is reported to be six. On this basis the process would have a Sigma Level of about 3.7. If the number of defects was reduced to 1 per 1000, the Sigma Level would increase to 5.1, which would indicate very high quality. However, even with no defects the total weight of the 1000 bars would be only 300 kg. The weight of raw materials was 350 kg and therefore almost 50 kg will still have been wasted during production. The 85 per cent resource efficiency measure therefore highlights opportunities for further waste reduction and cost savings, even in a high quality process.

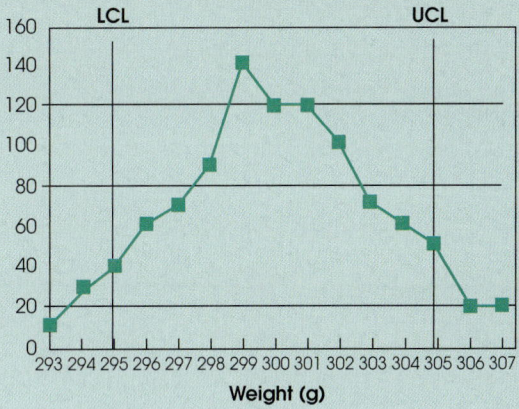

FIGURE 3 ■ Eighty chocolate bars were outside the upper and lower control limits

1) Define: The first stage is to define the project, including its problem statement, scope, objectives and timeline. It is useful at this stage to map the process so all materials and other utilities can be identified.

2) Measure: As noted earlier, the measuring stage should initially draw on existing data sets and then augmented with a planned sampling program to identify where wastes are being generated along the process. The costs of the raw material, energy and labour can also be collated at this stage so the full cost of waste can be calculated. Once the input and output data has been collated, a baseline resource efficiency estimate can be calculated.

3) Analyse: At the analysis stage the root causes of the various waste streams should be identified and priority areas for attention highlighted. This may involve benchmarking resource efficiency against other similar processes or businesses. While benchmarking has its limitations due to the variation in businesses, industry data may provide a useful context for the current performance.

4) Improve: The improvement stage will involve brainstorming sessions and various trials to identify optimal solutions for improving resource efficiency. This will include constructing financial models, forecasting any consequential impacts of the proposed changes and consulting people who may be affected by the changes. Once the solution has been identified an action plan should be prepared to detail the various tasks that must be completed, including the required resources and any timelines that need to be met, such as allowances for any shutdowns.

5) Control: The final stage is important as it will ensure that changes are integrated into the business, including updating of procedures, implementation of new monitoring and reporting systems, and the training of staff.

Source: Clay, S & Peyton, A 2006, *WME Magazine*, September, pp. 27–9.

Glossary

abnormal spoilage: spoilage that is not part of everyday operations (pp. 545, 584)

absorption costing: a system in which all manufacturing costs are recorded on the balance sheet as part of the cost of inventory and are then expensed as part of the cost of goods sold (COGS) when units are sold (p. 609)

accrual accounting rate of return: the expected increase in average annual operating income as a percentage of the initial increase in required investment (p. 367)

activity: a type of task or function performed in an organisation (p. 128)

activity-based budgeting: a budgeting process that uses activity cost pools and their related cost drivers to anticipate the costs for individual activities. A budget is developed for each activity in an entity's activity-based system. (p. 273)

activity-based costing (ABC): a system that assigns overhead costs to the specific activities performed in a manufacturing or service delivery process. It attempts to trace costs more accurately to products or other cost objects. (p. 128)

activity-based management (ABM): the process of using ABC information to evaluate the costs and benefits of production and internal support activities, and to identify and implement opportunities for improvements in profitability, efficiency and quality within an entity. (p. 135)

activity-based transfer prices: a transfer pricing method in which the purchasing unit is charged for the unit-level, batch-level and possibly some product-level costs for products transferred, plus an annual fixed fee that is a portion of the facility-level costs (p. 467)

activity drivers: factors that relate to the attributes of the individual activities and recognise that things other than volume cause indirect costs to be used by cost objects (p. 78)

actual costing: a method in which overhead is allocated using the actual volume of the allocation base times the actual allocation rate (p. 538)

actual operations: the various actions taken and results achieved over a period of time (p. 5)

actual overhead allocation rate: a method of allocating overhead calculated as follows: Actual allocation rate = Actual overhead cost ÷ Actual quantity of allocation base (p. 538)

agency costs: the costs that arise when agents fail to act in the interest of principals (p. 449)

agency theory: an analytical framework that examines potential conflicts between principals and agents (p. 448)

agents: people who act on behalf of others — the principals (p. 449)

allocation base: a measure of activity, preferably a cost driver, used to allocate costs to a cost object (p. 537)

allocation rate: the dollar amount per unit of allocation base used to allocate overhead to each cost object (p. 538)

analysis at the account level: a method used to create a cost function by reviewing the pattern of a cost over time in the accounting system and using knowledge of operations to classify the cost as variable, fixed or mixed (p. 33)

average cost (AC): computed as total costs (TC) divided by the quantity (Q) of activity or production (p. 48)

balanced scorecard: a formal method to incorporate both financial and non-financial performance measures into organisational management systems (p. 491)

batch-level activities: tasks or functions undertaken for a collection of goods or services that are processed as a group (p. 131)

bottleneck: any process, part or machine that limits overall capacity (p. 308)

budget: a formalised financial plan for the operations of an entity for a specified future period. Used to help the organisation coordinate the activities needed to carry out the plan. (p. 253)

budgetary slack: the practice of intentionally setting revenue budgets too low and cost budgets too high (p. 269)

budget assumptions: plans and predictions about the next period's operating activities (p. 254)

budget cycle: a series of steps that entities follow to develop and use budgets (p. 253)

budgeted financial statements: forecasts of the future income statement, balance sheet and cash flows, given an organisation's sales forecasts and expenditure plans for the next period (p. 254)

budgeted or expected capacity: the anticipated use of capacity over the next period. Based on management's planned operations in which customer demand is forecast. (p. 618)

budget variances: differences between budgeted and actual results (p. 266)

capital budgeting: a budgeting process in which managers choose among investment opportunities that have cash flows occurring over a number of years (p. 357)

cash budget: reflects the effects of management's plans on cash, and summarises the information that accountants gather about the expected amounts and timing of cash receipts and disbursements (p. 254)

collusive pricing: an illegal practice in which two or more organisations conspire to set prices above a competitive price (p. 192)

constant gross margin NRV method: allocates joint costs so that the gross margin percentage for each main product is identical (p. 315)

constraint: when limits in capacity, materials or labour restrict an entity's ability to provide enough products (goods or services) to satisfy demand (p. 307)

contribution margin: total revenue minus total variable costs (p. 212)

contribution margin budget variance: the difference between standard and actual contribution margins (p. 421)

contribution margin per unit: the selling price per unit minus the variable cost per unit (p. 212)

contribution margin ratio (CMR): the percentage by which the selling price (or revenue) per unit exceeds the variable cost per unit. Alternatively, the contribution margin as a percentage of revenue (p. 213)

contribution margin sales mix variance: examines the effects of changes in the sales mix, given the standard contribution margin and actual quantity of units sold (p. 423)

contribution margin sales quantity variance: examines the effects of changes in quantities sold, given the standard contribution margins and standard sales mix (p. 423)

contribution margin sales volume variance: indicates the effects of changes in units sold, given the standard contribution margins (p. 422)

contribution margin variance: indicates the effects of changes in contribution margins, given the actual level of sales (p. 422)

conversion costs: direct labour and production overhead costs (p. 567)

cost accounting: a technique or method for determining the cost of a project, process or thing (p. 6)

cost allocation: the allocation of indirect costs to specific cost objects (p. 77)

cost-based prices: selling prices determined by adding a mark-up to some calculation of the product's cost (p. 185)

cost-based transfer prices: transfer prices based on the cost of the good or service transferred. Cost can be computed in different ways, ranging from variable costs to fully allocated costs. (p. 467)

cost behaviour: the variation in costs relative to the variation in an organisation's activities at the operational level (p. 28)

cost-benefit analysis: the evaluation of costs and benefits (p. 11)

cost/benefit test: a comparison of the cost of tracing costs to cost objects against the benefits of a more detailed cost information tracing system (p. 76)

cost centres: responsibility centres in which managers are responsible only for the costs under their control (p. 454)

cost driver: an input or activity that causes changes in total cost for a cost object (pp. 14, 31, 78)

cost function: an algebraic representation of the total cost of a cost object over a relevant range of activity (p. 31)

cost object: a thing or activity for which we measure costs, e.g. a product, service, customer, department, business unit or geographic region (pp. 14, 75)

cost pool: a group of individual costs that are accumulated for a particular purpose. Cost pools can be grouped on a departmental basis, an activity basis or on some other criteria. (pp. 79, 536)

cost–volume–profit graph (CVP graph): a diagram that shows the relationship between total revenues and total costs, illustrating how an organisation's profits are expected to change under different volumes of activity (p. 215)

cost–volume–profit (CVP) analysis: a technique that examines changes in profits in response to changes in sales volumes, costs and prices. Often used to plan future levels of operating activity and provide information. (p. 212)

customer perspective: a method of analysing the entity in which managers identify the customers they want and develop strategies to get and keep them (p. 492)

customer-sustaining activities: tasks or functions undertaken to service past, current and future customers. These costs tend to vary with the needs of individual customers or groups of customers. (p. 131)

death spiral: a downward demand spiral that occurs in cost-based pricing when sales volumes inappropriately influence the price (p. 190)

decision rights: the responsibilities and financial decision-making authority of individual managers (p. 253)

deflation: an increase in the general purchasing power of the monetary unit; the opposite of inflation (p. 371)

degree of operating leverage: the extent to which the cost function is made up of fixed costs. Organisations with high operating leverage incur more risk of loss when sales decline. (p. 219)

direct cost: cost that can be directly linked to the cost object (p. 76)

direct labour efficiency variance: the difference between the standard amount of labour hours that should have been used and the amount actually used. The difference is valued at the standard labour price per hour. (p. 400)

direct labour price variance: the difference between the standard price and the actual price for labour (p. 399)

direct materials efficiency variance: the difference between the standard amount of materials that should have been used and the amount of materials actually used. The difference is valued at the standard price. (p. 400)

direct materials price variance: the difference between the standard price for direct materials and the actual price for the amount of direct materials purchased (p. 399)

direct method: allocates the costs of each support department only to the operating departments (p. 87)

discounted payback: future cash flows that have been discounted to reflect the opportunity cost of using funds for other projects (p. 367)

discount rate: the interest rate that is used across time to reduce the value of future dollars to today's dollars (p. 361)

dual-rate allocation: a method in which support costs are separated into fixed and variable cost pools, and cost drivers are identified for the variable cost pools to more accurately reflect the flow of resources (p. 96)

dual-rate transfer prices: transfer prices in which the selling department is credited for the market price, and the purchasing department is charged the variable cost (p. 468)

dumping: an illegal practice that occurs when a foreign-based entity sells products in Australia at prices below the market value in the country where the product is produced, and the price could harm an Australian industry (p. 192)

economic value added (EVA®): a type of residual income that incorporates a number of adjustments to reduce the disadvantages produced by using unadjusted residual income (p. 460)

efficiency variance: provides information about how economically direct resources such as materials and labour were used (p. 399)

engineered estimate of cost: a method used to estimate a cost function in which each activity is analysed according to the amount of labour time, materials and other resources used (p. 32)

equivalent units: resources used in partially completed units relative to the resources needed to complete the units (p. 569)

estimated allocation rate: a method of allocating overhead calculated as follows: Estimated allocation rate = Estimated overhead cost ÷ Estimated quantity of allocation base (p. 538)

external report: a document that presents information predominantly for use outside an organisation (p. 6)

facility-sustaining activities: tasks or functions undertaken to provide and manage an area, location or property. They occur regardless of the number of customers served, products sold, batches processed or units produced. (p. 130)

favourable variance: a variance in which actual revenues are larger than the budget, or actual costs are lower than the budget (p. 266)

financial accounting: the process of preparing and reporting financial information used most frequently by decision makers outside of the entity, such as shareholders and creditors (p. 6)

financial budgets: management's plans for capital expenditures, long-term financing and cash flows, resulting in a budgeted balance sheet and budgeted statement of cash flows (p. 254)

financial measures: performance measures that provide information measured in dollars or ratios of dollars, and also compare budget to actual results (p. 490)

financial perspective: a method of analysing the entity in which managers identify desired financial results, given the organisation's vision (p. 492)

first-in, first-out (FIFO) method: a method in which the current period's costs are used to allocate cost to work performed this period (p. 570)

fixed costs: costs that do not vary with small changes in activity levels such as production, sales and services provided (p. 29)

fixed overhead budget variance: the difference between allocated fixed overhead cost and actual fixed overhead cost (p. 405)

fixed overhead spending variance: the difference between estimated fixed overhead costs and actual fixed overhead costs (p. 406)

flexible budget: a budget that reflects a range of operations; fixed and variable costs are separated to more accurately reflect the effects of activity levels on cost. (p. 266)

full cost: the total costs incurred for a cost object (p. 75)

future value: the amount received in the future for a given number of years at a given interest rate, for a given investment today (p. 359)

general knowledge: information about volume of sales or product prices when organisations sell few products; such information is usually easy to transfer from one person to the next (p. 451)

generally accepted accounting principles (GAAP): a set of accounting methods and disclosures typically used to prepare financial statements for external parties (p. 461)

high-low method: a specific application of the two-point method using the highest and lowest data points of the cost driver (p. 34)

hybrid costing: the accounting approach used to assign product costs by applying a combination of both job and process costing (p. 569)

indifference point: the level of activity at which equal cost or profit occurs across multiple alternatives (p. 221)

indirect cost rate: the rate used to assign the cost to the cost object (p. 79)

indirect costs: costs that are used for the benefit of multiple cost objects (also referred to as **overheads**) (p. 76)

inflation: the decline in the general purchasing power of the monetary unit, meaning that more monetary units (such as dollars) are needed to purchase goods or services (p. 371)

innovation cycle: the first step in the value chain, it is concerned with processes to identify customer needs and to design goods and services that meet those needs (p. 493)

insourcing: the practice of providing the good or service from internal resources (p. 305)

internal business process perspective: a method of analysing the entity in which managers are concerned with the methods and practices used inside the entity to produce and deliver goods and services (p. 493)

internal rate of return (IRR): a method that determines the discount rate necessary for the present value of the discounted cash flows to be equal to the investment (p. 365)

internal report: a document that presents information for use only inside an organisation (p. 6)

inventoriable product costs: the direct and indirect costs of producing goods; includes costs incurred in the manufacturing process only (p. 532)

investment centres: responsibility centres in which managers are responsible for the revenues, costs and investments under their control (p. 454)

irrelevant information: information that does not vary with the action taken and therefore is not useful for decision making (p. 10)

job cost record: a record that contains all of the costs traced and assigned to a specific job (p. 536)

joint products: in the process of making one product, one or more other products or services are created (p. 312)

just-in-time (JIT) production and inventory control systems: systems in which materials are purchased and units are produced at the time customers demand them (p. 168)

kaizen budgets: budgets that set targeted cost reductions across time, anticipating market price reductions across the life of a product (p. 273)

kaizen costing: a system of continuous improvement in product cost, quality and functionality. Similar to target costing in that cost targets (goals) are set based on price predictions. (p. 180)

learning and growth perspective: a method of analysing the entity in which managers are concerned with achieving future success by discovering new and better strategies (p. 495)

life cycle analysis: a technique that evaluates all the activities involved in the design, development, production, sale, transportation and disposal of a product or service. The life cycle of a product or a service is often referred to as 'cradle to grave'. (p. 670)

life cycle costing: a decision-making method that considers changes in price and costs over the entire life cycle of a good or service, from the time the product is introduced through a number of years (pp. 184, 670)

make or buy: a decision to make a product or service inhouse, or to outsource it to outside vendors (p. 305)

management accounting: the process of gathering, summarising and reporting financial and non-financial information used internally by managers to make decisions (p. 6)

marginal cost: the incremental cost of an activity, e.g. producing a unit of goods or services (p. 30)

margin of safety: the excess of an organisation's expected future sales (in either revenue or units) above the breakeven point. Indicates the amount by which sales could drop before profits reach the breakeven point. (p. 219)

margin of safety percentage: the margin of safety divided by actual or estimated sales, in either units or revenues. Indicates the extent to which sales can decline before profits become zero. (p. 219)

market-based prices: selling prices determined using some measure of customer demand; managers strive to identify what customers are willing to pay for a good or service (p. 186)

market-based transfer prices: transfer prices based on competitors' prices or on the supply-and-demand relationship (p. 468)

master budget: a comprehensive plan for an upcoming financial period, usually a year. Often summarised in a set of budgeted financial statements. (p. 254)

mixed costs: costs that are partly fixed and partly variable (p. 29)

multiple regression analysis: a technique that develops a cost function by calculating values for the statistical relationship between total cost and two or more cost drivers (p. 39)

negotiated transfer prices: transfer prices based on an agreement reached between the managers of the selling and purchasing departments (p. 468)

net present value method (NPV): a method that determines whether an organisation would be better off investing in a project based on the net amount of discounted cash flows for the project (p. 359)

net realisable value (NRV) method: a method that allocates joint costs using the relative value of main products, taking into account both the additional sales value that is created and costs that are incurred after joint production ends (p. 315)

nominal method: a method in which cash inflows and outflows are forecast in nominal dollars (inflated) and discounted using a nominal discount rate (p. 371)

nominal rate of interest: the rate of return required on investments when inflation is present. Calculated by increasing the real rate of interest by the expected rate of inflation. (p. 371)

non-financial measures: provide performance information that cannot be measured in dollars, e.g. defect rates, throughput time and employee retention (p. 491)

non-value-added activities: activities that are unnecessary and therefore wasteful, and that the customer/client would not normally be prepared to pay for (pp. 13, 136)

normal capacity: an average use of capacity over time, or the typical volume of goods or services an entity produces to meet customer demand. (p. 618)

normal spoilage: defective units that arise as part of regular operations (pp. 544, 584)

operating budget: management's plan for revenues, production and operating costs (p. 254)

operating plans: specific short-term decisions that shape the organisation's day-to-day activities, e.g. drawing cash from a bank line of credit, hiring an employee or ordering materials. Often include specific performance objectives such as budgeted revenues and costs. (p. 5)

operational risk: the risk of loss resulting from inadequate or failed internal processes, people and systems, or from external events (p. 218)

operation costing: a particular type of hybrid method used when similar batches of identical products are manufactured. Units in each batch are identical, but the processing of each batch is different and may not include the same steps. (p. 569)

operations cycle: the second step in the value chain, it is concerned with the production and delivery of goods or services that are identified and designed in the innovation cycle (p. 494)

opportunity costs: the benefits forgone when one alternative is chosen over the next best alternative (p. 11)

organisational core competencies: the entity's strengths relative to competitors (p. 5)

organisational strategies: the tactics that managers use to take advantage of core competencies while working towards the organisational vision (p. 5)

organisational vision: the core purpose and ideology of the entity, which guides the entity's overall direction and approaches toward its various stakeholder groups (p. 4)

organisation-sustaining activities: tasks or functions undertaken to oversee the entire entity. They occur regardless of the number of facilities operated, customers served, products sold, batches processed or units produced. (p. 130)

outsourcing: the practice of finding outside vendors to supply products and services (p. 305)

overapplied overhead: occurs when actual costs are less than the total amount of overhead allocated to inventory accounts (p. 539)

overheads: costs that are used for the benefit of multiple cost objects; also referred to as **indirect costs** (p. 76)

participative budgeting: a budgeting process in which managers who are responsible for meeting budgets also prepare the initial budget forecasts, setting targets for themselves (p. 269)

payback method: measures the amount of time required to recover the initial investment (p. 367)

peak load pricing: the practice of charging different prices at different times to reduce capacity constraints (p. 190)

penetration pricing: the practice of setting low prices when new products are introduced to increase market share (p. 190)

performance objectives: the specific goals that managers choose to measure and monitor performance, helping employees carry out strategies and plans (p. 490)

period costs: all costs other than production costs that are assigned to the cost of inventory. GAAP requires that period costs be expensed when incurred because these costs are assumed to have no future benefit. (p. 610)

physical output method: allocates joint costs using the relative proportion of physical output for each main product. Used only when output for all main products can be expressed in the same physical measure, e.g. metres, kilograms or litres. (p. 314)

piecewise linear cost function: a cost function in which the variable cost per unit changes at some point but remains linear after the change (p. 31)

post-investment audit: provides feedback about whether operations are meeting expectations (p. 369)

post-sales service cycle: the final step in the value chain, it considers the service provided to customers after product delivery, e.g. providing warranty work, handling returns, correcting defects and collecting and processing payments (p. 494)

practical capacity: the upper capacity limit that takes into account the organisation's regularly scheduled times for production. Excludes potential production that could take place during anticipated and scheduled maintenance downtimes, holidays or other times in which production would normally be interrupted. (p. 618)

predatory pricing: an illegal practice of deliberately setting prices low to drive competitors out of the market and then raising prices. Low prices are not considered predatory if they can be justified by cost differences. (p. 191)

predetermined indirect cost rate: a method of allocating indirect costs using budgeted rather than actual indirect costs (p. 79)

present value: the value in today's dollars of a sum received in the future (p. 359)

price discrimination: an illegal practice of setting different prices for different customers (p. 191)

price elasticity of demand: the sensitivity of sales to price increases (p. 187)

price gouging: the practice of charging a price viewed by consumers as too high (p. 191)

price skimming: the practice of charging a higher price for a product or service when it is first introduced (p. 190)

price variance: the difference between standard and actual prices paid for resources purchased and used in the production of goods or services (p. 398)

principals: people or entities who hire agents to make decisions for them and act on their behalf (p. 448)

private impacts: effects that are internal or have a direct impact on the organisational value chain (p. 650)

process costing: the accounting approach for assigning product costs to mass-produced products (p. 566)

product costs: direct and indirect production costs that are assigned to the cost of inventory (p. 609)

production volume variance: the difference between the standard amount of fixed overhead cost allocated to products and the estimated fixed overhead costs (p. 407)

product-sustaining activities: tasks or functions undertaken to support the production and distribution of a single product or line of products. These activities are not related to units or batches, but to individual products or product lines. (p. 131)

profitability index: the ratio of the present value of the cash inflows to the present value of the investment cash outflows (p. 361)

profit centres: responsibility centres in which managers are responsible for both revenues and costs under their control (p. 454)

real method: an approach for calculating discounted cash flows in which cash inflows and outflows are forecast in real dollars (no inflation) and discounted using a real rate (p. 371)

real rate of interest: the rate of return required on investments when no inflation is a factor. Calculated as the sum of the risk-free rate and a risk premium. (p. 371)

reciprocal method: an approach that simultaneously allocates costs among support departments, and then from support departments to operating departments (p. 92)

relevant information: helps the decision maker to evaluate and choose among alternative courses of action (p. 9)

relevant range: a span of activity for a given cost object where both total fixed costs and variable costs per unit of activity remain constant (p. 30)

residual income: measures the dollar amount of profits in excess of a required rate of return (p. 459)

responsibility accounting: the process of assigning authority and responsibility to managers of subunits, and then measuring and evaluating their performance (p. 453)

responsibility centres: subunits (segments, divisions or departments) in which managers are accountable for specific types of operating activities. Four common types of responsibility centres are cost centres, revenue centres, profit centres and investment centres. (p. 453)

return on investment (ROI): the ratio of operating income to average operating assets (p. 455)

revenue budget variance: the difference between actual revenues and standard revenues (p. 419)

revenue centres: responsibility centres in which managers are responsible for the revenues under their control (p. 454)

revenue sales quantity variance: the difference between the standard and actual quantity of units sold at the standard selling price (p. 420)

rework: spoiled units that are repaired and sold as if they were originally produced correctly (p. 546)

risk-free rate: the 'pure' rate of interest paid on short-term government bonds without considering inflation (p. 371)

risk premium: an element above the risk-free rate that entities demand for undertaking risks (p. 371)

rolling budget: a budget that is prepared monthly or quarterly and reflects planning changes, often through the next 12 to 18 months. Often reflects the most recent results and incorporates significant changes in business strategy, operating plans and the economy. (p. 272)

sales mix: the proportion of different products or services that an organisation sells (p. 216)

sales price variance: the difference between standard and actual selling prices for the volume of units actually sold (p. 419)

sales value at split-off point method: allocates joint costs based on the relative sales value of main products at the point where joint production ends (p. 315)

scatter plot: a graphical technique in which data points for past costs are plotted against a potential cost driver (p. 33)

scrap: bits of direct material left over from normal manufacturing processes. Scrap sometimes has value and can be sold, and sometimes it is discarded. (p. 546)

simple regression analysis: a technique that develops a cost function by calculating values for the statistical relationship between total cost and a single cost driver (p. 39)

single-rate allocation: the practice of using only one base to allocate both fixed and variable costs (p. 96)

societal impacts: 'externalities', or those costs and benefits that are not generally accounted for in an entity's conventional accounting system (p. 650)

source documents: manual or electronic records created to capture and provide information about transactions or events (p. 533)

specific knowledge: detailed information about particular processes, customers or products; such information is costly to transfer within the entity (p. 451)

spoilage: units of product that are unacceptable and are discarded, reworked or sold at a reduced price (pp. 544, 584)

standard cost: the cost managers expect to incur to produce goods or services under operating plan assumptions (p. 394)

standard cost variance: the difference between a standard cost and an actual cost (p. 396)

standard fixed overhead allocation: the allocation of fixed costs to inventory and cost of goods sold (p. 404)

standard overhead allocation rate: an allocation rate used to allocate overhead; created at the beginning of each period to monitor overhead costs (p. 404)

standard variable overhead allocation rate: an allocation rate determined by estimating the variable amount of overhead cost per unit of an allocation base (p. 404)

static budget: a budget based on forecasts of specific volumes of production or services. All variable costs are calculated for a specific volume of operations. (p. 266)

step-down method: a method that allocates support department costs, one department at a time, to remaining support and operating departments in a cascading manner until all support department costs have been allocated (p. 90)

stepwise linear cost function: a cost function in which fixed cost changes at some point but remains constant after the change (p. 31)

strategies: tactics that relate to providing direction and guiding long-term decisions (p. 5)

supply chain: the flow of resources from the initial suppliers through the delivery of goods and services to customers and clients (pp. 13, 168)

sustainability management: the measuring, monitoring and simultaneous control of three important dimensions — the economic, environmental and social dimensions — to maximise corporate profits while reducing the environmental and social impact (p. 650)

sustainability management accounting: the tool used to attain the organisation's (or specific business unit's) sustainability goals. It simultaneously integrates the economic, environmental and social performance of an entity with strategic management. (p. 653)

target costing: the process of researching consumer markets to estimate an appropriate market price, then subtracting the desired return to determine a maximum allowable cost. This target cost is the maximum cost at which the entity can produce a good or service to generate the desired profit margin. (p. 175)

tax shield: a depreciation deduction in future years for investments such as buildings, land improvements, equipment and furnishings. The depreciation shields part of operating income from the payment of income taxes. (p. 370)

theoretical capacity: the upper capacity limit assuming continuous, uninterrupted production 365 days per year; or the maximum volume of goods or services that an entity could hypothetically produce (p. 618)

theory of constraints (TOC): a method of analysing the weakest link in the chain (the constraint) that limits the system from achieving higher performance (p. 173)

throughput accounting: a modified form of variable costing that measures the impact of bottlenecks and constraints on an organisation's goal achievement (p. 173)

throughput costing: a modified form of variable costing that treats direct labour and variable overhead as period expenses (p. 619)

time value of money: the idea that a dollar received today is worth more than a dollar received in the future (p. 357)

transfer price: the price used to record revenue and cost when goods or services are transferred between responsibility centres in an entity (pp. 191, 465)

two-point method: a method that uses any two sets of data points for cost and a cost driver to algebraically calculate a mixed cost function (p. 33)

underapplied overhead: occurs when actual costs are more than the amount of overhead allocated (p. 539)

unfavourable variance: a variance in which actual costs are greater than budgeted, or actual revenues are less than budgeted (p. 266)

unit-level activities: undertaken to produce individual units manufactured or services produced. Unit-level activities need to be performed for every unit of good or service, and therefore the cost should be proportional to the number of units produced. (p. 131)

value-added activities: activities that are necessary and increase the worth of an entity's goods or services to customers, and that the customer/client would normally be prepared to pay for (pp. 13, 136)

value chain: the key activities engaged in by the organisation or industry (p. 11)

variable costing: a costing method in which all variable costs are matched against revenues and fixed costs are treated as period costs. Product costs consist of only variable manufacturing costs such as direct materials, direct labour and variable manufacturing overhead. (p. 610)

variable costs: costs that change proportionately with changes in activity levels (p. 28)

variable overhead budget variance: the difference between allocated variable overhead cost and actual variable overhead cost (p. 405)

variable overhead efficiency variance: the difference between the flexible budget for variable overhead cost and the standard amount of variable overhead for the actual volume of the allocation base (p. 406)

variable overhead spending variance: the difference between the total expected variable overhead costs for the actual output and the actual variable overhead costs for that level of output (p. 405)

variance analysis: the process of calculating variances and then investigating the reasons they occurred (p. 396)

volume drivers: drivers that use a measure of output to assign the indirect costs, e.g. labour hours, machine hours or units of output (p. 78)

volume variance: the difference between the amount of estimated fixed overhead costs used to calculate the allocation rate and the amount of fixed overhead costs actually allocated to inventory during the period (p. 618)

weighted average contribution margin per unit: the average contribution margin per unit for multiple products weighted by the sales mix (p. 216)

weighted average contribution margin ratio: the combined contribution margin divided by combined revenue. Alternatively, it can be calculated by dividing the contribution margin per unit by the weighted average selling price (p. 217)

weighted average cost of capital: the weighted average rate for the costs of the various sources of financing such as debt and stock (p. 361)

weighted average method: a method in which costs from beginning WIP (performed last period) are averaged with costs incurred during the current period, and then allocated to units completed and ending WIP (p. 570)

zero-based budgeting: a budgeting process in which managers justify budget amounts as if no information about budgets or costs from prior budget cycles was available (p. 269)

Index